Selected Titles in This Series

57 **David C. Heath and Glen Swindle, Editors,** Introduction to mathematical finance (San Diego, California, January 1997)

56 **Jane Cronin and Robert E. O'Malley, Jr., Editors,** Analyzing multiscale phenomena using singular perturbation methods (Baltimore, Maryland, January 1998)

55 **Frederick Hoffman, Editor,** Mathematical aspects of artificial intelligence (Orlando, Florida, January 1996)

54 **Renato Spigler and Stephanos Venakides, Editors,** Recent advances in partial differential equations (Venice, Italy, June 1996)

53 **David A. Cox and Bernd Sturmfels, Editors,** Applications of computational algebraic geometry (San Diego, California, January 1997)

52 **V. Mandrekar and P. R. Masani, Editors,** Proceedings of the Norbert Wiener Centenary Congress, 1994 (East Lansing, Michigan, 1994)

51 **Louis H. Kauffman, Editor,** The interface of knots and physics (San Francisco, California, January 1995)

50 **Robert Calderbank, Editor,** Different aspects of coding theory (San Francisco, California, January 1995)

49 **Robert L. Devaney, Editor,** Complex dynamical systems: The mathematics behind the Mandlebrot and Julia sets (Cincinnati, Ohio, January 1994)

48 **Walter Gautschi, Editor,** Mathematics of Computation 1943–1993: A half century of computational mathematics (Vancouver, British Columbia, August 1993)

47 **Ingrid Daubechies, Editor,** Different perspectives on wavelets (San Antonio, Texas, January 1993)

46 **Stefan A. Burr, Editor,** The unreasonable effectiveness of number theory (Orono, Maine, August 1991)

45 **De Witt L. Sumners, Editor,** New scientific applications of geometry and topology (Baltimore, Maryland, January 1992)

44 **Béla Bollobás, Editor,** Probabilistic combinatorics and its applications (San Francisco, California, January 1991)

43 **Richard K. Guy, Editor,** Combinatorial games (Columbus, Ohio, August 1990)

42 **C. Pomerance, Editor,** Cryptology and computational number theory (Boulder, Colorado, August 1989)

41 **R. W. Brockett, Editor,** Robotics (Louisville, Kentucky, January 1990)

40 **Charles R. Johnson, Editor,** Matrix theory and applications (Phoenix, Arizona, January 1989)

39 **Robert L. Devaney and Linda Keen, Editors,** Chaos and fractals: The mathematics behind the computer graphics (Providence, Rhode Island, August 1988)

38 **Juris Hartmanis, Editor,** Computational complexity theory (Atlanta, Georgia, January 1988)

37 **Henry J. Landau, Editor,** Moments in mathematics (San Antonio, Texas, January 1987)

36 **Carl de Boor, Editor,** Approximation theory (New Orleans, Louisiana, January 1986)

35 **Harry H. Panjer, Editor,** Actuarial mathematics (Laramie, Wyoming, August 1985)

34 **Michael Anshel and William Gewirtz, Editors,** Mathematics of information processing (Louisville, Kentucky, January 1984)

33 **H. Peyton Young, Editor,** Fair allocation (Anaheim, California, January 1985)

32 **R. W. McKelvey, Editor,** Environmental and natural resource mathematics (Eugene, Oregon, August 1984)

31 **B. Gopinath, Editor,** Computer communications (Denver, Colorado, January 1983)

30 **Simon A. Levin, Editor,** Population biology (Albany, New York, August 1983)

(Continued in the back of this publication)

AMS SHORT COURSE LECTURE NOTES
Introductory Survey Lectures
published as a subseries of
Proceedings of Symposia in Applied Mathematics

Proceedings of Symposia in APPLIED MATHEMATICS

Volume 57

Introduction to Mathematical Finance

American Mathematical Society
Short Course
January 6–7, 1997
San Diego, California

David C. Heath
Glen Swindle
Editors

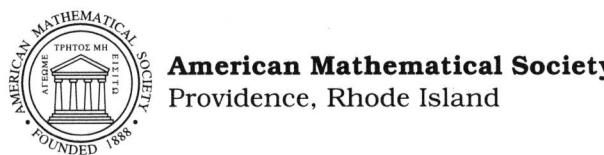

American Mathematical Society
Providence, Rhode Island

Editorial Board

Marsha J. Berger   Peter S. Constantin (Chair)   Eitan Tadmor

LECTURE NOTES PREPARED FOR THE
AMERICAN MATHEMATICAL SOCIETY SHORT COURSE
MATHEMATICAL FINANCE
HELD IN SAN DIEGO, CALIFORNIA
JANUARY 6–7, 1997

The AMS Short Course Series is sponsored by the Society's Program Committee for National Meetings. The series is under the direction of the Short Course Subcommittee of the Program Committee for National Meetings.

2000 *Mathematics Subject Classification.* Primary 91B28;
Secondary 60H30, 91B24, 93E20.

Library of Congress Cataloging-in-Publication Data
Introduction to mathematical finance : American Mathematical Society short course, January 6–7, 1997, San Diego, California / David C. Heath, Glen Swindle, editors.
    p. cm. — (Proceedings of symposia in applied mathematics, ISSN 0160-7634 ; v. 57. AMS short course lecture notes)
    ISBN 0-8218-0751-X
    1. Investments—Mathematical models. 2. Portfolio management. I. Heath, David C. II. Swindle, Glen. III. American Mathematical Society. IV. Proceedings of symposia in applied mathematics ; v. 57. V. Proceedings of symposia in applied mathematics. AMS short course lecture notes.
HG4515.2.I57 2000
332.6′01′51—dc21   99-056288

    Copying and reprinting. Material in this book may be reproduced by any means for educational and scientific purposes without fee or permission with the exception of reproduction by services that collect fees for delivery of documents and provided that the customary acknowledgment of the source is given. This consent does not extend to other kinds of copying for general distribution, for advertising or promotional purposes, or for resale. Requests for permission for commercial use of material should be addressed to the Assistant to the Publisher, American Mathematical Society, P. O. Box 6248, Providence, Rhode Island 02940-6248. Requests can also be made by e-mail to `reprint-permission@ams.org`.
    Excluded from these provisions is material in articles for which the author holds copyright. In such cases, requests for permission to use or reprint should be addressed directly to the author(s). (Copyright ownership is indicated in the notice in the lower right-hand corner of the first page of each article.)

© 1999 by the American Mathematical Society. All rights reserved.
The American Mathematical Society retains all rights
except those granted to the United States Government.
Printed in the United States of America.

∞ The paper used in this book is acid-free and falls within the guidelines
established to ensure permanence and durability.
Visit the AMS home page at URL: http://www.ams.org/
10 9 8 7 6 5 4 3 2 1   04 03 02 01 00 99

Contents

Preface	ix
Quantitative methods for portfolio management STEVEN E. SHREVE	1
An introduction to option pricing and the mathematical theory of risk MARCO AVELLANEDA	25
Non-arbitrage and the fundamental theorem of asset pricing: Summary of main results FREDDY DELBAEN AND WALTER SCHACHERMAYER	49
Introduction to models for the evolution of the term structure of interest rates DAVID HEATH	59
Transition densities for interest rate and other nonlinear diffusions YACINE AÏT-SAHALIA	65
Transaction costs in portfolio management and derivative pricing THALEIA ZARIPHOPOULOU	101
Index	165

Preface

Nearly 100 years ago Bachelier, in his fundamental work "Théorie de la spéculation," laid the foundation for the subject now known as Mathematical Finance. In the same work, he provided the first treatment of Brownian motion. The pace of work in this area has grown rapidly. About 50 years ago, Markowitz developed his mean-variance based model for portfolio selection. A little over 25 years ago, the works of Black, Merton, Scholes and Samuelson identified and illuminated the important (and shocking) consequences of assuming that markets present no opportunities for arbitrage. A few years later, Harrison and Kreps demonstrated the fundamental role of martingales and stochastic calculus in constructing and understanding models for financial markets. This connection opened the door for a virtual flood of mathematicians to contribute to developments over the past 20 years.

Concurrently with these mathematical developments, markets have developed and grown. For example, the Chicago Board Options Exchange (CBOE), founded in 1973, revolutionized options trading by creating standardized, listed stock options. Financial institutions now write custom (derivative) contracts for other firms allowing these firms to reduce their interest rate, foreign currency, and credit risks. The level of activity has grown rapidly. The total notional of derivatives written by U.S. commercial banks was $20 trillion in 1996, an order of magnitude greater than the federal budget.

Research activity in this area, both in academia and in industry, has continued to grow. There are now several journals devoted to this subject, and many universities have developed special programs to educate students in this area. One manifestation of this activity was the Short Course on Mathematical Finance, given in San Diego, CA in January of 1997; papers delivered at this course constitute the contents of this volume.

We would like to thank the AMS for their enthusiastic support and their encouragement of the publication of this collection.

Quantitative Methods for Portfolio Management

Steven E. Shreve

Abstract

This paper contains a derivation of the classic results of static mean-variance analysis, and presents the analogous results in a continuous-time model. To accomplish the latter, some basic results in stochastic calculus are developed.

1 Introduction

In his 1952 Ph.D. dissertation [8], Harry Markowitz constructed a mathematical model to quantify the trade-off between risk and expected return in a portfolio of stocks. Assuming that the actual returns of a set of stock are jointly normally distributed over some period of interest, one can compute the mean and variance of the return of a portfolio, whose actual return is a linear combinations of those of the individual stocks held in the portfolio. It is reasonable to hold only those portfolios whose mean return is highest among all portfolios with the same variance, and these are called *efficient*. *Mean-variance analysis* is devoted to finding such efficient portfolios.

Mossin [15], Sharpe [17] and Lintner [7] later developed the concept of the *market*, a portfolio which holds all stocks, and simplified the search for efficient portfolios by noting that the key parameters for a particular stock are its mean return and its correlation with the market. Furthermore, a formula (the so-called the *Capital Asset Pricing Model*) was obtained for the relationship between these two parameters. With the addition of the *riskless asset*, e.g., three-month treasury bonds, to this model, one obtains a *two-fund theorem*, i.e., every portfolio is dominated by a linear combination of

---

1991 *Mathematics Subject Classification*. Primary 90A09; Secondary 60H05, 60H10.
Work supported by National Science Foundation Grant DMS-9500626.

© 1999 American Mathematical Society

the riskless asset and the market portfolio. The optimal investment problem then *separates* into the problem of first constructing a market portfolio, and secondly chosing the market portfolio and risk-free asset weights appropriate for the risk/return preferences of a particular investor.

Using the geometric Brownian motion model of stock prices suggested by Samuelson, Robert Merton [11], [12] developed an elegant extension of the ideas of static mean-variance analysis to continuous-time dynamic models. In this extension, an investor may continuously vary her portfolio and does so in order to maximize the expected utility of her final wealth. Here "utility" is a concave, increasing function of wealth. Once again there are only two funds which matter, the risk-free asset and a particular mutual fund of stocks. Every investor can achieve her optimal investment policy by investing in a linear combination of these funds, with the weights for a particular investor determined by her wealth and utility function. A continuous-time version of the capital asset pricing model formula can also be obtained.

Section 2 of this paper contains a derivation of the classic results of static mean-variance analysis, and Section 4 presents the analogous results in a continuous-time model. Section 3 is a primer on stochastic calculus, necessary for the development in Section 4.

2 Mean-Variance Analysis

2.1 Stocks in a One-Period Model

In the *mean-variance model*, originally proposed by Markowitz [8] (see also [9], [10]), the return on an asset is a normal random variable X. That is to say, \$1 invested in the asset at the initial time will have a value of \$$(1+X)$ one period later. Of course, if the asset is a stock, then the return cannot be less than -1; the most which can be lost is the initial investment. Typically the mean of X is positive but near 0, say 5% to 30%, and the standard deviation is in a similar range, say 5% to 25%, so that in the model there is only a tiny probability that $1+X$ is negative. The mean and variance of the return on a stock, as well as its covariance with the return of other stocks, can be estimated from historical data. Although the distribution of these returns is not normal, the assumption of normality is made for reasons of tractability.

Consider an investor who has before her a vector of N assets with returns $S = (S_1, \ldots, S_N)'$, where these are jointly normally distributed with the vector of means $\mu = (\mu_1, \ldots, \mu_N)'$ and the symmetric, positive definite

covariance matrix
$$\Gamma = I\!\!E\left[(S-\mu)(S-\mu)'\right].$$
We denote by σ an $N \times N$ matrix square root of Γ, i.e., $\Gamma = \sigma\sigma'$. We do not require σ to be symmetric. At the initial time, the agent can divide her wealth among these assets. Generally the assets with the higher means also have the higher variances; to earn more on average one must accept more risk. Mean-variance analysis quantifies the trade-off between risk and mean return.

Figure 1 indicates the *mean/standard deviation profile* of two stocks, "Blue Chip" having return S_1, and "Young Growth," having return S_2. If the investor puts a fraction $0 < \alpha < 1$ of her wealth in "Blue Chip" and the remainder $1 - \alpha$ in "Young Growth", she will have a portfolio whose mean return $\mu(\alpha) = \alpha\mu_1 + (1-\alpha)\mu_2$ is a weighted average of that of the individual stocks. The standard deviation of the return of this portfolio is
$$\sigma(\alpha) = \sqrt{\alpha^2\sigma_1^2 + 2\rho\alpha(1-\alpha)\sigma_1\sigma_2 + (1-\alpha)^2\sigma_2^2},$$
where σ_i is the standard deviation of S_i and
$$\rho \stackrel{\Delta}{=} \frac{I\!\!E\left[(X_1-\mu_1)(X_2-\mu_2)\right]}{\sigma_1\sigma_2}$$

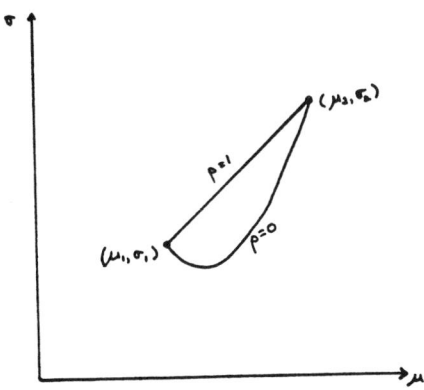

Figure 1

is the correlation between the two stock returns. In the case that $\rho = 1$, the stocks are perfectly correlated and $(\mu(\alpha), \sigma(\alpha))$ lies on the line segment connecting (μ_1, σ_1) and (μ_2, σ_2). However, if $\rho = 0$, so that the stock returns are independent, then $(\mu(\alpha), \sigma(\alpha))$ lies on the curve shown in Figure 1.

Note that by appropriate choice of α, one can achieve a portfolio with lower variance than either of the constituent stocks and a higher mean return than "Blue Chip"; this is the benefit of diversification. If ρ is negative, this diversification effect becomes more pronounced, and in the extreme case that $\rho = -1$, one can cause $\sigma(\alpha)$ to be zero by taking $\alpha = \sigma_2/(\sigma_1 + \sigma_2)$.

2.2 Efficient Frontier

Returning to the case of an N-dimensional normal random vector of returns $S = (S_1, \ldots, S_N)'$, we define the *set of mean/standard deviation portfolio profiles*

$$(2.1) \quad A \triangleq \left\{ \left(\mathbb{E}(\alpha'S), \sqrt{\mathbb{E}[\alpha'S - \mathbb{E}(\alpha'S)]^2} \right); \alpha \in \mathbb{R}^N, \alpha'e = 1 \right\},$$

where e is the N-dimensional column vector with each component equal to 1. In (2.1) we allow individual components of the vector α to be negative, so long as the sum of the components is 1. The portfolios thus constructed may involve selling some stocks "short" in order to invest in other stocks. This is the practice whereby one investor "borrows" stock from another investor and sells it; it must eventually be restored to its owner and the borrower must pay the owner any dividends declared in the interim.

Actually, not all of the set A is of interest. If two portfolios have the same standard deviation, the one with the higher mean is said to *dominate* the one with the lower mean. If two portfolios have the same mean, the one with the lower standard deviation is said to *dominate* the one with the higher standard deviation. An agent should prefer dominating portfolios to dominated ones. We define the *efficient frontier* of A to be the set of all portfolio/standard deviation pairs in A which are not dominated by any other portfolio in A.

To determine the efficient frontier of A, we first set a desired mean $m \in \mathbb{R}$ and then solve the standard deviation minimization problem

$$\text{Minimize} \quad \sqrt{\alpha'\Gamma\alpha}$$
$$(2.2) \quad \text{Subject to} \quad \alpha'e = 1,$$
$$(2.3) \quad \alpha'\mu = m.$$

As m ranges over $\mathbb{R}$, the efficient frontier (and more) will be swept out by the set of ordered pairs whose first component is m and whose second component is the minimizing standard deviation. Of course, if μ is a scalar multiple of e, then (2.2) does not allow m to range over the positive numbers and there is only one point in the efficient frontier. To avoid this triviality, we assume that μ and e are linearly independent.

It is easier and equivalent to minimize one-half the portfolio variance $\frac{1}{2}\alpha'\Gamma\alpha$ rather than the standard deviation, subject to (2.2) and (2.3), and for this problem the Lagrange multiplier equation is

$$(2.4) \qquad \Gamma\alpha = \lambda_1 e + \lambda_2 \mu.$$

The solution of (2.2)–(2.4) is

$$(2.5) \qquad \alpha = m\eta - \nu,$$

where

$$\eta \triangleq \frac{1}{\Delta}(\sigma')^{-1}\left[(e'\Gamma^{-1}e)\sigma^{-1}\mu - (e'\Gamma^{-1}\mu)\sigma^{-1}e\right],$$

$$\nu \triangleq \frac{1}{\Delta}(\sigma')^{-1}\left[(e'\Gamma^{-1}\mu)\sigma^{-1}\mu - (\mu'\Gamma^{-1}\mu)\sigma^{-1}e\right],$$

$$\Delta \triangleq \|\sigma^{-1}e\|^2 \|\sigma^{-1}\mu\|^2 - ((\sigma^{-1}e)'(\sigma^{-1}\mu))^2.$$

Because of our assumption that μ and e are linearly independent, the vectors $\sigma^{-1}\mu$ and $\sigma^{-1}e$ are linearly independent, the Cauchy-Schwarz inequality implies that $\Delta > 0$, and it is straight-forward to check that η and ν are linearly independent.

The convexity of the objective function $\frac{1}{2}\alpha'\Gamma\alpha$, together with the linearity of the constraints (2.2), (2.3), implies that the Lagrange multiplier conditions are sufficient as well as necessary. The function

$$(2.6) \qquad f(m) \triangleq \sqrt{(m\eta - \nu)'\Gamma(m\eta - \nu)}$$

provides the minimum standard deviation corresponding to a given mean m. We show below that this function is convex and the efficient frontier is

$$(2.7) \qquad \partial_+ A \triangleq \{(m, f(m)); m \geq m_0\},$$

where m_0 is the unique minimizer of f, given by (2.8) below.

Consider the derivatives

$$f'(m) = \frac{\eta'\Gamma(m\eta - \nu)}{f(m)},$$

$$f''(m) = \frac{1}{f^3(m)}\left[(m\eta - \nu)'\Gamma(m\eta - \nu) \cdot \eta'\Gamma\eta - (\eta'\Gamma'(m\eta - \nu))^2\right].$$

Because of the linear independence of η and ν, the vectors $\sigma(m\eta-\nu)$ and $\sigma\eta$ are linearly independent for all values of m, and according to the Cauchy-Schwarz inequality, $f''(m) > 0$ for all $m \in \mathbb{R}$. The unique minimizer of f is

$$(2.8) \qquad m_0 \triangleq \frac{\eta'\Gamma\nu}{\eta'\Gamma\eta} = \frac{e'\Gamma^{-1}\mu}{e'\Gamma^{-1}e},$$

and the efficient frontier is given by (2.7).

Let us assume henceforth that

$$(2.9) \qquad m_0 > 0,$$

so that the effecient frontier has the shape shown in Figure 2. We verify by direct computation the asymptotic formula

$$(2.10) \qquad \lim_{m \to \infty} \left(f(m) - m\sqrt{\eta'\Gamma'\eta} \right) = -m_0 \sqrt{\eta'\Gamma\eta}.$$

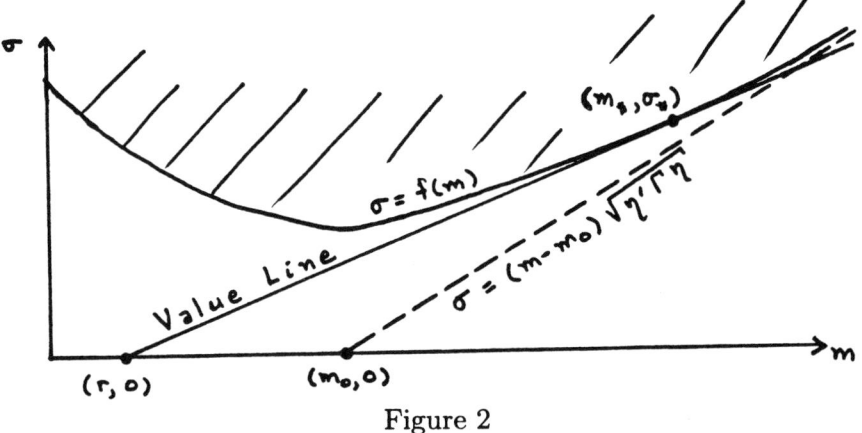

Figure 2

2.3 The Money Market

Following Tobin [18], we introduce a money market with interest rate r, assumed to satisfy $0 \leq r < m_0$. This asset has mean/standard deviation profile represented by the point $(r, 0)$ in Figure 2. We are interested in the point (m_*, σ_*) where the ray emanating from $(r, 0)$ is tangent to the efficient frontier, and we call the portfolio corresponding to this point the *market portfolio*. By distributing wealth between the money market and the market portfolio, the agent can construct a portfolio whose mean/standard deviation profile lies anywhere on the *value line* connecting the points $(r, 0)$ and

(m_*, σ_*). Indeed, by borrowing at interest rate r and investing the money in the market portfolio, the agent can have a portfolio whose mean/standard deviation profile is on the value line above and to the right of (m_*, σ_*). The portfolios on the value line dominate all other portfolios which can be constituted from stocks and the money market, including those on the efficient frontier. We summarize this discussion.

Separation Theorem. *Assume that Γ is positive definite, μ and e are linearly independent, and $0 \leq r < m_0$. The problem of choosing a best portfolio for a particular agent separates into two parts. First the agent should determine the market portfolio, a portfolio whose composition depends only on the asset parameters, not on the preferences of the individual agent. Secondly, the agent should allocate her wealth between the market portfolio and the money market according to her attitude toward risk.*

We denote by α_* the vector of proportions corresponding to the market portfolio, i.e., $\alpha_*'e = 1$ and

$$(2.11) \qquad m_* = \alpha_*'\mu, \quad f(m_*) = \sigma_* = \sqrt{\alpha_*'\Gamma\alpha}.$$

We can solve for m_* and α_* from the tangency condition

$$(2.12) \qquad f(m_*) = (m_* - r)f'(m_*),$$

which together with (2.5) leads immediately to the formulas

$$(2.13) \qquad m_* = \frac{(\nu - r\eta)'\Gamma\nu}{(\nu - r\eta)'\Gamma\eta}, \quad \alpha_* = m_*\eta - \nu.$$

From the Cauchy-Shwartz inequality, it is easily verified that $m_0 < m_* < \infty$ so long as $r < m_0$.

Sharpe [17], Lintner [7], and Mossin [15] discovered that within the mean-variance model, the mean return on each asset is related to the mean return of the market portfolio in a simple way, which we now describe. These authors showed how to use a single parameter for each stock, it's so-called "β", to construct efficient portfolios.

Capital Asset Pricing Theorem. *Assume that Γ is positive definite, μ and e are linearly independent, and $0 \leq r < m_0$. Let e_i denote the N-dimensional vector whose only nonzero component is a 1 in the i-th place, so that $\mu_i = e_i'\mu$ is the mean return of asset i. Then the risk premium $\mu_i - r$*

of the i-th asset is related to the risk premium $m_* - r$ of the market portfolio by the equation
(2.14) $$\mu_i - r = \beta_i(m_* - r),$$
where
(2.15) $$\beta_i = \frac{e_i' \Gamma \alpha_*}{\alpha_*' \Gamma \alpha_*},$$
is the covariance of the return on the i-th asset with the return of the market, divided by the variance of the market return.

PROOF: We form a portfolio of the i-th asset and the market portfolio by setting $\alpha_i(\epsilon) \triangleq (1-\epsilon)\alpha_* + \epsilon e_i$. The mean return of this portfolio is $\mu_i(\epsilon) \triangleq (1-\epsilon)m_* + \epsilon\mu_i$, and the standard deviation is $\sigma_i(\epsilon) \triangleq \sqrt{\alpha_i'(\epsilon)\Gamma\alpha_i(\epsilon)}$. As ϵ ranges over the real numbers, the pair $(\mu_i(\epsilon), \sigma_i(\epsilon))$ traces out a curve lying entirely above the efficient frontier in Figure 2, although the curve touches the efficient frontier at (m_*, σ_*) when $\epsilon = 0$. Indeed, the curve must be tangent to the efficient frontier, and therefore the value line, at this point. This observation leads to the equation

(2.16) $$\left. \frac{\frac{\partial}{\partial \epsilon}\sigma_i(\epsilon)}{\frac{\partial}{\partial \epsilon}\mu_i(\epsilon)} \right|_{\epsilon=0} = f'(m_*).$$

The left-hand side of this equation is

$$\left. \frac{\frac{\partial}{\partial \epsilon}\sigma_i(\epsilon)}{\frac{\partial}{\partial \epsilon}\mu_i(\epsilon)} \right|_{\epsilon=0} = \frac{(-\alpha_* + e_i)'\Gamma\alpha_*}{(\mu_i - m_*)\sqrt{\alpha_*'\Gamma\alpha_*}} = \frac{\sigma_*(\beta_i - 1)}{\mu_i - m_*},$$

and according to (2.12), the right-hand side is $\sigma_*/(m_* - r)$. Equating these two expressions, we obtain (2.14). ◇

Corollary. *The vector of stock proportions in the market portfolio is*

(2.17) $$\alpha_* = \frac{\Gamma^{-1}(\mu - re)}{e'\Gamma^{-1}(\mu - re)}.$$

PROOF: From (2.15) we have $\beta = \Gamma\alpha_*/\alpha_*'\Gamma\alpha_*$, and (2.14) in vector form is

$$\mu - re = \frac{m_* - r}{\alpha_*'\Gamma\alpha_*}\Gamma\alpha_*.$$

This implies $\alpha_* = \frac{\alpha'_* \Gamma \alpha_*}{m_* - r} \Gamma^{-1}(\mu - re)$, and because $e'\alpha_* = 1$, we have

$$\frac{\alpha'_* \Gamma \alpha_*}{m_* - r} = \frac{1}{e' \Gamma^{-1}(\mu - re)}.$$

3 Stochastic Calculus

3.1 Random Walk

In order to develop a continuous-time investment model, we need stochastic calculus, and for that we must introduce Brownian motion. We shall understand Brownian motion as a continuous-time analogue of random walk.

To construct a random walk, let us flip a fair coin, say 4 times. We get an outcome and then construct our random walk to step up one unit with each head (H) and down one unit with each tail (T). For example, if the outcome is $HTHT$, then the successive values of the random walk, denoted by R, are

$$R(0) = 0, R(1) = 1, R(2) = 0, R(3) = 1, R(4) = 0.$$

We plot the path of the random walk corresponding to the outcome $HTHT$ below, showing time on the horizontal axis and allowing each toss to consume one unit of time.

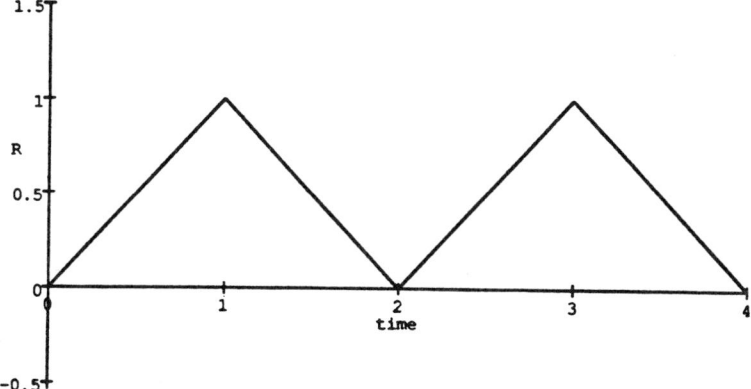

Figure 3

We could (and perhaps should) write

$$R(0; HTHT) = 0, \ R(1; HTHT) = 1, \ R(2; HTHT) = 0,$$

$$R(3; HTHT) = 1, \ R(4; HTHT) = 0$$

to explicitly indicate the dependence of the random walk on the outcome of the underlying coin tosses. It is customary, however, to suppress this dependence in the notation. Note that there are 16 possible outcomes from the four coin tosses, and there is a one-to-one correspondence between these outcomes and the possible paths of the random walk. We denote by Ω the set of these 16 possible outcomes. Each of the outcomes in Ω has probability 1/16 of occurring, and we can use this fact to construct a probability measure $I\!P$ on Ω which assigns to each subset of Ω a probability equal to the number of elements in the subset, divided by 16.

The *increments* of a random walk are statistically independent, i.e., if we choose integers $0 \leq k_1 < k_2 < \cdots < k_n$, then the increments $R(k_2) - R(k_1), R(k_3) - R(k_2), \ldots, R(k_n) - R(k_{n-1})$ are independent. Two important properties follow from the independence of increments.

First of all, random walk enjoys the *Markov property*. If you observe the random walk until some time k and are then asked to provide the (conditional) distribution of the random walk at a later time, the answer to this question depends only on the value of the random walk *at time* k, not on its values prior to time k. For example, if you know that $R(0) = 0$, $R(1) = 1$ and $R(2) = 0$, and you are asked, based on this information, to provide the the probability that $R(4) = 0$, the only information which is relevant is that $R(2) = 0$. (Incidentally, the probability requested here is $P[R(4) = 0|R(2) = 0] = 1/2$.)

The random walk also has the *martingale property*. If you observe the random walk until some time k and are then asked to compute its (conditional) expectation at a later time, the answer is its value at the current time. For example, if you know that $R(0) = 0$, $R(1) = 1$ and $R(2) = 0$, then based on this information, the conditional expectations of $R(3)$ and $R(4)$ are both 0. All you need to know to determine these conditional expectations of $R(3)$ and $R(4)$ is that $R(2) = 0$.

Finally, the random walk has *quadratic variation* up to time k equal to k. The quadratic variation up to time k is defined to be

$$\langle R \rangle(k) = \sum_{j=1}^{k} \Big(R(j) - R(j-1)\Big)^2,$$

and since $(R(j) - R(j-1))^2 = 1$ for all j, we have $\langle R \rangle(k) = k$. This last formula holds, regardless of the sequence of heads and tails obtained by the coin tosses underlying the random walk.

3.2 Brownian Motion

To obtain Brownian motion, we scale random walk so that its steps are smaller and they take place more rapidly. If we do the scaling properly and pass to the limit, we obtain Brownian motion. More specifically, let us toss a coin 400 rather than 4 times. With each head, let us step up $1/10$ unit; with each tail, let us step down $1/10$ unit. We plot a typical such path below, allowing each 100 tosses to consume one unit of time. Thus, $R(1/100)$ is $1/10$ or $-1/10$, depending on the outcome of the first toss, and $R(1) = R(100/100)$ records the cumulative effect of the first 100 tosses.

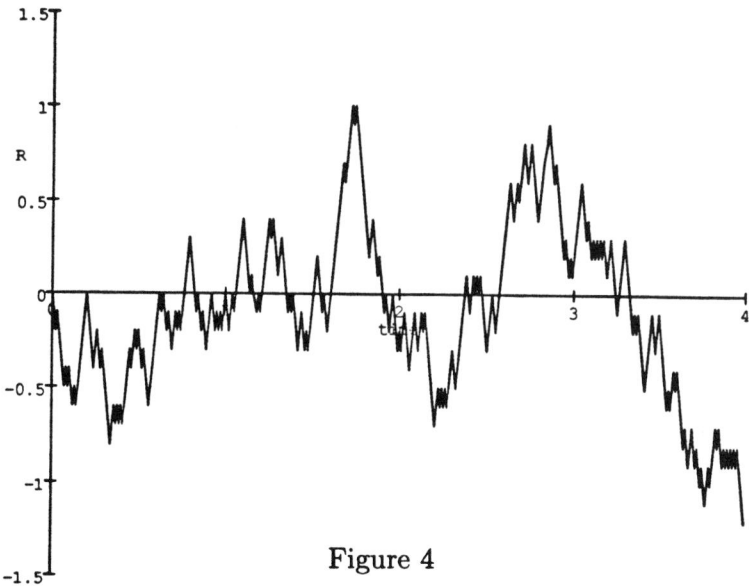

Figure 4

This scaled random walk still has independent increments, and consequently has the Markov property and the martingale property. Moreover, its quadratic variation over any time interval is still the length of the time interval. For

example,
$$\langle R\rangle(1) = \sum_{j=1}^{100}\left(R\left(\frac{j}{100}\right) - R\left(\frac{j-1}{100}\right)\right)^2 = 1,$$
because each term under the sum is 1/100 and there are 100 such terms.

To the naked eye, the plot in Figure 4 could very well be a path of a Brownian motion. Note that because $R(1)$ is the sum of 100 scaled binomial terms, each with mean zero and variance 1/100, the Central Limit Theorem guarantees that its distribution is approximately normal with mean zero and variance 1. Continuing this process of speeding up time and scaling down step-size, we can pass to the limit and obtain Brownian motion.

We shall use the symbol $B(t)$ for Brownian motion at time t, where now t can be any nonnegative number, not necessarily an integer. Underlying this Brownian motion, there is a sample space Ω, which one might think of as a set of coin tosses, although now infinitely many coin tosses take place in every positive interval of time. For this reason, it is more convenient to take Ω to be $C[0,\infty)$, the set of continuous functions on $[0,\infty)$. One could write $B(t;\omega) = \omega(t)$ to indicate explicitly the dependence of the Brownian motion on the underlying sample point $\omega \in \Omega = C[0,\infty)$, but this dependence is generally not shown explicitly in the notation. There is also a probability measure P on Ω, defined on the σ-algebra generated by the open subsets in the supremum norm topology. If $A \in \mathcal{F}$ is such that $P(A) = 1$, then we say that A occurs *almost surely*, which we shall sometimes abbreviate as *a.s.*

The key properties of Brownian motion are the following:

Continuity. Brownian motion has continuous paths.

Independent, normally distributed increments. If $0 \leq t_0 < t_1 < \cdots < t_k$, then the increments $B(t_1) - B(t_0), B(t_2) - B(t_1), \ldots, B(t_k) - B(t_{k-1})$ are independent, and each increment $B(t_j) - B(t_{j-1})$ is a normal random variable with mean zero and variance $t_j - t_{j-1}$. In particular, $B(t) = B(t) - B(0)$ is normally distributed with mean zero and variance t.

Markov property. If $0 \leq s < t$ are given, then conditioned on the information obtained by observing the Brownian motion until time s, the conditional distribution of $B(t)$ depends only on the value of $B(s)$.

Martingale property. If $0 \leq s < t$ are given, then conditioned on the information obtained by observing the Brownian motion until time s, the conditional expectation of $B(t)$ is $B(s)$.

Quadratic variation. If $t > 0$ is given, and one partitions the interval $[0, t]$ by choosing partition points $0 = t_0 \leq t_1 \leq \ldots \leq t_k = t$, then as the partition becomes finer (and k, the number of partition points, approaches infinity), the expression

$$\sum_{j=1}^{k} \left(B(t_j) - B(t_{j-1}) \right)^2$$

approaches t almost surely. We write $\langle B \rangle(t) = t, a.s.$

3.3 Quadratic Variation

Note that when working in continuous time, we define the quadratic variation of a process to be the *limit* of a sum of squares of increments. The quadratic variation computation for Brownian motion is in marked contrast to the computation of the quadratic variation for the usual functions we encounter. If $g(t)$ is a function of the variable $t \geq 0$ and g' exists and is continuous, then the quadratic variation of g on every interval is zero. Indeed, if we fix $t > 0$ and choose partition points $0 = t_0 \leq t_1 \leq \ldots \leq t_k = t$, then the Mean Value Theorem guarantees that in each interval $[t_{j-1}, t_j]$, there is a point τ_j such that $g(t_j) - g(t_{j-1}) = (t_j - t_{j-1}) g'(\tau_j)$. Consequently,

$$\left| \sum_{j=1}^{k} \left(g(t_j) - g(t_{j-1}) \right)^2 \right| = \left| \sum_{j=1}^{k} (t_j - t_{j-1})^2 \left(g'(\tau_j) \right)^2 \right|$$

$$\leq \max_{0 \leq \tau \leq t} |g'(\tau)|^2 \sum_{j=1}^{k} (t_j - t_{j-1})^2.$$

But

$$\sum_{j=1}^{k} (t_j - t_{j-1})^2 \leq \sum_{j=1}^{k} (t_j - t_{j-1}) \cdot \max_{1 \leq i \leq k} (t_i - t_{i-1})$$

$$= t \cdot \max_{1 \leq i \leq k} (t_i - t_{i-1}).$$

As the partition becomes finer, $\max_{1 \leq i \leq k}(t_i - t_{i-1})$ approaches zero, while t remains fixed. Therefore, the quadratic variation of g on $[0, t]$ is zero.

3.4 Stochastic Integral

The theory of stochastic calculus begins with Itô [1], [2], [3]. An accessible modern treatment is Oksendal [16]. A more comprehensive work, which includes applications to finance, is Karatzas & Shreve [5].

The first step in stochastic calculus is integration. One needs to make sense of the expression

$$(3.1) \qquad I(t) = \int_0^t \rho(s)\, dB(s),$$

where B is a Brownian motion and ρ is a random process whose value at time s depends only on the values of the Brownian motion up to time s. The problem is that paths of the integrator B have unbounded variation. However, they have finite quadratic variation, and this permits the following construction. Partition the time interval $[0,t]$ by choosing partition points $0 = t_0 \leq t_1 \leq \ldots \leq t_k = t$ and then approximate (3.1) by the sum

$$(3.2) \qquad \sum_{j=1}^{k} \rho(t_{j-1})\bigl(B(t_j) - B(t_{j-1})\bigr).$$

It is important in the above sum that the integrand $\rho(t_{j-1})$ is evaluated at the left-hand time point of the interval $[t_{j-1}, t_j]$ over which the increment $B(t_j) - B(t_{j-1})$ is taken. If ρ were a portfolio and B were a stock price, this corresponds to choosing the portfolio before seeing the increment in the stock price. With this restriction on how the approximating sums are set up, one can show that as the partition becomes finer, the approximating sums converge in mean square to a random variable, which we call $\int_0^t \rho(s)\, dB(s)$.

Stochastic integrals of the form (3.1) can be regarded as stochastic processes by varying the upper limit of integration t. These stochastic integrals have the martingale property precisely because the integrand $\rho(t_{j-1})$ in the approximating sum (3.2) is chosen not to depend on the increment $B(t_j) - B(t_{j-1})$ which multiplies it. Conditioned on the information available at time t_{j-1}, this increment has conditional mean zero. An important consequence of the martingale property for the stochastic integral $I(t)$ is that

$$(3.3) \qquad \mathbb{E} \int_0^t \rho(s)\, dB(s) = 0 \quad \forall t \geq 0.$$

3.5 Itô's Formula

The primary reason to work in continuous rather than discrete time is that there is a calculus for continuous-time processes. To get a feel for how this calculus works, let us consider the function $f(x) = \frac{1}{2}x^2$, for which $f'(x) = x$ and $f''(x) = 1$. Let x_j and x_{j-1} be numbers. By Taylor's Theorem,

$$(3.4) \quad f(x_j) - f(x_{j-1}) = (x_j - x_{j-1})f'(x_{j-1}) + \frac{1}{2}(x_j - x_{j-1})^2 f''(x_{j-1}).$$

In this case, the equation (3.4) is exact because the function f is quadratic. In the general case, this equation is only an approximation, but the error, which is of order $o((x_j - x_{j-1})^2)$, does not affect the outcome of the following argument. We next fix $t > 0$ and let $0 = t_0 \leq t_1 \leq \ldots \leq t_k = t$ be a partition of the interval $[0, t]$. Using (3.4), we may write

$$
\begin{aligned}
(3.5) \quad \frac{1}{2}B^2(t) - \frac{1}{2}B^2(0) &= f(B(t)) - f(B(0)) \\
&= \sum_{j=1}^{k}\left[f(B(t_j)) - f(B(t_{j-1}))\right] \\
&= \sum_{j=1}^{k}\left[B(t_j) - B(t_{j-1})\right] f'(B(t_{j-1})) \\
&\quad + \frac{1}{2}\sum_{j=1}^{k}\left[B(t_j) - B(t_{j-1})\right]^2 f''(B(t_{j-1})) \\
&= \sum_{j=1}^{k} B(t_{j-1})\left[B(t_j) - B(t_{j-1})\right] \\
&\quad + \frac{1}{2}\sum_{j=1}^{k}\left[B(t_j) - B(t_{j-1})\right]^2.
\end{aligned}
$$

As the partition becomes finer, the last two terms in this equation approach $\int_0^t B(s)\,dB(s)$ and $\frac{1}{2}\langle B\rangle(t) = \frac{1}{2}t$, respectively. This leads to the integral equation

$$\frac{1}{2}B^2(t) = \frac{1}{2}B^2(0) + \int_0^t B(s)\,dB(s) + \frac{1}{2}t.$$

We write this same equation in differential form as

$$(3.6) \quad \frac{1}{2}dB^2(t) = B(t)\,dB(t) + \frac{1}{2}dt.$$

Equation (3.6) is an instance of *Itô's formula*. If one were performing calculus with an ordinary function g which had a continuous derivative, then in contrast to (3.6), one would have the "chain rule"

$$\frac{1}{2}dg^2(t) = g(t)\,dg(t),$$

or in the more usual notation,

$$\frac{1}{2}\frac{d}{dt}g^2(t) = g(t)g'(t).$$

Itô's formula is the chain rule for stochastic processes. It contains an additional term (the term $\frac{1}{2}dt$ in (3.6)) because Brownian motion has a nonzero quadratic variation.

We now present Itô's formula for a function of the time variable and two stochastic processes. From this case, the formula for the general case is apparent. Let $f(t, x, y)$ be a function of three real variables, and denote its first partial derivatives by f_t, f_x, and f_y and its second partial derivatives by f_{xy}, etc. Let $X(t)$ and $Y(t)$ be stochastic processes. Then Itô's formula for this case is

$$\begin{aligned}
df(t, X(t), Y(t)) = {}& f_t(t, X(t), Y(t))\,dt \\
& + f_x(t, X(t), Y(t))\,dX(t) + f_y(t, X(t), Y(t))\,dY(t) \\
& + \frac{1}{2}f_{xx}(t, X(t), Y(t))\,dX(t)\,dX(t) \\
& + f_{xy}(t, X(t), Y(t))\,dX(t)\,dY(t) \\
& + \frac{1}{2}f_{yy}(t, X(t), Y(t))\,dY(t)\,dY(t).
\end{aligned} \quad (3.7)$$

One derives this result in integral form by first fixing a $t > 0$, letting $0 = t_0 \leq t_1 \leq \ldots \leq t_k = t$ be a partition of $[0, t]$, and writing

$$f(t, X(t), Y(t)) - f(0, X(0), Y(0))$$
$$= \sum_{j=1}^{k}\Big[f(t_j, X(t_j), Y(t_j)) - f(t_{j-1}, X(t_{j-1}), Y(t_{j-1}))\Big].$$

One works out a Taylor series expansion for the difference $f(t_j, X(t_j), Y(t_j)) - f(t_{j-1}, X(t_{j-1}), Y(t_{j-1}))$, passes to the limit as the partition becomes finer, and discovers Itô's formula. The term $\frac{1}{2}dX(t)\,dX(t)$ in (3.7) results from taking the limit of the term $\frac{1}{2}\sum_{j=1}^{k}\left(X(t_j) - X(t_{j-1})\right)^2$, the term $dX(t)\,dY(t)$

results from taking the limit of the term $\sum_{j=1}^{k}\bigl(X(t_j) - X(t_{j-1})\bigr)\bigl(Y(t_j) - Y(t_{j-1})\bigr)$, and the term $\tfrac{1}{2}dY(t)\,dY(t)$ results from taking the limit of the term $\tfrac{1}{2}\sum_{j=1}^{k}\bigl(Y(t_j) - Y(t_{j-1})\bigr)^2$.

Of course, in Itô's formula (3.7), one needs an easier way to compute terms like $dX(t)\,dY(t)$ than taking the limits which define them. When the processes X and Y can be written as integrals, these terms have simple formulas. Indeed, if

$$X(t) = X(0) + \int_0^t \mu_1(s)\,ds + \int_0^t \rho_1(s)\,dB(s) \tag{3.8}$$

$$Y(t) = Y(0) + \int_0^t \mu_2(s)\,ds + \int_0^t \rho_2(s)\,dB(s) \tag{3.9}$$

then

$$dX(t) = \mu_1(t)dt + \rho_1(t)dB(t), \tag{3.10}$$

$$dY(t) = \mu_2(t)dt + \rho_2(t)dB(t), \tag{3.11}$$

$$dX(t)\,dX(t) = \rho_1^2(t)\,dt, \tag{3.12}$$

$$dX(t)\,dY(t) = \rho_1(t)\rho_2(t)\,dt, \tag{3.13}$$

$$dY(t)\,dY(t) = \rho_2^2(t)\,dt. \tag{3.14}$$

One should understand here that we are not giving a mathematical definition for terms like $dX(t)dY(t)$, nor even $df(t, X(t), Y(t))$. These terms have meaning only in integrated form, i.e., when (3.7) is integrated so the left-hand side becomes $f(t, X(t), Y(t)) - f(0, X(0), Y(0))$ and the right-hand side is a sum of Lebesgue and Itô integrals, obtained by making the substitutions (3.10)–(3.14). It is, however, easier to remember and use the formulas in differential form, just as one learns to write $df(x) = f'(x)dx$ when changing variables in ordinary integrals.

3.6 Geometric Brownian motion

Let us now apply Itô's formula to geometric Brownian motion, defined by

$$S(t) = S(0)\exp\left\{\left(\mu - \frac{1}{2}\sigma^2\right)t + \sigma B(t)\right\}, \tag{3.15}$$

where the initial condition $S(0)$, the *mean rate of return* μ, and the *volatility* σ are nonrandom. We shall always assume that $\sigma > 0$. We let $f(t, x) =$

$\exp\{(\mu - \sigma^2/2)t + \sigma x\}$, so that $S(t) = f(t, B(t))$ and $f_t = (\mu - \sigma^2/2)f$, $f_x = \sigma f$ and $f_{xx} = \sigma^2 f$. According to the one-dimensional version of Itô's formula ((3.7) with no Y process),

$$\begin{aligned} dS(t) &= f_t(t, S(t))\,dt + f_x(t, S(t))\,dB(t) + \frac{1}{2}f_{xx}(t, S(t))\,dt \\ &= S(t)[\mu dt + \sigma dB(t)]. \end{aligned}$$
(3.16)

4 Continuous-Time Portfolio Optimization

With two landmark papers, Merton [11], [12] introduced stochastic calculus to portfolio optimization. (Despite its later publication date, Mirrlees [14] was a precursor to this work.) The two Merton papers and many others appear in [13].

4.1 Assets and Wealth in a Continuous-Time Model

Suppose there are N stocks, and the price per share of the i-th stock is given as the solution to the stochastic differential equation

$$dS_i(t) = S_i(t)\left[\mu_i dt + \sum_{j=1}^N \sigma_{ij} dB_j(t)\right],$$
(4.1)

where $B_1, \ldots, B_N$ are N independent Brownian motions. Because of this independence, when using Itô's formula, we will have

$$dB_i(t)dB_j(t) = \delta_{ij} dt,$$
(4.2)

where

$$\delta_{ij} = \begin{cases} 1 & \text{if } i = j, \\ 0 & \text{if } i \neq j, \end{cases}$$

is the Kronecker delta. In vector notation, we write $B(t) = (B_1(t), \ldots, B_N(t))'$. Although the driving Brownian motions are independent, the statistics of the stocks may be coupled through the $N \times N$ *volatility matrix* $\sigma = (\sigma_{ij})$. We assume that this matrix is nonsingular, so that $\Gamma \triangleq \sigma\sigma'$ is symmetric and positive definite.

Suppose also there is a *money market*, whose price per share at time t is

$$S_0(t) = e^{rt},$$
(4.3)

or in differential form,

$$(4.4) \qquad dS_0(t) = rS_0(t)dt.$$

Suppose at each time t, an agent distributes her wealth among the N-assets according to the N-dimensional vector $\alpha(t)$. The choice of this vector at time t is allowed to depend on present and past but not future stock prices. We do not require $\alpha'(t)e = 1$, but rather stipulate that any wealth not invested in stocks must be invested in the money market, i.e., the proportion $1 - \alpha'(t)e$ of the agent's wealth is invested in the money market. This proportion can be either positive or negative, representing investing or borrowing, respectively, at interest rate r.

Let $X(t)$ denote the *wealth* of the agent at time t. Changes in wealth, which result from interest earnings on the invesment in the money market and capital gains on the investments in stocks, are modelled by the stochastic differential equation

$$(4.5) \qquad dX(t) = rX(t)(1 - \alpha'(t)e)dt + X(t)\alpha'(t)[\mu\, dt + \sigma\, dB(t)].$$

4.2 Stochastic Control Problem

Let U be a strictly increasing, strictly concave *utility function* defined on $[0, \infty)$. Fix a planning horizon $T > 0$, and consider an agent endowed with wealth $x \geq 0$ at time $\tau \in [0, T]$. The agent desires to choose a portfolio process $\alpha(t), \tau \leq t \leq T$, so that when $X(\tau) = x$ and $X(t)$ for $\tau < t \leq T$ is given by (4.5), then $X(T) \geq 0$ almost surely and $\mathbb{E}U(X(T))$ is maximized. We denote by

$$(4.6) \qquad V(\tau, x) \triangleq \max_{\alpha(\cdot)} \mathbb{E}[U(X(T))|X(\tau) = x]$$

the *value function* for this problem.

Theorem 4.1 *Suppose there is a continuous function $v(t, x)$ defined on $[0, T] \times [0, \infty)$ such that the partial derivatives v_t, v_x and v_{xx} are defined and continuous on $[0, T) \times (0, \infty)$ and v satisfies the* **Hamilton-Jacobi-Bellman** *equation*

$$(4.7)\; v_t(t,x) + rxv_x(t,x) \\ + \max_{\alpha \in \mathbb{R}^N}\left[\alpha'(\mu - re)xv_x(t,x) + \tfrac{1}{2}\alpha'\Gamma\alpha x^2 v_{xx}(t,x)\right] = 0, \\ 0 \leq t < T, x > 0.$$

as well as the terminal condition

(4.8) $$v(T,x) = U(x), \quad x > 0.$$

Then v majorizes the value function V of (4.6). Furthermore, if there is an $\mathbb{R}^N$-valued function $a(t,x)$ satisfying

(4.9) $$\begin{aligned}\Big[a'(t,x)(\mu - re)xv_x(t,x) &+ \frac{1}{2}a'(t,x)\Gamma a(t,x)x^2 v_{xx}(t,x)\Big] \\ &= \max_{\alpha \in \mathbb{R}^N} \Big[\alpha'(\mu - re)xv_x(t,x) + \frac{1}{2}\alpha'\Gamma\alpha x^2 v_{xx}(t,x)\Big] \\ &\qquad\qquad 0 \leq t < T, x > 0,\end{aligned}$$

then with $X(t), \tau \leq t \leq T$, the solution of the stochastic differential equation (4.5) when $X(\tau) = x$ and $\alpha(t) = a(t, X(t))$, the portfolio process $\alpha(t) = a(t, X(t)), \tau \leq t \leq T$ attains the maximum in (4.6) and v agrees with V.

PROOF: Let $\alpha(t), \tau \leq t \leq T$, be any portfolio process and use Itô's formula to compute the differential

(4.10) $$\begin{aligned}dv(t, X(t)) &= \Big[v_t(t, X(t)) + rX(t)v(t, X(t)) + \alpha'(t)(\mu - re)X(t)v_x(t, X(t)) \\ &\qquad + \frac{1}{2}\alpha'(t)\Gamma\alpha(t)X^2(t)v_{xx}(t, X(t))\Big] dt \\ &\quad + X(t)v_x(t, X(t))\alpha'(t)\sigma dB(t) \\ &\leq X(t)v_x(t, X(t))\alpha'(t)\sigma dB(t),\end{aligned}$$

where we have used (4.7) to obtain the inequality. We integrate both sides of this inequality and take expectations, using (3.3) and (4.8), to derive the further inequality

(4.11) $$v(\tau, x) \geq \mathbb{E}v(T, X(T)) = \mathbb{E}U(X(T)).$$

Since $\alpha(\cdot)$ is an arbitrary portfolio process, we may maximize over $\alpha(\cdot)$ to obtain

(4.12) $$v(\tau, x) \geq V(\tau, x).$$

For the reverse inequality, with $\alpha(t) = a(t, X(t))$ as described in the theorem, we see that equality holds in (4.10), and thus also in (4.11). In particular, from (4.11) we observe that the final wealth $X(T)$ generated by this portfolio process $\alpha(\cdot)$ satisfies $\mathbb{E}U(X(T)) = v(\tau, x)$, and hence $v(\tau, x) = V(\tau, x)$ and $\alpha(\cdot)$ attains the maximum in (4.6). ◇

Like the utility function $U(\cdot)$, the value function $v(t, \cdot)$ is stricly increasing and concave, so the expression to be maximized in the Hamilton-Jacobi-Bellman equation (4.7) is a concave function of α. The maximizing α is easily seen to be

$$(4.13) \qquad a(t, x) = \Gamma^{-1}(\mu - re) \left(-\frac{v_x(t, x)}{xv_{xx}(t, x)} \right),$$

and substitution of this into (4.7) leads to the equation

$$(4.14) \quad v_t(t, x) + rxv_x(t, x) - \frac{1}{2}(\mu - re)'\Gamma^{-1}(\mu - re) \frac{v_x^2(t, x)}{v_{xx}(t, x)} = 0.$$

For the utility function $U(x) = \frac{1}{p}x^p$, where $p < 1$, $p \neq 0$, Merton solved this equation by guessing that $v(t, x)$ should be of the form $f(t)x^p$ and then determining $f(t)$ to be the solution to the constant-coefficient linear equation

$$(4.15) \qquad f'(t) + rf(t) + \frac{1}{2}(\mu - re)'\Gamma^{-1}(\mu - re)\frac{f(t)}{1 - p} = 0,$$

with the terminal condition $f(T) = \frac{1}{p}$. The solution to (4.7) for general utility functions can be deduced from Karatzas, Lehoczky, Sethi & Shreve [4], and these formulas are provided in Karatzas & Shreve [6].

4.3 Market Portfolio

The optimal portfolio process $a(t, x)$ given in feedback form (4.13) on the agent's wealth is the product of a vector $\Gamma^{-1}(\mu - re)$, which does not depend on the agent's utility function nor wealth, and the positive scalar

$$-\frac{v_x(t, x)}{(xv_{xx}(t, x))},$$

which depends on both of these. We assume as in Subsection 2.3 that

$$(4.16) \qquad 0 \leq r < m_0 \triangleq \frac{e'\Gamma^{-1}\mu}{e'\Gamma^{-1}e}.$$

Then $e'\Gamma^{-1}(\mu - re)$ is positive, and we can define the vector

$$(4.17) \qquad \alpha_* \triangleq \frac{1}{e'\Gamma^{-1}(\mu - re)}\Gamma^{-1}(\mu - re)$$

whose components sum of 1. This is the vector of relative weights in the market portfolio. In terms of this vector, we construct a *mutual fund* whose price per share at the intial time is $M(0) = 1$ and whose price evolves according to the stochastic differential equation

$$(4.18) \qquad dM(t) = M(t)\alpha'_*(\mu dt + \sigma dB(t)).$$

We have the following result.

Separation Theorem. *Assume that σ is nonsingular and $0 \leq r < m_0$. Then an agent seeking to maximize expected utility of wealth at the final time can realize her optimal policy by investing only in the mutual fund whose price per share evolves according to (4.18) and in the money market. The composition of the mutual fund depends only on the asset parameters, not on the utility function nor wealth of the agent. The optimal division of the agent's wealth between the mutual fund and the money market depends on her utility function and her wealth.*

4.4 Capital Asset Pricing Theorem

Just as in the one-period model, the risk premia of individual stocks are related to the risk premium of the mutual fund of (4.18). Note first that

$$(4.19) \qquad dM(t)dM(t) = \alpha'_*\sigma\sigma'\alpha_* dt = \alpha'_*\Gamma\alpha_* dt,$$

which justifies calling $\alpha'_*\Gamma\alpha_*$ the *instantanuous variance* of the mutual fund. Similarly, for the i-th stock,

$$(4.20) \qquad dS_i(t)dM(t) = e'_i\sigma\sigma'\alpha_* dt = e'_i\Gamma\alpha_* dt,$$

and $e'_i\Gamma\alpha_*$ is called the *instantaneous covariance* of the i-th stock with the mutual fund. Finally, the risk premium for the mutual fund is $m_* - r \triangleq \alpha'_*\mu - r$ and the risk premium for the i-th stock is $\mu_i - r$. These quantities are related in the following way.

Capital Asset Pricing Theorem *Assume that σ is nonsingular and $0 \leq r < m_0$. The risk premium of an arbitrary stock i is related to the risk premium of the mutual fund by the formula*

$$(4.21) \qquad \mu_i - r = \beta_i(m_* - r),$$

where
$$\beta_i = \frac{e_i'\Gamma\alpha_*}{\alpha_*'\Gamma\alpha_*}.$$

PROOF: Let us define
$$\delta \triangleq e'\Gamma^{-1}(\mu - re),$$
so that (4.17) becomes
$$\alpha_* = \frac{1}{\delta}\Gamma^{-1}(\mu - re).$$
Then
$$\begin{aligned}
\beta_i(m_* - r) &= \frac{e_i'\Gamma\alpha_*}{\alpha_*'\Gamma\alpha_*}(\mu'\alpha_* - r) \\
&= \frac{\frac{1}{\delta}e_i'(\mu - re)}{\frac{1}{\delta^2}(\mu - re)'\Gamma^{-1}(\mu - re)}\left(\frac{1}{\delta}\mu'\Gamma^{-1}(\mu - re) - r\right) \\
&= \frac{\mu_i - r}{(\mu - re)'\Gamma^{-1}(\mu - re)}\left(\mu'\Gamma^{-1}(\mu - re) - r\delta\right) \\
&= \mu_i - r.
\end{aligned}$$

◇

References

[1] Itô, K., *Stochastic integral*, Proc. Imperial Acad. Tokyo **20** (1944), 519–512.

[2] Itô, K., *On a stochastic integral equation*, Proc. Imperial Acad. Tokyo **22** (1946), 32–35.

[3] Itô, K., *On stochastic differential equations*, Mem. Amer. Math. Soc. **4**, 1–51.

[4] Karatzas, I., Lehoczky, J., Sethi, S. & Shreve, S., *Explicit solution of a general consumption/investment problem*, Math. Operations Research **11** (1986), 261–294.

[5] Karatzas, I. & Shreve, S., *Brownian Motion and Stochastic Calculus*, Second Ed., Springer-Verlag, New York, 1991.

[6] Karatzas, I. & Shreve, S., *Mathematical Finance*, Springer-Verlag, New York, to appear.

[7] Lintner, J., *The valuation of risky assets and the selection of risky investment in stock portfolios and capital budgets*, Rev. Economics Statistics **47** (1965), 13–37.

[8] Markowitz, H., *Portfolio selection*, J. Finance **8** (1952), 77–91.

[9] Markowitz, H. *Mean-variance analysis in portfolio choice and capital markets*, Basil Blackwell, New York, 1987.

[10] Markowitz, H. *Portfolio selection: efficient diversification of investments*, Basil Blackwell, Cambridge, MA, 1991.

[11] Merton, R. C., *Lifetime portfolio selection under uncertainty: the continuous time case*, Rev. Econom. Statist. **51** (1969), 247–257.

[12] Merton, R. C., *Optimum consumption and portfolio rules in a continuous-time model*, J. Economic Theory **3** (1971), 373–413. *Erratum*, J. Economic Theory **6** (1973), 213–214.

[13] Merton, R. C., *Continuous Time Finance*, Basil Blackwell, Cambridge, 1990.

[14] Mirrlees, J., *Optimal accumulation under uncertainty: the case of stationary returns to investment*, In J. Drêze, *Allocation under Uncertainty: Equilibrium and Optimality*, 36–50, Wiley, New York, 1974.

[15] Mossin, J., *Equilibrium in a capital asset market*, Econometrica **34** (1966), 768–783.

[16] Oksendal, B., *Stochastic Differential Equations*, Third Ed., Springer-Verlag, New York, 1992.

[17] Sharpe, W. F., *Capital asset prices: a theory of market equilibrium under conditions of risk*, J. Finance **19** (1964), 425–442.

[18] Tobin, J., *Liquidity preference as behavior towards risk*, Rev. Financial Studies **25** (1958), 68–85.

DEPARTMENT OF MATHEMATICAL SCIENCES, CARNEGIE MELLON UNIVERSITY, PITTSBURGH, PA 15139
E-mail address: shreve@cmu.edu

An Introduction to Option Pricing and the Mathematical Theory of Risk

Marco Avellaneda

This review paper discusses the topic of option pricing with emphasis on modeling financial risk. The Black-Scholes formula is derived using the classical dynamic hedging argument. Dynamic hedging justifies the valuation of contingent claims based on the use of risk-neutral, as opposed to "frequential", probabilities. This still leaves open – even in the simplest case of stock option contracts – the issue of specifying the volatility parameter or other charateristics of the model describing the evolution of market prices. This "specification problem" leads us to the issue of economic uncertainty, or risk, the *raison d'etre* of derivatives markets and financial intermediation. Thus, the valuation of contingent claims under uncertainty goes far beyond the exercise of computing expected values of cash-flows. After a discussion of the classical principles of option risk-management using differential sensitivities ("Greeks"), I review some more recent proposals for modeling uncertainty. The idea is to consider, as a starting point, a spectrum of risk-neutral probability measures spanning a set of beliefs and to construct option spreads to reduce uncertainty. This last part of the paper draws on work with my collaborators (Avellaneda, Levy and Parás (1995), Avellaneda and Parás (1996) and Avellaneda, Friedman, Holmes and Samperi (1997)).

2000 *Mathematics Subject Classification.* Primary 91B28; Secondary 60G35.

Reprinted with permission from "An introduction to option pricing and the mathematical theory of risk," Marco Avellaneda, *Probability Theory and Applications*, IAS/Park City Mathematics Series, vol. 6, pp. 349–374, 1999, Amer. Math. Soc. and the Inst. Adv. Study.

[1]Courant Institute-NYU, 251 Mercer Street, New York, NY 10012, and Morgan Stanley & Co., 1585 Broadway, New York, NY 10036

E-mail address: avellane@cims.nyu.edu

Mathematical Finance has produced a true convergence of ideas between different intellectual and applied fields. Presently, we see a strong collaboration between mathematicians, economists and financial professionals in academia and the financial industry. As financial markets become increasingly competitive, the demand for sophisticated ideas and creative solutions increases. Markets have thus benefited from the input of mathematics and this trend shows no signs of abating.

In this paper, I present a scientific perspective of one of the cornerstones of Mathematical Finance, the theory of options pricing. This theory was initiated by Fisher Black and Myron Scholes in their seminal 1973 paper (Black and Scholes, 1973) and has grown tremendously since. It would be impossible for me to do justice to this subject in only one lecture. After giving a a general introduction, I will discuss some aspects that have interested me the most. Therefore, the paper covers a lot of standard material as well as more advanced research ideas which use non-linear partial differential equations and ideas from optimal control theory to model risk. For a general introduction to financial markets and financial mathematics, I recommend Hull (1994).

1. Investments and Probability

Perhaps a good starting point would be to analyze the situation of an individual which faces the decision of investing money. The most common investments are in stocks, bonds and cash, or short-term deposits, often through mutual funds and pension funds. Even a "no-investment" decision, such as keeping the money in the bank or spending it, is a form of asset allocation. The typical parameters used to evaluate investment decisions are **yield**, or expected return on investment, and **risk** (which is less well defined). In a very schematic form, an investment in a particular asset over a time-period Δt starting at time t gives rise to a **return**

$$\frac{X(t + \Delta t) - X(t)}{X(t)} = \frac{\Delta X(t)}{X(t)}$$

where $X(t)$ is the amount initially invested and $X(t+\Delta t)$ the value of the investment at time $t + \Delta t$. A very rough measure of the quality of an investment is obtained if we study a historical time-series of returns and calculate the empirical mean and variance for this investment:

$$\mu = \frac{1}{N \Delta t} \sum_{n=1}^{N} \frac{X(n \Delta t) - X((n-1) \Delta t)}{X((n-1) \Delta t)},$$

and

$$\sigma^2 = \frac{1}{(N-1) \Delta t} \sum_{n=1}^{N} \left(\frac{X(n \Delta t) - X((n-1) \Delta t)}{X((n-1) \Delta t)} - \mu \right)^2.$$

Historical (long-term) numbers for these quantities are, more or less, $\mu = 16\%$, $\sigma \approx 15\%$ for stocks, $\mu = 10\%$, and $\sigma = 12\%$ for bonds, in annual terms. However, these numbers vary and are strongly dependent on the "time-window" or sample size.

Although investment is an art as much as a science, rational investment decisions are often based on evaluating the risk and return of different strategies.

Risk-averse individuals will keep their wealth mostly in bonds or in cash (not under the mattress, though!). Investors willing to bear some market risk in exchange of higher returns might invest in stocks or long-term bonds. Long-term bonds are, in principle, riskless instruments, since they have a well-defined return if held to maturity. However, the value of a bond changes because there is an "opportunity cost" in holding a bond that yields less than other instruments, *e.g.* cash or shorter-term notes.

It is important to take into consideration the fact that investment strategies can change across time. For example, investment advisors recommend "aggressive" stock portfolios to their younger clients and more "stable" portfolios consisting mostly of bonds, as these approach retirement age. Another form of time-dependent investing is "timing the market" – attempting to buy at the low and sell at the high. This is the goal of all investors, but is certainly not easy to do! The concept of **dynamic investment decision** or **dynamic asset allocation** is extremely important in Finance and Financial Mathematics. This principle applies even more so to firms and corporations in their management of capital and business decisions.

Nobel prize winner Harry Markowitz was one of the the first to propose a coherent theory of investment based on the use of probabilities (Markowitz, 1991). In his approach, the investor considers the **mean** and the **covariance matrix** of the returns of different investment lines. For instance, in the universe of a stock index, a bond index and cash, the investor would consider the 3-vector (μ_1, μ_2, μ_3) and the **covariance matrix**

$$\begin{pmatrix} \sigma_1^2 & \sigma_1\sigma_2\rho_{12} & \sigma_1\sigma_3\rho_{13} \\ \sigma_1\sigma_2\rho_{12} & \sigma_2^2 & \sigma_2\sigma_3\rho_{23} \\ \sigma_1\sigma_3\rho_{13} & \sigma_2\sigma_3\rho_{23} & \sigma_3^2 \end{pmatrix}$$

By allocating his resources among the three different assets in different proportions, the investor can construct a "portfolio" with yield

$$\sum_{i=1}^{3} w_i\, \mu_i \tag{1}$$

and variance

$$\sum_{i=1}^{3} w_i^2\, \sigma_i^2 \;+\; 2\sum_{i<j} w_i\, w_j\, \sigma_i\, \sigma_j\, \rho_{ij}\,. \tag{2}$$

The investor can choose the "portfolio weights" w_1, w_2, w_3 so as to maximize returns (1) holding the variance (2) fixed at a desired level. Here, the variance of the portfolio is identified with the risk of the investment. This is a classical quadratic optimization problem that can be solved with elementary linear algebra. The procedure, called **mean-variance optimization**, gives a rationale for targeting the maximum mean return for a given risk level. Mean-variance optimization and it many generalizations are the most widely used tools in modern asset allocation and money management.

Implicit in Markowitz's portfolio theory is the idea that the returns are governed by probabilities. We thus (i) regard the outcome of investing as a random variable, and (ii) assume that these probabilities can be inferred from historical data. This raises the fundamental question of to what extent can historical, or **frequential**[2], probabilities predict future returns. Can statistical analysis applied to financial markets predict the future? It is clear that the answer is ultimately no. Unlike physical (mechanical) systems, markets are not "closed systems" determined completely by their initial conditions. The future behavior of the market may depend on information not available at present or by future events that we cannot control and even less model. Furthermore, the market's dependence on a set initial conditions is often murky. The point is that there is a distinction to be made between probability (the calculation of outocmes based on known odds) and risk-analysis (the estimation of outcomes in the presence of odds that are not known with certainty). John Maynard Keynes (Keynes, 1936) put it like this:

> By "uncertain" knowledge...I do not mean merely to distinguish what is known for certain from what is only probable. The game of roulette is not subject, in this sense, to uncertainty. The sense in which I am using the term is that in which the prospect of a European war is uncertain, or the price of copper and the rate of interest twenty years hence, or the obsolescence of a new invention... About these matters, there is no scientific basis on which to form any calculable probability whatever. We simply do not know!

At first glance, this profound statement might lead us to the erroneous conclusion that quantitative tools are only of marginal use in finance and and economics. A deeper analysis – and reality – show that this is not so. The existence of financial risk leads to the need for hedging or diversifying it, hence to more sophisticated investment vehicles. In particular, the appearance and phenomenal growth of **derivatives** has prompted completely new applications of mathematics and probability to finance.

Derivatives are contracts that derive their value from other instruments (stocks, bonds, etc). They include options, which are the main topic of this paper. Derivatives exist because there is volatility, or risk. The effect of derivatives is what economists call "financial intermediation" : the transfer of financial risk from some individuals to others. There are people who, for a price, are willing to assume the investment risks on behalf of other investors who are risk-averse, more or less like an insurance company insures your home against casualty for a fee. The trading of derivative contracts implies that risk itself can be priced and transferred among investors in the marketplace. It is precisely in the area of modeling risk and risk-management that mathematics has proven to be extremely effective.

2. Options

An option is a contract that allows the holder to buy or sell a financial asset at a fixed price in the future. Unlike a forward contract, which consists in a commitment by two counterparties to enter into a transaction at a future date, an option needs not be **exercised** – the holder of the option will use it only if this is profitable. A **call** is an option to buy an asset and a **put** is an option to sell it. An option contract specifies the **exercise price** and the **expiration date** of the contract. For

---

[2]Based on the observed frequency of past events.

example, the 145 IBM Call of March 1997 gives the holder the right to buy 100 IBM shares at $ 145 anytime between now and the third Friday in March. This option is called **American** because it can be exercised anytime before its expiration date. Options that can be exercised *only* at the expiration date are called **European**.

Options increase the spectrum of investments. For instance, an investor holding shares of a given stock can use options in several ways. Suppose that he thinks that the market is "overvalued" and is due for a correction. He could choose to "take profits" by selling all or part of his stock holdings and perhaps buying bonds or keeping the proceeds in cash. If he does this, however, he might loose the opportunity of a further rally. With this in mind, he could choose instead to buy a put option, which gives him the right to sell the stock for a period of time at a predetermined exercise price, and maintain his stock position. In this way, he preserves the investment opportunity while insuring himself against a drop in price. This strategy is usually called a **protective put**. Note however that the purchase of the put implies paying up-front for this insurance (perhaps by selling some stock) and that this protection is valid only for a period of time. The investor who implements a protective put strategy reduces a fraction of his potential gains by purchasing the option. Another common strategy is the so called **buy-write** strategy. This is done by investors that hold stock and and believe that the market will not experience much volatility and wish to derive some "income" from the position they hold. In this case, the investor sells ("writes") calls on the stock and receives the option premium. He then becomes obliged to deliver the stock if the calls are exercised. Since he owns stock, he can meet the potential obligation implied by the option contract. There are infinitely many strategies for investment using options; the two mentioned above being the simplest. Puts and calls are traded esseantially like any other financial asset.

A longstanding problem in Finance was the valuation of option contracts. Is there a relationship between the price of the underlying asset, on the one hand, and an option contract written on this asset? This problem was solved by Fisher Black and Myron Scholes in 1973. Let us assume a **stochastic model** for the evolution of the price of the underlying asset:

$$(3) \qquad \frac{dS_t}{S_t} = \sigma\, dZ_t + \mu\, dt,$$

where Z_t is a Brownian motion and σ, μ represent respectively the volatility and mean of the returns for investing in the stock. This model is just the "continuous-time" version of the "stochastic returns" model of the previous section. We shall be purposely vague about how σ and μ are determined for now. The prevailing short-term interest rate will be denoted by r.

We shall make the initial guess that the value V_t of a call on the stock is given by

$$(4) \qquad V_t = C(S_t, t)\,,$$

where $C(S, t)$ is a smooth function of S and t.

Suppose that an investor sells one call option and buys Δ shares of the underlying asset at time t. The change in the value of his holdings over the interval $(t, t+dt)$ is

$$(5) \qquad (-V_{t+dt} + \Delta S_{t+dt}) - (-V_t + \Delta S_t) = -dV_t + \Delta dS_t .$$

Using equations (3) and (4) and applying **Itô's formula**, we can express the variation of the portfolio in terms of the variation of call price in terms of the variation of the price of the underlying asset, viz.,

$$(6) \qquad dV_t = C_S(S_t, t)\, dS_t + C_t(S_t, t)\, dt + \frac{1}{2} \sigma^2 S^2 C_{SS}(S_t, t)\, dt ,$$

to leading order in dt. Substituting this expression into (5), we arrive at the following expression for the change in the portfolio value

$$(7) \qquad (-C_S(S_t, t) + \Delta)\, dS_t - \left(C_t(S_t, t) + \frac{1}{2}\sigma^2 S_t^2 C_{SS}(S_t, t) \right) dt .$$

If the number of shares held in the portfolio was

$$\Delta = C_S(S_t, t)$$

then the dS_t term would vanish in equation (7), rendering the the return of the portfolio non-volatile over the period of time $(t, t+dt)$ (to leading order in dt). I claim that the rate of return of this portfolio should be exactly equal to the short-term interest rate. Indeed, if this were not so, there would be an opportunity for making money at no risk - an **arbitrage opportunity**. In fact, by investing in this portfolio (or its "mirror image"), an investor would effectively be able to borrow money at the cheapest rate and lend it out at the more expensive rate. Professionals would take advantage of this and, through the forces of supply and demand, would eventually drive the option price to a level where the return on the option-stock portfolio would be equal to the interest rate for cash.[3] Since the value of the option-stock portfolio at time t is $-C(S_t, t) + \Delta S_t = -C(S_t, t) + S_t C_S(S_t, t)$, the absence of arbitrage implies that

$$C_t + \frac{\sigma^2}{2} S^2 C_{SS} = r(C - SC_S)$$

or

$$(8) \qquad C_t + \frac{\sigma^2}{2} S^2 C_{SS} + rSC_S - rC = 0 .$$

This is the **Black-Scholes partial differential equation**. To determine the function $C(S, T)$ we must specify boundary conditions. In the case of a call with expiration date T we have

---

[3] An arbitrage is defined as a transaction in which one buys an asset and immediately sells it realizing a riskless profit. One of the consequences of an (ideal) equilibrium economy is the absence of arbitrage opportunities, or, at least, of "obvious" arbitrage opportunities.

(9) $$C(S, T) = (S - K)^+ = max(S - K, 0),$$

where K is the strike price (X^+ represents the positive part of X). Indeed, if $S_T \leq K$, the option is worthless, and if $S_T > K$, the holder of the call can buy the underlying asset for K dollars and sell it at market price, making a profit of $S_T - K$.

For a European-style call (which can be exercised only at the date T), $C(S, t)$ is determined by solving the Cauchy problem for the Back-Scholes PDE with final condition (8). The explicit solution is known as the **Black-Scholes formula**:

(10) $$C(S, t; K, T; r, \sigma) = S N(d_1) - K e^{-r(T-t)} N(d_2),$$

where

$$d_1 = \frac{1}{\sigma \sqrt{T-t}} \ln\left(\frac{S}{K e^{r(T-t)}}\right) + \frac{1}{2} \sigma \sqrt{T-t}; \qquad d_2 = d_1 - \sigma \sqrt{T-t},$$

and

$$N(z) = \frac{1}{\sqrt{2\pi}} \int_{-\infty}^{z} e^{-\frac{y^2}{2}} dy.$$

A similar formula exists for European puts, replacing the final condition in (9) by $(K - S)^+$.

American-style options, which allow for exercise anytime before the maturity date, can be evaluated in a similar way. However, the possibility of **early exercise** makes the contract more valuable, in principle. The "early exercise premium", or survalue of American options with respect to Europeans, depends on the income stream that can be derived by holding the underlying asset (e.g. stock dividends) and cash (interest rate) instead of waiting to exercise the option. The rule of thumb here is that *there is an early exercise premium whenever the asset that is "bought" has non-zero income stream.* So far, we have not assumed that the stock pays dividends. Therefore, call options on such assets would have no exercise premium. Puts do have early exercise premium since selling the stock is like "buying cash" and the interest rate (income for holding cash) is positive. The income earned by exercising the put option and investing the proceeds in cash may exceed the "speculative" value of holding a put expecting the underlying price to drop further. Therein lies the value of early exercise for puts.[4]

In the case of **stock index** options such as OEX options traded at the Chicago Mercantile Exchange, we must take into account the fact that the stocks composing the Standard & Poor 500 Index pay dividends (currently slightly below 2% on an annualized basis); therefore both puts and call have early exercise premium. It is well-known the value of an American S&P500 call (OEX contract of the CBOE) exceeds the value of the corresponding European contract (SPX).

---

[4]The Black-Scholes equation for assets that pay "continuous" dividends at a rate d, is analogous to (8). The only difference is that the drift term $r S C_S$ is replaced by $(r - d) S C_S$.

To value American options, the idea is that we should look for a function $C(S, t)$ that satisfies the Black-Scholes equation in regions of the (S, t)-plane where the option should not be exercised and provide additional boundary conditions along the region corresponding to price levels where the option should be exercised. One way to arrive at this region is to impose the additional conditions on option prices that should hold in the case of American-style options:

(11) $$C(S, t) \geq (S - K)^+ \text{ (calls)}, \quad P(S, t) \geq (K - S)^+ \text{ (puts)},$$

since the option is worth as least as much as what you would get by exercising it immediately. These constraints give rise to an **obstacle problem**, or differential inequality, for the Black-Scholes equation which can be solved numerically. The free boundary arising in this problem corresponds to the boundary of the "optimal exercise" region for the holder – the option should be exercised whenever equality holds in (11).

The free-boundary conditions for American options at the boundary of the exercise region are

$$C(S_t, t) = S_t - K, \quad \frac{\partial C(S_t, t)}{\partial t} = +1, \quad \text{(calls)}$$

(12) $$P(S_t, t) = K - S_t, \quad \frac{\partial P(S_t, t)}{\partial t} = -1. \quad \text{(puts)}$$

These are classical first-order contact free-boundary conditions for obstacle problems encountered in PDE texts.[5]

The story only begins here. The Black-Scholes PDE and its variants are used to value more general contracts which have payoffs depending on the value of another traded asset. Such contracts are generically called **contingent claims** in the Mathematical Finance literature. They include the class of **exotic options**, traded in the inter-bank market, which can have practically any conceivable payoff structure. The end-users of exotic options are banks, corporations and sophisticated investors that invest in "tailor-made" derivatives with special cash-flow structures especially suited to their needs. "Plain vanilla" stock options, on the other hand, are mostly traded in exchanges such as CBOE, CME, AMEX, etc., and over-the-counter as well.

3. Risk-Neutral Probabilities

Suppose that a contract gives rise to a series of cash-flows at different dates $T_1 < T_2 < ... < T_N$ and that these cash-flows are represented by functions $F_i(S_{T_i})$, $i = 1, 2..., N$. An argument similar to the one of the previous paragraph shows that the value of the corresponding contingent claim is $V_t = V(S_t, t)$, where $V(S, t)$ satisfies the PDE

$$\frac{\partial V}{\partial t} + \frac{1}{2} \sigma^2 S^2 \frac{\partial^2 V}{\partial S^2} + r S \frac{\partial V}{\partial S} - r V =$$

---
[5] These boundary conditions can be derived also from purely financial considerations (Avellaneda, NYU course notes).

$$(13) \qquad -\sum_{i:\, t< T_i} F_i(S)\,\delta(t-T_i)\,,$$

with $V(S, T_N + 0) = 0$. This formula also applies to option portfolios, i.e. to bundles of options held (long or short) by an investor.

The Black-Scholes PDE has a fundamental probabilistic interpretation. The correspondence between PDEs and probabilities via the Fokker-Plank formalism yields

$$(14) \qquad V(S_t, t) = \mathbf{E}\left\{\sum_{i:\, t< T_i} e^{-r(T_i - t)} F(S_{T_i})\,\big|\, I_t\right\},$$

where S_t is the diffusion process governed by the stochastic differential equation

$$(15) \qquad \frac{dS_t}{S_t} = \sigma\, dZ_t + r\, dt$$

and $\mathbf{E}\{\bullet \mid I_t\}$ represents the conditional expectation with respect to the σ-algebra generated by $\{Z_s,\, s \le t\}$.

If you compare equation (15) with the proposed statistics for the returns of the index (3), you will notice that the mean returns (drifts) are different. Indeed, in the latter equation, the mean return over the period $(t, t + \Delta t)$ is $r\,\Delta t$ instead of $\mu\,\Delta t$ (the "subjective" annual return on investment for the stock). Thus, the Black-Scholes theory tells us that the value of an option (or a more general contingent claim) is equal to the **expected future cash-flows**, calculated under a certain probability measure assigned to the future paths for the price of the underlying asset. This measure, however, is not the "subjective probability" that we started with!

Let us give a concrete example. Suppose that the interest rate is 5%, that the volatility of a stock XYZ is 16% and that it is expected to appreciate in price by 40% annually. The Black-Scholes value of a European-style option to buy this stock at today's price in 180 days is 5.75% of the price of the stock. This result is totally independent of the rate of return on the price of the stock (we assume that no dividends will be paid). On the other hand, the expected value of the cash-flows, $max\,(S_T - K)^+$, using 40% returns (equation (3)) is a whopping 21.46%. From an investor's point of view, this result may seem paradoxical, since the higher the expected returns, the higher the probability of profiting from holding the call. Therefore, he should be willing to pay more than 5.75% for the option. This argument, based on "frequential probabilities", is nevertheless wrong.

The explanation lies in the concept of dynamic hedging. Under the Black-Scholes assumptions, the holder of $\Delta_t = C_S(S_t, t)$ shares of stock and $C(S_t, t) - C_S(S_t, t) \cdot S_t$ dollars in a money-market account has a portfolio worth $C(S_t, t)$ dollars at time t. In the period $(t, t + dt)$, the change in the value of the shares plus the interest accrued in the cash account add up to the change in the function $C(S_t, t)$, because

$$dC(S_t, t) = C_S(S_t, t)\, dS_t + \left(C_t(S_t, t) + \frac{\sigma^2 S^2}{2} C_{SS}(S_t, t) \right) dt$$

$$= \Delta_t\, dS_t + r\, (\, C(S_t, t) - C_S(S_t, t) \cdot S_t\,)\, dt\, ,$$

by virtue of the Black-Scholes PDE. Therefore, by successively adjusting the number of shares, Delta after each trading period, it is possible to maintain a net portfolio value equal to $C(S_t, t)$. At the expiration date, the value of the portfolio is exactly equal to $C(S_T, T) = (S_T - K)^+$ which is the market value of the option.

The conclusion is that if you have an initial reserve at time t of $C(S_t, t)$ dollars, you can implement a dynamic trading strategy that generates a return identical to the one of the option at the expiration date. This strategy is called **option replication**, or **dynamic hedging**.

Referring back to the example, the point is that an individual that can engage in dynamic hedging, does not care if investing 21.46% of price of the underlying stock in the call will make him break even "in the long run". The option can be "manufactured" with only 5.75%, so why pay more? Conversely, if the expected return on the stock was less than 5% and the option was priced as a "statistical bet" instead of using Black-Scholes, the investor would probably buy but definitely not sell at that price! The probability measure on price paths (S_t) implied by (15) is called a **risk-neutral probability** because it has the property that the option premium corresponds to the value of a "statistical bet" (expectation) under this modified probability.

The Black-Scholes formula represents the *cost of of replicating the option*, rather than the expected value of the payoff under a subjective probability (as in a game of chance). It is a consequence of the absence of arbitrage opportunities: if the assumptions of the model are correct (volatility, interest rate) then if the market traded at another price, this would give rise to a profit at no risk. One would simply buy or sell the option and offset the risk by dynamic hedging.

An important caveat at this point is the ability of investors to engage in dynamic hedging in practice, which involves actively trading in the underlying security over the lifetime of the option. As some readers might know, the possibility of dynamic hedging is only available to professional option dealers, due to the large costs of execution, transaction costs, etc. However, option dealers, who compete for customers in the marketplace, estimate the cost of managing an option inventory using Black-Scholes and make prices accordingly. Since prices must be competitive with other dealers, they reflect the business costs of dynamic hedgers (risk-neutral valuation) rather than the expected value of the option payoff under subjective probabilities.

Let me also mention here that the use of risk-neutral probabilities for pricing contingent claims goes far beyond Black-Scholes theory. Harrison and Kreps (1979) formulated a general theory of **no-arbitrage pricing**, often called **Arbitrage Pricing Theory** (APT) which can be summarized as follows:

Suppose that a market has no arbitrage opportunities. Then, there exists a (risk-neutral) probability measure P defined on the paths of prices of traded assets such that

$$(16) \quad P_t = \mathbf{E}^P \left\{ e^{-\int_t^T r_s \, ds} P_T + \sum_{t < T_i < T} e^{-\int_i^T r_s \, ds} C_{T_i} \mid I_t \right\}.$$

Here, $P_\bullet$ represents the price of a traded asset, C_{T_i} represent cash-flows which are paid to the holder of the asset at different dates and r_s is a short-term interest rate. The measure P is called a **martingale measure** in the Mathematical Finance literature.

The significance of APT is that, *some* probability measure with the property (15), i.e a risk-neural probability, *must* exist in the absence of arbitrage. In other words, if such a measure would not exist, we would be able to find, in principle, a dynamic trading strategy that generates profits with no risk. Equation (15) can also be viewed as a formula for evaluating the price of securities, and it applies to all classes of financial assets. A complete discussion of the implications of APT is beyond the scope of this lecture. I recommend, for instance, Duffie (1992) for an in-depth discussion of this subject.

4. Risk-Management Using the "Greeks"

This section discusses practical uses of the Black-Scholes formula or, more generally, the Black-Scholes PDE, as a tool for for hedging an options portfolio. For simplicity, we consider a "pure" situation of a stock which pays no dividends between now and the expiration dates of the options.

Recall that the parameters that enter the Black-Scholes formula are (i) the exercise price, or strike price, K, (ii) the expiration date, T, (iii) the price of the underlying asset, S, (iv) the interest rate, r, and (v) the volatility, σ. Of these five parameters, the first four are observable at any given time (r is known for expiration dates which are less than 1 year away). In contrast, the volatility of the underlying asset is not directly observable. For each value of the volatilit y parameter we obtain a different theoretical option value. Conversely, it is easy to show that to each possible option value (in the range of the Black-Scholes formula) corresponds a unique volatility parameter. This is a consequence of the fact that the Black-Scholes option premium is a strictly increasing function of σ. The **implied volatility** of a traded call is, by definition, the value of σ that solves the equation

$$C(S, t; K, T; r, \sigma) = \text{ market price of the call},$$

where the left-hand side represents the BS theoretical value, with the same definition applying to puts.

The market price of the option defines its implied volatility, which is the volatility that "makes Black-Scholes true". We will assume henceforth that σ is the implied volatility. The main use of the Black-Scholes formula is to control the exposure of an options portfolio to different types of market risk. We already introduced the parameter Delta, which is the derivative of the portfolio value with respect to changes in S:

$$\Delta = \frac{\partial V(S, t)}{\partial S}.$$

Here, V represents the total value of the portfolio, i.e. the sum of the values of all the options in the portfolio). The portfolio Delta is the algebraic sum of the Deltas corresponding to each option computed with its own implied volatility. The fundamental result of BS is that a position in $-\Delta$ shares of the underlying asset renders the position "market-neutral" — the value of the portfolio will vary less than the stock price by an order of magnitude (dt rather than $dt^{1/2}$). Moreover, the Black-Scholes theory implies that the dt term is equal to the cost of funding the position at the riskless rate. (If funding is taken into account the variation of the total portfolio value is therefore $O(t^{3/2})$ - negligible even after adding all the variations over the life of the option).

For example, a 180-day European at-the-money call ($K = S$) with $r = 5\%$ and $\sigma = 16\%$ has a delta of 0.6086. This means that to hedge a short position in 100 calls (or, equivalently, one option to buy 100 shares), one should buy 60.86 shares of the underlying stock (say, 60 shares). Similarly, the holder of an option to buy 100 shares will be hedged by short-selling 60 shares. The same philosophy applies to option portfolios. At least in theory, Delta-hedging is a way of protecting an option portfolio against moves in the price of the underlying asset.

An important observation concerning **delta-hedged** option positions is that the distinction between owning a call and owning a put disappears completely! Indeed, the identity

$$(S - K)^+ - (K - S)^+ = S - K$$

implies that

$$C(S, t; K, T) - P(S, t; K, T) = S - K e^{-r(T-t)},$$

where the functions in the left-hand side of the equation represent the value of a call and a put with same strike and expiration date. The right-hand side can be interpreted as the fair value of a contract to buy the stock at K dollars at date T. This result is called **put-call parity**. It states that a put can be "synthesized" with a portfolio consisting of a call, one share held short, and a note with face value K. Differentiating this equation, we obtain obtain a relation between the Deltas of puts and calls:

$$\Delta_{call} - \Delta_{put} = 1.$$

The point is that unhedged option positions represent leveraged bets on the direction of the market and hedged positions are "non-directional". Delta-hedged option positions stand to profit or lose according to the behavior of volatility or interest rates.

The second-derivative of the BS price with respect to the spot price

$$\Gamma = \frac{\partial^2 V(S, t)}{\partial S^2},$$

is an important sensitivity for practical Delta-hedging. Gamma measures the change in Delta per change in the value of the underlying asset. This sensitivity does not enter the derivation of the Black-Scholes theory, which assumes continuous adjustments in Delta. However, in real life, adjustments to the hedge portfolio are done at discrete dates usually in response to changes in the price of the underlying asset). Discrete hedging gives rise to "hedge slippage": the option is no longer perfectly replicated an there are gains and losses at each time (relative to the Black-Scholes) fair value. The Gamma of an option (put or call) is given explicitly by

$$\Gamma = \frac{1}{S\sqrt{2\pi\sigma^2}} e^{-\frac{d_1^2}{2}}.$$

It is a positive quantity: the Delta of an option increases as the stock price increases. The graph of a hedged (long) option as a function of S is convex and has a minimum at the current spot price. It is easy to see that the graph at time $t+dt$ is also convex but it is uniformly lower in value for all S. This means that the holder of a hedged long option position will make money if $|S_{t+dt} - S_t|$ turns out to be large and will lose if the change in value of the stock is small. If we consider the reverse position, i.e., a short option hedged with the Black-Scholes delta, we see that the graph is now concave. Small stock moves give rise to a profit and large stock moves give rise to a loss, due to the negative convexity. Market professionals refer to the former situation as being "long Gamma" and the latter as being "short Gamma". This concept, like Delta, applies at the portfolio level. The Gamma of the portfolio is just the net Gamma obtained by adding all the option Gammas weighted by their sign (long/short) and by the number of contracts. Needless to say, positions with large Gammas are risky because they are difficult to hedge without introducing too much error with respect to theory. The size of Gamma, measures, in a sense, the risk exposure to missing the hedge by trading discretely. Managing Gamma is achieved by buying or selling options so as to to keep this sensitivity under prescribed limits, therefore limiting the risk of "hedge-slippage".

Gamma also becomes important when we take into account **transaction costs** incurred by hedging dynamically. For instance, traders that are short Gamma have to buy stock when its price goes up and sell when the price drops (always a painful proposition). On the other hand, hedging a long-Gamma position involves selling stock as the market rallies and buying when it drops. This creates a noticeable asymmetry in the expected cost of replicating long and short Gamma positions. In general, dynamic hedging in the presence of transaction costs is expensive and erodes traders' profits. A "compromise" must therefore be made between avoiding transaction costs and limiting the contract's risk-exposure. This subject leads to very interesting mathematics and is the object of numerous studies (Leland(1985), Davis, Panas and Zariphopolou (1993), Avellaneda and Parás (1994), Taleb(1997)).

Another important sensitivity of the BS equation is

$$\Theta = \frac{\partial V(S,t)}{\partial t},$$

known as the **time-decay**. It is of crucial importance in the risk-management of an options portfolio, because it tells the trader by how much the value of the position will change if the spot price stays the same. Theta and Gamma have opposite signs, as we argued above. We can see this more precisely by making the change of variables

$$\tilde{V} = e^{-rt} V \quad , \quad \tilde{S} = e^{-rt} S,$$

which expresses values in constant dollars, removing the effect of interest rates. In terms of these variables, the Black-Scholes PDE becomes

$$\frac{\partial \tilde{V}}{\partial t} + \frac{1}{2}\sigma^2 \tilde{S}^2 \frac{\partial^2 \tilde{V}}{\partial \tilde{S}^2} = 0,$$

or

$$\tilde{\Theta} = -\frac{1}{2}\sigma^2 \tilde{S}^2 \tilde{\Gamma},$$

where we use tildes to emphasize that values are computed in constant dollars. This relation can be rewritten as

$$\tilde{V}(t+dt) - \tilde{V}(t) \propto -\frac{1}{2}\tilde{\Gamma} \cdot \mathbf{E}\left\{\left(\tilde{S}(t+dt) - \tilde{S}(t)\right)^2\right\},$$

where we identified the variance with the square of the spot price increment. Thus, *the BS equation expresses a proportionality relation between time-decay, convexity and volatility.*

Let us illustrate this with a numerical example. The change in value a 180-day at-the-money call with $\sigma = 16\%$ over one day expressed in constant dollars is approximately $\Delta V = 0.01\%$ of the value of the underlying asset. This is what the holder of the option will lose over one day if the price of the underlying remains unchanged. On the other hand, the change in Delta for a 1% move in spot is 0.0357. A volatility of 16% represents approximately a $(\Delta \tilde{S})^2$ of $16 \times 16/365 = 0.71$ in percentage terms. Multiplying this by 0.5×0.0357 yields 0.012%. This is what the holder of the option expects to make if the spot price changes by one standard deviation.

As one might expect, the sensitivity of the BS value with respect to the volatility parameter plays a crucial role. This sensitivity is known as **Vega**:[6]

$$Vega = \frac{\partial V}{\partial \sigma}.$$

Traders often use other higher-order sensitivities of the Black-Scholes formula to analyze the risk of an option portfolio, such as

$$\frac{\partial^2 V}{\partial S \partial \sigma} = \frac{\partial \Delta}{\partial \sigma} = \frac{\partial (Vega)}{\partial S},$$

and

$$\frac{\partial^2 V}{\partial \sigma^2} = \frac{\partial (Vega)}{\partial \sigma}.$$

The intuition behind these higher-order sensitivities is probably mastered only by the most seasoned option professionals. For example, $\frac{\partial \Delta}{\partial \sigma}$ represents the change in the Delta, the amount of shares of the underlying asset to be held in the hedge under a change in the options implied volatility with all the other parameters

---

[6]The derivative of the stock price with respect to σ is now sometimes referred to as κ (Kappa), with the advantage that the latter is a Greek letter. Vega appears to be the terminology used by option traders in the "early days" and is currently widely used. The name Vega, on the other hand, corresponds to the name of a Chevrolet automobile model sold in this country in the 1970's, a somewhat amusing/nostalgic coincidence.

held constant. Another parameter often used to manage option positions is the sensitivity with respect to the short-term interest rate,

$$\rho = \frac{\partial V}{\partial r}.$$

Although, the effect of ρ is less important in general, considerations about changes in funding rates can be important in countries where interest rates are very high and/or fluctuate considerably over short periods of time.

By and large, option portfolio risk-management consists in neutralizing, or at least keeping with reasonable limits, the above-mentioned sensitivities in a portfolio. Thus, an options dealer will manage his Delta (usually set to zero), as well as Gamma, Theta, Vega and Rho. Except for Delta, which is managed by trading in the underlying asset, risk-management of other "Greeks" involves buying and selling options so as to keep the net sensitivities near target levels. This includes taking positions in these higher-order sensitivities as well. For example, a trader can gain exposure to a rise in implied volatility by having a positive-Vega portfolio for instance, but at the same time being neutral in Delta, Gamma and Rho. An obvious but important consideration is the opposite sign of Theta and Gamma – the "buyer of convexity" gets exposed naturally to time-decay, while "time is on the side" of the seller of convexity if the market remains quiet.

The management of volatility risk (and, in some cases, interest rate risk) of an options book is a highly non-trivial matter. Among other things, the implied volatilities of options with different maturities and strikes are generally not equal. Managing volatility risk requires therefore monitoring the joint movement of a "matrix" of implied volatilities

$$\sigma(K_i, T_j), \quad ij = 1, 2\ldots$$

where K_i and T_i represent different strikes and expiration dates. This implies frequent adjustments of the option portfolio to keep the Greek sensitivities in line and to design profitable option positions according to traders' expectations on the future behavior of volatilities and rates. In other words, professional option traders must evaluate the risk-return characteristics of **option spreads**, or different option combinations, in terms of volatility and interest-rate forecasts, price ranges, dividend pay-outs, liquidity of different contracts, etc. Natanberg (1988) and Taleb(1977) contain lucid analyses of option strategies from a practical point of view.

5. Uncertain Volatility Models

From a fundamental point of view, the assumption that volatility is constant and the use of Vega-hedging as a risk-management practice have several shortcomings. Specifically:

- The Black-Scholes model, (15), assumes implicitly that variations or the spot price are *homogeneous*, i.e. that price returns have the same statistics at different dates;

- Vega gives the sensitivity of an option only for *small changes* in the implied volatility;

- Vega-hedging is inconsistent with the fact that options with the same maturity and different strikes usually trade at different implied volatilities.

In mathematical parlance, one would say that Greek hedging corresponds to a "linearized" approach to managing risk. In particular, it is not expected to work in the event of a large move, or crash, or to a regime shift, in which market conditions change dramatically after some event.

The constant volatility assumption is actually inconsistent with APT. In fact, if two options with the same expiration date trade at different implied volatilities, which is often the case, then the "spot volatility" of the underlying asset

$$\frac{dS_t}{S_t} = \sigma_t \, dZ_t + r \, dt$$

cannot be constant, or even a deterministic function of time. If σ_t was constant or $\sigma_t = \sigma_0(t)$ where $\sigma_0(\cdot)$ is deterministic, at least one of the two options would be mispriced by the market. However, there is ample evidence that demonstrates that a difference in implied volatilities does not necessarily imply an arbitrage opportunity. Instead, it is currently believed that the implied volatility **smile** and **skew** observed in many markets, reflect traders' inhomogeneous volatility expectations. Traders estimate the cost of option replication conditionally on future events such as changes in market conditions, changes in the liquidity of the underlying asset, etc. There is no reason why the constant-volatility/lognormal assumptions of Black-Scholes should hold: only the *consequence* of the theory – the consequences of no-arbitrage – should hold, once a probabilistic model is specified.

Here, mathematics comes to the rescue in a big way. According to the No-Arbitrage Theorem of §2, no-arbitrage implies the existence of a probability measure on paths $\{S_t\}$ such that the prices of traded assets are *simultaneously* reproduced by taking expectations with respect to the same probability. The only restriction, dictated by APT, is that this probability should be such that that prices computed in constant dollars are martingales. By making the volatility σ_t a random process, or a function of S_t and t, for example, we can expect to satisfy the APT equation with a single probability measure for $S_\bullet$ and thus obtain therefore a more accurate valuation of option positions.

This prompted researchers to look for specifications of the volatility process that would reconcile Black-Scholes theory with observed behavior of implied volatility of option markets. One proposal has been to make the spot volatility a stochastic process, which may be statistically correlated with price shocks. Hull and White (1987) showed, among other things, that a negative correlation between volatility shocks and price shocks (as the market drops volatility rises) reproduces qualitatively (but, in my own experience, not quantitatively) the "volatility skew" observed in equity options markets. Typically, in these markets, out-of-the-money puts have a higher implied volatility than out-of-the-money calls. Other proposals for volatility modeling (Engle (1984), Noh *et al* (1994)) use **conditionally heteroskedastic models** (the ARCH-GARCH family) to model the behavior of the underlying asset. However, the use of stochastic volatility models or ARCH models raises the important problem of model specification (by econometric analysis or otherwise) and the relevance of historical data for managing future risk. Another critique of stochastic volatility models, with which Keynes would probably not disagree, is that the differential sensitivities with respect to the parameters of these more complicated models may not provide protection against large moves in the market. Making the model more elaborate may reflect better current options prices quoted in the market but still misses the notion of risk, or uncertainty about the model itself.

In an attempt to remedy these shortcomings of parametric models, I present here a new approach for managing volatility risk. This approach is based on the premise that we have little knowledge of the spot volatility process and that it may be preferable to use the concept of "uncertainty" or *lack of information*, rather than an elaborate specification the statistics of the volatility.

Let us assume that we have determined a **confidence interval** for the spot volatility process $\{\sigma_t, 0 \leq t \leq T\}$, without going into details of how this interval, or "cone" was obtained. We postulate therefore that the process of conditional volatility for the price of the underlying asset satisfies the inequalities

$$(17) \qquad \sigma_{min}(t) \leq \sigma_t \leq \sigma_{max}(t),$$

where $0 < \sigma_{min} < \sigma_{max}$ are deterministic functions. We shall consider the collection of all probability specifications on the underlying price process that satisfy the volatility bounds. Given this range of uncertainty, we cannot provide a single price for any given contract whose value is sensitive to volatility. Instead there is continuum of possible prices. We shall focus on the extreme model values, or upper and lower bounds on prices, which correspond to the **worst-case scenario replication costs** for short and long positions, respectively.

In this setting, the problem of calculating extreme prices is isomorphic to a stochastic control problem in which the volatility is the the control variable. Extremal prices can be computed using the Bellman dynamic programming principle. More specifically, the partial differential equation for the upper bound has the form

$$(18) \qquad \frac{\partial V}{\partial t} + \Phi_0 \left[\frac{S^2}{2} \frac{\partial^2 V}{\partial S^2} \right] + rS \frac{\partial V}{\partial S} - rV = - \sum_{i:\, t < T_i} F_i(S)\, \delta(t - T_i),$$

where

$$(19) \qquad \Phi_0\left[X\right] = \begin{cases} \sigma_{min}^2 X, & X < 0, \\ \sigma_{max}^2 X, & X \geq 0. \end{cases}$$

This equation constitutes a simple but important modification of the Black-Scholes PDE; it reduces to the latter when there is no uncertainty ($\sigma_{min} = \sigma_{max}$). The PDE (17) is known as the Uncertain Volatility Model (UVM) (Avellaneda, Levy and Paras, 1995). The Delta of the UVM equation can be used to immunize the portfolio against market risk, in the following sense: if the agent uses this Delta and starts with the reserves calculated with the UVM equation he or she will break even if the worst-case volatility scenario is realized and will otherwise make a profit (use less reserves than budgeted). This idea is known as a **dominating strategy** in Mathematical Finance. If the agent budgets initially less reserves that the UVM value, the strategy may lose money but losses are limited to the difference between the BS and UVM premia. It is intuitively clear that this method of valuation is robust with respect to volatility sepcification. However, this protection does not come for free, since UVM requires more reserves than Black-Scholes using, say, the center of the band as volatility parameter. In particular, UVM can generate option prices that are not competitive with those of a dealers using a volatility inside the band.

The difference between upper and lower extremal prices, or between the extremes and Black Scholes using the center of the band (16), is due to the fact that the new valuation provides protection against *all volatility paths in the band*. This gap in prices reflects our uncertainty about future volatility paths. One way to narrow this "uncertainty gap " is is to consider options as a partial alternative to dynamic hedging. An extension of UVM, which I describe now, provides a rational approach for doing this (Avellaneda and Parás, 1996). The method consists in using the UVM equation to price "packages" formed by the contingent claim of interest combined with traded options. Thus, the idea is to perform the UVM analysis on the new package package rather than on the original claim. Since the options can be bought/sold in the market we can concentrate on delta-hedging only the net exposure. Usually, this proposal gives rise to narrower price bands while, at the same time, hedges that perform well under a broad range of volatility scenarios.

Let me show how this works. Assume that there are M traded options in the market, with payoffs G_j, $j = 1, 2, ... M$ and expiration dates $\tau_1, \tau_2, ...\tau_M$. Assume also that each option trades at a price C_j respectively. If an agent sells the derivative security represented by the cash-flows $\{F_j\}$ and buys a portfolio of λ_1 contracts of the first option, λ_2 contracts of the second, and so forth, the amount of cash needed to hedge this position under the worst-case scenario is

$$\sup_P \mathbf{E} \left\{ \sum_{i=1}^N e^{-rT_i} F(S_{T_i}) - \sum_{j=1}^M \lambda_j e^{-r\tau_j} G(S_{\tau_j}) \right\},$$

where the sup is taken over all probabilities with volatility paths in the band (16). If we add to this the market price of the options portfolio, we obtain

$$(20) \quad V(\lambda_1, ... \lambda_M) = \sup_P \mathbf{E} \left\{ \sum_{i=1}^N e^{-rT_i} F(S_{T_i}) - \sum_{j=1}^M \lambda_j e^{-r\tau_j} G(S_{\tau_j}) \right\} + \sum_{j=1}^M \lambda_j C_j.$$

$V(\lambda_1, ... \lambda_M)$ can be interpreted as the worst-case scenario reserves necessary to hedge the contingent claim using a partial "static" options hedge and Delta-hedging the residual. If we minimize $V(\lambda_1, ... \lambda_M)$ over all combinations of the variables, we will have found the cheapest hedge using options that immunizes the portfolio over all possible volatility paths inside the band. This hedge will be represented by a vector of **option hedge-ratios** $(\lambda_1^*, ... \lambda_M^*)$. It is noteworthy that the function $V(\lambda_1, ... \lambda_M)$ is strictly convex, so that if a minimum exists, it must be unique. Moreover, the probability measure P^* which gives the worst-case scenario with these hedge-ratios satisfies the market price conditions

$$(21) \quad C_j = \mathbf{E} \left\{ e^{-r\tau_j} G(S_{\tau_j}) \right\}, \quad j = 1, 2, ... M.$$

To see this, it suffices to use the first-order conditions for the minimum in (19) taking into account that the partial derivatives of V satisfy

$$(22) \quad \frac{\partial V(\lambda_1, ...\lambda_M)}{\lambda_j} = C_j - \mathbf{E}^{P^*}\left\{ e^{-r\tau_j} G(S_{\tau_j}) \right\}, \quad j = 1, 2, ... M,$$

where P^* is the measure that realizes the supremum. In particular, the new worst-case scenario probability produces a **calibrated model**, matching the prices of all the traded options.

Let us illustrate the theory with an example. Suppose that the stock price is $S_0 = \$100$, and that $r = 5\%$. Suppose that a 180-day option on this stock with strike $K_1 = 100$ is trading with an implied volatility of 16%. Moreover, you expect the " spot" volatility σ_t to vary between the limits $\sigma_{min} = 8\%$ and $\sigma_{max} = 24\%$ How could you use this information to price and hedge an option with a strike $K_2 = 115$ expiring in 160 days?

In this problem, we have $M = N = 1$. The market price of the at-the-money option with $\sigma = 0.16$ is $5.75. Optimizing the function $V(\lambda_1)$ with $F_1(S) = (S-115)^+$, $G_1(S) = (S-100)^+$ and $C_1 = 5.75$ yields, for the short position,

$$\lambda_1 = 0.302, \quad V(\lambda_1) = 1.97, \quad \Delta = 0.06.$$

This means that optimal hedge consists in buying 0.302 at-the-money options for each 115-option sold. The UVM Delta hedge for the residual portfolio is 0.06, i.e., 6% of the notional amount of shares in the contract. The quantity $V(\lambda_1) = 1.97$ represents the cost of this hedge, which is broken down as follows: $5.75 \times 0.302 = \$1.73$ invested in the option hedge and $1.97 - 1.73 = \$0.24$ invested in reserves for dynamic hedging. We can compare this with the Black-Scholes premium with different values of σ. For $\sigma = 0.16$ we have a BS value of $ 0.75, which is much less than $V(\lambda_1) = 1.97$. On the other hand , if your worst-case fears materialize and the term volatility turned out to be 24% instead of 16%, the correct premium should have been $2.24! This is greater than the optimized value, 1.97. The price could be narrowed further if there were more options to add to the mix!

This hedging technique, called **Lagrangian Uncertain Volatility Model** ($\lambda-UVM$), can be used to systematically construct option hedges for exotic options and other non-standard derivatives which are more reliable with respect to changes in the volatility environment. They provide an alternative to hedging volatility risk using Vega and other σ-related Greeks. From a theoretical point of view, we see how the introduction of several risk-neutral measures (through a band of volatility paths) can be used to eliminate volatility risk by selecting a package of options that gives rise to a less risky net position. In my own opinion, this tradeoff between delta-hedging and buying option protection up-front is the key for managing volatility risk.

6. Relative Entropy: Combining Volatility Uncertainty with A-priori Beliefs

In this section, I sketch a generalization $\lambda - UVM$ which attempts to narrow the lack of information inherent in assumption (16) (Avellaneda, Friedman, Holmes, Samperi, 1997).

Let us assume now that we have a definite belief about the behavior of forward volatility, based upon historical analysis, expectations about future option prices, etc. This belief is expressed mathematically as a choice for the "most likely" risk-neutral probability measure, P_0, that will be realized, *e.g.*,

$$(23) \qquad \frac{dS_t}{S_t} = \sigma_0(S_t, t) \, dZ_t + r \, dt \, ,$$

where $\sigma_0(S, t)$ is a given function of (S, t). We now wish to price and hedge contingent claims taking into account also volatility risk – the possibility that the realized volatility will be differ from our a-priori belief σ_0. A natural approach is to compute a worst case-scenario probability measure, as before, introducing a penalization for probabilities which are "far away" from the prior measure (22) in some norm or distance and which we consider therefore unlikely to occur.

It turns out that a convenient notion of distance for this purpose is the **Kullback Leibler relative entropy distance**, given by

$$(24) \qquad \mathcal{E}(P; P_0) := \mathbf{E}^P \left\{ log\left(\frac{dP}{dP_0}\right) \right\} \, ,$$

where $\frac{dP}{dP_0}$ is the Radon-Nykodym derivative of P with respect to P_0. The KL relative entropy is a tool used in computer science to analyze the complexity of codes and in other fields of science as well, usually in connection with inverse problems and parameter estimation (Jaynes (1996, 1984)). It can be interpreted as a generalized likelihood ratio. To proceed along these lines, we must compute the relative entropy distance between P_0 and a generic probability measure (P) for S_t of the form

$$(25) \qquad \frac{dS_t}{S_t} = \sigma_t \, dZ_t + r \, dt \, .$$

As it turns out, the relative entropy of Ito processes with different volatilities is infinite. Nevertheless, this divergence can be removed by passing to a discrete lattice model and analyzing the asymptotic behavior of (23) as the mesh-size tends to zero. This yields the result

$$(26) \qquad \mathcal{E}(P; P_0) \approx \frac{\text{const.}}{\Delta t} \times \mathbf{E}^P \left\{ \int_0^T \eta\left(\frac{\sigma_t}{\sigma_0(S_t, t)}\right) dt \right\} \, ,$$

where ΔT represents the lattice time-time step and η is a convex function defined on non-negative real numbers. Equation (25) shows that the relative entropy of two measures defined on a lattice (trinomial tree) which approximate the Ito processes P and P_0 diverges at a rate inversely proportional to the lattice step, with a well-defined rate, given by the right-hand side of (25). The function η depends on the discretization scheme, unfortunately. However $\eta(Y)$ is, generically, a convex function of its argument, independently of the scheme used to approximate the diffusions. A possible choice for η, which is obtained from the standard trinomial lattice and is therefore useful for computations, is

(27) $$\eta(Y) = Y \log(Y) - Y + 1 \ .$$

This computation suggests that we consider the following variant of λ-UVM (compare with (20)):

$$V(\lambda_1, \dots \lambda_M) =$$

(28) $$\sup_P \mathbf{E}^P \left\{ -\epsilon \int_0^T \eta\left(\frac{\sigma_t}{\sigma_0(S_t, t)}\right) dt + \sum_{i=1}^N e^{-rT_i} F(S_{T_i}) - \sum_{j=1}^M \lambda_j e^{-r\tau_j} G(S_{\tau_j}) \right\} + \sum_{j=1}^M \lambda_j C_j \ ,$$

where the supremum is taken with respect to risk-netural measures such that σ_t lies in the band (16). In this equation, ϵ represents a numerical constant, which can be "tuned" in different ways. Large values of ϵ correspond to a large penalization for deviating from the a-priori measure P_0; small values of ϵ correspond to a weak effect of the relative entropy and hence to a larger volatility uncertainty.

For finite values of ϵ, minimization of (27) over all vectors $(\lambda_1, \dots \lambda_M)$ will give the best option hedge taking into account uncertain volatility and, at the same time, information about the "most likely risk-neutral measure" P_0. The minimization of the function in (27), which is convex in its arguments, is done using a non-linear PDE analogous to (17)-(18), but where the function Φ_0 is replaced by Φ_ϵ, given by

(29) $$\Phi_\epsilon(X) = \cdot \sigma_0^2 \cdot \sup_{\frac{\sigma_{min}}{\sigma_0} \leq Y \leq \frac{\sigma_{min}}{\sigma_0}} (XY - \epsilon \cdot \eta(Y)) \ .$$

A precise correspondence between this theory and λ-UVM can be made if we take $\eta(Y)$ to be a function equal to zero for $\sigma_{min}/\sigma_0 \leq Y \ \sigma_{max}/\sigma_0$, and to $+\infty$ otherwise (a degenerate convex function). In this case, the entropy term will be finite if and only if σ is inside the volatility band. A smooth, strictly convex function η which is finite in the interval and infinite outside this interval gives rise to a smooth transition, as a function of $Gamma$, between the extreme volatility values σ_{min}, σ_{max} which is equal to σ_0 when the Gamma of the portfolio vanishes (in the absence of volatility risk). For details on this theory and a variety of numerical results, see Avellaneda, Friedman, Holmes and Samperi (1997).

7. Conclusion

This paper sketched some of the main themes and results in the area of valuation of derivative securities. We have covered the principles underlying the valuation of options and contingent claims and also discussed the management of the risk of an options portfolio using differential sensitivities. This led us naturally to the original question of model specification and to managing the uncertainty as to which risk-neutral probability will be "realized" by the market in the future. We made a fundamental distinction between pricing contingent claims using a well-defined probabilistic model, and pricing in the presence of uncertainty with respect to model parameters. This uncertainty is ever-present in derivatives valuation, the argument being that if the pricing measure was known with certainty by all market participants, there would be ultimately no incentive for trading options. Option risk-management is therefore beyond the scope of linear models. Managing the "Greeks" is the preferred technique for handling model uncertainty, but we have shown that this method can be inconsistent with APT and, more importantly, that it will not provide protection against large changes in market conditions (*i.e.* large changes in risk-neutral probabilites). Proposals such as $\lambda - UVM$, which are based on the simultaneous consideration of different pricing scenarios, seem to be natural alternative to differential hedging.

I conclude by pointing out that the focus of this paper has been limited to a single risky asset. In reality, we are usually confronted with an economy with multiple sources of risk and multiple underlying assets, such as the universe of fixed-income instruments with different tenors. In the multidimensional case the complexity of the theory increases considerably, and even the apparently simple problem of evaluating expected cash-flows (under a single probability measure) presents difficulties. The need for exploring uncertainty in a multi-asset economy, such as correlation uncertainty, makes the analysis of risk under multiple probabilities even more relevant. I hope that some of the methods discussed here, or at least the ideas behind them, may prove useful for solving the challenging problems that still exist in this field.

BIBLIOGRAPHY

Avellaneda, M., Friedman, C., Holmes, R. and Samperi, D. (1997), Calibrating volatility surfaces via relative entropy minimization, *Applied Mathematical Finance*, vol 3, March issue.

Avellaneda, M., Levy, A. and Parás, A. (1995), Pricing and hedging derivative securities in markets with uncertain volatilities, *Applied Mathematical Finance*, vol 2, 73-88.

Avellaneda, M. and Parás, A. (1994), Dynamic hedging portfolios for derivative securities in the presence of large transaction costs, *Applied Mathematical Finance*, vol 1, 165-193.

Avellaneda, M. and Parás, A. (1996), Pricing and hedging derivative securities in markets with uncertain volatilities: the Lagrangian uncertain volatility model, *Applied Mathematical Finance*, vol 3, 21-52.

Black F. and Scholes, M. (1973), The pricing of options and corporate liabilities, *J. Pol. Econ.*, 81, 637-659.

Davis, M. H., Panas, V.G., and Zariphopolou, T. (1993), European option pricing with transaction costs, *SIAM J. Control and Optimization*, 31, 470-493.

Duffie, D. (1992), *Dynamical Asset Pricing Theory*, Princeton Univ. Press.

Engle, R., (1984), Wald likelihood ratio and Langrange multiplier tests in econometrics, in *Handbook of Econometrics*, vol II, Grilches and Intrilligator eds. North-Holland, Amsterdam; see also Noh, J. Engle, R. and Kane A. (1994), Forecasting volatility and options prices of the S&P 500 Index, *The Journal of Derivatives*, Fall issue.

Harrison, J.M., and Kreps, D. (1979), Martingales and arbitrage in multiperiod securities markets, *J. Econ. Theory*, 20, 381-408.

Hull, J. (1994), *Options, futures and other derivative securities*, 2nd ed., Prentice Hall, Englewod Hills, NJ.

Hull, J. and White, A., (1987), The pricing of options on assets with stochastic volatilities, *J. of Finance*, June, 281-300.

Jaynes, E. T. (1996), *Probability theory: The logic of science.* Unpublished Manuscript, Washington University, St. Louis, MO., see also article in *Inverse Problems*, vol 14, D. McLaughlin, ed., American Math. Soc., Providence, Rhode Island, 1984.

Keynes, J. M. (1936), *The General Theory of Investment Employment and Money*, Harcourt Brace and Co., New York.

Leland, H. (1985), Option pricing and replication in the presence of transaction costs, *J. of Finance*, 40, 1283-1301.

Markowitz, H. (1991), *Portfolio Selection*, J. Wiley and Sons, New York, 2nd edition.

Natanberg, S. (1988), *Option volatility and pricing strategies*, Probus.

Taleb, N. (1997), *Dynamic Hedging*, John Wiley and Sons, New York.

Non-Arbitrage and the Fundamental Theorem of Asset Pricing: Summary of Main Results

Freddy Delbaen and Walter Schachermayer

ABSTRACT. The concept of no arbitrage roughly says that it is impossible to make money out of nothing. The mathematical translation of this concept uses martingale theory and stochastic analysis. The paper gives an overview of the results obtained by the authors.

1. Introduction and Notation

Starting from the economically meaningful assumption that $(S_t)_{t \in \mathbb{R}_+}$ *essentially* does not allow arbitrage profits, the fundamental theorem of asset pricing allows the probability $\mathbf{P}$ on the underlying probability space $(\Omega, \mathcal{F}, \mathbf{P})$ to be replaced by an equivalent measure $\mathbf{Q}$ such that the process S becomes a (local) martingale under the new measure. This makes it possible to use the rich machinery of martingale theory. The present summary focuses on the question: "What is the precise meaning of the word essentially?" From a purely mathematical point of view, we remark that the proofs of the theorems below turn out to be surprisingly hard and require heavy machinery from the theory of stochastic processes, from functional analysis and also require some very technical estimates. The results are or will be published elsewhere where we will give references to related work of other authors. We apologise that in this summary no bibliographic references are given.

The $\mathbb{R}^d$-valued process S, sometimes denoted $(S_t)_{t \in \mathbb{R}_+}$, is supposed to satisfy mathematical properties that reflect economically meaningful ideas such as no arbitrage. There should be no trading strategy H for the process S, such that the final payoff described by the stochastic integral $(H \cdot S)_\infty$, is a nonnegative function, strictly positive with positive probability. The economic interpretation is that by betting on the process S and without bearing any risk, it should not be possible to make something out of nothing.

1991 *Mathematics Subject Classification.* Primary 60G44; Secondary 46N30, 46E30, 90A09, 60H05.

Key words and phrases. martingale, equivalent martingale measure, representing measure, risk neutral measure, hedging, stochastic integration, mathematical finance.

© 1999 American Mathematical Society

Mathematically a buy-and-hold strategy is described as an integrand of the form $H = f\mathbf{1}_{]T_1,T_2]}$, where $T_1 \leq T_2$ are finite stopping times and f is $\mathcal{F}_{T_1}$-measurable. The advantage of using such integrands is that they have a clear interpretation: when time $T_1(\omega)$ comes up, buy $f(\omega)$ units of the financial asset, keep them until time $T_2(\omega)$ and sell. The use of stopping times is interpreted as the use of signals coming from available, observable information. This explains why in financial theories the filtration and the derived concepts such as predictable processes, are important. A linear combination of such buy-and-hold strategies is called a simple integrand. Even if the process S is not a semi-martingale, the stochastic integral $(H \cdot S)$ for $H = f\mathbf{1}_{]T_1,T_2]}$ can be defined as the process $(H \cdot S)_t = (S_{\min(t,T_2)} - S_{\min(t,T_1)})f$.

We showed that in the general case simple integrands are not sufficient to characterise these processes that admit an equivalent martingale measure. On the other hand the use of general integrands leads to other problems. The first is that $H \cdot S$ has to exist. The hypothesis that S is a semi-martingale is therefore introduced. Earlier work shows that this property follows from very weak no-arbitrage properties. A second difficulty is the problem of doubling strategies ("les martingales" in French). To avoid these pathologies, a lower bound on the losses needs to be introduced. The resulting integrands are called *admissible*. In the general case, i.e., a time set of the form $[0, \infty[$ or $[0,1]$ and with a possibility of random jumps, the situation is very delicate.

The following notation will be used. The space $(\Omega, \mathcal{F}, \mathbf{P})$ as well as the filtration $(\mathcal{F}_t)_{t \in \mathbb{R}_+}$ will remain fixed. Economically this means that we are not considering important problems such as inside information or better/faster accessibility to (il)legal information. We suppose that the filtration satisfies the usual assumptions. The space L^0 denotes the vector space of all real-valued measurable functions defined on Ω, where as usual two functions equal a.s. are identified. Endowed with the topology of convergence in probability, this space becomes a complete, metrisable vector space (i.e. a Fréchet space). The space cannot be given an equivalent norm and there are, in general, no continuous linear functions from L^0 to $\mathbb{R}$. The space L^∞ is the subspace of L^0 of all bounded functions. Equipped with the obvious norm $\|f\|_\infty = \operatorname{ess\,sup}|f(\omega)|$, it becomes a Banach space that is the dual of L^1. The use of separation theorems in the space L^∞ poses the problem that the dual space of L^∞ is not L^1 and care has to be taken to work with sets that are weak*, i.e., $\sigma(L^\infty, L^1)$, closed. We remark that the two spaces L^∞ as well as L^0 are, among the L^p spaces, the only two spaces that remain the same when the original probability measure is replaced by an equivalent one.

S denotes an $\mathbb{R}^d$-valued semi-martingale, defined on the filtered probability space $(\Omega, (\mathcal{F}_t)_{t \in \mathbb{R}_+}, \mathbf{P})$. An $\mathbb{R}^d$-valued predictable process H is called a-admissible if it is S-integrable, if $H_0 = 0$, if the stochastic integral satisfies $H \cdot S \geq -a$ and if $\lim_{t \to \infty} (H \cdot S)_t$ exists a.s. If the integrand H is a-admissible for some a, then we simply call H admissible. It is understood that vector stochastic integration theory is used. We also need the following sets:

$$\mathcal{K} = \{ (H \cdot S)_\infty \mid H \text{ is admissible}\},$$
$$\mathcal{K}_a = \{ (H \cdot S)_\infty \mid H \text{ is } a\text{-admissible}\},$$
$$\mathcal{C}_0 = \mathcal{K} - L^0_+,$$
$$\mathcal{C} = \mathcal{C}_0 \cap L^\infty.$$

The following properties for S all reflect the idea that it is impossible to make something out of nothing. The bar denotes closure taken in the *norm* topology of L^∞. This means that we will have to take care of the particularities related to the duality (L^1, L^∞). We say that the process S satisfies the (NA) or No Arbitrage property if:

(NA) $$\mathcal{K} \cap L^0_+ = \{0\}$$

which is equivalent to:

$$\mathcal{C} \cap L^\infty_+ = \{0\}.$$

The process S is said to satisfy the (NFLVR) property or the No Free Lunch with Vanishing Risk property if:

(NFLVR) $$\overline{\mathcal{C}} \cap L^\infty_+ = \{0\}.$$

The latter property can be explained as follows. An element $f \in \overline{\mathcal{C}}$ is the limit in L^∞-norm of a sequence $(f_n)_{n\geq 1}$ taken in $\mathcal{C}$. If $f \geq 0$ then clearly the sequence of possible losses $(f_n^-)_{n\geq 1}$ tends to zero uniformly, i.e., the risk vanishes. The expression "No Free Lunch" is an old expression used already in the early days of the finance literature. Kreps gave the following technical definition of this concept. Let S be a bounded process and let $\mathcal{K}^{\text{simple}}$ be the set of all outcomes with respect to bounded simple integrands. We define $\mathcal{C}^{\text{simple}}$ in the same way,

$$\mathcal{C}^{\text{simple}} = \left(\mathcal{K}^{\text{simple}} - L^0_+\right) \cap L^\infty.$$

Kreps says that the càdlàg adapted process satisfies the property of "No Free Lunch," if

(NFL) $$\widetilde{\mathcal{C}^{\text{simple}}} \cap L^\infty_+ = \{0\},$$

where the tilde means the weak* closure. Unfortunately the weak* closure cannot be obtained by sequences. One has to use general concepts such as nets, generalised sequences and/or filters. The economic interpretation of these objects is unclear. It may happen that an element in the weak* closure can only be obtained by an *unbounded* generalised sequence. On the other hand the very strong requirement of (NFL) implies that S is a semi-martingale and that there is an equivalent martingale measure for the process S. The property (NFLVR) is a slightly stronger version than the no-arbitrage condition. However we pay a price (there is no free lunch as you know). We have to introduce the set of outcomes with respect to *general* admissible integrands. The construction of the stochastic integral has a lot of stability built in. Therefore we can do it with an assumption such as (NFLVR). The exploitation of this stability requires however the use of non-trivial arguments.

The following theorem relates the definition of (NFLVR) to a boundedness property in L^0.

THEOREM 1. *The process S satisfies the property* (NFLVR) *if and only if it satisfies*
  1. (NA) *and*
  2. $\mathcal{K}_1$ *is bounded in the space L^0.*

We remark that the boundedness of the set $\mathcal{K}_1$ has a direct economic interpretation. For outcomes that have a maximal loss bounded by 1, the profit is bounded in probability, this means that the probability of making a big profit can be estimated from above, uniformly over all such outcomes.

The following theorem gives a way to control the boundedness of the set $\mathcal{K}_1$.

THEOREM 2. *If there is a positive local martingale L such that $L_0 = 1$ and $L_\infty > 0$ a. s. as well as a strictly positive real-valued predictable process ϕ such that $(\phi \cdot S)L$ is a local martingale, then the set $\mathcal{K}_1$ is bounded in L^0.*

The multiplication with a function ϕ is done in order to take care of processes with big jumps. We will give more information on this in the last section. We remark that when ϕ is a bounded, nonzero real-valued predictable process, then the set of stochastic integrals with respect to S is the same as the set of stochastic integrals with respect to $\phi \cdot S$. So as long as only the stochastic integrals matter, we can always replace S by a "better" process $\phi \cdot S$. For locally bounded processes we usually can take $\phi = 1$. We also emphasize that in the above theorem we only require L to be a local martingale. See also the remark after Theorem 6.

2. The locally bounded case

The next theorem shows that, at least for locally bounded semi-martingales, the (NFLVR) property is equivalent to the existence of an equivalent probability measure that turns the price process S into a local martingale. It is easily seen that we may without loss of generality suppose that the process S is bounded, instead of locally bounded. Indeed if $(T_n)_{n \geq 0}$ is an increasing sequence of stopping times such that $T_0 = 0$, $\lim_{n \to \infty} T_n = \infty$ and such that every stopped processes S^{T_n} is bounded, by say k_n, then we can replace the process S by the process

$$S' = \sum_{n \geq 1} \mathbf{1}_{]T_{n-1}, T_n]} \frac{1}{k_n 2^n} (S^{T_n} - S^{T_{n-1}}) = \left(\sum_{n \geq 1} \frac{1}{k_n 2^n} \mathbf{1}_{]T_{n-1}, T_n]} \right) \cdot S.$$

Showing that there is an equivalent probability such that S becomes a local martingale is then the same as showing that there is a probability that turns S' into a martingale.

THEOREM 3. *The locally bounded semi-martingale S satisfies the (NFLVR) property if and only if there is an equivalent measure $\mathbf{Q}$ under which S becomes a local martingale. In this case the set $\mathcal{C}$ is closed in the weak* topology $\sigma(L^\infty, L^1)$.*

The key point is of course to show that the set $\mathcal{C}$ is weak* closed. Because of the (NA) property, the set $\mathcal{C}$ does not intersect the positive cone, and we can separate with a hyperplane given by a function in L^1. More precisely there is a strictly positive function g in L^1 such that for all $f \in \mathcal{C}$ we have $\mathbf{E}[fg] \leq 0$. This implies that for elements of the form $f = \mathbf{1}_A(S_t - S_s)$ where $s < t$ and $A \in \mathcal{F}_s$, we necessarily have $\mathbf{E}[fg] = 0$, since indeed both f and $-f$ are in $\mathcal{C}$. It is here that we use that the process S is bounded. Normalising g then gives us an equivalent probability $d\mathbf{Q} = g \, d\mathbf{P}$ that turns S into a martingale. The fact that $\mathcal{C}$ is weak* closed can be proved for general (i.e., not necessarily locally bounded) semi-martingales. However the last step of the proof, both f and $-f$ being in $\mathcal{C}$, fails! The proof of the weak* closure is based upon the following lemma. We first need a definition:

DEFINITION 4. An element $f \in \mathcal{K}$ is called maximal if for $g \geq f$ a.s. and $g \in \mathcal{K}$ we necessarily have that $f = g$.

It is easily seen that the (NA) property says that 0 is maximal. Also there are no maximal elements if the (NA) property is violated. Therefore we have that $f \in \mathcal{K}_1$ is maximal in $\mathcal{K}_1$ if and only if it is maximal in $\mathcal{K}$.

LEMMA 5. *Suppose that the process S satisfies the (NFLVR) property. If $(f_n)_{n \geq 1}$ is a sequence in $\mathcal{K}_1$, then there exists a sequence of convex combinations $g_n \in \operatorname{convex}\{f_n, f_{n+1}, \dots\}$ that converges in probability to some function $g \colon \Omega \to \mathbb{R}$. Moreover there is a maximal element $f \in \mathcal{K}_1$ such that $g \leq f$, i.e., $g \in \mathcal{C}$.*

From this lemma the weak* closure is easily deduced. One uses the property that a convex set in L^∞ is weak* closed if and only if the intersections with the balls of L^∞ are closed for the convergence in probability. We will not give a sketch of the proof of the lemma.

For continuous processes we can do a little bit better as the following theorem shows.

THEOREM 6. *Suppose that S is continuous with Doob–Meyer decomposition $S = M + A$. If S satisfies the (NA) property, then the following assertions hold:*
1. *The measure dA is for almost all $\omega \in \Omega$ absolutely continuous with respect to the matrix valued measure $d\langle M, M \rangle$.*
2. *The predictable density h defined as $dA = h \, d\langle M, M \rangle$ satisfies the property*

$$T = \inf\left\{ t > 0 \ \Big|\ \int_0^t h_u \, d\langle M, M\rangle_u h_u = +\infty \right\} > 0 \quad a.\,s.$$

3. *The exponential local martingale*

$$L_t = \exp\left(-\int_0^t h_u \, dM_u - \frac{1}{2} \int_0^t h_u \, d\langle M, M \rangle_u h_u \right) \quad \text{is defined.}$$

4. *There is $\mathbf{Q}$, a probability measure absolutely continuous with respect to $\mathbf{P}$, under which S becomes a local martingale and for which $\{d\mathbf{Q}/d\mathbf{P} > 0\} = \{L_\infty > 0\}$.*
5. *If $\mathbf{Q}$ is an absolutely continuous probability measure under which S becomes a local martingale, then necessarily $\{d\mathbf{Q}/d\mathbf{P} > 0\} \subset \{L_\infty > 0\}$.*

If L satisfies the property that $L_\infty > 0$ a.s., then we have a situation that is described by Theorem 2 and hence the set $\mathcal{K}_1$ is bounded in L^0. Indeed by using Itô's calculus and the fact that S and L are continuous, it is easily verified that LS is a local martingale. Together with the (NA) property this implies the (NFLVR) property and the theorem is proved. The case where L can become zero is more difficult to treat.

We remark that, except in the case of complete markets, the change of measure is not necessarily given by the local martingale L. There are examples of a strict local martingale Z such that there is an equivalent measure under which Z becomes a uniformly integrable martingale. This means that if we define $S = 1/Z$ and apply the construction above, we find $L = Z$ and hence $LS = 1$. However the process L does not define a new probability measure since $\mathbf{E}[L_\infty] < 1$. This also shows that for continuous processes S there is a strict separation between the (NA) property and the boundedness of $\mathcal{K}_1$. As an illustration of this loose statement, we take, on the time interval $[0,1]$, the Bessel process S in three dimensions, $S_0 = 1$ and with its natural filtration. It is easily seen that in this case the only candidate for a density is the strict local martingale $L = 1/S$. We conclude that the process S cannot have an equivalent local martingale measure and hence it cannot satisfy the (NA) property.

This example also shows that when we use L as a description of a foreign currency, there is no way of making arbitrage by betting on this currency. However the people living in the foreign country are faced with an exchange rate given by S and they have a possibility to make winning bets (also called investments)! Of course this paradoxical situation arises from the notion of admissible integrands. This notion is not invariant for currency changes. What is possible for the foreigners is not possible for the domestics! It also shows that a change of numéraire should be done with some extra care.

For the following theorems we need some extra notation. It is assumed that the bounded process S admits an equivalent local martingale measure. Define

$$\mathbf{M}^e(\mathbf{P}) = \left\{ \mathbf{Q} \mid \begin{array}{l} \mathbf{Q} \text{ is equivalent to } \mathbf{P} \\ \text{and the process } S \text{ is a } \mathbf{Q}\text{-local martingale} \end{array} \right\}$$

and

$$\mathbf{M}(\mathbf{P}) = \left\{ \mathbf{Q} \mid \begin{array}{l} \mathbf{Q} \text{ is absolutely continuous with respect to } \mathbf{P} \\ \text{and the process } S \text{ is a } \mathbf{Q}\text{-local martingale} \end{array} \right\}.$$

Because the process S is assumed to be bounded (or locally bounded), we can easily show that the set $\mathbf{M}(\mathbf{P})$ is the closure in L^1 of the set $\mathbf{M}^e(\mathbf{P})$. Again for non locally bounded processes this is false as an easy two period example, where $\mathbf{M}(\mathbf{P})$ is not closed, shows.

The weak* closedness of $\mathcal{C}$, the Hahn–Banach theorem, as well as the basic lemma yield:

THEOREM 7. *If $f \geq 0$, then*

$$\sup\{ \mathbf{E}_{\mathbf{Q}}[f] \mid \mathbf{Q} \in \mathbf{M}^e(\mathbf{P}) \} = \inf\{ \alpha \mid \text{There is } g \in \mathcal{K} \text{ with } f \leq \alpha + g \}.$$

Moreover when the expression is finite, the infimum is a minimum and g can be chosen to be a maximal element.

Using this equality and the characterisation of maximal elements given below, we can give an improvement of a result of Ansel–Stricker and Jacka. The theorem also says when a change of numéraire will not produce unwanted arbitrage opportunities.

THEOREM 8. *If $f = (H \cdot S)_\infty \in \mathcal{K}$, for H admissible, then are equivalent:*
1. *f is a maximal element in $\mathcal{K}$.*
2. *f is a maximal element in $\mathcal{K}_{\|f^-\|_\infty}$.*
3. *There is an element $\mathbf{Q} \in \mathbf{M}^e(\mathbf{P})$ for which the process $(H \cdot S)$ is a $\mathbf{Q}$-uniformly integrable martingale.*
4. *There is an element $\mathbf{Q} \in \mathbf{M}^e(\mathbf{P})$ for which $\mathbf{E}_{\mathbf{Q}}[f] = 0$.*

THEOREM 9. *If $f \geq 0$, then the following assertions are equivalent:*
1. *There is $\mathbf{Q} \in \mathbf{M}^e(\mathbf{P})$ such that $\mathbf{E}_{\mathbf{Q}}[f] = \sup\{ \mathbf{E}_{\mathbf{R}}[f] \mid \mathbf{R} \in \mathbf{M}^e(\mathbf{P}) \}$,*
2. *$f = \alpha + g$, where g is maximal in $\mathcal{K}$.*
3. *$f = \alpha + (H \cdot S)_\infty$ and $H \cdot S$ is a uniformly integrable martingale for some element $\mathbf{Q} \in \mathbf{M}^e(\mathbf{P})$.*

If $V = \alpha + H \cdot S$, H admissible and $f = V_\infty > 0$ a.s., then the above are also equivalent to:
  4. $(S/V, 1/V)$ satisfies the (NA) property.
  5. $(S/V, 1/V)$ has an equivalent local martingale measure.

Both these theorems are proved together and our proof does not use the H^1–BMO duality theory. Using the Bishop–Phelps theorem from functional analysis we obtain as a corollary:

THEOREM 10. *If $\mathbf{M}^e(\mathbf{P}) = \mathbf{M}(\mathbf{P}) \neq \varnothing$, then $\mathbf{M}^e(\mathbf{P})$ contains exactly one element.*

Because of the importance of the maximal elements, it is interesting to investigate the set $\mathcal{K}_1^{\max}$ of all these maximal elements.

THEOREM 11. *The set $\mathcal{K}_1^{\max}$ of maximal elements in $\mathcal{K}$ is a convex cone that is stable for countable convex combinations.*

COROLLARY 12. *If $(f_i)_{i \geq 1}$ is a countable family of maximal elements in $\mathcal{K}$, then there is an equivalent local martingale measure $\mathbf{Q}$ for S such that for all $i \geq 1$ we have $\mathbf{E}_\mathbf{Q}[f_i] = 0$. There are admissible strategies H^i, generating f_i, such that the processes $H^i \cdot S$ are uniformly integrable martingales under the measure $\mathbf{Q}$.*

It is a naive idea to think that for maximal elements f and for every element $\mathbf{Q} \in \mathbf{M}^e(\mathbf{P})$ we always have $\mathbf{E}_\mathbf{Q}[f] = 0$. The are examples where $\mathbf{E}_\mathbf{Q}[f] = 0$ for a well chosen measure $\mathbf{Q}$, but where $\mathbf{E}_\mathbf{R}[f] < 0$ for an even better chosen element $\mathbf{R} \in \mathbf{M}^e(\mathbf{P})$. Moreover we can show that in incomplete markets with continuous prices, such a situation is more the rule than the exception! However one can show that for a maximal element f the set $\{\mathbf{R} \mid \mathbf{R} \in \mathbf{M}(\mathbf{P}); \mathbf{E}_\mathbf{R}[f] = 0\}$ is a dense G_δ-set in $\mathbf{M}(\mathbf{P})$.

Given a convex cone, it is always a good idea to have a look at the vector space generated by it. So let us define

$$\mathcal{G} = \mathcal{K}^{\max} - \mathcal{K}^{\max}.$$

For an element $g \in \mathcal{G}$ we define the norm

$$\|g\|_\mathcal{G} = \inf\{a > 0 \mid \text{There exist } f, h \in \mathcal{K}_a \text{ with } g = h - f\}.$$

It is easy to see that it really defines a norm and that because of the properties of the cone $\mathcal{K}^{\max}$, the space $\mathcal{G}$ is complete for this norm.

THEOREM 13. *The space $\mathcal{G}$ with the above norm $\|\cdot\|_\mathcal{G}$ becomes a Banach space. We also have that*

$$2\|g\|_\mathcal{G} = \sup\{\|g\|_{L^1(\mathbf{Q})} \mid \mathbf{Q} \in \mathbf{M}^e(\mathbf{P})\}, \quad g \in \mathcal{G}.$$

Although the space $\mathcal{G}$ and its norm are defined in a natural way, we leave it as a challenge to give an economic interpretation of these results.

We end this section with a theorem that says that under a weak form of the (NFLVR) property, the process S is a semi-martingale. The theorem below therefore shows that in finance, the use of processes such as fractional Brownian motion, is not always appropriate.

THEOREM 14. *If for a bounded (or more generally a locally bounded) process S,*

$$\overline{\mathcal{C}^{\text{simple}}} \cap L^\infty = \{0\},$$

then S is a semi-martingale. (Again the bar denotes the norm closure in L^∞.)

3. The case of unbounded processes

The preceding section dealt with locally bounded processes. From a general viewpoint this is not satisfactory. Insurance models typically treat the case of unbounded claims that happen at totally inaccessible stopping times. Also from a mathematical viewpoint it would be nicer to have a result also for the case of unbounded jumps. The need is even greater if one compares the fundamental theorem with the Dalang–Morton–Willinger theorem. This theorem states that for processes indexed by a finite time-set, the no-arbitrage property implies the existence of an equivalent martingale measure. We remark that in the case of the Dalang–Morton–Willinger theorem, the no-arbitrage condition is written without any restriction to admissibility. More precisely they proved the following theorem.

THEOREM 15. *Let $(S_n)_{n=0,1,\ldots,N}$ be a d-dimensional process adapted to the filtration $(\mathcal{F}_n)_{n=0,1,\ldots,N}$. Let $\mathcal{K}^g$ be defined as*

$$\mathcal{K}^g = \left\{ \sum_{n=1}^N f_{n-1}(S_n - S_{n-1}) \;\bigg|\; \text{Each } f_n \colon \Omega \to \mathbb{R}^d \text{ is } \mathcal{F}_n\text{-measurable} \right\}.$$

If $\mathcal{K}^g \cap L^0_+ = \{0\}$, then there is an equivalent measure $\mathbf{Q}$ such that the process S is a $\mathbf{Q}$-martingale.

In the general case it turns out that there is no hope to prove the existence of an equivalent (local) martingale measure. We need a more general concept. We say that a semi-martingale X is a sigma-martingale if there is a strictly positive predictable process ϕ such that ϕ is X-integrable and such that $\phi \cdot X$ is a local martingale. In this case an easy—although not trivial—exercise shows that we can require that ϕ is bounded and that $\phi \cdot X$ is an $\mathcal{H}^1$-martingale. It is not difficult to see that a local martingale is a sigma-martingale and that a sigma-martingale is a local martingale if and only if the process ϕ can be taken to be decreasing. The concept of a sigma-martingale was introduced by Emery and Chou who called it "processus de la classe Σ_m." It is related to martingales in the same way as sigma-finite measures are related to finite measures.

Another easy exercise is to show that a sigma-martingale on a finite discrete time filtration (the case of the Dalang–Morton–Willinger theorem), is already a martingale.

We also remark that the set of all stochastic integrals with respect to a d-dimensional semi-martingale S is the same as the set of all stochastic integrals with respect to a process of the form $\phi \cdot S$. Hence, for applications in mathematical finance, the concept of sigma-martingales is, in most cases, as good as the more restrictive concept of local martingales.

We can now state the fundamental theorem in its most general form.

THEOREM 16. *Let $S = (S_t)_{t \in \mathbb{R}_+}$ be an $\mathbb{R}^d$-valued semi-martingale defined on the stochastic base $(\Omega, \mathcal{F}, (\mathcal{F}_t)_{t \in \mathbb{R}_+}, \mathbf{P})$. Then S satisfies the condition of* (NFLVR) if and only if there exists a probability measure $\mathbf{Q} \sim \mathbf{P}$ such that S is a sigma-martingale with respect to $\mathbf{Q}$.

The proof of this theorem starts in the same way as the proof in the locally bounded case. One first shows that the set $\mathcal{C}$ is weak* closed. But in this case such a statement can be trivial, since the set $\mathcal{K}$ of outcomes of admissible integrands can be reduced to the set $\{0\}$! Once the closedness is proved, we continue with the following result, interesting in itself.

THEOREM 17. *With the notation introduced above, let $\mathbf{Q}$ be an equivalent probability measure such that $\mathbf{E}_{\mathbf{Q}}[f] \leq 0$ for every element $f \in \mathcal{C}$. Then for each $\varepsilon > 0$ there is an equivalent probability measure $\mathbf{Q}_0$ such that $\|\mathbf{Q}_0 - \mathbf{Q}\| < \varepsilon$ and such that S is a sigma-martingale for the measure $\mathbf{Q}_0$.*

We remark that this theorem implies the Dalang–Morton–Willinger theorem and is in fact a little bit more general since we give somewhat more information about the distortion of the measure.

In the rest of this section we suppose that there is a sigma-martingale measure for the process S. Let us redefine:

$$\mathbf{M}^e(\mathbf{P}) = \left\{ \mathbf{Q} \ \middle| \ \begin{array}{l} \mathbf{Q} \text{ is equivalent to } \mathbf{P} \\ \text{and the process } S \text{ is a } \mathbf{Q}\text{-sigma-martingale} \end{array} \right\}.$$

As is easily seen, for locally bounded processes this set coincides with the set of equivalent local martingale measures.

The results on maximal elements shown above as well as the duality results can be restated also in the case of unbounded processes. But as observed above, the concept of admissible integrands is too restrictive. In order to solve this problem we introduce the concept of w-admissible integrands, where $w \geq 1$ is a weight function. The idea is to say that an integrand H is w-admissible if $H \cdot S \geq -w$. Here one has to be careful. If w is too small, then there might be no w-admissible integrands, this can be the case if we take e.g. $w = 1$ (the classical concept of admissibility) and if big jumps are present. If on the other hand we take w too big, then we might be able to use doubling strategies and there will be arbitrage opportunities. The good balance is to use weight functions $w \geq 1$ that satisfy the following properties:

1. There is a strictly positive predictable S-integrable function φ such that the maximal function of the vector-valued process $\varphi \cdot S$ satisfies $(\varphi \cdot S)^* \leq w$. In this case we are sure that there will be enough w-admissible integrands.
2. There is a sigma martingale measure $\mathbf{Q} \in \mathbf{M}^e(\mathbf{P})$ such that $\mathbf{E}_{\mathbf{Q}}[w] < \infty$. This will restrict the concept of w-admissibility and will prevent the use of doubling strategies.

It is clear that if $\mathbf{M}^e(\mathbf{P})$ is nonempty (as is the case here), then there are weight functions that satisfy both assumptions. We are now ready to define the concept of w-admissible integrands.

DEFINITION 18. *If $w \geq 1$ is a weight function that satisfies both assumptions above, then we say that an S-integrable predictable $\mathbb{R}^d$-valued process H is w-admissible if for each $\mathbf{Q} \in \mathbf{M}^e(\mathbf{P})$ we have*

$$(H \cdot S)_t \geq -\mathbf{E}_{\mathbf{Q}}[w \,|\, \mathcal{F}_t], \quad t \geq 0.$$

REMARK 19. We can show that in the preceding definition the requirement

$$(H \cdot S)_t \geq -\mathbf{E}_\mathbf{Q}[w|\mathcal{F}_t], \quad t \geq 0,$$

can be restricted to those elements $\mathbf{Q} \in \mathbf{M}^e(\mathbf{P})$ satisfying $\mathbf{E}_\mathbf{Q}[w] < \infty$. This yields an equivalent definition.

Let us also define

$$\mathcal{K}_w = \{ (H \cdot S)_\infty \mid (H \cdot S) \geq -nw \text{ for some } n \geq 0 \}.$$

It is easily seen that the limit exists. Indeed, if $\mathbf{E}_\mathbf{Q}[w] < \infty$, then the process $(H \cdot S)_t + \mathbf{E}_\mathbf{Q}[nw|\mathcal{F}_t]$, $t \geq 0$, is a positive supermartingale for the measure $\mathbf{Q}$.

With the set of admissible outcomes we can construct the set of dominated elements:

$$\mathcal{C}_w = \mathcal{K}_w - L^0_+.$$

The following theorem is the equivalent of the result that says that $\mathcal{C}$ is weak* closed.

THEOREM 20. *The set $\left(\frac{1}{w}\mathcal{C}_w\right) \cap L^\infty$ is weak* closed in L^∞.*

THEOREM 21. *The element $f \in \mathcal{K}_w$ is maximal if and only if there is an element $\mathbf{R} \in \mathbf{M}^e(\mathbf{P})$ such that $w \in L^1(\mathbf{R})$ and $\mathbf{E}_\mathbf{R}[f] = 0$.*

THEOREM 22. *If $f \geq -w$, then we have*

$$\sup\{\, \mathbf{E}_{\mathbf{R}'}[f] \mid \mathbf{E}_{\mathbf{R}'}[w] < \infty, \mathbf{R}' \in \mathbf{M}^e(\mathbf{P}) \,\}$$
$$= \inf\{\, \alpha \mid \text{There is } g \in \mathcal{K}_w \text{ with } f \leq \alpha + g \,\}.$$

The proofs of these results are a combination of the proofs for the locally bounded case together with compactness results of bounded sequences in the space $\mathcal{H}^1$. We remark that even in the case of locally bounded price processes S, the above results are more precise.

References

[DS94a] F. Delbaen and W. Schachermayer, *A general version of the fundamental theorem of asset pricing*, Math. Ann. **300** (1994), 463–520.
[DS94b] _____, *Arbitrage and free lunch with bounded risk for unbounded continuous processes*, Math. Finance **4** (1994), 343–348.
[DS95a] _____, *Arbitrage possibilities in Bessel processes and their relations to local martingales*, Probab. Theor. Relat. Fields **102** (1995), 357–366.
[DS95b] _____, *The no-arbitrage property under a change of numéraire*, Stochastics **53** (1995), 213–226.
[DS95c] _____, *The no arbitrage property for continuous processes*, Ann. of Appl. Probab. **5** (1995), 924–945.
[DS96a] _____, *The fundamental theorem of asset pricing for unbounded stochastic processes*, preprint (1996).
[DS96b] _____, *A compactness principle for bounded sequences of $\mathcal{H}^1$ martingales*, preprint (1996).
[DS97a] _____, *A simple counter-example to several problems in the theory of asset pricing, which arises generically in incomplete markets*, Math. Finance (1997).
[DS97b] _____, *The Banach space of workable contingent claims in arbitrage theory*, Ann. Inst. H. Poincaré. Probab. Statist. **33** (1997), 113–144.

DEPARTEMENT FÜR MATHEMATIK, ETH ZÜRICH, CH-8092 ZÜRICH, SWITZERLAND
E-mail address: `delbaen@math.ethz.ch`

INSTITUT FÜR STATISTIK, UNIVERSITÄT WIEN, BRÜNNERSTR. 72, A-1210 WIEN, AUSTRIA
E-mail address: `wschach@stat1.bwl.univie.ac.at`

Introduction to Models for the Evolution of the Term Structure of Interest Rates

David Heath

ABSTRACT. This expository paper introduces stochastic models for the evolution of the term structure of interest rates. We develop conditions for the absence of arbitrage and the existence and uniqueness of the martingale measure, and discuss valuation and model selection.

1. Introduction

Financial contracts whose payments depend upon the levels of interest rates are exceedingly important in today's financial markets. Such contracts allow, for example, manufacturing firms to finance new capacity without facing interest rate risk, which may have substantial economic benefits. The market for such instruments is large and continues to grow.

To understand these contracts and how to value them (and to hedge them) we shall begin with the simplest such contracts: default risk free pure discount bonds. A pure discount bond is an instrument which calls for a single payment, at a fixed date in the future (the maturity of the bond), of a fixed amount (the notional amount of the bond). Some such bonds (those issued by companies, for example) are risky in the sense that the issuing party may default, i.e., fail to make full payment on the specified date. A default risk free pure discount bond is one for which there is no possibility of default.

Although such pure discount bonds represent "ideal" instruments (because default is never really impossible), instruments very much like these do trade: U.S. Treasury Strips. Each such "strip" is a contract calling for the U.S. Government to pay a specified amount on a specified date, and is regarded by most as being default risk free. These are called "strips" because they are the result of "stripping" coupons from coupon bonds. This results in a separate contract for each coupon payment, and one for the repayment of the notional, or "principal", of the bond as well. If you look in the Wall Street Journal, you'll find that these strips are identified by their payment date and by "bp", "np", or "ci". The first two indicate that the payment arose from a bond principal or a note principal repayment; the last indicates that it arose from a coupon payment. In fact, these can be recombined

---

2000 *Mathematics Subject Classification.* 91B28, 91B70.

to produce one of the original coupon bonds, but to do this one must use an appropriate "np" or "bp" to reconstruct the principal repayment and "ci" payments for the coupons. (Because the different types of payments have these additional uses, strips with the same maturity may have different values. But we'll ignore this feature.)

Today's "term structure" is completely specified by the prices of all possible default risk free pure discount bonds. In a real market, we will observe the prices of only finitely many such bonds, but in principle there are infinitely many of them (one for every possible maturity from now on). If you look at a copy of the Wall Street Journal (and I urge you to do so), you'll see the prices of many strips.

Let $B(t,T)$ denote the price, at date t, for a default risk free pure discount bond maturing at date T, where $t \leq T$. The term structure observed at date t is the function which maps T to $B(t,T)$. The purpose of this note is to present sensible models for the evolution of the term structure. Because the evolution of the term structure seems unpredictable, we'll build models for which $B(t,T)$ is stochastic. For each fixed T, $B(t,T)$ will be a stochastic process (in t).

2. Sensible models for price processes

In one of the fundamental papers of mathematical finance [4], Harrison and Kreps develop the idea of a viable model (a model consistent with equilibrium in a simple economy) and the idea of no "free lunch" (ability to get something for nothing by trading in the market). They show that these concepts are necessary and sufficient for the existence of an equivalent martingale measure (a probability measure, equivalent to the model's probability measure, under which discounted market prices are martingales). These ideas were developed and expanded by many researchers including Dalang, Morton and Willinger [2], Lackner [7], and Delbaen and Schachermayer [3].

We shall consider only models for which there is an equivalent martingale measure. To construct such measures one can either attempt to build a model under the "real" (or "physical") probability measure and then show that there exists an equivalent martingale measure, or one can build models under the equivalent martingale measures and then replace the measure by any equivalent measure. (Actually, discounted security prices need to be martingales only during time periods within which these securities pay no cash flows.)

3. Constructing term structure models

We want to construct models for markets in which pure discount bonds and a "money market account" trade. Let $\{B(\cdot,T), 0 \leq T \leq T^*\}$ denote a family of bond price processes (indexed by T), and let $\beta(\cdot)$ be a stochastic process whose value at time t is the (random) amount an initial \$1 deposited in a money market account at date 0 would be worth at date t. We consider only smooth models: we require that these processes be defined on a probability space (Ω, F, Q) supporting a d-dimensional Brownian motion $\{W_t\}_{t \geq 0}$ with a filtration $\{F_t\}_{t \geq 0}$ generated by this Brownian motion, and that the above price processes are adapted to this filtration. Moreover, we consider these models under an equivalent martingale measure Q, so that the discounted price processes $\frac{B(t,T)}{\beta(t)}$ are, for each T, required to be martingales under the measure Q.

Traditionally these models were constructed by first specifying a stochastic process describing the evolution of the spot interest rate $r(\cdot)$ under an equivalent martingale measure Q. With minor restrictions, this process can be chosen arbitrarily. One then defines $\beta(t) = \exp(\int_0^t r(s)ds)$, and $B(t,T) = \beta(t)E_Q\{\frac{1}{\beta(T)}|F_t\}$. Clearly for each T the process Z given by $Z(t,T) = B(t,T)/\beta(t)$ is a Q-martingale for $0 \leq t \leq T$ as desired (provided $1/\beta(T)$ is in $L^1(Q)$).

This approach is both simple and elegant, but it ignores the necessity of ensuring that the distribution of the (discounted) price processes $Z(t,T) = B(t,T)/\beta(t)$ under Q must be equivalent to that which one observes under the "physical measure". (It is most definitely not sufficient to ensure that the distribution of the spot rate process r under Q be equivalent to that under P!)

The models we now present explicitly treat the entire term structure (the entire set of bond prices $B(t,T)$ for $T > t$, or something equivalent) as the description of the state of the system at date t, and prescribe the evolution of this term structure as t varies. These models are presented in [5] which contains a more complete exposition.

It is instructive to first consider how the term structure must evolve in a deterministic world if they are required not to allow arbitrage. (We omit a definition of "arbitrage" in this informal treatment, but roughly it means the existence of a strategy which gets something for nothing, with no risk of any loss.) In a deterministic world, the bond prices $B(t,T)$ are not random variables, but rather constants. Now suppose $s < t < T$, and consider two strategies which will deliver \$1 at date T:

Strategy 1: At date s, purchase one bond which matures at date T and hold it. This costs $B(s,T)$ at date s.

Strategy 2: At date s, purchase $B(t,T)$ (which is a constant, and hence is known at date t) shares of a bond maturing at date t. This results in the receipt of $B(t,T)$ units of cash at date t; use this cash to purchase one bond maturing at date T. Since one share of the bond maturing at t costs $B(s,t)$ at date s, this strategy costs $B(t,T)B(s,t)$.

Since these strategies produce the same result at date T and have no net cash flows except at dates s and T, to preclude arbitrage their date-s prices must be the same (assuming frictionless markets, short-selling allowed, etc.). Thus we conclude $B(t,T)B(s,t) = B(s,T)$. This means:

$$B(t,T) = \frac{B(s,T)}{B(s,t)}.$$

This specifies the term structure at date t in terms of that at date s. Our objective is to develop stochastic models for this evolution, and it is not immediately evident how one should introduce randomness into this simple deterministic model.

There are other ways to specify the term structure. Instead of specifying $B(t,T)$ for all $T > t$, one can specify the spot yields defined by: $y(t,T) = \frac{-\ln(B(t,T))}{T-t}$. Alternatively, assuming some smoothness of the bond prices, one can define the forward rates by $f(t,T) = -\frac{\partial(\ln(B(t,T)))}{\partial T}$ so that $B(t,T) = \exp(-\int_t^T f(t,u)du)$.

The "law of motion" for deterministic evolution (as described above) then becomes

$$y(t,T) = \frac{(T-s)y(s,T) - (t-s)y(s,t)}{T-t} \text{ for yields, or}$$

$$f(t,T) = f(s,T) \text{ for forward rates.}$$

Because of the simplicity of the evolution (in the deterministic case) expressed in terms of forward rates, we shall build our models in terms of the evolution of forward rates.

We assume given a probability space (Ω, F, P) and a standard (d-dimensional) Brownian motion $(W_t, t \geq 0)$ defined on it; we use the filtration $(F_t, t \geq 0)$ generated by the Brownian motion. (Our notation will suggest that $d = 1$ in this paper, but the higher-dimensional case is a simple extension.)

We take as our model $d_t f(t,T) = \sigma(t,T)dW_t + \alpha(t,T)dt$. More precisely, we assume

$$f(t,T,\omega) = f(0,T,\omega) + \int_0^t \sigma(s,T,\omega)dW_s + \int_0^t \alpha(s,T,\omega)ds.$$

REMARKS. We must of course assume that, for each T, the processes σ and α are adapted and suitably integrable stochastic processes. We define $r(t) = f(t,t)$. It follows that $B(t,T) = \exp(-\int_t^T (f(0,u) + \int_0^t \sigma(s,u)dW_s + \int_0^t \alpha(s,u)ds)du)$. Setting $\beta(t) = \exp(\int_0^t r(s)ds)$, one can use Ito's Lemma to compute

$$d_t\left(\frac{B(t,T)}{\beta(t)}\right) = B(t,T)\left\{\left(-\int_t^T \sigma(t,u)du\right)dW_t \right.$$
$$\left. + \left(-\int_t^T \alpha(t,u)du + \frac{1}{2}\left(\int_t^T \sigma(t,u)du\right)^2\right)dt\right\}.$$

(We note that this computation requires the use of a sort of "Fubini" theorem allowing the interchange of stochastic and Ito integrals, which is not difficult to prove.)

In order to ensure that the model does not allow arbitrage, we want to assure that there is an equivalent martingale measure. A converse of Girsanov's theorem (see Baxter and Rennie [1]) asserts that if Q is a probability measure equivalent to P, then there is an adapted, integrable process $\theta(\cdot)$ such that the process $\widetilde{W}_t = W_t + \int_0^t \theta(s)ds$ is a standard Brownian motion under Q. It follows that

$$d_t\left(\frac{B(t,T)}{\beta(t)}\right) = B(t,T)\left\{\left(-\int_t^T \sigma(t,u)du\right)d\widetilde{W}_t \right.$$
$$\left. + \left(\int_t^T (\sigma(t,u)\theta(t) - \alpha(t,u))du + \frac{1}{2}\left(\int_t^T \sigma(t,u)du\right)^2\right)dt\right\}.$$

This must be the differential of a martingale (under Q), and hence the coefficient of "dt" has to be 0. Thus we must have $\alpha(t,T) = \sigma(t,T)(\theta(t) + \int_t^T \sigma(t,u)du)$. And, finally, this means that $d_t f(t,T) = \sigma(t,T)d\widetilde{W}_t + \sigma(t,T)\int_t^T \sigma(t,u)du \, dt$.

Notice that α has vanished altogether! This means that the behavior of the price evolution under the equivalent martingale measure does not depend on α! (This corresponds to the "disappearance of μ" in the Black-Scholes formula.)

4. The pricing of contingent claims

The general method of pricing contingent claims arises from the fundamental theorem about no-arbitrage and the existence of equivalent martingale measures. Consider a market in which default risk free pure discount bonds trade together with another security with price process $\{X(t), t \geq 0\}$. Suppose we knew that for the bond prices alone (ignoring X) there is only one equivalent martingale measure Q. Then if Q' is any equivalent martingale measure for the whole market (including X), it must be equal to Q, since Q' would be an equivalent martingale for the bonds-only market. Thus $\frac{X(t)}{\beta(t)}$ must be a martingale for Q, and hence for $t < T$, $X(t) = \beta(t) E_Q(\frac{X(T)}{\beta(T)} | F_t)$. This gives the price for the claim at date t in terms of its (random) value at date T.

Thus we'd like to know conditions under which the martingale measure for our bond market is unique. To this end, suppose that Q^1 and Q^2 are equivalent martingale measures. Then there exist processes θ^1 and θ^2 as above. But then we must have $\alpha(t,T) = \sigma(t,T)(\theta^1(t) + \int_t^T \sigma(t,u)du) = \sigma(t,T)(\theta^2(t) + \int_t^T \sigma(t,u)du)$, which implies $\sigma(t,T)(\theta^1(t) - \theta^2(t)) \equiv 0$. Thus if $\sigma(t,\cdot)$ is not identically 0 (as a function of T) we must have $\theta^1(t) = \theta^2(t)$. And if this holds for almost every t, Q^1 and Q^2 are identical. (Actually, this argument works only for the 1-dimensional case. In higher dimensional models, the function σ is vector-valued, as is θ, and the situation is a little more complicated.)

5. Choosing a term structure model

We have seen above that choosing a term structure model is essentially the same as choosing a "volatility process" σ and an initial term structure $f(0, \cdot)$. For higher dimensional models (models for which the Brownian motion dimension d is greater than 1), σ must also be d-dimensional. More explicitly,

$$d_t f(t,T) = \sum_{i=1}^d \sigma_i(t,T) dW_t^i + \alpha(t,T) dt$$

or, under the equivalent martingale measure,

$$d_t f(t,T) = \sum_{i=1}^d \sigma_i(t,T) d\widetilde{W}_t^i + \sum_{i=1}^d \sigma_i(t,T) \int_t^T \sigma_i(t,u) du \, dt.$$

The simplest examples arise for $d = 1$ and simple choices for σ_1. For example, if σ_1 is taken to be a constant, say $\bar{\sigma}$, then

$$f(t,T) = f(0,T) + \bar{\sigma} \widetilde{W}_t + t\left(T - \frac{t}{2}\right)\bar{\sigma}^2.$$

This model is one in which the random shifts in forward rates affect rates of all maturities equally, i.e., the stochastic changes in forward rates result in "parallel shifts" of the forward curve. It is easy to see that this model produces negative forward rates (and negative spot rates) with positive probability. This model is essentially the continuous time version of the first full term structure model developed in discrete time by Ho and Lee [6]. It is also the simplest of a class of models introduced by Vasicek [8] corresponding to $\sigma_1(t,T) = \exp(-\lambda t)$.

In practice, models are often chosen based on estimation of historical term structure behavior and "adjusted" so that the model produces prices which agree with market prices for some marketed derivative instruments. Typically one assumes some model form and chooses model parameters either as estimates from historical data or to "calibrate" the model to match observed market prices. For example, one might choose the form $\sigma_i(t,T) = s(t)\bar{\sigma}_i(T-t)$. The univariate functions $\bar{\sigma}_i$ are estimated from historical data (using, for example, the method of principal components) and the function s is chosen to match prices of some options (like caps or swaptions). The estimated functions $\bar{\sigma}_i$ turn out to be remarkably similar when estimated over different time periods and even when estimated using data from different countries.

These models all produce negative interest rates with positive probability. To avoid this one is tempted to choose $\sigma_i(t,T,\omega) = s(t)\bar{\sigma}_i(T-t)f(t,T,\omega)$. Unfortunately, the solutions to the resulting stochastic differential equation for f explode with positive probability in any time interval. A form of this model sometimes used is:

$$\sigma_i(t,T,\omega) = s(t)\bar{\sigma}_i(T-t)\min(M, f(t,T,\omega))$$

for a large constant M. This prevents the undesired explosions, while keeping rates non-negative.

Valuation of claims (computed as expected discounted payoffs) under these models is often difficult since the motion of the term structure occurs in an infinite dimensional space. For simple models (like the Vasicek model) the motion stays in a low-dimensional subspace, so valuation is relatively easy, but for more interesting models the family of curves obtainable at date $t > 0$ is infinite dimensional. This means that valuation (i.e., computation of expected discounted values) is difficult, and techniques such as simulation must be used. In the simpler finite-dimensional settings, valuation can be carried out using standard numerical methods for partial differential equations.

References

[1] Baxter, Martin and Andrew Rennie, Financial Calculus, Cambridge University Press, 1994.
[2] Dalang, R.C., A. Morton and W. Willinger, Equivalent martingale measures and no-arbitrage in stochastic securities markets, Stoch. And Stoch. Reports, 29 (1990) 185-202.
[3] Delbaen, F., and W. Schachermayer, A general version of the fundamental theorem of asset pricing, Math. Ann., 300 (1994), 463-520.
[4] Harrison, M.J., and D. M. Kreps, Martingales and arbitrage in multiperiod securities markets, J. Economic Theory 29, (1979), 381-408
[5] Heath, D.C., R. Jarrow and A. Morton, Bond pricing and the term structure of interest rates: a new methodology, Econometrica, 60 (1992), 77-105.
[6] Ho, T.S.Y. and S-B Lee, Term structure movements and pricing interest rate contingent claims, Journal of Finance, 41 (1986), 1011-1029.
[7] Lackner, P., Martingale measure for a class of right-continuous processes, Math. Finance, 3 (1993), 43-53.
[8] Vasicek, O.A., An equilibrium characterization of the term structure, Journal of Financial Economics, 5 (1977), 177-188.

CARNEGIE MELLON UNIVERSITY

Transition Densities for Interest Rate and Other Nonlinear Diffusions

YACINE AÏT-SAHALIA*

ABSTRACT

This paper applies to interest rate models the theoretical method developed in Aït-Sahalia (1998) to generate accurate closed-form approximations to the transition function of an arbitrary diffusion. While the main focus of this paper is on the maximum-likelihood estimation of interest rate models with otherwise unknown transition functions, applications to the valuation of derivative securities are also briefly discussed.

CONTINUOUS-TIME MODELING IN FINANCE, though introduced by Louis Bachelier's 1900 thesis on the theory of speculation, really started with Merton's seminal work in the 1970s. Since then, the continuous-time paradigm has proved to be an immensely useful tool in finance and more generally economics. Continuous-time models are widely used to study issues that include the decision to optimally consume, save, and invest, portfolio choice under a variety of constraints, contingent claim pricing, capital accumulation, resource extraction, game theory, and more recently contract theory. Many refinements and extensions are possible, but the basic dynamic model for the variable(s) of interest X_t is a stochastic differential equation,

$$dX_t = \mu(X_t;\theta)dt + \sigma(X_t;\theta)dW_t, \qquad (1)$$

where W_t is a standard Brownian motion and the drift μ and diffusion σ^2 are known functions except for an unknown parameter[1] vector θ in a bounded set $\Theta \subset R^d$.

One major impediment to both theoretical modeling and empirical work with continuous-time models of this type is the fact that in most cases little can be said about the implications of the dynamics in equation (1) for longer

---

2000 *Mathematics Subject Classification.* Primary 60J35, 60J60, 91B28, 91B70.

Reprinted with permission from "Transition densities for interest rate and other nonlinear diffusions," Yacine Aït-Sahalia, *The Journal of Finance*, vol. LIV, No. 4, August 1999, Blackwell Publishers.

*Department of Economics, Princeton University. *Mathematica* code to implement this method can be found at http://www.princeton.edu/~yacine. I am grateful to David Bates, René Carmona, Freddy Delbaen, Ron Gallant, Lars Hansen, Per Mykland, Peter C. B. Phillips, Peter Robinson, Angel Serrat, Suresh Sundaresan, and George Tauchen for helpful comments. Robert Kimmel provided excellent research assistance. This research was conducted during the author's tenure as an Alfred P. Sloan Research Fellow. Financial support from the NSF (Grant SBR-9996023) is gratefully acknowledged.

[1] Non- and semiparametric approaches, which do not constrain the functional form of the functions μ and/or σ^2 to be within a parametric class, have been developed (see Aït-Sahalia (1996a, 1996b) and Stanton (1997)).

time intervals. Though equation (1) fully describes the evolution of the variable X over each infinitesimal instant, one cannot in general characterize in closed form an object as simple (and fundamental for everything from prediction to estimation and derivative pricing) as the conditional density of $X_{t+\Delta}$ given the current value X_t. For a list of the rare exceptions, see Wong (1964). In finance, the well-known models of Black and Scholes (1973), Vasicek (1977), and Cox, Ingersoll, and Ross (1985) rely on these existing closed-form expressions. In this paper, I describe and implement empirically a method developed in a companion paper (Aït-Sahalia (1998)) which produces very accurate approximations *in closed form* to the unknown transition function $p_X(\Delta, x | x_0; \theta)$, the conditional density of $X_{t+\Delta} = x$ given $X_t = x_0$ implied by the model in equation (1).

These closed-form expressions can be useful for at least two purposes. First, they let us estimate the parameter vector θ by maximum-likelihood.[2] In most cases, we observe the process at dates $\{t = i\Delta | i = 0, \ldots, n\}$, where $\Delta > 0$ is generally small, but fixed as n increases. For instance, the series could be weekly or monthly. Collecting more observations means lengthening the time period over which data are recorded, not shortening the time interval between successive existing observations.[3] Because a continuous-time diffusion is a Markov process, and that property carries over to any discrete subsample from the continuous-time path, the log-likelihood function has the simple form

$$\ell_n(\theta) \equiv n^{-1} \sum_{i=1}^n \ln\{p_X(\Delta, X_{i\Delta} | X_{(i-1)\Delta}; \theta)\}. \tag{2}$$

With a given Δ, two methods are available in the literature to compute p_X numerically. They involve either solving numerically the Kolmogorov partial differential equation known to be satisfied by p_X (see, e.g., Lo (1988)), or simulating a large number of sample paths along which the process is sampled very finely (see Pedersen (1995), Honoré (1997), and Santa-Clara (1995)). Neither method however produces a closed-form expression to be maximized

---

[2] A large number of new approaches have been developed in recent years. Some theoretical estimation methods are based on the generalized method of moments (Hansen and Scheinkman (1995) and Bibby and Sørenson (1995)) and on nonparametric density-matching (Aït-Sahalia (1996a, 1996b)), others are based on nonparametric approximate moments (Stanton (1997)), simulations (Duffie and Singleton (1993), Gouriéroux, Monfort, and Renault (1993), Gallant and Tauchen (1998), and Pedersen (1995)), the spectral decomposition of the infinitesimal generator (Hansen, Scheinkman, and Touzi (1998) and Florens, Renault, and Touzi (1995)), random sampling of the process to generate moment conditions (Duffie and Glynn (1997)), or, finally, Bayesian approaches (Eraker (1997), Jones (1997), and Elerian, Chib, and Shephard (1998)).

[3] Discrete approximations to the stochastic differential equation (1) could be employed (see Kloeden and Platen (1992)): see Chan et al. (1992) for an example. As discussed by Merton (1980), Lo (1988), and Melino (1994), ignoring the difference generally results in inconsistent estimators, unless the discretization happens to be an exact one, which is tantamount to saying that p_X would have to be known in closed form.

over θ, and the calculations for all the pairs (x, x_0) must be repeated separately every time the value of θ changes. By contrast, the closed-form expressions in this paper make it possible to maximize the expression in equation (2) with p_X replaced by its closed-form approximation.

Derivative pricing provides a second natural outlet for applications of this methodology. Suppose that we are interested in pricing at date zero a derivative security written on an asset with price process $\{X_t | t \geq 0\}$, and with payoff function $\Psi(X_\Delta)$ at some future date Δ. For simplicity, assume that the underlying asset is traded, so that its risk-neutral dynamics have the form

$$dX_t/X_t = \{r - \delta\}dt + \sigma(X_t; \theta)dW_t, \tag{3}$$

where r is the riskfree rate and δ is the dividend rate paid by the asset—both constant again for simplicity.

It is well known that when markets are dynamically complete, the only price of the derivative security that is compatible with the absence of arbitrage opportunities is

$$P_0 = e^{-r\Delta} E[\Psi(X_\Delta)|X_0 = x_0] = e^{-r\Delta} \int_0^{+\infty} \Psi(x) p_X(\Delta, x | x_0; \theta) \, dx, \tag{4}$$

where p_X is the transition function (or risk-neutral density, or state-price density) induced by the dynamics in equation (3).

The Black–Scholes option pricing formula is the prime example of equation (4), when $\sigma(X_t; \theta) = \sigma$ is constant. The corresponding p_X is known in closed-form (as a lognormal density) and so the integral in equation (4) can be evaluated explicitly for specific payoff functions (see also Cox and Ross (1976)). In general, of course, no known expression for p_X is available and one must rely on numerical methods such as solving numerically the PDE satisfied by the derivative price, or Monte Carlo integration of equation (3). These methods are the exact parallels to the two existing approaches to maximum-likelihood estimation that I described earlier.

Here, given the sequence $\{\tilde{p}_X^{(K)} | K \geq 0\}$ of approximations to p_X, the valuation of the derivative security would be based on the explicit formula

$$P_0^{(K)} = e^{-r\Delta} \int_0^{+\infty} \Psi(x) \tilde{p}_X^{(K)}(\Delta, x | x_0; \theta) \, dx. \tag{5}$$

Formulas of the type given in equation (4) where the unknown p_X is replaced by another density have been proposed in the finance literature (see, e.g., Jarrow and Rudd (1982)). There is an important difference, however, between what I propose and the existing formulas: the latter are based on calculating the integral in equation (4) with an ad hoc density $\tilde{p}_X$—typically adding free skewness and kurtosis parameters to the lognormal density, so as to allow for departures from the Black–Scholes formula. In doing so, these formulas ignore the underlying dynamic model specified in equation (3) for the asset price, whereas my method gives in closed form the option pricing formula (of order of precision corresponding to that of the approximation used) that corresponds to the given dynamic model in equation (3). Then one can, for instance, explore how changes in the specification of the volatility function $\sigma(x;\theta)$ affect the derivative price, which is obviously impossible when the specification of the density $\hat{p}_X$ to be used in equation (4) in lieu of p_X is unrelated to equation (3).

The paper is organized as follows. In Section I, I briefly describe the approach used in Aït-Sahalia (1998) to derive a closed-form sequence of approximations to p_X, give the expressions for the approximation, and describe its properties. In Section II, I study a number of interest rate models, some with unknown transition functions, and give the closed-form expressions of the corresponding approximations. Section III reports maximum-likelihood estimates for these models using the Federal funds rate, sampled monthly from 1963 through 1998. Section IV concludes, and a statement of the technical assumptions is in the Appendix.

I. Closed-Form Approximations to the Transition Function

A. Tail Standardization via Transformation to Unit Diffusion

The first step toward constructing the sequence of approximations to p_X consists of standardizing the diffusion function of X—that is, transforming X into another diffusion Y defined as

$$Y_t \equiv \gamma(X_t;\theta) = \int^{X_t} du/\sigma(u;\theta), \qquad (6)$$

where any primitive of the function $1/\sigma$ may be selected.

Let $D_X = (\underline{x},\bar{x})$ denote the domain of the diffusion X. I will consider two cases, where $D_X = (-\infty,+\infty)$ or $D_X = (0,+\infty)$. The latter case is often relevant in finance, when considering models for asset prices or nominal interest rates. Moreover, the function σ is often specified in financial models in such a way that $\sigma(0;\theta) = 0$ and μ and/or σ violates the linear growth conditions near the boundaries. The assumptions in the Appendix allow for this behavior.

Because $\sigma > 0$ on the interior of the domain D_X, the function γ in equation (6) is increasing and thus invertible. It maps D_X into $D_Y = (\underline{y},\bar{y})$, the domain of Y. For a given model under consideration, I will assume that the parameter space Θ is restricted in such a way that D_Y is independent of θ in Θ. This restriction on Θ is inessential, but it helps keep the notation simple. Again, in finance, most, if not all cases, will have D_X and D_Y be either the whole real line $(-\infty,+\infty)$ or the half line $(0,+\infty)$.

By applying Itô's Lemma, Y has unit diffusion as desired:

$$dY_t = \mu_Y(Y_t;\theta)dt + dW_t, \tag{7}$$

where

$$\mu_Y(y;\theta) = \frac{\mu(\gamma^{-1}(y;\theta);\theta)}{\sigma(\gamma^{-1}(y;\theta);\theta)} - \frac{1}{2}\frac{\partial\sigma}{\partial x}(\gamma^{-1}(y;\theta);\theta). \tag{8}$$

Finally, note that it can be convenient to define Y_t instead as minus the integral in equation (6) if that makes $Y_t > 0$, for instance if $\sigma(x;\theta) = x^\rho$ and $\rho > 1$. For example, if $D_X = (0,+\infty)$ and $\sigma(x;\theta) = x^\rho$, then $Y_t = (1-\rho)X_t^{1-\rho}$ if $0 < \rho < 1$ (so $D_Y = (0,+\infty)$), $Y_t = \ln(X_t)$ if $\rho = 1$ (so $D_Y = (-\infty,+\infty)$), and $Y_t = (\rho - 1)X_t^{-(\rho-1)}$ if $\rho > 1$ (so $D_Y = (0,+\infty)$ again). In all cases, Y has unit diffusion; that is, $\sigma_Y^2(y;\theta) = 1$. When the transformation $Y_t \equiv \gamma(X_t;\theta) = -\int^{X_t} du/\sigma(u;\theta)$ is used, the drift $\mu_Y(y;\theta)$ in $dY_t = \mu_Y(Y_t;\theta)dt - dW_t$ is, instead of equation (8),

$$\mu_Y(y;\theta) = -\frac{\mu(\gamma^{-1}(y;\theta);\theta)}{\sigma(\gamma^{-1}(y;\theta);\theta)} + \frac{1}{2}\frac{\partial\sigma}{\partial x}(\gamma^{-1}(y;\theta);\theta). \tag{9}$$

The point of making the transformation from X to Y is that it is possible to construct an expansion for the transition density of Y. Of course, this would be of little interest because we only observe X, not the artificially introduced Y, and the transformation depends on the unknown parameter vector θ. However, the transformation is useful because one can obtain the transition density p_X from p_Y through the Jacobian formula

$$p_X(\Delta,x|x_0;\theta) = \frac{\partial}{\partial x}\text{Prob}(X_{t+\Delta} \leq x|X_t = x_0;\theta)$$

$$= \frac{\partial}{\partial x}\text{Prob}(Y_{t+\Delta} \leq \gamma(x;\theta)|Y_t = \gamma(x_0;\theta);\theta)$$

$$= \frac{\partial}{\partial x}\left[\int_{\underline{y}}^{\gamma(x;\theta)} p_Y(\Delta,y|\gamma(y_0;\theta);\theta)dy\right]$$

$$= \frac{p_Y(\Delta,\gamma(x;\theta)|\gamma(x_0;\theta);\theta)}{\sigma(\gamma(x;\theta);\theta)}. \tag{10}$$

Therefore, there is never any need to actually transform the data $\{X_{i\Delta}, i = 0,\ldots,n\}$ into observations on Y (which depends on θ anyway). Instead, the transformation from X to Y is simply a device to obtain an approximation for p_X from the approximation of p_Y. Practically speaking, when the approximation for p_X has been derived once and for all as the Jacobian transform of that of Y, the process Y no longer plays any role.

B. Explicit Expressions for the Approximation

As shown in Aït-Sahalia (1998), one can derive an explicit expansion for the transition density of the variable Y based on a Hermite expansion of its density $y \mapsto p_Y(\Delta,y|y_0;\theta)$ around a Normal density function. The analytic part of the expansion of p_Y up to order K is given by

$$\tilde{p}_Y^{(K)}(\Delta,y|y_0;\theta) = \Delta^{-1/2}\phi\left(\frac{y-y_0}{\Delta^{1/2}}\right)\exp\left(\int_{y_0}^{y}\mu_Y(w;\theta)dw\right)\sum_{k=0}^{K}c_k(y|y_0;\theta)\frac{\Delta^k}{k!},$$

(11)

where $\phi(z) \equiv e^{-z^2/2}/\sqrt{2\pi}$ denotes the $N(0,1)$ density function, $c_0(y|y_0;\theta) = 1$, and for all $j \geq 1$,

$$c_j(y|y_0;\theta) = j(y-y_0)^{-j}\int_{y_0}^{y}(w-y_0)^{j-1}$$
$$\times \{\lambda_Y(w)c_{j-1}(w|y_0;\theta) + (\partial^2 c_{j-1}(w|y_0;\theta)/\partial w^2)/2\}\,dw, \quad (12)$$

where $\lambda_Y(y;\theta) \equiv -(\mu_Y^2(y;\theta) + \partial\mu_Y(y;\theta)/\partial y)/2$.

Tables I through V give the explicit expression of these coefficients for popular models in finance, which I discuss in detail in Section II. Before turning to these examples, a few general remarks are in order. The general structure of the expansion in equation (11) is as follows: The leading term in the expansion is Gaussian, $\Delta^{-1/2}\phi((y-y_0)/\Delta^{1/2})$, followed by a correction for the presence of the drift, $\exp(\int_{y_0}^{y}\mu_Y(w;\theta)\,dw)$, and then additional correction terms that depend on the specification of the function $\lambda_Y(y;\theta)$ and its successive derivatives. These correction terms play two roles: they account for the nonnormality of p_Y and they correct for the discretization bias implicit in starting the expansion with a Gaussian term with no mean adjustment and variance Δ (instead of $\text{Var}[Y_{t+\Delta}|Y_t]$, which is equal to Δ only in the first order).

In general, the function p_Y is not analytic in time. Therefore equation (11) must be interpreted strictly as the analytic part, or Taylor series. In particular, for given (y,y_0,θ) it will generally have a finite convergence radius in Δ. As we will see below, however, the series in equation (11) with $K = 1$ or 2 at most is **very** accurate for the values of Δ that one encounters in empirical work in finance.

The sequence of explicit functions $\tilde{p}_Y^{(K)}$ in equation (11) is designed to approximate p_Y. As discussed above, one can then approximate p_X (the object of interest) by using the Jacobian formula for the inverted change of variable $Y \to X$:

$$\tilde{p}_X^{(K)}(\Delta, x | x_0; \theta) \equiv \sigma(x; \theta)^{-1} \tilde{p}_Y^{(K)}(\Delta, \gamma(x; \theta) | \gamma(x_0; \theta); \theta). \tag{13}$$

The main objective of the transformation $X \to Y$ was to provide a method of controlling the size of the tails of the transition density. As shown in Aït-Sahalia (1998), the fact that Y has unit diffusion makes the tails of the density p_Y, in the limit where Δ goes to zero, similar in magnitude to those of a Gaussian variable. That is, the tails of p_Y behave like $\exp[-y^2/2\Delta]$ as is apparent from equation (11). However, the tails of the density p_X are proportional to $\exp[-\gamma(x;\theta)^2/2\Delta]$. So, for instance, if $\sigma(x;\theta) = 2\sqrt{x}$ then $\gamma(x;\theta) = \sqrt{x}$ and the right tail of p_X becomes proportional to $\exp[-x^2/2\Delta]$; this is verified by equation (13). Not surprisingly, this is the tail behavior for Feller's transition density in the Cox, Ingersoll, and Ross (1985) model. If now $\sigma(x;\theta) = x$, then $\gamma(x;\theta) = \ln(x)$ and the tails of p_X are proportional to $\exp[-\ln(x)^2/2\Delta]$: this is what happens in the log-Normal case (see the Black–Scholes model). In other words, while the leading term of the expansion in equation (11) for p_Y is Gaussian, the expansion for p_X will start with a deformed or "stretched" Gaussian term, with the specific form of the deformation given by the function $\gamma(x;\theta)$.

The sequence of functions in equation (11) solves the forward and backward Kolmogorov equations up to order Δ^K; that is,

$$\begin{cases} \dfrac{\partial \tilde{p}_Y^{(K)}}{\partial \Delta} + \dfrac{\partial}{\partial y}\{\mu_Y(y;\theta)\tilde{p}_Y^{(K)}\} - \dfrac{1}{2}\dfrac{\partial^2 \tilde{p}_Y^{(K)}}{\partial y^2} = O(\Delta^K) \\ \dfrac{\partial \tilde{p}_Y^{(K)}}{\partial \Delta} - \mu_Y(y_0;\theta)\dfrac{\partial \tilde{p}_Y^{(K)}}{\partial y_0} - \dfrac{1}{2}\dfrac{\partial^2 \tilde{p}_Y^{(K)}}{\partial y_0^2} = O(\Delta^K) \end{cases}. \tag{14}$$

The boundary behavior of the transition density $\tilde{p}_Y^{(K)}$ is similar to that of p_Y; under the assumptions made, $\lim_{y \to \underline{y} \text{ or } \bar{y}} p_Y = 0$. The expansion is designed to deliver an approximation of the density function $y \mapsto p_Y(\Delta, y | y_0; \theta)$ for a fixed value of conditioning variable y_0. Therefore, except in the limit where Δ becomes infinitely small, it is not designed to reproduce the limiting behavior of p_Y in the limit where y_0 tends to the boundaries.

Finally, note that the form of the expansion is compatible with the expression that arises out of Girsanov's Theorem in the following sense. Under the assumptions made, the process Y can be transformed by Girsanov's Theorem into a Brownian motion if $D_Y = (-\infty, +\infty)$, or into a Bessel process in dimension 3 if $D_Y = (0, +\infty)$. This gives rise to a formulation of p_Y in a form that involves the conditional expectation of the exponential of the integral of function of a Brownian Bridge (see Gihman and Skorohod (1972, Chap. 3) for the case where $D_Y = (-\infty, +\infty)$), or a Bessel Bridge if $D_Y = (0, +\infty)$. This conditional expectation term can either be expressed in terms of the conditional densities of the Brownian Bridge when $D_Y = (-\infty, +\infty)$ (see Dacunha-Castelle and Florens-Zmirou (1986)), or integrated by Monte Carlo simulation. Further discussion of these and other theoretical properties of the expansion is contained in Aït-Sahalia (1998).

II. Examples

A. Comparison of the Approximation to the Closed-Form Densities for Specific Models

In this section, I study the size of the approximation made when replacing p_X by $\tilde{p}_X^{(K)}$, in the case of typical examples in finance where p_X is known in closed form and sampling is at the monthly frequency. Since the performance of the approximation improves as Δ gets smaller, monthly sampling is taken to represent a worst-case scenario as the upper bound to the sampling interval relevant for finance. In practice, most continuous-time models in finance are estimated with monthly, weekly, daily, or higher frequency observations. The examples studied below reveal that including the term $c_2(y, y_0; \theta)$ generally provides an approximation to p_X which is better by a factor of at least 10 than what one obtains when only the term $c_1(y, y_0; \theta)$ is included. Further calculations show that each additional order produces additional improvements by an additional factor of at least 10.

I will often compare the expansion in this paper to the Euler approximation; the latter corresponds to a simple discretization of the continuous-time stochastic differential equation, where the differential equation (1) is replaced by the difference equation

$$X_{t+\Delta} - X_t = \mu(X_t; \theta)\Delta + \sigma(X_t; \theta)\sqrt{\Delta}\epsilon_{t+\Delta} \tag{15}$$

with $\epsilon_{t+\Delta} \sim N(0,1)$, so that

$$p_X^{\text{Euler}}(\Delta, x | x_0; \theta) = (2\pi\Delta\sigma^2(x_0; \theta))^{-1/2}$$
$$\times \exp\{-(x - x_0 - \mu(x_0; \theta)\Delta)^2 / 2\Delta\sigma^2(x_0; \theta)\}. \tag{16}$$

Example 1 (Vasicek's Model): Consider the Ornstein–Uhlenbeck specification proposed by Vasicek (1977) for the short-term interest rate:

$$dX_t = \kappa(\alpha - X_t)dt + \sigma dW_t. \tag{17}$$

X is distributed on $D_X = (-\infty, +\infty)$ and has the Gaussian transition density

$$p_X(\Delta, x | x_0; \theta) = (\pi\gamma^2/\kappa)^{-1/2}\exp\{-(x - \alpha - (x_0 - \alpha)e^{-\kappa\Delta})^2\kappa/\gamma^2\}, \tag{18}$$

Table I
Explicit Sequence for the Vasicek Model

This table contains the coefficients of the density approximation for p_Y corresponding to the Vasicek model in Example 1, $dX_t = \kappa(\alpha - X_t)dt + \sigma dW_t$. The terms in the expansion are evaluated by applying the formulas in equation (12). From equation (11), the $K = 0$ term in this expansion is $\tilde{p}_Y^{(0)}(\Delta, y|y_0; \theta)$, the $K = 1$ term is

$$\tilde{p}_Y^{(1)}(\Delta, y|y_0; \theta) = \tilde{p}_Y^{(0)}(\Delta, y|y_0; \theta)\{1 + c_1(y|y_0; \theta)\Delta\},$$

and the $K = 2$ term is

$$\tilde{p}_Y^{(2)}(\Delta, y|y_0; \theta) = \tilde{p}_Y^{(0)}(\Delta, y|y_0; \theta)\{1 + c_1(y|y_0; \theta)\Delta + c_2(y|y_0; \theta)\Delta^2/2\}.$$

Additional terms can be obtained in the same manner by applying equation (12) further. These computations and those of Tables II to V were all carried out in *Mathematica*.

$$\tilde{p}_Y^{(0)}(\Delta, y|y_0, \theta) = \frac{1}{\sqrt{\Delta}\sqrt{2\pi}} \exp\left[-\frac{(y-y_0)^2}{2\Delta} - \frac{y^2\kappa}{2} + \frac{y_0^2\kappa}{2} + \frac{y\alpha\kappa}{\sigma} - \frac{y_0\alpha\kappa}{\sigma}\right].$$

$$c_1(y|y_0,\theta) = -\frac{1}{6\sigma^2}\left(\kappa(3\alpha^2\kappa - 3(y+y_0)\alpha\kappa\sigma + (-3 + y^2\kappa + yy_0\kappa + y_0^2\kappa)\sigma^2)\right).$$

$$c_2(y|y_0,\theta) = \frac{1}{36\sigma^4}\left(\kappa^2(9\alpha^4\kappa^2 - 18y\alpha^3\kappa^2\sigma + 3\alpha^2\kappa(-6 + 5y^2\kappa)\sigma^2\right.$$
$$- 6y\alpha\kappa(-3 + y^2\kappa)\sigma^3 + (3 - 6y^2\kappa + y^4\kappa^2)\sigma^4$$
$$+ 2\kappa\sigma(-3\alpha + y\sigma)(3\alpha^2\kappa - 3y\alpha\kappa\sigma + (-3 + y^2\kappa)\sigma^2)y_0$$
$$+ 3\kappa\sigma^2(5\alpha^2\kappa - 4y\alpha\kappa\sigma + (-2 + y^2\kappa)\sigma^2)y_0^2 + 2\kappa^2\sigma^3(-3\alpha + y\sigma)y_0^3$$
$$\left.+ \kappa^2\sigma^4y_0^4)\right).$$

where $\theta \equiv (\alpha, \kappa, \sigma)$ and $\gamma^2 \equiv \sigma^2(1 - e^{-2\kappa\Delta})$. In this case, we have that $Y_t = \gamma(X_t; \theta) = \sigma^{-1}X_t$ and $\mu_Y(y; \theta) = \kappa\alpha\sigma^{-1} - \kappa y$, so that $\lambda_Y(y; \theta) = \kappa/2 - \kappa^2(\alpha - \sigma y)^2/2\sigma^2$.

Table I reports the first two terms in the expansion for this model, obtained from applying the general formula in equation (11). More terms can be calculated in equation (12) one after the other: once $c_2(y|y_0; \theta)$ has been obtained, calculate $c_3(y|y_0; \theta)$, etc. Starting from the closed-form expression, one can show directly that these expressions indeed represent a Taylor series expansion for the closed-form density $p_X(\Delta, x|x_0; \theta)$.

Figure 1A plots the density p_X as a function of the interest rate value x for a monthly sampling frequency ($\Delta = 1/12$), evaluated at $x_0 = 0.10$ and for the parameter values corresponding to the maximum-likelihood estimator from the Federal funds data (see Table VI in Section IV below). Figure 1B plots

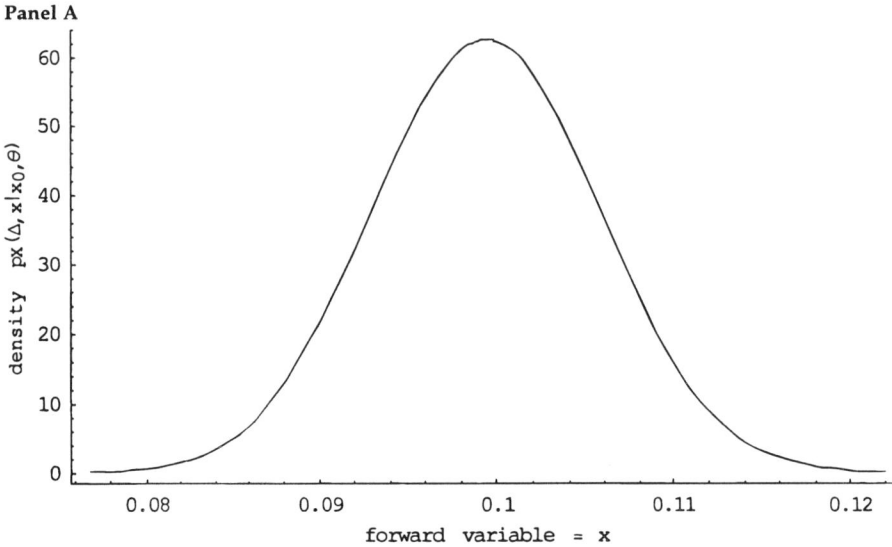

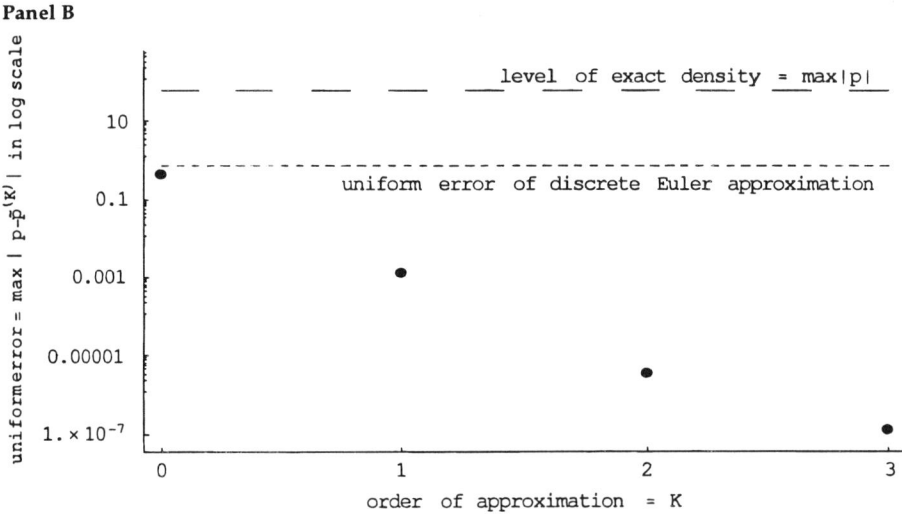

Figure 1. Exact conditional density and approximation errors for the Vasicek model. Figure 1A plots for the Vasicek (1977) model (see Example 1 and Table I) the closed-form conditional density $x \mapsto p_X(\Delta, x | x_0, \theta)$ as a function of x, with $x_0 = 10$ percent, monthly sampling ($\Delta = 1/12$) and θ replaced by the MLE reported in Table VI. Figure 1B plots the uniform approximation error $|p_X - \tilde{p}_X^{(K)}|$ for $K = 1, 2,$ and 3, in log-scale, so that each unit on the y-axis corresponds to a reduction of the error by a multiplicative factor of 10. The error is calculated as the maximum absolute deviation between p_X and $\tilde{p}_X^{(K)}$ over the range ± 4 standard deviations around the mean of the density. Both the value of the exact conditional density at its peak and the uniform error for the Euler approximation p_X^{Euler} are also reported for comparison purposes. This figure illustrates the speed of convergence of the approximation. A lower sampling interval than monthly would provide an even faster convergence of the density approximation sequence.

the uniform approximation error $|p_X - \tilde{p}_X^{(K)}|$ for $K = 1$, 2, and 3, *in log-scale*. The error is calculated as the maximum absolute deviation between p_X and $\tilde{p}_X^{(K)}$ over the range ± 4 standard deviations around the mean of the density, and is also compared to the uniform error for the Euler approximation. The striking feature of the results is the speed of convergence to zero of the approximation error as K goes from 1 to 2 and from 2 to 3. In effect, one can approximate p_X (which is of order 10^{+1}) within 10^{-3} with the first term alone ($K = 1$) and within 10^{-7} with $K = 3$, even though the interest rate process is only sampled once a month. Similar calculations for a weekly sampling frequency ($\Delta = 1/52$) reveal that the approximation error gets smaller even faster for this lower value of Δ.

In other words, small values of K already produce extremely precise approximations to the true density, p_X, and the approximation is even more precise if Δ is smaller. Of course, the exact density being Gaussian, in this case the expansion, whose leading term is Gaussian, has fairly little "work" to do to approximate the true density. In the Ornstein–Uhlenbeck case, the expansion involves no correction for nonnormality, which is normally achieved through the change of variable X to Y; it reduces here to a linear transformation and therefore does not change the nature of the leading term in the expansion. Comparing the performance of the expansion to that of the Euler approximation in this model (where both have the correct Gaussian form for the density) reveals that the expansion is capable of correcting for the discretization bias involved in a discrete approximation, whereas the Euler approximation is limited to a first-order bias correction. In this case, the Euler approximation can be refined by increasing the precision of the conditional mean and variance approximations (see Huggins (1997)). Of course, discrete approximations to equation (1) of an order higher than equation (15) are available, but they do not lead to explicit *density* approximations since, compared to the Euler equation (15), they involve combinations of multiple powers of $\epsilon_{t+\Delta}$ (see, e.g., Kloeden and Platen (1992)).

Example 2 (The CIR Model): Consider Feller's (1952) square-root specification

$$dX_t = \kappa(\alpha - X_t)dt + \sigma\sqrt{X_t}\,dW_t, \tag{19}$$

proposed as a model for the short-term interest rate by Cox et al. (1985). X is distributed on $D_X = (0, +\infty)$ provided that $q \equiv 2\kappa\alpha/\sigma^2 - 1 \geq 0$. Its transition density is given by

$$p_X(\Delta, x | x_0; \theta) = ce^{-u-v}(v/u)^{q/2}I_q(2(uv)^{1/2}), \tag{20}$$

with $\theta \equiv (\alpha, \kappa, \sigma)$ all positive, $c \equiv 2\kappa/(\sigma^2\{1 - e^{-\kappa\Delta}\})$, $u \equiv cx_0 e^{-\kappa\Delta}$, $v \equiv cx$, and I_q is the modified Bessel function of the first kind of order q. Here $Y_t = \gamma(X_t; \theta) = 2\sqrt{X_t}/\sigma$ and $\mu_Y(y; \theta) = (q + 1/2)/y - \kappa y/2$.

Table II
Explicit Sequence for the Cox–Ingersoll–Ross Model

This table contains the coefficients of the density approximation for p_Y corresponding to the Cox, Ingersoll, and Ross model in Example 2, $dX_t = \kappa(\alpha - X_t)dt + \sigma\sqrt{X_t}\,dW_t$. The expansion for p_Y in this table applies also to the model proposed by Ahn and Gao (1988) (see Example 3). The terms in the expansion are evaluated by applying the formulas in equation (12). From equation (11), the $K = 0$ term in this expansion is $\tilde{p}_Y^{(0)}(\Delta, y|y_0;\theta)$, the $K = 1$ term is

$$\tilde{p}_Y^{(1)}(\Delta,y|y_0;\theta) = \tilde{p}_Y^{(0)}(\Delta,y|y_0;\theta)\{1 + c_1(y|y_0;\theta)\Delta\},$$

and the $K = 2$ term is

$$\tilde{p}_Y^{(2)}(\Delta,y|y_0;\theta) = \tilde{p}_Y^{(0)}(\Delta,y|y_0;\theta)\{1 + c_1(y|y_0;\theta)\Delta + c_2(y|y_0;\theta)\Delta^2/2\}.$$

Additional terms can be obtained in the same manner by applying equation (12) further.

$$\tilde{p}_X^{(0)}(\Delta,y|y_0,\theta) = \frac{1}{\sqrt{\Delta}\sqrt{2\pi}} \exp\left[-\frac{(y-y_0)^2}{2\Delta} - \frac{y^2\kappa}{4} + \frac{\kappa y_0^2}{4}\right] y^{-(1/2)+(2\alpha\kappa/\sigma^2)} y_0^{(1/2)-(2\alpha\kappa/\sigma^2)}.$$

$$c_1(y|y_0\theta) = -\frac{1}{24yy_0\sigma^4}\left(48\alpha^2\kappa^2 - 48\alpha\kappa\sigma^2 + 9\sigma^4 + y\kappa^2\sigma^2(-24\alpha + y^2\sigma^2)y_0\right.$$
$$\left. + y^2\kappa^2\sigma^4 y_0^2 + y\kappa^2\sigma^4 y_0^3\right).$$

$$c_2(y|y_0\theta) = \frac{1}{576y^2 y_0^2 \sigma^8}\left(9(256\alpha^4\kappa^4 - 512\alpha^3\kappa^3\sigma^2 + 224\alpha^2\kappa^2\sigma^4 + 32\alpha\kappa\sigma^6 - 15\sigma^8)\right.$$
$$+ 6y\kappa^2\sigma^2(-24\alpha + y^2\sigma^2)(16\alpha^2\kappa^2 - 16\alpha\kappa\sigma^2 + 3\sigma^4)y_0$$
$$+ y^2\kappa^2\sigma^4(672\alpha^2\kappa^2 - 48\alpha\kappa(2 + y^2\kappa)\sigma^2 + (-6 + y^4\kappa^2)\sigma^4)y_0^2$$
$$+ 2y\kappa^2\sigma^4(48\alpha^2\kappa^2 - 24\alpha\kappa(2 + y^2\kappa)\sigma^2 + (9 + y^4\kappa^2)\sigma^4)y_0^3$$
$$\left. + 3y^2\kappa^4\sigma^6(-16\alpha + y^2\sigma^2)y_0^4 + 2y^3\kappa^4\sigma^8 y_0^5 + y^2\kappa^4\sigma^8 y_0^6\right).$$

The first two terms in the explicit expansion are given in Table II. When evaluated at the maximum-likelihood estimates from Fed funds data, the results reported in Figure 2 are very similar to those of Figure 1, again with an extremely fast convergence even for a monthly sampling frequency. The uniform approximation error is reduced to 10^{-5} with the first two terms, and 10^{-8} with the first three terms included.

Example 3 (Inverse of Feller's Square Root Model): In this example, I generate densities for Ahn and Gao's (1998) specification of the interest rate process as one over an auxiliary process that follows a Cox–Ingersoll–Ross specification. As a result of Itô's Lemma, the model's specification is

$$dX_t = X_t(\kappa - (\sigma^2 - \kappa\alpha)X_t)dt + \sigma X_t^{3/2} dW_t, \tag{21}$$

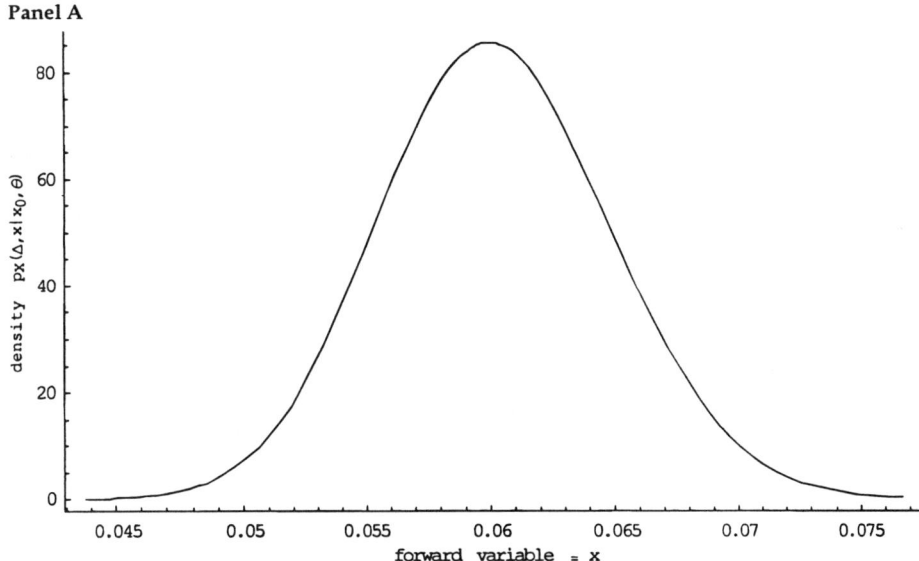
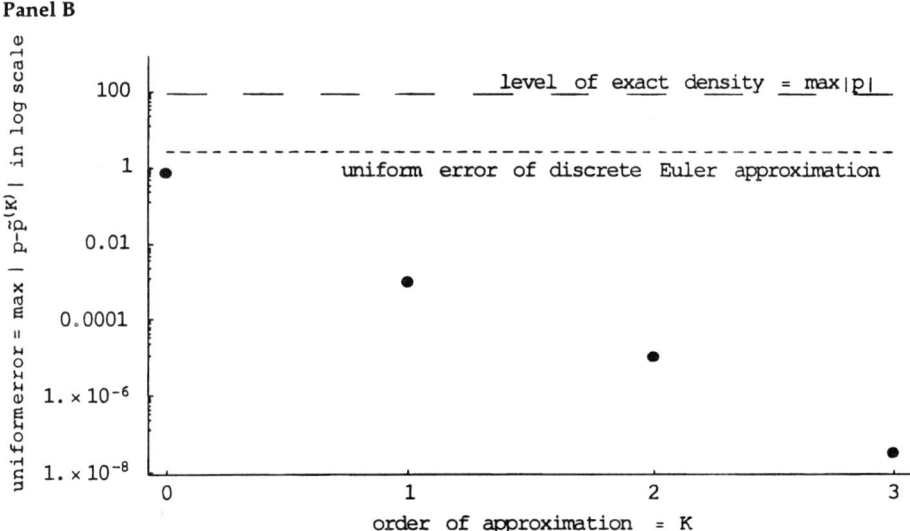

Figure 2. **Exact conditional density and approximation errors for the Cox–Ingersoll–Ross model.** Figure 2A plots for the CIR (1985) model (see Example 2 and Table II) the closed-form conditional density $x \mapsto p_X(\Delta, x|x_0, \theta)$ as a function of x, with $x_0 = 6$ percent, monthly sampling ($\Delta = 1/12$) and θ replaced by the MLE reported in Table VI. Figure 2B plots the uniform approximation error $|p_X - \tilde{p}_X^{(K)}|$ for $K = 1, 2$, and 3, in log-scale, so that each unit on the y-axis corresponds to a reduction of the error by a multiplicative factor of 10. The error is calculated as the maximum absolute deviation between p_X and $\tilde{p}_X^{(K)}$ over the range ± 4 standard deviations around the mean of the density. Both the value of the exact conditional density at its peak and the uniform error for the Euler approximation p_X^{Euler} are also reported for comparison purposes. This figure illustrates the speed of convergence of the approximation.

Panel A

μ(x)

Panel B

π(x)

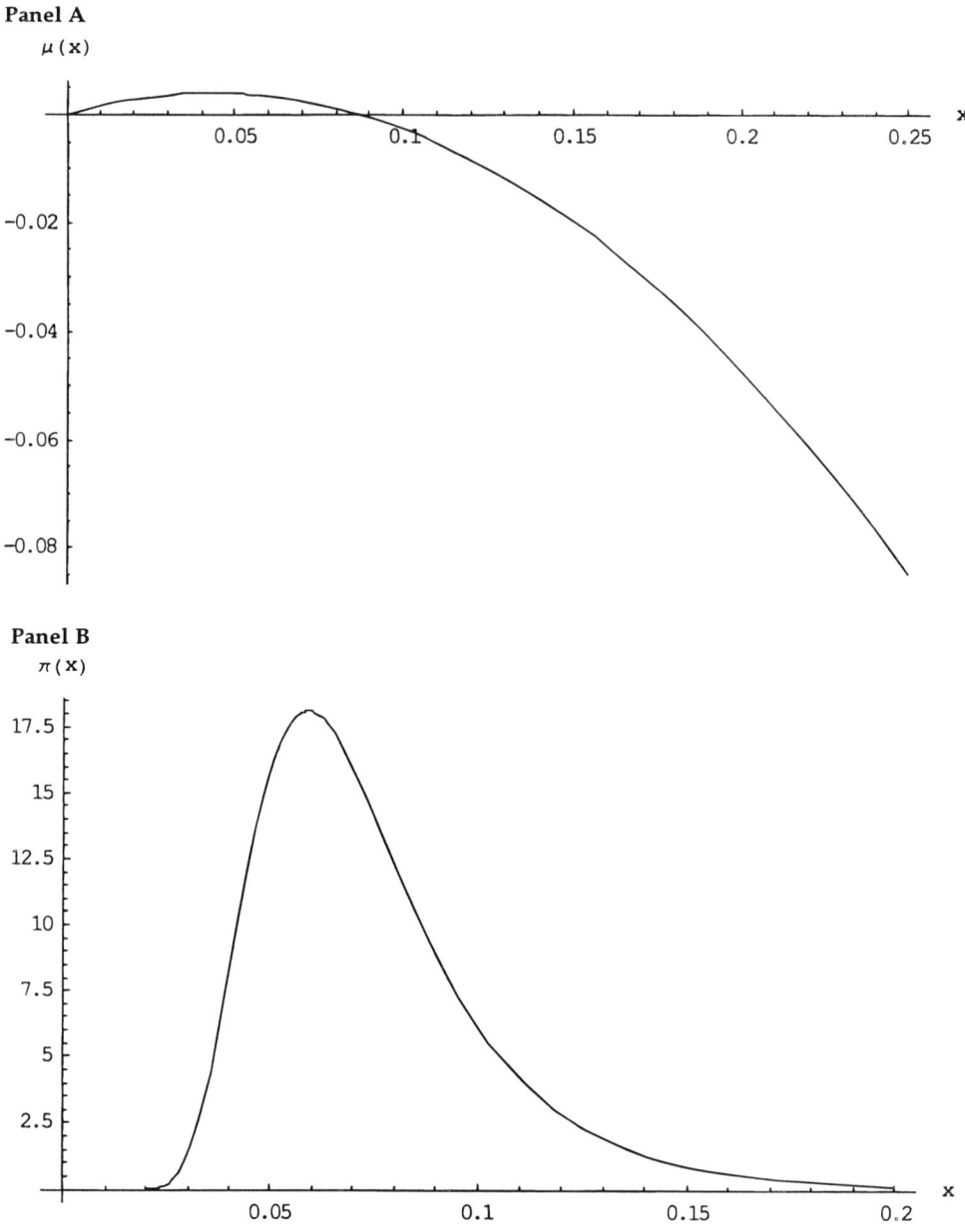

Figure 3. Drift, densities, and approximation errors for the inverse of Feller's process. Results for the model proposed by Ahn and Gao (1998) (see Example 3 and Table II) are reported: the drift $\mu(X_t,\theta) = X_t(\kappa - (\sigma^2 - \kappa\alpha)X_t)$ in Figure 3A, the marginal density $\pi(X_t,\theta)$ in Figure 3B, the exact and conditional density approximations, p_X, p_X^{Euler}, and $\tilde{p}_X^{(1)}$ as functions of the forward variable x, for $x_0 = 0.10$ in Figure 3C. The sampling frequency is monthly ($\Delta = 1/12$) and the parameter vector θ is evaluated at the MLE reported in Table VI. Figure 3D reports the uniform approximation error $|p_X - \tilde{p}_X^{(K)}|$ for $K = 1$, 2, and 3, in log-scale, as in Figures 1B and 2B.

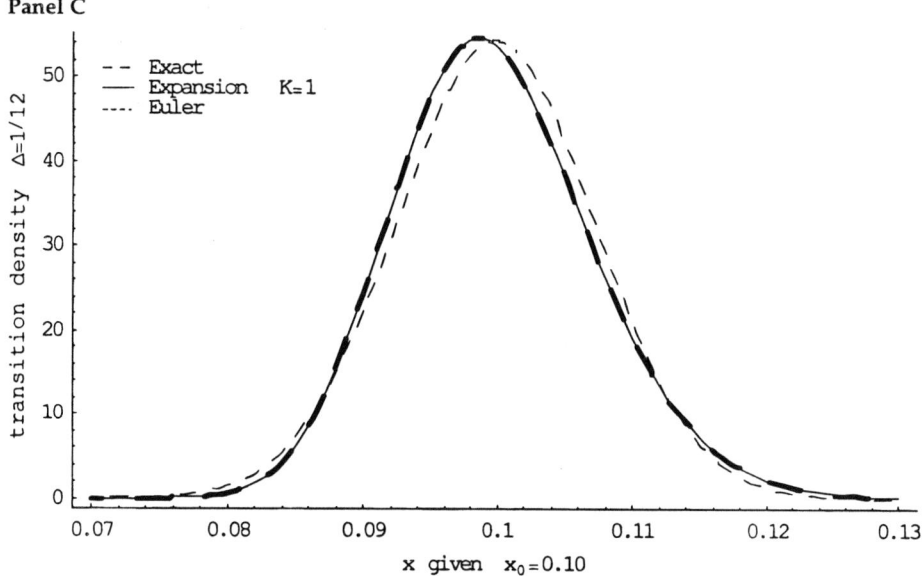

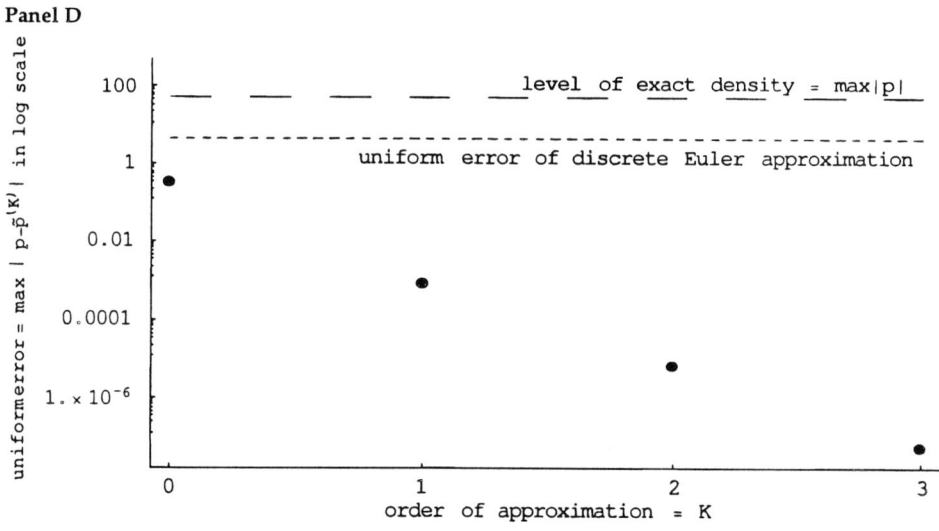

Figure 3. Continued

with closed-form transition density given by

$$p_X(\Delta, x|x_0; \theta) = (1/x^2)p_X^{\text{CIR}}(\Delta, 1/x|1/x_0; \theta), \tag{22}$$

where p_X^{CIR} is the density function given in equation (20). The expansion in equation (11) for p_Y is identical to that for the CIR model given in Table II (because the Y process is the same with the same transformed drift μ_Y and unit diffusion). To get back to an expansion for X, the change of variable $Y \to X$ however is different, and is now given by $Y_t = \gamma(X_t;\theta) = 2/(\sigma\sqrt{X_t})$; hence the expansion for p_X will naturally be different from that for the CIR model (it will now approximate the left-hand side of equation (22) rather than equation (20)).

Figure 3A reports the drift for this model, evaluated at the maximum-likelihood estimates from Table VI below. This model generates, in an environment where closed-form solutions are available, some of the effects documented empirically by Aït-Sahalia (1996b): almost no drift while the interest rate is in the middle of its range, strong mean-reversion when the interest rate gets large. Figure 3B plots the unconditional or marginal density, which is also the stationary density $\pi(x,\theta)$ for this process when the initial data point X_0 has π as its distribution. π is given by

$$\pi(y;\theta) \equiv \exp\left\{2\int^y \mu_Y(u;\theta)\,du\right\} \Big/ \int_{\underline{y}}^{\bar{y}} \exp\left\{2\int^v \mu_Y(u;\theta)\,du\right\} dv. \qquad (23)$$

Figure 3C compares the exact conditional density in equation (22), its Euler approximation, and the expansion with $K = 1$ for the conditioning interest rate $x_0 = 0.10$. It is apparent from the figure that including the first term alone is sufficient to make the exact and approximate densities fall on top of one another, whereas the Euler approximation is distinct. Finally, Figure 3D reports the uniform approximation error between the Euler approximation and the exact density on the one hand, and between the first three terms in the expansion and the exact density on the other. As can be seen from these figures, the expansion in equation (11) provides again a very accurate approximation to the exact density.

B. Density Approximation for Models with No Closed-Form Density

Of course, the usefulness of the method introduced in Aït-Sahalia (1998) lies largely in its ability to deliver explicit density approximations for models that do not have closed-form transition densities. The next two examples correspond to models recently proposed in the literature to describe the time series properties of the short-term interest rate, and the final example illustrates the applicability of the method to a double-well model where the stationary density is bimodal.

Example 4 (Linear Drift, CEV Diffusion): Chan et al. (1992) have proposed the specification

$$dX_t = \kappa(\alpha - X_t)\,dt + \sigma X_t^\rho\,dW_t, \qquad (24)$$

with $\theta \equiv (\alpha,\kappa,\sigma,\rho)$. X is distributed on $(0,+\infty)$ when $\alpha > 0$, $\kappa > 0$, and $\rho > 1/2$ (if $\rho = 1/2$; see Example 2 for an additional constraint). This model does not admit a closed-form density unless $\alpha = 0$ (see Cox (1996)), which

Table III
Explicit Sequence for the Linear Drift, CEV Diffusion Model

This table contains the coefficients of the density approximation for p_Y corresponding to the Chan et al. (1992) model in Example 4, $dX_t = \kappa(\alpha - X_t)dt + \sigma X_t^\rho dW_t$. The terms in the expansion are evaluated by applying the formulas in equation (12). From equation (11), the $K = 0$ term in this expansion is $\tilde{p}_Y^{(0)}(\Delta, y|y_0; \theta)$, the $K = 1$ term is

$$\tilde{p}_Y^{(1)}(\Delta, y|y_0; \theta) = \tilde{p}_Y^{(0)}(\Delta, y|y_0; \theta)\{1 + c_1(y|y_0; \theta)\Delta\}.$$

Additional terms can be obtained by applying equation (12) further.

$$\tilde{p}_Y^{(0)}(\Delta, y|y_0, \theta) = \frac{1}{\sqrt{\Delta}\sqrt{2\pi}} \exp\left[-\frac{(y-y_0)^2}{2\Delta} + \kappa(\rho - 1)\right.$$

$$\times (y^2(2\rho - 1) - 2y^{1+(\rho/(\rho-1))}\alpha(\rho - 1)^{\rho/(\rho-1)}\sigma^{1/(\rho-1)}$$

$$\left. + y_0(y_0 - 2\rho y_0 + 2\alpha(\rho - 1)^{\rho/(\rho-1)}\sigma^{1/(\rho-1)}y_0^{\rho/(\rho-1)}))/(4\rho - 2)\right]$$

$$\times y^{\rho/(-2+2\rho)}y_0^{\rho/(2-2\rho)}.$$

$c_1(y|y_0, \theta)$ for $y \neq y_0 = \left(-4y^4\kappa^2(\rho - 1)^4(2 - 9\rho + 9\rho^2)y_0 + 3\rho(4 + 20\rho + 27\rho^2 - 9\rho^3)\right.$

$$\times y_0 - 12y^2\kappa(\rho - 1)^2(13\rho - 27\rho^2 + 18\rho^3 - 2)$$

$$\times y_0 + 24y^{3+(\rho/(\rho-1))}\alpha\kappa^2(\rho - 1)^{4+(\rho/(\rho-1))}(3\rho - 1)\sigma^{1/(\rho-1)}$$

$$\times y_0 + 24y^{1+(\rho/(\rho-1))}\alpha\kappa(\rho - 1)^{3+(1/(\rho-1))}(2 - 9\rho + 9\rho^2)\sigma^{1/(\rho-1)}$$

$$\times y_0 - 12y^{2+2(\rho/(\rho-1))}\alpha^2\kappa^2(\rho - 1)^{5+(2/(\rho-1))}(3\rho - 2)\sigma^{2/(\rho-1)}$$

$$\times y_0 + y(3\rho(20\rho - 27\rho^2 + 9\rho^3 - 4)$$

$$+ 12\kappa(\rho - 1)^2(13\rho - 27\rho^2 + 18\rho^3 - 2)y_0^2$$

$$+ 4\kappa^2(\rho - 1)^4(2 - 9\rho + 9\rho^2)y_0^4$$

$$- 24\alpha\kappa(\rho - 1)^{3+(1/(\rho-1))}(2 - 9\rho + 9\rho^2)\sigma^{1/(\rho-1)}y_0^{1+(\rho/(\rho-1))}$$

$$- 24\alpha\kappa^2(\rho - 1)^{4+(\rho/(\rho-1))}(3\rho - 1)\sigma^{1/(\rho-1)}y_0^{3+(\rho/(\rho-1))}$$

$$+ 12\alpha^2\kappa^2(\rho - 1)^{5+(2/(\rho-1))}(3\rho - 2)\sigma^{2/(\rho-1)}$$

$$\left.\times y_0^{2+(2\rho/(\rho-1))}))/(24y(\rho - 1)^2(3\rho - 2)(3\rho - 1)(y - y_0)y_0\right).$$

$c_1(y|y_0, \theta)$ for $y = y_0 = \dfrac{1}{8(\rho - 1)^2 y_0^2}\left((\rho - 2)\rho - 4\kappa(\rho - 1)^2(2\rho - 1)y_0^2 - 4\kappa^2(\rho - 1)^4 y_0^4\right.$

$$+ 8\alpha\kappa(\rho - 1)^{2+(1/(\rho-1))}\rho\sigma^{1/(-1+\rho)}y_0^{1+(\rho/(\rho-1))}$$

$$+ 8\alpha\kappa^2(\rho - 1)^{3+(\rho/(\rho-1))}\sigma^{1/(\rho-1)}y_0^{3+(\rho/(\rho-1))}$$

$$\left.- 4\alpha^2\kappa^2(\rho - 1)^{4+(2/(\rho-1))}\sigma^{2/(\rho-1)}y_0^{2+(2\rho/(\rho-1))}\right).$$

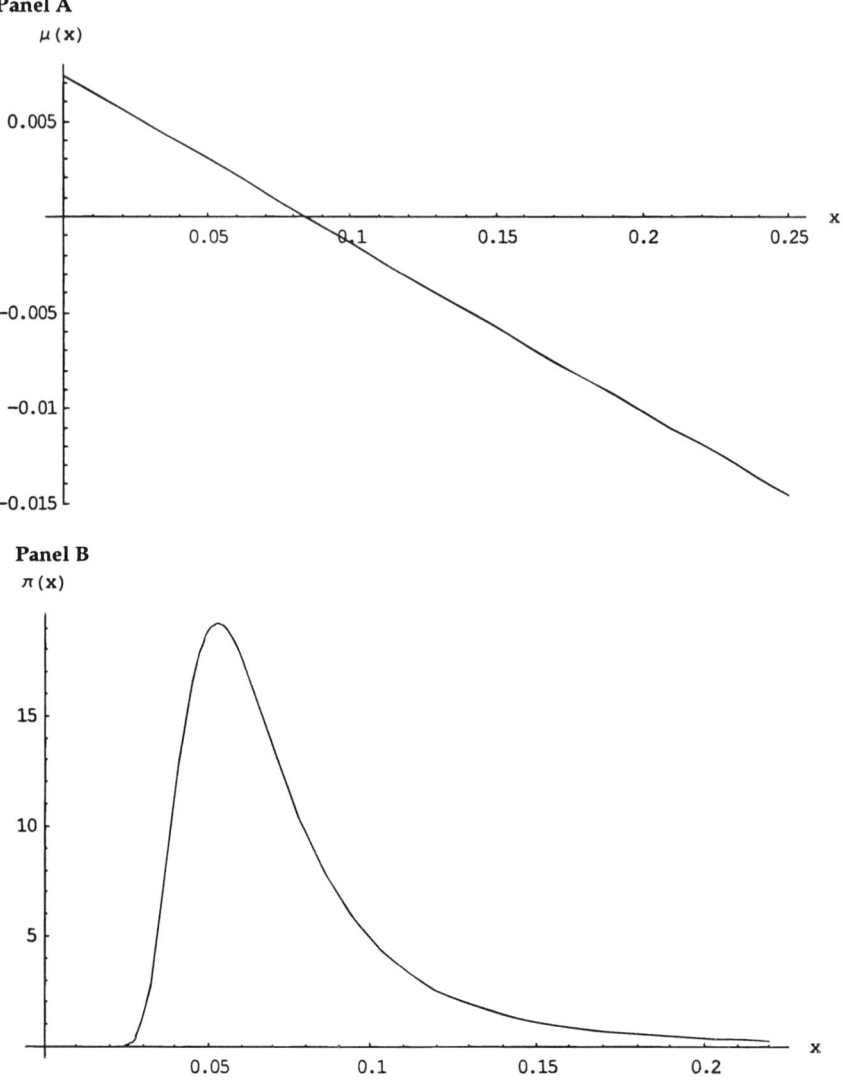

Figure 4. Conditional density approximations for the linear drift, CEV diffusion model.
These figures plot for the linear drift, CEV diffusion model of Chan et al. (1992) (see Example 4 and Table III) the drift function, $\mu(X_t, \theta) = \kappa(\alpha - X_t)$ (Figure 4A), the marginal density $\pi(X_t, \theta)$ (Figure 4B), and the conditional density approximations p_X^{Euler} and $\bar{p}_X^{(1)}$ as functions of the forward variable x, for two values of the conditioning variable x_0 in Figures 4C and 4D respectively. The sampling frequency is monthly ($\Delta = 1/12$) and the parameter vector θ is evaluated at the MLE reported in Table VI.

then makes it unrealistic for interest rates. I will concentrate on the case where $\rho > 1$, which corresponds to the empirically plausible estimate for U.S. interest rate data. The transformation from X to Y is given by $Y_t = \gamma(X_t; \theta) = X_t^{1-\rho}/\{\sigma(\rho - 1)\}$ and

Panel C

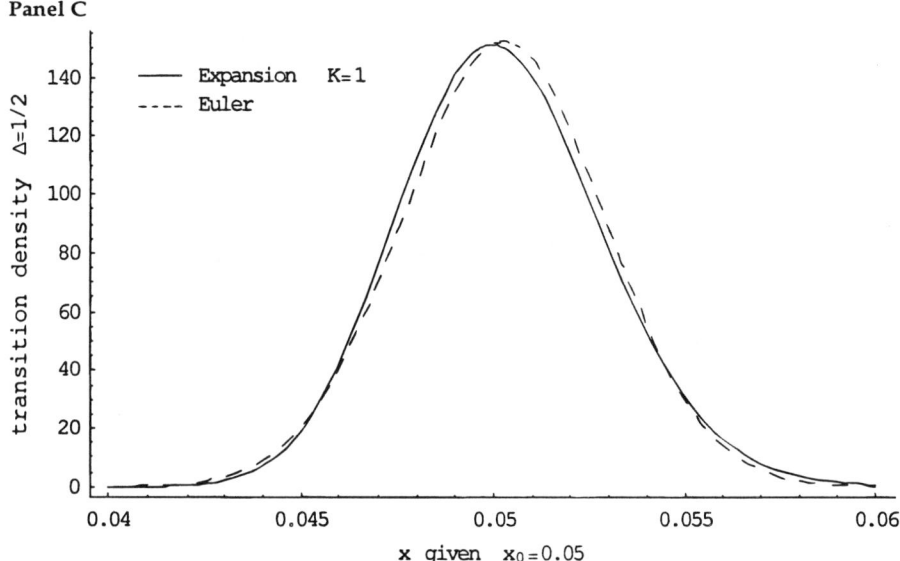

Panel D

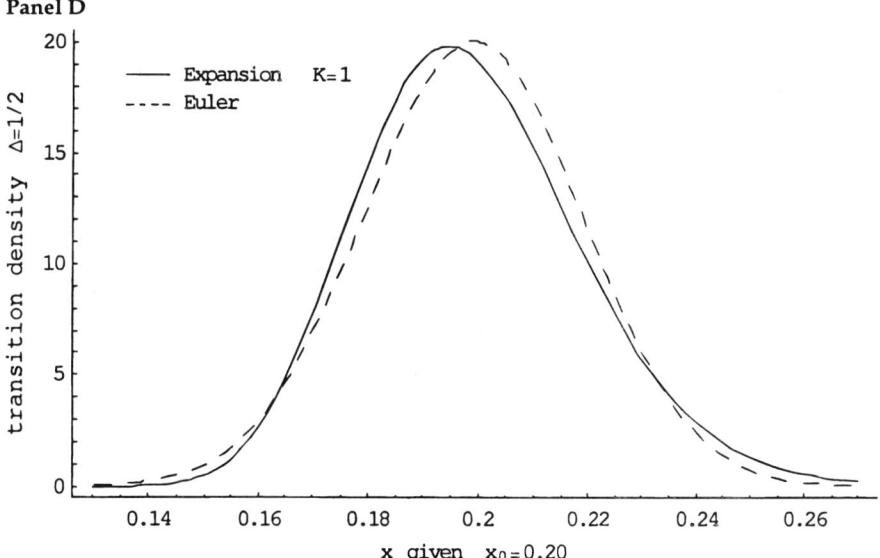

Figure 4. Continued.

$$\mu_Y(y;\theta) = \frac{\rho}{2(\rho-1)y} - \kappa(\rho-1)y + \alpha\kappa\sigma^{1/(\rho-1)}(\rho-1)^{\rho/(\rho-1)}y^{\rho/(\rho-1)}. \quad (25)$$

The first term in the expansion is given in Table III. The corresponding formulas can be derived analogously for the transformation $Y_t = \gamma(X_t;\theta) = X_t^{1-\rho}/\{\sigma(1-\rho)\}$, which is appropriate if $1/2 < \rho < 1$. I plot in Figure 4A the drift function corresponding to maximum-likelihood estimates (based on the expansion with $K = 1$, see Table VI below), in Figure 4B I plot the unconditional density, and in Figures 4C and 4D the conditional density approximations for monthly sampling at $x_0 = 0.05$ and 0.20, respectively.

Example 5 (Nonlinear Mean Reversion): The following model was designed to produce very little mean reversion while interest rate values remain in the middle part of their domain, and strong nonlinear mean reversion at either end of the domain (see Aït-Sahalia (1996b)):

$$dX_t = (\alpha_{-1}X_t^{-1} + \alpha_0 + \alpha_1 X_t + \alpha_2 X_t^2)\,dt + \sigma X_t^\rho\,dW_t, \qquad (26)$$

with $\theta \equiv (\alpha_{-1}, \alpha_0, \alpha_1, \alpha_2, \sigma, \rho)$. This model has been estimated empirically by Aït-Sahalia (1996b), Conley et al. (1997), and Gallant and Tauchen (1998) using a variety of empirical techniques. The new method in this paper makes it possible to estimate it using maximum likelihood. I again concentrate on the case where $\rho > 1$, and to save space I evaluate the formulas in Table IV for $\rho = 3/2$. This process has $D_X = (0, +\infty)$, $Y_t = \gamma(X_t; \theta) = 2/(\sigma\sqrt{X_t})$, and

$$\mu_Y(y;\theta) = \frac{3/2 - 2\alpha_2/\sigma^2}{y} - \frac{\alpha_1 y}{2} - \frac{\alpha_0 \sigma^2 y^3}{8} - \frac{\alpha_{-1} \sigma^4 y^5}{32}. \qquad (27)$$

Figure 5A plots the drift evaluated at the maximum-likelihood parameter estimates (corresponding to $K = 1$). Figure 5B plots the unconditional or marginal density of the process: in the specification test in Aït-Sahalia (1996b), this density is matched against a nonparametric kernel estimator. Figures 5C and 5D contain the conditional density approximations for $K = 1$, compared with the Euler approximation, for the two values $x_0 = 0.025$ and 0.20, respectively. As before, sampling is at the monthly frequency.

Example 6 (Double-Well Potential): In this example, I generate a bimodal stationary density through the specification

$$dX_t = (X_t - X_t^3)\,dt + dW_t. \qquad (28)$$

This model is distributed on $D_X = (-\infty, +\infty)$. Since the model is already set in unit diffusion, no transformation is needed ($Y = X$).

Table V contains the first two terms of the expansion; Figure 6A plots its drift, Figure 6B its marginal density, and Figures 6C and 6D the transition density for $K = 2$, monthly sampling, and $x_0 = 0.0$ and 0.5, respectively, with $\Delta = 1/2$. As is apparent from the figures, the densities in this model exhibit strong nonnormality, which obviously cannot be captured by the Euler approximation of equation (16).

Table IV
Explicit Sequence for the Nonlinear Drift Model

This table contains the coefficients of the density approximation for p_Y corresponding to the model in Aït-Sahalia (1996b), Conley et al. (1997), and Tauchen (1997) given in Example 5, $dX_t = (\alpha_{-1} X_t^{-1} + \alpha_0 + \alpha_1 X_t + \alpha_2 X_t^2) dt + \sigma X_t^\rho dW_t$ with $\rho = 3/2$. The terms in the expansion are evaluated by applying the formulas in equation (12). From equation (11), the $K = 0$ term in this expansion is $\tilde{p}_Y^{(0)}(\Delta, y | y_0; \theta)$ and the $K = 1$ term is

$$\tilde{p}_Y^{(1)}(\Delta, y | y_0; \theta) = \tilde{p}_Y^{(0)}(\Delta, y | y_0; \theta)\{1 + c_1(y | y_0; \theta)\Delta\}.$$

Additional terms can be obtained by applying equation (12) further.

$$\tilde{p}_X^{(0)}(\Delta, y | y_0, \theta) = \frac{1}{\sqrt{\Delta}\sqrt{2\pi}} \exp\left[-\frac{(y - y_0)^2}{2\Delta} + \frac{1}{192}\left(\sigma^4(-y^6 + y_0^6)\alpha_{-1}\right.\right.$$

$$\left.\left. - 6(y^2 - y_0^2)(\sigma^2(y^2 + y_0^2)\alpha_0 + 8\alpha_1))\right]$$

$$\times y^{(3/2)-(2\alpha_2/\sigma^2)} y_0^{-(3/2)+(2\alpha_2/\sigma^2)}.$$

$$c_1(y|y_0\theta) = -\frac{1}{7096320 y\sigma^4 y_0}\left(315y\sigma^{12}y_0(y^{10} + y^9 y_0 + y^8 y_0^2 + y^7 y_0^3 + y^6 y_0^4 + y^5 y_0^5 + y^4 y_0^6\right.$$

$$+ y^3 y_0^7 + y^2 y_0^8 + y y_0^9 + y_0^{10})\alpha_{-1}^2 + 88 y\sigma^6 y_0 \alpha_{-1}$$

$$\times \left(35\sigma^4(y^8 + y^7 y_0 + y^6 y_0^2 + y^5 y_0^3 + y^4 y_0^4 + y^3 y_0^5\right.$$

$$+ y^2 y_0^6 + y y_0^7 + y_0^8)$$

$$\times \alpha_0 + 36(-56 y^4 \sigma^2 - 56 y^3 \sigma^2 y_0 - 56 y^2 \sigma^2 y_0^2 - 56 y \sigma^2 y_0^3$$

$$- 56\sigma^2 y_0^4 + 5 y^6 \sigma^2 \alpha_1 + 5 y^5 \sigma^2 y_0 \alpha_1 + 5 y^4 \sigma^2 y_0^2 \alpha_1$$

$$+ 5 y^3 \sigma^2 y_0^3 \alpha_1 + 5 y^2 \sigma^2 y_0^4 \alpha_1 + 5 y \sigma^2 y_0^5 \alpha_1$$

$$+ 5\sigma^2 y_0^6 \alpha_1 + 28 y^4 \alpha_2 + 28 y^3 y_0 \alpha_2 + 28 y^2 y_0^2 \alpha_2$$

$$+ 28 y y_0^3 \alpha_2 + 28 y_0^4 \alpha_2))$$

$$+ 528(15 y \sigma^8 y_0 (y^6 + y^5 y_0 + y^4 y_0^2 + y^3 y_0^3 + y^2 y_0^4 + y y_0^5 + y_0^6)$$

$$\times \alpha_0^2 + 56 y \sigma^4 y_0 \alpha_0 (-30 y^2 \sigma^2 - 30 y \sigma^2 y_0 - 30 \sigma^2 y_0^2$$

$$+ 3 y^4 \sigma^2 \alpha_1 + 3 y^3 \sigma^2 y_0 \alpha_1$$

$$+ 3 y^2 \sigma^2 y_0^2 \alpha_1 + 3 y \sigma^2 y_0^3 \alpha_1 + 3 \sigma^2 y_0^4 \alpha_1$$

$$+ 20 y^2 \alpha_2 + 20 y y_0 \alpha_2 + 20 y_0^2 \alpha_2)$$

$$+ 560(9\sigma^4 - 24 y \sigma^4 y_0 \alpha_1 + y^3 \sigma^4 y_0 \alpha_1^2 + y^2 \sigma^4 y_0^2 \alpha_1^2$$

$$+ y \sigma^4 y_0^3 \alpha_1^2 - 48\sigma^2 \alpha_2 + 24 y \sigma^2 y_0 \alpha_1 \alpha_2 + 48\alpha_2^2))).$$

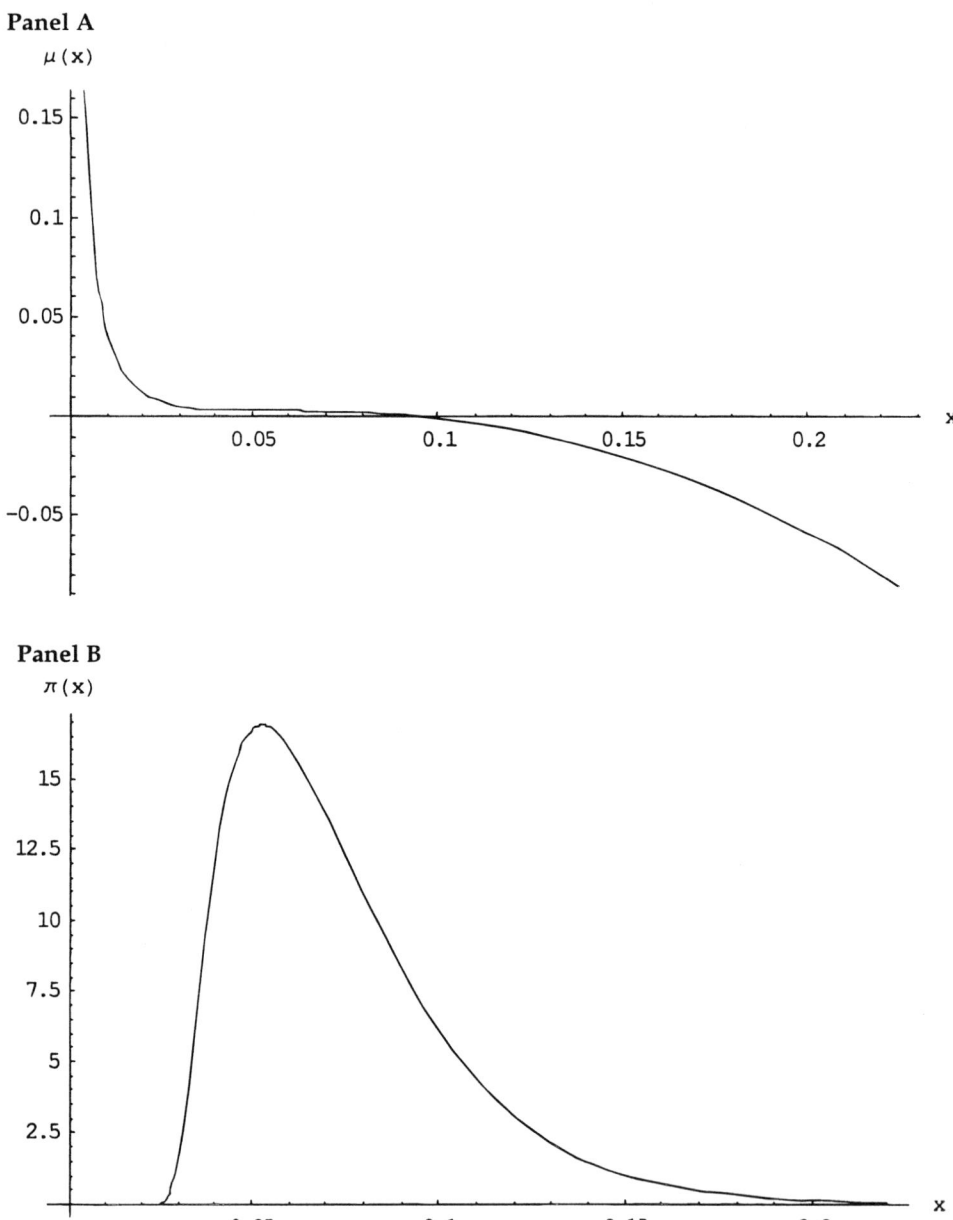

Figure 5. Drift and density approximations for the nonlinear drift model. These figures report results for the nonlinear drift model of Aït-Sahalia (1996b) (also estimated by Conley et al. (1997) and Gallant and Tauchen (1998)) described in Example 5 and Table IV. Figure 5A plots the drift function, $\mu(X_t, \theta) = \alpha_{-1} X_t^{-1} + \alpha_0 + \alpha_1 X_t + \alpha_2 X_t^2$ and Figure 5B the marginal density $\pi(X_t, \theta)$. This model does not have a closed-form solution for p_X. Figures 5C and 5D plot the conditional density approximations p_X^{Euler} and $\tilde{p}_X^{(1)}$ as functions of the forward variable x, for two different values of the conditioning variable x_0. The sampling frequency is monthly ($\Delta = 1/12$) and the parameter vector θ is evaluated at the MLE reported in Table VI.

Panel C

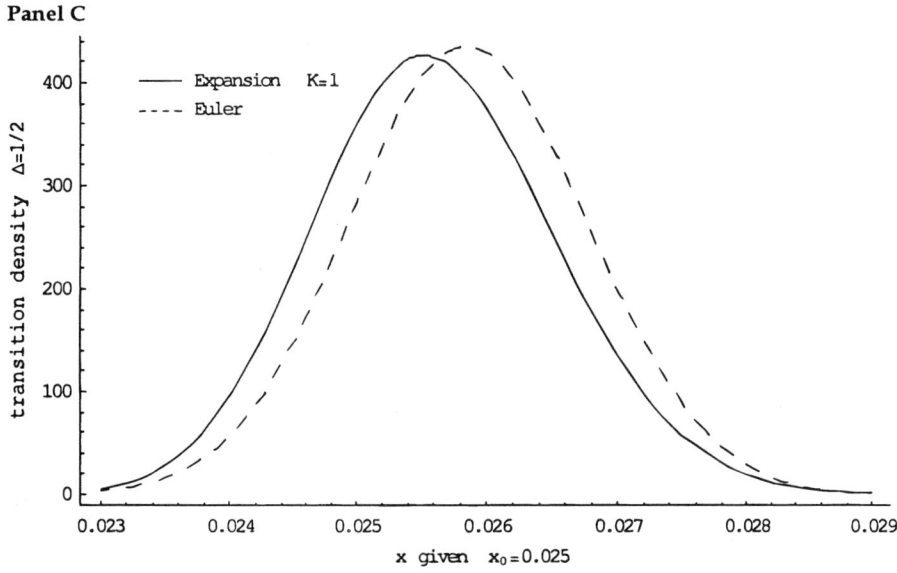

Panel D

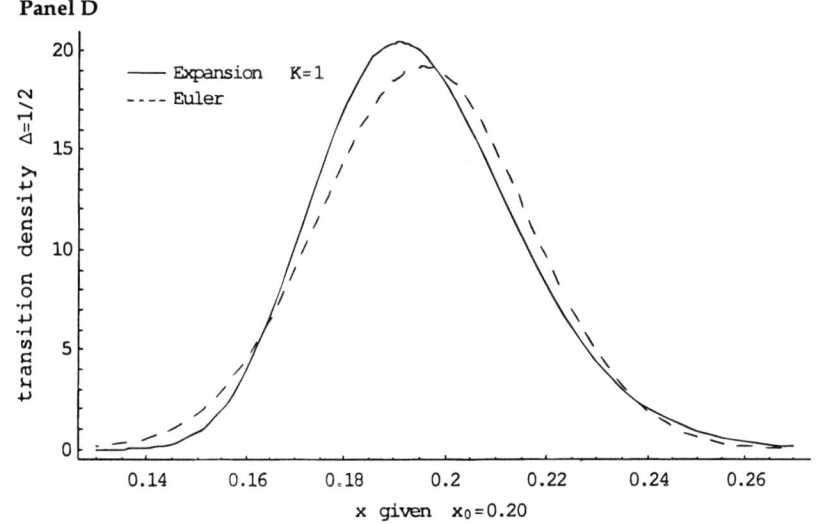

Figure 5. Continued

III. The Estimation of Interest Rate Diffusions

A. *The Data and Maximum-Likelihood Estimates*

To calculate approximate maximum-likelihood estimates, I maximize the approximate log-likelihood function

Table V
Explicit Sequence for the Double-Well Model

This table contains the coefficients of the density approximation for p_Y corresponding to the model in Example 6, $dX_t = (X_t - X_t^3)\,dt + dW_t$. The terms in the expansion are evaluated by applying the formulas in equation (12). From equation (11), the $K = 0$ term in this expansion is $\tilde{p}_Y^{(0)}(\Delta, y|y_0; \theta)$, the $K = 1$ term is

$$\tilde{p}_Y^{(1)}(\Delta, y|y_0; \theta) = \tilde{p}_Y^{(0)}(\Delta, y|y_0; \theta)\{1 + c_1(y|y_0; \theta)\Delta\},$$

and the $K = 2$ term is

$$\tilde{p}_Y^{(2)}(\Delta, y|y_0; \theta) = \tilde{p}_Y^{(0)}(\Delta, y|y_0; \theta)\{1 + c_1(y|y_0; \theta)\Delta + c_2(y|y_0; \theta)\Delta^2/2\}.$$

Additional terms can be obtained in the same manner by applying equation (12) further.

$$\tilde{p}_X^{(0)}(\Delta, y|y_0, \theta) = \frac{1}{\sqrt{\Delta}\sqrt{2\pi}} \exp\left[-\frac{(y - y_0)^2}{2\Delta} + \frac{y^2}{2} - \frac{y^4}{4} - \frac{y_0^2}{2} + \frac{y_0^4}{4}\right].$$

$$c_1(y|y_0, \theta) = \frac{1}{210}\left(-105 + 70y^2 + 42y^4 - 15y^6 + (70y + 42y^3 - 15y^5)y_0 + (70 + 42y^2 - 15y^4)y_0^2 \right.$$
$$\left. + (42y - 15y^3)y_0^3 + (42 - 15y^2)y_0^4 - 15yy_0^5 - 15y_0^6\right).$$

$$c_2(y|y_0, \theta) = \frac{1}{44100}\left(25725 + 11760y^2 - 19670y^4 + 9030y^6 - 336y^8 - 1260y^{10} + 225y^{12}\right.$$
$$+ 2y(10290 - 12110y^2 + 7455y^4 - 336y^6 - 1260y^8 + 225y^{10})y_0$$
$$+ 3(3920 - 7490y^2 + 6930y^4 - 336y^6 - 1260y^8 + 225y^{10})y_0^2$$
$$+ 2y(-12110 + 10395y^2 + 378y^4 - 2520y^6 + 450y^8)y_0^3$$
$$+ 5(-3934 + 4158y^2 + 504y^4 - 1260y^6 + 225y^8)y_0^4$$
$$+ 6y(2485 + 126y^2 - 1050y^4 + 225y^6)y_0^5$$
$$+ 21(430 - 48y^2 - 300y^4 + 75y^6)y_0^6 + 6y(-112 - 840y^2 + 225y^4)y_0^7$$
$$+ 3(-112 - 1260y^2 + 375y^4)y_0^8 + 180y(-14 + 5y^2)y_0^9$$
$$\left. + 45(-28 + 15y^2)y_0^{10} + 450yy_0^{11} + 225y_0^{12}\right).$$

$$\ell_n^{(K)}(\theta) \equiv n^{-1}\sum_{i=1}^{n} \ln\{\tilde{p}_X^{(K)}(\Delta, X_{i\Delta}|X_{(i-1)\Delta}; \theta)\} \tag{29}$$

(with the convention that $\ln(\alpha) = -\infty$ if $\alpha < 0$) over θ in Θ. This results in an estimator $\hat{\theta}_n^{(K)}$, which, as shown in Aït-Sahalia (1998), is close to the exact (but uncomputable in practice) maximum-likelihood estimator $\hat{\theta}_n$.

The data consist of monthly sampling of the Fed funds rate between January 1963 and December 1998 (see Figure 7). The source for the data is the H-15 Federal Reserve Statistical Release (Selected Interest Rate Series).

Panel A

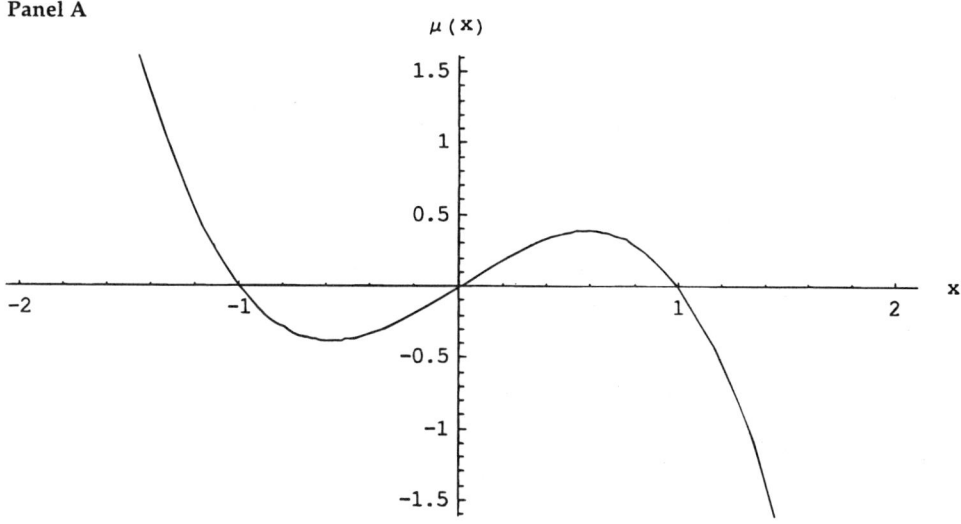

Panel B

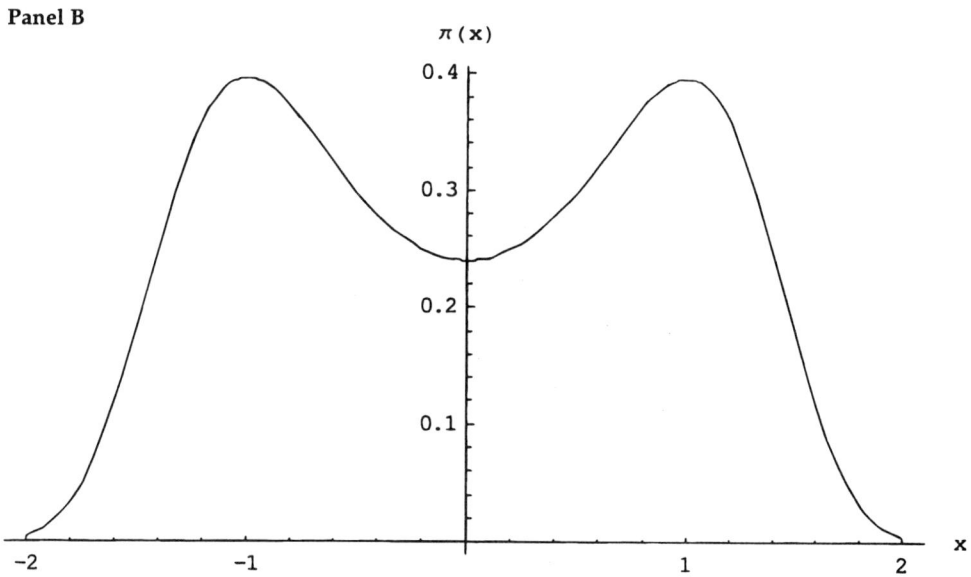

Figure 6. Drift and densities for the double-well model. Results for the double-well model of Example 6 and Table V are reported. The drift function $\mu(x) = x - x^3$ (Figure 6A) is such that the process avoids staying near 0 and is attracted to either -1 or $+1$, a fact reflected by the bimodality of the marginal density $\pi(x)$ in Figure 6B. This model does not have closed-form solutions for p_X. Figures 6C and 6D plot the conditional density approximations p_X^{Euler} and $\tilde{p}_X^{(2)}$ as functions of the forward variable x, for two different values of the conditioning variable x_0 with $\Delta = 1/2$. As is clear from these figures, the Euler approximation cannot reflect the substantial nonnormality captured by the density approximation of this paper. Figure 6E plots the conditional density surface, $(x, x_0) \mapsto \tilde{p}_X^{(2)}(\Delta, x | x_0, \theta)$ for $\Delta = 1/2$, and θ replaced by the MLE.

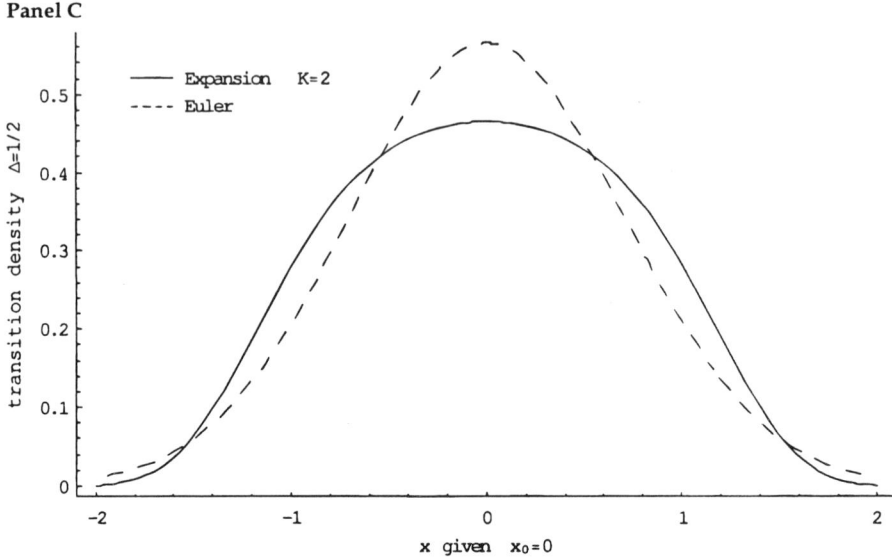

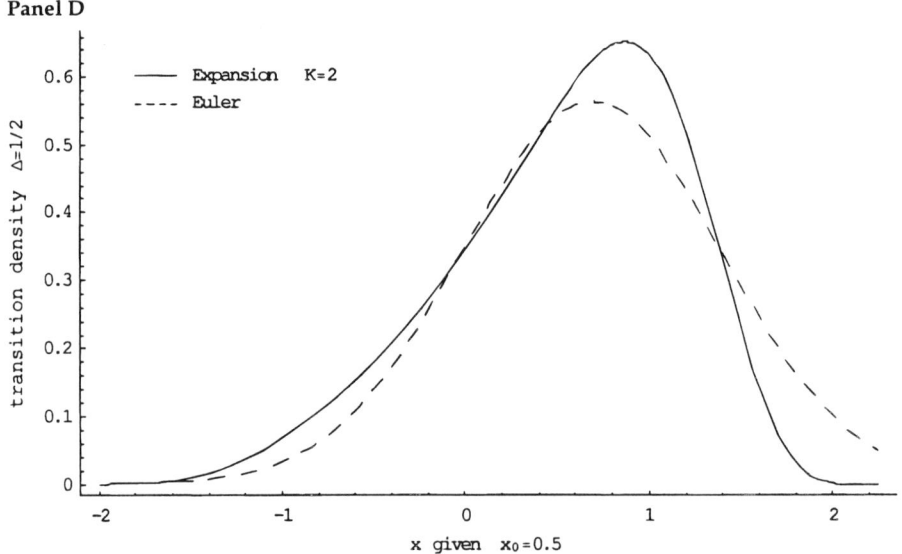

Figure 6. Continued.

Though the Fed funds rate series exhibits strong microstructure effects at the daily frequency (due for instance to the second Wednesday settlement effect; see Hamilton (1996)), these effects are largely mitigated at the monthly frequency. On the other hand, this rate represents one of the closest possible proxies for what is meant by an "instantaneous" short rate in theoretical models. Since the method in this paper does not rely on the sampling inter-

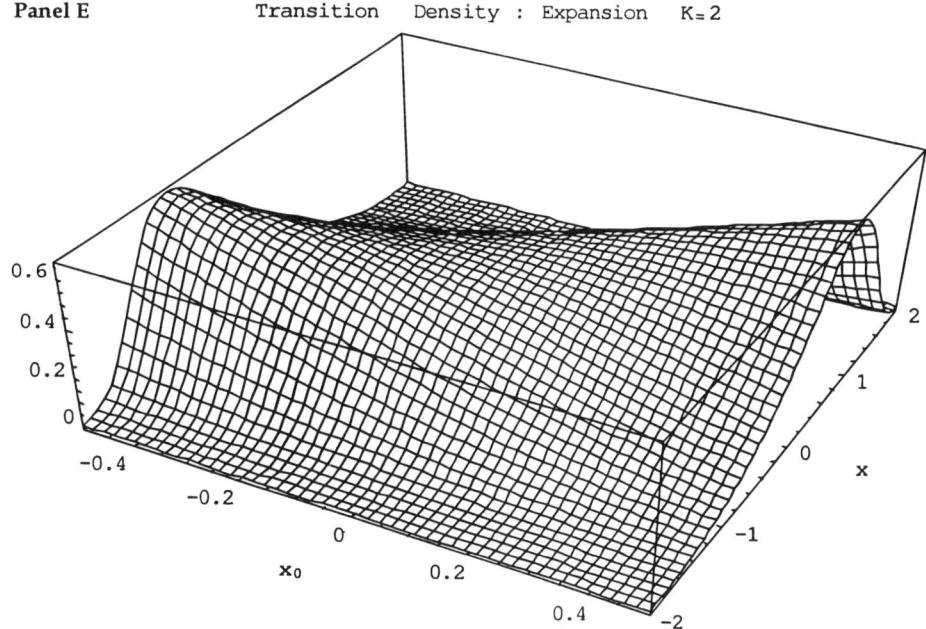

Figure 6. Continued

val being small, the trade-off between a larger sampling interval and the virtual absence of microstructure effects seems worthwhile. Of course, the implicit (unrealistic) assumption is made that a single diffusion specification can represent the evolution of the short rate for the entire period. Naturally, nothing prevents the estimation from being conducted on a shorter time period at the expense of reducing the sample size. One advantage of the long time series used here is that it contains different episodes of U.S. interest rate history, such as the Volcker period, as well as the low interest rate environments that preceded it and followed it. It is therefore interesting to see how different models would accommodate these different regimes.

The results for the five models of Examples 1 to 5 compared to the Euler approximation and, when available (Examples 1 to 3), the true log-likelihood, are reported in Table VI. The last column of the table reports the asymptotic standard deviations for the estimated parameters, derived as explained below.

The results in Table VI confirm those of Section II: the expansion used with $K = 1$ or 2 produces estimates $\hat{\theta}_n^{(K)}$ that are very close to $\hat{\theta}_n$. It is interesting to note that because the models evaluated at the true parameter values often display very little drift (hence their near unit root behavior), and because interest rates are not particularly volatile, the fitted densities over a one-month interval are often fairly close to a Gaussian density. In other words, for these data, $\Delta =$ one month is a "small" time interval. Hence, the Euler approximation performs relatively well in this specific context (except

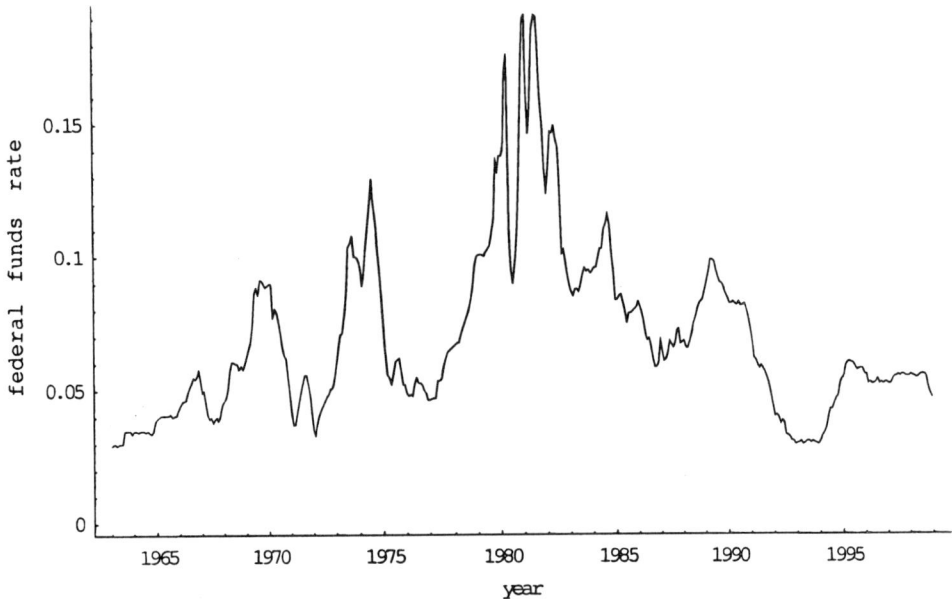

Figure 7. Federal funds rate, monthly frequency, 1963–1998. This figure plots the time series of the Federal funds data used for the estimation of the parameters in Table VI.

in the nonlinear drift model of Example 5, where the estimated parameters can be off by as much as 30 percent (although the standard deviation in this case is large), in the inverse Feller process of Example 3 where they are off by 5 to 10 percent, and in the Chan et al. (1992) specification of Example 4 where the drift parameters are off by 10 percent).

B. *Estimation of the Asymptotic Variance and How Many Terms to Include*

I consider here only the situation where the process admits a stationary distribution. For the more general case, see Aït-Sahalia (1998). The asymptotic variance of the maximum-likelihood estimator is given by the inverse of Fisher's Information Matrix, which is the lowest possible achievable variance among the competing estimators discussed in the Introduction.

Define $L(\theta) \equiv \ln(p_X(\Delta, X_\Delta | X_0; \theta))$, the $d \times 1$ vector $\dot{L}(\theta) \equiv \partial L(\theta)/\partial \theta$, and the $d \times d$ matrix $\ddot{L}(\theta) \equiv \partial^2 L(\theta)/\partial \theta \partial \theta^T$, where ^{T} denotes transposition. We have that

$$n^{1/2}(\hat{\theta}_n - \theta_0) \xrightarrow{d} N(0, i(\theta_0)^{-1}), \qquad (30)$$

where Fisher's Information Matrix is

$$i(\theta) \equiv E[\dot{L}(\theta)\dot{L}(\theta)^T] = -E[\ddot{L}(\theta)]. \qquad (31)$$

Table VI
Maximum-Likelihood Estimates for the Monthly Federal Funds Data, 1963–1998

This table reports the MLE for the parameters of five interest rate models estimated using the Fed funds data, monthly from January 1963 through December 1998. The estimates are calculated using the Euler approximation, the density approximation of this paper with $K=1$, and, when the transition density is available in closed-form (Examples 1, 2 and 3), the expansion with $K=2$ and the true density. In the table, "ln L" refers to the maximized value of the log-likelihood. The formulas for the density expansion can be found in the respective tables indicated in the third column. The asymptotic standard errors in the last column are computed from equation (30), with Fisher's Information Matrix in equation (31) replaced by the sample averages evaluated at the second derivative of the log-likelihood expansion with $K=1$, and confirmed with the average of the first derivative squared.

Model	Example Number	Density Expansion Table	Figure	Parameter Estimates: Euler	Parameter Estimates: Expansion $K=1$	Parameter Estimates: Expansion $K=2$	Parameter Estimates: True Density	Asymptotic Standard Error
$dX_t = \kappa(\alpha - X_t)dt + \sigma dW_t$	1	I	1	$\alpha = 0.0717$ $\kappa = 0.258$ $\sigma = 0.02213$ $\ln L = 3.634$	$\alpha = 0.0719$ $\kappa = 0.257$ $\sigma = 0.02237$ $\ln L = 3.634$	$\alpha = 0.0717$ $\kappa = 0.261$ $\sigma = 0.02237$ $\ln L = 3.634$	$\alpha = 0.0717$ $\kappa = 0.261$ $\sigma = 0.02237$ $\ln L = 3.634$	α: 0.014 κ: 0.12 σ: 0.00078
$dX_t = \kappa(\alpha - X_t)dt + \sigma\sqrt{X_t}dW_t$	2	II	2	$\alpha = 0.0732$ $\kappa = 0.145$ $\sigma = 0.06521$ $\ln L = 3.917$	$\alpha = 0.0742$ $\kappa = 0.189$ $\sigma = 0.06658$ $\ln L = 3.918$	$\alpha = 0.0742$ $\kappa = 0.189$ $\sigma = 0.06658$ $\ln L = 3.918$	$\alpha = 0.0721$ $\kappa = 0.219$ $\sigma = 0.06665$ $\ln L = 3.918$	α: 0.016 κ: 0.10 σ: 0.0023
$dX_t = X_t(\kappa - (\sigma^2 - \kappa\alpha)X_t)dt + \sigma X_t^{3/2} dW_t$	3	II	3	$\alpha = 15.019$ $\kappa = 0.177$ $\sigma = 0.8059$ $\ln L = 4.171$	$\alpha = 15.157$ $\kappa = 0.181$ $\sigma = 0.8211$ $\ln L = 4.158$	$\alpha = 15.150$ $\kappa = 0.182$ $\sigma = 0.8211$ $\ln L = 4.158$	$\alpha = 15.141$ $\kappa = 0.182$ $\sigma = 0.8211$ $\ln L = 4.158$	α: 2.9 κ: 0.1 σ: 0.03
$dX_t = \kappa(\alpha - X_t)dt + \sigma X_t^\rho dW_t$	4	III	4	$\alpha = 0.0808$ $\kappa = 0.0972$ $\sigma = 0.7224$ $\rho = 1.46$ $\ln L = 4.172$	$\alpha = 0.0844$ $\kappa = 0.0876$ $\sigma = 0.7791$ $\rho = 1.48$ $\ln L = 4.159$			α: 0.05 κ: 0.11 σ: 0.16 ρ: 0.08
$dX_t = (\alpha_{-1}X_t^{-1} + \alpha_0 + \alpha_1 X_t + \alpha_2 X_t^2)dt + \sigma X_t^{3/2} dW_t$	5	IV	5	$\alpha_{-1} = 0.00107$ $\alpha_0 = -0.0517$ $\alpha_1 = 0.877$ $\alpha_2 = -4.604$ $\sigma = 0.8047$ $\ln L = 4.173$	$\alpha_{-1} = 0.000693$ $\alpha_0 = -0.0347$ $\alpha_1 = 0.676$ $\alpha_2 = -4.059$ $\sigma = 0.8214$ $\ln L = 4.160$			α_{-1}: 0.002 α_0: 0.09 α_1: 1.3 α_2: 6.4 σ: 0.03

Note that it is necessary that the transition function p_X not be uniformly flat in the direction of any one of the parameters θ_m, $m = 1,\ldots,d$, otherwise $\partial p_X(\Delta, x|x_0;\theta)/\partial \theta_m \equiv 0$ for all (x,x_0) and the model cannot be identified. In other words, no parameter entering the likelihood function can be redundant. The asymptotic standard deviations from equation (30) are reported in the last column of Table VI for the interest rate models estimated above, with the expected values in equation (31) replaced by the sample averages evaluated at the MLE.

Test statistics can be derived. Suppose that the model is given by equation (1) and that we wish to test $H_0: \theta = \theta_0$ against the two-sided alternative $H_a: \theta \neq \theta_0$. The likelihood ratio test statistic evaluated behaves under H_0 as:

$$2\{\ell_n(\hat{\theta}_n) - \ell_n(\theta_0)\} \xrightarrow{d} \chi_d^2. \tag{32}$$

Distributional results can also be obtained for tests of a nested model that only allows for $\tilde{d}$ free parameters from the d parameters in θ, and one can also consider Rao's efficient score statistic, which depends only on the restricted estimator $\bar{\theta}_n$, and Wald's test statistic, which depends only on the unrestricted estimator $\hat{\theta}_n$.

In all the results above, one can then replace $\hat{\theta}_n$ (respectively $\bar{\theta}_n$) by $\hat{\theta}_n^{(K)}$ (respectively $\bar{\theta}_n^{(K)}$). As the examples above have shown, it is not necessary to go much beyond $K = 2$ in the relevant financial examples to estimate the true density with a high degree of precision. More generally, to select an appropriate K at which to stop adding terms to the expansion, the following approach can be adopted: take K large enough so that the *approximation error* made in replacing p_X by $\tilde{p}_X^{(K)}$ is smaller than the *sampling error* due to the random character of the data, by a predetermined factor.

That is, in

$$\|\hat{\theta}_n^{(K)} - \theta_0\| \leq \|\hat{\theta}_n^{(K)} - \hat{\theta}_n\| + \|\hat{\theta}_n - \theta_0\| \tag{33}$$

we can estimate the asymptotic standard variance of $\hat{\theta}_n$ about θ_0 by equation (30). By Chebyshev's Inequality, one can then bound the second term on the right-hand-side of equation (33). We can then stop considering higher order approximations at an order K such that the distance between the two successive estimates $\hat{\theta}_n^{(K)}$ and $\hat{\theta}_n^{(K-1)}$ is an order of magnitude smaller than the distance between $\hat{\theta}_n$ and θ_0. In practice, this is unlikely to make much of a difference and in most cases one can safely restrict attention to the first two terms, $K = 1$ and $K = 2$.

IV. Conclusion

This paper has demonstrated how to obtain very accurate closed-form approximations to the respective transition densities of a variety of models commonly used to represent the dynamics of the short-term interest rate.

Applications to derivative pricing, consisting of obtaining pricing formulas for any underlying price process, have been briefly outlined and will be developed in future work. Finally, an extension of these results to multivariate diffusions will be investigated.

Appendix: Regularity Conditions

ASSUMPTION 1 (Smoothness of the coefficients): *The functions $\mu(x;\theta)$ and $\sigma(x;\theta)$ are infinitely differentiable in x in D_X, and twice continuously differentiable in θ in the parameter space $\Theta \subset R^d$.*

ASSUMPTION 2 (Nondegeneracy of the diffusion):

1. *If $D_X = (-\infty, +\infty)$, there exists a constant c such that $\sigma(x;\theta) > c > 0$ for all $x \in D_X$ and $\theta \in \Theta$.*
2. *If $D_X = (0, +\infty)$, I allow for the possible local degeneracy of σ at $x = 0$: If $\sigma(0;\theta) = 0$, then there exist constants ξ_0, $\omega \geq 0$, $\rho \geq 0$ such that $\sigma(x;\theta) \geq \omega x^\rho$ for all $0 < x < \xi_0$ and $\theta \in \Theta$. Away from 0, σ is nondegenerate; that is, for each $\xi > 0$, there exists a constant c_ξ such that $\sigma(x;\theta) \geq c_\xi > 0$ for all $x \in [\xi, +\infty)$ and $\theta \in \Theta$.*

Assumption 3 below restricts the behavior of the function μ_Y and its derivatives near the boundaries of D_Y. It is formulated in terms of the function μ_Y for reasons of convenience, but the equivalent formulation directly in terms of the original functions μ and σ can be obtained from equation (8). Recall that $\lambda_Y(y;\theta) \equiv -(\mu_Y^2(y;\theta) + \partial \mu_Y(y;\theta)/\partial y)/2$.

ASSUMPTION 3 (Boundary behavior): *For all $\theta \in \Theta$, $\mu_Y(y;\theta)$, $\partial \mu_Y(y;\theta)/\partial y$, and $\partial^2 \mu_Y(y;\theta)/\partial y^2$ have at most exponential growth near the infinity boundaries and $\lim_{y \to \underline{y} \text{ or } \bar{y}} \lambda_Y(y;\theta) < +\infty$.*

1. *Left Boundary:*
   i. *If $\underline{y} = 0^+$, there exist constants ϵ_0, κ, α such that for all $0 < y \leq \epsilon_0$ and $\theta \in \Theta$, $\mu_Y(y;\theta) \geq \kappa y^{-\alpha}$ where either $\alpha > 1$ and $\kappa > 0$, or $\alpha = 1$ and $\kappa \geq 1$.*
   ii. *If $\underline{y} = -\infty$, there exist constants $E_0 > 0$ and $K > 0$ such that for all $y \leq -E_0$ and $\theta \in \Theta$, $\mu_Y(y;\theta) \geq Ky$.*
2. *Right Boundary: If $\bar{y} = +\infty$, there exist constants $E_0 > 0$ and $K > 0$ such that for all $y \geq E_0$ and $\theta \in \Theta$, $\mu_Y(y;\theta) \leq Ky$.*

The following remarks can help demonstrate the generality of these assumptions:

1. The upper bound $\lim_{y \to \underline{y} \text{ or } \bar{y}} \lambda_Y(y;\theta) < +\infty$ does not restrict λ_Y from going to $-\infty$ near the boundaries.
2. Similarly, Assumption 3 does not preclude μ_Y from going to $-\infty$ very fast near $\bar{y}$, and similarly, from going to $+\infty$ very fast near $\underline{y}$. Assumption 3 only restricts how large μ_Y can grow if it has the "wrong" sign;

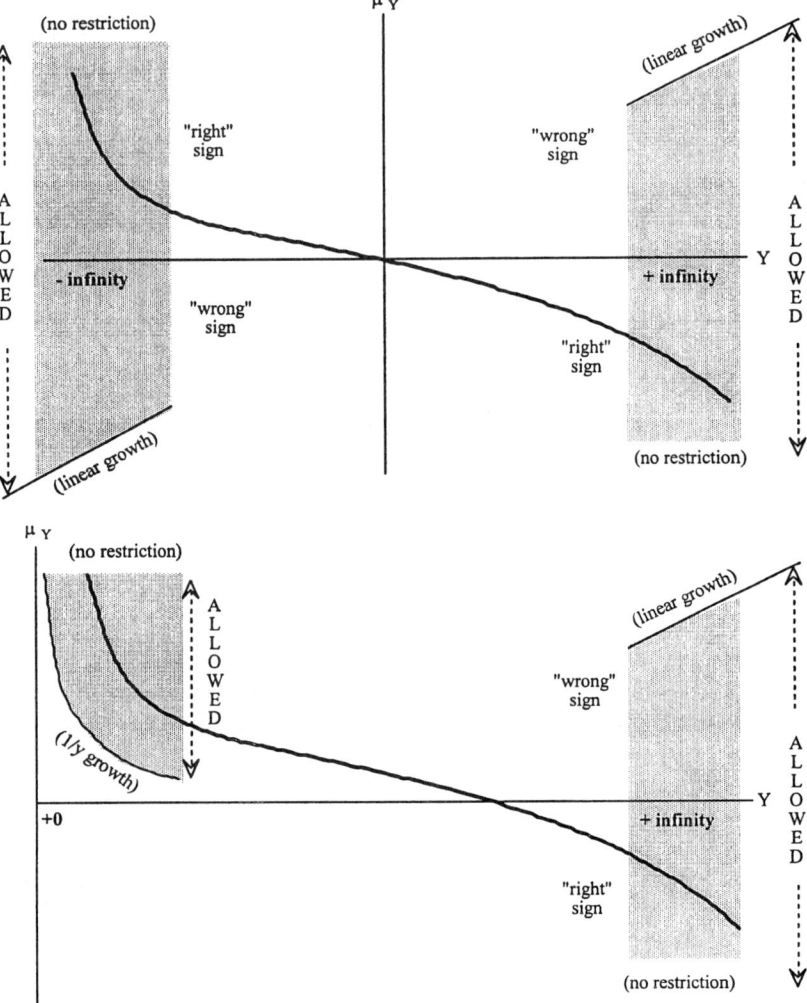

Figure A1. Growth conditions for the drift $\mu_Y(Y;\theta)$. This figure translates graphically the assumptions made in the Appendix regarding the shape of the function μ_Y. The admissible shape of the function is substantially less restricted than under the standard growth conditions. In particular, I only restrict the growth of μ_Y when it has the "wrong" sign (positive near $+\infty$, negative near $-\infty$).

that is, if it is positive near $\bar{y}$ and negative near $\underline{y}$ then linear growth is at the maximum possible growth rate. If μ_Y has the "right" sign then the process is being pulled back away from the boundary and I do not restrict how fast mean reversion occurs (up to an exponential rate for technical reasons). The admissible behavior of the drift function μ_Y under these assumptions is summarized in Figure A1.

3. The constraints on the behavior of the function μ_Y are essentially the best possible. For example, if μ_Y has the "wrong" sign near an infinity boundary, and grows faster than linearly, then Y explodes in finite time. Near a zero boundary at 0^+, if there exist $\kappa > 0$ and $\alpha < 1$ such that $\mu_Y(y;\theta) \leq ky^{-\alpha}$ in a neighborhood of 0^+ then 0 and negative values become attainable.
4. I can now fully characterize the boundary behavior of the diffusion Y implied by the assumptions made: if $+\infty$ is a boundary then it is natural if, near $+\infty$, $|\mu_Y(y;\theta)| \leq Ky$ and entrance if $\mu_Y(y;\theta) \leq -Ky^\beta$ for some $\beta > 1$. If $-\infty$ is a boundary then it is natural if, near $-\infty$, $|\mu_Y(y;\theta)| \leq K|y|$ and entrance if $\mu_Y(y;0) \geq K|y|^\beta$ for some $\beta > 1$. If 0^+ is a boundary, then it is entrance.

   Both entrance and natural boundaries are unattainable (see Feller (1952) or Karlin and Taylor (1981, Sec. 15.6) for the definition of boundaries). Natural boundaries can neither be reached in finite time, nor can the diffusion be started from there. Entrance boundaries, such as 0^+, cannot be reached starting from an interior point in $D_Y = (0,+\infty)$, but it is possible for Y to begin there. In that case, the process moves quickly away from 0 and never returns there. Typically, economic intuition says little about how the process would behave if it were to start at the boundary, or whether that is even possible, and hence it is sensible to allow both types of boundary behavior.
5. Assumption 3 neither requires nor implies that the process is stationary. When *both* boundaries of the domain D_Y are entrance boundaries then the process is necessarily stationary with unconditional (marginal) density,

$$\pi(y;\theta) \equiv \exp\left\{2\int^y \mu_Y(u;\theta)\,du\right\} \bigg/ \int_{\underline{y}}^{\bar{y}} \exp\left\{2\int^v \mu_Y(u;\theta)\,du\right\} dv,$$

(A.1)

provided that the initial random variable Y_0 is itself distributed with the same density π. When at least one of the boundaries is natural, stationarity is neither precluded nor implied. For instance, both an Ornstein–Uhlenbeck process, where $\mu_Y(y;\theta) = \kappa(\alpha - y)$, and a standard Brownian motion, where $\mu_Y(y;\theta) = 0$, satisfy the assumptions made, and both have natural boundaries at $-\infty$ and $+\infty$. Yet the former process is stationary, due to mean reversion, while the latter (null recurrent) is not.

Finally, the following assumption is needed for the purpose of maximizing the log-likelihood function only, not for the purpose of constructing the density expansion in equation (11).

ASSUMPTION 4 (Strengthening of Assumption 2 in the limiting case where $\alpha = 1$ and the diffusion is degenerate at 0): *Recall the constant ρ in Assumption 2(2), and the constants α and κ in Assumption 3(1.i). If $\alpha = 1$, then either $\rho \geq 1$ with no restriction on κ, or $\kappa \geq 2\rho/(1 - \rho)$ if $0 < \rho < 1$. If $\alpha > 1$, no restriction is required.*

REFERENCES

Ahn, Dong-Hyun, and Bin Gao, 1998, A parametric nonlinear model of term structure dynamics, Working paper, University of North Carolina at Chapel Hill.

Aït-Sahalia, Yacine, 1996a, Nonparametric pricing of interest rate derivative securities, *Econometrica* 64, 527–560.

Aït-Sahalia, Yacine, 1996b, Testing continuous-time models of the spot interest rate, *Review of Financial Studies* 9, 385–426.

Aït-Sahalia, Yacine, 1998, Maximum-likelihood estimation of discretely sampled diffusions: A closed-form approach, Working paper, Princeton University.

Bibby, Bo M., and Michael Sørenson, 1995, Martingale estimation functions for discretely observed diffusion processes, *Bernoulli* 1, 17–39.

Black, Fisher, and Myron Scholes, 1973, The pricing of options and corporate liabilities, *Journal of Political Economy* 81, 637–654.

Chan, K. C., G. Andrew Karolyi, Francis A. Longstaff, and Anthony B. Sanders, 1992, An empirical comparison of alternative models of the short-term interest rate, *Journal of Finance* 47, 1209–1227.

Conley, Timothy G., Lars P. Hansen, Erzo G. J. Luttmer, and José A. Scheinkman, 1997, Short-term interest rates as subordinated diffusions, *Review of Financial Studies* 10, 525–578.

Cox, John C., 1996, The constant elasticity of variance option pricing model, *The Journal of Portfolio Management*, Special issue.

Cox, John C., John E. Ingersoll, and Stephen A. Ross, 1985, A theory of the term structure of interest rates, *Econometrica* 53, 385–407.

Cox, John C., and Stephen A. Ross, 1976, The valuation of options for alternative stochastic processes, *Journal of Financial Economics* 3, 145–166.

Dacunha-Castelle, Didier, and Danielle Florens-Zmirou, 1986, Estimation of the coefficients of a diffusion from discrete observations, *Stochastics* 19, 263–284.

Duffie, Darrell, and Peter Glynn, 1997, Estimation of continuous-time Markov processes sampled at random time intervals, Working paper, Stanford University.

Duffie, Darrell, and Kenneth Singleton, 1993, Simulated moments estimation of Markov models of asset prices, *Econometrica* 61, 929–952.

Elerian, Ola, Sidartha Chib, and Neil Shephard, 1998, Likelihood inference for discretely observed non-linear diffusions, Working paper, Oxford University.

Eraker, Bjorn, 1997, MCMC analysis of diffusion models with application to finance, Working paper, Norwegian School of Economics, Bergen.

Feller, William, 1952, The parabolic differential equations and the associated semi-groups of transformations, *Annals of Mathematics* 55, 468–519.

Florens, Jean-Pierre, Eric Renault, and Nizar Touzi, 1995, Testing for embeddability by stationary scalar diffusions, *Econometric Theory*, forthcoming.

Gallant, A. Ronald, and George Tauchen, 1998, Reprojecting partially observed systems with an application to interest rate diffusions, *Journal of the American Statistical Association* 93, 10–24.

Gihman, I. I., and A. V. Skorohod, 1972, *Stochastic Differential Equations* (Springer-Verlag, New York).

Gouriéroux, Christian, Alain Monfort, and Eric Renault, 1993, Indirect inference, *Journal of Applied Econometrics* 8, S85–S118.

Hamilton, James D, 1996, The daily market for Federal funds, *Journal of Political Economy* 104, 26–56.

Hansen, Lars P., and José A. Scheinkman, 1995, Back to the future: Generating moment implications for continuous time Markov processes, *Econometrica* 63, 767–804.

Hansen, Lars P., José A. Scheinkman, and Nizar Touzi, 1998, Identification of scalar diffusions using eigenvectors, *Journal of Econometrics* 86, 1, 1–32.

Honoré, Peter, 1997, Maximum-likelihood estimation of non-linear continuous-time term structure models, Working paper, Aarhus University.

Huggins, Douglas J., 1997, Estimation of a diffusion process for the U.S. short interest rate using a semigroup pseudo-likelihood, Ph.D. Dissertation, University of Chicago.

Jarrow, Robert, and Andrew Rudd, 1982, Approximate option valuation for arbitrary stochastic processes, *Journal of Financial Economics* 10, 347–349.

Jones, Christopher S., 1997, Bayesian analysis of the short-term interest rate, Working paper, The Wharton School, University of Pennsylvania.

Karlin, Samuel, and Howard M. Taylor, 1981, *A Second Course in Stochastic Processes* (Academic Press, New York).

Kloeden, Peter E. and Eckhardt Platen, 1992, *Numerical Solution of Stochastic Differential Equations* (Springer-Verlag, New York).

Lo, Andrew W., 1988, Maximum likelihood estimation of generalized Itô processes with discretely sampled data, *Econometric Theory* 4, 231–247.

Melino, Angelo, 1994, Estimation of continuous-time models in finance; in Christopher S. Sims, ed.: *Advances in Econometrics, Sixth World Congress*, Vol. II (Cambridge University Press, Cambridge, England).

Merton, Robert C., 1980, On estimating the expected return on the market: An exploratory investigation, *Journal of Financial Economics* 8, 323–361.

Pedersen, Asger R., 1995, A new approach to maximum-likelihood estimation for stochastic differential equations based on discrete observations, *Scandinavian Journal of Statistics* 22, 55–71.

Santa-Clara, Pedro, 1995, Simulated likelihood estimation of diffusions with an application to the short term interest rate, Working paper, UCLA.

Stanton, Richard, 1997, A nonparametric model of term structure dynamics and the market price of interest rate risk, *Journal of Finance* 52, 1973–2002.

Vasicek, Oldrich, 1977, An equilibrium characterization of the term structure, *Journal of Financial Economics* 5, 177–188.

Wong, Eugene, 1964, The construction of a class of stationary Markov processes; in R. Bellman, ed.: *Stochastic Processes in Mathematical Physics and Engineering*, Proceedings of Symposia in Applied Mathematics, 16 (American Mathematical Society, Providence, RI).

Transaction costs in portfolio management and derivative pricing

Thaleia Zariphopoulou

ABSTRACT. This presentation provides an overview of valuation models in markets with transaction costs. Transaction costs are a realistic feature in numerous financial transactions and their presence affects considerably the theoretical asset and derivative prices.

In the area of optimal portfolio management, the valuation models give rise to singular stochastic control problems and the goal is to characterize the value function (maximal utility) and to specify the optimal control policies. The main characteristic of these optimization problems is the trading idleness at portfolio positions that are highly penalized by the transaction costs. The wealth space depletes into three regions: "no-trading", the "buy stock" and the "sell stock" regions. For the case of general utility functions, the location and the shape of the free boundries are in general unknown and they can be specified only through numerical schemes. In order to analyze the value function, one needs to work in a weak class of solutions, namely the viscosity solutions and this is the class of solutions used throughout the entire presentation.

In the area of derivative pricing, the classical Black and Scholes valuation theory, based on exact replication, breaks down completely when transaction costs are present. In fact, the Black and Scholes perfect hedging strategy requires to rebalance the portfolio continuously in time and this produces an infinite transaction volume due to the infinite variation of the diffusion price processes. Various approaches have been developed and they are discussed and compared in detail. These methods include among others, the method of super-replicating strategies (instead of exact replicating ones), the utility maximization theory and, finally, the implementation of imperfect hedging strategies.

1991 *Mathematics Subject Classification.* Primary 93E20, 60G40, 60H30; Secondary 90A09, 09A12.

Key words and phrases. transaction costs, optimal investment-consumption models, derivative pricing, singular stochastic control, Hamilton-Jacobi-Bellman equation, viscosity solutions.

Chapter A. Transaction costs in Portfolio Management

Section 1: Overview.

In his seminal papers, Merton ([**M1**], [**M2**]) introduced an optimal portfolio management model of a single agent in a stochastic setting. Trading takes place between a riskless security (e.g. a bond) and one or more stocks whose prices are modelled as diffusion processes. For each stock price, the mean rate of return and volatility are assumed to be constant and known. The investor, endowed with some initial wealth, trades dynamically between the available securities and consumes part of his wealth continuously in time. He is assumed to be a "small investor" in the sense that his actions do not influence the equilibrium prices of the underlying assets. His objective is to maximize the *expected utility function* which models his individual preferences as well as his attitude towards the risk inherent from the market uncertainty.

Merton studied, among others, the special case of power utility functions, known as *Constant Relevant Risk Aversion (CRRA) utilities* and produced closed-form solutions to the optimization problem of the single agent. An important consequence of these results is that all the risky securities can be replaced by a mutual fund with characteristics independent of the individual preferences. This feature facilitated the analysis of dynamic market equilibria which was developed by Merton [**M3**] and subsequently further generalized by others (Araujo and Montiero [**DH**], Dana and Pontier [**DPo**], Duffie [**D**], Duffie and Huang [**DH**], Huang [**H**], Karatzas, Lehoczky and Shreve ([**KLS1**] and [**KLS2**]), Mas-Collell ([**M-C1**] and [**M-C2**])).

A crucial simplification in Merton's work is the absence of *transaction costs* on the various trades. The first to incorporate proportional transaction costs in Merton's model were Magill and Constantinides [**MC**] in an effort to understand how these costs, affect the trading policies and also to explore if the equivalence between multiple stocks and the mutual fund is still preserved. Magill and Constantinides believed that transaction costs have an important impact on the trading activity of the investor; in fact, they argued that the individual must completely refrain from trading at portfolio states which are highly penalized by the transaction costs. These policies differ substantially from the ones recovered by Merton – for the same class of utility functions. Indeed, Merton's policies call for a continuous in time rebalancing of the security holdings so that a constant fraction of the current wealth remains always invested in the stock account(s). This wealth independent fraction is known as the *Merton ratio* and it depends on the market parameters and the risk aversion coefficient. Thus, in the absence of transaction costs, the optimal investment process turns out to be a diffusion process with values proportional to the ones of the current wealth process. In the presence of transaction costs, Magill and Constantinides brought out the important insight about the different nature of the optimal investment policies, the one of *singular trading policies*. Under these policies, lump-sum transactions take place which amount to instantaneously altering the portfolio holdings in the bond and the stock account(s). Even though Magill and Constantinides did not provide a *singular stochastic control* formulation of the underlying model, they paved the way to the correct formulation of the valuation models with transaction costs (see, also, Constantinides [**Co1**], [**Co2**]).

Taksar, Klass and Assaf [**TKA1**] were the first to formulate a transaction cost model as a singular stochastic control problem in the context of maximizing the long term expected rate of wealth. Subsequently, Davis and Norman [**DN**] provided a rigorous mathematical formulation and extensive analysis of the Merton problem in the presence of proportional costs for CRRA utilities. Their paper is considered a landmark in the literature on transaction costs and contains useful insights and fundamental results, both theoretic and numerical, for the value function and the optimal investment policies. Even though these results depend heavily on the homotheticity properties of the value function, inherited by the power form of the CRRA utilities, the model of David and Norman is viewed as the benchmark transaction costs model; it is presented and analyzed in detail in the next section.

Departing from the special class of CRRA utilities, Zariphopoulou ([**Z1**], [**Z2**]) was the first to study optimal portfolio management models with proportional transaction costs for general individual preferences. In [**Z1**], Zariphopoulou introduced a simple investment model with two securities, a riskless bond rate and a risky security whose rate of return is modelled as a continuous-time Markov chain, and she provided characterization results for the maximal utilities.

For the case of price processes modelled as diffusion processes and CRRA preferences, a considerable body of work has been produced with modifications and extensions of the Davis and Norman (DN) model. Shreve and Soner [**SS**] revisited the DN model and provided additional existence and regularity results for the optimal policies and the value function for a wide range of market parameters. A similar model, but in the case of finite trading horizon, was studied by Akian, Menaldi and Sulem in [**AMS1**] who allowed for more than one risky securities and provided some regularity results for the value function. Finally, the ergodic analogue of Akian, Menaldi and Sulem was subsequently analyzed by Akian, Sulem and Taksar in [**AST**].

As it will be apparent from the discussion in the next sections, the stochastic optimization problems with transaction costs do not have in general closed form solutions. Thus, it is highly desirable — mainly for the practical applications — to provide numerical results for their value function and the optimal investment policies and consumption plans. Such results were first provided by Davis and Norman [**DN**] and later by Tourin and Zariphopoulou [**TZ1**] for general utility functions. Other numerical schemes have been proposed by Akian, Menaldi and Sulem [**AMS2**] for a model of portfolio selection with more than one risky assets and by Sulem [**Su**] for a mixed portfolio problem with transaction costs. Pichler [**Pi**] developed a different class of schemes for the DN model and he also studied the probability distributions of the relevant expected gains.

In the entire volume of the aforementioned work, the mathematical analysis is carried out through the so-called *Hamiltonian-Jacobi-Bellman* (HJB) *equation*. This equation, as it will be discussed subsequently in detail, is the offspring of the optimality principle and stochastic analysis. Generally speaking, the value function (maximal utility) is expected to solve the HJB equation and the first order conditions in HJB usually give the candidate optimal policies in a feedback form. The verification that the solution of the HJB equation and the optimality of the candidate policies are established via classical verification results, provided that the value function has the appropriate regularity properties (for a general overview of the theory of controlled Markov processes, we refer the reader to the book of Fleming and Soner [**FS**]). In the majority of stochastic control problems arising in asset pricing models, the required regularity properties might not hold. This is the result of various characteristics of the particular nature of the involved financial models, like trading constraints, transaction costs, certain assumptions on the price processes as well as an imperfect information structure. Therefore, it is imperative to relax the notion of solutions of the associated HJB equation in order to develop a viable method to study this class of problems. It turns out that a rich class of weak solutions of the HJB equation are the so-called *viscosity solutions*. These solutions were introduced by Crandall and Lions [**CL2**] for first-order nonlinear partial differential equations and by Lions [**Li**] for the second-order case. The strength of this theory lies in the fact that it provides rigorous characterization of the value function as the unique viscosity solution of the HJB equation. Moreover, the strong stability properties of viscosity solutions provide excellent convergence results for a large class of numerical schemes for the value function and the optimal policies.

In stochastic optimization problems arising in optimal investment and consumption models, viscosity solutions were first employed by Zariphopoulou [**Z1**] for the Merton model with trading constraints (see also Zariphopoulou [**Z3**]) and for the aforementioned transaction cost model with the Markov chain parameters (see Zariphopoulou [**Z2**]) Subsequently, this class of solutions was used by Fleming and Zariphopoulou [**FZ**], Duffie and Zariphopoulou [**DuZ**], and in the context of transaction costs by Shreve and Soner [**SS**]. Shreve and Soner [**SS**] provided a viscosity characterization of the value function of the DN model for a broad range of market parameters. For general utilities, this characterization was provided by Tourin and Zariphopoulou [**TZ1**] and it was subsequently used to establish the convergence of the numerical schemes they developed (see also Tourin and Zariphopoulou [**TZ2**] and [**TZ3**]).

In other models with transaction costs, in particular in the area of derivative pricing, these solutions were used among others by Davis, Panas and Zariphopoulou [**DPZ**], Davis and Zariphopoulou [**DZ**], Barles and Soner [**BS**], Constantinides and Zariphopoulou [**CZ1**], Hodder and Zariphopoulou [**HZ**], Alvarez [**A**], Alvarez and Tourin [**ATo**], Barles et al [**BBRS**], Pichler [**Pi**] and Renault and Touzi [**RT**]. Being also employed by a number of authors in other valuation models with market imperfections, viscosity solutions gradually became a standard tool in the study of stochastic control problems arising in models of Mathematical Finance. Because of their important role, a considerable part of this manuscript is dedicated to their contribution in the analysis of optimization problems with transaction costs. Our presentation is strongly oriented towards this theory and the outlaid results follow closely the unified theme of viscosity solutions of the relevant HJB equations.

An alternative valuable approach to study optimal portfolio management models is based on the *martingale theory*. This powerful methodology is widely used in asset and derivative pricing and yields rich results under general assumptions on the market coefficients. We provide some of the basic references where this approach is used in subsequent sections.

This chapter is organized as follows: In Section 2, we introduce the fundamental optimal investment-consumption model for general utility functions and in Section 3, we analyze its associated HJB equation. Section 4 gives an overview of the results of Davis and Norman [**DN**] and Shreve and Soner [**SS**] for the case of preferences modelled as CRRA utilities. In Section 5 we present some numerical schemes and we conclude with Section 6 where we discuss variations and extensions of the basic model.

Section 2: The optimal investment-consumption model.

We start with the description of the benchmark optimal investment-consumption model of Davis and Norman incorporating general utilities in the payoff functional. This is a model of a single agent, or a small investor as it is otherwise known, in the sense that his/her actions cannot influence the prices of the underlying securities.

We consider an economy with two securities, a *bond* with price B_t and a *stock* with price S_t at date $t \geq 0$. Prices are denominated in units of a consumption good, say dollars.

The bond pays no coupons, is default free and has price dynamics

$$B_t = e^{rt} B_0, \qquad t \geq 0 \tag{2.1}$$

where r is the *constant rate of interest*.

We denote by W_t a one-dimensional standard Brownian motion which generates the filtration $\mathcal{F}_t$ on a fixed, complete probability space $(\Omega, \mathcal{F}, P)$. The stock price is the diffusion process

$$\begin{aligned} S_t &= S_0 + \int_0^t \mu S_\tau d\tau + \int_0^t \sigma S_\tau dW_\tau \\ &= S_0 \exp\left\{\left(\mu - \frac{\sigma^2}{2}\right) t + \sigma W_t\right\}, \end{aligned} \tag{2.2}$$

where μ is the *mean rate of return* and σ is the *volatility*; μ and σ are constants such that $\mu > r$ and $\sigma \neq 0$.

The investor holds x_t dollars of the bond and y_t dollars of the stock at date t. We consider a pair of right-continuous with left limits (CADLAG), non-decreasing processes (L_t, M_t) such that L_t represents the cumulative dollar amount transferred into the stock account and M_t the cumulative dollar amount transferred out of the stock account. By convention, $L_0 = M_0 = 0$. The stock account process is

$$y_t = y + \int_0^t \mu y_\tau d\tau + \int_0^t \sigma y_\tau dW_\tau + L_t - M_t \tag{2.3}$$

with $y_0 = y$.

Transfers between the stock and the bond accounts incur *proportional transaction costs*. In particular, the cumulative transfer L_t into the stock account reduces the bond account by βL_t and the cumulative transfer M_t out of the stock account increases the bond account by αM_t, where $0 < \alpha < 1 < \beta$.

The investor consumes at the rate c_t dollars out of the bond account. There are no transaction costs in transfers from the bond account into the consumption good.

The bond account process is

$$x_t = x + \int_0^t \{rx_\tau - c_\tau\} d\tau - \beta L_t + \alpha M_t \tag{2.4}$$

with $x_0 = x$. The integral represents the accumulation of interest and the drain due to consumption. The last two terms represent the cumulative transfers between the stock and bond accounts, net of transaction costs.

A policy is a $\mathcal{F}_t$-progressively measurable triple (c_t, L_t, M_t). We restrict our attention to the set of admissible policies $\mathcal{A}$ such that

$$\begin{cases} c_t \geq 0 \text{ and } E \int_0^t c_\tau d\tau < \infty \text{ a.s. for } t \geq 0 & (2.5) \\ \text{and} \\ w_t = x_t + \begin{pmatrix} \alpha \\ \beta \end{pmatrix} y_t \geq 0 \text{ a.s. for } t \geq 0, & (2.5)' \end{cases}$$

where we adopt the notation

$$\begin{pmatrix} \alpha \\ \beta \end{pmatrix} z = \begin{cases} \alpha z & \text{if } z \geq 0 \\ \beta z & \text{if } z < 0. \end{cases} \quad (2.6)$$

We refer to w_t as the *net worth*. It represents the investor's bond holdings, if the investor were to transfer the holdings from the stock account into the bond account, incurring in the process the transaction costs.

The investor has von Neumann-Morgenstern preferences

$$E\left[\int_0^{+\infty} e^{-\rho t} U(c_t) dt\right]$$

over the consumption stream $\{c_t, t \geq 0\}$, where ρ is the *subjective discount rate* and the *utility function* $U : R_0^+ \to R_0^+$ is assumed to have the following properties:

i) $U \in C([0, +\infty)) \cap C^1((0, +\infty))$ is increasing and concave.
ii) $U(c) \leq K(1+c)^\gamma$, $\forall c \geq 0$, for some positive constants K and γ with $0 < \gamma < 1$.

Given the initial endowment (x, y) in $\overline{D} = \left\{(x,y) \in \mathcal{R} \times \mathcal{R} : x + \begin{pmatrix} \alpha \\ \beta \end{pmatrix} y \geq 0 \right\}$, we define the *value function* V as

$$V(x,y) = \sup_{\mathcal{A}} E\left[\int_0^{+\infty} e^{-\rho t} U(c_t) dt \mid x_0 = x, y_0 = y\right]. \quad (2.7)$$

To guarantee that the value function is well defined, we either assume, as in Davis and Norman [**DN**], that

$$\rho > r\gamma + \frac{\gamma(\mu - r)^2}{2\sigma^2(1 - \gamma)} \quad (2.8)$$

or, assume, as in Shreve and Soner [**SS**], that

$$\rho > r\gamma + \gamma^2(\mu - r)^2 / 2\sigma^2(1 - \gamma)^2. \quad (2.9)$$

Either the set of conditions (2.8) and (2.9), yield that the value function which corresponds to $\alpha = \beta = 1$ and $U(c) = K(1+c)^\gamma$ is finite and, therefore, all functions with $0 \leq \alpha < 1, \beta \geq 1$ are finite.

We continue with some basic properties of the value function. (For other basic properties see Shreve and Soner [**SS**] or Tourin and Zariphopoulou [**TZ1**].)

PROPOSITION 2.1:. *The value function V is jointly concave in x and y, strictly increasing in x and increasing in y.*

Sketch of the proof: The joint concavity of the value function comes from the concavity of the utility function and the linearity of the dynamics. Indeed, if (C_1, L_1, M_1) and (C_2, L_2, M_2) are optimal policies for the points (x_1, y_1) and (x_2, y_2), then $(\lambda C_1 + (1-\lambda)C_2, \lambda M_1 + (1-\lambda)M_2, \lambda N_1 + (1-\lambda)N_2)$ is admissible for $(\lambda x_1 + (1-\lambda)x_2, \lambda y_1 + (1-\lambda)y_2)$.

The monotonicity of V follows from the same monotonicity of the utility function and the linear dynamics of the state trajectories. The strict monotonicity in x, comes from the fact that V is also concave. (For a detailed proof of a similar question, see Proposition 2.1 in Zariphopoulou [**Z3**].)

PROPOSITION 2.2. *The value function V is continuous on $\overline{D}$.*

PROOF. Since V is concave, it is obviously continuous in D. We next show that V is continuous on the boundary. The continuity at the point $(0,0)$ follows as in Proposition 2.2 in Zariphopoulou [**Z2**].

We now show that
$$\lim_{(x_n, y_n) \to (x_0, y_0)} V(x_n, y_n) = V(x_0, y_0)$$

where
$$(x_0, y_0) \in l_1 = \{(x,y) \in \mathcal{R}^+ \times \mathcal{R}^- : x + \beta y = 0\}$$

or
$$(x_0, y_0) \in l_2 = \{(x,y) \in \mathcal{R}^- \times \mathcal{R}^+ : x + \alpha y = 0\}.$$

We only examine the case $(x_0, y_0) \in l_1$ since the other is treated similarly. To this end, consider a point $(x_0, y_0) \in l_1$ and a sequence
$$(x_n, y_n) \in l_1^+ = \{(x,y) \in \mathcal{R}^+ \times \mathcal{R}^- : x + \beta y > 0\}$$

such that $\lim_{n \to +\infty} (x_n, y_n) = (x_0, y_0)$. First we observe that by suboptimality $V(x_0, y_0) \leq V(x_0 + \beta y_0, 0)$. Moreover the value function V is always bounded from above by the value function, say u, of the Merton problem without transaction costs and with the same preferences and price dynamics. Therefore, $V(x_0, y_0) \leq u(x_0 + \beta y_0) = 0$, for $x_0 + \beta y_0 = 0$ (see Merton [**M1**]). Thus to prove continuity of (x_0, y_0), it suffices to show that $\lim_{n \to \infty} V(x_n, y_n) = 0$; but this follows from the facts that $0 \leq V(x_n, y_n) \leq V(x_n + \beta y_n, 0)$, $V(x_n + \beta y_n, 0) \leq u(x_n + \beta y_n)$ and the continuity of u at zero (see Zariphopoulou [**Z1**]). (The author would like to thank D. Ocone for pointing out an error in a previous version.)

We conclude this section by stating a fundamental property of the value function known as the *Dynamic Programming Principle* (for a proof see, for example, Lions [**Li**]).

PROPOSITION 2.3. *If θ is a stopping time (i.e. a nonnegative, $\mathcal{F}$-measurable random variable), then*

$$V(x,y) = \sup_{\mathcal{A}} E\left\{ \int_0^\theta e^{-\rho t} U(c_t) dt + e^{-\rho \theta} V(x_\theta, y_\theta) \right\}. \tag{2.10}$$

Section 3: The HJB equation and viscosity solutions.

In this section we derive the Hamilton Jacobi Bellman equation and we characterize the value function as its *unique constrained viscosity solution*. The characterization of V as a constrained solution is natural because of the presence of state constraints given by (2.5)'.

The notion of *viscosity solutions* was introduced by Crandall and Lions [**CL2**] for first-order and by Lions [**Li**] for second order equations. For a general overview of the theory we refer to the "User's Guide" by Crandall, Ishii and Lions [**CIL**] and Fleming and Soner [**FS**].

Next, we recall the notion of *constrained viscosity solutions*, which was introduced by Soner [**Son**] and Capuzzo-Dolcetta and Lions [**C-DL**] for first-order equations and by Lions [**Li**] for second-order equations (see also Ishii and Lions [**IL**]). To this end, we consider a non-linear second order partial differential equation of the form

$$F(X, v, Dv, D^2v) = 0 \text{ in } D, \tag{3.1}$$

with the domain $\overline{D} \subset \mathcal{R}^N$, and Dv and D^2v standing respectively for the gradient vector and the second derivative matrix of v; F is continuous in all its arguments and *degenerate elliptic*, meaning that

$$F(X, p, q, A + B) \leq F(X, p, q, A) \text{ if } B \geq 0.$$

DEFINITION 3.1. A continuous function $v : \mathcal{R} \to \mathcal{R}$ is a *constrained viscosity solution* of (3.1) if

i) v is a *viscosity subsolution* of (3.1) on $\overline{D}$, that is for any $\phi \in C^2(\overline{D})$ and any local maximum point $X_0 \in \overline{D}$ of $v - \phi$

$$F(X_0, v(X_0), D\phi(X_0), D^2\phi(X_0)) \leq 0$$

and

ii) v is a *viscosity supersolution* of (3.1) in D, that is for any $\phi \in C^2(\overline{D})$ and any local minimum point $X_0 \in D$ of $v - \phi$

$$F(X_0, v(X_0), D\phi(X_0), D^2\phi(X_0)) \geq 0.$$

The following result was proved by Tourin and Zariphopoulou (in [**TZ1**]) and by Shreve and Soner (in [**SS**]) for the case of CRRA utilities (the proof below is from [**TZ1**]).

THEOREM 3.2. *The value function V is a constrained viscosity solution on $\overline{D}$ of the Hamilton–Jacobi–Bellman equation*

$$\min\left[\rho V - \frac{1}{2}\sigma^2 y^2 V_{yy} - \mu y V_y - rxV_x - \max_{c \geq 0}(-cV_x + U(c)),\right.$$

$$\left. \beta V_x - V_y, \ -\alpha V_x + V_y \right] = 0 \tag{3.2}$$

PROOF. i) We first show that V is a viscosity subsolution of (3.2) on $\overline{D}$. Let $\phi \in C^2(D)$ and $X_0 = (x_0, y_0) \in \overline{D}$ be a maximum of $V - \phi$; without loss of generality we may assume that

$$V(X_0) = \phi(X_0) \text{ and } V \leq \phi \text{ on } \overline{D}. \tag{3.3}$$

We need to show that

$$\min\left[\rho\phi(X_0) - \frac{1}{2}\sigma^2 y_0^2 \phi_{yy}(X_0) - \mu y_0 \phi_y(X_0) - rx_0\phi_x(X_0) - \max_{c\geq 0}(-c\phi_x(X_0) + U(c)),\right.$$

$$\left.\beta\phi_x(X_0) - \phi_y(X_0), -\alpha\phi_x(X_0) + \phi_y(X_0)\right] \leq 0. \quad (3.4)$$

We argue by contradiction and we assume that

$$\beta\phi_x(X_0) - \phi_y(X_0) > 0, \quad (3.5)$$

$$-\alpha\phi_x(X_0) + \phi_y(X_0) > 0, \quad (3.6)$$

and

$$\rho\phi(X_0) - \frac{1}{2}\sigma^2 y_0^2 \phi_{yy}(X_0) - \mu y_0 \phi_y(X_0) - rx_0\phi_x(X_0)$$
$$- \max_{c\geq 0}(-c\phi_x(X_0) + U(c)) > \theta \quad (3.7)$$

for some $\theta > 0$.

From the fact that ϕ is smooth, the above inequalities become

$$\beta\phi_x(X) - \phi_y(X) > 0, \quad (3.8)$$

$$-\alpha\phi_x(X) + \phi_y(X) > 0, \quad (3.9)$$

and

$$\rho\phi(X) - \frac{1}{2}\sigma^2 y^2 \phi_{yy}(X) - \mu y\phi_y(X) - rx\phi_x(X) - \max_{c\geq 0}(-c\phi_x(X) + U(c)) > \theta \quad (3.10)$$

for some $\theta > 0$, where $X = (x,y) \in \mathcal{B}(X_0)$ a neighborhood of X_0.

We now consider the optimal trajectory $X_{0,t}^* = (x_{0,t}^*, y_{0,t}^*)$ where $X_{0,0}^* = (x_0, y_0)$ with optimal policies (c_t^*, L_t^*, M_t^*) being used. (The existence of optimal policies was shown in Zhu [**Zh**] (Th. (iv) 2)). We will need the following lemma which shows that $X_{0,t}^*$ has no jumps a.s. at $t = 0^+$.

LEMMA 3.3. *Assume that inequality (3.5) (resp. (3.6)) holds and let A be the event that the optimal trajectory $X_{0,t}^*$ has a jump at least of size ϵ at $t = 0^+$ along the direction $(-\beta, 1)$ (resp. $(\alpha, -1)$). If $(x_0 - \beta\epsilon, y_0 + \epsilon) \in \mathcal{B}(X)$ (resp. $(x_0 + \alpha\epsilon, y_0 - \epsilon) \in \mathcal{B}(X_0)$) then $P(A) = 0$.*

The proof can be found in Lemma 1 in Davis, Panas and Zariphopoulou [**DPZ**], and it is not presented here.

We now continue the proof of the theorem. We define the random time τ to be $\tau(\omega) = \inf\{t \geq 0 : X_{0,t}^* \notin \mathcal{B}(X_0)\}$. Notice that by the preceding Lemma, $\tau(\omega) > 0$ a.s. Combining (3.8), (3.9) and (3.10) we get

$$E\int_0^\tau \theta e^{-\rho s}ds < E\int_0^\tau e^{-\rho s}[\rho\phi(X_s^*) - \tfrac{1}{2}\sigma^2(y_s^*)^2\phi_{yy}(X_s^*)$$
$$-\mu y_s^*\phi_y(X_s^*) - rx_s^*\phi_x(X_s^*) - \{-c_s^*\phi_x(X_s^*) + U(c_s^*)\}]ds$$
$$+E\int_0^{\tau(\omega)} e^{-\rho s}[\beta\phi_x(X_s^*) - \phi_y(X_s^*)]dL_s^* \quad (3.11)$$
$$+E\int_0^{\tau(\omega)} e^{-\rho s}[-\alpha\phi_x(X_s^*) + \phi_y(X_s^*)]dM_s^*$$
$$= E(I_1(\tau)) - E\int_0^\tau e^{-\rho s}U(c_s^*)ds + E(I_2(\tau)) + E(I_3(\tau)).$$

Applying Itô's formula to $e^{-\rho\tau}\phi(X_{0,\tau}^*)$ gives

$$E\{e^{-\rho\tau}\phi(X_{0,\tau}^*)\} = \phi(X_0) - [E(I_1(\tau)) + E(I_2(\tau)) + E(I_3(\tau))]. \quad (3.12)$$

Combining (3.3), (3.11) and (3.12) we get

$$E\{V(X_{0,\tau}^*)\} \leq V(X_0) - \left[E\int_0^\tau e^{-\rho s}U(c_s^*)ds + \theta\frac{1-Ee^{-\rho\tau}}{\rho}\right], \quad (3.13)$$

which violates the dynamic programming principle, together with the optimality of the policy (c_t^*, L_t^*, M_t^*). Therefore, at least one of the arguments of the minimum operator in (3.4) must be non-positive and hence the value function is a viscosity subsolution of (3.2).

ii) In the second part of the proof, we show that V is a viscosity supersolution of (3.2) in D; for this we must show that, for all smooth functions $\varphi(X)$, such that $V - \varphi$ has a local minimum at $X_0 \in D$, the following holds:

$$\min\left[\rho\varphi(X_0) - \frac{1}{2}\sigma^2 y_0^2\varphi_{yy}(X_0) - \mu y_0\varphi_y(X_0) - rx_0\varphi_x(X_0)\right.$$
$$\left. - \max_{c\geq 0}(-c\varphi_x(X_0) + U(c)), \beta\varphi_x(X_0) - \varphi_y(X_0), -\alpha\varphi_x(X_0) + \varphi_y(X_0)\right] \geq 0$$

where, without loss of generality, $V(X_0) = \varphi(X_0)$ and $V \geq \varphi$ on $\overline{D}$. In this case, we prove that each argument of the above minimum operator is nonnegative.

Consider the trading strategy $L_t = L_0 > 0$ and $M_t = 0$ for $t \geq 0$. By the Dynamic Programming Principle,

$$V(x_0, y_0) \geq V(x_0 - \beta L_0, y_0 + L_0).$$

This inequality holds for φ as well, and, by taking the left-hand side to the right-hand side, dividing by L_0 and sending $L_0 \to 0$, we get

$$\beta\varphi_x(X_0) - \varphi_y(X_0) \geq 0.$$

Similarly, by using the trading strategy $L(t) = 0$ and $M(t) = M_0 > 0$, for $t \geq 0$, we obtain

$$-\alpha\varphi_x(X_0) + \varphi_y(X_0) \geq 0.$$

Finally, consider the case where the investor does not trade but consumes at a constant rate $c_t = c$ for $0 < t \leq \tau$ where $\tau = n \wedge \tau_1 \wedge \tau_2$ with $n \in N$

$$\tau_1 = \inf\{t : x_t + \beta y_t \geq 0 \text{ a.s. if } y_t \leq 0\},$$

$$\tau_2 = \inf\{t : x_t + \alpha y_t \geq 0 \text{ a.s. if } y_t \geq 0\}$$

and x_t, y_t are the state trajectories, given by (2.4) and (2.3), under policy $(c, 0, 0)$. The Dynamic Programming Principle yields

$$V(x_0, y_0) \leq E\left[\int_0^\tau e^{-\rho s} U(c) ds + e^{-\rho \tau} V(x_\tau, y_\tau)\right].$$

The same inequality holds for φ which, in turn, combined with the Itô's rule applied to $e^{-\rho \tau} \varphi(x_\tau, y_\tau)$ gives

$$E \int_0^\tau e^{-\rho s}[-\rho\varphi(X_s) + \frac{1}{2}\sigma^2 y_s^2 \varphi_{yy}(X_s) - \mu y_s \varphi_y(X_s) - r x_s \varphi_x(X_s)$$

$$+ c\varphi_x(X_s) - U(c)] ds \leq 0.$$

Dividing by n, and sending $n \to +\infty$ we get

$$\rho\varphi(X_0) - \frac{1}{2}\sigma^2 y_0^2 \varphi_{yy}(X_0) - \mu y_0 \varphi_y(X_0) - r x_0 \varphi_x(X_0)$$

$$- \max_{c \geq 0}(-c\varphi_x(X_0) + U(c)) \geq 0$$

(for a detailed argument, see Zariphopoulou [**Z3**]). This completes the proof.

We conclude this section by presenting a comparison result for constrained viscosity solutions of (3.2) which appears in Tourin and Zariphopoulou [**TZ1**]. This result will be used in subsequent sections to obtain convergence of the numerical schemes employed for the value function and the optimal policies and also to derive bounds on derivative prices.

THEOREM 3.4 (TZ). *Let u be an upper semi-continuous viscosity subsolution of (3.2) on $\overline{D}$ with sublinear growth and v be a bounded from below uniformly continuous viscosity supersolution of (1.8) in D. Then, $u \leq v$ on $\overline{D}$.*

Sketch of the proof: We first construct a positive strict supersolution of (3.2) in D. To this end, let $w(x,y)$ be the value function defined as in (2.7) with U replaced by some U_1 such that $U_1(c) > U(c)$ for $c > 0$, $U_1(0) = U(0) \geq 0$ and $\alpha = \beta = 1$. This value function is the solution to the classical Merton optimal consumption-portfolio problem in the absence of transaction costs and satisfies $w(x,y) = v(z)$, where $z = x + y$ and v solves

$$\begin{cases} \rho v = -\dfrac{(\mu - r)^2}{2\sigma^2} \dfrac{v'^2}{v''} + rzv' + \max_{c \geq 0}\{-cv' + U_1(c)\} & (z > 0) \\ v > 0, v' > 0 \text{ and } v'' < 0, \quad (z > 0). \end{cases} \quad (3.14)$$

We now let

$$G(x,y) = v(x+ky) + K + C_1 x + C_2 y \qquad ((x,y) \in D)$$

where the constants K, C_1, C_2 and k are positive and C_1, C_2 and k satisfy

$$\alpha < k < \beta, \quad \beta C_1 \geq C_2 \geq \frac{\rho - r}{\rho - \mu} \alpha C_1,$$

and we claim that G is a positive strict supersolution of (3.2).

The choice of k implies $x + ky > 0$ whenever $(x,y) \in \overline{D}$ which combined with (3.14) yields $v > 0$ and $v' > 0$ on D. The choice of the constants C_1 and C_2 also gives that $C_1 x + C_2 y > 0$ and therefore G is positive. It then follows that

$$\begin{cases} \beta G_x(x,y) - G_y(x,y) = (\beta - k)v'(x+ky) + [\beta C_1 - C_2] \\ \\ -\alpha G_x(x,y) + G_y(x,y) = (-1 - \alpha + k)v'(x+ky) + [-\alpha C_1 + C_2]. \end{cases} \qquad (3.15)$$

Also,

$$\rho G(x,y) - \tfrac{1}{2}\sigma^2 y^2 G_{yy}(x,y) - \mu y G_y(x,y) - rx G_x(x,y) - \max_{c \geq 0}\{-c V_x(x,y) + U(c)\}$$

$$= \rho v(z) - \tfrac{1}{2}\sigma^2 (ky)^2 v''(z) - \mu(ky)v'(z) - rxv'(z)$$

$$- \max_{c \geq 0}\{-c(v'(z) + C_1) + U(c)\} + \rho K + \rho C_1 x + \rho C_2 y - \mu C_2 y - r C_1 x.$$

Next, observe that, because $C_1 > 0$,

$$\max_{c \geq 0}\{-c(v'(z) + C_1) + U(c)\} \leq \max_{c \geq 0}\{-cv'(z) + U(c)\}.$$

Moreover, the choice of the constants C_1 and C_2, together with the fact that $\mu > r$, yields

$$(\rho - r)C_1 x + (\rho - \mu)C_2 y \geq 0 \qquad ((x,y) \in \overline{D})$$

as well as,

$$(1 + \beta)C_1 \geq C_2 \geq \alpha C_2.$$

Combining the above inequalities and (3.14) we get,

$$\rho v(z) - \tfrac{1}{2}\sigma^2(ky)^2 v''(z) - \mu(ky)v'(z) - rxv'(z) - \max_{c \geq 0}\{-c(v'(z)+C_1)+U(c)\}$$

$$+ \rho K + (\rho - r)C_1 x + (\rho - \mu)C_2 y \geq$$

$$\geq \rho K + \left\{ -\frac{(\mu - r)^2}{2\sigma^2}\frac{(v'(z))^2}{v''(z)} - \tfrac{1}{2}\sigma^2(ky)^2 v''(z) - (\mu-r)kyv'(z) \right\}$$

$$+ \left\{ \max_{c \geq 0}[-cv'(z) + U_1(c)] - \max_{c \geq 0}[-cv'(z) + U(c)] \right\}$$

$$= \rho K + g_1(z,y) + g_2(z).$$

We now observe that the term g_1 in the above sum is nonnegative, since the maximum value of the quadratic $\mathcal{D}(q) = \tfrac{1}{2}\sigma^2 q^2 v'' + (\mu - r)qv'$ is $-\dfrac{(\mu-r)^2}{2\sigma^2}\dfrac{(v')^2}{v''}$, achieved at the point $q = ky$. Moreover

$$g_2(z) = g_2(x+ky) = \max_{c \geq 0}\{-cv'(x+ky) + U_1(c)\} - \qquad(3.16)$$

$$\max_{c \geq 0}\{-cv'(x+ky) + U(c)\} > 0,$$

due to the choice of U_1.

Introduce the notation

$$H(X, G, DG, D^2G) = \min\left\{ \rho G - \tfrac{1}{2}\sigma^2 y^2 G_{yy} - \mu y G_y - rxG_x - \right.$$

$$\left. - \max_{c\geq 0}\{-cG_x + U(c)\}, \beta G_x - G_y, -\alpha G_x + G_y \right\}.$$

Combining (3.15) and (3.16) yields

$$H(X, G, DG, D^2G) \geq \min\{\rho K, \beta C_1 - C_2, -\alpha C_1 + C_2\} = \delta > 0 \text{ in } D.$$

To conclude the proof of the theorem we will need the following lemma. Its proof follows along the lines of Theorem VI.5 in Ishii and Lions [**IL**] and therefore it is omitted.

LEMMA 3.5. *Let V be an upper semi-continuous with sublinear growth viscosity subsolution of (3.2) on D and v be bounded from below, uniformly continuous viscosity supersolution of $H(X, u, Du, D^2u) - h(X)$, where $h \geq \delta > 0$ in D, for some constant δ. Then $V \leq v$ on D.*

We now conclude the proof of the theorem. We define the function $w^\theta = \theta v + (1-\theta)G$ where $0 < \theta < 1$ and we observe that w^θ is a viscosity supersolution of $H - h = 0$ with $h(X) \equiv \delta$. (See also Davis, Panas and Zariphopoulou

[**DPZ**] for a similar argument). Applying the above Lemma to V and w^θ we get $V \leq w^\theta$ on D; sending θ to 1 concludes the proof.

Section 4: The case of CRRA utilities.

A special class of utility functoons are the so called Constant Relative Risk Aversion utilities. These functions $U : \mathcal{R}^+ \to \mathcal{R}$ have the form

$$\begin{cases} U(c) = \frac{1}{\gamma}c^\gamma & \text{for } \gamma < 1, \gamma \neq 0 \\ U(c) = \log c & \text{for } \gamma = 0, \end{cases} \quad (4.1)$$

where the variable c typically plays the role of the consumption stream or the state wealth. The main characteristic of these utilities is that their *Relative Risk Aversion coefficient*, defined as $-\dfrac{cU''(c)}{U'(c)}$, is constant across consumption (or wealth) levels.

The CRRA utilities have been widely used in stochastic models of portfolio management and asset pricing. Not only, a fact supported by empirical evidence, these utilities capture effectively the investors' preferences and their attitudes towards risk, they also facilitate considerably the analysis of the various economic valuation models. Indeed, in the absence of transaction costs and when the asset prices are modelled as geometric Brownian motions, explicit (or closed form) solutions can be readily derived for optimal portfolio management policies and consumption plans as well as for equilibrium prices. (See, among others, Merton [**M1**], [**M2**], Karatzas et al [**KLLS**], Cox and Huang [**CH**], Vila and Zariphopoulou [**VZ**]). This derivation mainly comes from the fact that the value function turns out to be homothetic of the same degree as the utility function. The homotheticity properties are in turn used in producing explicit solutions for the value function together with its first and second order derivatives which enter in the (feedback) formulae of the optimal policies.

In models with proportional transaction costs, the homotheticity properties are primarily used to reduce the dimensionality of the relevant optimization problem. This is the central feature in the benchmark work of Davis and Norman who reduced the dimensionality of (3.2) via the transformation

$$V(x,y) = y^\gamma F(\frac{x}{y}). \quad (4.2)$$

The function F solves the one-dimensional Variational Inequality

$$\min\left\{\tilde{\rho}F - \frac{1}{2}\sigma^2 z^2 F'' - \tilde{\mu}zF' - \frac{1-\gamma}{\gamma}(F')^{\frac{\gamma}{\gamma-1}},\right.$$

$$\left.(\beta\gamma + z)F' - \gamma F, \ -(\alpha\gamma + z)F' + \gamma F\right\} = 0 \quad (4.3)$$

for $z = \dfrac{x}{y}$ and $\tilde{\rho} = \rho - \mu\gamma + \frac{1}{2}\sigma^2\gamma(1-\gamma)$ and $\tilde{\mu} = \rho - r - \sigma^2(1-\gamma)$; the non-linear term $\dfrac{1-\gamma}{\gamma}(F')^{\frac{\gamma}{\gamma-1}}$ comes from the reduced form of $\max_{c \geq 0}\left\{-cV_x + \dfrac{c^\gamma}{\gamma}\right\}$ using that $V_x(x,y) = y^{\gamma-1}F'\left(\dfrac{x}{y}\right)$.

Davis and Norman analyzed the above equation and under certain assumptions on the market coefficients, they constructed a solution ψ satisfying, for some positive constants A and B, and points z_1 and z_2

$$\begin{cases} \psi(z) = A(\alpha\gamma + z)^\gamma & z \leq z_1 \\ \tilde{\rho}\psi = \dfrac{1}{2}\sigma^2 z^2 \psi'' + \tilde{\mu}z\psi' + \dfrac{1-\gamma}{\gamma}(\psi')^{\frac{\gamma}{\gamma-1}} & z_1 < z < z_2 \\ \psi(z) = B(\beta\gamma + z)^\gamma & z \geq z_2. \end{cases} \quad (4.4)$$

The function ψ was constructed as the solution of a two point boundary problem of second order with endpoints z_1 and z_2. These endpoints were specified by the so-called "principle of smooth fit" which is used to produce a smooth solution of (4.3).

The set of equations (4.4) indicates that when the ratio of account holdings $\dfrac{x}{y}$ is between the threshold levels z_1 and z_2, then it is optimal not to rebalance the portfolio but only to consume. In other words, the individual must refrain from trading in the region $\mathcal{NT} = \{(x,y) \in D : z_1 \leq \dfrac{y}{x} \leq z_2\}$.

If the holdings ratio, say $\dfrac{y_0}{x_0}$, is below z_1 then it is optimal to instantaneously rebalance the portfolio components by moving from the original point to the point $(\overline{y}, \overline{x})$ with $\overline{y} = z_1 \overline{x}$ with $\overline{x} = \dfrac{x_0 + \beta y_0}{1 + \beta z_1}$. This corresponds to a transaction of *buying shares of stock* and this is the optimal policy that one should apply to all points $(x,y) \in \overline{D}$ with $\dfrac{y}{x} < z_1$. Similarly, if the holdings ratio $\dfrac{y_0}{x_0}$ is above z_2, then it is optimal to instantaneously rebalance the portfolio components by moving to the point $\tilde{y} = z_2 \tilde{x}$ with $\tilde{x} = \dfrac{x_0 + \alpha y_0}{1 + \alpha z_2}$. This corresponds to a transaction of *selling stock shares* and this is the optimal policy for all point $(x,y) \in \overline{D}$ such that $\dfrac{y}{x} > z_2$.

The above analysis shows that the state space $\overline{D} = \{(x,y) : x + \begin{pmatrix} \alpha \\ \beta \end{pmatrix} y \geq 0\}$ depletes into three regions: the so-called *sell* ($\mathcal{S}$) and *buy* ($\mathcal{B}$) regions (sales and purchases of stock shares occur instantaneously) and the *no trading* ($\mathcal{NT}$) region (no trading takes place but only consumption from the bond account holdings). The $\mathcal{NT}$ region lies in between the $\mathcal{B}$ and the $\mathcal{S}$ region and the common boundaries are straight lines emanating from the origin; the latter properties are dictated by the homotheticity of the value function (see Figure 1). Davis and Norman showed that the existence of a smooth solution of (4.4) provides a sufficient condition for the optimality of a policy, say (c_t^*, L_t^*, M_t^*) such that the associated state process (x_t^*, y_t^*) is a *reflecting diffusion* in the $\mathcal{NT}$ region and L_t^* and M_t^* are given from the relevant *local times* at the lower and upper boundaries, respectively.

As it was mentioned in the Introduction, the work of Davis and Norman is a landmark in the area of transaction costs. A number of key ideas and insights were gained from their work which influenced a number of papers in the area. In particular, Shreve and Soner [**SS**] studied the same model and extended the DN results in several directions. Below, we present the main parts of the analysis of Shreve and Soner [**SS**] together with some relevant results of Davis and Norman. We choose to proceed this way mainly because Shreve and Soner used viscosity methods and therefore, we are able to continue our exposition, in a unified manner, following the previous chapter.

First, using convex analysis arguments, Shreve and Soner [**SS**] proved the following result.

THEOREM 4.1 (SS). *For $\gamma < 1, \gamma \neq 0$, there exist constants $A > 0, B > 0$ such that*
$$\begin{cases} V(x,y) = \frac{1}{\gamma} A^{\gamma-1}(x+\alpha y)^\gamma & \text{for } (x,y) \in \mathcal{S} \\ V(x,y) = \frac{1}{\gamma} B^{\gamma-1}(x+\beta y)^\gamma & \text{for } (x,y) \in \mathcal{B}. \end{cases}$$

For $\gamma = 0$, there exist constants A, B such that
$$\begin{cases} V(x,y) = \frac{1}{\rho}\log(x+\alpha y) + A & \text{for } (x,y) \in \mathcal{S} \\ V(x,y) = \frac{1}{\rho}\log(x+\beta Y) + B & \text{for } (x,y) \in \mathcal{B}. \end{cases}$$

To explore the regularity of the value function in the $(\mathcal{NT})$ region, Shreve and Soner employed, as in [**DN**], its homotheticity properties. They used a different scaling transformation, namely

$$V(x,y) = \begin{cases} (x+y)^\gamma u\left(\frac{y}{x+y}\right) & \text{for } \gamma < 1, \gamma \neq 0 \\ \frac{1}{\rho}\log(x+y) + u\left(\frac{y}{x+y}\right) & \text{for } \gamma = 0. \end{cases} \quad (4.5)$$

They subsequently studied the regularity properties of the above function $u(z)$ where the variable z is given by $z = \frac{y}{x+y}$. Using that (x,y) have the property $x + \binom{\alpha}{\beta} y \geq 0$, (see $(2.5)'$), one gets that $z \in J = \left[-\frac{1}{\beta-1}, \frac{1}{1-\alpha}\right]$.

Below we adopt the notation of Shreve and Soner [**SS**] and we state their main results. To this end, we introduce the quantities,

$$d_1(z) = r + (\mu - r)z - \frac{1}{2}\sigma^2(1-\gamma)z^2$$
$$d_2(z) = (\mu - r)z(1-z) - \sigma^2(1-\gamma)z^2(1-z)$$
$$d_3(z) = \frac{1}{2}\sigma^2 z^2(1-z)^2$$
$$d_4(z) = \frac{1}{1-\alpha}(1-(1-\alpha)z)$$
$$d_5(z) = \frac{\beta}{\beta-1}\left(1 - \frac{\beta-1}{\beta}(1-z)\right).$$

Direct computations in (4.5) show that the value function V is a smooth solution of the HJB equation (3.2) if and only if u is a classical solution of the second-order ordinary differential equation

$$\min \left\{ \rho u - d_1(z)\gamma u - d_2(z)u' - d_3(z)u'' - \tilde{U}_\gamma(-zu' + \gamma u), \right.$$

$$\left. \gamma u + d_1(z)u', \gamma u - d_5(z)u' \right\} = 0 \quad \text{for} \quad \gamma \neq 0, \gamma < 1, \tag{4.6}$$

or

$$\min \left\{ \rho u - \frac{1}{\rho}d_1(z) - d_2(z)u' - d_3(z)u'' - \tilde{U}_0(-zu' + \frac{1}{\rho}), \right.$$

$$\left. \frac{1}{\rho} + d_1(z)u', \frac{1}{\rho} - d_5(z)u' \right\} = 0 \quad \text{for} \quad \gamma = 0, \tag{4.7}$$

where

$$\tilde{U}_\gamma(\tilde{c}) = \sup_{c>0} \{-c\tilde{c} + U(c)\} = \begin{cases} \frac{1-\gamma}{\gamma} \tilde{c}^{\frac{\gamma}{\gamma-1}} & \text{for } \gamma < 1, \gamma \neq 0 \\ -1 - \log \tilde{c} & \text{for } \gamma = 0, \end{cases}$$

with U as in (4.1).

Using arguments from the theory of viscosity solutions, the following result was established.

THEOREM 4.2 (SS). *The function u is C^1 on $J \setminus \{0\}$. If u is not also C^1 at $\{0\}$, then for every $x > 0$*

$$V(x,0) = \begin{cases} \dfrac{1}{\gamma} M^{\gamma-1} x^\gamma & \text{for } \gamma \neq 0 \\ \dfrac{1}{\rho} \log x + \dfrac{1}{\rho} \log \rho + \dfrac{r-\rho}{\rho^2} & \text{for } \gamma = 0, \end{cases}$$

where $M = \dfrac{\rho - r\gamma}{1 - \gamma} > 0$. Furthermore, even if u is not C^1 at $\{0\}$, its one-sided derivatives exist and are limits of its derivatives from the appropriate sides at 0.

Subsequently, Shreve and Soner [**SS**] argued that $\mathcal{NT} \neq \phi$ and therefore there exist two numbers, say θ_1 and θ_2, such that

$$\mathcal{NT} = \left\{ (x,y) \in \overline{D} : \theta_1 < \frac{y}{x+y} < \theta_2 \right\} \tag{4.8}$$

Using elements from viscosity theory, the following regularity result was established.

THEOREM 4.3 (SS). *The function u is C^2 on $(\theta_1, \theta_2)\setminus\{0,1\}$ and, on this set satisfies, in the classical sense, the equation*

$$\begin{cases} \rho u(z) - d_1(z)\gamma u(z) - d_2(z)u'(z) - d_3(z)u''(z) - \\ \quad -\tilde{U}_\gamma(-zu'(z) + \gamma u(z)) = 0 & \text{for } \gamma \neq 0, \gamma < 1 \\ \rho u(z) - \dfrac{1}{\rho}d_1(z) - d_2(z)u'(z) - d_3(z)u''(z) \\ \quad -\tilde{U}_0\left(-zu'(z) + \dfrac{1}{\rho}\right) = 0 & \text{for } \gamma = 0. \end{cases} \quad (4.9)$$

Therefore, V is C^2 in the set $\mathcal{NT}\setminus\{(x,y): x=0 \text{ or } y=0\}$ and satisfies, in the classical sense, the equation

$$\rho V = \frac{1}{2}\sigma^2 y^2 V_{yy} + \mu y V_y + rx V_x + \max_{c>0}\{-cV_x + U(c)\}$$

with U as in (4.1). Moreover, the regions $\mathcal{S} \neq \phi$ and $\mathcal{B}$ contains the cone $G = \{(x,y) \in \overline{D}; y < 0\}$.

The following theorem provides a *verification result* for the optimal policies.

THEOREM 4.4 (SS). *The quantities θ_1 and θ_2 satisfy*

$$0 \leq \theta_1 < \theta_2 < \frac{1}{1-\alpha}. \quad (4.10)$$

Furthermore, if $(x,y) \in \overline{D}$, then there is a triple $(c, L, M) \in \mathcal{A}$ such that with the processes x_t and y_t, as defined in (2.4) and (2.3), the following conditions hold almost surely:

i) If $(x,y) \notin \mathcal{NT}$, then $(x_0, y_0) \in \partial \mathcal{NT}$ \hfill (4.11)

ii) the processes $(x_t, y_t) \in \overline{\mathcal{NT}}$, $\forall t \geq 0$ \hfill (4.12)

iii) $L_t^* = \int_0^t \mathbf{1}_{\{\frac{y_s}{x_s+y_s} = \theta_1\}} dL_s$, $\forall t \geq 0$ \hfill (4.13)

iv) $M_t^* = \int_0^t \mathbf{1}_{\{\frac{y_s}{x_s+y_s} = \theta_2\}} dM_s$, $\forall t \geq 0$ \hfill (4.14)

v) $c_t^* = [V_x(x_s, y_s)]^{\frac{1}{\gamma-1}}$, $\forall t \geq 0$. \hfill (4.15)

The triple is optimal, i.e.

$$V(x,y) = E\int_0^{+\infty} e^{-\rho t} U(c_t^*) dt.$$

Next, we consider the two boundaries of the $\mathcal{NT}$ wedge region

$$\partial_1 \mathcal{NT} = \{(x,y) \in D : y \geq 0, -\theta_1 x - (\theta_1 - 1)y = 0\}$$

and

$$\partial_2 \mathcal{NT} = \{(x,y) \in D : y > 0, \theta_2 x + (\theta_2 - 1)y = 0\},$$

we define the reflection direction index

$$\tilde{\gamma}(x,y) = \begin{cases} (-\beta, 1) & \text{if } (x,y) \in \partial_1 \mathcal{NT} \\ \\ (\alpha, -1) & \text{if } (x,y) \in \partial_2 \mathcal{NT} \end{cases}$$

and we let $\widetilde{\gamma}(x,y) = (\widetilde{\gamma}_1(x,y), \widetilde{\gamma}_2(x,y))$.

The above theorem states that for any pair of portfolio positions $(x,y) \in \overline{\mathcal{NT}}$, there is a solution to the *Skorohod problem*:

Skorohod problem: Find continuous processes x_t, y_t, k_t such that $x_0 = x$, $y_0 = y$, $k_0 = 0$, k is nondecreasing and the following assertions hold

i) $(x_t, y_t) \in \overline{\mathcal{NT}} \quad \forall t \geq 0$ (4.16)

ii) $dx_t = [rx_t - (V_x(x_t, y_t))^{\frac{1}{\gamma-1}}]dt + \widetilde{\gamma}_1(x_t, y_t)dk_t$ (4.17)

iii) $dy_t = \mu y_t dt + \sigma y_t dW_t + \widetilde{\gamma}_2(x_t, y_t)dk_t$ (4.18)

iv) $k_t = \int_0^t \mathbf{1}_{\{(x_t, y_t) \in \partial \mathcal{NT}\}} dk_t$. (4.19)

The above conditions, (4.16)-(4.19), correspond to (4.11)–(4.15) with the identification

$$\begin{cases} L_t = \int_0^t \mathbf{1}_{\{(x_t, y_t) \in \partial_1 \mathcal{NT}\}} dk_t \\ \\ M_t = \int_0^t \mathbf{1}_{\{(x_t, y_t) \in \partial_2 \mathcal{NT}\}} dk_t, \end{cases}$$

where

$$\partial_i \mathcal{NT} = \{(x,y) \in \overline{\mathcal{NT}} : \frac{y}{x+y} = \theta_i\}, \quad i = 1, 2. \quad (4.20)$$

Shreve and Soner [**SS**] used control theory arguments to establish additional regularity results for the value function across the interfaces $\partial_i \mathcal{NT}$ defined in (4.20) above. Finally, they produce various results for the *location of the optimal exercise boundaries*; these results are stated below in terms of the slopes θ_1 and θ_2.

THEOREM 4.5 (SS). *The partial derivative V_{yy} is continuous across $\partial_2 \mathcal{NT}$, and if $\theta_2 \neq 1$, then V is C^2 across $\partial_2 \mathcal{NT}$. If $\theta_1 \neq 0$, then V_{yy} is continuous across $\partial_1 \mathcal{NT}$, and if $\theta_1 \neq 0$ and $\theta_1 \neq 1$, then V is C^2 across $\partial_1 \mathcal{NT}$.*

PROPOSITION 4.1 (SS). *i) The value function V is C^2 in $\mathcal{S} \setminus \{(x,y) : x = 0 \text{ or } y = 0\}$.*
ii) The functions V, V_x and V_y are continuous in $D \setminus \{(x, 0) : x > 0\}$.

The next Propositions provide information about the location of the exercise boundaries and closed-form solutions for the value function.

PROPOSITION 4.2 (SS). *If $\gamma < 1$, $\gamma \neq 0$ then there is a positive constant A with $\frac{A}{\gamma} < \frac{(\rho - r\gamma)}{\gamma(1-\gamma)}$ such that, for $(x,y) \in \mathcal{S}$,*

$$V(x,y) = \frac{1}{\gamma} A^{\gamma-1}(x + \alpha y)^\gamma.$$

If $\gamma = 0$, then there is a constant $\widehat{A}$ with $\widehat{A} > (\log \rho)/\rho + (r - \rho)/\rho^2$ such that, for $(x,y) \in \mathcal{S}$,

$$V(x,y) = \frac{1}{\rho} \log(x + \alpha y) + \widehat{A}.$$

PROPOSITION 4.3 (SS). *For all $\gamma < 1$, the slope θ_2 satisfies*

$$\theta_2 < \frac{2(\mu - r)}{\alpha \sigma^2 (1-\gamma) + 2(1-\alpha)(\mu - r)}.$$

Moreover, if $\sigma^2(1-\gamma) \neq \mu - r$ and the quantity $M(\gamma) = \dfrac{\rho - r\gamma}{1-\gamma} - \dfrac{\gamma(\mu-r)^2}{2\sigma^2(1-\gamma)^2} > 0$, then

$$\theta_2 > \frac{\mu - r}{\alpha\sigma^2(1-\gamma) + (1-\alpha)(\mu - r)}.$$

If $\sigma^2(1-\gamma) = \mu - r$ and $M(\gamma) > 0$, then $\theta_2 = 1$. Finally if $M(\gamma) > 0$ and $\sigma^2(1-\gamma) > \dfrac{\beta - 1}{\beta}(\mu - r)$ then the slope of the low exercise boundary satisfies

$$\theta_1 < \frac{\mu - r}{\beta\sigma^2(1-\gamma) - (\beta - 1)(\mu - r)}.$$

THEOREM 4.6 (SS). *The slope $\theta_1 > 0$, i.e. the positive x-axis belongs to the $\mathcal{B}$ region.*

Besides the above results, Shreve and Soner provided conditions for the value function to be well defined; these conditions are considerably more general than the ones of Davis and Norman.

Section 5: Numerical Schemes.

Due to the wide applicability of the models with transaction costs, it is highly desirable to obtain information about the value function and, in particular, the optimal exercise boundaries. As it is apparent from the previous sections, in the case of general utilities, minimal information is available about the solutions, besides some general characterization arguments. In the case of CRRA utilities, even though considerably more information is available, still it is not known what the exact slopes of the transaction rays are as well as how the transaction interphases change in terms of the various market parameters.

Davis and Norman [**DN**] developed a numerical algorithm for the case of CRRA utilities. They analyzed the one-dimensional reduced problem as a two-point boundary value one with the endpoints corresponding to the desired boundaries of the $\mathcal{NT}$ region. They considered a system of equations related to the second-order differential part and they searched for its solutions via backwards numerical integration (in order to gain on the stability of the approximation). Then, they determined the interphase points (free boundaries) by equating the solutions to specific values corresponding to the smooth-pasting conditions across the interphase. Davis and Norman (1990) validated their scheme for a range of market parameters and studied in terms of the latter the behavior of the transaction regions.

Other numerical schemes of the same problem, but with exponential utilities were developed by Davis, Panas and Zariphopoulou [**DPZ**] and by Davis and Panas [**DP**] in the context of derivative pricing with transaction costs. Davis, Panas and Zariphopoulou [**DPZ**] used a two state Markov-chain approximation of the stock price to discretize the problem and they produced numerical results for the value function which in turn determined bounds for the prices of European calls. Davis and Panas [**DP**], extending the work of [**DPZ**], studied numerically the problem of specifying the price of the writer of the derivative for general utilities. They developed a suitable discretization scheme, using stochastic difference equations and established the weak convergence of the discrete-time model to its continuous-time counterpart.

Besides the numerical work of Davis and Norman, Tourin and Zariphopoulou ([**TZ1**], [**TZ2**]) used a different approach to develop numerical schemes for models with general utilities. These schemes compute effectively the unique viscosity solution of the HJB equation (3.2) and they have the desirable properties of *monotonicity*, *stability* and *consistency*. Barles and Souganidis [**BSou**] established that such schemes converge to the correct solution which coincides with the value function.

Following our general plan to outline the use and contribution of viscosity solutions, we state these fundamental properties and the basic convergence result below (see Theorem 5.1). We also mention that convergence of such schemes was originally proved in some situations by Crandall and Lions [**CL1**] and Souganidis [**Sou**]. More recently, it was proved for parabolic equations, arising in problems of option pricing, by Barles, Daher and Romano in [**BDR**] and by Davis, Panas and Zariphopoulou in [**DPZ**].

We continue with the definition of the three key properties of the numerical schemes presented herein. We use a generic notation for the equation (3.2) in order to simplify the presentation.

To this end, we consider a nonlinear equation $F(w, u(w), Du(w), D^2u(w)) = 0$ for $w \in \overline{D}$, where Du and D^2u denote respectively the gradient and the second order derivative matrix of the solution u; F is continuous in all its arguments and the equation is degenerate elliptic meaning that $F(w, p, q, A + B) \leq F(w, p, q, A)$ if $B \geq 0$.

DEFINITION 5.1. *We consider a sequence of approximations*
$S : \mathcal{R}^+ \times \overline{D} \times \mathcal{R} \times \mathcal{B}_{\text{loc}}(\overline{D}) \to \mathcal{R}$ *where* $S = S(\theta, w, u^\theta(w), u^\theta)$.

We say that S is:

i) *monotone* if
$$S(\theta, w, t, u) \leq S(\theta, w, t, v) \quad \text{for } u \geq v,$$

ii) *consistent* if
$$\limsup_{(\theta, y, \xi) \to (0, w, 0)} \frac{S(\theta, w, \phi(w) + \xi, \phi + \xi)}{\theta} =$$

$$\liminf_{(\theta, y, \xi) \to (0, w, 0)} \frac{S(\theta, w, \phi(w) + \xi, \phi + \xi)}{\theta} = F(w, \phi(w), D\phi(w), D^2\phi(w)),$$

and

iii) *stable* if

$\forall \theta > 0$, there exists a solution $u^\theta \in \mathcal{B}_{\text{loc}}(\overline{D})$ of $S(\theta, w, u^\theta(w), u^\theta) = 0$ and its (local) bound is independent of θ.

The motivation to use such schemes for our model comes from the fact that these schemes exhibit excellent convergence properties to the (viscosity) solution of fully nonlinear degenerate elliptic partial differential equations, like the HJB equation at hand, as long as the latter has a unique solution. This result was established by Barles and Souganidis [**BSou**] and it is stated below for completeness.

THEOREM 5.1 (BS). *Assume that the equation $F(w, u, Du, D^2u) = 0$ admits the strong uniquess property, i.e. if u (resp. v) is a viscosity subsolution (resp. supersolution) of $F = 0$, then $u \leq v$. If the approximation sequence $\{S^\theta\}$ satisfies the monotonicity, consistency and stability properties then the solution u^θ of $S(\theta, w, u^\theta(w), u^\theta) = 0$ converges locally uniformly to the unique viscosity solution of $F(w, u, Du, D^2u) = 0$.*

In the scheme constructed by Tourin and Zariphopoulou [**TZ1**], the first-order operators are approximated by a monotone finite difference scheme. As far as the second-order operator is concerned, the first-order part is approximated by a monotone explicit scheme based on the Dynamic Programming Principle whereas the second-order term is approximated by an implicit Cranck-Nickolson scheme. Thus splitting into two half iterations allows one to choose a time step of the same order as the mesh size. This method is known as the *time splitting* method or method of *fractional steps*.

To facilitate the exposition, we write the HJB equation (3.2) in the concise form

$$\min\left\{L_0(x, y, u, u_x, u_y, u_{yy}), L_1(u_x, u_y), L_2(u_x, u_y)\right\} = 0 \tag{5.1}$$

where

$$L_0(x, y, u, u_x, u_y, u_{yy}) = \rho u - \frac{1}{2}\sigma^2 y^2 u_{yy} - \mu y u_y - rx u_x - \max_{c \geq 0}\{-cu_x + U(c)\}$$

and

$$L_1(u_x, u_y) = \beta u_x - u_y, \quad L_2(u_x, u_y) = -\alpha u_x + u_y.$$

Tourin and Zariphopoulou [**TZ1**] studied the problem under the state constraints $x_t \geq 0$ and $y_t \geq 0$ a.s. $\forall t \geq 0$ instead of $x + \binom{\alpha}{\beta} y \geq 0$. Therefore the relevant domain is $\widetilde{D} = \{(x, y) : x \geq 0, y \geq 0\}$ and not $\overline{D}$. They also assumed that the non-transaction region belongs entirely to the interior of $\widetilde{D}$. Note that in this case, the values of the value function in $\widetilde{D}\backslash\mathcal{NT}$ can be approximated as follows. In the *sell region* ($\mathcal{S}$), V is constant along the lines $x + \alpha y = c > 0$ and therefore, $V(x, y) = V(0, y_0)$ for all (x, y) such that $x + \alpha y = \alpha y_0$ and $y \geq y_0$. Similarly, in the *buy region* ($\mathcal{B}$), V is constant along the lines $x + \beta y = c > 0$ and therefore $V(x, y) = V(x_0, 0)$ for all (x, y) such that $x + \beta y = x_0$ and $x \geq x_0$.

Next, we consider the rectangular domain $\mathcal{D} \subset \mathcal{R}^2$

$$\mathcal{D} = [0, (M-1)\Delta x] \times [0, (L-1)\Delta y],$$

where M and L denote the number of grid points on the x and y axis and $\Delta x, \Delta y > 0$ are the mesh sizes. The value of the numerical approximation at the point $((i-1)\Delta x, (j-1)\Delta y)$, for $i = 1, \ldots, M-1$ and $j = 1, \ldots, L-1$, will be denoted by V_{ij}.

We then define the first order differences

$$D_x^+ V_{ij} = \frac{V_{i+1,j} - V_{ij}}{\Delta x}, \quad D_y^+ V_{ij} = \frac{V_{i,j+1} - V_{ij}}{\Delta y},$$

and

$$D_x^- V_{ij} = \frac{V_{ij} - V_{i-1,j}}{\Delta x}, \quad D_y^- V_{ij} = \frac{V_{ij} - V_{i,j-1}}{\Delta y}.$$

Inside the domain, the first-order operators L_1 and L_2 are approximated in a monotone way using the appropriate backward and forward finite differences

$$g_1(D_x^- V_{ij}, D_y^+ V_{ij}) = \beta D_x^- V_{ij} - D_y^+ V_{ij} \tag{5.2}$$

$$g_2(D_x^+ V_{ij}, D_y^- V_{ij}) = -\alpha D_x^+ V_{ij} - D_y^- V_{ij}. \tag{5.3}$$

Next, we consider the first-order operator L_0' obtained by eliminating the second-order term from L_0, i.e.

$$L_0'(x, y, V, V_x, V_y) = \rho V - \mu y V_x - r x V_x - \max_{c \geq 0}\{-c u_x + U(c)\}.$$

The solution of the equation $L_0'(x, y, \overline{V}, \overline{V}_x, \overline{V}_y) = 0$ can be characterized (see, for example Lions [**Li**]) as the value function of the deterministic control problem

$$\overline{V}(x, y) = \max_{c \geq 0}\left\{\int_0^\infty e^{-\rho t} U(c_t) dt\right\} \tag{5.4}$$

where the state trajectories $\overline{x}_t$ and $\overline{y}_t$ solve

$$\begin{cases} d\overline{x}_t = (r x_t - c_t) dt - \beta dL_t + \alpha dM_t \\ \\ d\overline{y}_t = \mu y_t dt + dL_t - dM_t \\ \\ \overline{x}_0 = x, \ \overline{y}_0 = y. \end{cases}$$

The next step is to construct a monotone scheme to approximate the value function $\overline{V}$. Such deterministic control problems have been examined by a number of authors, see for example Alziary de Roquefort [**Al**], Capuzzo-Dolcetta [**C-D**], Capuzzo-Dolcetta and Falcone [**C-DF**], Falcone [**F1**], [**F2**], Tourin [**Tou**], and Rouy and Tourin [**RT**]. To this end, we apply the Dynamic Programming Principle to (5.4) to get

$$\overline{V}(x, y) = \max_{c \geq 0}\left\{\int_0^T e^{-\rho t} U(c_t) dt + e^{-\rho T} \overline{V}(\overline{x}_T, \overline{y}_T)\right\}.$$

We choose $T = \Delta \tau$ arbitrarily small and assume that the control remains constant in the time interval $[0, T]$. The above equality then yields

$$\sup_{c \geq 0}\left\{U(c) + \frac{\overline{V}(x + \Delta\tau(rx - c), y + \Delta\tau \mu y) - \overline{V}(x, y)}{\Delta\tau} e^{-\rho\Delta\tau}\right.$$
$$\left. + \overline{V}(x, y) \frac{e^{-\rho\Delta\tau} - 1}{\Delta\tau}\right\} = 0.$$

In order to approximate the operator L_0', one has to find an explicit formulation for the following optimum:

$$\max\{\sup_{0 \leq c \leq r(i-1)\Delta x}(U(c) - \rho V_{ij} + D_x^+ V_{ij}(r(i-1)\Delta x - c) + D_y^+ V_{ij} \mu(j-1)\Delta y),$$

$$\sup_{c \geq r(i-1)\Delta x}(U(c) - \rho V_{ij} + D_x^- V_{ij}(r(i-1)\Delta x - c) + D_y^+ V_{ij} \mu(j-1)\Delta y)\}.$$

Finally, inside the rectangular domain, a numerical approximation V of the solution $\overline{V}$ of the equation $L'_0(x,y,\overline{V},\overline{V}_x,\overline{V}_y) = 0$ will satisfy

$$g(D_x^- V_{ij}, D_x^+ V_{ij}, D_y^+ V_{ij}) = 0$$

for all $1 < i < M$ and $1 < j < L$; the function g is described below.

Below and only to simplify the presentation, we restrict ourselves to the case of the CRRA utility functions. We note, however, that all our arguments can be easily extended to general utilities.

When U is a CRRA utility function, given by $U(c) = \frac{1}{\gamma}c^\gamma$ with $\gamma \in (0,1)$, g takes the following form:

i) if $(D_x^+ V_{ij})^{\frac{1}{\gamma-1}} < r(i-1)\Delta x$ and $(D_x^- V_{ij})^{\frac{1}{\gamma-1}} < r(i-1)\Delta x$ then

$$g(D_x^- V_{ij}, D_x^+ V_{ij}, D_y^+ V_{ij}) = -\rho V_{ij} +$$
$$\frac{1-\gamma}{\gamma}(D_x^+ V_{ij})^{\frac{\gamma}{\gamma-1}} + r(i-1)\Delta x D_x^+ V_{ij} + \mu(j-1)\Delta y D_y^+ V_{ij},$$

ii) if $(D_x^+ V_{ij})^{\frac{1}{\gamma-1}} < r(i-1)\Delta x$ and $(D_x^- V_{ij})^{\frac{1}{\gamma-1}} > r(i-1)\Delta x$ then

$$g(D_x^- V_{ij}, D_x^+ V_{ij}, D_y^+ V_{ij}) = -\rho V_{ij} +$$
$$\frac{1-\gamma}{\gamma}(D_x^- V_{ij})^{\frac{\gamma}{\gamma-1}} + r(i-1)\Delta x D_x^- V_{ij} + \mu(j-1)\Delta y D_y^+ V_{ij},$$

iii) if $(D_x^+ V_{ij})^{\frac{1}{\gamma-1}} > r(i-1)\Delta x$ and $(D_x^- V_{ij})^{\frac{1}{\gamma-1}} > r(i-1)\Delta x$ then

$$g(D_x^- V_{ij}, D_x^+ V_{ij}, D_y^+ V_{ij}) = -\rho V_{ij} +$$
$$\frac{1-\gamma}{\gamma}(D_x^+ V_{ij})^{\frac{\gamma}{\gamma-1}} + r(i-1)\Delta x D_x^+ V_{ij} + \mu(j-1)\Delta y D_y^+ V_{ij},$$

iv) if $(D_x^+ V_{ij})^{\frac{1}{\gamma-1}} > r(i-1)\Delta x$ and $(D_x^- V_{ij})^{\frac{1}{\gamma-1}} < r(i-1)\Delta x$ then

$$g(D_x^- V_{ij}, D_x^+ V_{ij}, D_y^+ V_{ij}) = -\rho V_{ij} +$$
$$\frac{1-\gamma}{\gamma}(r(i-1)\Delta x)^{\frac{\gamma}{\gamma-1}} + \mu(j-1)\Delta y D_y^+ V_{ij}.$$

In addition to the above approximations one has to construct an approximation for the points located on the boundary of the discretized domain $\mathcal{D}$. We first consider the x and the y-axis which, by assumption, belong respectively to the *sell* and the *buy* region; therefore, the value function solves $L_1(\overline{V}_x,\overline{V}_y) = 0$, on the x-axis and $L_2(\overline{V}_x,\overline{V}_y) = 0$, on the y-axis.

At the points located on the x-axis, V_{i1} satisfies

$$g_1(D_x^- V_{i1}, D_y^+ V_{i1}) = 0 \quad \text{for} \quad 1 < i \leq M,$$

where g_1 is given by (5.2). At the points located on the y-axis, the function V_{1j} satisfies

$$g_2(D_x^+ V_{1j}, D_y^- V_{1j}) = 0 \quad \text{for} \quad 1 < j \leq L,$$

where g_2 is given by (5.3).

One may notice that this method could not be applied to the real boundaries $x + \alpha y = 0$ $(y \geq 0)$ and $x + \beta y = 0$ $(y \leq 0)$. Indeed, the monotone approximation of

L_2 requires the backward finite difference along the y-axis and the approximation of L_1 requires the backward finite difference along the x-axis and these values are not available at the boundaries of $\tilde{D}$ due to the presence of the state constraint (1.4).

Next, at the point $i = 1$, $j = 1$, we impose the Dirichlet condition $V_{11} = 0$. Actually this value follows directly from the Variational Inequality itself evaluated at the origin.

We impose Neumann conditions at the points located on $x = (M-1)\Delta x$ and $y = (L-1)\Delta y$. We have to assign specific values to the normal derivatives but the results may vary strongly with the prescribed values, especially the results that describe the location of the free boundaries. In fact, we recall that the value function is unique only in the class of concave functions. Therefore, the following situation may occur: if one imposes over-estimated conditions that allow the approximation to loose its concavity, the scheme may converge to another solution of the Variational Inequality instead of the value function. Moreover, it turns out that even if normal derivatives are set to reasonable values, the location of the free boundaries is still sensitive to the given values. Actually, it appears that the error is essentially concentrated near the boundary. Such a phenomenon has been already noticed by Barles, Daher and Romano [**BDR**] for the heat equation and the Black and Scholes formula, and by Fitzpatrick and Fleming [**FF**] for an optimal investment-consumption model with borrowing constraints. Finally, we impose some reasonable values on the boundary of a sufficiently large domain and compute the corresponding value function and the free boundaries. Then, we only take into account the results obtained inside the domain.

In the second half iteration, we solve the one dimensional heat equation using a Cranck Nickolson scheme. Such a scheme requires boundary conditions which are chosen as follows: on the x-axis, we impose Dirichlet conditions whose values are provided by the formula: $g_1(D_x^- V_{ij}, D_y^- V_{ij}) = 0$. At the points located on $y = (L-1)\Delta y$, we have already imposed Neumann conditions. Thus, the second half-iteration consists of inverting a tridiagonal matrix.

Let us recall that we have to choose the time step in order that the scheme be monotone. At each step, we may add a sufficient condition for the monoticity. Finally, at each step, we choose the greatest value among those which preserve the monotonicity of the scheme. Actually, it yields a time step which is not far from being constant but may evolve a little during the convergence.

Finally, we compute the approximation using the following algorithm:

Algorithm

1st **step:**
- $V_{ij}^0 = (i-1)\Delta x + (j-1)\Delta y,\ 1 \leq i \leq M, 1 \leq j \leq L$
- C given

$(n+1)^{\text{st}}$ **step:**
- V^n is given
- Construction of V_1:

$$V_{1,ij}^{n+1} = V_{ij}^n - (\min(g_1, g_2))\Delta t, \quad 1 < i < M, 1 < j < L.$$

- Construction of V on the boundaries $x = (M-1)\Delta x$ and $y = (L-1)\Delta y$:

$$V_{i1}^{n+1} = V_{i1}^n - g_1 \Delta t, \quad 1 < i \leq M,$$
$$V_{1j}^{n+1} = V_{1j}^n - g_2 \Delta t, \quad 1 < j \leq L,$$
$$V_{11}^{n+1} = 0.$$

- Construction of V_2.

First half-iteration:
$$V_{2,ij}^{n+1/2} = V_{ij}^n + \Delta t g(D_x^- V_{ij}^n, D_x^+ V_{ij}^n, D_y^+ V_{ij}^n), \quad 1 < i < M, \ 1 < j < L.$$

Second half-iteration:
$$\frac{V_{2,ij}^{n+1} - V_{2,ij}^{n+1/2}}{\Delta t} = \frac{1}{2}(\Delta y)^2 (j-1)^2 \left[\frac{1}{2} \left(V_{2,ij+1}^{n+\frac{1}{2}} + V_{2,ij-1}^{n+\frac{1}{2}} - 2V_{2,ij}^{n+\frac{1}{2}} \right) \right.$$

$$\left. + \frac{1}{2} \left(V_{2,ij+1}^{n+1} + V_{2,ij-1}^{n+1} - 2V_{2,ij}^{n+1} \right) \right],$$

given that $V_{2,iL}^{n+1} = V_{2,iL-1}^{n+1} + C$ for $1 < i < M$, $1 < j < L$.

- Construction of V^{n+1} from V_1^{n+1} and V_2^{n+1}:

$$V_{ij}^{n+1} = \max\left(V_{1,ij}^{n+1}, V_{2,ij}^{n+1} \right) \quad 1 < i < M, 1 < j < L,$$

$$V_{iL}^{n+1} = V_{iL-1}^{n+1} + C \quad 1 < i \leq M,$$

$$V_{Mj}^{n+1} = V_{M-1j}^{n+1} + C \quad 1 < j \leq L.$$

- If $\sup_{ij} |V_{ij}^n - V_{ij}^{n+1}| < \epsilon$ then stop, where ϵ is a tolerance bound prescribed by the user.
- After the convergence is established, find the non-transaction region:

$$(\mathcal{NT}) = \left\{ ((i-1)\Delta x, (j-1)\Delta y) \text{ where } \min\{L_0, L_1, L_2\} = L_0 \right\}.$$

The algorithm has been implemented on a HP 735 workstation. In order to obtain satisfactory free boundaries, one has to let the algorithm converge for a few hours, the time depending highly on the choice of the utility function and the initial condition. To improve the efficiency of the algorithm, second-order schemes for Hamilton-Jacobi equations were tried based on ideas developed by Osher and others for problems of Conservation Laws (see Harten, Engquist, Osher and Chakravarthy [**HEOC**]). Moreover, adaptive mesh size techniques might be used to make the algorithm more efficient. Finally, the precision near the origin has been really improved but the approximation of the free boundaries for large values is not yet satisfactory; actually, for some utility functions, the free boundaries almost desegregate. To improve this, one may use ideas based on second-order filtered schemes whose convergence has been recently proved by Lions and Souganidis [**LiSou**].

Numerical experiments: Next, we present numerical experiments corresponding to three different classes of utility functions

i) $U(c) = \frac{1}{\gamma} c^\gamma$ with $\gamma < 1$,

ii) $U(c) = \frac{1}{\gamma_1} c^{\gamma_1} + \frac{1}{\gamma_2} c^{\gamma_2}$ with $0 < \gamma_1, \gamma_2 < 1$,

iii) $U(c) = M - c^{-\alpha}$ with $\alpha > 0$.

Figures 2–4 show the computed non-transaction ($\mathcal{NT}$) regions corresponding to the utility functions $U_1(c) = 2\sqrt{c}, U_2(c) = 3c^{\frac{1}{3}} + \frac{3}{2} c^{\frac{2}{3}}$ and $U_3(c) = 100 - \frac{1}{\sqrt{c}}$. The schemes were validated for the market parameters $\mu = 0.12$, $r = 0.07$, $\sigma = 0.4$ and $\rho = 0.1$ and indices $L = M = 401$. Other numerical schemes have been proposed for the same model by Pichler [**Pi**], and also for its variations, see Sulem [**Su**]. In the latter, Sulem provides numerical approximations for two models: the finite horizon analogue of (2.7) in which utility comes only from terminal wealth without intermediate consumption and also an ergodic analogue of (2.7) in which one maximizes the long-run rate of expected wealth. In these models the utilities are, respectively, of power and of logarithmic type. In the finite horizon case, Sulem assumes that there are two risky assets and provides accurate characterizations of the exercise boundaries and also numerical values for the rates of return of the optimal portfolio positions.

Section 6: Other models of portfolio management with transaction costs.

Departing from the benchmark optimal investment-consumption model of Davis and Norman, other valuation models with transaction costs have been introduced and analyzed with alternative analytical methods. The main incentive to develop such models comes from the absence of closed form expressions for the optimal investment strategies in the DN model, a feature highly desirable for practical applications. In fact, as the outlaid analysis indicates, in order to analyze the transaction costs portfolio problems one needs to solve a free boundary problem. The free boundaries define the no-transaction ($\mathcal{NT}$) region in which trading is prohibited due to the high penalties from the transaction costs. The precise characterization and the accurate computation of these interphases are imperative for the practical importance of the model. In addition, more realistic models incorporate more than one risky securities as these models look at larger portfolios or at "books" of options. In this case, the regions of trading idleness have a rather complex structure. To solve such problems is a formidable task both from the theoretic as well as the numerical point of view.

To overcome these difficulties, alternative models were introduced which, from one hand, can be analyzed more effectively and, from the other hand, produce optimal trading strategies which do not deviate considerably from their theoretical counterpart. The first models in this direction are the models of Morton and Pliska [**MP**] and Pliska and Selby [**PSe**]; Schroder [**Sch**] independently obtained similar results for some special cases. The key features in the approach of Morton, Pliska and Selby are the possibility of investing in more than one stock and the fact that the transaction costs are proportional to a fixed fraction of the (dynamic) portfolio value.

In the models of Morton, Pliska and Selby, the risky securities are modelled as correlated geometric Brownian motions and there is no intermediate consumption drainage. The optimality criterion differs from the DN payoff in that the aim is to maximize the long-run expected growth rate of the total portfolio value, $\liminf_{T \to \infty} E \frac{(\ln V_T)}{T}$. The transaction costs are considered fixed in the sense that, each time funds are shifted between two or more securities (riskless or risky ones), a penalty is imposed equal to the fraction $(1-\epsilon)$ times the current value of the entire portfolio. Aside from the current portfolio value, the penalty is independent of the prices and the positions in the individual securities.

In Morton and Pliska [**MP**] the trading strategy which maximizes the relevant criterion is fully determined by an M-dimensional vector, say $\vec{b}$ and an optimal stopping time τ. The dimension of $\vec{b}$ coincides with the number of risky securities (assuming that their variance-covariance matrix is of full rank) and its components are strictly positive and sum to less than one. The optimal solution $\vec{b}^*$ and the stopping time τ are found by solving a free boundary problem which can be reduced to a linear complimentarity problem. In the case of only one risky security, the free boundary consists of only two points and the optimal solution can be achieved easily. The numerical method becomes much more complex when there are two or more risky securities because, in this case, the optimal exercise boundary consists of infinitely many points. Pliska and Selby [**PSe**] addressed this issue by employing a novel transformation to the original free boundary problem of Merton and Pliska (1994), for the case of two risky securities. This transformation makes the problem considerably easier to solve but still does not address the issue of more than two risky securities, both from the analytic as well as the numerical point of view.

Atkinson and Wilmott [**AW**] studied the multi-dimensional case under the assumption that the *transaction costs are small* — but still of realistic size. They used asymptotic methods and a local analysis in the original Merton problem which is free of transaction costs. This asymptotic approach showed that the continuation region resembles an ellipsoid which actually resembles the region obtained by Morton and Pliska [**MP**]. This property holds in a certain part of the state space, related to the local behavior of the Merton solution but the approximation breaks down in the other parts. This key difficulty was successfully addressed in Atkinson, Pliska and Wilmott [**APW**] who studied the non-constant coefficient version of the Atkinson and Wilmott model. By handling the non-constant coefficient case, Atkinson, Pliska and Wilmott succeeded in by-passing the difficulties in the asymptotic analysis of Atkinson and Wilmott. Asymptotic results for small transaction costs for the DN model in the case of many risky assets was performed by Atkinson and Al–Ali [**AA**].

Optimal investment models in which the stock price structure is similar to the Davis and Norman but with alternative optimization criteria have been analyzed by a number of authors. Portfolio models with *finite trading horizon* and utilities depending on the terminal wealth were studied, analytically and/or numerically, by Fleming et al [**FGVZ**], Akian, Menaldi and Sulem ([**AMS1**], [**AMS2**])Akian et al [**ASSA**], Akian, Sulem and Séquier [**ASS**], Sulem [**Su**] and more recently by Tiu and Zariphopoulou [**TiZ**]. Other models with "long-run" type criteria have been examined first by Taksar, Klass and Assaf [**TKA**] and subsequently by Dumas and Luciano [**DL**], Fleming et al [**FGVZ**], Sulem [**Su**], Akian, Sulem and Taksar [**AST**].

So far, in all the above models and the ones discussed in the previous section, the common avenue of obtaining information about the value function and the optimal investment and consumption plans is via the HJB equation. An alternative and rather powerful approach is the one that uses results from *martingale theory*. The majority of the results obtained through this approach are found in models of derivative pricing with transaction costs and they are discussed in the second chapter. In the context of portfolio optimization, this methodology, together with tools from convex and functional analysis and duality theory, was employed by Cvitanic and Karatzas [**CK**] (we also refer the reader to the monograph of Karatzas [**Kar**]).

Transaction costs have also been incorporated in other kinds of asset pricing models. In many of these models, financial trades are charged by "adjustment" or "shipping" costs which can have more complex structure. The economic considerations are different and the mathematical analysis is overall less rigorous as one moves to more applied areas of finance. Optimal consumption models of durable goods have been examined by Caballero ([**Ca1**], [**Ca2**]), Bertola and Caballero [**BeCa**], Grossman and Laroque [**GLa**], Eberly [**Eb2**] and empirically by Lam ([**La1**], [**La2**]) and Eberly [**Eb1**]. Other capital asset pricing models with transactions costs for divident policies, stock returns, term structure, exchange rates and asset demands are listed in the references.

In summary, transaction costs result in *irreversible losses* which in most cases cannot be valuated with the classical existing theories. There are still may challenging questions in equilibrium asset pricing theory which do not have a satisfactory answer. The difficulties come not only from the lack of a coherent modelling structure but also from the absence of good analytic and numerical techniques needed to attack the related stochastic optimization models.

Chapter B. Transaction costs in Derivative Pricing

Section 7: Overview.

The area of derivative securities has been one of the fastest growing areas of Finance as well as one of the most active areas of research on stochastic analysis, stochastic control and computations. Derivatives are financial instruments whose values depend on the price levels of the so-called primitive securities, like stocks. The fundamental problem of derivative valuation amounts in determining the derivative's fair value and in specifying the hedging policy which eliminates the risk inherent to the contract. Derivative contracts had always existed in financial environments but it was after the seminal work of Fisher Black and Myron Scholes [**BSc**] (in collaboration with Robert Merton) that this area blossomed and started expanding rapidly. The Black and Scholes valuation approach brought to the modern finance the powerful methodologies of martingale theory and stochastic calculus. Today, numerous different kinds of derivative instruments are traded all around the world and various new contracts are being created every day. The valuation of these contracts gives rise to a number of challenging problems in the areas of stochastic analysis, martingale theory, stochastic control and partial differential equations.

Despite the ever growing activity in derivatives' markets, very few questions have been successfully addressed to date when derivatives are produced, traded and hedged in *markets with frictions*. The most important kind of frictions comes from the stochastic nature of the volatility of the primitive stock security. Other market frictions come from trading constraints, incomplete information and finally from transaction costs. This chapter is dedicated to the existing derivative valuation theories in markets with transaction costs. As it will be demonstrated below, the available theories have various flaws and none gives a completely satisfactory answer. Many problems are still open both for the theorists as well as the practitioners.

The fundamental difficulty for pricing derivatives in the presence of transaction costs lies in the fact that the Black and Scholes approach breaks down completely. In fact, in a frictionless market, Black and Scholes [**BSc**] and Merton [**M4**] relied on an ingenious no-arbitrage argument to price an option on a stock when the interest rate is constant and the stock price follows a geometric brownian motion. They presented a self-financing, dynamic trading policy between the bond and stock accounts which replicates the payoff of the option. They then argued that absence of arbitrage dictates that the option price is equal to the cost of setting up the replicating portfolio. The appeal of the argument lies in its reliance on the absence of arbitrage alone and is independent of other aspects of the equilibrium, such as a particular asset pricing model. The precise derivation arguments of Black and Scholes are discussed in the next section.

The Achilles' heel of the argument is that the frictionless market assumption must be taken literally. The dynamic replication policy incurs an *infinite volume* of transactions over any finite trading interval, given the fact that the brownian motion which drives the stock price has infinite variation. In a market with proportional transaction costs, the dynamic replication policy incurs infinite transaction costs over any finite trading interval and cannot be self-financing, no matter how small the finite transaction costs rate is.

Merton ([**M5**], Chapter 14) maintained the goal of a dynamic trading policy as that of replicating the option payoff and modelled the path of the stock price as a two-period binomial process. The initial cost of the replication policy is finite and serves as an upper bound to the write price of a call which is arbitrage-free. Shen [**Sh**] and Boyle and Vorst [**BoV**] extended Merton's model to a multiperiod binomial process for the stock price and provided numerical solutions to the initial cost of the replicating portfolio. As the number of periods increases within the given lifetime of the call option, the initial cost of the replicating portfolio tends to infinity.

Bensaid et. al. [**BLPS**] and Edirisinghe, Naik and Uppal [**ENU**] noted that a tighter upper bound on the write price of a call option is obtained by replacing the goal of replicating the payoff of the option with the goal of *dominating the payoff*. For example, the payoff of one share of stock dominates the payoff of a call option and, therefore, the cost of initially buying one share provides an upper bound to the cost of a minimum-cost dominating policy as the number of periods increases within the given lifetime of the option. Davis and Clark [**DCl**] conjectured and Soner, Shreve and Cvitanic [**SSC**] proved, that the cost of initially buying one share of stock is indeed the cost of the cheapest dominating policy in the presence of finite proportional transaction costs. Their result on feasible *super-replicating strategies* was subsequently generalized by Leventhal and Skorohod [**LSk**].

Leland [**Le**] initiated a novel approach by introducing a class of *imperfectly replicating policies* in the presence of proportional transaction costs. He calculated the total cost, including transaction costs, of an imperfectly replicating policy and the "tracking error", that is the standard deviation of the difference between the payoff of the option and the payoff of the imperfectly replicating policy. Imperfectly replicating policies were further studied by Figlewski [**Fi**], Flesaker and Hughston [**FlH**], Grannan and Swindle [**GrSw**], Henrotte [**Hen**], Hoggard, Whalley and Wilmott [**HoWhWi**] and Toft [**To**]. Avellaneda and Parás [**AvPa1**] extended the notion of imperfectly replicating policies to that of imperfectly dominating policies.

An alternative approach, initiated by Hodges and Neuberger [**HN**] and developed further by Davis, Panas and Zariphopoulou [**DPZ**], is the so-called *utility maximization method*. The fundamental ideas for this method stem from the economic principles of *stochastic dominance* (see, for relevant results, Perrakis and Ryan [**PeRy**], Levy [**Lev**] and Ritchken [**Ri**]). In this approach, the price of the derivative is determined by comparing the value functions of an investor with and without the opportunity to trade the available derivative. The individual preferences are modelled via an exponential utility and the derivative is a European call. By considering the utility functionals (with and without the derivative), this methodology incorporates the individual's attitude towards the risk which cannot be eliminated, in contradistinction to the case of no transaction costs. The above results were considerably generalized by Constantinides and Zariphopoulou [**CZ2**] who applied utility methods to establish price bounds for all types of European claims and for general preferences.

Besides the claims of European-type, the valuation of American options was examined by Davis and Zariphopoulou [**DZ**] for the class of exponential utilities. More recently, Constantinides and Zariphopoulou [**CZ2**] extended their results to the cases of American-type and path-dependent claims, written on many stocks and for CRRA utilities. Other path-dependent claims were priced by Dewynne, Whalley and Wilmott [**DeWhWi**] using ideas from the Leland's valuation approach.

Finally, a considerable volume of work has been produced under the assumption that the *transaction costs are "small"*. This assumption is not far from reality for a sizeable class of models and produces adequate results for the prices and, in particular for the hedging strategies. To most extent, the relevant analysis imitates the Black and Scholes methodology together with various elements from the above methods. We mention among others, the work of Whalley and Wilmott [**WhWi3**], Barles and Soner [**BSo**] and Albanese and Tompaidis [**AT**].

This chapter is organized as follows: In Section 8, we present the seminal valuation arguments of Black and Scholes, and the Sections 9, 10 and 11 are dedicated to the various approaches for pricing derivatives with transaction costs, namely the super-replication approach, the utility maximization theory and the method of imperfectly replicating strategies. We conclude with Section 12 where we discuss other valuation models.

Section 8: The Black and Scholes valuation formula.

In their seminal paper, Black and Scholes [**BSc**] developed a theory for the valuation of derivative securities in frictionless markets. They considered the problem of determining the value of a *European call* which is written on an underlying stock whose price S_s follows the diffusion process, as described in (2.2). The market is also endowed with a riskless security whose price is given by (2.1). The European claim is written at the time say $t > 0$ and expires at maturity time T. Its payoff, at expiration, is given by $(S_T - K)^+$ where K is the (prespecified) *exercise price*.

The valuation problem amounts to specifying the *fair value* of the security at its birth time t.

Black and Scholes had the novel idea of constructing a dynamic portfolio whose value coincides with the terminal payoff, $(S_T - K)^+$, of the call. Then they argued that the amount needed to set up this hedging portfolio, at time t, yields the correct price of the European call. Moreover, the components of this portfolio, across time, give the *perfectly replicating (hedging) strategies* which reproduce the value of the security.

Black and Scholes postulated that the call price is a smooth function of the current stock price and time. Therefore, there exists a smooth function $C : [0, +\infty) \times [0, T] \to \mathbb{R}^+$ such that the call price process h_s, $t \leq s \leq T$ can be represented as $h_s = C(S_s, s)$ with S_s being given in (2.1).

Applying Itô's formula to h_s yields

$$dh_s = \left[\frac{\partial C}{\partial t}(S_s, s) + \frac{1}{2}\sigma^2 S_s^2 \frac{\partial^2 C}{\partial S^2}(S_s, s)\right.$$
$$\left. + \mu S_s \frac{\partial C}{\partial S}(S_s, s)\right] ds + \sigma S_s \frac{\partial C}{\partial S}(S_s, s) dW_s. \tag{8.1}$$

Next, we assume that the riskless interest rate is $r > 0$ and that the components of the replicating portfolio are β_s and δ_s. In other words, at any time s, we would have to purchase β_s shares of the riskless security and δ_s shares of the underlying stock. According to the perfect replication idea of Black and Scholes, the following equalities must hold

$$\beta_s B_s + \delta_s S_s = h_s \quad \text{a.e. } t \leq s < T \tag{8.2}$$

$$\beta_T B_T + \delta_T S_T = (S_T - K)^+. \tag{8.3}$$

Taking into account the price equations (2.1) and (2.3), (8.2) yields

$$dh_s = (\mu \delta_s S_s + r\beta_s B_s) ds + \sigma \delta_s S_s dW_s$$

or, equivalently,

$$dh_s = [(\mu + r)\delta_s S_s - rh_s] ds + \sigma \delta_s S_s dW_s. \tag{8.4}$$

We recall that the processes β_s and δ_s satisfy certain "self-financing" assumptions which in turn justify the above differential forms. Equating formally the coefficients in (8.1) and (8.4) yields

$$\begin{cases} \delta_s = \dfrac{\partial C}{\partial S}(S_s, s) \\ \beta_s = \dfrac{h_s - \delta_s S_s}{B_s}, \end{cases} \tag{8.5}$$

as long as the following condition holds a.e.

$$rh_s = \frac{\partial C}{\partial t}(S_s, s) + \frac{1}{2}\sigma^2 S_s^2 \frac{\partial^2 C}{\partial S}(S_s, s) + rS_s \frac{\partial C}{\partial S}(S_s, s). \tag{8.6}$$

Therefore, in order to specify the components (β_s, δ_s) of the replicating portfolio, it suffices for $C = C(S, t)$ to solve the second order nonlinear partial differential

equation
$$rC = \frac{\partial C}{\partial t} + \frac{1}{2}\sigma^2 S^2 \frac{\partial^2 C}{\partial S^2} + rS\frac{\partial C}{\partial S} \qquad (8.7)$$
together with the boundary and terminal conditions, for $0 \leq t \leq T$, $S \geq 0$,
$$C(0,t) = 0 \text{ and } C(S,T) = (S-K)^+. \qquad (8.8)$$

The solution of (8.7) and (8.8) is given by
$$C(S,t) = S\mathcal{N}(d_1) - e^{-r(T-t)}K\mathcal{N}(d_2)$$
where $\mathcal{N}$ is the cumulative standard normal distribution and the quantities d_1 and d_2 are defined as
$$d_1 = \frac{\ln(S/K) + \left(r + \frac{\sigma^2}{2}\right)(T-t)}{\sigma\sqrt{T-t}}$$
and
$$d_2 = \frac{\ln(S/K) + \left(r - \frac{\sigma^2}{2}\right)(T-t)}{\sigma\sqrt{T-t}} = d_1 - \sigma\sqrt{T-t}.$$

Equation (8.7) is the celebrated *Black and Scholes* equation for European type claims written on a stock with constant volatility and when the riskless interest rate is $r > 0$. The first partial derivative of the call price, $\frac{\partial C}{\partial S}(S,t)$ is known as the *delta* of the option and it provides the needed number of stock shares in the replicating portfolio. The important consequence of the diffusion nature of the stock price is that both components of the hedging portfolio turn out to be *diffusion processes*, given by
$$\beta_s = \frac{h_s - S_s\frac{\partial C}{\partial S}(S_s,s)}{B_s} \quad \text{and} \quad \delta_s = \frac{\partial C}{\partial S}(S_s,s). \qquad (8.9)$$

Therefore, the Black and Scholes valuation analysis dictates that rebalancing of the hedging portfolio must take place *infinitely often*. It is for this reason that in the presence of transaction costs, these replicating strategies *are not feasible*. Continuous rebalancing would produce an infinite volume of transactions no matter how small the transaction costs are.

Section 9: Super-replicating strategies.

The strategies of Black and Scholes demonstrate that both components of the replicating portfolio, see (8.9), are diffusion processes as it follows from the diffusion nature of the underlying stock price. Clearly, these hedging strategies will immediately produce an infinite volume of transactions no matter how small the transaction costs are. Therefore, a *perfectly replicating portfolio no longer exists!*

Abandoning the idea of exact replication, one might look for a portfolio strategy which results, at expiration time T, in portfolio value at least as great as the value of the European call. Such strategies are known as *super-replicating* strategies.

Bensaid, Lesne, Pagès and Scheinkman [**BLPS**] uncovered the intriguing idea that super-replication may be feasible, in the sense that the cost of the super-replicating portfolio is actually finite. This cost then may provide a sensible bound on the price of the option. Bensaid et al [**BLPS**] constructed super-replicating policies in a discrete-time framework. (See also, Ediriskinghe, Naik and Uppal [**ENU**].)

Unfortunately, in the (limiting) case of continuous time, the super-replication approach cannot form the basis of a viable valuation theory. In fact, Davis and Clark [**DCl**] conjectured that the *minimal* cost of the super-replication of a European call is the *value of one share* of the underlying stock. Therefore, even though super-replication techniques might provide finite values, their minimal value yields a trivial bound, the value of one stock of share, which is of little economic interest.

Using convex analysis arguments, Soner, Shreve and Cvitanic [**SSC**] established the conjecture of Davis and Clark. Below we state their result by adopting the notation used in the previous Chapter. The bond and stock account processes, x_s and y_s, are given by the state equations (2.4) and (2.3). The European call has exercise time T, strike price K and it is written on the underlying stock whose price is given in (2.2).

THEOREM 9.1 (SSC). *Consider the payoff* $(S_T - K)^+$ *of a European call written of a stock with price* S_s, $t \leq s \leq T$, *as in (2.2). Then in order to have at* $t = T$,

$$x_T + \binom{\alpha}{\beta} y_T \geq (S_T - K)^+ \quad a.e. \tag{9.1}$$

the following constraint must hold for <u>*all*</u> $t \leq s < T$

$$x_s + \binom{\alpha}{\beta}\left(y_s - \frac{S_s}{\alpha}\right) \geq 0 \quad a.e. \tag{9.2}$$

The above result on *trivial super-replicating strategies* was later established by Leventhal and Skorohod [**LSk**] in a general framework. Leventhal and Skorohod assumed that the underlying stock price is a continuous semimartingale and under mild non-degenerate and stability properties, they carried out the analysis for European and American claims. Their method is based on considering a discrete-time version of the underlying model which is free of transaction costs. We refer the reader to their paper for the general super-replication results; below, we state a variation of one of their Propositions (see Section 5 on European options in Leventhal and Skorohod [**LSk**]), adopting the existing notation. This is done only in order to be able to refer to their results from subsequent sections and to preserve the continuity of the exposition.

PROPOSITION 9.1. *Consider a European claim with payoff* $g(S_T)$ *at expiration time* T, *where* g *is increasing, convex and* $g(0) = 0$ *with* $\lim_{S \to \infty} \frac{g(S)}{S} = \ell > 0$. *The stock price* S_s, $t \leq s \leq T$ *is the diffusion process described in (2.2). Then in order to have*

$$x_T + \binom{\alpha}{\beta} y_T \geq g(S_T) \quad a.e. \tag{9.3}$$

the following constraint must hold for <u>*all*</u> $t \leq s < T$

$$x_S + \binom{\alpha}{\beta}\left(y_s - \ell\frac{S_s}{\alpha}\right) \geq 0 \quad a.e. \tag{9.4}$$

Even though super-replicating strategies produce price bounds of little economic interest, these results are of fundamental importance in the utility maximization theory. In fact, the *state constraints* (9.2) and (9.4) essentially characterize the set of *feasible strategies* that the writer, or the buyer of the derivative may use in their valuation strategies. As it will be demonstrated in the next section, even under the stringent constraints (9.2), (9.4), the presence of risk aversion — through the utility functionals — allows us to derive non-trivial bounds for the so-called reservation derivative prices.

Finally, from the previous results an interesting question arises, namely, how can the constraints (9.2) and (9.4) be relaxed, if at all, when the super-replication requirements (9.1) or (9.3) are allowed to hold with probability $1 - \epsilon$, instead of almost surely. This problem is interesting especially from the practical point of view where some "slipage" might be tolerated. Numerical results for the case of European calls can be found in Tourin and Zariphopoulou [**TZ4**].

Section 10: The utility maximization theory.

The Black and Scholes valuation method produces derivative prices which are *independent* of the individual portfolio holdings as well as the individual attitude towards risk. Clearly, these universal properties stem from the ability to exactly replicate the payoff of the security, in the absence of market frictions. As it was discussed earlier, this possibility disappears in the presence of transaction costs and thus, these universal features might not be preserved. Indeed, the utility maximization approach brings in the individual attitude towards the derivative-inherent risk which cannot be any more eliminated.

Even though one of the main ingredients of the Black and Scholes price cannot be retrieved, this method relies on the fundamental economic principles of *stochastic dominance* which still provide adequate viable valuation conclusions. The strengths of this approach are that it can be applied to a large class of derivatives, departing from the European ones; for this class very little is known through the other existing pricing methods with transaction costs. Moreover, the derivative prices are determined via two utility maximization models which give rise to two (singular) stochastic control problems. The powerful theory of viscosity solutions facilitates considerably the analysis by providing essential comparison results for the utilities of the buyer, the writer and the one of the plain investor.

Hodges and Neuberger [**HN**] were the first to apply the utility approach to price European calls when the agents are endowed with exponential utilities. Their results were further developed by Davis, Panas and Zariphopoulou [**DPZ**] for the same class of options, and by Davis and Zariphopoulou [**DZ**] for American options. Note that the exponential utilities of wealth, say $U(z) = 1 - e^{-\gamma z}$ have the property of constant (wealth independent) Absolute Risk Aversion, i.e. $-\dfrac{U''(z)}{U'(z)} = \gamma$.

Before we present the main results, we discuss the simple case of a one-period model, where the end of the period coincides with the expiration date of the option. The purpose of this is two-fold; first, the exposition brings out the fundamental economic ideas of stochastic dominance and secondly, the analysis demonstrates that the stochastic dominance argument breaks when *intermediate trading* is allowed as it is the case in dynamic models. The seemingly innocuous generalization of the model to allow for intermediate trading activities makes the valuation problem far more difficult.

The following arguments come from a modification of the stochastic dominance arguments of Perrakis and Ryan [**PeRy**], Levy [**Lev**] and Ritchen [**Ri**] to account for proportional transaction costs (see also Reisman [**Re**]).

i) Bounds on European options via Stochastic Dominance: single-period models

We consider an economy with two securities, a riskless bond and a risky stock. We denote by B and S the bond and the stock prices, respectively, at the beginning of the (single) period and by B_T and S_T the prices at the end of the period which is assumed to have length T.

Trading in the bond and the stock accounts occurs only at the beginning and end of the period and is subject to transaction costs. As in the continuous time model, β dollars of the bond may be converted into one dollar of the stock and, one dollar of the stock may be converted into α dollars of the bond; the constants α and β satisfy $0 < \alpha < 1 < \beta$.

The important simplifying assumption is that no trading may occur at intermediate times. This assumption is relaxed later and the implications are fully explored therein.

The investor's pre-trade endowment consists of x_0 dollars in the bond account and y_0 dollars in the stock account. The investor trades at the beginning of the period incurring transaction costs and attains a post-trade endowment of x dollars in the bond account and y dollars in the stock account.

We assume that $y > \dfrac{S}{\alpha}$, that is the investor invests in at least $\dfrac{1}{\alpha}$ shares of the stock. At the end of the period, the investor converts the stock account into the bond account and consumes

$$c(S_T) = xR_F + y\frac{S_T}{S}$$

where $R_F = \dfrac{B_T}{B}$.

We assume that the investor's expected utility is the expectation of $u(c(S_T))$, where $u: \mathcal{R} \to \mathcal{R}$ is increasing and concave. In the absence of the opportunity to invest in an option, the investor chooses (x, y) to maximize the expected utility.

Given (x, y), we now present the investor with the opportunity to write one cash-settled, European-style call option with expiration at the end of the period and strike price K. Let C denote the post-transaction-cost price at which the investor may write the call: if the investor writes the call, the bond account increases by C dollars at the beginning the the period and decreases by $[S_T - K]^+$ dollars at the end of the period.

To provide an upper bound to the reservation write price of a call, we adopt the stochastic dominance arguments of Perrakis and Ryan [**PeRy**], Levy [**Lev**] and Ritchken [**Ri**], modified to account for transaction costs.

Consider the zero-net-cost portfolio which consists of a short position in one call and a long position in $\dfrac{C}{\beta S}$ shares of stock. The net payoff in the bond account at the end of the period is $z(S_T)$ where

$$z(S_T) = \frac{\alpha C S_T}{\beta S} - [S_T - K]^+.$$

Note that $z(S_T) \gtrless 0$ as $S_T \lessgtr \hat{S}$ where $\hat{S}$ is defined by

$$\frac{\alpha C \hat{S}}{\beta S} - S_T + K = 0.$$

The investor has post-trade endowment (x,y) and contemplates whether to write the call. If the investor writes the call and invests the proceeds in the stock, the expected utility is

$$E[u(c(S_T) + z(S_T))] \geq E[u(c(S_T))] + E[z(S_T)u'(c(S_T) + z(S_T))]$$

(by the concavity of u)

$$\geq E[u(c(S_T))] + E[z(S_T)u'(c(\hat{S}) + z(\hat{S}))]$$

(since $z(S_T) \gtreqless 0$ and $u'(c(s_T) + z(S_T)) \gtreqless u'(c(\hat{S}) + z(\hat{S}))$ as $S_T \lesseqgtr \hat{S}$)

$$\geq E[u(c(S_T))] + u'(c(\hat{S}) + z(\hat{S}))E[z(S_T)]$$

and exceeds the expected utility from refraining to write the call, unless $E[z(S_T)] < 0$, i.e.

$$(\alpha/\beta)CE[S_T/S] - E[[S_T - K]^+] < 0.$$

Therefore,

$$C < \beta E[[S_T - K]^+]/\alpha E[S_T/S_0] \equiv \bar{C}_1$$

and $\bar{C}_1$ is an upper bound to the reservation write price of a call option.

We consider next a different zero-net-cost portfolio which consists of a short position in one call and a long position in C dollars in the bond. Proceeding as before, we conclude that the expected utility in writing the call exceeds the expected utility in not writing the call, unless

$$C < E[[S_T - K]^+]/R_F \equiv \bar{C}_2.$$

Combining the above equations we conclude that $\bar{C}$ is an upper bound to the reservation write price of a call option, where

$$\bar{C} = E[[S_T - K]^+] \min\left[R_F^{-1}, \frac{\beta/\alpha}{E[S_T/S]}\right].$$

To derive a lower bound to the reservation purchase price of a call option, let C denote the post-transaction-cost price at which the investor may purchase the call. Consider the zero-net-cost portfolio which consists of

(a) a long position in one call;

(b) a short position in $1/\beta$ shares of stock; and

(c) investment of $\alpha S_T/\beta - C$ dollars in the bond account.

Denote by $z(S_T)$ the net payoff in the bond account at the end of the period, where

$$z(S_T) = [S_T - K]^+ - S_T + \left\{\alpha\frac{S}{\beta} - C\right\}R_F.$$

Repeating the earlier argument, we conclude that the expected utility in purchasing the call exceeds the expected utility in refraining from purchasing the call, unless $E[z(S_T)] < 0$, which yields $\underline{C}$ as a lower bound to the reservation purchase price of a call, where

$$\underline{C} = \frac{E[[S_T - K]^+]}{R_F} - \frac{E[S_T]}{R_F} + \frac{\alpha S}{\beta}.$$

It is easily shown that $\underline{C} \leq \bar{C}$. In equilibrium, transaction prices of a call option must lie in the region $[\underline{C}, \bar{C}]$. For, if a transaction occurs at a price $C < \underline{C}$, then the writer is acting suboptimally as the writer could have found a willing buyer of the call at a price as high as $\underline{C}$. Likewise, if a transaction occurs at a price $C > \bar{C}$, then the buyer of the call is acting suboptimally as the buyer could have found a willing writer of the call at a price as low as $\bar{C}$.

The stochastic dominance bounds are appealing in that they apply for any increasing and concave utility function. It turns out, however, that the derivation of these bounds breaks down when intermediate trading is permitted in the open interval $(0, T)$.

Let us reconsider the stochastic dominance argument for the reservation write price of a call. The plausible assumption was made that the investor's endowment satisfies the condition $y > \dfrac{S}{\alpha}$. Without intermediate trading, the consumption at the end of the period is $c(S_T)$ and has two crucial properties:

(1) it is monotone increasing in S_T with slope greater than one; and

(2) given S_T, $c(S_T)$ is independent of the stock price path ω_T over $(0, T)$.

The first property is crucial in the proof in that it implies that $c(S_T) + z(S_T)$ is increasing in S_T and therefore $u'(c(S_T) + z(S_T))$ is decreasing in S_T. The second property is crucial in the step which allowed us to take $u'(c(S_T) + z(S_T))$ outside the expectation: if c is a function of the price path ω_T, $[u'(c(\omega_T) + z(S_T)) \mid S_T]$ is a random variable and cannot be taken outside the expectation. Another problem is that, in the presence of intermediate trading, $c(\omega_T) + z(S_T)$ is not even bounded from below and expected utility is undefined for utility functions which are only defined for consumption bounded from below. Similar problems arise in attempting to generalize the stochastic dominance argument in the derivation of a lower bound to the reservation purchase price when intermediate trading is allowed.

ii) Bounds on prices of European-type claims via utility maximization: continuous-time models

The utility maximization approach looks at the value functions of the investor with and without the opportunity to trade (write or buy) the derivative security.

If the investor chooses not to trade the available claim, his value function is given by $V(x, y)$, as it is defined in (2.7). Suppose now that a third asset is introduced, a cash settled European-style contingent claim with expiration at date T and payoff $g(S_T)$ at expiration. If the investor writes the claim at date t with $0 \leq t \leq T$, the bond account is credited with an amount, say C dollars, which represents the price of the claim, and is debited $g(S_T)$ dollars at the expiration date T. To keep the problem tractable we assume that the investor may not trade the claim in the open interval $(0, T)$.

Let x_t and y_t be the initial endowment at time t *after* the bond account has been credited with the proceeds from writing the claim. Once the claim is written, the writer's objective is to maximize his expected utility from consumption, as in case *(i)* with the extra obligation to surrender to the buyer $g(S_T)$ dollars at time T. Therefore the utility payoff of the writer is

$$E\left[\int_t^T e^{-\rho(s-t)} U(c_s) ds + e^{-\rho(T-t)} V(x_T - g(S_T), y_T) \mid x_t = x, y_t = y, S_t = S\right]$$

where V is defined in (2.7) and S_s is given by (2.2).

The *value function of the writer* is

$$J(x,y,S,t) = \sup_{\mathcal{A}_1} E\left[\int_t^T e^{-\rho(s-t)}U(c_s)ds \right. \tag{10.1}$$
$$\left. + e^{-\rho(T-t)}V(x_T - g(S_T), y_T) \mid x_t = x, y_t = y, S_t = S\right]$$

where $\mathcal{A}_1$ is the set of admissible policies defined below.

It is assumed that the payoff function g satisfies the following assumptions

$$\begin{cases} g : [0, +\infty) \to [0, +\infty) \quad \text{is convex} \\ \\ g(0) = 0 \\ \\ \lim_{S \to \infty} \dfrac{g(S)}{S} = 1. \end{cases} \tag{10.2}$$

The previous exposition on feasible super-replication strategies suggests that the set of the writer's admissible policies must be determined as follows. From (10.1) we have that the writer's terminal (liquidated) wealth must be nonnegative; in other words, the terminal constraint

$$x_T + \binom{\alpha}{\beta} y_T \geq g(S_T) \quad \text{a.e.} \tag{10.3}$$

must be fulfilled. The payoff function g satisfies the assumptions of Leventhal and Skorohod [**LSk**]. Therefore, Proposition 10.2 yields that at *all* previous times $t \leq s < T$, the state wealth of the writer must satisfy the stringent constraint

$$x_s + \binom{\alpha}{\beta}\left(y_s - \frac{S_s}{\alpha}\right) \geq 0 \quad \text{a.e..} \tag{10.4}$$

So, we define the set $\mathcal{A}_1$ of admissible policies of the investor who has written a contingent claim, as the set of $\mathcal{F}_t$-progressively measurable processes (c_t, L_t, M_t), with L_t and M_t being CADLAG which also satisfy the conditions

$$\begin{cases} c_s \geq 0 \text{ and } E\int_t^s c_\tau d\tau < \infty \text{ a.s. for } t \leq s \leq T \tag{10.5} \\ \\ \text{and} \\ \\ w_s = x_s + \binom{\alpha}{\beta}\left(y_s - \dfrac{S_s}{\alpha}\right) \geq 0 \text{ a.s. for } t \leq s < T, \end{cases} \tag{10.6}$$

and we define the set of admissible policies $\{c_t, L_t, M_t; T < t\}$ of the investor who has written a claim by $\mathcal{A}$, as given in (2.5) and (2.5)'. Note that for $s > T$, the option has expired and settled and the investor's problem is indistinguishable from that of an investor who has not written the claim. Thus it is natural to define the set of admissible policies for $s > T$ as $\mathcal{A}$.

The set $\mathcal{A}_1$ is a subset of $\mathcal{A}$ for $t \leq s \leq T$ in the sense that the second restriction ensures that the investor will have nonnegative net worth upon closing up the short position in the call option and, therefore, that it is feasible to write a call option in the first place. The results of Soner, Shreve and Cvitanic [**SSC**], et. al. (for $g(S) = (S - K)^+$) and Leventhal and Skorohod [**LSk**] (for general g) state that the set of policies in $\mathcal{A}_1$ is not overly restrictive given the goal of ensuring that it is feasible to write the claim option.

The value function $J(x, y, S, t)$ is given by (10.1) and is defined for $(x, y, S) \in \overline{D}_1$ where

$$\overline{D}_1 = \left\{ (x, y, S) : x + \binom{\alpha}{\beta}\left(y - \frac{S}{\alpha}\right) \geq 0,\ S \geq 0 \right\}.$$

Consider now the writer with endowment $(x, y) \in \overline{D}$ at time t before writing the claim. If the writer chooses to write the claim at price C, the endowment becomes $(x + C, y)$ and by Theorem 9.1 and Proposition 9.1, the price C must be such that $(x + C, y, S) \in \overline{D}_1$. In the case of *zero-transaction costs*, the function $C = C(S, t)$ is determined as the price that makes the writer *indifferent* between writing the claim or refraining from writing it, i.e.

$$V(x, y) = J(x + C(S, t), y, S, t).$$

In the special case $g(S) = (S - K)^+$, one can show that $C(S, t)$ is the Black and Scholes price which is of course independent of the current portfolio holdings (x, y) and the utility function. Moreover, because of the absence of transaction costs, perfect replication is possible and the constraints (10.3) and (10.4) are not binding.

In the case of *non-zero transaction costs*, the above equality *is not feasible for all* $(x, y, S) \in \overline{D}_1$ if C is allowed to depend *only* on (S, t); this fact motivates the following definitions.

DEFINITION 10.1. *The reservation write price* $C(x, y, S, t)$, *for initial endowment* (x, y), *is defined as the minimum value at which the investor is willing to write the claim. Therefore, C satisfies for* $(x + C(x, y, S, t), y, S) \in \overline{D}_1$

$$V(x, y) = J(x + C(x, y, S, t), y, S, t). \tag{10.7}$$

DEFINITION 10.2. *The write price* $\overline{C}(S, t)$ *is defined as the maximum of reservation write prices across all admissible states* (x, y, S). *Therefore, $\overline{C}$ satisfies for all* $(x + \overline{C}(S, t), y, S) \in \overline{D}_1$,

$$V(x, y) \leq J(x + \overline{C}(S, t), y, S, t). \tag{10.8}$$

The above inequality guarantees that the *writer will be willing to write the option at any price higher than* $\overline{C}(S, t)$, independently of his current portfolio position.

The case of exponential utilities was first examined by Hodges and Neuberger [**HN**] and subsequently by Davis, Panas and Zariphopoulou [**DPZ**]. Constantinides and Zariphopoulou [**CZ1**] generalized all previous results on the subject for general individual preferences and they derived an upper bound $h = h(S, t)$ for the write price which satisfies (10.8) on D_1. The main steps for the construction and characterization of the upper bound are presented below. The proof of their main result can be found in Constantinides and Zariphopoulou [**CZ1**].

THEOREM 10.1 (CZ). *The value function is a constrained viscosity solution on $\overline{D}_1 \times [0,T)$ of the Variational Inequality*

$$\min\left[\mathcal{L}J - \overline{\mathcal{L}}J, \beta\frac{\partial J}{\partial x} - \frac{\partial J}{\partial y}, -\alpha\frac{\partial J}{\partial x} + \frac{\partial J}{\partial y}\right] = 0, \qquad (10.9)$$

with

$$J(x,y,S,T) = V(x - g(S), y), \qquad (10.10)$$

where the operators $\mathcal{L}$ and $\overline{\mathcal{L}}$ are given by

$$\begin{cases} \mathcal{L}J = \rho J - \dfrac{1}{2}\sigma^2 y^2 \dfrac{\partial^2 J}{\partial y^2} - \mu y \dfrac{\partial J}{\partial y} - rx\dfrac{\partial J}{\partial x} - \max_{c\geq 0}\left(-c\dfrac{\partial J}{\partial x} + U(c)\right) \\ \overline{\mathcal{L}}J = \dfrac{\partial J}{\partial t} + \dfrac{1}{2}\sigma^2 S^2 \dfrac{\partial^2 J}{\partial S^2} + \sigma^2 yS \dfrac{\partial^2 J}{\partial y \partial S} + \mu S \dfrac{\partial J}{\partial S}. \end{cases} \qquad (10.11)$$

Moreover, J is the unique constrained viscosity solution of (10.9) in the class of uniformly continuous and concave functions, with respect to the state variables (x, y, S).

The underlying idea for the derivation of *analytic bounds* for the write price of a European-type claim, is to construct suitable subsolutions of the HJB equations (3.2) and (10.9) in order to use a comparison result to establish (10.7). The main difficulty stems from the fact that the value functions V and J are defined on different domains and that there are no explicit or closed-form solutions for the two associated free-boundary problems (2.7) and (10.1).

We start with a formal discussion in order to motivate the construction of the analytic bound. To ease the presentation, we recall that the value functions V and J solve, respectively,

$$\min\left\{\mathcal{L}V, \beta\frac{\partial V}{\partial x} - \frac{\partial V}{\partial y}, -\alpha\frac{\partial V}{\partial x} + \frac{\partial V}{\partial y}\right\} = 0$$

in

$$\overline{D} = \left\{(x,y) : x + \binom{\alpha}{\beta} y \geq 0\right\}$$

and

$$\min\left\{\mathcal{L}J - \overline{\mathcal{L}}J, \beta\frac{\partial J}{\partial x} - \frac{\partial J}{\partial y}, -\alpha\frac{\partial J}{\partial x} + \frac{\partial J}{\partial y}\right\} = 0$$

in

$$\overline{D}_1 = \left\{(x,y,S) : x + \binom{\alpha}{\beta}\left(y - \frac{S}{\alpha}\right) \geq 0\right\}.$$

with the differential operators $\mathcal{L}$ and $\overline{\mathcal{L}}$ given in (10.11). The domains $\overline{D}$ and $\overline{D}_1$ are illustrated in Figures 5 and 6.

The goal is to construct a function $h = h(S,t)$, *independent* of (x,y), such that, for $(x+h, y, S) \in \overline{D}_1$

$$V(x,y) \leq J(x + h(S,t), y, S, t) \qquad (10.12)$$

Using the suboptimality inequality

$$J(x + h(S,t), y, S, t) \geq J\left(x, y + \frac{h(S,t)}{\beta}, S, t\right)$$

and a simple transformation, we observe that (10.11) follows if we find an h such that

$$V\left(x, y - \frac{h(S,t)}{\beta}\right) \leq J(x,y,S,t) \qquad (10.13)$$

for $(x,y,S) \in \overline{D}_1$.

The basic idea of Constantinides and Zariphopoulou [**CZ1**] for the choice of the candidate bound is first to find a price that satisfies (10.13) in the case that $(x,y,S) \in \partial D_1$, i.e. when the writer holds the *minimal allowed position* which amounts to the value of one stock share, taking into account the transaction costs. We then need to show that this price works for all wealth levels greater than the minimal one.

To this end, we start with the following lemma which gives us information about the value function J on $\partial D_1 = \left\{ (x,y,S) : x + \left(\frac{\alpha}{\beta}\right)\left(y - \frac{S}{\alpha}\right) = 0 \right\}$.

LEMMA 10.1 (CZ). *For* $(x,y,S) \in \partial D_1$, *the value function J is given by*

$$J(x,y,S,t) = E\left[e^{-\rho(T-t)} V\left(-g(S_T), \frac{S_T}{\alpha}\right) \mid S_t = S \right]. \qquad (10.14)$$

PROOF. The proof follows directly from the fact that the only admissible policy for the boundary points (x,y,S) is to move instantaneously at time t, to the point $\left(0, \frac{S}{\alpha}, S\right)$ and remain there until time T.

The next result gives the main ingredient for the construction of the candidate solution. Its proof can be found in Constantinides and Zariphopoulou [**CZ1**].

LEMMA 10.2 (CZ). *If $h_{\hat{\rho}} = h_{\hat{\rho}}(S,t)$ is such that*

$$V\left(\frac{\beta}{\alpha}S, -\frac{h_{\hat{\rho}}}{\beta}\right) = E\left[e^{-\hat{\rho}(T-t)} V(S_T - g(S_T), 0) \mid S_t = S \right] \qquad (10.15)$$

with $0 \leq h_{\hat{\rho}} \leq \frac{\beta}{\alpha}S$ and $\hat{\rho} \geq \rho$, then (10.13) holds for $(x,y,S) \in \partial D_1$.

Next, we observe that if the $\mathcal{NT}$ region is a proper subset of the first quadrant, then the points $\left(\frac{\beta}{\alpha}S, 0\right)$ and $(S - g(S), 0)$ belong to the $\mathcal{B}$ region (see Figures 5 and 6).

In the $\mathcal{B}$ region, the value function V satisfies $\beta V_x = V_y$, which implies that there exists a function, denoted as G such that V can be *expressed in terms of G* as

$$V(x_0, y_0) = G(x_0 + \beta y_0) \quad \text{for} \quad (x_0, y_0) \in \mathcal{B}.$$

Therefore,

$$V\left(\frac{\beta}{\alpha}S, -\frac{h(S,t)}{\beta}\right) = G\left(\frac{\beta}{\alpha}S - h(S,t)\right) \qquad (10.16)$$

and

$$V(S_T - g(S_T), 0) = G(S_T - g(S_T)) \qquad (10.17)$$

Combining the above equalities and (10.15) yields

$$G\left(\frac{\beta}{\alpha}S - h(S,t)\right) = E\left[e^{-\hat{\rho}(T-t)}G(S_T - g(S_T)) \mid S_t = S\right].$$

It follows easily from the monotonicity properties of the value function V (see, for example, Tourin and Zariphopoulou [**TZ1**]) that G is strictly increasing and therefore invertible. This in turn yields that the function h is well defined and given by

$$h(S,t) = \frac{\beta}{\alpha}S - G^{-1}\left(E\left[e^{-\hat{\rho}(T-t)}G(S_T - g(S_T)) \mid S_t = S\right]\right). \tag{10.18}$$

It will turn out that the above function is a candidate upper bound for the write price.

The next result is the key step in establishing the validity of $h(S,t)$ being a reservation price bound. Its proof is rather tedious and technical and can be found in Constantinides and Zariphopoulou [**CZ1**].

PROPOSITION 10.1. *Assume that the $\mathcal{NT}$ region for the utility maximization problem (2.7) satisfies $\mathcal{NT} \subseteq \{(x,y) : Ax \leq y \leq Bx, x \geq 0 \text{ with } B > A > 0\}$. Also, assume that the utility function U satisfies $\lambda_1 \frac{c^\gamma}{\gamma} \leq U(c) \leq \lambda_2 \frac{c^\gamma}{\gamma}$ for some positive constants λ_1 and λ_2. Let*

$$m = \left[\left(\frac{\lambda_2\left(\beta + \frac{1}{A}\right)}{\lambda_1\left(\alpha + \frac{1}{B}\right)^\gamma}\right)^{\frac{1}{1-\gamma}} \frac{\rho - r\gamma}{\alpha\gamma} + \left(\mu + \frac{r}{\alpha A}\right) - \frac{\rho}{2}\left(1 + \frac{1}{\beta B}\right)\right]\sigma^{-2}$$

and consider the discount factor $\hat{\rho}$ in (10.18) given by

$$\hat{\rho} = \max\left[\rho, \mu + \frac{m\sigma^2(1-\beta A)}{2\beta A}\right]. \tag{10.19}$$

Then, for the candidate price h, defined in (10.18) with $\hat{\rho}$ as above, the function $F : D_1 \times [0,T] \to [0,+\infty)$ given by

$$F(x,y,S,t) = V\left(x, y - \frac{h(S,t)}{\beta}\right) \tag{10.20}$$

is a viscosity subsolution of the HJB equation (3.19).

The next theorem establishes that the candidate $h(S,t)$ is indeed a price bound.

THEOREM 10.2 (CZ). *Let h be given by*

$$h(S,t) = \frac{\beta}{\alpha}S - G^{-1}\left(E\left[e^{-\hat{\rho}(T-t)}G(S_T - g(S_T)) \mid S_T = S\right]\right)$$

where $\hat{\rho}$ is defined in (10.19). Then the function $h(S,t)$ is an upper bound to the reservation write price.

PROOF. In order to prove the theorem, it suffices to show that inequality (10.13) holds on $\overline{D}_1 \times [0, T]$, i.e. that

$$V\left(x, y - \frac{h(S,t)}{\beta}\right) \leq J(x, y, S, t).$$

First, we observe that at $t = T$ the above inequality holds. In fact, from (10.10) and (10.18) we have

$$J(x, y, S, T) = V(x - g(S), y)$$

$$V\left(x, y - \frac{h(S,T)}{\beta}\right) = V\left(x, y - \frac{\beta - \alpha}{\alpha \beta} S - \frac{g(S)}{\beta}\right).$$

Therefore, it suffices to show

$$V\left(x, y - \frac{\beta - \alpha}{\alpha \beta} S - \frac{g(S)}{\beta}\right) \leq V(x - g(S), y)$$

which, by suboptimality, reduces to showing

$$V\left(x, y - \frac{\beta - \alpha}{\alpha \beta}(S - g(S))\right) \leq V(x, y).$$

Using that V is increasing and that, $g(S) \leq S$ (see Remark 3.1), we easily conclude.

Next, recall that by the special choice of h, (see Lemma 10.2), the desired inequality holds for $(x, y, S) \in \partial D_1$. Moreover, from Proposition 10.2 we have that the function $V\left(x, y - \frac{h(S,t)}{\beta}\right)$ is a viscosity subsolution of the (HJB) equation (10.9) whose unique solution is the value function J. Finally, routine arguments can be used to show that the rest of the conditions for the comparison results for solutions of (10.9) hold. We therefore conclude that the subsolution $V(x, y - \frac{h(S,t)}{\beta})$ is dominated by the solution $J(x, y, S, t)$ and the validity of the price bound h is established.

From the above results, one can see that the "trivial" super-replicating price bound — of one stock share — is substantially improved once one employs the utility maximization method. As a matter of fact, the latter method relies on the risk aversion attitude of the investors as opposed to the super-replicating approach which is based on risk-neutrality. The weak point of the utility method is that little information is available for the hedging strategies and this can be actually retrieved only through the optimal investment strategies for the utility maximization problems (2.7) and (10.1). On the other hand, the utility method can be easily extended to other kinds of derivatives like American options, path-dependent and exotics written, actually, one more than one stock. For these kinds of derivatives very little is known through the other valuation methods for markets with transaction costs (for a complete study of these cases, we refer the reader to Constantinides and Zariphopoulou [**CZ2**]). Moreover, even though the utility maximization method departs from the fundamental and classical risk-neutral valuation theory, it could still contribute in a number of custom-made derivatives or real options, and also serve as the basis line for developing improved methods based on *general risk functionals*. Finally, the utility maximization approach can be easily applied to valuation problems with other kinds of frictions, like stochastic volatility (see, for example, Mazaheri [**Ma**]). An interesting application of the utility method which relates small transaction costs and modified volatility can be found in Barles and Soner [**BSo**]).

Section 11: Imperfect hedging strategies.

An appealing alternative approach for the valuation of derivatives in the presence of transaction costs, is to *relax* the requirement of continuous rebalancing by allowing the adjustment of the "hedging" portfolio to take place at *discrete times*. Clearly, a correct valuation procedure based on discrete hedging is highly desirable for the practical applications since continuous rebalancing is practically impossible. Generally speaking, even in the absence of transaction costs, discrete in time rebalancing does not lead to perfect hedging but nevertheless, *imperfect hedging strategies* have become a standard vehicle in valuating derivatives in practice.

Two important papers on discrete hedging without transaction costs were produced by Boyle and Emanuel [**BoE**] and Wilmott [**Wi**]. In both papers, rebalancing takes place at fixed time intervals. Boyle and Emanuel [**BoE**] provided a thorough study on *the hedging error* which is defined as the *discrepancy* between the discrete hedging strategy and the continuous in time strategy dictated by the Black and Scholes formula. They established that rehedging in fixed time intervals produces a hedging error which is proportional to the gamma of the option and chi-squared distributed. Wilmott [**Wi**] used asymptotic expansions and found improved hedging strategies which are also related to an adjusted option value. One of the underlying ideas was to use the number of shares which minimize the variance of the hedging portfolio over the next time step. By equating the expected value on the hedged portfolio with the riskless interest rate, Wilmott [**Wi**] found that the option should be priced at a modified constant volatility. The latter depends on the rehedging time-interval as well as the mean rate of return of the stock price.

The phenomenon of getting an *enhanced volatility* when discrete hedging takes place is rather common in derivative pricing, especially when discrete hedging is used to accomodate the effects of transaction costs. The groundwork on this subject was originated by Leland [**Le**] and his results are considered a benchmark in the area of imperfect hedging.

Imitating the Black and Scholes analysis and proceeding in a rather ad-hoc way, Leland [**Le**] produced a valuation formula for European options in the presence of proportional transaction costs. He showed that the equation satisfied by the new option price resembles the Black and Scholes one (8.7) but with increased volatility (see equation (11.7) below). The enhanced volatility explodes, and so does the derivative price as the size of the hedging time intervals goes to zero.

Below, we continue with the construction of Leland's price for a European option; in order to be consistent with his calculations, we assume that the transaction costs are symmetric which corresponds, in our notation to $\alpha = \dfrac{1}{\beta} = 1 - k$; to simplify the exposition we also assume that the interest rate is zero. Following the Black and Scholes analysis, Leland postulated that the price of the call, say C_t, at time t, can be represented as a convex function of the stock price S_t and time, i.e. $C_t = h(S_t, t)$ with $h : [0, +\infty) \times [0, T] \to [0, +\infty)$.

Let us denote the increments of the underlying stock price as $\Delta S_s \triangleq S_{s+\Delta s} - S_s$. From equation (2.1) we have, for $t \leq s \leq T$,

$$\Delta S_s \simeq S_s(\mu \Delta s + \sigma \Delta W_s). \tag{11.1}$$

Proceeding formally, we suppose — as in the Black and Scholes case — that there exists a replicating strategy, say δ_s, with δ_s denoting the number of stocks needed at time s. Then the price of the option will change according to

$$\begin{cases} \Delta h_s \simeq \delta_s \Delta S_s - k S_s \\ \\ \simeq S_s(\mu \delta_s \Delta s - k|\Delta \delta_s|) + \sigma S_s \delta_s \Delta W_s. \end{cases} \quad (11.2)$$

Assuming that all the necessary derivatives exist, Itô's formula yields

$$\Delta h_s \simeq \left(\frac{\partial h}{\partial t}(S_s, s) + \mu S_s \frac{\partial h}{\partial S}(S_s, s) + \right.$$

$$\left. + \frac{1}{2}\sigma^2 S_s^2 \frac{\partial^2 h}{\partial S^2}(S_s, s) \right) \Delta s + \sigma S_s \frac{\partial h}{\partial S}(S_s, s) \Delta W_s. \quad (11.3)$$

Equating the coefficients in (11.2) and (11.3) gives,

$$\begin{cases} \sigma S_s \delta_s = \sigma S_s \frac{\partial h}{\partial S}(S_s, s) \\ \\ S_s \left(\mu \delta_s - k \frac{|\Delta \delta_s|}{\Delta s} \right) = \frac{\partial h}{\partial t}(S_s, s) + \mu S_s \frac{\partial h}{\partial S}(S_s, s) \\ \\ + \frac{1}{2}\sigma^2 S_s^2 \frac{\partial^h}{\partial S^2}(S_s, s). \end{cases} \quad (11.4)$$

The first equation above implies $\delta_s = \frac{\partial h}{\partial S}(S_s, s)$ which in turn yields

$$|\Delta \delta_s| \simeq \left| \sigma S_s \frac{\partial^2 h}{\partial S^2}(S_s, s) \Delta W_s \right| + m(s) \quad (11.5)$$

where $m(s)$ includes terms of order s or higher. Leland based his derivation of the assumption that

$$|\Delta W_s| \simeq \sqrt{\frac{2}{\pi}} \sqrt{\Delta s} \quad (11.6)$$

without really justifying his choice. Nevertheless, using this approximation together with (11.4) and (11.5) yields that the option price function $h(S, t)$ must solve

$$\frac{\partial h}{\partial t} + \frac{1}{2}\sigma^2 S^2 \left(1 + \frac{2k}{\sigma\sqrt{\Delta t}} \sqrt{\frac{2}{\pi}} \right) \frac{\partial^2 h}{\partial S^2} = 0. \quad (11.7)$$

Leland's *enhanced volatility* is then given by

$$\tilde{\sigma} = \sigma \left(1 + \frac{2k}{\sigma\sqrt{\Delta t}} \sqrt{\frac{2}{\pi}} \right)^{1/2}. \quad (11.8)$$

The above analysis was carried out for the case of call options. Similar arguments can lead for the case of put positions to a pricing equation of the same form as (11.7) but with different enhanced volatility, namely $\underline{\sigma} = \sigma \left(1 - \frac{2k}{\sigma\sqrt{\Delta t}} \sqrt{\frac{2}{\pi}} \right)^{1/2}$. Therefore, in Leland's approach, "short and long" positions have different values.

As it was mentioned earlier, even though Leland did not justify his choice of approximation in (11.6), his formula became rather popular in practical applications mainly because it relies on discrete in time rebalancing and it also requires an implementation similar to the Black and Scholes one. Moreover, in contradistinction to the utility maximization method, Leland's approach is able to produce a specific trading strategy, albeit imperfect.

A number of researchers modified or extended Leland's work by choosing different approximations and encountering modified errors. Boyle and Vorst [**BoV**] applied Leland's techniques to a binomial valuation model and maintained the obligation to rehedge at constant time steps. They obtained a perfectly hedging strategy and an associated option price. Additionally, they examined the behavior of the option price as the time step $\Delta t \downarrow 0$ assuming that the proportional transaction costs, λ and μ, decrease to zero at a $\sqrt{\Delta t}$ rate. With these limiting assumptions, Boyle and Vorst found that the limiting price equation preserves the Black and Scholes and Leland structure but with a different enhanced volatility, namely

$$\hat{\sigma} = \sigma \left(1 + \frac{2k}{\sigma\sqrt{\Delta t}}\right)^{1/2}. \tag{11.9}$$

The above volatility can be obtained directly from Leland's arguments provided one chooses the approximation $|\Delta W_s| \simeq \sqrt{\Delta s}$, instead of (11.6). Whalley and Wilmott [**WhWi2**] provide a nice discussion on the similarities and differences between the various approximations and how they affect the long and short positions, attributing them mostly to the asymmetries inherent from the transaction costs.

A different valuation model, for arbitrary option payoffs, was introduced by Hoggard, Whalley and Wilmott [**HWhWi**] who used the same idea of rehedging at fixed time intervals Δs but they imposed a *generalized shares costs structure*. In fact, they assume that their cost structure is of the form $k_1 + k_2\delta_s + k_3\delta_s S_s$, i.e. there is a component of fixed costs, k_1, a second component of cost $k_2\delta_s$ proportional to the number of shares rehedged and a third one, $k_2\delta_s S_s$, proportional to the current traded value. Working along the basic Leland valuation analysis, Hoggard, Whalley and Wilmott derived the following option price equation (stated for non-zero interest rates)

$$\frac{\partial h}{\partial t} + \frac{1}{2}\sigma^2 S^2 \frac{\partial^2 h}{\partial S^2} + rS\frac{\partial h}{\partial S} = rh + \frac{k_1}{\Delta t} + \left[\sqrt{\frac{2}{\pi \Delta t}}\sigma S(k_2 + k_3 S)\right]\left|\frac{\partial^2 h}{\partial S^2}\right|.$$

As with Leland's analysis, the above equation yields different values for short and long positions. Moreover its solution may attain negative values, a feature not desirable for an option valuation model. Hoggard, Whalley and Wilmott argued that this issue stems mainly from the ad hoc obligation to rehedge at every time step and it can be corrected by *regulating the rehedging process* taking into account the current option values. This modification calls for dynamically ceasing the rebalancing as soon as the call price goes to levels that any further rehedging would lead to negative values. This approach gives rise to a free-boundary valuation problem with similar characteristics to an American put.

Departing from the obligation to rehedge at fixed time-intervals, Whalley and Wilmott [**WhWi1**] developed a model in which rebalancing takes place whenever the current position deviates considerably from the position of perfect hedging. To fix the notation, we denote by $C(S,t)$ the Black and Scholes price, with perfect hedging and by $h(S,t)$ the price under imperfect hedging. Recall that the perfect hedging position at time s, is given by the delta position $d_s(S_s, s) = \dfrac{\partial C}{\partial S}(S_s, s)$. In an effort to control the big losses from frequent rehedging in the presence of transaction costs, one might decide to hold $-\widetilde{d}_s(S_s, s)$ shares of the underlying without considering the extra cost of selling (or buying) for rehedging. If the variance of this position is used to measure the inherent risk exposure, one gets a risk exposure of size $\sigma^2 S_s^2 (\widetilde{d}_s(S_s, s) - d_s(S_s, s))^2 \Delta s$. Since choosing $\widetilde{d}_s = d_s$ is not feasible, Whalley and Wilmott [**WhWi1**] introduced an *index of tolerance* by considering the maximum expected risk in the portfolio, say H_0 and by requiring the constraint

$$|\widetilde{d}_s(S_s, s) - d_s(S_s, s)| \leq \frac{H_0}{\sigma S_s}$$

to hold at all times. Therefore, any time the above condition is violated, the position should be rebalanced.

Avellaneda and Parás [**AvPa1**] studied the illposedness of the replication strategies by Hoggard, Whalley and Wilmott [**HWhWi1**] and proposed an explanation in the case of large transaction costs which intensifies the difference between the (asymmetric) short and long positions. They argued that the writer of the derivative is always obliged to rehedge dynamically his market exposure independently of the effects from the transaction costs. The buyer does not face the same stringency as all he risks is the initial premium and, after all, "hedging is done primarily to offset time-decay". Large transaction costs alter irreversibly the adjusted delta strategies and the value of the positions become eroded. Avellaneda and Parás [**AvPa1**] proposed a new scheme for the valuation of the derivatives which is based on solving an obstacle problem for the Leland partial differential equation (11.7) with enhanced volatility. The obstacle problem arises from optimal stopping rules dictating when the rehedging must temporarily stop.

In a more recent paper, Avellaneda and Parás [**AvPa2**], considered the issue of minimizing the total cost of the hedging strategies of option portfolios. They followed the discrete in time approach by Bensaid et al [**BLPS**] and they examined the limit of the positions as the number of trading periods becomes large. Generally speaking, Avellandea and Parás showed that, in the limit, the cost function satisfies a non-linear, diffusion equation. In particular, if the rehedging interval Δs, the volatility σ and the "roundtrip" transaction costs k satisfy $m = \dfrac{k}{\sigma \Delta s} < 1$, then the cost function converges to the solution of a non-linear Black and Scholes type equation. The volatility parameter of the latter depends on the local convexity of the cost function and it is adjusted either to $\sigma\sqrt{1+m}$ or to $\sigma\sqrt{1-m}$. If $m < 1$, the optimal hedging strategy *replicates* the final payoff via delta-hedging directly from the solution of the nonlinear Black and Scholes type equation. On the other hand, if $m \geq 1$ the hedging strategy of minimal cost is path-dependent and *super-replicates* the final payoff.

Henrotte [**Hen**] also used ideas from Leland's approach and extended the concept of diffusion limits of replicating positions to hedging policies based on changes in the stock price. In [**Hen**], Henrotte considers the asymptotic replication error and compres the performance of hedging strategies based on rebalancing at equal time steps, to strategies depending on prespecified changes of the underlying stock price. Grannan and Swindle [**GrSw**] extended the use of limiting hedging strategies by optimizing over different classes of strategies, like for example, strategies which allow for varying time intervals. They also explored the induced *replication errors* and compared them to the ones of the standard approach based on constant in time intervals. The work of Grannan and Swindle [**GrSw**] was subsequently generalized by Ahn et al [**ADGS**] who considered rather general hedging strategies which include all other existing ones, like for example "time-interval" strategies, "price change" strategies, renewal policies and delta-strategies based on local deviations.

As it was mentioned at the beginning of the section, Leland's analysis was not mathematically rigorous as some rather ad-hoc assumptions were used. Some of his limiting results and conjectures were later revisited and corrected by Lott [**Lo**] and more recently by Kabanov and Safarian [**KSa**].

Section 12: Other models of derivative pricing with transaction costs.

Various other valuation techniques have been developed besides the ones mentioned in the previous sections.

Martingale theory, convex analysis and duality results have been used by a number of authors to obtain derivative prices and to construct appropriate strategies. A general approach to characterize arbitrage-free models with transaction costs was developed in Jouini and Kallal [**JK**]. Along the lines of the super-replication method, martingale techniques were used by Cvitanic and Karatzas [**CK**] and by Cvitanic, Pham and Touzi [**CPhT**] for continuous time models and by Koehl, Pham and Touzi [**KPT**] for the discrete case; see also Kusuoka [**Ku**] for some convergence results.

A different method which relies on insights from both the utility maximization as well as the Leland's approach, uses as optimality criterion the *minimization of the "local risk"*. It is based on a *local quadratic loss criterion* which was first introduced by Schweizer [**Schw**]. This method has been extensively used in the frictionless case by a number of authors, but for the case of transaction costs, it was first employed by Mercurio and Vorst [**MV**] for some special cases (see also Mercurio [**Me**]). Recently, Lamberton, Pham and Schweizer [**LPS**] provided rigorous results for the existence of locally risk-minimizing strategies in the class of square-integrable contingent claims. The strength of this new approach is that, besides its mathematical tractability, it produces hedging strategies whose initial costs are *much lower* than those produced by the super-replicating strategies and whose replicating errors are relatively small.

In a different direction, various authors considered the derivative valuation problem assuming that the transaction costs are finite but *arbitrarily small*. The majority of these models use key insights from the utility maximization approach, see for example Barles and Soner [**BSo**], Whalley and Wilmott [**WhWi4**], Albanese and Tompaidis [**AT**]. The model of Whalley and Wilmott was successfully tested against others in the Monte Carlo simulations of Mohamed [**Mo**]. In arbitrary transaction cost structure was allowed by Whalley and Wilmott [**WhWi3**] when the costs are either proportional or fixed. Whalley and Wilmott produced a simple expression for the "hedging bandwidth" around the Black and Scholes delta strategies and argued that in this region rehedging is not optimal. They used asymptotic analysis to specify explicit points of optimal rehedging in the case of proportional, fixed and mixed transaction costs.

The accurate valuation of derivatives in the presence of transaction costs has become more and more desirable as new derivatives are being created every day and custom-made instruments have a rising demand. Some kinds of path-dependent derivatives, including Asians and look-backs have been examined by Dewynne, Whalley and Wilmott [**DeWhWi**]; their valuation method is based on Leland's approach of imperfect hedging and the mathematical analysis is mostly relying on the associated non-linear Black and Scholes type equations. Using utility maximization methods, Constantinides and Zariphopoulou [**CZ2**] recently priced various kinds of exotic options as well as American instruments written on more than one securities for investors with CRRA utilities.

13. References

[ADGS] H. Ahn, M. Dayal, E. Grannan and G. Swindle, *Option replication with transaction costs: general diffusion limits*, Annals of Applied Probability **8(3)** (1998), 676–707.

[AMS1] M. Akian, J. L. Menaldi and A. Sulem, *Multi-asset portfolio selection problem with transaction costs. Probabilités numériques*, Mathematics and Computers in Simulation **38** (1992), 163–172.

[AMS2] M. Akian, J. L. Menaldi and A. Sulem, *On an investment-consumption model with transaction costs*, SIAM Journal on Control and Optimization **34** (1996), 329–364.

[ASS] M. Akian, P. Séquier and A. Sulem, *A finite horizon multidimensional portfolio selection problem with singular transactions*, Proceedings CDC, New Orleans, vol. 3, (1996), pp. 2193–2198.

[ASSA] M. Akian, P. Séquier, A. Sulem and A. Aboulalaa, *A finite horizon portfolio selection problem with multi risky assets and transaction costs: the domestic asset allocation example*, Proceedings Association Française de Finance, Bordeaux, June 1995.

[AST] M. Akian, A. Sulem and M. Taksar, *Dynamic optimisation of a long-term growth rate for a mixed portfolio with transaction costs*, Preprint (1996).

[AT] C. Albanese and S. Tompaidis, *Small transaction costs asymptotics for the Black and Scholes models*, Preprint (1998).

[A] O. Alvarez, *A singular stochastic control problem in an unbounded domain*, Communications in Partial Differential Equations **19** (1994), 2075–2089.

[ATo] O. Alvarez and A. Tourin, *Viscosity solutions of nonlinear integro-differential equations*, Ann. Inst. Henri Poincaré **13(3)** (1996), 203–317.

[Al] B. Alziary de Roquefort, *Jeux differentiels et approximátion de fonction valeur*, RAIRO (1991) (to appear).

[AM] A. Araujo and P. K. Montiero, *Equilibrium without uniform conditions*, Journal of Economic Theory **48** (1989), 416–427.

[AA] C. Atkinson and B. Al–Ali, *On an investment-consumption model with transaction costs: an asymptotic analysis.*, Preprint (1995).

[APW] C. Atkinson, S. Pliska and P. Wilmott, *Portfolio management with transaction costs*, Proc. Roy. Soc. A (1999) (to appear).

[AW] C. Atkinson and P. Wilmott, *Portfolio management with transaction costs: an asymptotic analysis of the Morton and Pliska model*, Mathematical Finance **5** (1995), 357–367.

[AvPa1] M. Avellaneda and A. Parás, *Optimal hedging portfolios for derivative securities in the presence of large transaction costs*, Applied Mathematical Finance **1**, 165–193.

[AvPa2]   M. Avellaneda and A. Parás, *Hedging financial derivatives in the presence of transaction costs: dynamic programming, nonlinear volatility and free boundary problems*, Preprint (1997).

[BBRS]   G. Barles, J. Burdeau, M. Romano and N. Samsoen, *Critical stock price near expiration*, Mathematical Finance **5(2)** (1995), 77–95.

[BDR]   G. Barles, C. Daher and M. Romano, *Convergence of numerical schemes for parabolic equations arising in finance theory*, Report, Caisse Autonome de Refinancement. (1991).

[BS]   G. Barles and H. M. Soner, *Option pricing with transaction costs and a nonlinear Black and Scholes equation*, Finance and Stochastics **2** (1998), 369–397.

[BSou]   G. Barles and P. E. Souganidis, *Convergence of approximation schemes for fully nonlinear second order equations*, Journal of Asymptotic Analysis **4** (1991), 271–283.

[BLPS]   B. Bensaid, J. Lesne, H. Pages and J. Scheinkman, *Derivative asset pricing with transaction costs*, Mathematical Finance **2** (1992), 63–86.

[BeSm]   G. J. Benston and C. W. Smith, Jr., *A transactions cost approach to the theory of financial intermediation*, Journal of Finance **31(2)** (1976), 215–231.

[BLN]   S. A. Berkowitz, D. E. Logue and E. A. Noser, Jr, *The total cost of transactions on the NYSE*, Journal of Finance **43(1)** (1988), 97-112.

[BeCa]   G. Bertola and R. Caballero, *Kinked adjustment costs and aggregate dynamics*, NBER Macroeconomics Annual, National Bureau of Economic Research (1990), 237–288.

[BiPl]   T. Bielecki and S. Pliska, *Risk sensitive asset management with transaction costs*, Finance and Stochastics (to appear).

[BSc]   F. Black and M. Scholes, *The pricing of options and corporate liabilities*, Journal of Political Economy **81** (1973), 637–654.

[Bl]   L. E. Blume, *Equilibrium and optimality in a sequence of markets with transaction costs*, Contributions to Mathematical Economics (1986), North-Holland, Amsterdam–New York, 103–118.

[BoE]   P. P. Boyle and D. Emanuel, *Discretely adjusted option hedges*, Journal of Financial Economics **8** (1980), 259–282.

[BoV]   P. Boyle and T. Vorst, *Option replication in discrete time with transaction costs*, Journal of Finance **47** (1992), 271–293.

[Bren]   M. J. Brennan, *The optimal number of securities in a risky asset portfolio when there are fixed costs of transacting: Theory and some empirical results*, Journal of Financial and Quantitative Analysis **10** (1975), 483–496.

[BC]   M. Brennan and T. E. Copeland, *Stock splits, stock prices, and transaction costs*, Journal of Financial Economics **22(1)** (1988), 83–102..

[Ca1]   R. J. Caballero, *On the sign of the investment-uncertainty relationship*, American Economic Review **81(1)**, 279–288.

[Ca2]   R. J. Caballero, *Durable Goods: An explanation for their slow adjustment*, Journal of Political Economy **101(2)**, 351–383.

[C-D]   I. Capuzzo-Dolcetta, *On a discrete approximation of the Hamilton-Jocobi equation of dynamic programming*, Journal of Applied Mathematics and Optimization **10** (1983), 367–377.

[C-DF]   I. Capuzzo-Dolcetta and M. Falcone, *Discrete dynamic programming and viscosity solutions of the Bellman equation*, Annales de l'Institut Henry Poincaré Analyse Non Linéaire **6** (1989), 161–181.

[C-DL]   I. Capuzzo-Dolcetta and P.-L. Lions, *Hamilton-Jacobi equations with state constraints*, Transactions of the American Mathematical Society **318** (1990), 543–583.

[Con] K. A. Condon, *Measuring equity transaction costs*, Financial Analysis Journal **37(5)** (1981), 57–60.

[Co1] G. M. Constantinides, *Multiperiod consumption and investment behavior with convex transactions costs*, Management Science **25** (1979), 1127–1137.

[Co2] G. M. Constantinides, *Capital market equilibruim with transaction costs*, Journal of Political Economy **94** (1986), 842–862.

[CZ1] G. M. Constantinides and T. Zariphopoulou, *Bounds on prices of contingent claims in an intertemporal economy with proportional transaction costs and general preferences*, in press, Finance and Stochastics (1999).

[CZ2] G. M. Constantinides and T. Zariphopoulou, *Price bounds on a general class of derivatives written on multi-securities*, Preprint (1998).

[CH] J. Cox and C. Huang, *Optimal consumption and portfolio policies when asset prices follow a diffusion process*, Journal of Economic Theory **49** (1989), 33–83.

[CIL] M. G. Crandall, H. Ishii and P.-L. Lions, *User's guide to viscosity solutions of second order partial differential equations*, Bulletin of the American Mathematical Society **27** (1992), 1–67.

[CL1] M. G. Crandall and P.-L. Lions, *Two approximations of solutions of Hamilton-Jacobi equations*, Mathematics of Computation **43** (1984), 1–19.

[CL2] M. G. Crandall and P.-L. Lions, *Viscosity solutions of Hamilton-Jacobi equations*, Transactions of the American Mathematical Society **277** (1983), 1–42.

[CK] J. Cvitanić and I. Karatzas, *Hedging and portfolio optimization under transaction costs: a martingale approach*, Mathematical Finance **6** (1996), 133–165.

[CPT] J. Cvitanić, H. Pham and N. Touzi, *A closed-form solution to the problem of super-replication under transaction costs*, Preprint (1997).

[DPo] R.-A. Dana and M. Pontier, *On existence of an Arrow-Radner equilibrium in the case of complete markets. Two remarks*, Mathematics of Operations Research **17** (1992), 148–163.

[DCl] M. H. A. Davis and J. M. C. Clark, *A note on super-replicating strategies*, Philosophical Transactions of the Royal Society of London A (1994), 485–494.

[DN] M. H. A. Davis and A. R. Norman, *Portfolio selection with transaction costs*, Mathematics of Operations Research **15** (1990), 676–713.

[DP] M. H. A. Davis and V. Panas, *The writing price of a European contingent claim under proportional transaction costs*, Mat. Apl. Comput. **13** (1994), 115–157.

[DPZ] M. H. A. Davis, V. Panas and T. Zariphopoulou, *European option pricing with transaction costs*, SIAM Journal on Control and Optimization **31** (1993), 470–493.

[DPr] J. C. Dermody and E. Z. Prisman, *Term structure multiplicity and clientele in markets with transactions costs and taxes*, Journal of Finance **43(4)** (1988), 893-911.

[DeWhWi] J. N. Dewynne, A. E. Whalley and P. Wilmott, *Path-dependent options and transactions costs*, Philosophical Transaction of the Royal Society of London A **347** (1994), 517–529.

[D] D. Duffie, *Stochastic equilibria: existence, spanning number, and the "no expected gain from trade" hypothesis*, Econometrica **54** (1986), 1161–1183.

[DH] D. Duffie and C. F. Huang, *Implementing Arrow-Debreu equilibria by continuous trading of few long-lived securities*, Econometria **53** (1985), 1337–1356.

[DuZ] D. Duffie and T. Zariphopoulou, *Optimal investment with undiversifiable income risk*, Mathematical Finance **3** (1993), 135–148.

[DL] B. Dumas and E. Luciano, *An exact solution to a dynamic portfolio choise problem under transaction costs*, Journal of Finance **46** (1991), 577–595.

[Eb1] J. Eberly, *Adjustment of consumers' durables stocks: Evidence from automobile purchases*, Journal of Political Economy **102(3)**, 403–436.

[Eb2] J. Eberly, *Optimal Consumption under uncertainty with durability and transaction costs*, Journal of Economic Dynamics and Control (1999) (to appear).

[ENU] C. Edirisinghe, V. Naik and R. Uppal, *Optimal replication of options with transaction costs and trading restrictions*, Journal of Finance **28** (1993), 117–138.

[F1] M. Falcone, *Numerical solution of deterministic continuous control problems*, Proceedings of the International Symposium on Numerical Analysis, Madrid, (1985).

[F2] M. Falcone, *A numerical approach to the infinite horizon problem of deterministic control theory*, Applied Mathematics and Optimization **15** (1987), 1–13.

[FY] J. Fellingham and R. A. Young, *Special allocations, investment decisions, and transactions costs in partnerships*, Journal of Accounting Review **27(2)** (1989), 179-200.

[Fi] S. Figlewski, *Options arbitrage in imperfect markets*, Journal of Finance **44** (1989), 1289–1311.

[FF] B. G. Fitzpatrick and W. H. Fleming, *Numerical methods for an optimal investment/consumption model*, Mathematics of Operations Research **16** (1991), 823–841.

[FGVZ] W. H. Fleming, S. Grossman, J. L. Vila, J. L. and T. Zariphopoulou, *Optimal portfolio rebalancing with transaction costs*, Preprint (1989).

[FS] W. H. Fleming and H. M. Soner, *Controlled Markov Processes and Viscosity Solutions*, Springer Verlag, New York, 1993.

[FZ] W. H. Fleming and T. Zariphopoulou, *An optimal investment/consumption model with borrowing*, Mathematics of Operations Research **16** (1991), 802–822.

[FlH] B. Flesaker and L. P. Houghton, *Contingent claim replication in continuous time in the presence of transaction costs*, Merril Lynch working paper (1994).

[GO] M. B. Garman and J. A. Ohlson, *Valuation of risky assets in arbitrage-free economies with transactions costs*, Journal of Financial Economics **9(3)** (1981), 271-280.

[GL] J. E. Gilster, Jr. and W. Lee, *The effects of transaction costs and different borrowing and lending rates on the option pricing model: A note*, Journal of Finance **39(4)** (1984), 1215–1221.

[Gla] D. Glassman, *Exchange rate risk and transactions costs: evidence from bid-ask spreads*, Journal of International Money and Finance **6(4)** (1987), 479-490.

[Go2] D. Goldsmith, *Transactions costs and the theory of portfolio selection*, Journal of Finance **31(4)** (1976), 1127-1139.

[Goo] A. C. Goodman, *Modeling and computing transactions costs for purchasers of housing services*, American Real Estate and Urban Economics Association **18(1)** (1990), 1-21.

[GG] J. P. Gould and D. Galai, *Transactions costs and the relationship between put and call prices*, Journal of Financial Economics **1(2)** (1974), 105-129.

[GrSw] E. R. Grannan and G. H. Swindle, *Minimizing transaction costs of option hedging strategies*, Mathematical Finance (to appear).

[GWh] D. Grant and R. Whaley, *Transactions costs on government bonds: A respecification*, Journal of Business **51(1)** (1978), 57-64.

[Gro] H. I. Grossman, *Expectations, transactions costs, and asset demands*, Journal of Finance **24(3)** (1969), 491-506.

[GLa] S. Grossman and G. Laroque, *Asset pricing and optimal portfolio choice in the presence of illiquid durable consumption goods*, Econometrica **58(1)** (1990), 25–51.

[HS] A. Haller and H. R. Stoll, *Market structure and transaction costs: implied spreads in the german stock market*, Journal of Business, Finance and Accounting **13(4/5)** (1989), 697–708.

[HEOC]   A. Harten, B. Engquist, S. Osher and S. Chakravarthy, *Some results on uniformly high-order accurate nonoscillatory schemes*, Applied Numerical Mathematics **2** (1986), 347–377.

[Hen]   P. Henrotte, *Transactions costs and duplication strategies*, Preprint (1993), Graduate School of Business, Stanford University.

[HZ]   J. E. Hodder and T. Zariphopoulou, *Transaction costs in portfolio and asset pricing model*, Applications of Stochastic Control (Q. Zhang and G. Yin, ed.), Volume in Honor of W. H. Fleming, Springer-Verlag (to appear).

[HN]   S. D. Hodges and A. Neuberger, *Optimal replication of contingent claims under transactions costs*, The Review of Futures Markets **8(2)** (1989), 222-239.

[HWhWi]   T. Hoggard, E. Whalley and P. Wilmott, *Hedging option portfolios in the presence of transaction costs*, Advances in Futures and Options Research **7** (1994), 21–35.

[H]   C. F. Huang, *An intertemporal general equilibrium asset pricing model: the case of diffusion information*, Econometrica **55** (1987), 117–142.

[Hub]   G. Huberman, *Dividend neutrality with transaction costs*, Journal of Business **63(1)**, Part (1990), S93–S106.

[IL]   H. Ishii and P.-L. Lions, *Viscosity solutions of fully nonlinear second-order elliptic partial differential equations*, Journal of Differential Equations **83** (1990), 26–78.

[JK]   E. Jouini and H. Kallal, *Martingales and arbitrage in securities markets with transaction costs*, Journal of Economic Theory **66** (1995), 178–197.

[KSa]   Y. M Kabanov and M. M. Safarian, *On Leland's strategy of option pricing with transactions costs*, Finance and Stochastics **1** (1997), 239–250.

[Kar]   I. Karatzas, *Lectures on the Mathematics of Finance*, CRM Monograph Series, AMS, (1997).

[KLSS]   I. Karatzas, J. Lehoczky, S. Sethi and S. Shreve, *Explicit solution of a general consumption/investment problem*, Mathematics of Operations Research **11** (1987), 261–294.

[KLS1]   I. Karatzas, J. P. Lehoczky and S. E. Shreve, *Existence and uniqueness of multi-agent equilibrium in a stochastic, dynamic consumption/investment model*, Mathematics of Operations Research **125** (1990), 80–128.

[KLS2]   I. Karatzas, J. P. Lehoczky and S. E. Shreve, *Equilbrium models with singular asset prices*, Mathematical Finance **15** (1991), 11–29.

[KR]   S. Kandel and S. A. Ross, *Some intertemporal models of portfolio selection with transaction costs*, Working paper, No. 107, Grad. School Bus., Center Res. Security Prices, University of Chicago, (1983).

[Kim]   K. P. Kimbrough, *Inflation, employment, and welfare in the presence of transactions costs*, Journal of Money, Credit, and Banking **18(2)** (1986), 127-140.

[KPT]   P.-F. Koehl, H. Pham and N. Touzi, *Option pricing under transaction costs: a martingale approach*, Preprint (1996), CREST, Paris.

[K1]   M. Kurz, *Equilibrium in a finite sequence of markets with transaction cost*, Econometrica **42** (1974), 1–20.

[K2]   M. Kurz, *Arrow-Debreu equilibrium of an exchange economy with transaction cost*, International Economic Review **15** (1974), 699–717.

[Ku]   S. Kusuoka, *Limit theorem on option replication cost with transaction costs*, Annals of Applied Probability **5** (1995), 198–221.

[La1]   P. Lam, *Irreversibility and consumer durables expenditures*, Journal of Monetary Economics **23(1)** (1989), 135–150.

[La2]   P. Lam, *Permanent income, liquidity, and adjustments of automobile stocks: Evidence from panel data*, Quarterly Journal of Economics **106** (1991), 203–230.

[LPS] D. Lamberton, H. Pham and M. Schweizer, *Local risk-minimization under transaction costs*, Mathematics of Operations Research **23** (1998), 585–612.

[Le] H. E. Leland, *Option pricing and replication with transaction costs*, Journal of Finance **40** (1985), 1283–1301.

[L-W] U. Leopold-Wildburger, *Equilibrium selection in a bargaining problem with transaction costs*, International Journal of Game Theory **14** (1985), 151–172.

[LSk] S. Levental and A. Skorohod, *On the possibility of hedging options in the presence of transaction costs*, Annals of Applied Probability **7** (1997), 410–443.

[Lev] H. Levy, *Equilibrium in an imperfect market: A constraint on the number of securities in the portfolio*, American Economic Review **68** (1978), 643–658.

[Li] P.-L. Lions, *Optimal control of diffusion processes and Hamilton-Jacobi-Bellman equations 1: The dynamic programming principle and applications; 2: Viscosity solutions and uniqueness*, Communications in Partial Differential Equations **8** (1983), 1101–1174; 1229–1276.

[LiSou] P.-L. Lions and P. E. Souganidis, *Convergence of MUSCL and filtered schemes for scalar conservation laws and Hamilton-Jacobi equations*, Numeritsche (1995) (to appear).

[LR] R. H. Litzenberger and J. Rolfo, *Arbitrage pricing, transaction costs and taxation of capital gains: A study of government bonds with the same maturity date*, Journal of Financial Economics **13(3)** (1984), 337–351.

[Lo] K. Lott, *Ein Verfahren zur Replikation von Optionen unter Transaktionskosten in stetiger Zeit*, Ph.D. Thesis, Universitat der Bundeswehr, Müchen, (1993).

[MC] M. J. P. Magill and G. Constantinides, *Portfolio selection with transaction costs*, Journal of Economic Theory **13** (1976), 245–263.

[M-C1] A. Mas-Colell, *The theory of general economic equilibrium: A differentiable approach*, Econometric Society Monograph, Cambridge University Press, (1985).

[M-C2] A. Mas-Colell, *The price equilibrium existence problem in topological vector lattices*, Econometrica **54** (1986), 1039–1053.

[May] J. Mayshar, *Transaction costs and the pricing of assets*, Journal of Finance **36(3)** (1981), 583–597.

[Ma] M. Mazaheri, *Derivative pricing with stochastic volatility via a utility method*, Preprint (1998).

[Me] F. Mercurio, *Options pricing and hedging in discrete time with transaction costs*, Mathematics of derivative securities, Newton Institute, Cambridge Univ. Press, Cambridge, (1997).

[MV] F. Mercurio and T. C. F. Vorst, *Option pricing and hedging in discrete time with transaction costs and incomplete markets*, M. A. H. Dempster and S. R. Pliska, eds, Mathematics of Derivative Securities, Cambridge University Press, (1997), pp. 190–215.

[M1] R. C. Merton, *Lifetime portfolio selection under uncertainty: the continuous-time case*, Journal of Economic Theory **3** (1969), 247–257.

[M2] R. C. Merton, *Optimum consumption and portfolio rules in a continuous-time model*, Journal of Economic Theory **3** (1971), 373–413.

[M3] R. C. Merton, *An intertemporal capital asset pricing model*, Econometrica **41** (1973), 867–887.

[M4] R. C. Merton, *Theory of rational option pricing*, Bell Journal of Economics and Management Science **4** (1973a), 141–183.

[M5] R. C. Merton, *Continuous Time Finance*, Basil Blackwell, Oxford, UK, (1990).

[MS] F. Milne and C. Smith, Jr., *Capital asset pricing with proportional transaction costs*, Journal of Financial and Quantitative Analysis **15(2)** (1980), 253–266.

[Mo] B. Mohamed, *Simulations of transaction costs and optimal rehedging*, Applied Mathematical Finace (1994) (to appear).

[MP] A. Morton and S. Pliska, *Optimal portfolio management with fixed transaction costs*, Mathematical Finance **5** (1995), 337–356.

[PS] N. Patel and M. G. Subrahmanyam, *A simple algorithm for optimal portfolio selection with fixed transaction costs*, Management Science **28** (1982), 303–314.

[PeRy] S. Perrakis and P. J. Ryan, *Option pricing bounds in discrete time*, Journal of Finance **39** (1984), 519–525.

[Pet] R. R. Pettit, *Taxes, transaction costs and the clientele effect of dividends*, Journal of Financial Economics **5(3)** (1977), 419–436.

[Pi] A. Pichler, *On transaction costs and HJB equations*, Preprint (1996).

[PSe] S. Pliska and M. Selby, *On a free boundary problem that arises in portfolio management*, Mathematical Models in Finance, Edited by D. Howison, F. P. Kelly and P. Wilmott, Chapman and Hall, The Royal Society, (1995).

[Po] G. A. Pogue, *An extension of the markowitz portfolio selection model to include variable transactions' costs, short sales, leverage policies and taxes*, Journal of Finance **25(5)** (1970), 1005-1027.

[Pr] J.-L. Prigent, *Incomplete markets: Convergence of options values under the minimal martingale measure*, Preprint (1995), University of Cergy-Pontoise.

[Re] H. Reisman, *Black and Scholes pricing and markets with transaction costs: an example*, Technion-Israel Institute of Technology, Haifa, Preprint, (1998).

[RT] E. Renault and N. Touzi, *Option hedging and implicit volatilities in a stochastic volatility model*, Mathematical Finance **6** (1996), 279–302.

[R1] R. Repullo, *The existence of equilibrium without free disposal in economies with transaction costs and incomplete markets*, International Economic Review **28** (1987), 275–290.

[R2] R. Repullo, *The core of an economy with transaction costs*, Review of Economic Studies **55** (1988), 447–458.

[Ri] P. H. Ritchken, *On option pricing bounds*, Journal of Finance **40** (1985), 1219–1233.

[Rit] L. S. Ritter, *On The fundamental role of transactions costs in monetary theory: Two illustrations from casino gambling*, Journal of Money, Credit, and Banking **10(4)** (1978), 522-528.

[RT] E. Rouy and A. Tourin, *A viscosity solutions approach to shape-from-shading*, SIAM Journal of Numerical Analysis (1995) (to appear).

[Ru] M. Rutkowski, *Optimality of replication in the CRR model with transaction costs*, Applied Mathematics (Warsaw) **25** (1998), 29–53.

[SWa] T. J. Sargent and Neil Wallace, *Market transaction costs, asset demand functions, and the relative potency of monetary and fiscal policy*, Journal of Money, Credit, and Banking **3(2), Part 2** (1971), 469–506.

[Sau] D. S. Saurman, *Transactions costs, foreign exchange demands, and the expected rates of change of exchange rates*, Journal of Money, Credit, and Banking **14(1)** (1982), 20-32.

[Sav1] T. R. Saving, *Transaction costs and the demand for money*, Journal of Money, Credit, and Banking **4(2)** (1972), 245–259.

[Sav2] T. R. Saving, *Transactions cost function and the Inventory-theoretic approach to money demand*, Journal of Money, Credit, and Banking **8(3)** (1976), 339-345.

[Scha]   M. Schäl, *On quadratic cost criteria for option hedging*, Mathematics of Operations Research **19** (1994), 121–131.

[Schn]   J. A. Schnabel, *Variable transactions costs, the capital asset pricing model and the corporate dividend decision: A comment*, Journal of Business, Finance and Accounting **8(4)** (1982), 559-562.

[Sch]   M. Schroder, *Optimal portfolio selection with fixed transaction costs*, Preprint (1993).

[Schu]   P. Schultz, *Transaction costs and the small firm effect: A comment*, Journal of Financial Economics **12(1)** (1983), 81–88.

[Schw]   M. Schweizer, *Hedging of options in a general semimartingale model*, Diss. ETH Zürich **8615** (1988).

[Sh]   Q. Shen, *Bid-ask prices for call options with transaction costs*, Working paper, University of Pennsylvania (1990).

[SK]   H. Shirakawa and H. Konno, *Pricing of options under the proportional transaction costs*, Preprint, Tokyo Institute of Technology, (1996).

[SS]   S. E. Shreve and H. M. Soner, *Optimal investment and consumption with transaction costs*, Annals of Applied Probability **4(3)** (1994), 206–236.

[Sin]   T. Sinha, *The effects of survival probabilities, transactions costs and the attitude towards risk on the demand for annuities*, Journal of Risk and Insurance **53(2)** (1986), 301-307.

[Sko]   G. Skogh, *The transactions costs theory of insurance: Contracting impediments and costs*, Journal of Risk and Insurance **56(4)** (1989), 726-732.

[Son]   H. M. Soner, *Optimal control with state space constraints*, SIAM Journal on Control and Optimization **24** (1986), 552–562, 1110–1122.

[SSC]   H. M. Soner, S. Shreve and J. Cvitanic, *There is no nontrivial hedging portfolio for option pricing with transaction costs*, Annals of Applied Probability **5(2)** (1995), 327–355.

[Sou]   P. E. Souganidis, *Convergence of approximation schemes for viscosity solutions of Hamilton-Jacobi equations*, Journal of Differential Equations **57** (1985), 15–29.

[SW]   H. R. Stoll and Robert E. Whaley, *Transaction costs and the small firm effect*, Journal of Financial Economics **12(1)** (1983), 57–80.

[Su]   A. Sulem, *Dynamic optimization for a mixed portfolio with transaction costs*, Numerical methods in finance, Newton Institute, Cambridge Univ. Press, Cambridge, (1997).

[Tak]   S. Takagi, *Transactions costs and the term structure of interest rates in the OTC bond market in Japan*, Journal of Money, Credit, and Banking **19(4)** (1987), 515-527.

[TKA]   M. Taksar, M. J. Klass and D. Assaf, *A diffusion model for optimal portfolio selection in the presence of brokerage fees*, Mathematics of Operations Research **13** (1988), 277–294.

[Th1]   M. Theobald, *A note on variable transactions costs, the capital asset pricing model and the corporate dividend decision*, Journal of Business, Finance and Accounting **6(1)** (1979), 9-16.

[Th2]   M. Theobald, *Variable transactions costs, the capital asset pricing model and the corporate dividend decision: A reply*, Journal of Business, Finance and Accounting **8(4)** (1982), 563-564.

[TiZ]   C. Tiu and T. Zariphopoulou, *Level curves in transaction costs models*, Preprint (1998).

[To]   K. B. Toft, *On the mean-variance tradeoff in option replication with transactions costs*, Journal of Financial and Quantitative Analysis **31** (1996), 233–263.

[Tou]   A. Tourin, *Thèse de Doctorat*, Université Paris IX-Dauphine, Paris, (1992).

[TZ1] A. Tourin and T. Zariphopoulou, *Numerical schemes for investment models with singular transactions*, Computational Economics **7** (1994), 287–307.

[TZ2] A. Tourin and T. Zariphopoulou, *Portfolio selection with transactions costs*, Progress in Probability **36** (1995), 385–391.

[TZ3] A. Tourin and T. Zariphopoulou, *Viscosity solutions and numerical schemes for investment/ consumption models with transaction costs*, Numerical methods in finance, Newton Institute, Cambridge Univ. Press, Cambridge, (1997), pp. 245–269.

[TZ4] A. Tourin and T. Zariphopoulou, *Super-replicating strategies with probability less than one in the presence of transaction costs*, Preprint (1998).

[UC] J. Umbeck and R. E. Chatfield, *The structure of contracts and transaction costs*, Part 1, Journal of Money, Credit, and Banking **14(4)** (1982), 511–516.

[VZ] J. L. Vila and T. Zariphopoulou, *Optimal consumption and portfolio choice with borrowing constraints*, Journal of Economic Theory **7** (1997), 402–431.

[WhWi1] A. E. Whalley and P. Wilmott, *Hedge with an edge*, Risk Magazine (October 1994).

[WhWi2] A. E. Whalley and P. Wilmott, *A review of key results in the modeling of discrete hedging and transaction costs*, Frontiers in Derivatives, Ed. Konishi and Dattatreya, (1996).

[WhWi3] A. E. Whalley and P. Wilmott, *Optimal hedging of options with small but arbitrary transaction cost structure*, Preprint (1997).

[WhWi4] A. E. Whalley and P. Wilmott, *An asymptotic analysis of the Davis, Panas and Zariphopoulou model for option pricing with transaction costs*, Mathematical Finance **7** (1997), 307–324.

[Wil] S. Williamson, *Transactions costs, inflation, and the variety of intermediation services*, Journal of Money, Credit, and Banking **19(4)** (1987), 484–498..

[Wi] P. Wilmott, *Discrete charms*, Risk (March 1994).

[WC] P. N. Wilson and R. I. Cummin, *Saving management and transaction costs*, Financial Analysis Journal **33(2)** (1977), 58–62.

[WT] D. Wrightsman and J. Terninko, *On the measurement of opportunity cost in transactions demand models*, Journal of Finance **26(4)** (1971), 947–950.

[Z1] T. Zariphopoulou, *Investment-consumption models with constraints*, Ph.D. Thesis, Brown University, (1989).

[Z2] T. Zariphopoulou, *Investment/consumption model with transaction costs and markov-chains parameters*, SIAM Journal on Control and Optimization **30** (1992), 613–636.

[Z3] T. Zariphopoulou, *Investment and consumption models with constraints*, SIAM Journal on Control and Optimization **32** (1994), 59–84.

[Zh] H. Zhu, *Characterization of variational inequalities in singular control*, Ph.D. Thesis, Brown University, Providence, RI, (1986).

Department of Mathematics and School of Business, University of Wisconsin–Madison, Madison, Wisconsin 53706

Current address: Department of Mathematics and School of Business, University of Wisconsin–Madison, Madison, Wisconsin 53706

E-mail address: `zariphop@math.wisc.edu`

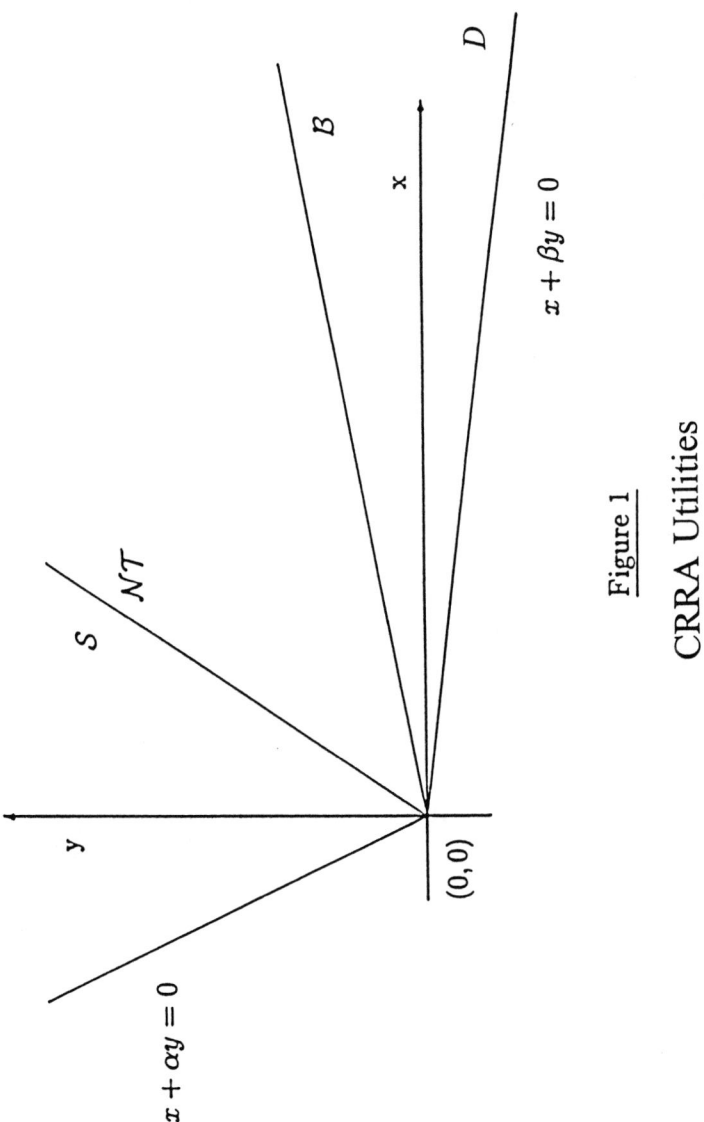

Figure 1
CRRA Utilities

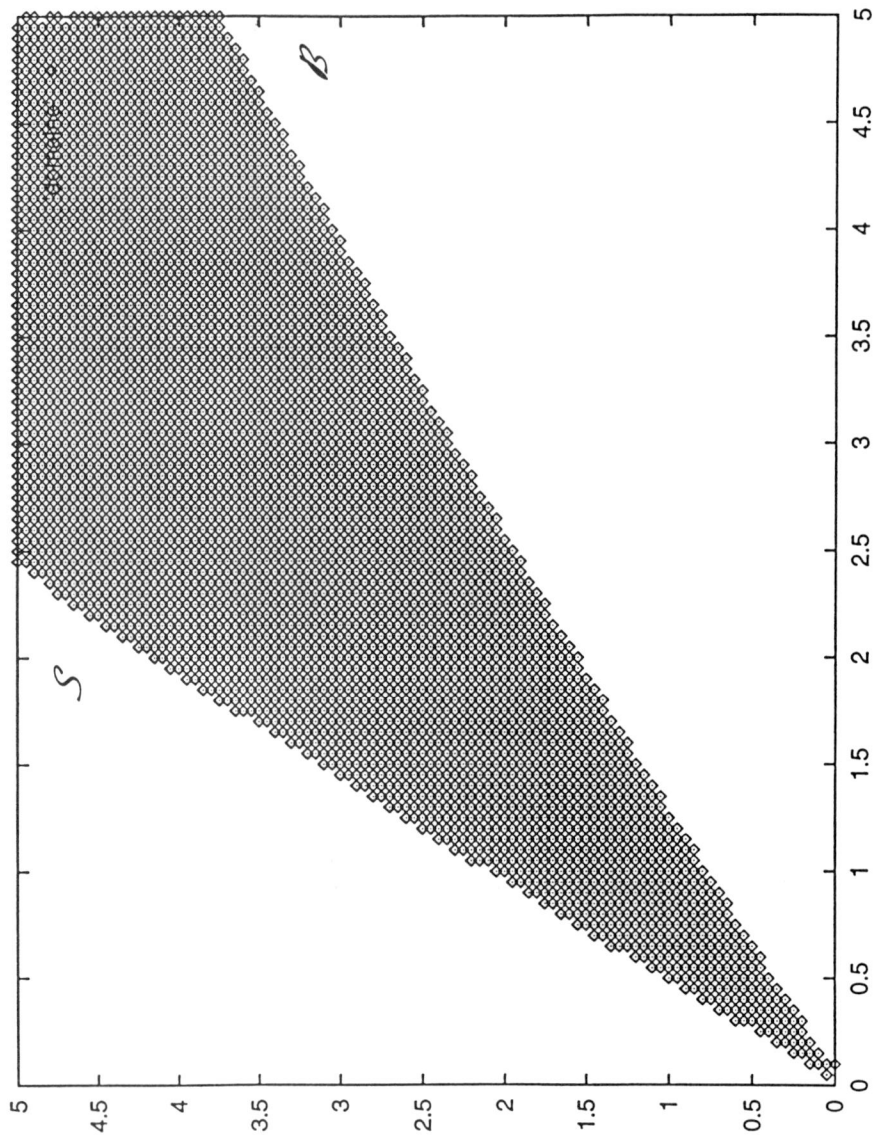

Figure 2

$U(c) = 2\sqrt{c}$

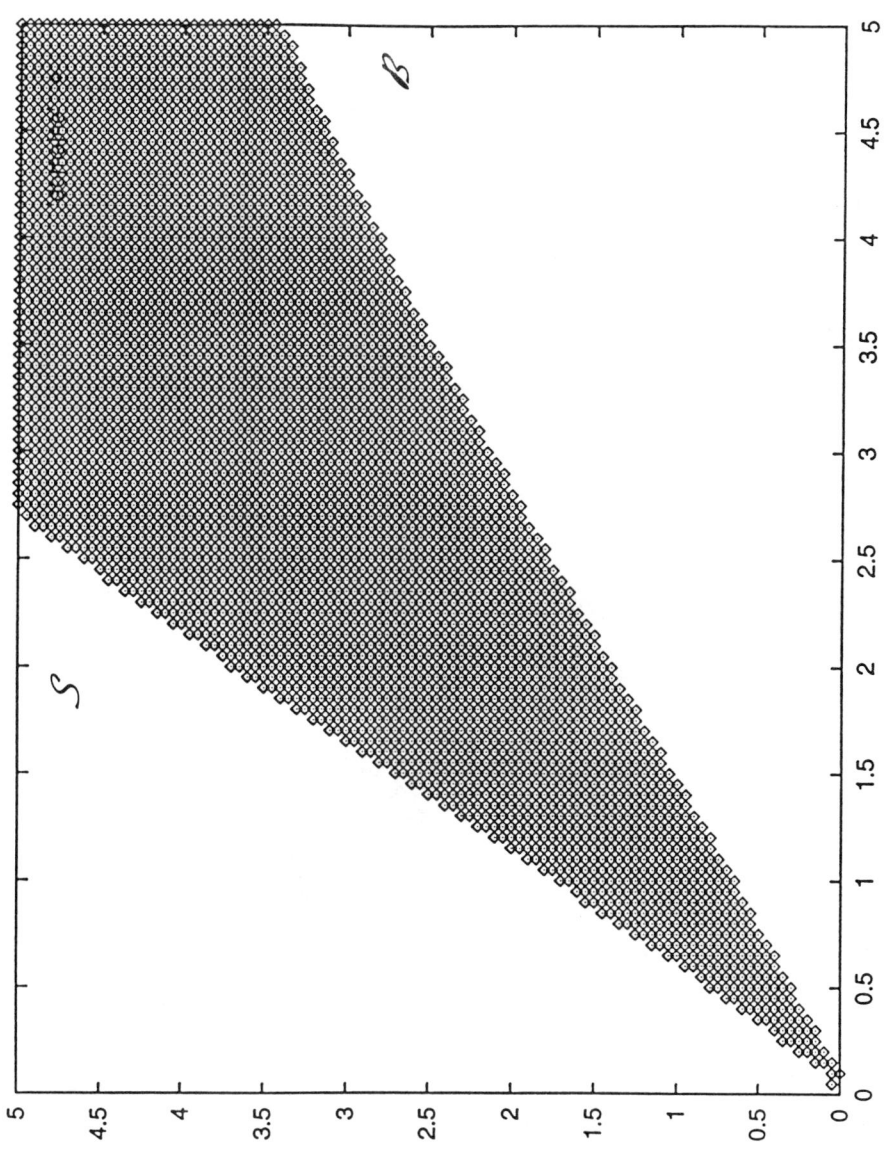

Figure 3

$$U(c) = 3c^{1/3} + \frac{3}{2} c^{2/3}$$

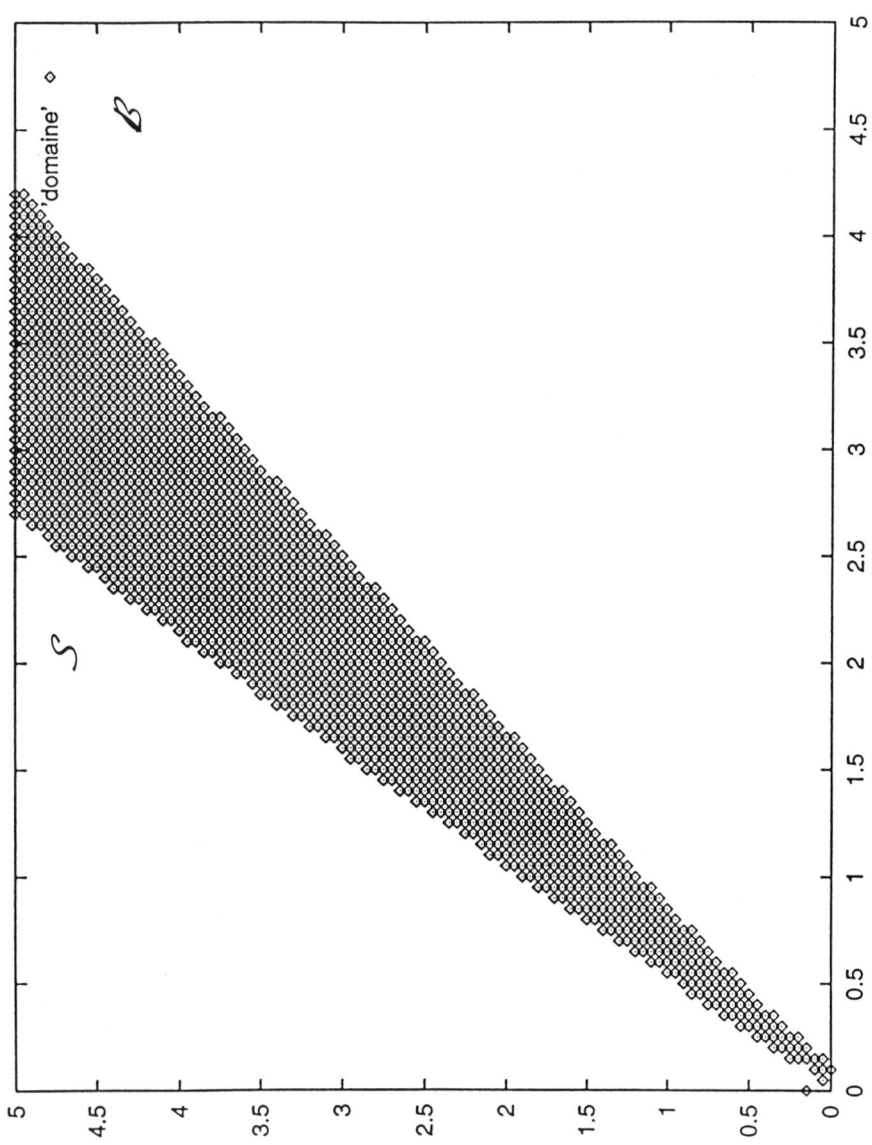

Figure 4

$$U(c) = 100 - \frac{1}{\sqrt{c}}$$

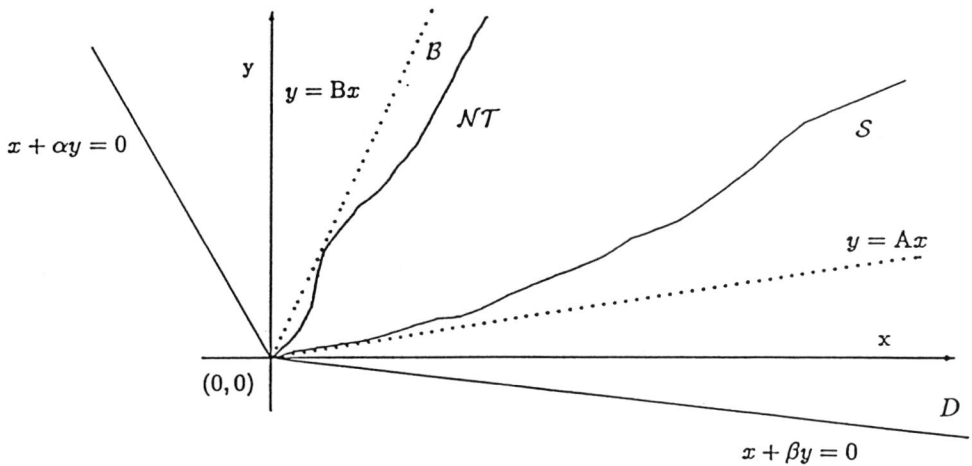

Figure 5

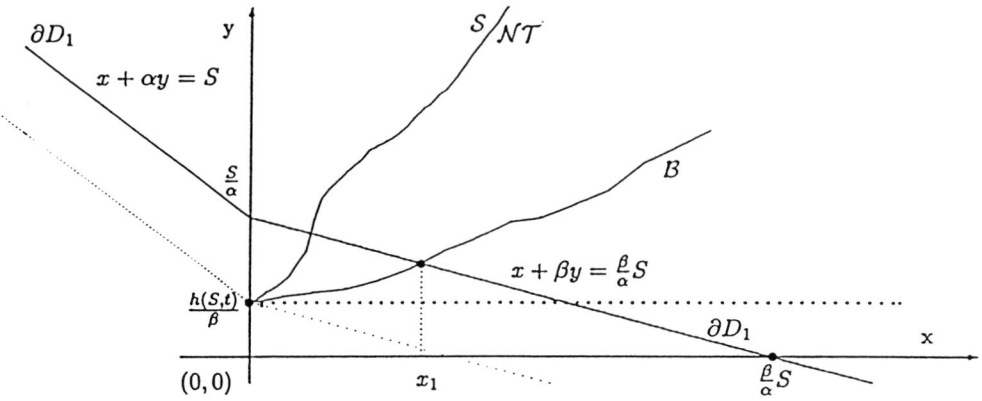

Figure 6

Index

β, 7, 22, 23
a-admissible, 52
w-admissible, 59
"buy region, 117
"no-trading region, 117
"sell region, 117
"static" options hedge, 44

admissible, 52
American, 29
Ansel-Stricker and Jacka, 56
arbitrage opportunity, 31
Arbitrage Pricing Theory, 35
ARCH-GARCH, 42

Bessel process, 56, 73
Bishop-Phelps theorem, 57
Black and Scholes valuation formula, 133
Black-Scholes, 31
Black-Scholes formula, 31
bounds to reservation prices, 145
Brownian motion, 9, 11–14, 16, 73
Brownian motions, 18
buy-and-hold strategy, 52

Capital Asset Pricing Model, 1
capital asset pricing model, 2
Capital Asset Pricing Theorem, 7, 22
Central Limit Theorem, 12
change of measure, 55
change of numéraire, 56
closed-form approximations, 67
conditional volatility, 42
conditionally heteroskedastic models, 42
confidence interval, 42
consistency, 123
consistent scheme, 123
Constant Relative Risk Aversion utilities, 116
constrained viscosity solutions, 110
contingent claims, 33
continuous-time, 67
convex combinations, 57
convex cone, 57
covariance matrix, 27
Cox, Ingersoll, and Ross, 73

Dalang-Morton-Willinger theorem, 58
degenerate elliptic, 110
Delta, 37
Derivative pricing, 69
derivatives, 29
diffusion, 67
dominating strategy, 43
Doob-Meyer decomposition, 55
double-well, 86
doubling strategies, 52, 59
dynamic hedging, 25, 35
Dynamic Programming Principle, 109

efficient frontier, 4, 6–8
efficient portfolios, 1
Emery and Chou, 58
enhanced volatility, 147
equivalent local martingale measure, 57
equivalent martingale measure, 51, 53, 62
European, 29
European call, 133
exercise price, 29
exotic options, 33
expiration date, 29
exponential local martingale, 55
exponential utilities, 137

fixed transaction costs, 130
foreign currency, 56
forward rates, 63
fractional Brownian motion, 57
Fundamental Theorem of Asset Pricing, 51

general admissible integrands, 53
general risk functionals, 146
geometric Brownian motion, 2, 17
Girsanov's Theorem, 73

Hamilton-Jacobi-Bellman equation, 19, 21, 110
hedging, 51
hedging error, 147
Hermite expansion, 72
Ho and Lee, 65
homotheticity properties, 116

imperfect hedging strategies, 147
imperfectly replicating policies, 132

implied volatility, 36
instantaneous covariance, 22
insurance models, 58
interest rate models, 67
intermediate trading, 137
Itô's formula, 15–18, 20, 30

Kreps, 53
Kullback-Leibler relative entropy distance, 46

Lagrangian uncertain volatility model, 45
Leland's approach, 148
Leland's enhanced volatility, 148
local martingale, 54
local quadratic loss criterion, 151
local times, 117
locally bounded semi-martingales, 54
long-run expected growth rate, 130

market portfolio, 6–8, 21
markets with frictions, 131
Markov process, 68
Markov property, 10–12
Martingale, 12
martingale, 10, 11, 14
martingale measure, 36
martingale theory, 51
mathematical finance, 51
maximal element, 55
maximum-likelihood, 68
mean reversion, 86
mean-variance analysis, 1–3
mean-variance optimization, 28
method of fractional steps, 124
minimal super-replicating strategies, 136
minimization of the "local risk", 151
modeling financial risk, 25
money market account, 62
monotone scheme, 123
monotonicity, 123
mutual fund, 2, 22

no arbitrage property (NA), 53
No Free Lunch (NFL), 53
No Free Lunch with Vanishing Risk Property (NFLVR), 53
no trading region, 129
non-arbitrage, 51

obstacle problem, 33
option hedge-ratios, 44
option replication, 35
option spreads, 41
options, 29
Ornstein-Uhlenbeck, 74

paradoxical situation, 56
perfectly replicating (hedging) strategies, 134

physical measure, 63
portfolio optimization, 18
pricing of contingent claims, 64
proportional transaction costs, 107
pure discount bound, 61
put-call parity, 37

quadratic variation, 10, 11, 13, 14, 16

random walk, 9–11
reflecting diffusion, 117
relative entropy, 46
representing measure, 51
reservation write price, 142
return, 26
risk, 26
risk neutral measure, 51
risk premia, 22
risk premium, 7, 8, 22
risk-neutral probability, 35
risk-neutral probability measures, 25

semi-martingale, 52
separation theorem, 7, 22
sigma martingale measure, 59
sigma-martingale, 58
skew, 42
Skorohod problem, 121
small transaction costs, 130, 151
smile, 42
spot interest rate, 62
spot yields, 63
stability, 123
stable scheme, 123
static mean-variance, 1
stochastic calculus, 1, 2, 9, 14, 18
stochastic differential equation, 18, 20, 22
stochastic differential equations, 67
stochastic dominance, 137, 138
stochastic integral, 14
stochastic integration, 51
stochastic model, 30
stock index, 32
strict local martingale, 55
subjective discount rate, 108
super-replicating strategies, 132, 135

term structure, 62
the utility maximization theory, 137
time splitting method, 124
time-decay, 39
totally inaccessible stopping times, 58
transaction costs, 38
transaction costs are "small", 133
transition function, 68
two-fund theorem, 1

U.S. Treasury Strips, 61
unbounded claims, 58
unbounded jumps, 58

uncertain volatility models, 41
uniformly integrable martingales, 57
utility, 2, 19, 21, 22
utility function, 108

valuation of contingent claims under uncertainty, 25
value line, 6, 8
Vasicek, 65
Vasicek's Model, 74
Vega, 40
viscosity solutions, 110
viscosity subsolution, 110
viscosity supersolution of (3.1), 110
volatility, 17, 18
volatility uncertainty beliefs, 45

weak* closure, 53
weight function, 59
worst-case scenario, 43
write price, 142

yield, 26

Selected Titles in This Series

(Continued from the front of this publication)

29 **R. A. DeMillo, G. I. Davida, D. P. Dobkin, M. A. Harrison, and R. J. Lipton,** Applied cryptology, cryptographic protocols, and computer security models (San Francisco, California, January 1981)

28 **R. Gnanadesikan, Editor,** Statistical data analysis (Toronto, Ontario, August 1982)

27 **L. A. Shepp, Editor,** Computed tomography (Cincinnati, Ohio, January 1982)

26 **S. A. Burr, Editor,** The mathematics of networks (Pittsburgh, Pennsylvania, August 1981)

25 **S. I. Gass, Editor,** Operations research: mathematics and models (Duluth, Minnesota, August 1979)

24 **W. F. Lucas, Editor,** Game theory and its applications (Biloxi, Mississippi, January 1979)

23 **R. V. Hogg, Editor,** Modern statistics: Methods and applications (San Antonio, Texas, January 1980)

22 **G. H. Golub and J. Oliger, Editors,** Numerical analysis (Atlanta, Georgia, January 1978)

21 **P. D. Lax, Editor,** Mathematical aspects of production and distribution of energy (San Antonio, Texas, January 1976)

20 **J. P. LaSalle, Editor,** The influence of computing on mathematical research and education (University of Montana, August 1973)

19 **J. T. Schwartz, Editor,** Mathematical aspects of computer science (New York City, April 1966)

18 **H. Grad, Editor,** Magneto-fluid and plasma dynamics (New York City, April 1965)

17 **R. Finn, Editor,** Applications of nonlinear partial differential equations in mathematical physics (New York City, April 1964)

16 **R. Bellman, Editor,** Stochastic processes in mathematical physics and engineering (New York City, April 1963)

15 **N. C. Metropolis, A. H. Taub, J. Todd, and C. B. Tompkins, Editors,** Experimental arithmetic, high speed computing, and mathematics (Atlantic City and Chicago, April 1962)

14 **R. Bellman, Editor,** Mathematical problems in the biological sciences (New York City, April 1961)

13 **R. Bellman, G. Birkhoff, and C. C. Lin, Editors,** Hydrodynamic instability (New York City, April 1960)

12 **R. Jakobson, Editor,** Structure of language and its mathematical aspects (New York City, April 1960)

11 **G. Birkhoff and E. P. Wigner, Editors,** Nuclear reactor theory (New York City, April 1959)

10 **R. Bellman and M. Hall, Jr., Editors,** Combinatorial analysis (New York University, April 1957)

9 **G. Birkhoff and R. E. Langer, Editors,** Orbit theory (Columbia University, April 1958)

8 **L. M. Graves, Editor,** Calculus of variations and its applications (University of Chicago, April 1956)

7 **L. A. MacColl, Editor,** Applied probability (Polytechnic Institute of Brooklyn, April 1955)

6 **J. H. Curtiss, Editor,** Numerical analysis (Santa Monica City College, August 1953)

For a complete list of titles in this series, visit the
AMS Bookstore at www.ams.org/bookstore/.

ISBN 0-8218-0751-X

Synopsis of Orthopaedics

Synopsis of Orthopaedics

Howard S. An, M.D.
Assistant Professor, Director of Reconstructive Spine Surgery
Department of Orthopaedic Surgery
The Medical College of Wisconsin
Milwaukee, Wisconsin

1992
Thieme Medical Publishers, Inc., New York
Georg Thieme Verlag, Stuttgart • New York

Thieme Medical Publishers, Inc.
381 Park Avenue South
New York, New York 10016

Synopsis of Orthopaedics
Howard S. An, M.D.

Library of Congress Cataloging-in-Publication Data
An, Howard S.
    Synopsis of orthopaedics / Howard S. An.
        p.   cm.
    Includes bibliographical references and index.
    ISBN 0-86577-383-1
    1. Orthopedics. I. Title.
    [DNLM: 1. Orthopedics. WE 168 A531s]
RD731.A557   1991
617.3 — dc20
DNLM/DLC
for Library of Congress   91-530
                                  CIP

Copyright © 1992 by Thieme Medical Publishers, Inc. This book, including all parts thereof, is legally protected by copyright. Any use, exploitation or commercialization outside the narrow limits set by copyright legislation, without the publisher's consent, is illegal and liable to prosecution. This applies in particular to photostat reproduction, copying, mimeographing or duplication of any kind, translating, preparation of microfilms, and electronic data processing and storage.

Important note: Medicine is an ever-changing science. Research and clinical experience are continually broadening our knowledge, in particular our knowledge of proper treatment and drug therapy. Insofar as this book mentions any dosage or application, readers may rest assured that the authors, editors, and publishers have made every effort to ensure that such references are strictly in accordance with the state of knowledge at the time of production of the book. Nevertheless, every user is requested to carefully examine the manufacturers' leaflets accompanying each drug to check on his own responsibility whether the dosage schedules recommended therein or the contraindications stated by the manufacturers differ from the statements made in the present book. Such examination is particularly important with drugs that are either rarely used or have been newly released on the market.

Some of the product names, patents, and registered designs referred to in this book are in fact registered trademarks or proprietary names even though specific reference to this fact is not always made in the text. Therefore, the appearance of a name without designation as proprietary is not to be construed as a representation by the publisher that it is in the public domain.

Printed in the United States of America.

5 4 3 2 1

TMP ISBN 0-86577-383-1
GTV ISBN 3-13-764701-0

Dedicated to my Parents

Contents

Contributors ix
Foreword xi
Preface xiii

Section 1: Anatomy

Howard S. An, Anthony Frogameni
1. Shoulder 3
2. Arm 7
3. Elbow 11
4. Forearm 16
5. Wrist and Hand 20
6. Spine 27
7. Hip 35
8. Thigh 39
9. Knee 42
10. Leg 47
11. Foot and Ankle 50

Section 2: Basic Sciences and Pathology

Howard S. An, Donald A. Hackbarth
12. Bone: Structure and Function 59
13. Metabolic Bone Diseases 63
14. Fracture Healing and Nonunion 70
15. Osteonecrosis, Osteochondroses, and Osteochondritis Dissecans 74
16. Bone Grafting 79
17. Articular Cartilage and Arthritis and Synovial Diseases 82
18. Muscle, Nerve, Tendon, Ligament, and Collagen 93
19. Orthopaedic Infections 98
20. Tumors 109
21. Genetics 141

Section 3: Pediatric Orthopaedics

Howard S. An, John G. Thometz
22. Foot Problems 145
23. Angular and Torsional Deformities of Lower Extremities in Children 154
24. Congenital Hip Dislocation 158
25. Legg-Calvé-Perthes Disease (Coxa Plana) 163
26. Slipped Capital Femoral Epiphysis 167
27. Neuromuscular Problems 170
28. Congenital Disorders, Skeletal Dysplasias, and Connective Tissue Disorders 181
29. Miscellaneous Pediatric Disorders 193
30. Pediatric Fractures 198

Section 4: Adult Orthopaedics

Howard S. An, James B. Stiehl, Kevin P. Black, Michael J. Shereff, John S. Gould
31. Shoulder Problems 217
32. Elbow Problems 231
33. Hip Problems 238
34. Knee Problems 246
35. Sports Injuries of the Lower Extremities 255
36. Foot and Ankle Problems 268

Section 5: Orthopaedic Trauma

Howard S. An, Michael J. Brennan
37. Principles of Orthopaedic Trauma 283

38. Fractures of the Radius and Ulna   287
39. Fractures and Dislocations of the Elbow   290
40. Fractures of the Humeral Shaft   295
41. Fractures and Dislocations of the Shoulder   298
42. Fractures of the Pelvis and Acetabulum   302
43. Fractures and Dislocations of the Hip   310
44. Fractures of the Shaft of the Femur   316
45. Fractures and Dislocations of the Knee   318
46. Fractures of the Tibia   322
47. Fractures and Dislocations of the Ankle and Foot   327

Section 6: Hand

Howard S. An, Douglas P. Hanel

48. Fingertip and Soft Tissue Coverage of the Hand   339
49. Tendon Injuries   345
50. Fractures and Dislocations of the Hand   352
51. Replantation   357
52. Wrist Injuries and Disorders   359
53. Nerve Injuries and Compression Neuropathies   366
54. Tendon Transfers of the Hand   372
55. Tenosynovitis, Osteoarthritis, and Rheumatoid Arthritis   376
56. Contractures and Reflex Sympathetic Dystrophy   384
57. Congenital Anomalies of the Hand   391
58. Tumors of the Hand and Amputation Surgery   396

Section 7: Spine

Howard S. An, J. Michael Simpson

59. Congenital and Developmental Anomalies of the Cervical Spine   403
60. Scoliosis   408
61. Kyphosis   417
62. Spondylolysis and Spondylolisthesis   423
63. Cervical Disc Disease   428
64. Lumbar Disc Disease and Spinal Stenosis   435
65. Spinal Trauma   445
66. Tumors of the Spine   460
67. Arthritis of the Spine (Rheumatoid Arthritis and Seronegative Spondylitis)   467

Section 8: Biomechanics and Biomaterials

Howard S. An, Jeffrey P. Schwab, David Skrade

68. Essential Concepts   473
69. Mechanics of Structures   482
70. Biomaterials   485
71. Biologic Tissues and Functional Biomechanics   491

Section 9: Orthopaedic Rehabilitation

Kenneth M. Morrison, Howard S. An

72. Lower Limb Amputation   499
73. Lower Limb Prosthetics   503
74. Lower Limb Orthotics in Adults   509
75. Lower Limb Prosthetics and Orthotics in Children   512
76. Upper Limb Amputation Surgery   514
77. Upper Limb Prosthetics   516
78. Upper Limb Orthotics   519
79. Spinal Orthoses   521
80. Sports Orthoses   525

Index   527

Contributors

Howard S. An, M.D.
Assistant Professor, Director of
 Reconstructive Spine Surgery
Department of Orthopaedic Surgery
The Medical College of Wisconsin
Milwaukee, Wisconsin

Kevin P. Black, M.D.
Assistant Professor, Director of Sports
 Medicine
Department of Orthopaedic Surgery
The Medical College of Wisconsin
Milwaukee, Wisconsin

Michael J. Brennan, M.D.
Assistant Professor, Director of
 Orthopaedic Trauma
Department of Orthopaedic Surgery
The Medical College of Wisconsin
Milwaukee, Wisconsin

Anthony Frogameni, M.D.
Orthopaedic Resident
Department of Orthopaedic Surgery
The Medical College of Ohio
Toledo, Ohio

John S. Gould, M.D.
Professor and Chairman
Department of Orthopaedic Surgery
The Medical College of Wisconsin
Milwaukee, Wisconsin

Donald A. Hackbarth, M.D.
Assistant Professor, Director of
 Orthopaedic Oncology
Department of Orthopaedic Surgery
The Medical College of Wisconsin
Milwaukee, Wisconsin

Douglas P. Hanel, M.D.
Assistant Professor, Director of Hand and
 Microsurgery
Department of Orthopaedic Surgery
The Medical College of Wisconsin
Milwaukee, Wisconsin

Kenneth Morrison, M.D.
Assistant Professor, Department of
 Orthopaedics
Michigan State University
East Lansing, MI

J. Michael Simpson, M.D.
Spine Fellow
Department of Orthopaedic Surgery
Thomas Jefferson University and
 Rothman's Institute
Philadelphia, PA

Michael J. Shereff, M.D.
Associate Professor, Director of Foot and
 Ankle Service
Department of Orthopaedic Surgery
The Medical College of Wisconsin
Milwaukee, Wisconsin

Jeffrey P. Schwab, M.D.
Associate Professor, Vice-chairman,
 Director of Orthopaedic Education
Department of Orthopaedic Surgery
The Medical College of Wisconsin
Milwaukee, Wisconsin

David Skrade, M.S.
Biomedical Engineer
Department of Orthopaedic Surgery
Orthopaedic Biomechanical Laboratory
The Medical College of Wisconsin
Milwaukee, Wisconsin

James B. Stiehl, M.D.
Assistant Professor, Director of Adult
　Reconstructive Joint Surgery
Department of Orthopaedic Surgery
The Medical College of Wisconsin
Milwaukee, Wisconsin

John G. Thometz, M.D.
Assistant Professor, Director of Pediatric
　Orthopaedics
Department of Orthopaedic Surgery
The Children's Hospital of Wisconsin
The Medical College of Wisconsin
Milwaukee, Wisconsin

Foreword

Perhaps the quintessential element of success for the contemporary orthopaedic surgeon is no longer intellectual brilliance or digital dexterity but rather the efficient handling and assimilation of new data. With the recent explosive growth of medical and orthopaedic literature, it is becoming increasingly difficult for the orthopaedic surgeon to efficiently distill and absorb the monumental amount of new information available in the scientific literature. It is, therefore, critical that monographs such as Dr. An's *Synopsis of Orthopaedics* evolve and be available for a global review of orthopaedic principles.

Dr. An has called upon a scholarly and capable panel of chapter authors who crystallize and review in a lucid and timely fashion the essential knowledge in each of the main specialty areas within orthopaedic surgery. Beginning with a careful foundation of basic science information focused on anatomy and pathology, Dr. An then proceeds to apply this information and other clinical data to the major contemporary issues that must be mastered in the clinical realm by today's orthopaedic practitioner.

Students, residents, and young orthopaedic surgeons preparing for their board examinations will find this volume an invaluable asset to their learning process. It is timely, carefully prepared, and contains the core knowledge of today's orthopaedic world. It should find a place on every orthopaedic surgeon's bookshelf.

Richard H. Rothman, M.D., Ph.D.
James Edwards Professor and
Chairman, Department of Orthopaedic Surgery
Thomas Jefferson University

Preface

Synopsis of Orthopaedics outlines the scientific data and principles of orthopaedic surgery that are essential to the successful management of orthopaedic patients. Great advances in the field of orthopaedic surgery during the last several years have made it increasingly difficult for the orthopaedic surgeon or resident to keep up with the literature. In this book, essential facts and current advances in orthopaedics are distilled so that the reader can review the materials efficiently in a minimal amount of time. This book is particularly valuable to those who are preparing for boards or in-training examinations.

This book is also useful for medical students, family practice physicians, internists, rheumatologists, physical medicine physicians, physical therapists, and emergency physicians as a reference source, since all aspects of orthopaedics are covered.

The text is organized in nine sections, which represent the various subspecialties of orthopaedic surgery. Each section is subdivided into individual chapters, each of which has been carefully edited by subspecialists to give the most current information.

I wish to extend thanks to my colleagues who edited these chapters. This text could not have been completed without their contributions. I extend great thanks to my teachers, Dr. W. Thomas Jackson, Dr. Richard H. Rothman, and Dr. Jerome M. Cotler, who have given me knowledge and encouragement throughout. Special thanks go to Dr. John S. Gould, who gave me an opportunity to pursue my academic career at the Medical College of Wisconsin and who greatly encouraged me to finish this project. I also thank Kandy Kettling for her professional help on figures and line drawings. Finally, I express my deep appreciation to my wife for her understanding and encouragement during the 5 years that I spent writing this book.

Howard S. An, M.D.

Synopsis of Orthopaedics

SECTION 1: ANATOMY

Howard S. An
Anthony Frogameni

1. Shoulder
2. Arm
3. Elbow
4. Forearm
5. Wrist and Hand
6. Spine
7. Hip
8. Thigh
9. Knee
10. Leg
11. Foot and Ankle

1
Shoulder

I. Bony

A. Clavicle
1. Ossification: two centers, 5th to 6th fetal week (first bone to ossify). Acromial epiphysis unites during 20th year. Sternal epiphysis unites during 25th year
2. Articulations
   a. Sternoclavicular (synovial): articular disc, anterior and posterior ligaments
   b. Costoclavicular (fibrous)
   c. Acromioclavicular (synovial): articular disc, weak capsule
   d. Coracoclavicular (fibrous): trapezoid, conoid ligaments

B. Scapula
1. Ossification: seven centers, beginning 8th fetal week and unites during 14th to 20th year
2. Posterior surface is divided by spine into supraspinous and inferior spinous fossae
3. Spine of scapula ends in the flattened acromion, and the great notch of scapula joins the infraspinous and supraspinous fossae
4. Scapular notch is in the superior border
5. Anterior surface of subscapular fossa is concave

C. Humerus
1. Ossification: eight centers, 8th fetal week
2. Parts (proximal): head, anatomic neck, surgical neck, greater and lesser tuberosities, bicipital groove

II. Joint

A. Type: ball and socket
B. Motion: flexion, extension, abduction, adduction, internal rotation, external rotation, and circumduction
C. Ligaments
1. Articular capsule: edge of glenoid to anatomic neck
2. Glenohumeral: superior, middle, inferior
3. Coracohumeral: coracoid to greater tuberosity
4. Transverse humeral: bridges intertubercular sulcus
5. Glenoid labrum: fibrocartilage attached to edges of glenoid fossa to deepen it and continuous with long head of biceps

III. Muscles

A. Flexors
1. Pectoralis major: from medial clavicle and lateral sternum to crest of greater tubercle of humerus. Innervated by medial and lateral pectoral nerves
2. Deltoid (anterior): from anterior clavicle and lateral acromion to deltoid tubercle of humerus. Innervated by axillary nerve
3. Coracobrachialis: from coracoid process to middle of humeral shaft. Innervated by musculocutaneous nerve

B. Extensors
1. Latissimus dorsi: from spines T6 to T12 and iliac crest to intertubercular groove of humerus. Innervated by thoracodorsal nerve
2. Teres major: from dorsal inferior scapula to lesser tubercle of humerus. Innervated by lower subscapular nerve
3. Deltoid (posterior)
4. Triceps (long head): from infraglenoid tubercle to olecranon. Innervated by radial nerve

C. Abductors
1. Deltoid
2. Supraspinatus: from medial supraspinatous fossa to greater tuberosity of

humerus. Innervated by suprascapular nerve
D. Adductors
   1. Pectoralis major
   2. Latissimus dorsi
   3. Teres major
   4. Subscapularis: from medial subscapular fossa to lesser tuberosity of humerus. Innervated by upper and lower subscapular nerves
   5. Triceps (long head)
E. Internal Rotators
   1. Pectoralis major
   2. Latissimus dorsi
   3. Teres major
   4. Subscapularis
   5. Deltoid
F. External rotators
   1. Infraspinatus: from medial infraspinatous fossa to greater tuberosity of humerus. Innervated by suprascapular nerve
   2. Teres minor: from upper dorsal scapular to greater tuberosity of humerus. Innervated by axillary nerve
   3. Deltoid

IV. Anatomy of the Brachial Plexus (Fig 1-1)
A. Anterior rami of the spinal nerves from C5 to T1. (spinal nerves are bound to the transverse processes by prevertebral fascia)
B. Trunks: between scalene muscles
   1. Upper trunk (C5, C6)
   2. Middle trunk (C7)
   3. Lower trunk (C8, T1)
C. Prefixed (C4 contribution) or postfixed (T2 contribution)
D. Cords: middle third of the clavicle
   1. Lateral: formed by anterior divisions of upper and middle trunks
      a. Lateral pectoral nerve: pectoralis major
      b. Lateral head of median nerve
      c. Musculocutaneous nerve
   2. Medial: formed by anterior division of lower trunk
      a. Medial pectoral: pectoralis major and minor
      b. Medial brachial cutaneous
      c. Medial antebrachial cutaneous
      d. Medial head of median nerve
      e. Ulnar nerve
   3. Posterior: formed by posterior divisions of all trunks
      a. Upper subscapular: subscapularis
      b. Thoracodorsal: latissimus dorsi
      c. Lower subscapular: subscapularis and teres major
      d. Axillary: deltoid and teres minor
      e. Radial: triceps and extensors
E. Nerves from plexus itself
   1. Suprascapular: from upper trunk. Innervates supraspinatus and infraspinatus
   2. Long thoracic: from C5, C6, and C7. Innervates serratus anterior
   3. Phrenic: from C4 and C5. Innervates the diaphragm

V. Surgical Approaches
A. Anterior (Fig 1-2)
   1. Surgery
      a. Incision from coracoid 10 cm in deltopectoral groove
      b. Locate cephalic vein and retract medially with pectoralis major
      c. Retract conjoined tendon medially
      d. Rotate arm laterally to reveal subscapularis and divide muscle 1 cm from its insertion
      e. Incise capsule longitudinally
   2. Dangers
      a. Abduction brings axillary artery close to coracoid
      b. Musculocutaneous nerve enters coracobrachialis 5–8 cm distal to coracoid medially
B. Lateral
   1. Surgery
      a. Incision 5 cm from lateral border of acromion down to the lateral aspect of arm
      b. Split deltoid in line of fibers
      c. Lateral aspect of upper humerus

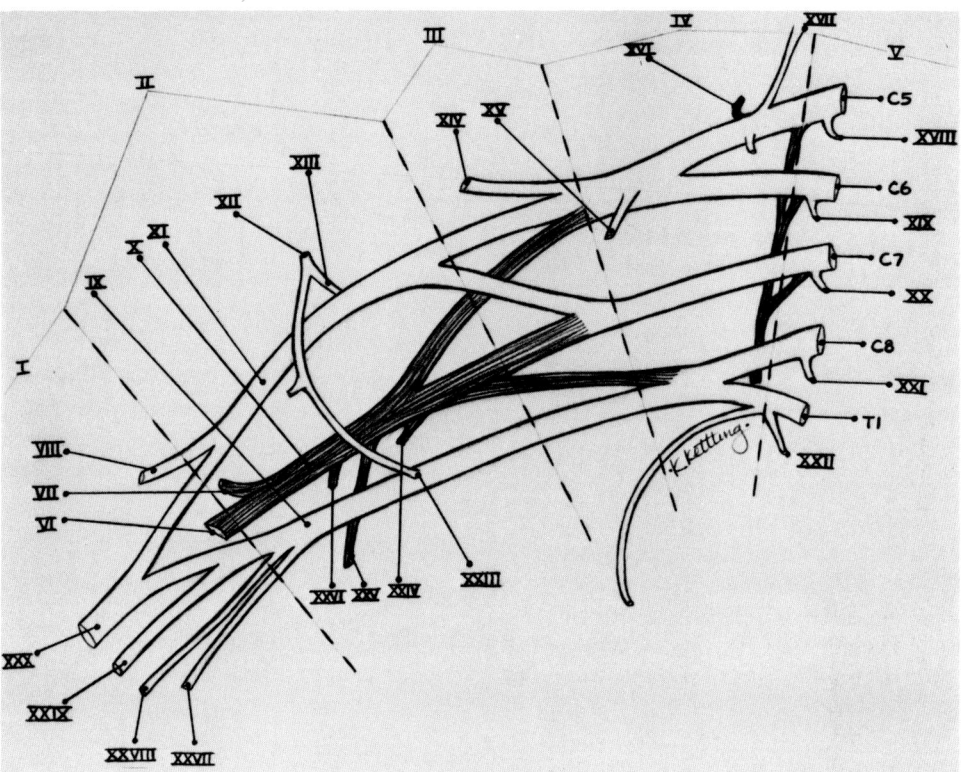

Figure 1-1. The brachial plexus, consisting of anterior rami (V), trunks (IV), divisions (III), cords (II), and terminal nerves (I). Trunks: Upper trunk (C5, C6), Middle trunk (C7), Lower trunk (C8, T1). Lateral cord (XI) formed by anterior divisions of upper and middle trunks (Branches are Lateral pectoral nerve or lateral anterior thoracic (XIII), Lateral head of median nerve (XXX), and Musculocutaneous nerve (VIII). Medial cord (IX) formed by anterior division of lower trunk (Branches are Medial pectoral nerve or medial anterior thoracic nerve (XXIII), Medial brachial cutaneous nerve (XXVII), Medial antebrachial cutaneous nerve (XXVIII), Medial head of median nerve (XXX), and Ulnar nerve (XXIX). Posterior cord (X) formed by posterior divisions of all trunks (Branches are Upper subscapular nerve (XXIV), Thoracodorsal nerve (XXV), Lower subscapular nerve (XXVI), Axillary nerve (VII), Radial nerve (VI). Other branches off the upper trunk are suprascapular nerve (XIV), nerve to rhomboides (XVI), and nerve to subclavius (XV). C5, C6, C7, and C8 rami gives off branches to the longus colli and scaleni (XVIII, XIX, XX. XXI). Long thoracic nerve gets contribution from C5, C6, and C7.

  and rotator cuff under the subacromial bursa
 2. Dangers
  a. Axillary nerve enters quadrangular space with posterior humeral circumflex artery. Nerve enters deltoid posteriorly from deep surface about 7 cm below tip of the acromion
C. Posterior
 1. Surgery
  a. Incision along the entire length of scapular spine to acromion
  b. Detach deltoid from origin on scapular spine
  c. Retract deltoid inferiorly to find plane between deltoid and infraspinatus
  d. Develop plane between infraspinatus superiorly and teres minor inferiorly
  e. Incise joint capsule longitudinally
 2. Dangers
  a. Axillary nerve in quadrangular space
  b. Suprascapular nerve passes around base of scapular spine

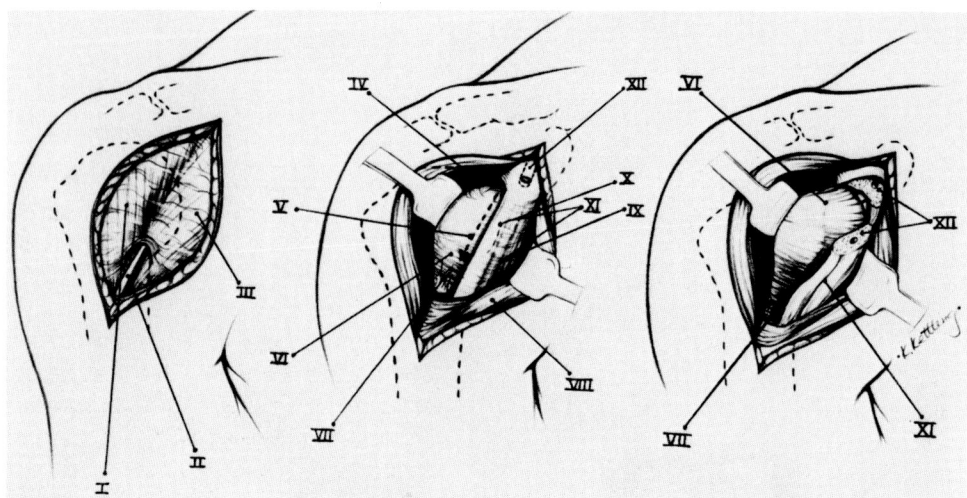
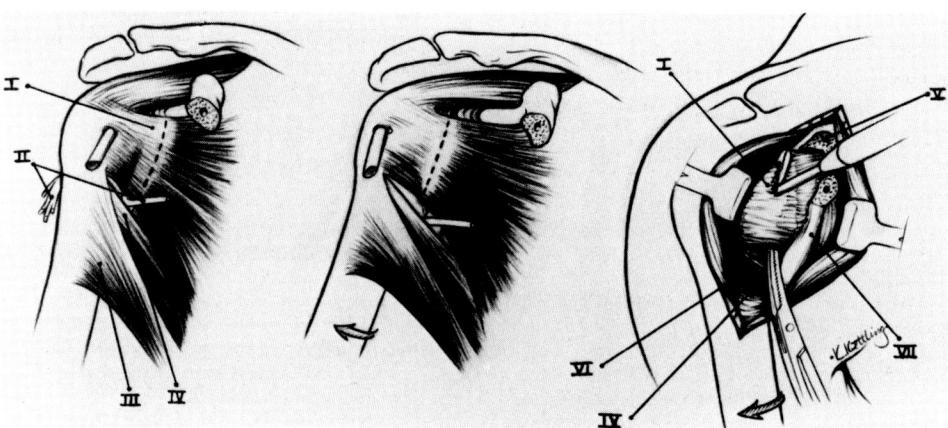

Figure 1-2. Anterior approach to the shoulder. Top left: Skin incision over the deltoid (I) and pectoralis major (III). The cephalic vein (II) is located in the groove. Top center: Retract the pectoralis major (VIII) medially and deltoid (IV) laterally to expose the conjoined tendon (XI), consisting of biceps tendon (X) and coracobrachialis (IX). If coracoid osteotomy is necessasry, predrilling (XII) is done. The fascia (V) is divided over the subscapularis (VI) just lateral to the conjoined tendon. Note the vessels (VII) on the inferior aspect of the subscapularis. Top right: Osteotomy of coracoid (XII) exposes the subscapularis (VI) better. Bottom left: The axillary nerve (II) is at risk in the caudal end of subscapularis (I). The axillary nerve exits above the teres major (IV) and latissimus dorsi (III). Bottom center: External rotation of the humerus places the axillary nerve away from the subscapularis incision. Bottom right: Incision of the subscapularis (I) is done by separating it from the underlying capsule. Other structures in view are coracoid process (V), conjoined tendon (VII), vessels (VI), and teres major (IV). (Redrawn from Hoppenfeld S, deBoer P: Surgical Exposures in Orthopaedics. Philadelphia, J. B. Lippincott Inc, 1984)

2
Arm

I. Bony: Humeral Shaft
A. Surfaces: anterolateral, anteromedial, posterior
B. Radial sulcus for the radial nerve
C. Lateral supracondylar ridge distally

II. Muscles
A. Coracobrachialis
B. Biceps
   1. Long head: from supraglenoid tuberosity to radial tuberosity. Innervated by musculocutaneous nerve (flexion of forearm)
   2. Short head: from coracoid to radial tuberosity. Innervated by musculocutaneous nerve (supination of forearm)
C. Brachialis: from lower ⅔ of humerus to coronoid process of ulna. Innervated by musculocutaneous nerve
D. Triceps
   1. Long head: from infraglenoid tuberosity to olecranon. Innervated by radial nerve (extends and adducts arm)
   2. Lateral head: from posterolateral humerus to olecranon. Innervated by radial nerve (extends the elbow)

III. Vascular
A. Brachial artery from axillary artery, which terminates as radial and ulnar arteries
B. Brachial artery courses anterior to triceps and brachialis, posterior to biceps aponeurosis, medial to coracobrachialis, lateral to ulnar nerve
C. Deep branch enters radial sulcus behind humerus and terminates as radial and middle collateral arteries

IV. Nervous (Fig 1-3)
A. Median nerve: begins lateral to brachial artery, then crosses and runs medial to brachial artery at distal humerus (no branches)
B. Musculocutaneous nerve: pierces coracobrachialis proximally and continues to become lateral antebrachial cutaneous nerve
C. Radial nerve: pierces lateral intermuscular septum and divides into superficial and deep branches in front of lateral epicondyle. Branches to arm consist of posterior brachial, lateral brachial, posterior antebrachial, and cutaneous nerves
D. Ulnar nerve: staying medial to brachial artery, it pierces the medial intermuscular septum and runs with superior ulnar collateral artery to groove behind medial epicondyle

V. Surgical Approaches
A. Anterior
   1. Surgery
      a. Incision from coracoid in deltopectoral groove along lateral border of biceps
      b. Deltopectoral intermuscular plane proximally and divide periosteum lateral to pectoralis insertion and lateral to long head of biceps
      c. Develop plane between biceps and brachialis distally
      d. Split brachialis longitudinally, which is innervated by the radial nerve laterally and the musculocutaneous nerve medially
   2. Dangers
      a. Radial nerve: vulnerable in groove behind middle third of humerus; also in distal third anteriorly as nerve pierces intermuscular septum; lies between brachialis and brachioradialis
      b. Axillary nerve: underneath deltoid
      c. Anterior humeral circumflex artery:

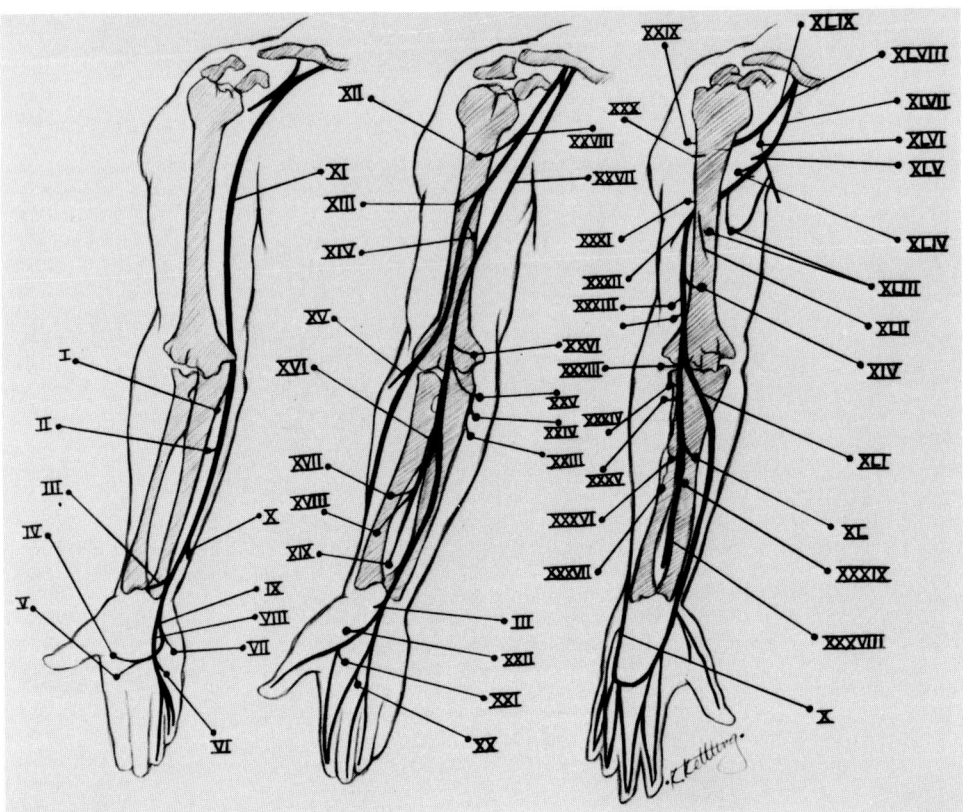

Figure 1-3. Nervous structures of the upper extremities. Left: Ulnar nerve (XI) distribution. Flexor carpi ulnaris (I), Flexor digitorum profundus (II), Palmar cutaneous branch (III), Adductor pollicis and deep head of flexor pollicis brevis (IV), Interossei and third and fourth lumbricales (V), Palmaris brevis (VI), Abductor digiti minimi, flexor digiti minimi brevis, opponens digiti minimi (VII), superficial branch (VIII), deep branch (IX), dorsal branch (X). Middle: Median nerve (XXVII) and musculocutaneous (XXVIII) distributions. Coracobrachialis (XII), biceps brachii (XIII), brachialis (XIV), lateral antebrachia cutaneous nerve (XV), anterior interosseus nerve (XVI), flexor digitorum profundus (XVII), flexor pollicis longus (XVIII), pronator quadratus (XIX), second lumbricalis (XX), first lumbbricalis (XXI), abductor pollicis brevis, opponens pollicis, and superficial head of flexor pollicis brevis (XXII), flexor carpi radialis (XXIII), palmaris longus (XXIV), flexor digitorum superficialis (XXV), pronator teres (XXVI). Right: The radial nerve (XLVII) distributions. Lateral head of triceps (XXXI), posterior antebrachial cutaneous nerve (XXXII), brachioradialis, extensor carpi radialis longus, and extensor carpi radialis brevis (XXXIII), supinator (XXXIV), extensor digitorum, extensor digiti minimi, and extensor carpi ulnaris (XXXV), extensor pollicis longus (XXXVI), Extensor indicis (XXXVII), dorsal branch of ulnar nerve (X), posterior interosseus nerve (XXXVIII), extensor pollicis brevis (XXXIX), abductor pollicis longus (XL), superficial branch of radial nerve (XLI), brachialis (XIV), Anconeus (XLII), medial head of triceps (XLIII), long head of triceps (XLIV), and posterior brachial cutaneus nerve (XLV). Axillary nerve (XLIX) from the posterior cord (XLVIII) and deltoideus (XXIX), lateral brachial cutaneus nerve (XXX) and teres minor (XLVI) are shown as well.

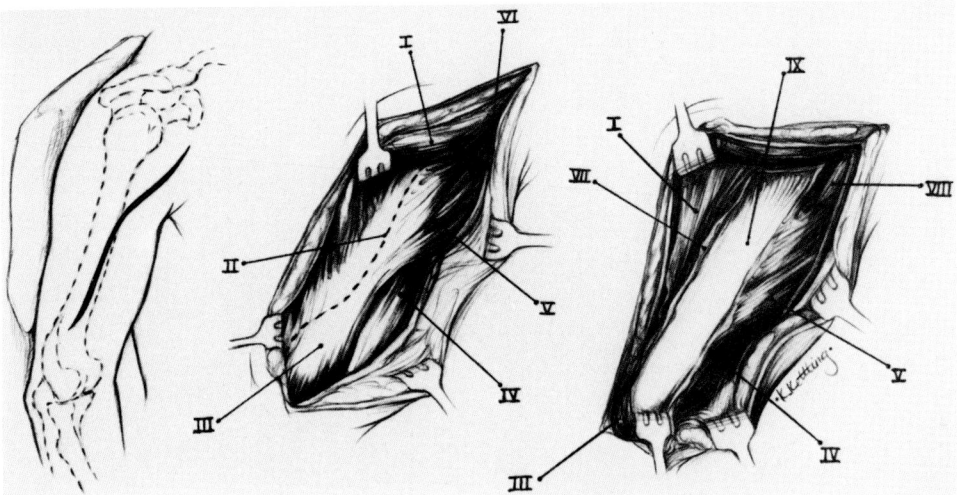

Figure 1-4. Anterolateral exposure of the humeral shaft. Left: Incision from 2 cm below the coracoid process and extends toward the lateral condyle of the humerus. Middle: The cephalic vein (VI) is retracted medially and the deltoid (I) laterally in the proximal aspect of the dissection. The incision (II) is made between pectoralis major (V) and deltoid (I) and continues distally on the lateral aspect of the brachialis (III). The biceps (IV) is medial to the brachialis. Right: Subperiosteal dissection is done, while taking great care not to injure the radial nerve, which extends downward in the lateral groove behind the bone. Structures in view are deltoid (I), humerus (IV), short head of biceps (VIII), periosteum (VII), pectoralis major (V), biceps (IV), and brachialis (III). (Modified from Banks SW, Laufman H: Atlas of Surgical Exposures of the Extremities, Philadelphia, WB Saunders Inc, 1953)

crosses field between pectoralis major and deltoid in upper arm
- B. Anterolateral (Fig 1-4)
    1. Surgery
        a. Curved incision over lateral border of biceps starting 10 cm above flexor crease of elbow
        b. Develop plane between brachioradialis and brachialis; locate radial nerve and trace proximally
        c. Retract nerve and brachioradialis laterally, and retract biceps and brachialis medially
    2. Dangers
        a. Musculocutaneous nerve between biceps and brachialis
        b. Radial nerve between brachialis and brachioradialis
- C. Posterior (Fig 1-5)
    1. Surgery
        a. Make incision in midline of posterior arm to the olecranon fossa
        b. Develop plane between lateral and long heads of triceps
        c. Incise along deep fibers of triceps
    2. Dangers
        a. Radial nerve: lies in spiral groove just proximal to origin of medial head of triceps
        b. Ulnar nerve: lies deep to medial head of triceps on lower third of arm
        c. Profunda brachii artery lies with radial nerve in the spiral groove
- D. Lateral approach to the distal humerus
    1. Skin incision over the lateral supracondylar ridge and dissection between brachioradialis and triceps
    2. Danger: the radial nerve pierces the lateral intermuscular septum on distal third of humerus

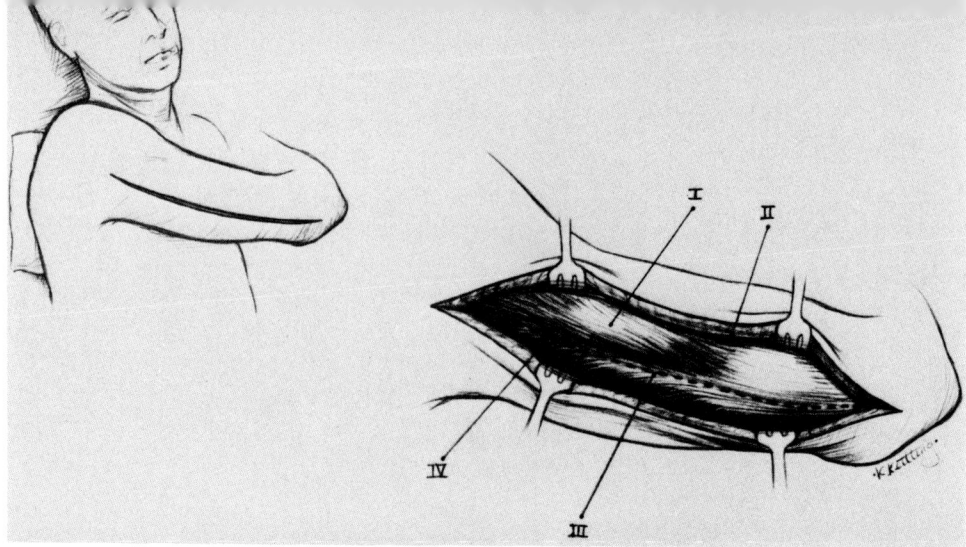
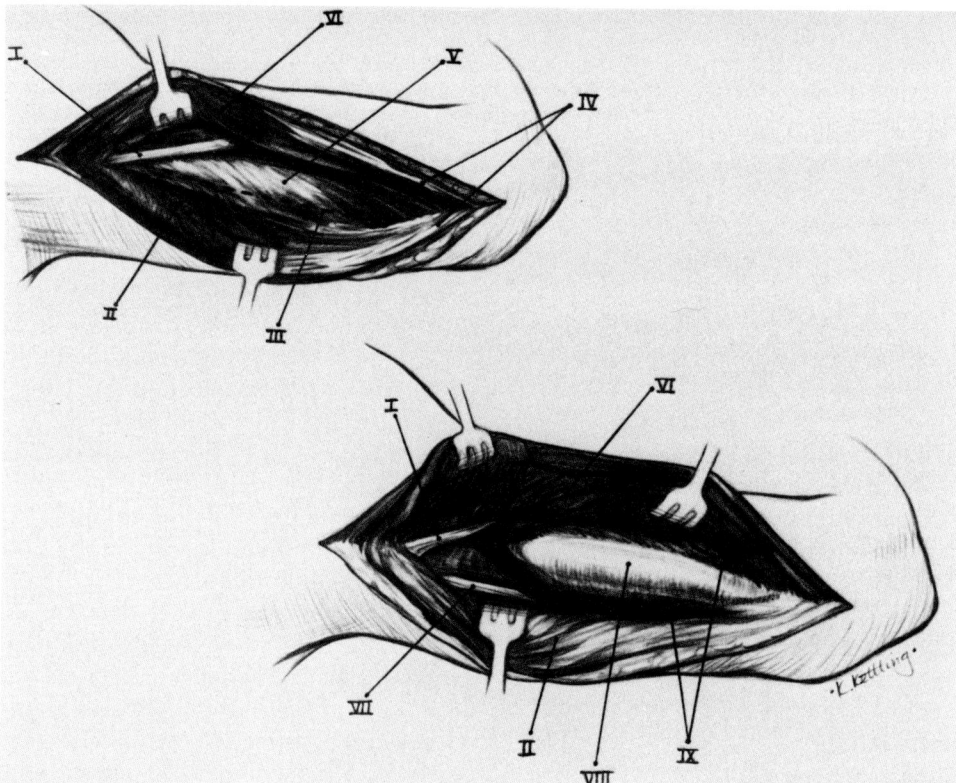

Figure 1-5. Posterior approach of the humerus. Top left: Midline incision to the olecranon fossa. Top right: After incising the fascia (II), the triceps is splitted (III) between the lateral head (I) and long head (IV). Bottom left: This is followed by incision along the deep head of the triceps (V), taking care to protect the radial nerve (I) proximally. Bottom right: The humeral shaft (VIII) is exposed. Other structures in view are radial nerve (I), lateral head of the triceps (VI), long head of triceps (II), deep fibers of triceps (IX), and the ulnar nerve (VII). (Modified from Banks SW, Laufman H: Atlas of Surgical Exposures of the Extremities, Philadelphia, WB Saunders Inc, 1953)

3
Elbow

I. Bony
A. Ossification
1. Capitellum: 1–2 years
2. Radial head: 3–4 years
3. Medial epicondyle: 5 years
4. Trochlea: 7 years
5. Olecranon: 9 years
6. Lateral epicondyle: 11 years

B. Epiphyses fuse to each other and to metaphysis between 10 and 12 years, and the medial epicondyle closes last

II. Joint
A. Humeroulnar
1. Type: hinge
2. Motion: flexion and extension
3. Ligaments
   a. Ulnar collateral: anterior, oblique, posterior; from front and back of medial epicondyle to medial side of coronoid process and olecranon
   b. Radial collateral: from below lateral epicondyle to annular ligament and lateral margin of ulna

B. Radioulnar
1. Type: pivot
2. Motion: pronation, supination
3. Ligaments
   a. Annular ligament encircles radial head; attached to ends of radial notch of ulna
   b. Quadrate ligament is between neck of radius and lower part of radial notch of ulna

III. Muscles
A. Flexion: biceps, brachialis, brachioradialis, pronator teres, flexor carpi radialis (FCR), flexor carpi ulnaris (FCU), palmaris longus (PL), flexor digitorum superficialis (FDS)
B. Extension: triceps, anconeus, extensor carpi radialis longus (ECRL), extensor carpi radialis brevis (ECRB), extensor digitorum communis (EDC), extensor digiti minimi (EDM), extensor carpi ulnaris (ECU), supinator
C. Supination: biceps, supinator
D. Pronation: pronator teres, pronator quadratus

IV. Antecubital Region
A. Boundaries
1. Base: between two humeral condyles
2. Lateral: brachioradialis
3. Medial: pronator teres
4. Roof: aponeurosis of biceps
5. Floor: brachialis and supinator

B. Superficial
1. Veins
   a. Cephalic vein at lateral edge along brachialis
   b. Basilic vein along medial edge over biceps
2. Nerves
   a. Medial antebrachial cutaneous nerve sends branches superficial and deep to basilic vein
   b. Lateral antebrachial cutaneous nerve lies deep to cephalic vein

C. Deep
1. Arteries
   a. Brachial artery runs through middle of fossa and divides into two branches
   b. Radial artery lies on tendon of biceps
   c. Ulnar artery passes beneath pronator teres
2. Nerves
   a. Median nerve lies on medial side of brachial artery in upper fossa and lies between heads of pronator teres
   b. Radial nerve lies beneath brachio-

radialis and splits in front of lateral epicondyle
- (1) Superficial nerve continues under brachioradialis
- (2) Deep radial nerve curves around lateral radius between layers of the supinator

c. Ulnar nerve stays behind medial epicondyle

V. Surgical Approaches

A. Posterior
  1. Surgery
     a. Begin incision 5 cm above olecranon in the midline and curve laterally just above tip of olecranon. Complete incision by curving medially over ulna
     b. Expose ulnar nerve behind epicondyle
     c. For olecranon osteotomy, predrill and pretap and perform transverse osteotomy 2 cm from olecranon tip
     d. Elevate triceps with olecranon
  2. Dangers
     a. Ulnar nerve behind medial epicondyle
     b. Median nerve anterior to distal humerus
     c. Radial nerve is in danger if dissection is carried proximally above distal ¼ of the humerus
     d. Brachial artery lies adjacent to median nerve

B. Medial (Fig 1-6)
  1. Surgery

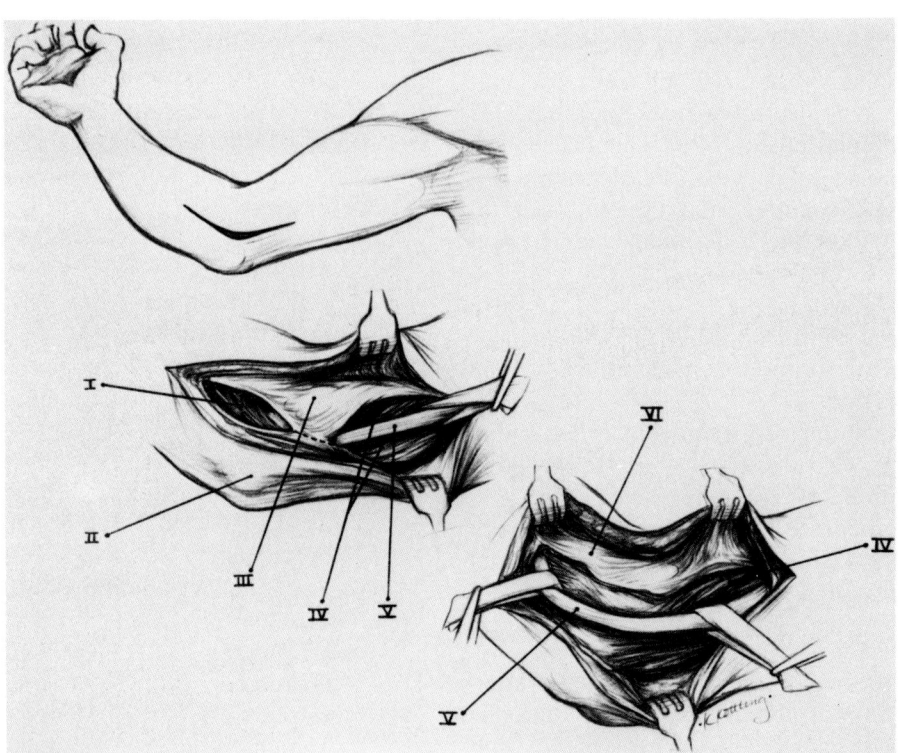

Figure 1-6. Medial approach to the ulnar nerve. Top: Incision along the medial epicondyle Middle: Isolate ulnar nerve (V), which is just posterior to the medial epicondyle (III). Flexor carpi ulnaris (I), olecranon (II), and triceps (IV) are shown. Bottom: Division of the fascia (VI) is followed by the dissection along the ulnar nerve (Modified from Banks SW, Laufman H: Atlas of Surgical Exposures of the Extremities, Philadelphia, WB Saunders Inc, 1953)

a. Curved 10 cm incision centered on medial epicondyle
b. Isolate ulnar nerve
c. Define interval between pronator teres and brachialis
    (1) Median nerve goes medially
    (2) Ulnar nerve retracted inferiorly
d. Osteotomize medial epicondyle and reflect with attached muscles distally
e. Proximally, develop plane between brachialis (retract anteriorly) and triceps (retract posteriorly)
f. Incise medial capsule and collateral ligament

2. Dangers
a. Ulnar nerve must be identified. It courses behind the medial epicondyle and comes to the anterior compartment by passing between two heads of flexor carpi ulnaris and travels along the anterior surface of the flexor digitorum profundus in forearm
b. Median nerve and its major branch, the anterior interosseus, may have a traction injury

C. Anterolateral approach
1. Surgery
a. Dissection between lateral border of biceps-brachialis and medial border of brachioradialis proximally and between brachioradialis and pronator teres distally
b. Be careful of the lateral antebrachial cutaneous nerve between biceps and brachialis
c. Identify the radial nerve between brachioradialis and brachialis
d. The radial nerve splits into three branches
    (1) Posterior interosseous nerve to supinator
    (2) Sensory branch underneath brachioradialis
    (3) Motor branch to extensor carpi radialis brevis
e. After developing plane between brachioradialis and pronator teres, cut supinator insertion just lateral to the

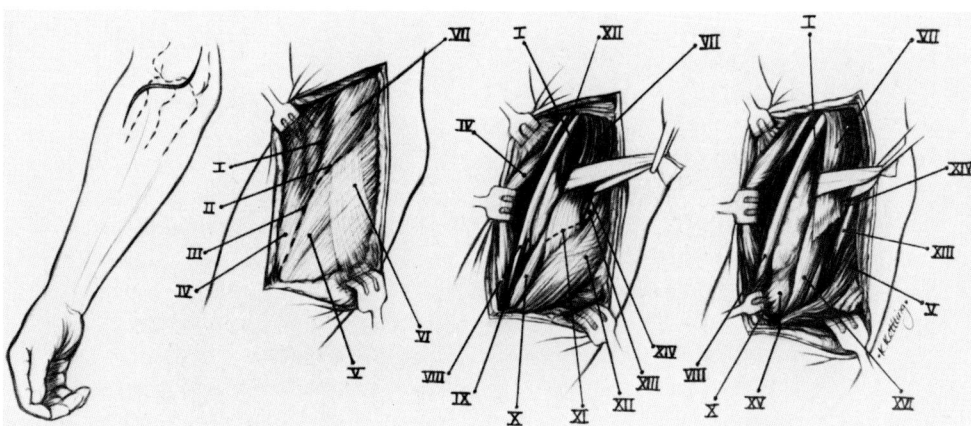

Figure 1-7. Exposure of the antecubital fossa. Left: Incision from the medial aspect of the biceps above the elbow and extends distally to the lateral margin of the brachioradialis Left center: The fascial incision (II) follows on the medial aspect of the biceps (VII), across the biceps aponeurosis (VI), and between brachioradialis (IV) and pronator teres (V). Brachialis (I) is lateral to the biceps. Right center: Divide the bicipital aponeurosis (XI) and identify median nerve (XIII), brachial artery (XIV), and the biceps tendon (X) from medial to lateral and from superficial to deep locations. Other structures in view are brachialis (I), biceps (VII), deep fascia (XII), radial nerve (VIII), deep branch of radial nerve (IX), brachioradialis (IV), and pronator teres (XII). Right: The radial nerve (VIII) is between the brachialis (I) and brachioradialis. Other structures in view are biceps (VII), brachial artery (XIV), median nerve (XIII), biceps tendon (XVI), pronator teres (V), supinator (X), and radial head (XV). (Modified from Banks SW, Laufman H: Atlas of Surgical Exposures of the Extremities, Philadelphia, WB Saunders Inc, 1953)

biceps tendon while supinating the forearm in order to expose the radial head and capitellum
2. Dangers: radial nerve, posterior interosseus nerve, lateral cutaneous nerve of forearm, and recurrent branches of radial artery
D. Anterior approach to cubital fossa (Fig 1-7)
  1. Surgery
     a. Make incision along the medial border of biceps and brachioradialis
     b. Dissect between biceps and brachialis proximally and brachioradialis and pronator teres distally
     c. Divide bicipital aponeurosis and identify median nerve, brachial artery, and biceps tendon from medial to lateral and from superficial to deep locations
  2. Dangers

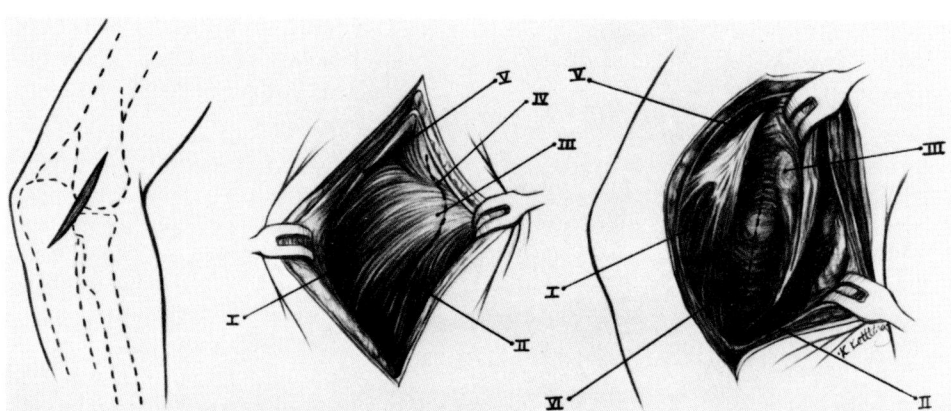

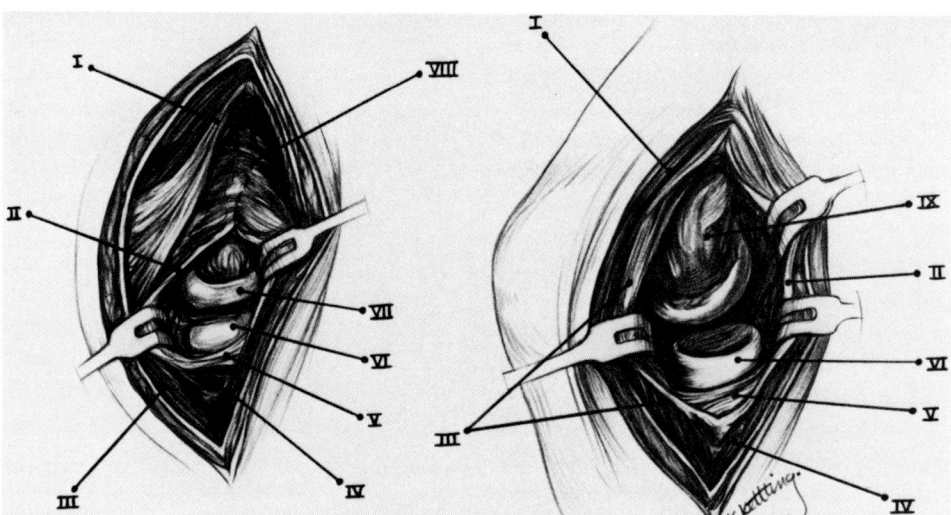

Figure 1-8. Posterolateral approach to the radial head. Top left: Incision from the lateral epicondyle to the posterior aspect of the radial head. Top center: Dissection (IV) between extensor carpi ulnaris (II) and anconeus (I). Lateral epicondyle (III) and triceps (V) are also shown. Top right: Capsular incision (VI) over the radial head. The radial head (VI) and capitellum (VII) are shown. Triceps (I), capsule (II), anconeus (III), supinator (IV), annular ligament (V), and extension along the lateral epicondyle are shown. (Modified from Banks SW, Laufman H; Atlas of Surgical Exposures of the Extremities, Philadelphia, WB Saunders Inc, 1953)

a. Brachial artery runs just lateral to median nerve and divides into two branches
   (1) Radial artery: on top of biceps insertion and courses between pronator teres and brachioradialis and travels between flexor carpi radialis and brachioradialis and on top of flexor digitorum longus in the forearm
   (2) Ulnar artery: crosses underneath the median nerve at the musculotendinous junction of pronator teres and courses just lateral to ulnar nerve in the forearm
      i. Anterior interosseus artery: a branch of ulnar artery that courses along with anterior interosseus nerve in forearm
   b. Median nerve
E. Posterolateral approach to radial head (Fig 1-8)
   1. Surgery
      a. Dissect between extensor carpi ulnaris and anconeus
      b. Divide supinator while pronating forearm
   2. Danger: posterior interosseus nerve

4
Forearm

I. Bony
A. Radius and ulnar shafts: appear at 8th fetal week
B. Radius and ulna are connected by proximal and distal radioulnar joints and interosseus membrane

II. Compartments
A. Volar compartment: flexors
B. Dorsal compartment: extensors
C. Lateral or mobile wad compartment: ECRL, ECRB, brachioradialis (BR)

III. Volar Forearm
A. Muscles
  1. Superficial group: from medial epicondyle
     a. Pronator teres: to lateral midradius
     b. Flexor carpi radialis (FCR): to second and third metacarpal bases
     c. Palmaris longus (PL): to palmar aponeurosis
     d. Flexor carpi ulnaris (FCU): to pisiform, hamate, and fifth metacarpal (the only superficial flexor supplied by ulnar nerve; others by median nerve)
     e. Flexor digitorum superficialis (FDS): to sides of middle phalanx of four fingers (flex proximal interphalangeal [PIP] joint, metacarpophalangeal [MCP] joint, and wrist)
  2. Deep Group
     a. Flexor digitorum profundus (FDP): upper anteromedial ulna and interosseus membrane to bases of terminal phalanges of four fingers
        (1) Flexes all phalanges (distal interphalangeal [DIP] joint and wrist)
        (2) Medial half innervated by ulnar nerve; lateral half by anterior interosseous branch of median nerve
     b. Flexor pollicis longus (FPL): anterior radial shaft and interosseus membrane to base of distal thumb phalanx
        (1) Flexes thumb: adducts first metacarpal
        (2) Innervated by anterior interosseus nerve
     c. Pronator quadratus: distal anterior ulnar shaft to distal anterolateral radius
        (1) Pronates hand
        (2) Innervated by anterior interosseus nerve
B. Vascular
  1. Radial artery
     a. From neck of radius to medial side of radial styloid
     b. Deep to brachioradialis, above superficial flexor group, just lateral to FCR
     c. Branches: radial recurrent, muscular, palmar carpal, superficial palmar
  2. Ulnar artery
     a. From neck of radius to flexor retinaculum
     b. Branches: anterior and posterior recurrent, muscular, common interosseus
  3. Common interosseus artery
     a. Anterior interosseus artery: travels on interosseus membrane along with anterior interosseus nerve
     b. Posterior interosseus artery: lies between supinator and abductor pollicis longus and descends between superficial and deep flexors

C. Nervous
   1. Radial nerve
      a. Superficial branch runs lateral to radial artery under brachioradialis
      b. Deep branch: posterior forearm
   2. Median nerve
      a. Passes between heads of pronator teres and lies between FDS and FDP. Becomes superficial near wrist, between tendons of FDS and FCR. Passes deep and medial to tendon of PL
      b. Branches: muscular, anterior interosseus
   3. Ulnar nerve
      a. Enters forearm through FCU and becomes medial to ulnar artery and FCU near wrist
      b. Branches: muscular, palmar cutaneous, posterior branch

IV. **Posterior Forearm**
A. Muscles
   1. Superficial group
      a. Brachioradialis: lateral humeral supracondylar ridge to lateral base of radial styloid
         (1) Flexes forearm
         (2) Innervated by radial nerve
      b. Extensor carpi radialis longus (ECRL): from lateral supracondylar ridge to posterior base of second metacarpal
         (1) Extends and abducts wrist
         (2) Innervated by radial nerve
      c. Extensor carpi radialis brevis (ECRB): lateral epicondyle to posterior base of third metacarpal
         (1) Extends and abducts wrist
         (2) Innervated by radial nerve
      d. Extensor digitorum communis (EDC): lateral epicondyle to bases of middle and distal phalanges of four fingers
         (1) Extends fingers, wrist
         (2) Innervated by deep radial nerve
      e. Extensor digiti minimi (EDM): lateral epicondyle to posterior proximal phalanx of little finger
         (1) Extends little finger
         (2) Innervated by deep radial nerve
      f. Extensor carpi ulnaris (ECU): lateral epicondyle and posterior ulna to tubercle at fifth metacarpal base
         (1) Extends, adducts wrist
         (2) Innervated by deep radial nerve
      g. Anconeus: lateral epicondyle to olecranon
         (1) Extends elbow
         (2) Innervated by radial nerve
   2. Deep group (innervated by deep radial nerve)
      a. Supinator: lateral epicondyle and ulna to radial tubercle
      b. Abductor pollicis longus (APL): lateral posterior ulna, posterior radius to lateral base of first metacarpal
      c. Extensor pollicis brevis (EPB): posterior radius to base of proximal thumb phalanx
      d. Extensor pollicis longus (EPL): posterolateral ulna to base of distal thumb phalanx
      e. Extensor indicis proprius (EIP): posterior ulna to tendon of EDC to index finger
B. Vascular: posterior interosseus artery passes between borders of supinator and APL. Descends between superficial and deep layers. Gives muscular branches, interosseus recurrent, inferior ulnar recurrent, posterior ulnar recurrent
C. Nervous
   1. Radial nerve between brachialis and brachioradialis divides in front of lateral epicondyle
      a. Superficial branch under brachioradialis
      b. Deep branch curves around lateral radius between layers of supinator and continues between superficial and deep layers. In middle of forearm, deep branch becomes posterior in-

terosseus nerve and lies between interosseus nerve, interosseus membrane and EPL

V. Surgical Approaches

A. Anterior approach to radius (Fig 1-9)
   1. Surgery
      a. Incision from anterior flexor crease of elbow lateral to biceps tendon down to radial styloid
      b. Develop plane between brachioradialis and FCR
      c. For proximal third, develop plane between brachioradialis and pronator teres; cut supinator insertion just lateral to biceps tendon while supinating forearm
      d. For middle third of radius, pronate forearm and detach insertion of pronator teres from lateral aspect of radius. This will also detach origin of FDS
      e. For distal third, partially supinate forearm and incise periosteum of the lateral radius lateral to pronator quadratus and FPL. Retract muscles medially
      f. For very distal radius exposure, an interval between FCR and PL can be used. Retract PL, median nerve, FDS, and FDP medially, and retract FPL radially, followed by cutting quadratus
   2. Dangers

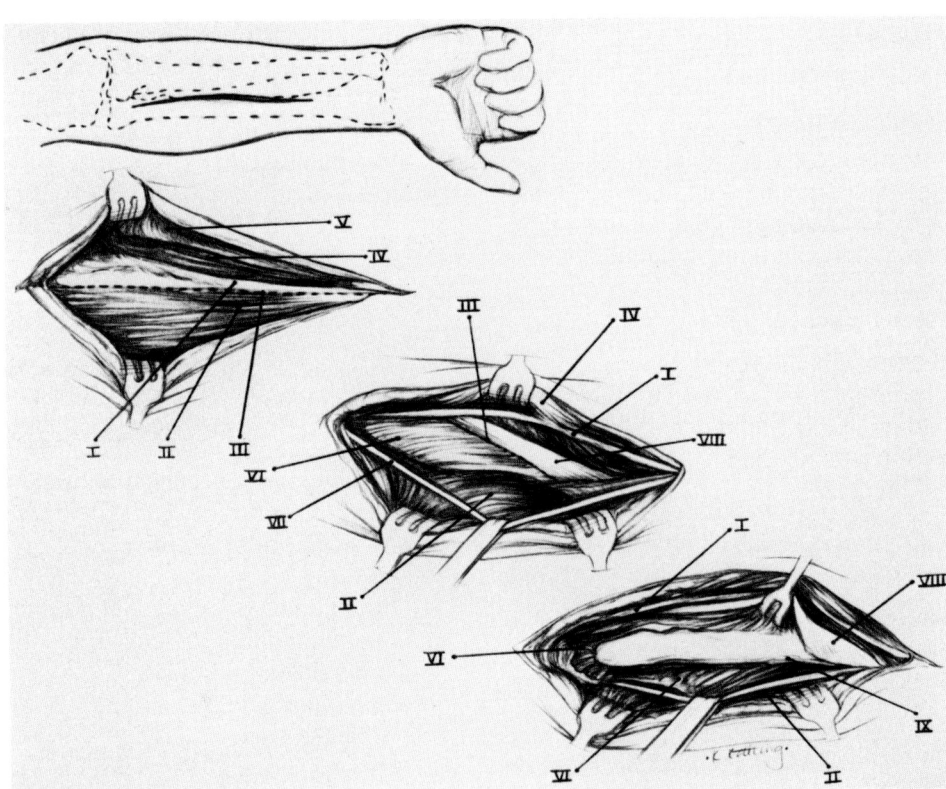

Figure 1-9. Anterior approach to the forearm. Top: Incision from anterior flexor crease of elbow lateral to biceps tendon down to radial styloid. Top center: Develop plane (III) between brachioradialis (II) and FCR (IV), taking great caution not to injure the radial artery (I). Bottom center: Superficial branch of the radial nerve (VII) should also be protected. Pronate the forearm and detach insertion (III) of pronator teres (VIII) from lateral aspect of radius. Bottom: Subperioteal exposure (IX) may be done. (Modified from Banks SW, Laufman H: Atlas of Surgical Exposures of the Extremities, Philadelphia, WB Saunders Inc, 1953)

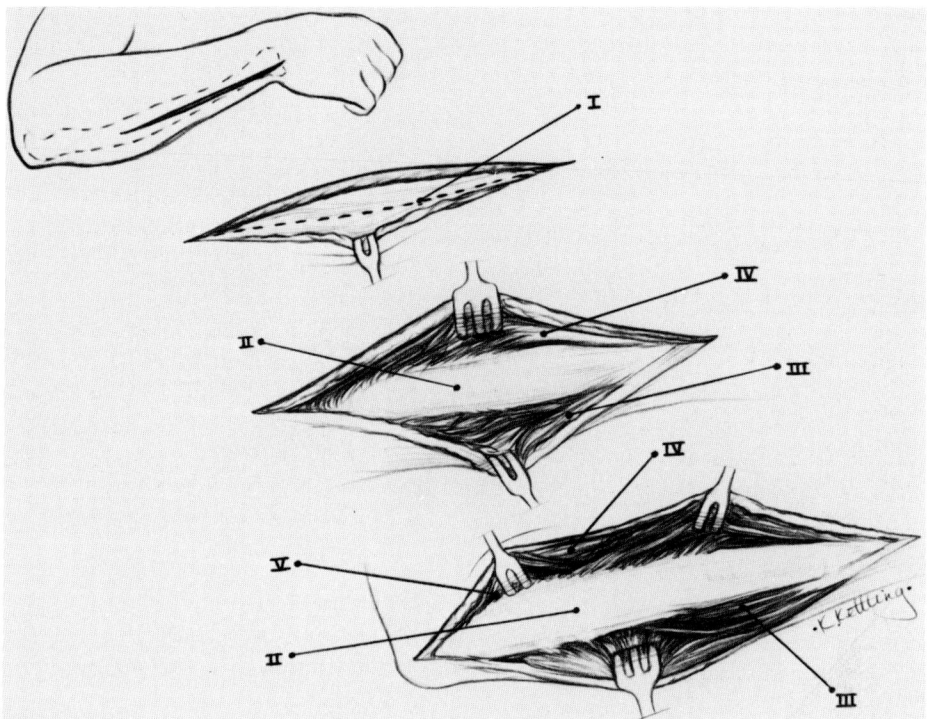

Figure 1-10. Ulnar approach to the forearm. Top: Linear incision over subcutaneous border of the ulna. Top center: Fascial incision. Bottom center: Dissection is between ECU (IV) and FCU (III). Subperiosteal dissection to bone (II). Bottom: Proximal extension by reflecting the anconeus (V). (Modified from Banks SW, Laufman H: Atlas of Surgical Exposures of the Extremities, Philadelphia, WB Saunders Inc, 1953)

    a. Posterior interosseus nerve: vulnerable as it winds around neck of radius within supinator
    b. Superficial radial nerve under brachioradialis
    c. Radial artery down middle of forearm
B. Approach to ulna (Fig 1-10)
  1. Surgery
    a. Linear incision over subcutaneous border of ulna between ECU and FCU
    b. Incise periosteum over bone
  2. Dangers
    a. Ulnar nerve lies on FDP under FCU
    b. Ulnar artery radial to ulnar nerve
C. Posterior approach to radius
  1. Surgery
    a. Incision from lateral humeral epicondyle along dorsal forearm to ulnar side of Lister's tubercle
    b. Develop plane between ECRB and EDC
    c. Identify posterior interosseus nerve as it emerges between superficial and deep heads of supinator 1 cm proximal to distal edge of muscle
    d. Detach supinator insertion from anterior aspect of radius and strip it subperiosteally while supinating forearm
    e. To gain access to radial diaphysis, separate APL and EPB from underlying bone and retract distally and separate ECRB and EPL for distal exposure
  2. Danger: posterior interosseus nerve

5
Wrist and Hand

WRIST

I. Bony
A. Distal radius
  1. Ossification: appears 2nd year; closes 20th year
  2. Three dorsal grooves for tendons
  3. Lister's tubercle: EPL
B. Distal ulna
  1. Ossification: appears 4th year; closes 20th year
  2. Head with styloid process
C. Carpus
  1. Proximal row
    a. Scaphoid
      (1) Ossification: 6th year
      (2) Blood supply from branches of radial artery, which enter dorsally and distally
    b. Lunate: ossifies 5th year
    c. Triquetrum: ossifies 3rd year
    d. Pisiform: ossifies 12th year (last)
  2. Distal row
    a. Trapezium: ossifies 5th year
    b. Trapezoid
      (1) Ossification: 8th year
      (2) Smallest bone in distal row
    c. Capitate
      (1) Ossification: 1st year (first)
      (2) Largest carpal bone
    d. Hamate: ossifies 1st year

II. Joints
A. Radiocarpal
  1. Motion: flex, extend, abduct, adduct
  2. Ligaments
    a. Dorsal and palmar radiocarpal
    b. Radial and ulnar collateral
  3. Triangular fibrocartilage between distal ulna and carpus
B. Distal radioulnar
  1. Type: pivot
  2. Motion: pronation and supination
  3. Ligaments
    a. Dorsal and palmar radioulnar
    b. Articular disc
C. Intercarpal
  1. Arthrodial joints with dorsal, palmar, and interosseus ligaments
  2. Midcarpal
    a. Type: hinge
    b. Dorsal, palmar, and interosseus ligaments

III. Muscles
A. Flexion: FCU, FCR, PL, FDS, FDP
B. Extension: ECRL, ECRB, ECU, EDC
C. Abduction: FCR, ECRL, ECRB, EPL, EPB
D. Adduction: FCU, ECU, EIP
E. Supination: biceps, supinator, EPL, EPB
F. Pronation: pronator teres, pronator quadratus

IV. Anterior Wrist Features
A. Fascia: palmar carpal ligament with transverse fibers extending between radial and ulnar styloids; crosses superficial to all superficial flexors
B. Tendons
  1. FCR just lateral to PL, which is in anterior midline of the wrist
  2. Tendons of FDS are arranged so that those to long and ring fingers pass superficial to those of index and little finger
C. Neurovascular
  1. Ulnar nerve just lateral to ulnar artery, both of which are lateral to FCU
  2. Radial artery just lateral to FCR
  3. Superficial radial nerve just lateral to radial artery
  4. Median nerve deep to PL and medial to FCR

V. Dorsal Wrist Features (Fig 1-11)
A. Fascia: Extensor retinaculum attached to ulnar styloid, triquetrum, pisiform, radius; forms six osseus canals or compartments for tendon passage
   1. APL, EPB (most radial)
   2. ECRL, ECRB
   3. EPL (passes ulnar to Lister's tubercle)
   4. EDC, EIP
   5. EDM (passes between radius and ulna)
   6. ECU
B. Neurovascular: dorsal branch of ulnar nerve and lateral antebrachial cutaneous nerve reach the wrist but do not cross into the hand

VI. Surgical Approaches
A. Dorsal
   1. Surgery
      a. Begin 3 cm proximal to wrist joint and make an 8 cm incision distally
      b. Incise extensor retinaculum over EDC and EIP and mobilize tendons
      c. Incise joint capsule longitudinally
      d. Continue dissection subcapsularly
   2. Dangers: superficial radial nerve emerges from underneath brachioradialis tendon to travel to dorsum of hand
B. Volar
   1. Surgery
      a. Begin incision just ulnar to thenar crease, third of the way into the hand; curve around crease and then curve ulnarward to cross wrist crease obliquely
      b. Expose PL and retract ulnarward; identify median nerve
      c. Identify motor branch of median nerve as it arises in the carpal tunnel and retract laterally
      d. To access volar wrist joint, mobilize median nerve in the carpal tunnel and retract laterally
      e. Incise base of carpal tunnel to expose carpus
   2. Dangers
      a. Palmar cutaneous branch of median nerve arises 5 cm proximal to wrist joint and runs along ulnar side of FCR; then crosses flexor retinaculum
      b. Motor branch of median nerve
      c. Superficial palmar vascular arch

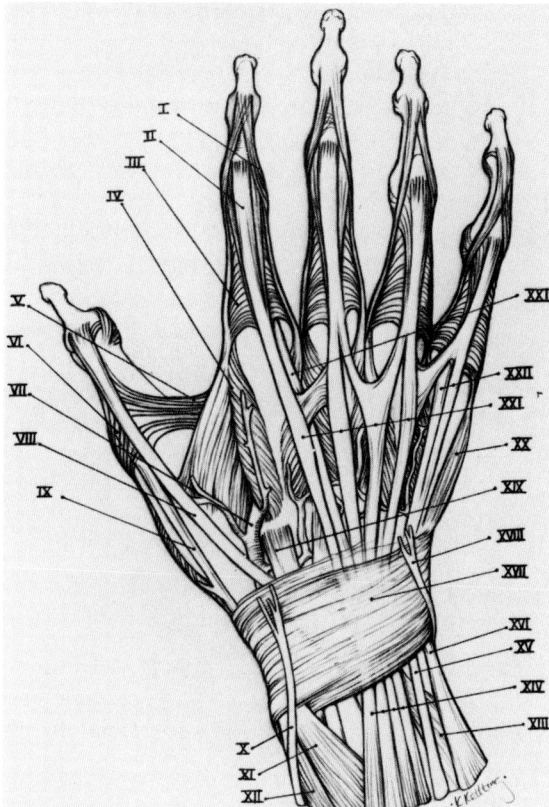

Figure 1-11. Dorsal anatomy of the wrist and hand. Lateral bands (I), Central slip (II), dorsal digital expansion (III), first dorsal interosseus (IV), abductor pollicis (V), expansion of abductor pollicis (VI), dorsal branch of radial artery (VII), extensor pollicis longus (VIII), abductor pollicis longus (IX), superficial radial nerve (X), extensor pollicis brevis (XI), abductor pollicis longus (XII), extensor indicis (XIII), extensor digitorum communis (XIV), extensor digiti minimi (XV), extensor carpi ulnaris (XVI), extensor retinaculum (XVII), dorsal cutaneous branch of the ulnar nerve (XVIII), extensor carpi radialis longus and brevis (XIV), abductor digiti minimi (XX), extensor digiti communis (XXI), extensor digiti minimi (XXII), extensor indicis (XXIII). (Redrawn from Hoppenfeld S, deBoer P: Surgical Exposures in Orthopaedics. Philadelphia, JB Lippincott Inc, 1984)

crosses palm at the level of the distal end of the outstretched thumb
C. Volar approach to scaphoid
   1. Surgery
      a. Make 3 cm incision (curvilinear) from scaphoid tubercle proximally between FCR and radial artery
      b. Identify radial artery and retract laterally
      c. Retract FCR medially
      d. Incise wrist capsule over scaphoid to expose it
   2. Dangers: radial artery

HAND

I. Bony
A. Metacarpals
   1. Ossification
      a. Body appears 8th fetal week; closes 20th year
      b. Distal end of second to fifth and base of first appear 3rd year and close 20th year
B. Phalanges: body appears 8th week, and base appears at 3–4 years and unite in 20th year

II. Joints
A. Carpometacarpal
   1. Type: all arthrodial except thumb, which is a saddle joint permitting flexion, extension, abduction, adduction, and opposition
   2. All have dorsal, palmar, and interosseus ligaments
B. Intermetacarpal: arthrodial
C. Metacarpophalangeal (MCP)
   1. Type: condyloid
   2. All have palmar and collateral ligaments
D. Interphalangeal (IP; proximal, PIP; distal, DIP)
   1. Type: hinge
   2. Palmar and collateral ligaments

III. Muscles
A. Thenar
   1. Abductor pollicis brevis (APB): from scaphoid tuberosity and trapezium to lateral base of proximal thumb phalanx. Innervated by median nerve
   2. Opponens pollicis: from trapezium to radial side of first metacarpal; abducts, flexes, rotates first metacarpal. Innervated by median nerve
   3. Flexor pollicis brevis (FPB): From trapezium to lateral and medial base of proximal thumb phalanx; flexes and adducts thumb. Innervated by median and deep ulnar nerves
   4. Adductor pollicis
      a. Oblique: from capitate, bases of second and third metacarpals to medial base of proximal thumb phalanx; adducts thumb
      b. Transverse: from third metacarpal shaft to medial base of proximal thumb phalanx; adducts thumb
      c. Innervated by ulnar nerve
B. Hypothenar
   1. Palmaris brevis: from palmar aponeurosis to skin of medial border of palm; builds up hypothenar eminence. Innervated by ulnar nerve
   2. Abductor digiti minimi: from pisiform and tendon of FCU to medial base of proximal phalanx of small finger; abducts small finger. Innervated by ulnar nerve
   3. Flexor digiti minimi brevis: from hamate to medial base of proximal phalanx of small finger; flexes proximal phalanx. Innervated by ulnar nerve
   4. Opponens digiti minimi: from hamate to medial shaft of fifth metacarpal; opposes small finger. Innervated by ulnar nerve
C. Intrinsics (Fig 1-12)
   1. Lumbricals
      a. First and second: radial side of deep flexor tendons to index and middle finger and insert into tendon of EDC

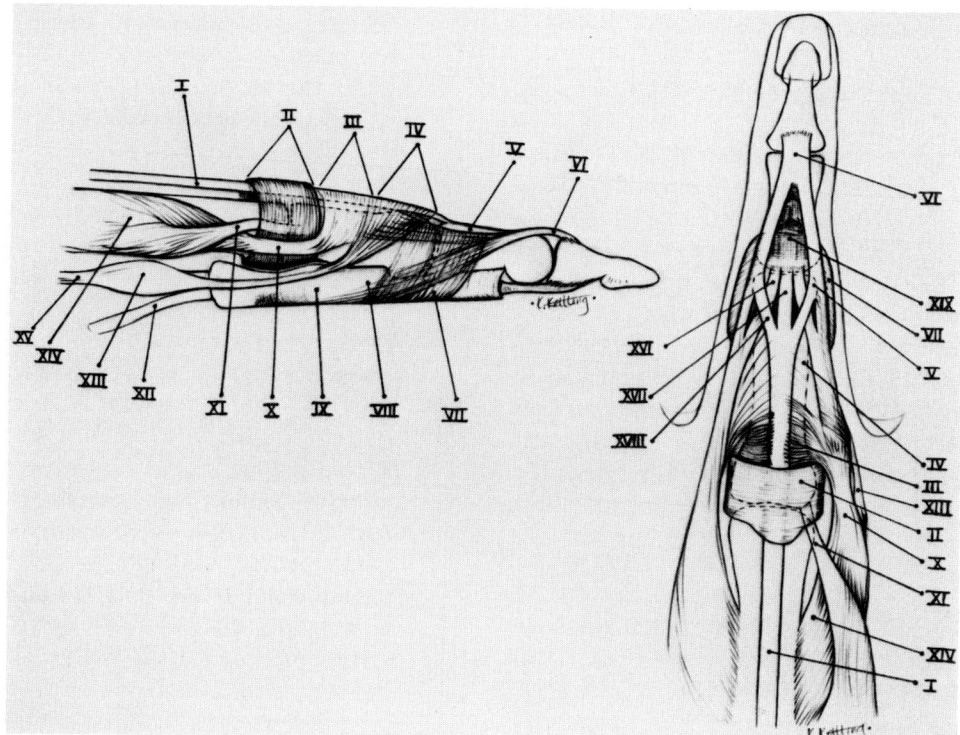

Figure 1-12. Extensor mechanism of the long finger. Common extensor tendon (I), Sagittal bands (II), Transverse fibers of the interossei (III), Oblique fibers of the interossei (IV), lateral conjoined tendon (V), terminal tendon (VI), Flexor digitorum profundus tendon (VII), Interosseus muscle (second dorsal) deep head (VIII), Lumbrical muscle (IX), Tendon of flexor digitorum superficialis (X), Medial tendon, superficial head of second dorsal interosseus (XI), Lateral tendon of deep head of second dorsal interosseus (XII), Fibrous flexor pulley (XIII), Oblique retinacular ligament (XIV), Transverse retinacular ligament (XV), Medial interosseus band (XVI), Central slip of the common extensor (XVII), Lateral slip of the common extensor (XVIII), Triangular ligament (XIX). (Redrawn from The American Society for surgery of the Hand, Regional Review Course in Hand Surgery, 1985)

on dorsum of proximal phalanx of index and middle fingers; flex MCP and extend PIP and DIP. Innervated by median nerve
  b. Third and fourth: adjoining sides of deep flexor tendons to middle and ring fingers and insert into tendon of EDC on dorsum of proximal phalanx of ring and little fingers; same action as first and second. Innervated by deep ulnar nerve
 2. Interossei (innervated by ulnar nerve)
  a. First, second, and fourth dorsal interossei are subdivided into superficial and deep groups, and superficial interossei insert at bases of proximal phalanges to abduct fingers
  b. Deep group and third dorsal interosseus insert into proximal dorsal hood or aponeurosis to flex MCP and extend IP joints
  c. Three volar interossei insert to dorsal aponeurosis to adduct fingers

IV. Superficial Palmar Hand
 A. Arteries
  1. Ulnar
   a. Passes deep to palmar carpal ligament, but superficial to flexor reti-

naculum, and lies lateral to pisiform bone
    b. Superficial palmar arch runs beneath palmar aponeurosis, but superficial to long flexor tendons, lumbricals, ulnar and median nerves. Arch is completed by a superficial palmar branch of the radial artery
   2. Radial: superficial branch helps make up superficial palmar arch
B. Nerves
   1. Radial nerve: superficial to lateral side of thumb; deep but does not enter hand
   2. Ulnar nerve: superficial to palmar cutaneous and palmar digitalis; runs deep with deep palmar arch to supply all interossei and adductor pollicis

V. Compartments
A. Thenar: contains short thumb muscles, except adductor, tendon of FPL, and palmar branch of radial artery
B. Hypothenar: contains all short muscles of small finger
C. Central: contains lumbricals, superficial volar arch, palmar branch of median nerve, superficial branch of ulnar nerve, and all the flexor tendons
D. Interossei/Adductor: contains interossei, adductor pollicis, second to fourth metacarpals, deep volar arch, deep ulnar nerve

VI. Tendon Sheaths, Nerves, and Vessels of the Fingers
A. Vincula (Fig 1-13)
   1. Short: 2 for each finger; from superficial to first IP joint and head of first phalanx; from deep tendon to second IP joint and head of second phalanx
   2. Long: 2 for each finger: under side of profunda to superficialis and from superficial tendon to proximal end of first phalanx
B. Sheaths
   1. Extensors: terminate in proximal third of hand and are not found in fingers
   2. Flexors: continuous with radial and ulnar bursae to thumb and index; for 3rd to 5th fingers, origins at heads of metacarpals and continue to insertions of deep flexors
C. Arteries
   1. Proper palmar digital: extend on either side of finger, dorsal to corresponding nerves. Cross anastomoses exist at fingertips and IP joint
   2. Dorsal digital: run just ventral to their corresponding nerves but reach only to the PIP joint
D. Nerves
   1. Proper palmar digital: lie just ventral to arteries; supply skin at end of finger, nail bed, and skin over dorsum of distal phalanx
   2. Dorsal digital: lie just above corresponding artery; extend to near the DIP joint

VII. Extensor Apparatus (Fig 1-12)
A. Junctura tendinae
   1. Commonly arise from extensor tendon of ring finger and insert to extensor tendons of middle and small digits
   2. Extension of ring finger, which may help extension of middle and small finger via juncturae if tendons are cut proximally
B. Sagittal band at MCP joint
   1. Arise from extensor central tendon and course between medial (superficial head) and lateral (deep head) tendons of dorsal interossei and attach to the volar plate and periosteum of the proximal phalanx
   2. Function as extension of the proximal phalanx and stabilization of the central tendon against ulnar subluxation and limit extensor excursion
C. Central tendon: divides into three slips
   1. Central slip inserts into the middle phalanx and joined by interossei medial bands

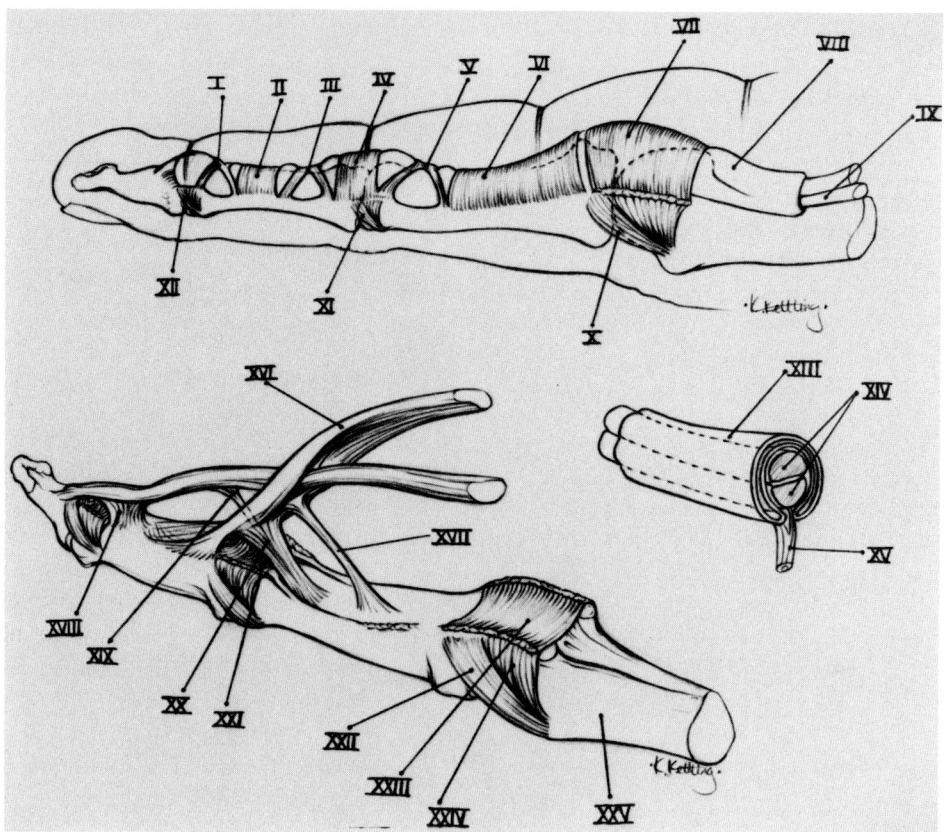

Figure 1-13. Pulleys and vincula anatomy of the flexor tendon. C3 pulley (I), A4 pulley (II), C2 pulley (III), A3 pulley (IV), C1 pulley (V), A2 pulley (VI), A1 pulley (VII), flexor digitorum superficialis (VIII), Flexor digitorum profundus (IX), Accessory ligament of metacarpo-phalangeal joint (X), Collateral ligament of the PIP joint (XI), Collateral ligament of DIP joint (XII), Synovial flexor sheath (XIII), Flexor tendons (XIV), Vinculum (XV), Flexor digitorum superficialis (XVI), Vinculum longus to superficialis (XVII), Vinculum brevis to profundus (XVIII), Vinculum longus to profundus (XIX), Vinculum brevis to superficialis (XX), Volar plate (XXI), Lateral collateral ligament (XXII), Volar plate (XXIII), Accessory ligament (XXIV), metacarpal (XXV). (Redrawn from Hoppenfeld S, deBoer P: Surgical Exposures in Orthopaedics. Philadelphia, JB Lippincott Inc, 1984)

    2. Two lateral slips insert into the distal phalanx via the lateral bands
    3. Rupture or attenuation leads to boutonnière deformity
  D. Aponeurotic expansion
    1. Proximal transverse fibers from interossei: flexion of MCP joints
    2. Distal oblique fibers from interossei and lumbricals: extension of PIP joints
    3. Adherence or contracture leads to intrinsic-plus deformity
  E. Lateral bands
    1. Conjoined tendon from lateral slips of common extensor tendon and lateral interossei band
    2. At 55° flexion, lateral bands act as flexors due to change of the central axis
  F. Triangular ligament
    1. Transverse directed fibers bounded proximally by insertion of central tendon slip, laterally by lateral bands
    2. Prevents excessive volar shift of lateral bands
    3. Attenuation leads to boutonnière deformity

G. Terminal extensor tendon
  1. The two conjoined lateral bands insert in dorsal base of distal phalanx
  2. Rupture leads to mallet deformity and hyperextension of DIP joint in boutonnière deformity
H. Transverse retinacular ligament
  1. From edge of flexor tendon sheath at PIP joint to lateral band
  2. Prevents excessive dorsal shift of lateral band
  3. Attenuation leads to swan-neck deformity
I. Oblique retinacular ligament
  1. From lateral crest of proximal phalanx, along volar to axis of PIP joint, to lateral extensor tendon
  2. DIP joint extension and all DIP joint flexion when PIP joint is flexed
  3. DIP joint flexion exercise is encouraged in boutonnière deformity to stretch this ligament before reconstruction
  4. May be involved in Dupuytren's contracture, causing PIP joint flexion and DIP joint extension
J. Cleland's ligament
  1. Origin from osseus flexor tendon gutter at PIP joint and insert to digital fascia (dorsal to neurovascular bundle)
  2. Hold skin in position during flexion and extension
K. Grayson's ligament
  1. Origin from volar aspect of flexor tendon sheath and insert to skin (volar to neurovascular bundle)
  2. Hold skin and neurovascular bundle (NVB) in place
  3. Frequently involved in Dupuytren's contracture

VIII. Surgical Approaches
A. Volar
  1. Surgery
     a. Zigzag incision crossing palm creases at 45° angle, making 90° angles to each limb of the zig
     b. To expose flexor tendons, incise subcutaneous tissue in a longitudinal fashion
     c. To expose NVB, separate subcutaneous tissue at lateral border of fibrous flexor sheath. NVB is separated from volar subcutaneous flap by Grayson's ligament
B. Midlateral approach
  1. Make a longitudinal incision on lateral aspect of finger, starting at most dorsal point of proximal finger crease
  2. Incise fibrous flexor sheath longitudinally to expose underlying tendon

6
Spine

I. Cervical Spine
A. Bony anatomy
  1. Atlas
     a. No body, anterior tubercle (longus collis attachment), posterior tubercle (rectus minor and suboccipital membrane attachment), and large transverse processes with transverse foramen (superior and inferior oblique muscle attachment)
     b. Posterior neural arch fuses at 3 years, and anterior neural arch (two sites) fuses at 7 years
  2. Axis
     a. Odontoid process with oval articular facet anteriorly, making a synovial joint with anterior arch facet and large spinous process (rectus major and inferior oblique muscle attachment)
     b. Synchondrosis between dens and arch and neurocentral cleft between the body and arch fuse at 3–6 years
  3. C3–C6 vertebrae: bifid spinous processes, pedicle, laminae, articular processes, lateral mass (between the articular processes), transverse processes with anterior and posterior tubercles and transverse foramen (carotid tubercle for C6 anterior tubercle and vertebral artery in foramen), uncinate processes (joints of Luschka) and triangular vertebral foramen
  4. C7 vertebra: large thick spinous process and not bifid
B. Ligamentous anatomy and articulation
  1. Atlantooccipital articulation: articulation between condyles of occipital bone superior facets of atlas; supported by anterior and posterior occipital membranes (continuation of anterior longitudinal membranes and ligamentum flavum, respectively) and capsule (flexion, extension, and lateral motion)
  2. Atlantoaxial articulation
     a. Rotational movement between the odontoid process and anterior arch of the atlas
     b. Ligaments
        (1) Anterior and posterior atlantoaxial ligaments
        (2) Transverse ligament: across the arch of atlas to hold dens against anterior arch of atlas (cruciform ligament of atlas: transverse ligament plus superior and inferior extension)
        (3) Alar ligament (sides of dens to condyles of occipital bone) and apical ligament (from apex of dens to foramen magnum as remnant of notocord in this area)
        (4) Tectoral membrane: continuation of posterior longitudinal membrane
  3. C2–C7 articulation
     a. Flexion and extension motion
     b. Facet joint and capsule: horizontal plane (45° oblique) of joint and weak capsule allow more mobility than lumbar and thoracic vertebrae
     c. Ligaments
        (1) Anterior and posterior longitudinal ligaments
        (2) Ligamenta flava: from posterior aspect of lamina below to anterior aspect of lamina above with deficiency in midline
        (3) Interspinous ligament: oblique orientation from posterior superior aspect to anterior inferior aspect

- (4) Supraspinous ligament
- (5) Ligamentum nuchae: fibroelastic septum from the occiput to C7
- d. Intervertebral discs: annulus fibrosus and nucleus pulposus

C. Muscles
1. Muscles
   a. Posterior muscles
      (1) Superficial: trapezius (from external occipital protuberance and C7 to T12 spinous processes to lateral clavicle, acromion, and spine of scapula)
      (2) Intermediate: splenius capitis and splenius cervicis
      (3) Deep: semispinalis capitis, semispinalis cervicis, and multifidus spinae with rotators
   b. Suboccipital muscles
      (1) Rectus capitis posterior major: C2 spinous process to inferior nuchal line
      (2) Rectus capitis posterior minor: C1 posterior tubercle to inferior nuchal line
      (3) Obliquus capitis inferior: C2 spinous process to transverse process of C1
      (4) Obliquus capitis superior: C1 transverse process to occipital bone between superior and inferior nuchal lines
   c. Anterior muscles
      (1) Platysma: from deltoid and pectoral fascia to mandible and skin. Innervated by facial (VII) nerve
      (2) Sternocleidomastoid: from sternum and clavicle to mastoid process
      (3) Strap muscles of larynx: sternohyoid and sternothyroid muscles
      (4) Omohyoid: superior and inferior bellies to depress the hyoid bone
      (5) Longus colli: anterior aspect of vertebral bodies

D. Approaches
1. Posterior approach to occiput and C1–C2
   a. Midline incision from external occipital protuberance to C2 spinous process (6–8 cm)
   b. Ligamentum nuchae and paravertebral muscle dissection to the posterior elements of C1 and C2
   c. Lateral exposure should not go beyond 1.5 cm on C1 ring (cervical ganglion and vertebral artery) and should be done with care so as not to fracture the C1 ring
   d. Separate occipitoatlantal and atlantoaxial membranes from bone for wiring
   e. Occiput: make drill holes above foramen magnum and remove bone distally for decompression (do not reach under edge of foramen magnum for possible uncontrolled bleeding). External occipital protuberance can be used for wiring
   f. Neurovascular structures
      (1) Suboccipital nerve (C1): within suboccipital triangle (motor)
      (2) Greater occipital nerve (C2): beneath and over inferior oblique muscle (sensory)
      (3) Third occipital nerve: lateral to suboccipital triangle (sensory)
      (4) Vertebral artery: from C6 transverse foramen to atlas transverse foramen to pierce the lateral angle of the posterior atlantooccipital membrane
2. Posterior approach to the cervical spine
   a. Midline incision down to spinous processes
   b. Lateral exposure to beginning of transverse processes, exposing the lateral masses
   c. Ligamenta flava excision from the midline
   d. Laminectomy or foraminotomy: re-

section of the medial aspect of superior and inferior facets or excision of disc or osteophytes of the joints of Luschka to decompress the nerve roots
  (1) C5 nerve root forms about a 45° angle with spinal cord; this angle increases as one descends to about a 90° angle at C8 level
  (2) Nerve roots: discs and joints of Luschka anteriorly, zygapophyseal articulations posteriorly, and pedicles superiorly and inferiorly. Also, vertebral artery is anterior to the roots

3. Anterior medial approach to midcervical spine (Fig 1-14)
  a. Landmarks
    (1) Hard palate: arch of atlas
    (2) Lower border of mandible: C2–C3
    (3) Hyoid bone: C3
    (4) Thyroid cartilage: C4–C5
    (5) Cricoid cartilage: C6
    (6) Carotid tubercle: C6
  b. Transverse incision from midline to posterior border of the sternocleidomastoid
  c. Split platysma longitudinally

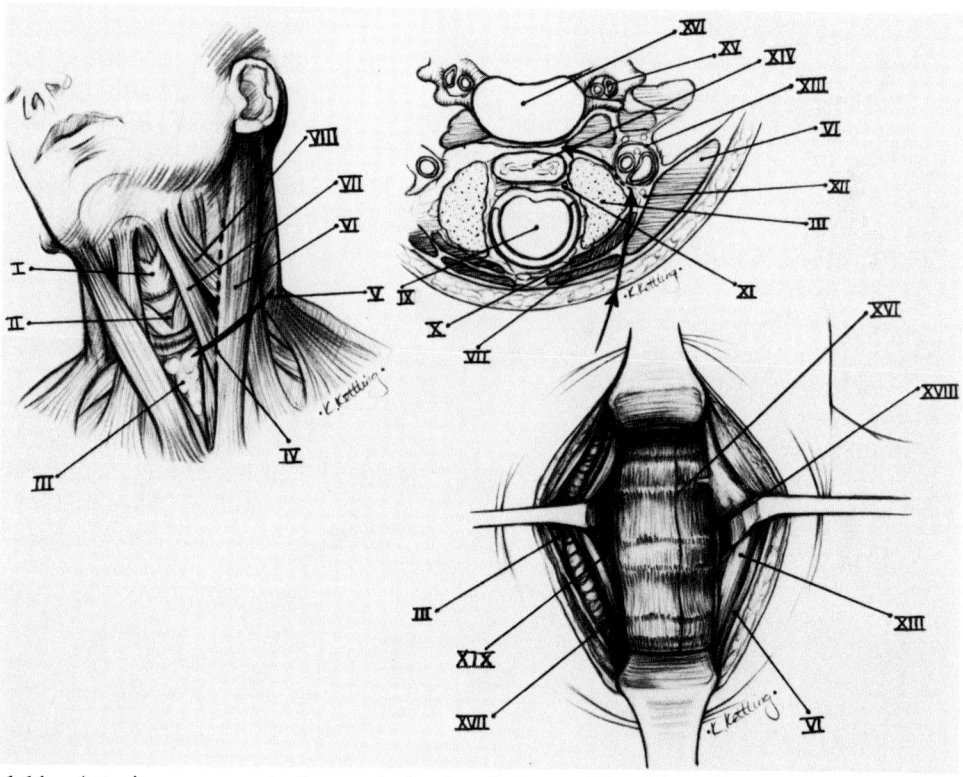

Figure 1-14. Anterior exposure to the cervical spine. Left top: Thyroid cartilage (I), Cricoid cartilage (II), Thyroid gland (III), Longitudinal incision for extensive exposure (IV), Transverse incision for most 1–3 level exposure (V), Sternocleidomastoid (VI), Sternohyoid (VII), Omohyoid (VIII), Right top: Trachea (IX), Sternothyroid (X), Recurrent laryngeal nerve (XI), Pretracheal fascia (XII), Carotid sheath (XIII), Esophagus (XIV), Vertebral artery (XV), Sternohyoid (VII). Bottom: Anterior longitudinal ligament (XVI), Esophagus (XVII), Sympathetic chain (XVIII), Longus colli (XIX), Sternocleidomastoid (VI), Trachea (III), and Carotid sheath (XIII). (Modified from Southwick WO, Robinson RA: Surgical approaches to the vertebral bodies in the cervical and lumbar regions. J Bone Joint Surg 39A:634, 1957)

d. Incise pretracheal fascia immediately anterior to sternocleidomastoid, followed by blunt finger dissection to vertebral bodies, retracting carotid sheath (carotid artery, internal jugular vein, and vagus nerve) laterally and strap muscles, trachea, and esophagus medially
e. Superior thyroid arteries may limit dissection above C3–C4, and inferior thyroid artery below C6 (may ligate and divide)
f. With a cautery, divide prevertebral fascia and anterior longitudinal ligament in midline, retracting the longus colli laterally
g. Bone graft insertion after discectomy is a common procedure (Fig 1-15)
h. Neurovascular and vital structures
  (1) Recurrent laryngeal nerve: ascends in the neck between the trachea and esophagus from the arch of the aorta on the left side; runs along the trachea after hooking around the subclavian artery on the right side. It crosses from lateral to medial to the midline of trachea in the lower part of the neck, making the right-sided approach slightly more vulnerable. Protect it by placing the retractor below longus colli muscles
  (2) Sympathetic nerves and stellate ganglion: avoid dissection out onto transverse processes and keep dissection subperiosteal
  (3) Carotid sheath contents: carotid artery, internal jugular vein, and vagus nerve anterior to the sternocleidomastoid muscle
  (4) Esophagus: take precaution on deep medial retraction
4. Other anterior approaches to the cervical spine

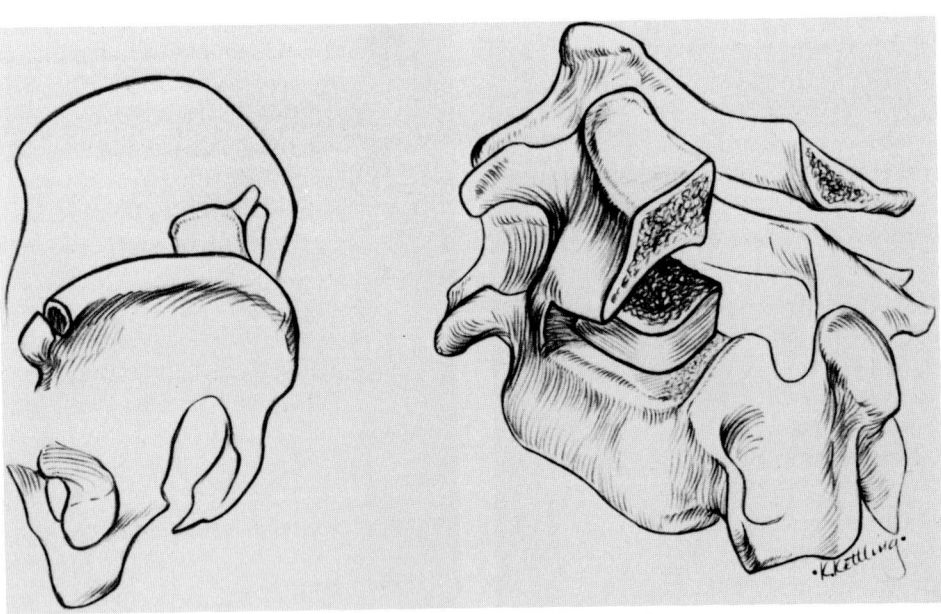

Figure 1-15. Illustration of anterior cervical fusion. Left: Tricortical bone graft from the iliac crest Right: The graft is countersunk about 2 mm posterior to the anterior lip of the vertebrae.

a. Transoral approach to C1–C2
b. Anteromedial approach to C1, C2, C3
c. Anterolateral approach to upper cervical spine
d. Lateral approach to cervical spine (Verbiest)
e. Lateral approach to cervical spine (Hodgson)
f. Supraclavicular approach
g. Lincoln highway approach to cervical spine

II. Thoracolumbar Spine, Sacrum, and Coccyx

A. Bony and ligamentous anatomy
 1. Thoracic vertebrae
    a. Mechanically stiffer and less mobile because of rib attachment
    b. Physiologic kyphosis
    c. Upper and middle thoracic vertebrae are stabilized against anteroposterior translation, and lower thoracic vertebrae are stabilized against rotation by facet joint orientation
    d. Transverse processes decrease from T1 to T10 in size
    e. Spinal canal is round and has less free space for the spinal cord than the cervical and lumbar regions
    f. Articular facets for ribs: body and transverse process and ligaments (radiate and costovertebral ligaments between the body and rib and costotransverse and intertransverse ligaments between the transverse process and rib)
 2. Lumbar vertebrae
    a. Strong facet joint and capsule for rotational stability and superior articular processes are lateral (mammillary process) and anterior to inferior articular process below
    b. Pedicles: located at 1 mm inferior to tip of inferior articular process and in line with the middle of transverse processes
    c. Triangular spinal canal
    d. Ligaments
       (1) Supraspinous ligament: ends around L3
       (2) Interspinous ligament: oriented obliquely from superior to inferior, from posterior to anterior
       (3) Posterior longitudinal ligament
       (4) Anterior longitudinal ligament
       (5) Ligamenta flava: from posterior aspect of lamina below to anterior aspect of lamina above
 3. Sacrum and coccyx
    a. Bony structures of sacrum: ala, promontory, median sacral crest, sacral foramina, articular surface
    b. Coccyx
    c. Sacroiliac joint
       (1) Articular process: sacral hyaline cartilage and iliac fibrocartilage
       (2) Ligaments: interosseous sacroiliac ligament, posterior sacroiliac ligament, anterior sacroiliac ligament
    d. Connecting ligaments
       (1) Sacrotuberous ligament: sacrum to ischial tuberosity
       (2) Sacrospinous ligament: divides pelvis into greater and lesser sciatic notches
       (3) Iliolumbar ligaments: L5 transverse processes to ala of sacrum
B. Soft tissue structures
 1. Muscles
    a. Superficial
       (1) Latissimus dorsi: origin from T6–T12, lumbar spine, sacrum and posterior iliac crest, and lower four ribs to insert at bottom of intertubercular groove of the humerus
       (2) Levator scapulae: origin from C1–C4 transverse processes to insert at the medial border of scapula above the spine
       (3) Rhomboid minor: origin from C7–

T1 to insert at medial border of scapula at the root of the spine
    (4) Rhomboid major: origin from T2–T5 to insert at medial border of the scapula below spine
  b. Deep muscles of the back
    (1) Superficial layer (costotransverse group or erector spinae): iliocostalis, longissimus, spinalis
    (2) Deeper layer (transversospinal group): semispinalis, multifidus, rotatores
    (3) Deepest layer: interspinales and intertransversarii
2. Neural structures
  a. Spinal cord
    (1) Begins at cephalic border of atlas and ends in filum terminale at L1 or L2
    (2) H-shaped gray matter and peripheral white matter
  b. Meninges
    (1) Dura mater: outer covering of spinal cord
    (2) Arachnoid: thin membrane containing spinal fluid
    (3) Pia mater: thin covering of spinal cord, containing small vessels
  c. Spinal nerves (Fig 1-16)
    (1) Dorsal sensory and ventral motor roots merge to become spinal nerve
    (2) Each nerve root exits below the pedicle and above the disc
    (3) Dorsal root ganglion in intervertebral foramen below the pedicle
    (4) Three branches: ventral ramus for motor, sinu-vertebral nerve to the annulus of the disc, dorsal ramus for facets and posterior muscles
  d. Sacral plexus (Fig 1-17)
    (1) Lumbosacral trunk (L4, L5) and S1, S2, S3, and S4 anterior rami
    (2) Sciatic (L4–S3) and pudendal (S2–S4) nerves
    (3) Branches: superior gluteal (L4–S1), inferior gluteal to obturator internus and quadratus femoris (L5–S2), and posterior cutaneous nerve of the thigh (S1–S3)
    (4) Anterior coccygeal plexus: S5 and coccygeal anterior rami to become anterior caudal nerve

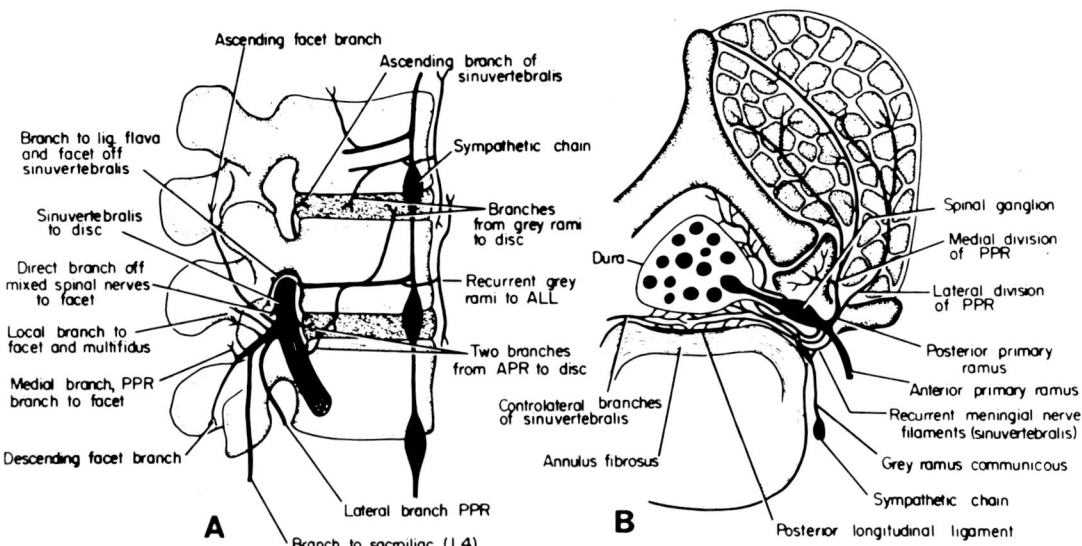

Figure 1-16. Neuroanatomy of the lumbar spine. (From Dupuis PR, Kirkaldy-Willis WH: The spine: integrated function and pathophysiology. In Cruess RL, Rennie WRJ: Adult Orthopaedics. New York, Churchill Livingstone, 1984)

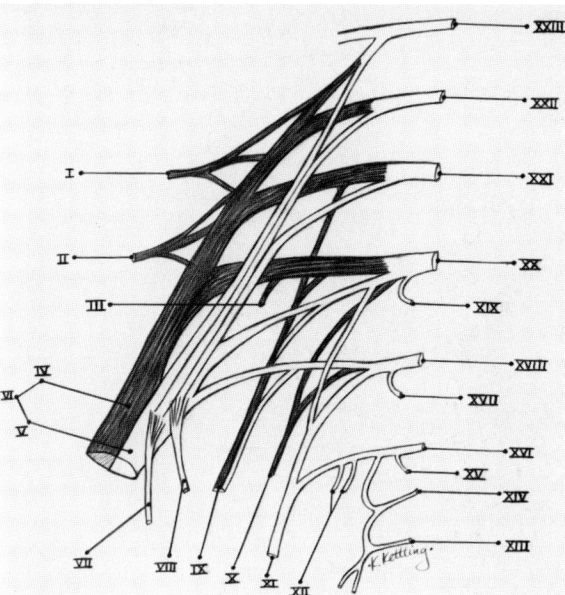

Figure 1-17. Lumbosacral plexus. Superior gluteal (I), inferior gluteal (II), piriformis (III), common peroneal (IV), tibial (V), sciatic (VI), quadratus femoris and inferior gemellus (VII), obturator internus and superior gemellus (VIII), posterior cutaneous femoris (IX), perforating cutaneus (X), pudendal (XI), levator ani, coccygeus, and sphincter ani externus (XII), coccygeal (XIII), fifth sacral (XIV), visceral branch (XV, XVII, IX), fourth sacral (XVI), third sacral (XVIII), second sacral (XX), first sacral (XXI), fifth lumbar (XXII), fourth lumbar (XXIII).

C. Approaches
  1. Posterior approaches
    a. Thoracic spine: midline exposure of posterior elements (spinous process, lamina, facets, and transverse processes)
    b. Lumbar spine
      (1) Laminotomy and discectomy: unilaterally expose spinous process, lamina, and ligamenta flava (Fig 1-18)
      (2) Excise ligamenta flava to enter the epidural space
      (3) Nerve root is medially retracted to remove offending disc material
    c. Transpedicular approach
      (1) Thoracic spine: pedicle is located by crossing a horizontal line at the midportion of transverse process and a vertical line at junction between the lamina and transverse process ("valley")
      (2) Lumbar spine: pedicle is located by crossing a horizontal line at the midportion of the transverse

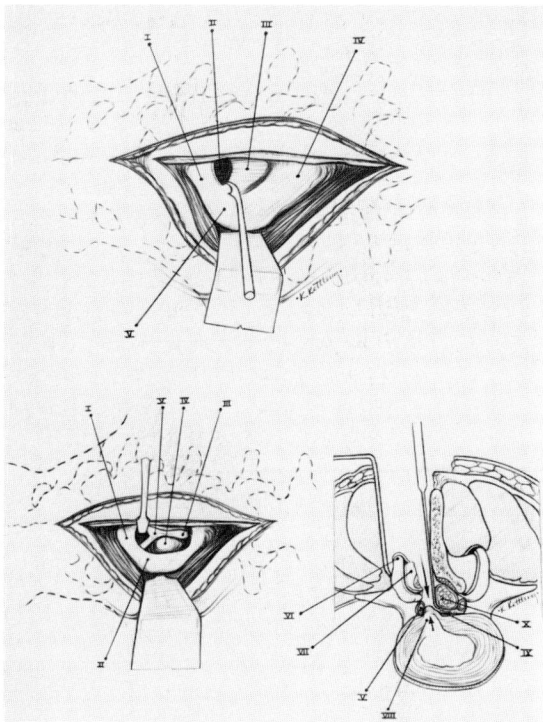

Figure 1-18. Top: Unilateral exposure for excision of herniated lumbar disc. Removal of ligamentum flavum (III) by cutting its caudal attachment to the inferior lamina (I) or cephalad attachment to the superior lamina (IV). Epidural space (II) is shown under the ligamentum flavum. The facet joint and capsule (V) are lateral to the lamina. Bottom left: Following excision of ligamentum flavum, exposure of the lateral aspect (V) of the nerve root (III) is exposed by bone removal and the nerve root is retracted medially. Herniated disc (IV) is visualized. Part of the facet joint (II) may have to be undercut to visualize the lateral aspect of the nerve root. Bottom right: Cross section revealing a herniated lumbar disc (VIII) prior to medial retraction of the spinal nerve (V). In order to safely retract this spinal nerve, part of the superior articular process of the distal vertebra (VI) should be undercut first. The inferior articular process of the proximal vertebra (VII) is left alone. The thecal sac with cauda equina (X) and venous structures overlying the posterior longitudinal ligament (IX) are also shown (Redrawn from Hoppenfeld S, deBoer P: Surgical Exposures in Orthopaedics. Philadelphia, JB Lippincott Inc, 1984)

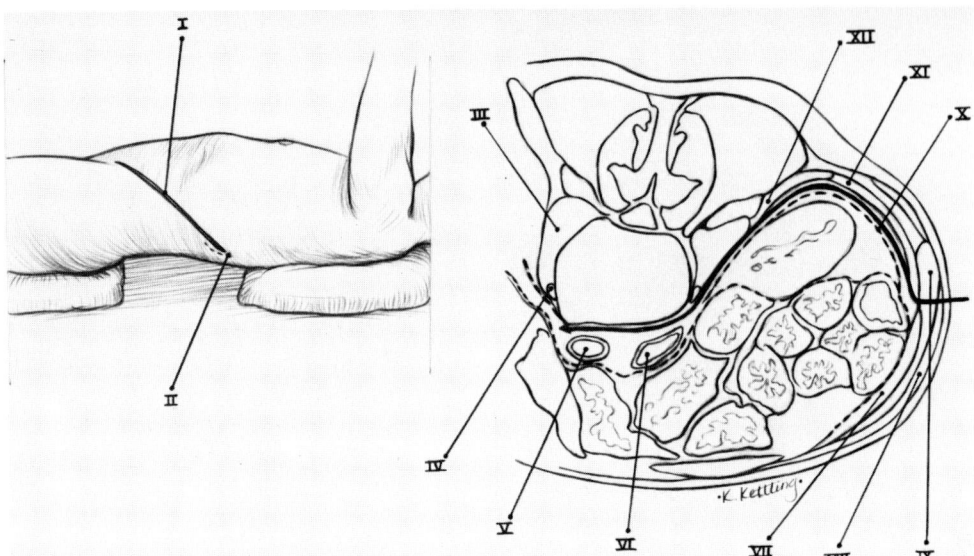

Figure 1-19. Anterolateral approach to the lumbar vertebrae. Left: Oblique flank incision (I) between the inferior rib cage (II) and the iliac crest. Right: Cross section revealing the plane of dissection between renal fascia (X) and the retroperitoneal fat pad (XI), quadratus lumborum (XII), and psoas muscle (III). Dissection involves cutting through the external oblique (VIII), internal oblique (IX), and transverse abdominis (VII) muscles. Sympathetic trunck (IV), inferior vena cava (V), and aorta (VI) are also shown.

   processes and a vertical line at the lateral edge of the superior facet
2. Anterior approaches
   a. Thoracic spine: transthoracic approach by removing a rib and dividing the pleura
   b. Thoracolumbar junction: thoracoabdominal approach by removing 10th rib and dividing diaphragm and dissecting retroperitoneal space
   c. Lumbar spine: retroperitoneal approach (Fig 1-19)
      (1) Dissection is through external oblique, internal oblique, and transversus abdominis muscles
      (2) Retroperitoneal space is entered laterally by identifying retroperitoneal fat, taking care to avoid penetration of peritoneum just lateral to rectus sheath
      (3) Blunt finger dissection anterior to psoas muscle should lead to spine. Identify genitofemoral nerve on anterior surface of psoas muscle and sympathetic chains medial to muscle
      (4) Ureter is under peritoneum anteriorly
      (5) Vessels (aorta or vena cava) are mobilized, and segmental vessels are identified in middle portion of vertebral bodies and are ligated as necessary
      (6) For exposure of lumbosacral junction, iliac vessels are mobilized, or transperitoneal approach may be used

7
Hip

I. Bony
A. Acetabulum: formed superiorly by ilium, posteroinferiorly by ischium, and anteroinferiorly by pubis
  1. Ossification
     a. Lower ilium appears 8th fetal week; closes 18th year
     b. Superior ramus appears 3rd fetal month; closes 18th year
     c. Acetabulum appears 12th year; closes 18th year
B. Proximal femur
  1. Ossification
     a. Head appears 1st year; closes after puberty
     b. Greater trochanter appears 4th year; closes after puberty
     c. Lesser trochanter appears 13th year; closes after puberty
  2. Blood supply
     a. Medial femoral circumflex artery: upper capsular arteries (posterior branch) supply 65–80% of epiphysis
     b. Obturator artery: arises from internal iliac; gives branch to acetabulum (ligamentum teres); supplies 20% of epiphysis
     c. Lateral femoral circumflex artery: supplies lateral metaphysis and muscles

II. Joint
A. Type: ball and socket
B. Motion: flexion, extension, abduction, adduction, external rotation, internal rotation
C. Ligaments
  1. Acetabular labrum: deepens socket
  2. Transverse acetabular: completes acetabulum inferiorly
  3. Articular capsule: from acetabular rim to intertrochanteric crest
  4. Iliofemoral (ligament of Bigelow): anterior inferior iliac spine to intertrochanteric line
  5. Ischiofemoral: posterior ischium to blend with capsule
  6. Pubofemoral: superior pubic ramus to join iliofemoral
  7. Ligamentum teres: acetabular notch and transverse ligament to fovea of femur

III. Muscles
A. Flexors
  1. Iliopsoas: from iliac crest and L1–L5 transverse processes to lesser trochanter (L2, L3 nerve)
  2. Sartorius: from anterior superior iliac spine (ASIS) to upper medial tibia (femoral nerve)
  3. Pectineus: from pubis to pectineal line (femoral nerve)
  4. Rectus femoris: from anterior inferior iliac spine to patellar base (femoral nerve)
B. Extensors
  1. Gluteus maximus: from ilium to gluteal tuberosity (inferior gluteal nerve)
  2. Hamstrings (tibial portion of sciatic nerve)
     a. Semitendinosus: ischial tuberosity to pes anserinus
     b. Semimembranosus: ischial tuberosity to posteromedial tibia
     c. Biceps femoris (long head): ischial tuberosity to head of fibula
C. Abductors
  1. Gluteus medius: from outer ilium to lateral greater trochanter (superior gluteal nerve)
  2. Gluteus minimus: from outer ilium to anterior greater trochanter (superior gluteal nerve)
  3. Tensor fascia lata: from anterior iliac

crest to iliotibial band (superior gluteal nerve)
   4. Piriformis: from anterior sacrum to upper greater trochanter (nerve to piriformis)
D. Adductors
   1. Adductor group (obturator nerve)
      a. Adductor longus: from front of pubis to linea aspera
      b. Adductor brevis: from inferior pubic ramus to pectineal line, linea aspera
      c. Adductor magnus: from inferior ischiopubic rami to adductor tubercle
   2. Gracilis: from lower symphysis to proximal medial tibia or pes anserinus (obturator nerve)
   3. Pectineus
   4. Obturator externus: ischiopubic rami to trochanteric fossa (obturator nerve)
   5. Quadratus femoris: ischial tuberosity to quadrate line (nerve to quadratus femoris)
E. Internal rotators
   1. Gluteus medius
   2. Gluteus minimus
   3. Tensor fascia lata
F. External rotators
   1. Piriformis
   2. Obturator internus: from ischiopubic rami to greater trochanter (nerve to obturator internus)
   3. Gemellus superior: from ischial spine to tendon of obturator internus (nerve to obturator internus)
   4. Gemellus inferior: from ischial tuberosity to tendon of obturator internus (nerve to quadratus femoris)
   5. Obturator externus
   6. Quadratus femoris
   7. Gluteus maximus
   8. Adductors

IV. Surgical Approaches
A. Anterior (Smith-Petersen) (Fig 1-20)
   1. Surgery
      a. Long incision following anterior half of iliac crest across ASIS and curve down vertically for 10 cm, aiming for lateral patella
      b. Externally rotate leg and develop plane between tensor fascia lata and sartorius (retract lateral femoral cutaneous nerve medially)
      c. Detach iliac origin of tensor fascia lata and retract laterally
      d. Detach both heads of rectus femoris and retract medially
      e. Retract gluteus medius laterally
      f. Retract iliopsoas medially; then adduct and externally rotate leg
      g. Incise hip joint capsule and dislocate hip with external rotators
   2. Dangers
      a. Lateral femoral cutaneous nerve: passes over sartorius 2.5 cm below ASIS
      b. Femoral nerve: directly over hip joint, medial to rectus
      c. Ascending branch of lateral femoral circumflex artery: crosses field between sartorius and tensor fascia lata and must be ligated
B. Anterolateral (Watson-Jones)
   1. Surgery
      a. Flex thigh into 30° angle and adduct it
      b. Center a 15 cm incision on greater trochanter
      c. Incise fascia lata distally to expose vastus lateralis
      d. Bluntly develop plane between tensor fascia lata and gluteus medius
      e. Retract gluteus medius proximally and laterally
      f. Externally rotate leg and reflect vastus lateralis origin inferiorly for 1 cm
      g. Detach abductor mechanism
      h. Detach reflected head of rectus femoris
      i. Incise anterior capsule longitudinally
   2. Dangers
      a. Femoral nerve: injured when retrac-

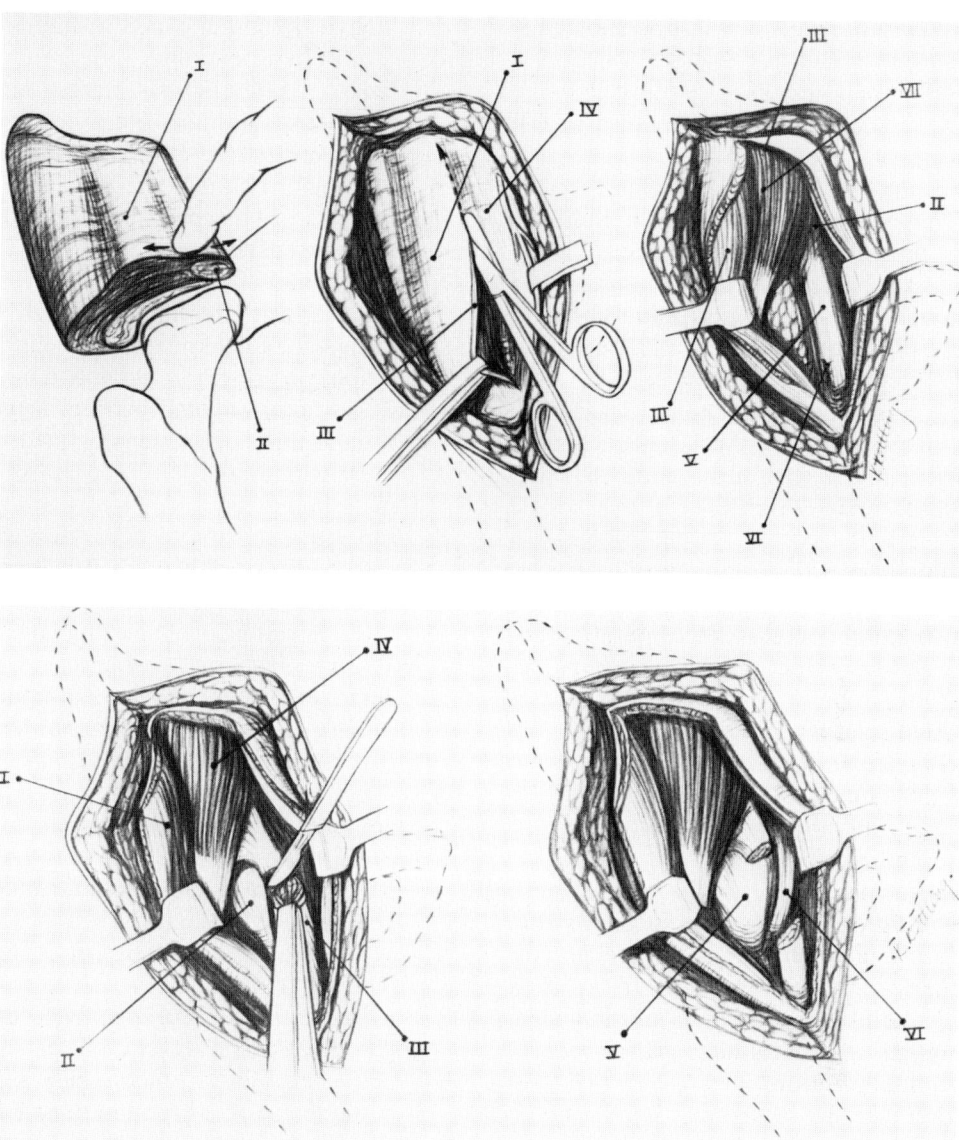

Figure 1-20. The anterior Smith-Peterson approach to the hip. Top left: Dissection is between tensor fasciae latae (I) and the sartorius (II) Top center: After diviing the tascia lata (III), develop a plane between tensor fascia lata (I) and sartorius (IV) Top left: The deeper layer shows the gluteus medius (VII), rectus femoris (V), and ascending branch of the lateral femoral circumflex artery (VI). Bottom left: Detach both heads of rectus femoris (III) and retract medially. Anterior capsule (II) of the joint is visible. Bottom right: Retract gluteus medius laterally and iliopsoas (VI) medially. Incise hip joint capsule (V) and dislocate hip with external rotation (Redrawn from Hoppenfeld S, deBoer P: Surgical Exposures in Orthopaedics. Philadelphia, JB Lippincott Inc, 1984.)

tors are placed within the substance of iliopsoas
  b. Femoral vessels
C. Posterior (Southern or Moore approach)
  1. Surgery
    a. Center a 15 cm curved incision on posterior aspect of the greater trochanter, curving across buttock
    b. Incise fascia lata and continue proximally in line with skin incision
    c. Split fibers of gluteus maximus
    d. Internally rotate and place stay sutures in piriformis and obturator internus and detach muscles near their insertion into greater trochanter. Lay muscles over the sciatic nerve
    e. T-shaped incision in capsule
  2. Dangers
    a. Sciatic nerve: exits sciatic notch and enters field under piriformis before traveling on top of short external rotators
    b. Inferior gluteal artery: under gluteus medius
D. Straight lateral approach (Hardinge or Liverpool approach)
  1. Surgery
    a. Make a straight line incision from proximal femoral shaft over greater trochanter and midportion between anterior and posterior superior iliac spines with patient in lateral decubitus position
    b. Divide the fascia lata, exposing the gluteus medius
    c. Split the gluteus medius in line with muscle fibers and reflect it along with its tendinous attachment and gluteus minimus anteriorly, while leaving the posterior ⅔ tendon attachment intact
    d. Divide or resect the capsule for exposure of the joint
  2. Dangers
    a. Superior reflection of gluteus medius must be done without damaging superior gluteal vessels and nerves
    b. Retractor is placed anteriorly and must not damage femoral neurovascular structures
E. Medial approach
  1. Surgery
    a. Incision over the adductor longus
    b. Dissect interval between adductus longus anteriorly and gracilis posteriorly
    c. Dissect deeper between adductor brevis and adductor magnus
    d. Anterior branch of obturator nerve is between adductor longus and adductor brevis, and posterior branch of obturator nerve is between adductor brevis and adductor magnus
    e. Medial capsulotomy leads to the joint
  2. Dangers
    a. Branches of obturator nerve
    b. Medial femoral circumflex artery that passes around medial side of the distal psoas tendon must be preserved

8
Thigh

I. Bony: Femur
A. Ossification
  1. Body appears 7th fetal week
  2. Distal portion appears 9th fetal week; closes 20th year
B. Neck or shaft angle: 125°
C. Normal anteversion: 5°–15° in adults (greater in females)

II. Muscles
A. Anterior
  1. Sartorius
  2. Quadriceps
    a. Rectus femoris
    b. Vastus medialis
    c. Vastus lateralis
    d. Vastus intermedius
B. Medial
  1. Pectineus
  2. Adductors
    a. Adductor longus
    b. Adductor magnus
    c. Adductor brevis
  3. Gracilis
C. Posterior
  1. Biceps femoris
  2. Semitendinosus
  3. Semimembranosus

III. Septa
A. Medial: divides extensors and adductors; extends inward between quadriceps and adductor longus
B. Lateral: separates vastus lateralis from biceps femoris

IV. Vascular
A. Femoral artery: branches into superficial epigastric, superficial circumflex iliac, external pudendal, deep femoral, genicular arteries
B. Profunda femoris artery
  1. Courses medial to femur, behind adductor longus, and ends as fourth perforator
  2. Branches
    a. Medial circumflex: medial femur between pectineus and psoas
    b. Lateral circumflex: arises laterally behind sartorius
    c. Three perforators arise and pierce adductor magnus to reach back of thigh
C. Obturator artery
D. Femoral vein: begins at hiatus of adductor magnus and receives tributaries from deep femoral and great saphenous

V. Nervous (Fig 1-21)
A. Femoral: lateral to artery and cutaneous to anterior and medial thigh
B. Saphenous: runs with femoral artery, crossing from lateral to medial in adductor canal
C. Obturator
  1. Anterior: lies between adductor longus and brevis
  2. Posterior: lies between adductor brevis and magnus
D. Sciatic: lies behind ischium and short external rotators, lies on adductor magnus, and is crossed by long head of biceps femoris. Splits above popliteal fossa into tibial and common peroneal

VI. Adductor (Hunter's) Canal
A. Begins at apex of femoral triangle and ends in hiatus of adductor magnus
B. At caudal end (adductor hiatus), femoral vessels enter popliteal space

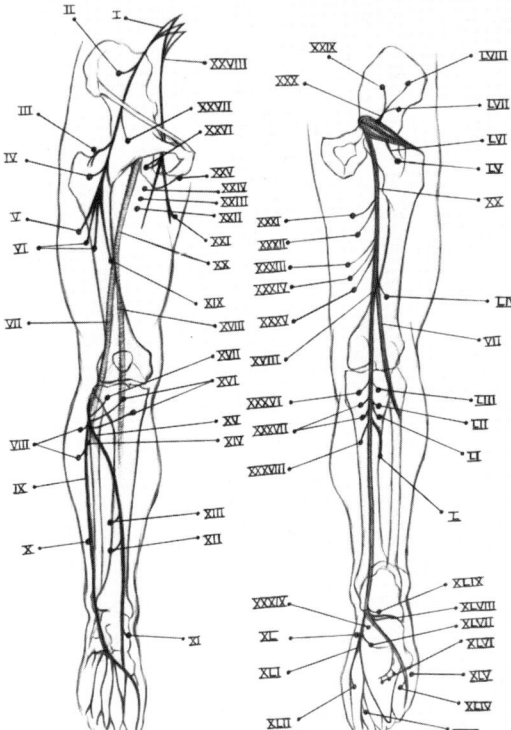

Figure 1-21. Nerves of the lower extremities. Femoral nerve (I), iliacus (II), sartorius (III), rectus femoris (IV), vastus lateralis (V), vastus intermedius (VI), common peroneal nerve (VII), peronius longus (VIII), superficial peroneal nerve (IX), peroneus brevis (X), extensor digitorum brevis (XI), peronius tertius (XII), extensor hallucis longus (XIII), extensor digitorum longus (XIV), deep peroneal nerve (XV), tibialis anterior (XVI), extensor digitorum longus (XVII), tibial nerve (XVIII), vastus medialis (XIX), sciatic nerve (XX), adductor magnus (XXI), adductor longus (XXII), adductor brevis (XXIII), gracilis (XXIV), obturator externus (XXV), pectineus (XXVI, XXVII), obturator nerve (XXVIII), gluteus minimus (XXIX), superior gluteal nerve (XXX), semitendinosus (XXXI), long head of biceps femoris (XXXII), adductor magnus (XXXIII), semimembranosus (XXXIV), semitendinosus (XXXV), medial head of gastrocnemius (XXXVI), soleus (XXXVII), flexor digitorum longus (XXXVIII), flexor accesorius (XXXIX), abductor hallucis (XL), medial plantar nerve (XLI), flexor hallucis brevis (XLII), lumbricalis (XLIII), interosseus (XLIV), flexor digiti minimi brevis (XLV), interossei, lumbricalis, adductor hallucis (XLVI), flexor digitorum brevis (XLVII), lateral plantar nerve (XLVIII), abductor digiti minimi (XLIX), flexor hallucis longus (L), tibialis posterior (LI), popliteus (LII), lateral head of gastrocnemius (LIII), short head of biceps femoris (LIV), gluteus maximus (LV), inferior gluteal nerve (LVI), gluteus medius (LVII), tensor fasciae latae (LVIII).

VII. Surgical Approaches

A. Lateral
  1. Surgery
     a. Incise skin over greater trochanter and extend down lateral aspect of thigh
     b. Incise fascia lata and incise vastus lateralis fascia
     c. Split vastus in line with its fibers
     d. Incise periosteum
  2. Dangers: perforators of profunda femoris must be coagulated

B. Anterolateral
  1. Surgery
     a. Linear incision 5 cm below ASIS to lateral border of patella
     b. Incise fascia lata
     c. Identify plane between vastus lateralis and rectus femoris
     d. Split fibers of vastus intermedius and incise periosteum
  2. Dangers
     a. Nerve to vastus lateralis enters medial side of muscle at upper part of the femoral shaft
     b. Branches of lateral femoral circumflex artery cross field

C. Anteromedial
  1. Surgery
     a. Incision 10 cm over interval between rectus femoris and vastus medialis
     b. Incise fascia lata and cut through medial patellar retinaculum
     c. Continue proximally, splitting quadriceps
     d. Split vastus intermedius in line with its fibers
     e. Incise periosteum
  2. Dangers: Medial superior genicular artery winds around lower end of medial femur

D. Posterior
  1. Surgery
     a. Incision 20 cm down midline of posterior thigh

- b. Incise deep fascia lateral to line of skin incision
- c. Develop plane between biceps femoris and vastus lateralis, covered by lateral intermuscular septum
- d. Detach origin of biceps short head from linea aspera and reflect it medially
- e. Retract long head of biceps laterally in distal aspect of wound to expose sciatic nerve

2. Dangers
   - a. Sciatic nerve lies medial to biceps in upper part of incision
   - b. Nerve to biceps femoris enters muscle from medial side proximally

E. Approaches to the distal femur
   1. Posterolateral approach
      - a. Dissect between vastus lateralis and lateral intermuscular septum
      - b. Reflect vastus lateralis anteriorly and divide periosteum along shaft
      - c. Be careful not to perforate branches of deep femoral artery
   2. Medial approach
      - a. Medial incision and dissection between vastus medialis and adductor magnus
      - b. Be careful of saphenous nerve and femoral artery

9
Knee

I. **Bony**
  A. Distal femur
    1. Attachment for anterior cruciate ligament (ACL) and posterior cruciate ligament (PCL)
    2. Attachment for tibial and fibular collateral ligaments
    3. Patellofemoral sulcus
    4. Femoral condyles (medial larger)
  B. Tibia (proximal)
    1. Ossification: appears at birth; closes at 20th year
    2. Tibial plateau
      a. Posterior inclination of 10°
      b. Medial plateau is larger and concave
      c. Lateral plateau is smaller and convex
    3. Gerdy's tubercle for iliotibial band attachment
    4. Menisci and cruciate attachments
  C. Patella
    1. Ossification: appears 2nd year; closes at puberty
    2. Largest sesamoid bone
    3. Facets
      a. Lateral facet is concave and larger
      b. Medial facet is convex and smaller but varies
      c. Odd facet makes contact in extreme flexion
    4. Largest contact with femur at 45°

II. **Joint**
  A. Type: hinge between femur and tibia and arthrodial between femur and patella
  B. Motion: flexion, extension, slight rotation; patella allows sliding
  C. Ligaments
    1. Medial (divided into thirds) (Fig 1-22)
      a. Anterior: capsule (weak)
      b. Middle: superficial collateral ligament, deep collateral ligament
      c. Posterior: posterior capsule, posterior oblique ligament, oblique popliteal ligament (semimembranosus), medial head of gastrocnemius
    2. Lateral (Fig 1-23)
      a. Anterior: capsule (weak), lateral retinaculum
      b. Middle: iliotibial band, deep capsule
      c. Posterior: fibular collateral, arcuate ligament, popliteal aponeurosis, lateral head of gastrocnemius
  D. Intra-articular structures (Fig 1-24)
    1. Synovial membrane: suprapatellar pouch attached superiorly by genu articularis; invests cruciate ligaments and popliteal tendon
    2. Cruciate ligaments
      a. Anterior
        (1) Forty by 10 mm, intra-articular, extrasynovial
        (2) Posterior intercondylar surface of lateral femoral condyle to anterolateral tibial spine
        (3) Anteromedial bundle: tense in entire arc of motion, especially flexion
        (4) Posterolateral bundle: tense in extension (greater bulk and length)
        (5) Blood supplied by medial geniculate artery and medial or lateral fat pads
      b. Posterior
        (1) Thirty-eight by 13 mm
        (2) Attach at posterior part of lateral surface of medial femoral condyle and at depression behind posterior tibia
    3. Menisci
      a. Crescent-shaped fibrocartilages with vascular periphery; attached to borders of tibia by coronary ligaments

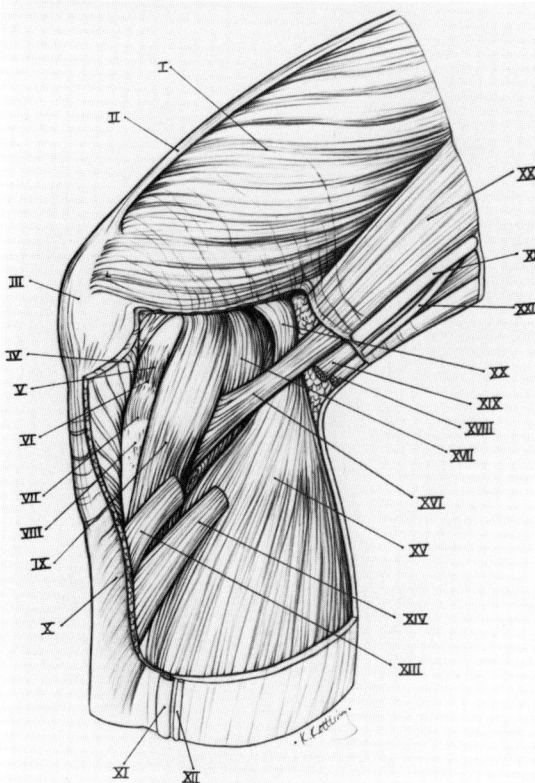

Figure 1-22. Structures of the medial aspect of the knee. Vastus medialis (I), Quadriceps tendon (II), Patella (III), Medial patellar retinaculum (IV), Anterior joint capsule (V), Medial meniscus (VI), Coronary ligament (VII), Medial tibial plateau (VIII), Superficial medial ligament (IX), Pes anserinus (X), Long saphenous vein (XI), Saphenous nerve (XII), Gracilis (XIII), Semitendinosus (XIV), Medial head of gastrocnemius (XV), Semimembranosus (XVI), Posteromedial joint capsule (XVII), Semditendinosus (XVIII), Gracilis (XIX), Medial head of gastrocnemius (XX), Saphenous nerve (XXI), Long saphenous vein (XXII), Sartorius (XXIII). (Redrawn from Hoppenfeld S, deBoer P: Surgical Exposures in Orthopaedics. Philadelphia, JB Lippincott Inc, 1984)

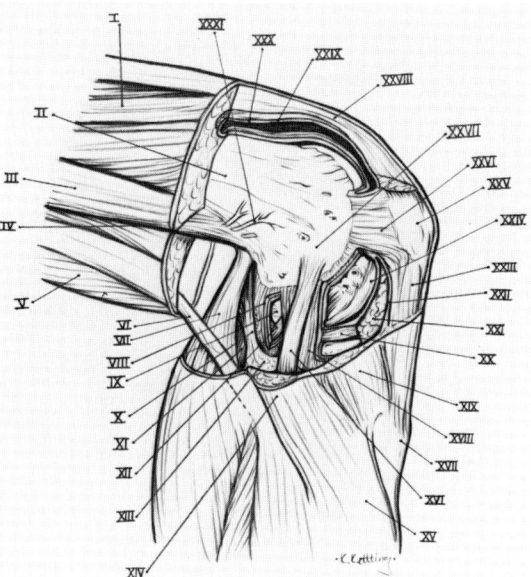

Figure 1-23. Structures of the lateral aspect of the knee. Vastus lateralis (I), Femur (II), Iliotibial band (III), Lateral intermuscular septum (IV), Biceps femoris (V), common peroneal nerve (VI), Lateral head of gastrocnemius (VII), Posterolateral joint capsule (VIII), Lateral femoral condyle (IX), Arcuate ligament (X), Popliteus (XI), Popliteus tendon (XII), Fibular head (XIII), Tendon of biceps femoris (XIV), Tibia (XV), Superficial lateral collateral ligament (XVI), Tibial tubercle (XVII), Joint capsule (XVIII), Iliotibial band (XIX), Lateral meniscus (XX), Infrapatellar fat pad (XXI), Joint capsule (XXII), Patellar tendon (XXIII), Lateral femoral condyle (XXIV), Patella (XXV), Lateral patellar retinaculum (XXVI), Lateral epicondyle (XXVII), Quadriceps tendon (XXVIII), Suprapatellar pouch (XXIX), Articularis genus (XXX), Lateral superior genicular artery (XXXI). (Redrawn from Hoppenfeld S, deBoer P: Surgical Exposures in Orthopaedics. Philadelphia, JB Lippincott Inc, 1984)

    b. Moves slide forward on extension and backward on flexion
    c. Functions of meniscus
       (1) Stability; limits extremes of flexion and extension
       (2) Joint congruity and reduce space for lubrication
       (3) Joint nutrition
       (4) Load transmission and shock absorption
    d. Medial meniscus
       (1) Wider posterior and anterior
       (2) Insert anterior to ACL anteriorly and anterior to PCL posteriorly
       (3) Attachments: anterior, meniscopatellar ligament; middle, deep capsule; posterior, posterior oblique ligament and expansion
       (4) Less mobile than lateral meniscus
    e. Lateral meniscus
       (1) More circular shape
       (2) Inserts posterior to ACL ante-

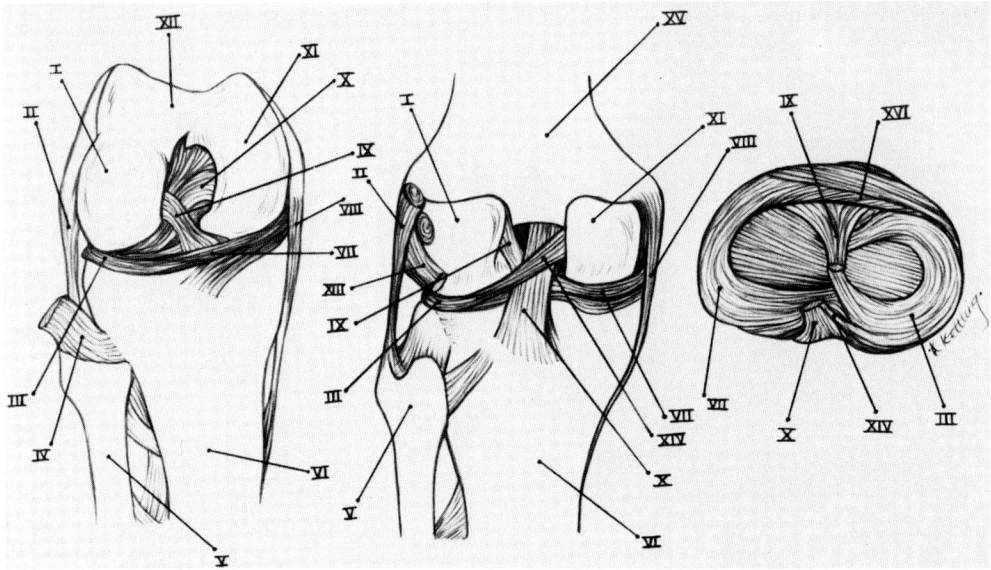

Figure 1-24. Intra-articular structures of knee. Left: Anterior view: Lateral condyle (I), lateral collateral ligament (II), lateral meniscus (III), biceps femoris (IV), fibula (V), tibia (VI), medial meniscus (VII), medial collateral ligament (VIII), anterior cruciate ligament (IX), posterior cruciate ligament (X), medial condyle (XI), and patellar surface (XII). Middle: Posterior view: tendon of popliteus (XIII), ligament of wrisberg (XIV), femur (XV). Right: Coronal view showing menisci, cruciate ligaments and transverse ligament (XVI).

riorly and anterior to posterior horn of medial meniscus
   (3) Attachments: weaker attachment to lateral capsule and lack of attachment where popliteus tendon passes through and therefore more mobile
   (4) Ligaments of Humphry and Wrisberg (anterior and posterior meniscofemoral ligaments): from posterior aspect of lateral meniscus to embrace PCL

III. Muscles

A. Flexion
   1. Semimembranosus
   2. Semitendinosus
   3. Biceps femoris
   4. Sartorius
   5. Gracilis
   6. Popliteus: from lateral condyle of femur to posterior tibia above soleal line; flexes leg and rotates leg medially. Innervated by tibial nerve
   7. Gastrocnemius: from upper posterior medial and lateral femoral condyles to tendo Achillis into midposterior calcaneus; flexes leg and plantar flexes foot. Innervated by tibial nerve
   8. Plantaris: from lower lateral supracondylar line to posterior calcaneus; flexes leg and plantar flexes foot. Innervated by tibial nerve
B. Extension
   1. Quadriceps femoris
   2. Tensor fascia lata
C. Medial rotation
   1. Popliteus
   2. Semimembranosus
   3. Semitendinosus
   4. Sartorius
   5. Gracilis
D. Lateral rotation: biceps femoris

IV. Surgical Approaches

A. Medial parapatellar
   1. Surgery
      a. Begin incision on medial side of quadriceps tendon 3 to 5 cm above superior pole of patella

b. Curve around medial patella and then run just medial to patellar ligament
c. Open joint capsule in line with skin
d. Dislocate patella laterally; rotate it 180° and flex knee to 90°
2. Dangers
a. Anterior horn of medial meniscus is vulnerable during opening of synovium at the joint line
b. Infrapatellar branch of saphenous nerve is often cut with this approach, since it runs 8 cm posterior to medial edge of patella
B. Medial approach to the knee (Fig 1-25)
1. Surgery
a. Curved incision from adductor tubercle toward medial aspect of proximal tibia
b. Incise fascia along the anterior aspect of the sartorius and retract it posteriorly (infrapatellar branch of the saphenous nerve crosses over the sartorius muscle)
c. Expose anterior capsule and medial meniscus anterior to superficial medial collateral ligament; expose semimembranosus, posterior joint capsule, and medial head of the gastrocnemius posterior to the medial collateral ligament. Semitendinosus and gracilis are superficial to the collateral ligament and insert distal to the collateral ligament onto the proximal tibia
d. Arthrotomy may be made posterior to the collateral ligament to expose posteromedial corner of the joint, or arthrotomy may be made anteriorly over the parapatellar retinaculum to expose anterior intra-articular structures

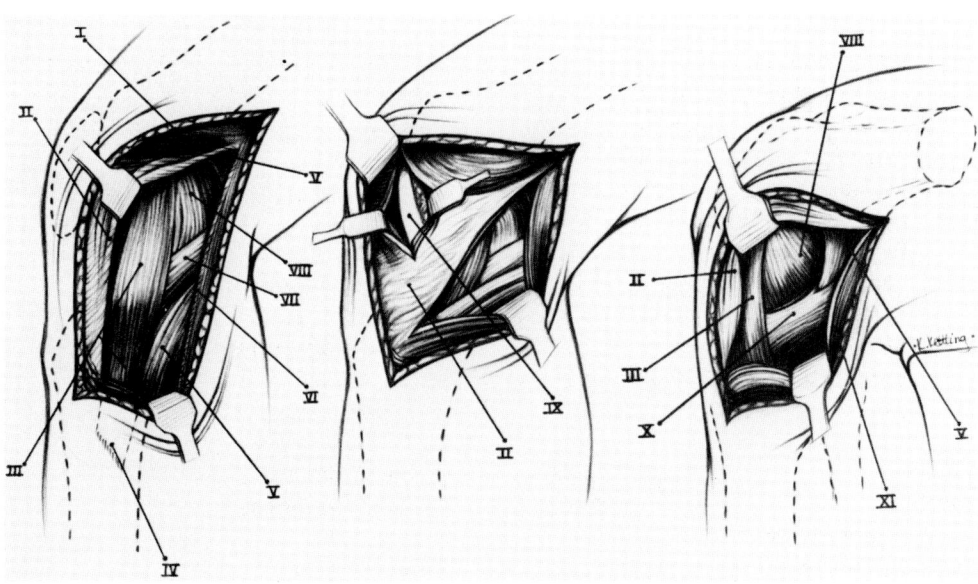

Figure 1-25. Medial approach to the knee. Left: Curved incision from the adductor tubercle toward the medial aspect of the proximal tibia. Incise the fascia along the anterior aspect of the sartorius (VI) and retract it posteriorly. Structures shown are Fascia over vastus medialis (I), Medial patellar retinaculum (II), Superficial medial ligament (III), Tibial insertion of superficial ligament (IV), Medial head of gastrocnemius (V), Tendon of semimembranosus (VII), Posteromedial capsule (VIII), Medial head of gastrocnemius (IX). Center: Expose medial femoral condyle (IX) and intraarticular structures anteriorly by dividing medial patellar retinaculum (II). Right: Expose the posteromedial corner of the joint by retracting sartorius (XI) posteriorly and medial patellar retinaculum (II) anteriorly. Structures shown are superficial medial collateral ligament (III), Semimembranosus (X), Medial head of gastrocnemius (V), and Posteromedial joint capsule (VIII). (Redrawn from Hoppenfeld S, deBoer P: Surgical Exposures in Orthopaedics. Philadelphia, JB Lippincott Inc, 1984)

2. Dangers
   a. Infrapatellar branch of saphenous nerve, which emerges from between gracilis and sartorius, should be preserved if possible or buried in fat if cut to prevent painful neuroma
   b. Vessels: saphenous vein, medial inferior genicular artery, popliteal artery
C. Lateral approach to the knee
   1. Surgery
      a. Curved incision from the lateral condyle to Gerdy's tubercle
      b. Incise fascia between iliotibial band and biceps femoris, exposing the lateral collateral ligament (common peroneal nerve is posterior to biceps femoris)
      c. Arthrotomy may be done over the posterolateral capsule just posterior to the lateral collateral ligament or anterior to the lateral head of the gastrocnemius, exposing the lateral joint and intra-articular portion of the popliteus tendon. Arthrotomy may be done anteriorly over the parapatellar retinaculum to expose anterolateral joint structures
   2. Dangers
      a. Common peroneal nerve lies posterior to biceps tendon, and injury or traction should be avoided
      b. Lateral genicular artery runs between lateral head of gastrocnemius and posterolateral capsule, and ligation is often necessary for exposure
D. Posterior approach
   1. Surgery
      a. Use S-shaped incision starting laterally over biceps femoris and curve obliquely across popliteal fossa
      b. Turn downward over medial head of gastrocnemius
      c. Incise fascia of popliteal fascia
      d. To gain access to posteromedial joint, detach tendinous origin of medial head of gastrocnemius
      e. To gain access to posterolateral joint, detach lateral head of gastrocnemius
   2. Dangers
      a. Sural cutaneous nerve lies lateral to the small saphenous vein in the midline of the calf
      b. Small saphenous vein
      c. Common peroneal nerve runs along posterior border of biceps femoris
      d. Popliteal artery and vein lie deep and medial to the tibial nerve between the semimembranosus (medially) and biceps femoris (laterally)

10
Leg

I. Bony
A. Tibia ossifies at 7th fetal week
B. Fibula ossifies at 8th fetal week; proximal end appears by 4th year; and closes 25th year

II. Compartments (Fig 1-26)
A. Four compartments: anterior, lateral, superficial posterior, deep posterior
B. Intermuscular septa
  1. Anterior: between peronei and extensor digitorum longus (EDL)
  2. Posterior: between peronei and soleus
C. Anterior, lateral, and posterior compartments formed by septae, bones, and interosseus membrane

III. Muscles
A. Anterior (innervated by deep peroneal nerve)
  1. Tibialis anterior: from lateral tibial condyle to medial aspect of first cuneiform and base of first metatarsal; dorsiflexes and inverts foot

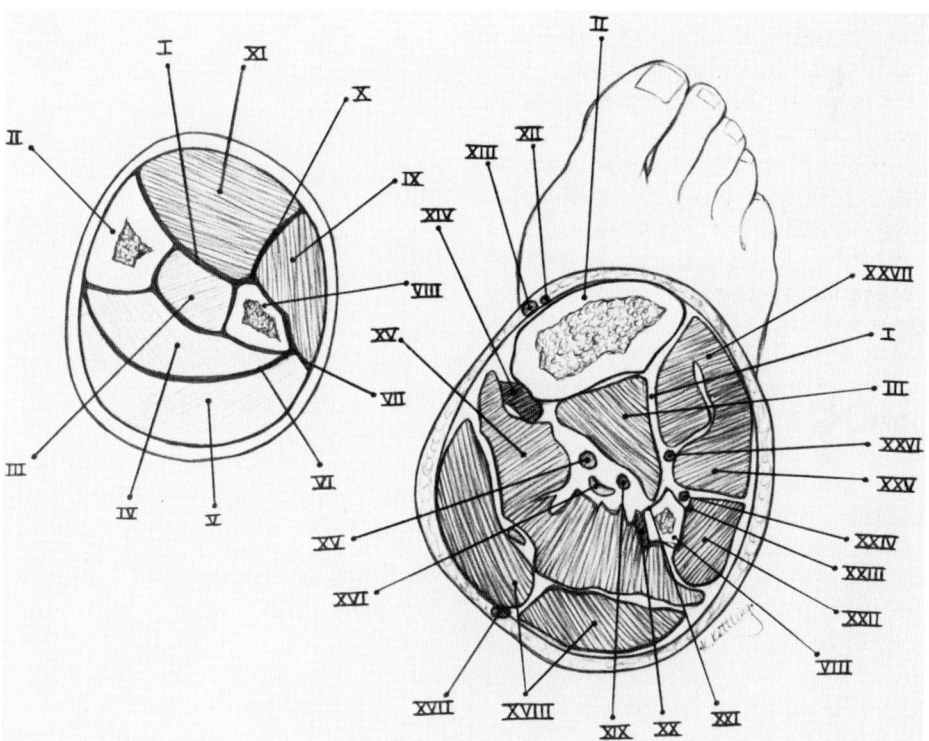

Figure 1-26. Cross-sections of the tibia. Left: Interosseus membrane (I), tibia (II), tibialis posterior (III), deep flexors (IV), triceps surae (V), deep transverse fascia (VI), posterior intermuscular septum (VII), fibula (VIII), peronei (IX), anterior intermuscular septum (X), extensors (XI). Right: Saphenous nerve (XII), large saphenous vein (XIII), flexor digitorum longus (XIV), soleus and posterior tibial artery (XV), tibial nerve (XVI), small saphenous vein (XVII), gastrocnemius (XVIII), peroneal artery (XIX), flexor hallucis longus (XX), medial crest (XXI), peroneus longus (XXII), superficial peroneal nerve (XXIII), deep peroneal nerve (XXIV), extensor digitorum longus (XXV) anterior tibial artery (XXVI), and tibialis anterior (XXVII).

2. Extensor digitorum longus (EDL): from lateral tibial condyle and anterior fibula to bases of middle and distal phalanges of lateral four toes; extends toes and dorsiflexes foot
3. Peroneus tertius (PT): from distal fibula to base of fifth metatarsal; dorsiflexes and everts foot
4. Extensor hallucis longus (EHL): from middle anterior fibula to base of distal phalanx of great toe; extends great toe and everts foot
B. Lateral (innervated by superficial peroneal)
   1. Peroneus longus: from lateral tibial condyle and fibular head to first cuneiform and lateral first metatarsal; plantar flexes and everts foot
   2. Peroneus brevis: from middle lateral fibula to dorsal surface of fifth metatarsal; everts and plantar flexes foot
C. Superficial posterior (innervated by tibial nerve)
   1. Gastrocnemius: from medial and lateral posterior femoral condyles to tendo Achillis into posterior calcaneus; flexes leg and plantar flexes foot
   2. Soleus: from upper fibula and upper tibia to tendo Achillis; plantar flexes foot
   3. Plantaris: from lateral supracondylar line to posterior calcaneus; flexes leg and plantar flexes foot
D. Deep posterior (innervated by tibial nerve)
   1. Popliteus: from lateral femoral condyle and popliteal ligament to posterior tibia; flexes and internally rotates leg
   2. Flexor hallucis longus (FHL): from inferior ⅔ of fibula to base of distal phalanx of great toe; flexes great toe and plantar flexes or inverts foot
   3. Flexor digitorum longus (FDL): from posterior tibia to base of distal phalanx of lateral four toes; flexes toes and plantar flexes or inverts foot
   4. Tibialis posterior: posterior upper tibia or fibula to navicular tuberosity, sustentaculum tali, three cuneiforms, cuboid, bases of second, third, and fourth metatarsals; plantar flexes, adducts, and inverts foot

IV. Vascular
A. Anterior tibial artery: from lower border of popliteus, passes between heads of tibialis posterior through interosseus membrane to front of leg. Joins deep peroneal nerve. Passes between EHL and EDL at ankle
B. Posterior tibial artery: direct continuation of popliteal artery; passes behind medial malleolus with posterior tibial nerve
C. Peroneal artery: arises from posterior tibial artery; lies in a fibrous canal between PT and FHL

V. Nervous
A. Anterior compartment: deep peroneal nerve between fibular neck and peroneus longus and runs deep to EDL
B. Lateral compartment: superficial peroneal nerve between fibular neck and peroneus longus; lies anterolateral to fibula between peronei and EDL
C. Superficial posterior compartment: sural nerve runs laterally within fascia of leg
D. Deep posterior compartment: tibial nerve passes posterior to vein and artery in popliteal fossa and passes deep to soleus and runs inferiorly on posterior tibialis

VI. Surgical Approaches
A. Anterior
   1. Surgery
      a. Longitudinal incision over anterior tibia, parallel but lateral to bone
      b. Reflect tibialis anterior laterally
      c. Incise periosteum over tibia
   2. Dangers: long saphenous vein runs up medial side of calf, and deep peroneal nerve runs between tibialis anterior and EHL

B. Posterolateral
 1. Surgery
    a. Longitudinal incision over lateral border of fibula
    b. Develop plane between lateral head of gastrocnemius and soleus posteriorly and peroneus longus anteriorly
    c. Detach lower origin of soleus and origin of FHL from the fibula and retract them along with tibialis posterior posteriorly from the interosseus membrane and posterior aspect of the tibia
    d. Continue dissection just posterior to interosseus membrane
 2. Dangers
    a. Short saphenous vein runs up posterolateral aspect of leg
    b. Peroneal artery branches cross plane between gastrocnemius and peroneus brevis
    c. Posterior tibial artery and nerve are posterior to bulk of tibialis posterior muscle
C. Approach to the fibula
 1. Surgery
    a. Incision on posterior aspect of fibula
    b. Dissect between peronei and soleus FHL
 2. Dangers
    a. Common peroneal nerve around fibula neck just posterior to biceps
    b. Superficial peroneal nerve emerges between EDL and peronei at junction between distal and middle third of the shaft
    c. Peroneal artery in deep posterior compartment
    d. Sural nerve posterior to distal fibula

11
Foot and Ankle

ANKLE

I. Bony
A. Talus
1. Ossification: appears 7th fetal month
2. Bony: posteriorly has medial and lateral tubercle with intervening groove for flexor hallucis longus (FHL); inferiorly has deep groove-sulcus tali
3. Head: articulates with navicular and calcaneus

B. Tibia (medial malleolus): ossification appears at 7–8 years
C. Fibula (lateral malleolus): ossification appears at 18 months

II. Joint
A. Type: hinge
B. Motion: flexion and extension
C. Ligaments
1. Articular capsule
2. Medial: deltoid ligament consisting of anterior tibiotalar, posterior tibiotalar, tibionavicular, tibiocalcaneal
3. Lateral: anterior and posterior talofibular, calcaneofibular

III. Muscles (Figs 1-27, 1-28, 1-29)
A. Dorsiflexion
1. Tibialis anterior
2. EDL
3. Peroneus tertius
4. EHL

B. Plantar flexion
1. Peroneus longus
2. Peroneus brevis
3. Gastrocnemius
4. Soleus
5. Plantaris
6. FHL
7. Flexor digitorum longus (FDL)
8. Tibialis posterior

IV. Neurovascular
A. Anterior tibial artery and deep peroneal nerve travel between tibialis anterior and EHL
B. Posterior tibial artery and nerve pass behind medial malleolus between FDL and FHL
C. Sural nerve located halfway between lateral malleolus and lateral edge of tendo Achilles
D. Greater saphenous vein just anterior to medial malleolus

V. Surgical Approaches
A. Anterior
1. Surgery
   a. Incision 15 cm over anterior aspect of ankle, beginning 10 cm proximal to joint
   b. Incise deep fascia, cutting through extensor retinaculum
   c. Develop plane between EHL and EDL
   d. Identify neurovascular bundle and retract medially with EHL
   e. Incise tissues over anterior aspect of the tibia and cut through the capsule of the ankle joint
2. Danger: anterior neurovascular bundle (anterior tibial artery and deep peroneal nerve)

B. Medial and posteromedial
1. Surgery
   a. Incision 10 cm centered on tip of medial malleolus. Distally, curve toward medial malleolus
   b. Divide flexor retinaculum and identify tibialis posterior tendon. Retract tendon posteriorly
   c. Perform malleolar osteotomy to expose the joint if necessary

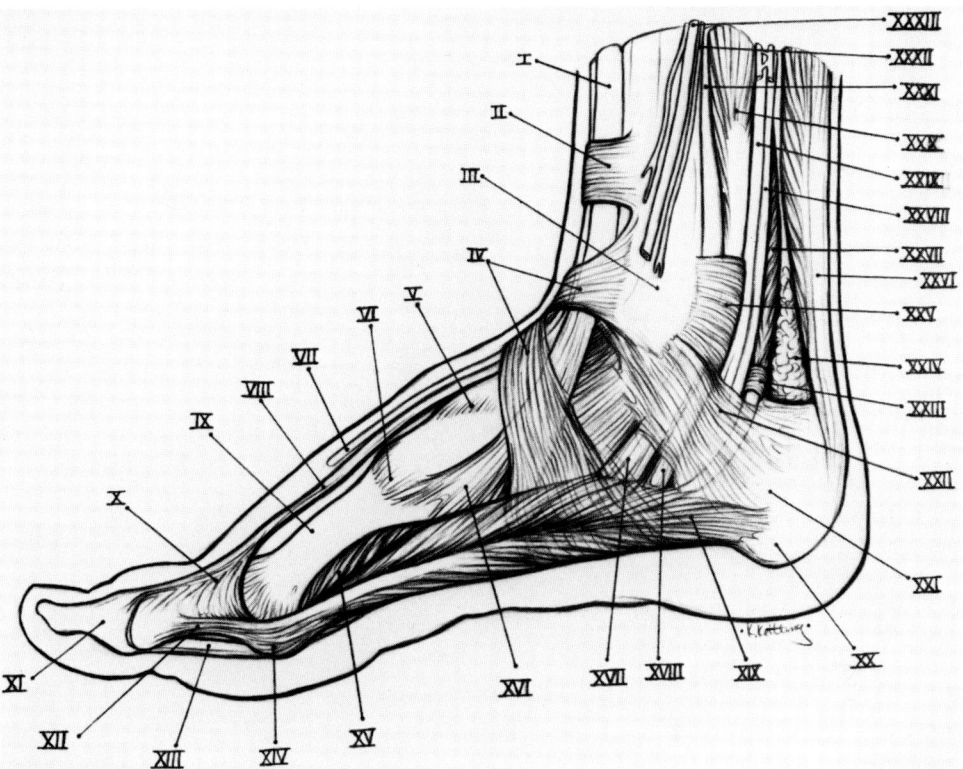

Figure 1-27. Structures of the medial aspect of the foot. Tibialis anterior (I), Superior extensor retinaculum (II), Medial malleolus (III), Inferior extensor retinaculum (IV), Navicular-first cuneiform joint (V), First cuneiform metatarsal joint (VI), Extensor digitorum longus (VII), Extensor hallucis longus (VIII), First metatarsal (IX), Extensor expansion (X), Distal phalanx of great toe (XI), Abductor hallucis (XII), Flexor hallucis longus (XIII), Medial sesamoid (XIV), Medial belly of flexor hallucis brevis (XV), Tibialis anterior (XVI), Tibialis posterior (XVII), Flexor digitorum longus (XVIII), Abductor hallucis (XIX), Medial tuberosity of calcaneus (XX), Calcaneus (XXI), Flexor retinaculum (XXII), Fibrous pulley for flexor hallucis longus (XXIII), Fat pad (XXIV), Achilles tendon (XXV), Flexor retinaculum (XXVI), Flexor hallucis longus (XXVII), Tibial nerve (XXVIII), Posterior tibial artery (XXIX), Extensor digitorum longus (XXX), Tibialis posterior (XXXI), Saphenous nerve (XXXII), Long saphenous vein (XXXIII). (Redrawn from Hoppenfeld S, deBoer P: Surgical Exposures in Orthopaedics. Philadelphia, JB Lippincott Inc, 1984)

      d. In posteromedial approach, FDL, posterior tibial artery, tibial nerve, and FHL (fibro-osseus tunnel) are identified from anterior to posterior direction. Retract FHL anteriorly to the joint
  2. Dangers
      a. Saphenous nerve and vein just anterior to medial malleolus
      b. Posterior tibialis tendon and neurovascular structures

C. Posterolateral
  1. Surgery
      a. Incision 10 cm halfway between lateral malleolus and tendo Achilles
      b. Incise deep fascia
      c. Identify peroneus brevis (anterior) and peroneus longus; incise peroneal retinaculum
      d. Make longitudinal incision through lateral fibers of FHL and retract muscle medially

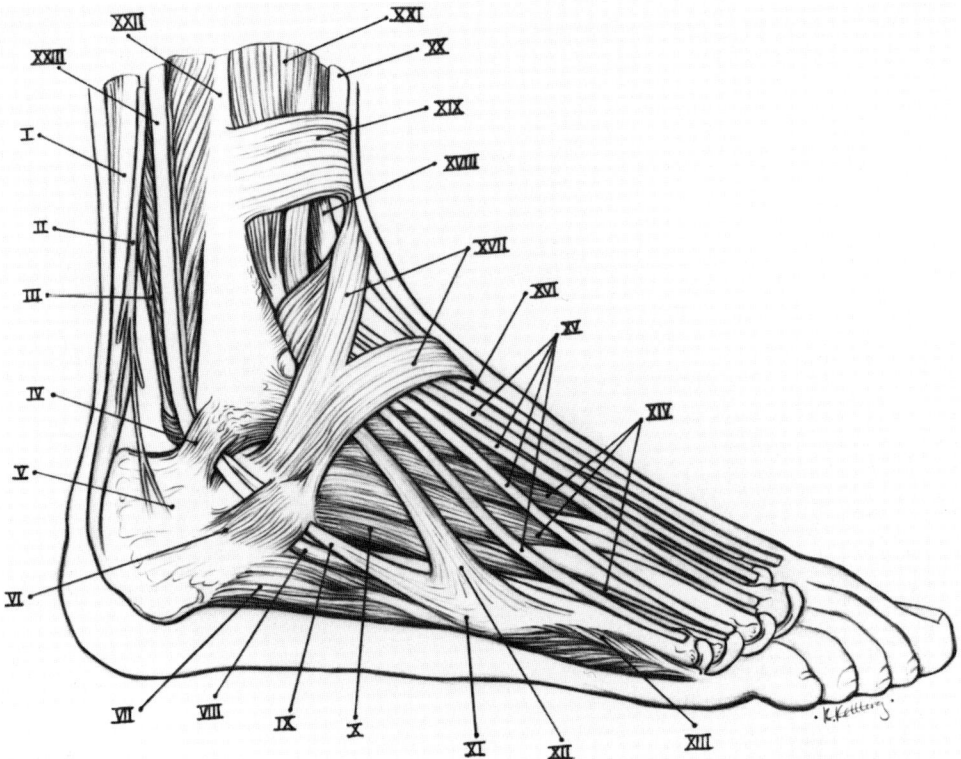

Figure 1-28. Structures of the lateral aspect of the foot. Achilles tendon (I), Sural nerve (II), Flexor hallucis longus (III), Superficial peroneal retinaculum (IV), Calcaneus (V), Inferior peroneal retinaculum (VI), Abductor digiti minimi (VII), Peroneus longus (VIII), Peronius brevis (IX), Extensor digitorum brevis (X), Styloid process of fifth metatarsal (XI), Peronius tertius (XII), Abductor digiti minimi (XIII), Extensor digitorum brevis (XIV), Extensor digitorum longus (XV), Extensor hallucis brevis (XVI), Inferior extensor retinaculum (XVII), Extensor hallucis longus (XVIII), Superior extensor retinaculum (XIX), Tibialis anterior (XX), Extensor digitorum longus (XXI), Fibula (XXII), Peroneus longus (XXIII). (Redrawn from Hoppenfeld S, deBoer P: Surgical Exposures in Orthopaedics. Philadelphia, JB Lippincott Inc, 1984)

      e. Follow posterior aspect of tibia to enter ankle joint
   2. Dangers: short saphenous vein and sural nerve lateral to lateral malleolus
D. Anterolateral ankle and lateral hindfoot
   1. Surgery
      a. Curved incision 15 cm on anterolateral aspect of ankle, beginning 5 cm proximal to joint
      b. Cross ankle joint 2 cm medial to lateral malleolus, ending 2 cm medial to fifth metatarsal base
      c. Cut through superior and inferior retinacula
      d. Incise down to bone, just lateral to peroneus tertius and EDL
      e. Identify extensor digitorum brevis (EDB) and detach its origin from calcaneus
      f. Identify capsules of calcaneocuboid and talonavicular joints as well as the fat in sinus tarsi
   2. Dangers: Superficial peroneal nerve, deep peroneal nerve, and anterior tibial artery

FOOT

I. Bony
A. Tarsals (7)
   1. Talus
   2. Calcaneus

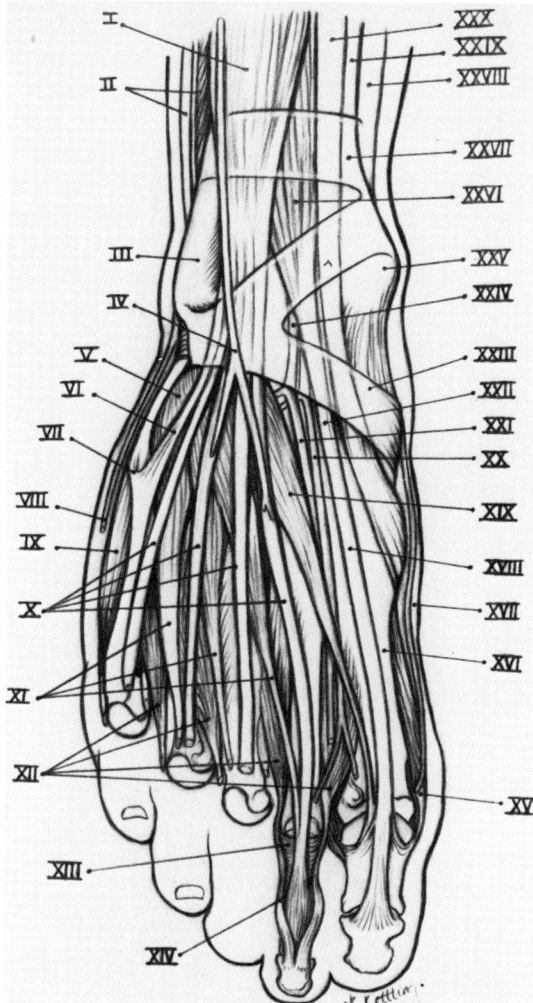

Figure 1-29. Structures of the anterior aspect of the foot and ankle. Extensor digitorum longus (I), Peronei (II), Lateral malleolus (III), Superficial peroneal nerve (IV), Extensor digitorum brevis (V), Peroneus tertius (VI), Styloid process of fifth metatarsal (VII), Sural nerve (VIII), Abductor digiti minimi (IX), Extensor digitorum longus (X), Extensor digitorum brevis (XI), Dorsal interossei (XII), Extensor hood (XIII), Lateral band (XIV), Abductor hallucis (XV), First metatarsal (XVI), Saphenous nerve (XVII), Extensor hallucis longus (XVIII), Extensor hallucis brevis (IX), Deep peroneal nerve (XX), Dorsalis pedis artery (XXI), Extensor hallucis longus (XXII), Inferior extensor retinaculum (XXIII), Tibialis anterior artery (XXIV), Medial malleolus (XXV), Extensor hallucis (XXVI), Superior extensor retinaculum (XXVII), Tibialis posterior (XXVIII), Tibia (XXIX), Tibialis anterior (XXX). (Redrawn from Hoppenfeld S, deBoer P: Surgical Exposures in Orthopaedics. Philadelphia, JB Lippincott Inc, 1984)

      a. Ossification: appears 6th fetal month; has second center for heel
      b. Parts
         (1) Sustentaculum tali: medial shelf to hold head of talus; below is groove for FHL
         (2) Medial and lateral plantar tubercles
         (3) Groove associated with sulcus tali to form sinus tarsi
    3. Navicular: appears 4th year
    4. Cuboid
      a. Ossification: appears 9th fetal month
      b. Has plantar groove for peroneus longus
    5. Cuneiforms
      a. Lateral ossifies 1st year
      b. Medial ossifies 3rd year
      c. Intermediate ossifies 4th year
  B. Metatarsals (5)
    1. Ossification: 9th week, body; 3rd year, base of first metatarsal; 5–8 years, heads of lateral four metatarsals
    2. Base of second metatarsal extends farther proximally than the others to lock into mortise of tarsometatarsal joint
  C. Phalanges (14): body appears 10th fetal week; bases appear 4–10 years of age

II. Joints and Ligaments

  A. Subtalar joint
    1. Type: arthrodial (gliding)
    2. Ligaments
      a. Anterior, posterior, medial, and lateral talocalcaneal
      b. Interosseus talocalcaneal
  B. Talocalcaneonavicular joint
    1. Type: arthrodial (gliding, rotation)
    2. Ligaments
      a. Dorsal talonavicular
      b. Plantar calcaneonavicular (spring ligament) supports head of talus
  C. Calcaneocuboid
    1. Type: arthrodial (gliding, rotation)
    2. Ligaments
      a. Dorsal, plantar calcaneocuboid
      b. Bifurcate (calcaneocuboidnavicular)

c. Long plantar
D. Tarsometatarsal
1. Type: arthrodial (slight gliding)
2. Ligaments: Dorsal, plantar, interosseus
E. Metatarsophalangeal (MTP)
1. Type: condyloid (flexion, extension, abduction)
2. Ligaments: plantar, two collateral
F. Interphalangeal (IP)
1. Type: ginglymus (flexion, extension)
2. Ligaments: plantar, two collateral

III. Muscles

A. Dorsal: innervated by deep peroneal nerve except for interossei (Fig 1-29)
1. Extensor hallucis longus
2. Extensor digitorum longus
3. Peroneus tertius
4. Tibialis anterior
5. Extensor digitorum brevis: from lateral, superior calcaneus to lateral side of long extensor tendons and bases of first phalanx of medial four toes; extends medial four toes
6. Dorsal interossei: adjacent side and bases of first four metatarsals to both sides of first and second metatarsals and lateral side of third and fourth metatarsals; abduct toes; flex proximal phalanx; extend distal two phalanges. Innervated by deep branch of lateral plantar nerve

B. Plantar (Fig 1-30)
1. Superficial layer
a. Abductor hallucis: from medial calcaneal tuberosity to medial base of great toe proximal phalanx; flexes and abducts great toe. Innervated by medial plantar nerve
b. Flexor digitorum brevis: from medial calcaneal tuberosity to middle phalanges of lateral four toes; flexes

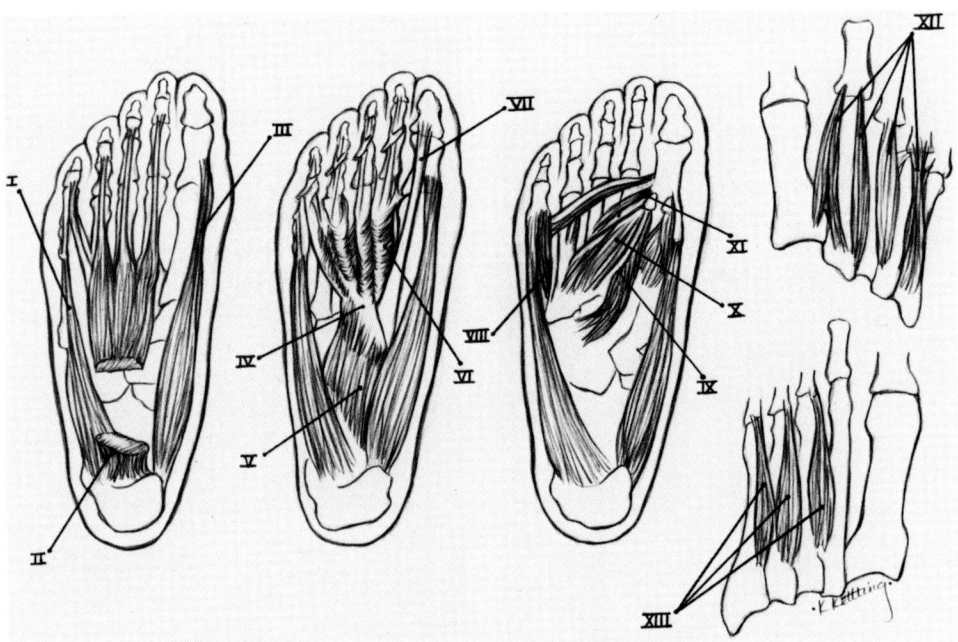

Figure 1-30. Muscles of the plantar aspect of the foot. Left: First layer: abductor digiti minimi (I), flexor digitorum brevis (II), abductor hallucis (III). Left center: Second layer: flexor digitorum longus (IV), quadratus platae (V), lumbricales (VI), flexor hallucis longus (VII), Right center. Third layer: flexor digiti minimi brevis (VIII), flexor hallucis brevis (IX), oblique head of adductor hallucis (X), transverse head of adductor hallucis (XI), Right: Fourth layer: dorsal interossei (XII), and plantar interossei (XIII).

toes. Innervated by medial plantar nerve
  c. Abductor digiti minimi: from calcaneal tuberosities to lateral surface of small toe proximal phalanx; flexes and abducts small toe. Innervated by lateral plantar nerve
 2. Second layer
  a. Quadratus plantae: from medial and lateral calcaneal tuberosities to lateral border of long flexor tendons; flexes toes. Innervated by lateral plantar nerve
  b. Lumbricals: from medial side of long flexor tendons to proximal phalanx of toes 2–5; flexes proximal and extends distal phalanges. Innervated by medial (first) and lateral (second, third, fourth) plantar nerves
  c. Tendons of FDL
  d. Tendon of FHL
 3. Third layer
  a. Flexor hallucis brevis: from cuboid and third cuneiform to base of proximal phalanx; flexes proximal phalanx of great toe. Innervated by medial plantar nerve
  b. Adductor hallucis
   (1) Oblique head: from bases of metatarsals 2, 3, 4 to flexor hallucis brevis; adducts and flexes proximal phalanx of great toe. Innervated by lateral plantar nerve
   (2) Transverse head: from MTP joint capsules of third, fourth, and fifth metatarsals to lateral side of base of proximal phalanx of great toe. Innervated by lateral plantar nerve
  c. Flexor digiti minimi brevis: from peroneus longus tendon and base of fifth metatarsal to base of proximal phalanx of small toe; flexes proximal phalanx, small toe. Innervated by lateral plantar nerve
 4. Deep layer
  a. Plantar interossei: from proximal shaft and base of metatarsals 3, 4, 5 to base of extensor tendons of proximal phalanx and of toes 3, 4, 5; adducts toes and flexes proximal, and extends distal part of toes 3–5. Innervated by lateral plantar nerve
  b. Tendon of tibialis posterior
  c. Tendon of peroneus longus

IV. Dorsal Neurovascular Anatomy
A. Arteries: Dorsalis pedis passes between EHL and EDL into the dorsum of foot and runs in first intermetatarsal space; terminates as first dorsal metatarsal and deep plantar arteries. Gives branches: medial and lateral tarsals, arcuate
B. Nerves: Most of dorsum of foot supplied by superficial peroneal, which crosses over distal fibula and enters foot laterally. Deep peroneal nerve (sensation to first web space) travels with dorsalis pedis artery

V. Plantar Neurovascular Anatomy
A. Arteries: Posterior tibial artery runs beneath origin of abductor hallucis and divides into medial and lateral plantar arteries
 1. Medial plantar artery runs along medial side of foot
 2. Lateral plantar artery joins deep branch of dorsalis pedis to form plantar arch
B. Posterior tibial nerve runs with posterior tibial artery and divides in a similar fashion. Medial plantar nerve supplies most of the sole to middle of fourth ray; lateral foot supplied by lateral plantar nerve
C. Saphenous nerve runs with greater saphenous vein and supplies sensation to part of medial sole
D. Sural nerve runs posterolaterally with lesser saphenous vein and gives sensation to part of lateral sole

VI. Surgical Approaches
A. Lateral approach to the subtalar joint (Kocher approach, ie, triple arthrodesis)

1. Surgery
   a. Incision begins 2 cm proximal to tip of lateral malleolus, curves around malleolus, and extends to talonavicular joint level
   b. Fascial incision is made to expose peroneal tendons
   c. Calcaneofibular ligament is cut to expose posterior facet of subtalar joint
2. Dangers
   a. Small saphenous vein and nerve posterior to incision
   b. Intermediate dorsal cutaneous nerves should be protected

B. Medial approach to calcaneus (ie, tarsal tunnel, rupture of posterior tibial tendon)
   1. Surgery
      a. Begin incision at superior aspect of calcaneus and 1 cm posterior to medial malleolus, curve around malleolus, and extend to tuberosity of navicula
      b. Divide retinaculum to expose tendons and neurovascular bundles if necessary
      c. Exposure of medial side of the calcaneus does not require division of the retinaculum
   2. Dangers
      a. Saphenous vein and nerve anterior to incision
      b. Posterior tibialis, flexor digitorum longus, posterior tibial artery, posterior tibial nerve, and flexor hallucis longus beneath the retinaculum

C. Dorsal approach to the midfoot
   1. Surgery
      a. Dorsomedial incision to expose talonavicular, naviculocuneiform, and dorsal tendons
      b. Dorsolateral incision to expose calcaneocuboid and base of fifth metatarsal
      c. Cut down directly onto structures that are to be exposed
   2. Dangers: extensor tendons and neurovascular structures

D. Dorsal or dorsomedial approach to the great toe
   1. Surgery
      a. Dorsal or dorsomedial skin incision and avoid injury to dorsal digital nerve
      b. Incise deep fascia and develop a distal-based flap, exposing metatarsophalangeal joint
      c. Resect bunion in line with shaft
      d. Adductor release and capsulorrhaphy are done in hallux valgus patients
   2. Danger: dorsal sensory branch, which is a branch of saphenous nerve

E. Dorsal approach to the lesser toes
   1. Longitudinal or transverse incision over proximal phalangeal joint
   2. Tendon of EDL is retracted or split for exposure of PIP joint

REFERENCES

Anderson JE: *Grant's atlas of anatomy,* ed 8. Baltimore, Williams and Wilkins, 1983

Clemente CD: *Anatomy. A regional atlas of the human body.* Philadelphia, Lea & Febiger, 1975

Hoppenfeld S, de Boer P: *Surgical exposures in orthopaedics. The anatomic approach.* Philadelphia, JB Lippincott, 1984

McMinn RMH, Hutchings RT: *Color atlas of human anatomy.* Chicago, Year Book, 1977

Moore KL: *Clinically oriented anatomy.* Baltimore, Williams & Wilkins, 1980

Pansky B, House EL: *Review of gross anatomy,* ed 3. New York, Macmillan, 1975

Warfel JH: *The extremities,* ed 4. Philadelphia, Lea & Febiger, 1974

Warfel JH: *The head, neck and trunk,* ed 4. Philadelphia, Lea & Febiger, 1974

SECTION 2: BASIC SCIENCES AND PATHOLOGY

Howard S. An
Donald A. Hackbarth

12. Bone: Structure and Function
13. Metabolic Bone Diseases
14. Fracture Healing and Nonunion
15. Osteonecrosis, Osteochondroses, and Osteochondritis Dissecans
16. Bone Grafting
17. Articular Cartilage and Arthritis and Synovial Diseases
18. Muscle, Nerve, Tendon, Ligament, and Collagen
19. Orthopaedic Infections
20. Tumors
21. Genetics

12
Bone: Structure and Function

I. Structure of Bone

A. Cortical and cancellous bone (gross structure)
1. Eighty percent cortical bone and 20% cancellous bone are present in the body
2. More surface area is available in the cancellous bone for metabolic interaction
3. Cortical bone has greater density for strength and stiffness

B. Woven and lamellar bone (microscopic structure)
1. Woven bone is immature and unorganized in loose arrangement of collagen and found in fetus, fracture callus, Paget's disease, neoplasm, etc.
2. Lamellar bone
   a. Starts to form 1 month after birth
   b. Mature, remodeled and mostly in cortical bone
   c. Collagen oriented along the line of stress (anisotrophic collagen)
   d. Cortical bone contains haversian complex with osteon and Volkmann's canal, and cancellous bone is arranged in trabecular lamellae

C. Blood supply of bone: arterial and venous system
1. Growing bone contains epiphyseal, perichondrial, and metaphyseal arteries
   a. Epiphyseal and metaphyseal arteries anastomose at about 18 months
   b. Hypertrophic zone is avascular
2. Metaphyseal region has greater blood flow
3. Diaphyseal bone has an endosteal (nutrient artery) and periosteal blood supply
4. There is anastomosis and drainage between endosteal and periosteal systems

D. Nervous supply to bone
1. Intraosseous vessels are supplied by adrenergic nerves
2. Autonomic or sympathetic innervation also exists in bone

E. Periosteum
1. Fibrous layer for tendon, ligament, and capsule attachment
2. Cambium layer contains cells that can produce bone or cartilage
3. Periosteum becomes more fibrous, less cellular, and less vascular with age

II. Microscopic Composition of Bone

A. Cells
1. Osteoprogenitor cells (undifferentiated mesenchymal cells)
   a. Become osteoblasts and osteocytes if immobilized
   b. Found on periosteal and endosteal surfaces of bone and in perimysium of myositis ossificans
   c. Influenced by numerous factors, such as bone morphogenic protein, oxygen, electricity, and pH
   d. Differentiate to chondroblasts if motion is present or to fibroblasts if tensile forces exist
2. Osteoblasts
   a. Origin: marrow stromal cells
   b. Responsible for matrix synthesis for repair and growth
   c. Contain many endoplasmic reticulum, Golgi apparatus, and canaliculi
   d. Abundant alkaline phosphatase but little acid phosphatase

e. Become round to oval when active but flattened when inactive
3. Osteocytes
   a. Buried in mineralized matrix (>90% of cells are osteocytes in the mature skeleton)
   b. Extensive projections and canaliculi are present
   c. Important function in nutrition and homeostasis
   d. Some function in matrix production and resorption of bone
   e. Osteocytes and osteoblasts are connected by "bone membrane" for communication and regulation of calcium and phosphate content
4. Osteoclasts
   a. Larger cells derived from macrophages or hematopoietic system
   b. Contain lysosomal enzymes such as acid phosphatase, collagenase, and cathepsin
   c. Ruffled border is active site for bony resorption
   d. Influenced by parathyroid hormone, 1,25-dihydroxyvitamin D ($1,25(OH)_2D$), vitamin A, osteoclast activating factor, prostaglandins
   e. Osteopetrosis is due to failure of osteoclasts to resorb calcified cartilage, and Paget's disease is from overactivity of the osteoclasts
B. Extracellular matrix and minerals
1. Bone mineral
   a. Comprises about ⅔ of bone mass and is responsible for stiffness or compressive strength of bone
   b. Hydroxyapatite crystal [$Ca_{10}(PO_4)6(OH)_2$] is the chief mineral compound
   c. Calcium can be exchanged by strontium, lead, and magnesium and chelated by tetracycline
   d. Fluoride can exchange with hydroxyl anion (OH^{-1})
   e. Diphosphonates can prevent $CaPO_4$ incorporation
   f. Technetium pyrophosphate scan uptake occurs in mineralization region
2. Organic bone matrix
   a. Comprises about ⅓ of bone mass and is responsible for viscoelasticity and tensile strength of bone
   b. Type I collagen comprises 90% of the matrix, and hydroxyproline is a degradation product
   c. Matrix vesicle and surface of collagen are initial sites for calcification
   d. Acidophilic pink staining is due to reduced chondroitin sulfate and basic collagen
   e. Noncollagenous proteins or calcium binding proteins are also present in the matrix
      (1) Phosphoproteins are localized between "holes" of collagen and may function in nucleation process
      (2) Gamma-carboxyglutamic acid containing proteins: clotting factors and osteocalcin have affinity to calcium and may play a role in mineralization
      (3) Osteonectin function is to bind between collagen and hydroxyapatite mineral

III. Mineralization and Remodeling
A. Mineralization
1. Initiation and nucleation
   a. High concentration of ions present
   b. Formation or exposure of mineral nucleators occurs
   c. Removal or modification of mineralization inhibitors takes place
   d. Noncollagenous protein act as nucleators
   e. Alkaline phosphatase hydrolyzes pyrophosphate, which inhibits calcification
   f. Matrix vesicles and "hole zones" of collagen are involved in initial mineralization

2. Crystal growth is by multiplication of minerals
3. Secondary nucleation: more mineral is added to osteoid
B. Ossification (types)
 1. Endochondral bone formation
  a. Primary center of ossification occurs by vascular invasion to cartilagenous anlage
  b. Secondary center of ossification: epiphysis (Fig 2-1)
   (1) Reserve zone: store lipids and nutrition
   (2) Proliferative zone: matrix production and cellular proliferation (high oxygen tension and aerobic metabolism)
   (3) Hypertrophic zone
    i. Three subzones: maturation or columnation, degeneration, and provisional calcification
    ii. Inhibition of calcification becomes less effective due to decrease in subunits of proteoglycans
    iii. Matrix calcification first occurs in the matrix vesicles
    iv. This zone is avascular, has low oxygen tension, and primarily anaerobic metabolism
   (4) Metaphysis
    i. Central 80% is supplied by nutrient artery and periphery by metaphyseal vessels
    ii. Vascular invasion of calcified cartilage, bone formation, and remodeling follows
   (5) The groove of Ranvier is for circumferential growth, and perichondral ring of LaCroix function is a fibrous supporting structure
 2. Intramembranous ossification: bone laid down directly from mesenchymal cells to osteoblasts
C. Remodeling: removal of bone followed by formation according to biologic stress
 1. It is a stress-related phenomenon (Wolff's law)
 2. Cortical bone remodels 50% per year in the child and 2–5% per year in the elderly
 3. "Cutting cone" with osteoclasts is seen histologically for resorption of haversian canal
 4. Five to 10 times more remodeling occurs in the trabecular bone than cortical bone, and Howship's lacunae with osteoclasts are seen histologically
 5. Remodeled bone is generally weaker than the previously formed bone
D. Modeling: appositional growth on the loaded surface without removal of bone first (examples are periosteal bone formation, aseptic necrosis followed by bone growth, and external fracture callus)
E. Regulation of calcium and phosphate
 1. Parathyroid hormone (PTH)
  a. Increases renal calcium absorption and phosphate excretion in the distal convoluted tubule and osteoclastic bone resorption
  b. Indirectly enhances calcium absorption across gut by stimulating conversion of 25(OH) vitamin D to 1,25-(OH)$_2$D in the mitochondria of the proximal tubule of the kidney. (In

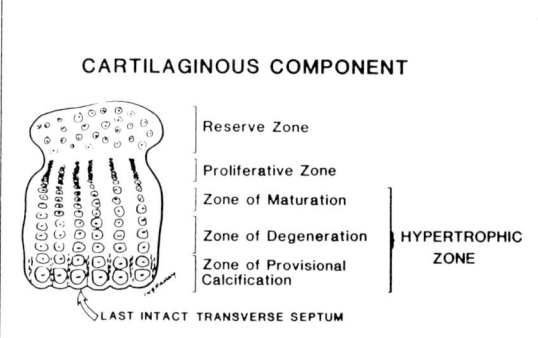

Figure 2-1. Various zones of the growth plate. (From Simon SR, Riggins RS, Wirth CR, Fox ML, eds. Orthopaedic science. American Academy of Orthopaedic Surgeons, 1986, p 11. Reprinted with permission.)

the absence of PTH, conversion is to 24,25-(OH)$_2$D, which is an inactive form)
   c. PTH release is stimulated by hypocalcemia, prostaglandin E, and beta-adrenergic agonists, and propranolol can block its secretion
2. 1,25-dihydroxyvitamin D
   a. Stimulates intestinal absorption of calcium and phosphate by activation of calcium-binding protein for transport
   b. Also enhances renal calcium absorption in states of hypocalcemia, low PTH level, or total body volume expansion, and augments renal phosphate absorption, but these effects may be secondary to increased filtered calcium and phosphate from the intestine
   c. It can also potentiate PTH for osteoclastic bone resorption
   d. 24,25-dihydroxyvitamin D inhibits 1,25-(OH)$_2$D by feedback mechanism
3. Calcitonin inhibits osteoclastic and renal resorption of calcium and phosphate, and its action is stimulated by hypercalcemia and inhibited by hypocalcemia
4. Growth hormone, insulin, testosterone, and estrogen stimulate bone formation, but thyroid hormone and corticosteroid increase bony resorption
5. Only 1% of calcium is outside the bone and 50% is bound to albumin, 20% of calcium is absorbed through duodenum and jejunum, and 98% of filtered calcium is reabsorbed in the kidney
6. Phosphate is stored in bone (85%)
7. Either diet ergocalciferol (vitamin D$_2$) or cholecalciferol (vitamin D$_3$) converted from 7-dehydrocholestrol by exposure to ultraviolet light is converted to 25-(OH)$_2$D in the liver and converted to 1,25-(OH)$_2$D in the mitochondria of kidney cells

REFERENCES

Bonucci E: New knowledge on the origin, function, and fate of osteoclasts. Clin Orthop 158:252–269, 1981

Boskey AL: Current concepts of the biochemistry and physiology of calcification. Clin Orthop 157:165–196, 1981

Boskey AL, Posner AS: Bone structure, composition, and mineralization. Orthop Clin North Am 15:597–612, 1984

Brighton CT: The growth plate. Orthop Clin North Am 15:571–595, 1984

Goodship AE, Lanyon LE, McFie H: Functional adaptation of bone to increased stress: An experimental study. J Bone Joint Surg 61A:539–546, 1979

Kanis JA: Vitamin D metabolism and its clinical application. J Bone Joint Surg 64B:542–560, 1982

Messer HH: Bone cell membranes. Clin Orthop 166:256–276, 1982

Raisz LG, Kream BE: Regulation of bone formation. N Engl J Med 309:29–35, 1983

Vaes G: Cellular biology and biochemical mechanism of bone resorption. A review of recent developments on the formation, activation, and mode of action of osteoclasts. Clin Orthop 231:239–271, 1988

Wuthier RE: A review of the primary mechanism of endochondral calcification with special emphasis on the role of the cells, mitochondria and matrix vesicles. Clin Orthop 169:219–242, 1982

13
Metabolic Bone Diseases

I. Classification (Mankin) (Table 2-1)
  A. Deficiency rickets and osteomalacia
    1. Vitamin D deficiency
    2. Calcium deficiency
    3. Phosphorus deficiency
    4. Chelators in diet
  B. Absorptive rickets and osteomalacia
    1. Gastric abnormalities
    2. Biliary disease
    3. Enteric absorptive defects
  C. Renal tubular rickets and osteomalacia
    1. Proximal tubular lesions
    2. Proximal and distal tubular lesions
    3. Distal tubular lesions (renal tubular acidosis)
       a. Primary
       b. Secondary
  D. Renal osteodystrophy
  E. Unusual forms of rickets and osteomalacia
    1. Rickets with fibrous dysplasia
    2. Rickets with neurofibromatosis
    3. Rickets associated with soft tissue and bone neoplasms
    4. Hypophosphatasia
    5. Drugs (such as phenytoin, aluminum, antacids)

II. Deficiency Rickets and Osteomalacia
  A. Pathogenesis
    1. Lack of vitamin D (nutrition or solar) results in decreased $1,25(OH)_2D$, which affects gastrointestinal absorption of calcium and leads to hypocalcemia and mild secondary hyperparathyroidism (causing slight decrease in phosphorus)
    2. Malabsorption: sprue, Billroth II procedure
    3. Drug induced: phenytoin induces P450 hydrolase, which competes with 25-vitamin D hydroxylase in the liver
  B. Clinical findings
    1. Rickets: apathetic, irritable, short stature, muscle weakness, laxities, frontal bossing, genu varus (younger) or valgus (older child), kyphosis, scoliosis, smaller and narrow pelvis, and frequent fractures (6 months to 2 years old)
    2. Osteomalacia: bone pain and fractures
  C. Laboratory findings: low phosphorus, low or normal calcium, and high alkaline phosphatase, low 25-(OH) vitamin D
  D. X-rays
    1. Rickets: thin cortices, splayed, enlarged, flared, cupping and irregular metaphysis, biconcave vertebrae, funnel-shaped pelvis, and rachitic "rosary" of the ribs
    2. Osteomalacia: osteopenia, coarse trabeculae, "looser zones" in the cortices, ground-glass trabeculae in severe cases
  E. Pathology
    1. Rickets
       a. Thick hypertrophic zone with poor provisional calcification and mineralization of the primary trabeculae in the epiphysis
       b. Increased uncalcified osteoid seam and prominent osteoblastic and osteoclastic activities
    2. Osteomalacia: abundant uncalcified osteoid seam
  F. Treatment
    1. Deficiency
       a. Vitamin D
       b. Elemental calcium: 1000–1500 mg/day
    2. Malabsorption
       a. Vitamin D
       b. Elemental calcium: 1500 mg/day
       c. $1,25(OH)_2D$

Table 2-1 Summary of Features of Various Metabolic Bone Disorders

Disease	Pathology	Clinical Feature	X-Ray Findings	Laboratory Findings	Comments
Nutritional deficiency rickets	Deficient vitamin D, calcium	Genu varus or valgus prone to kyphosis, scoliosis, bowing of bones, enlarged ends of bones	Thin cortex, irregular splayed, enlarged metaphysis, biconcave vertebrae, rachitic "rosary"	$Ca\downarrow$, $PO_4\downarrow$, Alk P$\uparrow$* PTH$\uparrow$, 25-(OH)D$\downarrow$	Treatment with vitamin D and calcium
Vitamin D resistant rickets (hypophosphatemic rickets)	Deficient renal absorption of PO_4 at PCT*	Dwarf with normal upper extremities, craniosynostosis genu varus, enlarged bone ends	Similar to vitamin D deficient rickets	Ca normal, $PO_4\downarrow$, Alk P$\uparrow\uparrow$	Treatment with high dose of vitamin D and PO_4
Fanconi syndrome	Renal tubular defect (PCT & DCT*)	Very ill, severe osteopenia and rickets picture	Severe ricketic changes, "ground glass"	$Ca\downarrow$, $PO_4\downarrow$, Alk P$\uparrow$, and AA and glucose in urine	Treatment with vitamin D and PO_4
Renal tubular acidosis	Renal tubular defect (DCT)	Renal stones, hypokalemia, infantile and acquired types	Ricketlike pathologic fractures	$PO_4\downarrow$, $K^+\downarrow$, $Ca\downarrow$	Treatment with vitamin D, PO_4, bicarbonate and K^+
Renal osteodystrophy	Renal failure	Dwarf, genu valgus, enlarged bone ends, and bowing. Epiphyseal separation and metaphysical fractures	Similar to vitamin D deficient rickets. Also osteitis fibrosa cystica	$Ca\downarrow$, $PO_4\uparrow$, Alk P normal or high PTH$\uparrow$, 25-(OH)D normal	Treatment of renal failure, PO_4, vitamin D, and calcium supplement

Disease	Cause	Clinical	Radiographic	Laboratory	Treatment
Hypophosphatasia	Genetic error of Alk P synthesis	Growth retardation, severe ricketlike picture, deformities, 50–90% mortality	Ricketlike, especially wrist and knees and costochondral junction	Alk P↓, and phosphoethanolamine in urine	
Adult osteomalacia	Deficient vitamin D and calcium. Multiple fractures. Defect in mineralization Abundant uncalcified osteoid (biopsy)	Bone pain, fractures	Osteopenia, "looser zone," ground glass in severe cases	Ca↓, PO$_4$↓, Alk P↑	Treatment with vitamin D and calcium
Osteoporosis	Postmenopausal and senile, multiple factors, decreased bone mass	Fractures (spine, radius, and hip)	Osteopenia	Calcium normal or high, PO$_4$ normal, Alk P normal or low	Treatment with vitamin D, calcium, fluoride, estrogen
Hyperparathyroidism	Adenoma (1°), hyperplasia (2°)	Bone pain, fractures, hypercalcemia	Osteitis fibrosa cystica, brown tumor (1°), ectopic calcification	Ca↑, PO$_4$↓ (1°) Alk P↑, Ca↓ (2°)	Treatment by parathyroidectomy
Paget's disease	Abnormal osteoclast	Bone pain, deformities, 95% asymptomatic	Pelvis, spine, femur, and skull (osteolytic, osteoblastic, and sclerotic)	Alk P↑↑, hydroxyproline in urine	Treatment with etidronate, calcitonin, plicamycin

*AA: amino acids; Alk P: alkaline phosphatase; Ca: calcium; DCT: distal convoluted tubule; K$^+$: potassium ion; PCT: proximal convoluted tubule; PO$_4$: phosphate; PTH: parathyroid hormone.

3. Drug induced
   a. Vitamin D
   b. Elemental calcium: 1500 mg/day

III. Vitamin D Resistant Rickets (Hypophosphatemic Rickets)

A. Pathogenesis
   1. Inherited (sex-linked dominant or autosomal recessive) condition with deficient renal absorption of phosphorus at the proximal convoluted tubules
   2. May also be due to decreased synthesis of $1,25\text{-}(OH)_2D$ or end-organ insensitivity
B. Clinical findings: dwarf similar to achondroplasia but normal upper extremities, genu varus, enlarged bone ends, and craniosynostosis
C. Laboratory finding: normal calcium but very low phosphorus (<2.5 mg/dL), and very high alkaline phosphatase
D. X-ray and pathology: similar to severe vitamin deficient rickets
E. Treatment: high-dose vitamin D or $1,25\text{-}(OH)_2D$ and phosphorus supplementation

IV. Fanconi Syndrome

A. Pathogenesis: renal tubular defects (more in the proximal than distal convoluted tubules) causing decreased absorption of calcium and phosphorus
B. Clinical findings: very ill, severe osteopenia, clinically similar to severe rickets
C. Laboratory findings: low calcium, very low phosphorus, and high alkaline phosphatase. Amino acids and glucose in urine
D. X-ray and pathology: similar to severe rickets
E. Treatment: vitamin D, calcium, and phosphorus

V. Renal Tubular Acidosis (Classic)

A. Pathogenesis: congenital defect of the distal convoluted tubule resulting in failure to acidify urine and spillage of calcium, phosphorus, and potassium
B. Clinical findings: ricketlike picture, renal stones, growth retardation, nephritis, and fractures
C. Laboratory findings: low calcium, phosphorus and potassium, high chloride, and secondary hyponatremia (secondary hyperaldosteronism)
D. X-rays and pathology: similar to rickets
E. Treatment: vitamin D, phosphorus, potassium, and bicarbonate

VI. Renal Osteodystrophy

A. Pathogenesis
   1. Renal parenchymal damage resulting in decreased synthesis of $1,25\text{-}(OH)_2D$ and phosphorus retention
   2. Hypocalcemia causes secondary hyperparathyroidism
B. Clinical findings: dwarf, genu valgus, enlarged epiphysis, fractures, and prone to slipped capital femoral epiphysis
C. Laboratory findings: low calcium, high phosphorus, and normal or high alkaline phosphatase
D. X-rays and pathology: ricketlike picture, osteosclerosis ("rugger jersey" spine), metastatic calcification, and osteitis fibrosa cystica
E. Treatment: correct renal failure, calcium (750–1500 mg/day) and low phosphate diet

VII. Hypophosphatasia

A. Pathogenesis: genetic defect of alkaline phosphatase synthesis (autosomal recessive)
B. Clinical findings: growth retardation, craniosynostosis, severe rickets picture, 50–90% mortality
C. Laboratory findings: low alkaline phosphatase and positive phosphoethanolamine in the urine
D. X-ray and pathology: severe ricketlike picture
E. Treatment: transfusion of Paget's pa-

tients' blood (alkaline phosphatase replacement from patients with Paget's disease is experimental)

VIII. Osteoporosis

A. General considerations
  1. Pathogenesis: decreased skeletal mass due to multiple factors
     a. Bone resorption is greater than bone formation
        (1) Bone mass peaks and gradual loss occurs normally by 25 years of age
        (2) Bone loss about 0.5% per year after 30 years of age, and postmenopausal women lose at 2% per year (8% trabecular, and 0.5% cortical bone)
     b. Postmenopausal: low estrogen level may retard its inhibitory effect on bony resorption
     c. Endocrine: hyperthyroidism, hyperadrenalism, hyperparathyroidism, hypogonadism (Kleinfelter, Turner, castration, panhypopituitarism), diabetes mellitus, hyperglucocorticosteroid, estrogen deficiency
     d. Disuse: 30–40% in 6 months' immobilization and 7% of lumbar vertebra loss after only 3 weeks of bed rest
     e. Neoplastic: multiple myeloma, leukemia and lymphoma (circulating osteoclastic-activating factors)
     f. Collagen defects: scurvy, osteogenesis imperfecta, homocystinuria
     g. Idiopathic osteoporosis: juvenile and adult (osteoblastic defect)
     h. Hematologic: sickle cell anemia, thalassemia
     i. Cigarette smoking and alcohol intake
     j. Osteomalacia associated: nutritional, drugs, renal
     k. Medications: corticosteroids, dilantin, calcium losing diuretics
  2. Incidence
     a. Most common in postmenopausal white females over 65 years old (15% over 65 years)
     b. Eight percent of postmenopausal women also have osteomalacia
     c. Osteomalacia found in 25% intertrochanteric and 35% femoral neck fractures
     d. Fifty percent of females over 80 years old have compression thoracic fractures
B. Clinical findings
  1. Fractures: vertebral bodies, ribs, proximal femur and humerus, distal radius and pubic ramus
  2. Laboratory: normal or slightly high calcium, normal phosphorus, and normal or low alkaline phosphatase
  3. Diagnosis
     a. X-ray: 30–40% bone loss before visible
     b. Singh index
        (1) Grade 6: normal
        (2) Grade 5: Ward's triangle has lost trabeculae
        (3) Grade 4: secondary tension and compression, trabeculae lost
        (4) Grade 3: primary tension, trabeculae lost across the greater trochanter
        (5) Grade 2: primary tension, trabeculae absent
        (6) Grade 1: primary compression, trabeculae thin
     c. Single beam absorptiometry: distal radius
     d. Dual photon absorptiometry: very sensitive test (1–2% precision)
     e. Quantitative computed tomography (CT) scan: good correlation with vertebral osteoporosis (3–15% precision, high radiation)
     f. Bone biopsy
        (1) Taken 2 cm posterior and inferior to the anterior inferior iliac spine (6–10 mm bore)

- (2) Double tetracycline labeling: decreased labeling rate and smudging and increased osteoid in osteomalacia
- (3) Differentiate osteoporosis from osteomalacia and assess activity of osteoporosis
4. Treatment
   a. Activity and exercise (eg, swimming, walking)
   b. Daily calcium maintenance and vitamin D
      (1) Children: 400–700 mg of calcium and 400 U of vitamin D
      (2) Adolescent: 1300 mg of calcium and 400 U of vitamin D
      (3) 25 years to 50 years of age: 500–750 mg of calcium and 400 U of vitamin D
      (4) Pregnancy: 1500 mg of calcium and 400–800 U of vitamin D
      (5) Lactating: 2000 mg of calcium and 400–800 U of vitamin D
      (6) Postmenopausal: 1500 mg of calcium and 400–800 U of vitamin D
      (7) Men >50 years of age: 1200 mg of calcium and 400–800 U of vitamin D
      (8) Fracture: 1500 mg of calcium and 400–800 U of vitamin D
   c. Estrogen: usually for premature menopausal women, and women with low bone mass or rapidly decreasing bone densities (should cycle with progesterone to decrease incidence of uterine cancer)
   d. Sodium fluoride: may increase bone mass
   e. Calcitonin: if estrogen treatment is contraindicated (50–100 Units/day)

IX. Paget's Disease of Bone
A. General considerations
   1. Incidence: 3–4% over 40 years and 10% over 70 years
   2. More common in males and in England
   3. Location: pelvis, sacrum, spine, skull, femur, tibia
B. Pathogenesis
   1. Abnormal osteoclast hyperactivity and secondary increase in osteoblastic activity
   2. Etiology: unknown (viral origin is suspected)
   3. Phases
      a. Osteolytic: increase in osteoclastic activity and vascularity
      b. Mixed: increase in osteoblastic and osteoclastic activity with mosaic x-ray picture and net increase of bone may occur
      c. Sclerotic: irregular cement lines and hard bone
   4. Bone deformities along the line of stress
C. Clinical findings
   1. Asymptomatic in 95%
   2. Symptoms: apathy, lethargy, pain, deformity
   3. Complications: pathologic fracture, osteoarthritis, neurologic involvement (spinal cord), high cardiac output leading to cardiac failure, nonunions, neoplasms (osteosarcoma, fibrosarcoma, and malignant fibrous histiocytoma)
   4. X-rays
      a. Lytic, mixed (mosaic), and sclerotic
      b. Thick and irregular long boned, vertebral enlargement, and platybasia
      c. Bowing deformities, pathologic fractures, and sarcomatous degeneration
      d. Bone scan: positive
   5. Laboratory findings: increased alkaline phosphatase and urinary hydroxyproline
D. Treatment: if symptomatic
   1. Calcitonin: inhibit osteoclasts and decrease blood flow especially during osteolytic phase
   2. Diphosphonate: binds to hydroxyapatite crystals and inhibits mineralization
   3. Plicamycin: only if impending paraplegia

X. Hyperparathyroidism

A. General considerations
1. Types
   a. Primary: excess production of parathyroid hormone by adenomas (80%) or hyperplasia
   b. Secondary: stimulation of increased parathyroid secretion from hypocalcemia (renal, malabsorption, or hepatic causes)
2. Malignant carcinoma of the chief cells: rare
3. Parathyroid hormone: increase serum calcium by osteoclastic resorption and renal absorption

B. Clinical findings
1. Asymptomatic hypercalcemia
2. Symptomatic hypercalcemia: general malaise, loss of appetite, nausea, vomiting, polydipsia, abdominal pain, muscle weakness, and associated with pancreatitis and renal stones
3. Bone pain, brown tumors, and fractures
4. X-rays
   a. Bone resorptions: subperiosteal resorption of bone (especially medial aspect of middle phalanx of the hand, erosion of distal tufts, marginal joint erosion), endosteal bone resorption, subchondral bone resorption, and intracortical bone resorption
   b. Trabecular resorption within medullary bone (especially in the cranium known as "salt and pepper skull")
   c. Brown tumor (fibrous tissue and giant cells): more common in primary hyperparathyroidism
   d. Osteosclerosis: increased amount of trabecular bone formation, more common in secondary type
   e. Ectopic calcification: more common in secondary type
5. Laboratory findings
   a. Primary hyperparathyroidism: increased serum calcium, decreased phosphate, increased alkaline phosphatase, and increased PTH
   b. Secondary hyperparathyroidism: hyperphosphatemia
6. Histology: osteoclastic trabecular resorption and osteocytic lacunar cortical resorption

C. Treatment
1. Adenoma removal or subtotal parathyroid glands removal in hyperplasia
2. Secondary type
   a. Treat the cause (ie, renal disease)
   b. Calcium, vitamin D or $1,25-(OH)_2D$ when indicated

REFERENCES

Barth RW, Lane JM: Osteoporosis. Orthop Clin North Am 19:845–858, 1988

Doppelt SH: Vitamin D, rickets and osteomalacia. Orthop Clin North Am 15:671–686, 1984

Kanis JA: Vitamin D metabolism and its clinical application. J Bone Joint Surg 64B:542–560, 1982

Kaplan FS, August CS, Fallon MD, et al: Successful treatment of infantile malignant osteopetrosis by bone-marrow transplant: A case report. J Bone Joint Surg 70A:617–623, 1988

Klein KL, Maxwell MH: Renal osteodystrophy. Orthop Clin North Am 15:687–696, 1984

Lane, JM, Vigorta VJ: Osteoporosis. Orthop Clin North Am 15:711–728, 1984

Lane JM, Healey JH, Schwartz E, et al: Treatment of osteoporosis with sodium fluoride and calcium: Effects pm vertebral fracture incidence and bone histomorphometry. Orthop Clin North Am 15:729–746, 1984

Maldague B, Malghem J: Dynamic radiographic patterns of Paget's disease of bone. Clin Orthop 217:126–151, 1987

Mankin HJ: Rickets, osteomalacia and renal osteodystrophy, Part I and II. J Bone Joint Surg 56A:101–128, 352–386, 1974

Merkow RL, Lane JM: Current concepts of Paget's disease of bone. Orthop Clin North Am 15:747–764, 1984

Raisz LG: Local and systemic factors in the pathogenesis of osteoporosis. N Engl J Med 318:818–828, 1988

Riggs BL, Melton LJ III: Involutional osteoporosis. N Engl J Med 314:1676–1686, 1986

Schnitzler CM, Sweet MB, Blumenfeld TS, et al: Radiographic features of the spine in fluoride therapy for osteoporosis. J Bone Joint Surg 69B:190–194, 1987

14

Fracture Healing and Nonunion

I. Fracture Healing
A. Stages of long bone healing (Brighton)
 1. Stage of impact
 2. Stage of inflammation (1–3 days)
    a. Hemorrhage
    b. Hematoma: polymorphonuclear neutrophils (PMNs), macrophages, and mast cells with fibrin clot
    c. Bone necrosis at ends of fracture site
    d. Granulation tissue replaces hematoma with invading capillaries and fibroblasts. Osteoclasts remove dead bone
    e. Induction (stage of subperiosteal and endosteal cellular proliferation): cambium layer of periosteum and mesenchymal cells or osteoprogenitor cells from bone marrow, endosteum and soft tissue differentiate into osteoblasts and chondroblasts
 3. Stage of soft callus (3 weeks): primary callus and external bridging callus
    a. Fibrocartilagenous tissue: low oxygen tension, high proteoglycan content, anaerobic glycolytic process, and negative bioelectricity
    b. Progressive calcification
       (1) Mineral deposition occurs on the collagen fibrils
       (2) Matrix vesicles are found in the fracture callus
       (3) This fails to occur in nonunion
    c. Vascular invasion and vascularity peaks at 2 weeks
 4. Stage of hard callus (3–4 months): late medullary callus
    a. Ossification is an aerobic process
    b. Clinical healing when no gross movement and no tenderness
    c. Radiologic healing follows later
 5. Stage of remodeling (Wolff's law): lamellar structure
B. Cancellous bone healing
 1. Inflammation stage: hematoma, granulation tissue, and induction
 2. Callus stage: osteoblasts lay down matrix (woven bone)
 3. Remodeling stage: trabecular bone in lamellar structure
C. Types of callus
 1. Primary callus response: fractures that are not rigidly fixed
 2. External bridging callus: if bony ends are not in continuity
 3. Late medullary callus: osteogenic cells from ends of bones
 4. Primary cortical healing: rigid fixation and perfect apposition
D. Vascularity
 1. The presence of periosteal vessels alone is sufficient for fracture healing
 2. Nutrient or endosteal vessels constitute ⅔ of cortical circulation and therefore are important as vascular supply
 3. Intraosseous vein reconstituted about 12 weeks after fracture
E. Electricity
 1. Piezoelectricity: stress-generated electric potential
    a. Electronegativity in compression
    b. Electropositivity in tension
 2. Biopotential: negative charge on cell membrane
    a. Metaphysis is electronegative compared to diaphysis
    b. Medulla is electronegative compared to the cortex
    c. Fracture callus is electronegative
 3. Negative potential promotes osteo-

genesis, whereas positive potential causes resorption

II. Types of Nonunion
A. Hypertrophic
  1. Viable or biologic activity on both sides of the fracture sites but no bridging due to motion
  2. Union can be obtained with reduction and compression stabilization alone
B. Atrophic
  1. Nonviable or avascular fracture site
  2. No change over time in callus formation
  3. Stimulus for further healing is necessary, such as electricity or bone graft
C. Synovial pseudarthrosis
  1. Separated by synovia-like joint due to excess motion
  2. Pseudojoint
  3. More common in humerus, clavicle, and femur
  4. Excision of this membrane is necessary in addition to rigid immobilization

III. Factors Associated with Nonunion
A. Local
  1. Devascularization
  2. Discontinuity: distracting force and fibrous tissue
  3. Inadequate immobilization (especially cyclic tensile loading)
  4. Infection
B. Systemic: nutrition, steroids, anticoagulants, anemia, radiation, hormones, etc.

IV. Clinical Findings
A. Pain and tenderness
B. Motion at fracture site
C. Plain x-ray, tomogram, fluoroscopy, magnetic resonance imaging (MRI)
D. Bone scan can differentiate types
  1. Hypertrophic: increased uptake around the fracture site
  2. Atrophic: no increased uptake or minimally increased uptake only in the proximal fragment
  3. Synovial: cold spot in the cleft

V. Treatment
A. Surgery
  1. Undisplaced diaphyseal nonunion
     a. Hypertrophic: compression plate on tension side or intramedullary rod (excision of pseudarthrosis or bone grafting is not necessary)
     b. Atrophic: compression plate or intramedullary rod (shingling the cortex and bone grafting are necessary, but excision of fibrous nonunion is not)
  2. Displaced or malaligned diaphyseal nonunion: resect pseudarthrosis and correct malalignment and bone grafting and stabilization with plate or rod
  3. Metaphyseal pseudarthrosis: rigid fixation with or without bone grafting and early range of motion
  4. Synovial pseudarthrosis: excision of pseudarthrosis is mandatory and compression fixation with bone grafting
  5. Infected pseudarthrosis: if no evidence of active infection for 3 months, primary stabilization and bone grafting is advisable
     a. Meticulous removal of dead bone and use of pure cancellous bone grafting
     b. Papineau bone grafting for osteomyelitis
     c. Active drainage: incision and drainage, and external fixator and posterolateral bone grafting in tibia
  6. Large defects: vascularized graft
B. Bone grafting
  1. Cancellous: osteosynthetic (mesenchymal cells differentiate to osteoblasts)
  2. Cortical: osteoconductive (vascular granulation invasion and resorption followed by bone deposition; initially strong and fills the defect, but weak until 6 months to 2 years
  3. Osseous bed preparation: decortication and drilling of the sclerotic bone for vascularity
     a. Graft survival better after 7–10 days
     b. Graft thickness: about 5 mm and

cancellous bone should face the surrounding soft tissue for vascular penetration
      c. Soak the graft in blood (not in saline or antibiotic) and shorter time between donor and recipient sites is better for graft survival
  C. Electric stimulation
    1. Types: invasive, semi-invasive, noninvasive (pulsing electromagnetic fields)
    2. Mechanism
      a. Stimulate fibrocartilage for mineralization
      b. May increase vascularity
    3. Clinical indications
      a. Patient cooperation: noninvasive and semi-invasive types
      b. Not for synovial pseudarthrosis, atrophic types (dead bone at bone ends), large gap (1 cm or half the diameter), and active infection (invasive and semi-invasive types)
      c. Nonweight-bearing status: noninvasive and semi-invasive types
      d. Overall success varies depending on regions and types of pseudarthrosis
  D. Regional considerations
    1. Cervical spine
      a. Type II fracture of the odontoid frequently fails to unite and treated with Brooks C1–C2 wiring/fusion
      b. Anterior interbody pseudarthrosis: revision anterior fusion or posterior wiring and fusion is successful
    2. Thoracolumbar spine: surgical exposure of nonunion, decortication of bone mass, cancellous bone grafting, and stable instrumentation
    3. Humerus
      a. Nonunion if no healing in 4 months
      b. Transverse fractures are more commonly ununited
      c. Treatment with electricity gives poor results
      d. Synovial pseudarthrosis type is common
      e. Surgical excision, bone grafting, and internal fixation with compression plating or intramedullary rod are necessary
    4. Forearm
      a. Compression plating with bone graft: 90% success
    5. Scaphoid of the wrist: Russe bone graft or electricity gives good results
    6. Hip
      a. Subcapital fractures: hemiarthroplasty in older patients and aseptic necrosis cases. Osteotomy and bone grafting in younger patients with viable femoral head
      b. Intertrochanteric fractures: hip compression screw and bone grafting
      c. Subtrochanteric fractures: stable fixation with bone grafting
    7. Femur
      a. The incidence is about 1% but higher in open fractures
      b. Intramedullary rod is preferred with or without bone grafting
    8. Knee
      a. Distal femur: compression lag screw and plate with bone grafting
      b. Patella: excision of nonunion and tension band wiring
    9. Tibia
      a. Nondisplaced stable nonunion: consider electricity
      b. Displaced
        (1) Correct malalignment, bone grafting and fixation (intramedullary rod or plate)
        (2) Fibular osteotomy if distracting force or deformity needs to be corrected
        (3) Posterolateral bone grafting, especially in infected nonunions
    10. Medial malleolus and metatarsals: bone grafting with fixation or electricity

REFERENCES

Bassett CA: The development and application of pulsed electromagnetic (PEMFs) for ununited fractures and arthrodesis. Orthop Clin North Am 15:61–88, 1984

Blick SS, Brumback RJ, Lakatos R, et al: Early prophylactic bone grafting of high-energy tibial fractures. Clin Orthop 240:21–41, 1989

Brighton CT: The semi-invasive method of treating nonunion with direct current. Orthop Clin North Am 15:33–46, 1984

Brighton CT: Principles of fracture healing: Part I: The biology of fracture repair. In AAOS instructional course lectures 33. St Louis, CV Mosby, 1984

Gordon L, Chiu EJ: Treatment of infected non-unions and segmental defects of the tibia with staged microvascular muscle transplantation and bone grafting. J Bone Joint Surg 70A:377–386, 1988

Heppenstall RB: The present role of bone graft surgery in treating nonunion. Orthop Clin North Am 15:113–124, 1984

Johnson EE, Marder RA: Open intramedullary nailing and bone grafting for non-union of tibial diaphyseal fracture. J Bone Joint Surg 69A:375–380, 1987

Johnson EE, Urist MR, Finerman GAM: Repair of segmental defects of the tibia with cancellous bone grafts augmented with human bone morphogenetic protein: A preliminary report. Clin Orthop 236:249–257, 1988

Osterman AL, Bora FW: Free vascularized bone grafting for large gap nonunion of long bones. Ortho Clin North Am 15:131–143, 1984

Paterson D: Treatment of nonunion with a constant direct current: A totally implantable system. Orthop Clin North Am 15:47–60, 1984

Saliban AH, Anzel SH, Salyer WA: Transfer of vascularized grafts of iliac bone to the extremities. J Bone Joint Surg 69A:1319–1327, 1987

15

Osteonecrosis, Osteochondroses, and Osteochondritis Dissecans

I. General Considerations

A. Osteonecrosis: avascular necrosis of bone
B. Osteochondrosis: idiopathic condition characterized by disorders of both chondrogenesis and osteogenesis, which arises on a formerly normal growth mechanism
C. Osteochondritis dissecans: avascular necrosis of a segment of subchondral bone causing symptoms in the joint (implies fracture first and subsequent necrosis)
D. Locations: articular or subchondral (ie, avascular necrosis [AVN] of the hip and Freiberg's disease), diaphysis (ie, bone infarct) and tendon or ligament attachment (ie, Osgood-Schlatter disease and Sever's disease)

II. Ischemic Necrosis of the Femoral Head

A. General Considerations
 1. Less than 5% are idiopathic
 2. Risk factors include femoral neck fracture, hip dislocation, acetabular fracture, caisson's disease, sickle cell disease, Gaucher's disease, and postirradiation necrosis. Probable risk factors are gout and hyperuricemia, postvenous thrombosis, hip dysplasia, serum lipid disorders (alcoholism), connective tissue disease, and osteoporosis or osteomalacia
 3. Percentage of patients taking steroids who develop AVN is small

B. Pathogenesis
 1. Infarction theory: under a variety of circumstances, blood supply to the femoral head becomes incompetent, leading to infarction. Clinical presentation, however, is delayed until revascularization occurs, followed by trabecular resorption, microfracture, and eventual collapse
 2. Progressive ischemia theory: bone functions as a closed, nondistensible compartment. Any increase in the bone marrow pressure will therefore lead to a subsequent decrease in bone blood flow as the thin-walled vessels collapse. This in turn can lead to a progressive ischemic event within the femoral head

C. Histologic findings
 1. Plasmostasis: eosinophilic material is initially found separating the lipocytes within the bone marrow. This probably represents edematous fluid
 2. Lipocyte degeneration: as this occurs, fat-filled histiocytes (or foam cells) are seen
 3. Medullary fibrosis
 4. Trabecular necrosis

D. Diagnosis
 1. Early diagnosis is the single most important factor in the treatment of AVN
 2. Unfortunately, many patients are asymptomatic during the early clinical stages
 3. Pain is the usual presenting complaint but is usually representative of advanced disease

4. The range of motion is preserved as opposed to arthritic joint
5. Radiographic findings
   a. Radiographic changes lag far behind histopathologic changes
   b. Frog leg lateral view is best in delineating any changes in the trabecular pattern of the femoral head
   c. Comparison views are often helpful in the early stages
   d. Subchondral lucency and loss of sphericity represent the earliest radiographic features of morphologic failure
   e. Bone scan and sulfur colloid testing can be done when plain x-rays are normal but suspicion is high. However, false-negative rates are unacceptably high
   f. MRI scanning is currently the test of choice in diagnosing AVN in its early stages
6. Radiographic classification (Ficat)
   a. Stage I: normal joint line and femoral head with osteoporosis
   b. Stage II: normal joint line and femoral head with mixed osteoporosis and sclerosis
   c. Stage III: normal joint line and flattened subchondral collapse with sclerotic sequestrum
   d. Stage IV: narrow joint line, collapsed head, and destruction of superior pole
7. Bone marrow pressure (BMP) measurement
   a. Elevated BMP may be the common pathway for the various pathogenic entities
   b. Baseline pressure is obtained by placing a cannula into the proximal femur
   c. Stress test is done by injecting 5 cc of saline intraosseously and remeasuring the pressure: in the normal situation this will provoke only a slight change in the BMP, but in AVN, BMP will exhibit a prolonged elevation
   d. Intraosseous venography in the patient with AVN will show poor filling of the metaphyseal veins, diaphyseal reflux, and stasis
E. Treatment options
   1. Core decompression
      a. Indicated primarily for stages I and II. This may be used as a palliative measure in more advanced cases
      b. Technique consists of removing an 8–10 mm core of bone from the anterolateral portion of the femoral head
      c. Postoperatively, patient should be kept nonweight bearing for at least 6 weeks
      d. Ficat and Arlet have reported 92% good to excellent results in stages I and II disease with 8-year follow-up
   2. Bone grafting: fibular or tibial strut grafts have been used to augment structural integrity of proximal femur. Recently, vascularized fibular strut graft has gained popularity
   3. Flexion varus osteotomy for stages II and III: principle is to bring the collapsed segment out of the weight-bearing region of the acetabulum
   4. Arthrodesis
      a. Stage IV in the young and active patient without ipsilateral knee or back problems
      b. Not commonly done because of lower fusion rate and the availability of uncemented arthroplasty

III. Osteonecrosis of Other Bones
A. Body of the talus
   1. Blood supply of the talar body is from anastomotic sling between the artery of the tarsal canal (a branch of the posterior tibial artery) and artery of the tarsal sinus (anastomotic loop between dorsalis pedis and perforating branch of the peroneal artery); many branches

enter the neck and course posterolaterally, and the medial quarter of the body is supplied by the deltoid branch from the posterior tibial artery
2. Post-traumatic: 13% incidence after nondisplaced fracture of the talar neck, but 50% incidence after displaced fracture with subtalar dislocation and 84% incidence after fracture with subtalar and ankle dislocation
3. Not all avascular necrosis of the talus becomes symptomatic to require surgery
4. Conservative nonweight-bearing treatment or patellar tendon bearing brace may be effective in some cases
5. Subtalar fusion or pantalar fusion may be done

B. Humeral head
1. Blood supply is from intraosseous vessels fed by periosteal vessels penetrating at the greater and lesser tuberosities and humeral shaft
2. Greatest risk is with four-part fracture of the proximal humerus and displaced fracture of the anatomic neck
3. Associated with corticosteroid use
4. Symptomatic AVN can be treated by arthroplasty in older patients and fusion in younger active patients

C. Carpal scaphoid
1. Vascular supply (radial artery)
   a. Artery to dorsal ridge of scaphoid: proximal 80%
   b. Volar radial branch: distal 20% (volar approach is less traumatic to proximal scaphoid)
2. Associated with nonunion
3. Incidence is greater with proximal pole fractures
4. Treatment varies, depending on degenerative changes of involved joints

D. Femoral condyles
1. Medial is more common than lateral condyle
2. Usually occurs in patients over 60 years of age, and sudden onset of pain is common
3. More frequent in women (3:1)
4. Osteonecrosis of the medial tibial plateau may also cause pain in the medial aspect of the knee
5. Treatment: conservative if minimally symptomatic, high tibial osteotomy if varus deformity, unicondylar arthroplasty if one compartment involvement, and total knee arthroplasty if tricompartment involvement

IV. Osteochondroses
A. Types
1. Articular osteochondroses (ie, Freiberg's and Perthes' diseases)
2. Nonarticular osteochondroses (Osgood-Schlatter and Sever's diseases)
3. Physeal osteochondroses (Scheuermann's and Blount's diseases)

B. Freiberg's disease
1. Osteochondrosis of the metatarsal head, usually second and occasionally third and fourth metatarsals
2. Usually age 12–15 prior to closure of the physis
3. Symptoms appear before x-ray changes (pain, tenderness, swelling)
4. X-ray findings: sclerosis, fragmentation and widening of epiphysis, narrowing of the joint
5. Treatment: rest, no weight-bearing ambulation, cast, arch support, and occasionally excision of loose bodies or dorsiflexion osteotomy

C. Panner's disease
1. Osteochondrosis of capitellum of humerus
2. Mostly males around 8–9 years of age
3. Symptoms: pain following mild trauma and inability to extend elbow fully
4. X-ray findings: fragmentation and irregularity of capitellum
5. Treatment: rest and conservative treatment. Occasionally excision of loose bodies

D. Kohler's disease
1. Osteochondrosis of the tarsal navicular
2. Seventy-five to 80% males and com-

mon during 4 to 10 years of age, with a third being bilateral
   3. Clinical findings: local pain, swelling, tenderness
   4. X-ray findings: sclerosis, flattening and fragmentation of the navicular
   5. Usually self-limited process, and spontaneous reconstruction is the rule
   6. Treatment: rest, observation, occasional short walking cast
  E. Osgood-Schlatter syndrome
   1. Traction osteochondrosis of tibial tubercle
   2. More common in active boys during puberty and often bilateral
   3. Clinical findings: pain, tenderness, and swelling; symptoms may last for months to years
   4. X-ray findings: fragmentation of the tibial tubercle with dense-appearing ossicles and soft tissue swelling
   5. Treatment: conservative treatment and occasionally a cylinder cast. Rarely is surgery necessary, such as drilling or excision of ununited fragment
  F. Sinding-Larsen's syndrome
   1. Traction osteochondrosis of the inferior pole of the patella
   2. Clinical findings: local pain and tenderness
   3. X-ray findings: sclerosis and fragmentation of the inferior pole of the patella
   4. Treatment: symptomatic
  G. Sever's disease
   1. Pressure osteochondrosis or traction apophysitis of the Achilles tendon insertion
   2. More common in boys between 8 and 15 years of age
   3. Frequently asymptomatic and may be normal variant
   4. Treatment: symptomatic and heel lift

V. Osteochondritis Dissecans

  A. AVN of segment of subchondral bone and partially or totally detached osteochondral fragment
  B. Associated with trauma (50%)
  C. Clinical findings: pain, joint effusion, locking episodes, arthritis
  D. Common in the lateral aspect of the medial femoral condyle, posteromedial or anterolateral aspects of the talar dome, anterolateral aspect of the capitellum and femoral head after Perthes' disease
  E. Treatment
   1. Children and in early adolescence: activity modification and immobilization
   2. Older patients
      a. Rest and protection if small size and stable lesions and minimally symptomatic
      b. Symptomatic lesions
         (1) Intact lesion: multiple drill holes through the articular surface into the subchondral fragment and into vascularized bone
         (2) Early separation: percutaneous wire fixation
         (3) Partially detached: gentle debridement of fibrous interposed tissue and securing flap with K-wires
         (4) Loose fragment: if large enough, attempt to reattach and secure with K-wires (bone grafting may be used)

REFERENCES

Canale ST, Belding RH: Osteochondral lesions of the talus. J Bone Joint Surg 62A:97–102, 1980

Cruess RL, Ross D, Crawshaw E: The etiology of steroid-induced avascular necrosis of bone. Clin Orthop 113:178, 1975

Ficat RP, Arlet J: In Hungerford DS, ed. *Ischemia and necrosis of bone*. Baltimore, Williams & Wilkins, 1980

Fisher DE, Bickel WH: Corticosteroid induced avascular necrosis. A clinical study of 77 patients. J Bone Joint Surg 53A:859–873, 1971

Genant HK, Jergeson HE, Heller M, et al: Magnetic resonance imaging of the hip. Hip 13:150–156, 1985

Glimcher MJ, Kenzora JE: The biology of osteonecrosis of the human femoral head and its clinical implications III. Clin Orthop 140:273, 1979

Guhl JF: Arthroscopic treatment of osteochondritis dissecans. Clin Orthop 167:65–74, 1982

Hungerford DS, Zizic TM: The treatment of ischemic necrosis of the femoral head. Clin Orthop 130:144, 1978

Ippolito E, Pollini PTR, Falex F: Kohler's disease of the tarsal navicular: Long-term follow-up of 12 cases. J Pediatr Orthop 4:416–417, 1984

Medlar RC, Lyne ED: Sinding-Larsen-Johansson disease. It etiology and natural history. J Bone Joint Surg 60A:1113–1116, 1978

Meyers MH: The treatment of osteonecrosis of the hip with osteochondral allografts and with the muscle pedicle graft technique. Clin Orthop 130:202, 1978

Mital MA, Matza RA, Cohen J: The so-called unresolved Osgood-Schlatter lesion: A concept based on fifteen surgically treated lesions. J Bone Joint Surg 62A:732–739, 1980

O'Farrell TA, Costello BG: Osteochondritis dissecans of the talus. J Bone Joint Surg 64B:494–498, 1982

Ogden JA, Southwick WO: Osgood-Schlatter's disease and tibial tuberosity development. Clin Orthop 116:180, 1976

Williams GA, Cowell HR: Kohler's disease of the tarsal navicular. Clin Orthop 158:53–58, 1981

16
Bone Grafting

I. General Considerations
A. Types of bone grafts
  1. Autograft: autogenous bone from the same individual
  2. Isograft: isogenic bone from genetically same individuals (ie, identical twins)
  3. Allograft: between members of the same species
  4. Xenograft: between different species
B. Preservation methods are many: fresh, frozen, freeze-dried (with or without irradiation), or dimineralized
C. Bone grafts differ in size, shape, and tissue composition (cortical or cancellous) for different application
D. Synthetic grafts are also being developed (such as bone morphogenic protein, hydroxyapatite, tricalcium phosphate, collagen, combinations)
E. Bone graft incorporation
  1. Host-graft interaction: host factors such as vascularity of soft tissue, underlying bone quality, infection, chemotherapy, radiation treatment, and nutrition are all important in graft incorporation
  2. Graft may act as osteoconductive or osteoinductive material
    a. Osteoconduction: passive template for the influx of vessels and preexisting cells (ie, ceramics, frozen allografts)
      (1) Blood supply comes from the host bed: revascularization and microanastomosis occur in cancellous autograft to a depth of 1 mm, but bone resorption and ingrowth of capillaries occur in allograft
      (2) Osteoclasts come from circulating monocytes of hemopoietic system
      (3) Osteoblasts come from precursor cells found in the marrow and soft tissues
      (4) Cells such as osteoprogenitor cells may survive within autografts and proliferate to form bone
      (5) Close contact with the donor tissue is important in osteoconduction
    b. Osteoinduction: induce differentiation of fibroblast-like mesenchymal cells into osteoprogenitor cells to produce bone (such as bone matrix and bone morphogenic protein)
  3. Stages of bone graft incorporation (Urist)
    a. Stage 1: inflammation, activation of mesenchymal cells (within minutes to hours)
    b. Stage 2: surface surviving osteoblasts secrete matrix for early bone formation, particularly in cancellous autograft, but resorption and osteocyte necrosis occur first in allograft
    c. Stage 3: osteoinduction occurs simultaneously with inflammation and osteoblast differentiation, and consists of mesenchymal cell differentiation to bone-forming cells by donor bone matrix
      (1) Osteoinductive properties of donor's matrix are destroyed by autoclaving or irradiation
      (2) Osteoinductive properties are decreased by immune response (delayed hypersensitivity response) as in frozen or freeze-dried allograft
    d. Stage 4: osteoconduction occurs over periods of months to years as ingrowth of sprouting capillaries

and bone take place into porous structures
      e. Stage 5: remodeling takes place over years according to biomechanical factors

II. Autograft
A. Cortical bone
   1. Osteonecrosis and removal of necrotic bone occur via osteoclastic channels through haversian canal along with vascular invasion
   2. Revascularization is slow
   3. The graft becomes porous and weaker initially (3–6 months)
   4. Osteoblastic response takes over later via creeping substitution up to 2 years
   5. Less than half of the preexisting cortex is replaced eventually
   6. Good for structural support in the clinical setting
B. Cancellous bone
   1. Osteoblasts and osteoclasts function simultaneously in the initial period of bone graft incorporation
   2. Revascularization is quicker due to intrinsic porosity
   3. Cancellous bone is replaced more completely and rapidly
   4. Superior to cortical bone in nonunions and in primary fusions where structural support is not important
C. Vascularized bone
   1. No cell necrosis and rapid healing
   2. Graft remains viable and healing at the junction is similar to fracture healing
   3. Technically difficult but clinical application is wide (such as nonunions and segmental defects)

III. Allograft
A. Cortical bone
   1. Provides good strength
   2. Little vascular invasion and replacement take place; therefore the bone does not become porous and weak in the initial period as opposed to autogenous cortical bone
   3. Very slow healing at the junction
   4. Clinically used if autogenous cortical bone is not available and should be used with cancellous chips to promote faster union
B. Cancellous bone
   1. Generally a good osteoconductive source, but poor osteoinductive agent
   2. Combination with inductive materials such as bone marrow or autogenous cancellous bone is frequently utilized in the clinical setting
   3. Commonly used as a supplementary bone graft to autogenous cancellous bone graft
C. Preservation techniques
   1. Frozen allografts
      a. Deep freezing at $-70°C$ is recommended
      b. Maintains the biomechanical property better than freeze-dried method
      c. Easy storage and readily available
      d. Permits cartilage preservation with glycerol or dimethyl sulfoxide
      e. Decreased, but not elimination of, immunogenicity with freezing
      f. Potential for bacteria or virus transmission
   2. Freeze-dried (lyophilization) allografts
      a. Indefinite storage at room temperature
      b. Biomechanical strength is slightly decreased
      c. Immunogenicity is decreased (slightly better than freezing method)
      d. Potential for bacteria or virus transmission
      e. Must soak in saline before use
      f. Irradiation lessens the virus transmission and immunogenicity but further decreases strength and inductivity
   3. Demineralized matrix preparation
      a. Potent osteoinductor
      b. Little intrinsic strength
      c. Bone morphogenic protein
         (1) Low molecular weight noncollagenous protein

(2) Stimulate DNA synthesis and undifferentiated cell replication
(3) Isolation, purification, and synthesis are being investigated
4. Synthetic bone substitutes
   a. Hydroxyapatite or calcium phosphate crystal (ceramic)
   b. Osteoconductive materials
   c. May be used with osteoinductors such as bone morphogenetic protein or bone marrow
   d. Currently under investigation

REFERENCES

Bucholz RW, Carlton A, Holmes R: Interporous hydroxyapatite as a bone graft substitute in tibial plateau fractures. Clin Orthop 240:53–62, 1989

Burchardt H: The biology of bone graft repair. Clin Orthop 174:28–42, 1983

Burwell RG: The function of bone marrow in the incorporation of a bone graft. Clin Orthop 200:125–14, 1985

Czitrom AA, Langer F, McKee N, et al: Bone and cartilage allotransplantation: A review of 14 years of research and clinical studies. Clin Orthop 208:141–145, 1986

Dell PC, Burchardt H, Glowczewskie FP Jr: A roentgenographic, biochemical and histological evaluation of vascularized and nonvascularized segmental fibular canine autografts. J Bone Joint Surg 67A:105–112, 1985

Einhorn TA, Lane JM, Burstein AH, et al: The healing of segmental bone defects induced by demineralized bone matrix. A radiographic and biomechanical study. J Bone Joint Surg 66A:274–279, 1984

Flately TJ, Lynch KL, Benson M: Tissue response to implants of calcium phosphate ceramic in the rabbit spine. Clin Orthop 179:246, 1983

Friedlaender GE: Bone banking: In support of reconstructive surgery of the hip. Clin Orthop 225:17–21, 1987

Friedlaender GE: Bone grafts: The basic science rationale for clinical applications. J Bone Joint Surg 69A:786–790, 1987

Friedlaender GE, Mankin HJ: Bone banking: Current methods and suggested guidelines. In Instructional course lectures, Vol 30, The academy of orthopaedic surgeons. St Louis, CV Mosby, 1981

Friedlaender GE, Mankin HJ, Sell KW (eds): Osteochondral allografts: Biology, banking, and clinical applications. Boston, Little, Brown, 1983

Friedlaender GE, Strong DM, Sell KW: Studies on antigenicity of bone. I. Freeze-dried and deep frozen allografts in rabbits. J Bone Joint Surg 58A:854–885, 1976

Gepstein R, Weiss RE, Saba K, et al: Bridging large defects in bone by demineralized bone matrix in the form of a powder. J Bone Joint Surg 69A:984–992, 1987

Goldberg VM, Stevenson S: Natural history of autografts and allografts. Clin Orthop 225:7–16, 1987

Harakas NK: Demineralized bone-matrix-induced osteogenesis. Clin Orthop 188:239–251, 1984

Holmes RE, Bucholz RW, Mooney F: Porous hydroxyapatite as a bone graft substitute in diaphyseal defects: A histometric study. J Orthop Res 5:114–121, 1987

Horowitz MC, Friedlaender GE: Immunologic aspects of bone transplantation: A rationale for future studies. Orthop Clin North Am 18:227–233, 1987

Lane JM, Sandhu HS: Current approaches to experimental bone grafting. Orthop Clin North Am 18(2):213–225, 1987

Mankin HJ, Doppelt S, Tomford W: Clinical experience with allograft implantation. The first ten years. Clin Orthop 174:69–86, 1983

Moore DC, Chapman MW, Manske D: The evaluation of a biphasic calcium phosphate ceramic for use in grafting long-bone diaphyseal defects. J Orthop Res 5:356–365, 1987

Nasca RJ, Whelchel JD: Use of cyropreserved bone in spinal surgery. Spine 12:222–227, 1987

Nilsson OS, Urist MR, Dawson T, et al: Bone repair induced by bone morphogenetic protein in ulnar defects in dogs. J Bone J Surg 68B:635, 1986

Prolo DJ, Rodrigo JJ: Contemporary bone graft physiology and surgery. Clin Orthop 200:322–342, 1985

Shaffer JW, Field GA, Goldberg VM, et al: Fate of vascularized and nonvascularized autografts. Clin Orthop 197:32–43, 1985

Stevenson S: The immune response to osteochondral allografts in dogs. J Bone Joint Surg 69A:573–582, 1987

Stevenson S, Hohn RB, Templeton JW: Effects of tissue antigen matching on the healing of fresh cancellous bone allografts in dogs. Am J Vet Res 44:201–206, 1983

Takagi K, Urist MR: The role of bone marrow in bone morphogenetic protein induced repair of massive femoral diaphyseal defects. Clin Orthop 171:224, 1982

Tomford WW, Ploetz JE, Mankin HJ: Bone allografts of femoral heads: Procurement and storage. J Bone Joint Surg 68:534–537, 1986

Tomford WW, Starkweather RJ, Goldman MH: A study of the incidence of infection in the use of banked allograft bone. J Bone Joint Surg 63A:244–248, 1981

Urist ME, Delange RJ, Finerman GAM: Bone cell differentiation and growth factors. Science 220:680–686, 1983

Urist MR, Dawson E: Intertransverse process fusion with the aid of chemosterilized autolyzed allogeneic (AAA) bone. Clin Orthop 154:97–113, 1981

Urist MR, Lietz A, Mizutani H, et al: Bovine low molecular weight bone morphogenetic protein (BMP) fraction. Clin Orthop 162:219, 1982

Weiland AJ, Moore JR, Daniel RK: Vascularized bone autografts: Experience with 41 cases. Clin Orthop 174:87–95, 1983

17
Articular Cartilage and Arthritis and Synovial Diseases

ARTICULAR CARTILAGE

I. General Considerations
A. Cartilage is a highly specialized form of connective tissue that forms independently during embryonic development of mesenchymal and cartilaginous precursors of the rest of the bone
B. Cartilage has the fewest cells of any tissue but it is biologically active
C. Function of chondrocytes: synthesize and maintain proteoglycan (PG) and collagen
D. Cartilage is avascular and aneural: dependent primarily on diffusion of synovial fluid for nutrition
E. Composed primarily of water (80%), collagen type II (15%), and proteoglycans (5%)
F. Functionally, cartilage enables articulating surfaces to transmit high loads while maintaining contact stresses at low levels
G. Interaction of the different macromolecules
   1. Collagen: cohesion to tissue
   2. Proteoglycans: viscoelastic properties of cartilage
H. Thickness of the articular cartilage varies from joint to joint. Generally, it is thicker in the weight-bearing joints, averaging 2.0–4.0 mm

II. Histology
A. Four distinct zones (Fig 2-2)
   1. Superficial tangential
   2. Intermediate
   3. Deep
   4. Calcified
B. Superficial tangential zone (10%)
   1. Only several microns thick
   2. Chondrocytes are flattened and elongated, lying parallel to the surface. These cells have little endoplasmic reticulum (ER) and generally are inactive
   3. Collagen fibers are packed in bundles parallel to the joint surface, with a paucity of intervening ground substance
   4. Most superficially, there is a "lamina splendens"
C. Middle zone (40%)
   1. Chondrocytes are larger and spheroidal, tend to be randomly arranged, and appear more active than the cells in the superficial zone with well-developed ER and Golgi apparatus
   2. Collagen fibers become more vertically oriented as they approach the deep zone. This arrangement of the collagen fibers allows for loads to be transmitted to the subchondral bone
   3. Collagen bundles are larger in this zone, measuring 300–800 Å compared to the thin fibrils of the superficial zone. These bundles are associated with larger concentrations of PGs
   4. Structure of the collagen has been shown to change with load. The open network actually becomes obliterated with constant load lining up at right angles to the direction of the load applied
D. Deep zone (40%)
   1. Chondrocytes are arranged in palisades of 4–8 cells in a columnar fashion, perpendicular to the joint surface. The cells along with those of the middle zone appear to be the most active

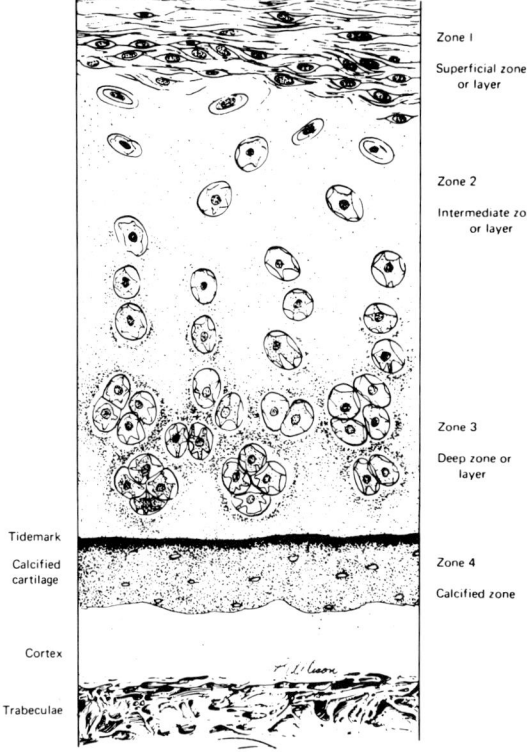

Figure 2-2. Distinct zones of the adult articular cartilage. (From Turek SL. Orthopaedics, Philadelphia, JB Lippincott, 1984, p 19. Reprinted with permission.)

  2. Collagen bundles are thick here as well, measuring as much as 1400 Å in diameter
  3. Concentration of PG is markedly increased over the more superficial regions
 E. Calcified zone (10%)
  1. Represents a transitional zone between bone and cartilage. Cartilage is infiltrated with calcium salts. Function is to anchor tissue securely to the subchondral bone and to protect it from shear forces
  2. Cells are very small, stain poorly, and appear to have no activity. This is a distinct zone, separate from the underlying subchondral bone
  3. Collagen bundles are discontinuous with those of the underlying bony end plate
 F. The tidemark is the region between the calcified and deep zones demarcated as a blue line on hematoxylin-eosin staining. This may represent an area of active remodeling
 G. Chrondrocyte
  1. Chondrocytes that are present at maturity persist throughout adult life
  2. They are responsible for the synthesis, degradation, and remodeling of matrix components throughout life
  3. Cells near the articular surface are less active than those in the deep and middle zones
  4. Most active cells are rich in rough ER, have characteristic multiple nucleoli, and a well-organized Golgi apparatus responsible for post-translational modification
  5. Chondrocyte is occupied within a lacunae, in which chondrocyte secretes products that diffuse out to matrix components

III. Surface Morphology
 A. Surface has distinct irregularities
 B. These are grouped into four types, depending on the size of the irregularity
  1. Primary: correspond to the general contour of the joint
  2. Secondary: 1 mm in size and correspond to asperities in the subchondral plate
  3. Tertiary: 20–40 μm in diameter. These may in fact represent artifact
  4. Quarternary: 1–2 μm in diameter. These are found in parallel rows in the same direction as the motion of the joint. These are reflective of collagen bundles

IV. Biochemistry of the Matrix
 A. Physiologic and mechanical properties of articular cartilage depend primarily on the physical properties of the matrix

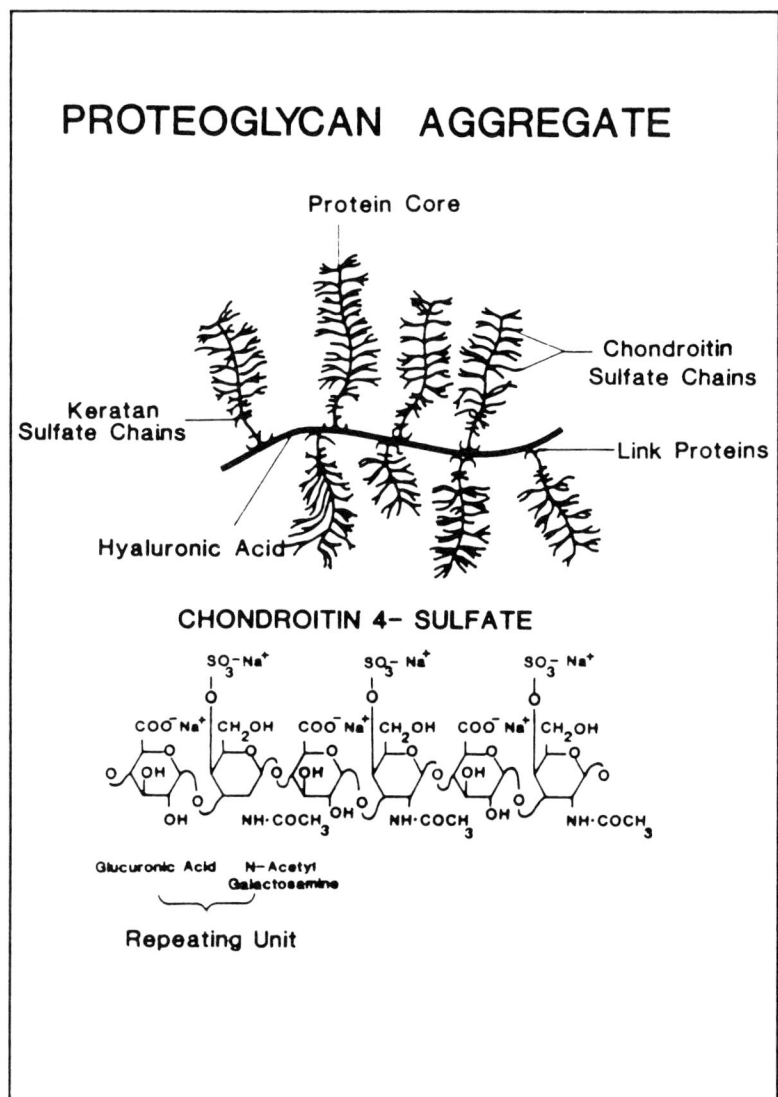

Figure 2-3. Diagram of proteoglycan aggregate, showing glycosaminoglycan side chains (keratin sulfate and chondroitin 6-sulfate) attached to a central protein core. (From Simon SR, Riggins RS, Wirth CR, Fox ML, eds. Orthopaedic science. American Academy of Orthopaedic Surgeons, 1986, p 21. Reprinted with permission.)

B. Proteoglycans: important in supporting collagen fibers (Fig 2-3)
  1. PG subunit consists of a glycosaminoglycan (GAG) side chain attached to a central core protein. Subunits usually contain a sulfated group giving them a strong negative charge
  2. Subunits in turn form large aggregates as the core protein attaches itself to hyaluronic acid. This bond is stabilized by a special link protein. In solution, only a small percentage exists as a free subunit
  3. GAG side chains include chondroitan 4-sulfate, chondroitan 6-sulfate, and keratin sulfate. PG attaches from its end rich in keratin sulfate
  4. These aggregates help to immobilize

PGs and to provide a more ordered structure within the extracellular matrix. Primary function of PG is to withstand compressive loads
   5. Concentration of keratin sulfate increases with age and in osteoarthritis
   6. In solution, aggregates tend to expand and resist compression because the polyanionic nature of GAGs is strongly electronegative, invoking resistance to compressive force and contributing materially to the resiliency of the tissue
C. Collagen
   1. Articular cartilage contains type II collagen fibrils. These are composed of a high concentration of hydroxylysine in the typical sequence of x-y-glycine
   2. Collagen acts as a discontinuous membrane resisting the flow of PG. Collagen is relatively inextensible, existing as taut structure because of swollen ground substance
   3. Primary mechanical function of collagen fibrils is to withstand tensile stresses. Surface layer of articular cartilage is the stiffest, with a high density of small diameter bundles. Deepest layer is the least stiff, being composed of widely spaced, haphazardly arranged fibrils
D. Cartilage water
   1. Comprises 70–80% of the weight of the tissue: decreases with aging and increases with prolonged immobilization, denervation, and osteoarthritis
   2. Vital to nutrition of cartilage cells, as well as in disposal of waste products
   3. Water plays an important role in the "weeping lubrication" in which water flows out during loading of tissue and back through the surface as the load is decreased, as well as to resiliency of the tissue
   4. Cartilage creep is a measure of progressive deformation of a material with time and is probably due to the expression of fluid from normal cartilage

V. Biomechanical Functions of Articular Cartilage

A. Two main functions of articular cartilage are mechanical load carriage and lubrication
B. Load carriage: PG and collagen are responsible for resistance of compressive and tensile stresses, respectively
C. Compressive stress by PG work by several mechanisms
   1. Electrostatic repulsion among the closely packed, negatively charged groups and the associated osmotic swelling pressure
   2. Intrinsic rigidity of PG aggregate
   3. Frictional resistance of fluid flow through molecular pores of intramolecular space
D. Compressive stiffness of solid matrix of cartilage is directly proportional to amount of PGs present in the tissue
E. When load is applied to articular cartilage, an instantaneous deformation develops and is followed by a time-dependent creep phase
F. When the load is removed, cartilage recovers original thickness as a result of an initial instantaneous (elastic) recovery followed by a time-dependent recovery phase (reimbibition of water)
G. Lubrication
   1. Fluid lubrication: when a film of fluid completely separates the opposing bearing surfaces, resistance to motion arises from the viscosity of the fluid
   2. Boundary lubrication: coated with a thin layer of molecules that slide on the opposing surface more readily than they are sheared off the underlying one. This acts best in low load situations
   3. Under a load, the cartilage surface undergoes deformation, creating a depression narrower at its periphery than at its center, trapping the fluid so that fluid lubrication occurs
   4. Compressed articular cartilage weeps

fluid through small pores. This is known as weeping lubrication, which is a form of hydrostatic lubrication. This mechanism works best under high loads

VI. Immature Cartilage and the Effect of Aging

A. Immature cartilage is a bluish white tissue, considerably thicker than mature cartilage. Increased thickness is due to dual functions as articular surface and microepiphyseal plate for endochondral ossification
B. Considerably more cellular than adult tissue
C. In lower zones the orientation changes drastically, and at about midway through the cartilage, the chondrocytes are arranged in irregular columns
D. Mitotic cells seen in the early stages of life in two distinct zones within the middle zone, one for growth of the articular cartilage, the other for endochondral ossification
F. Chemical changes with maturity
  1. PG content is highest at birth and diminishes with age. Concentration of chondroitin sulfate falls and keratin sulfate increases
  2. Water content of aging cartilage is decreased

VII. Response of Articular Cartilage to Mechanical Trauma

A. Response to superficial lacerative injury
  1. In injuries confined to cartilage (no violation of junction between calcified zone and underlying bony end plate), response clearly lacks an inflammatory component of the repair process
  2. Chondrocytes adjacent to the cut undergo necrosis and form ghost cells, followed by mitotic activity at the margins
  3. No evidence of chondromalacia or osteoarthritis 2 years later
B. Response to a deep penetrating injury
  1. Laceration violates the vascular, underlying bony end plate, and the response is more characteristic of vascularized tissues
  2. Organized clot is followed by undifferentiated cells turning into fibroblasts and vascular ingrowth forming granulation tissue. Fibrous tissue will subsequently fill the cartilage gap, which then undergoes progressive hyalinization and subsequently becomes chondrified to produce a fibrocartilaginous mass
  3. Early repair tissue is similar to normal hyaline cartilage tissue. However, by 12 months, PG concentration decreases and tissue appears more fibrous. Surface becomes fibrillated
  4. Continuous motion may have an effect on improving the cartilage

ARTHRITIS AND SYNOVIAL DISEASES

I. Osteoarthritis

A. Etiology unknown: aging, trauma, loss of joint sensation, immobilization, immune or cartilageous problems
B. Secondary osteoarthritis: traumatic, avascular necrosis, inflammatory, infectious, metabolic (ochronosis, gout) and hemorrhagic (hemophilia)
C. Pathogenesis unknown
  1. Chondrocytes more active and immature forms initially, but become inactive and less matrix synthesis later
  2. Matrix
    a. Collagenous disruption with increased amount of collagenase
    b. Proteoglycan: synthesis is increased initially with higher chondroitin sulfate to keratin sulfate ratio and increased amount of hyaluronic acid but decreased synthesis later with less PG-hyaluronic acid aggregate

3. Water content: increased possibly secondary to increased extensibility of collagen network
D. Pathology
   1. Compressibility of matrix is lost and minute fractures of the matrix with fibrillation and fissuring (chondromalacia)
   2. Subchondral marrow reparative process with granulation and fibrous connective tissue and subchondral trabecular bone hypertrophy
   3. Small bodies of cartilage free in the joint and capsule and immunologic and inflammatory processes (infiltration of lymphocytes, plasmacytes, synovitis, and increased production of synovial fluid with higher viscosity-decreased effective lubrication)
   4. Osteophytes: to broaden weight-bearing surface and attempt repair (begins as granulation tissue forms where capsule attaches to peripheral articular cartilage and matures to fibrocartilage first, which undergoes endochondral ossification to become bone spurs)
   5. Subchondral cysts: minute fractures of subchondral trabeculae with necrosis and resorption
E. Radiologic findings
   1. Joint space narrowing (cartilage)
   2. Subchondral bone hypertrophy
   3. Osteophyte formation
   4. Subchondral cyst formation
F. Treatment
   1. Conservative: nonsteroidal anti-inflammatory drugs (NSAIDs), activity modification, physical therapy range of motion and muscle strengthening
   2. Surgery: arthroscopy, osteotomies, arthroplasty, or arthrodesis when appropriate

II. Rheumatoid Arthritis

A. Pathogenesis
   1. Unknown antigens (Epstein-Barr virus, bacteria cell wall products, collagen II, mycoplasma, etc.)
   2. Genetically susceptible individuals (HLA-DR4 type)
   3. Antibody formation and cellular interaction (monocyte, B and T lymphocytes) and immune complex formation (rheumatoid factor, IgM)
   4. Phagocytosis of immune complexes (synovial cells type A and PMNs) and complement activation along with coagulation, kinin, and fibrinolytic system
   5. Chemotaxis of inflammatory cells and synovitis by monokines and production of proteolytic enzymes and prostaglandins
   6. Cartilage destruction (collagenase, proteolytic enzymes from PMNs, synovial cells, and chondrocytes)
   7. Periarticular osteoporosis: disuse and prostaglandins
   8. Subluxation, dislocation, deformity, and ankylosis
B. Pathology
   1. Synovium: synovitis with villi, infiltrated with lymphocytes and plasmacyte and surrounding edema and fibrin
   2. Pannus: proliferation of mesenchymal cells and vascular granulation, invading the cartilage from the periphery
   3. Rheumatoid nodules: fibrinous necrosis in the center with surrounding layer of palisading epithelial cells
C. Clinical findings
   1. Most common during 30–40 years of age and 3:1 female to male ratio
   2. Insiduous onset, symmetrical polyarthritis, constitutional symptoms, and variable clinical course
   3. X-ray: soft tissue swelling, juxta-articular ostoporosis, and bone erosion
   4. Laboratory: rheumatoid factor (75%), rheumatoid arthritis nuclear antigen (50%), rheumatoid arthritis precipitin (67% in seropositive patients)
D. Treatment: aspirin or NSAIDs, rest, gold, chloroquine, D-penicillamine, steroids

III. Seronegative Arthritis

A. Ankylosing spondylitis
   1. General considerations
      a. Age: between 15 and 24 years
      b. Sex: males to females ratio 9:1
   2. Pathogenesis
      a. Inflammatory arthritis of the spine that also involves sacroiliac joints and peripheral joints
      b. Cartilage destruction and bony erosion
   3. Clinical findings
      a. Incidious onset: 1–3 years of symptoms before diagnosis
      b. Symptoms: low-back pain and stiffness, which is worse in the morning and better with activity
      c. Peripheral joint arthritis in 15–25%
      d. Physical findings:
         (1) Limitation of lumbar motion (Shober test)
         (2) Decreased chest expansion
         (3) Positive sacroiliac stress maneuver (Patrick)
      e. X-rays
         (1) Sacroiliitis: erosion, reactive bone and fusion of the joint (on the lower portion of iliac side first)
         (2) Spine: paravertebral ossification and syndesmophytosis from the margins of the vertebral bodies ("bamboo spine") and erosion of the vertebrae ("squaring of the vertebral body"), osteoporosis, disc and apophyseal joint narrowing
      f. Laboratory findings: increased erythrocyte sedimentation (ESR) rate, negative rheumatoid factor, HLA-B27 positive (96%)
   4. Treatment
      a. Breathing exercise and isometric exercise of the muscles, range of motion and posture exercise of the spine, swimming
      b. Nonsteroidal anti-inflammatory medications or aspirin
      c. Surgery: spinal osteotomy, peripheral joint reconstructions

B. Reiter's syndrome
   1. General consideration
      a. Sex: males
      b. Age: 20–40 years
      c. Questionable relationship to infectious agents (chlamydiae, mycoplasma, etc.) and sexual contact
   2. Clinical findings
      a. Triad: urethritis, conjunctivitis, and polyarthritis (large weight-bearing joints in asymmetrical pattern)
      b. Skin lesions: balanitis circinata, ulcers in the oral mucosa, and keratoderma blennorrhagicum
      c. Laboratory findings: increased ESR, HLA-B27 positive in 70%, and sterile pyuria
      d. X-rays: periosteitis in the heel and toes, sacroiliitis, and occasionally unilateral syndesmophytes in the spine
      e. Self-limited disease from 6 weeks to 6 months, but recurrence is common (50%)
   3. Treatment: physical therapy and medications (aspirin or nonsteroidal anti-inflammatory drugs [NSAIDs])

C. Psoriatic arthritis
   1. General considerations
      a. Affects about 5–7% of psoriatic patients
      b. Five types
         (1) Asymmetrical peripheral polyarthritis, especially distal interphalangeal joints
         (2) Arthritis mutilans: osteolysis of fingers and toes
         (3) Symmetrical polyarthritis: resembles rheumatoid arthritis but rheumatoid factor negative
         (4) Oligoarticular disease: hand and feet with swelling ("sausage digits") — most common type
         (5) Psoriatic spondyloarthritis: spine involvement

2. Clinical findings
      a. Variable, but fingers and toes are most commonly involved. Back pain and other joint pain and stiffness may occur
      b. Laboratory: increased ESR and positive HLA-B27 (40% in spondylitic group)
      c. X-ray: erosions, ankylosis of distal interphalangeal joints of hands and feet, unilateral sacroiliitis and syndesmophytes in the spine (unilateral and start from midvertebral body rather than margins as in ankylosing spondylitis)
   3. Treatment
      a. Physical therapy
      b. Medications: NSAIDs, gold, cautious use of antimalarial and immunosuppressive agents
D. Enteropathic arthritis
   1. General considerations
      a. Peripheral arthritis in 20% of regional enteritis and 12% of ulcerative colitis and spondylitis in 6% of both groups
      b. Slightly more common in males in axial disease
      c. Whipple disease: nonspecific peripheral arthritis and sacroiliac involvement
   2. Clinical findings
      a. Oligoarticular pattern and knees and ankles are common and back pain (spondylitis is indistinguishable from ankylosing spondylitis and spondylitis may precede primary disease in 25%)
      b. Laboratory: increased ESR and HLA-B27 is positive in 70% of spondylitic patients
      c. X-ray: inflammatory arthritic pattern of involved joints and sacroiliitis and spondylitis indistinguishable from ankylosing spondylitis
   3. Treatment: of underlying disease and NSAIDs

IV. Crystal-Induced Arthritis

A. Gout
   1. General considerations
      a. Age: most common during 5th decade
      b. Sex: more common in males (90%)
      c. Types
         (1) Underexcretion of uric acid: idiopathic, lead intoxication, drugs such as diuretics, alcohol, and nicotinic acid, renal disease, and organic aciduria, such as lactic acid and ketoacidosis
         (2) Overproduction of uric acid (>900 mg/24 hr urine): idiopathic, lymphoproliferative or myeloproliferative diseases and enzyme defects
      d. Hereditary predisposition
   2. Pathology: deposition of urate crystal, articular cartilage erosion (depolymerization of PG), subchondral cyst and pannus formation
   3. Clinical findings
      a. Painful acute monoarthritis, most commonly in the first metatarsophalangeal joint but may occur in any joint
      b. Fever and leukocytosis
      c. Hyperurecemia (>8mg/dL), erythema, and tenderness of the joint, previous similar attacks and good response to colchicine
      d. Tophi: helix of the ears, olecranon bursae and distal joints
      e. Diagnosis: aspiration of joint fluid (leukocytosis in the range of 10,000–25,000/mm^3 and slender needle-shaped negative birefringence urate crystals)
   4. Treatment
      a. Indomethacin or intravenous colchicine for acute gout attacks
      b. Avoid allopurinol during acute gout
      c. Prophylaxis: oral colchicine for 3–6 months and either uricosuric drugs (probenecid or sulfinpyrazone for

gout with urate underexcretion and normal renal function) or allopurinol (xanthine oxidase inhibitor for gout with urate overproduction, urate lithiasis, and renal problems)
- B. Chondrocalcinosis and pseudogout
  1. General considerations
     a. Age: more prevalent in older patients
     b. Associated diseases: osteoarthritis, hyperparathyroidism, hemochromatosis, neuropathic arthropathy, hypothyroidism, and hypophosphatasia
  2. Pathogenesis
     a. Crystal deposition in the tissues: most commonly calcium pyrophosphate dihydrate (CPPD) in fibrocartilage, hyaline cartilage, synovium, tendon, and ligament
     b. Phagocytosis of crystals by leukocytes and inflammatory response
  3. Clinical findings
     a. Acute monoarthritis, especially the knee, and frequently precipitated by medical or surgical illness
     b. Inflammatory synovitis and effusion
     c. Laboratory: increased ESR, aspiration (leukocytosis in the range of 3000–50,000/mm^3, and weak positive rhomboid-shaped CPPD crystals)
     d. X-ray: chondrocalcinosis in the knee menisci, symphysis pubis, and triangular fibrocartilage of the wrist
  4. Treatment: indomethacin or other NSAIDs

V. Other Miscellaneous Rheumatic Conditions

- A. Systemic lupus erythematosus
  1. General considerations
     a. Age: 2nd to 4th decades
     b. Sex: female to male ratio 9:1
     c. HLA-DR2 and HLA-DR3 association and familial incidence
  2. Pathogenesis: multisystem disease with a spectrum of clinical manifestations and abnormalities of humoral and cellular immune system
  3. Clinical findings
     a. Fever, skin lesions (discoid lesions, alopecia, and mucous membrane lesions), arthritis, synovitis, myositis, cardiac problems (pericarditis, myocardial and endocardial lesions), pleuritis, and kidney involvement
     b. Laboratory findings: positive antinuclear antibody (ANA; anti-DNA and diffuse and peripheral immunofluorescence pattern), lupus erythematosus (LE)-cells, low serum complement, anemia, lymphopenia, thrombocytopenia, and increased ESR
  4. Treatment: NSAIDs, corticosteroids, and cytotoxic medications when appropriate
- B. Scleroderma (progressive systemic sclerosis)
  1. General considerations
     a. Sex: female to male ratio 4:1
     b. Pathogenesis: excessive fibrosis and vascular changes in multiple organs, but exact underlying immune abnormalities are unclear
  2. Clinical findings
     a. Skin involvement: taut, hidebound skin with thinning of the epidermis, especially on the extensor surface of the hand
     b. Vascular involvement: Raynaud's phenomenon and digit vascular changes like telangiectasia
     c. Gastrointestinal, renal, and cardiopulmonary involvement
     d. Calcinosis cutis, Raynaud's phenomenon, esophageal dysfunction, sclerodactyly, and telangiectasia: CREST syndrome
     e. Laboratory: speckled or nucleolar ANA pattern
  3. Treatment: vasodilators for vascular problems and other medical treatment as indicated

C. Mixed connective tissue disease (MCTD)
1. Clinical and serologic overlap of numerous rheumatic diseases
2. Clinical findings: polyarthralgia, Raynaud's phenomenon, sclerodactyly, esophageal disease, myositis, renal disease, positive ANA (speckled and nuclear ribonucleoprotein [nRNP]), and hyperglobulinemia
3. Treatment: medical

D. Sicca syndrome
1. General considerations
   a. Sex: 90% women
   b. Age: over 40 years
   c. Associated with other diseases, such as rheumatoid arthritis, scleroderma, and systemic lupus erythematosus
   d. Pathogenesis: chronic inflammatory disease associated with lymphocytic infiltration of exocrine glands
2. Clinical findings
   a. Xerostomia (parotid gland enlargement) and keratoconjunctivitis sicca
   b. Laboratory: positive ANA (speckled or nucleolar pattern) and SS-A (Ro) and SS-B (Ha, La) positive rheumatoid factor (90%)
3. Treatment: medical

VI. Synovial Diseases and Miscellaneous Joint Disorders

A. Pigmented villonodular synovitis
1. General considerations
   a. Age: young adult
   b. Sex: more common in males
   c. Pathology: monoarticular synovial proliferation most often in the knee
2. Clinical findings
   a. Painless bloody effusion
   b. Normal articular cartilage
   c. X-ray: joint swelling and lytic subchondral lucency if subchondral bone is invaded
3. Biopsy: reddish-brown, thickened nodular appearance and villous synovium with capillaries, giant cells, and hemosiderin on histologic examination
4. Treatment: complete synovectomy (extracapsular margin)

B. Synovial chondromatosis
1. General considerations
   a. Age: young adults to middle age
   b. Sex: more common in males
   c. Metaplastic cartilage formation in joint and cartilage may undergo endochondral ossification
2. Clinical findings:
   a. Internal derangement and pain
   b. X-ray: speckled calcification within the lobulated masses within the joint
   c. Differential diagnosis
      (1) Tumoral calcinosis: associated with scleroderma, dermatomyositis, etc., and calcified mass occurs along fascial plane and periarticular regions (intracapsular or marginal removal is adequate)
      (2) Chondrosarcoma: clinical and radiographic staging is more important than histologic findings
      (3) Heterotopic ossification
3. Biopsy: active hyaline cartilage resembling low-grade chondrosarcoma
4. Treatment: synovectomy and removal of loose bodies

C. Ochronosis
1. Inborn error of pyridine metabolism in which excess homogentisic acid accumulates
2. Hyperpolymerization of PG of the articular cartilage, where grayish black pigmentation of the cartilage occurs and makes it more brittle
3. Alkaptonuria: dark urine
4. Arthropathy and spondylosis (intervertebral calcification and osteophytes)

REFERENCES

Beary JF, Christian CL, Sculco TP: Manual of rheumatology and outpatient orthopaedic disorders. Boston, Little, Brown

Cooke TDV, Scudamore RA: Rheumatoid arthritis and allied conditions. In Cruess RL, Rennie WRJ, eds: Adult orthopedics. New York, Churchill Livingstone

Kelley WN, Harris ED, Ruddy S, Sledge CB: Textbook of rheumatology. Philadelphia, WB Saunders, 1981

Mankin HJ: The articular cartilage, cartilage healing, and osteoarthritis. In Cruess RL, Rennie WRJ, eds. Adult orthopaedics. New York, Churchill Livingstone

Moskowitz RW, Howell DS, Goldberg VM, Mankin HJK: Osteoarthritis: Diagnosis and management. Philadelphia, WB Saunders, 1984

18
Muscle, Nerve, Tendon, Ligament, and Collagen

I. Skeletal Muscle
A. Structure
1. Fascicles: group of parallel muscle fibers. Group of fascicles make up muscle
2. A muscle fiber is made up of myofibrils (Fig 2-4)
   a. Myofibril is 1–2 μm in diameter
   b. Sarcomere is a structural unit within myofibrils
   c. Many mitochondria and sarcoplasmic reticulum around myofibrils
   d. T-tubule (transverse tubule) is an extension of sarcolemma (cell membrane), located at the "A"–"I" junction between pair of terminal cisternae
   e. Terminal cisternae are an extension of transversely oriented saccular portion of sarcoplasmic reticulum
   f. The pair of terminal cisternae and T-tubule make up the triad, which is the location of calcium exchange to activate actin-myosin contraction (adenosine triphosphatase [ATPase] split ATP on heavy meromyosin and release energy for actin-myosin contraction mechanism)
3. A myofibril is made up of myofilaments such as actin and myosin (Fig 2-5)
   a. A band consists of myosin and does not change its length during contraction
   b. I band consists of unoverlapped portion of actin, which shortens during contraction
   c. H zone consists of the middle portion of unoverlapped myosin, which shortens during contraction
   d. Z line is at the half of I band on each side: a sarcomere is from one Z line to another
   e. Actin is a thin filament, consisting of globular actin, tropomyosin, and troponin
      (1) Hexagonally arranged around each myosin filament
      (2) Responsible as calcium receptor protein
   f. Myosin is a thick filament, consisting of heavy and light meromyosin:

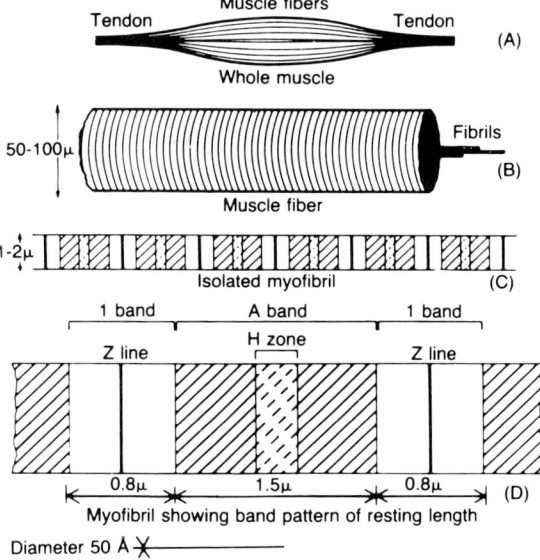

Figure 2-4. Dimensions and arrangement of the contractile components in a muscle. The whole muscle (A) is made of fibers (B) that contain cross-striated myofibrils (C, D). These are constructed of two kinds of protein filaments (E). (From Huxley HE: The molecular basis of contraction. In Bourne GH, ed. The structure and function of muscle. New York, Academic Press, 1972. Reprinted with permission.)

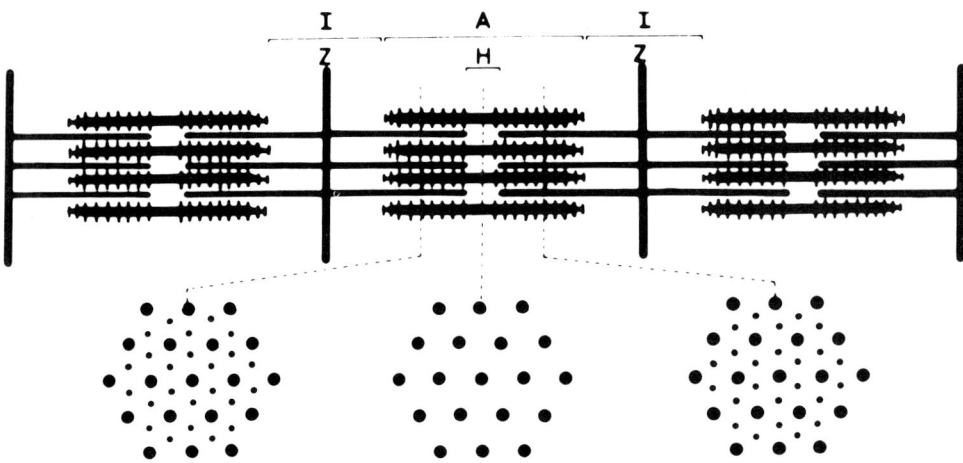

Figure 2-5. Structure of striated muscle, showing the relationship between actin and myosin filaments. (From Huxley HE: The molecular basis of contraction. In Bourne GH, ed. The structure and function of muscle. New York, Academic Press, 1972. Reprinted with permission.)

heavy meromyosin has globular projections at ends to form cross-bridges during contraction
B. Muscle physiology
  1. Muscle fiber types
    a. Type I: slow contraction, no fatigue, oxidative metabolism, low glycogen content, many mitochondria, low myofibril ATPase, and high lipids and myoglobulins
    b. Type IIA: fast contraction, no fatigue, both oxidative and anaerobic metabolism, high glycogen content, many mitochondria, high myofibril ATPase, and high lipids and myoglobulins
    c. Type IIB: fast contraction, fatigue, anaerobic metabolism, high glycogen content, little mitochondria, high myofibril ATPase, and low lipids and myoglobulins
  2. Exercise
    a. During exercise, respiration and cardiac output (stroke volume and heart rate) increase
    b. Immediate source for energy during fast-twitch muscle exercise is ATP phosphagen and anaerobic metabolites (lactic acid), but slow twitch endurance exercise utilize aerobic metabolism
    c. During exercise, glycogen in the muscle is utilized first, followed by triglycerides in the muscle, blood glucose, and blood-free fatty acids
    d. Conditioning exercise (training) increases the maximum rate of oxygen consumption, induces a higher rate of lipid utilization, a decreased rate of carbohydrated utilization, slower lactate increase, and an increased utilization of fatty acid oxidation
    e. Muscle hypertrophy is due to increase in the number of myofibrils, whereas the number of muscle fibers does not change. More rapid increase in muscle bulk occurs with isometric than isotonic exercise
    f. Muscle atrophy may be due to immobilization or denervation, and type II fibers are particularly prone to denervation after immobilization
C. Muscle diseases
  1. Motor neuron diseases: poliomyelitis, spinal muscular atrophy, and amyotrophic lateral sclerosis

    a. Small group atrophy initially due to single motor neuron death
    b. Large group atrophy later as many fibers or even whole fascicles degenerate
  2. Peripheral neuropathies
    a. Many conditions affect the peripheral nerves, such as entrapment syndromes and metal poisoning
    b. Myelin sheath involvement results in decrease of nerve conduction velocity
    c. Axonal involvement results in decrease in amplitude of electrical potential during electromyography
    d. Recovering neuropathy may give predominant type grouping on muscle biopsy
  3. Disorders of neuromuscular junction: myasthenia gravis, Eaton-Lambert syndrome, botulism, and tick paralysis
  4. Myopathic disorders: muscular dystrophies, congenital myopathies (central core disease, nemaline myopathy, myotubular myopathy, congenital fiber type disproportion, and centronuclear myopathy), inflammatory myopathy, endocrine myopathy, toxic or drug-induced myopathy, and disuse atrophy
    a. Abnormal muscle enzymes, central nuclei, rounded muscle fibers of varying size
    b. Fiber splitting may occur
    c. Polyphasic and low voltage potentials during electromyography
    d. Prevalence of type I fibers

II. Nerve

A. Structure
  1. Neuron: large surface areas with cytoplasmic extensions and contains nucleus and Nissl bodies: When the nerve fiber is injured, the neuronal nucleus moves to the cell periphery and Nissl bodies are reduced in number
  2. Axons
    a. Contains microtubules for axoplasmic transport, particularly important in developing axons, and neurofilaments that are responsible for maintenance of axonal configuration
    b. Myelinated nerve fiber
      (1) Myelin is produced by Schwann cell or neurilemma cell, which surrounds the axon
      (2) Length of an axon wrapped by a single neurilemma cell is an internodal segment
      (3) Node of Ranvier is the place where two successive neurilemma cells meet
    c. Unmyelinated nerve fiber: smaller axon that is embedded around the periphery of Schwann cells
    d. Types
      (1) Type Ia: proprioception, muscle spindle and alpha and gamma motor to muscle
      (2) Type Ib: afferent fibers from Golgi apparatus
      (3) Type II: touch, pressure, and motor fibers to muscle spindle
      (4) Type III: pain and temperature sensation and sympathetic preganglionic fibers
      (5) Type IV: cutaneous pain and sympathetic postganglionic fibers (these are only unmyelinated fibers)
  3. Organization of peripheral nerves
    a. Endoneurium: very fine connective tissue around each myelinated axon or group of unmyelinated axons
    b. Perineurium: connective tissue around each fascicle of nerve fibers
    c. Epineurium: areolar connective tissue around the entire nerve, which commonly includes several fascicles (contains vasa nervorum and lymphatics)
B. Nerve injuries
  1. Neuropraxia: transient paralysis in which localized conduction block without distal axonal degeneration

a. Demyelination with decrease in conduction velocity
   b. Traction or mild compression injuries
  2. Axonotemesis: segregation of axon and wallerian degeneration (crush injuries)
  3. Neurotemesis: disruption of axon and connective tissue (lacerations)

III. Collagen
A. Biosynthesis
  1. Protein is synthesized within the rough ER; the Golgi is responsible for the addition of any sugar moiety and the condensation of these products. The vesicles that bud from the Golgi then fuse with the plasma membrane, releasing the products into the matrix. The collagen is released as procollagen, which polymerizes to tropocollagen once procollagen peptidase removes an inhibitory segment
  2. Tropocollagen is the basic unit of collagen (Fig 2-6). It is composed of three alpha chains, each about 1000 amino acids long. This molecule has an inherent structure that allows it to form fibrils. Interfibrillar cross-linking provides structural stability
  3. Collagen is degraded by collagenase, which is activated in disease states, such as in rheumatoid synovial fluid
B. Types of collagen
  1. Type I: skin, bone tendon
  2. Type II: cartilage
  3. Type III: Blood vessels, skin, spleen
  4. Type IV: Basement membrane
  5. Type V: Placenta, smooth muscle
C. Collagen disorders
  1. Osteogenesis imperfecta
  2. Ehlers-Danlos syndrome
  3. Marfan syndrome

IV. Tendons and Ligaments
A. Tendon
  1. Dense, regularly arranged connective tissue composed of fibroblasts, collagen, and proteoglycan
  2. The major constituent is type I collagen
  3. Great resistance to tensile forces
  4. Fascicles within the tendon are bound together by loose connective tissue or endotenon, which permit movement of the collagen bundles and presence of blood vessels, lymphatics, and nerves
  5. Tendon coverings
    a. Paratenon: loose areolar connective tissue that is not enclosed within a sheath
    b. Tendon sheath: flexor tendon sheath to prevent bowstring and to provide a gliding mechanism
  6. Tendon repair
    a. Inflammation initially
    b. Granulation tissue between the cut tendon ends by paratenon tissue
    c. Tendon callus formation as fibroblasts with collagen fibers unite the gap at 3 weeks
    d. Collagen fibers orient parallel to the long axis of the tendon as stress is placed on the healing tendon
    e. Continuation of remodeling and increasing tensile strength to near normal at 3 months
    f. Tendons enclosed by a sheath are repaired both intrinsically and extrinsically
      (1) Tenoblasts are capable of generating collagen
      (2) Tendon sheaths aid in the formation of granulation tissue and collagen formation
      (3) Synovial fluid diffusion is also important as part of nutrition
      (4) Early mobilization is important in preventing adhesions and increasing tensile strength
B. Ligament
  1. Immobilization decreases the strength, particularly at the bone-ligament junction

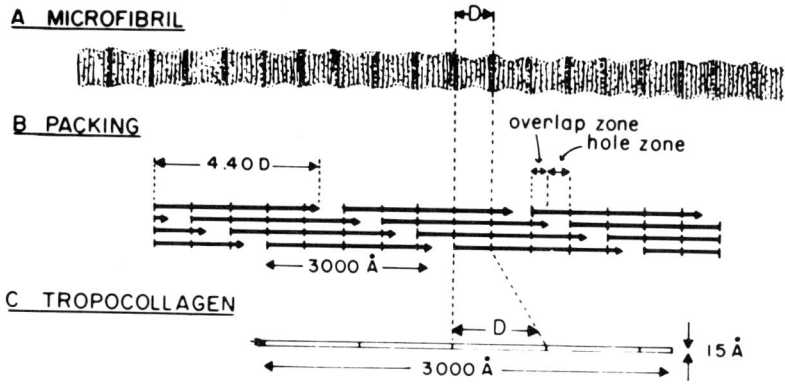

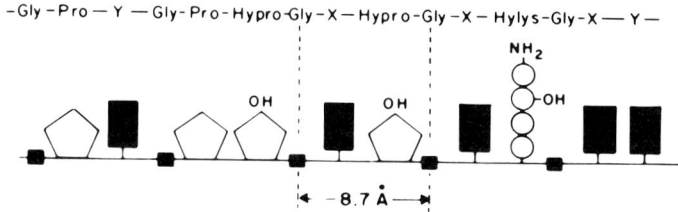

Figure 2-6. Microstructure of collagen. **A.** Microfibril of collagen showing cross-striation with a regular repeat period. **B.** Packing arrangement of tropocollagen. **C.** Each tropocollagen has large numbers of darkly staining bands, and five of these are separated by a regular distance of 680A. **D.** Each tropocollagen consists of three polypeptides. **E.** Typical sequence in polypeptide chains. (From Grant ME, Prockop DJ: The biosynthesis of collagen. N Engl J Med 286:194, 242, 291, 1972. Reprinted with permission.)

2. Sensory function: mechanoreceptors are present for proprioception function
3. Ligament healing
   a. Ligament healing is better if exposed to stress and strain (controlled mobilization)
   b. Stages: clot formation, inflammation, collagen synthesis and degradation, and contraction (actin)

REFERENCES

Cooper RR: Skeletal muscle and muscle disorders. In Cruess RL, Rennie WRJ, eds. Adult orthopaedics. New York, Churchill Livingstone, 1984

Gelberman RH, Vande Berg JS, Lundborg GN, et al: Flexor tendon healing and restoration of the gliding surface: An ultrastructural study in dogs. J Bone Joint Surg 65A:70–80, 1983

Jokle P, Konstadt S: The effects of limb immobilization on muscle function and protein composition. Clin Orthop 174:222–229, 1983

Manske PR, Gelberman RH, Vande Berg JS, et al: Intrinsic flexor-tendon repair: A morphological study in vitro. J Bone Joint Surg 66A:385–396, 1984

Orgel MG: Experimental studies with clinical application to peripheral nerve injury: A review of the past decade. Clin Orthop 163:98–106, 1982

Woo SL-Y, Buckwalter JA, eds: Injury and repair of the musculoskeletal soft tissues. Park Ridge, IL, American Academy of Orthopaedic Surgeons, 1988

19
Orthopaedic Infections

ANTIMICROBIAL DRUGS

I. Actions of Antibiotics
A. Inhibit cell wall synthesis: beta-lactam antibiotics such as penicillins and cephalosporins
B. Inhibit cell membrane function: polymyxin, amphotericin B, and nystatin
C. Inhibit protein synthesis: aminoglycosides, clindamycin, chloroamphenicol, tetracycline, and erythromycin
D. Inhibit nucleic acid synthesis: vancomycin and sulfonamides

II. Side Effects of Antibiotics
A. Penicillins and cephalosporins
   1. Hypersensitivity or allergy (5–20% cross hypersensitivity between penicillin and cephalosporin)
   2. Hematologic: dose-dependent granulocytopenia and platelet dysfunction (carbenicillin, ticarcillin, pipercillin, methicillin, ampicillin)
   3. Gastrointestinal: pseudomembranous colitis
   4. Interstitial nephritis (methicillin)
B. Aminoglycosides: nephrotoxicity and ototoxicity
C. Clindamycin: diarrhea and pseudomembranous colitis (treatment with oral vancomycin)
D. Chloroamphenicol: bone marrow suppression and gray baby syndrome
E. Vancomycin: renal and ototoxicity. Skin rash, fever, pruritus, and hypotension may develop if given rapidly intravenously
F. Tetracyclin: staining and deformity of teeth in the fetus

III. Choice of Antibiotics
A. Prophylaxis
   1. Cefazolin is the best agent in orthopaedics, because it covers *Staphylococcus aureus,* which is the most common organism in postoperative infections, and also gram-negative organisms and gives a high serum value and longer half-life
   2. Postoperative infection is decreased fourfold if prophylactic antibiotic is used
   3. *Staphylococcus epidermidis* and anaerobes are common organisms when perioperative antibiotic is given
B. Antibiotic selection (Table 2-2)
   1. Choice depends on what organism is most likely in a given circumstance while culture is pending
   2. Definitive selection depends on culture and sensitivity
      a. Nafcillin, oxacillin, or first-generation cephalosporin for *S. aureus*
      b. Penicillin G or ampicillin for streptococci and gonococci
      c. Ampicillin or chloramphenicol or cephamandole or third-generation cephalosporin for *Haemophilus*
      d. Aminoglycosides for gram-negative bacilli
      e. Aminoglycosides, ticarcillin (or mezlocillin, piperacillin) or ciprofloxacin for *Pseudomonas*
      f. Vancomycin for methicillin-resistant *S. aureus* or other gram-positive organisms in patients with penicillin allergy
      g. Clindamycin for anaerobes
      h. Primaxin for broad coverage in unknown cases in adults

Table 2-2 General Recommendations of Antibiotic Use

Bacteria	Antibiotics
Gram-positive organisms	Penicillins (nafcillin, oxacillin, dicloxacillin) Cephalosporins (first generation is better than second or third generations) **First generation**: Cefazolin, Cephalothin, Cephradine, Cephalexin, Cefaclor, Cefadroxil **Second generation**: Cefamandole, Cefoxitin, Cefuroxime, Cefotiam, Cefmetazole **Third generation**: Cefotaxime, Ceftizoxime, Ceftriaxone, Ceftazidime, Cefoperazone, Moxalactam, Cefsulodin Clindamycin Vancomycin (methicillin-resistant staphylococci or penicillin allergy)
Gram-negative organisms	Aminoglycosides (gentamicin, tobramycin, amikacin) Cephalosporins (third generation better than second and first generations) Expanded spectrum penicillins (ticarcillin, mezlocillin, piperacillin) Primaxin Quinolones (ciprofloxacin)
Mixed organisms	Nafcillin or cephalosporin and aminoglycoside Add clindamycin if anaerobes Primaxin

ACUTE HEMATAGENOUS OSTEOMYELITIS

I. Pathogenesis

A. Different organism, depending on age and circumstance
   1. Premature infants and neonatal: gram-negative organisms (*Escherichia coli*), beta-hemolytic *Streptococcus* group B and *S. aureus*
   2. Infancy and young children: *Haemophilus influenzae*, *S. aureus* and group A streptococci
   3. Older children and adolescents: *S. aureus*, streptococci, and *Neisseria gonorrhoeae*
   4. Uncommon in adults
B. Onset may be acute, subacute, or chronic (stages)
   1. Vascular: metaphyseal sinusoid localization due to sledging of blood flow (trauma may also play a role)
   2. Abscess formation: thrombosis of veins and arteries to disrupt endosteal blood supply followed by pus subperiosteally to disrupt periosteal blood supply
   3. Intra-articular extension may occur in the neonates, in which epiphyseal ossification is not completed as a natural barrier, but the hip, shoulder, and the ankle regions are at greater risk because the metaphysis is intra-articular
   4. Sequestrum and involucrum formation if persistent infection
C. Route may be hematogenous, local extension, or direct inoculation: direct inoculation frequently causes *Pseudomonas* infection, and most of the *H. influenzae* osteomyelitis are secondary from septic arthritis
D. Granulomatous infection: tuberculosis, fungus, and syphilis are rare
E. *Salmonella* infection is found in increased frequency in sickle cell anemic patients, and *Brucella* in farming community

II. Clinical Findings

A. Sudden onset with fever and localized pain and tenderness
B. Elevated white blood cell count (WBC), ESR, and blood culture (50% positive)
C. X-ray: soft tissue swelling, obliteration of translucent areolar tissue plane between muscle layers early, periosteal new bone in 10–14 days, and positive bone scan early (15% false negative)
D. Aspiration: 16 or 18 gauge spinal needle for subperiosteal aspiration and Gram's stain and culture

III. Treatment

A. Control sepsis (intravenous fluid)
B. Antibiotic treatment depends on likely organism and results of culture
   1. Neonates: aminoglycosides and nafcillin or cefazolin for staphylococci and gram-negative organisms
   2. Young children: ampicillin or chloroamphenicol to cover *Haemophilus* and cefazolin for staphylococci
   3. Sexually active adolescents: penicillin for gonococci
   4. Sickle cell patients: ampicillin and aminoglycosides to cover *Salmonella* and staphylococci
C. Antibiotics should be administered intravenously for 4–6 weeks
D. Immobilization with splints to prevent fractures
E. Surgical drainage if x-ray changes are seen or symptoms for many days or failure of medical management for 48 hours
F. Sequestrectomy and bone graft for chronic osteomyelitis

SEPTIC ARTHRITIS

I. Pathogenesis

A. Most common during 1–2 years old and 2–3 times more common in males
B. The hip is most common site involved, followed by the knee and elbow
C. Different organism, depending on the age and circumstance (similar to osteomyelitis)
D. Route may be hematogenous (especially neonate), direct extension from osteomyelitis (especially hip, shoulder, and ankle) and direct inoculation
E. Stages
   1. Synovitis: hyperemia and edema of synovial membrane and excess synovial fluid production with decreased hyaluronic acid content
   2. Pus formation
   3. Cartilage breakdown
      a. Proteolytic enzymes from inflammatory cells, synovial cells, and chondrocytes
      b. Bacterial enzymes (staphylokinase and streptokinase activate protease and plasminogen)
      c. Mechanical breakdown
      d. Bacterial cell wall products may cause antibody formation and immunologic reaction to destroy the cartilage
F. Complications
   1. Subluxation and dislocation
   2. Osteomyelitis
   3. Contracture or ankylosis
   4. Avascular necrosis
   5. Degenerative arthritis
   6. Deformities and limb length discrepancy

II. Clinical Findings

A. Frequent antecedent: infection and fever
B. Pain, tenderness, and swelling
C. Elevated WBC with left shift (not reliable)
D. ESR is usually elevated and higher than in osteomyelitis (>60 mm/hr), and C-reactive protein is elevated
E. Blood culture positive (50%)
F. Counterimmunophoresis (CIE) assay for certain organisms, such as *Haemophilus*
G. X-rays: soft tissue swelling, subluxation, widening of joint (initially) and narrowing

of joint (later), and osteomyelitic focus if present
H. Technetium bone scan (if osteomyelitis is suspected) or gallium scan (specific for inflammatory or infected focus) can be utilized

III. Aspiration

A. Anterior approach: 18 gauge spinal needle is inserted 1 cm lateral to the femoral artery and 1 cm distal to the inguinal ligament (often requires general anesthesia and fluoroscopy)
B. Fluid
  1. Decreased viscosity and poor mucin clot
  2. Gram's stain and culture
  3. WBC >50,000 and 90% PMNs
  4. May get glucose value (30–50 mg) and protein (>4 g/dL)

IV. Treatment

A. Control sepsis (intravenous fluid)
B. Intravenous antibiotics (depending on suspected organism and aspiration) 4–6 weeks; switch to oral if bactericidal titer is greater than 1:8 and 1:2, compliance and oral tolerance
C. Immobilization acutely first and mobilization later
D. Surgical drainage
  1. Hip joint regardless of organism
  2. Purulent *Staphylococcus* on aspiration for any joint
  3. Poor response to medical treatment (antibiotics and repeated aspiration) within 48 hours
  4. Sepsis in hips is best drained anteriorly, especially if lateral subluxation is present. A drain is left in for 24–48 hours postoperatively. Drilling of the femoral neck is done if osteomyelitic focus is present. Postoperative immobilization is important
E. Arthroscopy may be considered in selected cases
F. Unusual organisms
  1. Brucellosis: usually the knee is affected after the spine, and tetracycline is the antibiotic of choice
  2. Lyme disease: spirochete *Borrelia burgdorferi*
    a. In 3–30 days after tick bite, erythema chronicum migrans appear
    b. Bell's palsy and cardiac involvement may follow
    c. Arthritis occurs later: the knee is most frequently affected

V. Prognosis

A. Timing of treatment is most important
B. Hip joint has a worse prognosis
C. Younger age is worse
D. Associated osteomyelitis is worse
E. Organisms: *Staphylococcus* and gram-negative organisms are worse than streptococci and gonococci

VERTEBRAL OSTEOMYELITIS

I. Incidence

A. Rare (1–4% of all osteomyelitis)
B. Lumbar > thoracic > cervical
C. Males > females (2:1) and more common after 5th decade
D. Most commonly hematogenous route
E. Organisms: *Staphylococcus* and gram-negative bacteria (*E. coli, Proteus, Klebsiella*) and less often *Pseudomonas* and tuberculosis

II. Pathology

A. Hematogenous spread to vertebral metaphysis adjacent to anterior longitudinal ligament (nutrient artery and rich vascular supply)
B. Spread to intervertebral discs and neural arch
C. Soft tissue extension: paravertebral abscesses, psoas, retropharyngeal, and epidural collections
D. Neurologic involvement: compression of

the spinal cord and roots (4–13% paralysis)

III. Clinical Findings
A. Delayed diagnosis is common and unfortunate
B. Acute, subacute, and chronic types
C. Localized pain and tenderness are most consistent findings
D. Fever, malaise, and associated infection
E. Complete blood count, ESR (−80 mm/hr), blood culture (25% positive), and urine culture should be ordered

IV. X-ray Findings
A. Bone scan and/or gallium scan detects at early stage
B. Plain films: paravertebral soft tissue swelling, lytic and sclerotic changes, disc space narrowing, disc destruction, collapse and kyphosis of vertebrae (x-ray changes are seen in late stage of disease)
C. CT scan (disc hypodensity in early stage and helpful in soft tissue extension and neurologic involvement)
D. Myelogram: should be ordered if neurologic deficit
E. MRI: detects osteomyelitis early and may distinguish from neoplasms

V. Biopsy
A. Closed: 71% positive and unsafe in cervical and thoracic regions unless CT-guided technique is used
B. Open: most accurate method and debridement can be done simultaneously

VI. Treatment
A. Intravenous antibiotic: early cases
B. Surgery: late or failure to respond to medical treatment or abscess formation
  1. Preoperative antibiotic, 3 weeks
  2. Anterior approaches
     a. Cervical (Southwick and Robinson)
     b. Thoracic (transthoracic or costotransversectomy)
     c. Lumbar (retroperitoneal)
     d. Thoracolumbar (thoracoabdominal or retroperitoneal)
  3. Debridement until bleeding cancellous bone
  4. Autogenous bone grafting (rib or iliac crest)
  5. Drainage, 48 hours
  6. Secondary posterior stabilization in unstable cases
  7. Intravenous antibiotic (6 weeks) and oral (3–6 months)
  8. Body cast or jacket, 6 months
C. Surgical emergency: epidural abscess

DISC SPACE INFECTIONS

I. General Considerations
A. The blood supply: to the intervertebral disc in childhood is from the surfaces of the adjacent vertebral bodies, and discitis may arise hematogenously
B. Lumbar spine is most frequently affected

II. Clinical Findings
A. Typical patient is between 2 and 7 years old
B. One to 2 weeks of back pain
C. Limping, refusal to walk, or referred hip pain may be presenting symptoms
D. Back tenderness and paravertebral spasm are noted
E. ESR and WBC are elevated
F. Bone scan or MRI are positive at early stages
G. Plain x-ray: narrowing of the intervertebral space, sclerosis, or bony erosion

III. Treatment
A. Immobilization with brace
B. Antibiotic treatment to cover *Staphylococcus* and *E. coli* and follow clinically, and ESR
C. Biopsy: if does not respond to treatment

D. Rarely need surgery (ie, paravertebral abscess)

TUBERCULOSIS OF THE SPINE

I. General Considerations
A. Tuberculosis: is still common in developing countries
B. Psoas abscess or severe kyphosis may result

II. Diagnosis
A. Not difficult because of known history and frequent associated pulmonary findings and positive skin tests

III. Treatment
A. Antibiotics and ambulatory treatment have good long-term results
B. Anterior debridement and fusion
   1. Indications: resistance to medical treatment, progressive deformity, abscess, or neurologic deficits
   2. Earlier fusion and less kyphosis than nonoperative patients

HAND INFECTIONS

I. General Considerations
A. Organisms responsible for infection may be bacteria, *Mycobacterium tuberculosis*, atypical mycobacterium, fungus, or virus
B. Immunocompromised or diabetic patients are prone to serious hand infections
C. General treatment considerations: rest, elevation, culture, antibiotic treatment, and prompt surgery when required

II. Specific Hand Infections
A. Felon
   1. Infection of the terminal pulp spaces of the finger
   2. Throbbing pain and erythema
   3. Usually *Staphylococcus*
   4. Treatment should include incision and drainage (high incision) and antibiotics
B. Paronychia
   1. Most common infection of the finger
   2. Symptoms: cellulitis, erythema about nail, pain, and abscess
   3. Treatment
      a. Soaks and antibiotics in early cases
      b. Incision and removal of portion of the nail plate in severe or late cases
C. Acute suppurative tenosynovitis
   1. Kanavel's four cardinal signs
      a. Pain on passive extension
      b. Flexed digits
      c. Symmetrical swelling often includes the hand
      d. Tendon sheath tenderness
   2. Infection may extend to the thenar, midpalmar space, and horseshoe abscess (radial and ulnar bursae)
   3. Treatment: midlateral or Brunner incision and leave open or limited incision with closed irrigation
D. Web space abscess
   1. Dorsal and palmar with swelling and erythema in the web space, usually from a puncture
   2. Treatment: incision and drainage and antibiotics
E. Herpetic whitelow
   1. More common in medical personnel who care for orotracheal region
   2. Painful vesicles on fingertips
   3. Herpes simplex: rise in complement fixing antibody titer
   4. Splint and elevate 10–14 days
   5. No surgery
   6. Superinfection with *S. aureus* may require antibiotic treatment
F. Bites
   1. Human bite (*Eikenella corrodens*): penicillin, or ampicillin
   2. Cat or dog bite (*Pasteurella multocida*): penicillin or ampicillin
G. Erysipeloid (*Erysipelothrix rhusiopathiae*)
   1. Circumscribed erythema, and pruritus
   2. Penicillin gives prompt improvement

INFECTED TOTAL JOINT ARTHROPLASTY

I. General Considerations
A. Incidence: 1–2%, less with antibiotic prophylaxis and laminar flow room and space suits
B. Etiologies: direct contamination, airborne bacteria, and hematogenous seeding
C. Increased susceptibility with use of implants
   1. Metal debris
   2. Methyl-methacrylate: bone necrosis and inhibition of PMNs phagocytosis and migration
   3. Glycocalyx: bacteria's protective film of polysaccharide
D. Organisms
   1. Gram-positive organisms: *S. aureus, S. epidermidis, Streptococcus,* etc.
   2. Gram-negative organisms: *E. coli, Proteus, Pseudomonas, Enterobacter,* etc.
   3. Mixed infection
   4. Anaerobic infection
E. Patients at higher risk
   1. Rheumatoid arthritis, corticosteroid use, revision surgery, dental abscess, diabetes, obesity, skin lesions, urinary tract infection, and poor nutrition
   2. Postoperative hematoma, drainage, and dehiscence

II. Diagnosis
A. Symptoms and signs: pain, erythema, fever, drainage
B. X-rays: 3–6 months postoperative
   1. Radiolucent zone at bone-cement interphase
   2. Scalloping of endosteum
   3. Periosteal reaction
   4. Component migration
C. Increased ESR
D. Scans: technetium is positive in both mechanical loosening and in infection, and gallium and indium scans are more specific for infection
E. Hip aspiration
   1. Arthrogram: filling of pseudocapsule
   2. Gram's stain: organisms or more than 5 PMNs per high power field
   3. Culture: negative culture does not rule out infection

III. Treatment
A. Prevention
   1. Meticulous surgical technique
   2. Clean operating room environment (laminar flow, minimal traffic, space suits)
   3. Prophylactic antibiotics (cefazolin or cefamandole at the time of anesthesia induction and 1–3 days postoperatively)
B. Hip
   1. Removal of prosthesis, all cement and thorough debridement followed by delayed reinsertion of prosthesis
      a. Timing: 2–3 months for low virulence gram-positive organism and 1 year for gram-negative or mixed infections
      b. One-stage reimplantation with antibiotics in the cement may be performed in clean wounds and low virulence organism
      c. Repeat debridement as necessary
      d. Systemic antibiotics: 6 weeks intravenous and 6 months oral
      e. Suction-irrigation may be done for 3 days
      f. Prosthesis may be left alone in acute cases (days)
   2. Resection (Girdlestone) arthroplasty: if draining sinus, gram-negative, mixed, or anaerobic organisms, pelvic osteomyelitis or fracture, poor femoral bone stock, frailty, and old age
   3. Arthrodesis: salvage technique in the young patient with a failed total hip arthroplasty
C. Knee
   1. Debridement, removal of prosthesis and cement and delayed reimplanta-

tion (4–6 weeks) for low virulence organisms: antibiotic impregnated cement block can be used
2. Debridement, removal of prosthesis and cement and arthrodesis for resistent organisms, revision failure, poor skin and quadriceps problem: external fixator, intramedullary rod, or plate can be used

POST-TRAUMATIC INFECTIONS AND OSTEOMYELITIS

I. General Considerations
A. Prevention of infection is key to success because functional results may be impaired with infections. Infection also has deleterious effect on healing of the fracture
B. Soft tissue coverage, fracture stability, and vascularity are all important in the prevention of nonunion and infection

II. Principles of Open Fractures
A. Tetanus prophylaxis is mandatory
B. Gram's stain and culture should be taken before and after debridement and irrigation
C. Systemic antibiotics
   1. Cefazolin or oxacillin to cover *S. aureus*
   2. Add aminoglycosides if grade III wounds for 3 days
   3. Add penicillin for farm injuries
D. Irrigation and debridement: 10 L of saline and 2 L of bacitracin and polymyxin. Repeat debridement and irrigation for grade III open fractures
E. Obtain soft tissue coverage: delay closure, skin graft, local flap, or free flap may be necessary to obtain early soft tissue coverage
   1. Partial closure may be done in grade I or II open injuries but leave wound open initially for grade III injuries
   2. Soft tissue coverage should be done within 1 week
F. Obtain stability of fracture
   1. External fixator is the best method for grade III open fracture of the tibia
   2. Intramedullary nails may be used in grade I or II open fractures, but increased risk of infection for grade III open fractures of the tibia
   3. Unreamed nails are preferred to reamed nails if intramedullary rods are chosen for management of open fractures
   4. Intramedullary rods are probably preferred to external fixators for the management of open femoral fractures
G. Obtain union
   1. Bone grafting should be done in 3–6 weeks for comminuted fractures with bony defects
   2. Early posterolateral bone grafting is beneficial in grade III open fractures to prevent delayed or nonunions

III. Infected Nonunions
A. Etiologies: ununited fracture, sequestrum, or foreign body
B. First objective is to decontaminate wound: cultures, antibiotics, debridement, and irrigation
C. Second objective is to stabilize the fracture
   1. If the metal is providing stability, then do not remove
   2. If the metal is not providing any stability, it should be removed and replaced by internal or external fixation
D. Third objective is to obtain union
   1. Posterolateral bone grafting: procedure of choice for infected nonunion of the tibia (over 90% success)
   2. Other options may be Papineau grafting, free vascularized bone graft, noninvasive electrical stimulation, tibia-profibula bone graft
E. If soft tissue defect is part of the problem,

local or free flaps may be utilized for bone coverage

IV. Chronic Osteomyelitis

A. General considerations
1. Patients with diabetes mellitus and peripheral vascular disease are more susceptible to osteomyelitis
2. Intravenous drug abusers and sickle cell patients are at greater risk
3. *Staphylococcus* is the most common organism
4. Gram-negative bacilli and streptococci are infrequent organisms
5. Mixed organisms and anaerobes are common in chronic cases
B. Staging of osteomyelitis (Cierny) (Fig 2-7)
    1. Anatomic type
        a. I: Medullary
        b. II: Superficial
        c. III: Localized
        d. IV: Diffuse
    2. Physiologic class
        a. A: host, normal systemic defenses, metabolic capabilities, vascularity
        b. B: host, local, systemic, or combined wound healing deficiencies
        c. C: host, minimal disability, high treatment morbidity, treatment palliative
    3. Clinical staging by combination of type I–IV and class A, B, or C
C. Treatment
    1. Nutritional and metabolic improvement
    2. Optimal biopsy technique
    3. Aggressive debridement of necrotic bone and soft tissue
    4. Appropriate antibiotics
    5. Creation of a well-vascularized soft tissue bed and obliteration of dead space
    6. Adequate stability of involved bone
    7. Good bone grafting techniques

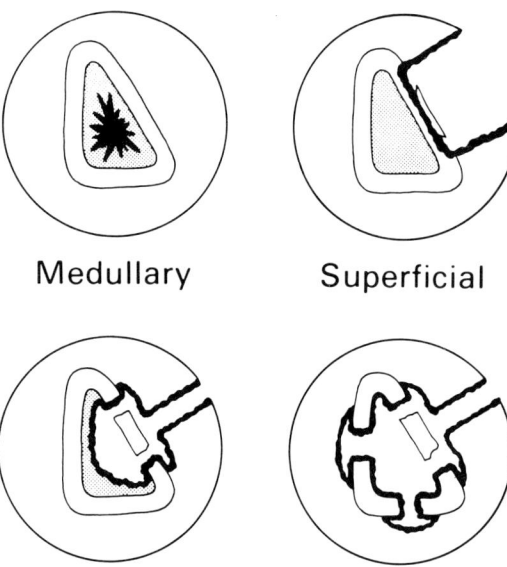

Figure 2-7. Anatomic classification of adult osteomyelitis. (From Cierny G III: Chronic osteomyelitis: results of treatment. In Greene WB, ed. Instructional Course Lectures, vol. XXXIX. Park Ridge, IL, American Academy of Orthopaedic Surgeons, 1990, p 495. Reprinted with permission.)

OTHER INFECTIONS

I. Atypical and Fungal Orthopaedic Infections

A. Mycobacterium
1. Tuberculosis
2. Atypical mycobacteria: *M. kansasii* and *M. marinum* cultured at 30–32°C
3. Treatment: isoniazid, rifampin, and ethambutol (streptomycin)
B. Fungal
1. Actinomycosis: sulfa
2. Sporotrichosis (rose gardener): amphotericin B
3. Blastomycosis: amphotericin B
4. Histoplasmosis: amphotericin B
5. Coccidioidomycosis (Southwestern United States): amphotericin B

II. Anaerobes

A. Gas gangrene
1. *Clostridium perfringens* (gram-positive bacillus)

2. Treatment: wide debridement, intravenous penicillin G 4 million U intravenously every 4 hours, hyperbaric oxygen, and amputation if necessary
B. Tetanus
 1. *Clostridium tetani* (death rate up to 50%)
 2. Treatment: antitoxin and supportive
 3. Prevention is the key

III. Necrotizing Fasciitis (Meleny's Infection)
A. Hemolytic staphylococci, microaerophilic nonhemolytic streptococci
B. Treatment: wide surgical excision deep to fascia, and penicillin

IV. Toxic Shock Syndrome
A. Unexplained fever postoperatively
B. Serosanguinous exudate from the wound
C. Mortality rate: 7–10%
D. Culture the wound
E. Open debridement and antibiotics if staphylococci are found

V. Acquired Immune Deficiency Syndrome
A. One million people infected with HIV in the United States
B. Five to 7% per year progress to AIDS among HIV-positive individuals
C. High-risk patients: homosexuals, intravenous drug users, hemophiliacs
D. Precautions for preventing acquisition of HIV are important in the hospital setting

VI. Lyme Arthritis
A. Multisystem inflammatory disorder caused by tick bites
B. Rash appears 3 days to 3 weeks after bite (erythema chronicum migrans)
C. Constitutional symptoms may accompany skin rash (such as malaise, fatigue, lymphadenopathy, headache, meningeal irritation, musculoskeletal pain)
D. Neurologic or cardiac involvement in 10–15%
E. Arthritis in 60%
 1. Migratory musculoskeletal pain
 2. Arthritis and swelling months after onset of illness
 3. Joint destruction in 10% of patients with arthritis
F. Diagnosis: Antibody titer to spirochete
G. Treatment: Penicillin, erythromycin, or dicloxacillin

REFERENCES

Bartlett P, Reingold AL, Graham DR, et al: Toxic shock syndrome associated with surgical wound infection. JAMA 247:1448–1451, 1982

Canner GC, Steinberg ME, Heppenstall RB, et al: The infected hip after total hip arthroplasty. J Bone Joint Surg 66A:1393–1399, 1984

Culp RW, Eichenfield AH, Davidson RS, et al: Lyme arthritis in children; an orthopaedic perspective. J Bone Joint Surg 69A:96–99, 1987

Digby JM, Kersley JB: Pyogenic nontuberculous spinal infection. An analysis of thirty cases. J Bone Joint Surg 64B:32–35, 1982

Eismont FJ, Bohlman HH, Prasanna LS, et al: Pyogenic and fungal vertebral osteomyelitis with paralysis. J Bone Joint Surg 65A:19–29, 1983

Fitzgerald RH Jr, Ruttle PE, Arnold PG, et al: Local muscle flaps in the treatment of chronic osteomyelitis. J Bone Joint Surg 67A:175–185, 1985

Fountain SS: A single stage combined surgical approach for vertebral resections. J Bone Joint Surg 61A:1011–1017, 1979

Frederickson B, Yuan H, Olans R: Management and outcome of pyogenic vertebral osteomyelitis. Clin Orthop 131:160–167, 1978

Gordon L, Chiu EJ: Treatment of infected non-unions and segmental defects of the tibia with staged microvascular muscle transplantation and bone-grafting. J Bone Joint Surg 70A:377–386, 1988

Griffith HED, Jones DM: Pyogenic infection of the spine. A review of twenty-eight cases. J Bone Joint Surg 53B:383–391, 1971

Gristina AG, Costerton JW: Bacterial adherence to biomaterials and tissue: The significance of its role in clinical sepsis. J Bone Joint Surg 67A:264–273, 1985

Grogan TJ, Dorey F, Rollins J, et al: Deep sepsis following total knee arthroplasty: Ten-year experience at the University of California at Los Angeles Medical Center. J Bone Joint Surg 68A:226–234, 1986

Irvine GW, Kling TF, Hensinger RN: Postoperative toxic shock syndrome following osteoplasty of the hip: A case report. J Bone Joint Surg 66A:955–958, 1984

Johnson KD, Johnston DW: Orthopaedic experience with methicillin-resistant *Staphylococcus aureus* during a hospital epidemic. Clin Orthop 21:281–288, 1988

Kemp, HBS, Jackson JW, Jeremiah JD, et al: Anterior fusion of the spine for infective lesions in adults. J Bone Joint Surg 55B:715–734, 1973

Lord CF, Gebhardt MC, Tomford WW, et al: Infection in bone allografts: Incidence, nature, and treatment. J Bone Joint Surg 70A:369–376, 1988

Maderazo EG, Judson S, Pasternak H: Late infections of total joint prostheses: A review and recommendations for prevention. Clin Orthop 229:131–142, 1988

Medical research council working party on tuberculosis of the spine: A 10-year assessment of a controlled trial comparing debridement and anterior spinal fusion in the management of tuberculosis of the spine in patients on standard chemotherapy in Hong Kong. J Bone Joint Surg 64B:393–398, 1982

Miskew DBW, Lorenz MA, Pearson RL, et al: *Pseudomonas aeruginosa* bone and joint infection in drug abusers. J Bone Joint Surg 65A:829–832, 1983

Petty W, Spanier S, Shuster JJ, et al: The influence of skeletal implants on incidence of infection: Experiments in a canine model. J Bone Joint Surg 67A:1236–1244, 1985

Sheftel TG, Mader JT, Pennick JJ, et al: Methicillin resistant *Staphylococcus aureus* osteomyelitis. Clin Orthop 198:231–239, 1985

Shutzer SF, Harris WH: Deep-wound infection after total hip replacement under contemporary aseptic conditions. J Bone Joint Surg 70A:724–727, 1988

Weiland AJ, Moore JR, Daniel RK: The efficacy of free tissue transfer in the treatment of osteomyelitis. J Bone Joint Surg 66A:181–193, 1984

20
Tumors

PRINCIPLES OF TUMOR TREATMENT

I. Clinical Information
A. Age
  1. Less than 10 years: unicameral bone cysts, eosinophilic granuloma, fibrous dysplasia, osteosarcoma, Ewing's sarcoma, and leukemia
  2. Ten to 20 years: fibrous dysplasia, osteoid osteoma, fibroma, osteochondroma, chondroblastoma, chondromyxoid fibroma, osteosarcoma, and Ewing's sarcoma
  3. Twenty to 40 years: aneurysmal bone cysts, giant cell tumor, osteoblastoma, chondromyxoid fibroma, adamantinoma, parosteal osteosarcoma, fibrosarcoma, lymphoma, and malignant fibrous histiocytoma
  4. Forty to 80 years: Paget's disease, hemangioma, metastatic diseases, multiple myeloma, chondrosarcoma, fibrosarcoma, malignant fibrous histiocytoma, and lymphoma
B. Location
  1. Diaphysis of long bone: fibrous dysplasia, adamantinoma (cortex of tibia), ossifying fibroma (tibia), histiocytosis X, Ewing's sarcoma, and lymphoma
  2. Metaphysis of long bone: aneurysmal bone cyst, unicameral bone cyst, fibrous dysplasia, osteoblastoma, chondromyxoid fibroma, osteosarcoma and periosteal chondroma (proximal humerus)
  3. Epiphysis of long bone: chondroblastoma and giant cell tumor
  4. Spine
      a. Anterior elements: metastases, multiple myeloma, histiocytosis X ("vertebral plana"), chordoma (sacrum), Paget's disease, and hemangioma
      b. Posterior elements: aneurysmal bone cyst, osteoblastoma, osteoid osteoma
  5. Ribs: metastases, multiple myeloma, Ewing's sarcoma, chondrosarcoma, and fibrous dysplasia
  6. Pelvis: metastases, multiple myeloma, Ewing's sarcoma, chondrosarcoma, and Paget's disease
  7. Surface lesions: myositis ossificans, parosteal osteosarcoma, periosteal osteosarcoma, periosteal chondroma, periosteal chondrosarcoma, osteochondroma
  8. Multiple lesions: metastases, multiple myeloma, fibrous dysplasia, enchondroma, hemangioma, histiocytosis X, and hereditary exostosis

II. Radiographic Considerations
A. Lytic patterns or margins
  1. Geographic lesions: 1A (well-defined margin with sclerosis), 1B (well-defined margin without sclerosis), and 1C (ill-defined margin)
  2. Moth-eaten: trabecular defects
  3. Permeative: cortical resorption
B. Reactive tissue
  1. In situ
  2. Reactive rim
  3. Scallop (endosteum)
  4. Codman's triangle
  5. Onion skinning
  6. Sunburst patterns
C. Mineralized matrix patterns
  1. Solid
  2. Cloud-like
  3. Ivory-like
  4. Stippled

5. Flocculent
6. Rings and arcs

III. Staging and Grading of Tumors (Enneking)
A. Benign bone tumors
   1. Stage 1: latent
   2. Stage 2: active
   3. Stage 3: aggressive
B. Malignant bone tumors
   1. Surgical grading (Table 2-3)
      a. Stage I: low-grade tumors
      b. Stage II: high-grade tumors
      c. Stage III: metastasis
   2. Surgical sites (Table 2-4)
      a. A: intracompartmental
      b. B: extracompartmental
   3. Surgical staging: based on grade, site, and metastasis (Table 2-5)
C. Skip lesions and Stage IIB with aggressive involvement of adjacent compartmental tissue have a worse prognosis than stage II A lesions

IV. Diagnostic Work-up
A. History, physical examination, and laboratory (ESR, calcium, phosphorus, alkaline phosphatase, serum electrophoresis, etc.)
B. X-rays; plain films, chest film, tomograms, CT scan (bone and lungs), arteriography (vascular lesions), myelography, arthrogram, bone scan (margins, skip lesions, and metastasis), and MRI (soft tissue extension and skip lesions)

V. Biopsy
A. Staging done prior to biopsy, because staging may be difficult after biopsy by decrease in imaging specificity

Table 2-3 Surgical Grade (G)

Low (G_1)	High (G_2)
Parosteal osteosarcoma	Classic osteosarcoma
Endosteal Osteosarcoma	Radiation sarcoma
	Paget's sarcoma
Secondary chondrosarcoma	Primary chondrosarcoma
Fibrosarcoma, Kaposi's sarcoma	Fibrosarcoma
Atypical malignant fibrous histiocytoma	Malignant fibrous histiocytoma
	Undifferentiated primary sarcoma
Giant-cell tumor, bone	Giant-cell sarcoma, bone
Hemangioendothelioma	Angiosarcoma
Hemangiopericytoma	Hemangiopericytoma
Myxoid liposarcoma	Pleomorphic liposarcoma
	Neurofibrosarcoma
	Rhabdomyosarcoma
	Synovial sarcoma
Clear cell sarcoma, tendon sheath	
Epithelioid sarcoma	
Chordoma	
Adamantinoma	
Alveolar cell sarcoma	Alveolar cell sarcoma
Other and undifferentiated	Other and undifferentiated

From Enneking WF: Musculoskeletal tumor surgery. New York, Churchill Livingstone, 1983, p 72. Reprinted with permission.

Table 2-4 Surgical Sites (T)

Intracompartmental (T_1)	Extracompartmental (T_2)
Intraosseous	Soft tissue extension
Intra-articular	Soft tissue extension
Superficial to deep fascia	Deep fascial extension
Paraosseous	Intraosseous or extrafascial
Intrafascial compartments	Extrafascial planes or spaces
Ray of hand or foot	
Posterior calf	Midfoot and hindfoot
Anterolateral leg	Popliteal space
Anterolateral thigh	Groin—femoral triangle
Medial thigh	Intrapelvic
Posterior thigh	Midhand
Buttocks	Antecubital fossae
Volar forearm	Axilla
Dorsal forearm	Periclavicular
Anterior arm	Paraspinal
Posterior arm	Head and neck
Periscapular	

From Enneking WF: Musculoskeletal tumor surgery. New York, Churchill Livingstone, 1983, p 72. Reprinted with permission.

  B. Incision should be placed so that it can be removed en bloc with tumor if necessary (crucial for limb salvage)
  C. Vertical incision and fewest number of compartments and do not dissect between fascial planes
  D. Types of biopsy
    1. Excisional: marginal removal of tumor (appropriate for obviously benign small tumors)
    2. Incisional biopsy
      a. Open: better specimen and appropriate for primary malignant tumors and nondiagnostic radiographs but more complications (tumor spillage, hematoma, infection, pathologic fractures)
      b. Closed: better for homogeneous tumors, such as metastasis, myeloma, and infection, and diagnostic radio-

Table 2-5 Surgical Stages

Stage		Grade	Site		Metastases
I	A	Low (G_1)	Intracompartmental	(T_1)	None (M_0)
	B	Low (G_1)	Extracompartmental	(T_2)	None (M_0)
II	A	High (G_2)	Intracompartmental	(T_1)	None (M_0)
	B	High (G_2)	Extracompartmental	(T_2)	None (M_0)
III	A	Low (G_1)	Intra- or extracompartmental	(T_1-T_2)	Regional or distant (M_1)
	B	High (G_2)	Intra- or extracompartmental	(T_1-T_2)	Regional or distant (M_1)

From Enneking WF: Musculoskeletal tumor surgery. New York, Churchill Livingstone, 1983, p 81. Reprinted with permission.

graphs, but poorer sample and need x-ray guidance (more appropriate for pelvis and spine lesions, especially with fluoroscopy or CT scan)
E. Procedure
1. Least mineralized tissue is most diagnostic
2. Soft tissue component is better than bone
3. Longitudinal incision
4. Do not use Esmarch for exsanguination
5. Release tourniquet and obtain meticulous hemostasis
6. Bone biopsy: oval shape hole and may pack the site with polymethyl methacrylate
7. Closure: close-placed sutures and drains
8. Frozen section:
   a. Should be done whenever possible
   b. Definitive surgery based on frozen section can be done if perfect clinical, radiologic, and pathologic correlations are found (redraping and prepping and new instrumentations should be used)
   c. If in doubt, wait for permanent section

VI. Treatment

A. Surgical margins (Figs 2-8, 2-9)
1. Intralesional: incisional biopsy, curettage, debulking excision or debulking amputation (for benign self-healing bone tumors, ie, nonossifying fibroma, unicameral bone cyst, fibrous dysplasia, histiocytosis X, and osteoid osteoma)
2. Marginal: excisional biopsy, marginal excision or marginal amputation (surgery through pseudocapsule for benign soft tissue tumors, locally aggressive bone tumors such as osteoblastoma, chondroblastoma, aneurysmal bone cyst, chondromyxoid fibroma, and giant cell tumor)
3. Wide: wide excision or wide amputation (through normal cuff of tissue but intracompartmental surgery for low-grade sarcomas parosteal osteosarcoma, adamantinoma, low-grade chondrosarcoma, etc.)
4. Radical: radical resection or radical disarticulation (extracompartmental surgery for high-grade sarcomas)

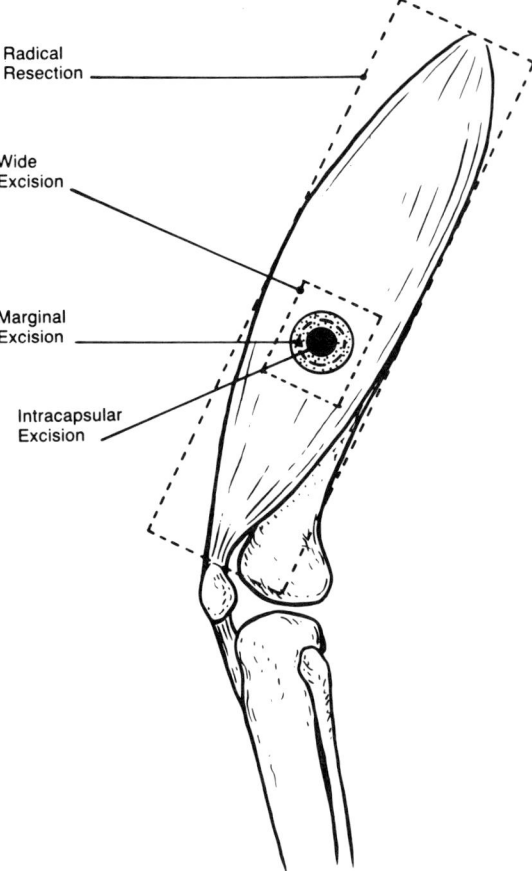

Figure 2-8. Diagrammatic classification of local procedures. (From Enneking WF: Musculoskeletal tumor surgery. New York, Churchill Livingstone, 1983, p 93. Reprinted with permission.)

B. Surgical treatment of bone tumors
1. Curettage: for benign tumors (latent or active) and bone graft
2. Extended curettage: for aggressive benign tumors
   a. Curettage plus burr, the wall to normal tissue
   b. Phenol cauterization, cementation,

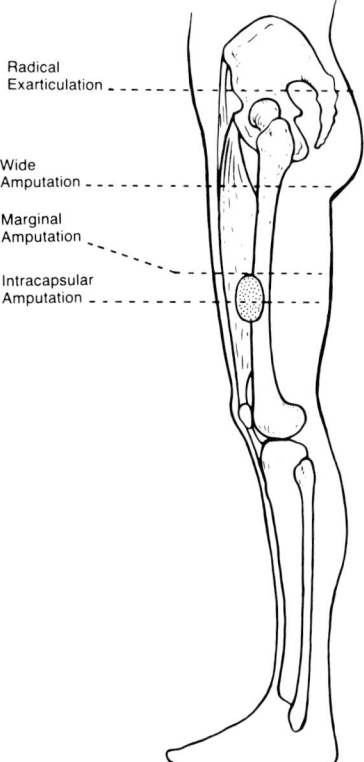

Figure 2-9. Diagrammatic classification of amputations. (From Enneking WF: Musculoskeletal tumor surgery. New York, Churchill Livingstone, 1983, p 94. Reprinted with permission.)

      cryotherapy, or bone grafting can be considered for adjunctive treatment
- 3. Wide excision: for very aggressive benign tumors or low-grade sarcomas (IA or IB lesions)
  - a. Limb salvaging techniques: arthrodesis with intercalary autograft or allograft, osteoarticular allograft, custom prosthesis, or composite allograft-prosthesis
  - b. Adjuvant chemotherapy or radiation therapy for IIA or IIB lesions with wide margins
- 4. Radical: high-grade sarcomas (IIA or IIB lesions)
  - a. Amputation or disarticulation
  - b. Consider chemotherapy or radiation treatment
- 5. Thoracotomy: for stage III lung metastasis

VII. Histologic Types of Benign Bone Tumors

- A. Fibrous lesions
  1. Nonossifying fibroma (fibrous cortical defect)
  2. Periosteal desmoid (avulsive cortical irregularity)
  3. Ossifying fibroma
  4. Desmoplastic fibroma
  5. Fibrous dysplasia
- B. Cartilagenous lesions
  1. Enchondroma
  2. Exostosis (osteochondroma)
  3. Periosteal chondroma
  4. Chondroblastoma
  5. Chondromyxofibroma
- C. Osseous lesions
  1. Osteoma
  2. Osteoid osteoma
  3. Osteoblastoma
- D. Vascular tumors
  1. Hemangioma
- E. Lesions simulating bone tumors or unknown origin
  1. Unicameral bone cyst
  2. Aneurysmal bone cyst
  3. Giant cell tumor
  4. Histiocytosis X (round cell tumor)
  5. Bone infarcts
  6. Mastocytosis (mast cells)
  7. Bone islands
  8. Disappearing bone disease (Gorham)
  9. Heterotopic ossification

VIII. Histologic Types of Malignant Tumors

- A. Fibrous lesions
  1. Fibrosarcoma
  2. Malignant fibrous histiocytoma
- B. Cartilagenous lesions
  1. Chondrosarcoma
- C. Osseous lesions
  1. Osteosarcoma
- D. Round cell sarcomas
  1. Ewing's sarcoma

    2. Lymphoma of bone
    3. Myeloma
    4. Neuroblastoma
    5. Rhabdomyosarcoma
  E. Vascular lesions
    1. Hemangioendothelioma (angiosarcoma)
    2. Hemangiopericytoma
  F. Unknown origin
    1. Giant cell sarcoma
    2. Adamantinoma
  G. Notochord (chordoma)
  H. Metastatic bone tumors

IX. Histologic Type of Soft Tissue Neoplasm

  A. Fibrous lesions
    1. Fibroma
    2. Fibromatosis
    3. Pseudosarcomatous fasciitis
    4. Fibrosarcoma
    5. Malignant fibrous histiocytoma
  B. Cartilagenous lesions
    1. Chondroma
    2. Extraosseous chondrosarcoma
    3. Tumoral calcinosis
    4. Synovial chondromatosis
  C. Osseous lesions
    1. Extraosseous osteosarcoma
    2. Pseudomalignant myositis ossificans
  D. Synovial lesions
    1. Giant-cell tumor of tendon sheath
    2. Synovial sarcoma
    3. Ganglion cyst
    4. Pigmented villonodular synovitis
  E. Vascular lesions
    1. Hemangioma
    2. Congenital hemangiomatosis
    3. Massive osteolysis
    4. Glomus tumor
    5. Malignant vascular tumors
  F. Fat lesions
    1. Lipoma
    2. Angiolipoma
    3. Spindle cell lipoma
    4. Liposarcoma
    5. Fat necrosis
  G. Neural lesions
    1. Neurilemmoma
    2. Neurofibroma
    3. Neurosarcoma
    4. Neuroma
  H. Muscular lesions
    1. Leiomyoma
    2. Leiomyosarcoma
    3. Rhabdomyoma
    4. Rhabdomyosarcoma
  I. Uncertain origin
    1. Epithelioid sarcoma
    2. Clear cell sarcoma
    3. Mesenchymoma
    4. Undifferentiated sarcoma

NONOSSIFYING FIBROMA

I. General Considerations

A. Age: 2nd decade
B. Sex: males > females
C. Location: metaphysis adjacent to epiphysis and may be multiple
D. Most common benign skeletal lesion
E. Usually asymptomatic and spontaneous healing is the rule but enlargement or pathologic fracture may occur

II. Pathology

A. Developmental defect by failure of ossification occupied by fibrous connective tissue
B. Tan (active and immature) or yellow fat (mature and latent) or brown (hemosiderin)

III. Diagnosis

A. Asymptomatic
B. X-ray: eccentric, oval-shaped radiolucency with scalloped line of sclerosis of the overlying cortex (Fig 2-10A)
C. Phases: active (nonossifying fibroma), remodeling (fibrous cortical defect) and quiescent (benign metaphyseal bone scar)
D. Histology: whorled fibrous tissue, loosely textured cells with giant cells and histio-

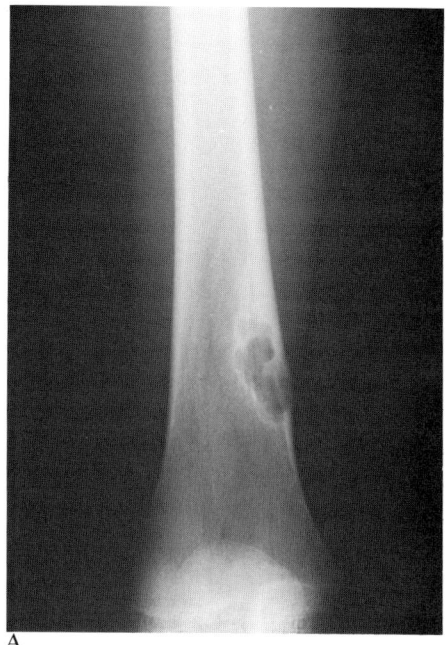
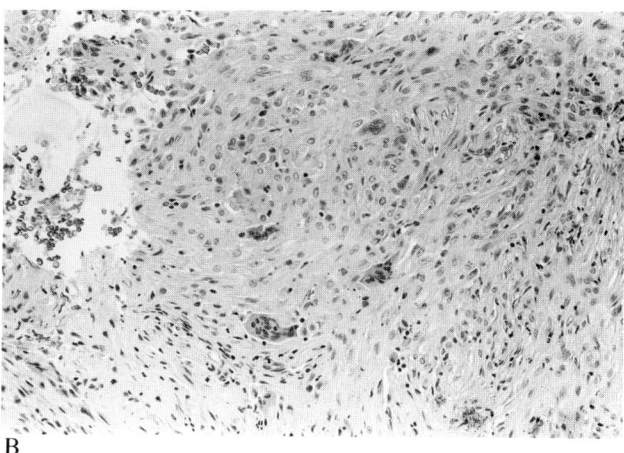

Figure 2-10. A. Roentgenographic appearance of typical nonossifying fibroma, showing eccentric, oval-shaped radiolucency with scalloped line of sclerosis of the overlying cortex. **B.** High-power histologic examination shows whorled fibrous tissue, loosely textured cells, with giant cells and histiocytes.

cytes (similar to giant cell tumor and indicates maturing process) (Fig 10B)

IV. Treatment
A. Observation
B. Doubtful cases: intracapsular curettage for diagnosis and cure

V. Periosteal Desmoid: Avulsive Cortical Irregularity
A. Medial supracondylar fibrous lesion of the femur at the adductor insertion
B. Male adolescents are commonly affected, and usually asymptomatic
C. Shallow scooped-out center with well demarcated margin
D. Treatment: observation

VI. Jaffe-Campanacci Syndrome
A. Multiple nonossifying fibroma of long bones and jaw
B. Café-au-lait spots
C. Mental retardation
D. Endocrine abnormalities

OSSIFYING FIBROMA

I. General Considerations
A. Age: first 10 years (most often 5 years)
B. Sex: males > females (slight)
C. Location: exclusively in the anterior cortex of the middle third of the tibia and distal third of the fibula
D. Considered as a variant of fibrous dysplasia or adamantinoma and also known as Campanaci's disease

II. Pathology
A. Recurrence is high, especially with surgical intervention
B. Occasionally pathologic fractures and pseudarthrosis

III. Diagnosis
A. May present as enlargement of tibia and anterior bowing
B. X-ray: single or multiple lucent area surrounded by dense sclerosis with narrow-

ing of the medullary canal (similar to adamantinoma)
C. Histology: bony trabeculae scattered through a fibrous stroma bordered by osteoblasts

IV. Treatment
A. Surgery: delay until skeletal maturity because of high recurrence (osteotomies for deformities)

DESMOPLASTIC FIBROMA

I. General Considerations
A. Age: 50% in second decade
B. Rare tumor
C. Location: metaphyseal region of long bones, pelvis

II. Pathology
A. Pathologic fractures can occur
B. Dense, rubbery, firm white mass of fibrous tissue, considered as intraosseous counterpart of the desmoid tumor in the soft tissue
C. Encapsulated by a shell of reactive bone but cohesive and aggressive

III. Diagnosis
A. Pain, swelling, and functional disability
B. X-ray: radiolucent central defect, well-demarcated margins but often irregular radiodense borders (x-ray looks deceivingly benign) (Fig 2-11)
C. Bone scan: minimally increased uptake
D. Angiogram: negative
E. MRI: may be helpful for soft tissue extension
F. Histology: hypocellular with slender spindle-shaped cells with abundant collagen formation (lack of giant cells and osseous metaplasia)
G. Stage: often 3 and soft tissue extension
H. Differential diagnosis: fibromatosis, fibrosarcoma

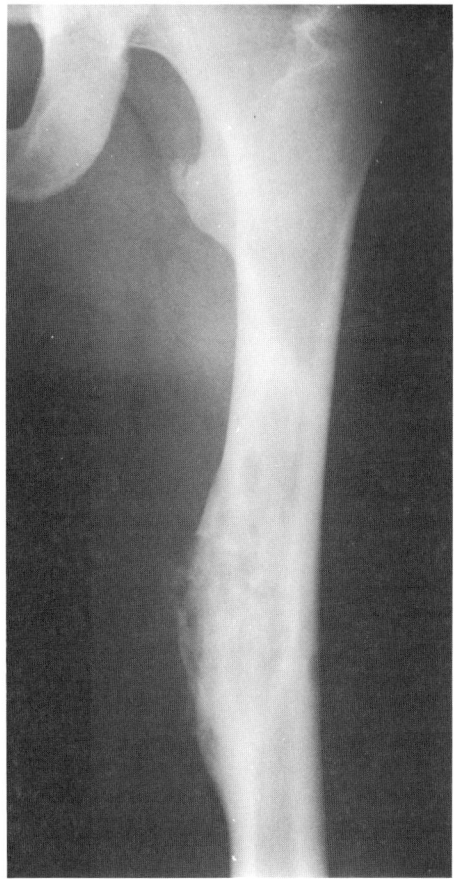

Figure 2-11. Roentgenographic appearance of desmoplastic fibroma, showing osseous defect with irregular radiodense borders.

IV. Treatment
A. Wide excision is preferable to prevent recurrence
B. Clinical staging is not accurate (pathologic diagnosis is important as far as treatment is concerned)

FIBROUS DYSPLASIA

I. General Considerations
A. Age: more common during second and third decades
B. Sex: male = female

C. Location: medullary portion of the metaphysis, diaphysis, and ribs
D. Albright syndrome: precocious puberty in the female, café-au-lait spots (irregular "coast of Maine" contour) and fibrous dysplasia

II. Pathology

A. Developmental failure of normal bone maturation, replaced by fibrous tissue
B. Common in the jaw, base of the skull, ribs, and long bones
C. Mono-ostotic or polyostotic (worse prognosis, greater deformities)
D. Fibrosarcomatous degeneration is rare if radiation is avoided
E. Spontaneous regression at puberty is common
F. Variable disability: pathologic fractures, progressive deformity ("shephard's crook" deformity of the proximal femur with leg shortening)

III. Diagnosis

A. Usually asymptomatic unless deformity or fractures are created
B. X-ray: oval-shaped radiolucent lesion in the central aspect of the metaphysis (Fig 2-12A). Often homogeneous increased density (ground-glass appearance), endosteal erosion and expansion and poor distinction between the cortex and medulla as opposed to unicameral bone cyst
C. Bone scan is positive
D. Histology: irregular foci of woven bone trabeculae with osteoid seam but little osteoblastic rimming and fibrous stroma with sharp stellate shape of fibroblasts (Fig 2-12B)

IV. Treatment

A. Conservative: observation and prevention of deformity
B. Surgery if unrelenting pain and progressive deformity. Curettage and cortical au-

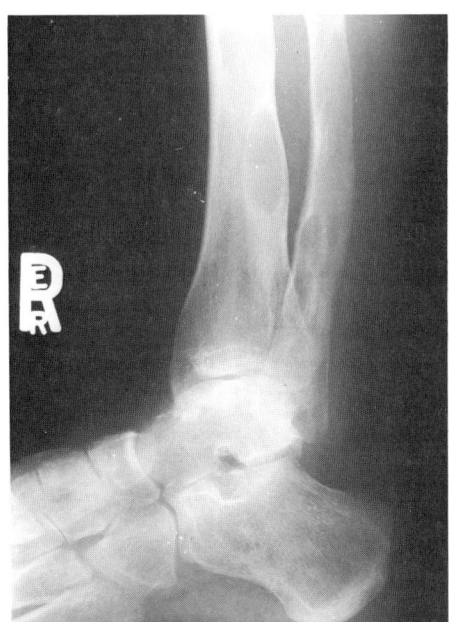

A

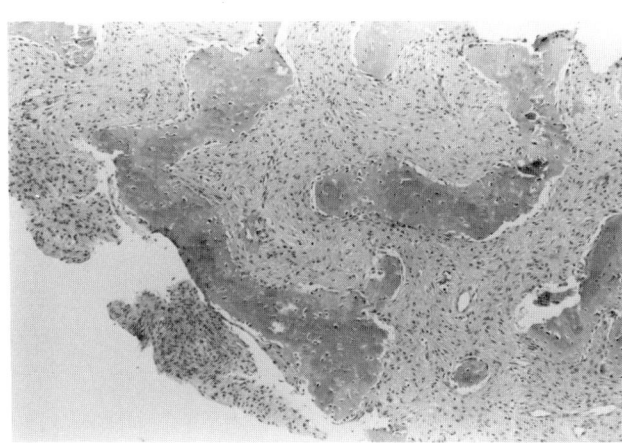

B

Figure 2-12. **A.** Roentgenographic appearance of fibrous dysplasia, showing oval-shaped radiolucent lesions in the metaphysis with increased density (ground-glass appearance). **B.** Low-power histologic examination shows fibrous stroma and irregular foci of woven bone trabeculae with osteoid seam but little osteoblastic rimming.

tograft or allograft (stability and prevention of deformity)

ENCHONDROMA

I. General Considerations
A. Age: even (60% second through fourth decades)
B. Sex: equal
C. Location: within shafts of tubular bones (40% occur in the hands and feet)
D. Ollier's disease: multiple enchondromatosis or chondrodysplasia
E. Maffucci's syndrome: multiple enchondromas with skin angiomas
F. Higher incidence of sarcomatous degeneration in Ollier's disease and Maffucci's syndrome (30%)

II. Pathology
A. Lesion of mature hyaline cartilage occurring in bone
B. Slow growing cartilage mass
C. Lobulated masses of bluish, semitranslucent cartilage

III. Diagnosis
A. Usually asymptomatic
B. X-ray: rarefaction and stippled calcification (similar to bone infarct — generally shows central rarefaction and peripheral calcification) (Fig 2-13)
C. Bone scan is negative
D. Histology: masses of hyaline cartilage with chondrocytes separated by septae of fibrous tissue (difficult to differentiate from low-grade chondrosarcoma). Look for cellularity, replicating nuclei, and extension to surrounding tissue and myxoid or mucinous changes in addition to clinical findings (pain, increase in size, positive bone scan, and x-ray findings of surrounding zone lucency, internal buttressing and increase in endosteal scalloping, pointing toward chondrosarcoma)

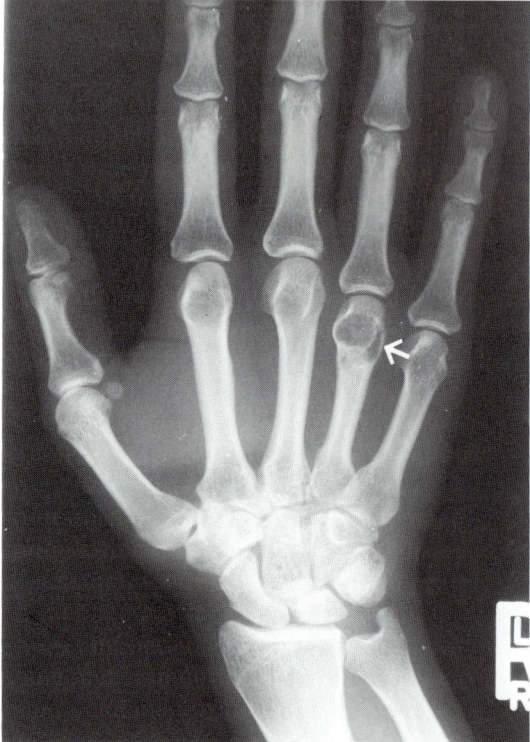

Figure 2-13. Roentgenographic appearance of enchondroma, showing a radiolucent defect in the metaphysis of the metacarpal (arrow).

IV. Treatment
A. Asymptomatic: observation
B. Curettage and bone graft in symptomatic, structurally weakened areas (recurrence is rare)
C. Pathologic fractures: let fracture heal first
D. Wide resection if chondrosarcoma is suspected

EXOSTOSIS (OSTEOCHONDROMA)

I. General Considerations
A. Age: 2nd and 3rd decades
B. Sex: males > females (slightly)
C. Location: metaphysis of long bones, particularly distal femur, proximal humerus and proximal tibia
D. Most common tumor of bone

II. Pathology

A. Outgrowth of bone and cartilage (endochondral ossification) at the edge of physis
B. Arises at tendon insertions and grows along line of tendon pull
C. Exostosis continues to grow away from the physis and the cartilagenous cap persists (usually 2–3 mm thick, up to 1 cm in adolescents, and >2 cm is suspicious for malignancy)
D. May form a bursa overlying the lesion (this lesion may be confused as soft tissue tumor from chondrosarcomatous degeneration. Aspiration may be done to rule it out)
E. Multiple osteochondromatosis: autosomal dominant heredity, and higher risk of malignant transformation
F. Trevor's disease: intraarticular osteochondroma

III. Diagnosis

A. Age, location, and exostotic x-ray appearance are usually characteristic of the lesion (Fig 2-14)
   1. Sessile or pedunculated
   2. Continuity of cortex and cancellous bone with adjacent bone
B. Bone scan may be necessary in doubtful cases and if chondrosarcoma is suspected
C. Biopsy
   1. Trabecular woven bone with cartilage resembling the epiphysis but more disorderly with persistent calcified cartilage without remodeling
   2. Cartilage cap: persistent indefinitely, similar to epiphyseal side of normal physeal-bone interphase
   3. No tidemark after maturity

IV. Treatment

A. Extracapsular marginal excision: biopsy purpose symptomatic lesions (remove cartilage cap), or if suspicious for malignancy

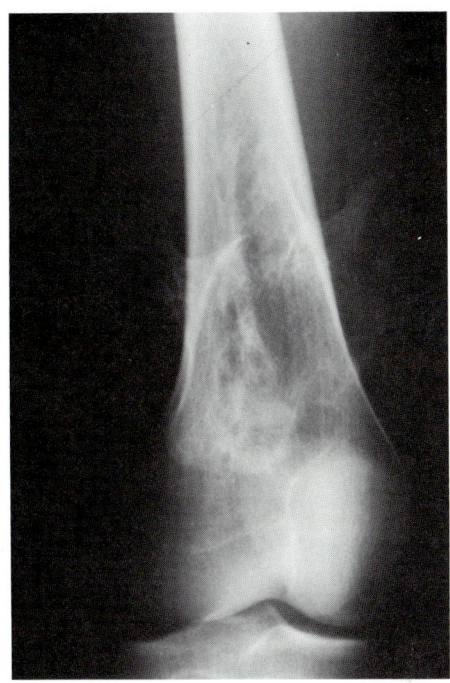

Figure 2-14. Roentgenographic appearance of a typical osteochondroma arising from the distal femur.

B. Recurrence: 2%
C. Malignant transformation: <1% in single lesion and 10% in multiple hereditary osteochondromatosis

PERIOSTEAL CHONDROMA

I. General Considerations

A. Less common than enchondromas or exostoses
B. Location: lateral aspect of the proximal metaphysis of the humerus, other long bones along the periosteal surface

II. Pathology

A. Active proliferating cartilage mass beneath periosteum
B. Well-encapsulated by outer fibrous layer of periosteum
C. Enlargement continues long after maturity
D. No calcification or ossification

III. Diagnosis
A. Asymptomatic mass
B. X-ray: shallow, craterlike defect lined by thin rim of reactive bone
C. Bone scan: increased uptake about the reactive edge
D. Histology: cellular cartilage and may mimic low-grade chondrosarcoma
D. Stage: active stage 2

IV. Treatment
A. En bloc marginal or wide excision
B. Labeling with tetracycline is helpful

CHONDROBLASTOMA

I. General Considerations
A. Age: 50% in the 2nd decade
B. Sex: males > female (3:2)
C. Location: epiphysis (especially proximal humerus, proximal tibia, and distal femur) and secondary ossification center
D. Metaphyseal expansion may occur and secondary aneurysmal bone cyst may occur

II. Pathology
A. Grayish pink lesion with hemorrhage, necrosis, or calcification (softer and reddish than enchondroma)
B. May be surrounded by thin rim of reactive bone
C. May cross the physis in aggressive cases
D. Recurrence is less than giant cell tumors and chondromyxoid fibroma but recurrence can be more devastating because of intra-articular extension

III. Diagnosis
A. Local pain
B. X-ray: localized destructive lesion of the epiphysis with occasional metaphyseal extension. Margin is well defined with thin rim of reactive bone (Fig 2-15A)
C. Bone scan: positive
D. Histology: mononuclear cells in sheetlike arrangement, chondroid islands, giant cells and lacy calcification ("chicken wire" — calcification of chondroid matrix around the cells) (Fig 2-15B)
E. Staging: majority are stage 2, but often stage 3 in the pelvis

IV. Treatment
A. Stage 1: curettage and bone graft
B. Stage 2: marginal extracapsular resection
C. Stage 3: wide surgical margin
D. Surgery should be through the physeal plate rather than the joint to prevent intra-articular extension, if possible
E. Attempt to preserve the joint and epiphysis
F. Cryosurgery can be utilized
G. Aggressive curettage and cementation may be utilized
H. No radiation: may transform to chondrosarcoma

CHONDROMYXOFIBROMA

I. General Considerations
A. Age: 2nd and 3rd decades
B. Sex: males > females
C. Location: metaphysis in the long bones, especially proximal tibia
D. Very rare tumor

II. Pathology
A. Firm, lobulated, and well-circumscribed lesion with occasional satellite nodules
B. Microscopic fields similar to chondroblastoma
C. Small, up to 5 cm diameter

III. Diagnosis
A. Not painful
B. X-ray: eccentric, well-circumscribed radiolucent lesion with diffuse sclerotic scalloped margin (differential diagnosis includes nonossifying fibroma) (Fig 2-16A)
C. Bone scan: increased uptake about the edge

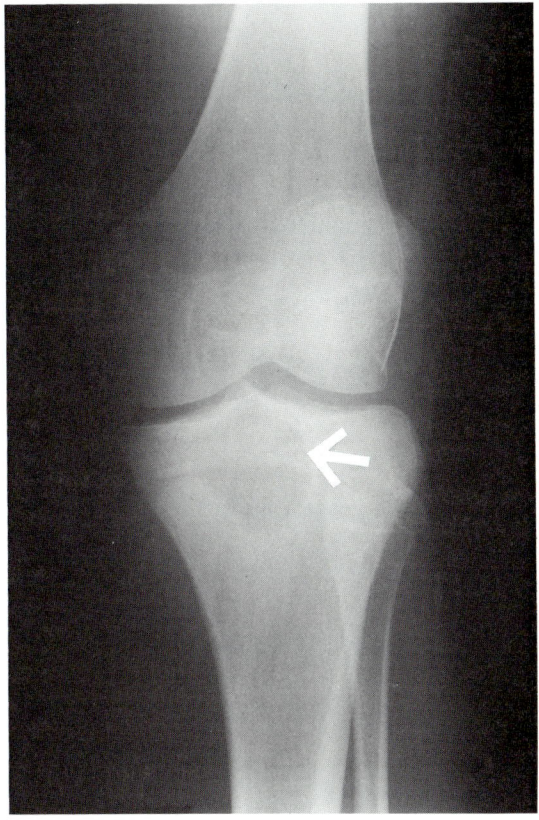

Figure 2-15. A. Roentgenographic appearance of chondroblastoma, showing a lytic lesion of the proximal tibial with well-defined margin and thin rim of reactive bone (arrow). **B.** High-power histologic examination shows mononuclear cells in sheetlike arrangement, chondroid islands, giant cells, and lacy calcification, resembling "chicken wire."

D. CT scan: presence or absence of soft tissue mass
E. Pathologic fracture may occur
F. Histology: chondroid, myxoid, and fibrous areas in a lobulated pattern (spindle cells, chondroblasts in chondroid stroma) (Fig 2-16B)

IV. Treatment

A. Curettage and bone graft: 15–25% recurrence
B. Marginal or wide resection is preferred

OSTEOMA

I. General Considerations

A. Age: Adolescents and early adults
B. Location: mandible, skull, middle third of the anterior tibia
C. Uncommon lesion

II. Pathology

A. Proliferation of bone beneath the periosteum or endosteum
B. Slowly enlarging mass but seldom exceeds 10 cm

III. Diagnosis

A. Painless enlarging hard mass
B. X-ray: dense mature cortical bone well-outlined from the underlying normal bone
C. Bone scan: positive in active lesions
D. Histology: Admixture of osteons, haversian systems, and active mesenchymal ossification in the periphery
E. Stage: active stage 2 early, then latent afterward

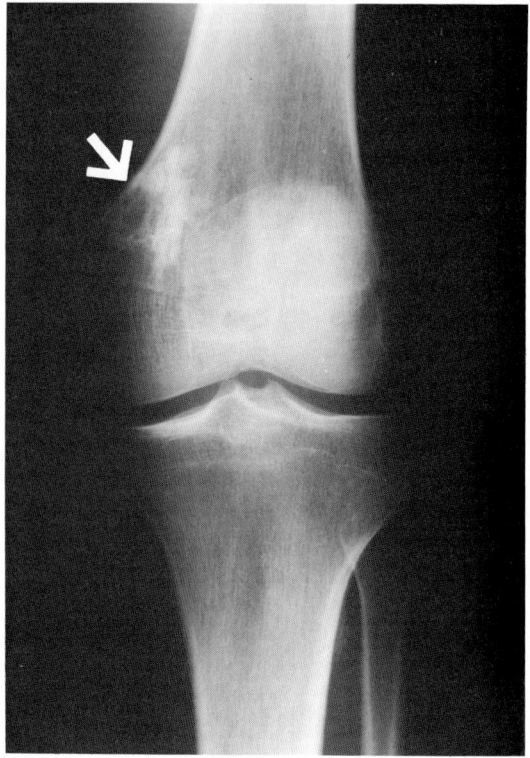

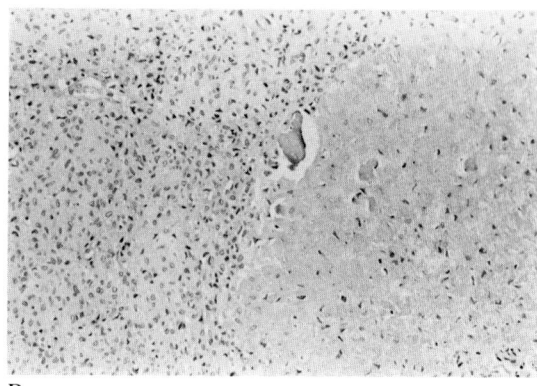

Figure 2-16. A. Roentgenographic appearance of chondromyxofibroma, showing an eccentric metaphyseal lesion of the distal femur with diffuse sclerotic scalloped margin (arrow). **B.** Low-power histologic examination shows fibrous stroma with spindle cells and myxomatous-like chondroid area with chondroblasts.

IV. Treatment

A. Removal: for biopsy purposes or cosmesis
B. Marginal resection

OSTEOID OSTEOMA

I. General Considerations

A. Age: 2nd decade
B. Sex: males > females (2:1)
C. Location: anywhere in skeleton, especially in cortices of long bones. Posterior elements of the spine, lesser trochanter (differential diagnosis, stress fracture), and capsular insertions with minimal reactive rims (eg, talus, femoral neck; arthrogram or MRI may be helpful)

II. Pathology

A. Central nidus and reactive bone
B. Nidus
　1. Mesenchymal vascularized granulation tissue with spindle stromal cells surrounding unossified osteoid (thick and nonstressed osteoid bars with no cement lines)
　2. Soft early but dense later with calcification
　3. Ossification of the center portion of the nidus occurs later
　4. The size is usually <1.5cm
C. Reactive bone: 2–3 times as thick as nidus (less in intracapsular lesions)

III. Diagnosis

A. History: painful especially at night, relieved by aspirin
B. X-ray: lucent nidus with sclerotic reactive bone
C. Tomogram, CT scan, or MRI may be helpful (Fig 2-17)
D. Bone scan: positive
E. Arthrogram: intracapsular lesions
F. Histology
　1. Nidus: vascular primitive mesenchy-

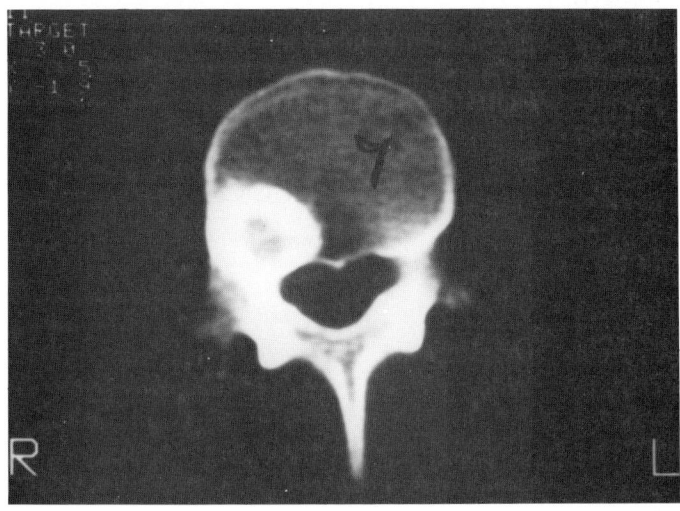

Figure 2-17. Computed tomography scan of an osteoid osteoma arising from the posterior aspect of the vertebra.

mal tissue (calcification or ossification in mature lesions, and occasional nerve endings and giant cells)
2. Reactive bone: benign immature bone with no mitosis or chondroid element
G. Differential diagnosis: stress fracture, intracortical abscess, osteomyelitis, osteochondritis dissecans, osteoblastoma

IV. Treatment

A. Observation if asymptomatic (spontaneous healing is frequent) or aspirin
B. Complete resection of nidus and bone grafting
C. Curettage should be discouraged to avoid leaving nidus
D. Tetracycline labeling may be helpful

OSTEOBLASTOMA

I. General Considerations

A. Age: first 3 decades and peaks at 2nd decade
B. Sex: males > females
C. Location: 50% in cancellous bone in spine (posterior elements) and sacrum
D. Rare tumor

II. Pathology

A. Large lucent lesion with thin rim of reactive bone
B. Do not spontaneously heal and local invasion may occur
C. Larger size than osteoid osteoma: >1–2 cm

III. Diagnosis

A. Less painful than osteoid osteoma
B. X-ray: large lucent lesion with thin reactive bone
C. Bone scan: (increased uptake proportional to the lesion)
D. Angiogram: increased vascularity
E. Histology: similar to osteoid osteoma but vascularity is greater with many osteoblasts. Histology may resemble osteogenic sarcoma
F. Stage: usually 2, but 3 in the pelvis

IV. Treatment

A. Curettage alone leads to high recurrence
B. Wide resection is best for local control

ANEURYSMAL BONE CYST

I. General Considerations

A. Age: 2nd and 3rd decades
B. Location: metaphyseal; any region, including the posterior element of the spine
C. Difficult to predict clinical course

II. Pathology
A. Cystic cavities containing blood, lined by thick, flesh brownish staining membrane
B. Primary (50%) versus secondary (simple bone cyst, giant cell tumor, chondroblastoma, chondromyxoid fibroma, eosinophilic granuloma, osteosarcoma, etc.)
C. Expansile lesion erodes the cortex and contained by thin reactive bone

III. Diagnosis
A. Pain and swelling of variable duration
B. X-ray: lytic and expansile and well circumscribed but lacks a sclerotic border (Fig 2-18A). Types (Campanacci): I, center of bone; II, inflated; III, eccentric; IV, periosteal; V, periosteal and cortical erosion
C. Positive bone scan (larger uptake peripherally), CT scan (mass lesion with thin reactive rim, fluid level after 30 minutes in dependent position), and angiogram (hypervascular margin with cold center)
D. Histology: vascular lakes containing red blood cells and giant cells with admixture of immature bone and mesenchymal tissue (Fig 2-18B)
E. Staging: mostly stage 2 but stage 3 is common
F. Differential diagnosis: unicameral bone cyst, giant cell tumor, or malignant tumors, such as fibrosarcoma, malignant fibrous histiocytoma, and telangiectatic osteosarcoma

IV. Treatment
A. Curettage alone gives high recurrence (30%), and therefore marginal extracapsular excision with bone grafting is preferred
B. Curettage and adjunctive cryotherapy, methyl methacrylate (especially older patients and large lesions), or bone graft (autogenous and allograft) can be used in selected cases. Curettage should be aggressive, using a large window, high-speed burr, water pick lavage, and local phenol may be used as an adjuvant

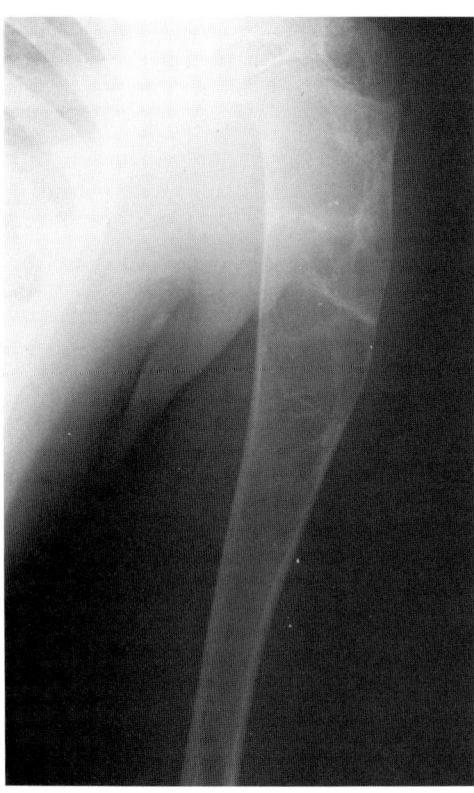

Figure 2-18. Roentgenographic appearance of an active unicameral bone cyst, showing eccentric lucency in the metaphysis of the proximal humerus with cortical thinning.

HEMANGIOMA

I. General Considerations
A. Age: one third in the 5th decades
B. Sex: females > males
C. Location: two thirds in calvarium or vertebrae
D. Gorham's disease: hemangioma-like proliferation in bone or "disappearing bone" disease

II. Pathology
A. Widely dilated channels with flattened endothelial cells or conglomerations of small vessels

B. Histology may be confused with low-grade sarcoma or hematomous malformation

III. Diagnosis
A. Many are asymptomatic
B. Local pain, particularly with compression fracture of vertebra
C. X-ray: osteopenic lesion with exaggerated vertical striation in the vertebrae
C. CT scan: honeycomb appearance
D. Angiogram: may reveal increased vascularity and feeding vessels

IV. Treatment
A. Curettage and grafting in symptomatic lesions
B. Vascularity makes any procedure hazardous
C. Preoperative embolization should be considered
D. Radiation treatment for inaccessible lesions

UNICAMERAL BONE CYST

I. General Considerations
A. Age: active (<10 years), latent (>10 years)
B. Location: metaphyseal adjacent to epiphyseal plate or physis (especially proximal humerus, proximal and distal femur, and proximal tibia and fibula) and migrate away with time
C. Pathologic fractures are common

II. Pathology
A. Fluid-filled lesion lined by a fibrous membrane
B. Etiology: unknown (may be secondary to aberrant growth of bone at the epiphyseal plate from trauma)
C. As the bone grows, cyst "migrates" away from the epiphyseal plate
D. Some heal spontaneously 25% in active cysts

III. Diagnosis
A. Asymptomatic unless pathologic fracture occurs
B. X-ray: elongated eccentric lucency in the metaphysis with reactive rim. Cortical thinning in active cysts (Fig 2-19)
C. Active versus latent
  1. Active
     a. Less than 8 years of age
     b. Abutting the epiphyseal plate (<1 cm)
     c. X-ray: single cavity with cortical thinning but not larger than the physeal width
     d. Cyst aspiration pressure: >30 cm H_2O and pulsatile column and increases with valsalva maneuver
     e. Venography: quick venous filling and clearing in 1–2 minutes
     f. Bone scan: increased uptake
     g. Histology: thin shiny membrane with few histiocytes and little hemosiderin and osteoclasts
  2. Latent
     a. Age: >8 years
     b. Located away from the epiphyseal plate
     c. X-ray: multiloculated cavity with thick cortical margin similar to aneurysmal bone cyst (remodeled around the lesion as opposed to abrupt expansile lesions, such as eosinophilic granuloma and osteomyelitis)
     d. Cyst aspiration pressure: 6–10 cm H_2O
     e. Venography: nonpulsatile and slow filling and clearing of the dye
     f. Bone scan: negative
     g. Histology: thick membrane with frequent giant cells, hemosiderin, cholesterol slits, and osteoclasts
D. Differential diagnosis
  1. Fibrous dysplasia: blending of the lesion to the cortical rim with ground-glass appearance
  2. Aneurysmal bone cyst: dilation of

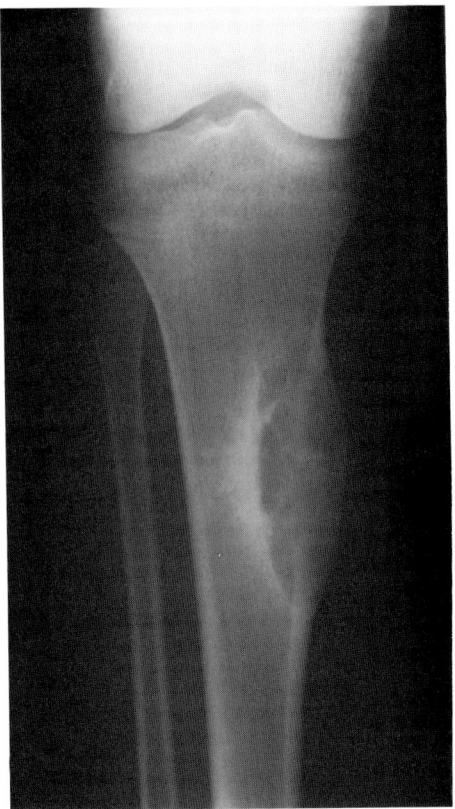

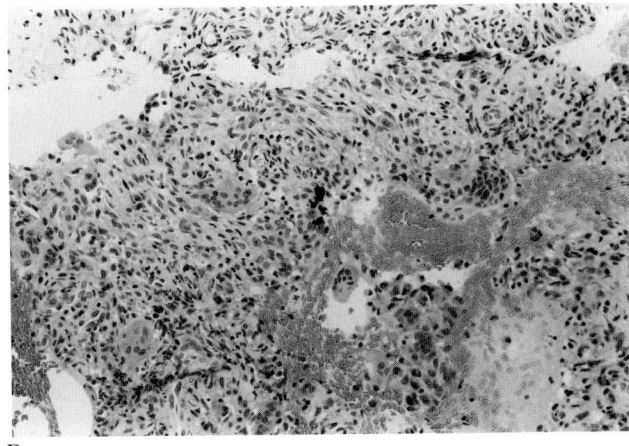

Figure 2-19. **A.** Roentgenographic appearance of an eccentric aneurysmal bone cyst, showing lytic and expansile processes. **B.** Low-power field histologic examination shows vascular lakes containing red blood cells and giant cells with admixture of immature bone and mesenchymal tissue.

bone with region of the lesion wider than the width of physis

IV. Treatment

A. Methylprednisolone: 80–200 mg (40 mg/cc) and may repeat a few times (15–50% recurrence in active cysts and 0% in latent cysts, overall, 85% healing in 12 months)
   1. Two-needle technique
   2. Renografin injection
   3. Pressurized injection of steroid
   4. Repeat up to two to three times until increased density seen on x-ray every 4–6 months
B. Curettage and bone graft:
   1. Recurrent cases despite corticosteroids
   2. If jeopardy of fracture because of location, patient activity
   3. 30–50% recurrence in active cysts and 0% in latent cysts
C. Treat pathologic fractures first
D. Observation in typical calcaneus cyst and most mature resolving latent cysts

GIANT CELL TUMOR

I. General Considerations

A. Age: 85% after 19 years old and peak at 3rd decade
B. Sex: females > males (3:2)
C. Location: secondary ossification centers after physeal closure (especially knee, distal radius, ulna, sacrum, ilium); sometimes multicentric variant

II. Pathology

A. Benign locally aggressive lesion of bone (unknown origin and wide spectrum)

B. Distant pulmonary metastasis may occur (2%)
C. Gray (necrotic tissue and histiocytes) to red-brown (viable stroma and giant cells) lesion, abutting subchondral bone plate and may show cystic changes
D. Destroys articular cartilage

III. Diagnosis

A. Aching pain, local swelling, tenderness, limitation of motion, and a limp
B. X-ray: lytic and eccentric in the subarticular portion of the bone with no sclerosis at margins and rare periosteal reaction (Fig 2-20). Grades (Campanacci): 1, intraosseous; 2, erosion of the cortex; and 3, broken through the cortex
C. Bone scan: homogenously increased
D. Angiogram: hypervascular
E. Histology
   1. Cellular stroma (giant cells and mononuclear cells with nuclei of identical appearance) of fibrous connective tissue with vascularity and areas of necrosis and histiocytes
   2. Histology similar to hyperparathyroidism
   3. Grading: not reliable and clinical correlation is poor
F. Staging: more reliable, 15% stage 1, 70% stage 2, and 15% stage 3

IV. Treatment

A. Stage 1: aggressive curettage and removal of reactive bone (recurrence is 5%)
B. Stage 2: marginal to en bloc excision or aggressive curettage with cryotherapy, methyl methacrylate, or phenol and alcohol (30% recurrence with curettage alone)
C. Stage 3: wide en bloc excision (70–80% recurrence with curettage alone)
D. Adjunct radiation treatment in inaccessible area
E. Complete excision of fibula, ulna, ribs, hand and foot, and distal tibia (difficult for limb salvage)
F. Wide excision of pulmonary metastasis
G. Treat fractures first, followed by neoplasm

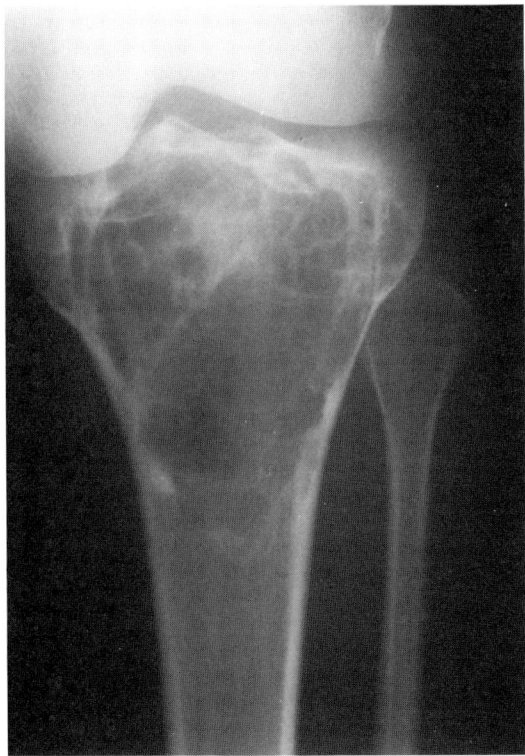

Figure 2-20. Roentgenographic appearance of typical giant cell tumor showing lytic lesion in the subarticular region with little sclerosis or periosteal reaction.

HISTIOCYTOSIS X

I. General Considerations

A. Age: eosinophilic granuloma (first 3 decades especially 5–10 years), Hand-Schüller-Christian disease (5–10 years), and Letterer-Siwe disease (<3 years)
B. Sex: males > females
C. Location: eosinophilic granuloma (single or occasionally multiple bones, including skull, spine, femur, flat bones, ribs, and mandible), Hand-Schüller-Christian (jaw with loose teeth and skull), and Letterer-Siwe (no bony lesion)

D. Pathogenesis: unknown cause with no evidence of metabolic, lipid storage, or hereditary pattern

II. Pathology
A. Eosinophilic granuloma: benign bony lesion with good prognosis and self-healing potential
B. Hand-Schüller-Christian disease: skeletal and visceral involvement (splenohepatomegaly, lymphadenopathy, and anemia) and classic triad of exophthalmos, diabetes insipidus, and bony lesions
C. Letterer-Siwe disease: acute fulminating disease with poor prognosis

III. Diagnosis
A. Local bone pain in eosinophilic granuloma and systemic signs in Hand-Schüller-Christian and Letterer-Siwe diseases
B. X-ray: radiolucent bone defects with expansion and endosteal scalloping (no smooth remodeling as seen in latent unicameral bone cyst)
C. Bone scan may be normal
D. Histology: histiocytes, eosinophils, and Birbeck granule on electron microscopy
E. Differential diagnosis: osteomyelitis, Ewing's tumor, and unicameral bone cysts

IV. Treatment
A. Eosinophilic granuloma: observation or incisional biopsy and optional corticosteroid injection (curettage and bone grafting not necessary in most isolated lesions)
B. Hand-Schüller-Christian and Letterer-Siwe diseases: chemotherapy
C. Consider low dose radiation treatment in inaccessible lesions that are progressive

BONE INFARCT

I. General Considerations
A. Common
B. Etiology: trauma, dysbarism, sickle cell disease, corticosteroid therapy, alcohol abuse, idiopathic
C. Locations: femoral head, humeral head, femoral condyle talus, carpal navicular, and metaphysis of long bones

II. Pathology
A. Dense, white, chalky hard area of heavy trabecular bone firmly embedded within normal cancellous bone
B. Malignant degeneration: infarct becomes loose, enveloped by malignant tissue

III. Diagnosis
A. Asymptomatic in metaphysis unless malignant degeneration occurs
B. X-ray: irregular increased density with sharp transition
C. Bone scan: slight increased uptake in the periphery
D. Malignant transformation possible: symptomatic, osteolytic, increased uptake on bone scan, neovascularity on angiogram and tumor mass on CT scan (usually stage II fibrosarcoma or malignant fibrous histiocytoma)
E. Histology: empty lacunae in the necrotic bone with areas of calcified acellular fibrous tissue
F. Differential diagnosis: enchondroma, chondrosarcoma

IV. Treatment
A. Observation
B. Malignant degeneration should be managed according to staging studies

MASTOCYTOSIS

I. General Considerations
A. Age: 50% are less than 6 months old, 25% are adolescents, and 25% are adults
B. Rare

II. Pathology
A. Proliferative disorder of mast cells
B. Urticaria pigmentosa (pruritic rash, pigmented and urticaria)
C. Systemic involvement: rare but may af-

fect the liver, lymph nodes, spleen, skeleton, and gastrointestinal tract

III. Diagnosis
A. Skin lesion: urticaria pigmentosa
B. Asymptomatic skeletal involvement: 10% with uticaria pigmentosa and 70% with systemic mastocytosis (skull, vertebrae, pelvis, and ends of long bones) — no destructive changes and no pathologic fractures
C. X-ray: irregular patches of increased density or oval radiolucencies surrounded by sclerotic halo
D. Histology: a small cell infiltrate and fibrosis of the marrow, metachromatic cytoplasmic granules in mast cells under high magnification or special staining

IV. Treatment
A. Observation for skeletal lesions
B. Thirty percent die of leukemia in 5 years

FIBROSARCOMA OF BONE

I. General Considerations
A. Rare
B. Age: adolescence to middle age
C. Location: metaphysis and shaft of long bones and occasionally flat bones
D. More common in the soft tissue than in the bone

II. Pathology
A. Low-grade, more common than aggressive
B. May be associated with old infarct, fibrous dysplasia, or irradiation
C. Twenty-five percent 5-year survival

III. Diagnosis
A. Pain and pathologic fractures
B. X-ray: nondiagnostic mottled erosion with soft tissue extension with poor margins (similar to metastatic or marrow cell tumors or osteogenic sarcoma)
C. Histology: sheets of immature mesenchymal cells from low (stage I) to high grade (stage II), but intermediate grade is staged according to clinical and x-ray findings
D. Stage: over 50% as IIB

IV. Treatment
A. Stage I: wide resection
B. Stage II: Radical resection
C. Wide resection plus adjuvant radiation may be considered

MALIGNANT FIBROUS HISTIOCYTOMA

I. General Considerations
A. Formerly known as high-grade or undifferentiated fibrosarcoma
B. Age: similar to fibrosarcoma and older age group associated with Paget's disease and infarcts
C. More ominous prognosis than fibrosarcoma

II. Pathology
A. Aggressive fibrous tumor
B. Malignant fibroblasts and histiocytes in a storiform pattern and anaplasia

III. Diagnosis
A. Pain and aggressive clinical progression
B. X-ray: permeative lesion with destruction (Fig 2-21)
C. Bone scan: increased uptake beyond the x-ray margin
D. Angiogram: nodal involvement and soft tissue extension
E. Histology: storiform collagen, foamy histiocytes, and bizarre undifferentiated spindle cells
F. Stage: mostly IIB

IV. Treatment
A. Radical margin
B. Wide margin with adjunctive radiation or chemotherapy

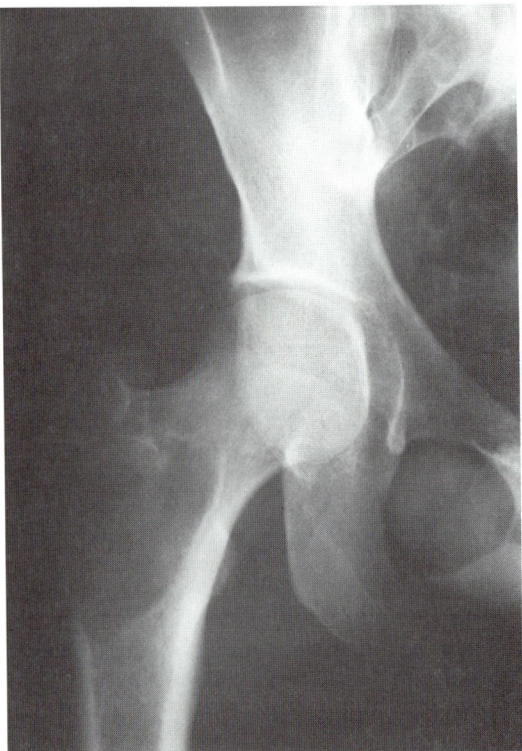

Figure 2-21. Roentgenographic appearance of malignant fibrous histiocytoma, showing permeative lesion with poor margins.

CHONDROSARCOMA

I. General Considerations
A. Age: adult to old age
B. Location: flat bones of pelvis and shoulder girdle and proximal humerus and femur

II. Pathology
A. Malignant lesions of cartilage cells (large cauliflower-like mass of glistening cartilage)
B. Primary versus secondary
  1. Primary: older age group, flat bones and low to high grades
  2. Secondary: younger age group, 5 to 25% from multiple exostosis and 85% low grade
C. Central versus peripheral: peripheral has better prognosis
D. Variants
  1. Mesenchymal: high grade, 2nd or 3rd decades, osteolytic and hemangiopericytoid and chondroid bimorphic pattern on histologic examination, poor prognosis
  2. Dedifferentiated: very aggressive and poor prognosis
  3. Clear cell: old epiphyseal and metaphyseal, osteolytic with histologic clear cells
E. Metastasis late but local invasion is the rule

III. Diagnosis
A. Local pain or swelling (insidious onset)
B. X-ray: endosteal scalloping, uneven calcification, and bone destruction (Fig 2-22A)
C. Bone scan: if cold bone scan changes to hot, malignant transformation is suspected
D. Angiogram, CT scan, and MRI for soft tissue extension and malignant transformation (Fig 2-22B)
E. Histology
  1. Difficult to distinguish low-grade malignancy from aggressive benign cartilage lesions (must correlate with clinical and radiographic findings)
  2. Cellularity, mitotic figures, and double nuclei are suggestive of malignancy (Fig. 2-22C)

IV. Treatment
A. Wide surgical margin
B. No chemotherapy or radiation

OSTEOSARCOMA

I. General Considerations
A. Age: second decade except secondary to Paget's and radiation
B. Sex: males > females
C. Location: 50% around the knee, metaphysis
D. Second most common malignant tumor of bone after multiple myeloma

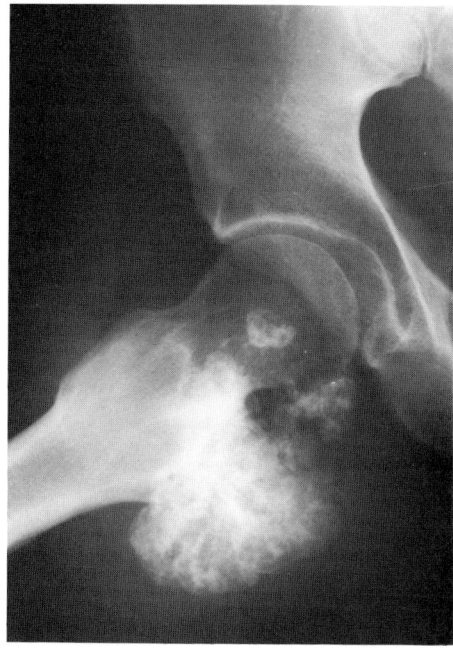

Figure 2-22. A. Roentgenographic appearance of chondrosarcoma showing destructive process with characteristic flocculent calcification. **B.** Computed tomography scan of chondrosarcoma defines the bony destruction and soft tissue extension. **C.** High-power field histologic examination shows poor differentiated malignant cells with mitosis.

II. Pathology

A. Spindle cell stroma with osteoid bone formation
B. Flesh area with vascularity and hemorrhage
C. Local invasion to normal tissue
D. Distant metastasis common
E. Types and variants
   1. Conventional
      a. Osteoblastic
      b. Chondroblastic
      c. Fibroblastic
   2. Clinical variants: jaw, post-irradiation, Paget's sarcoma, multifocal
   3. Morphological variants
      a. Well-differentiated intraosseous osteosarcoma
      b. Osteosarcoma resembling osteoblastoma
      c. Telangiectatic osteosarcoma
      d. Small cell osteosarcoma
   4. Surface variants
      a. Parosteal
      b. Dedifferentiated parosteal
      c. Periosteal
      d. High grade surface osteosarcoma
   5. Telangiectatic osteosarcoma
   6. Paget's sarcoma: 15–20% of polyostotic Paget's disease, 6th–7th decades, and poor prognosis
   7. Radiation-induced osteosarcoma: poor prognosis
   8. Jaw osteosarcoma
   9. Low-grade well-differentiated intraos-

seous osteosarcoma: 20–30 years of age, usually stage IA
10. Small cell osteosarcoma

III. Diagnosis: Conventional Type

A. Pain, swelling, and enlarging mass
B. X-ray: destructive (lytic and sclerotic) and ill-defined margins. Breaks through the cortex and soft tissue invasion. "Sunburst" (tumor bone) and Codman's triangle (periosteal elevation) and "onion skinning" (reactive bone). (Fig 2-23A)
C. CT scan, tomogram, bone scan, MRI, and angiogram are helpful (Fig 2-23B)
D. Laboratory: alkaline phosphatase and antisarcoma antibody
E. Biopsy: incisional (malignant spindle stromal cells with numerous mitosis with osteoid) (Fig 2-23C)
F. Staging: mostly IIB

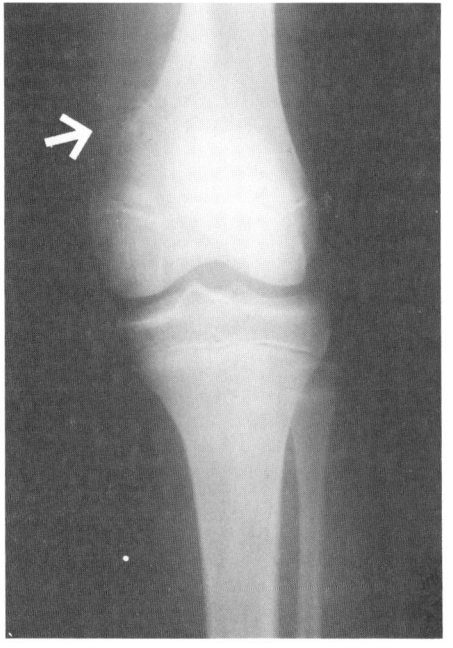
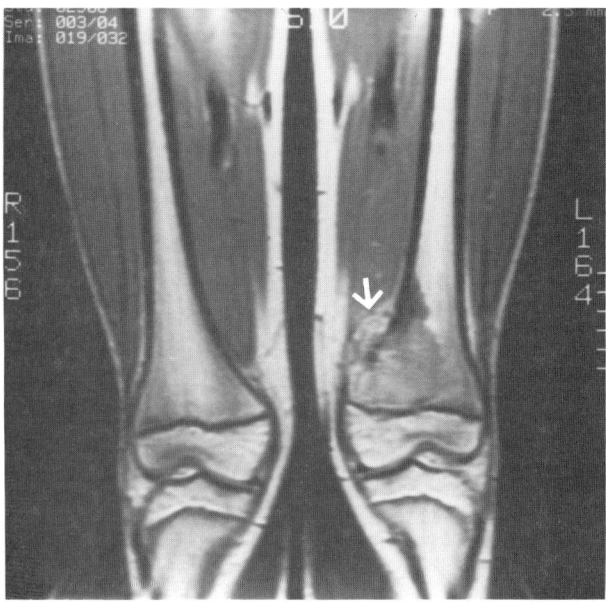
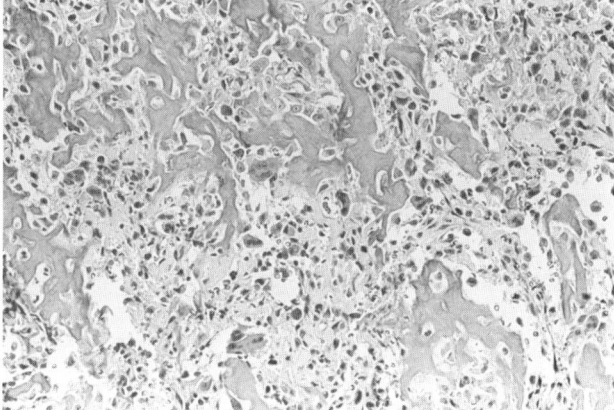

Figure 2-23. A. Roentgenographic appearance of osteosarcoma, showing destructive process with ill-defined margins (arrow). **B.** Magnetic resonance imaging shows soft tissue extension. **C.** Low-power histologic examination shows undifferentiated spindle stromal cells and mitosis with osteoid seam.

IV. Treatment
A. Wide resection (limb salvage) or radical amputation or disarticulation
B. Adjuvant or neoadjuvant chemotherapy (50–60% 5-year survival)

EWING'S SARCOMA

I. General Considerations
A. Age: common during the 2nd decade
B. Sex: males are slightly more affected
C. Location: any bone but more common in long tubular bones, especially fibula, femur, tibia, and flat bones
D. Rare in blacks

II. Pathology
A. A round cell sarcoma (medullary stem cell as origin)
B. Grayish white tumor mass involving the marrow space and haversian canals with soft tissue extracortical mass
C. Intense periosteal reactive bone (Codman's triangle)
D. Metastasis via bloodstream (15% metastasis at onset)

III. Diagnosis
A. Pain, swelling, tenderness, fever, leukocytosis, and elevated ESR
B. X-ray: lytic destruction, extension through the cortex, and multiple layers of subperiosteal reactive new bone ("onion skin") (Fig 2-24A)
C. Bone scan: increased uptake beyond the x-ray margins
D. Angiogram: hypervascular reaction and neoplastic vasculature
E. CT scan or MRI: soft tissue extension
F. Histology: sheets of small uniform cells (pseudorosettes) with inconspicuous nucleoli and little stroma (glycogen granule

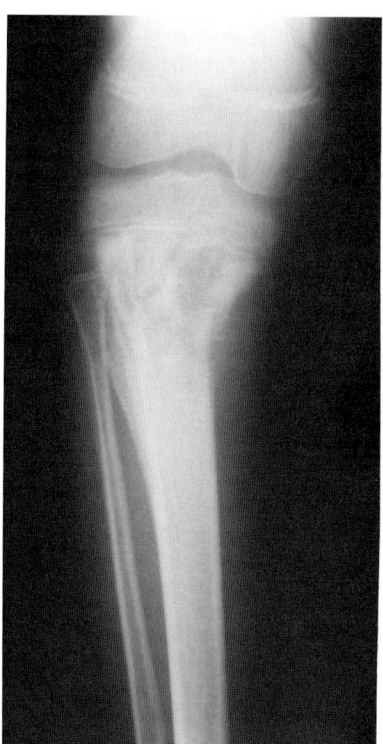
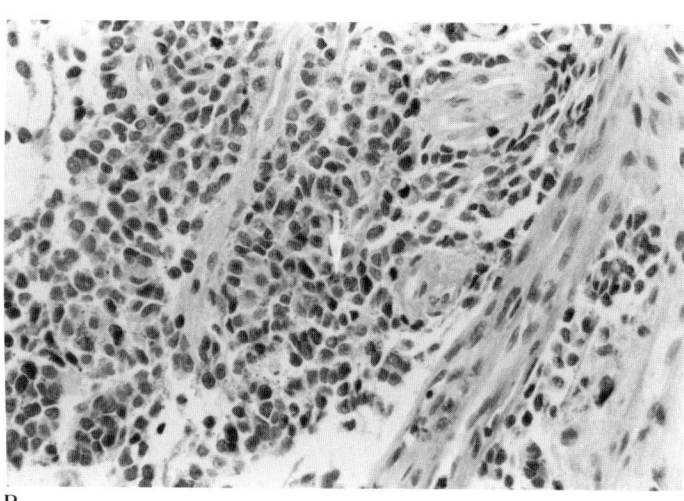

Figure 2-24. **A.** Roentgenographic appearance of Ewing's sarcoma, showing destruction, extension through the cortex, and periosteal reactive new bone. **B.** Periodic acid–Schiff staining shows sheets of small uniform cells (pseudorosettes), little stroma, and glycogen granule (arrow).

and periodic acid–Schiff stain positive) (Fig 2-24B)
G. Electron microscopy: intracytoplasmic glycogen granules
H. Staging: mostly solitary extraosseous (IIB) but occasionally present with multicentric or distant metastasis
I. Differential diagnosis
   1. Clinical: osteomyelitis, osteosarcoma
   2. Histology
      a. Neuroblastoma: < 5 years of age, rosette cells
      b. Lymphoma (reticulum cell sarcoma): no glycogen and no intercellular junction on electron microscopy
      c. Small cell osteosarcoma: osteoid and positive alkaline phosphatase stain
      d. Rhabdomyosarcoma: positive actin and myosin
      e. Eosinophilic granuloma: histiocytes and eosinophils and lacks malignant features

IV. Treatment
A. Multiagent chemotherapy
B. Radiation treatment
   1. Dose of 4000–6000 rads in areas inaccessible, such as spine, pelvis, and trunk
   2. Lesions where amputations would be necessary to obtain wide or radical margins
   3. Radiation-induced sarcoma after 5 years may be as high as 40%
C. Surgery
   1. Chemotherapy and surgery
      a. Expendable areas, such as fibula, rib, clavicle and pelvis
      b. Amputation: children with distal femur physeal involvement, very large lesions, pathologic fractures, and recurrence after radiation treatment
      c. Primary excision (wide or radical margin) plus chemotherapy
   2. Chemotherapy, radiation, and adjunctive surgery
      a. Pelvis, spine lesions
      b. Multicentric or disseminated lesions
      c. Primary excision (marginal resection) plus radiation and chemotherapy
D. Prognosis: 40–50% 5-year survival, but worse in males, younger children, pelvis involvement, and in patients with metastasis

LYMPHOMA OF BONE

I. General Considerations
A. Histiocytic lymphoma or recticulum sarcoma
B. Age: middle age to elderly
C. Sex: males > females
D. Location: pelvis, proximal femur, rib, and distal femur

II. Pathology
A. Histiocytic origin
B. Forty percent of all lymphomas of bone arise from bone

III. Diagnosis
A. Pain and swelling
B. X-ray: diffuse, permeative, and destructive lesion with small amount of reactive bone
C. Laboratory examination: complete blood count and blood smear, ESR, lymphangiography, CT scan, and bone marrow aspirate should be done to rule out other lymphomas and leukemia and staging
D. Histology: masses of large, bizarre, and polymorphic cells with frequent mitosis and foamy appearance (reticular network by special staining)
E. Other hematopoietic tumors
   1. Hodgkin's disease
   2. Malignant lymphoma (lymphoblastic lymphosarcoma)
   3. Leukemia: microscopic bony infiltration

IV. Treatment
A. Radiation treatment

B. Chemotherapy in disseminated lesions
C. Surgery in expendable areas, pathologic fractures and acetabular reconstruction (cement), followed by chemotherapy or radiation

MYELOMA

I. General Considerations
A. Age: rare before 5th decade
B. Sex: males more affected than females
C. Location: vertebrae, skull, thoracic cage, pelvis, proximal humerus, and femur
D. Most common primary bony malignancy

II. Pathology
A. Plasma cell malignancy involving bone marrow
B. Overproduction of monoclonal immunoglobulins
C. Types
   1. Multiple myeloma (most common)
   2. Solitary plasmacytoma (25%)
   3. Extramedullary plasmacytomas (usually upper airway and oral cavity)

III. Diagnosis
A. Skeletal pain (back pain and pathologic fractures)
B. Anemia, hypercalcemia, impaired renal function, infection, and amyloidosis
C. Laboratory findings: anemia, hypercalcemia, increased ESR (>50 mm/hr), rouleou formation of erythrocytes on peripheral smear, gamma-globulin peak on serum electrophoresis (85%), Bence Jones proteinuria (50%), immunoelectrophoresis (light versus heavy chain myeloma), and positive bone marrow aspirate (92%)
D. X-ray: multiple osteolytic lesions ("punched out" lesions), osteoporosis, vertebral collapse (pedicles are usually preserved initially as opposed to metastasis) (Fig 2-25)
E. Bone scan: usually negative unless pathologic fractures occur
F. Angiogram: hypervascular in the periphery
G. Histology: plasma cells (eccentrically located nuclei with a characteristic clumped, chromatin pattern that produces a cartwheel pattern) and little stroma and occasional amyloid

IV. Treatment
A. Radiation (pain and localized tumor) and chemotherapy (cyclophosphamide and prednisone)
B. Surgery: compressive paraplegia, impending or actual pathologic fractures

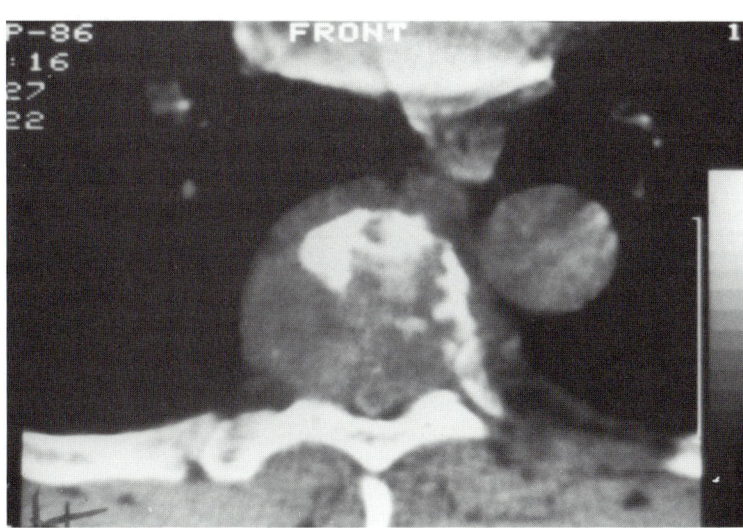

Figure 2-25. Computed tomography scan of multiple myeloma arising from the vertebral body with extension to the pedicles and spinal canal.

NEUROBLASTOMA

I. General Considerations
A. Age: usually <3 years old
B. Sex: males more frequently affected than females
C. Location: skull, spine, and long bones

II. Pathology
A. Arise from the adrenal medulla or sympathetic tissue
B. Skeletal metastasis usually bilateral and symmetrical

III. Diagnosis
A. Usually with known neuroblastoma with skeletal metastasis later
B. X-ray: destructive lesion similar to Ewing's sarcoma or osteomyelitis or diffuse osteoporosis
C. Laboratory findings: urinary excretion of catecholamine
D. Histology: small round cells in rosette

IV. Treatment
A. Excision of tumor
B. Radiation and chemotherapy

GIANT CELL SARCOMA

I. General Considerations
A. Age: 3rd and 4th decades
B. Sex: more frequently in males
C. Location: epiphyseal regions of the major long bones

II. Pathology
A. Malignant sarcoma from the onset (not as malignant transformation from the benign giant cell tumor)
B. Destructive and invasive malignant tumor penetrating the cortex, soft tissue, and joint

III. Diagnosis
A. Rapidly growing mass with pain and occasional fractures
B. X-ray: large, radiolucent and poorly marginated lesion with early extension to cortex and soft tissue (Fig 2-26)
C. Bone scan: intense uptake beyond the x-ray lesion
D. Angiogram: intralesional and reactive neovasculature
E. Histology: malignant spindle cells with mitotic figures and multinucleated giant cells (giant cells are smaller and more uniform in size compared to benign giant cells)

IV. Treatment
A. Radical margin
B. Wide margin plus radiation and chemotherapy

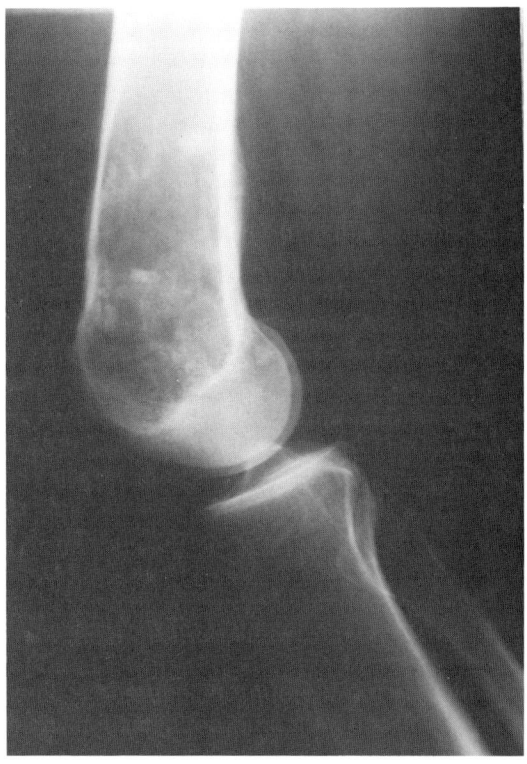

Figure 2-26. Roentgenographic appearance of giant cell sarcoma in the distal femur, showing radiolucent and poorly marginated lesion extension to cortex and soft tissue.

CHORDOMA

I. General Considerations
A. Age: young adults
B. Sex: males more frequently affected
C. Location: midline of the spine, especially in the sacrum and base of the skull

II. Pathology
A. Arise from the remnants of the notochord
B. Slow, indolent growth and many years before metastasis
C. Gelatinous, grayish white vascular material, displacing the surrounding tissue and invasion later

III. Diagnosis
A. Chronic intermittent low-back pain, neurologic signs, urinary and sphincter dysfunction, and palpable mass on rectal examination
B. X-ray: radiolucent defect in the sacrum with minimal reactive bone
C. CT scan and MRI: assess anatomic extent of the lesion (commonly invade neural canal and extradural space) (Fig 2-27)
D. Myelogram: extradural extension
E. Angiogram: hypervascular
F. Histology: great masses of large cells with definite cell membrane with clear cytoplasm, small central nucleus (physilliferous cells similar to target cells)
G. Staging: usually IB
H. Differential diagnosis: giant cell tumor, aneurysmal bone cyst, metastatic hypernephroma, and chondrosarcoma

IV. Treatment
A. Wide surgical resection
B. The first surgery is the best time for good success, and adequate excision is necessary without too much regard to the nerve roots
   1. One stage: posterior, small low lesion
   2. Two stages: anterior excision with ligation of internal iliac artery, followed by posterior incision

ADAMANTINOMA

I. General Considerations
A. Age: early adulthood
B. Sex: males more common
C. Location: anterior cortex of the middle third of the tibia and occasionally jaw and fibula
D. Rare

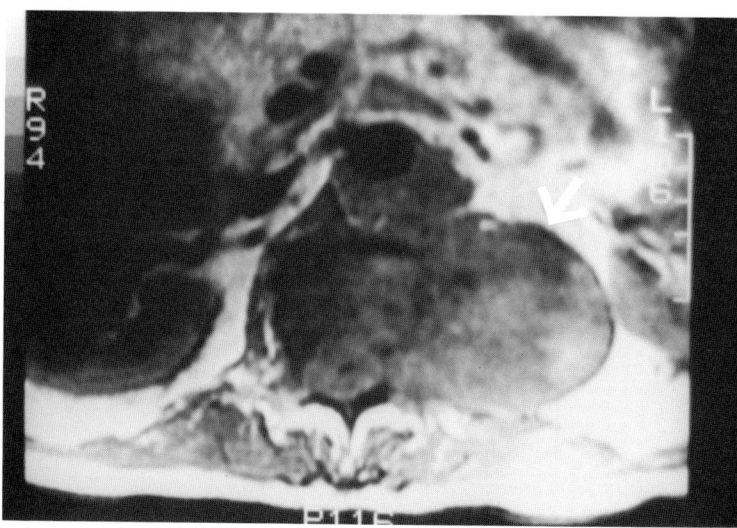

Figure 2-27. Magnetic resonance imaging of chordoma at L1 vertebra, showing intraspinal as well as large extraspinal extensions (arrow).

II. Pathology
A. Unknown origin
B. Slow-growing malignancy

III. Diagnosis
A. Slow-growing mass with modest discomfort
B. X-ray: a long, shallow, craterlike, radiolucent defect in the anterior aspect of the tibia, marginated by a thin shell of subperiosteal reactive bone (diagnostic)
C. CT and bone scan: extension of the lesion for surgical planning
D. Histology: cords of epithelial-like cells in pseudoglandular pattern in a background stroma of spindle cells
E. Stage: usually IB

IV. Treatment
A. Wide surgical margin
　1. Wide resection if no intramedullary extension
　2. Segmental resection or amputation if intramedullary extension
B. No radiation or chemotherapy

METASTATIC BONE DISEASE

I. General Considerations
A. Most common tumors: lung, breast, prostate, kidney, thyroid
B. Most common sites: vertebrae, pelvis, femur, ribs, skull (70% of cancer patients have osseous metastasis at autopsy)
C. Metastasis by arterial or venous (Batson's plexus)

II. Diagnosis
A. Clinical suspicion if constant pain in the bone or vertebral column
B. X-rays may be negative initially: prostate metastasis is usually osteoblastic (Fig 2-28A,B), lung, renal, and thyroid tumors

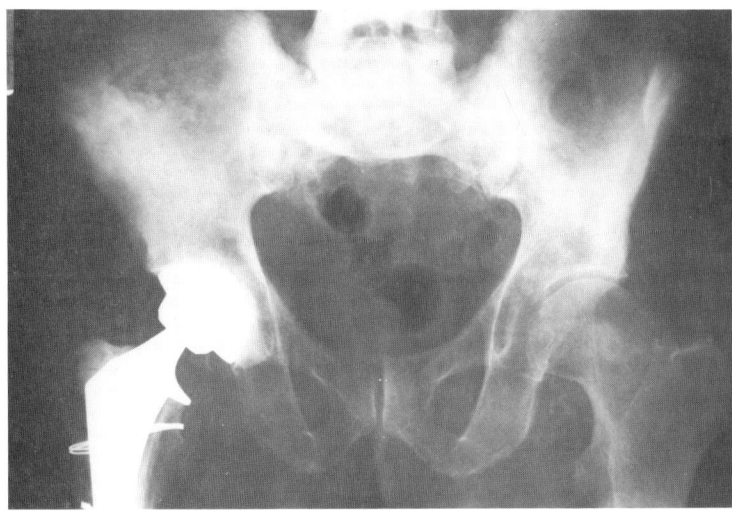
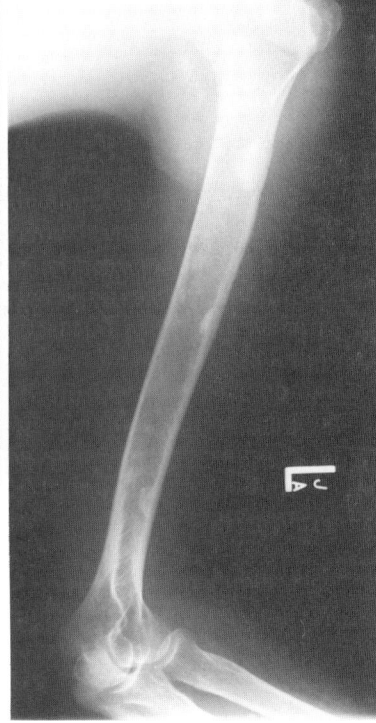

Figure 2-28. A. Roentgenographic appearance of prostate metastasis to the pelvis. **B.** Osteoblastic metastasis to the humerus secondary to prostate carcinoma.

are primarily osteolytic with variable osteoblastic response. Breast carcinoma may be osteoblastic or osteolytic
C. Bone scan is quite helpful to assess areas of involvement
D. CT scan or MRI: helpful in the spine or sacrum
E. Biopsy: unless the diagnosis is certain, biopsy should be done prior to treatment

III. Treatment

A. Medical and radiation oncology consultation
B. Radiation therapy is particularly helpful for pain relief and myelopathy cases, in which the structural stability is not of concern
C. Prophylactic fixation
  1. Intractable pain despite radiation treatment
  2. Osteolytic lesion more than 3 cm in diameter and 50% cortex is destroyed in the lower extremity
D. Pathologic fractures: most patients deserve stable fixation and early mobilization to make rest of their life as comfortable as possible
E. Vertebral involvement
  1. Pain with or without neurologic involvement: radiation treatment and bracing if no structural deformity or no bony impingement
  2. Neurologic involvement: anterior corpectomy and stabilization (anterior, or both anterior and posterior) if resistant to radiation or bony deformity
  3. Palliative treatment for patients with neurologic involvement with limited life span: posterior laminectomy, transpedicular decompression, and posterior stabilization

REFERENCES

Bogmill GP, Shwamm HA: *Orthopaedic pathology.* Philadelphia, WB Saunders, 1984

Boland PJ, Lane JM, Sundaresan N: Metastatic disease of the spine. Clin Orthop 169:95, 1982

Bullough PG, Vigorta VJ: *Atlas of orthopaedic pathology.* Baltimore, University Park Press, 1984

Campanacci M, Capanna R, Picci P: Unicameral and aneurysmal bone cysts. Clin Orthop 204:25–36, 1986

Dahlin DC: *Bone tumors: General aspects and data on 6221 cases,* ed 3. Springfield, Ill, Charles C Thomas, 1978

Eckhardt JJ, Grogan TJ: Giant cell tumor of bone. Clin Orthop 204:45–58, 1986

Enneking WF: A system of staging musculoskeletal neoplasms. Clin Orthop 204:9–24, 1986

Enneking WF: *Musculoskeletal tumor surgery.* New York, Churchill Livingstone, 1983

Enneking WF, Spanier SS, Goodman MA: A system for the surgical staging of musculoskeletal sarcoma. Clin Orthop 153:106, 1980

Frassica FJ, Unni KK, Beaubout J, Sim FH: Dedifferentiated chondrosarcoma: A report of the clinicopathologic features and treatment of seventy-eight cases. J Bone Joint Surg 68A:1197–1205, 1986

Harrington KD: Current concepts review. Metastatic disease of the spine. J Bone Joint Surg 68A:1110, 1986

Harrington KD: The management of acetabular insufficiency secondary to metastatic malignant disease. J Bone Joint Surg 63A:653, 1981

Harrington KD: Metastatic diseases of bone. In Chapman MW, ed. *Operative orthopaedics,* vol 2. Philadelphia, JB Lippincott, 1988

Healy JH, Ghelman B: Osteoid osteoma and osteoblastoma. Current concepts and recent advances. Clin Orthop 204:76–86, 1986

Huvos A: *Bone tumors: Diagnosis, treatment and prognosis.* Philadelphia, WB Saunders, 1979

Huvos A, Marcove RC: Chondroblastoma of bone. A critical review. Clin Orthop 95:300–312, 1973

Johnston JO: Principles of limb salvage surgery. In Chapman MW, ed. *Operative orthopaedics,* vol 2. Philadelphia, JB Lippincott, 1988, pp 893–909

Lane JM, Duane K, Glasser DB: Benign bone tumors. In Chapman MW, ed. *Operative orthopaedics,* vol 2. Philadelphia, JB Lippincott, 1988, pp 929–940

Lane JM, Hurson B, Boland PJ, Glasser DB: Osteogenic sarcoma. Clin Orthop 204:93, 1986

Li WK, Lane JM, Roen G, et al: Pelvic Ewing's sarcoma: Advances in treatment. J Bone Joint Surg 65A:738–747, 1983

Localio SA, Eng K, Ranson JHC: Abdominosacral approach for tetrorectal tumors. Ann Surg 191:555–559, 1980

Makley JJ, Carter JR: Eosinophilic granuloma of bone. Clin Orthop 204:37–44, 1986

Mankin HJ, Lange TA, Spannier SS: The hazards of biopsy in patients with malignant primary bone and soft tissue tumors. J Bone Joint Surg 64A:1121, 1982

Moon NF, Mori H: Adamantinoma of the appendicular skeleton — updated. Clin Orthop 204:215–237, 1986

Pritchard DJ, Dahlin DC, Dauphine RT, et al: Ewing's sarcoma: A clinicopathological and statistical analysis of patients surviving five years or longer. J Bone Joint Surg 57A:10–16, 1975

Shives TC: Clinical evaluation, biopsy, and staging of bone tumors. In Chapman MW, ed. *Operative orthopaedics,* vol 2. Philadelphia, JB Lippincott, 1988, pp 887–892

Sim FH: *Diagnosis and treatment of bone tumors: A team approach* (Mayo Clinic Monograph). Thorofare, NJ, Slack, 1983

Sim FH, McDonald DJ, Wold LE: Malignant bone tumors. In Chapman MW, ed. *Operative orthopaedics,* vol 2. Philadelphia, JB Lippincott, 1988, pp 941–958

Simon MA: Biopsy of musculoskeletal tumors. J Bone Joint Surg 64A:1253, 1982

21
Genetics

I. General Considerations

A. There are three major mechanisms for the production of genetic abnormalities
   1. Chromosomal imbalance such as Down syndrome (trisomy 21), Turner's syndrome (XO), and Kleinfelter's syndrome (XXY), polydactyly in trisomy 13, radioulnar synostosis in multiple X syndromes, vertical talus in trisomy 18, and clubfeet in several of the deletion syndromes
   2. Gene mutation: genes that change their characteristics, giving rise to new genes
   3. Polygenic mechanisms: multifactorial and familial tendency, such as congenital dislocation of the hip, clubfoot, and scoliosis
B. Congenital means only that it is present at birth and does not imply a genetic cause
C. Many genetic diseases are not apparent at birth

II. Inheritance Patterns

A. Autosomal dominant pedigree
   1. Condition is manifest in the heterozygous state
   2. Fifty percent of offspring are affected, with no sex preference
   3. Normal offspring do not transmit the condition
   4. Male to male transmission is required to confirm this pattern of inheritance
   5. Every affected person will have at least one affected parent
   6. In general, dominant traits tend to cause structural deformities with less functional loss than recessive traits
   7. There is considerable variation in expressivity
B. Autosomal recessive inheritance
   1. The homozygous state demonstrates the condition
   2. Parents are unaffected, who are heterozygous for a single mutant gene
   3. Twenty-five percent of the offspring will be affected with no sex preference, but 50% will be heterozygous carriers of the gene
   4. Classically, a single enzymatic deficiency causes more threat to life and functional loss
   5. There is little variation in expressivity
C. Sex-linked dominant inheritance
   1. The heterozygote manifests the condition
   2. Affected females who are heterozygous transmit X-linked gene to half their daughters and half their sons (vertical transmission)
   3. Affected females who are homozygous will transmit to all their children
   4. Affected males transmit X-linked gene to all daughters and to none of their sons
   5. Father to son transmission does not occur
   6. There will be more affected females, but males tend to be more severely affected
D. Sex-linked recessive inheritance
   1. Heterozygous male is clinically affected
   2. Affected male transmits gene to all daughters, who are carriers, and to none of his sons
   3. Carrier female transmits gene to one half of her daughters, who are carriers, and one half of her sons, who are affected
   4. There is no male to male transmission

E. Polygenic inheritance
 1. There is a low level of risk in the population
 2. There is an increased risk in relatives of affected individuals
 3. Threshold of risk is affected by race, sex, and geography
 4. Risk level and severity relate to family pattern of involvement
    a. If parent and child are involved, risk of subsequent children being involved is greater
    b. If the deformity is greater in severity, the greater likelihood of children being affected
    c. If affected parent is of less likely affected sex, risk for subsequent children increases

REFERENCES

Jackson LG, Schimke RN: *Clinical genetics: A source book for physicians.* New York, John Wiley & Sons, 1979

McKusick VA: *Heritable disorders of connective tissue,* ed 3. St Louis, CV Mosby, 1966

SECTION 3: PEDIATRIC ORTHOPAEDICS

Howard S. An
John G. Thometz

22. Foot Problems
23. Angular and Torsional Deformities of Lower Extremities in Children
24. Congenital Hip Dislocation
25. Legg-Calvé-Perthes Disease (Coxa Plana)
26. Slipped Capital Femoral Epiphysis
27. Neuromuscular Problems
28. Congenital Disorders, Skeletal Dysplasias, and Connective Tissue Disorders
29. Miscellaneous Pediatric Disorders
30. Pediatric Fractures

22
Foot Problems

CLUBFOOT

I. Etiology
Unknown, possibly multiple factors, including polygenic inheritance, persistence of fetal positioning, primary germ plasma defect, and neuromuscular factors

II. Incidence
A. In whites, 1.2/1000, male > female (2:1); 50% bilateral

III. Embryology
A. Embryonic position: 30 mm embryo with equinovarus foot
B. Fetal position: 50 mm embryo with mild adducted equinovarus foot secondary to tibial growth

IV. Pathology
A. Histologic abnormalities in muscle, tendon, and ligament in addition to contracture
B. Equinus, hindfoot varus, and foot varus (talonavicular)
C. Calcaneus rotates through subtalar joint in a medial direction and inverts (varus tilting or supination)
D. Body of talus may be directed laterally and neck of talus is directed medially (lateral rotation of the talus)
E. Navicula is displaced medially
F. Cuboid is often subluxated medially
G. Plantar fascia is tight

V. X-Ray Findings
A. Increased lateral calcaneotibial angle (>125°) secondary to ankle equinus
B. Decreased lateral talocalcaneal angle (<35°, 35–50° normal) and anteroposterior (AP) talocalcaneal angle (<20°, 20–40° normal) secondary to hindfoot varus
C. Abnormal AP talo-first metatarsal angle (zero is normal) secondary to talonavicular subluxation

VI. Prognosis
A. Condition worse if
  1. Teratogenic (eg, arthrogryposis, myelodysplasia)
  2. Short, fat, rigid foot with severe midfoot crease
  3. Boat-shaped heel, severe adductus varus, atavistic short first toe
  4. Delayed treatment and failure to respond

VII. Treatment
A. Postnatal: corrective manipulation and casting (correct adduction, heel varus, and then equinus) every 1–2 weeks for 3 months, then holding cast or brace until surgery (50% effective)
B. Surgery
  1. One-stage posteromedial release of tight structures
  2. Ideally, 4–8 months but up to 6 years of age
  3. Turco posteromedial or extensive subtalar release by Mckay or Simon techniques
  4. Cincinnati incision is often utilized (Fig 3-2)
  5. Structures that are released
    a. Achilles tendon Z-lengthening
    b. Posterior release of ankle and subtalar joints, including calcaneofibular and posterior talofibular ligaments
    c. Z-lengthening or release of posterior tibialis
    d. Superficial medial release of the subtalar joint: superficial deltoid (calcaneotibial and tibionavicular ligament),

    calcaneonavicular (spring ligament) and talonavicular ligament dorsally
    e. Deep medial release: the bifurcated ligament (calcaneonavicular and calcaneocuboid) and enough talocalcaneal interosseous ligament
    f. Plantar release and lateral release of dorsal calcaneocuboid joint if necessary
  C. Postoperative management
    1. Smooth K-wire through talonavicular joint and talocalcaneal joint, occasionally calcaneocuboid joint
    2. Three months postoperative casting
    3. Many months of splinting, particularly if tibialis anterior and peroneal muscles are weak

VIII. Salvage Procedures
A. Resistant deformity of the foot
  1. Forefoot: Heyman-Herndon tarsometatarsal capsulotomies or metatarsal osteotomies
  2. Midfoot
    a. Midtarsal osteotomies (Japas or Dome)
    b. Open wedge of first cuneiform or talus (medial column lengthening)
    c. Close wedging of os calcis and/or cuboid (lateral column shortening)
  3. Hindfoot: Dwyer osteotomy of os calcis, sliding osteotomy
B. Triple arthrodesis: resistant foot 12 years old
  1. Residual deformities
  2. Overcorrected planovalgus deformity

METATARSUS ADDUCTUS

I. Pathogenesis
A. The forefoot adducted and supinated at the tarsometatarsal joint (present at birth)
B. Incidence: 1/1000, 2/3 bilateral
C. Affected by intrauterine position and prone posture
D. Association with internal tibial torsion and hip dysplasia
E. Spontaneous correction is usually the case, although some remain rigid and become fixed
F. Abnormal abductor hallucis or posterior tibialis insertion may be pathogenic

II. Clinical Findings
A. The forefoot adducted and supinated at the tarsometatarsal joint with the convex lateral border and frequently wide space between first and second toes
B. Bleck's heel bisector severity: the line points to second toe, normal; third toe, mild; fourth toe, moderate; and fifth toe, severe
C. Flexibility: **flexible** if corrects beyond neutral, **partial** if corrects to neutral, and **rigid** if cannot correct to neutral
D. X-rays: medial angulation at the tarsometatarsal joint, and there may be increased talocalcaneal angle because of hindfoot valgus (a differentiating feature from clubfoot) (Fig 3-1)

III. Treatment
A. Mild and flexible type: observation if corrects with stroking the foot and proper stretching by parents if the foot does not correct with stroking
B. Moderate and severe type: serial casting
  1. Hold the forefoot in abduction and pronation with the axis of rotation at the cuboid and keep the heel in slight equinus to prevent valgus deformity
  2. Casting is appropriate at 1–8 months of age and 6–8 weeks of treatment is usually necessary (change the cast every 2 weeks): casting less effective after 8 months of age
  3. Complications: valgus heel and hallux valgus
  4. Surgical methods
    a. Rarely done. For painful, severe, rigid foot and cosmesis

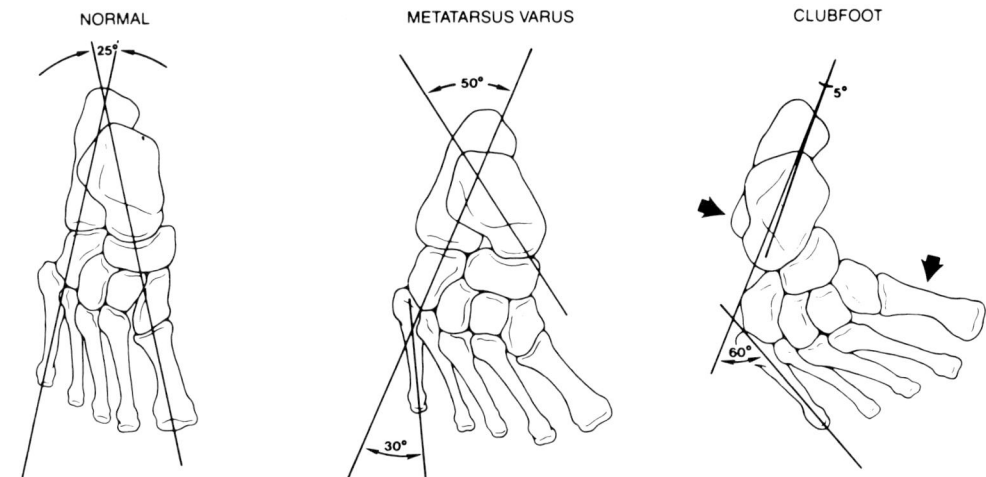

Figure 3-1. Anteroposterior talocalcaneal angle (Kite's angle) is increased in metatarsus varus but decreased in clubfoot. (From Wenger DR: Children's orthopaedics. In Bucholz RW, Lippert FG, Wenger DR, Ezaki M, eds. Orthopaedic decision making. Philadelphia, BC Decker, and St. Louis, CV Mosby, 1984, p 222. Reprinted with permission.)

b. Tenotomy of abductor hallucis with or without first cuneiform-metatarsal release and casting in resistant cases (<2 years)
c. Tarsometatarsal release (Heyman-Herndon)
  (1) Age between 3 and 7 years
  (2) Divide only tarsometatarsal and intermetatarsal ligaments, not the lateral capsules
  (3) Avoid damage to the articular surfaces
  (4) Immobilize at least 4 months
  (5) Use K-wires (first metatarsal to cuneiform and fifth metatarsal to cuboid)
  (6) Minimal and careful dissection
  (7) Complications: prominence of fifth metatarsal if lateral ligament released, prominence of the base of the third metatarsal, avascular necrosis of the second cuneiform secondary to total release, articular damage, and degenerative joint changes
d. Metatarsal osteotomy
  (1) Age >6 years
  (2) Dome-shaped osteotomy
  (3) Immobilize for 6 weeks
  (4) Complication: shortening, first metatarsal epiphyseal arrest, nonunion, malunion, wound slough

CONGENITAL VERTICAL TALUS (Congenital convex pes valgus)

I. Types
A. Group I: supple feet resembling calcaneovalgus feet
B. Group II: rigid feet (may be associated with nail-patellar syndrome, multiple pterygium syndrome, Marfan's syndrome, arthrogryposis. Calcaneocuboid dislocation may be present
C. Group III: vertical talus associated with trisomy 13–15 or 18
D. Group IV: vertical talus associated with neuromuscular problems (eg, spina bifida)

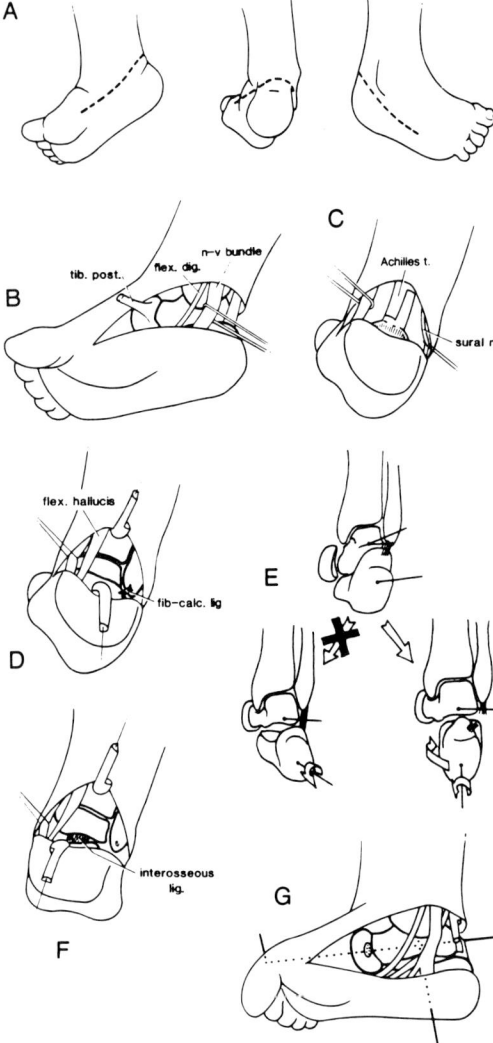

Figure 3-2. **A.** Cincinnati incision. **B.** Dissection of neurovascular bundle and posterior tibial tendon. **C.** Z-plasty of Achilles tendon. **D.** Posterior release of ankle and subtalar joints, including posterior talofibular ligaments. **E.** Release of posterolateral structures, including calcaneofibular ligament, allows external rotation of the os calcis. **F.** Release of interosseous ligament may be partial or complete. **G.** Pin fixation through talonavicular and subtalar joints. (From Rab GT. Congenital deformities of the foot. In Chapman MW, ed. Operative orthopaedics, vol 3. Philadelphia, JB Lippincott, 1988, p 2149. Reprinted with permission.)

E. True vertical talus is usually associated with other anomalies

II. Pathology

A. Bony deformities
 1. Os calcis is in equinus and rotated posterolaterally
 2. Talus is plantar-flexed and rotated medially
 3. Anterior articular facet and sustentaculum are hypoplastic
 4. Navicular is dislocated dorsolaterally (the head of talus palpable medially)
 5. Cuboid is subluxed dorsally and laterally on calcaneus

B. Joint capsules and ligaments
 1. Posterior capsule of ankle and subtalar joint contracted
 2. Dorsal talonavicular, tibionavicular, bifurcated ligament, and calcaneofibular ligaments contracted
 3. Plantar calcaneonavicular ligament (spring) elongated

C. Tendons
 1. Tendo Achilles, tibialis anterior, extensors, and peroneals contracted
 2. Peroneus longus and posterior tibialis may be displaced anteriorly

III. Clinical

A. Equinus and valgus of hindfoot, abducted and dorsiflexed forefoot (convex or rocker bottom sole)

B. Differential diagnosis: calcaneovalgus of foot (os calcis is in calcaneus position and hindfoot is supple)

IV. X-Ray Findings

A. Lateral: increased talocalcaneal angle, axis of talus parallel to long axis of tibia, and os calcis in equinus and plantar-flexed talus

B. AP: increased talocalcaneal angle

C. To differentiate from supple hindfoot valgus, obtain a forced plantar-flexed lateral view: talometatarsal axis is corrected in congenital oblique talus but not in congenital vertical talus because the navicular remains dislocated

V. Treatment
A. Casting: first 3–4 months (hold forefoot in equinus, varus, and supination and subtalar joint in inversion and ankle in equinus) to stretch soft tissues prior to surgery
B. Surgery: one-stage release at 4–12 months ideal up to 2.5 years (separate incisions): earlier the surgery, better the outcome
   1. Posterior release: posterior incision over Achilles tendon and Z-plasty of Achilles tendon and release of posterior capsule (posterior tibiofibular and talofibular ligaments) — may do as a separate stage
   2. Lateral release: separate lateral incision and release of calcaneocuboid capsule and bifurcate ligament (calcaneonavicular and calcaneocuboid) and calcaneofibular ligament — pin calcaneocuboid joint if dislocated (type II, S. Coleman)
   3. Anterior release: separate medial incision and cut tibialis posterior and plantar calcaneonavicular (spring) ligament distally and tighten during closure. Release of dorsal talonavicular, deltoid (anterior tibiotalar, tibionavicular) ligaments, and interosseous talocalcaneal ligament and elevate the talus and Z-lengthening of extensors. Insertion of K-wire in the center of talar head and reduction of talonavicular joint and pinning
   4. Transfer of the tibialis anterior to the neck of the talus if neurogenic imbalance is present
   5. Other procedures
      a. Subtalar bone block (Grice arthrodesis): 3–6 years
      b. Triple arthrodesis in older children
      c. Excision of navicular may be necessary in those over 3 years old and in severe neuromuscular deformities

TARSAL COALITION
(peroneal spastic flatfoot)

I. Incidence
A. Less than 1%, males > females (4:1), common during 8–16 years, > 50% bilateral

II. Pathogenesis
A. Failure of segmentation of mesenchyme
B. Familial tendency: autosomal dominant (14%)
C. Calcaneonavicular > talocalcaneal (middle facet more frequently fused than anterior facet). Talonavicular fusion is rare
D. Types of fusion: bone, cartilage, fibrous

III. Clinical Findings
A. Decreased subtalar motion, local tenderness
B. Peroneal spasm on inversion
C. Pronated rigid flat foot
D. Increased incidence of ankle sprain
E. Calcaneonavicular fusion usually presents about 8–12 years of age, whereas talocalcaneal fusion presents about 12–16 years of age
F. Differential diagnosis of peroneal spasm: juvenile rheumatoid arthritis, osteoid osteoma, infection, and trauma

IV. X-Ray Findings
A. Lateral view: calcaneal beak suggests calcaneonavicular coalition
B. On 45° oblique view: calcaneonavicular bar is best seen
C. On 45° axial view of the calcaneus (Harris view): middle facet fusion of talocalcaneal fusion is seen
D. Computed tomography (CT) is better than Harris view
E. Dorsal beaking of talonavicular joint may be present secondary to lack of hindfoot motion
F. Magnetic resonance imaging (MRI) may be useful in fibrous or cartilaginous coalitions

V. Treatment

A. Nonoperative: always try first short leg cast for acute symptoms, University of California Biomechanics Laboratory (UCBL) orthosis for increased valgus
B. Calcaneonavicular bar: if no significant arthritic changes in the talonavicular joint, resection of the bar and interposition of extensor brevis tendon or fat is recommended even with talar breaking. If arthritis is present, triple arthrodesis is recommended
C. Talocalcaneal coalition: if detected early and no talonavicular arthritis, and if the coalition occupies less than 50% of the middle facet on CT, then resection with interposition arthroplasty (fat) can be done. Triple arthrodesis may be necessary in advanced disease or failed resection cases. Subtalar arthrodesis may be attempted if pain results from micromotion at the talocalcaneal coalition

PES PLANUS (flat foot)

I. Etiology (Unknown)

A. Ligament laxity, which may be part of a syndrome: Down and Marfan syndromes, etc.
B. Muscle imbalance
C. Contracture of gastrocnemius
D. Residual of calcaneovalgus foot

II. Pathogenesis

A. Normal longitudinal arch usually develops by 3–5 years
B. The arch may sag at the talonavicular and/or naviculocuneiform joint

III. Clinical Features

A. "Foot strain" rarely occurs in severe cases with excessive use
B. Mild contracture of the heel cord is often present (secondary to long-standing heel valgus)
C. Hindfoot is flexible (longitudinal arch present when sitting as opposed to rigid flatfoot, as in tarsal coalition)

IV. X-Ray Findings

A. AP talocalcaneal angle increased (heel valgus)
B. Loss of arch on lateral view (sagging at the talonavicular or naviculocuneiform joint)
C. Decreased calcaneal pitch

V. Treatment

A. Only if symptomatic (shoes with good arch support and stretch contractures of Achilles tendon)
B. Scaphoid pad, Thomas heel (medial heel wedge and longitudinal arch support), plastic heel cup (especially heel valgus), UCBL orthosis, Plastizote orthosis (older children) may be used but effectiveness not proven
C. Surgery rarely necessary
   1. Indicated for persistent pain or excessive shoewear problems
   2. Procedures
      a. Miller: distal advancement of plantar calcaneonavicular ligament and posterior tibial tendon (Kidner procedure if associated with accessory navicular)
      b. Talonavicular fusion
      c. Hoke: naviculocuneiform fusion
      d. Fowler: lengthen lateral column
      e. Dwyer osteotomy
      f. Subtalar arthrodesis
      g. Triple arthrodesis

PES CAVUS

I. General Considerations

A. Definition: fixed equinus deformity of the forefoot on the hindfoot
B. Frequently associated with claw toes (clawfoot) and hindfoot varus (cavovarus), and

may be seen with hindfoot calcaneus (calcaneocavus) or hindfoot equinus (equinocavus)
C. Most often the result of underlying neurologic or muscular disease

II. Pathogenesis
A. Muscle imbalance
  1. Weak anterior tibialis versus strong peronus longus
  2. Paralysis of intrinsics
  3. Weak peroneus brevis versus strong peronus longus and posterior tibialis
  4. Triceps surae weakness and strong long toe flexors
B. Neuromuscular diseases
  1. Muscular dystrophy
  2. Peripheral nerve: Charcot-Marie-Tooth disease, polyneuritis, sciatic nerve injury, Dejerine-Sottas interstitial hypertrophic neuritis
  3. Spinal cord: poliomyelitis, myelomeningocele (especially L5 level), diastematomyelia
  4. Spinocerebellar tract: Friedreich's ataxia, Roussy–Lévy syndrome
  5. Cortical: cerebral palsy, dystonia musculorum deformans
C. Idiopathic

III. Clinical
A. Patients with cavus foot must have muscle examination, electromyography/nerve conduction study (EMG/NCS), spine x-rays, and often pediatric neurology consultation
B. Types
  1. Simple pes cavus: plantar flexion deformity is equal on medial and lateral borders
  2. Pes cavovarus: medial column of the forefoot is in plantar flexion (first metatarsal in equinus and pronation) and varus of the heel. Check flexibility of heel with Coleman block test
  3. Calcaneocavus: hindfoot in calcaneus, mostly seen in flaccid paralysis (ie, poliomyelitis, myelomeningocele)
  4. Pes equinocavus: residual clubfoot

IV. Treatment
A. Conservative therapy only in mild cases: stretching, metatarsal pads, lateral wedge (heel varus)
B. Surgery: consider position of hindfoot, appearance of toes, flexibility of foot, and muscle imbalance for possible tendon transfer and correct the deformity at its apex
  1. Release of plantar aponeurosis
  2. Release of plantar aponeurosis and flexor digiti brevis (FDB), abductor hallucis brevis (AHB), abductor digiti minimi (ADM) (Steindler stripping)
  3. Transfer of long toe extensors to heads of metatarsals: for flexible paralytic deformity, especially the first ray
  4. Opening wedge osteotomy of the medial cuneiform and transfer of the anterior tibialis to dorsum of the cuneiform: if hindfoot is flexible
  5. Dorsal wedge resection (naviculocuneiform and cuboid) or dome osteotomy: may combine with plantar release
  6. Japas V-osteotomy of the tarsus: children over 6 years of age
  7. Metatarsotarsal dorsal wedge resection with fusion and dorsal wedge resection of lateral four metatarsals at their bases: skeletal immature patients with greatest deformity at the metatarsal area
  8. Osteotomy of os calcis: if heel varus or calcaneus is present (up to 10 years)
     a. Lateral closing wedge (Dwyer)
     b. Posterior superior displacement osteotomy (for calcaneocavus)
     c. Dorsal wedge osteotomy: for calcaneus deformity
  9. Triple arthrodesis: after 12 years

ADOLESCENT HALLUX VALGUS

I. Pathogenesis
A. Metatarsus primus varus and hallux valgus
B. Secondary bunion and metatarsalgia

II. Clinical Findings
A. Pain and difficulty of shoe wearing
B. Tenderness to palpation

III. Treatment
A. Conservative: wide forefoot shoe, pads of felt, bunion splints, metatarsal pads or bar: relieve symptoms but no correction of deformity
B. Surgery rarely indicated in children
  1. Painful feet with failure of conservative treatment
  2. Not before 10 years of age
  3. Procedures: Wilson or Chevron osteotomy for milder deformities and proximal osteotomy with distal release for greater deformities
  4. High recurrence rate before skeletal maturity, especially when associated with flatfoot

MISCELLANEOUS FOOT PROBLEMS

I. Curly Toe
A. Tight Toe Flexors
B. Many Improve with Time
C. Tenotomy if Deformity Persists

II. Polydactyly/Syndactyly
A. Operate 1–3 Years
B. Avoid Surgery on Simple Syndactyly

III. Osteochondrosis
A. Freiberg's (second metatarsal head), Kohler's (navicular), and Sever's (calcaneal apophysitis) diseases
B. Treatment of Freiberg's disease
  1. Conservative and symptomatic
  2. May need removal of loose bodies and/or resection of proximal half of the proximal phalanx in late cases (avoid metatarsal resection)

IV. Toe Walking
A. Diagnosis
  1. Rule out neuromuscular etiologies, such as cerebral palsy, diastematomyelia, spinal dysraphism, muscular dystrophy, or spinal cord tumor
B. Clinical Findings
  1. If normal neurologic examination, consider idiopathic contracture of tendo Achilles (autosomal dominant)
C. Treatment
  1. Usually responds to serial casting, occasionally requires surgical lengthening

REFERENCES

Berg EE: A reappraisal of metatarsus adductus and skewfoot. J Bone Joint Surg 68A:1185–1196, 1986

Bleck EE: Metatarsus adductus: Classification and relationship to outcomes of treatment. J Pediatr Orthop 3:2–9, 1983

Bordelon RL: Hypermobile flatfoot in children: Comprehension, evaluation, and treatment. Clin Orthop 181:7–14, 1983

Chamber RB, Cook TM, Cowell HR: Surgical reconstruction for calcaneonavicular coalition. Evaluation of function and gait. J Bone Joint Surg 64A:829–836, 1982

Cowell HR: Talocalcaneal coalition and new causes of peroneal spastic flatfoot. Clin Orthop 85:16, 1972

Crawford AH, Marxen JL, Oterfeld PL: The Cincinnati incision: A comprehensive approach for surgical procedures of the foot and ankle in childhood. J Bone Joint Surg 64A:1355–1358, 1982

Dwyer FC: Osteotomy of the calcaneus for pes cavus. J Bone Joint Surg 41B:80, 1959

Dwyer FC: The treatment of relapsed clubfoot by the insertion of a wedge into the calcaneus. J Bone Joint Surg 43B:67, 1961

Hamanishi C: Congenital vertical talus: Classification with 69 cases and new measurement system. J Pediatr Orthop 4:318–326, 1984

Helal B: Surgery of adolescent hallux valgus. Clin Orthop 157:50–63, 1981

Herzenberg JE, Carroll NC, Christoferson MR: Clubfoot analysis with three-dimensional computer modeling. J Pediatr Orthop 3:257–262, 1988

Irani RN, Sherman MS: The pathological anatomy of clubfoot. J Bone Joint Surg 45A:45–52, 1963

Jahss MH: Tarsometatarsal truncated-wedge arthrodesis for pes cavus and equinovarus deformity of the fore part of the foot. J Bone Joint Surg 62A:713–722, 1980

Luba R, Rosman M: Bunions in children: Treatment with a modified Mitchell osteotomy. J Pediatr Orthop 4:44–47, 1984

McKay DW: New concept of and approach to clubfoot treatment. J Pediatr Orthop 3:10–21, 3:141–148, 1983

Olney BW, Asher MA: Excision of symptomatic coalition of the middle facet of the talocalcaneal joint. J Bone Joint Surg 69A:539–544, 1987

Paulos L, Coleman SS, Samuelson KM: Pes cavovarus: Review of a surgical approach using selective soft-tissue procedures. J Bone Joint Surg 62A:942–953, 1980

Scranton PE Jr: Treatment of symptomatic talocalcaneal coalition. J Bone Joint Surg 69A:533–539, 1987

Scranton PE Jr, Zuckerman JO: Bunion surgery in adolescents: Results of surgical treatment. J Pediatr Orthop 4:39–43, 1984

Sherman F, Westin G: Plantar release in the correction of deformities of the foot in childhood. J Bone Joint Surg 63A:1382–1389, 1981

Simons GW: Complete subtalar release in clubfoot. J Bone Joint Surg 67A:1144–1655, 1985

Staheli LT, Chew DE, Corbett M: The longitudinal arch: A survey of eight hundred and eighty-two feet in normal children and adults. J Bone Joint Surg 69A:426–428, 1987

Swionkowski MF, Scranton DE, Hansen S: Tarsal coalition: Long term results of surgical treatment. J Pediatr Orthop 3:287–292, 1983

Turco VJ: Resistant congenital clubfoot — one-stage posterolateral release with internal fixation: A follow-up report of a 15-year experience. J Bone Joint Surg 61A:805–814, 1979

Turco VJ: Surgical correction of the resistant clubfoot. One-stage posteromedial release with internal fixation. A Preliminary report. J Bone Joint Surg 53A:477, 1971

Walker AP, Ghali NN, Silk FF: Congenital vertical talus: The results of staged operative reduction. J Bone Joint Surg 67B:117–121, 1985

Wilcox PG, Weiner DS: The Akron midtarsal dome osteotomy in the treatment of rigid pes cavus: A preliminary review. J Pediatr Orthop 5:333–338, 1985

Williams GA, Cowell HR: Kohler's disease of the tarsal navicular. Clin Orthop 158:53–58, 1981

23
Angular and Torsional Deformities of Lower Extremities in Children

I. **Normal Variation and Growth Patterns**
A. Foot
   1. Differentiate positional equinovarus and metatarsus adductus from clubfoot
   2. Differentiate positional calcaneovalgus from congenital vertical talus
   3. Early pronated and valgus heel (flat foot) is normal until 5 years of age
B. Tibia
   1. Tibia normally rotates externally with age (tibiomalleolar axis [TMA] is 5° at birth, 15° in children, and 20° at maturity)
   2. Tibiofemoral angle changes with age: (15° varus at 1 year, 0° at 18 months, 12° valgus at 2–3 years, and 7°–9° valgus at adulthood) (Fig 3-3)
C. Femur
   1. Anteversion greatest at birth (40°); 15° in adult females and 10° in adult males
   2. External rotation contracture of the hip at birth resolves at 2–3 years, and therefore clinical anteversion is most apparent around 3 years

II. **Evaluation**
A. History
   1. Age at which torsional deformity is most frequent: metatarsus adductus (0–18 months), internal tibial torsion (18–36 months), anteversion of the femur (>36 months)
   2. Family history: some familial tendency in metatarsus adductus and femoral anteversion
   3. Sleeping and sitting posture: prone position aggravates metatarsus adductus and internal tibial torsion and "W" posture aggravates femoral anteversion
B. Examination
   1. Common causes of intoeing are femoral anteversion, internal tibial torsion, and metatarsus adductus
   2. Common causes of out-toeing are external contracture of the hip, external tibial torsion, and calcaneovalgus of foot
   3. When assessing genu varum or valgum, rule out pathologic causes (eg, metabolic rickets, skeletal dysplasia)
   4. Rule out neuromuscular causes also when assessing torsional problems
   5. Record the torsional profiles of Staheli
      a. Foot progression angle (FPA)
      b. Medial rotation (MR)
      c. Laternal rotation (LR)
      d. Thigh-foot axis (TFA)
      e. Transmalleolar axis (TMA)

III. **Internal Tibial Torsion**
A. Most common cause of intoeing
B. Common during 6–36 months of age, usually asymmetrical, mostly detected after walking
C. Consider TFA equals 5° internal at birth, 10° external at 12 months, 15° external as child, and 20° external at maturity
D. X-rays not necessary
E. Treatment
   1. Correct posture (ie, no "W" sitting)
   2. Observation until 15–18 months and

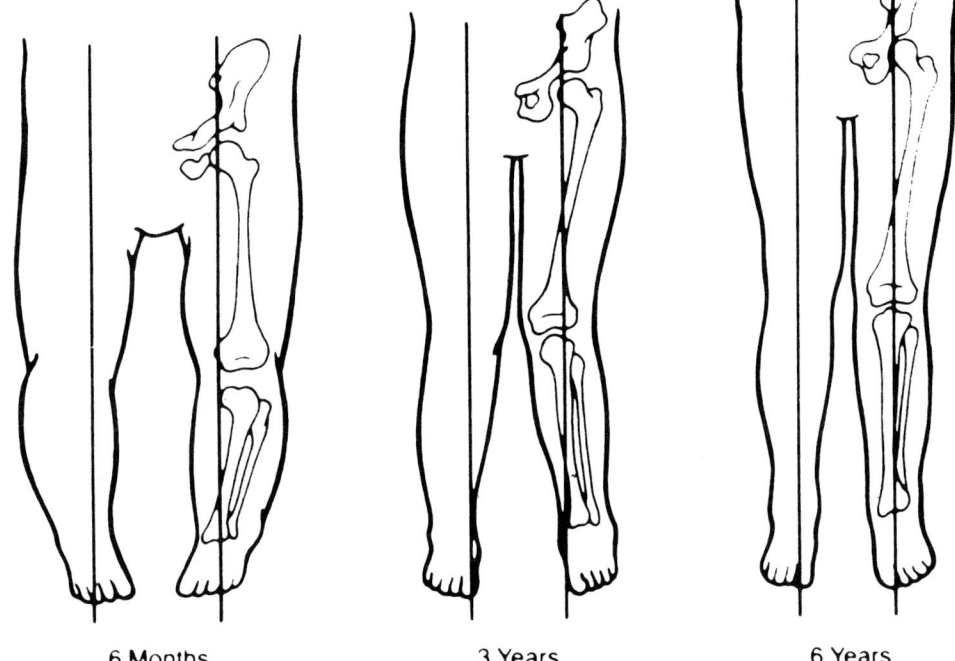

Figure 3-3. Tibiofemoral angle changes with age: normal progression from bowlegs in the first year to knock knees at 3 years to normal slightly valgus knees at 6 years. (From Wenger DR: Children's orthopaedics. In Bucholz RW, Lippert FG, Wenger DR, Ezaki M, eds. Orthopaedic decision making. Philadelphia, BC Decker, and St. Louis, CV Mosby, 1984, p 210. Reprinted with permission.)

      natural history favors spontaneous correction
- 3. Dennis-Brown brace >18 months until 3 years (some use it earlier)
    - a. Indication: >30°–40° deformity and no spontaneous correction
    - b. The length of bar equals width of pelvis
    - c. Genu valgus may result, especially if the width of the bar is too long
- 4. Derotation osteotomy: >8 years and do distal osteotomy (a higher incidence of compartment syndrome with proximal osteotomy)

IV. Internal Femoral Torsion

- A. Detected after 2–3 years, especially 5–6 years
- B. Familial tendency
- C. Aggravated by "W" sitting posture
- D. Females > males (2:1)
- E. Usually bilateral and symmetrical
- F. Examination
    1. Internal rotation > external rotation with hip extension
    2. Medially directed patella
    3. Compensatory external tibial torsion present in 50%
- G. X-rays: CT scan
- H. Treatment (femoral anteversion)
    1. Orthotics do not work
    2. Derotation osteotomy: especially for females with external hip rotation <0°–15°, presenting with gait difficulty and cosmetic problems
        - a. Supracondylar osteotomy: after 8 years of age, followed by hip spica cast for 2–3 months (2 cm above distal femoral epiphysis, medial ap-

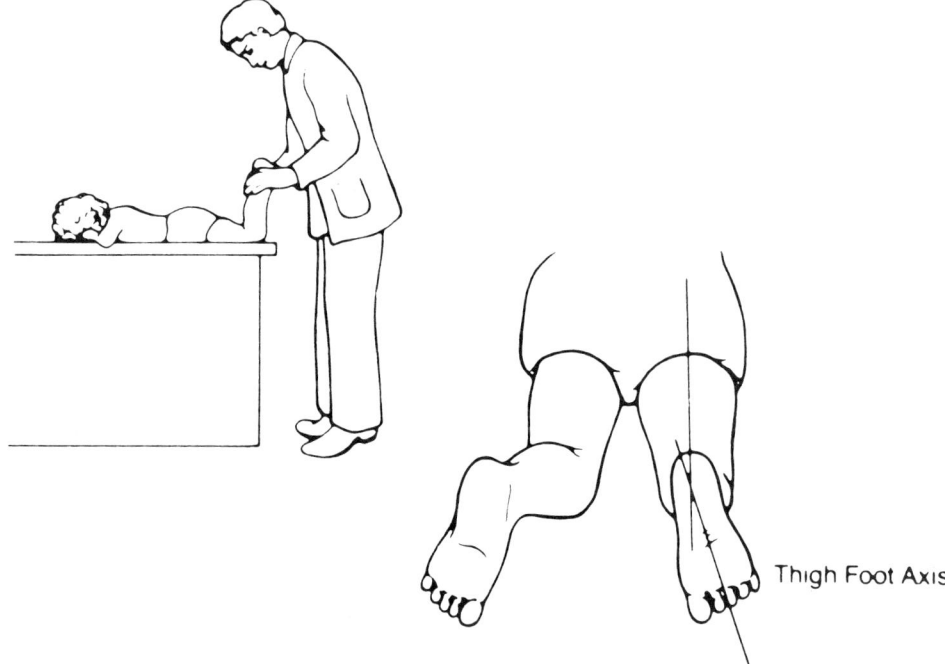

Figure 3-4. Thigh-foot axis decribes tibial torsion (positive values equal external or lateral torsion and negative values equal internal or medial torsion). (From Wenger DR: Children's orthopaedics. In Bucholz RW, Lippert FG, Wenger DR, Ezaki M, eds. Orthopaedic decision making. Philadelphia, BC Decker, and St. Louis, CV Mosby, 1984, p 208. Reprinted with permission.)

proach, hip spica in extension, percutaneous approach possible)
  b. Intertrochanteric osteotomy: severe deformity especially associated coxa varus or valgus and external tibial torsion and older age group

V. External Rotation Gait (Toeing Out)
A. Normal FPA equals 0°–25°
B. Hip
  1. External rotation contracture: usually resolves by 18 months of age
  2. Femoral retroversion: rare
C. External tibial torsion: usually secondary to internal femoral torsion (malalignment syndrome) and inappropriate use of Dennis-Brown splint
D. Foot
  1. Calcaneovalgus
  2. Congenital vertical talus
  3. Pes planus (flat foot)

VI. Angular Malalignment
A. Physiologic: 15° genu varus at 1 year, 0° at 18 months, 12°–15° valgus from 2–6 years, and 7°–9° valgus at maturity
B. Pathologic deformities
  1. Most important entity to distinguish is Blount's disease (tibia vara)
  2. Other disorders may cause angular malalignment, such as congenital bowings (benign posteromedial bowing or more serious anterolateral bowing associated with pseudarthrosis), metaphyseal dysplasia, osteochondromatosis, hemihypertrophy, paraxial fibular hemimelia, multiple epiphyseal dysplasia, rickets, fibrous dysplasia, epiphyseal trauma, etc.

VII. Tibia Vara (Blount's Disease)
A. Growth disturbance of posteromedial corner of the proximal tibial epiphysis

B. Bilateral in 60%, internal tibial torsion common
C. Obese, early-walking children with genu varum place excessive stress on the posteromedial physis, causing growth inhibition
D. Types: infantile, juvenile, and adolescent
E. X-rays
  1. Langenskiold's six radiographic stages (progression from fragmentation to bony bridge)
  2. Metaphyseal-diaphyseal angle: >11° likely to progress
F. Treatment
  1. Less than 18 months of age: observation (cannot easily distinguish from physiologic varus)
  2. From 18–36 months: orthosis, especially for grades 1 and 2
  3. More than 3 years and stage II: valgus external rotation osteotomy before 4 years of age
  4. More advanced cases may require elevation of medial tibial plateau
  5. Adolescent tibia vara
    a. Starts >9 years old
    b. Progressive tibia vara or valgus due to premature closure of the growth plate
    c. Tibial osteotomy and evaluate leg-length discrepancy

REFERENCES

Balthazar DA, Pappas AM: Acquired valgus deformity of the tibia in children. J Pediatr Orthop 4:538–541, 1984

Beck CL, Burke SW, Roberts JM, et al: Physeal bridge resection in infantile Blount disease. J Pediatr Orthop 7:161–163, 1987

Bowen JR, Leahey JL, Zhang Z, MacEwen GD: Partial epiphysiodesis at the knee to correct angular deformity. Clin Orthop 188:184, 1985

Fabry G, MacEwen GD, Shands AR Jr: Torsion of the femur: A follow-up study in normal and abnormal conditions. J Bone Joint Surg 55A:1726, 1973

Kling TF Jr, Hensinger RN: Angular and torsional deformities of the lower limbs in children. Clin Orthop 176:136–147, 1983

Langenskiold A, Riska EB: Tibia vara. J Bone Joint Surg 46A:1405, 1964

Levine AM, Drennan JC: Physiological bowing and tibia vara: The metaphyseal-diaphyseal angle in the measurement of bowleg deformities. J Bone Joint Surg 64A:1158–1163, 1982

Loder RT, Johnston CE II: Infantile tibia vara. J Pediatr Orthop 7:639–646, 1987

Ogata K, Goldsand EM: A simple biplanar method of measuring femoral anteversion and neck-shaft angle. J Bone Joint Surg 61A:846–851, 1979

Schoenecker PL, Meade WC, Pierron RL, et al: Blount's disease: A retrospective review and recommendations for treatment. J Pediatr Orthop 5:181–186, 1985

Staheli LT, Clauson DK, Hubbard DD: Medial femoral torsion: Experience with operative treatment. Clin Orthop 146:222–225, 1980

Staheli LT, Corbett M, Wyss C, et al: Lower extremity rotational problems in children. Normal values to guide management. J Bone Joint Surg 67A:39–47, 1985

Stahehi LT, Engle GM: Tibial torsion: A method of assessment and a survey of normal children. Clin Orthop 86:183, 1972

24
Congenital Hip Dislocation

I. Incidence
A. Occurs in 4–10 per 1000 cases, considerable racial variation
B. Sixty percent are first born, female > males (6:1)
C. Increased in breech delivery and oligohydramnios
D. The left hip in 60%, bilateral in 20%
E. Associated conditions: muscular torticollis, metatarsus adductus, calcaneovalgus
F. Postnatal influence: increased incidence when hips are kept in extended and adducted positions
G. Associated diseases: Ehlers-Danlos syndrome, Larsen's syndrome, myelomeningocele, arthrogryposis, etc.

II. Pathology of Late Cases
A. Defective acetabulum growth (frontal acetabular inclination)
B. Femoral anteversion
C. Capsular constriction
D. Inverted labrum in dislocation and everted in subluxation
E. Shortened inferior transverse ligament
F. Pulvinar and tight Iliopsoas

III. Clinical Findings
A. Ortolani test: reduction maneuver by gently abducting and lifting the involved femur
B. Barlow test: a provocative test to detect a dislocatable or subluxable hip
C. Decreased abduction (the best test after age of 2 months)
D. Galeazzi sign: apparent shortening of the femur when hips flexed to 90°
E. Prominent and higher greater trochanter
F. Extra skin folds and widened perineum in bilateral cases
G. Increased lordosis, particularly with bilateral cases and positive Trendelenburg sign (hip should be held in extension to prevent false-negative by iliopsoas muscle in hip flexion)
H. Hip dysplasia associated with abduction contracture of the contralateral hip
   1. Pelvic obliquity and apparent leg length discrepancy
   2. Secondary to intrauterine packing problem
   3. Positive Ober test: abduction contracture of the hip
I. Teratologic dislocation (1%)
   1. Arthrogryposis, paralytic, sacral agenesis, chromosomal abnormalities, etc.
   2. Generally do not respond to nonoperative management

IV. X-Ray Findings (Fig 3-5)
A. Unreliable before 4–6 weeks, may be taken to rule out teratologic dislocations or proximal femoral focal deficiency
B. Von Rosen view (45° abduction and 25° internal rotation) may be more useful for infants but there can be false negative results
C. Acetabular index: <30° is normal, but there is a wide variation during the first year
D. Lateral and superior migration of the femoral head (ie, proximal femoral metaphysis is lateral to Perkin's line)
E. Delayed ossification of the femoral head (should appear during first 6–12 months; compare with the opposite side)
F. Shenton's line is broken in the dislocated hip
G. Center edge (CE) angle of Wiberg: <20°–25° indicates subluxation of the femoral head (use after 4 years of age)
H. Arthrogram
   1. Very useful in ruling out mechanical

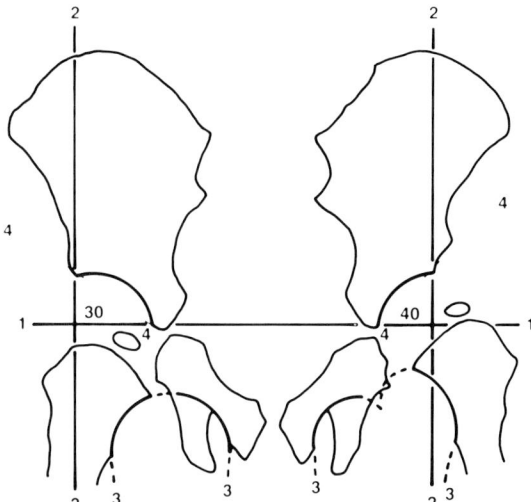

Figure 3-5. Diagram of the various lines for measuring reduction. 1: Hilgenreiner's line; 2: Perkin's lines; 3: Shenton's lines. The angle between 1 and 4 equals the acetabular index. (From Gruebel Lee DM. Disorders of the hip. Philadelphia, JB Lippincott 1983, p 114. Reprinted with permission.)

blocks to reduction of the infant hip, such as hourglass constriction of the capsule by the psoas muscle
2. Confirms the shape and congruence of the femoral head and the acetabulum
3. Medial space >3–5 mm indicates failure of closed reduction
I. Ultrasound
1. Most effective prior to ossification of the proximal femoral head
2. Can be used to diagnose subluxable hip or to confirm concentric reduction in the Pavlik harness
3. Gaining increasing use
J. CT scan: can be used to document concentric reduction in a cast

V. Treatment

A. Newborn to 6 months of age: Pavlik harness
1. Minimum 2 months' duration or about twice the child's age
2. Obtain an x-ray or ultrasound 1 week after being in brace
3. A 95° flexion using the anterior strap, and safe zone abduction (45°–60°) using the posterior strap
4. Wean if the hip is stable in extension
5. Discontinue Pavlik harness if it does not relocate the hip after 1 month of use
6. Avoid extreme positions to prevent osteonecrosis

B. Between 4 and 6 months and 18 months of age
1. Traction is required because hip contracture is developed and the hip does not reduce
2. Closed reduction under anesthesia with adductor tenotomy if necessary and spica cast: may be appropriate until 3 years of age in selected individuals
3. Traction: skin traction with 30°–45° flexion and 30° abduction. Two to 3 pounds of weight is used until the head is down to the level of triradiate cartilage (home traction can be done for about 3 weeks)
4. Percutaneous adductor tenotomy may be done if the adductors are tight or safe zone is narrow
5. Hip spica cast: 110° flexion and safe zone abduction (30°–60°) and 10°–20° internal rotation for 6 months' duration
   a. Fiberglass cast preferred
   b. Single cut CT scan may be done to confirm reduction in doubtful cases
6. Occasional open reduction may be necessary in 12- to 18-month-old children if closed reduction fails or when extreme positioning is required to maintain reduction

C. Between 18 months and 3 years: open reduction
1. Traction and gentle reduction may be attempted but open reduction is usually necessary in this age group
2. Distal femoral skeletal traction may be dangerous in producing avascular necrosis
3. Medial approach
   a. If the hip is reducible but difficult to

maintain, concentric reduction in a child <24 months old
b. Not for lax ligaments or teratologic cases
c. Release of the hourglass constriction of the capsule, iliopsoas tendon, the transverse acetabular ligament, and infolded labrum can be done, but capsulorrhaphy cannot be performed with this approach
4. Anterolateral approach: between sartorius and tensor fascia lata (most widely used)
a. Excise ligmentum teres and pulvinar
b. Release inferior transverse ligament
c. Capsulorrhaphy to tighten the lax capsule
d. Adductor tenotomy
e. Postoperative: 6–12 weeks of hip spica cast and 6–12 weeks of abduction splint
5. Femoral shortening or acetabular augmentation can be done (usually after 3 years of age)
6. Femoral varus derotation osteotomy if excess femoral anteversion
7. Pelvic osteotomy is rarely indicated in this age group
D. Greater than 3–4 years
1. Femoral varus derotation osteotomies
a. Results are better in younger patients
b. Derotation correct excess anteversion, and varus alignment improves containment
2. Pelvic osteotomies
a. Indications
(1) Inability to obtain stability at open reduction
(2) Failure of acetabulum to remodel: the acetabulum has capacity to remodel with concentric reduction until 8 years
(3) More effective than femoral osteotomy after 4 years of age
b. Types
(1) Reconstruction procedures
i. Salter (Fig 3-6)
(a) Mild to moderate acetabular dysplasia
(b) Femoral head centers on abduction and internal rotation maneuver

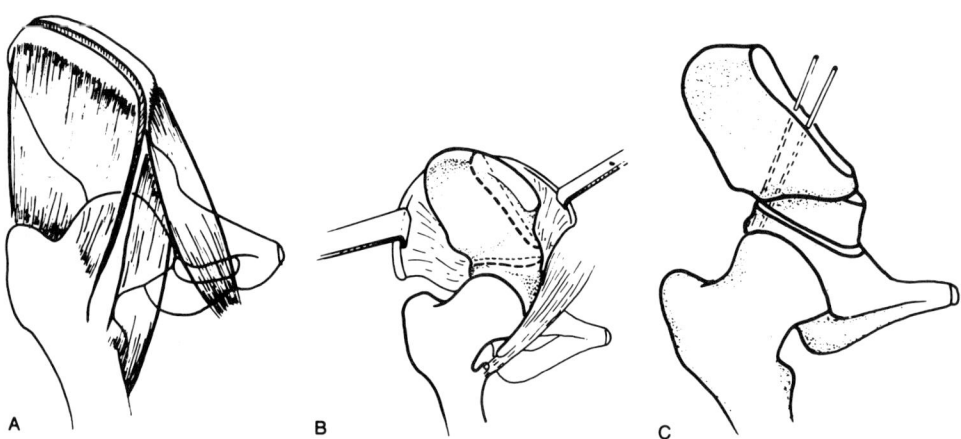

Figure 3-6. Surgical technique for Salter innominate osteotomy. (From Rab GT, Congenital deformities of the foot. In Chapman MW, ed. Operative orthopaedics, vol 3. Philadelphia, JB Lippincott, 1988, p 2124. Reprinted with permission.)

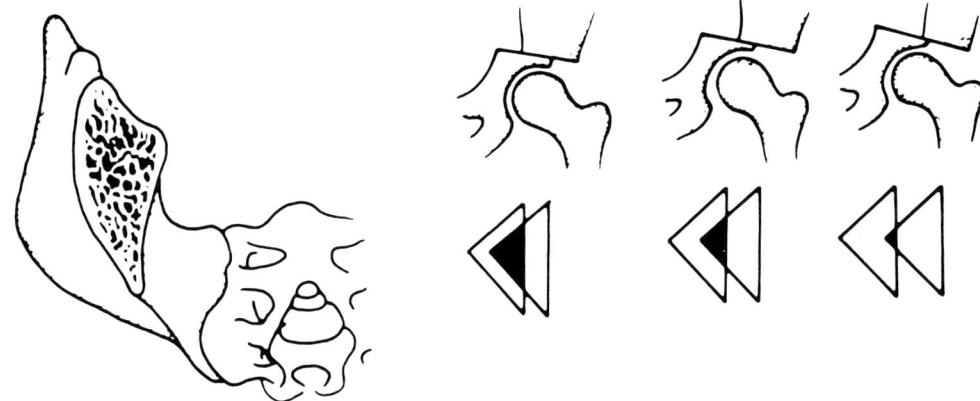

Figure 3-7. Chiari osteotomy cut is through a triangular section of the ilium. Excessive displacement of distal fragment will reduce the contact area. (From Rab GT: Congenital deformities of the foot. In Chapman MW, ed. Operative orthopaedics, vol 3. Philadelphia, JB Lippincott, 1988, p 2225. Reprinted with permission.)

- (c) Increases the anterior (20° to 30°) and lateral coverage (10° to 15°)
- (d) Affected limb is made longer and may increase the hip joint force
- (e) Not indicated in paralytic dislocations
- (f) Age: 18 months to teens

ii. Pemberton
  - (a) Moderate to severe deformity
  - (b) Good for large or flattened acetabulum because this procedure makes the acetabulum smaller
  - (c) Can be effective in paralytic dislocations
  - (d) Age: 18 months to 6 years
  - (e) Technically more difficult than Salter procedure

iii. Steele (triple innominate osteotomy) or Sutherland (double innominate osteotomy): for adolescent subluxating hips that are congruous but symphysis pubis is less flexible

iv. Wagner or Eppright: dial osteotomy with direct rotation of the acetabulum is technically demanding

(2) Salvage procedures
  i. Chiari (Fig 3–7)
    - (a) For adolescent subluxated hip with incongruity
    - (b) Particularly effective for shallow acetabulum
  ii. Shelf procedure: slotted acetabular augmentation (Staheli)

REFERENCES

Berkely ME, Dickson JH, Cain TE, et al: Surgical therapy for congenital dislocation of the hip in patients who are twelve to thirty-six months old. J Bone Joint Surg 66A:412–420, 1984

Castelein RM, Sauter AJM: Ultrasound screening for congenital dysplasia of the hip in newborns: Its value. J Pediatr Orthop 8:666–670, 1988

Gage JR, Winter RB: Avascular necrosis of the capital femoral epiphysis as a complication of closed reduction of congenital dislocation of the hip: A critical review of twenty years' experience at Gillette Children's Hospital. J Bone Joint Surg 54A:373, 1972

Kalamchi A, MacEwen GD: Avascular necrosis following treatment of congenital dislocation of the hip. J Bone Joint Surg 62A:876–888, 1980

Linstrom JR, Ponseti IV, Wenger DR: Acetabular development after reduction in congenital dislocation of the hip. J Bone Joint Surg 61A:112–118, 1979

Pemberton PA: Capsular arthroplasty for congenital dislocation of the hip: Indications and techniques. Some long-term results. J Bone Joint Surg 47A:607, 1965

Ramsey PL, Lasser S, MacEwen GD: Congenital dislocation of the hip: Use of the Pavlik harness in the child during the first six months of life. J Bone Joint Surg 58A:1000, 1976

Salter RB, Dubos J: The first fifteen years' personal experience with innominate osteotomy in the treatment of congenital dislocation and subluxation of the hip. Clin Orthop 98:72, 1974

Schoenecker PL, Strecker WB: Congenital dislocation of the hip in children: Comparison of the effects of femoral shortening and of skeletal traction in treatment. J Bone Joint Surg 66A:21–27, 1984

Steel HH: Triple osteotomy of the innominate bone. J Bone Joint Surg 55A:343, 1973

Sutherland DH, Greenfield R: Double innominate osteotomy. J Bone Joint Surg 59A:1082, 1977

Zionts LE, MacEwen GD: Treatment of congenital dislocation of the hip in children between the ages of one and three years. J Bone Joint Surg 68A:829–846, 1986

25

Legg-Calvé-Perthes Disease (Coxa Plana)

I. Incidence
A. Occurs during 4–8 years of age (80%)
B. Incidence: 1:10,000 (varies by region and race)
C. Males > females (4:1)
D. Ten percent bilateral but usually not simultaneous
E. Increased incidence in children with older parents, mother smoking during pregnancy, breech delivery, low birth weight, delayed skeletal maturation, and low socioeconomic group

II. Pathogenesis
A. Idiopathic avascular necrosis (AVN) of the femoral head, followed by subchondral fracture (clinical onset), revascularization and healing ossification processes
B. Etiology of AVN is unknown: inflammatory, synovitis, generalized disorder, growth hormone or somatomedin deficiency, traumatic, cartilaginous disorder, vascular or infections are possibilities

III. Stages
A. Avascular necrotic stage
  1. Failure of the ossific nucleus to grow, but the whole head is larger because of increased cartilagenous growth
  2. Increased medial joint space is seen radiologically secondary to synovitis, decreased ossific nucleus, and continued cartilage hypertrophy
  3. Subchondral lucency (crescent sign)
  4. Increased density of the femoral head secondary to marrow calcification and collapse
B. Fragmentation stage
  1. Fragmentation of the ossific nucleus and rarefaction of the femoral head
  2. Irregular physis and metaphyseal lucency and cysts can be seen
C. Reparative stage
  1. Ossification and healing period
  2. Head deformities can be seen (coxa magna, vara, plana)

IV. Clinical and X-ray Findings
A. Varies in intensity
B. Limping, pain in hip and knee
C. Decreased range of motion (abduction and internal rotation)
D. X-ray findings
  1. Plain x-ray: increased joint space, subchondral lucency, increased density, fragmentation, deformities
  2. Arthrogram: assess femoral head deformity and subluxation whether containable or hinged with abduction and internal rotation
  3. MRI (arthrogram-like image and can differentiate live versus dead marrow) and bone scan (early detection) but not always predictive

V. Differential Diagnosis
A. Transient synovitis (may develop to Perthes)
B. Sickle cell, infection, tuberculosis, Gaucher's disease, rheumatic fever, trauma, and tumors, such as lymphoma and eosinophilic granuloma of the hip
C. Bilateral (multiple epiphyseal dysplasia, spondyloepiphyseal dysplasia, trichorhinophalangeal syndrome, pseudoachon-

droplasia congenita and tarda, sickle cell disease, hypothyroidism)

VI. Prognosis
A. Clinical prognostic factors
  1. More than 6–8 years of age (most important factor)
  2. Obesity
  3. Decreased range of motion (adduction contracture)
  4. Females (have more Catterall type III and IV)
  5. Sixty percent with degenerated hip at 5th decade
B. Roentgenographic prognostic signs
  1. Gage's sign: lytic area in lateral epiphysis and adjacent metaphysis
  2. Calcification lateral to the epiphysis
  3. Diffuse metaphyseal reaction
  4. Lateral subluxation
  5. Horizontal physis
  6. Physeal damage
C. Epiphyseal extrusion index: uncovering of the femoral head >20% is a bad prognostic indicator
D. Extent of involvement
  1. Catterall classification (Fig 3-8)
    a. Group I: anterior head involvement, no sequestrum, no subchondral fracture
    b. Group II: anterior and central ½ head involvement with intact lateral margin (V shaped defect on lateral view). Sequestrum and subchondral fracture and anterolateral metaphyseal lesions
    c. Group III: large ¾ head involvement, including posterior ½ epiphysis (only posteromedial segment spared). Large sequestrum and subchondral fracture and diffuse metaphyseal changes
    d. Group IV: whole head involvement
  2. Salter: based on the extent of the subchondral fracture
    a. Group A: <½ involvement
    b. Group B: >½ involvement

VII. Treatment: Motion and Containment
A. Catterall I: no treatment
B. Catterall II or Salter group A (<50% head involvement) and <6 years old
  1. Observation if good range of motion
  2. Intermittent traction and active range of motion (especially abduction and internal rotation) if limitation of motion
  3. Traction and bracing if recurrent limitation of motion or symptoms
C. Catterall II and >6 years old: traction and bracing
D. Catterall III and IV or Salter group B (>50% head involvement): achieve good range of motion and containment
  1. Preliminary traction or Petrie cast for motion (for 6 weeks' duration — 45° abduction and 5° internal rotation)
  2. Two alternatives: orthosis or surgery
    a. Scottish Rite or other orthosis
      (1) Wean off of daytime orthosis and nighttime traction combination when reossification is visible in lateral column in about 18 months
      (2) Unsuitable if >10 years old
    b. Surgery for containable hip
      (1) Salter innominate osteotomy
        i. Only after full range of motion
        ii. The femoral head centers with abduction and internal rotation
        iii. Congruent round head without coxa magna, plana
        iv. Best indicated for patients between 6 and 8 years old, who have Catterall III or IV types without head deformity
        v. Disadvantage: may increase hip joint pressure and stiffness
      (2) Femoral osteotomy
        i. Only after full range of motion, especially abduction
        ii. Containable with abduction or internal rotation
        iii. Best indicated for patients between 6 and 9 years who have

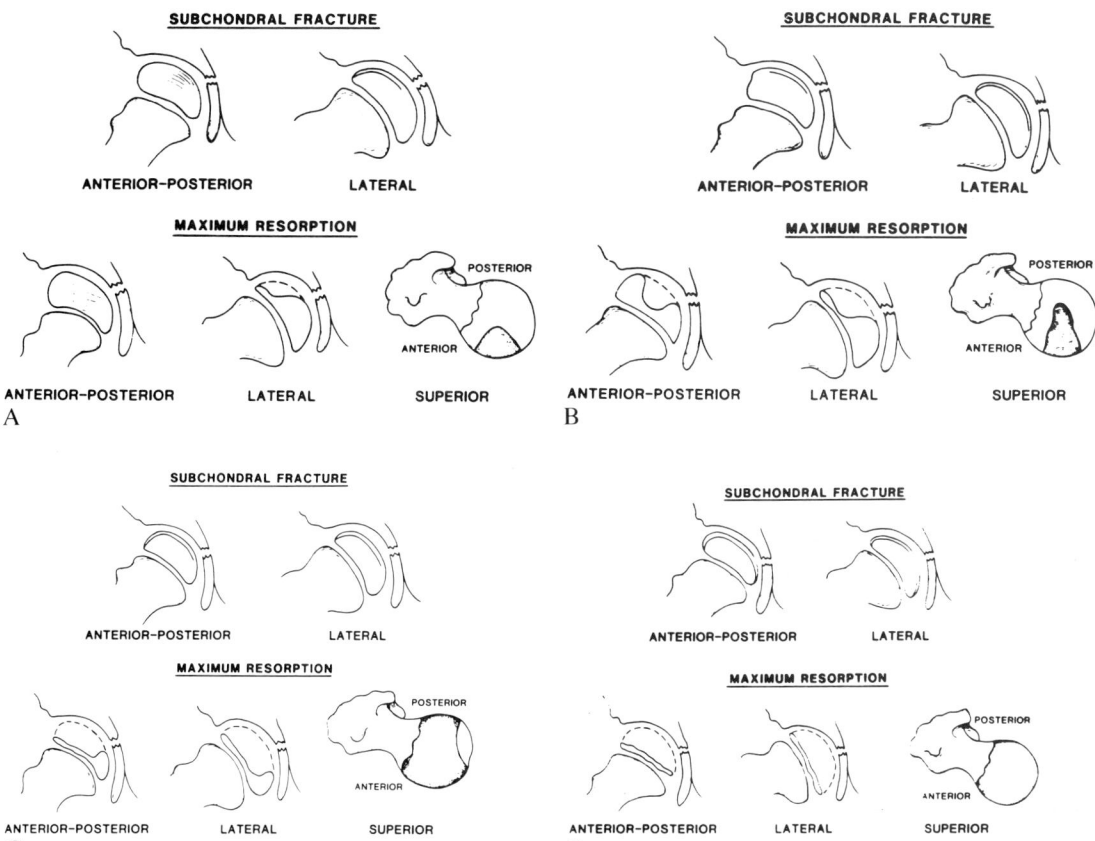

Figure 3-8. Catterall classification of Legg-Calvé-Perthes disease. **A.** Group 1: involvement limited to only the anterior portion of the epiphysis with no metaphyseal reaction, no sequestrum, and no subchondral fracture line. **B.** Group 2: sequestrum with clear junction, anterolateral metaphyseal reaction, and subchondral fracture on the anterior half, with the intact lateral epiphyseal margin. **C.** Group 3: large sequestrum with sclerotic junction, diffuse anterolateral metaphyseal reaction, and subchondral fracture on the posterior half (involvement of the lateral margin of the epiphysis). **D.** Group 4: whole head involvement, diffuse metaphyseal reaction, and posterior remodeling. (From Salter RB, Thompson GH: Legg-Calve-Perthes disease: The prognostic significance of the subchondral fracture and a two-group classification of the femoral head involvement. J Bone Joint Surg 66A:479–489, 1984. Reprinted with permission.)

Catterall type III with extruded or subluxated head and no femoral head deformity
   iv. Disadvantages: shortening and Trendelenburg gait
  c. Salvage procedures for noncontainable hip or hinge-abduction hip
     (1) Valgus extension osteotomy of the femur to improve range of motion
     (2) Chiari osteotomy to increase coverage (older than 12 years)
     (3) Cheilectomy: painful coxa magna and plana deformities in 10- to 13-year-old patients with impingement on abduction
  d. Other procedures
     (1) Trochanteric advancement: children 8 years or older who have arrest of the physeal growth of

the femoral head with abductor pain and a positive Trendelenburg test due to abductor inefficiency

(2) Resection of osteochondritis dissecans

(3) Epiphysiodesis of longer leg if necessary

REFERENCES

Catterall A: Legg-Calve-Perthes syndrome. Clin Orthop 158:41–52, 1981

Catterall A: The natural history of Perthes disease. J Bone Joint Surg 53B:37, 1971

Clancy M, Steel HH: The effect of an incomplete intertrochanteric osteotomy on Legg-Calve-Perthes disease. J Bone Joint Surg 67A:213–216, 1985

Evans IK, Deluca PA, Gage JR: A comparative study of ambulation-abduction bracing and varus derotation osteotomy in the treatment of severe Legg-Calve-Perthes disease in children over 6 years of age. J Ped Orthop 8:676–682, 1988

Hoikka V, Linholm TS, Poussa M: Intertrochanteric varus osteotomy in Legg-Calve-Perthes disease: A report of 112 hips. J Pediatr Orthop 6:600–604, 1986

McAndrew MP, Weinstein SL: A long-term follow-up of Legg-Calve-Perthes disease. J Bone Joint Surg 66A:860–869, 1984

Petrie JG, Bitenc I: The abduction weight-bearing treatment in Legg-Perthes' disease. J Bone Joint Surg 53B:54, 1971

Quain S, Catterall A: Hinge abduction of the hip: Diagnosis and treatment. J Bone Joint Surg 68B:61–64, 1986

Salter RB: The pathogenesis of deformity in Legg-Calve-Perthes' disease. J Bone Joint Surg 48B:389, 1966

Salter RB, Thompson GH: Legg-Calve-Perthes disease: The prognostic significance of the subchondral fracture and a two-group classification of the femoral head involvement. J Bone Joint Surg 66A:479–489, 1984

Sponseller PD, Desai SS, Millis MB: Comparison of femoral and innominate osteotomies for the treatment of Legg-Calve-Perthes disease. J Bone Joint Surg 70A:1131–1139, 1988

26
Slipped Capital Femoral Epiphysis

I. General Considerations
A. One to 3/100,000 incidence
B. Males > females (2.5:1)
C. Twenty-five percent bilateral (15–50% of these present simultaneously)
D. Common during 13–16 years (males) and 11–13 years (females)
E. Increased incidence in overweight or Froelich-type body habitus, slender tall type, black females; also occurs in hypothyroidism, hypopituitarism, especially treated with growth hormone, renal osteodystrophy patients, Down syndrome, positive family history
F. Suspect endocrine abnormalities if age of onset is <10 years or >16 years of age
G. Etiology is unknown

II. Classification
A. Acute: associated with acute traumatic injury resulting in a sudden displacement of femoral head
B. Acute on chronic: acute exacerbation of symptoms >3 weeks due to minor trauma
C. Chronic: history of pain >3 weeks

III. Pathogenesis
A. Slippage through the zone of hypertrophy
B. Relative retroversion may be present
C. The epiphysis slips posteriorly and inferiorly, and the leg rotates externally (anteriorly and superiorly)
D. Progressive apparent coxa vara and shortening of the leg result

IV. Clinical Findings
A. Chronic or intermittent pain in groin and referred down the medial aspect of the knee
B. Antalgic gait with externally rotated foot progression angle
C. Decreased internal rotation, abduction, and flexion
D. Hip flexion produces external rotation
E. Shortening of the femur in severe cases

V. X-Ray Findings (Fig 3-9)
A. Early change seen only on lateral x-ray view in 15%
B. On AP projection, there is loss of overhang of epiphysis at the superolateral aspect of femoral neck (Kline's line)
C. Posterior displacement of the epiphysis: 50% slip in one plane gives 39% overlap of the femoral head on the neck, and 50% slip in both planes gives only 18% overlap
D. "Metaphyseal blanch sign of Steel": early sign of posterior slipping
E. The proximal and medial part of the femoral neck does not overlap on the ischium
F. Chronic changes: widening of the physis, sclerosis, and ossification at the junction of the medial femoral neck
G. Narrowed joint space and osteopenia of femoral head and acetabulum in chondrolysis
H. Increased bone density and segmental collapse of femoral head in avascular necrosis

VI. Treatment
A. Acute
  1. Traction temporarily until surgery (split Russell skin traction is adequate with internal rotation vector)
  2. In situ pin fixation
    a. One pin is adequate for chronic slip and helps to avoid pin penetration

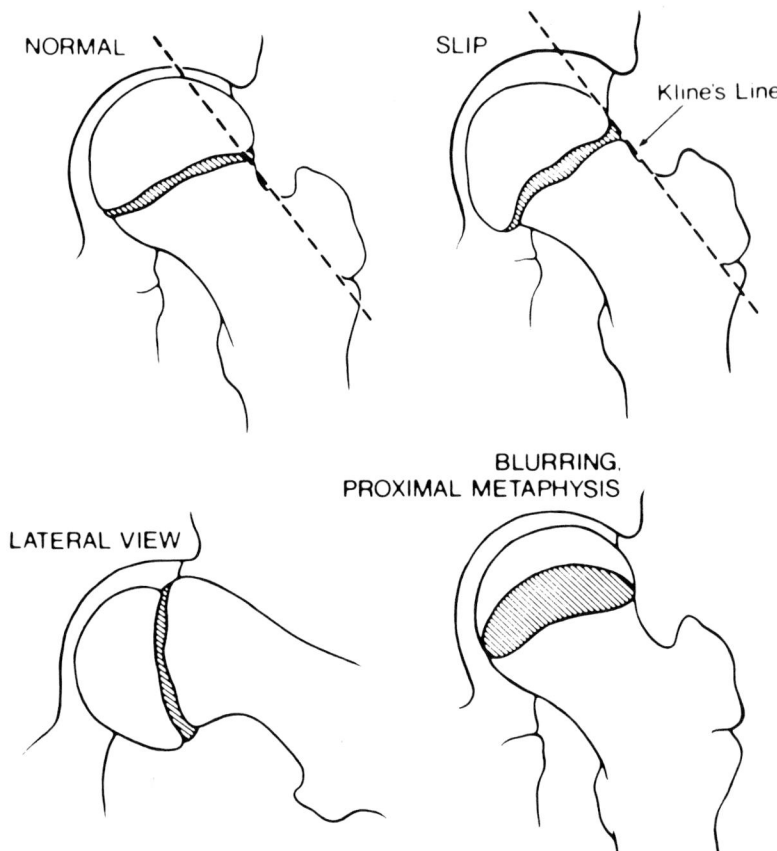

Figure 3-9. Radiographic changes in slipped capital femoral epiphysis. (From Wenger DR: Children's orthopaedics. In Bucholz RW, Lippert FG, Wenger DR, Ezaki M, eds. Orthopaedic decision making. Philadelphia, BC Decker, and St. Louis, CV Mosby, 1984, p 194. Reprinted with permission.)

      b. Start anteriorly from base of the neck and aim posteroinferiorly under fluoroscopic imaging
      c. Avoid superolateral quadrant of the femoral head where the posterosuperior retinacular vessels enter
      d. Percutaneous method is possible
   3. Crutch ambulation and partial weight bearing for 6 weeks
B. Acute on chronic
   1. Pinning in situ is accepted by most authors
   2. Reduction increases the risk of avascular necrosis
   3. If reduction is performed, only the acute displacement should be reduced in a gentle manner
C. Chronic
   1. Pinning in situ without reduction
   2. Primary epiphysiodesis is also acceptable, particularly for moderate to severe degrees of slippage
   3. Possible delayed reconstruction osteotomy can be done later in severe cases
   4. Transcervical and basal neck osteotomies are associated with increased incidence of avascular necrosis

VII. Complications
A. Chondrolysis
   1. Increased in blacks and more common in females
   2. Associated with pin penetration

3. Clinical: stiffness and muscle spasm: laboratory findings such as erythrocyte sedimentation rate (ESR) and complete blood count (CBC) are normal
4. X-rays: joint space narrowing and positive bone scan with increased uptake of acetabulum and femoral head
5. Prognosis: may recover in 6–12 months but may cause degenerative or ankylosis of the joint
6. Treatment
   a. Traction, range of motion exercise, continuous passive motion, nonsteroidal anti-inflammatory drugs (NSAIDs)
   b. Soft tissue release and continuous range of motion
   c. Salvage operations: arthrodesis or arthroplasty
B. Avascular necrosis of femoral head
1. Rarely due to slip itself
2. Associated with manipulation for reduction or osteotomies especially in femoral neck
3. Treatment
   a. Nonweight-bearing and range of motion exercise
   b. Osteotomies such as valgus, varus, or rotational types can be considered for focal femoral head involvement
   c. Salvage operations: arthroplasties or arthrodesis

VIII. Prophylactic Pinning

A. Not indicated
B. Follow contralateral hip radiographically closely until the physeal closure
C. Bilaterality increased in renal osteodystrophy; may consider prophylactic pinning here

REFERENCES

Bennet GC, Koreska J, Rang M: Pin placement in slipped capital femoral epiphysis. J Pediatr Orthop 4:574–578, 1984

Boyer DW, Mickelson MR, Ponseti IV: Slipped capital femoral epiphysis: Long-term follow-up study of 121 patients. J Bone Joint Surg 63A:85–95, 1981

Gelberman RH, Cohen MS, Shaw BA, et al: The association of femoral retroversion with slipped capital femoral epiphysis. J Bone Joint Surg 68A: 1000–1007, 1986

Ingram AJ, Clarke MS, Clark CS Jr, et al: Chondrolysis complicating slipped capital femoral epiphysis. Clin Orthop 165:99–109, 1982

Southwick WO: Osteotomy through the lesser trochanter for slipped capital femoral epiphysis. J Bone Joint Surg 49A:807, 1967

Stambough JL, Davidson RS, Ellis RD, et al: Slipped capital femoral epiphysis: An analysis of 80 patients as to pin placement and number. J Pediatr Orthop 6:265–273, 1986

Weiner DS, Weinrer S, Melby A, et al: A 30 year experience with bone graft epiphysiodesis in the treatment of slipped capital femoral epiphysis. J Pediatr Orthop 4:145–152, 1984

27
Neuromuscular Problems

CEREBRAL PALSY

I. Definition
A. Result of damage to the developing brain (prenatally, at birth, or early in postnatal period), producing a disorder of movement and posture that is static

II. Etiology
A. Incidence: 1–5/1000
B. Etiology
  1. Genetic
  2. Pregnancy complications: drugs, alcohol, infections
  3. Perinatal: anoxia, jaundice
  4. Postnatal: trauma, meningitis, hydrocephalus
C. Prematurity is biggest single association with cerebral palsy
D. Forty percent of cases are potentially preventable

III. Classification
A. Geographic
  1. Hemiplegia
  2. Diplegia: most walk by age 7 years
  3. Quadriplegia: 10% chance of walking and if cannot walk by age 7 years, they never will
B. Physiologic
  1. Spastic: pyramidal involvement — hypertonic, especially flexors, most common type seen by orthopedic surgeons
  2. Athetoid: basal ganglia involvement — involuntary movement, writhing and speech difficulty
  3. Ataxic: cerebellar and brainstem involvement — tremor, nystagmus, and balance difficulties
  4. Other types: rigid, floppy, mixed, hemiballismus

C. Clinical Findings
  1. Careful history and examination: birth and developmental history, gait, range of motion, muscle strength, spinal contour
  2. Rule out metabolic problems, tethered cord, Charcot-Marie-Tooth, and Friederick's diseases
  3. Walkers versus nonwalkers: can be predicted at 2 years of age by Bleck's criteria
     a. Nonambulators: sitters or transfer only
     b. Ambulators: exercise, household, or community ambulators
  4. Muscle shortening
     a. Muscle growth is also retarded, because stimulus for muscle growth (stretch of the relaxed muscle) is hindered by increased stretch reflex
     b. Number of sarcomere (determination of muscle length) decreases when muscle is held at shortened position
     c. Excursion decreases, which is determined by length of fibers
     d. Strength also decreases as muscle bulk (number of fibers) decreases

IV. Treatment
A. Goals: socialization, school attendance, pain relief, improved mobility and function, prevent joint dislocations, sitting and satisfactory gait
B. Types of treatment
  1. Physical therapy: prevent contractures, especially 0–3 years
  2. Bracing
     a. Not used to correct fixed deformity and difficult to control strong dynamic deformity

b. Two purposes: prevention of contractures (especially postoperatively) and tone control
c. Less orthotics are better and use light plastic materials if possible
3. Surgery
 a. Spastic types: control static and dynamic deformity
 b. Foot/ankle usually precedes hip and knee
 c. Scoliosis and pelvic obliquity should be corrected before hip correction, if possible
 d. Early surgical intervention before contractures and dislocations occur
 e. Pay attention to linkage (hip-knee-ankle)
C. Spine involvement
 1. Twenty-five percent incidence and more in nonambulatory patients
 2. Orthosis (thoracic suspension or thoracosacrolumbar orthosis [TSLO]) if <50° to control curve before adolescence
 3. Spinal fusion to balance spine over pelvis
  a. Posterior fusion with Luque rods and sublaminar wires and Galveston pelvic fixation (upper thoracic spine to ilium for nonambulatory patients with pelvic obliquity)
  b. Anterior release and fusion with or without instrumentation (Zielke), followed by posterior fusion with Luque rods for severe stiff curves and when preoperative traction x-rays do not show the spine balanced over the pelvis
  c. Ambulatory patients without significant pelvic obliquity should have fusion posteriorly without extending down to the sacrum
D. Foot and ankle involvement
 1. Equinus deformity
  a. Heel cord stretching initially: stretch with foot in varus and knee in extension
  b. Bracing or casting to maintain correction
  c. Sliding or Z-plasty heel cord lengthening if failure of conservative therapy
 2. Equinovalgus
  a. Heel cord stretching and bracing
  b. Aponeurosis or tendo Achilles lengthening for mild flexible deformities
  c. Intramuscular lengthening of peroneus brevis in milder cases
  d. Peroneus brevis to posterior tibialis transfer may be effective in muscle imbalance cases
  e. Grice subtalar arthrodesis in severe cases (4–8 years of age)
  f. Triple arthrodesis in adolescents
 3. Equinovarus
  a. Dynamic electromyography to assess dynamic deformity muscles
  b. Varus is tolerated less than valgus and earlier surgery is indicated
  c. Posterior tibialis tendon lengthening with TAL if dynamic EMG reveals marked myoelectric activity of posterior tibialis and abnormal activity in gastrocnemius-soleus. Split posterior tibialis transfer should be considered if the anterior tibialis is active
  d. Split transfer of anterior tibialis transfer if varus hindfoot, supinated forefoot with weight bearing over the lateral aspect of the foot on walking and if dynamic EMG reveals marked myoelectric activity of anterior tibialis and abnormal activity in gastrocnemius-soleus muscles
  e. Transfer of tibialis posterior if its activity is out of phase with the predominant myoelectric signal recorded during the swing phase of the gait cycle and nonfunctioning anterior tibialis
  f. Lateral closing wedge calcaneal osteotomy or triple arthrodesis in fixed varus deformities of hind foot
  g. Forefoot deformities: cavus, meta-

tarsus adductus, hallux valgus, dorsal bunion, toe flexor contractures
E. Hip involvement
1. Hip at risk: femoral head uncovered ⅓ of diameter, <45° combined abduction, and break in Shenton line
   a. Do early soft tissue release to prevent dislocation (adductor release and iliopsoas release or recession or transfer to greater trochanter)
   b. Neurectomy of the anterior branch of the obturator nerve can be done in nonambulators
2. Subluxed hip: femoral head uncovered ⅓ or more
   a. Adductor release and psoas recession
   b. Subtrochanteric varus derotation osteotomy to correct coxa valga and excess anteversion at 8–10 years old
   c. Chiari, Shelf, or Pemberton osteotomy if acetabular dysplasia is present
      (1) Pemberton is preferred over Salter osteotomy, but Salter osteotomy can be modified to increase lateral coverage without uncovering posteriorly
      (2) Femoral and pelvic osteotomy can be done simultaneously in severe cases
      (3) Chiari or acetabular augmentation procedures are done in older children
3. Dislocation requires combined procedures
   a. Adductor, psoas release, and capsulorrhaphy
   b. Subtrochanteric varus derotation osteotomy
   c. Pelvic osteotomy
   d. Femoral shortening may be necessary
4. One must rule out apparent hip flexion contracture by rectus femoris or sartorius contracture by performing Ely prone test, and rule out apparent adduction contracture by medial hamstring by performing Phelps-Baker test
   a. Positive Ely test: passive flexion of the knee will elevate the pelvis in prone position
   b. Positive Phelps-Baker test: adduction contracture disappears on flexion of the knee (relaxing of the medial hamstring)
5. Unilaterally dislocated hips should be reduced even in nonambulatory patients because pelvic obliquity, sitting imbalance, and pain may ensue
F. Knee involvement
1. Flexion deformity
   a. Frequent association with hip flexion and equinus
   b. Ankle-foot orthosis (AFO) is preferable to knee-ankle-foot orthosis (KAFO) for more efficient ambulation
   c. Lengthening of semitendinosus and gracilis release or lengthening and aponeurotic lengthening of semimembranosus and biceps femoris
2. Internal rotation
   a. Dynamic: transfer of semitendinosus to lateral intermuscular septum if medial hamstrings are the cause
   b. Osteotomy may be necessary if osseous deformity

MYELOMENINGOCELE

I. Spina Bifida Types
A. Spina bifida occulta
B. Meningocele
C. Myelomeningocele
D. Myelocele

II. Pathoetiology
A. Etiology
   1. Failure of neural tube to close
   2. Rupture of normally closed neural tube secondary to relative hydrocephalus
B. Incidence: 1/1000

C. Familial: 1/20 risk if one sibling and ½ chance if two siblings are affected
D. Alpha-fetoprotein detection in the amniotic fluid by 16–18 weeks of gestation
E. Associated conditions: Arnold-Chiari malformation, hydrocephalus, cerebellar hypoplasia, syringomyelia, diastematomyelia, hydromyelia

III. Deformities Depending on Levels
A. Levels: difficult to determine accurately and may be asymmetrical
B. Deformities
  1. T12: no deformity (flail) except flexion, abduction, and external rotation of the limbs from posture
  2. L1: Hip flexed and externally rotated
  3. L2: Hip flexed and adducted
  4. L3: Hip flexed, adducted, and knee extended
  5. L4: Hip flexed, adducted, and knee extended. Dorsiflexion of ankle and varus of the foot
  6. L5: Hip extended, knee flexed and cavus foot
  7. S1: Knee flexed and equinus of the foot

IV. Spine
A. Congenital kyphosis
  1. At birth: generally not recommended to correct the major spine deformity because of lack of bone stock and associated problems
  2. Posterior resection of kyphosis
    a. Two to three vertebrae proximal to apex
    b. Posterior stabilization with wires or Luque rods
    c. Better results if done before 3 years of age
B. Developmental or paralytic kyphoscoliosis
  1. Deformity is progressive, because the extensors of the spine (sacrospinalis and quadratus lumborum muscles) rotate anteriorly to increase flexion force
  2. Rule out hydromyelia or tethered cord in progressive deformities
  3. Treatment
    a. Bracing for young patients and mild deformity
    b. Posterior fusion: long fusion to the sacrum
    c. Anterior release with or without Zielke instrumentation and fusion followed by posterior fusion with instrumentation for severe cases

V. Hip
A. Etiology of developmental hip dislocation
  1. Muscle imbalance
    a. L1–L2: frequent early dislocation
    b. L3–L4: highest incidence of hip dislocation
  2. Pelvic obliquity and scoliosis can lead to windblown deformity of the legs
  3. Acetabular dysplasia
  4. Valgus of the neck
B. Treatment
  1. Birth to 18 months: range of motion exercise to prevent contractures and maintain reduction with brace, traction, or occasional soft tissue release
  2. Soft tissue release (adductors and psoas)
  3. Varus osteotomy with or without muscle transfer, posterior iliopsoas transfer (Sharrard or Mustard procedures), external oblique transfer or adductor to ischium transfer

VI. Knee
A. Flexion contractures
  1. Brace (AFO with plantar flexion)
  2. Lengthening or transfer of hamstrings
  3. Osteotomy of the distal femur
B. Extension deformities (recurvatum): treat with AFO with slight dorsiflexion or quadriceps lengthening
C. Valgus
  1. Tight iliotibial band or secondary to weak abductors of the hip

2. Treatment: KAFO, release, or osteotomy

VII. Foot and Ankle
A. Deformities: equinovarus > calcaneus > equinovalgus, cavus and claw toes
B. Equinovarus: casting for 2–3 months and surgery at 4–6 months (release contracted structures rather than lengthening to prevent recurrences)
C. Calcaneus: manipulation until 2 years and transfer of anterior tibialis and peroneus tertius to os calcis; also consider tenotomies
D. Equinovalgus: associated with external tibial torsion, knee valgus, and weak hip abductors
   1. Partial Achilles tenodesis to the fibula if <1 cm fibular shortening in young children
   2. Supramalleolar tibial osteotomy or epiphyseal stapling of the medial tibia epiphysis in older children
   3. Tibial osteotomy and triple arthrodesis in adolescent

OTHER NEUROMUSCULAR DISEASES

I. Classification
A. Primary upper motor neuron (ie, cerebral palsy)
B. Primary anterior horn cell disease (ie, spinal muscular atrophy)
C. Primary peripheral neuropathy (ie, Charcot-Marie-Tooth disease)
D. Primary disease of neuromuscular junction (ie, myasthenia gravis)
E. Primary muscle disorders (ie, Duchenne's muscular dystrophy)

II. Evaluation
A. History: developmental milestones
B. Physical examination and careful neurologic examination
C. Laboratory data: creatine phosphokinase (CPK), aldolase, and SGOT
D. Electromyography
   1. Electromyographic components
      a. Amplitude: low in myopathy
      b. Duration: prolonged in chronic neuropathy
      c. Phases: polyphasic in myopathy
      d. Rate: increased in neuropathy
   2. Denervation and myopathic disorders
      a. Lower motor neuron diseases: fibrillation potentials
      b. Spinal muscular atrophy: fibrillation and fasciculation with decreased number of recordings
         (1) Early stage: brief, biphasic, low voltage
         (2) Chronic stage: prolonged, polyphasic, high voltage potentials
      c. Myopathic: polyphasic and low voltage potentials. Myotonia dystrophica has characteristic "dive bomber sound"
E. Nerve conduction studies
   1. Measurement of conduction velocities
      a. Amplitude: decreased in axonal lesions
      b. Latency: myelin disorders
      c. Velocity: decreased in demyelination and normal in anterior horn cell, root, and myopathies
   2. Peripheral neuropathies: Charcot-Marie-Tooth and spinocerebellar diseases
F. Muscle biopsy
   1. Choose muscle that is involved but still has function: rectus femoris, vastus lateralis, biceps, deltoids, or gastrocnemius
   2. Atraumatic, no cautery technique
   3. Rectangular piece (5–10 by 2–3 mm thick)
   4. Preparation
      a. Moist saline gauze
      b. Liquid nitrogen for histologic examination
      c. Glutaraldehyde for electron microscopy

        d. Enzyme histochemical tests
    5. Fiber type
        a. Normal: 1:2 (type 1 and type 2)
        b. Myopathic: type 1 predominates
        c. Neuropathy: small group atrophy, fiber-type grouping, and greater than 80% type 2 in lower motor neuron disease

III. Muscular Dystrophy

A. Classification (Walton)
    1. Sex linked
        a. Severe Duchenne type
        b. Benign Becker type (adult)
    2. Autosomal recessive
        a. Limb-girdle
        b. Childhood except Duchenne
        c. Congenital
    3. Autosomal dominant: facioscapulohumeral
    4. Distal
    5. Ocular
    6. Oculopharyngeal
    7. Myotonia
        a. Myotonia congenita
        b. Dystrophia myotonica
        c. Paramyotonia congenita
B. Duchenne's pseudohypertrophic muscular dystrophy
    1. General consideration
        a. Sex-linked inheritance
        b. Incidence: 13–33/100,000 males
        c. Age: diagnosable at birth, clinically apparent at 3 years
    2. Clinical findings
        a. Lumbar hyperlordosis, waddling gait, positive Gower's sign, hip flexion, knee flexion, equinovarus, and tensor fascia contractures
        b. Proximal muscles involved first, then distal. Lower extremities first, then upper extremities
        c. Loses independent ambulation at 10–11 years
        d. Cardiac problems
        e. Muscle bulk is initially pseudohypertrophic, then atrophy
    f. Diagnosis
        (1) CPK markedly elevated (50–100 times)
        (2) EMG: myopathic (low amplitude, polyphasic, short duration)
        (3) Biopsy: fibrosis, degeneration, and variation of sizes. Fatty tissue and centralization of nuclei. Prevalence of type I fibers
    g. Progressive flexion contractures, scoliosis, and death from respiratory failure in 2nd or 3rd decade
    3. Treatment
        a. Bracing and physical therapy
        b. Surgery
            (1) Achilles tendon lengthening for equinus contracture at appropriate time
            (2) Posterior tibialis transfer: equinovarus
            (3) Hip and knee flexion contracture releases
            (4) Scoliosis: Long spinal fusion when >30° using Luque technique
C. Adult muscular dystrophy (Becker)
    1. Inheritance: X-linked recessive
    2. Clinical findings:
        a. Sex: males
        b. Age: adolescence
        c. Muscle: weakness of proximal muscle
        d. Prognosis: better than Duchenne's muscular dystrophy
    3. Biopsy: similar to Duchenne's except type 2B fibers are preserved
    4. Treatment: nonspecific

IV. Myotonia and Other Myopathies

A. Myotonia: inability of skeletal muscle to relax
    1. Myotonia dystrophica (Steinert's disease)
        a. Steadily progressive systemic disease in which myotonia and muscle weakness are present
        b. Gonadal atrophy, cataracts, frontal

baldness, heart disease, and mental deficiency are associated findings
   c. Autosomal dominant and usually occurs during late adolescence
   d. Distal muscles earlier and lower extremities more involved
   e. Difficulty in relaxing muscle (myotonia) tends to disappear as muscle weakness and atrophy progress and inability to ambulate after 15–20 years
   f. Decreased deep tendon reflexes and scoliosis
   g. Treatment: cervical collar for weak neck muscles, orthosis for the extremities, and brace for scoliosis
   h. Myotonia dystrophica in infancy: hypotonia, facial diplegia, and diminished sucking at birth and myotonia and muscle weakness later during 5–10 years of age (contractures of the foot and ankle are common)
  2. Myotonia congenita (Thomsen's disease)
   a. Myotonia without muscle weakness
   b. Generalized muscle hypertrophy
   c. Normal life span
   d. Treatment: phenytoin and procainamide in severe cases of myotonia
  3. Paramyotonia congenita (Eulenburg's disease)
   a. Paradoxical myotonia and flaccid paresis
   b. Precipitated by cold exposure
   c. Potassium level may be abnormal
   d. Treatment: quinine sulfate and potassium balance
 B. Congenital myopathies: floppy baby (hypotonia) and muscle weakness, especially in shoulder and pelvic muscles (autosomal dominant)
  1. Central core disease: center of the muscle fiber (type I fibers) is replaced by amorphous substance devoid of oxidative and glycolytic enzymes (malignant hyperthermia is a potential complication)
  2. Nemaline myopathy: more common in females, skeletal changes similar to arachnodactyly, and rod body requires special stains (ie, Gomori trichome) or electron microscopy
  3. Myotubular myopathy: axial weakness, including facial and extraocular involvement (central zone devoid of adenosine triphosphatase [ATPase] reaction)
  4. Congenital fiber-type disproportion: type I fibers are smaller (lower extremity contractures and scoliosis are common in addition to hypotonia)
  5. Mitochondrial myopathies: metabolic abnormalities and weakness of neck flexors and extraocular motor weakness
  6. Pompe's disease (glycogen storage disease IIA): hypotonia, enlarged heart, liver, and tongue (progressive disease with death within 1 year, in milder forms patient may survive several years)
 C. Inflammatory myopathies
  1. Polymyositis and dermatomyositis
  2. Systemic lupus erythematosus
  3. Scleroderma
  4. Myositis ossificans

V. Hereditary Motor and Sensory Neuropathies (Dyck) (Table 3-1)

A. Type I: Charcot-Marie-Tooth (peroneal muscular atrophy)
 1. Roussy-Lévy syndrome: hereditary areflexic dystaxia, clinically similar to Charcot-Marie-Tooth except tremor of the hands
 2. Inheritance: autosomal dominant
 3. Pathology: demyelinating peripheral neuropathy, hypertrophic type
 4. Clinical findings
  a. Onset in the first decade
  b. Females worse than males
  c. Symmetrical weakness beginning distally, especially peroneals, anterior musculature, and extensor digitorum brevis

Table 3-1 Classification of Hereditary Sensory-Motor Neuropathies*

Type	Other Names	Heredity	Nerve Conduction	Orthopaedic Problems
I	Hypertrophic form of Charcot-Marie-Tooth Peroneal muscular atrophy Roussy-Lévy syndrome	Autosomal dominant	Delayed	Pes cavus Claw hands Hip dysplasia Scoliosis Claw toes
II	Neuronal form of Charcot-Marie-Tooth disease Peroneal muscular atrophy	Autosomal dominant	Near normal	Pes calcaneovarus Claw toes Claw hands Scoliosis Hip dysplasia
III	Dejerne-Sotta disease Hereditary neuropathy of infancy Peroneal muscular atrophy	Autosomal recessive	Very delayed	Trunk ataxia Delayed milestones Scoliosis Pes cavus Dropped foot
IV	Refsum's disease Phytanic acid storage neuropathy	Autosomal recessive	Delayed	Epiphyseal dysplasia Shortened metacarpals Pes cavus Pes equinus Scoliosis
V	Neuropathy with spastic paraplegia	Autosomal dominant	Slightly delayed	Spastic paraplegia Contractures

*From Bowen JR, MacEwen GD; Muscle and nerve disorders. In Chapman MW, Ed. Operative Orthopaedics, vol 3. Philadelphia, JB Lippincott, 1988, p. 2187. Reprinted with permission.

     d. Areflexic, decreased vibration, and position sense
     e. Lower extremity earlier and more especially cavovarus
     f. Scoliosis: 10%
  5. Laboratory findings
     a. Nerve conduction velocity (NCV) extremely slow (<60%), distal latency prolonged, and EMG gives neuropathic pattern
     b. Nerve biopsy: "onion bulb" demyelination, increased fibrosis, remyelinization (hypertrophic neuropathy)
  6. Treatment: cavovarus of the foot (plantar release, posterior tibialis transfer, triple arthrodesis)

B. Type II: Charcot-Marie-Tooth neuronal type
  1. Inheritance: autosomal dominant
  2. Pathology: anterior horn cell degeneration
  3. Clinical findings
     a. Onset in the 2nd and 3rd decades
     b. "Stork-legged"
     c. Reflexes diminished and lower extremity more involved
  4. Laboratory findings
     a. NCS normal or slightly delayed and EMG gives denervation pattern
     b. Nerve biopsy: axonal degeneration but myelin persists
C. Type III: Dejerine-Sottas disease (hypertrophic neuropathy of infancy)

1. Inheritance: autosomal recessive
2. Pathology: Schwann cell hypertrophy
3. Clinical findings
    a. Seen early in infancy and childhood
    b. Enlarged peroneal and ulnar peripheral nerves
    c. Areflexic and "stocking/glove" sensory loss
    d. Truncal ataxia and spasmodic finger movements
4. Laboratory findings
    a. NCS markedly slowed and EMG shows denervation
    b. Nerve biopsy: "onion bulb" formation with Schwann cell hypertrophy and segmental demyelination and perineural fibrosis
    c. Protein elevated in cerebrospinal fluid

D. Type IV: Refsum's disease
1. Inheritance: autosomal recessive
2. Pathology: serum phytanic acid elevated with hypertrophic neuropathy
3. Clinical findings
    a. Onset in childhood or at puberty
    b. Repeated attacks of distal sensory and motor loss in the hands and feet
    c. Anosmia, progressive deafness, night blindness (retinitis pigmentosa), ichthyosis, cardiac abnormalities
    d. Cerebellar abnormalities — ataxia and nystagmus
4. Laboratory findings
    a. Serum phytanic acid elevated
    b. NCS slow
    c. Protein markedly elevated in cerebrospinal fluid
    d. Nerve biopsy: hypertrophic nerves with fat deposits (increased endoneurium)

E. Type V: Neuropathy with spastic paraplegia
1. Inheritance: autosomal dominant
2. Rare with infrequent orthopaedic problems
3. Spastic paraplegia
4. NCS/EMG shows peripheral neuropathy

VI. Spinal Muscular Atrophy (SMA) (Table 3-2)

A. Classifications
1. Infantile SMA (Werdnig-Hoffmann) — type I

Table 3-2 Types of Spinal Muscular Atrophy*

Form	Age at Onset	Progression	Inheritance
Type I	<3 months	Rapid	Autosomal recessive
Type II	6 mo. to 3 yr	Moderately rapid	Autosomal recessive
Type III	1–15 yr	Moderate	Autosomal recessive
Adult	18–50 yr	Slow	Probably recessive
Scapular peroneal atrophy	Variable	Slow	Autosomal dominant
Charcot-Marie-Tooth disease, neuronal	Variable	Slow	Autosomal dominant
Facioscapulohumeral, neurogenic	Variable	Slow	Autosomal dominant
Distal	Variable	Slow	Autosomal recessive

*From Bowen JR, MacEwen GD: Muscle and nerve disorders. In Chapman MW, ed. Operative orthopaedics, vol 3. Philadelphia, JB Lippincott, 1988, p 2193. Reprinted with permission.

    a. Diagnosed at 2–6 months of age
    b. No sitting balance and head control
  2. Juvenile SMA (Kugelberg-Welander) — type II
    a. Onset after 2 years of age
    b. Almost normal life span, but proximal weakness later
    c. Differential diagnosis: muscular dystrophy, especially limb-girdle type
B. Inheritance: autosomal recessive
C. Pathology: chronic progressive degeneration of the anterior horn cells in the spinal cord
D. Clinical findings
  1. Symmetrical hypotonia that affects the lower extremities and proximal muscle groups more
  2. Areflexia, tongue fasciculation, tremor of the hand
  3. Laboratory findings
    a. Normal NCS and EMG with denervation pattern
    b. Muscle biopsy: neuropathy pattern with group atrophy and persistent group of hypertrophic fibers
  4. Functional groups
    a. Group I: bulbar involvement (poor suck and swallow)
    b. Group II: life expectancy early to middle adulthood
    c. Group III: upper extremity weakness in the 2nd decade, neck muscle involved in 3rd and 4th decades and life expectancy often beyond 45 years
    d. Group IV: almost normal life span but usually wheelchair ambulators by mid-30s

VII. Arthrogryposis Multiplex Congenita

A. Periarticular soft tissue structures become fibrotic, developing an incomplete fibrous ankylosis
B. Syndrome of nonprogressive multiple congenitally rigid joints
C. Abnormalities in the central nervous system, anterior horn cells, and muscle and joints are reported
D. Clinical findings: rigid joints, adducted and internal rotation of the shoulder, flexion or extension of the elbow, flexed and ulnarly deviated wrist, dislocated hips, clubfeet, and dislocated patella
E. Treatment:
  1. Neonatal contractures: serial casting and manipulation
  2. Physical therapy, splints and braces to maintain correction and prevent deformities
  3. Surgery: correct lower extremity deformities before 2 years of age to help ambulation
    a. Clubfoot: complete subtalar release at 6 months or talectomy at 12–18 months of age
    b. Knee: posterior capsulotomy with hamstring release for flexion contractures and anterior capsulotomy and quadriceps lengthening for hyperextension contractures
    c. Hip: flexion, abduction, and external contractures and dislocation. Open reduction is indicated at 1 year of age for unilateral dislocations only. For flexion contractures, casting at a young age or subtrochanteric osteotomy at near skeletal maturity
    d. Scoliosis: posterior instrumentation and fusion if >40°
    e. Upper extremities: various surgical procedures to enhance functions (feeding, toilet use, handling objects)

VIII. Neurofibromatosis

A. Incidence: 1/2500 to 3000
B. Genetics: autosomal dominant trait with variable penetrance and a high rate of spontaneous mutation
C. Clinical findings
  1. Café-au-lait spots: usually >6 and

≥1.5 cm in diameter and smooth edges (coast of California)
2. Nodules: dermal neurofibroma, 12% in childhood
3. Nevus: 6% incidence and 10% of plexiform neuroma result in malignant transformation (treatment is early surgical excision)
4. Elephantiasis: 10% incidence and quite characteristic of neurofibromatosis
5. Verrucous hyperplasia: overgrowth of skin and thickening (grotesque and can get infected)
6. Neoplasia: 7–20% incidence of malignant transformation of neural mass

D. Skeletal manifestation
1. Scoliosis: 60% incidence
   a. Nondystrophic: similar to idiopathic type
   b. Dystrophic: short, sharply angulated curvature and progression is the rule (early spinal fusion is recommended and myelogram preoperatively to rule out dural ectasia or intraspinal neurofibroma)
2. Kyphoscoliosis
   a. High incidence of paraplegia
   b. Both anterior and posterior fusion is recommended
3. Cervical spine disorders: torticollis, neck mass, bony anomalies, deformity
4. Congenital bowing and pseudarthrosis: tibia, ulna, femur, clavicle, radius, humerus
5. Subperiosteal bone proliferation: superiosteal calcifying hematoma

REFERENCES

Asher M, Olson J: Factors affecting the ambulatory status of patients with spina bifida cystica. J Bone Joint Surg 65A:350–356, 1983

Bleck EE: Orthopaedic management of cerebral palsy. Philadelphia, WB Saunders, 1979

Bunch WH, Hakala MW: Iliopsoas transfers in children with myelomeningocele. J Bone Joint Surg 66A:224–227, 1984

Burkus JK, Moore DW, Raycroft JF: Valgus deformity of the ankle in myelodysplastic patients. Correction by stapling of the medial part of the distal tibial physis. J Bone Joint Surg 65A:1157–1162, 1983

Crawford AH Jr, Bagamery N: Osseous manifestations of neurofibromatosis in childhood. J Pediatr Orthop 6:72–88, 1986

Drenann JC: Orthopaedic management of neuromuscular disorders. Philadelphia, JB Lippincott, 1983

Drummond DS, Moreau M, Cruess RL: The results and complications of surgery for the paralysis hip and spine in myelomeningocele. J Bone Joint Surg 62B:49–53, 1980

Green N, Griffin P, Shiavi R: Split posterior tibial tendon transfer in cerebral palsy. J Bone Joint Surg 65A:748–754, 1983

Hoffer MM, Barakat G, Koffman M: 10-year follow-up of split anterior tibial tendon transfer in cerebral palsy patients with spastic equinovarus deformity. J Pediatr Orthop 5:432–434, 1985

Hoffer MM, Brink J: Orthopaedic management of acquired cerebrospasticity in childhood. Clin Orthop 110:244, 1975

Kling TF, Kaufer H, Hensinger RN: Split posterior tibial-tendon transfers in children with cerebral spastic paralysis and equinovarus deformity. J Bone Joint Surg 67A:186–194, 1985

Linseth RE, Stelzer L Jr: Vertebral excision for kyphosis in children with myelomeningocele. J Bone Joint Surg 61A:699–704, 1979

Lonstein JE, Akbarnia BA: Operative treatment of spinal deformities in patients with cerebral palsy or mental retardation. An analysis of one-hundred-and-seven cases. J Bone Joint Surg 65A:43–55, 1983

Nicol RO, Menelaus MB: Correction of combined tibial torsion and valgus deformity of the foot. J Bone Joint Surg 65B:641–645, 1983

Root L, Miller SR, Kirz P: Posterior tibial-tendon transfer in patients with cerebral palsy. J Bone Joint Surg 69A:1133–1139, 1987

Shafer MF, Dias LS: Myelomeningocele. Orthopaedic treatment. Baltimore, Williams & Wilkins, 1983

Stevens PM, Toomey E: Fibular-Achilles tenodesis for paralytic ankle valgus. J Pediatr Orthop 8:169–175, 1988

Zucherman JD, Staheli LT, McLaughlin JF: Acetabular augmentation for progressive hip subluxation in cerebral palsy. J Pediatr Orthop 4:436–442, 1984

28
Congenital Disorders, Skeletal Dysplasias, and Connective Tissue Disorders

CONGENITAL DISORDERS

I. Proximal Femoral Focal Deficiency (PFFD)
A. Wide spectrum from simple shortening to complete aplasia
B. Ilium and proximal femur develop from the same cartilage anlage and a cleft develops to form the hip joint
C. Flexion (if absent hip) or external rotation deformity (if hip present) of the hip is clinically seen
D. Classification (Aitken) (Fig 3-10)
   1. Type A: congenital short femur with adequate acetabulum (pseudarthrosis may be present, but bony connection is present between the shaft and femoral head at maturity)
   2. Type B: congenital short femur with adequate femoral head and acetabulum but no continuity between the femoral head and the shaft at maturity
   3. Type C: no femoral head is present with dysplastic acetabulum
   4. Type D: femoral head and acetabulum are absent
E. Treatment: individualized
   1. Short femur: leg lengthening or epiphysiodesis as appropriate or knee arthrodesis and Syme's amputation in severe short femurs
   2. Hip stabilizing procedures: bone grafting or valgus osteotomy may be indicated in type A or B
   3. Syme's amputation and knee arthrodesis and above knee prosthesis are standard in severe cases (if hip is present and stable, lengthening of the femur is an option instead of Syme's amputation)
   4. Modified prosthesis or no treatment for bilateral PFFD
   5. Van Ness turnaround operation and below knee amputation is an alternative to Syme's

II. Congenital or Developmental Coxa Vara
A. Growth plate cartilage is unable to form normal trabeculae and triangular metaphyseal fragment forms in the inferior femoral neck adjacent to the physis
B. Incidence: rare (1/13,000) and bilateral in 25%
C. Clinical findings
   1. Age at 3–4 years
   2. Short stature, Trendelenburg gait, or waddle
   3. Decreased abduction and internal rotation of the hip
D. X-rays
   1. Progressing varus deformity
   2. Femoral head may become flat and acetabular dysplasia may occur with eventual degenerative joint changes
   3. Pseudarthrosis of the fissure may occur
E. Treatment
   1. Observation: neck shaft angle >110° and Hilgenreiner epiphyseal angle <45°

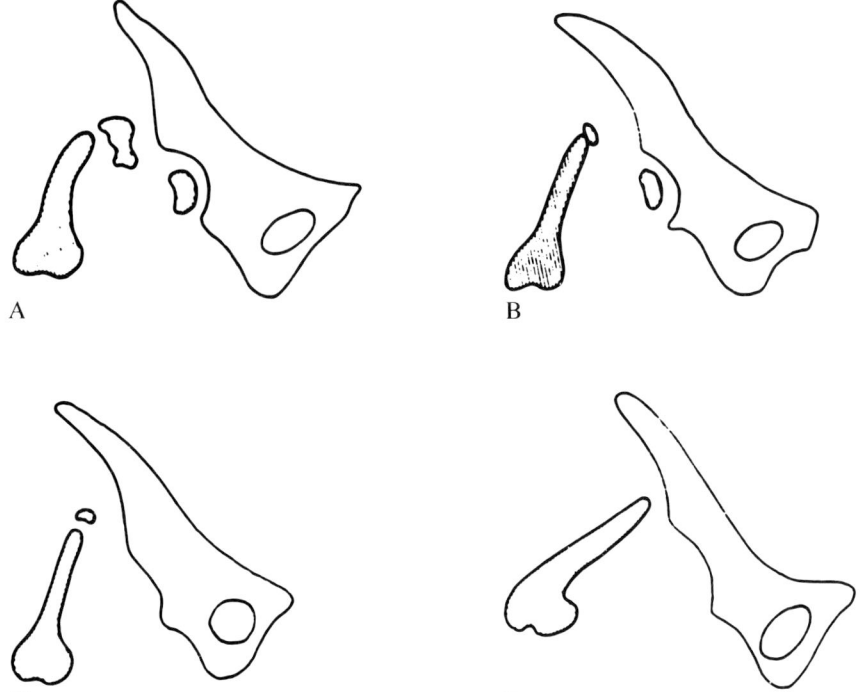

Figure 3-10. Aitken classification of proximal femoral focal deficiency. Type A: congenital short femur with adequate acetabulum (pseudarthrosis may be present, but bony connection is present between the shaft and femoral head at maturity). Type B: congenital short femur with adequate femoral head and acetabulum but no continuity between the femoral head and the shaft at maturity. Type C: no femoral head is present with dysplastic acetabulum. Type D: femoral head and acetabulum are absent. (From Grogan DP, Love SM, Ogden JA: Congenital malformations of the lower extremities. Orthop Clin North Am 18:538, 1987. Reprinted with permission.)

2. Surgery
   a. Varus <100° and Hilgenreiner epiphyseal angle >60°
   b. Marked abductor lurch
   c. Vertical neck defect with varus progression
   d. Valgus osteotomy and adductor release are standard and greater trochanter epiphysiodesis for varus from 90°–100° in children between 5 and 7 years old can be considered

III. Congenital Deficiency of the Fibula
A. Classification (Fig 3-11)
   1. Type I: partial fibular absence
      a. Type A: proximal and distal physis closer together than normal
      b. Type B: partial proximal absence with distal epiphysis proximal to ankle
   2. Type II: Complete fibular absence
B. Associated anomalies: short femur, lateral condyle hypoplasia of the knee, AP laxity of the knee, patella alta, valgus deformity of the ankle, ball and socket ankle joints with tarsal coalitions (type I), and anteromedial bow of the leg (type II)
C. Treatment
   1. Lengthening: for shortening of ≤15% or with good ball and socket ankle
   2. Osteotomy: deformity of the tibia
   3. Syme's amputation: severe shortening with marked foot deficiency about 1 year old

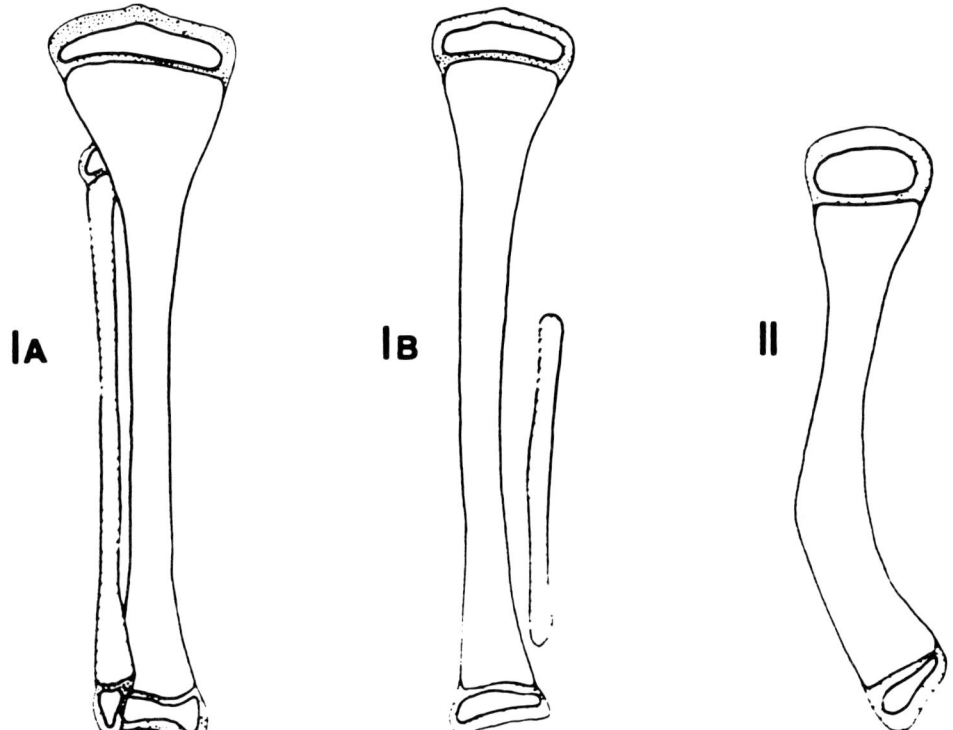

Figure 3-11. Classification of longitudinal deficiency of the fibula. Type IA: partial fibular absence with proximal and distal physes closer together than normal. Type IB: partial fibula absence with partial proximal absence and distal epiphysis proximal to ankle. Type II: complete fibular absence. (From Grogan DP, Love SM, Ogden JA: Congenital malformations of the lower extremities. Orthop Clin North Am 18:542, 1987. Reprinted with permission.)

IV. Congenital Deficiency of the Tibia
A. A wide spectrum
B. Types
   1. Type I: total absence
   2. Type II: Distal half of tibia absent
   3. Type III: Dysplastic distal tibia, diastasis of ankle joint
C. Clinical findings
   1. Short and bowed leg, knee flexion contracture, equinovarus foot deformity, and medial ray defects
   2. Associated with upper extremity anomalies, such as supernumerary digits and lobster claw deformity
D. Treatment
   1. Complete: knee disarticulation and prosthesis (fibular transposition is rarely successful)
   2. Partial: proximal fusion of fibula and tibia and Syme's to have below-knee prosthesis
   3. Syme's amputation for severe foot and ankle problems

V. Angular Deformities of the Tibia
A. Types
   1. Anterolateral angulation with eventual pseudarthrosis
   2. Anteromedial angulation usually associated with other leg anomalies (fibular hemimelia)
   3. Posteromedial angulation
B. Congenital pseudarthrosis of the tibia
   1. Types (Fig 3-12)
      a. Type I: increased cortical density but normal medullary canal

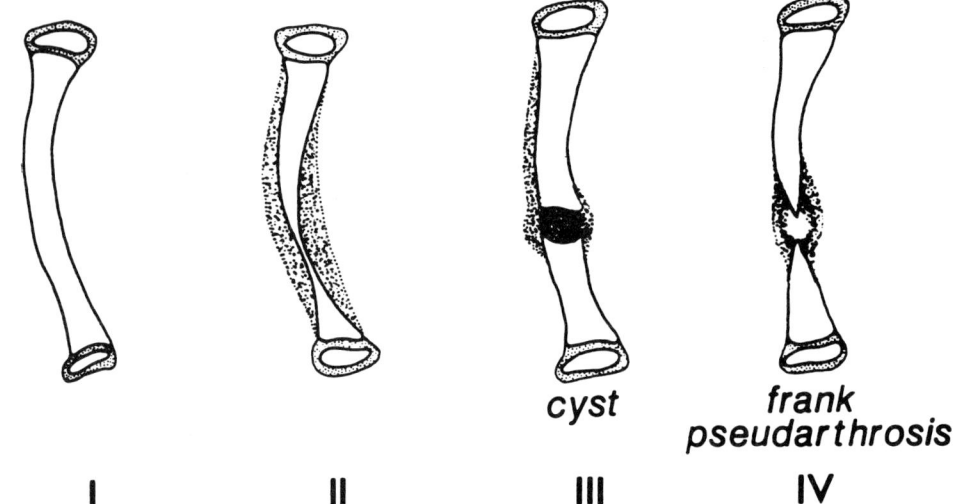

Figure 3-12. Classification of pseudarthrosis of the tibia. Type I: increased cortical density but normal medullary canal. Type II: a failure of tubulation and a narrowed, sclerotic narrowed canal. Type III: a cystic lesion or prefracture. Type IV: frank fracture or pseudarthrosis. (From Grogan DP, Love SM, Ogden JA: Congenital malformations of the lower extremities. Orthop Clin North Am 18:548, 1987. Reprinted with permission.)

     b. Type II: failure of tubulation and a narrowed, sclerotic narrowed canal
     c. Type III: cystic lesion or prefracture
     d. Type IV: frank fracture or pseudarthrosis
  2. Pathogenesis: unknown, but fibrous dysplasia, neurofibroma, or hemartoma are possible
  3. Segmental weakening in the tibia with anterior bowing and eventual pseudarthrosis
  4. Forty percent are associated with neurofibromatosis
  5. Treatment
     a. Prolonged orthotic support, and tibiofibular synostosis may be necessary to prevent ankle valgus
     b. Intramedullary rodding crossing ankle and subtalar joints and massive bone grafting (fibula also if involved) and the rod should not be removed
     c. Timing of surgery should be as late as possible to have better success of surgery and use orthosis to maintain alignment and prevent fractures
     d. Iliazarov bone transport or free vascularized graft
     e. Syme's amputation: failure to unite after three surgeries, leg length discrepancy >5 cm and functionless foot
C. Posteromedial bowing of the tibia
  1. Congenital bowing at the distal third of the tibia with shortening
  2. Calcaneovalgus foot
  3. Bowing corrects with time, but leg length discrepancy may be a problem (3.3–6.9 cm at maturity)
  4. Treatment
     a. Observation but no casting
     b. Leg length discrepancy: epiphysiodesis
     c. If the medial bow or internal tibial torsion is not corrected by 4 years of age, osteotomy may be necessary

VI. Deformities of the Knee

A. Congenital dislocation/subluxation of the knee
  1. Dislocation (uncommon, about 1/100,000), subluxation is more common

2. Bilateral in >50%
3. Sixty percent associated with other congenital anomalies, such as clubfeet and congenital hip dislocation
4. Pathology: tibia is displaced anteriorly and laterally with hyperextension with or without valgus, rotatory deformity, or tibial bowing
5. Treatment
   a. Serial casting for 6 weeks to 6 months (subluxation cases do well)
   b. Surgery may be necessary in resistant dislocated cases (<45° flexion after 3 months casting): V-Y quadriplasty, capsular release or posterior transfer of hamstrings and iliotibial band (successful up to 2 years)

B. Discoid lateral meniscus
   1. May cause snapping
   2. Not always associated with disability
   3. If torn: partial or complete excision

SKELETAL DYSPLASIAS

I. General Considerations

A. Dwarf (disproportionate shortness) and midget (proportionate shortness)
   1. Short trunk dwarfism: greater axial skeleton involvement (ie, Morquio and spondyloepiphyseal dysplasia)
   2. Short limb dwarfism: greater appendicular skeleton involvement
      a. Rhizomelic: proximal segment shortening (ie, diastrophic dwarfs and achondroplasia)
      b. Mesomelic: middle segment shortening (ie, dyschondrosteosis)
      c. Acromelic: distal segment shortening
   3. Proportionate change during growth (ie, metatropic dwarfs)

B. Classification
   1. Epiphysis
      a. Articular cartilage
         (1) Spondyloepiphyseal dysplasia
         (2) Mucopolysaccharidoses
         (3) Pseudoachondroplasia
         (4) Dysplasia epiphysealis hemimelica (Trevor's disease)
      b. Secondary ossification center
         (1) Multiple epiphyseal dysplasia
         (2) Dysplasia epiphysealis punctata (Conradi's syndrome)
   2. Physis
      a. Zone of proliferation
         (1) Achondroplasia
         (2) Chondroectodermal dysplasia (Ellis-van Creveld syndrome)
         (3) Hyperchondroplasia (Marfan syndrome)
      b. Zone of hypertrophy
         (1) Metaphyseal dysostosis (metaphyseal chondrodysplasia — Schmid, Spahr-Hartman, McKusick, and Jansen types)
         (2) Multiple enchondromatosis
   3. Metaphysis
      a. Zone of primary spongiosa
         (1) Hypophosphatasia
         (2) Osteopetrosis
         (3) Pyknodysostosis
      b. Zone of secondary spongiosa
         (1) Metaphyseal dysplasia (Pyle's disease)
         (2) Osteopathia striata (Voorhoeve's disease)
         (3) Multiple exostosis
         (4) Osteopoikilosis
   4. Diaphysis
      a. Periosteal bone formation
         (1) Osteogenesis imperfecta
         (2) Progressive diaphyseal dysplasia (Engelmann's disease)
      b. Endosteal bone formation
         (1) Idiopathic juvenile osteoporosis
         (2) Hyperphosphatasia (child's form of Paget's disease)
         (3) Endosteal hyperostosis
   5. Mixed dysfunction
      a. Physeal-epiphyseal
         (1) Diastrophic dwarfism
         (2) Metatropic dwarfism

b. Entire bone
     (1) Melorheostosis

II. Specific Dysplasias

A. Spondyloepiphyseal dysplasia
  1. Congenital
     a. Autosomal dominant and presents at birth
     b. Short neck and trunk dwarfism. Rhizomelic shortening of limbs and normal hands and feet
     c. Flattened midface, sternal protrusion, and ocular anomalies
     d. Thoracic kyphoscoliosis and lumbar lordosis and C1–C2 instability due to odontoid hypoplasia
     e. X-rays: delayed bone maturation, trapezoidal vertebral body, squared ilium, hypoplastic hip, coxa vara
     f. Treatment for spine and coxa vara
  2. Tarda
     a. X-linked recessive, presents around 10 years of age
     b. Short neck, trunk shortening
     c. Barrel-shaped chest
     d. Hip arthritis or ankylosis
     e. X-rays: mild flattening of the vertebrae, sclerosis of superior and inferior end plates, ovoid vertebral bodies, small pelvis, and hypoplastic hip
B. Mucopolysaccharidoses: enzyme defects causing inability to metabolize one of several proteoglycans leading to an abnormal chondroid scaffolding for secondary trabeculae formation during endochondral ossification
  1. Type I: Hurler syndrome
     a. Autosomal recessive and presents at infancy
     b. Hepatosplenomegaly, cardiopulmonary involvement, mental retardation, and dies during first decade
     c. Multiple joint contractures, gibbus, and anterior breaking of the lumbar vertebrae
     d. Dermatan sulfate B and heparin sulfate in urine
  2. Type II: Hunter's syndrome
     a. X-linked recessive and presents at infancy
     b. Hepatosplenomegaly, cardiopulmonary involvement, deafness, mild mental retardation and dies during 3rd decade; some have normal life span
     c. Spine and bone anomalies are less severe
     d. No clouding of cornea or lumbar kyphosis
     e. Dermatan sulfate and heparin sulfate in urine
  3. Type III: Sanfilippo's syndrome
     a. Autosomal recessive and presents at early childhood
     b. Mental retardation and life expectancy around 4th decade and bony changes are rare
     c. Heparin sulfate in urine
  4. Type IV: Morquio syndrome
     a. Autosomal recessive and presents at 12–18 months
     b. Orthopedic involvements:
        (1) Basilar impression with odontoid hypoplasia and C1–C2 instability: occiput to C2 fusion with tibial graft may be needed (iliac crest is a source of graft bone)
        (2) Kyphosis of spine
        (3) Flexion deformities, genu valgus, epiphyseal hypertrophy, and irregular ossification with secondary broadening and flattening, tapering short broad metacarpals, glass-shaped inner pelvis, and coxa valga
     c. Keratan sulfate in urine
     d. Realignment of genu valgus may be necessary at age 8–10 years
  5. Type V: Scheie syndrome
     a. Autosomal recessive and presents at adolescence

    b. Cornea and heart involvement
    c. Bony changes are rare
    d. Dermatan sulfate and heparin sulfate in urine
  6. Type VI: Maroteaux-Lamy syndrome
    a. Autosomal recessive and presents at birth
    b. Mild hepatosplenomegaly and dwarfism
    c. Dermatan sulfate in urine
C. Pseudoachondroplasia
  1. Autosomal dominant or recessive
  2. Due to abnormal proteoglycans
  3. Rhizomelic dwarfism, lumbar lordosis, scoliosis, or kyphosis may develop. Varus or valgus knees may occur. Normal face
  4. X-rays: small epiphyses inserting into metaphysis via a depression, diaphyseal coarseness and irregular metaphyseal lines. Short metacarpals, ovoid vertebral bodies with tonguelike projections
  5. Treatment: may need tibial osteotomies
D. Dysplasia epiphysealis hemimelica (Trevor's disease)
  1. Asymmetrical abnormal proliferation of cartilage and associated enchondral ossification
  2. Pathology is same as osteochondroma
  3. Most commonly talus, distal femur, and proximal tibia
  4. Periarticular masses, decreased range of motion, and deformity and leg length discrepancy
E. Multiple epiphyseal dysplasia (Fairbank)
  1. Autosomal dominant and affect epiphyseal ossification centers in the appendicular skeleton
  2. Clinical manifestation: presents at 5–10 years and short stature and eventual joint stiffness and arthritis. Hips may look like Perthes'
  3. Physeal plate shows poor columnation and calcification and the articular cartilage deforms later because of lack of osseous support
  4. X-rays: irregular fragmented epiphyses especially humeral and femoral heads, coxa vara and breva, oblique distal tibia, and occasional odontoid hypoplasia
F. Dysplasia epiphysealis punctata (stippled epiphyses or Conradi's syndrome or chondrodysplasia punctata)
  1. Autosomal dominant condition characterized by an irregular vascularization of the epiphyses leading to a disturbance of chondroblastic maturation and mucoid degeneration of the epiphyseal cartilage with irregular amorphous calcification
  2. Clinical findings: flat facies, flattened nasal bridge, asymmetrical shortening of the limbs, congenital cataracts in 20%, hyperkeratoic dermatoses, scoliosis, and joint contractures
  3. X-rays: punctate calcifications in the vertebral column and epiphyses of long bones, carpals, tarsals, and pelvic bones and dysplastic deforming epiphyses
  4. Treatment: limb length inequality and scoliosis
G. Achondroplasia
  1. Commonest type of dwarfism (3 per million)
  2. Autosomal dominant and failure of endochondral ossification resulting from a primary germ plasma defect appearing at the second month of fetal life
  3. Physis: very small zone of proliferation, erratic provisional calcification, and trabecular irregularity of the spongiosa
  4. Clinical manifestation: rhizomelic short limb dwarfness, large head with a broad face, prominent frontal region, prognathic and flattened nasal bridge. Thoracolumbar kyphosis, lumbar lordosis, and abdominal protrusion. Broad and

short fingers and trident hands. Genu varus and decreased range of motion
5. X-rays: short tubular bones, thickened cortices and splayed metaphysis. The physes are centrally notched or V-shaped. A champagne glass appearance of pelvis, concave posterior vertebral bodies, short and thick pedicles, and decreasing interpedicular distance in the lumbar spine
6. Treatment: Genu varus may be corrected with shortening osteotomy of fibula or epiphysiodesis of proximal fibula, or occasionally osteotomy of the tibia. Kyphosis usually balances out with lumbar lordosis, but spinal stenosis and herniated discs may give myelopathy, which requires decompression
7. Hypochondroplasia: a distinct form of dwarfism, which is also considered as a mild form of achondroplasia (normal head and face, rhizomelic and short trunk, and short limbs with minimal bowing)

H. Chondroectodermal dysplasia (Ellis-van Creveld syndrome)
1. Autosomal recessive and failure of chondroblast proliferation and chondroid production
2. Physis: marked physeal disorganization
3. Clinical manifestation: postaxial polydactyly (10%), absent and deformed nails, mesomelic dwarfism, and frequent atrial septal defect
4. X-rays: plump metaphyses, square ilia and horizontal acetabulae. Fusion of the capitate and hamate, lateral tibial plateau hypoplasia and genu valgus
5. Treatment: removal of supernumerary digits and tibial osteotomies for genu valgus

I. Metaphyseal dysostosis (metaphyseal chondrodysplasia)
1. Four major types: Schmid, Spahr-Hartman, McKusick, and Jansen
2. Improper mineralization of the metaphysis is pathogenic
3. Schmid type
   a. Most common type and autosomal dominant pattern
   b. Present with growth deficits, bowing, and limping
   c. Normal face and spine
   d. X-ray: physeal cupping, metaphyseal streaking, short and thick diaphyses, particularly of the femur, proximal tibia, and humerus
   e. Differential diagnosis: vitamin D resistant rickets
4. Spahr-Hartman type
   a. Autosomal recessive
   b. Similar to Schmid type, except hands and feet are involved instead of proximal femur and humerus
5. McKusick type (cartilage-hair-hypoplasia)
   a. Autosomal recessive pattern
   b. Clinical manifestations: sparse fine hair, hyperextensibility of wrist and fingers, short and pudgy fingers, flexion contracture of the elbow, and varus ankle deformity due to excessive length of distal fibula. Megacolon (10%) and decreased cellular immunity (chickenpox prone)
6. Jansen type: rare and severe dwarfism, contractures, and mental retardation

J. Pyknodysostosis
1. Autosomal recessive condition of unclear etiology but pathogenesis is similar to osteopetrosis in that there is a lack of formation and resorption of spongiosa
2. Clinical manifestations
   a. Short extremities, large skull with frontal bossing, persistent fontanelles, hypoplastic mandible, persistent fontanelles and wide cranial sutures, short and broad hands and feet, and crowding or maloccluded teeth

b. Increased bone density similar to osteopetrosis
  c. Fractures and deformities of the limbs may occur
  d. Scoliosis, kyphosis, and increased lumbar lordosis may be present
K. Metaphyseal dysplasia (Pyle's disease)
  1. Autosomal recessive condition caused by remodeling defect of the metaphysis of unknown pathogenesis
  2. Clinical manifestations: mild deformity such as genu valgus, pes planus, long legs, and mild decreased range of motion
  3. X-rays: Erlenmeyer flask appearance with thin metaphyseal cortices and thick diaphyseal cortices
  4. No orthopaedic treatment
L. Osteopathia striata (Voorhoeve's disease)
  1. Failure of osteoclastic remodeling
  2. Incidental findings and no symptoms
  3. Symmetrical fanlike streaks of bone through the metaphysis and into the diaphysis
M. Osteopoikilosis
  1. Autosomal dominant condition with hyperplasia of secondary spongiosa
  2. Incidental findings of the lentil-shaped osseous densities on x-ray, particularly around joints
N. Progressive diaphyseal dysplasia (Engelmann's disease)
  1. Autosomal dominant condition with increased osteoblastic activity of periosteal and endosteal bone and possible decreased activity of osteoclastic activity
  2. Clinical findings
    a. Walking delays, easy fatigue, a waddling gait, or leg pain may occur
    b. Slender with long extremities and normal facies
    c. Pes planus, genu valgus, and increased lumbar lordosis
    d. Delayed puberty
    e. Myeloid metaplasia may develop later in life
  f. X-ray: symmetrical fusiform appearance of the diaphyses with increased cortical diameter and decreased intramedullary canal diameter
  g. Treatment: observation of leg length and correct bowing as needed
O. Diastrophic dwarfism
  1. Autosomal recessive condition with a mixture of both epiphyseal and physeal dysplasia
  2. Failure of formation of normal chondroid and lack of normal columnation and calcifications
  3. Clinical manifestations
    a. Severe micromelia, clubfeet, joint contractures, "hitchhiker's thumb," and cauliflower ears
    b. Severe kyphosis of cervical spine and kyphoscoliosis of thoracolumbar spine
    c. Short, deformed, and curved extremities
    d. Coxa vara and hip dislocations
    e. X-ray: similar to achondroplasia at birth with short broad bones and metaphyseal flaring. Delayed epiphyseal ossifications and flattened vertebrae
  4. Treatment
    a. Early aggressive treatment of clubfeet
    b. Treat knee contractures and spinal deformities as needed
P. Metatropic dwarfism
  1. Autosomal recessive condition with mixed epiphyseal-physeal dysplasia
  2. Clinical manifestations
    a. Similar to achondroplasia with short extremities and normal trunk but has normal facies
    b. Progressive kyphoscoliosis and shortened trunk similar to Morqui syndrome
    c. X-ray: bulbous metaphyseal enlargement and knobby joints, "barbell" bones, platyspondylisis
  3. Guarded prognosis

Q. Melorheostosis
1. Asymmetrical hyperplasia of the entire bone
2. "Candle wax dripping" appearance on x-ray and periarticular enchondral ossification
3. Pain in affected bones, decreased range of motion, and flexion contractures
4. Tense and shiny skin with induration of the soft tissues and compression neuropathies may develop
5. Treatment: leg length discrepancy and joint contractures

R. Osteopetrosis
1. Autosomal recessive condition, also known as Albers-Schönberg's disease
2. Failure of primary spongiosa absorption
3. Calcified chondroid persists because of nonfunctional osteoclasts (no collagenase and no response to hyperparathyroid hormone)
4. Clinical findings
   a. Infancy: pallor, fever, purpura, ecchymoses, optic atrophy, hepatosplenomegaly, extremity bowing and rib rosary
   b. Pancytopenia due to hypoplastic marrow
   c. X-ray: generalized skeletal density, cone-shaped bone ends (defective metaphyseal remodeling) and "bone in bone" appearance
   d. Very brittle and fracture-prone
   e. Slow healing of fractures
   f. Usually dies within 2 years unless bone marrow transplantation is performed
5. Osteopetrosis tarda: autosomal dominant condition with a better prognosis

CONNECTIVE TISSUE DISORDERS

I. Osteogenesis imperfecta

A. Pathogenesis
1. Genetically determined
2. Abnormal codes for regulation and synthesis of procollagen I (underproduction and abnormal structure)
3. Affects skeleton, skin, ligament, eye, ear, and teeth
4. Pathology: osteoporosis (thin cortex and disorganized trabeculae), close cement lines and decreased and irregularly oriented collagen and physeal involvement (matrix with decreased collagen and poor primary spongiosa and fragmentation of the plate with trauma)

B. Classification
1. Type I: autosomal dominant with blue sclera (most common)
2. Type II: autosomal recessive and lethal
3. Type III: autosomal recessive, progressively deforming type, and normal sclerae
4. Type IV: autosomal dominant and normal sclerae (moderate skeletal deformity and growth retardation)
5. Less severely affected are tarda types in which tarda I patients have deformities usually confined to the lower limbs that limit ambulation, and tarda II patients are without significant deformities except short stature

C. Clinical findings
1. Disproportionate shortening of limbs, large heads, soft calvarium, wide fontanelle, and dwarfism
2. Multiple fractures of extremities and deformity (anterolateral bow of the femur and anteromedial bow of the tibia)
3. Spine: biconcave and kyphoscoliosis and elongated spondylolisthesis
4. Frequent respiratory infection

D. Treatment
1. Orthotics: early mobility and weight bearing and postoperatively
2. Surgery: delay until 4–5 years of age if possible
   a. Sofield osteotomy and Bailey-Dubow rodding: 30°–40° angulation with interference with ambulation of the

tibia (occasionally femur and humerus)
b. Forearm: do not attack surgically
c. Spinal fusion for >50° scoliosis

II. Marfan Syndrome

A. Autosomal dominant: abnormal production of alpha$_1$ chain of collagen may be pathogenic
B. Clinical manifestations
 1. Positive family history
 2. Cardiac valve abnormalities by echocardiography
 3. Scoliosis, arachnodactyly, pectus excavatum, joint laxity and tall stature
 4. Inferior lens dislocation
C. Treatment: scoliosis (brace or surgery), patellofemoral subluxation (exercise), foot problems (orthosis), and protrusio acetabuli (possible early operative closure of the triradiate cartilage if significant protrusio is identified early)

III. Homocystinuria

A. Deficiency of cystathione synthase and abnormally high concentration of homocystine in the blood and urine
B. Autosomal recessive condition with mental retardation, osteoporosis, fracture, thromboembolic phenomenon, and ectopic lens
C. Clinically resembles Marfan syndrome, but the diagnosis is made by urine screen of homocystine
D. Stiffness and contractures may be found as opposed to Marfan syndrome
E. Treatment
 1. Pyridoxine hydrochloride (vitamin B$_6$, and methionine-restricted diet)
 2. Bracing or osteotomy of genu valgus
 3. Careful observation of scoliosis and lens dislocation

IV. Ehlers-Danlos Syndrome

A. Heterogenous group of disorders affecting skin, joint ligaments, and other connective tissues
B. At least 11 types known, based on clinical, genetic, and biochemical differences
C. Orthopaedic manifestations include arthralgias, joint dislocations, such as the patella, shoulder, thumb
D. Orthopaedic treatment
 1. Muscle strengthening exercise
 2. Ligament surgery is temporarily beneficial
 3. Arthrodesis of the trapeziometacarpal joint is beneficial
 4. Scoliosis: bracing or surgery
 5. Clubfoot may be present and require surgery

REFERENCES

Beals RK: Orthopaedic care for patients with skeletal dysplasias. In Akeson WH, Bornstein P, Glimcher MJ, eds. AAOS symposium on heritable disorders of connective tissue. St Louis, CV Mosby, 1982

Beighton P, Horan F: Orthopaedic aspects of Ehlers-Danlos syndrome. J Bone Joint Surg 51B:444–453, 1969

Bethem D, Winter RB, Lutter L, et al: Spinal disorders of dwarfism. J Bone Joint Surg 63A:1412–1425, 1981

Finsterbush A, Pogrund H: The hypermobility syndrome. Clin Orthop 168:124–127, 1982

Gamble JG, Rinsky LA, Strudwick J, et al: Nonunion of fractures in children who have osteogenesis imperfecta. J Bone Joint Surg 70A:439–443, 1988

Goldberg MJ: The dysmorphic child: An orthopaedic perspective. New York, Raven Press, 1987

Horan F, Beighton P: Orthopaedic problems in inherited skeletal disorders. Berlin, Springer-Verlag, 1982

Jacobsen ST, Crawford AH, Miller HA, et al: The Syme amputation in patients with congenital pseudarthrosis of the tibia. J Bone Joint Surg 65A:533–537, 1983

Kalamchi A, Dawe RV: Congenital deficiency of the tibia. J Bone Joint Surg 67B:581–584, 1985

Kopits SE: Orthopaedic complications of dwarfism. Clin Orthop 114:153–179, 1976

Kruger LM: Recent advances in surgery of lower limb deficiencies. Clin Orthop 148:97–105, 1980

Lange DR, Schoenecker PL, Baker CL: Proximal femoral focal deficiency; treatment and classification in forty-two cases. Clin Orthop 135:15–25, 1978

Loder RT, Herring JA: Fibular transfer for congenital absence of the tibia: A reassessment. J Pediatr Orthop 7:8–13, 1987

McKusick VA: Heritable disorders of connective tissue, ed 4. St Louis, CV Mosby, 1972

McKusick VA, Scott CI: A nomenclature for constitutional disorders of bone. J Bone Joint Surg 53A:978–986, 1971

Morrissy RT: A symposium: Congenital pseudarthrosis. Clin Orthop 166:1–61, 1982

Shapiro F: Consequences of an osteogenesis imperfecta diagnosis for survival and ambulation. J Pediatr Orthop 5:456–462, 1985

Shapiro F, Glimcher MJ, Holtrop ME, et al: Human osteopetrosis. J Bone Joint Surg 62A:384–399, 1980

Smith DW: Recognizable patterns of human malformation: Genetic, embryologic, and clinical aspects, ed 3. Philadelphia, WB Saunders, 1982

Steel HH, Lin PS, Betz RR, et al: Iliofemoral fusion for proximal femoral focal deficiency. J Bone Joint Surg 69A:837–843, 1987

Thomas IH, Williams PF: The Gruca operation for congenital absence of the fibula. J Bone Joint Surg 69B:587–592, 1987

Tiley F, Albright JA: Osteogenesis imperfecta: Treatment by multiple osteotomy and intermedullary insertion. J Bone Joint Surg 55A:701, 1973

Westin GW, Sakai DN, Wood WL: Congenital longitudinal deficiency of the fibula. J Bone Joint Surg 58A:492–496, 1970

Wynne-Davis R, Gormley J: The prevalence of skeletal dysplasias: An estimate of their minimum frequency and the number of patients requiring orthopaedic care. J Bone Joint Surg 67B:133–137, 1985

Yong-Hing K, MacEwen GD: Scoliosis associated with osteogenesis imperfecta. J Bone Joint Surg 64B:36, 1982

29
Miscellaneous Pediatric Disorders

CHRONIC JUVENILE ARTHRITIS

I. Systemic Onset JRA
A. Twenty percent
B. Equal sex ratio
C. Polyarticular and 25% severe arthritis
D. Associated with fever, rash, splenomegaly, serositis, leukocytosis, anemia, and growth retardation
E. Rheumatoid factor (RF) negative and antinuclear antigen (ANA) negative

II. Polyarticular JRA
A. RF negative
   1. Twenty-five percent
   2. More common in females
   3. Severe arthritis in 15%
   4. Mild systemic signs
   5. RF negative, ANA positive in 20%
B. RF positive
   1. Five percent
   2. More common in females
   3. Late childhood
   4. Fifty percent with severe arthritis
   5. Rheumatoid nodules and weight loss
   6. RF positive, ANA positive in 75%
   7. HLA-DR4 related

III. Pauciarticular JRA
A. Type I
   1. Thirty to 35%
   2. Early childhood
   3. Few large joints involved
   4. Associated with chronic iridocyclitis (30–50%) and ocular damage (10–20%)
   5. RF negative, ANA positive (60%)
B. Type II
   1. Ten to 15%
   2. More common in males
   3. Late childhood (8 years or older)
   4. Few large joints (especially hips, knees, and sacroiliac joints)
   5. Five to 10% with acute iridocyclitis
   6. Features of Reiter's inflammatory bowel disease and psoriasis
   7. RF negative, ANA negative, HLA-B27 related

IV. Treatment
A. Salicylates (20–30 mg/dL)
B. NSAIDs
C. Remitting agents: gold, antimalarials, and D-penicillamine

V. Orthopaedic Management
A. Splints, traction, and orthosis
B. Physical therapy
C. Synovectomy
D. Soft tissue release for stiffness and contracture
E. Osteotomies, total joint replacements, or arthrodesis

HEMOPHILIA

I. Pathogenesis
A. Factor VIII deficiency (classic hemophilia A, sex-linked recessive), Factor IX deficiency (Christmas disease, hemophilia B), and Factor XI deficiency (mild hemophilia C, autosomal dominant)
B. Von Willebrand's disease: rare musculoskeletal involvement
C. Acquired inhibitors in 15% of cases
D. Pathology
   1. Hemarthrosis (especially knee, elbow, ankle, and shoulder)

2. Synovitis and chondrocyte necrosis (immunologic reaction)
   3. Degenerative arthritis
   4. Subperiosteal and muscle hemorrhage may occur

II. Radiology (Stages)
A. Grade I: soft tissue swelling
B. Grade II: osteopenia in the epiphysis
C. Grade III: bony changes (squaring of the patella, widening of intercondylar femoral notch, and subchondral cysts)
D. Grade IV: narrowing of articular cartilage and osteophyte formation
E. Grade V: destructive joint changes

III. Diagnosis
A. Careful history of bleeding and family history (sex-linked transmission in hemophilia A and B)
B. Physical examination: hemathrosis and joint contracture
C. Partial thromboplastin time (PTT) elevated and specific factor assays
D. Radiographic changes

IV. Treatment
A. Prophylaxis
   1. Physical therapy and avoid contact sports
   2. Perioperative restoration of factor levels
B. Acute hemarthrosis
   1. Replacement therapy: 30–50% activity
   2. Immobilization and gradual range of motion exercise
   3. Arthrocentesis if large hemarthrosis and painful (within 24 hours of bleeding and not for patients with antibodies)
C. Subacute hemarthropathy: >3 bleeding episodes in 6 weeks
   1. Immobilization for 3 weeks and prophylactic replacement for 6 weeks and gradual range of motion exercise
   2. Synovectomy if persistent for 6 months
D. Chronic hemarthropathy
   1. Physical therapy and orthotics
   2. Synovectomy and soft tissue corrections of contractures
   3. Arthrodesis
   4. Total joint replacement
E. Other treatments
   1. Excision of pseudotumor
   2. Fasciotomies for compartment syndrome
   3. Knee: arthroscopy (menisectomy, synovectomy, and evacuation of hematoma) and manipulation under anesthesia
   4. Fractures: usually conservative management
   5. Muscle hemorrhage: factor replacement, immobilization, elevation, and compression
F. Surgical principles
   1. Use tourniquet
   2. Meticulous hemostasis with electrocautery
   3. Coaptation tissue closure with hemostatic continuous Dexon sutures
   4. No drains
   5. Bulky compression dressing and postoperative immobilization
   6. Factor replacement pre- and postoperative period

SICKLE CELL ANEMIA

I. Types
A. Sickle cell disease: hemoglobin SS and 1% incidence among blacks
B. Sickle cell trait: hemoglobin SA and 7% incidence among blacks

II. Pathogenesis
A. Inherited defect in the synthesis of hemoglobin
B. Erythroid hyperplasia results from hypoxia caused by sickle cell hemolysis
C. Sickle cell crisis usually begins about 2–3 years of age

D. Infarction of affected organs results (abdominal organs and skeleton)

III. Clinical Findings
A. Bone infarction is difficult to distinguish from osteomyelitis clinically
B. Blood culture and aspiration biopsy may be needed
C. Bone infections by *Salmonella* or staphylococci are common
D. Osteonecrosis of the femoral head is common in adolescents

IV. Treatment
A. Aggressive diagnosis and prompt treatment of osteomyelitis
B. Avascular necrosis of the femoral head is managed conservatively with crutch ambulation initially, but arthroplasty may be needed in resistant cases in adults.

GAUCHER'S DISEASE

I. General Considerations
A. Cereboside reticulocytosis due to lipid metabolic disturbance
B. Familial tendency and more common in Jews

II. Types
A. Acute: rare and involves the central nervous system in the infant with resultant death within 18 months
B. Chronic: insidious onset during first 2 decades

III. Clinical Findings
A. Splenomegaly, lymph node enlargement
B. Thrombocytopenia, leukopenia, and anemia due to bone marrow infiltration
C. Skeletal changes: metaphyseal expansion, erosion of cortex, and avacular necrosis of femoral head or humeral head
D. Pathologic fractures are common

IV. Treatment
A. Splenectomy may be indicated
B. Conservative treatment for pathologic fractures except femoral neck fractures
C. Avascular necrosis of the hip: conservative with partial or nonweight bearing. Arthroplasty in the adult

CHROMOSOMAL ABNORMALITIES

I. Down Syndrome
A. General considerations
  1. Incidence of 1/660
  2. Frequency increases with maternal age
  3. Ninety-five percent due to trisomy 21
B. Clinical features
  1. Mental retardation varies widely
  2. Congenital anomalies: gastrointestinal and cardiac
  3. Leukemia develops in 1%
  4. Other problems may be seizures, hypothyroidism, diabetes mellitus, and dementia
  5. Musculoskeletal abnormalities: disproportionately short legs, hip instability, slipped capital femoral epiphysis, ligamentous laxity (patellofemoral joint, pes planovalgus, hallux valgus, atlantoaxial instability), odontoid hypoplasia or ossicle terminale, scoliosis, and spondylolisthesis
C. Treatment
  1. Atlantoaxial instability
    a. Fifteen percent have >5 mm instability
    b. Instability and neurologic symptoms require posterior C1–C2 fusion
    c. Asymptomatic instability should be followed and patients should be restricted from contact sports
  2. Patellofemoral instability: surgery should be avoided if possible because recurrence and complications are common

II. Turner's Syndrome
A. Females with XO chromosome abnormality
B. Clinical features: short stature, sexual infantilism, web neck without vertebral anomalies, cubitus valgus, genu valgus, scoliosis
C. Treatment: bracing or surgery for scoliosis

III. Noonan's Syndrome
A. Phenotypically similar to Turner's syndrome with short stature, web neck, and cubitus valgus
B. Occurs in both males and females with normal sex chromosomes
C. Associated with mental retardation, right-sided congenital heart defects, chest wall deformities, and scoliosis

IV. Prader-Willi Syndrome
A. Deletion of part of the long arm of chromosome 15
B. Hypotonic floppy infant and delay in developmental milestones
C. Obesity, small hands and feet, hypoplastic genitalia
D. Mental retardation
E. Congenital hip dislocation (10%) and scoliosis (50–90%)

OTHER SYNDROMES

I. Rett Syndrome
A. Progressive dysfunction of the brain in the female, probably due to abnormal X chromosome
B. Motor and intellectual deterioration starting 6–12 months of age (autistic)
C. Complex stereotypic movement of the hands
D. Spasticity, ataxia, and scoliosis develop as in patients with severe cerebral palsy
E. Orthopedic treatment may include surgery for dislocated hip or scoliosis

II. Larsen's Syndrome
A. Usually autosomal dominant trait, manifesting as multiple congenital dislocations of large joints
B. Affected joints: knee, hips, elbow, and clubfeet
C. Facial feature: flattened with prominent forehead
D. Cervical kyphosis may be severe to cause quadraplegia
E. Scoliosis is frequently present
F. Treatment: joint reduction and maintenance is difficult

LEG LENGTH DISCREPANCY

I. Etiologies
A. Increased length: congenital hemihypertrophy, local stimulation of the physis, such as juvenile arthritis, infection, and fracture of the midshaft
B. Decreased length: congenital shortening, growth plate fractures, tumors, and neurologic diseases

II. Assessment
A. Measurement of leg length
   1. From the anterior superior iliac spine to the medial malleolus
   2. Block method
   3. X-rays: orthoroentgenogram or CT scanogram
B. Prediction at maturity
   1. Ideally follow for 2–3 years with x-rays and bone age
   2. Green-Anderson growth inhibition
   3. Mosley straight line chart
   4. Roughly $3/8$ inch/year for the femur and $1/4$ inch/year for the tibia until 15 years for females and 17 years for males

III. Treatment
A. Depends on predicted discrepancy at maturity
   1. Less than 2–3 cm: shoe lift

2. If 3–5 cm: epiphysiodesis at appropriate time or shortening in mature skeleton
3. If 5–17 cm: lengthening (6 cm at a time in femur and 5 cm at a time in tibia)
4. More than 17 cm: amputation

B. Epiphysiodesis
1. Sufficient growth left: 2 cm or 2 years
2. Less than 50% physis involved
3. Percutaneous or open methods
4. Complications secondary to inaccurate calculation

C. Shortening
1. Skeletally mature
2. Femur only (up to 6 cm)
3. Usually at the midshaft of the femur
4. Open or closed techniques

D. Lengthening
1. Diaphyseal
   a. Wagner device with large pins and immediate distraction and gradual lengthening of 1.4 mm once a day
   b. Requires secondary plate and bone grafting
   c. High incidence of complication
2. Metaphyseal
   a. Ilizarov: small pins and delayed distraction (both ends possible and no graft)
   b. De Bastiani (orthofix): large pins and delayed distraction of 0.25 mm four times a day (callostasis with no graft)
3. Epiphyseal: possible with De Bastiani or Ilizarov but may cause early closure of the physis

REFERENCES

Canale ST, Russell TA, Holcomb RL: Percutaneous epiphyseodesis: Experimental study and preliminary clinical results. J Pediatr Orthop 6:150–156, 1986

De Bastiani G, Aldegheri R, Renzi-Brivio L, et al: Limb lengthening by callus distraction (callostasis). J Pediatr Orthop 7:129–134, 1987

Dugdale TW, Renshaw TS: Instability of the patellofemoral joint in Down syndrome. J Bone Joint Surg 68A:405–413, 1986

Engh CA, Hughes JL, Abrams RC, et al: Osteomyelitis in patients with sickle cell disease: Diagnosis and management. J Bone Joint Surg 53A:1–15, 1971

French HG, Burke SW, Robert JM, et al: Upper cervical ossicles in Down syndrome. J Pediatr Orthop 7:69–71, 1987

Goldblatt J, Sacks S, Beighton P: The orthopaedic aspects of Gaucher disease. Clin Orthop 137:208–214, 1978

Grill F: Distraction of the epiphyseal cartilage as a method of limb lengthening. J Pediatr Orthop 4:105–108, 1984

Habermann ET, et al: Larsen's syndrome. J Bone Joint Surg 58A:558, 1976

Jacobsen ST, Levinson JE, Crawford AJ: Late results of synovectomy in juvenile rheumatoid arthritis. J Bone Joint Surg 67A:8–15, 1985

Lachiewicz PF: Gaucher's disease. Orthop Clin North Am 15:765–774, 1984

Mallouh A, Talb Y: Bone and joint infection in patients with sickle cell disease. J Pediatr Orthop 5:158–162, 1985

McMillan CW, Greene WB, Blatt PM, et al: The management of musculoskeletal problems in hemophilia. In AAOS instructional course lectures 32: 210–241, 1983

Mezhenina EP, Roulla EA, Pechesky AG, et al: Methods of limb elongation with congenital inequality in children. J Pediatr Orthop 4:201–207, 1984

Monticelli G, Spinelli R: Distraction epiphysiolysis as a method of limb lengthening. III. Clinical application. Clin Orthop 154:274–285, 1981

Paley D: Current techniques of limb lengthening. J Pediatr Orthop 8:73–92, 1988

Pueschel SM, Herndon JH, Gelch MM, et al: Symptomatic atlantoaxial subluxation in persons with Down syndrome. J Pediatr Orthop 4:682–688, 1984

Schaller J: Chronic arthritis in children: Juvenile rheumatoid arthritis. Clin Orthop 182:79–89, 1984

Shapiro F: Developmental patterns in lower extremity length discrepancies. J Bone Joint Surg 64A:639–651, 1982

Speer DP: Early pathogenesis of hemophilic arthropathy: Evolution of the subchondral cyst. Clin Orthop 185:260–265, 1984

Stephens DC: Femoral and tibial lengthening. J Pediatr Orthop 3:424–430, 1983

30
Pediatric Fractures

I. Epiphyseal Fractures and Growth Mechanism Injuries
A. Fifteen percent of childhood fractures
B. Distal radius is most common site
C. More common in males
D. Classification (Salter-Harris, Rang [Fig 3-13], and Ogden)
   1. Type 1: fractures extend transversely across the hypertrophic and calcified zones of the physis
      a. Difficult to diagnose in nondisplaced fractures
      b. Most common injury pattern in infants and young children
      c. Good prognosis after closed reduction and immobilization at most but not all locations
   2. Type 2: fracture along the physeal-metaphyseal interface and into the metaphysis (Thurstan-Holland fragment)
      a. Most common injury pattern, especially after 4 years
      b. Closed reduction and immobilization
   3. Type 3: fracture along the physeal-metaphyseal interface and through epiphysis and through the articular cartilage
      a. Open reduction and internal fixation is necessary for displaced fractures, pinning the epiphyseal fragment to the uninjured fragment without crossing the physis
      b. Partial growth arrest, articular incongruity, and nonunion may occur
   4. Type 4: fracture from the articular surface through the epiphysis to the metaphyseal area, crossing the physis
      a. Open reduction and internal fixation necessary in displaced fractures
      b. Highest incidence of partial growth arrest
   5. Type 5: microscopic splitting, linear disruption and microvascular compromise of the physis from loading
      a. Diagnosis is made retrospectively
      b. If suspected, nonweight bearing and immobilization are prescribed
      c. Total growth arrest is common
   6. Type 6: peripheral region of the growth plate (zone of Ranvier) is injured and peripheral osseous bridge may occur with angular deformity
   7. Type 7: intraepiphyseal fractures such as malleoli, capitellum, osteochondral fractures of the distal femur, and Osgood-Schlatter tibial tuberosity lesion
   8. Type 8: metaphyseal fractures affecting metaphyseal growth and remodeling mechanisms, such as proximal tibial metaphysis
   9. Type 9: diaphyseal growth is affected after periosteal stripping injury

II. Partial Physeal Arrest
A. Trauma accounts for 80% (others are infection, tumor, iatrogenic, irradiation, burns)
B. Location: distal femur is most common site, followed by distal tibia, proximal tibia, distal radius, and distal ulna. (Other rarer sites are distal fibula, proximal phalanx of the great toe, proximal humerus, triradiate cartilage)
C. Evaluation includes constructing a map with tomograms
D. Treatment: excision if 2 years of growth left and <50% involvement
   1. Peripheral bar is excised from periphery
   2. Central bar is removed through a window made in the metaphysis
   3. Fill cavity with fat, methyl methacrylate or Silastic

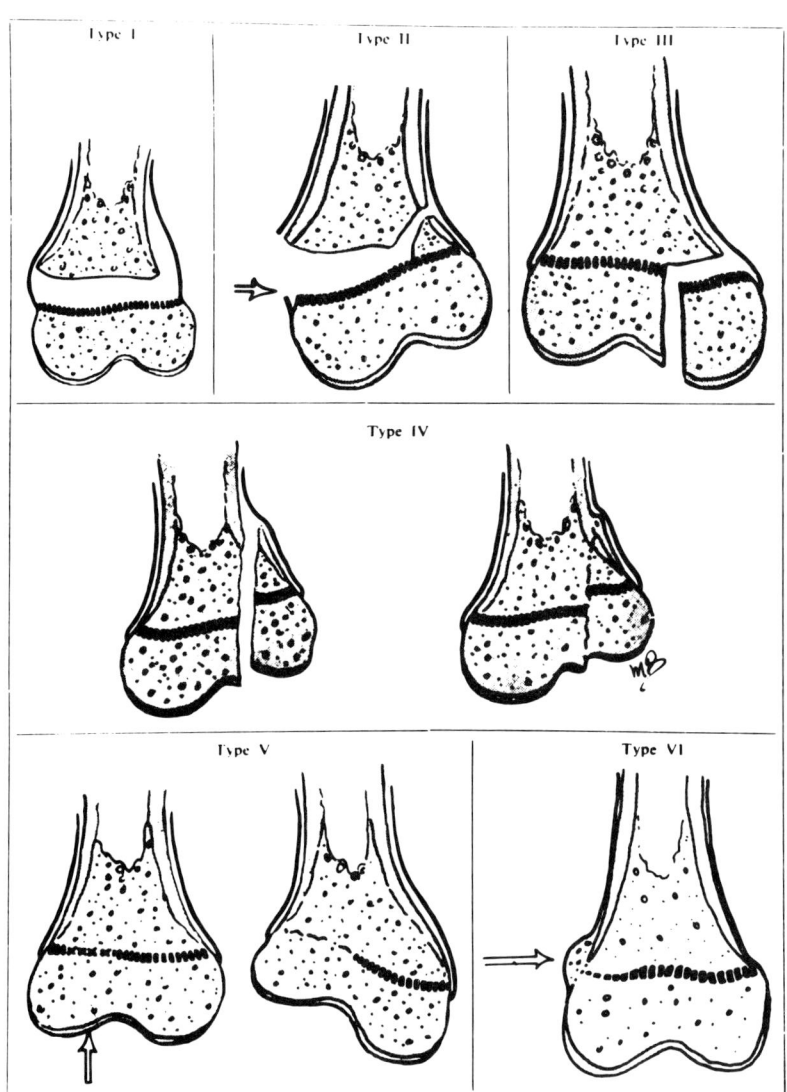

Figure 3-13. Rang's version of the Salter-Harris classification. (Rang M: *The growth plate and its disorders*. Baltimore, Williams & Wilkins, 1969. Reprinted with permission.)

III. General Principles

A. Remodeling is favorable if ≥2 years of growth left, fractures are close to the growth plate, and angulation is in the plane of joint motion
B. Remodeling is poor if rotational deformity, displaced intra-articular fractures, and fractures across the growth plate
C. Suspect child abuse in uncared child, delay in seeking care, inappropriate child behavior, lack of parent and infant bonding, vague inconsistent history, and physical examination revealing burns, bite marks, hand imprints, head injury, or sexual molestation. (Fractures are typically multiple in various stages of healing, posterior rib fractures, growth plate separation with "corner fractures," "bucket

handle" and periosteal new bone formation, spiral fractures of the humerus, femur, tibia, or forearm)

IV. Fractures of the Hand and Wrist
A. Fractures of the phalanges
   1. Fractures of the distal phalanx
      a. Hyperflexion injuries: Salter I or II in younger patient and Salter III in the preadolescent (mallet equivalents) — closed reduction and immobilization in extension or open reduction and pinning
      b. Crushed fingertip: nailbed should be carefully repaired if lacerated and soft tissue care is important to prevent infection
   2. Phalangeal physeal fractures
      a. Involves proximal ends of phalanges
      b. Proximal phalanges remodel better than middle phalanges
      c. Treatment: Salter II fractures are reduced closely and immobilized. If significant angulation that cannot be reduced closely, then open reduction is necessary. Open reduction is frequently necessary for Salter III fractures and articular incongruity
   3. Phalangeal neck and shaft fractures
      a. Phalangeal neck fractures can be significantly rotated, which is best seen on lateral x-ray view
      b. Closed reduction, percutaneous pinning, or open reduction is done, depending on reducibility. (Open reduction is frequently necessary for rotated neck fractures)
   4. Intra-articular fractures: open reduction and K-wire fixation if displaced (dorsal tendon splitting approach)
B. Fractures of the metacarpals
   1. Metacarpal neck fractures: closed reduction or open reduction if physis or epiphysis is injured and displaced
   2. Metacarpal shaft fractures: closed reduction and well-padded splint or percutaneous pinning if unstable
   3. Metacarpal base fractures: most fractures are undisplaced and treated by splinting but intra-articular fractures of the base of the thumb needs open reduction (equivalent of adult Bennett's fractures)
C. Dislocations in the hand
   1. Thumb metacarpophalangeal or interphalangeal dislocations can usually be reduced closed
   2. Metacarpophalangeal dislocations (index and little fingers) require open reduction (volar approach to extract the volar plate)
D. Wrist carpal navicular fractures
   1. Avulsion fracture of the distal pole is most common
   2. Thumb spica cast if snuff box tenderness
   3. Ischemic necrosis is rare
E. Fractures of the distal radius and ulna
   1. Ulnar styloid fractures may give rise to nonunion
   2. Distal metaphyseal fractures may be torus or completely displaced
   3. Distal fractures often involve the physis (radius or ulna)
   4. Closed reduction and casting is done and gentle reduction is stressed in physeal displaced fractures. Completely displaced ulnar physeal fractures may need open reduction. Completely displaced fractures of the distal radius and ulna are reduced closed and a long arm cast is applied with the forearm supinated and wrist slightly flexed (bayonet apposition is acceptable if angulation is acceptable)
   5. Greenstick fractures should be gently reduced and immobilized in a long arm cast (reduction is done while pronating the forearm and immobilized in pronation for volarly angulated fractures, whereas reduction and immobilization

are in supination for dorsally angulated fractures)

V. Fractures of the Shafts of the Radius and Ulna

A. Types (greenstick, compression, or complete) and locations (proximal, middle, and distal third)
B. Radiographic determination of rotation
   1. AP view: the bicipital tuberosity is medially located and the radial styloid is radially located when taken in full supination
   2. Lateral view: midpronation should reveal the coronoid process anteriorly and radial tuberosity posteriorly as well as radial styloid anteriorly and ulnar styloid posteriorly
C. General treatment principles
   1. Reduction: more than 15° angulation is unacceptable for children 6–10 years old and near anatomic reduction should be done for older children
   2. Rotation should be anatomic to prevent supination or pronation loss (minimum 50° motion necessary, especially supination)
   3. Remodeling is less for the older child and proximal shaft fractures and dorsal angulation
D. Greenstick fractures
   1. More common before 10 years
   2. Both rotation and angulation must be corrected
   3. Pronation for reduction if volar angulation and supination if dorsal angulation
   4. Long arm casting in supination or pronation, depending on angulation
E. Complete fractures
   1. Correct angulation, rotation, and length
   2. Fractures proximal to pronator teres insertion should be supinated and distal to pronator teres should be pronated for reduction. Neutral position is for middle third fractures
   3. Look at the bicipital tuberosity on x-rays to determine correct amount of rotational deformity
   4. Use finger traps for reduction and casting with the forearm in neutral in most cases
   5. Children older than 10 years may need open reduction and internal fixation
      a. Four hole plates are commonly used, especially for distal fractures
      b. Intramedullary rods may be used for proximal radius or ulnar fractures
F. Plastic deformation
   1. Both radius and ulna or either may occur
   2. Treatment: gradual force to correct the deformity and long arm cast for 6–8 weeks (general or regional anesthesia)
   3. Children <4 years can be treated by observation alone in cases of mild deformity because of remodeling potential
G. The Monteggia lesion
   1. Fractures of the proximal ulna and dislocation of the radial head
   2. Reduction of the radial head and fracture is important
   3. Closed reduction and long arm cast for 4–6 weeks
   4. Open reduction may be necessary in unstable oblique or comminuted fractures or irreducible radial head, especially in the older child
   5. Classification and treatment
      a. Type I: anterior dislocation of the radial head with anteriorly angulated fracture of the ulna (most common type) — long arm casting with the elbow in 100° flexion and the forearm supination
      b. Type II: posterior or posterolateral dislocation of the radial head with posteriorly angulated fracture of the ulna — elbow extension and forearm neutral position for long arm casting
      c. Type III: lateral or anterolateral dis-

location of the radial head with ulnar metaphyseal fracture (treatment same as type I)
d. Type IV: anterior dislocation of the radial head with fractures of the proximal thirds of the radius and ulna (treatment same as type I)
H. Galeazzi fracture-dislocation
1. Fractures or the distal radial shaft with radioulnar joint dislocation
2. Ulnar angulation and pronation of the distal fragment is a usual pattern
3. Treatment: longitudinal traction and reduction and long arm cast in 90° elbow flexion and forearm supination

VI. Fractures and Dislocations of the Elbow

A. General considerations
1. Eight to 9% of all fractures
2. Most common during 5–10 years of age
3. Carrying angle: 15° at 1–4 years and 17.8° in the adult
4. Comparison radiograph to the opposite elbow is important for the carrying angle and ossification
B. Average secondary ossification of the elbow (Fig 3-14)
1. Capitellum: 1 year
2. Radial head: 3 years
3. Medial epicondyle: 5 years
4. Trochlea: 7 years
5. Olecranon: 9 years
6. Lateral epicondyle: 11 years
7. Epiphyses fuse to each other and to the metaphysis during 10–12 years of age and the medial epicondyle closes
C. Blood supply
1. Lateral condyle: from inferior ulnar collateral artery and enters the capitellum from the posteromedial aspect in the olecranon fossa region (disruption of blood supply may lead to AVN or nonunion)
2. Medial condyle: two vessels supplying two ossification centers
D. Supracondylar fractures
1. Sixty-nine percent of elbow fractures, most common during 5–10 years of age (peak, 6.5 years)
2. Two types by mechanism of injury
a. Extension (97.7%)

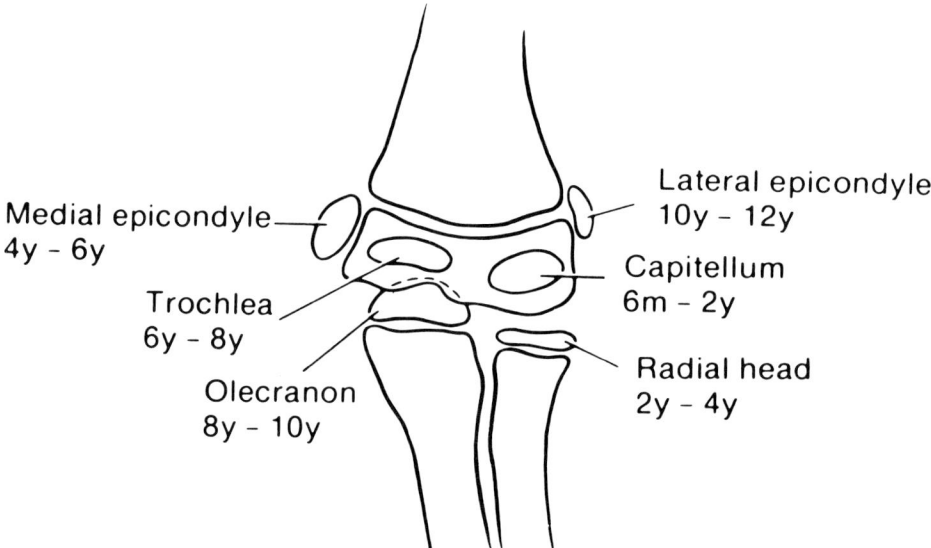

Figure 3-14. Secondary ossification centers of the elbow. (From Bucholz RW: Orthopaedic trauma. In Bucholz RW, Lippert FG, Wenger DR, Ezaki M, eds. Orthopaedic decision making. Philadelphia, BC Decker and St. Louis, CV Mosby, 1984, p 78. Reprinted with permission.)

b. Flexion (2.3%)
3. Classification
   a. Undisplaced
   b. Displaced with intact posterior cortex
   c. Displaced with no cortical contact
      (1) Posterior medial displacement with varus angulation: more common by pull of the triceps and biceps attaching more medially
      (2) Posterior lateral displacement with valgus angulation
4. Treatment
   a. Undisplaced fractures: posterior splint in 120° elbow flexion for 3 weeks
   b. Displaced fractures
      (1) Closed reduction: traction, correct medial/lateral displacement, correct varus angulation, correct rotation, and gradual gentle flexion to 120° flexion and pronation for posteromedial fractures (posterolaterally displaced fractures are more stable in supination)
      (2) Long arm splint or cast
      (3) Most displaced fractures need percutaneous pinning for stability (two lateral pins or crossed pins)
      (4) Open reduction and pinning if cannot reduce closely or associated vascular injury: lateral or anterior approach
      (5) Traction (olecranon pin): if significant soft tissue swelling
      (6) Flexion type: anteromedial displacement and ulnar nerve may be injured and immobilization in near extension is required unless percutaneous fixation is done
5. Complications
   a. Neurologic compromise: 7%
      (1) The radial nerve injury is most common
      (2) Posterolateral displacement may cause injuries to brachial artery and median nerve
      (3) Flexion type is associated with ulnar nerve injury
      (4) Exploration if no recovery in 3 months
   b. Vascular injury: may cause Volkmann's ischemic contractures (prompt exploration is necessary)
   c. Angular deformity
      (1) Cubitus varus is most common and is a cosmetic problem (lateral closing wedge operation can be done when skeletally mature or earlier)
      (2) Cubitus valgus: less common and may occur after posterolateral type of injury and malreduced posteromedial type fractures with pronated position
E. Fractures of the lateral condyle
   1. Occurs in 16.8% of elbow fractures and 54.2% of elbow physeal fractures and common during 4–8 years of age
   2. Types
      a. Milch type II (Salter II): impaction by the olecranon and fracture includes the lateral trochlear ridge and more unstable
      b. Milch type I (Salter IV): impaction by the radial head
   3. Mechanism: extension and varus force
   4. Treatment
      a. Nondisplaced fractures: posterior splint in 90° flexion for 3 weeks
      b. Displace 2 mm: open reduction and pinning
   5. Complications
      a. Delayed union or nonunion
      b. AVN (avoid extensive soft tissue dissection)
      c. Valgus malunion
      d. Premature physeal arrest
      e. Lateral condylar overgrowth
      f. Neurologic problems, especially tardy ulnar nerve palsy in nonunion cases with valgus

g. Fishtail deformity of the trochlea secondary to underdevelopment of the later crista of the trochlea
F. Fractures of the medial condyle
 1. Rare, and more common during 8–14 years of age
 2. Mechanism: extension and valgus
 3. Types
    a. Milch II: impaction by olecranon
    b. Milch I: impaction by the radial head
 4. Anteromedial displacement by pull of flexors and medial collateral ligament
 5. Confused with fractures of the medial epicondyle in younger children because the trochlea ossify later than the medial epicondyle (arthrogram may be done)
 6. Treatment: open reduction and fixation if displaced
G. Transcondylar fractures
 1. Usually type I injury, especially <3 years but type II may occur in the older child
 2. Displacement is posteromedial, whereas elbow dislocation is usually posterolaterally displaced
 3. Treatment: closed reduction and immobilization in flexion and pronation (usually successful). Pinning or open reduction and fixation may be necessary
H. Fractures of the medial epicondyle
 1. More common during 9–14 years of age
 2. Associated with elbow dislocation (50%)
 3. Mechanism: valgus pull with extension (avulsion by flexor muscle mass and collateral ligament)
 4. "Little league elbow syndrome": chronic stress to the medial epicondyle or osteochondritis of the capitellum (tension stress medially and compression loading laterally)
 5. Treatment: closed treatment if <2 mm displacement, but open reduction and pinning for significant displaced or intra-articular entrapped fractures
I. Fractures of the lateral epicondyle
 1. Very rare
 2. May be confused with normal physeal line: distal part of the lateral epicondyle fuses to capitellum before proximal part fuses to the metaphysis
 3. Closed treatment if <2 mm displacement
J. Fractures of the radial head and neck
 1. Metaphyseal compression is most common but physeal injuries can occur
 2. May be associated with elbow dislocation or elbow reduction or medial epicondylar fractures or olecranon fractures (50% associated injuries)
 3. Mechanism: valgus or extension
 4. Treatment: closed reduction (supination and traction, followed by flexion and direct pressure on the radial head) and immobilize in 90° elbow flexion and forearm pronation for 2–3 weeks. Open reduction and pinning if reduction cannot achieve <45° angulation or <2 mm displacement or displaced physeal fractures
K. Olecranon fractures
 1. Mechanism: avulsion (flexion), extension (varus or valgus) or direct force
 2. Associated fractures such as radial head, medial epicondyle, or radial dislocation
 3. Open reduction and tension band fixation if displaced
L. Elbow dislocations
 1. Usually older child (13–14 years)
 2. Associated medial epicondylar fractures, radial head, or coronoid process
 3. Mechanism: extension and valgus
 4. Displacement: posterolateral is most common
 5. Treatment: closed reduction and early range of motion in most cases. Surgery for irreducible cases or unstable dislocations with associated fractures
M. Nursemaid elbow
 1. Hyperpronation injury resulting in subluxation of the radial head and partial displacement of the annular ligament
 2. Occurs in the younger child because of

ligamentous laxity (2–3 years)
   3. Treatment: supination and flexion and pressure on the radial head to feel for reduction

VII. Fractures and Dislocations of the Humerus and Shoulder

A. Anatomy
   1. The radial nerve winds around the humerus at the junction of the middle and distal third of the diaphysis
   2. Blood supply is generous
   3. Supracondylar process may be present in the anteromedial aspect of the distal humerus (1%)
B. Fractures of the humeral shaft or metaphysis
   1. Types: greenstick, transverse, oblique, or spiral
   2. Radial nerve injury is common
   3. Treatment
      a. Neonate: soft bandage or splint for 7–14 days (should rule out birth palsy)
      b. Neonates to 3 years: usually greenstick type and rule out child abuse. Posterior splint and collar and cuff sling
      c. At 3–12 years: usually proximal metaphysis. Posterior splint and collar and cuff or sugar tong
      d. Over 12 years
         (1) Coaptation splints, sugar tong, hanging arm cast, or cast-brace for shaft fractures
         (2) Shoulder spica cast may be used for proximal fractures that cannot be controlled by other means
         (3) Traction or open reduction and internal fixation may be necessary in open fractures or multiple trauma patient
      e. Closed reduction should be done to keep angulation <20° and 1–2 cm shortening is acceptable
C. Fractures of the proximal humerus physis
   1. In 80% humeral growth occurs at the proximal physis
   2. Ossification: proximal epiphysis at 6 months and greater tuberosity (7 months to 3 years) and lesser tuberosity (2–5 years) and fusion of the epiphysis at 5–7 years and physeal closure at 17–18 years
   3. The periosteum in the posteromedial region is stronger and displacement tends to be anterolateral
   4. The medial aspect of the physis is intra-articular
   5. Types: type I in the neonate and younger children, type II in older children
   6. Treatment
      a. Neonates: manual reduction if completely displaced and keep the arm abducted and flexed (often misinterpreted as shoulder dislocation)
      b. Closed reduction and immobilization in sling and swathe or cast (keep the arm abducted in unstable cases in bed)
      c. Pinning or open reduction is rarely necessary
D. Shoulder dislocation
   1. Unusual prior to skeletal maturity
   2. Anterior is much more common than posterior dislocation
   3. Treatment: closed reduction and immobilization
   4. Recurrent dislocation is common in younger patients
E. Fractures of the clavicle
   1. In 80% occur within the shaft
   2. Membranous bone
   3. Sternal end of the physeal plate accounts for 80% of longitudinal growth
   4. Ossifications: two primary centers in the shaft, which grow until 5 years, and secondary ossification in the sternal end occur 12–19 years and fuse at 25 years
   5. Anatomy: the medial ⅔ is convex anteriorly and the nutrient artery is just medial to the attachment of the coracoclavicular ligament
   6. Function: stabilize the shoulder and

link the trunk and arm and protect the lungs and neurovascular structures
7. Displacement: distal part is medial, anterior, and inferior
8. Treatment
   a. Shaft
      (1) Neonates: symptomatic treatment (rule out congenital pseudarthrosis or cleidocranial dysostosis)
      (2) Figure-of-eight clavicle strap
   b. Distal end
      (1) Usually type 1 or 2 injury
      (2) Inferior periosteal sleeve is intact and attached to the coracoclavicular ligament
      (3) Conservative treatment (sling)
      (4) If significantly displaced and unstable, closed reduction and percutaneous pinning may be done
   c. Medial end
      (1) Type 1 or 2 injury
      (2) Anterior or posterior displacement
      (3) 40° cephalic tilt x-ray shows anterior displacement of the clavicle above the sternum and posterior displacement below the sternum
      (4) Treatment: closed reduction. Open reduction and stabilization may be required if posterior displacement

VIII. Fractures of the Spine

A. Normal roentgenographic variants
   1. The apical ossification center of the odontoid
   2. Secondary ossification centers at the tips of the transverse and spinous processes
   3. Incomplete ossification, especially of the odontoid process, with apparent "superior subluxation of the anterior arch of C1"
   4. Persistence of the synchondrosis at the base of the odontoid (fuses around 8–10 years of age)
   5. Anterior wedging of a young child's vertebral body may simulate compression fracture or a subluxation
   6. Pseudosubluxation of C2 over C3
   7. Increase in the atlantodens interval up to 4 mm
   8. Absence of the ossification center of the anterior arch of C1 in the first year of life may suggest posterior displacement of C1 on the odontoid
   9. Physiologic variations in the width of the vertebral soft tissue swelling
   10. Angulation of the odontoid in 4% of normal children
   11. Horizontally placed facets in the younger child, creating the illusion of a pillar fracture
B. Fractures of the atlas and occiput-C1 disruption
   1. Rare
   2. Occiput-C1 dislocation is usually fatal
   3. Normal synchondrosis (one anteriorly and two posteriorly in the atlas and disappear by 4–5 years of age)
   4. CT scan is the best for diagnosis of C1 fractures
   5. Treatment: Minerva jacket for C1 fractures
C. C1–C2 rotatory subluxation
   1. Presents as torticollis
   2. CT scan imaging is excellent
   3. Rule out torticollis due to other etiologies, such as inflammation
   4. Types
      a. Simple rotatory subluxation: most common
      b. Rotatory subluxation with anterior shift <5 mm
      c. Rotatory subluxation with anterior shift >5 mm
      d. Rotatory subluxation with posterior shift
   5. Treatment: traction and gentle manipulation without anesthesia or C1–C2 fusion if neurologic involvement, anterior displacement, failure to obtain cor-

rect alignment after 3 months of treatment, and recurrent deformity
D. Odontoid fractures
1. Synchondrotic slips (undisplaced fractures may be confused with dentocentral synchondrosis)
2. May be complicated by development of os odontoideum
3. Treatment: reduction by recumbancy and hyperextension and Minerva jacket or halo
E. Lower cervical spine fractures
1. Rare
2. Anterior displacement of the ring apophysis may occur
3. Anterior sloping of the superior margin and pseudosubluxation secondary to hypermobility must not be confused with fractures or dislocation
4. Treatment: collar, Minerva cast, or posterior fusion if indicated (anterior fusions are contraindicated)
F. Fractures of the thoracolumbar spine
1. Relatively uncommon
2. Types: compression injuries are more common than distraction or fracture-dislocation injuries
3. Posterior apophysis may be fractured, mimicking herniated disc (often seen in teenage lifters)
4. Spinal cord injuries: a high incidence of late scoliosis (80–100%) or kyphosis if injury occurs when skeletally immature
5. Treatment: body cast if significant body involvement or posterior instrumentation and fusion if ligamentous involvement. Removal of posterior apophysis if fractured fragment is impinging on the nerve root

IX. Pelvis and Hip Fractures

A. Pelvic fractures
1. Multiple trauma protocol
2. Assess major vessel laceration, retroperitoneal bleed, rectal tears, urethral laceration, and bladder rupture
3. Fractures tend to occur adjacent to joints rather than separation of symphysis pubis or sacroiliac joint
4. Avulsion fractures of iliac spines or ischium may occur
5. Treatment
   a. Stable fractures are treated with bed rest and early ambulation
   b. Unstable injuries: may need external fixator
   c. Avulsion fractures are treated symptomatically and rehabilitation
B. Acetabulum fractures
1. Triradiate cartilage may be affected
2. Growth abnormality can occur if <9 years old
3. Treatment: bed rest and no weight bearing for 6 weeks if minimally displaced. Infrequently requires surgery
C. Fractures and dislocations of the hip
1. Fractures of the hip
   a. Incidence: rare; more common in males around 11–12 years of age
   b. Anatomy
      (1) Ossification: capital femoral epiphysis appears at 4–6 months, the greater trochanter appears at 4 years and the lesser trochanter appears during adolescence and fuse around 18 years of age
      (2) Blood supply: posterior superior and inferior branches from the medial circumflex artery provides blood supply to most of the head and lateral circumflex artery provides blood supply to the greater trochanter, intracapsular metaphysis, and small part of the head
      (3) Growth: longitudinal growth is from the subcapital femoral epiphysis, and the latitudinal growth is from the superior posterior part of the neck, where the epiphyseal cartilage is continuous
   c. Classification (Ratliff)
      (1) Transepiphyseal fractures (8%)
      (2) Transcervical fractures (45–50%)

            (3) Cervicotrochanteric fracture (36%)
            (4) Intertrochanteric fracture (11%)
        d. In the neonate, septic arthritis or congenital hip dislocation must be ruled out for transepiphyseal fractures
        e. Complications
            (1) Avascular necrosis
                i. Leading cause of poor results, especially in displaced transepiphyseal and displaced transcervical fractures
                ii. Types: entire femoral head (type I), anterolateral part (type II), and neck region (type III)
                iii. Treatment: early anatomic reduction, and consider capsulotomy to decrease pressure. Trochanteric epiphysiodesis to prevent coxa vara
            (2) Premature closure of the physis
                i. Associated with threaded pin across the physis and avascular necrosis
                ii. Treat coxa vara (subtrochanteric osteotomy or greater trochanteric epiphysiodesis) and leg length discrepancy
            (3) Nonunion: less common, but does occur, particularly with transcervical fractures
        f. Treatment
            (1) Closed reduction and hip spica cast if nondisplaced intertrochanteric fractures and transepiphyseal fractures
            (2) Internal fixation and hip spica if displaced transcervical or cervicotrochanteric fractures
            (3) Internal fixation for nondisplaced transcervical fractures
    2. Hip dislocation
        a. Posterior dislocation is much more common
        b. Avascular necrosis rate: 8–10%
        c. Treatment: closed reduction and non-weight bearing for 3–4 weeks
    3. Fractures of the greater and lesser trochanters
        a. Traction apophysis of the greater trochanter may be fractured or lesser trochanter may be avulsed
        b. Sports-related injuries are common
        c. Treatment: crutches and progressive weight bearing and open reduction for severely displaced greater trochanteric fragment

X. Fractures of the Femoral Shaft
A. General considerations
    1. Proximal fragment tends to go into flexion, abduction, and external rotation
    2. Deformities
        a. Varus due to adductors and hamstrings
        b. Flexion of proximal fragment by iliopsoas and unopposed abductors
        c. Shortening secondary to hamstrings and quadriceps
        d. External rotation of the proximal fragment
B. Treatment
    1. Neonates and infants
        a. Rule out child abuse
        b. Immediate spica cast in human position (90° flexion, 45° abduction, and 20° external rotation)
    2. Children (2–9 years)
        a. Immediate hip spica if original shortening is <2 cm
        b. Split Russell traction for weeks if >2 cm shortening and hip spica
        c. Hip spica: about 30° abduction, 30° flexion, and 20° external rotation and some knee flexion
        d. Shortening of 1–1.5 cm is ideal
        e. Angulation up to 10°–15° frontal plane, 20° sagittal plane and transverse plane is acceptable, more in younger children

3. Older child (10–12 years)
   a. A 90–90 femoral skeletal traction
   b. Hip spica cast
4. Adolescent
   a. Skeletal traction vs surgery
   b. Surgery: intramedullary nailing
5. Surgery if head injury, pathologic fracture, or severe soft tissue loss even in younger age groups

XI. Fractures and Dislocations Around the Knee

A. Fractures of the distal femoral physis
   1. Greatest incidence between 11 and 15 years; growth arrest is common because of undulating physis
   2. Types
      a. Abduction-adduction (Salter type II and often collateral ligament laxity)
      b. Hyperextension: anterior displacement of epiphysis (risk of neurovascular compromise)
      c. Hyperflexion: rare
      d. Salter type III or IV fractures
   3. Treatment
      a. Closed reduction and casting
      b. Percutaneous pinning or open reduction and pinning
      c. Anatomic reduction is important
B. Fractures of the proximal tibial physis
   1. Rarely type I and most often type II
   2. In 50% type I is nondisplaced and stress view is helpful
   3. Popliteal artery is at risk and peroneal nerve injury
   4. Treatment: casting for 6 weeks. Open reduction if displaced type III or IV
C. Fractures of the intercondylar eminence
   1. Mostly anterior cruciate avulsion
   2. Types (Fig 3-15)
      a. Type I: nondisplaced
      b. Type II: anterior rim lifted
      c. Type IIIa: entire fragment displaced
      d. Type IIIb: entire fragment displaced and rotated
   3. Diagnosis by drawer or Lachman test and lateral x-ray
   4. Medial collateral ligament may be torn
   5. Treatment: closed reduction by full extension for 6 weeks and if unsuccessful arthroscopic or open reduction (meniscus may be interposed)
D. Tibial tubercle elevation
   1. Not common, but occurs more in males between 14 and 16 years of age when epiphysiodesis has begun

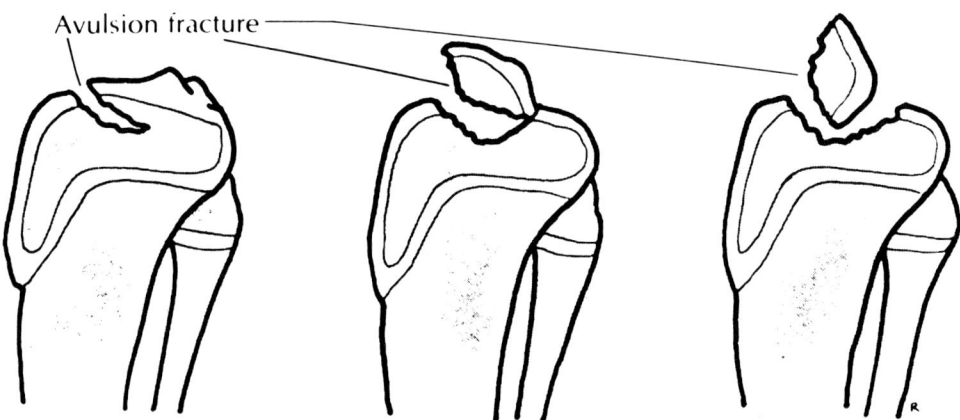

Figure 3-15. Classification of fractures of the anterior intercondylar eminence of the tibia. Left: Type 1 nondisplaced fracture. Center: Type 2 hinged fracture. Right: Type 3 completely displaced fracture. (From Roberts JM: Fractures and dislocations of the knee. In Rockwood CA, Wilkins KE, King RE, eds. Fractures in Children, vol. 3. Philadelphia, JB Lippincott, 1984, p. 943. Reprinted with permission.)

2. Types
      a. Fracture across secondary ossification center
      b. Fracture at junction of primary and secondary ossification centers
      c. Intra-articular fractures
   3. Treatment: open reduction and fixation if cannot actively fully extend
  E. Fractures of the patella
   1. Bipartite patella may be present
   2. Treatment: closed reduction if nondisplaced and open reduction and tension band wiring if displaced
   3. Sleeve fractures: a small part of distal pole is avulsed with a relatively large portion of the articular surface (requires open reduction and fixation)

XII. Fractures of the Tibia and Fibula
  A. Fractures of the proximal metaphysis
   1. Medial greenstick fractures are common
   2. Progressive valgus angulation is possible (malreduction, soft tissue interposition, or overgrowth may be pathogenic)
   3. Most commonly between 2 and 5 years of age
   4. Treatment
      a. Long leg cast with knee extended and varus mold
      b. If persistent medial gap, surgery should be done to remove interposed pes and periosteum
      c. Valgus deformity: may correct spontaneously or osteotomy if persistent angulation >10°
  B. Fractures of the tibial shaft
   1. Fractures of the shafts
      a. Neurovascular status check is important
      b. Treatment: closed reduction and long leg cast
      c. A 10° recurvatum, 5° varus or valgus angulation is acceptable; avoid malrotation
   2. Toddler's fracture
      a. Spiral fractures of the tibia
      b. Radiologic diagnosis is often not obvious initially
      c. Treatment: cast immobilization
   3. Fractures of the distal tibial and fibular physes
      a. Common during 11–15 years of age
      b. The physis closes in the central portion first, followed by medial and lateral parts
      c. A high incidence of physeal arrest, especially Salter IV fractures of the medial malleolus
      d. Classification (Fig 3-16)
         (1) Supination-inversion: Salter I fracture of the lateral malleolus and Salter III or IV fracture of the medial malleolus
         (2) Pronation-eversion: Salter II fracture of the distal tibial physis and high fibular fracture
         (3) Supination-plantar flexion: Salter type II fracture of the distal tibial physis
         (4) Supination-external rotation
            i. Stage 1: Salter II fracture (anterolateral part of the distal tibial epiphysis is avulsed by anterior inferior tibiofibular ligament)
            ii. Stage 2: periosteal detachment of the distal tibia superior to the anterior inferior tibiofibular ligament
            iii. Stage 3: Triplane fractures (two or three parts and medial or lateral triplane types)
            iv. Stage 4: distal fibular metaphyseal fracture
      e. Treatment
         (1) Closed reduction and casting
         (2) Open reduction and internal fixation if >2 mm displacement of Salter III or IV fractures

XIII. Fractures and Dislocations of the Foot
  A. Fractures of the talus
   1. Blood supply

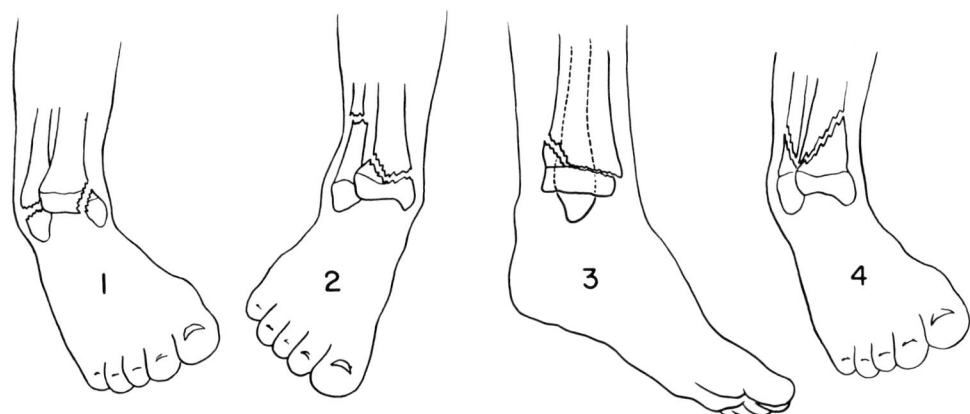

Figure 3-16. Classification of physeal injuries of the distal tibia and fibula. 1: Supination-inversion; 2: pronation-eversion-external rotation; 3: supination-plantar flexion; 4: supination-external rotation. (From Dias LS: Fractures of the tibia and fibula. In Rockwood CA, Wilkins KE, King RE, eds. Fractures in children, vol. 3. Philadelphia, JB Lippincott, 1984, p 1016. Reprinted with permission.)

- a. The artery of the tarsal canal: from the posterior tibial artery and anastomoses with branches from the dorsalis pedis over the neck of the talus (supplies the part of the head and midbody)
- b. The artery of the tarsal sinus (an anastomotic loop between perforating peroneal and lateral tarsal branches of the dorsalis pedis) forms an anastomosis with the artery of the tarsal canal at the neck to supply most of body
- c. Talar head supplied by the artery of the sinus tarsi and branches from the dorsalis pedis
- d. Deltoid branch from the artery of the tarsal canal: supply the medial ¼ of the body
2. Types
   - a. Fractures of the neck: forced dorsiflexion
   - b. Osteochondritis of the articular margin: anterolateral or posteromedial lesions
   - c. Os trigonum fracture
3. Treatment
   - a. Neck fractures: immobilization and nonweight bearing if nondisplaced and closed reduction or open reduction if displaced (<5 mm and <5° AP displacement is adequate)
   - b. Immobilization or surgery for osteochondritis and immobilization for os trigonum fractures
4. Complications: ischemic necrosis and joint pain

B. Fractures of the calcaneus
1. Extra-articular or intra-articular
2. Closed treatment unless displacement is severe

C. Foot metatarsals
1. Proximal physis in the first metatarsals and distal physis in other metatarsals
2. Shaft fractures are more common than physeal injuries and tarsometatarsal fractures/dislocations may occur
3. Apophyseal injury to the base of the fifth metatarsal secondary of pull of peronius brevis
4. Treatment
   - a. Tarsometatarsal fractures/dislocation: reduction of the second metatarsal is important and percutaneous fixation can be done to the first and fifth metatarsals as well
   - b. Metatarsal fractures: walking cast for minimally displaced fractures

and closed reduction (finger traps) and casting for displaced fractures
c. Base of the fifth metatarsals: immobilization (nonunion may occur in transverse fractures through fifth metatarsal metaphysis)

REFERENCES

Balthazar DA, Pappas AM: Acquired valgus deformity of the tibia in children. J Pediatr Orthop 4:538–541, 1984

Baxter MP, Wiley JJ: Fractures of the tibial spine in children: An evaluation of knee stability. J Bone Joint Surg 70B:228–230, 1988

Canale ST, Belding RH: Osteochondral lesions of the talus. J Bone Joint Surg 62A:97–102, 1980

Christie MJ, Dvanch VM: Tibial tuberosity avulsion fracture in adolescents. J Pediatr Orthop 1:391–394, 1981

DeLee JC, Wilkins KE, Rogers LF, et al: Fracture separation of the distal humeral epiphysis. J Bone Joint Surg 67A:46–51, 1980

Ertl JP, Barrack RL, Alexander AH, et al: Triplane fracture of the distal tibial epiphysis: Long-term follow-up. J Bone Joint Surg 70A:967–976, 1988

Fielding JW, Hawkins RJ: Roentgenographic diagnosis of the injured neck. In AAOS instructional course lectures 25:149–170, 1976

Flynn JC, Richards JF: Non-union of minimally displaced fractures of the lateral condyle of the humerus in children. J Bone Joint Surg 53:1096–1101, 1971

Fowles JV, Kassab MT: Displaced fractures in the medial humeral condyle in children. J Bone Joint Surg 62A:1159–1163, 1980

Friddian NJ, Grace DL: Traumatic dislocation of the hip in adolescence with separation of the capital femoral epiphysis. J Bone Joint Surg 65B:148–149, 1983

Gross RH, et al: Cast brace management of the femoral shaft fracture in children and young adults. J Pediatr Orthop 3:572–582, 1983

Irani RN, Nicholson JT, Chung SMK: Long-term results in the treatment of femoral shaft fractures in young children by immediate spica immobilization. J Bone Joint Surg 58A:945–951, 1976

Jeffrey CC: Fracture of the head of the radius in children. J Bone Joint Surg 53B:429–439, 1971

Karrholm J, Hansson LI, Svensson K: Prediction of growth pattern after ankle fractures in children. J Pediatr Orthop 3:319–325, 1983

King J, Diefendorf D, Apthorp J, et al: Analysis of 429 fractures in 189 battered children. J Pediatr Orthop 8:585–589, 1988

Kling TF, Bright RW, Hensinger RN: Distal tibial physeal fractures in children that may require open reduction. J Bone Joint Surg 66A:647–657, 1984

Kohler R, Trillaud JM: Fracture and fracture separation of the proximal humerus in children: Report of 136 cases. J Pediatr Orthop 3:326–332, 1983

Langenskiold A: Surgical treatment of partial closure of the growth plate. J Pediatr Orthop 1:3–11, 1981

Letts RM, Gibeaut D: Fractures of the neck of the talus in children. Foot Ankle 1:74–77, 1980

Lombardo SJ, Harvey JP: Fractures of the distal femoral epiphysis. Factors influencing prognosis. J Bone Joint Surg 59A:742–751, 1977

Mass DP, Spiegel PG, Laros GS: Dislocation of the hip with traumatic separation of the capital femoral epiphysis. Clin Orthop 146:184–187, 1980

Molander ML, Wallin G, Wikstad I: Fracture of the intercondylar eminence of the tibia: A review of 35 patients. J Bone Joint Surg 63B:89–91, 1981

Ogden JA: Skeletal injury to the child. Philadelphia, Lea & Febiger, 1982

Ogden JA, Tross RB, Murphy MJ: Fractures of the tibial tuberosity in adolescents. J Bone Joint Surg 62A:205–215, 1980

Oppenheim WL, et al: Supracondylar humeral osteotomy for traumatic childhood cubitus varus deformity. Clin Orthop 188:34–39, 1984

Peterson HA: Operative correction of post-fracture arrest of the epiphyseal plate: Case report with 10-year follow-up. J Bone Joint Surg 62A:1018–1020, 1980

Ratliff AHC: Fractures of the neck of the femur in children. In The Hip. Proceedings of the ninth open scientific meeting of the Hip Society. St. Louis, CV Mosby, 1981

Riseborough EJ, Barrett EJ, Shapiro F: Growth disturbance following distal physeal fracture-separations. J Bone Joint Surg 65A:885–893, 1983

Rockwood CA: Dislocations of the sternoclavicular joint. In AAOS instructional course lectures 24:144–159, 1975

Rockwood CA: Fractures of the outer clavicle in children and adults. J Bone Joint Surg 64B:642, 1982

Rockwood CA, Wilkins KE, King RE, eds: Fractures in children, vol 3. Philadelphia, JB Lippincott Co, 1984

Salter RB, Harris WR: Injuries involving epiphyseal plates. J Bone Joint Surg 45A:587–622, 1963

Sander WE, Heckman JD: Traumatic plastic deformation of the radius and ulna. Clin Orthop 188:56–67, 1984

Schmidt TL, Weiner DS: Calcaneal fractures in children. An evaluation of the nature of the injury in 56 children. Clin Orthop 171:150–155, 1982

Shapiro F: Fractures of the femoral shaft in children. The overgrowth phenomenon. Acta Orthop Scand 52:649–655, 1981

Shelton WR, Canale ST: Fractures of the tibia through the proximal tibial epiphyseal cartilage. J Bone Joint Surg 61A:167–173, 1979

Sherk HH, Nicholson JT: Fractures of the odontoid process in young children. J Bone Joint Surg 60A:921–924, 1978

Siberstein MJ, et al: Some vagaries of the olecranon. J Bone Joint Surg 63A:722–725, 1981

Spiegel PG, et al: Triplane fractures of the distal tibial epiphysis. Clin Orthop 188:74–81, 1984

Staheli LT, Sheridan GW: Early spica cast management of femoral shaft fractures in young children. Clin Orthop 126:162–166, 1977

Tomkins DG: The anterior Monteggia fracture. J Bone Joint Surg 53A:1109–1114, 1971

Tredwell SJ, Van Peteghem K, Clough M: Patterns of forearm fractures in children. J Pediatr Orthop 4:604–608, 1984

Watts HG: Fractures of the pelvis in children. Orthop Clin North Am 7:615–624, 1976

Wiley JJ: Tarsometatarsal joint injuries in children. J Pediatr Orthop 1:255–260, 1981

Zionts LE, MacEwen GD: Spontaneous improvement of post-traumatic tibia valga. J Bone Joint Surg 68A:680–687, 1986

Ziv I, Rang M: Treatment of femoral fracture in the child with head injury. J Bone Joint Surg 65B:276–278, 1983

SECTION 4: ADULT ORTHOPAEDICS

Howard S. An
James B. Stiehl
Kevin P. Black
Michael J. Shereff
John S. Gould

31. Shoulder Problems
32. Elbow Problems
33. Hip Problems
34. Knee Problems
35. Sports Injuries of the Lower Extremities
36. Foot and Ankle Problems

31
Shoulder Problems

IMPINGEMENT SYNDROME AND ROTATOR CUFF TEAR OF THE SHOULDER

I. General Considerations
A. Repetitive irritation between the rotator cuff and the undersurface of the acromion is pathogenic
B. Tendons of rotator cuff (particularly the supraspinatus tendon) and biceps impinge against coracoacromial ligament, antero-inferior surface of the acromion, and undersurface of acromioclavicular joint (Fig 4-1)
C. Supraspinatus tendon proximal to its insertion onto the greater tuberosity is hypovascular
D. Rotator cuff is important for dynamic stability, whereas ligaments are important for static stability
E. Eighty to 90% power of external rotation is provided by the rotator cuff
F. Deltoid provides 50% power of abduction
G. Etiologies of rotator cuff diseases
  1. Degenerative joint disease with osteophytes and subacromial impingement
  2. Inflammatory synovitis (crystalline induced or systemic)
  3. Post-traumatic: displaced fractures of the acromion, proximal humerus and anterior dislocations (50–80% of anterior dislocations are associated with rotator cuff tear in older patients)
  4. Congenital skeletal malformation (os acrominale)
  5. Paralysis of the trapezius (spinal accessory nerve injury)
H. Spectrum of disease
  1. Inflammatory tendinitis: edema and hemorrhage, common during 20–40 years of age and reversible
  2. Impingement syndrome (painful arc syndrome): thickening and fibrosis of the cuff and progressive
  3. Degenerated tear of rotator cuff (>40 years of age): associated with bony changes and biceps tendon rupture
I. Differential diagnosis
  1. Cervical disc disease (C5–C6)
  2. Frozen shoulder
  3. Instability
  4. Acromioclavicular or glenohumeral arthritis
  5. Calcific tendinitis
  6. Suprascapular nerve palsy

II. Clinical Findings
A. Inflammatory tendinitis (subacromial bursitis) and impingement syndrome
  1. Tenderness to rotator cuff insertion at the greater tuberosity
  2. Painful arc motion
    a. Impingement sign: pain by forward hyperflexion of the humerus
    b. Pain and crepitus on abduction of the internally rotated humerus against acromial arch between 90° and 120°
  3. Biceps resistance test (Yergason's test): if associated biceps tendinitis
  4. External rotation strength test with 90° abduction (rotator cuff muscles provide 80–90% of external rotation power but only 50% abduction power)
  5. Impingement test: subacromial lidocaine injection should diminish pain from inflammatory origin and acromioclavicular injection can be done to distinguish pain from it
B. Rotator cuff tears
  1. Acute: inability to abduct the arm
  2. Chronic: weak and painful abduction

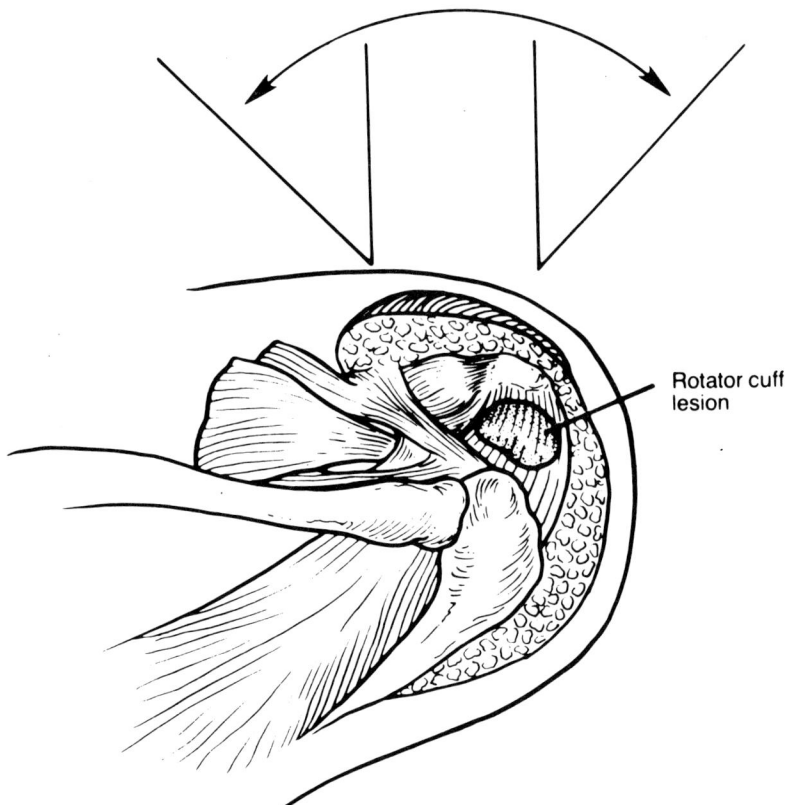

Figure 4-1. Rotator cuff lesion just anterior to the acromion on forward flexion. (From Lippert FG III: Adult orthopaedics. In: Bucholz RW, Lippert FG, Wenger DR, Ezaki M, eds. Orthopaedic decision making, Philadelphia, B.C. Decker, and St Louis, CV Mosby, 1984, p 100. Reprinted with permission.)

and external rotation (range of motion is often good)
3. X-ray findings:
   a. Superior subluxation of the humeral head: acromiohumeral distance <6 mm is abnormal
   b. Sclerosis and cystic changes at the greater tuberosity in chronic cases
   c. Positive arthrogram: presence of dye in the subdeltoid bursa
      (1) Single and double contrast arthrography
      (2) Highly accurate for full-thickness tears
      (3) Less useful for partial tears
      (4) Invasive, painful
   d. Ultrasonography
      (1) Reliable in detecting full-thickness tears
      (2) Less reliable in partial-thickness tears <1 cm
      (3) Highly dependent on skill of ultrasonographer
   e. Magnetic resonance imaging (MRI)
      (1) Accurate at determining extent of tears
      (2) Confusion between partial-thickness tears and inflammation/degeneration

III. Treatment
A. Impingement syndrome
   1. Nonoperative approach for 6 months: nonsteroidal anti-inflammatory drugs (NSAIDs), rest, injection, strengthening
   2. Surgery

a. Resection of the coracoacromial ligament
   b. Anteroinferior acromioplasty (Neer)
   c. Acromioclavicular arthroplasty (Mumford): if radiographically involved, preoperative tenderness, or preoperative injection relieve pain
   d. Tenodesis of the biceps if necessary
   e. Arthroscopic decompression may give equally good (80–90%) results if properly performed
B. Rotator cuff tear
   1. Acute tear: surgical repair within 3 weeks if massive tear, and for those who are younger (<50 years), and for those who have normal functioning of preinjury shoulder
   2. Chronic tear
      a. Primary indication for surgery is pain, and secondary indications are improving function and preventing cuff tear arthropathy
      b. Rest, NSAIDs, rehabilitation, subacromial steroid injection
      c. If patient remains significantly disabled, surgery should be considered
   3. Surgery
      a. Treat impingement syndrome
      b. Goals of cuff repair
         (1) Provide cuff stability
         (2) Restore strength of external rotation and abduction
         (3) Restore humeral head depression
         (4) Seal synovial cavity for articular nutrition
      c. Techniques of repair
         (1) Small and medium tears: Tendon-to-tendon or tendon-to-bone.
         (2) Large and massive tears: Difficult to repair due to quality of tissue and retraction of cuff. Options include
            i. Mobilization and transposition of existing cuff tissue — preferred technique
            ii. Less satisfactory results with allograft cuff, fascia lata, carbon fiber
            iii. Acromioplasty and debridement alone for massive cuff tears have been reported but conflicting results reported. Cuff repair should be performed whenever possible
      d. Results after cuff repair
         (1) Overall, approximately 85% of patients note significant improvement in pain and 70% note improvement in function
         (2) Poor results associated with
            i. Significant preoperative weakness
            ii. Long-standing massive tears
            iii. Lack of compliance with rehabilitation postoperatively
            iv. Workman's compensation
            v. Missed diagnosis
            vi. Inadequate bone removal
            vii. Deltoid detachment
         (3) Revision surgery for failed acromioplasty/cuff repair should be considered for pain relief, not functional improvement. Technically more demanding, results more variable

IV. Cuff Tear Arthropathy

A. Definition: coexistence of massive rotator cuff tears and nonrheumatoid shoulder arthritis
B. History: usually suggestive of long history of rotator cuff disease, which preceded onset of articular surface degenerative changes
C. Pathology: rotator cuff tear, articular cartilage degeneration, and bone loss of humeral head, glenoid, and acromion
D. Radiographs
   1. Superior subluxation of humeral head
   2. Joint space narrowing
   3. Abnormal bony contour of humeral head, glenoid, and acromion

E. Differential Diagnosis
  1. Osteoarthritis
  2. Rheumatoid arthritis
  3. Infection
  4. Avascular necrosis
  5. Charcot joint
F. Treatment: Resurfacing total shoulder arthroplasty, rotator cuff reconstruction, rehabilitation. If rotator cuff is not reconstructible, prosthesis is usually unstable and results in glenoid loosening. Hemiarthroplasty should be considered in these cases. Primary indication for surgery in these patients is pain relief. Functional improvement is secondary
G. Milwaukee shoulder (basic calcium pyrophosphate deposition disease). Unknown if this is same phenomenon as cuff tear arthropathy, but end result is basically the same. Characterized by
  1. Large rotator cuff tears
  2. Glenohumeral arthritis
  3. Joint effusions: few leukocytes, basic calcium phosphate crystals, particulate collagen of types I, II, III, and collagenase and neutral protease particles
  4. Treatment: same as cuff tear arthropathy

V. Other Conditions Affecting the Shoulder

A. Inflammation and degeneration of the long head of the biceps
  1. Usually associated with the inflammatory conditions of shoulder. Isolated biceps disease uncommon
  2. Synovial lining, which is continuous with glenohumeral joint, surrounds biceps for varying distances in bicipital groove
  3. Physical examination: Tenderness of bicepital groove, positive Speed (resisted forward flexion) and Yergason (resisted supination) tests
  4. Treatment: Careful patient selection essential. If isolated disease, tenodesis/transfer can be successful. If other disease present, biceps tenodesis alone unsuccessful
B. Acromioclavicular disease
  1. May be chronic degenerative process or post-traumatic (following acromioclavicular (AC) separation)
  2. Plain radiographs underestimate frequency; physical examination (tenderness) most sensitive diagnostic tool
  3. Nonsurgical treatment: Rest, NSAID, injection (for both diagnostic and therapeutic reasons)
  4. Surgical treatment: distal clavicle excision (Mumford) has high success rate. Weaver-Dunn procedure (distal clavicle excision plus coracoacromial ligament transfer) can be performed if clavicle unstable
C. Calcific tendinitis
  1. Often incidental X-ray finding
  2. Usually responds well to nonoperative treatment
  3. Occasionally tendon debridement required (arthroscopic vs open)
D. Entrapment neuropathies
  1. Spinal accessory: may be injured in cervical node dissection, blunt trauma, etc. Eden-Lange procedure successful if trapezius paralysis results in significant disability
  2. Suprascapular: may be injured proximal or distal to supraspinatus innervation. Usually improves with rest, rehabilitation. Further work-up and surgery may be required in select cases
  3. Long thoracic: serratus paralysis results in scapular winging. (However, scapular winging may result from a variety of etiologies.) Symptoms often resolve with rehabilitation. Surgical stabilization of scapula required in select cases
E. Adhesive capsulitis
  1. General considerations
    a. Pathogenesis: inflammatory process of the rotator cuff or immune-mediated response
    b. More common in females, age 45–60 years

c. Patients with cardiovascular or cerebrovascular disease, diabetes mellitus, and thyroid disease or certain personality traits are at increased risk
d. Differential diagnosis: missed posterior shoulder dislocation, cervical spondylosis, rotator cuff tear, glenohumeral arthritis, biceps tendinitis, and calcific tendinitis
2. Pathomechanics
   a. Contracture of the subscapularis and coracohumeral ligament results in restriction of external rotation and thus abduction
   b. The normally lax inferior capsular recess becomes contracted secondary to prolonged adduction
   c. Scapulothoracic motion attempts to compensate for this loss of motion. It may result in stretching or tethering of the suprascapular nerve at the suprascapular ligament, increasing pain
   d. Normal joint capacity of 25 cc is diminished to 7–12 cc
3. Clinical findings
   a. Gradual onset of stiffness and pain with functional limitation
   b. Motion loss, particularly abduction, internal rotation and external rotation
   c. Natural history: most patients will have complete restoration of movement and resolution of pain within 18 months
   d. Arthrogram: decreased volume and loss of axillary fold
4. Treatment
   a. Conservative: rest and anti-inflammatory medications (including oral corticosteroids) are typically used in the early stages with passive range of motion exercises. Once pain subsides, active motion may be initiated, stressing external rotation
   b. Hydraulic distension
   c. Manipulation does not result in the release of adhesions but, in fact, results in tearing of the subscapularis at its musculotendinous junction
   d. Complications: manipulation may result in fracture of the proximal humerus or radial nerve adhesion to teres major at time of manipulation
   e. Surgery indicated in select patients without psychiatric disorder who have failed nonoperative treatment. Open release of contracted structures required. Contracture of coracohumeral ligament and rotator interval appears to be main lesion in chronic adhesive capsulitis

INSTABILITIES OF THE SHOULDER

RECURRENT ANTERIOR DISLOCATION

I. General Considerations
A. Anatomy
   1. Inherently unstable joint that sacrifices stability for motion
   2. Stability: static and dynamic restraints
      a. Static: bony architecture, labrum, and capsule. Superior, middle, and inferior glenohumeral ligaments comprise capsular ligaments. Incompetency of inferior glenohumeral ligament is major pathologic lesion of anterior instability
      b. Dynamic: musculature
B. Classification
   1. Frequency: acute, recurrent, and fixed
   2. Etiology: single traumatic event, microtrauma/overuse, and atraumatic
   3. Direction: anterior, posterior, inferior, multidirectional
   4. Degree: dislocation, subluxation
C. Most athletic shoulder injuries fall into one of two groups
   1. Acute (recurrent), traumatic, anterior dislocation

2. Recurrent, microtrauma/overuse, anterior subluxation

II. Acute, Traumatic, Anterior Dislocation

A. Mechanism: abduction, external rotation load
B. Diagnosis
   1. Check for neurovascular injury, particularly for the axillary nerve function
   2. X-ray
      a. Anteroposterior (AP) and lateral (scapular Y) view in all cases
      b. Axillary view for Bankart lesion
      c. Internal rotated view (50°–80°) for Hill-Sach lesion
C. Prognosis
   1. Length of immobilization has no effect on recurrence
   2. Major prognostic factor is age at first dislocation
      a. Twelve to 22 years of age: 55% recurrence
      b. Twenty-three to 29 years of age: 37% recurrence
      c. Thirty to 40 years of age: 12% recurrence
D. Treatment
   1. Reduction: many techniques but the basic principle is adequate relaxation and gentle traction
   2. Nonsurgical treatment
      a. Rest and strengthening
      b. Indications for surgery in the past have generally been several involuntary dislocations, but more aggressive approach may be considered in young athlete with high demand shoulder
   3. Surgical treatment
      a. Bankart reconstruction: the gold standard
      b. Putti-Platt or Magnuson-Stack: subscapularis procedures that limit external rotation
      c. Bristow procedure: high complication/reoperation rate
      d. Osteotomies: proximal humerus rotation
      e. Arthroscopic procedures: early results demonstrate significantly higher failure rates
   4. Recurrent, traumatic, anterior subluxation is also very common and frequently misdiagnosed
      a. Patient may be more disabled than the recurrent dislocation
      b. Physical examination: positive apprehension sign
      c. Computed tomographic (CT) arthrography is the most accurate test that demonstrates labral avulsion and anterior capsular redundancy

III. Recurrent, Microtrauma/Overuse, Anterior Subluxation

A. Usually affect athletes in overhead activities (pitcher, swimmer, tennis, quarterback, volleyball)
B. Mechanism: overuse of shoulder musculature can result in
   1. Weakening of humeral head depressors, impingement
   2. Compromised function of muscles that contribute dynamically to shoulder instability
   3. Vicious cycle: muscle overuse, fatigue, and weakening causes loss of dynamic stabilizers and subluxation, which in turn affects motion of the shoulder and produces tendinitis or impingement
C. Diagnostic dilemma: how to distinguish shoulder pain secondary to pure tendinitis/impingement from pain resulting secondary to instability and tendinitis (Table 4-1)
D. Treatment
   1. Rest, NSAIDs
   2. Strengthening program for rotator cuff and parascapular muscles
   3. Strengthening
      a. Isometrics
      b. Isotonics
      c. Isokinetics

Table 4-1 Distinction Between Instability and Impingement of the Shoulder

	Instability	Impingement
Age	16–35 years	>35 years
Pain	Late cocking and acceleration ("dead arm")	No specific location/phase
Location of pain	Posterior shoulder	Diffuse
X-ray	Usually normal	Frequently abnormal
Examination	Impingement sign frequently present Positive apprehension sign and relocation test	Impingement sign always present Negative apprehension and relocation tests

   d. Endurance exercises
      (1) High repetition
      (2) Low load
   e. Throwing program (between 3 and 6 months after rest)
 4. Surgical reconstruction
   a. Indicated for failed rehabilitation
   b. Capsular type repair is best for throwing athlete
   c. Results less successful than non-throwing athlete

IV. Posterior Instability

A. General considerations
 1. Relatively rare (approximately 4% of all shoulder dislocations) and frequently missed
 2. Associated with motor vehicle accidents, seizures, electric shock treatment, and alcohol-related injuries
B. Clinical findings: internally rotated deformity with inability to externally rotate the arm.
C. X-rays
 1. AP view
   a. Vacant glenoid sign: empty glenoid
   b. Daylight sign: gap between the glenoid and head
   c. Trough line: impaction fracture of the head
   d. Cystic and hollow appearance of the humeral head and loss of profile of the humeral neck because of internal rotation of the arm
 2. Axillary view is diagnostic, and usually not taken in those cases that are initially missed
 3. Impaction fractures of the head may be seen
 4. Lesser tuberosity fracture may be seen
 5. CT arthrography may demonstrate posterior labral lesion (posterior Bankart) in recurrent instability
D. Treatment
 1. Options: no treatment, closed reduction (with general anesthesia if necessary), subscapularis transfer, hemiarthroplasty, and total joint arthroplasty
   a. Acute traumatic posterior subluxation: may require posterior reconstruction if it becomes a chronic, recurrent problem
   b. Recurrent traumatic posterior dislocation: immobilize in most stable position. Reconstruction for recurrent instability
   c. Unreduced posterior dislocation
      (1) Open reduction is usually required for large anteromedial humeral head defect or several week-old dislocations
      (2) If dislocation is missed for months or years, and patient has minimal pain and functional loss,

a nonoperative approach should be considered
- d. Surgical indications
  - (1) Acute traumatic posterior dislocation: need for surgical intervention is unlikely. Indications are major displacement of the lesser tuberosity, large posterior glenoid fracture, irreducible cases, and open dislocations
  - (2) Recurrent traumatic posterior dislocation: rule out voluntary dislocation or psychiatric disorder. Procedures may be reverse Bankart, Putti-Platt, and glenoid osteotomy. McLaughlin procedure is indicated in presence of large anteromedial humeral head defect
  - (3) Unreduced posterior dislocation: reconstruction is indicated if significant disability and good bone stock. Indications for arthroplasty include a humeral head defect of more than 45% of the articular surface or chronic dislocation. Glenoid fossa destruction necessitates total shoulder arthroplasty (humeral component should be placed in neutral version)

V. Multidirectional Instability

A. General considerations
1. Implies inferior component of instability along with anterior and/or posterior instability
2. Capsular tissues are very lax; generalized ligamentous laxity is frequently present
3. Most patients can recall a specific episode that initiated the instability

B. Clinical findings
1. Aching shoulder pain with lifting activities frequently present in addition to instability complaints
2. Physical examination: "Sulcus sign" demonstrates inferior instability
3. X-rays are usually negative
4. Examination under anesthesia and arthroscopy may be helpful in determining directions of instability and intra-articular pathologic conditions

C. Treatment
1. Rule out psychiatric disorder/voluntary instability
2. Strengthening shoulder musculature and patient counseling may allow a return to acceptable life-style
3. Surgery indicated for involuntary instability in patients who have failed rehabilitation and have significant disability
4. "Inferior capsular shift" or similar type of procedure is preferred surgical technique

ARTHRODESIS AND TOTAL SHOULDER REPLACEMENT

I. Glenohumeral Arthrodesis

A. General considerations
1. Diseases for which arthrodesis was commonly performed have become relatively uncommon
2. Improvements in fixation methods have eliminated need for extra-articular approaches and improved fusion rates

B. Indications
1. Infection with significant loss of articular cartilage
2. Paralysis of deltoid and rotator cuff
3. Severe rotator cuff deficiencies (failed repair of massive cuff tears)
4. Traumatic arthritis with severe rotator cuff disease
5. Recurrent subluxations dislocations with continuing instability and arthritis
6. Failed prosthetic reconstructions (infection, severe bone loss, rotator cuff disease)

7. Arthrodesis may rarely be indicated in rheumatoid patients with severe rotator cuff disease and minimal ipsilateral involvement of other joints

C. Contraindications
1. Strength of the scapulothoracic muscles must be evaluated. Trapezius and serratus anterior should be present to give good results. The additional presence of active rhomboids will better stabilize the scapula while pectoralis will add power in flexion
2. Acromioclavicular, sternoclavicular, and distal joints of the involved extremity must be evaluated because additional stresses will be placed on them after fusion. If the acromioclavicular joint is found to be diseased, a distal claviculectomy may be considered
3. The presence or potential presence of a prosthetic elbow is an absolute contraindication

D. Treatment options
1. Extra-articular fusion: used in the past when chronic active tuberculous infections were common
2. Intra-articular fusion: improved fixation techniques with either large cancellous screws or compression plating make this the preferred method
3. Position: classically 45° of each abduction, flexion, and internal rotation (salute position) has been described. More recently, however, most believe that 30° of abduction, 30° of flexion, and 30° of internal rotation are best

E. Resectional arthroplasty
1. Should be considered only as a salvage procedure
2. Resection of the humeral head with or without musculotendinous reconstruction has generally given poor results. (35–50% have pain and 45% have only 30°–40° motion and overall poor function)
3. Partial glenoidectomy has been reported to give fair results in the rheumatoid patient

II. Total Shoulder Replacement

A. General considerations
1. Pain relief is the primary indication in total shoulder arthroplasty
2. Limitation of function should be considered a secondary indication because improvement is less predictable
3. Anatomic considerations: humeral head is 35°–40° retroverted and the glenoid is 5° anteverted to the scapula body (Fig 4-2)
4. Three types of prostheses: constrained, semiconstrained, and unconstrained
5. Biomechanical considerations: the peak compressive joint reaction force is 10 times arm weight at 90° flexion and 60° abduction. The rotator cuff functions to decrease cephalad migration of the axis of rotation as the arm flexes and abducts, and therefore decreases shear stress

B. Specific indications
1. Rheumatoid arthritis: one must consider other joint involvement in the patient. A high incidence of rotator cuff problem
2. Osteoarthritis
3. Fractures: acute, severe three and four part fractures or impression fractures involving >50% of the humeral articular surface
4. Malunion with a resultant irregular, painful joint surface
5. Nonunion: endoprosthesis may be considered, especially in an elderly, osteoporotic patient
6. Avascular necrosis
7. Cuff tear arthropathy

C. Contraindications
1. Extreme osteoporosis and medial resorption of the glenoid are common problems in the rheumatoid patient that may preclude the use of a total

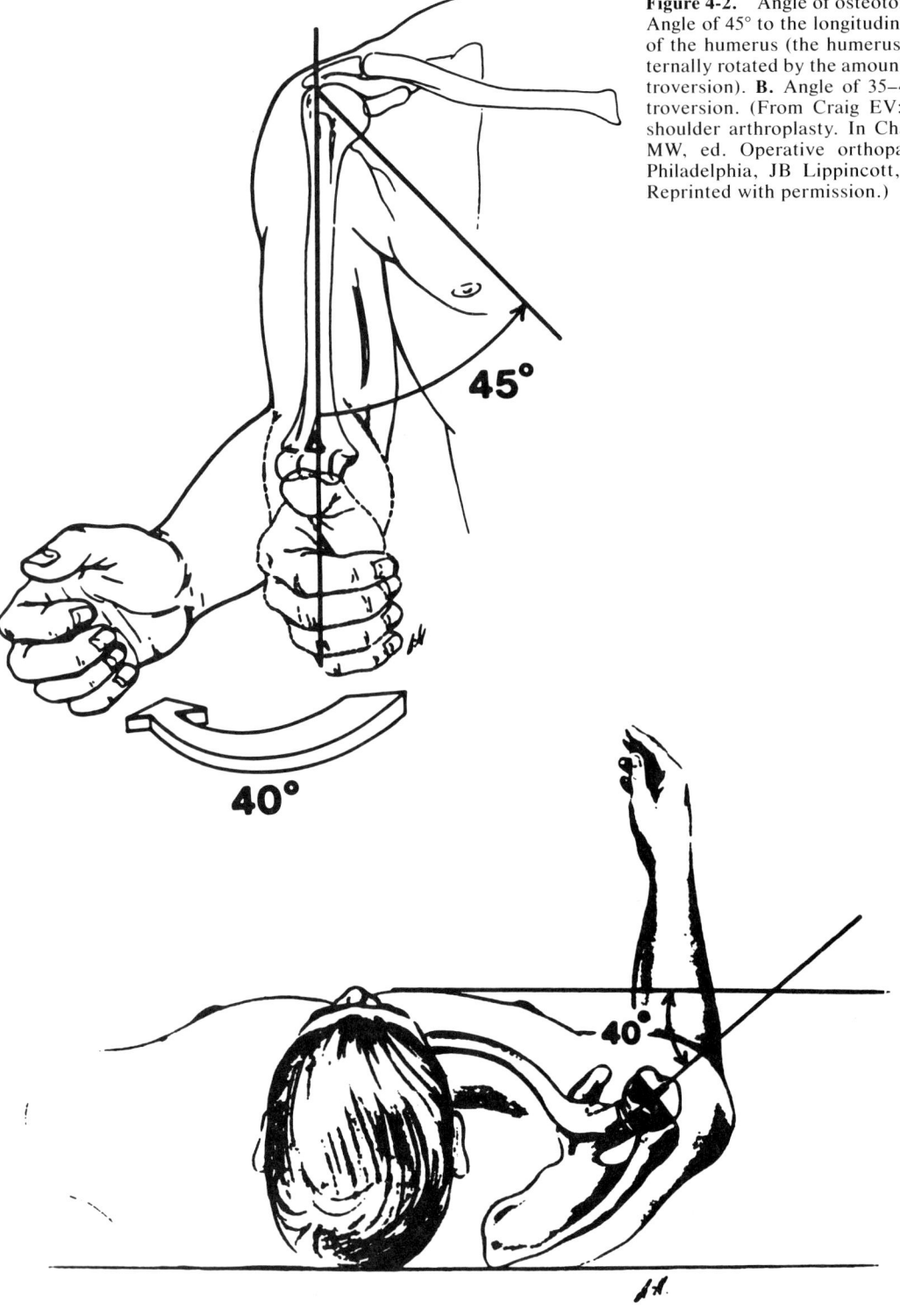

Figure 4-2. Angle of osteotomy. **A.** Angle of 45° to the longitudinal axis of the humerus (the humerus is externally rotated by the amount of retroversion). **B.** Angle of 35–40° retroversion. (From Craig EV: Total shoulder arthroplasty. In Chapman MW, ed. Operative orthopaedics. Philadelphia, JB Lippincott, 1988. Reprinted with permission.)

shoulder arthroplasty (may consider hemiarthroplasty)
   2. Paralysis of the deltoid and rotator cuff or deltoid paralysis with severe rotator cuff disease
   3. Neuropathic joint
   4. Acute or recent infection. History of an ancient infection is not necessarily a contraindication
D. Prosthetic designs
   1. Most present-day designs are relatively unconstrained, surface replacement implants
   2. More constrained devices can be used, especially when it is necessary to support or replace the stabilizing functions of the rotator cuff or capsule. Long-term follow-up with these devices does show a higher rate of radiographic loosening
E. Results of unconstrained prosthesis
   1. Ninety-two percent satisfactory pain relief in 73 shoulders, using the unconstrained Neer prosthesis with 2–6.5 year follow-up. Range of motion was found to improve an average of 44°–141° in the osteoarthritic patient, 103° in the rheumatoid, and 109° in the traumatic arthritic patient (Cofield, 1984)
   2. Neer emphasized the necessity of a full postoperative therapy program to obtain optimal results
   3. Radiographic loosening is seen in approximately 30% of glenoid components, but only a small number of these patients are symptomatic, requiring revision (3–4% clinical loosening after 3–5 years)
   4. Other complications include infection, nerve injuries (axillary and musculocutaneous), rotator cuff tears, and joint instability. Overall, 5–8% of patients will require a second procedure
F. Results of constrained prostheses
   1. Post, 1983: 95% pain relief, but have a higher complication rate with 10% dislocation, 50% humeral radiographic loosening, and 30% glenoid radiographic loosening
   2. Indications may be rotator cuff insufficiency, capsular insufficiency, and tumor (even for those with rotator cuff deficiency, nonconstrained prosthesis can be used if pain relief only is of concern)
   3. Must have trapezius and deltoid function

SURGERY OF THE PALSIED SHOULDER

I. General Considerations
A. Paralysis about the shoulder girdle greatly diminishes function of the entire upper extremity
B. Careful and exact diagnosis is needed in order to plan surgical treatment
C. Strength and function of each shoulder girdle muscle must be assessed by palpation and strength against resistance
D. The glenohumeral joint should be stabilized without fusion whenever possible. However, one must consider patient activity levels, occupation, and stress requirements

II. Classification (Goldner)
A. Group I: partial deficiency of abduction and external rotation
B. Group II: complete paralysis of abduction and external rotation, biceps, triceps, and brachialis
C. Group III: deltoid weakness and weak or absent external rotators
D. Group IV: primary scapulothoracic muscle deficiency

III. Etiology
A. Brachial plexus injury involving either roots, trunk, cords, or peripheral nerves
B. Muscle damage secondary to trauma or tumor
C. Poliomyelitis

D. Brachial plexitis (Pillane-Parsonage-Turner syndrome)
E. Guillain-Barré syndrome

IV. Treatment
A. Group I
  1. Muscle strength in this group is considered to be less than 30% of normal
  2. Birth trauma is considered to be the major cause of disease in this group
  3. Surgery
     a. Transfer of the teres major and lattismus dorsi posteriorly to the humerus to change their function to external rotators
     b. Elongation of the short head of the biceps with fascia lata graft and transfer to the acromion anteriorly to improve flexion
     c. Elongate pectoralis major with fascia lata if necessary and transfer superiorly to the anterolateral shoulder cuff, improving abduction-flexion of the shoulder
     d. It may be necessary to elongate the subscapularis if contracture is severe
B. Group II
  1. In this group complete paralysis of the deltoid, supraspinatus, infraspinatus, and teres minor is seen. The subscapularis is usually normal
  2. Surgical procedures performed singly or in combination include the following
     a. Transfer of the trapezius with a bony segment from the acromion to the shoulder cuff to augment abduction and stabilize the proximal humerus
     b. Transfer of the short head of the biceps, latissimus dorsi, and teres major, as described for Group I
     c. Transfer of the long head of the triceps from the scapular neck to the acromion. This aids glenohumeral extension, external rotation, and abduction
C. Group III
  1. Deltoid, biceps, brachialis, and triceps weakness combined with weak or absent external rotators
  2. Goal of treatment in this group is to decrease painful subluxation and diminish instability
  3. Shoulder arthrodesis may be best method of treatment, depending on patient needs
  4. Other procedures include creation of an abduction contracture by plicating and advancing the subscapularis superiorly, advancing supraspinatus and infraspinatus to the anatomic neck of the humerus, and elongation and transfer of the trapezius to the greater tuberosity. With this alteration, scapulothoracic muscles may function sufficiently to move the humerus
D. Group IV
  1. Lesions may be isolated or combined, affecting serratus anterior, rhomboid muscles, and trapezius
  2. These lesions result in severe limitation of scapular motion and cause scapular malrotation, thus indirectly limiting glenohumeral motion
  3. If the serratus anterior is paralyzed, transfer of the pectoralis major or minor may be done
  4. If trapezius is paralyzed, transfer of the levator scapulae to the acromion is done
  5. With bilateral rhomboid paralysis, fascia lata strips may be taken and secured to the medial border of both scapulae. This is reinforced with trapezius which is displaced caudally to provide additional support to the medial, inferior scapular segment

REFERENCES

Adler JB, Patterson RL Jr: Erb's palsy, long term results of treatment in eighty-eight cases. J Bone Joint Surg 49A:1052, 1967

Andrew S Jr, Carson WG Jr, McLeod WD: Glenoid labrum tears related to the long head of the biceps. Am J Sports Med 13:337–341, 1985

Barret WP, Franklin JL, Jackins SE, et al: Total shoulder arthroplasty. J Bone Joint Surg 69A:865–872, 1987

Barton NJ: Arthrodesis of the shoulder for degenerative conditions. J Bone Joint Surg 54A:1759, 1972

Becker DA, Cofield RH: Tenodesis of the long head of the biceps brachii for chronic bicipital tendinitis: Long-term results. J Bone Joint Surg 71A:376–381, 1989

Beltran JE, Trilla JC, Barjau R: A simplified compression arthrodesis of the shoulder. J Bone Joint Surg 57A:538, 1975

Bigliani LV, Morrison DS, April EW: The morphology of the acromion and its relationship to rotator cuff tears. Orthop Trans 10:228, 1986

Bigliani LV, Perel-Sanz JR, Wolfe IN: Treatment of trapezius paralysis. J Bone Joint Surg 67A:871–877, 1985

Bigliani LV, D'Alessandro DF, Duralde XA, et al: Anterior acromioplasty for subacromial impingement in patients younger than 40 years of age. Clin Orthop 246:111–116, 1989

Black KPJ, Lombardo JA: Suprascapular nerve injuries with isolated paralysis of the infraspinatus. Am J Sports Med 17:788, 1990

Charnley J, Houston JK: Compression arthrodesis of the shoulder. J Bone Joint Surg 46B:614, 1964

Cofield RH: Total shoulder arthroplasty with the Neer prosthesis. J Bone Joint Surg 66A:899, 1984

Cofield RH, Briggs BT: Glenohumeral arthrodesis: Operative and long term functional results. J Bone Joint Surg 61A:668, 1979

DeOrio JK, Cofield RH: Results of a second attempt at surgical repair of a failed initial rotator-cuff repair. J Bone Joint Surg 66A:563–567, 1984

Duncan BF: The frozen shoulder syndrome: Rehabilitation approach to treatment. Contemp Orthop 6:69, 1983

Edmonson A, Crenshaw A: Campbell's operative orthopaedics, ed 6. St Louis, CV Mosby, 1980

Ellman H: Arthroscopic subacromial decompression: Analysis of one- to three-year results. Arthroscopy 3:173–181, 1987

Ellman H, Hanker G, Bayer M: Repair of the rotator cuff: End-result study of factors influencing reconstruction. J Bone Joint Surg 68A:1136–1144, 1986

Fareed DO, Gallivan WR: Office management of frozen shoulder syndrome: Treatment with hydraulic distension under local anesthesia. Clin Orthop 242:177–183, 1989

Garth WP Jr, Allman FL Jr, Armstrong WS: Occult anterior subluxations of the shoulder in noncontact sports. Am J Sports Med 15:579–585, 1987

Gartsman GM, Blair ME Jr, Noble PC, et al: Arthroscopic subacromial decompression: An anatomical study. Am J Sports Med 16:48–50, 1988

Goldner JL: Muscle-tendon transfers for paralysis of the shoulder girdle. In Evarts CM, ed: Surgery of the musculoskeletal system, vol 3. New York, Churchill Livingstone, 1983

Ha'eri GB, Wiley AM: Advancement of the supraspinatus muscle in the repair of ruptures of the rotator cuff. J Bone Joint Surg 63A:232–238, 1981

Hawkins RJ, Brock RM, Abrams JS, et al: Acromioplasty for impingement with an intact rotator cuff. J Bone Joint Surg 70B:795–797, 1988

Hawkins RJ, Chris T, Bokor D, et al: Failed anterior acromioplasty: A review of 51 cases. Clin Orthop 243:106–111, 1989

Hawkins RJ, Misamore GW, Hobieka PE: Surgery for full thickness rotator cuff tears. J Bone Joint Surg 67A:1349–1355, 1985

Hawkins RJ, Neer CS II, Pianta RM, et al: Locked posterior dislocation of the shoulder. J Bone Joint Surg 69A:918, 1987

Hawkins RJ, Neer CS II: A functional analysis of shoulder fusions. Clin Orthop 223:65–76, 1987

Hernandez A, Drez D: Operative treatment of posterior shoulder dislocations by posterior glenoidplasty, capsulorrhaphy and infraspinatus advancement. Am J Sports Med 14:187–191, 1986

Hovelius L: Anterior dislocation of the shoulder in teenagers and young adults: Five-year prognosis. J Bone Joint Surg 69A:393–399, 1987

Howell SM, Imobersteg AM, Seger DH, et al: Classification of the role of the supraspinatus in shoulder function. J Bone Joint Surg 68A:398–404, 1986

Matthews LS, Vetter WL, Oweida SJ, et al: Arthroscopic staple capsulorraphy for recurrent anterior shoulder instability. Arthroscopy 4:106–111, 1988

McCarty DJ, Halverson PB, Carrera GF, et al: Milwaukee shoulder — association of micro spheroids containing hydroxyapatite crystals, active collagenase, and neutral protease with rotator cuff defects. I. Clinical aspects. Arthritis Rheum 24:464–473, 1981

McGlynn FJ, Caspari RB: Arthroscopic findings in the subluxating shoulder. Clin Orthop 183:173–178, 1984

McMaster WC: Anterior glenoid labrum damage: A painful lesion in swimmers. Am J Sports Med 14:383–387, 1986

Morgan CD, Bodenstab AB: Arthroscopic Bankart suture repair: Technique and early results. Arthroscopy 3:111–122, 1987

Mosely HF: Arthrodesis of the shoulder in the adult. Clin Orthop 20:156, 1961

Neer CS II: Impingement lesions. Clin Orthop 173:70–77, 1983

Neer CS II, Craig EV, Fukuda H: Cuff tear arthropathy. J Bone Joint Surg 65A:1232–1244, 1982

Neer CS II, Foster CR: Inferior capsular shift for involuntary inferior and multidirectional instability of the shoulder: A preliminary report. J Bone Joint Surg 62A:897–908, 1980

Neer CS II, Kirby RM: Revision of humeral head and total shoulder arthroplasties. Clin Orthop 170:189–195, 1982

Neer CS II, Morrison DS: Glenoid bone-grafting in total shoulder arthroplasty. J Bone Joint Surg 70A:1154–1162, 1988

Neer CS II, Watson KC, Stanton FJ: Recent experience in total shoulder replacement. J Bone Joint Surg 64A:319, 1982

Nevaiser RJ, Nevaiser TJ, Nevaiser JS: Concurrent rupture of the rotator cuff and anterior dislocation of the shoulder in the older patient. J Bone Joint Surg 70A:1308–1311, 1988

Ozak J, Fujimoto S, Nakagawa Y, et al: Tears of the rotator cuff of the shoulder associated with pathological changes in the acromion: A study in cadavera. J Bone Joint Surg 70A:1224–1230, 1988

Ozak J, Nakagawa Y, Sakura G, Tamai S: Recalcitrant chronic adhesive capsulitis of the shoulder. J Bone Joint Surg 71A:1511–1515, 1989

Post M, Jablon M: Constrained total shoulder arthroplasty: Long term follow-up observations. Clin Orthop 173:109, 1983

Post M, Mayer J: Suprascapular nerve entrapment: Diagnosis and treatment. Clin Orthop 223:126–136, 1987

Rafii M, Minkoff J, Bonamo J, et al: Computed tomography (CT) arthrogram of shoulder instabilities in athletes. Am J Sports Med 16:352–361, 1988

Richards RR, Sherman RM, Hudson AR, et al: Shoulder arthrodesis using a pelvic-reconstruction plate: A report of eleven cases. J Bone Joint Surg 70A:416–421, 1988

Rowe CR: Arthrodesis of the shoulder used in treating painful conditions. Clin Orthop 173:92, 1983

Rowe CR: Reevaluation of the position of arthrodesis of the shoulder in the adult. J Bone Joint Surg 56A:913, 1974

Rowe, CR, Patel D, Southmayd WW: The Bankart procedure, a long-term end result study. J Bone Joint Surg 60A:1, 1978

Rybka V, Raunio P, Vainio K: Arthrodesis of the shoulder in rheumatoid arthritis: A review of 41 cases. J Bone Joint Surg 61B:155, 1979

Seeger LL, Gold RH, Basset LW, et al: Shoulder impingement syndrome; MR findings in 53 shoulders. AJR 150:343–347, 1988

Stenlund B, Marions O, Engstrom KJ, et al: Correlation of macroscopic osteoarthrotic changes and radiographic findings in the acromioclavicular joint. Acta Radiol 29:571–576, 1988

Tanner MW, Cofield RH: Prosthetic arthroplasty for fractures and fracture-dislocations of the proximal humerus. Clin Orthop 179:116, 1983

Tibone JE, Elrod B, Jobe FW, et al: Surgical treatment of tears of the rotator cuff in athletes. J Bone Joint Surg 68A:887–891, 1986

Tibone JE, Jobe FW, Kerlan RK, et al: Shoulder impingement syndrome in athletes treated by an anterior acromioplasty. Clin Orthop 198:134, 1985

Wainwright D: Glenoidectomy in the treatment of the painful arthritic shoulder. J Bone Joint Surg 58B:377, 1976

Warren RF: Instability of shoulder in throwing sports. In Stauffer ES, ed. American academy of orthopaedic surgeons instructional course lectures, XXXIV, St Louis, CV Mosby, 1985

Watson M: Major ruptures of the rotator cuff: The results of surgical repair in 89 patients. J Bone Joint Surg 67B:618–624, 1985

32
Elbow Problems

ARTHRITIS OF THE ELBOW

I. Biomechanics and Stability of the Elbow Joint

A. Bony elements
  1. Humeroulnar articulation imparts considerable stability but is dependent on ligamentous support to prevent lateral displacement
  2. Humeroradial articulation has intrinsic stability
B. Ligamentous elements
  1. Medial collateral ligament (MCL)
     a. MCL originates slightly posterior and distal to the axis of rotation at the medial condyle, and thus shows increased tension with increased flexion
     b. With valgus stress applied, the MCL provides 55% of elbow stability; with distractive forces it supplies 78%
  2. Lateral collateral ligament (LCL)
     a. LCL originates in the center of the lateral epicondyle and is therefore isometric with respect to elbow position
     b. LCL provides little to the stability of the elbow joint; only 10% with varus stress and 10% with distractive forces
  3. Annular ligament: essential for proximal radioulnar stability
C. Capsule provides significant amount of stability, especially anteriorly
D. Musculotendinous support is provided by the triceps, biceps, brachialis, and flexor and extensor masses; is much less important than the above-stated structures
E. Elbow range of motion is normally 0°–150°; however, functional range of flexion is only 30°–130°

II. Arthrodesis of the Elbow

A. Motion at the elbow is absolutely necessary for proper functioning of the entire upper extremity, and thus arthrodesis is rarely indicated
B. This procedure is rarely indicated and reserved for patients who suffer from painful arthrosis and have high activity demands (ie, heavy laborer)
C. Adequate bony stock is an absolute requirement to successful arthrodesis. As a rule, these are difficult fusions to achieve, requiring bone graft and rigid fixation
D. In general, 90° of flexion is the position of arthrodesis. However, this may be altered to fit patient needs
E. Techniques
  1. Steindler: a posterior tibial cortical graft is keyed into the olecranon through a posterolateral approach
  2. Brittain: utilizes a crossed tibial graft technique in attempts to obtain more rigid fixation

III. Synovectomy

A. Procedure may be used in the rheumatoid patient with elbow pain refractory to conservative medical management. Loss of motion is not an indication for synovectomy. Range of motion is not improved as a general rule
B. Unlike the knee, synovectomy of the elbow can be effective even when there is significant loss of articular cartilage
C. Results show 90% effectiveness in stages I and II rheumatoid patients. This drops to 50% effectiveness in stages III and IV of the disease
D. Other, much less frequent indications include hemophiliacs with recurrent elbow hemorrhage and patients who have developed fungal infections

E. Contraindications include
   1. Patients with ankylosing forms of rheumatoid arthritis
   2. Instability or severe bone loss
F. Most surgeons recommend excision of the radial head if crepitus is present. Replacement of the radial head with a Silastic implant is encouraged by some if lateral instability develops

IV. Resectional Arthroplasty

A. Because of the recent advances in total elbow arthroplasty, soft tissue resectional arthroplasty is rarely performed as a primary procedure
B. However, in young patient with disabling symptoms of pain and loss of motion, resectional arthroplasty should be considered. Long-term results of prosthetic replacement are unknown
C. There are two major problems with resectional arthroplasty
   1. Instability
   2. Resorption of the bony ends, which can lead to secondary development of instability and progressive loss of motion
D. Removal of too little bone can lead to reankylosis
E. Skin, fascia, muscle, and silicone sheets all have been used as interpositional materials
F. Elbow distraction arthroplasty is a relatively new concept with encouraging results. A pin is placed into the distal humerus along its axis of rotation and in the ulna to distract the joint. If the pins are placed properly, motion can be maintained during the 3–6 week distraction period

V. Radial Head Replacement

A. Radial head replacement has been combined with synovectomy in patients with rheumatoid arthritis, as noted earlier. It may also be used in an acute or late setting for fracture of the radial head. Radial head excision alone is the procedure of choice for acute, comminuted, uncomplicated radial head fractures
B. Other indications
   1. An associated dislocation leads to elbow instability
   2. Essex-Lopresti injury
   3. An associated ulnar collateral ligament injury leads to instability after excision of the radial head

VI. Total Elbow Arthroplasty

A. General considerations
   1. Essential arc of motion for activities of daily living is flexion of 30°–130° and 50° of each pronation and supination
   2. Constrained designs offer intrinsic stability compared to semiconstrained or nonconstrained devices but are accompanied by an increased incidence of mechanical loosening
   3. Rebalancing of any soft tissue deficiency is absolutely necessary to maintain stability
   4. Rheumatoid arthritis and post-traumatic arthritis comprise the two largest groups requiring total elbow arthroplasty
   5. Timing is essential in the rheumatoid patient. Lower extremity joint surgery should be completed first to help avoid stress on the elbow implant while crutch walking
   6. The post-traumatic patient is typically younger with single joint involvement. Post-traumatic changes in the anatomy of the region pose great problems and may require custom prostheses. Additionally, high activities predispose this group to earlier prosthetic failure. Interpositional arthroplasty or arthrodesis should be considered
B. Elbow biomechanics
   1. Biomechanical investigations have led to improved designs
   2. Normally, there is some axial rotation

about the humeroulnar articulation. This fact may lead to early failure of constrained devices
3. Flexion and extension of the elbow imparts a cyclic force pattern on the distal humerus. With increased flexion, the direction of force changes direction from anterior to posterior and approaches nearly 3 times body weight. This indicates a need for secure humeral fixation

C. Indications
1. Rheumatoid arthritis and post-traumatic arthritis are most common diagnoses
2. Primary indications include pain, loss of motion, or inability to use the extremity secondary to instability
3. Gross deformity or significant cartilage erosion should be evident prior to contemplating surgery

D. Contraindications
1. Active or subacute infectious process
2. Elbow arthrodesis
3. Ankylosed rheumatoid arthritis as patients have a high percentage of reankylosis
4. Poor bone stock

E. Complications
1. Transient ulnar nerve paresthesias: seen in 10–15% of patients. Many now advocate simultaneous anterior transposition of the nerve
2. Wound hematoma and incisional necrosis: 10%. Important to use a straight incision and keep elbow in <90° to avoid pressure on the incision from the ulna
3. Triceps weakness, 10%
4. Infection, 6%
5. Epicondylar fracture, 10–15%
6. Loosening: 22% of components are found to be loose by radiographic criteria at 3 years in constrained devices
7. Instability/dislocation
8. Failure rate of 27% after 3–9 years (Roper)

SPORTS OR OVERUSE INJURIES TO THE ELBOW

I. Tennis Elbow (Lateral Epicondylitis)
A. Etiology: most feel that this is an overuse syndrome related to episodic or repetitive stress to wrist and digit extensors, especially extensor carpi radialis brevis (ECRB). Others believe that it represents a periostitis secondary to repeated strains
B. Symptoms and findings: pain and tenderness over the lateral epicondyle exacerbated by stress of the extensors
C. Differential diagnosis: radial nerve entrapment, cervical radiculopathy, and compartment syndrome of the anconeus
D. Pathology
1. Nirschl: angiofibroblastic proliferation at the origin of the extensor carpi radialis brevis (ECRB)
2. Others have found tears in the capsule or radial collateral ligament and believe this to be the cause of symptoms
E. Treatment
1. Conservative: rest, avoidance of aggravating activities, followed by strengthening exercises of the involved muscle group is the treatment of choice
2. Surgery: indicated only when conservative measures fail or the patient experiences recurrent disabling episodes of pain. Surgery involves the excision of the angiofibroblastic lesion and repair of the extensor aponeurosis

II. Olecranon Bursitis
A. Acute olecranon bursitis
1. Usually due to mechanical irritation
2. Avoidance of irritating factors, splinting, and use of anti-inflammatory agents will usually suffice in the treatment
3. Occasionally, aspiration followed by injection of a corticosteroid will help
4. Aspiration to rule out the possibility of infection is sometimes indicated
B. Chronic olecranon bursitis: more likely to

necessitate surgical excision because recurrence is frequent

III. Biceps Tendon Rupture

A. Proximal
1. Typically occurs at the proximal portion of the bicipital groove under the anterior acromion
2. Most of these patients have manifestations of an underlying impingement syndrome. A large percentage of these are found to have concurrent rotator cuff tears
3. Treatment
   a. Active patient with biceps rupture and rotator cuff tear should undergo repair of the cuff with biceps tenodesis
   b. Repair of an isolated rupture in an otherwise asymptomatic patient should be treated conservatively unless the patient is young and active. Biceps tenodesis may be performed if cosmesis is of concern

B. Distal
1. Distal rupture of the biceps tendon is relatively rare, but probably necessitates repair as 40% of flexion and supination strength will be lost
2. Radial nerve is at risk during the repair as it passes through the supinator muscle. The two-approach technique of Boyd and Anderson is the safest and thus preferred method
3. Early repair within 7–10 days after injury will provide nearly full recovery of strength and function

IV. Throwing Injuries to the Elbow

A. Classification (Slocum) (Fig 4-3)
1. Medial tension overload
   a. Muscular (flexor-pronator group)
      (1) Strain (minor tears)
      (2) Rupture
      (3) Fascial compartment syndrome
      (4) Medial epicondylitis
      (5) Avulsion of the medial epicondyle
   b. Ligamentous
      (1) Ulnar traction spurs (coronoid process)
      (2) Calcium deposits
      (3) Medial ligamentous laxity
      (4) Loose bodies
2. Lateral compression injuries
   a. Osteochondral fractures of the capitellum
   b. Loose bodies
   c. Post-traumatic arthritis
3. Extension overload
   a. Triceps muscle overload
   b. Avulsion fracture tip of olecranon
   c. Olecranon hypertrophy
   d. Loose bodies in the olecranon fossa
   e. Tears of brachialis and anterior capsule
   f. Fixed flexion contractures

B. Medial epicondylitis (flexor origin syndrome)
1. Etiology: an overuse syndrome of the flexor-pronator group, especially the pronator teres
2. Symptoms and findings: pain and tenderness at the medial epicondyle exacerbated by flexor-pronator stress. Syndrome is commonly confused with peripheral nerve entrapment, particularly the median nerve
3. Differential diagnosis
   a. Median nerve entrapment: patients will complain of night pain and have palpable tenderness over the median nerve. Electromyograms (EMGs) may help but cannot exclude the diagnosis
   b. Chronic flexor compartment syndrome: especially in heavily muscled individuals. These patients present with diffuse compartment tenderness and episodes of swelling and induration
   c. Stress fracture at the epiphysis of the medial condyle in adolescents
4. Treatment: conservative treatment is again the treatment of choice. If unsuccessful or the patient suffers from re-

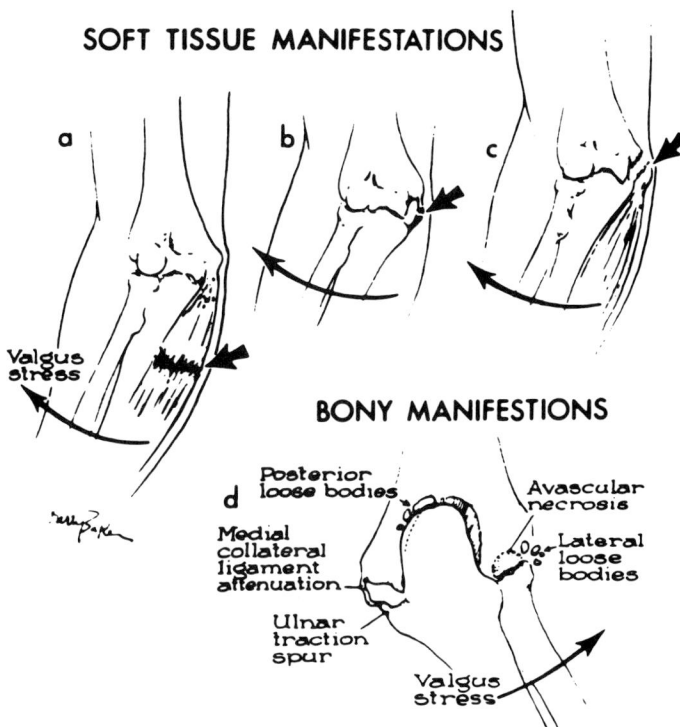

Figure 4-3. Illustration of various injuries in the throwing elbow. **a.** Flexor-pronator muscle strain. **b.** Medial ligament instability. **c.** Avulsion of the medial epicondyle. **d.** Bony manifestations from valgus or extension overload. (From Barnes DA, Tullos HS: An analysis of 100 symptomatic baseball players. Am J Sports Med 6:62–67, 1978. Reprinted with permission.)

peated injury, surgical intervention is indicated. This involves removal of granulation tissue and repair of the pronator teres tendon

C. Ulnar nerve neuritis
1. Repeated mechanical stretching and friction secondary to tensile forces
2. Other causes of ulnar neuritis: direct trauma, recurrent subluxation, osteophytes, progressive cubitus valgus, and developmental anomalies
3. Diagnosis: ulnar nerve sensory/motor dysfunctions and EMG/nerve conduction velocity (NCV)
4. Treatment: conservative initially and surgery if persistent symptoms (submuscular transposition of the nerve)

D. Ulnar collateral ligament sprain
1. Due to valgus stress and medial tension
2. Symptoms: medial elbow pain, particularly during the cocking and acceleration stage of throwing
3. Tenderness along the medial aspect of the joint and increased pain with valgus stress
4. Rupture of the ligament is possible with continued stress
5. Treatment
    a. Conservative program: rest, NSAIDs, strengthening program
    b. Surgery: failure of conservative treatment in a motivated athlete or gross valgus instability
        (1) Primary repair if acute tear
        (2) Reconstruction of anterior oblique band of MCL with palmaris longus tendon graft
        (3) Ulnar nerve transposition

E. Osteochondritis dissecans
1. Osteochondral fracture of the capitellum, loose body formation, and capitellar deformity

2. Treatment
   a. Rest and no throwing activities if fragment is intact
   b. Arthroscopic removal if loose fragment
   c. Drilling and bone grafting may be helpful in select cases

THE PALSIED ELBOW

I. General Considerations
A. Etiology
   1. Inflammatory conditions, such as Guillain-Barré syndrome, poliomyelitis, and brachial plexitis
   2. Brachial plexus trauma
   3. Direct muscle damage
B. Elbow and hand should be reconstructed before shoulder

II. Surgical Procedures to Restore Elbow Flexion
A. Steindler flexorplasty: Steindler first described a procedure to improve elbow flexion with a proximal and medial advancement of the flexor mass on the humerus. This improves flexion of the elbow, but weak, and also fixes the forearm in pronation (not recommended commonly)
B. Pectoralis major and minor transfer: good procedure and strong
   1. Elongation of the tendon with fascia lata graft and insertion to the radial tubercle
   2. Detach the lateral ⅔ of the pectoralis major from sternal and costal attachments and reattach the muscle belly to the biceps region. The tendon is inserted at the radial tubercle. This method provides improved mechanical advantage but does risk damage to the neurovascular pedicle
C. Latissimus dorsi transfer: involves isolation and mobilization of the entire muscle on its neurovascular pedicle to the humerus (especially good if upper brachial palsy is present since latissimus dorsi is innervated by C6, C7, and C8)

III. Surgical Procedures to Restore Elbow Extension
A. Use of posterior third of deltoid transfer to the triceps
B. Postoperative cast in extension of the elbow for 6 weeks and gradual increase of flexion over next 6 weeks

REFERENCES

Andrew JR, St. Pierre RK, Carson WG Jr: Arthroscopy of the elbow. Clin Sports Med 5:653–662, 1986

Andrews JR: Bony injuries about the elbow in the throwing athlete. In Stauffer ES, ed. American academy of orthopaedic surgeons instructional course lectures, XXXIV. St Louis, CV Mosby, 1985, pp 323–331

Arafiles RP: A new technique of fusion of tuberculous arthritis of the elbow. J Bone Joint Surg 63A:1396, 1981

Baker BE, Bierwagen D: Rupture of the distal tendon of the biceps brachii: Operative versus non-operative treatment. J Bone Joint Surg 67A:414–417, 1985

Beckenbaugh RD: Resectional arthroplasty and arthrodesis of the elbow. In Evarts MC, ed. Surgery of the musculoskeletal system. New York, Churchill-Livingstone, 1983

Brooks D, and Sedden HJ: Pectoral transplantation for paralysis of the flexors of the elbow. J Bone Joint Surg 41B:36, 1959

Brumfield RH Jr, Resnick CT: Synovectomy of the elbow in rheumatoid arthritis. J Bone Joint Surg 67A:16–20, 1985

Bunnell S: Restoring flexion to the paralytic elbow. J Bone Joint Surg 33A:556, 1951

Carroll RE, Kleinmann WB: Pectoralis major transplantation to restore elbow flexion to the paralytic limb. Hand Surg 4:501–507, 1979

Davis RF, Weiland AJ, Hungerford DS, et al: Nonconstrained total elbow arthroplasty. Clin Orthop 171:156, 1982

Deland JT, Walker PS, Sledge CB, Farberov A: Treatment of posttraumatic elbows with a new hinge-distractor. Orthopaedics 6:732–737, 1983

Edmonson A, Crenshaw, A: Campbell's operative orthopaedics, ed 7. St Louis, CV Mosby, 1987, pp 1139–1142

Ewald FC, Jacobs MA: Total elbow arthroplasty. Clin Orthop 182:137–142, 1984

Figgie HE III, Inglis AE, Ranawat CS, et al: Results of total elbow arthroplasty as a salvage procedure for failed elbow reconstructive operations. Clin Orthop 219:185–193, 1987

Friedman RJ, Ewald FC: Arthroplasty of the ipsilateral shoulder and elbow in patients who have rheumatoid arthritis. J Bone Joint Surg 69A:661–666, 1987

Goldner JL: Elbow flexion restoration with muscle-tendon transfers. In Evarts CM, ed. Surgery of the musculoskeletal system. New York, Churchill-Livingstone, 1983

Goldner JL: Restoration of partial or complete loss of elbow flexion by muscle and tendon transfers. In AAOS symposium on tendon surgery in the hand. St Louis, CV Mosby, 1976

Jobe FW, Nuber G: Throwing injuries of the elbow. Clin Sports Med 5:621–636, 1986

Jobe FW, Stark H, Lombardon SJ: Reconstruction of the ulnar collateral ligament in athletes. J Bone Joint Surg 68A:1158–1163, 1986

Johnson JR, Getty CJM, Lettin AWF, Glasgow MMS: The Stanmore total elbow replacement for rheumatoid arthritis. J Bone Joint Surg 66B:732–736, 1984

Josefsson P, Gentz C, Johnell O, et al: Surgical versus nonsurgical treatment of ligamentous injuries following dislocation of the elbow. J Bone Joint Surg 69A:605, 1987

Kudo H, Iwano K, Watanabe S: Total replacement of the rheumatoid elbow with a hingeless prosthesis. J Bone Joint Surg 62A:277, 1980

Linclau LA, Winia WPCA, Korst JK: Synovectomy of the elbow in rheumatoid arthritis. Acta Orthop Scand 54:935–937, 1983

Lowe, LW, Miller AJ, Allum RL, Higginson DW: The development of an unconstrained elbow arthroplasty. A clinical review. J Bone Joint Surg 66B:243–247, 1984

McManama GB Jr, Micheli LJ, Berry MV, et al: The surgical treatment of osteochondritis of the capitellum. Am J Sports Med 13:11–21, 1985

Morrey BF: Arthroscopy of the elbow. In Anderson LD, ed. American academy of orthopaedic surgeons instructional course lectures. St Louis, CV Mosby, 1986, pp 102–107

Morrey BF: The elbow and its disorders. Philadelphia, WB Saunders, 1985

Morrey BF, An KN: Articular and ligamentous contributions to the stability of the elbow joint. Am J Sports Med 11:315–319, 1983

Morrey BF, An KN: Functional anatomy of the ligaments of the elbow. Clin Orthop 201:84–90, 1985

Morrey BF, Askew LJ, An KN, et al: Rupture of the distal tendon of the biceps brachii: A biomechanical study. J Bone Joint Surg 67A:418–421, 1985

Morrey BF, Bryan RS: Complications of total elbow arthroplasty. Clin Orthop 170:204, 1982

Morrey BF, Bryan RS: Infection after total elbow arthroplasty. J Bone Joint Surg 65A:330, 1983

Morrey BF, Bryan RS: Prosthetic arthroplasty of the elbow. In Evarts MC, ed. Surgery of the musculoskeletal system. New York, Churchill Livingstone, 1983

Morrey BF, Bryan RS: Revision total elbow arthroplasty. J Bone Joint Surg 69A:523–532, 1987

Nirschl RP: Soft-tissue injuries about the elbow. Clin Sports Med 5:637–652, 1986

Nirschl RP, Pettrone FA: Tennis elbow: The surgical treatment of lateral epicondylitis. J Bone Joint Surg 61A:832–839, 1979

Oyemade GAA: Fascial arthroplasty for elbow ankylosis. Int Surg 68:81–84, 1983

Rosenberg GM, Turner RH: Nonconstrained total elbow arthroplasty. Clin Orthop 187:154–162, 1984

Staples OS: Arthrodesis of the elbow joint. J Bone Joint Surg 34A:207, 1952

Steindler A: Muscle and tendon transplantation at the elbow. In Instructional course lectures on reconstruction surgery, The american academy of orthopaedic surgeons. Ann Arbor, JW Edwards, 1944, pp 276–283

Takami H, Takahashi S, Ando M: Latissimus dorsi transplantation to restore elbow flexion to the paralysed limb. J Hand Surg 9B:61–63, 1984

Trancik T, Wilde AH, Borden LS: Capitellocondylar total elbow arthroplasty: Two to eight year experience. Clin Orthop 223:175–180, 1987

Tsai TM, Kalisman M, Burns J, Kleinert HE: Restoration of elbow flexion by pectoralis major and pectoralis minor transfer. J Hand Surg 8:186–190, 1983

33
Hip Problems

SURGICAL TREATMENT OF ARTHRITIS OF THE HIP

I. Osteotomy
A. Seventy-five percent good results at 1-year, 40–50% good results at 5-year, and 25% good results at 10-year follow-up
B. Goal: reduce joint reaction force by increasing weight-bearing surface and restore joint congruity
C. Indication: young (<50–65 years), 80° flexion arc and 15° adduction and abduction, nonobese patients, and nondeformed femoral head and preserved joint space
D. Varus osteotomy
 1. If excellent coverage with abduction is present
 2. Extension osteotomy may be combined
 3. Greater trochanteric advancement if more than 15°–20° correction
 4. Best for residual subluxation and neck-shaft angle greater than 140°
E. Valgus osteotomy: varus deformed hips with nonspherical femoral head and medial osteoarthritis
F. Extension (bring undiseased anterior part of the femoral head under acetabulum)
G. Pelvic osteotomies if acetabular deficiency center edge (CE) angle of Wiberg is <20° in adults between 20 and 50 years of age: acetabular osteotomy (Ganz), triple osteotomy (Steel)

II. Arthrodesis
A. Indication
 1. Infection (tuberculosis, pyogenic)
 2. Arthritis in young active patients, especially bilateral involvement (arthrodesis on one side and total hip arthroplasty [THA] on the other side)
 3. Freely mobile joints in ipsilateral knee, back, and contralateral hip (contraindicated in stiff and arthritic)
B. Long-term results: 60% with back pain and knee arthritis and 25% with contralateral hip pain 20 years later
C. Operative techniques
 1. Fuse 35°–45° flexion and 0°–5° adduction and 0°–5° external rotation (abduction causes more back and knee problems later)
 2. Cobra head plate: rigid fixation but significant dissection and abductors are compromised
 3. Preserve hip abductors if possible to convert to total hip arthroplasty later if necessary (use Barr bolts)
 4. Postoperative hip spica cast
D. Results
 1. Eighty percent satisfactory after 20 years
 2. Eight percent pseudoarthrosis, mild sexual dysfunction (24% in men and 38% in women)
 3. Back pain and ipsilateral knee laxity are common

III. Resectional Arthroplasty
A. A salvage procedure
B. Bilateral procedure is possible
C. Eighty percent pain relief and results may improve with time
D. Two to 5 cm shortening is expected
E. Useful in cerebral palsy patients to improve sitting

IV. Total Hip Arthroplasty
A. Goal: eliminate pain and restore function
B. Biomechanical goals
 1. Minimize abductor muscle effort during ambulation: lateral transfer of the

greater trochanter theoretically increases the hip abduction moment but trochanteric osteotomy may give nonunion and bursitis problems
2. Decrease joint contact force at the hip: the center of acetabulum is placed medially, inferiorly, and anteriorly (superior and lateral positioning of acetabulum produce higher bone-cement stress)
3. Decrease the bending moment at the prosthetic neck-stem junction
   a. Increase the femoral shaft-neck angle, but this increases the hip joint force
   b. Shorter neck length decreases the bending moment

C. Femoral prosthesis design
   1. Broad medial and lateral surfaces and increased cross-sectional size of the stem is desirable for stress distribution and decreases compressive and tensile stresses of the cement and the stem
   2. Length: increases stress in the stem if too long and increases stress of the cement if too short
   3. Modulus: flexible stem increases stress in the proximal cement but decreases stress in the stem. Stiffer stem transfers load distally and protects proximal cement but may cause stress shielding of the proximal femur
   4. Collar design: increases stress in the calcar region but prevents subsidence: precise fit of the collar over large surface area of the calcar gives best results but difficult to achieve
   5. Head size: larger size gives less stress, more motion and less dislocation but more torque and more wear or friction on polyethylene (smaller head size gives less acetabular loosening rate)

D. Cement fixation techniques of femur
   1. Pulsating lavage
   2. Brushing and cleaning and drying
   3. Pressurization and cement plug about 1–2 cm distally: failure at the bone-cement junction is increased without the plug
   4. Centrifugation or vacuum to reduce air voids and increase strength
   5. Low viscosity cement: increase intrusion but decrease strength
   6. Even cement mantle, 5–10 mm proximal and medial, 2 mm distal; avoiding distal contact of the stem tip with the cortical bone is important
   7. Remove all loose cancellous bone in the femoral canal

E. Cement fixation techniques of the acetabulum
   1. Subchondral bone should be preserved
   2. Complete socket coverage is important to lower loosening rate
   3. Keyholes in the socket are important for additional stability
   4. Remove osteophytes and excess cement to prevent impingement, pain, and dislocation
   5. Metal-backed prosthesis may increase failure rate with cement fixation
   6. Extended wall on the acetabular prosthesis is helpful in reducing dislocations

F. Long-term results of cemented prosthesis
   1. Femoral component: 30–41% radiographic loosening and 3–20% revision rate at 10 years
   2. Acetabular component: 10–29% radiographic loosening and 1.3 to 12% revision rate at 10 years
   3. Results vary, depending on types of prosthesis, techniques, age, and activity of the patient
   4. Overall 90% satisfactory results can be expected in 10-year follow-ups

G. Loosening and prosthetic failure
   1. Young age, heavier weight, male sex, and increased level of activity predispose to loosening
   2. Poor techniques: varus positioning of the stem, poor cement technique, poor

bone stock, small stem with inadequate press fit
3. Bone-cement interface loosening by micromotion that creates fibrous membrane and activates macrophages, prostaglandins (especially PGE_2) and osteolysis occurs that is also known as "cement disease"
   a. Prosthetic subsidence: cement-bone lucent zone >2 mm and cement fractures
   b. Four modes of femoral loosening
      (1) Piston mode with distal migration due to poor cement technique
      (2) Medial midstem pivot mode: rocking in proximal medial and distal lateral direction due to varus position and insufficient medial cement
      (3) Calcar pivot mode with distal loosening due to inadequate distal cement support
      (4) Cantilever fatigue mode with proximal loosening and eventual stem fracture due to poor proximal cement support
4. Acetabular loosening
   a. Incidence of femoral loosening may increase over 10 years, but earlier acetabular loosening is observed in patients <30 years of age
   b. Associated with protrusio acetabuli, inadequate bony coverage, perforation and failed cups, and poor technique and malposition (metal-backed cup decreases peak cement and bone stresses)
5. Polyethylene wear: high molecular compound and metal-backed acetabulum decrease the wear and peak stresses (increased wear if <7 mm thick and 32 mm head)
6. Stem fracture: associated with varus positioning, sharp medial edge, and metallic defect, heavy males, and decreased range of motion (mostly due to proximal loosening and cantilever fatigue mode and fatigue fracture through middle ⅓ stem)
   a. Metallurgic defects: first 3 years
   b. Fixation failure: 4–7 years
   c. Stress fracture: 8 years or longer
   d. Removal is difficult: cortical window or high-speed burr to create an offset hole in the broken stem or use of a large circular trephine saw
H. Noncemented prosthesis
   1. Porous coat of 250–400 μm beads for bone ingrowth in 6 weeks: sintering technique on titanium or cobalt-chromium alloys
   2. Intimate contact or fit and adequate postoperative immobilization are important
   3. Bone ingrowth may be inhibited by radiation and indomethacin and promoted by hydroxyapatite
   4. Stress shielding with cortical osteoporosis may be a long-term problem
   5. Indicated for younger active patients at this time
   6. Retrieval studies show minimal bone ingrowth (10%). Bone ingrowth does not preclude pain
   7. Anterior thigh pain may be a significant clinical problem
   8. Metal toxicity and malignancy are potential problems
   9. Recent trend is to use a hybrid total hip arthroplasty: cemented femoral stem and pressfit acetabulum for patients >65 years of age
I. Implant considerations of noncemented femoral prosthesis
   1. Bone quality is important for long-term fixation
   2. Optimal proximal fit and canal fill is important for stress transfer
   3. Distal porous coating causes proximal stress shielding
   4. Low modulus material reduces stress shielding and distal tip off loading
   5. Thigh pain is common (up to 30%) and

may be related to micromotion of the stem and activity level of the patient
6. Collared device may decrease subsidence and increase load to failure but proximal calcar stress resorption is possible if contact force is not evenly distributed
7. Definite risk of iatrogenic femur fracture (6.7%) due to technical difficulties

J. Implant considerations of noncemented acetabular cup
   1. Hemispherical pressfit cup with biologic ingrowth on the surface is an optimal design
   2. Supplementary fixation with screws may increase the risk of neurovascular damage
   3. Orientation should be 45° abduction, 20°–25° anteversion
   4. Acetabular position: medial contact with quadralateral plate, complete superolateral coverage, rim seating with adequate bone stock anteriorly, superiorly, and posteriorly

K. Infection
   1. Higher in rheumatoid arthritis, steroid-dependent patients, sickle cell anemia patients, revision cases, and cases in which major bone grafting is performed
   2. Prophylactic antibiotics should be given when dental or urologic procedures are performed
   3. Ultraclean air and body exhaust system and ultraviolet light decrease infection rate
   4. Prophylactic antibiotics should be given for every total joint operation: cefazolin or others, such as nafcillin, vancomycin, and cephalosporins (the incidence of infection is <1% with prophylaxis)
   5. Add aminoglycoside and gentamycin-impregnated cement for revision cases
   6. Infection may be superficial vs deep, acute (days) vs chronic (>2 weeks)
   7. Organism may be less virulent, such as gram-positive bacteria, or more virulent, such as methicillin-resistant staphylococci and gram-negative organisms. Mixed infections are difficult to treat
   8. Technetium bone scan: uptake is increased in both mechanical loosening and infection, but gallium or indium-111 uptake are increased in infection
   9. Needle aspiration: most definitive if positive but false-negative rate is high
   10. Treatment
       a. Acute stage: debridement and irrigation if superficial infection or nonvirulent organism, but removal of prosthesis and cement if deep or virulent organism
       b. Chronic stage (>2 weeks)
           (1) Nonvirulent organism: removal of prosthesis and cement and reimplantation at 3 months or one-stage exchange with antibiotic-impregnated cement if the wound is clean after debridement
           (2) Two-staged operations: removal of prostheses and cement and implant gentamycin-impregnated polymethyl-methacrylate (PMMA) beads. Reimplantation at 6–12 months if the wound is clean, erythrocyte sedimentation rate (ESR) is <20 mm/hr, and 1–2 white blood cells per high-power field on frozen section
           (3) Girdlestone procedure for persistently infected wounds with virulent organisms, such as methicillin-resistant staphylococci and gram-negative organisms

L. Thromboembolism
   1. Associated with higher plasma-free fatty acids and fibrinogen to serum antithrombin III ratio
   2. Peak onset of thrombosis is fourth postoperative day
   3. Obesity and long hours of surgery are associated increased risks

4. The incidence of deep vein thrombosis is about 50%, and the incidence of fatal pulmonary embolism is 2.3% in unprotected patients
5. The incidence of symptomatic and asymptomatic deep vein thrombosis is slightly lower (30%) with adjusted dose of warfarin to maintain prothrombin time around 14–16 seconds, and the incidence of silent pulmonary embolism is still 19% with warfarin, but the incidence of fatal pulmonary embolism is significantly decreased with the use of warfarin (0.2%)
6. Dextran plus external pneumatic compression are better than aspirin alone
7. Dihydroergotmine/heparin combination may be effective
8. Antithrombin III and low-dose heparin give only 4.9% incidence of deep vein thrombosis with no bleeding complications
9. Combined B mode/Doppler (duplex) scan is highly sensitive (>90%) for proximal thigh vein clots. Venogram remains the gold standard but difficult to interpret in pelvis
10. Calf vein thrombosis: 50% propagates to thigh, 20% cause asymptomatic or symptomatic pulmonary embolism (whether to treat calf vein thrombosis or not is controversial)
11. Thigh vein thrombosis: 50% cause pulmonary embolism, therefore warfarin therapy is indicated for 3–6 months
12. All at-risk patients should be monitored with noninvasive studies and treated for proximal thigh vein thrombosis if detected
13. If ventilation perfusion (V/Q) scan shows high probability and positive venogram, then start heparin for 5 days and warfarin for 6 months. If low probability V/Q scan and positive venogram, pulmonary angiogram should be done

M. Other complications
1. Nerve injury
   a. Incidence of 0.3–4%: sciatic nerve is most common, followed by femoral and obturator nerves
   b. Leg lengthening over 3 cm is associated with increased risk
   c. Treatment: observation for 8 weeks
2. Vascular injury
   a. Incidence of 0.1–0.2%: profunda femoris artery is most common, followed by iliac arteries
   b. Avoid excessive traction, retractor malposition, and iliac intrapelvic penetration
   c. Avoid acetabular screw fixation in the anterior column
3. Dislocation
   a. Incidence of 0.5–4%
   b. More often after revision surgery, patients with neuromuscular disease, posterior approaches
   c. Malpositioning of components (retroversion and vertical cups) is the principal cause of early dislocation
   d. Late dislocations may be due to capsule/scar laxity and increased range of motion
   e. Treatment: reduction and immobilization to allow pseudocapsule healing, but component repair and/or trochanteric advancement may be necessary
4. Heterotopic ossification
   a. Incidence of 5–61% but 1–5% symptomatic (higher risk in ankylosing spondylitis, Paget's disease, Parkinson's disease, and older patients)
   b. Prevention by minimizing tissue trauma, hemostasis, and prophylaxis in high-risk patients with postoperative radiation therapy about 1000 rads
   c. Indomethacin and diphosphonates are of questionable value
5. Femoral fracture and perforation: intraoperative or postoperative
   a. The incidence is higher with uncemented prosthesis and revision surgery

- b. Revision with a long stem is needed in fractures distal to the tip of the stem (at least 3 cm or one cortical diameter beyond the fracture site), and fractures around the stem may be treated with traction if good alignment but early mobilization is prohibited
- c. Bone graft is often necessary with internal fixation, such as wire, Parham bands, and specially designed plates
6. Bleeding
  - a. Transfusion-related risks: hepatitis and AIDS
  - b. Hypotensive anesthesia, patient donation of blood, and red blood cell recovery system, and stopping NSAIDs help to reduce blood loss
N. Congenital hip dislocations
  1. Technically more demanding and complications higher
  2. Anatomic placement of the acetabulum is desired
  3. Small femoral head is usually required (22 mm)
  4. Superolateral bone grafting is often necessary
  5. Adductor, psoas, and abductor release may be needed
  6. Osteotomy of the proximal femur with segmental bone removal may prevent excess stretch of neurovascular structures
O. Conversion of arthrodesed hip
  1. If disabling back or knee pain
  2. Incidence of dislocation is higher and abductor weakness is common
  3. Good results can be expected if surgery properly performed: failure is more common in surgically arthrodesed hips than spontaneously ankylosed hips
P. Acetabulum protrusio
  1. Anatomic placement of the acetabulum is important
  2. Cement with wire mesh, bone grafting or special rim prosthesis can be used, depending on the defect
  3. Uncemented: rim seat up on periphery of the acetabulum and fill defect with bone
Q. Other diseases
  1. Sickle cell disease: 50% failure rate after 5 years, high perioperative complications, particularly with blood loss
  2. Renal transplantation patients: higher complication rate (both medical and infection)
  3. Rheumatoid arthritis: good indications but higher wound and infection complications
  4. Paget's disease: higher bleeding and heterotopic bone problems
  5. Developmental or acquired deformity: requires corrective osteotomy and cementless implant

IV. Revision Total Hip Replacement

A. General considerations
  1. Pain is usual with loosening but significant radiologic loosening should also alert one to consider revision despite mild symptoms
  2. Results are generally worse than in the primary surgery
  3. Technically more demanding
  4. Bone-cement interface strength is decreased by 70% with first revision and 80% decrease with second revision
  5. Cemented revisions are generally effective in the short term
B. Surgical techniques
  1. Good exposure is mandatory (trochanteric osteotomy may be necessary)
  2. Removal of all cement from the acetabulum is mandatory and avoid iliac vessels when the floor is penetrated
  3. Careful removal of cement from the femoral shaft to prevent penetration
     - a. A cortical window may be necessary
     - b. A new femoral stem should bypass the large hole at least two to three diameters to prevent fractures
  4. Either cemented or uncemented stems can be inserted

5. Uncemented cups and stems must be rigidly stabilized. May require a custom implant for femoral stem
6. Bone grafting is frequently necessary for defects
   a. Morselized bone graft for small defects in the acetabulum
   b. Block allograft with cemented or uncemented socket with major bone loss (must be rigidly stabilized)
   c. Block proximal allograft with uncemented prosthesis with major bone loss in the femur (stable fixation and local autograft is necessary at the allograft-host bone interface)

REFERENCES

Agins HJ, Alcock NW, Bansal M, et al: Metallic wear in failed titanium-alloy total hip replacements: A histological and quantitative analysis. J Bone Joint Surg 70A:347–356, 1988

Ayers DC, Evarts CM, Parkinson JR: The prevention of heterotopic ossification in high risk patients by low-dose radiation therapy after total hip arthroplasty. J Bone Joint Surg 68A:1423–1430, 1986

Beisau NE, Camerota HJ, Groth HE, et al: Dihydroergotamine/heparin in the presentation of deep vein thrombosis after total hip replacement: A controlled, prospective, randomized multicenters trial. J Bone Joint Surg 70A:2–10, 1988

Burke DW, Gates EI, Harris WH: Centrifugation as a method of improving tensile and fatigue properties of acrylic bone cement. J Bone Joint Surg 66A:1265–1273, 1984

Callaghan JJ, Brand RA, Pederson DR: Hip arthrodesis: A long term followup. J Bone Joint Surg 67A:1328–1335, 1985

Callaghan JJ, Dysart SH, Savaory CG: The uncemented porous-coated anatomic total hip prosthesis: Two-year results of a prospective consecutive series. J Bone Joint Surg 70A:337–346, 1988

Canner GC, Steinberg ME, Heppenstall RB, et al: The infected hip after total hip arthroplasty. J Bone Joint Surg 66A:1393–1399, 1984

Collier JP, Mayor MB, Chae JL, et al: Macroscopic and microscopic evidence of prosthetic fixation with porous coated materials. Clin Orthop 235:173–180, 1988

Collis DK: Cemented total hip replacement in patients who are less than fifty years old. J Bone Joint Surg 66A:353–359, 1984

Collis DK: Long-term radiographic follow-up of total hip replacements. Hip 10:1–26, 1982

Cook SD, Thomas KA, Haddod RJ, Jr: Histologic analysis of retrieved human porous-coated total joint components. Clin Orthop 234:90–101, 1988

Detenbeck L, Coventry M, Kelly P: Intertrochanteric osteotomy for degenerative osteoarthritis of the hip. Clin Orthop 86:73, 1972

Engh CA, Bohyn JD, Glassman AH: Porous-coated hip replacement: The factors governing bone ingrowth, stress shielding and clinical results. J Bone Joint Surg 69B:45–55, 1987

Ganz R, Klaus K, Vinh TS, Mast JW: A new periacetabular osteotomy for the treatment of hip dysplasia. Clin Orthop 232:26–36, 1988

Gerber SD, Harris WH: Femoral head autografting to augment acetabular deficiency in patients requiring total hip replacement: A minimum five-year and average seven-year follow-up study. J Bone Joint Surg 68A:1241–1248, 1986

Goldring SR, Schiller AL, Roelke M, et al: The synovial-like membrane at the bone-cement interface in loose total hip replacements and its proposed role in bone lysis. J Bone Joint Surg 65A:575–584, 1983

Harris WH, White RE Jr: Advantages of metal backed acetabular components for a total hip replacement: A clinical assessment with a minimum 5-year follow-up. Hip 11:240–246, 1983

Jofe MH, Gebhardt MC, Tomford WW, et al: Reconstruction for defects of the proximal part of the femur using allograft arthroplasty. J Bone Joint Surg 70A:507–516, 1988

Kavanagh BF, Ilstrup DM, Fitzgerald RH, et al: Revision total hip arthroplasty. J Bone Joint Surg 67A:517–526, 1985

Lidwell OM: Clean air at operation and subsequent sepsis in the joints. Clin Orthop 211:91, 1986

Linder L, Lindberg L, Carlsson A: Aseptic loosening of hip prostheses: A histologic and enzyme histochemical study. Clin Orthop 175:93–104, 1983

Ling RSM: Complications of total hip replacement. Edinburgh, Churchill Livingstone, 1984

Maquet P, Radin EL: Osteotomy as an alternative to total hip replacement in young adults. Clin Orthop 123:138, 1977

Morscher EW: Intertrochanteric osteotomy in osteoarthritis of the hip. In The Hip Society, The hip: Proceedings of the eighth open scientific meeting of the hip society. St Louis, CV Mosby, 1980

Muller MM: Intertrochanteric osteotomies. In Evarts MC, ed. Surgery of the musculoskeletal system. New York, Churchill Livingstone, 1983

Paiement G, Wessnyer G, Waltman AC, et al: Low dose warfarin versus external pneumatic compression for prophylaxis against various thromboembolism following total hip replacement. J Arthroplasty 2:23, 1987

Pellici PM, Wilson PD, Sledge CB, et al: Long-term results of revision total hip replacements: A follow-up report. J Bone Joint Surg 67A:513–516, 1985

Poss R: The role of osteotomy in the treatment of osteoarthritis of the hip. J Bone Joint Surg 66A:144–151, 1984

Poss R, Brick GW, Wright J, et al: The effects of modern cementing techniques in the longevity of total hip arthroplasty. Orthop Clin North Am 19:591, 1988

Poss R, Maloney JP, Ewald FC, et al: Six to 11 year results of total hip arthroplasty in rheumatoid arthritis. Clin Orthop 182:109–116, 1984

Ranawat CS, Atkinson RE, Salvati EA, Wilson PD Jr: Conventional hip arthroplasty for degenerative joint disease in patients between the ages of forty and sixty years. J Bone Joint Surg 66A:745–752, 1984

Roberts JM, Fu FH, McClain EJ, Ferguson AB Jr: A comparison of the posterolateral and anterolateral approaches to total hip arthroplasty. Clin Orthop 187:1205–1210, 1984

Russell TA: Arthrodesis of the lower extremity and the hip. In Crenshaw AH, ed. Campbell's operative orthopaedics, ed 7. St Louis, CV Mosby, 1987

Salter RB, Hansson G, Thompson GH: Innominate osteotomy in the management of residual congenital subluxation of the hip in young adults. Clin Orthop 182:53–68, 1984

Santore RF, Bombelli R: Long term follow-up of the Bombelli experience with osteotomy for osteoarthritis: Results at 11 years with the hip. Proceedings of the eleventh open scientific meeting. St Louis, CV Mosby, 1983

Schatzker J: The intertrochanteric osteotomy. New York, Springer Verlag, 1984

Schutzer SF, Harris WF: Deep wound infection after total hip replacement under contemporary aseptic conditions. J Bone Joint Surg 70A:724–727, 1988

Sponseller PD, McBeath AA, Perpich M: Hip arthrodesis in young patients. J Bone Joint Surg 66A:853–859, 1984

Steel HH: Triple osteotomy of the innominate bone. J Bone Joint Surg 55A:1343–1351, 1973

Stillwell W: Total hip arthroplasty. Orlando, FL, Grune & Stratton, 1987

Stone RG, Werks LE, Hajdu M, et al: Evaluation of sciatic nerve compression during total hip arthroplasty. Clin Orthop 201:26–31, 1985

Thomas BJ, Salvati EA, Small RR: The CAD hip arthroplasty: Five to ten year followup. J Bone Joint Surg 68A:640–646, 1986

Trippel SB: Current concepts review: Antibiotic impregnated cement in total hip arthroplasty. J Bone Joint Surg 68A:1297–1302, 1986

Tullos HS, McCaskill BL, Dickey R, et al: Total hip arthroplasty with a low-modulus porous-coated femoral component. J Bone Joint Surg 66A:888–898, 1984

Urbaniak JR: Microsurgery for major lumbar reconstruction. St Louis, CV Mosby, 1987, pp 178–184

Vicar AJ, Coleman CR: A comparison of the anterolateral, transtrochanteric and posterior surgical approaches in primary total hip arthroplasty. Clin Orthop 188:152–159, 1984

Weisl H: Intertrochanteric osteotomy for osteoarthritis, a long term follow-up. J Bone Joint Surg 62B:37, 1980

Wroblewski BM: 15–21-year results of the Charnley low friction arthroplasty. Clin Orthop 211:30–35, 1986

34
Knee Problems

ARTHRITIS

I. General Considerations
A. The knee is commonly involved in degenerative and inflammatory joint disease
B. Early changes tend to be focal (ie, limited to one compartment)
C. With advanced changes, varus and valgus deformities arise, which secondarily produce soft tissue alterations and instability
D. Rheumatoid patients are an exception because they tend to develop panarticular disease

II. Osteoarthritis of the Patellofemoral Joint
A. Usually is seen in conjunction with tibiofemoral disease, but may be isolated
B. Diagnosis easily made by physical and radiographic examination
C. Treatment: isolated patellofemoral disease is a difficult entity to treat
  1. Nonoperative measures include anti-inflammatory agents, exercise, activity alteration, and bracing
  2. Operative measures include debridement, excisional or replacement arthroplasty, and realignment procedures
  3. Contraindications to operative intervention include:
     a. Extensive disease in other compartments
     b. Restricted motion (<90°)
     c. Unmotivated or debilitated patients
  4. Debridement: may work well in early or localized cases but results are unpredictable
  5. Patellectomy
     a. Continuity of the extensor mechanism must be preserved to prevent extensor lag
     b. Reduced power of knee extension is a common complaint
     c. Ninety percent good to excellent results have been reported when a tube is fashioned from the remainder of the quadriceps mechanism
  6. Realignment procedures
     a. Lateral retinacular release
     b. Transfer of patellar tendon insertion (Roux, Goldthwait)
     c. Tibial tubercle elevation such as Maquet can be done but not without significant morbidity, including wound healing problems, compartment syndrome, tibial fracture, and poor cosmesis
  7. Replacement arthroplasty: available designs include a hemiarthroplasty and total patellofemoral replacement. Results have been inconsistent with a high complication rate

III. Osteoarthritis of the Knee Joint
A. Treatment options in the patient with arthritis of the knee joint include conservative measures, synovectomy, osteotomy, or total joint replacement
  1. Conservative: Anti-inflammatory agents, modified activity, and use of heel wedges may help
  2. Synovectomy
     a. Indications include chronic synovitis for at least 6 months' duration, which does not respond to conservative measures
     b. X-ray should show good preservation of cartilage
     c. Standard total knee approach should be used
     d. Arthroscopic synovectomy is possible
     e. At 2 years, approximately 80% of

patients have relief of pain and swelling
3. High tibial osteotomy
   a. Indications
      (1) Active patient, <65 years old with unicompartment disease
      (2) Stable knee ligaments and no subluxation
      (3) At least 100° of flexion and no flexion deformity greater than 15°
      (4) Ideally less than 10° varus and no rest pain
   b. Contraindications
      (1) Rheumatoid arthritis
      (2) Varus deformity >15°
      (3) Valgus deformity >15°. Here, a distal femoral osteotomy is preferred
   c. Anatomic axis is normally 5°–7° (center of the proximal shaft, center of the knee, center of the ankle)
      (1) Should restore the knee to anatomic 8°–10° of valgus for an initial varus deformity and neutral or 2°–3° valgus for an initial valgus deformity
      (2) Realignment unloads the degenerative compartment and probably decreases the intraosseous vascular pressure in the proximal tibia, thus diminishing pain
   d. Techniques: two most commonly utilized techniques are the Coventry (closing wedge) and Macquet (dome) (Figs 4-4, 4-5)
   e. Complications
      (1) Undercorrection: usually represents inaccurate preoperative measurements. Macquet procedure offers some advantages in that some alteration can be made
      (2) Loss of correction: usually due to poor fixation
      (3) Phlebitis or pulmonary embolism
      (4) Peroneal nerve palsy: most cases occur when percutaneous pins and compression fixation are used. Osteotomy of the fibula, which is necessary with severe deformities, is also associated with a high percentage of palsy
      (5) Infection: generally infrequent. Pin sites have increased risk at 10%
   f. Results
      (1) 80% good to excellent results at 5 years but 40% at 10 years
      (2) Most failures are due to overcorrection and undercorrection

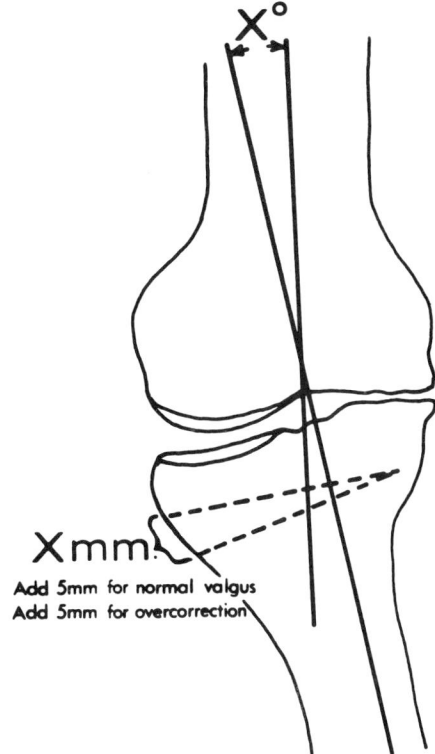

Figure 4-4. Coventry closing tibial wedge osteotomy. The upper cut should parallel the articular surface, and the amount of wedge resection (X mm) should exceed the angle of deformity (X°) so that the final valgus of 9° is attained. (From Turek SL: Orthopaedics, ed. 4. Philadelphia, JB Lippincott, 1984, p 1373. Reprinted with permission.)

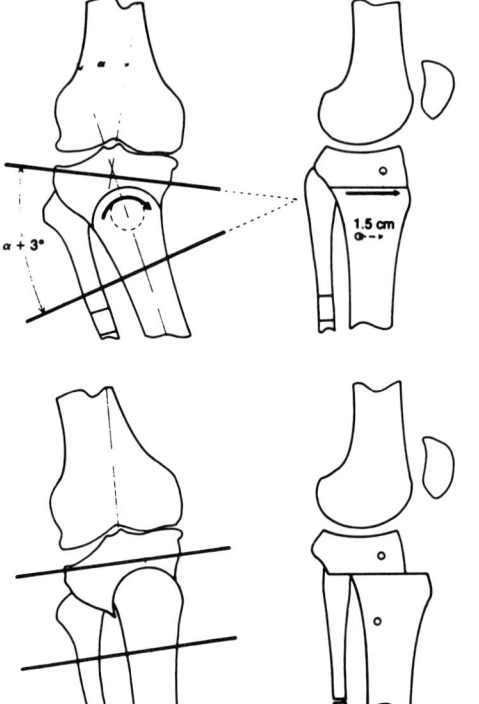

Figure 4-5. Macquet dome osteotomy. The fixation of pins above and below the dome osteotomy site allows correction, and anterior translation of the distal part can be done for patellofemoral arthritis. (Macquet PGJ: Biomechanics of the knee: with application to the pathogenesis and the surgical treatment of osteoarthritis. New York, Springer-Verlag, 1976. Reprinted with permission.)

4. Varus osteotomy of the distal femur
   a. Indications: young, active patient with isolated lateral compartment disease and valgus deformity >10°–15°
   b. High tibial osteotomy with an excessive valgus deformity will result in significant joint obliquity and predispose to medial-lateral subluxation
   c. Medial closing wedge is preferred method
   d. No large series with long-term results has been reported

5. Unicompartmental total knee replacement
   a. Excellent alternative to the high tibial osteotomy for unicompartmental disease, especially in the older patient (>60 years for medial compartment and even younger patient for lateral compartment)
   b. Contraindicated in the rheumatoid or hemophiliac
   c. Procedure has fewer complications associated with it than a tibial osteotomy
   d. Preserves both the anterior and posterior cruciate ligaments
   e. Knees with deformities >10° varus or 15° valgus should not have unicompartmental replacement
   f. Results: 90% good to excellent at 10 years in properly selected patients
   g. Undercorrection of any existing deformity will lead to excessive wear and stress on the prosthetic component
   h. Overcorrection may lead to accelerated degenerative changes in the opposite compartment

6. Tricompartmental total knee replacement
   a. Goal: relieve pain and restore knee function
   b. Contraindications: charcot joint and infection
   c. Biomechanical considerations
      (1) Femur has an anterior articular surface for the patella and medial and lateral condyles, which have a decreasing radius of curvature from anterior to posterior. The lateral condyle is smaller
      (2) Tibia with the menisci provides a partially congruent surface for the rounded femoral condyles. The articular surface of the tibia declines anteriorly to posteriorly approximately 7°. This inclination creates a translational stress

on the tibia when an axial load is applied in the extended position. This stress diminishes as the knee is flexed, however, as the resultant forces at the tibiofemoral contact points become more perpendicular to the tibial articular surface
(3) Patella increases the efficiency of the extensor mechanism by providing a longer moment arm, and secondarily reduces the weight-bearing load of the tibiofemoral joint in the flexed position
(4) Tibiofemoral joint motion is three dimensional, with flexion-extension being the most important. This particular motion is polycentric. A normal gait pattern requires approximately 65° of flexion, 10° of adduction-abduction and 15° of rotation

d. Component design: most bicondylar, minimally constrained knee systems have evolved into a common design, with the following features
  (1) Femoral component shape mimics the normal shape of the distal femur, including a trochlear flange for the patellofemoral joint
  (2) Tibial component is typically one piece or two modular pieces with metal-backed component with a polyethylene insert. This tends to distribute the weight-bearing forces more evenly (central stem with about 70 mm length provides better stability and share about 30% axial loading)
  (3) Most designs allow for retention of the posterior cruciate ligament, which gives increased anterior-posterior stability, aids in femoral rollback, and reduces the tibial interface stress
  (4) Posterior cruciate retaining tibial implants have gently posterior slope of 5°–7° and have flat posterior surfaces that tend to increase polyethylene wear from point contact than more constrained designs
  (5) Metal-backed patellar prosthesis tends to wear polyethylene more because of smaller amount of polyethylene, so use is suspect at this time
  (6) One should place the joint line about the same as that preoperatively to avoid patellofemoral problems
  (7) If significant bone loss is encountered, bone grafting is preferred over methyl methacrylate

e. Component fixation
  (1) Polymethyl methacrylate: present cementing techniques have lowered incidence of aseptic loosening to 3% at 5–10 year follow-up
  (2) Porous coated: short-term results are excellent, but tibial fixation is a problem
  (3) Most recommend cemented components in patients >65 years old, and uncemented for younger patients

f. Operative techniques
  (1) Femoral component
    i. Femoral implant should be made so that it approximates normal anatomy
    ii. Normal valgus angle of the distal femur is 7° (anatomic axis)
    iii. Normal mechanical axis of the knee joint (straight line from the center of the hip to center of the ankle) passes through the center of the knee and center of the ankle) (Fig 4-6)
    iv. Femoral cuts should be 90° with respect to the mechani-

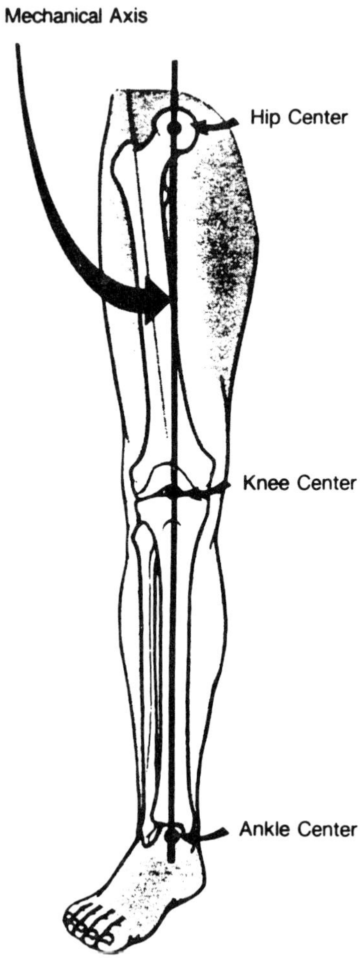

Figure 4-6. Mechanical axis is from the hip center, knee center, and the ankle center. (From Rohr WL Jr: Primary total knee arthroplasty. In Chapman MW, ed. Operative orthopaedics. Philadelphia, JB Lippincott, 1988, p 718. Reprinted with permission.)

       cal axis in the frontal and sagittal planes (Fig 4-7)
- v. Femoral component should be neutral or externally rotated for patellar tracking
- vi. Avoid notching of the anterior femoral cortex to prevent fractures
- vii. Both intramedullary and extramedullary alignment jigs are needed

(2) Tibial component
- i. Is 90° perpendicular to tibial shaft axis with 10° posterior inclination (Fig 4-8A)
- ii. Tibial base plate must cover the entire proximal tibial surface
- iii. Maximum tibial resection should be no more than 8 mm to avoid soft metaphyseal bone and the thickness should equal the thickness of tibial component (Fig 4-8B)
- iv. Soft tissue balance must be physiologic throughout range of motion (soft tissue release should be distal in varus knees and proximal in valgus knees)
- v. Most frequent causes of loosening are component malposition, malalignment, and instability, all of which create exaggerated forces at the interphase

(3) Patellar component
- i. Symmetrical cut in medial or lateral plane is necessary to avoid patellar tilt and subluxation
- ii. Must restore normal sagittal thickness of patella because too thin patella is prone to fracture and too thick patella may produce polyethylene wear and poor range of motion
- iii. Lateral reticular release should be done in patients with abnormal patella tracking and avoid superior lateral genicular artery
- iv. Medial subfascial approach by leaving the vastus medialis oblique insertion intact preserves medial geniculate artery
- v. Patella position should be near anatomic in cephalad-caudad direction

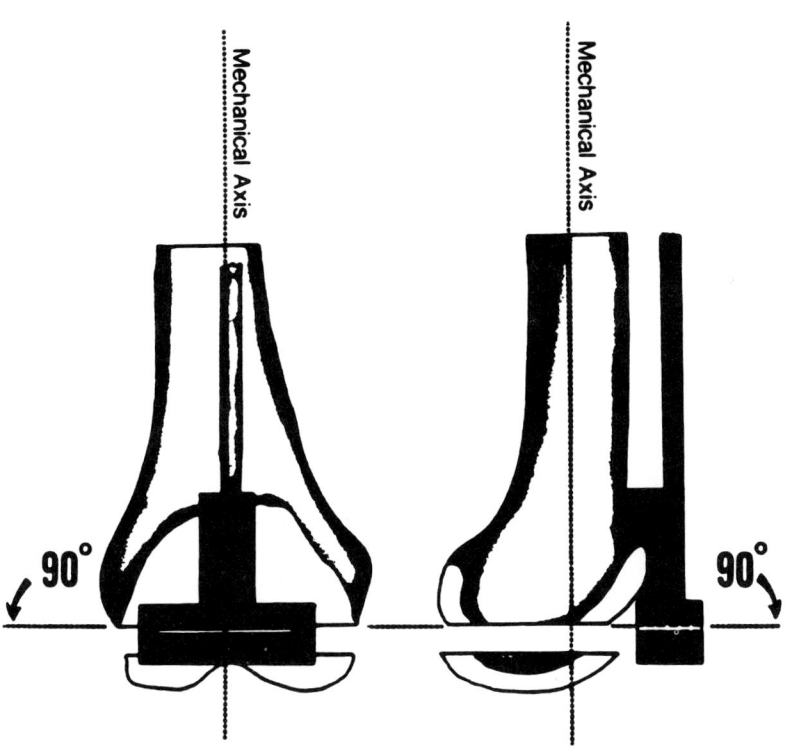

Figure 4-7. The femoral cut should be 90° with respect to the mechanical axis in the frontal and sagittal planes. (From Rohr WL Jr: Primary total knee arthroplasty. In Chapman MW, ed. Operative orthopaedics. Philadelphia, JB Lippincott, 1988, p 723. Reprinted with permission.)

    (a) Malposition of patella is associated with pain
    (b) Normal distance between the inferior pole of the patellar prosthesis and the weight-bearing surface of the tibial component is 10–13 mm
    (c) Patella infera may result if too much femoral resection and large plateau thickness of tibial component as the patellar height decreases (avoid smaller femoral prosthesis and take more bone from tibia if possible and place the patellar component slightly higher)
  g. Complications
    (1) Thrombophlebitis: 40% of patients will have positive postoperative venograms; however, most are asymptomatic. In view of these findings most surgeons use prophylactic anticoagulation therapy
    (2) Infection: approximately 1% of primary condylar knee replacements. *Staphylococcus aureus* is most common. If acute, surgical debridement and antibiotics may suffice. For delayed infection, the components must be removed, with reimplantation at 4–6 weeks if the infecting organism is nonvirulent and controlled. With virulent organisms, one should wait about 1 year after infection is controlled for reimplantation or consider fusion or resectional arthroplasty
    (3) Loosening: femoral component loosening is rarely a problem. With

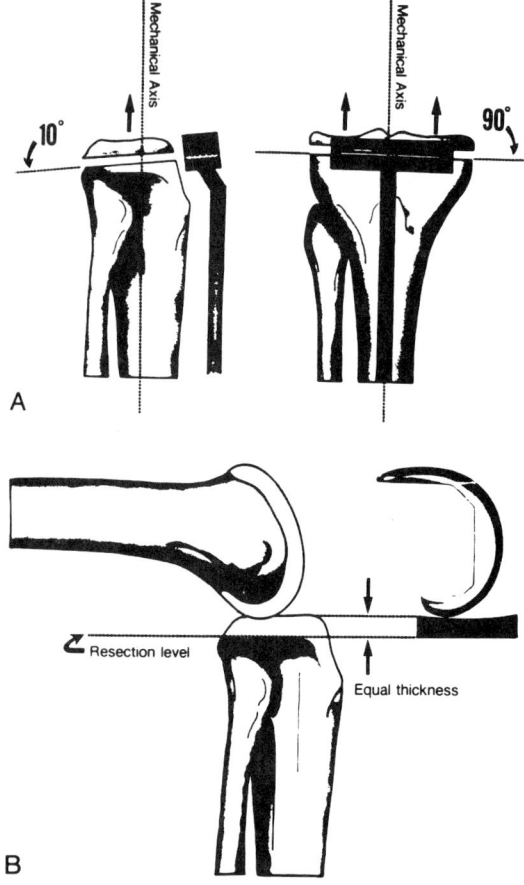

Figure 4-8. **A.** Tibial cut should be perpendicular to tibial shaft axis and 10° posterior inclination. **B.** Resection should equal the thickness of tibial component. (From Rohr WL Jr: Primary total knee arthroplasty. In Chapman MW, ed. Operative orthopaedics. Philadelphia, JB Lippincott, 1988, p 722. Reprinted with permission.)

well-aligned, less constrained designs and better cementing techniques, tibial loosening frequency has diminished to approximately 15% at 2 years and 7% reoperation rate after 5–9 years. No long-term results are yet available on the uncemented knees
(4) Nerve injury: peroneal nerve (keep knee in flexion, and observation)

(5) Femoral fractures: conservative or operative treatment, depending on fracture pattern and patient
(6) Patellar problems
   i. Malalignment: lateral subluxation, patella baha
   ii. Fractures; patellectomy or open reduction and fixation if active extension is absent
   iii. Prepatellectomized patient: posterior stabilized knee prosthesis is recommended
   iv. Skin slough: early soft tissue coverage with gastrocnemius or free tissue transfer is needed

IV. Arthrodesis of the knee
A. Indications
   1. Rarely indicated as a primary procedure
   2. Infected total knee arthroplasty is the most common indication. Others include septic arthritis or neuropathic joint
B. Contraindications
   1. Bilateral knee disease
   2. Ipsilateral hip or ankle disease
C. Operative technique
   1. Best performed using an external fixator to give compression with the knee in 10°–15° flexion and 5°–10° valgus
   2. With an active infection, 2–3 debridements may be necessary prior to bone grafting
   3. In the most severe infections with severe bone loss Papineau grafting is indicated
   4. Fixation device must be kept in as long as possible because the healing process is slow (10–12 weeks)
   5. Alternative method is 75 cm intramedullary rod with supplementary compression plate
D. Results
   1. A 98% success rate in the unoperated, non-neuropathic joint
   2. An 80% success rate in the postarthro-

plasty patient with minimal bone loss, but 56% after hinged type prosthesis failure
E. Complications
1. Pseudoarthrosis: usually painful with ambulation
2. Fibrous ankylosis
3. Shortening: 3–5 cm is expected
4. Malalignment
5. Increased energy expenditure: 20% more

V. Osteonecrosis

A. Osteonecrosis of the femoral condyle
1. Painful knee, particularly at night
2. More common in elderly females
3. Mild effusion, synovitis, and local tenderness. Range of motion is well preserved
4. X-ray findings: negative initially and later sclerosis and collapse
5. Bone scan and MRI: positive early
6. Treatment
   a. Small lesions heal without surgery
   b. Large lesions go on to collapse and require surgery (unicompartmental arthroplasty)
B. Tibial osteonecrosis
1. Painful knee on the medial side
2. More common in elderly women
3. Mild to moderate effusion and tender medial proximal tibia
4. Positive bone scan and MRI
5. Treatment
   a. Conservative treatment for 6–12 months with good success
   b. If collapse of the tibial plateau occurs, arthroplasty is required

REFERENCES

Aaron RK, Scott R: Supracondylar fracture of the femur after total knee arthroplasty. Clin Orthop 219:136–139, 1987

Bae DK, Guhl JF, Keane SP: Unicompartmental knee arthroplasty for single compartment disease: Clinical experience with an average four-year follow-up study. Clin Orthop 176:233–238, 1983

Bartel DL, Bicknell VL, Wright TM: The effect of conformity, thickness, and material on stresses in ultra-high molecular weight, components for total joint replacement. J Bone Joint Surg 68A:1041–1051, 1986

Bayley JC, Scott RD, Ewald FC: Failure of the metal-backed patellar component after total knee replacement. J Bone Joint Surg 70A:668–674, 1988

Bourne RB, Finlay JB: The influence of tibial component intramedullary stems and implant-cortex contact on the strain distribution of the proximal tibia following total knee arthroplasty: An in vitro study. Clin Orthop 208:95–99, 1986

Brick GW, Scott RD: The patellofemoral component of total knee arthroplasty. Clin Orthop 231:163–178, 1988

Coventry MB: Proximal varus osteotomy for osteoarthritis of the lateral compartment of the knee. J Bone Joint Surg 69A:32–38, 1987

Coventry MB: Upper tibial osteotomy. Clin Orthop 182:46–52, 1984

Coventry MB: Upper tibial osteotomy for osteoarthritis. J Bone Joint Surg 67A:1136–1140, 1985

Dorr LD, Boiardo RA: Technical considerations in total knee arthroplasty. Clin Orthop 205:5–11, 1986

Dorr LD, Ranawat CS, Sculco TA, et al: Bone graft for tibial defects in total knee arthroplasty. Clin Orthop 205:153–165, 1986

Falahee MH, Matthews LS, Kaufer H: Resection arthroplasty as a salvage procedure for a knee with infection after a total arthroplasty. J Bone Joint Surg 69A:1013–1021, 1987

Figgie HE, Goldberg VM, Heiple KG, et al: The influence of tibial-patellofemoral location on function of the knee in patients with the posterior stabilized condylar knee prosthesis. J Bone Joint Surg 68A:1035–1040, 1986

Freeman MAR, McCleod HC, Levai JP: Cementless fixation of prosthetic components in arthroplasty of the knee and hip. Clin Orthop 176:88–94, 1983

Goldberg VM, Figgie MP, Figgie HE III, et al: The results of revision of total knee arthroplasty. Clin Orthop 226:86–92, 1988

Goldberg VM, Figgie MP, Figgie HE III, et al: Use of a total condylar knee prosthesis for treatment of osteoarthritis and rheumatoid arthritis: Long term results. J Bone Joint Surg 70A:802–811, 1988

Grace JR, Sim FH: Fracture of the patella after total knee arthroplasty. Clin Orthop 230:168–175, 1988

Grogan TJ, Dorey F, Rollin J, et al: Deep sepsis following total knee arthroplasty: Ten year experience at the UCLA Medical Center. J Bone Joint Surg 68A:226–234, 1986

Haddad RJ, Cooke SD, Thomas KH: Biological fixation of porous-coated implants. J Bone Joint Surg 69A:1459–1466, 1987

Hagemann WF, Woods GW, Tullos, HS: Arthrodesis in failed total knee replacement. J Bone Joint Surg 60-A:790, 1978

Holden DL, James DL, Larson RL, et al: Proximal tibial osteotomy in patients who are fifty years old or less: A long-term follow-up study. J Bone Joint Surg 70A:977–982, 1988

Insall JR: Surgery of the knee. New York, Churchill Livingstone, 1984

Insall JN, Hood RW, Flawn LB, Sullivan DJ: The total

condylar knee prosthesis on gonarthrosis: A five to nine-year follow-up of the first one hundred consecutive replacements. J Bone Joint Surg 65A:619–628, 1983

Insall JN, Joseph DM, Msika C: High tibial osteotomy for varus gonarthrosis: A long term follow-up study. J Bone Joint Surg 66-A:1040–1048, 1984.

Insall JN, Kelly M: The total condylar prosthesis. Clin Orthop 205:43–48, 1986

Ishikawa H, Ohno O, Hirohata K: Long-term results of synovectomy in rheumatoid patients. J Bone Joint Surg 68A:198–205, 1986

Johnson EW Jr, Bodell LS: Corrective supracondylar osteotomy for painful genu valgum. Mayo Clin Proc 56:87–92, 1981

Knutson K, Lindstrand A, Lidgren L: Arthrodesis for failed total knee arthroplasty: A report of 20 cases. J Bone Joint Surg 67-B:47, 1985

Larsson S-E, Larsson S, Lundkvist S: Unicompartmental knee arthroplasty: A prospective consecutive series following for six to 11 years. Clin Orthop 232:174–181, 1988

Lotke PA, Ecker ML, Alavi A, et al: Indications for the treatment of deep venous thrombosis following total knee replacement. J Bone Joint Surg 66A:202–208, 1984

Marmor L: Unicompartmental arthroplasty of the knee with a minimum ten year follow-up period. Clin Orthop 228:171–177, 1988

Mazet R Jr, Urist MR: Arthrodesis of the knee with intramedullary nail fixation. Clin Orthop 18:43, 1960

Merkow RL, Soudry M, Insall JN: Patellar dislocation following total knee replacement. J Bone Joint Surg 67A:1321–1327, 1985

Morrey BF, Adams RA, Ilstrup DM, et al: Complications and motility associated with bilateral or unilateral total knee arthroplasty. J Bone Joint Surg 69A:484–488, 1987

Rand JA, Bryan RS: Results of revision of total knee arthroplasties using condylar prosthesis. J Bone Joint Surg 70A:738–745, 1988

Rand JA, Bryan RS, Chao EY: Failed total knee arthroplasty treated by arthrodesis of the knee using the Ace-Fischer apparatus. J Bone Joint Surg 69A:39–45, 1987

Rorabeck CH, Bourne BB, Nott L: The cemented Kinematic II and the noncemented porous-coated anatomic prosthesis for total knee replacement. J Bone Joint Surg 70A:483–490, 1988

Rydholm U, Elborgh R, Ranstam J, et al: Synovectomy of the knee in juvenile chronic arthritis. A retrospective, consecutive follow-up study. J Bone Joint Surg 68B:223–228, 1986

Schurman DJ, Parker JN, Ornstein D: Total condylar knee replacement: A study of factors influencing range of motion as late as two years after arthroplasty. J Bone Joint Surg 67A:1006–1014, 1985

Scott RD, Joyce MJ, Ewald FC, et al: McKeever metallic hemiarthroplasty of the knee in unicompartmental degenerative arthritis: Long-term clinical follow-up and current indications. J Bone Joint Surg 67A:203–207, 1985

Scott WN, Rubinstein M, Scuderi G: Results after knee replacement with a posterior cruciate substituting prosthesis. J Bone Joint Surg 70A:1163–1173, 1988

Sledge CB, Walker PS: Total knee arthroplasty in rheumatoid arthritis. Clin Orthop 182:127–136, 1984

Staeheli JW, Cass JR, Morrey BF: Condylar total knee arthroplasty after failed proximal tibial osteotomy. J Bone Joint Surg 69A:28–31, 1987

Stuart MJ, Rand JA: Total knee arthroplasty in young adults who have rheumatoid arthritis. J Bone Joint Surg 70A:84–87, 1988

Stulberg SD: Arthrodesis in failed total knee replacements. Orthop Clin North Am 13:213, 1982

Swanson AB, Swanson GdeG, Powers T, et al: Unicompartmental and bicompartmental arthroplasty of the knee with a finned metal tibial-plateau implant. J Bone Joint Surg 67A:1175–1182, 1985

Tooms RE: Arthroplasty of ankle and knee. In Crenshaw AH, ed. Campbell's operative orthopaedics. St Louis, CV Mosby, 1987

Vander Griend R: Arthrodesis of the knee with intramedullary fixation. Clin Orthop 181:146, 1983

35
Sports Injuries of the Lower Extremities

I. General Considerations
A. Running injuries are common due to overuse phenomenon
B. Tremendous advances have been made in the past decade in the diagnosis and treatment of knee injuries
C. Injuries of foot/ankle will be discussed under foot section

II. Running Injuries
A. Classification of runners
  1. Jogger: 3–20 miles/week
  2. Sports runner: 20–40 miles/week
  3. Long distance runner: 40–70 miles/week
  4. Elite marathoner: 70–200 miles/week
B. Estimated 20 million runners in North America
C. Factors to consider in evaluation of training
  1. Mileage (rate of increase)
  2. Surface (asphalt preferred over hard cement)
  3. Banked surface or hills give more problems
  4. Flexibility exercises are important
  5. Shoe wear
     a. Provides varying degrees of shock absorption, support, and flexibility, depending on the type of shoe
     b. Shoe terminology
        (1) Leather or nylon **upper** is built on a wooden or plastic **last**
        (2) "Slip lasted": if upper is sewn to itself on last
        (3) "Board lasted": if the upper is sutured to a cardboard on the undersurface
        (4) Last can be straight, curved (7°) or intermediate
        (5) Board and straight-lasted shoes are more stable; curved and slip-lasted shoes provide more flexibility
     c. Excessive pronation: use more stable shoe
     d. Cavus foot: use more flexible shoe
     e. Inserts
        (1) Flexible, semirigid, or rigid
        (2) Rigid inserts are rarely indicated for a runner
        (3) Soft inserts provide maximal cushioning but wear out easily
        (4) Semirigid are most frequently used
D. Mechanism of injury
  1. Training error: 60%
  2. Biomechanical factors: 40%
     a. Normal walking has stance (60%) and swing (40%) phases: as speed of walking increases and progresses to jogging and running, stance phase decreases, swing phase increases, and float phase occurs in which both feet are off the ground
     b. During walking, there is about 115–120% body weight of force, and 275% of body weight during running at heel strike
     c. Running involves complex motion of upper extremities, spine, pelvis, femur, knee, leg, ankle, and foot
     d. From heel strike to midstance, the lower extremity rotates internally as subtalar eversion, "unlocking" of the transverse tarsal joint, and arch collapse occur simultaneously
     e. From midstance to toe off, lower extremity externally rotates, as subtalar inversion, "locking" of trans-

verse tarsal joint, and reconstitution occur
  f. Cyclic arch collapse (pronation) is important in dissipating energy
  g. Hyperpronation may cause persistent internal tibial torsion, genu valgus, and medial knee pain
  h. Hyperpronation may be a compensatory mechanism for tibia vara, tight Achilles tendon, and hindfoot and forefoot varus
E. Evaluation
  1. History: training methods, mechanism of injury
  2. Examination
    a. Spine, pelvis and lower extremities and neurovascular status
    b. Structural abnormalities: wide pelvis, genu valgus or varus, tibia vara, internal or external tibial torsion, ankle varus or valgus, pronated or cavus foot
    c. Malalignment syndrome: broad pelvis, femoral anteversion, genu valgus, excess Q angle, external tibial torsion, and pronated feet
F. Treatment
  1. Prevention: appropriate shoe wear, maintenance stretching and strengthening program, and avoidance of sudden changes in training
  2. Three principles of treatment
    a. Acute symptom management: ice, activity modification, NSAIDs
    b. Bimechanical alteration: shoewear, inserts, etc.
    c. Training pattern: distance, surface, terrain, etc.

III. Patellofemoral Pain

A. Diffuse, aching anterior knee pain, which is made worse by running, stairs, kneeling, squatting, or other "flexed-knee types of activities." Not arthritis
B. Patellofemoral disease
  1. Stage I: swelling and softening of cartilage
  2. Stage II: fissuring
  3. Stage III: fasciculation ("crab meat")
  4. Stage IV: erosion and exposure of subchondral bone
C. Etiology: trauma (fracture or dislocation), malalignment syndrome, patella alta, weak vastus medialis, tight vastus lateralis, or retinaculum
D. Clinical findings
  1. Retropatellar pain, retropatellar crepitus, subpatellar tenderness pseudolocking and giving way, and positive patellar inhibition test for chondromalacia
  2. Tight lateral retinaculum: patellar tilt is zero or negative (normal is about 15°)
  3. Loose medial retinaculum: patellar translation is >50% (passive patellar glide test)
  4. Malalignment or abnormal tracking of patella: active quadriceps contraction with the knee flexed at 20° reveals greater lateral excursion than superior excursion of the patella
  5. Patellar subluxation: positive apprehension test
E. X-ray findings
  1. Tangential view at 20° flexion to look for patellar tilt (Fig 4-9)
  2. Bone scan or CT scan may be helpful in special circumstances
F. Treatment
  1. Conservative: rest, NSAIDs, and isometric or short arc quadriceps strengthening exercise
  2. Arthroscopic shaving: short-term benefit
  3. Lateral retinacular release (open or arthroscopic) if lateral tilt
  4. Proximal medial reefing: if passive patellar glide is greater than 75%
  5. Distal tibial tubercle realignment: if high Q angle and excess lateral excursion
  6. Tibial elevation: patellofemoral arthritis

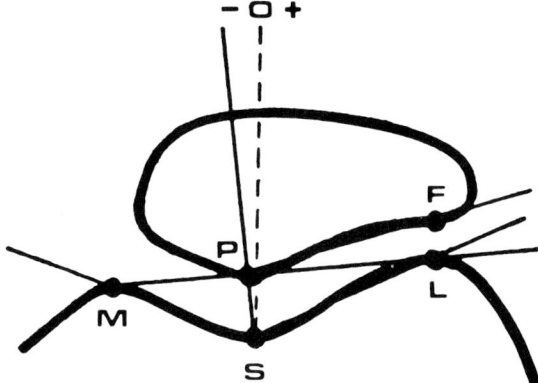

Figure 4-9. Measurements of patellofemoral congruence. SO is the zero reference line that bisects the sulcus angle formed by medial condyle, lateral condyle, and the sulcus. Line PF (patellar ridge to lateral facet) and line ML should diverge laterally (lateral patellofemoral angle). Angle PSO is the congruence angle (average is $-8°$ with standard deviation of $6°$). (From Merchant AC: Patellofemoral disorders. In Chapman MW, ed. Operative orthopaedics. Philadelphia, JB Lippincott, 1988, p 1703. Reprinted with permission.)

IV. Iliotibial Band Friction Syndrome

A. Friction between lateral femoral condyle and iliotibial band
B. Pain in the region of the lateral epicondyle of the femur
C. Excess hill running, especially downhill
D. Associated with tibia vara, cavus, or hyperpronated foot
E. Treatment: rest, NSAIDs, orthotics (if hyperpronated foot)

V. Leg Pain in Runners

A. Stress fracture
  1. Well-localized pain present that usually develops after sudden increase in training intensity
  2. Physical examination: tenderness of well-localized area of bone affected
  3. X-ray findings: cortical thickening, fracture line, or callus formation may be seen on plain X-rays. If diagnosis is made early, plain X-rays may be normal but bone scan will demonstrate localized area of increased uptake
  4. Treatment: rest, immobilization, low impact exercise for conditioning
B. Chronic, exertional compartment syndrome
  1. Reported in both upper and lower extremities, but much more common in leg
  2. Four compartments — anterior, lateral, superficial posterior, deep posterior
  3. Pathophysiology: exercise results in increased pressure within enclosed fascial compartment. Increased tissue pressure results in corresponding elevation in venous pressure and decreased local blood flow. Symptoms develop secondary to muscle ischemia (pain) and nerve ischemia (numbness, paresthesias). Neurologic symptoms distally correspond to compartment(s) affected and neural structures contained within
  4. Physical examination: negative or tenderness of involved compartment
  5. Diagnosis: document pressure increase using slit catheter
    a. Resting pressure
      (1) Normal: 0–15 mmHg
      (2) Exertional compartment syndrome: 0–15 mmHg or greater
    b. Exercise pressure
      (1) Normal: 30–40 mmHg
      (2) Exertional compartment syndrome: ≥40 mmHg
    c. Return to resting pressure
      (1) Normal: 3–4 minutes
      (2) Exertional compartment syndrome: ≥15 minutes
  6. Treatment: rest usually does not result in improvement of symptoms after return to athletics. Surgical treatment preferred and should result in release of all compartments with elevated pressures
C. "Shin splints" (tibial periostitis)
  1. Pain in distal third of tibia posteromedially
  2. Examination: tenderness of postero-

medial tibial cortex along diffuse area in distal third
3. Pain and tenderness are not as localized as in stress fracture
4. X-ray findings are negative. Bone scan may demonstrate linear streaking
5. Treatment: nonsurgical. Rarely is surgery necessary. Involves fasciotomy and periosteal cauterization

VI. Miscellaneous Leg Conditions

A. Tear of medial head of gastrocnemius. Common in individuals 30–50 years old playing racquet sports. Treatment is rest, heel lift, stretching, and strengthening
B. Pes bursitis: medial knee pain and tenderness below joint line. Treatment is nonsurgical, occasionally steroid injection
C. Patellar and quadriceps tendon problems
   1. Point tenderness of well-localized area of quadriceps or patellar tendon attachment to patella. Also known as patellar tendinitis or jumper's knee. Treatment is nonsurgical, rarely is surgical debridement necessary
   2. Sindig-Larsen-Johansson syndrome: avulsion fractures at inferior pole of patella

VII. Meniscus and Osteochondral Knee Injuries

A. Meniscus
   1. Fibrocartilaginous structure with collagen fibers oriented in circumferential manner
   2. Function: Load bearing, stress distribution, nutrition, and lubrication of articular cartilage. Medial meniscus contributes to stability in anterior cruciate ligament (ACL) deficient knee
B. Localized pain present. Mechanical symptoms such as "catching," locking, may be present to variable degree. Physical examination: Joint line tenderness and pain with circumduction maneuvers
C. Types of tears
   1. Stable (5 mm) vs unstable (10 mm): tears that are 5–10 mm in length must be judged individually
   2. Vertical vs horizontal, radial vs longitudinal
   3. Vascular (peripheral 10–33%) vs avascular zones
   4. Buckle handle tears, peripheral tears, flap tears, extensive tears, etc. (Fig 4-10)
D. Treatment: Preserve as much meniscus as possible while removing unrepairable portions of meniscus that are contributing to clinical symptoms. Peripheral rim of meniscus resists hoop stresses generated during weight bearing, should be preserved if at all possible
   1. Partial meniscectomy of tears in avascular zone
   2. Repair of tears in vascular zone
      a. Excellent results reported using open and arthroscopic techniques
      b. ACL laxity that is not addressed at time of surgery jeopardizes results (retear rate at 5 years increases from 4–5% to almost 40%)
   3. Repair of tears in avascular zone
      a. Fibrin clot used to stimulate healing response
      b. Early results inferior to repair of peripheral tears
   4. Meniscal transplantation or regeneration: experimental techniques under investigation in animal model
E. Osteochondritis dissecans
   1. Etiology unknown. Ischemia of subchondral bone vs trauma. Note also that accessory ossification centers are a normal finding in the skeletally immature. Seventy to 80% involve medial femoral condyle
   2. Aching pain. Mechanical symptoms may develop as lesion becomes displaced
   3. Most commonly found in the lateral aspect of the medial femoral condyle near the posterior cruciate attachment

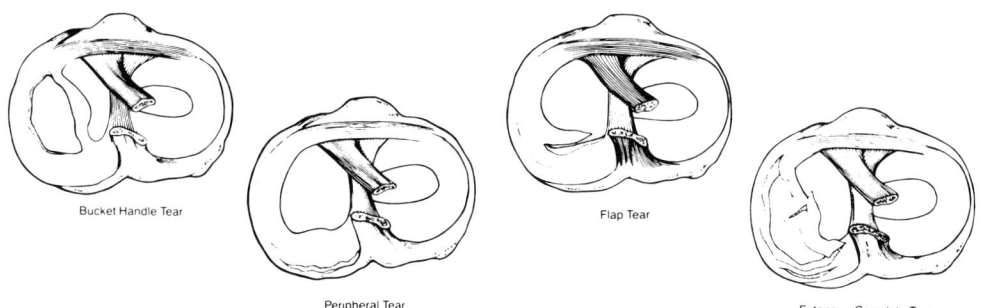

Figure 4-10. Typical meniscal tears. (From Bucholz RW: Orthopaedic trauma. In Bucholz RW, Lippert FG, Wenger DR, Ezaki M, eds. Orthopaedic decision making. Philadelphia, BC Decker and St Louis, CV Mosby, 1984, p 52. Reprinted with permission.)

4. Treatment
   a. Skeletally immature: symptomatic treatment or immobilization. If radiographs do not demonstrate healing and symptoms persist after 3–4 months, surgery may be considered
   b. Skeletally mature: more aggressive treatment indicated. Treatment depends on status of lesion
      (1) Intact: drilling from inside-out or outside-in
      (2) Partly to completely detached fragment: same principle of treatment of fracture nonunion apply
         i. Assure blood supply to fracture site
         ii. Reduce fragments
         iii. Securely fix fragments
      (3) Bone graft may be required to fill defect prior to replacement of fragment

VIII. Knee Ligament Injuries
A. Anatomy of ACL
   1. Is 4 × 1 cm, intra-articular, extrasynovial
   2. Composed of collagen fibrils, which then form fibers that run parallel to long axis of ligament
      a. Collagen fibers then merge to form subfascicular unit, which is surrounded by loose connective tissue called endotenon
      b. Large amount of endotenon in humans makes ligament appear to consist of several bundles
      c. Subfasciculi combine to form collagen fasciculus, which is then surrounded by epitenon. Paratenon surrounds and blends with entire ligament. Synovium covers ligament making it extrasynovial
   3. Attachment of cruciate ligament to bone is mediated by a transitional zone of fibrocartilage and mineralized cartilage, resulting in gradual increase in stiffness, which helps to prevent stress concentration at attachment site
   4. Vascular supply
      a. Predominant source is middle geniculate artery, which pierces the posterior capsule after leaving the popliteal artery
      b. Significant blood supply from fat pad via inferior medial and lateral geniculate arteries
      c. Osseous attachments contribute little to vascularity
   5. Neural innervation
      a. Pain fibers in intrafascicular spaces
      b. Three types of mechanoreceptors
   6. Fiber orientation and insertion site anatomy

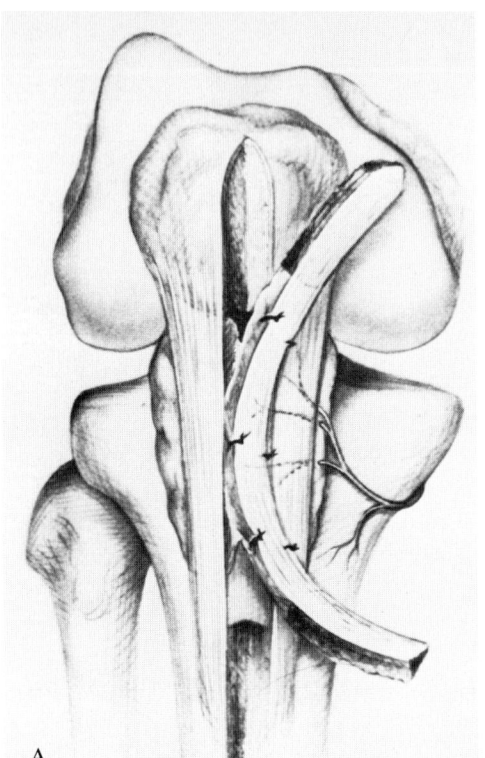
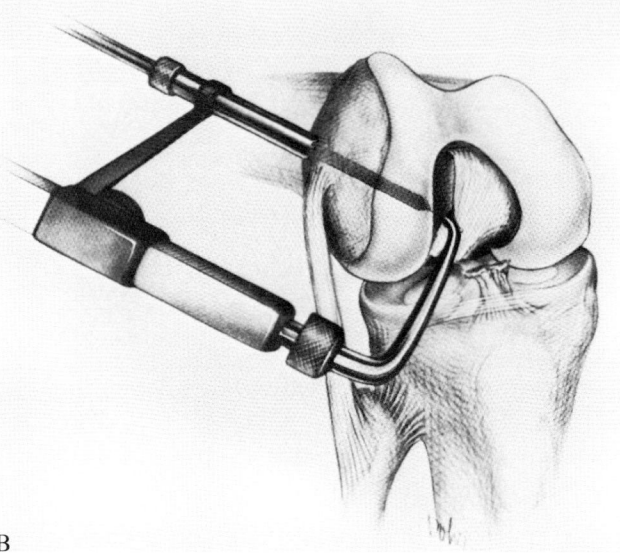
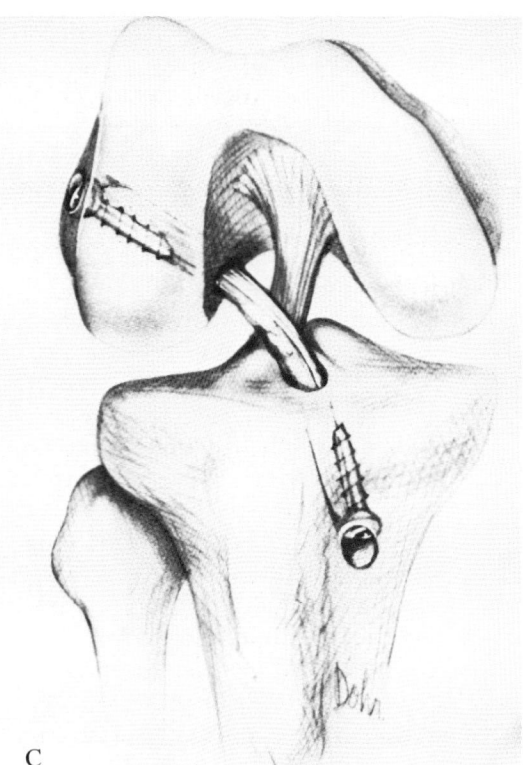

Figure 4-11. Intra-articular reconstruction of the anterior cruciate ligament, using the patellar tendon. **A.** Midthird patellar tendon is harvested. **B.** A drill guide is used to make a tunnel at the anatomic site. **C.** Isometric positioning and secure fixation of bone plugs are done. (From Feagin JA, Lambert KL, Cunningham RR: Repair and reconstruction of the anterior cruciate ligament. In Chapman MW, ed. Operative orthopaedics. Philadelphia, JB Lippincott, 1988, pp 1644–1646. Reprinted with permission.)

a. Anteromedial, posterolateral, and, in some cases, intermediate bands present
b. Functional bands varying fiber tension with range of motion. Anteromedial band is tight in flexion and posterolateral band is tight in extension
c. Attachment in longitudinal axis of femur; tibial attachment (broad) is longitudinal in AP axis. This results in "twist" of ACL fibers as knee moves from flexion to extension. Fibers also externally rotate 90° in coronal plane as they approach tibial surface

B. Associated structural anatomy
 1. Medial
    a. Anterior third: anterior capsule, lateral retinaculum
    b. Middle third: superficial collateral ligament, deep collateral ligament
    c. Posterior third: posterior capsule, posterior oblique ligament, oblique popliteal ligament (semimembranosus) and medial head of gastrocnemius
 2. Lateral
    a. Anterior third: anterior capsule, lateral retinaculum
    b. Middle third: iliotibial band, deep capsule
    c. Posterior third: fibular collateral ligament arcuate ligament, popliteal aponeurosis dynamic (popliteus, biceps, lateral head of gastrocnemius)

C. Biomechanics
 1. Primary restraint to anterior tibial translation
 2. Secondary restraint to internal (major) and external (minor) rotation, and varus or valgus stress (minor)
 3. Hamstrings complement ACL, whereas quadriceps increase anterior tibial translation
 4. Loading
    a. Fast: injury in midsubstance (80%)
    b. Slow: avulsion (at mineralized fibrocartilage zone), off femur (18%), off tibia (2%), especially in immature, old, or immobilized patients
 5. Failure of ACL
    a. 400 pounds of force
    b. Continuous serial pattern (30% elongation before failure) — incomplete tears may occur 10–20%
    c. Thicker fibers are stronger, longer fibers are less stiff, oblique oriented fibers, as opposed to parallel fibers, are less stiff but weaker
    d. ACL insufficiency displaces the instant center of motion and causes more friction: normal rolling or gliding mechanism is disrupted

D. Mechanism of injury
 1. Football and skiing injuries are common
 2. Mechanism
    a. Valgus or external rotation (60%): often associated with MCL injury
    b. Hyperextension/internal rotation: posterolateral bundle torn first and isolated ACL may occur
    c. Severe internal rotation
 3. Sudden deceleration and change of direction are important history

E. Classification of knee instabilities
 1. Straight instabilities
    a. Medial: medial structures and posterior cruciate ligament (PCL) rupture and usually ACL torn
    b. Lateral: lateral structures and PCL ruptures and usually ACL torn
    c. Anterior: ACL rupture with medial and lateral capsular tear
    d. Posterior: PCL and arcuate complex tear
 2. Rotatory instabilities
    a. Anteromedial: ACL and medial structures affected (positive anterior drawer test with the foot externally rotated)
    b. Anterolateral: ACL and lateral structures affected (pivot shift tests)
    c. Posterolateral: arcuate complex with or without PCL rupture (positive

external rotation recurvatum and reverse pivot shift tests and posterior drawer in 30° flexion is positive if arcuate complex tear and is also positive in 90° flexion if PCL is torn. Posterior drawer with the knee externally rotated is also positive)
 3. Combined injuries and global instability
F. Evaluation of knee ligament injuries
 1. History
    a. Direct blow vs rotational
    b. Snap, pop
    c. "Shifting" sensation
    d. Swelling
    e. Previous injury
 2. Physical examination
    a. May be difficult in acutely injured knee but gentle examination puts patient at ease and facilitates evaluation
    b. Specific tests for instability
       (1) ACL
           i. Lachman's test: 20° flexion, posterior to anterior force applied to tibia
           ii. Anterior drawer: 70°–90° flexion, posterior to anterior force applied to tibia
           iii. Pivot shift
       (2) PCL
           i. Posterior drawer: 70°–90° flexion, anterior to posterior force applied to tibia
           ii. Posterior sag: hip and knee flexed 90°
       (3) Posterolateral rotatory instability
           i. External rotation, recurvatum
           ii. "Reverse pivot"
           iii. Tibial external rotation
       (4) MCL
           i. Valgus stress at 30° flexion (cruciates relaxed and full extension cruciates taught)
           ii. Laxity in full extension suggests intra-articular injury in addition to MCL
       (5) LCL
           i. Varus stress at 30° flexion and full extension
           ii. Laxity in full extension suggests intra-articular injury
 3. Radiographs
    a. Usually negative
    b. Lateral capsular sign or "Segund's nubbin," which represents bony avulsion from proximal tibia by anterolateral capsule, is indicative of ACL injury
    c. Intercondylar eminence fracture more often seen in skeletally immature
    d. MRI should not be routinely utilized to evaluate ligament injury
 4. Description of ligament injury
    a. Laxity has been described as increased motion relative to normal side: 1+ equals 1–5 mm of increased motion compared to uninjured side; 2+ equals 6–10 mm, 3+ equals 11–15 mm, 4+ equals 16–20 mm
    b. Traditionally, terms such as anterolateral rotatory instability, anteromedial instability, etc., have been used
    c. Effort is currently underway to develop a more accurate and descriptive way of describing abnormal knee motion associated with ligament injury
G. Treatment of torn ACL
 1. General agreement that a history from a reliable patient should reveal the following
    a. Closed growth plates
    b. Significant instability
    c. Vigorous participation in high-risk sports that require jumping or hard cutting maneuvers
 2. Each case must be considered individually
 3. Unwillingness or inability on patient's part to participate in rehabilitation program argues against stabilization

4. Nonoperative treatment
   a. Allow swelling to decrease, regain range of motion
   b. Vigorous quadriceps and hamstring rehabilitation program
   c. Use of functional knee brace for athletes
   d. Activity modification
   e. In general, less active patients without significant instability are good candidates for nonoperative treatment
   f. No harm in nonsurgical approach as long as repeated injury does not occur
   g. Repeated episodes of giving way result in articular surface and meniscal injury and subsequently degenerative changes
5. Operative treatment
   a. Goal is to restore normal motion and stability to knee with minimal morbidity
   b. Surgical options
      (1) Repair torn ACL: unreliable due to poor quality tissue and fixation
      (2) Reconstruct ACL is more reliable
   c. Extra-articular reconstructive procedures
      (1) Variety of techniques available, but does not restore normal stability to knee and reconstruction tends to stretch with time
      (2) The role of extra-articular procedures in ACL reconstruction surgery is currently believed to be extremely limited
   d. Intra-articular reconstructive procedures
      (1) Intra-articular tissue
         i. Autogenous tissue: Most frequently used tissues are central third patellar tendon, hamstrings (semitendinosis, gracilis) and iliotibial (IT) band. Center third patellar tendon (13–14 mm diameter) has about 170% of the strength of normal ACL. Due to concerns about extensor mechanism pathology after using patellar tendon, some surgeons prefer to use other sources of tissues (hamstrings, IT band), which although weaker can be folded back on itself to increase strength
         ii. Allograft: patellar tendon most frequently used. Deep freezing or freeze drying required for graft processing, but additional processing such as gamma irradiation is necessary for graft sterilization. Allografts seem to undergo a remodeling process similar to autograft with progressive revascularization, cellular repopulation, and eventual collagen fiber reorganization. Early clinical results are promising but concern remains about immunologic response to tissue and risk of transmittable disease
         iii. Synthetic: may be used as an ACL substitute (Gore-Tex) on load-sharing device to protect ACL graft in early postoperative period (ligament augmentation device [LAD]). Gore-Tex has had promising early results but results have deteriorated with time (complications: infection, aseptic synovitis, laxity). LAD may improve stability when used in an over-the-top reconstruction
      (2) Graft fixation: "Weak link" in femur-graft-tibia preparation immediately postoperatively is at fixation site. Therefore more secure fixation allows more aggressive rehabilitation postoperatively. Most secure fixation involves

bone plug fixation in tunnel using interference fit screw. Less rigid fixation techniques are tying sutures in bone plug over a button or under a "post" (cancellous screws). If a bone plug is not attached to graft, fixation can be achieved with a screw and spiked plate combination. Use of a staple for soft tissue fixation results in tissue necrosis and poor fixation
- (3) Graft placement
    - i. ACL is not isometric. Different areas have varying tension throughout range of motion. Theoretically, a line of fibers exists in ACL which is isometric. Femoral and tibial attachment sites of this theoretical band should be intra-articular attachment sites of ACL substitute, which does not have the same collagen fiber orientation as ACL and needs to be as isometric as possible
    - ii. Different tensiometers currently available to evaluate length changes between femoral and tibial sites prior to drilling and graft placement
    - iii. Since tibial attachment site of ACL is farther from joint axis of rotation than femoral site, it has less effect on length changes between attachment sites during range of motion than femoral hole. If distance between attachment sites increases during knee flexion (as happens in over-the-top reconstruction), graft is too posterior (when viewing from anterior with knee flexed 90°). Moving the femoral site anteriorly decreases the distance between attachment sites during flexions
- (4) Role of notchplasty: Amount of notchplasty required is uncertain. If graft positioned at anteromedial zone of ACL origin, impingement of graft on roof of intercondylar notch will occur if notchplasty not performed. An adequate notchplasty allows full extension without graft impingement
- (5) Postoperative rehabilitation: Many different protocols exist but a general trend exists toward early motion to minimize morbidity, which develops secondary to immobilization and atrophy

H. PCL injuries
1. Anterolateral and posteromedial bands: anterolateral band is tight in flexion, and posteromedial band is tight in extension
2. Femoral attachment in longitudinal axis of femur in AP plane and more at apex of intercondylar notch than inner wall. Tibial attachment below joint line in middle of tibia
3. Ligaments of Humphry and Wrisberg: meniscofemoral ligaments that run from the posterior horn of the lateral meniscus to blend with PCL and femoral attachment. Humphry is anterior and Wrisberg is posterior
4. Primary restraint to posterior tibial translation. Major secondary restraint to external tibial rotation, minor secondary restraint to varus/valgus angulation
5. Distinguish "isolated" PCL injury from PCL injury with associated capsuloligamentous injury
6. Mechanism
    a. Fall on flexed knee with ankle plantar flexed
    b. Hyperextension
7. Examination

a. Positive posterior drawer test with 90° knee flexion
b. Posterior sag or gravity tests are positive
c. A 90° active drawer test is also positive
d. Both medial and lateral instabilities in full extension indicate PCL deficiency
e. External rotation recurvatum and reverse pivot shift tests are positive if posterolateral rotatory instability
8. Bony avulsion occasionally seen at PCL insertion on tibia
9. Majority of patients with isolated PCL injury do well with nonoperative treatment at even the elite athlete level of activity, despite the objective laxity present on physical examination. The minority of patients who do poorly develop patellofemoral and medial compartment degenerative changes
10. Relative indicators for surgical reconstruction
    a. Additional capsuloligamentous injury: arcuate complex
    b. Medial/lateral collateral ligaments
    c. ACL injury
    d. Bony avulsion should be repaired if ligament itself is intact
11. Surgery: multiple procedures described. Most frequently performed procedure currently uses central third patellar tendon (bone-tendon-bone)

I. Collateral ligament injury
   1. MCL, including third degree
      a. Isolated MCL injury heals well without surgical intervention
      b. MCL injury in conjunction with ACL or PCL: controversial. No clear evidence supports surgical treatment of both ACL and MCL vs operating on only ACL. There is a trend toward stabilizing only the intra-articular structure
      c. When ACL and MCL injuries occur together, attempts at regaining motion are more difficult if surgery is performed shortly after injury occurs. Difficulty in regaining motion if surgery is delayed 3 weeks
   2. LCL: isolated injury much less common than MCL and disruption of LCL complex is usually associated with cruciate ligament injury. Surgical repair is recommended for complete LCL complex injury

J. Multiple ligament injury
   1. Represent severe injuries with severe soft tissue and often articular surface injury. Careful neurovascular examination and follow-up required
   2. High incidence (40%) of intraluminal tear or arterial thrombus, which can compromise circulation immediately or days after injury
   3. If joint dislocation has been documented or both cruciates and a collateral ligament have been injured, an arteriogram should be performed
   4. Treatment
      a. In a young, active, reliable patient ligament reconstruction (or repair if bone avulsion) should be performed. Posterolateral complex injuries should be repaired as well
      b. Risk of joint stiffness is quite high and ligament repair and graft fixation must be strong so early motion program can be initiated
      c. Postoperative rehabilitation is extremely difficult and time consuming. Patient must be committed to rehabilitation or poor result can be expected

REFERENCES

Andrew JR, Carson WG Jr, eds: The anterior cruciate ligament, Part I and II (Symposium). Orthop Clin North Am 16:1,165, 1985

Arnoczky SP, Warren RF, Spivak JM: Meniscal repair using an exogenous fibrin clot: An experimental study in dogs. J Bone Joint Surg 70A:1209–1217, 1988

Cassidy RE, Shaffer AJ: Repair of peripheral meniscus tears. Am J Sports Med 9:209, 1981

Cerullo G, Puddu G, Conteduca F, et al: Evaluation of the results of extensor mechanism reconstruction. Am J Sports Med 16:93–96, 1988

Clancy WG Jr, Nelson DA, Reider B, et al: Anterior cruciate ligament reconstruction using one-third of the patellar ligament, augmented by extraarticular tendon transfers. J Bone Joint Surg 64A:353, 1982

Clancy WG Jr, Ray M, Zoltan DJ: Acute tears of the anterior cruciate ligament: Surgical versus conservative treatment. J Bone Joint Surg 70A:1483–1488, 1988

Clancy WG Jr, Shelbourne KD, Zoellner GB, et al: Treatment of knee joint instability secondary to rupture of the posterior cruciate ligament. J Bone Joint Surg 65A:310–322, 1983

Cox JS: Patellofemoral problems in runners. Clin Sports Med 4:699–715, 1985

Daniel DM, Stone ML, Barnett P, et al: Use of the quadriceps active test to diagnose posterior cruciate-ligament disruption and measure posterior laxity of the knee. J Bone Joint Surg 70A:386–391, 1988

Daniel DM, Stone MA, Sachs R, et al: Instrumented measurement of anterior knee laxity in patients with acute anterior cruciate ligament disruption. Am J Sports Med 13:401–407, 1985

Davey JR, Rorabeck CH, Fowler PJ: The tibialis posterior muscle compartment. An unrecognized cause of exertional compartment syndrome. Am J Sports Med 12:391–397, 1984

DeHaven KE, Black KP, Griffith HS: Meniscus repair. Technique and 2 to 9 year results. Am J Sports Med 17:788, 1989

DeHaven KE, Dolan WA, Mayer PJ: Chondromalacia patellae in athletes. Clinical presentation and conservative management. Am J Sports Med 7:5, 1979

DeLee JC, Riley MB, Rockwood CA Jr: Acute straight lateral instability of the knee. Am J Sports Med 11:404–411, 1983

Detmer DE: Chronic shin splints: Classification and management of medial tibial stress syndrome. Sports Med 3:436–446, 1986

Ficat P, Hungerford DS: Disorders of the patellofemoral joint. Baltimore, Williams & Wilkins, 1977

Gillquist J, Odensten M: Arthroscopic reconstruction of the anterior cruciate ligament. Arthroscopy 4:5–9, 1988

Gollehon DL, Torzilli PA, Warren RF: The role of the posterolateral and cruciate ligaments in the stability of the human knee: A biomechanical study. J Bone Joint Surg 69A:233–242, 1987

Grood ES, Stowers SF, Noyes FR: Limits of movement in the human knee: Effect of sectioning the posterior cruciate ligament and posterolateral structures. J Bone Joint Surg 70A:88–97, 1988

Hamberg P, Gillquist J, Lysholm J: Suture of new and old peripheral meniscus tears. J Bone Joint Surg 65A:193–197, 1983

Hawkins RJ, Misamore GW, Merritt TR: Follow-up of the acute nonoperated isolated anterior cruciate ligament tear. Am J Sports Med 14:205–210, 1986

Hughston JC: Subluxation of the patella. J Bone Joint Surg 50A:1003, 1968

Hughston JC, Andrews JR, Cross MN, et al: Classification of knee ligament instabilities. Part I. The medial compartment and cruciate ligament. J Bone Joint Surg 58A:159, 1976

Hughston JC, Andrews JR, Cross MN, et al: Classification of knee ligament instabilities. Part II. The lateral compartment. J Bone Joint Surg 58A:173, 1976

Hughston JC, Bowden JA, Andrews JR, et al: Acute tears of the posterior cruciate ligament. Results of operative treatment. J Bone Joint Surg 62A:438, 1980

Hughston JC, Deese M: Medial subluxation of the patella as a complication of lateral retinacular release. Am J Sports Med 16:383–388, 1988

Hughston JC, Jacobson KE: Chronic posterolateral rotatory instability of the knee. J Bone Joint Surg 67A:351–359, 1985

Indelicato PA: Non-operative treatment of complete tears of the medial collateral ligament of the knee. J Bone Joint Surg 65A:323–329, 1983

Inoue M, McGurk-Burleson E, Hollis JM, et al: The treatment of medial collateral ligament injury: The importance of anterior cruciate ligament on the varus-valgus knee laxity. Am J Sports Med 15:15, 1987

Insall JN: Current concepts review: Patellar pain. J Bone Joint Surg 64A:147, 1982

Jackson DW, Jennings LD, Maywood RM, et al: Magnetic resonance imaging of the knee. Am J Sports Med 16:29–38, 1988

Jakob RP, Staubli HU, Zuber K, et al: The arthroscopic meniscal repair: Techniques and clinical experience. Am J Sports Med 16:137–142, 1988

Kannus P, Jarvinen M: Long-term prognosis of non-operatively treated acute knee distortions having primary hemarthrosis without clinical instability. Am J Sports Med 15:138–143, 1987

Kurosaka M, Yoshiya S, Anokish JT: A biomechanical comparison of different surgical techniques of graft fixation in anterior cruciate ligament reconstruction. Am J Sports Med 15:225, 1987

Lutter LD: Surgical decisions in athletes' subcalcaneal pain. Am J Sports Med 14:481–485, 1986

Manco LG, Kavanaugh JH, Lozman J, et al: Diagnosis of meniscal tears using high-resolution computed tomography: Correlation with arthroscopy. J Bone Joint Surg 69A:498–502, 1987

McBryde AM Jr: Stress fractures in runners. Clin Sports Med 4:737–752, 1985

McKenzie DC, Clement DB, Taunton JE: Running shoes, orthotics, and injuries. Sports Med 2:334–347, 1985

Morgan CD, Casscells SW: Arthroscopic meniscal repair: A safe approach to the posterior horns. Arthroscopy 2:3–12, 1986

Mubarek SJ, Owen CA: Double incision fasciotomy of the leg for decompression in compartment syndrome. J Bone Joint Surg 59A:1811, 1977

Northmore-Ball MD, Dandy DJ, Jackson RW: Arthroscopic, open partial, and total menisectomy: A comparative study. J Bone Joint Surg 65B:400–404, 1983

Noyes FR, Grood ES, Torzilli PA: Current concepts review: The definitions of terms for motion and position of the knee and injuries of the ligaments. J Bone Joint Surg 71A:465–472, 1989

O'Connor RL, Shahriaree H: Arthroscopic technique and normal anatomy of the knee. In Shahriaree H, ed. O'Connor's textbook of arthroscopic surgery. Philadelphia, JB Lippincott, 1984

Ogilvie-Harris DJ, Jackson RW: The arthroscopic treatment of chondromalacia patellae. J Bone Joint Surg 66B:660–665, 1984

Parolie JM, Bergfeld JA: Long-term results of nonoperative treatment of isolated posterior cruciate ligament injuries in the athlete. Am J Sports Med 14:35, 1986

Paulos LE, Butler DL, Noyes FR, et al: Intra-articular cruciate reconstruction. II. Replacement with vascularized patellar tendon. Clin Orthop 172:78–84, 1983

Paulos LE, Rosenberg TD, Drawbert J, et al: Infrapatellar contracture syndrome: An unrecognized cause of knee stiffness with patella entrapment and patella infera. Am J Sports Med 15:331–341, 1987

Robertson DB, Daniel DM, Biden E: Soft tissue fixation to bone. Am J Sports Med 14:398, 1986

Rorabeck CH, Bourne RB, Fowler PJ: The surgical treatment of exertional compartment syndrome in athletes. J Bone Joint Surg 65A:1245, 1983

Schepsis AA, Leach RE: Surgical management of Achilles tendinitis. Am J Sports Med 15:308–315, 1987

Scott GA, Jolly BL, Henning CE: Combined posterior incision and arthroscopic intra-articular repair of the meniscus. J Bone Joint Surg 68A:847, 1986

Shoemaker SC, Markolf KL: The role of the meniscus in the anterior-posterior stability of the loaded anterior cruciate-deficient knee: Effects of partial versus total excision. J Bone Joint Surg 68A:71–79, 1986

Silva I Jr, Silver DM: Tears of the meniscus as revealed by magnetic resonance imaging. J Bone Joint Surg 70A:199–202, 1988

Simpson LA, Barrett JP Jr: Factors associated with poor results following arthroscopic subcutaneous lateral retinacular release. Clin Orthop 186:165–171, 1984

Sisto DJ, Warren RF: Complete dislocation: A follow-up study of operative treatment. Clin Orthop 198:94–101, 1985

Woo SL-Y, Inoue M, McGurk-Burleson E, et al: Treatment of the medial collateral ligament injury. II. Structure and function of canine knees in response to differing treatment regimens. Am J Sports Med 15:22–29, 1987

Zarins B, Rowe CR: Combined anterior cruciate-ligament reconstruction using semitendinosus tendon and iliotibial tract. J Bone Joint Surg 68A:160, 1986

36
Foot and Ankle Problems

GREAT TOE PROBLEMS

I. Hallux Valgus

A. General considerations
 1. More common in females (5–15:1)
 2. Associated deformities: metatarsus primus varus, prominent medial eminence, pronated hallux, hammered second toe, arthritic first metatarsophalangeal (MTP) joint
 3. Etiology: high heel shoes with narrow toe box, trauma, inflammation, and familial

B. Pathoanatomy
 1. Abductor hallucis is laterally displaced and plantarly rotated
 2. Adductor hallucis aggravates deformity by pulling proximal phalanx and lateral sesamoid into valgus position
 3. Flexor hallucis brevis and insertion to sesamoids are laterally displaced
 4. Extensor hallucis and flexor hallucis longus aggravate the deformity with bowstring effect
 5. Pronation of the great toe by adductor and displaced abductor pull (usually if valgus $>35°$)
 6. Oblique metatarsocuneiform joint and metatarsus primus varus predispose to hallux valgus (normal intermetatarsal angle is $<9°$)
 7. Medial capsule stretches and the lateral capsule contracts as hallux valgus progress (normal MTP angle $<15°$)

C. Severity
 1. Mild: $<20°$
 2. Moderate: $20°–40°$
 3. Severe: $>40°$

D. Treatment
 1. Shoe modification: high wide toe box, rubber wedge soles, soft leather uppers
 2. Surgery
  a. Excision of the prominent medial eminence (1 mm medial to sagittal groove) especially for patients with minimal deformity with large exostosis that impinges against the toe box shoe
  b. Soft tissue procedure (DuVries modification of McBride): simple exostectomy, adductor hallucis release, and medial capsular reefing (Fig 4-12)
   (1) Hallux valgus $<40°$ and metatarsus primus varus $<15°$
   (2) The major complication is hallux varus (correct by rerouting lateral $2/3$ of extensor hallucis longus through the proximal phalanx or MTP arthrodesis)
  c. Distal metatarsal osteotomies
   (1) Chevron: for patients <50 years and intermetatarsal angle $<15°$ and <30 MTP angle
   (2) Mitchell: for patients <50 years, intermetatarsal angle $<18°$, especially with metatarsalgia of lesser metatarsals
   (3) Complications: nonunion, dorsal angulation, and avascular necrosis
  d. Proximal metatarsal osteotomy (Fig 4-13)
   (1) Used with distal soft tissue procedure
   (2) If metatarsus primus varus is $>15°$ or cannot reduce lateral sesamoid
   (3) Crescenteric osteotomy is preferred to preserve length
  e. Akin proximal phalangeal osteot-

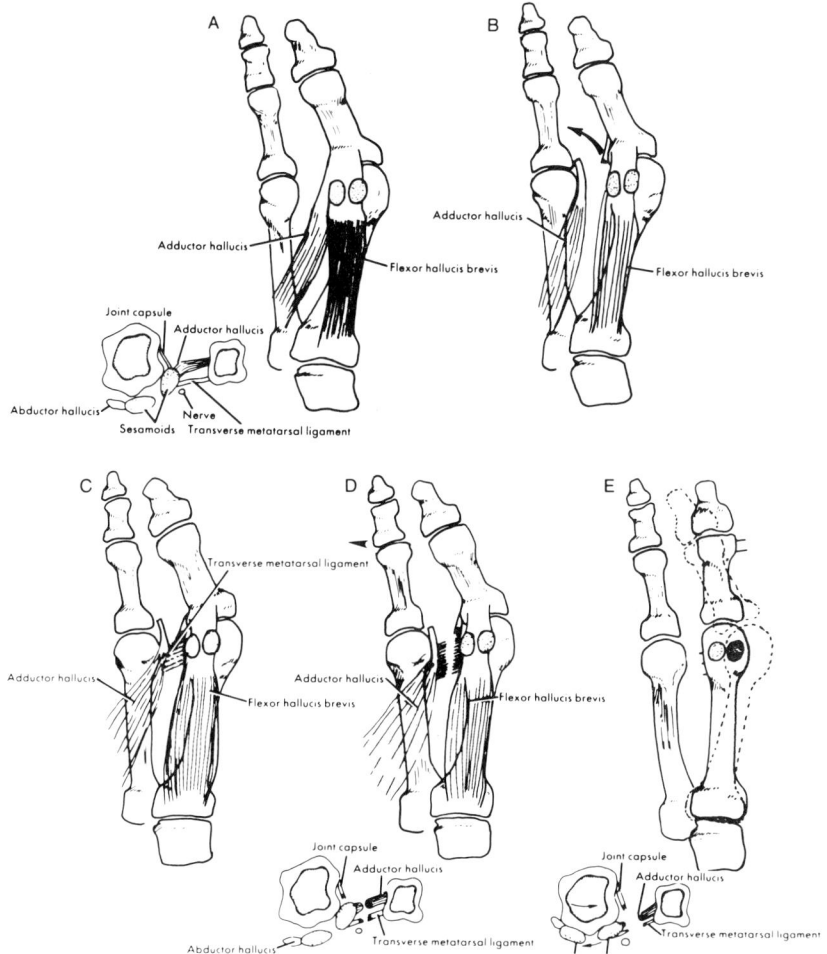

Figure 4-12. Soft tissue procedure (DuVries modification of McBride procedure). **A.** Adductor hallucis, joint capsule, and the transverse metatarsal ligament are contracted. **B.** Release of adductor hallucis. **C.** Transverse metatarsal ligament is released. **D.** Lateral capsule is released. **E.** Realignment is checked and the sesamoids should be reduced normally. (From Mann RA: Surgery of the foot. St Louis, CV Mosby, 1986. Reprinted with permission.)

omy if significant hallux interphalangeus or hallux valgus without metatarsus primus varus
f. Resection arthroplasty (Keller): resect proximal third of the proximal phalanx
   (1) Indications are elderly patients with arthritic MTP joint or as salvage surgery for failed bunion procedure
   (2) Complications may be unstable joint and transfer of weight to other metatarsal heads
g. MTP arthrodesis
   (1) Position of fusion: 15°–20° valgus, 10° dorsiflexion to floor, or 25° with respect to metatarsal shaft
   (2) Indication is arthritic MTP joint in patients <60 years of age

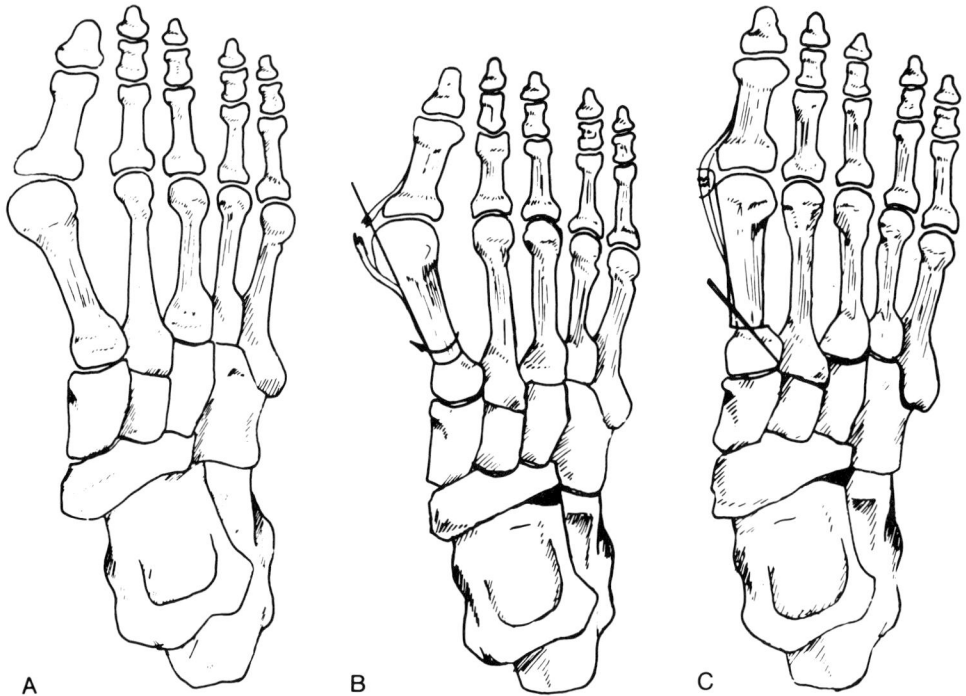

Figure 4-13. Proximal metatarsal osteotomy. **A.** Metatarsus primus varus. **B.** Basal osteotomy. **C.** Pin fixation. (From Mann RA: Surgery of the foot. St Louis, CV Mosby, 1986. Reprinted with permission.)

II. Hallux Rigidus

A. Definition: MTP disorder of the great toe characterized by pain and decreased motion, especially dorsiflexion

B. Etiology
1. Congenital or juvenile: early teenagers, usually osteochondritic defect of the metatarsal head (trauma or abnormal MTP joint, such as flat metatarsal head, may be associated)
2. Post-traumatic arthritis
3. Arthridites: osteoarthritis, gout, or psoriatic arthritis

C. Clinical findings
1. Symptoms: painful MTP joint, prominent dorsal exostosis, decreased motion
2. Physical examination: tenderness and decreased dorsiflexion of the MTP joint
3. X-ray: dorsal degenerative changes of first MTP and dorsal osteophyte in the metatarsal head

D. Treatment
1. NSAIDs
2. Shoe modifications to decrease MTP joint motion: rigid sole or rocker sole
3. Surgery
   a. Cheilectomy: removal of the osteophytes up to dorsal third metatarsal head to allow 60°–80° of dorsiflexion
      (1) Indicated for relatively young patients with good remaining articular cartilage
      (2) Best initial procedure with good results
   b. Arthrodesis: fuse at 15°–20° valgus and 15°–20° dorsiflexion relative to the metatarsal shaft and fixation with a screw

(1) Indicated for young patients with advanced arthritis
(2) Good primary or salvage operation
  c. Keller procedure
  (1) Resection of the proximal third of the base of proximal phalanx
  (2) Indicated in older patients with decreased activity level
  (3) Shortening and loss of function of the great toe and lateral transfer of metatarsalgia may occur

LESSER TOE DEFORMITIES

I. Hammer Toes
A. Pathologic anatomy
  1. MTP joint is hyperextended
  2. Proximal interphalangeal (PIP) joint is hyperflexed
  3. Distal interphalangeal (DIP) joint is hyperextended
B. Etiology may be familial, traumatic, neuromuscular, inflammatory, shoe wear (short narrow toe box or high heel), or idiopathic
C. Clinical findings
  1. Bony prominences on the dorsum of PIP joint
  2. Tender corns overlying prominences
  3. Difficulty fitting shoes
  4. Flexible or fixed deformities
D. Treatment
  1. Conservative: shaving corns, hammer toe shields, splinting devices, and high wide toe box shoes
  2. Surgery
    a. Flexible: flexor to extensor transfer
    b. Fixed deformities
      (1) Resection of distal portion of proximal phalanx (Fig 4-14)
      (2) Diaphysectomy of proximal phalanx
    c. Dislocation of MTP joint: Extensive soft tissue release of first MTP joint

II. Clawed Toes
A. Pathologic anatomy
  1. MTP joint is hyperextended
  2. PIP joint is hyperflexed
  3. DIP joint is hyperflexed

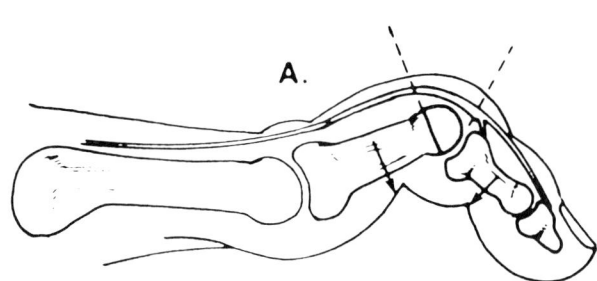
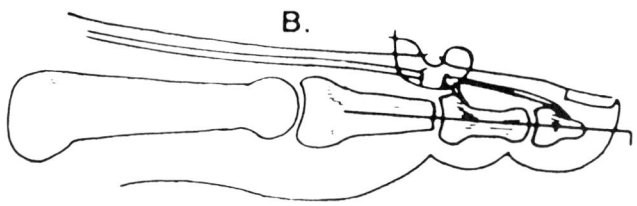

Figure 4-14. Resection of the distal portion of the proximal phalanx for hammer toe repair. (From Coughlin MJ: Lesser toe abnormalities. In Chapman MW, ed. Operative orthopaedics. Philadelphia, JB Lippincott, 1988, p 1767. Reprinted with permission.)

B. Etiology may be familial, traumatic, neuromuscular, inflammatory, idiopathic, or shoe wear (short narrow toe box shoes or high heel)
C. Clinical findings
   1. Bony prominences of the dorsum of the PIP joint
   2. Corns on the dorsum of the PIP joint
   3. Distal tip corn
   4. Deformity is flexible early and becomes fixed later
D. Treatment
   1. Conservative treatment: high wide toe box shoes, dynamic splinting (if flexible), and toe crest (if fixed)
   2. Surgical treatment
      a. Flexible: flexor to extensor transfer
      b. Fixed
         (1) Distal hemiphalangectomy
         (2) Distal hemiphalangectomy and flexor to extensor transfer
         (3) Diaphysectomy

III. Mallet Toe
A. Definition: flexion deformities of DIP joint
B. Etiology may be traumatic or idiopathic
C. Clinically distal tip corn and difficulty fitting shoes
D. Treatment
   1. Pads and splints
   2. Resection of middle phalanx (partial or total)

IV. Bunionette (tailor's bunion)
A. Prominence of the fifth metatarsal head with pain and tenderness: associated with hallux valgus, and splay foot or lateral deviation of metatarsal
B. Treatment
   1. Conservative: adequate shoes, float pad
   2. Surgery
      a. Excision of the lateral portion of the metatarsal head with or without lateral condyle of the proximal phalanx
      b. Osteotomy of the neck shaft or base if lateral deviation of the metatarsal shaft

DISEASES OF THE NERVES OF THE FOOT

I. Interdigital Neuroma
A. Definition: enlargement of one of the common digital nerves of the foot at the level of the metatarsal heads
B. Etiology: nerve compression, microtrauma
C. Incidence
   1. Male to female ratio: 1:4
   2. Average age: 40–60 years
   3. Unilateral: 85–90%
   4. Third web space (85%), second web space (15%)
D. Predisposing factors: high-heeled shoes and prolonged standing on inflexible surfaces
E. Clinical findings
   1. Burning type pain at the third web space
   2. Occasional radiation pain to tips of toes
   3. Pain that increases on weight bearing
   4. Numbness and paresthesias of third and fourth toes
   5. Physical examination: tenderness at third web space and pain on lateral compression of metatarsal heads
F. Differential diagnosis
   1. Neuritis elsewhere: herniated disc, tarsal tunnel syndrome, and peripheral neuritis
   2. Metatarsalgia: synovitis, subluxation and dislocation of MTP joint, Freiberg's disease, and degenerative plantar pad
   3. Tumors: synovial cyst, ganglion, bony growths
G. Treatment
   1. Conservative: NSAIDs, metatarsal pad, local or steroid injections
   2. Surgery: excision of the nerve at least

3 cm or more proximal to the intermetatarsal ligament

II. Tarsal Tunnel Syndrome
A. Pathogenesis
   1. Entrapment of posterior tibial nerve or its branches (medial, lateral plantar nerves, and medial calcaneal nerve)
   2. Local pathologic condition may be the cause: ganglion, lipoma, exostosis or scar (previous calcaneus fracture or trauma), tarsal coalition, venous plexus, hypertrophy of abductor hallucis (runner), neurilemmoma and rheumatoid arthritis
B. Clinical findings
   1. Diffuse burning pain on the plantar aspect of the foot (usually unilateral)
   2. Paresthesia and Tinel's sign
   3. EMG findings
      a. Abductor hallucis (medial plantar nerve)
      b. Abductor digiti quinti (lateral plantar nerve): affected earlier
C. Treatment
   1. Conservative: NSAIDs, orthosis, and injection
   2. Surgery: release of the entire tarsal tunnel for decompression of the tibial nerve and its branches and resection of flexor retinaculum (be careful of medial calcaneal branch)

KERATOTIC LESIONS AND METATARSALGIA

I. Corns
A. Pathogenesis
   1. Localized keratoses from pressure between underlying bones or shoes
   2. Types
      a. Hard: exposed surface of the toes
      b. Soft: between the toes over condyles of the phalanx or also known as clavus
B. Treatment
   1. Conservative: shoe modification, orthotics for weight-bearing areas, toe protectors, splinting devices
   2. Surgery
      a. Corn on the dorsolateral aspect of the fifth toe: condylectomy of the proximal phalanx or resection of distal portion of proximal phalanx with or without syndactyly
      b. Corn over dorsum of middle three toes: correct hammer toes or mallet toes
      c. Corn in web space between toes
         (1) Head of fifth proximal phalanx: impinge against base of fourth proximal phalanx: excise offending bony condyles or resection of distal portion of proximal phalanx with or without syndactyly (fourth and fifth toes)
         (2) Soft corn elsewhere: condylectomy

II. Callus and Metatarsalgia
A. Pathogenesis
   1. Hyperkeratotic skin on the plantar aspect of the foot
   2. Localized underneath tibial sesamoid or fibular condyle of a metatarsal head
   3. Etiology (metatarsalgia)
      a. Faulty footwear (narrow-pointed toed shoes)
      b. Osseous abnormalities (plantar flexed metatarsals)
      c. Foot deformities (varus or valgus, cavus and pronated feet)
      d. Iatrogenic: Keller procedure, osteotomies with dorsal angulation
      e. Malunion of metatarsal fractures
      f. Rheumatoid arthritis
      g. Morton's toe
B. Differential diagnosis of metatarsalgia
   1. Morton's neuroma
   2. Freiberg's infarction
   3. Metatarsal stress fracture
   4. Plantar warts

5. Synovitis or inflammatory diseases
6. Sesamoiditis
7. Second metatarsalgia
8. Intractable plantar keratosis
9. Cavus foot

III. Treatment

A. Conservative: trimming, shoe modification (soft sole, low heel, wide toe box), metatarsal pads inserted to elevate proximal to metatarsal heads
B. Surgery
  1. Under tibial sesamoid: shaving of plantar half of the sesamoid is superior to excision (Mann)
  2. Under metatarsal heads
     a. Small discrete plantar callus as in intractable planter keratosis: condylectomy on the fibular and plantar aspect (DuVries) — 85% good result (Fig 4-15)
     b. Other options: distal or proximal metatarsal osteotomies
  3. Must correct the underlying problems if present (ie, osteotomy for plantar flexed metatarsal)

OTHER DISORDERS OF THE FOOT AND ANKLE

I. Diabetic Foot

A. General considerations
  1. Infected foot is the most common septic complication leading to hospitalization of the diabetic patient
  2. Second foot: amputation of one foot leads to contralateral foot problems in 50% of patients
  3. Neuropathy is common
     a. Peripheral neuropathy
     b. Intrinsic weakness with claw toes

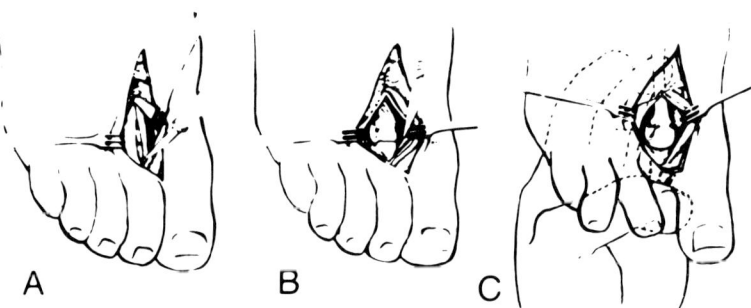

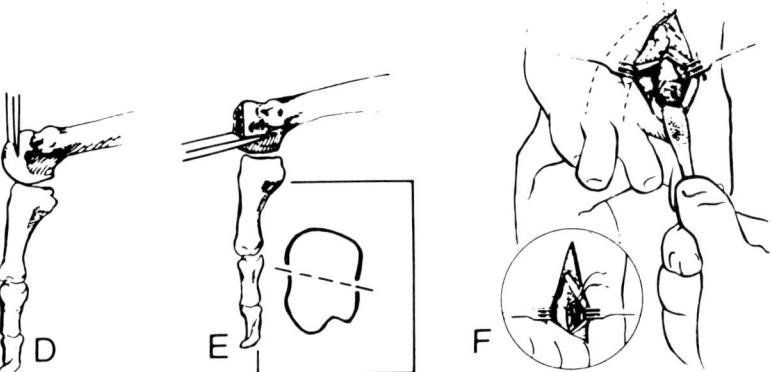

Figure 4-15. Procedure for arthroplasty and plantar condylectomy for a discrete intractable keratosis under the lesser metatarsal heads. **A.** Incision. **B.** Capsulotomy. **C.** Exposure of the metatarsal head. **D.** A 2 mm section of articular surface is removed. **E.** Removal of plantar condyle. **F.** Smooth surface with a rasp. (From Mann RA, DuVries HL: Keratotic disorders of the plantar skin. In Mann RA, ed. DuVries surgery of the foot, ed. 4. St Louis, CV Mosby, 1978. Reprinted with permission.)

c. Charcot joint (80% in the midfoot)
4. Vascularity
   a. Lower leg systolic divided by arm systolic blood pressure is the ischemic index
   b. If ischemic index >0.45 (systolic pressure usually >70 mmHg), healing will occur after surgery. If ankle pressure is >90 mmHg, spontaneous healing is expected
   c. Toe pressure >40 mmHg is needed for healing
5. Calcified arteries distal to ankle joint is diagnostic of diabetes mellitus
B. Classification of foot lesions
1. Grade 0: skin intact
2. Grade 1: localized superficial ulcer
3. Grade 2: deep ulcer to tendon, bone, ligament, or joint
4. Grade 3: Deep abscess, osteomyelitis
5. Grade 4: gangrene of toes or forefoot
6. Grade 5: gangrene of whole foot
C. Treatment
1. Prevention
   a. Daily foot inspection by patient and family
   b. Early recognition of problems
   c. Good hygiene
   d. Good shoe wear (extra depth and thick sole) or orthotics
2. Surgery
   a. Prophylactic surgery in grade 0: bunionectomy, claw toes, metatarsal resection, or osteotomies
   b. Grade 1: debridement, iodoform packs, antibiotics, walking cast (skin graft or porcine graft may be needed)
   c. Grade 2: surgical debridement and closure over drain or skin graft if >2 cm size, and walking cast
   d. Grade 3: surgical debridement, irrigation-suction system, partial amputations, and cast
   e. Grade 4 or 5: amputation where involved and surgical levels depend on ischemic index
   f. Procedures: ray or toe amputations, transmetatarsal amputation, Syme's amputation, calcaneus excision (partial or complete), below knee or above knee amputations
D. Vascular consideration: if Doppler pressures are significantly lowered, arteriography and vascular bypass surgery should be considered prior to foot surgery

II. Charcot Joint

A. Etiology
1. Diabetes mellitus
2. Syphilis
3. Syringomyelia
4. Other neuropathic causes
B. Clinical findings
1. Heat, swelling, redness
2. Insensate foot with repeated trauma
3. Midfoot (80%), hindfoot, forefoot, or ankle deformities (valgus)
4. X-ray findings: destructive and maligned joint
C. Treatment
1. Long-term cast or orthotic protection (4–6 months and even up to 18 months)
2. Surgical correction of deformities, bony prominences
3. Arthrodesis is not predictable but may be only alternative in late resistant cases

III. Rheumatoid Foot and Ankle

A. Forefoot
1. Common deformities
   a. Hallux valgus
   b. Claw or hammer toes
   c. Hypertension of MTP and prominent metatarsal heads
2. Treatment
   a. Conservative: medications, extra depth shoes, orthosis, and range of motion exercise
   b. Surgical treatment
      (1) Hoffman: resection of all 1–5 metatarsal heads
      (2) Clayton: resection of all 1–5

metatarsal heads plus resection of bases of proximal phalanges (good for dislocated or severely involved foot)
(3) Mann: fusion of the great toe and resection of metatarsal heads 2–5 (fusion rate, 94%) (Fig 4-16)
(4) Alternative: Keller arthroplasty hallux resection of metatarsal heads from second to fifth toes with or without resection of base of proximal phalanges from second to fifth toes and with or without syndactyly of second-third and fourth-fifth toes

B. Hindfoot
 1. Valgus deformity common
  a. Ligament laxity with subluxation of subtalar joint
  b. Loss of cartilage and bone
  c. Rupture of posterior tibialis tendon
 2. Clinical findings
  a. Pes planovalgus
  b. Tenderness in the sinus tarsi
  c. Decreased subtalar motion
  d. Pain with ambulation
 3. Treatment
  a. Conservative: medications, shoes, and University of California Biomechanics Laboratory (UCBL) hindfoot orthosis
  b. Surgery: subtalar or triple arthrodesis

C. Ankle
 1. Ankle involvement in 45% but usually mild
 2. Tenosynovitis common
 3. Articular involvement: synovitis and joint destruction
 4. Treatment
  a. Conservative: shoes and brace
  b. Surgery: synovectomy, arthrodesis, or total ankle arthroplasty

IV. Degenerative Arthritis of the Ankle

A. Etiologies: primary osteoarthritis (rare), trauma, osteochondritis dissecans, avascular necrosis, synovial chondromatosis, and rheumatoid arthritis

B. Treatment
 1. Nonoperative: orthotics to limit ankle motion and reduce pain, and NSAIDs

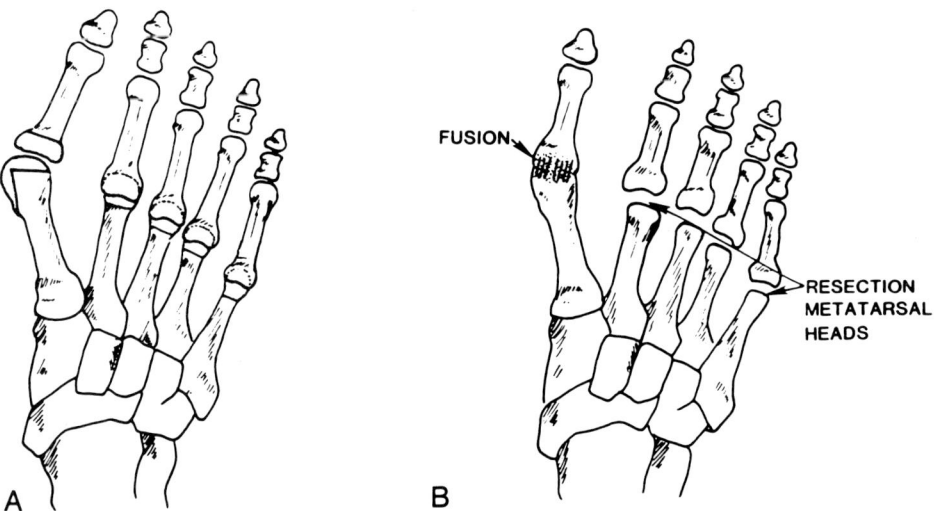

Figure 4-16. Fusion of the metatarsophalangeal joint of the great toe and symmetrical resection of lesser metatarsals for rheumatoid forefoot problems. (From Coughlin MJ: Lesser toe abnormalities. In Chapman MW, ed. Operative orthopaedics. Philadelphia, JB Lippincott, 1988, p 1852. Reprinted with permission.)

2. Surgery
   a. Excision of osteophytes from the talus and tibia if the disease is limited to the anterior joint
   b. Arthrodesis
      (1) Position: neutral plantar flexion, 5°–7° valgus and neutral or 5° external rotation
         i. If too much externally rotated: hallux valgus complication
         ii. If internally rotated: lateral border of the foot becomes painful
      (2) Trend is to use internal fixation: anteromedial and anterolateral approach with maximum contact of joint surface (compression screw fixation is helpful)
      (3) Anterior tibial graft slide may be performed
   c. Total ankle arthroplasty
      (1) Rheumatoid arthritis or older less active patient
      (2) Contraindications: significant laxity, deformity >20°, history of previous infection, failed fusion, lack of bone stock, osteonecrosis of talus
      (3) Complications are many and results are poor

V. Overuse Disorders or Injuries of the Foot and Ankle

A. Achilles tendinitis
   1. Associated with tight hamstring, tibia vara, tight heel cord, valgus heel, and pronated feet
   2. Running on hills and low-heel shoes
   3. Tenderness along course of the tendon and limited dorsiflexion
   4. Treatment: NSAIDs, heel lift, heel cord stretching exercise
   5. Partial rupture
      a. Often acute pain
      b. Diagnosis aided by MRI
      c. Treatment: conservative first or surgery if resistant
   6. Achilles tendon rupture
      a. Sudden pop and pain
      b. Squeeze test (Thompson test): the most reliable test
      c. Treatment: below knee nonweight-bearing cast in plantar flexion for 4 weeks followed by walking cast for 4 weeks in elderly or sedentary patients and surgery for active young patients
   7. Retrocalcaneal bursitis
      a. Heel counter rubs against the posterolateral prominence of the calcaneus
      b. Treatment
         (1) Removal of pressure (remove the heel counter or heel lift to elevate heel above counter)
         (2) Surgery: rare except persistent problems associated pump bump or Haglund's deformity (excision of posterolateral bony prominence of the calcaneus)
B. Plantar fasciitis
   1. Pain at the plantar surface of the heel, worse in the morning
   2. Associated with tight Achillis tendon, cavus, and hyperpronated feet
   3. Tenderness at the plantar medial aspect of the calcaneus where the plantar fascia attach
   4. Entrapment of the calcaneal branch of the posterior tibial nerve or nerve to the abductor digiti quinti at the origin of the abductor hallucis (a branch of lateral plantar nerve) has been implicated
   5. Examination: tenderness and pain produced by dorsiflexion
   6. Treatment: heel cord stretching, heel lift (1.25 to 2 cm), NSAIDs, orthotics (heel cup, arch support), and injection of steroid if resistant
   7. Surgery: rarely if conservative treatment fails after 18 months (release of

the fascia, excision of heel spur, or release of the medial calcaneal nerve has been described)
C. Ankle sprain
   1. Types
      a. Lateral (most common)
      b. Medial: deep deltoid ligament attach to the posterior colliculus and superficial to the anterior colliculus
      c. Anterior capsular: impact on a plantar flexed ankle (long rehabilitation is needed)
   2. Lateral sprain; anterior talofibular and calcaneofibular ligaments are most frequently involved (subtalar sprain may be present)
   3. Diagnosis
      a. Anterior drawer test (>5 mm) and talar tilt (>5° in patients without previous injury) suggest injury to the anterior talofibular ligament
      b. Talar tilt suggests injury of the calcaneofibular ligament as well as anterior talofibular ligament
   4. Treatment
      a. Casting for short period of time (2 weeks), early motion, and strengthening program
      b. Occasionally repair the lateral collateral ligament in young athletic patients
      c. Chronic instability: Chrisman-Snook or other procedures
D. Peroneal subluxation and dislocation
   1. Forced dorsiflexion or inversion causes peroneus brevis to sublux anteriorly and tear the peroneal retinacular sheath and spontaneous reduction often occurs
   2. Swelling and tenderness behind the lateral malleolus if acute and snapping if chronic
   3. X-ray: thin cortical fracture of the posterior lateral malleolus
   4. Treatment: short leg cast for 3 weeks if acute and reconstruction of the retinaculum augmented with part of Achilles tendon or calcaneofibular ligament if chronic
E. Tibiofibular syndesmosis injury
   1. External rotation or forced dorsiflexion
   2. Spectrum from isolated anterior inferior tibiofibular ligament tear to severe widening of the syndesmosis
   3. Treatment: syndesmotic screw if widening is not reduced
F. Posterior tibialis tendon rupture
   1. Most common in women in ≥5th decades
      a. History of trauma in 50%
      b. Insidious development of unilateral flatfoot
   2. Posterior tibialis tendinitis may precede the injury
   3. Examination: pes valgus with forefoot abducted on standing. Inversion strength is decreased and can elicit tenderness along the tibialis tendon
   4. Treatment
      a. Repair and augmentation with flexor digitorum longus tendon. Direct repair through drill hole in the navicular if avulsed
      b. Chronic with hindfoot degeneration with deformity: talonavicular, subtalar, or triple arthrodesis
      c. Orthosis can be tried on old ruptures before surgery
G. Fractures
   1. Posterior talus fractures: plantar flexion and inversion cause fracture of the posterior eminence of the body of the talus or os trigonum (an accessory ossicle can be separated from the talus by synostosis)
      a. Os trigonum is present in 5%, is bilateral in 65%, and fused by synostosis in 46%
      b. Pain can be acute or related with activity
      c. Treatment: casting if acute and con-

servative if chronic. Excision if symptoms >6 months
2. Osteochondral talar dome fractures
   a. Lateral lesion: dorsiflexion and eversion and located anteriorly. More likely to be displaced
   b. Medial lesion: plantarflexion and eversion. Located posteriorly and usually nondisplaced
   c. Diagnosis: plain x-rays, tomogram
   d. Treatment: conservative if nondisplaced and surgery if displaced
3. Lateral process fractures of the talus
   a. Inversion and dorsiflexion
   b. Pain and swelling anterior and inferior to the tip of the lateral malleolus
   c. Late cases may present with bony overgrowth limiting valgus and dorsiflexion of the hindfoot, posterior subtalar degeneration, or nonunion
   d. Treatment: casting if acute and reconstruction or fusion in late cases
4. Fracture of sustenaculum tali
   a. Landing on the heel with inversion of the heel
   b. Pain and tenderness below the medial malleolus
   c. Treatment: casting if nondisplaced and open reduction and fixation if displaced (nonunion and subtalar arthritis may occur)
5. Anterior process fracture of the calcaneus
   a. Inversion of the ankle
   b. Anterior process attaches the bifurcate ligament and articulates the cuboid
   c. Tenderness along the sinus tarsi and oblique x-ray
   d. Treatment: casting if acute and 28% take >1 year to become asymptomatic
6. Avulsion fractures of the navicular
   a. Adduction causes avulsion of the navicular off tibialis posterior attachment
   b. Tenderness and pain with adduction
   c. Associated with fracture of cuboid and midtarsal subluxation
   d. Treatment: casting
7. Base of the fifth metatarsal
   a. Avulsion (peronius brevis) vs Jones fracture
   b. Symptomatic treatment for avulsion fractures but no weight-bearing cast for Jones fractures (92% healing if treated acutely)
   c. Nonunion: common after stress fractures and delayed treatment (surgery with cancellous screw and bone grafting is needed)

REFERENCES

Barbari SG, Brevig K: Correction of clawtoes by the Girdlestone-Taylor flexor-extensor transfer procedure. Foot Ankle 5:67–73, 1984

Beauchamp CG, Kirby T, Rudge SR, et al: Fusion of the first metatarsophalangeal joint in forefoot arthroplasty. Clin Orthop 190:249–253, 1984

Bordelon RL: Subcalcaneal pain: A method of evaluation and plan for treatment. Clin Orthop 177:49–53, 1983

Coughlin MJ, Mann RA: Arthrodesis of the first metatarsophalangeal joint as salvage for the failed Keller procedure. J Bone Joint Surg 69A:68–75, 1987

Cracchiolo A: Management of the arthritic forefoot. Foot Ankle 3:17–23, 1982

Evans GA, Hardcastle P, Frenyo AD: Acute rupture of the lateral ligament of the ankle: To suture or not to suture? J Bone Joint Surg 66B:209–212, 1984

Funk DA, Cass JR, Johnson KA: Acquired adult flat foot secondary to posterior tibial tendon pathology. J Bone Joint Surg 68A:95–102, 1986

Gainor BJ, Epstein GR, Henstorf JE, et al: Metatarsal head resection for rheumatoid deformities of the forefoot. Clin Orthop 230:207–213, 1988

Hattrup SJ, Johnson KA: Chevron osteotomy: Analysis of factors in patients' dissatisfaction. Foot Ankle 5:327–332, 1985

Johnson KA: Tibialis posterior tendon rupture. Clin Orthop 177:140–147, 1983

Johnson KA, Cofield RH, Morrey BF: Chevron osteotomy for hallux valgus. Clin Orthop 142:44–47, 1979

Johnson JE, Johnson KA, Unni KK: Persistent pain after excision of an interdigital neuroma: Results of reoperation. J Bone Joint Surg 70A:651–657, 1988

Johnson KA, Spiegl PV: Extensor hallucis longus transfer for hallux varus deformity. J Bone Joint Surg 66A:681–686, 1984

Love TR, Whynot AS, Farine I, et al: Keller arthroplasty: A prospective review. Foot Ankle 8:46–54, 1988

Mann RA: Surgery of the Foot, ed 5. St Louis, CV Mosby, 1986

Mann RA: Treatment of the bunion deformity. Orthopedics 10:49–55, 1987

Mann RA, Clanton TO: Hallux rigidus: Treatment by cheilectomy. J Bone Joint Surg 70A:400–406, 1988

Mann RA, Coughlin MJ: Hallux valgus: Etiology, anatomy, treatment and surgical considerations. Clin Orthop 157:31–41, 1981

Mann RA, Thompson FM: Arthrodesis of the first metatarsophalangeal joint for hallux valgus in rheumatoid arthritis. J Bone Joint Surg 66A:687–692, 1984

Mann RA, Thompson FM: Rupture of the posterior tibial tendon causing flat foot. J. Bone Joint Surg 67A:556–561, 1985

Morgan CD, Henke JA, Bailey RW, et al: Long-term results of tibiotalar arthrodesis. J Bone Joint Surg 67A:546–550, 1985

Scranton PE Jr: Use of internal compression in arthrodesis of the ankle. J Bone Joint Surg 67A:550–555, 1985

Snook GA, Chrisman OD, Wilson TC: Long-term results of the Chrisman-Snook operation for reconstruction of the lateral ligaments of the ankle. J Bone Joint Surg 67A:1–7, 1985

SECTION 5: ORTHOPAEDIC TRAUMA

Howard S. An
Michael J. Brennan

37. Principles of Orthopaedic Trauma
38. Fractures of the Radius and Ulna
39. Fractures and Dislocations of the Elbow
40. Fractures of the Humeral Shaft
41. Fractures and Dislocations of the Shoulder
42. Fractures of the Pelvis and Acetabulum
43. Fractures and Dislocations of the Hip
44. Fractures of the Shaft of the Femur
45. Fractures and Dislocations of the Knee
46. Fractures of the Tibia
47. Fractures and Dislocations of the Ankle and Foot

37
Principles of Orthopaedic Trauma

I. Multiple System Trauma

A. Initial evaluation and resuscitation
   1. Establish an airway
      a. Intubate if inadequate ventilation, flail chest, or deterioration of oxygenation and severe head injury
         (1) Suction, chin lift, and oropharyngeal airway initially
         (2) Nasotracheal intubation if airway is not established
         (3) Cricothyroidotomy may be necessary in certain situations
      b. Improve ventilation and insert chest tube if pneumothorax, hemothorax, or tension pneumothorax
         (1) Open pneumothorax (sucking chest wound), tension pneumothorax and large flail chest are life-threatening injuries
         (2) Large bore angiocatheter is used to alleviate tension pneumothorax temporarily, followed by chest tube insertion
         (3) Open chest wound should be covered by a sterile semiocclusive dressing
   2. Immobilize the cervical spine: gentle traction, sand bags, or collar
   3. Ensure cardiovascular function
      a. Hemorrhagic shock
         (1) Ringer's lactate if <25% loss of blood volume
         (2) Blood and Ringer's lactate if >25% loss of blood volume (use type O blood if type specific or cross-matched blood is not available)
         (3) For every 6 U of blood, give 2 U of fresh frozen plasma, and after 10 U of blood, add platelets
         (4) Palpable radial pulse begins at 80 mmHg, femoral pulse over 70 mmHg, and carotid pulse over 60 mmHg
         (5) Two large bore peripheral lines should be established
      b. Pump failure
         (1) Pericardial tamponade: pericardiocentesis
         (2) Arrhythmia or myocardial infarction: appropriate drugs
      c. Arrest hemorrhage
         (1) Arterial bleeding: direct pressure
         (2) Retroperitoneal or intra-abdominal bleeding: antishock trousers or other pneumatic splints
         (3) Pelvic bleeding: external fixation
   4. Rapid evaluation of neurologic status
      a. Alert, responds to verbal stimuli, responds to painful stimuli, or unresponsive
      b. Gross voluntary movement and pupil status are assessed
   5. Expose the patient and look for penetrating injuries and evaluate blood pressure

B. Complete assessment or secondary survey
   1. Head injuries
      a. Intubate and hyperventilate
      b. Mannitol or corticosteroids
      c. Computed tomography (CT) to diagnose subdural or epidural hematoma, which is a medical emergency

2. Spinal injuries
   a. Lateral C-spine x-ray down to T1 level
   b. Complete neurologic examination, including rectal and bulbocavernosus reflex
   c. Neck immobilization with collar or tongs
3. Thoracic and abdominal injuries
   a. Chest x-ray
      (1) Look for wide mediastinum, suggesting aortic rupture
      (2) Look for pneumothorax, hemothorax, and rib fractures
   b. Peritoneal lavage if suspected abdominal bleeding: red blood cells >100,000/mm^3, white blood cells >500/mm^3, or amylase >175 U/dL
   c. CT is as helpful as peritoneal lavage
4. Urologic injuries
   a. Gross hematuria requires intravenous pyelogram
   b. Pelvic fractures are associated with urologic injuries in 5–15%
   c. Urethrogram, cystogram, or intravenous pyelogram may be necessary
   d. High-riding prostate indicates urethral injury
5. Pelvic injuries
   a. Pneumatic antishock garment: hypovolemic shock due to peritoneal or retroperitoneal hemorrhages (may cause tissue anoxia or compartment syndrome if used >30 minutes >30 mmHg)
   b. External fixation to reduce venous bleeding and to stabilize the fractures is preferred to pneumatic antishock garment
   c. Arteriogram and embolization if persistent arterial bleeding
   d. Open pelvic fractures: high mortality and diverting colostomy should be done routinely
6. Extremity injuries
   a. Assess vascular status
      (1) Gentle traction should be applied if no pulse
      (2) If no pulse after reduction maneuver, arteriogram should be done
      (3) Fix the fracture first, followed by repair of the vessel only if ischemic time has been short
      (4) Be aware of compartment syndrome
      (5) Obtain arteriogram in all knee dislocations
   b. Assess and document neurologic status
   c. Open wounds
      (1) Tetanus prophylaxis: 0.5 cc tetanus toxoid if >5 years since last tetanus toxoid, and 250 U of human tetanus immunoglobulin if not immunized in the past
      (2) Grading: type I, <1 cm; type II, >1 cm without significant tissue destruction; type IIIA, >10 cm wound with significant soft tissue damage and high energy injuries; type IIIB, extensive soft tissue injury with bone exposure and contamination; and type IIIC, open fracture with vascular injury
      (3) Antibiotic coverage: cephalosporins for type I or II wounds and add aminoglycosides for type III wounds

II. Orthopaedic Management of Polytrauma Patient

A. Goal: early fracture stabilization and mobilization of the patient
B. Pulmonary failure is the most common cause of death and early mobilization is the key
C. Aggressive nutritional support is important for patient's general status as well as fracture healing
D. Immediate fixations
   1. Intramedullary rodding of the femur

2. Intramedullary rodding of the femur or external fixation of the tibia
3. Rigid fixation for all intra-articular fractures even if they are open fractures
4. External fixation of the pelvic fractures
5. Plating of the forearm fractures
6. Intramedullary rodding or internal fixation of the humerus if floating elbow, open fractures, vascular injuries, head injuries, or multiple extremity injuries

E. Delayed fixations
1. Open reduction and internal fixation of the pelvis and sacrum
2. Acetabular fractures
3. Spine fractures can usually be fixed a few days after injury, unless progressive neurologic deficit or multiple extremity trauma that necessitates movement of the patient to jeopardize neurologic status

III. Complications

A. Fat embolism
1. Acute respiratory insufficiency as a result of fat emboli in patients with fractures of long bones and pelvis
2. Free fatty acids have a toxic effect on the lung parenchyma, causing chemical pneumonitis as well
3. Disturbance in hemostatic mechanism by thromboplastin, which is released from damaged tissue
4. Incidence: 0.5–2.0% of all long bone fractures and 5–10% in multiple trauma patients with pelvic fractures
5. Usually manifested within 48 hours
6. Fatal in 10–15%
7. Clinical presentation
   a. Fever, tachypnea, tachycardia, agitation, and altered mentation
   b. Petechiae on the chest and conjuntiva
   c. Thrombocytopenia
8. Treatment
   a. Cardiopulmonary support (positive end-expiratory pressure [PEEP], oxygen)
   b. Consider methylprednisolone (9 mg/kg)
   c. Early stabilization of fractures

B. Adult respiratory distress syndrome
1. Acute respiratory failure due to non-cardiogenic pulmonary edema
2. Occurs in 2% of patients with multiple trauma, particularly in those with massive trauma, burns, severe head injuries, fat embolism, acute pancreatitis, sepsis, and aspiration pneumonitis
3. Clinical findings
   a. Tachypnea, dyspnea, hypoxemia, and increased pulmonary secretion
   b. Chest x-ray shows bilateral diffuse infiltrates
   c. Thrombocytopenia
4. Treatment
   a. Prevention by early fracture fixation, mobilization, pulmonary oxygenation, nutritional support, and prevention of shock and sepsis
   b. Respiratory support with positive PEEP

C. Compartment syndrome
1. Definition: circulation and function of tissues within a closed space are compromised by increased pressure within that space
2. Compartment syndrome is most common in the leg and the forearm but can occur anywhere, such as the thigh, arm, hand, and foot
3. Irreversible damage to muscle then nerve after ischemia of 6 hours and 12 hours, respectively
4. High index of suspicion is very important
5. Compartment syndrome may occur in open fractures as well
6. Symptoms and signs
   a. Pain that is out of proportion is the most important symptom
   b. Passive movement of the involved muscle and joint that causes pain

and tender swollen hard muscle are the most important signs
c. Paresthesia is frequently present at an early stage of compartment syndrome
d. Paralysis: motor deficit is a late finding and should have done fasciotomy before this stage
e. Pulselessness is rare and a very late finding: must rule out vascular injury if present
7. Wick catheter measurement is important in borderline cases and altered sensorium
a. Do fasciotomy if increasing compartment pressures are noted above 30–40 mmHg range
b. False high reading may be obtained in the hematoma
c. Clinical judgment is the key
8. Risk injuries
a. Fractures of the distal humerus, forearm, and tibia
b. Dislocations of the knee and the elbow
c. Crush injuries, particularly of the hands and feet
d. Prolonged ischemic injuries with vascular compromise
9. Do not elevate the limb
10. Surgery
a. Fasciotomy should be done if clinically suspicious or when the compartment pressure is above 30–40 mmHg
b. Forearm: anterior release including the carpal tunnel. Dorsal compartment or mobile wad compartments need not be released routinely unless they are specifically involved
c. Tibia
(1) Anterior compartment is most commonly involved, but all four compartments should be released in general unless the specific compartment is completely supple and has normal intracompartment pressure
(2) Two-incision technique is favored by most authors: medial incision adjacent to the medial border of the tibia to decompress superficial posterior and deep posterior compartments and lateral incision anterior to the fibular to release the anterior and lateral compartments

REFERENCES

Barbagli G, Selli C, Stomaci N: Urethral trauma: Radiological aspects and treatment options. J Trauma 27:256–261, 1987

Bone LB, Bucholz R: The management of fractures in the patient with multiple trauma. J Bone Joint Surg 68A:945–949, 1986

Bone LB, Johnson KD, Weigelt J: Early versus delayed stabilization of femoral fractures: A prospective randomized study. J Bone Joint Surg 71A:336–340, 1989

Gomez GA, Alvarez R, Plasencia G: Diagnostic peritoneal lavage in the management of blunt abdominal trauma: A reassessment. J Trauma 27:1–5, 1987

Johnson KD, Cadambi A, Seibert GB: Incidence of adult respiratory distress syndrome in patients with multiple musculoskeletal injuries; Effect of early operative stabilization of fractures. J Trauma 24:375–384, 1985

Kallenbach J, Lewis M, Zaltzman M, et al: "Low-dose" corticosteroid prophylaxis against fat embolism. J Trauma 27:1173–1176, 1987

38
Fractures of the Radius and Ulna

I. General Considerations
A. Anatomy
  1. Bony anatomy: radius and ulna are parallel to each other, touching only at the proximal and distal ends of the bones
  2. The radius is mobile and the ulna is static on supination and pronation (120°–140°)
  3. Interosseus membrane: thick fibrous band runs obliquely from distal to proximal and from ulna to radius, preventing upward displacement of the radius (function is still good after radial head excision)
  4. Fractures of upper radius between the biceps-supinator and pronator teres result in supination rotation of the proximal fragment
  5. Fractures distal to the pronator teres will have minimal supination or neutral rotation
B. Treatment principles
  1. Anatomic reduction is essential: length, angulation, rotation
     a. Tuberosity of radius: project medially in supination, posteriorly in midposition, and laterally in full pronation in anteroposterior (AP) view, and project posteriorly in midposition in lateral view
     b. Radial styloid: project laterally in supination in AP view and project anteriorly in midposition seen on lateral view
     c. Coronoid process is directed anteriorly and ulnar styloid is directed posteriorly in midposition on lateral view
     d. Therefore take AP view in full supination and look for radial tuberosity medially and radial styloid laterally and take lateral view in midpronation to look for coronoid process anteriorly and radial tuberosity posteriorly as well as radial styloid anteriorly and ulnar styloid posteriorly
  2. Supination loss is more devastating than pronation because shoulder motion can compensate for lack of pronation (minimum of 50° of motion is required and >20° angulation will result in significant rotational loss)
  3. Open reduction and internal fixation is necessary in displaced forearm fractures in adult

II. Specific Fractures
A. Undisplaced fractures of radius and ulna shafts
  1. Rare
  2. Treatment: long arm cast with elbow in 90° flexion and forearm in neutral position
  3. Close follow-up is important
B. Displaced fractures of radius and ulnar shafts
  1. Closed treatment: 71% poor result and 12% of delayed or nonunion
  2. Open reduction and internal fixation
     a. Dynamic compression plate (DCP) and 3.5 mm screws
        (1) Anatomic reduction
        (2) Mechanical rigid fixation
        (3) Rapid mobilization of joints

b. Anterior approach for the distal radial shaft (between brachioradialis and flexor carpi radialis) and plating on the volar side
  c. Posterior Thompson approach for proximal radial shaft (between extensor digitorum communis and extensor carpi radialis brevis) and plating on the dorsal surface
  d. Subcutaneous border incision for the ulnar shaft between flexor carpi ulnaris and extensor carpi ulnaris
  e. Six cortices in both sides
  f. Bone grafting if comminution greater than 1/3 of the cortex but avoid synostosis
  g. Extraperiosteal dissection and do not close fascia
  h. Removal of plates after 12–18 months except proximal radial plate and protect for 6 weeks
  i. Segmental fractures: double plates for radius and intramedullary nail for ulna or plating
  j. Severe comminuted fractures can be managed with intramedullary nail and cerclage wires and bone grafting
 3. Complications
  a. Infection: more if plated for grade III open fractures
  b. Nonunion: rare if at least 6 screws are used with DCP and bone graft used for comminution and often associated with infection
  c. Compartment syndrome
  d. Neurovascular compromise
  e. Cross-union
C. Open fractures
 1. Debridement and irrigation
 2. Primary fixation and delayed primary closure or delayed primary closure, followed by internal fixation 2 weeks later for types I and II
 3. External fixator or internal fixation for type III after debridement and irrigation
D. Fracture of the ulna alone (nightstick fracture)
 1. Nondisplaced (more common)
  a. Long arm cast for 3 months in 90° elbow flexion and slight supination of the forearm
  b. Functional Sarmiento cast brace or sleeve is probably better (after acute symptoms subside, remove the long arm cast and use functional sleeve and range of motion of the elbow, wrist, and pronation-supination can be done)
 2. Displaced
  a. If >25% and >15°, open reduction and internal fixation with DCP is necessary (plating on the ulnar aspect of ulna)
  b. Intramedullary nail can be considered in distal and middle thirds, especially comminuted fractures
E. Monteggia fractures
 1. Classification (Bado)
  a. Type I: anterior dislocation of the radial head with anteriorly angulated fracture of the ulna (most common type)
  b. Type II: posterior or posterolateral dislocation of the radial head with posteriorly angulated fracture of the ulna
  c. Type III: lateral or anterolateral dislocation of the radial head with ulnar metaphyseal fracture
  d. Type IV: anterior dislocation of the radial head with fractures of the proximal thirds of the radius and ulna
 2. Deep branch of the radial nerve may be injured
 3. Not difficult to miss radial head dislocation
 4. Treatment
  a. Open reduction and rigid internal fixation (DCP) of the ulna
  b. Bone grafting if comminuted
  c. Reduction of the radial head (not

necessary to open the radial head unless infolding of the labrum or telescoping of the radial head behind the lateral epicondyle prevents anatomic reduction)
  d. Long arm cast in 110° elbow flexion except in type II injury only 70° flexion for 6 weeks
F. Fracture of the radius alone (proximal ⅔)
  1. Undisplaced fractures or proximal ⅕ fractures can be treated with long arm cast in supination
  2. Displaced fractures: open reduction and internal fixation (DCP)
G. Fracture of the distal third of radius (Galeazzi)
  1. Associated with dorsal subluxation of the distal ulna
  2. Treatment: open reduction and internal fixation (anterior approach and DCP) and long arm cast in supination for 6 weeks

REFERENCES

Anderson LD, Sisk TD, Tooms RE, et al: Compression plate fixation in acute diaphyseal fractures of the radius and ulna. J Bone Joint Surg 57A:287–297, 1975

Bado JL: The Monteggia lesion. Clin Orthop 50:71–86, 1967

DeLuca PA, Linsey RW, Ruwe PA: Refracture of bones of the forearm after removal of compression plates. J Bone Joint Surg 70A:1372–1376, 1988

Lange RH, Foster RJ: Skeletal management of humeral shaft fractures associated with forearm fractures. Clin Orthop 195:173–177, 1985

Matthews LS, Kaufer H, Garver DF, et al: The effect on supination-pronation of angular malalignment of fractures of both bones of the forearm. J Bone Joint Surg 64A:14–17, 1982

Moed BR, Kellam JF, Foster RJ, et al: Immediate internal fixation of open fractures of the diaphysis of the forearm. J Bone Joint Surg 68A:1008–1016, 1986

Reckling FW: Unstable fracture-dislocations of the forearm (Monteggia and Galeazzi lesions). J Bone Joint Surg 64A:857–863, 1982

Stern PJ, Drury WJ: Complications of plate fixation of forearm fractures. Clin Orthop 175:25–29, 1983

Tarr RR, Garfinkel AI, Sarmiento A: The effects of angular and rotational deformities of both bones of the forearm. J Bone Joint Surg 66A:65–70, 1984

Vince KG, Miller JE: Cross-union complicating fracture of the forearm: Part I. Adults. J Bone Joint Surg 69A:640–653, 1987

39
Fractures and Dislocations of the Elbow

I. Fractures of the Distal End of the Humerus
A. General considerations
1. Types: supracondylar, transcondylar, intercondylar, condyles, capitellum, trochlear, and epicondyles
2. Classification
   a. ASIF (Fig 5-1)
      (1) A2: transverse supracondylar fracture
      (2) A3: comminuted supracondylar fracture
      (3) C1: intercondylar fracture
      (4) C2: comminuted supracondylar and noncomminuted intercondylar fracture
      (5) C3: comminuted supracondylar and comminuted intercondylar fracture
   b. Riseborough and Radin for intercondylar fractures (Fig 5-2)
      (1) Type I: Undisplaced fracture
      (2) Type II: Displaced fracture without rotatory deformity
      (3) Type III: Displaced fracture with rotatory deformity
      (4) Type IV: Comminuted fracture
3. Most displaced fractures are unstable and require open reduction and internal fixation
4. Early motion of the elbow is important (2–3 weeks)
B. Treatment
1. Undisplaced or displaced stable supracondylar fractures: closed reduction and posterior splint with the elbow in 90° flexion and the forearm pronation for the extension type
2. Unstable supracondylar and intercondylar fractures: open reduction and internal fixation
   a. Surgical exposure: prone position and posterior approach
      (1) Campbell: triceps splitting approach for supracondylar area
      (2) Cassebaum: olecranon osteotomy for distal humerus and intra-articular fractures
      (3) Combined approach: olecranon osteotomy and splitting the triceps leaving the ulnar side intact
   b. Internal fixation
      (1) Cancellous type screw to reduce the articular surface anatomically
      (2) Contoured plates are applied either posteriorly, medially, or laterally, depending on the fracture pattern
      (3) Additional K-wire fixation can be done
      (4) The plates must not encroach on the olecranon fossa and screws must not protrude in the coronoid fossa anteriorly
3. Fractures of condyles
   a. Lateral condyle
      (1) Type I: varus stress and avulsion fracture of the lateral condyle with the fracture line lateral to the trochlear ridge
         i. Undisplaced: long arm cast with flexion of the elbow and supination of the forearm
         ii. Displaced: Closed reduction in extension and long arm cast in flexion and supination
      (2) Type II: valgus stress and unsta-

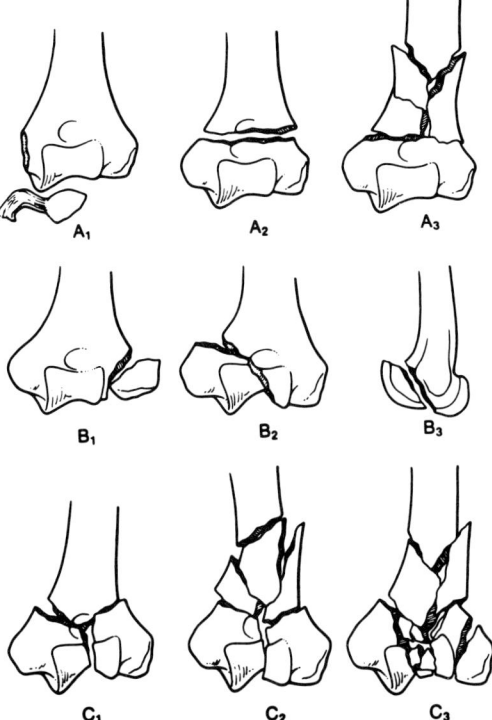

Figure 5-1. AO/ASIF classification of the distal humerus fracture. (From Muller ME, Allgower M, Schneider R, et al: Manual of internal fixation: techniques recommended by the AO group, ed 2. New York, Springer-Verlag, 1979. Reprinted with permission.)

ble fracture of the condyle with the fracture line medial to the trochlear ridge and medial collateral ligament is torn (open reduction and internal fixation with a screw and consider repair of the medial collateral ligament)
   b. Medial condyle
      (1) Type I: lateral trochlear ridge remains intact
         i. Undisplaced: long arm cast with the forearm pronated and wrist and elbow flexed
         ii. Displaced: open reduction and internal fixation if closed reduction cannot be done
      (2) Type II: lateral trochlear ridge is a part of the fractured medial condyle and torn lateral collateral ligament secondary to varus stress (open reduction and internal fixation and rarely repair of the collateral ligament is necessary)
4. Fractures of the articular surface of the distal humerus
   a. Fractures of the capitellum: anterior shear stress from the radial head with anterior and proximal displacement of the fragment
      (1) Type 1 (Hahn-Steinthal): large capitellum fragment and may involve part of the trochlea

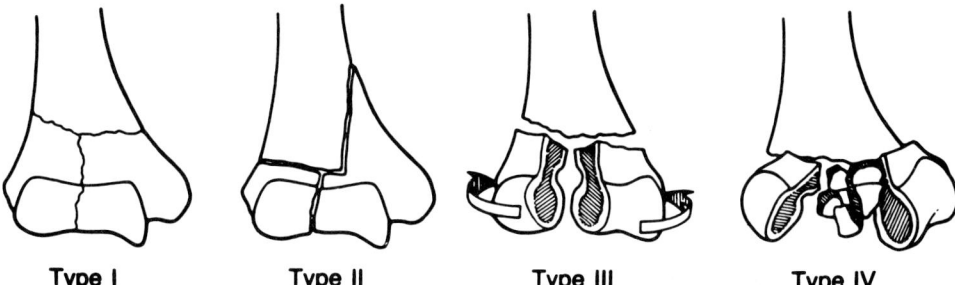

Figure 5-2. Riseborough and Radin's classification of intercondylar fractures. (From Henley MB: Intra-articular distal humeral fractures in adults, Orthop Clin North Am 18:14, 1987. Reprinted with permission.)

(2) Type 2 (Kocher-Lorenz): articular cartilage with small amount of subchondral bone
(3) Treatment
    i. Nondisplaced: posterior splint with elbow flexed and pronated for 2–3 weeks
    ii. Displaced: open reduction and internal fixation for large fragment and excision for small fragment
b. Fractures of the trochlea: "Laugier's fracture"
    (1) Very rare
    (2) Open reduction and internal fixation or excision as appropriate and early motion
5. Fractures of the epicondyles
    a. Fractures of the medial epicondyle
        (1) Closed reduction and long arm cast with the forearm pronated and the elbow and wrist flexed to reduce tension of the pronator-flexors
        (2) Entrapped in the joint associated with the elbow dislocation: arthrotomy and K-wire fixation
    b. Fractures of the lateral epicondyle: extremely rare and long arm cast with the forearm supinated and the wrist dorsiflexed is applied

II. Dislocation of the Elbow

A. General considerations
1. Third most common dislocation after shoulder and finger
2. Most commonly posterior or posterolateral type (80–90%)
3. Anterior oblique portion of the medial collateral ligament is most important for stability
4. Classification
    a. Dislocation of both the radius and ulna
        (1) Posterior (lateral or medial)
        (2) Medial
        (3) Lateral
        (4) Anterior
        (5) Divergent (anteroposterior or divergent)
    b. Dislocation of the radius alone
        (1) Anterior
        (2) Posterior
        (3) Lateral
    c. Dislocation of ulna alone
        (1) Anterior
        (2) Posterior
B. Posterior dislocation of the elbow
1. Mechanism: fall on the outstretched hand with the arm extended and abducted
2. Brachialis artery and nerve (ulnar or median) injuries can occur
3. Ligamentous (both collaterals), muscular (brachialis and triceps) and joint capsule injuries are extensive
4. Associated fractures
    a. Radial head
    b. Coronoid: avulsion of brachialis muscle
    c. Entrapped medial epicondyle
5. Treatment
    a. Prompt reduction is important (slight extension, distraction, pressure on the olecranon)
    b. Posterior splint in 90° flexion and early motion (1 week)
6. Complications
    a. Ligamentous calcification
    b. Myositis ossificans
    c. Neurovascular compromise
    d. Compartment syndrome
    e. Recurrent dislocations
    f. Stiffness

III. Olecranon Fractures

A. General considerations
1. Mechanism: direct blow or indirect as a fall on the outstretched hand with the elbow flexed and contraction of the triceps muscle
2. Swelling and hemarthrosis, inability to extend the elbow and occasional ulnar nerve injury

3. Anatomy: anterior oblique medial collateral ligament attaches to the coronoid process (if the fracture line is proximal to the coronoid process, excision of the fragment and attachment of the triceps tendon to the bone may be done without significant loss of stability)
B. Classification
  1. Undisplaced
  2. Displaced
     a. Avulsion fractures
     b. Oblique and transverse
     c. Comminuted
     d. Fracture-dislocations
C. Treatment
  1. Undisplaced: long arm cast with the elbow about 45°–90° flexion and early range of motion (3 weeks)
  2. Avulsion: excision of the fragment and repair of the triceps
  3. Transverse fractures: tension band wiring or screw plus a figure-of-eight wire
  4. Oblique fractures: cancellous screw plus tension band wiring
  5. Comminuted: excision of the fragments and repair of the triceps or open reduction and internal fixation, using combination of screws, plate, and tension band wire
  6. Fracture-dislocations: open reduction and internal fixation with screws or intramedullary device

IV. Radial Head Fractures
A. Mechanism: indirect as a fall on the outstretched hand with longitudinal thrust of the radius against the capitellum or direct force
B. Classification (Mason)
  1. Type I (undisplaced)
  2. Type II (marginal fractures with displacement, including impaction, depression, angulation)
  3. Type III (comminuted fractures involving the entire head)
  4. Type IV (associated elbow dislocation)
C. Treatment
  1. Type I: aspiration of the joint and early range of motion (2–3 days)
  2. Type II: controversial
     a. Trial of conservative treatment (early motion) for 3 weeks and assess excision of the radial head if symptomatic (late excisions are successful in 80%)
     b. Primary fixation (K-wires or Herbert screws) if half of the radial head remains to provide stability
  3. Type III: Early primary excision
  4. Type IV: Reduction of elbow dislocation and excision or repair of the radial head
  5. Radial head prosthesis is controversial but may be used if
     a. Posterior dislocation of the elbow combined with radial head or capitellum comminution
     b. Essex-Lopresti type injury, where distal radioulnar joint is injured and proximal migration of the radius is expected
     c. Medial collateral ligament is injured along with comminuted fracture of the radial head
     d. Long-term results are unpredictable

REFERENCES

An KN, Morrey BF, Chao EY: The effect of partial removal of proximal ulna on elbow constraint. Clin Orthop 209:270–279, 1986

Broberg MA, Morrey BF: Results of delayed excision of the radial head after fracture. J Bone Joint Surg 68A:669–674, 1986

Cassebaum WH: Open reduction of T and Y fractures of the lower end of the humerus. J Trauma 9:915–925, 1969

Coleman DA, Blair WF, Shurr D: Resection of the radial head for fracture of the radial head: Long-term follow-up of seventeen cases. J Bone Joint Surg 69A:385–392, 1987

DeLee JC, Green DP, Wilkin KE: Fractures and dislocations of the elbow. In Rockwood CA, Green DP, eds. Fractures in Adults, ed 2, vol 1. Philadelphia, JB Lippincott, 1984, pp 559–652

Fyfe IS, Mossad MM, Holdsworth BJ: Methods of fixation of olecranon fractures: An experimental mechanical study. J Bone Joint Surg 67B:367–372, 1985

Goldberg I, Peylan J, Yosipovitch Z: Late results of excision of the radial head for an isolated closed fracture. J Bone Joint Surg 68A:675–679, 1986

Josefsson PO, Gentz CF, Johnell O: Surgical versus nonsurgical treatment of ligamentous injuries following dislocations of the elbow joint. Clin Orthop 214:165–169, 1987

Josefsson PO, Johnell O, Gentz CF: Long-term sequelae of simple dislocation of the elbow. J Bone Joint Surg 66A:927–930, 1984

Jupiter JB, Neff U, Hozach P, et al: Intercondylar fractures of the humerus: An operative approach. J Bone Joint Surg 67A:226–239, 1985

McArthur RA: Herbert screw fixation of fracture of the head of the radius. Clin Orthop 224:79–87, 1987

Mehlhoff TL, Noble PC, Bennett JB, et al: Simple dislocation of the elbow in the adult: Results after closed treatment. J Bone Joint Surg 70A:244–249, 1988

Miller GK, Drennan DB, Maylahn DJ: Treatment of displaced segmental radial-head fractures. J Bone Joint Surg 63A:712–717, 1981

Morrey BF, Askew L, Chao EY: Silastic prosthetic replacement for the radial head. J Bone Joint Surg 63A:454–458, 1981

Mueller ME, Allgower M, Schneider R, et al: Manual of internal fixation. New York, Springer-Verlag, 1979

Murphy DF, Greene WB, Dameron TB Jr: Displaced olecranon fractures in adults: Clinical evaluation. Clin Orthop 224:215–223, 1987

Riseborough EJ, Radin EL: Intercondylar T fractures of the humerus in the adult: A comparison of operative and nonoperative treatment in 29 cases. J Bone Joint Surg 51A:130–141, 1969

Wolfgang G, Burke F, Bush D, et al: Surgical treatment of displaced olecranon fractures by tension-band wiring technique. Clin Orthop 224:192–204, 1987

Zagorsi JB, Jennings JJ, Burkhalter WE, et al: Comminuted intra-articular fractures of the distal humeral condyles: Surgical vs nonsurgical treatment. Clin Orthop 202:197–204, 1986

40
Fractures of the Humeral Shaft

I. General Considerations
A. Anatomy (Fig 5-3)
   1. Fracture line between the rotator cuff insertion and pectoralis major: abduction and internal rotation of the proximal fragment
   2. Fracture line between the pectoralis major insertion and deltoid: adduction of proximal fragment
   3. Fracture line below the deltoid attachment: abduction of the proximal fragment
B. Mechanism of injury: falls and direct blow
C. Radial nerve palsy with distal shaft fracture: Lewis-Holstein type

II. Treatment
A. Hanging cast
   1. Cast from 1 inch proximal to the fracture site to the wrist
   2. Erect or semierect position
   3. Best for displaced fractures with shortening and spiral type and not good for proximal shaft fractures and transverse and distracted types
   4. Loop on the dorsum of the wrist
      a. Anterior angulation: shorten the suspension
      b. Posterior angulation: lengthen the suspension
      c. Varus angulation: place the loop on the dorsum of the wrist
      d. Valgus angulation: place the loop on the more volar aspect of the wrist
B. Coaptation splint
   1. U-shaped coaptation splint with a collar and cuff
   2. Best for transverse and distraction types
   3. Easier to reapply when swelling subsides
C. Skin or skeletal traction: severe open fractures and patients who require bed rest
D. Shoulder spica cast: unstable fractures with comminution and delayed union cases
E. Functional bracing: orthoplast or polypropylene with Velcro straps or cast brace
F. External fixation: severe open fractures, infected nonunion, bone loss, burn patients, and concomitant fracture in the forearm when early mobilization is necessary
G. Operative methods
   1. Indication
      a. Multiple trauma patients (ipsilateral forearm or elbow fractures, bilateral humerus fractures, and lower extremity fractures)
      b. Inadequate reduction after closed treatment
      c. Head or spinal cord injury patients
      d. Parkinson patients
      e. Pathologic fractures
      f. Open fractures
      g. Vascular injury
      h. Neurologic injury: if manipulation or closed treatment caused the neurologic deficit
   2. Plate fixation: rigid and good for nonunion cases and distal shaft fractures
   3. Intramedullary rods
      a. Enders, Rush, or Küntscher

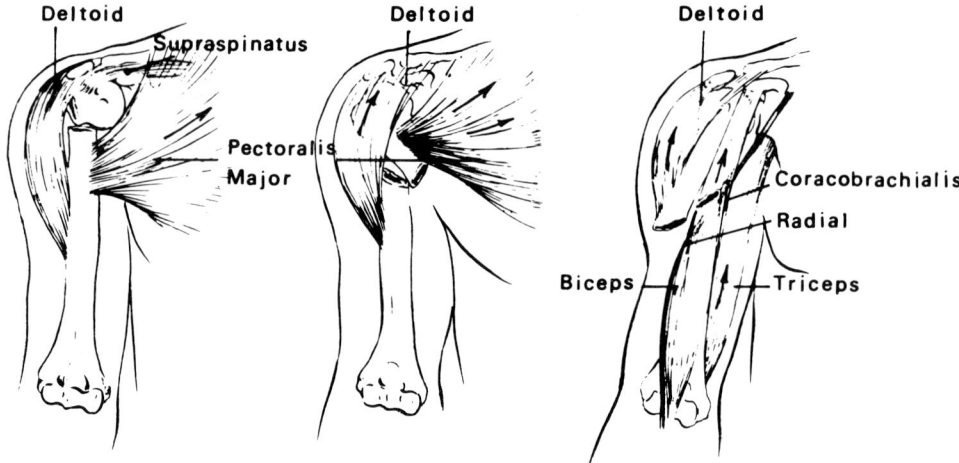

Figure 5-3. Anatomic factors that influence deformities in fractures of the humeral shaft. Left: Proximal fracture causes adduction and slight internal rotation. Center: Fracture between pectoralis major and deltoid produces adduction of proximal fragment. Right: Fracture below deltoid insertion causes abduction of proximal fragment. (From Epps CH: Fractures of the shaft of the humerus. In Rockwood CA, Green DP, eds. Fractures in adults, ed 2. Philadelphia, JB Lippincott 1984, p 654. Reprinted with permission.)

b. Good for proximal fractures and when alignment is the critical factor

III. Prognostic Factors

A. Type of fracture: transverse or segmental fractures heal slower
B. Fractures close to the elbow or shoulder joint are more difficult to manage
C. Open fractures: infection, osteomyelitis, or nonunion
D. Interposition of soft tissue
E. Neurovascular compromise
F. Ipsilateral fracture of the shoulder or forearm

IV. Complications

A. Radial nerve palsy: 5–10% but surgical exploration not necessary unless no improvement in 3 months
B. Vascular complications: stabilize the fracture first then repair the artery unless the ischemic time is prolonged
C. Nonunion: especially in transverse type, distraction at the fracture site and soft tissue interposition. Treatment for nonunion should be done if no healing in 4 months (plating or intramedullary nailing with bone grafting)
D. Malunion: up to 20° anterior angulation and 30° varus angulation and shortening of 1 inch may be acceptable

REFERENCES

Balfour GW, Mooney V, Ashby M: Diaphyseal fractures of the humerus treated with a ready-made fracture brace. J Bone Joint Surg 64A:11–13, 1982

Brumback RJ, Bosse MJ, Poka A, et al: Intramedullary stabilization of humeral shaft fractures in patients with multiple trauma. J Bone Joint Surg 68A:960–970, 1986

Christensen NO: Kuntschner intramedullary reaming and nail fixation for nonunion of the humerus. Clin Orthop 116:222–226, 1976

Dubin RA, Gottesman MJ, Saunders KC: Hackenthal stacked nailing of humeral shaft fractures. Clin Orthop 179:168–174, 1983

Epps CH; Fractures of the shaft of the humerus. In Rockwood CA, Green DP, eds. Fractures in adults, ed 2, vol 1. Philadelphia, JB Lippincott, 1984

Foster RJ, Dixon GL, Back AW, et al: Internal fixation of fractures and nonunions of the humeral shaft. Indications and results in a multicenter study. J Bone Joint Surg 67A:857–864, 1985

Hall RJ Jr, Pankovich AM: Ender nailing of acute fractures of the humerus: A study of closed fixation by intramedullary nails without reaming. J Bone Joint Surg 69A:558–567, 1987

Healy WL, Whiter GM, Mick CA, et al: Nonunions of the humeral shaft. Clin Orthop 219:206–213, 1987

Holstein A, Lewis G: Fractures of the humerus with radial nerve paralysis. J Bone Joint Surg 45A: 1382–1388, 1963

Klenerman L: Fractures of the shaft of the humerus. J Bone Joint Surg 48B:105–111, 1966

Lange RH, Foster RJ: Skeletal management of humeral shaft fractures associated with forearm fractures. Clin Orthop 195:173–177, 1985

Pollock FH, Drake D, Bovill DG, et al: Treatment of radial neuropathy associated with fractures of the humerus. J Bone Joint Surg 63A:239–243, 1981

Sarmiento A, Kinman PB, Calvin EG, et al: Functional bracing of fractures of the shaft of the humerus. J Bone Joint Surg 59A:596–601, 1977

Stern PJ, Mattingly DA, Pomeroy DL, et al: Intramedullary fixation of humeral shaft fractures. J Bone Joint Surg 66A:639–646, 1984

41
Fractures and Dislocations of the Shoulder

I. Fractures About the Shoulder
A. Fractures of the proximal humerus
 1. Mechanism: fall on outstretched arm
 2. Classification (Neer) (Fig 5-4)
    a. Parts: anatomic neck, greater tuberosity, lesser tuberosity, and surgical neck
    b. Displacement: significant if >45° angulation or 1 cm displacement
 3. X-ray: AP, scapular Y, and axillary views
 4. Treatment
    a. Minimal displacement: sling and swathe and early range of motion
    b. Two-part
       (1) Displaced anatomic neck: open reduction and internal fixation with screw
       (2) Shaft displacement (surgical neck fractures): closed reduction and immobilization or may need percutaneous pinning, Enders nailing or buried Rush rods or open reduction in unstable fractures
       (3) Greater tuberosity: open reduction and internal fixation (heavy sutures or wires) with cuff repairs
       (4) Lesser tuberosity: Velpeau sling
    c. Three part: open reduction and internal fixation but consider prosthesis in older patients (>70 years old) with poor bone stock
    d. Four part: prosthesis with tuberosity fixation and cuff repair
    e. Fracture-dislocation
       (1) Anterior: closed or open reduction and internal fixation and cuff repair for two part and three part and prosthesis for four part
       (2) Posterior: reduction and immobilization at side in slight external rotation for two part and reduction and fixation for three part and prosthesis for four part
    f. Articular fractures (impression fractures)
       (1) If 20%, cast in slight external rotation
       (2) If 20–40%, closed reduction, transplant lesser tuberosity with subscapularis into the humeral defect
       (3) If >50%, prosthesis
    g. Head-splitting fractures: prosthesis with cuff repair
 5. Complications
    a. Joint stiffness
    b. Malunion, nonunion
    c. Avascular necrosis
    d. Myositis ossificans
    e. Neurovascular compromise
B. Fractures of the clavicle
 1. Mechanism: lateral force causes shear force
 2. Classification (Neer)
    a. Middle third: 80%
    b. Proximal third: 5%
    c. Distal third: 15%
       (1) Type I: minimal displacement with intact coracoclavicular ligament
       (2) Type II: displaced and the coracoclavicular ligament is detached proximally
       (3) Type III: fracture into the acroclavicular joint

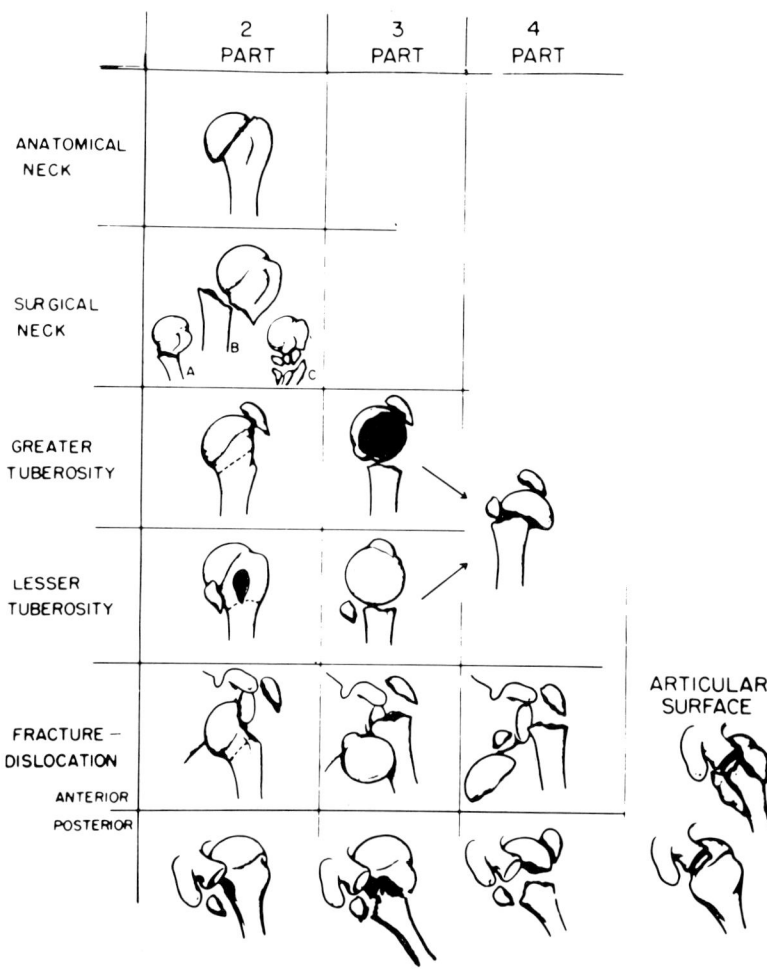

Figure 5-4. Neer classification of fractures of the proximal humerus (Neer CS II, Rockwood CA: Fractures and dislocations of the shoulder. In Rockwood CA, Green DP, eds. Fractures in adults, ed 2. Philadelphia, JB Lippincott, 1984, p 678. Reprinted with permission.)

   3. Treatment
     a. Middle: figure-of-eight splint or sling
     b. Proximal and distal type I: sling
     c. Distal type III: late excision if symptomatic
     d. Distal type II: coracoclavicular fixation with screw or tape and supplemented with transacromial pin
C. Fractures of the scapula
   1. Body and spine
     a. Associated with other injuries such as thorax, ribs, and clavicle (up to 87%)
     b. Treatment: sling and swathe and early motion
   2. Intrathoracic scapular dislocation (locked scapula)
     a. Lower angle locked between ribs
     b. Treatment: closed reduction and scapular taping and sling
   3. Neck fractures: olecranon pin traction vs early functional exercises
   4. Glenoid
     a. In 20% of traumatic shoulder dislocation
     b. Treatment: open reduction for intra-articular incongruity

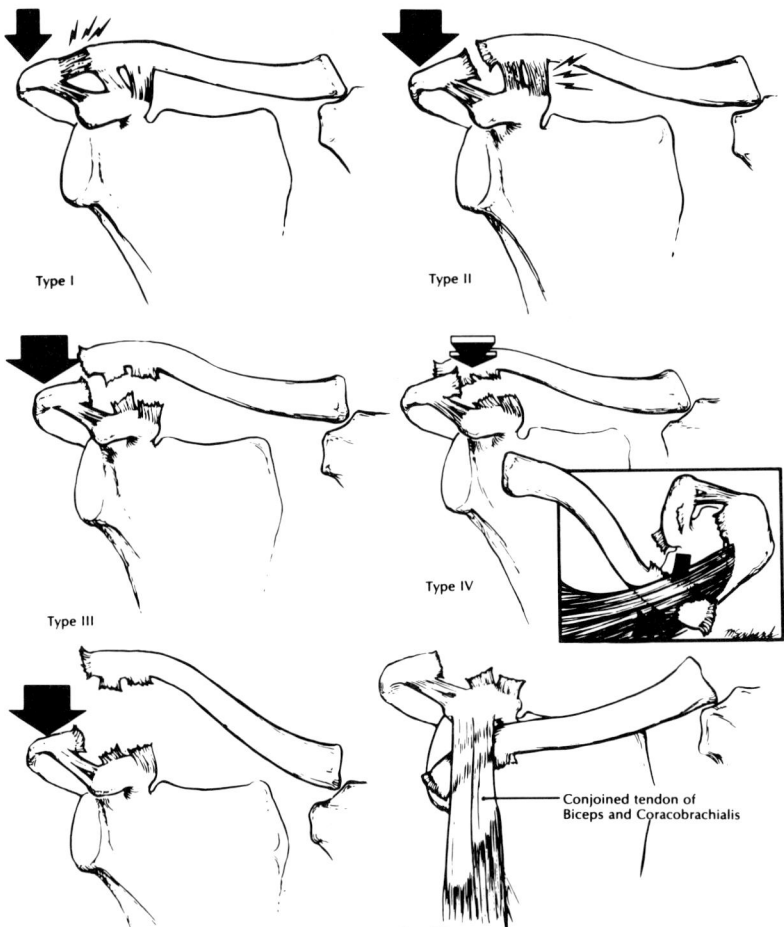

Figure 5-5. Neer classification of injuries to the acromioclavicular injuries. (Neer CS II, Rockwood CA, Fractures and dislocations of the shoulder. In Rockwood CA, Green DP, eds. Fractures in adults, ed 2. Philadelphia, JB Lippincott, 1984, p 871. Reprinted with permission.)

    5. Acromion
       a. Associated with rotator cuff tears
       b. Treatment: sling and early range of motion. Displaced fractures require elevation and K-wire fixation
    6. Coracoid
       a. Suprascapular nerve may be involved and early exploration is recommended
       b. Conservative treatment in most cases except associated acromioclavicular separation

D. Acromioclavicular separation
    1. Classification (Neer) (Fig 5-5)
       a. Type 1: Sprain of acromioclavicular ligament
       b. Type II: Rupture of acromioclavicular ligament with intact coracoclavicular ligament
       c. Type III: Rupture of both acromioclavicular and coracoclavicular ligaments
       d. Type IV: Posterior displacement into the trapezius muscle

  e. Type V: Severe superior displacement with deltoid and trapezius detached from the distal clavicle
  f. Type VI: Inferior dislocation of the distal clavicle
 2. Treatment
  a. Nonoperative treatment for types I to III (sling or Kenny-Howard splint)
  b. Surgery for types IV to VI
  c. Occasionally, surgery may be performed in patients with type III injuries, who are thin, active, and do overhead activities
   (1) Open reduction, excision of the intra-articular disc
   (2) Two-threaded pin fixation
   (3) Capsular and ligament repair
E. Injuries to the sternoclavicular joint
 1. Anterior dislocation (95%) and posterior dislocation (5%)
 2. Fracture of the physis of the distal clavicle (Salter type I or II) until 20 years old
 3. X-ray view: 40° inclination view (serendipity view)
  a. Anterior dislocation: clavicle is seen above
  b. Posterior dislocation: clavicle is seen below
 4. Treatment
  a. Anterior dislocation: conservative treatment (reduction maneuver usually fails to maintain and surgical stabilization should be avoided)
  b. Posterior dislocation: urgent problem with high complication rate such as pneumothorax, superior vena cava injury, and subcutaneous emphysema
   (1) Closed reduction: arm over side of the table and abduction and extension maneuver
   (2) Towel clip may be necessary
   (3) Stable reduction is usual
F. Scapulothoracic dissociation
 1. Severe lateral traction injury to the shoulder girdle
 2. Underlying brachial plexus and vascular injuries with intact skin
 3. Three types: sternoclavicular disruption, clavicle fractures, and acromioclavicular dissociation
 4. Prompt recognition and exploration of the neurovascular structures are important

REFERENCES

Ebraheim NA, An HS, Jackson WT, et al: Scapulothoracic dissociation. J Bone Joint Surg 70A:428–433, 1988

Galpin RD, Hawkins RJ, Grainger RW: A comparative analysis of operative versus nonoperative treatment of grade III acromioclavicular separations. Clin Orthop 193:150–155, 1985

Hardegger FH, Simpson LA, Weber BG: The operative treatment of scapular fractures. J Bone Joint Surg 66B:725, 1984

Hawkins RJ, Bell RH, Gurr K: The three-part fracture of the proximal part of the humerus: Operative treatment. J Bone Joint Surg 68A:1410–1414, 1986

Jupiter JB, Leffert RD: Non-union of the clavicle: Associated complications and surgical management. J Bone Joint Surg 69A:753–760, 1987

Larsen E, Bjerg-Nielsen A, Christensen P: Conservative or surgical treatment of acromioclavicular dislocation: A prospective, controlled, randomized study. J Bone Joint Surg 68A:552–555, 1986

Manske DJ, Szabo RM: The operative treatment of mid-shaft clavicular non-unions. J Bone Joint Surg 67A:1367–1371, 1985

Neer CS II: Displaced proximal humeral fractures. I. Classification and evaluation. J Bone Joint Surg 52A:1077–1090, 1970

Neer CS II, Rockwood CA: Fractures and dislocations of the shoulder. In Rockwood CA, Green DP, eds. Fractures in adults, ed 2, vol 1. Philadelphia, JB Lippincott, 1984

Selesnick FH, Jablon M, Frank C, et al: Retrosternal dislocation of the clavicle. J Bone Joint Surg 66A:287–291, 1984

Stableforth PG: Four-part fractures of the neck of the humerus. J Bone Joint Surg 66B:104–108, 1984

Taft TN, Wilson FC, Oglesby JW: Dislocation of the acromioclavicular joint: An end-result study. J Bone Joint Surg 69A:1045–1051, 1987

Tanner NW, Cofield RH: Prosthetic arthroplasty for fractures and fracture-dislocations of the proximal humerus. Clin Orthop 179:116–128, 1983

Wilkins RM, Johnston RM: Ununited fractures of the clavicle. J Bone Joint Surg 65A:773–778, 1983

42

Fractures of the Pelvis and Acetabulum

PELVIC FRACTURES

I. Anatomy

A. Pelvis is a ring made up of innominate bones and sacrum connected by ligaments
B. Innominate is made up of ilium, ischium, and pubis
C. Structural stability
   1. Major weight-bearing lines transmitted across sacroiliac joints into neck of femurs, therefore major stabilization is posterior
   2. Anterior stability is by the symphysis pubis acting as a strut (opening >2.5 cm disrupts the sacrospinous ligament) or the ischiopubic ramus
   3. Posterior sacroiliac joint: most critical structure for pelvic stability (disrupted in shear injuries)
      a. Hyaline cartilage between ilium and sacrum but not truly synovial
      b. Movement markedly restricted by ligaments
         (1) Interosseous sacroiliac ligaments
         (2) Posterior sacroiliac ligament bands
         (3) Anterior sacroiliac ligaments
D. Connecting ligaments
   1. Sacrotuberous ligament: from dorsal sacrum and posterior superior or inferior iliac spines to ischial tuberosity (resists shear force)
   2. Sacrospinous ligament: from lateral sacrum and coccyx, deep to sacrotuberous ligament, and to ischial spine (divides ischial area into greater and lesser sciatic foramens and resists external rotation force)
   3. Iliolumbar ligaments: from fifth lumbar transverse process to iliac crests, and is the thickened portion of the fascia of the quadratus lumborum
   4. Lateral lumbosacral ligament: fifth lumbar transverse process to ala of the sacrum (its sharp medial edge may abut against the anterior ramus of the fifth lumbar root)
   5. All the posterior-placed ligaments resist tension, acting as a tension band, transversely-placed bands resist rotation, and vertical bands resist shear
E. Injury patterns (Fig 5-6)
   1. External rotation (open book type)
      a. Anterior or posterior force
      b. Opening of the symphysis pubis
      c. Sacrospinous ligament may be disrupted if >2.5 cm opening
   2. Lateral compression
      a. Either via iliac crest or greater trochanter
      b. Associated with acetabular fracture and internal rotation of the pelvis
      c. Major lateral thrust is through the posterior sacroiliac ligaments. Bone tends to compress before the ligaments rupture, resulting in a stable injury
   3. Shear
      a. Force that crosses perpendicular to trabecular pattern of the posterior pelvic complex (sacrum, sacroiliac joint, or adjacent ilium) in the vertical plane
      b. Marked displacement with unstable pelvic ring
      c. Posterior displacement of sacroiliac

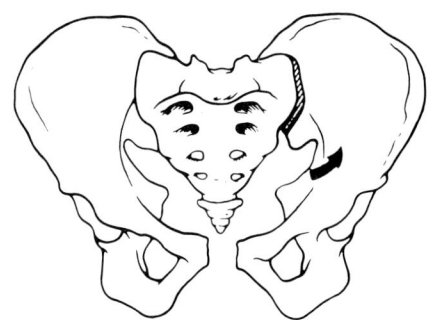 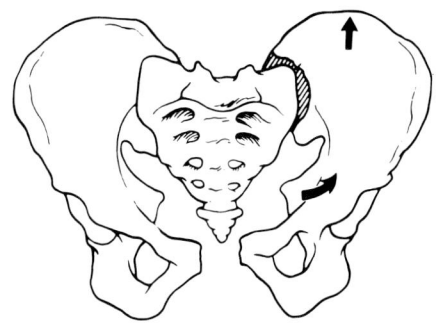

Figure 5-6. Pelvic fractures. Left: Stable open book injury. Right: Unstable shear injury. (From Bucholz RW, Orthopaedic trauma. In Bucholz RW, Lippert FG, Wenger DR, Ezaki M, eds. Orthopaedic decision making. Philadelphia, BC Decker, and St Louis, CV Mosby, 1984, p 28. Reprinted with permission.)

joint >1 cm indicates complete ligamentous disruption

II. Clinical Findings

A. History is important in finding out the mechanism of injury
B. Physical examination
  1. Open wounds, contusions
  2. Genitorectal examination to diagnose occult open fractures, urethral injury in males, and sphincter problems
  3. Neurovascular examination: lumbosacral plexus or cauda equina injuries
  4. Lower extremity internally rotated in lateral compression injury, whereas lower extremity tends to be externally rotated in shear type fracture
  5. Pelvic manipulation may help to assess the stability of the fracture
C. Radiologic assessment
  1. AP view
     a. Good in acute situation but often insufficient
     b. Look for avulsion of fifth lumbar transverse process, which often indicates posterior instability
     c. Avulsion of the ischeal spine is sometimes seen in AP injuries
  2. Inlet view
     a. With patient supine, 60° from cephalad to caudad
     b. Best view of AP displacement
  3. Outlet view
     a. Patient supine, 45° directed from foot to symphysis
     b. Shows superior displacement of posterior pelvis and inferior displacement of anterior pelvis
     c. Sacral fractures are also detected
  4. CT scan: an excellent complementary test, particularly to define the sacroiliac disruptions
  5. Urethrogram prior to Foley insertion if blood at the meatus or high-riding prostate. Cystogram and postvoiding view to diagnose bladder injuries

III. Classification (Tile)

A. Type A
  1. A1: fractures of the pelvis not involving the ring, such as avulsion injuries in adolescents and pubic rami fractures in the elderly
  2. A2: stable, minimally displaced fractures of the ring
B. Type B: rotationally unstable but vertically stable
  1. B1: open book
     a. Stage 1: <2.5 cm
     b. Stage 2: >2.5 cm (sacrospinous and anterior part of sacroiliac ligament is disrupted)
     c. Stage 3: bilateral lesion

2. B2: lateral compression
3. B3: contralateral (bucket handle)
C. Type C: rotationally and vertically unstable
   1. C1: unilateral
   2. C2: bilateral
   3. C3: associated with an acetabular fracture

IV. Treatment
A. Resuscitation of hemorrhagic patients
   1. Pneumatic antishock garment (PASG)
      a. Hemostatic (tamponade)
      b. Increased peripheral vascular resistance
      c. Disadvantage: decreased access to abdomen, lower extremities, and may cause compartment syndromes of the leg
   2. Reduction and external stabilization of the fracture is the best
   3. Angiography and embolization if arterial bleeding is persistent despite external fixation
   4. Open surgery
      a. Open fracture may be associated with mortality rate up to 50%, but mortality rate is dropping with better care
      b. Diverting colostomy or suprapubic bladder catheter should be considered in open injuries
      c. Emergency open surgery may be necessary if hemorrhage cannot be controlled by other means (avoid decompression of retroperitoneal hematoma)
B. Management of pelvic fracture
   1. Minimal displacement
      a. Bed rest
      b. Prevent bedsores (turning) and deep vein prophylaxis
   2. Significant displacement
      a. AP compression — reduction, close the book
         (1) Stage I: usually bed rest will suffice
         (2) Stage II or III (>2.5 cm opening): pelvic sling is difficult for nursing care and hip spica is awkward. External skeletal fixator is method of choice. Internal fixation is indicated, especially if laparotomy is done and no contamination
      b. Lateral compression
         (1) B2: elastic recoil of the pelvis usually restores the anatomy to near normal and no form of stabilization is required
         (2) B3: reduction could make the fracture unstable. An unacceptable amount of shortening (>1.5 cm) and significant malrotation may call for reduction and stabilization
            i. Closed reduction and external fixator
            ii. Open reduction and internal fixation: rare (only in young patient with severe shortening and malrotation, or if acetabulum involved or symphysis locked)
   3. Grossly unstable fractures: shear injuries
      a. Partial anterior stabilization with external fixation or plate followed by posterior stabilization with internal fixation
      b. Screws, sacral bar, or fluoroscopic or CT-guided percutaneous methods
         (1) Unilateral fractured ilium: interfragmentary compression and neutralization plate
         (2) For unilateral sacroiliac dislocation: cancellous screws through the joint or anterior plate fixation
         (3) For sacral fracture: two sacral bars from the posterior superior iliac spines
         (4) Bilateral disruptions: must fix into the sacrum

FRACTURES OF THE ACETABULUM

I. Anatomy
A. Posterior column is strong and most suitable for internal fixation
   1. Inner surface: quadrilateral area
   2. Posterior surface: nonarticular posterior wall
   3. Anterior surface: posterior articular surface
B. Anterior column: from iliac crest to pubis, including anterior wall but not the anterior inferior iliac spine
C. Superior dome: from the anterior inferior iliac spine to posterior column

II. Biomechanics
A. Fractures caused by driving femoral head into pelvis
   1. Look for damage to the femoral head
   2. Associated patella and/or posterior cruciate injuries
B. Position of femoral head important
   1. Flexion: posterior wall fracture and/or posterior dislocated hip
   2. External rotation: anterior wall damage
   3. Internal rotation: posterior damage
   4. Abducted: inferomedial wall damage
   5. Adducted: superolateral area damage

III. Classification (Letournel) (Fig 5-7)
A. Posterior types with or without posterior dislocation (frequent dashboard injury, and associated with sciatic palsy and avascular necrosis)
   1. Posterior column fractures
      a. Greater sciatic notch through acetabulum to inferior pubic ramus
      b. Displacement seen on obturator and iliac oblique views
      c. Hip incongruency common; therefore open reduction and internal fixation recommended

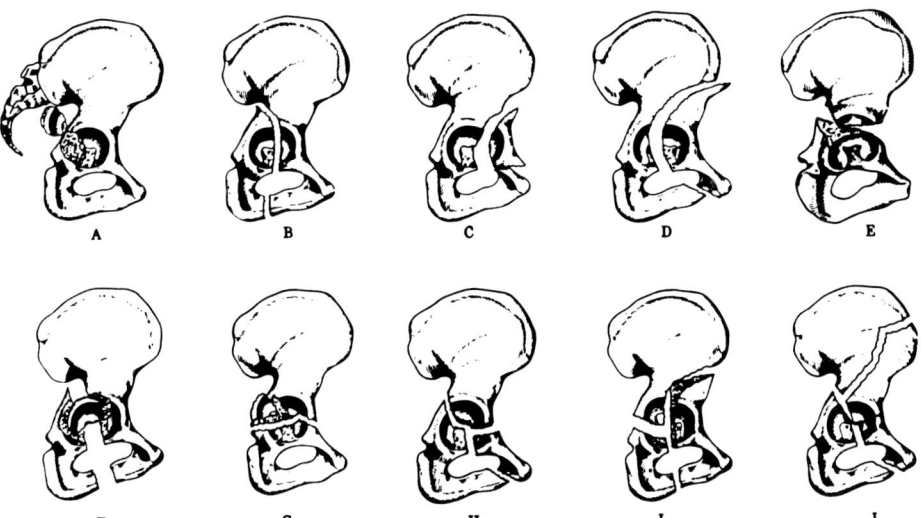

Figure 5-7. Classification of Letournel. **A.** Posterior wall fracture. **B.** Posterior column fracture. **C.** Anterior wall fracture. **D.** Anterior column fracture. **E.** Transverse fracture. **F.** Associated posterior column and posterior wall fracture. **G.** Associated transverse and posterior wall fracture. **H.** T-shaped fracture. **I.** Associated anterior column and posterior hemitransverse fracture. **J.** Both column fracture. (From Matta JM, Merritt PO: Trauma: Pelvis and acetabulum. In American Academy of Orthopaedic Surgeons, Orthopaedic Knowledge Update 2. 1987, p 348. Reprinted with permission.)

2. Posterior wall fractures
   a. Involves portion of posterior articular surface
   b. Open reduction and internal fixation mandatory if fragment large
3. Posterior wall with posterior column: open reduction and internal fixation
4. Posterior wall with transverse fractures
   a. Common: 20% of all cases
   b. Open reduction and internal fixation needed
   c. Identification of posterior injury important because of risk of avascular necrosis and sciatic problems

B. Anterior types with or without anterior dislocation
   1. Anterior column fractures
      a. Through superior pubic ramus
      b. Prognosis good because not weight bearing
      c. If extends to superior dome, then open reduction and internal fixation
   2. Anterior wall fractures: rare
   3. Anterior wall fractures and anterior column and/or transverse fractures (anterior column posterior hemitransverse)

C. Transverse types with or without central dislocation
   1. Pure transverse fractures
      a. A division through both columns
      b. Displacement can be mild to complete central dislocation of femoral head into the pelvis
   2. T-fractures
      a. With the transverse fracture, usually splits the acetabulum vertically
      b. Vertical component may go anterior or posterior to the obturator foramen
      c. More violent injury than pure transverse type
      d. "T" component is of great significance because the reduction of one column will not reduce the other, as it would in a pure transverse type
   3. Transverse and acetabular wall fractures
      a. Characteristics determined by the wall injury rather than the transverse component
      b. Superior dome involvement is significant
   4. Double column fractures
      a. "Floating acetabulum" not attached to axial skeleton
      b. Fracture divides both columns above level of acetabulum
      c. Spur sign is characteristic
      d. Reduction of the ilium is the key

IV. Radiographic Examination
A. AP pelvic view
B. Acetabular views (AP and Judet views)
   1. AP view — all major landmarks can be seen (Fig 5-8)
   2. Obturator oblique view (internal rotation) (Fig 5-9)
      a. Outlines anterior column
      b. Posterior lip or wall
      c. Iliac wing in lateral — see spur sign in double-column injuries
   3. Iliac oblique view (external rotation) (Fig 5-10)
      a. Outlines posterior column
      b. Anterior wall of acetabulum
      c. Full expansion of iliac wing
C. CT scan or three-dimensional CT
   1. Fractures of the wall and fragments in the joint
   2. Degree of comminution is better appreciated
D. Indications for surgery
   1. Joint incongruity
   2. Superior dome fractures
   3. Hip instability
   4. If a sciatic lesion develops with reduction of the hip
   5. If associated with ipsilateral femur fracture
   6. Polytraumatized patient

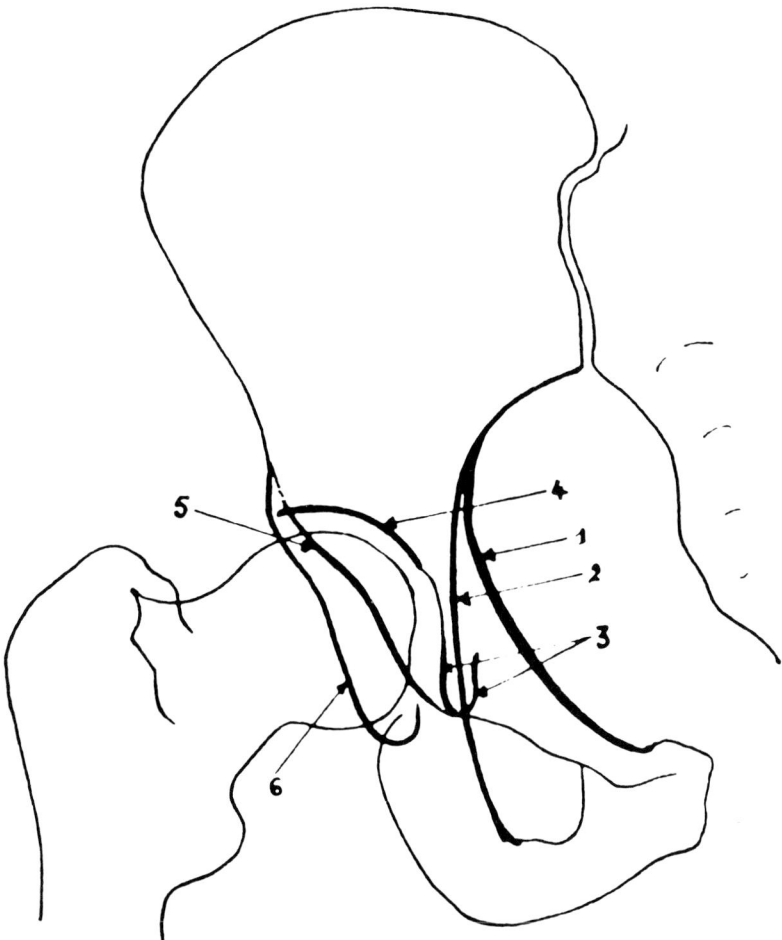

Figure 5-8. Anteroposterior view of the acetabulum. 1: Iliopectineal line; 2: ilioischial line; 3: radiographic "U" or "tear drop," 4: acetabular roof; 5: anterior rim; 6: posterior rim (From Matta JM, Merritt PO: Trauma: pelvis and acetabulum. In: American Academy of Orthopaedic Surgeons, Orthopaedic Knowledge Update 2. 1987, p 347. Reprinted with permission.)

E. Contraindications
 1. Medically unstable
 2. Severely comminuted fracture
 3. Inexperienced surgical team

V. Management

A. Undisplaced and stable fractures: conservative management
B. Prompt reduction if associated hip dislocation
 1. Any dislocation, especially posterior, is an emergency
 2. Ideally closed reduction should be done under general anesthesia and fluoroscopy
 3. Open reduction and internal fixation in 2–5 days
C. Skeletal traction while awaiting surgery
D. Fractures in which closed methods may maintain congruity are low anterior column, low transverse, double column, medial wall fractures, and fractures where closed methods are likely to fail are all posterior types, high transverse or T

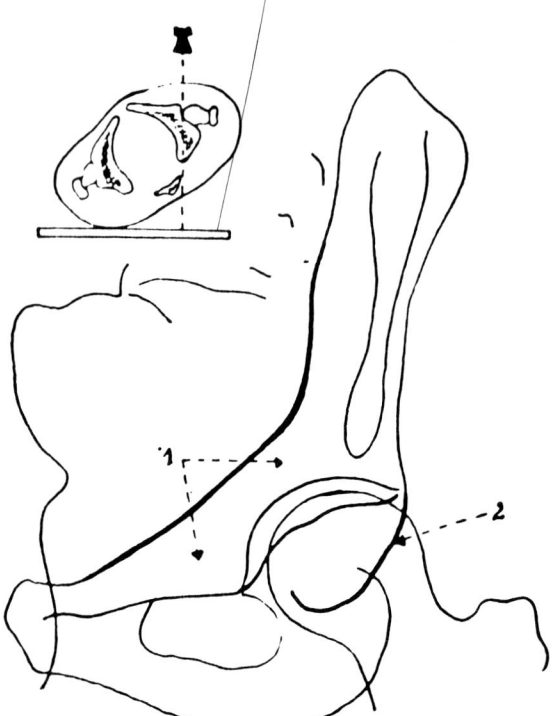

Figure 5-9. Judet obturator (internal oblique) view of the acetabulum. 1: Anterior column; 2: posterior rim. (From Matta JM, Merritt PO: Trauma: Pelvis and acetabulum. In American Academy of Orthopaedic Surgeons, Orthopaedic Knowledge Update 2. 1987, p 349. Reprinted with permission.)

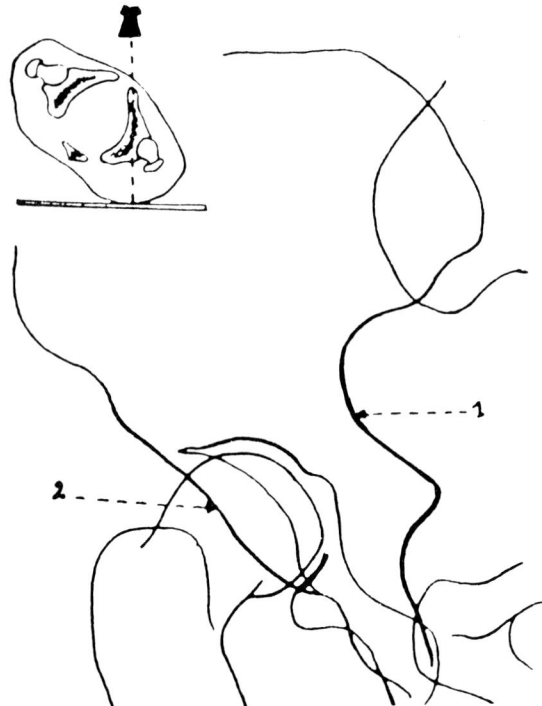

Figure 5-10. Judet iliac (external oblique) view of the acetabulum. 1: Posterior column; 2: anterior rim. (From Matta JM, Merritt PO: Trauma: pelvis and acetabulum. In American Academy of Orthopaedic Surgeons, Orthopaedic Knowledge Update 2. 1987, p 349. Reprinted with permission.)

types, superior weight-bearing dome, and fractures with interposition with bone or soft tissue
E. Surgical technique
  1. Approaches depend on the type of fracture
     a. Posterior wall fractures: posterior Kocher-Langenbeck
     b. Posterior wall associated with posterior column or transverse: Kocher-Langenbeck with trochanteric osteotomy
     c. Transverse or T fracture: transtrochanteric or ilioinguinal
     d. Anterior types, including anterior column anterior wall with or without transverse component: ilioinguinal
     e. Double-column fractures: ilioinguinal, extended iliofemoral, or combined anterior plus posterior approach
  2. Triradiate incision by Mears is useful in posterior column fractures and most transverse or T fractures
  3. Use of pelvic reduction clamp and reconstruction plates are routine

REFERENCES

Bray TJ, Esser M, Fulkerson L: Osteotomy of the trochanter in open reduction and internal fixation of the acetabular fractures. J Bone Joint Surg 69A: 711–717, 1987

Bucholz RW: The pathologic anatomy of Malgaigne fracture-dislocation of the pelvis. J Bone Joint Surg 63A:400, 1981

Denis F, Davis S, Comfort T: Sacral fractures: An important problem. Retrospective analysis of 236 cases. Clin Orthop 227:67–81, 1988

Judet R, Judet J, Letournel E: Fractures of the acetabulum: Classification and surgical approaches for open reduction. J Bone Joint Surg 46A:1615, 1964

Kellam JF, McMurtry RY, Paley D, et al: The unstable pelvic fracture: Operative treatment. Orthop Clin North Am 18:25–41, 1987

Letournel E: Acetabular fractures: Classification and management. Clin Orthop 151:81–106, 1980

Letournel E: Fractures of the acetabulum. New York, Springer-Verlag, 1981

Matta JM, Anderson LM, Epstein HC, et al: Fractures of the acetabulum. A retrospective analysis. Clin Orthop 205:230–240, 1986

Matta JM, Mehne DK, Roffi R: Fractures of the acetabulum: Early results of a prospective study. Clin Orthop 205:230–240, 1986

Matta J, Merritt P: Displaced acetabular fractures. Clin Orthop 230:83–97, 1988

Matta JM, Saucedo T: Internal fixation of pelvic ring fractures. Clin Orthop 242:83–97, 1989

McMurtry R, Walton D, Dickenson D, et al: Pelvic disruption in the polytraumatized patient: A management protocol. Clin Orthop 151:22, 1980

Mears DC, Fu FH: Modern concepts of external skeletal fixation of the pelvis. Clin Orthop 151:65–72, 1980

Pennal GF, Tile M, Waddell JP, et al: Pelvic disruption. Assessment and classification. Clin Orthop 151:12, 1980

Reinert CM, Bosse MJ, Poka A, et al: A modified extensile exposure for the treatment of complex or malunited acetabular fractures. J Bone Joint Surg 70A:329–337, 1988

Tile M: Fractures of the pelvis and acetabulum. Baltimore, Williams & Wilkins, 1984

Tile M: Pelvic ring fractures: Should they be fixed. J Bone Joint Surg 70B:1–12, 1988

43
Fractures and Dislocations of the Hip

I. Femoral Neck Fractures
A. Anatomy
1. Capsule: attached anteriorly at the intertrochanteric line; however, posteriorly the lateral half of the femoral neck is extracapsular
   a. No cambium layer to allow for peripheral callus
   b. Healing must take place by endosteal healing
2. Arterial supply
   a. Extracapsular arterial ring at base of neck
      (1) Formed posteriorly by large branch of medial femoral circumflex artery
      (2) Anteriorly by lateral femoral circumflex artery
   b. Ascending cervical branches of extracapsular ring on surface of neck (retinacular arteries from the medial and lateral circumflex arteries)
      (1) Four groups: lateral, medial, anterior, posterior with the lateral epiphyseal vessels providing the greatest blood supply
      (2) At the articular margin, they form a ring: subsynovial arterial ring, which then send arteries into the femoral head called epiphyseal arteries
   c. Arteries of ligamentum teres
      (1) Branch of obturator or the medial femoral circumflex artery
      (2) Fairly insignificant supply in most studies
B. Classification (Garden) (Fig 5-11)
1. Garden I: incomplete or impacted fracture
2. Garden II: complete fracture without displacement
3. Garden III: complete fracture with partial displacement (frequently shortened and externally rotated but continuity maintained)
4. Garden IV: complete fracture with total displacement (femoral head assumes normal relationship with acetabulum so that trabeculi line up normally)
C. Diagnosis
1. Stress and impacted fractures
   a. Pain with range of motion or percussion over the trochanter
   b. X-ray is often negative initially; therefore tomograms or bone scan may be needed in some cases
2. Displaced fractures
   a. Shortened or externally rotated extremity
   b. AP and lateral x-rays reveal Garden classification
D. Risk for nonunion or avascular necrosis
1. Primarily depends on the type of fracture and amount of displacement
   a. Five percent of nonunion in Garden I and II vs 30% in Garden III and IV types
   b. Sixteen percent avascular necrosis in Garden I and II and 28% in Garden III and IV types
   c. Posterior comminution and inadequate reduction or stabilization increase the risk of nonunion
   d. Delay in reduction is another factor in producing avascular necrosis
2. Age and medical status: older patients and patients with Paget's disease have a higher nonunion rate

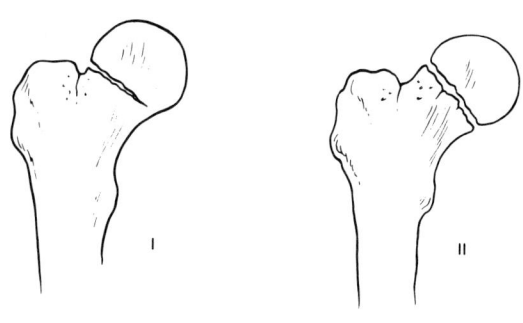

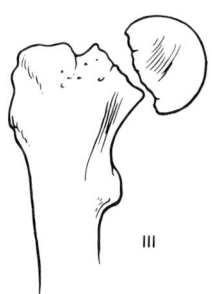 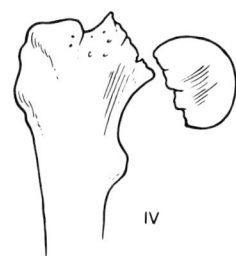

Figure 5-11. Garden classification of femoral neck fractures. I: Incomplete or impacted fracture; II: complete fracture without displacement; III: complete fracture with partial displacement; IV: complete fracture with total displacement. (From Bucholz RW, Orthopaedic Trauma. In Bucholz RW, Lippert FG, Wenger DR, Ezaki M, eds. Orthopaedic decision making. Philadelphia, BC Decker, and St Louis, CV Mosby, 1984, p 36. Reprinted with permission.)

    3. Bone scan can help predict avascular necrosis (90%)
  E. Treatment
    1. Garden I (15–20% of neck fractures)
      a. Nonoperative: displacement (8–20%) and avascular necrosis may develop
      b. Internal fixation is therefore recommended to mobilize the patient early without risk of fracture displacement
      c. Multiple pins or sliding screw and supplementary cancellous screw
    2. Garden II: internal fixation (consider hip aspiration to increase blood flow to the femoral head)
    3. Displaced fractures (Garden III or IV)
      a. Closed reduction (slight hip flexion, traction in abduction and external rotation and internal rotation and hip extension) and internal fixation
        (1) Relatively younger patients (<70 years old)
        (2) The femoral head is thought to be viable (bone scan)
        (3) Nonambulatory senile patients and those with lack of muscle control, since arthroplasty in these patients may result in postoperative dislocations
      b. Hemiarthroplasty (Austin-Moore or bipolar prosthesis)
        (1) Older ambulatory patients (>70 years)
        (2) Patients with inadequate closed reduction due to posterior comminution
        (3) Arthroplasty is generally preferred in patients with arthritis, Paget's disease, severe osteopenia, pathologic fractures, or failed internal fixation
        (4) Lateral approach and/or adductor tenotomy should be considered if postoperative dislocation is of concern, as in patients with Parkinson's disease

II. Intertrochanteric Fractures
  A. General considerations
    1. Extracapsular fractures with better healing potential
    2. Age group is about 10 years older than in subcapital fractures, and female to male ratio is 3.5:1
    3. Degree of osteoporosis is important to consider in attaining implant stability
    4. Hospital mortality is 5–10%, and mortality increases up to 20% 6–12 months later

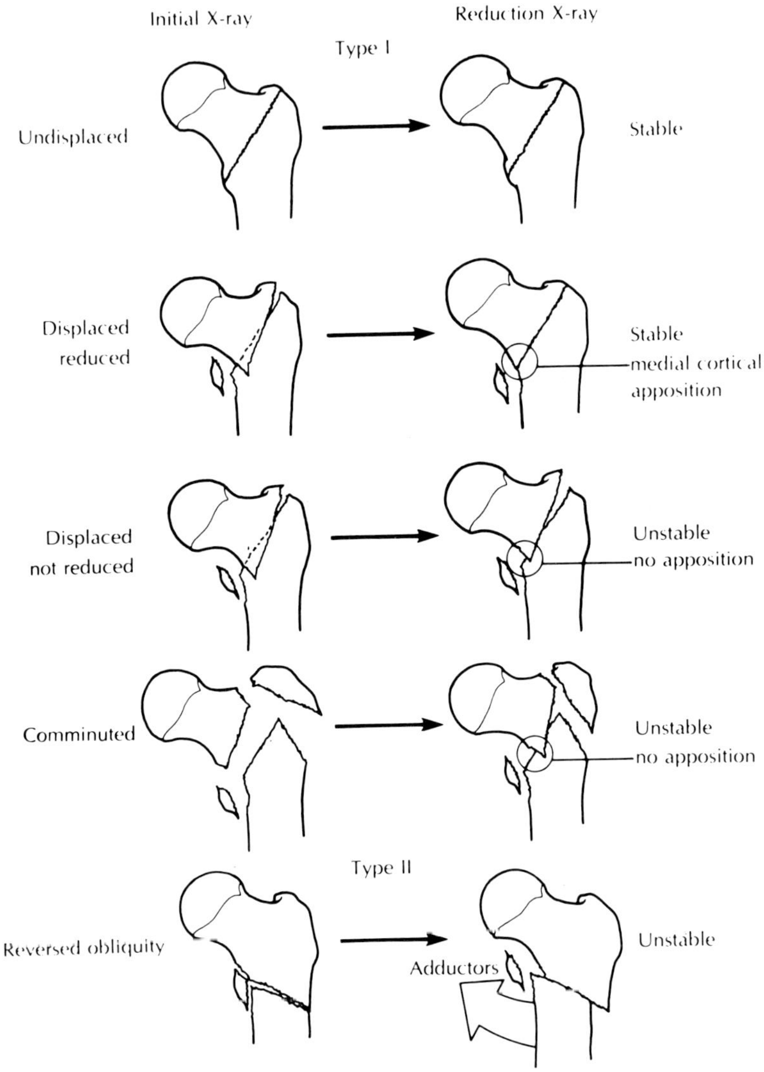

Figure 5-12. Evan's classification of intertrochanteric fractures. (From DeLee JC: Fractures and dislocations of the hip. In Rockwood CA, Green DP, eds. Fractures in adults, ed 2. Philadelphia, JB Lippincott, 1984, p 1262. Reprinted with permission.)

B. Classification (Evans) (Fig 5-12)
1. Type I: Fracture line extends upward and outward from the lesser trochanter
   a. Two part: fracture along the intertrochanteric line without comminution (undisplaced or displaced)
   b. Three part: intertrochanteric fracture with comminution of the lesser trochanter (apposition of the medial cortex is important in reduction)
   c. Four part or comminuted: fracture with fragments of greater and lesser trochanters
2. Type II: Reverse obliquity fractures with greater instability
C. Stability of fracture
1. Integrity of the medial cortex is the most important factor for stability
2. Reverse obliquity fracture is more unstable and there is tendency toward

medial displacement of the distal fragment
3. Comminuted fractures such as three or four part types are obviously more unstable
4. Stability of surgical construct depends on bone quality, fragment geometry, reduction quality, implant types, and implant placement

D. Treatment
1. Closed treatment in traction is contraindicated in most patients due to complications associated with prolonged bed rest
2. Operative treatment within the first 48 hours significantly reduces mortality
3. Surgery
   a. Closed reduction on the fracture table: traction, slight abduction, and external rotation under fluoroscopy
   b. Anatomic reduction and stable fixation
      (1) Sliding compression hip screw is the gold standard
         i. Screw should be within the center of the femoral head
         ii. Head of screw should be within 1 cm of the subchondral bone
         iii. Obtain anatomic or valgus reduction
         iv. Avoid superior or anterior positions of the femoral head
         v. Methyl methacrylate may be utilized to enhance fixation of the screw in severely osteoporotic patients
      (2) Short intramedullary fixation with distal interlocking device is experimental
   c. Osteotomies can also be done to obtain stability in four-part fractures if anatomic reduction cannot be obtained
      (1) Medial displacement osteotomy: Dimon and Hughston
      (2) Valgus osteotomy: Sarmiento

III. Subtrochanteric Fractures

A. Difficult fracture in terms of obtaining stable construct because of increased moment arm
B. Classification (Seinsheimer) (Fig 5-13)
   1. Type I: nondisplaced
   2. Type II: displaced transverse or oblique fractures without comminution
   3. Type III: three-part fractures
   4. Type IV: four-part fractures
   5. Type V: Comminuted fractures involving the greater trochanter

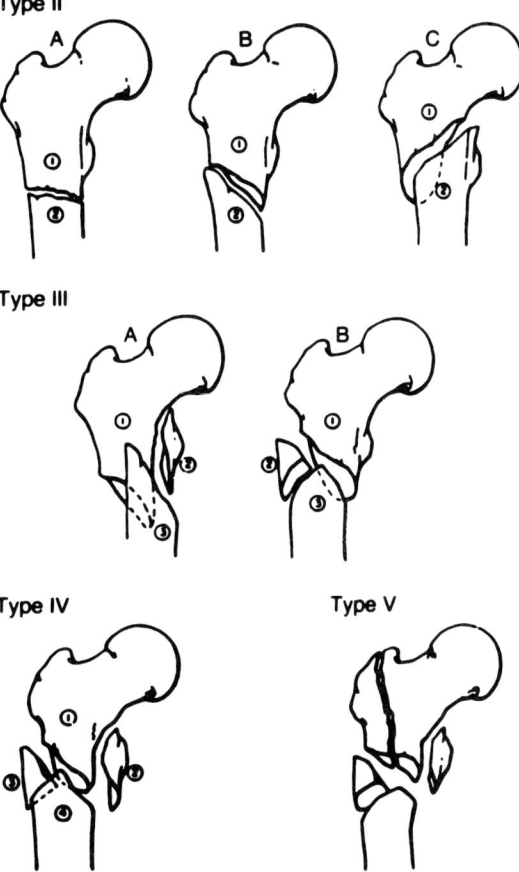

Figure 5-13. Seinsheimer classification of subtrochanteric fractures. (From Seinsheimer F III: Subtrochanteric fractures of the femur. J Bone Joint Surg 60A:300, 1978. Reprinted with permission.)

C. Treatment
   1. Traction may be associated with prolonged bed rest
   2. Surgery: compression screw, Zickel nail, interlocking femoral rod, or AO plate, depending on fracture types and surgeon's preference

IV. Hip Dislocations
A. Posterior dislocation
   1. Most common type
   2. Leg is shortened, internally rotated, and adducted
   3. Ten percent incidence of sciatic complications and >15% avascular necrosis
   4. Classification (Epstein)
      a. Type I: no or only minor fractures
      b. Type II: large posterior acetabular rim fractures
      c. Type III: Comminuted fracture of posterior rim with or without major fragment
      d. Type IV: fracture of both acetabular rim and floor
      e. Type V: fracture of femoral head with or without other fragment
   5. Treatment
      a. Immediate reduction: adduction, flexion, traction then abduction, and external rotation under sedation or general anesthesia, followed by ambulation in 10 days and graduated weight bearing
      b. Open reduction if closed reduction not possible or old dislocation after 3 weeks: capsule or piriformis muscle may block acute reduction
      c. Arthrotomy if loose fragment in the joint
B. Posterior dislocation with femoral head fracture (Epstein type V)
   1. Mechanism: posterior force with hip flexed <50°
   2. Classification (Pipkin)
      a. Pipkin I: posterior dislocation of hip and head fracture fragment caudad to fovea
      b. Pipkin II: posterior dislocation of hip and head fracture fragment cephalad to the fovea
      c. Pipkin III: type I or II with femoral neck fracture
      d. Pipkin IV: head fracture associated with fracture of the acetabulum
   3. Treatment
      a. Closed reduction for types I, II, and IV injuries
      b. Open reduction for type III injuries
      c. Assess the quality of reduction with CT scan
         (1) If concentric reduction, skeletal traction for 8 weeks followed by mobilization with protected weight bearing
         (2) If nonconcentric reduction, open reduction is needed
      d. Fragments in type I or fragments in type II with less than $\frac{1}{3}$ of articular surface involvement can be excised (large size fragments are fixed)
      e. Type IV injuries in elderly can be managed with replacement prosthesis
C. Anterior dislocation
   1. Ten percent incidence of hip dislocation
   2. Avascular necrosis in 4% of cases
   3. Indentation fractures of the femoral head: 4 mm or more indentation with poorer prognosis
   4. Types
      a. Superior (pubic or iliac): hip is abducted, externally rotated, flexed
      b. Inferior (obturator): hip is abducted, externally rotated, and extended
   5. Treatment
      a. Closed reduction: traction, extension, and internal rotation (add adduction for obturator type)
      b. Open reduction: if loose bodies or nonconcentric reduction (anterior approach)

REFERENCES

Bartucci EJ, Gonzalez MH, Cooperman DR, et al: The effect of adjunctive methylmethacrylate on failures of fixation and function in patients with intertrochanteric fractures and osteoporosis. J Bone Joint Surg 67A:1094–1107, 1985

Bergman GD, Winquist RA, Mayo KA, et al: Subtrochanteric fracture of the femur; fixation using the Zickel nail. J Bone Joint Surg 69A:1032–1040, 1987

Bochner RM, Pellici PM, Lyden JP: Bipolar hemiarthroplasty for fracture of the femoral neck. J Bone Joint Surg 70A:1001–1010, 1988

Bray TJ, Smith-Hoefer E, Hooper A, et al: The displaced femoral neck fracture: Internal fixation versus bipolar endoprosthesis. Results of a prospective randomized comparison. Clin Orthop 230:127–140, 1988

Doppelt SH: The sliding compression screw: Today's best answer for stabilization of intertrochanteric hip fractures. Orthop Clin North Am 11:507–523, 1980

Epstein HC: Traumatic dislocation of the hip. Baltimore, Williams & Wilkins, 1980

Epstein HC, Wiss DA, Cozen L: Posterior fracture dislocation of the hip with fractures of the femoral head. Clin Orthop 201:9–17, 1985

Garden RS: Reduction and fixation of subcapital fractures of the femur. Orthop Clin North Am 5:683–712, 1974

Hougaard K, Thomsen PB: Traumatic posterior fracture-dislocation of the hip with fracture of the femoral head or neck or both. J Bone Joint Surg 70A:233–239, 1988

Kyle RF, Gustilo RB, Premer RF: Analysis of six hundred and twenty-two intertrochanteric hip fractures. J Bone Joint Surg 61A:216–221, 1979

Kyle RF, Wright TM, Burstein AH: Biomechanical analysis of the sliding characteristics of compression hip screws. J Bone Joint Surg 62A:1308–1314, 1980

Schatzker J, Waddell JP: Subtrochanteric fractures of the femur. Orthop Clin North Am 11:539–554, 1980

Seinsheimer F: Subtrochanteric fractures of the femur. J Bone Joint Surg 60A:300–306, 1978

Stern MB, Angerman A: Comminuted intertrochanteric fractures treated with a Leinbach prosthesis. Clin Orthop 218:75–80, 1987

Swinkowski MF, Hansen ST Jr, Kellam J: Ipsilateral fractures of the femoral neck and shaft: A treatment protocol. J Bone Joint Surg 66A:260–268, 1984

Swinkowski MF, Winquist RA, Hansen ST Jr: Fractures of the femoral neck in patients between the ages of twelve and forty-nine years. J Bone Joint Surg 66A:837–846, 1984

Tooke SM, Favero KJ: Femoral neck fractures in skeletally mature patients, fifty years old or less. J Bone Joint Surg 67A:1255–1260, 1985

Zickel RE: Subtrochanteric femoral fractures. Orthop Clin North Am 11:555–568, 1980

44
Fractures of the Shaft of the Femur

I. General Considerations
A. Femur: strongest and longest bone in the body
B. Deforming forces
   1. Abduction and flexion and external rotation deformities by abductors and iliopsoas
   2. Varus deformity by adductor attachment
   3. Posterior angulation by gastrocnemius
C. Blood supply
   1. Femoral artery perforates at adductor hiatus and vascular damage may occur at this point
   2. Four perforating branches from deep femoral artery: course posteriorly to enter adjacent to linea aspera
   3. Endosteal vessels are more important, but periosteal vessels constitute multitude of tiny transverse vessels and wiring does not greatly obstruct blood flow

II. Classification (Winquist) (Fig 5-14)
A. Grade 0: noncomminuted (transverse, oblique, or spiral)
B. Grade 1: small fragment broken off
C. Grade 2: large fragment <50% of the cortex
D. Grade 3: large fragment >50% of the cortex
E. Grade 4: comminution precludes contact between proximal and distal fragments

III. Treatment
A. Skeletal traction
   1. Tibial pin
      a. Easier insertion with less risks for neurovascular injuries
      b. More difficult to control varus and internal rotation malalignment
      c. Contraindicated in unstable ipsilateral knee
      d. Better for temporary preoperative traction, especially if distal interlocking intramedullary rod is to be used
   2. Femoral pin
      a. Stronger pull and control malalignment better
      b. Increased risks for vascular injury
      c. Possible subsequent mechanical block or infection if distal locking screw is used for intramedullary rodding
      d. Consider two pins (distal femoral and proximal tibial for early range of motion of the knee, especially when conservative treatment is selected)
B. Cast brace
   1. May be indicated for certain distal ½ fractures
   2. Some comminuted fractures
   3. Simple fractures in young patients
   4. Complications: shortening ≥1 cm in 25% and varus angulation
C. External fixation
   1. May be used as a temporary device
   2. Severe open fractures
   3. Shotgun injury
   4. Osteomyelitis or draining infection
   5. Multiple injuries on the ipsilateral side
D. Intramedullary fixation
   1. Treatment of choice for most fractures
   2. Early mobilization is advantageous
   3. Types of intramedullary rods
      a. Reamed intramedullary rod for noncomminuted midshaft fractures
      b. Interlocking rods for proximal or distal shaft fractures, comminuted fractures with <50% cortical apposition (grade III or IV) and long spiral fractures. Interlocking is gener-

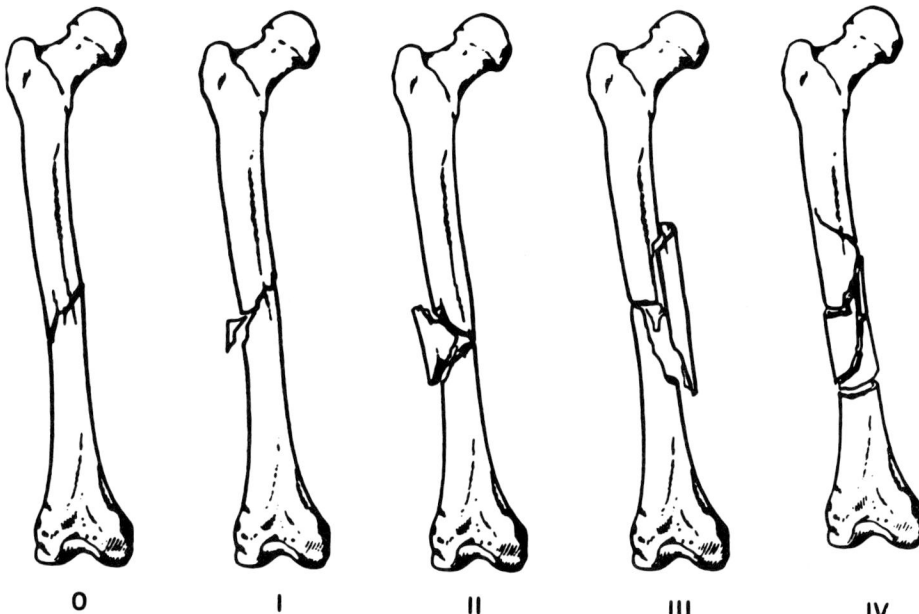

Figure 5-14. Winquist classification of the femoral shaft. (From Johnson KD, Johnson DWC, Parker B: Comminuted femoral-shaft fractures: Treatment by roller traction, cerclage wires and an intramedullary nail, or interlocking intramedullary nail. J Bone Joint Surg 66A:1222, 1984. Reprinted with permission.)

      ally preferred over noninterlocking nails to control rotation and length better
  c. Flexible unreamed rods may not be rigid enough to give stable fixation and early mobilization

REFERENCES

Bone LB, Johnson KD, Weiglet J, et al: Early versus delayed stabilization of femoral fractures: A prospective randomized study. J Bone Joint Surg 71A:336–340, 1989

Browner BD, Cole JD: Current status of locked intramedullary nailing: A review. J Orthop Trauma 1:183–195, 1987

Brumback RJ, Reilly JP, Poka A, et al: Intramedullary nailing of femoral shaft fractures: Part I. Decision-making errors with interlocking fixation. J Bone Joint Surg 70A:1453–1463, 1988

Brumback RJ, Uwagie-Eros S, Lakatos RP, et al: Intramedullary nailing of femoral fractures: Part II. Fracture-healing with static interlocking fixation. J Bone Joint Surg 70A:1453–1462, 1988

Hansen ST Jr, Winquist RA: Closed intramedullary nailing of the femur. Kuntscher technique with reaming. Clin Orthop 138:56–61, 1979

Hardy AE: The treatment of femoral fractures by cast-brace application and early ambulation: A prospective review of one hundred and six patients. J Bone Joint Surg 65A:56–65, 1983

Johnson KD, Johnson DWC, Parker B: Comminuted femoral shaft fractures: Treatment by roller traction, circlage wires and an intramedullary nail. J Bone Joint Surg 66A:1222–1235, 1984

Kempf I, Grosse A, Beck G: Closed locked intramedullary nailing. J Bone Joint Surg 67A:709, 1985

Lhowe DW, Hansen ST: Immediate nailing of open fractures of the shaft. J Bone Joint Surg 70A:812–820, 1988

Thoresen BO, Alho A, Ekeland A, et al: Interlocking intramedullary nailing in femoral shaft fractures. J Bone Joint Surg 67A:1313–1320, 1985

Veith RG, Winquist RA, Hansen ST Jr: Ipsilateral fractures of the femur and tibia: A report of fifty-seven consecutive cases. J Bone Joint Surg 66A:991–1002, 1984

White GM, Healy WL, Brumback RJ, et al: The treatment of fractures of the femoral shaft with the Brooker-Wills distal locking intramedullary nail. J Bone Joint Surg 68A:865–876, 1986

Winquist RA, Hansen ST, Clawson DK: Closed intramedullary nailing of femoral fractures: A report of five hundred and twenty cases. J Bone Joint Surg 66A:529–539, 1984

Wiss DA, Fleming CH, Matta JM, et al: Comminuted and rotationally unstable fractures of the femur treated with an interlocking nail. Clin Orthop 212:35–47, 1986

45

Fractures and Dislocations of the Knee

I. Fractures of the Distal Femur
A. General considerations
   1. Supracondylar and intercondylar fractures are considered
   2. Gastrocnemius pull causes posterior displacement, and varus and internal rotational displacement are frequent
   3. Careful neurovascular assessment is required
B. Classification
   1. Supracondylar fractures (AO/ASIF) (Fig 5-15)
      a. Type A: extra-articular fractures
      b. Type B: intra-articular noncomminuted fractures
      c. Type C: Comminuted fractures
   2. Intercondylar fractures (Neer)
      a. I: undisplaced T or Y fractures
      b. IIa: T or Y fractures with medial displacement
      c. IIb: T or Y fractures with lateral displacement
      d. III: comminuted fractures
C. Treatment
   1. Supracondylar fractures
      a. Conservative: balanced skeletal traction with knee flexed 30° using proximal tibial pin and 10–20 pounds of weight for 4–6 weeks, followed by cast brace for 3–4 months
         (1) May utilize distal femoral pin plus the proximal tibial pin to align the fracture
         (2) Knee motion during traction is important
         (3) Prevent excess shortening, distraction, varus, and internal rotational deformities
      b. Surgery is preferred if significant displacement cannot be controlled conservatively
         (1) Blade plate or supracondylar sliding nail-plate devices (consider bone grafting if defect or comminution is present)
         (2) Early knee motion is important
   2. Intercondylar fractures
      a. Surgery is required if any displacement is present
      b. Blade plate or rigid internal fixation is required with anatomic reduction for early motion
   3. Femoral condylar fractures
      a. May be one or both condyles with displacement, and coronal plane fracture is known
      b. Open reduction and internal fixation with cancellous screws or bolts is preferred

II. Fractures of the Patella
A. General considerations
   1. Largest sesamoid bone in the body
   2. Bipartite patella: anomaly of ossification, located in the superolateral corner of the patella
   3. Blood supply: superior pole is least vascularized and may be susceptible to avascular necrosis
   4. Undisplaced fractures are common: medial and lateral retinacula are intact
   5. Most common during 4th and 5th decades and more common in males than females (2:1)
B. Classification
   1. Undisplaced
   2. Transverse or oblique (50–80%)

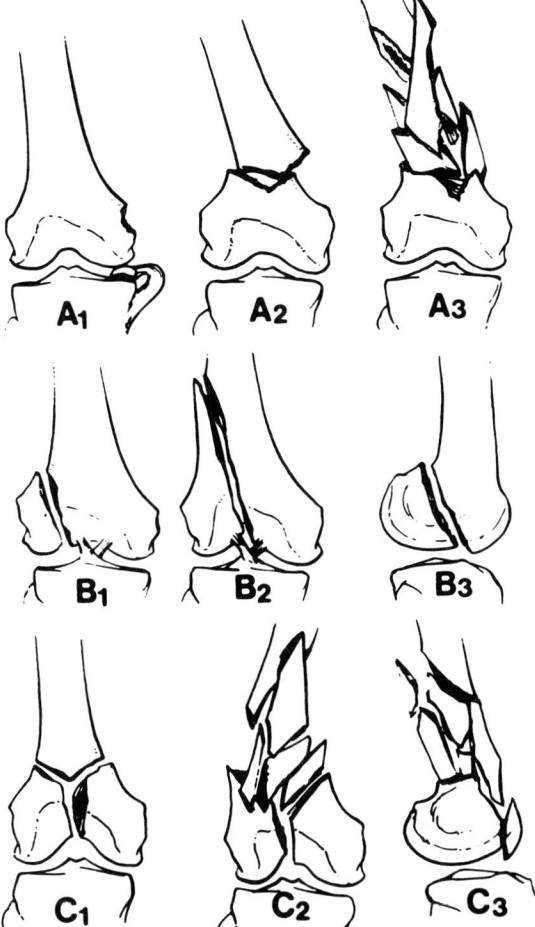

Figure 5-15. AO/ASIF classification of supracondylar fractures (AO/ASIF). (From Muller ME, Allgower M, Schneider R, et al: Manual of internal fixation: techniques recommended by the AO group, ed 2. New York, Springer-Verlag, 1979. Reprinted with permission.)

   3. Lower pole or upper pole
   4. Comminuted (30–35%)
   5. Vertical (12–27%)
C. Treatment
   1. Undisplaced fractures: cylinder cast for 6 weeks with partial weight bearing
   2. Lower pole or upper pole or comminuted: excision if small fragments and reattachment of the extensor mechanism
   3. Transverse or oblique types: AO tension band technique and immobilization for 2 weeks and early motion
      a. Patellofemoral pain and arthritis are common
      b. Avascular necrosis of the proximal fragment is rare

III. Fractures of the Proximal Tibia
A. Mechanism
   1. Motor vehicle accident or falls
   2. Axial loading
      a. Knee in extension: anterior tibial plateau disrupted and usually milder injuries
      b. Knee in flexion: middle to posterior tibial plateau is disrupted and usually severe injuries
   3. Concomitant ligament injuries to the knee are common
B. Classifications
   1. Hohl (Fig 5-16)
      a. Type I: minimally displaced
      b. Type II: local compression
      c. Type III: split compression
      d. Type IV: total condylar depression
      e. Type V: bicondylar
   2. Schatzker
      a. Type I: pure cleavage fracture of the lateral plateau
      b. Type II: cleavage combined with depression of the lateral plateau
      c. Type III: pure central depression of the lateral plateau
      d. Type IV: medial plateau fracture
      e. Type V: pure bicondylar fracture
      f. Type VI: tibial fracture with dissociation of the tibial metaphysis and diaphysis
C. X-rays: plain films, tomograms, and stress views
D. Treatment
   1. Minimally displaced: posterior splint or casting, followed by early range of motion (1–3 weeks) and no weight bearing until healing (3 months)

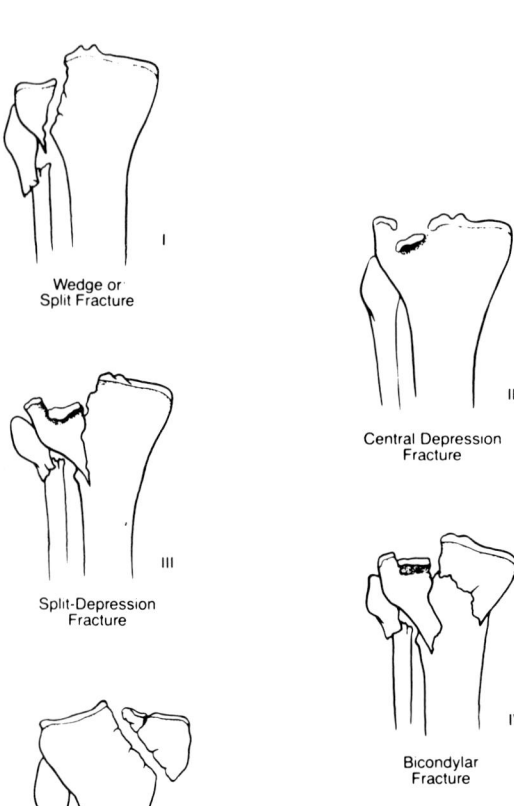

Figure 5-16. Mason classification of tibial plateau fractures. (Hohl M, Larson RL, Jones DC: Fractures and dislocations of the knee. In Rockwood CA, Green DP, eds. Fractures in adults. Philadelphia, JB Lippincott, 1984, p 1455. Reprinted with permission.)

2. Local compression
   a. Open reduction and internal fixation if 8 mm or more depression (in younger patients 4 mm or more)
   b. Bone grafting, tibial bolts and early motion in 3 weeks using cast brace
3. Split compression
   a. Nonoperative treatment if split fragment is in good position supporting the femoral condyle and depression is <8 mm
   b. Open reduction and internal fixation if significantly displaced and depressed (rigid fixation with screws, bolts or plates, and bone grafting if necessary)
4. Total condylar depression
   a. Nonoperative treatment if depression is <4–6 mm
   b. Open reduction and internal fixation if significant depression with plates (more aggressive for medial condylar fractures)
5. Bicondylar fractures
   a. Nonoperative treatment: comminuted osteoporotic fractures (distal tibial traction and range of motion exercise)
   b. Open reduction and internal fixation if reduction is not acceptable

IV. Fracture/Dislocation of the Knee
A. Classification (Hohl)
   1. Split fracture
   2. Entire plateau fracture
   3. Rim avulsion: high incidence of ligamentous injury
   4. Rim compression: high incidence of ligamentous injury
   5. Four-part fracture
B. Treatment: almost all types require open reduction and internal fixation with repair of ligaments if torn

V. Fractures of the Tibial Spine
A. Classification (Meyers and McKeever)
   1. Type I: undisplaced or only anterior margin displacement
   2. Type II: the anterior margin is lifted completely with only posterior apposition
   3. Type IIIA: complete displacement
   4. Type IIIB: complete displacement and rotated
B. Treatment: closed reduction and casting in extension and if unsuccessful open reduction or arthroscopic reduction and stabilization

REFERENCES

Hohl M: Tibial condylar fractures. J Bone Joint Surg 49A:1455, 1967

Lotke PA, Ecker ML: Transverse fractures of the patella. Clin Orthop 158:180, 1981

Mize RD, Bucholz RW, Grogan DP: Surgical treatment of displaced comminuted fractures of the distal end of the femur. J Bone Joint Surg 64A:871–879, 1982

Neer CS, Grantham S, Shelton L: Supracondylar fracture of the adult femur. J Bone Joint Surg 49A:591–613, 1967

Schatzker J, Lambert DC, Shelton L: Supracondylar fracture of the adult femur. Clin Orthop 138:77–83, 1979

Schatzker J, McBroom R, Bruce D: The tibial plateau fracture: The Toronto experience 1968–1975. Clin Orthop 138:94, 1979

46
Fractures of the Tibia

I. Introduction
A. Most commonly fractured long bone in the body
B. These fractures are associated with a high rate of complications, including compartment syndromes, infection, and nonunion because tibia has poor soft tissue coverage and tenuous blood supply

II. Anatomic Considerations
A. Anterior medial surface and anterior crest are covered only by skin and subcutaneous, leading to a high incidence of open fractures
B. Neurovascular structures are at highest risk in proximal third of the tibial shaft
  1. Popliteal artery goes from midline position between heads of gastrocnemius and then sweeps laterally to go beneath the soleus. It then divides into the anterior and posterior tibial arteries and peroneal artery
  2. Common peroneal nerve curves around the fibular neck and divides into the superficial and deep peroneal nerves
  3. Anterior compartment structures are enclosed in an unyielding compartment with the interosseous membrane posteriorly and anterior fascia leading to a relatively high incidence of compartment syndrome
     a. Tibialis anterior
     b. Extensor hallucis longus
     c. Peroneus tertius
     d. Anterior tibial artery
     e. Peroneal nerve
  4. Lateral compartment
     a. Peroneus brevis
     b. Peroneus longus
     c. Superficial peroneal nerve may be at risk with fibular neck fractures
  5. Posterior compartments (superficial and deep)
     a. Soleus
     b. Gastrocnemius
     c. Tibialis posterior
     d. Flexor hallucis longus
     e. Flexor digitorum longus
     f. Posterior tibial artery
     g. Posterior tibial nerve
C. Blood supply
  1. A single nutrient artery (supplied by the posterior tibial artery) entering the posterolateral cortex
  2. This artery divides into three ascending branches and single descending branch responsible for 90% of normal cortical blood flow
  3. Injury to the single descending branch will result in a reversal of flow from the periosteal system. Therefore preservation of soft tissue attachments in surgery is extremely important

III. Mechanism of Injury
A. Direct trauma resulting in transverse or comminuted fractures due to high energy forces
B. Indirect trauma commonly results in spiral or oblique fracture pattern from low energy forces
C. Prognosis depends on initial displacement and angulation comminution, soft tissue injury, and mechanism of injury
D. Classifications
  1. Rockwood and Green
     a. Minor: horizontal displacement of <50% with or without comminution
     b. Moderate: horizontal displacement of >50% with or without comminution
     c. Severe: completely displaced frac-

ture with a major open wound or comminution
2. Winquist classification (Fig 5-17)
   a. Type I: very small butterfly fragment
   b. Type II: comminution up to 50% of the bone width
   c. Type III: butterfly fragment >50%
   d. Type IV: comminution of complete bone segment
   e. Type V: segmental bone loss
3. AO classification (Johner and Wruhs): this classification is based on fracture morphology with main emphasis on the degree of comminution and strict differentiation between spiral and nonspiral fractures (Fig 5-18)
4. Classification for open injuries (Gustilo and Anderson)
   a. Grade I: low energy injury causing a spiral or oblique fracture pattern. Clean wound <1 cm in length
   b. Grade II: moderate energy with displaced fracture pattern or comminuted. Soft tissue injury generally >1 cm but without devitalized tissue
   c. Grade III: high energy significant displacement comminuted or with bone loss. Grossly contaminated with significant soft tissue devitalization and >10 cm wound
      (1) IIIa: adequate coverage of the fracture by soft tissue despite

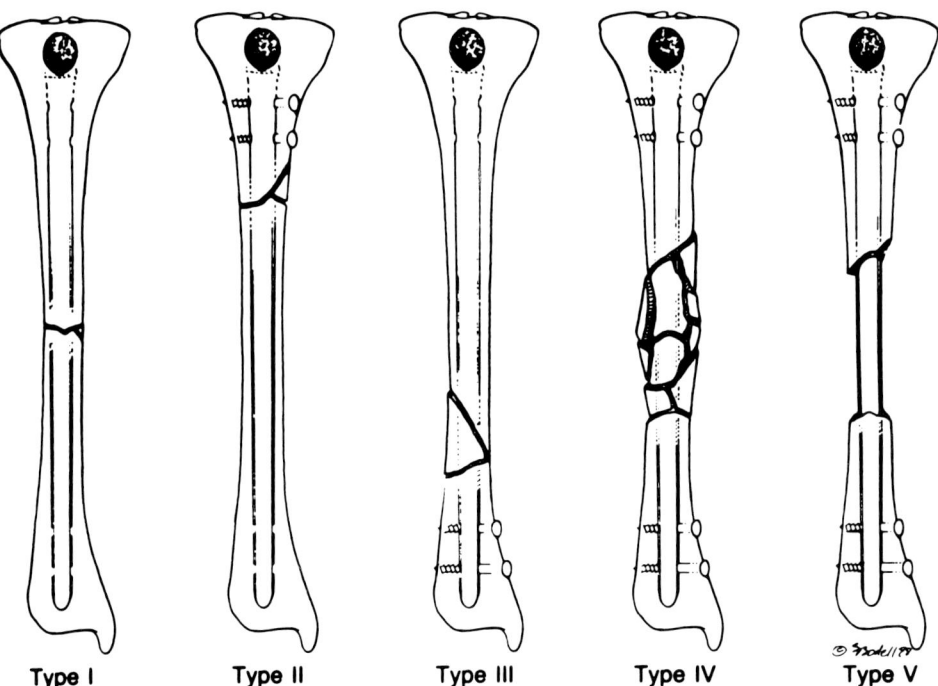

Figure 5-17. Winquist classification of tibial comminution and the recommended treatment. (From Henley MB: Intramedullary devices for tibial fracture stabilization. Clin Orthop 240:91, 1989. Reprinted with permission.)

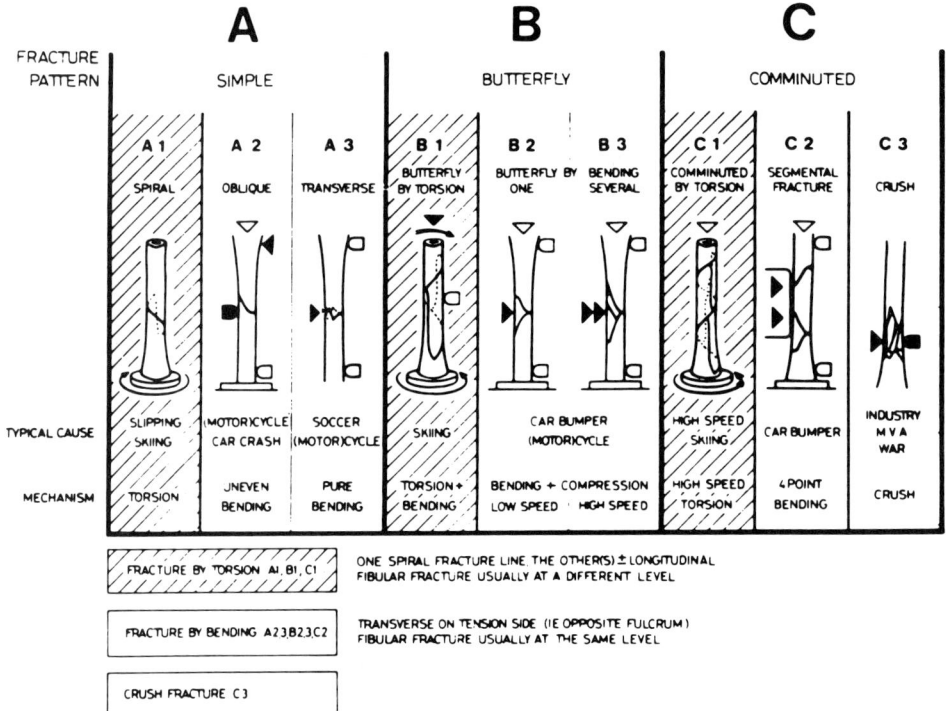

Figure 5-18. AO/ASIF classification of tibial fractures. (From Johner R, Wruhs O: Classification of tibial fractures and correlation with results after rigid internal fixation. Clin Orthop 178:7, 1983. Reprinted with permission.)

extensive lacerations or flaps of tissue
   (2) IIIb: extensive soft tissue injury with stripping of the periosteum and exposure of bone
   (3) IIIc: arterial injury

IV. Treatment Options for Closed Fractures

A. Acceptable reduction
   1. AP view: only 5° of varus or valgus acceptable (valgus is better than varus)
   2. Lateral view: 10° of anterior or posterior bowing acceptable
   3. Rotation should be almost perfect
   4. Shortening of ≤1 cm acceptable
B. Closed methods
   1. Plaster immobilization with a long leg cast is adequate for many tibial fractures
      a. The knee is routinely put in slight flexion and kept on no weight bearing for at least 10–14 days and then allowed to bear weight if the fracture pattern permits. More severe injuries will need longer immobilization periods
      b. Dependent on type of injury and degree of severity, the leg is eventually put into a patellar tendon bearing or total contact below knee functional brace. This is only done after several weeks when the fracture is stable
      c. Additional closed methods of treatment may include pins and plaster and skeletal traction
C. Indications for surgical treatment
   1. Unstable fracture with displacement of the main fragment of the full width of the shaft
   2. Shortening of >1 cm

3. Angulation of >5° varus/valgus or 10° anterior or posterior
4. Segmental fractures
5. Fractures in polytraumatized patients
6. Fractured tibia associated with intra-articular fracture at the knee or ankle
7. Ipsilateral femoral shaft fracture producing a "floating knee"

D. Types of fixation
1. Interfragmentary screw and compression plating for metaphyseal and intra-articular fractures involving the knee or ankle
2. Intramedullary nailing
   a. Unreamed nails with or without interlocking may be used in grade I or II open fractures
   b. Reamed nails with or without interlocking provide much more rigid fixation with improved rotational control in most cases

V. Management of the Open Fracture

A. High energy wounds with a high rate of infection and nonunion
1. Infection rate is 10–20 times higher than for other open skeletal fractures
2. Fifty percent of all patients who sustain a grade III injury will have an impaired functional end result

B. Steps in management
1. Tetanus prophylaxis
2. Immediate debridement and irrigation (6–10 L)
3. Antibiotics (add penicillin in farm injuries and aminoglycosides in grade III injuries in addition to cephalosporins)
4. Early rigid fixation and wound coverage
   a. External fixator in grade III fractures
   b. Unreamed nails may be used in grade I or II fractures
   c. Unreamed interlocking nails may also be used
   d. Intramedullary fixation for type III injuries is controversial
5. Delay secondary closure
   a. Goal is to obtain wound closure within 5–10 days
   b. Delayed primary closure vs split skin graft usually will suffice for most injuries
   c. Type IIIb injuries may require local flaps or free tissue transfer
      (1) Proximal third defects: Gastrocnemius
      (2) Middle third: soleus
      (3) Distal third: free flaps
6. Repair of bony discontinuity
   a. Early posterolateral bone grafting now recommended for high energy tibial fractures
   b. Anteromedial grafting limited by the amount of graft that can be placed and complicated by further soft tissue destruction and skin problems
   c. Shortening of the tibia may be utilized in cases where significant bone loss has occurred; 2 cm is acceptable
   d. Vascularized grafts or Ilizarov are recommended for segmental bone losses exceeding 8 cm
   e. Early amputation should be considered in patients who sustain type IIIc injuries complicated by severe crush injury, loss of soft tissue, and a nerve injury
   f. External fixator to intramedullary rod exchange can be considered as staged procedure

VI. Complications

A. Delayed union >20 weeks. Most advocate use of cancellous grafting at 12–16 weeks
B. Nonunion
1. Increased risk in severely displaced fractures, open fractures, and if inadequately stabilized
2. Treatment
   a. Posterolateral bone grafting is the treatment of choice in infected nonunion cases and may be used in non-infected cases with good results

    b. Electrical treatment is an option if the nonunion is relatively stable, minimal deformity, and no synovial layer is present
    c. Intramedullary reaming and rodding is quite successful in noninfected cases
    d. Displaced or significant deformity present: open reduction and internal fixation with plating or rodding
    e. Fibular osteotomy if distracting force is contributing to delayed healing but do not resect the fibula routinely because it contributes to stability of the fracture
C. Malunion: may require osteotomy
D. Neurovascular injury
  1. Stretch palsy of the common peroneal nerve most common
  2. Weakness of extensor hallucis longus (EHL) and diminished sensation at the first dorsal web space
  3. Most common vascular injury occurs at trifurcation of popliteal artery
E. Compartment syndrome: most common in the anterior compartment followed by lateral, deep, and superficial posterior compartments. Compartment syndrome is also possible after open fractures
F. Infection: stable fixation or bone healing often helps to resolve infection

REFERENCES

Behrens F, Comfort TH, Searls K, et al: Unilateral external fixation for severe open tibial fractures-primary report of a prospective study. Clin Orthop 178:111, 1983

Blick SS, Brumback RJ, Poka A, et al: Compartment syndrome in open tibial fractures. J Bone Joint Surg 68A:1348–1353, 1986

Bone LB, Johnson KD: Treatment of tibial fractures by reaming and intramedullary nailing. J Bone Joint Surg 68A:877–887, 1986

Brighton CT, Black J, Friedenberg ZB, et al: A multicenter study of the treatment of non-union with constant direct current. J Bone Joint Surg 63A:2–13, 1981

Brown PW, Urban JG: Early weight-bearing treatment of open fractures of the tibia. J Bone Joint Surg 51A:59–75, 1969

Caudle RJ, Stern PJ: Severe open fractures of the tibia. J Bone Joint Surg 69A:801–807, 1987

Chapman MW, Mahoney M: The role of internal fixation in the management of open fractures. Clin Orthop 138:120, 1979

Clancey CJ, Hansen ST: Open fractures of the tibia. J Bone Joint Surg 60A:118–122, 1978

Edwards CC: Staged reconstruction of complex open tibial fractures using Hoffman external fixation-clinical decisions and dilemmas. Clin Orthop 178:130, 1983

Galpin RD, Veith RG, Hansen ST: Treatment of failures after plating of tibial fractures. J Bone Joint Surg 68A:1231–1236, 1986

Gustilo RB, Anderson JT: Prevention of infection in the treatment of 1025 open fractures of long bones. J Bone Joint Surg 58A:453, 1976

Gustilo RB, Mendoza RM, Williams DN: Problems in the management of type III (severe) open fractures: A new classification of Type III open fractures. J Trauma 24:742–746, 1984

Gustilo RB, Simpson L, Nixon R, et al: Analysis of 511 open fractures. Clin Orthop 66:148, 1969

Johnson EE, Marder RA: Open intramedullary nailing and bone-grafting for non-union of tibial diaphyseal fracture. J Bone Joint Surg 69A:375–380, 1987

Lange RH, Bach AW, Hansen ST, et al: Open tibial fractures with associated vascular injuries: Prognosis for limb salvage. J Trauma 25:203–208, 1985

Mayer L, Werbie T, Schwab JP, et al: The use of Ender nails in fractures of the tibial shaft. J Bone Joint Surg 67A:446–454, 1985

Pankovich AM, Tarabishy IE, Yelda S: Flexible intramedullary nailing of tibial-shaft fractures. Clin Orthop 160:185, 1981

Patzakis MJ, Harvey JP, and Ivler D: The role of antibiotics in the management of open fractures. J Bone Joint Surg 56A;532, 1974

Reckling FW, Waters CH III: Treatment of nonunions of fractures of the tibial diaphysis by posterolateral cortical cancellous bone-grafting. J Bone Joint Surg 62A:936–941, 1980

Ruedi T, Webb JK, Allgower M: Experience with the dynamic compression plate (DCP) in 418 recent fractures of the tibial shaft. Injury 7:252, 1976

Sarmiento A: Functional bracing of tibial fractures. Clin Orthop 105:202–219, 1974

Sarmiento A, Sobol PA, Sew Hoy AL, et al: Prefabricated function braces for the treatment of the tibial diaphysis. J Bone Joint Surg 66A:1328, 1984

Simpson JM, Ebraheim NA, An HS, et al: Posterolateral bone graft of the tibia. Clin Orthop 251:200–206, 1990

Velazco A, Fleming LL: Open fractures of the tibia treated by the Hoffman external fixator. Clin Orthop 180:125, 1983

Velazco A, Fleming LL, Nahai F: Soft-tissue reconstruction of the leg associated with the use of the Hoffman external fixator. J Trauma 223:1052, 1983

Winquist RA, Hansen ST Jr, Clawson DK: Closed intramedullary nailing. J Bone Joint Surg 66A:877, 1986

47
Fractures and Dislocations of the Ankle and Foot

I. Pilon Fractures (Tibial Plafond Fractures)
A. Fracture of distal tibial metaphysis involving the ankle joint
B. Mechanism: axial loading, rotation, or both
C. High energy injury or twisting injury in osteoporotic bone
D. Soft tissue problems may be little or significant with vascular compromise
E. Classification (Ruedi/Allgower) (Fig 5-19A,B,C)
   1. Grade I: articular fracture without displacement
   2. Grade II: articular fracture with significant articular incongruity
   3. Grade III: severely comminuted and impacted articular fracture
F. Treatment
   1. Soft tissue treatment
      a. Provisional management with os calcis skeletal traction or external fixator in open wounds
      b. Fibular fixation may be done to hold the fracture out to length
   2. Definitive management
      a. Hold fibular out to length by plating it
      b. Skin bridge between the anteromedial and lateral incision should be at least 7 cm
      c. Reconstruct articular surface (K-wires)
      d. Plate on the medial aspect of the tibia
      e. Bone grafting of the defect
      f. Closure of the skin may be difficult and split thick skin graft may be used

II. Ankle Fractures
A. Classification
   1. Lauge-Hanson (first category refers to the position of the foot and second category refers to the direction of deforming force) (Fig 5-20)
      a. Supination-adduction (stages I and II)
      b. Supination-eversion (stages I–IV)
      c. Pronation-abduction (stages I–III)
      d. Pronation-eversion (stages I–IV)
   2. Danis-Weber (AO classification): fracture line of the fibula (Fig 5-21)
      a. Type A: below joint line
      b. Type B: at joint level
      c. Type C: above joint level
   3. Maisonneuve's fractures: fracture of the proximal third of the fibula with deltoid ligament rupture, involving the anterior tibiofibular and interosseus ligament disruption
   4. Injuries to the medial aspect of the ankle
      a. Deltoid ligament tear: widening between the medial malleolus and talus over 4 mm
      b. Medial malleolus fractures: anterior and posterior colliculi (deep deltoid attaches to the posterior colliculus)
   5. Treatment
      a. Minimally displaced fractures: anatomic closed reduction and casting (must prevent shortening, widening of the mortise, and malrotation)
      b. Displaced fractures: anatomic reduction and internal fixation
         (1) Distal fibula should be fixed first except in supination adduction type or laterally comminuted fractures

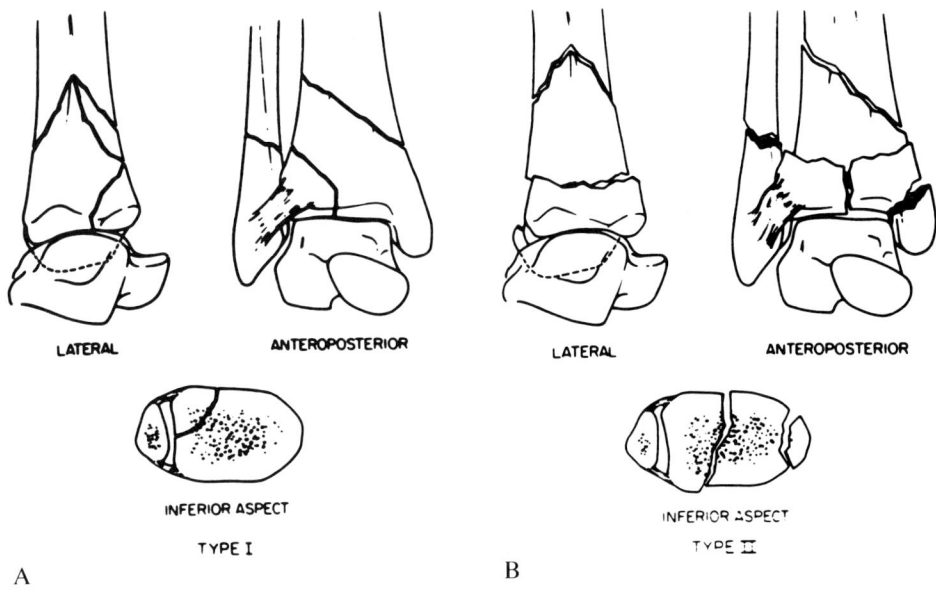

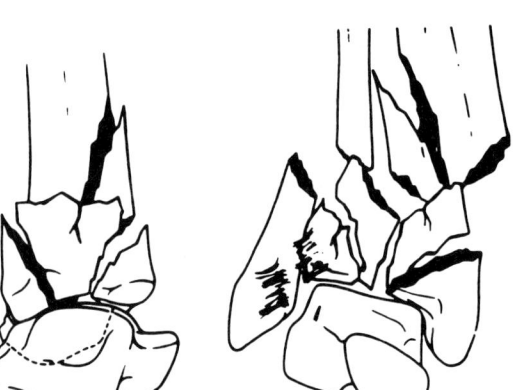

Figure 5-19. Ruedi and Allgower classification of pylon fractures of the distal tibia. **A.** Type I: undisplaced cleavage fractures. **B.** Type II: moderate comminution with some incongruity of the articular surface. **C.** Type III: gross comminution and articular surface incongruity. (From Bourne RB: Pylon fractures of the distal tibia. Clin Orthop 240:43, 1989. Reprinted with permission.)

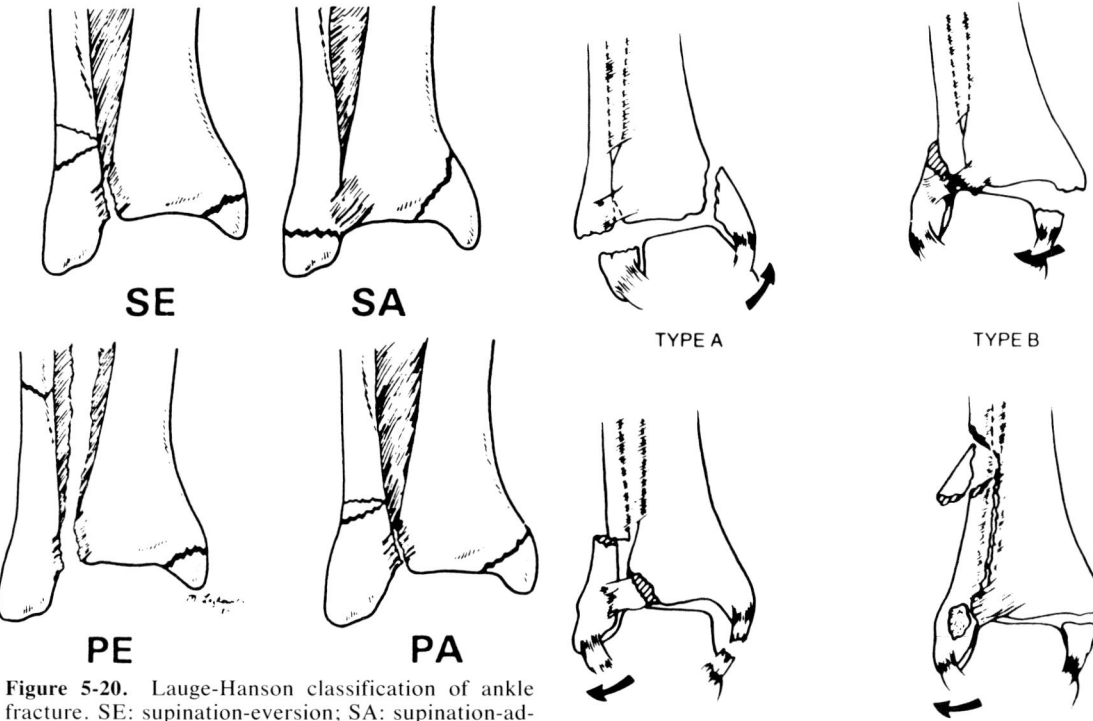

Figure 5-20. Lauge-Hanson classification of ankle fracture. SE: supination-eversion; SA: supination-adduction; PE: pronation-eversion; PA: pronation-adduction. (From Orthopaedic Knowledge Update II, Park Ridge, Illinois, 1987. Reprinted with permission.)

Figure 5-21. Weber classification of ankle fracture. Type A: below the joint line. Type B: at the joint level. Type C: above the joint level. (From Bucholz RW, Orthopaedic Trauma. In Bucholz RW, Lippert FG, Wenger DR, Ezaki M., eds. Orthopaedic decision making. Philadelphia, BC Decker, and St Louis, CV Mosby, 1984, p 64. Reprinted with permission.)

    (2) Most deltoid ligamentous ruptures do not need repair if the mortise is normal
    (3) Syndesmotic screw if unstable fibular secondary to ruptured syndesmotic ligament (use 3.5 mm cortical screw with the ankle in full dorsiflexion and no lagging about 3 cm above joint line)
    (4) Posterior malleolar fragment: >25% need open reduction and fixation
    (5) Open fractures: irrigation and debridement and immediate internal fixation and primary or secondary wound management

III. Calcaneal Fractures

A. Mechanism: fall from a height
B. Associated thoracolumbar or pelvic fractures
C. X-rays: anteroposterior, lateral, tangential, Broden's views, CT scan
D. Normal Bohler's angle: 25°–40° (Fig 5-22)
E. Classification (Essex-Lopresti)
    1. Extra-articular fractures: anterior process, tuberosity, medial process, sustentaculum tali and body
    2. Intra-articular fractures: 70–75% of calcaneal fractures

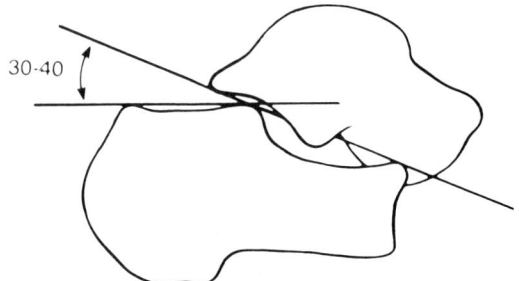

Figure 5-22. Bohler's angle. (From Bucholz RW, Orthopaedic trauma. In Bucholz RW, Lippert FG, Wenger DR, Ezaki M, eds. Orthopaedic decision making. Philadelphia, BC Decker, and St Louis, CV Mosby, 1984, p 66. Reprinted with permission.)

      a. Tongue type
      b. Joint depression type (Fig 5-23)
  F. Treatment
    1. Extra-articular fractures: short leg non-weight-bearing cast for 6 weeks
    2. Intra-articular fractures: controversial
      a. Minimally displaced fractures: early range of motion and no weight bearing for 2 months
      b. Tongue type: Essex-Lopresti reduction and pinning
      c. Joint depression type: either lateral or medial approaches (Fig 5-24)
    3. Complications: subtalar joint pain, peroneal tendonitis, plantar heel spur, arthritis of calcaneocuboid joint, and nerve entrapment (medial or lateral plantar nerves or sural nerves)

IV. Fractures/Dislocations of the Talus

  A. Anatomy
    1. Body of the talus: wider anteriorly
    2. Neck of the talus: constructed and deviates medially 15°–20°
    3. Head of the talus: articulates with the navicula anteriorly, spring ligament inferiorly, sustentaculum tali posteroinferiorly and deltoid ligament medially
    4. Bony processes
      a. Posterior: medial and lateral tubercles separated by flexor hallucis longus and os trigonum may arise from the lateral tubercle posteriorly (50%)
      b. Lateral process: wedge-shaped and articulates with posterior facet and distal fibula

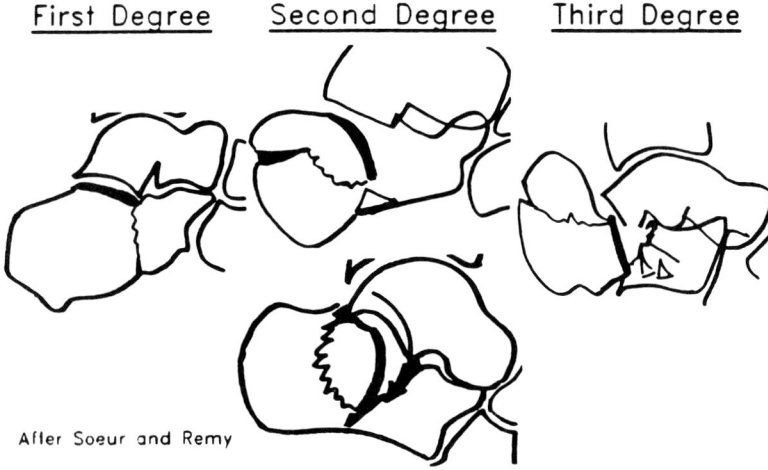

Figure 5-23. Degrees of joint-depression type fractures expanded from Essex-Lopresti's original classification by Soeur and Remy. (From Miller ME: Surgical management of calcaneus fractures: Indications and techniques. In Greene WB, ed. Instructional Course Lectures, Park Ridge, Illinois, American Academy of Orthopaedic Surgeons, 1990, p 162. Reprinted with permission.)

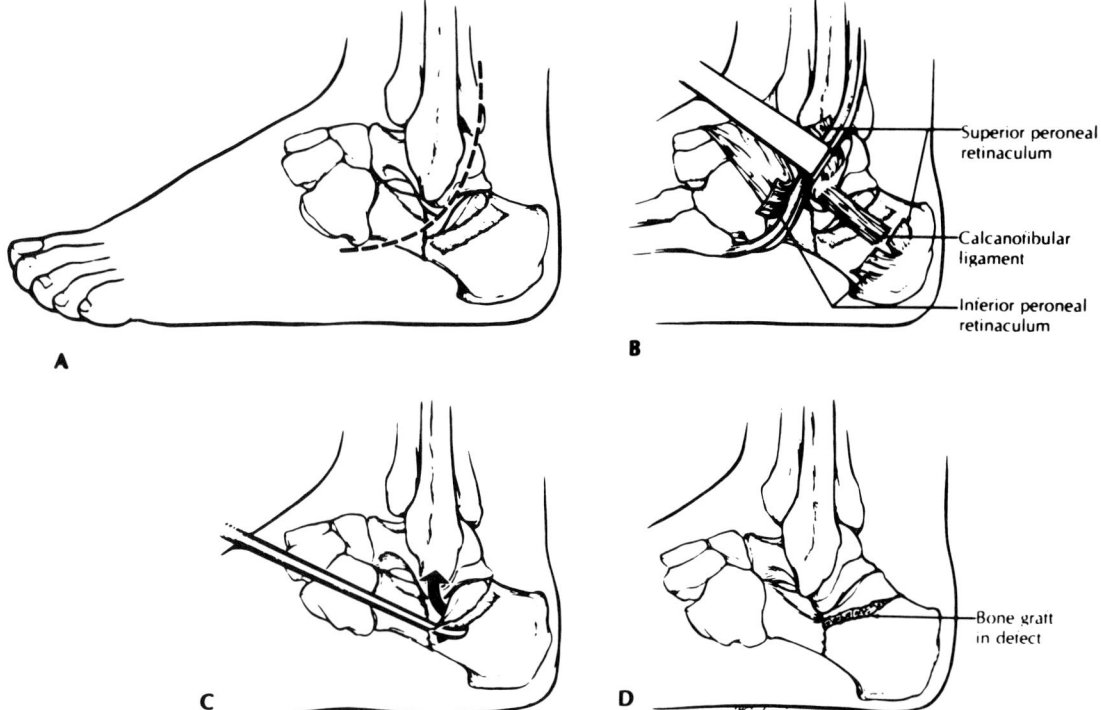

Figure 5-24. Open reduction and bone grafting of displaced intra-articular fractures of the calcaneus. **A.** Posterolateral incision. **B.** Peroneal tendons are retracted anteriorly and calcaneofibular ligament is detached distally. **C.** Posterior facet is reduced anatomically. **D.** Bone grafting in the defect. (From Heckman JD: Fractures and dislocations of the foot. In Rockwood CA, Green DP, eds. Fractures in adults, ed 2. Philadelphia, JB Lippincott, 1984, p 1783. Reprinted with permission.)

    5. No muscular and tendinous attachment and 60% covered by articular cartilage
- B. Blood supply (Fig 5-25)
    1. Talar head: branches of the dorsalis pedis and the artery of the tarsal sinus
    2. Talar body: anastomic sling between the artery of the tarsal canal (a branch of the posterior tibial artery) and artery of the tarsal sinus (anastomotic loop between dorsalis pedis and perforating branch of the peroneal artery) gives many branches entering the neck and coursing posterolaterally
    3. Medial quarter of the body: deltoid branch from the posterior tibial artery
    4. Posterior process: branches of the peroneal artery
- C. Fractures of the neck of the talus
    1. Mechanism: hyperdorsiflexion of the foot
    2. Classification (Hawkins) (Fig 5-26)
        a. Type I: nondisplaced
        b. Type II: displaced fracture of the talar neck with subluxation or dislocation of the subtalar joint
        c. Type III: displaced fracture of the talar neck with dislocation of the body of the talus from both subtalar and ankle joint
        d. Type IV: type III with an additional dislocation at the talonavicular joint

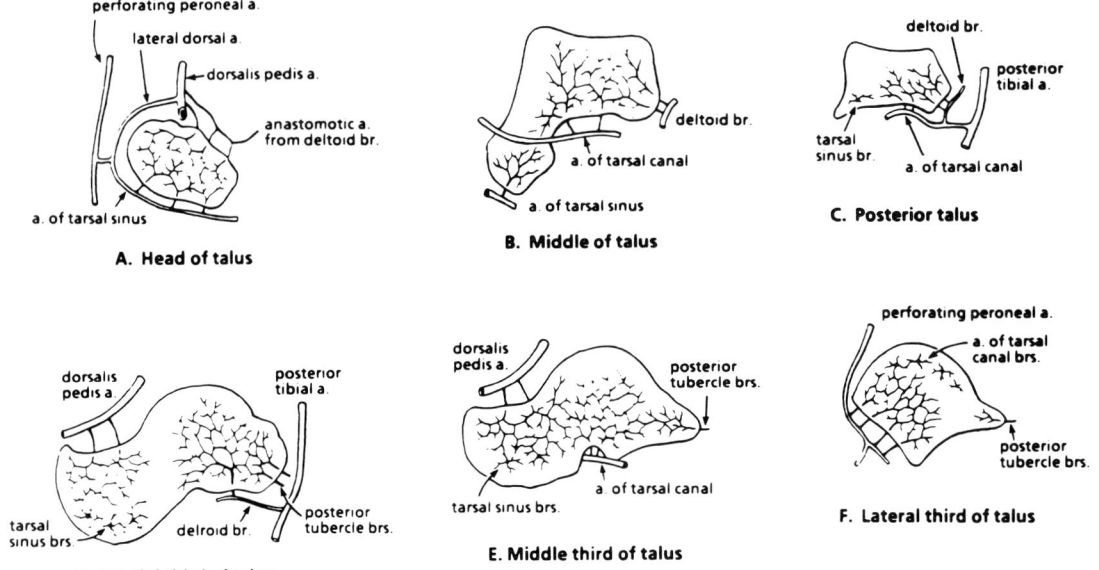

Figure 5-25. Blood supply of the talus. (From Adelaar RS: Fractures of the talus. In Greene WB, ed. In Instructional Course Lectures, Park Ridge, Illinois, American Academy of Orthopaedic Surgeons, 1990, p 148. Reprinted with permission.)

3. X-rays: 15° pronated and 75° angle projection for anteroposterior view of the talus
4. Treatment
   a. Closed reduction by plantar flexion and casting and 8–10 weeks of nonweight bearing if minimally displaced
   b. Open reduction and internal fixation: posteromedial or anterolateral approaches
      (1) If medial malleolus is fractured or the body is posteriorly dislocated, use posteromedial approach and malleolar osteotomy, preserving deltoid branch of the posterior tibial artery (a screw from posterior to anterior direction)
      (2) Anterolateral approach is between the extensor hallucis longus with neurovascular bundle and extensor digitorum longus
      (3) Cancellous screws or malleolar screws, 4.0
5. Complications
   a. Avascular necrosis
      (1) Incidence: 0–13% (type I), 20–50% (type II), and 83–100% (type III)
      (2) Diagnosis: negative Hawkins sign (disuse osteoporosis in the body of the talus if viable), bone scan or magnetic resonance imaging
      (3) Not all avascular necrosis is going to be problematic
      (4) Treatment: nonweight bearing, brace, or ankle fusion
   b. Skin necrosis, infection, malunion
D. Fractures of the body of the talus
   1. Relatively rare
   2. High incidence of avascular necrosis
   3. Treatment: nonweight-bearing cast for nondisplaced fractures and open reduction and internal fixation for displaced fractures
   4. Comminuted fractures: arthrodesis
E. Fractures of the head of the talus
   1. Rare

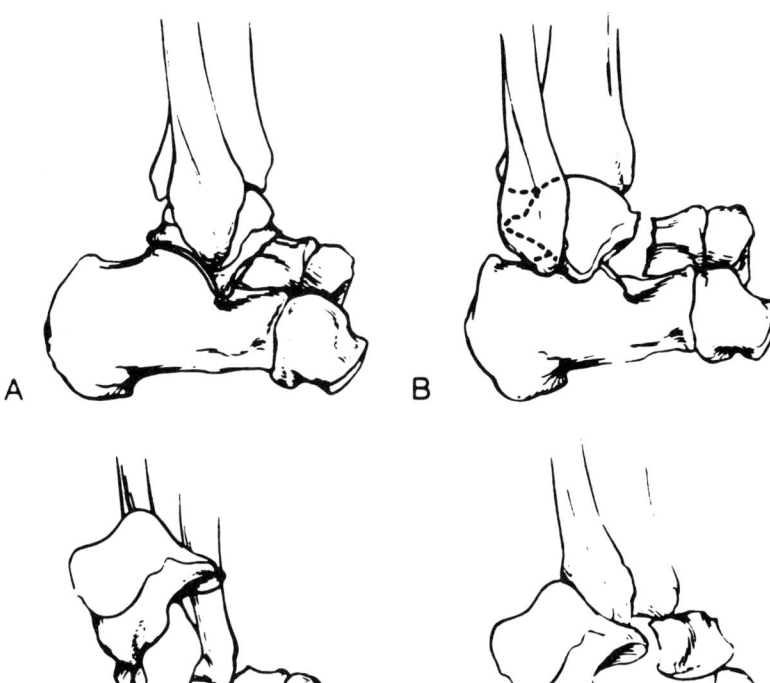

Figure 5-26. Hawkins classification of talus neck fractures. **A.** Type I: nondisplaced. **B.** Type II: displaced fracture of the talar neck with subluxation or dislocation of the subtalar joint. **C.** Type III: displaced fracture of the talar neck with dislocation of the body of the talus from both subtalar and ankle joint. **D.** Type IV: type III with an additional dislocation at the talonavicular joint. (From Mann RA, ed. Surgery of the foot. ed 5. St Louis, CV Mosby, 1986, p 684. Reprinted with permission.)

      2. Treatment: short leg cast for 6–8 weeks and arch support for 6 months and open reduction and pinning if displaced
  F. Fractures of the talar processes
      1. Lateral process, posterior process (lateral tubercle) and rarely medial tubercle of the posterior process
      2. Treatment: mostly short leg casting for 6 weeks and open reduction for large lateral process fractures, which are displaced
  G. Subtalar dislocation
      1. Types
         a. Medial: more common (85%) and inversion mechanism
         b. Lateral: 15% incidence and eversion mechanism
      2. Associated fractures are common
      3. Treatment
         a. Closed reduction and casting for 3 weeks and range of motion exercise
            (1) Lateral dislocation is more difficult to reduce closed than medial dislocation, and posterior tibialis tendon may be entrapped
            (2) In medial dislocation, head of the talus may be trapped by talonavicular capsule, extensor digitorum brevis muscle, or transverse fibers of the cruciate-crural ligament and impaction by the navicular
         b. Open reduction if irreducible (anteromedial incision) and internal fixation

V. Tarsometatarsal Injuries (Lisfranc Joint)

A. General considerations
 1. Second metatarsal is the key to reduction
 2. Maintain longitudinal and transverse arches
 3. Arterial injury or compartment syndrome may develop
 4. Reflex sympathetic dystrophy may develop later
B. Classification (Hardcastle) (Fig 5-27)
 1. Type I or homolateral: entire metatarsal group is shifted in one direction
 2. Type II or isolated: either the first metatarsal is displaced medially or lateral four metatarsals are displaced laterally
 3. Type III or divergent: first metatarsal and the lateral four metatarsals diverge in opposite directions
C. Treatment
 1. Closed reduction: reduce the second metatarsal, followed by the first and lateral metatarsals
 2. Percutaneous pins are used both medially and laterally
 3. Open reduction and either K-wire or screw fixation if closed reduction is not possible

VI. Fractures of the Forefoot

A. Usually conservative treatment
B. Fractures of the base of the fifth metatarsal: nonweight-bearing short leg cast for 6 weeks (nonunion is common)
C. Longitudinal wires if multiple fractures
D. Small interfragmentary screws or AO plate may be used in selected cases with appropriate fracture configurations

REFERENCES

Arntz CT, Veith RG, Hansen ST: Fracture and fracture dislocations of the tarsometatarsal joint. J Bone Joint Surg 70A:173–181, 1988

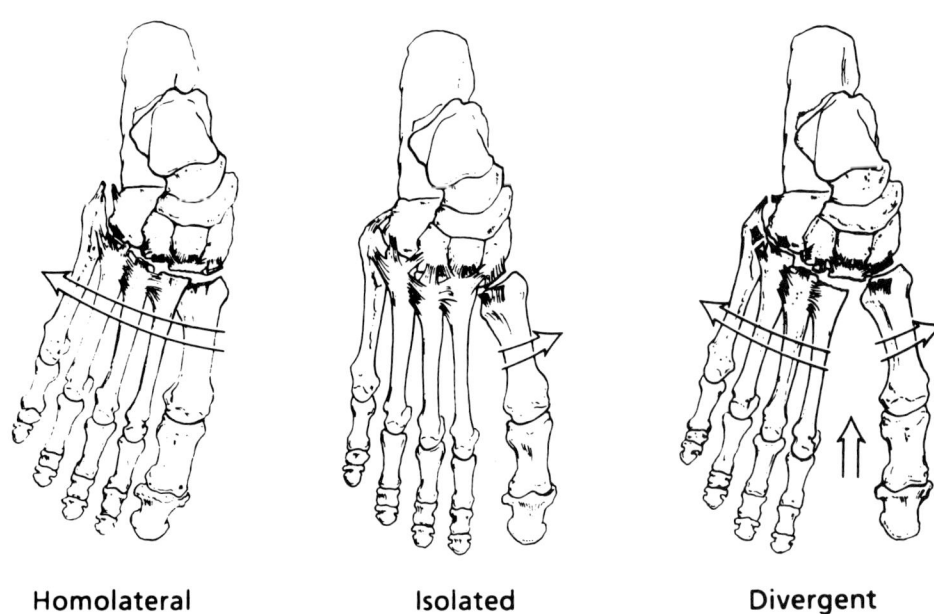

Figure 5-27. Classification of tarsometatarsal injuries. (From Adelaar RS: The treatment of tarsometatarsal fracture-dislocation. In Greene WB, ed. In Instructional Course Lectures, Park Ridge, Illinois, American Academy of Orthopaedic Surgeons, 1990, p 142. Reprinted with permission.)

Bauer M, Bergstron B, Hemborg A, et al: Malleolar fractures. Nonoperative versus operative treatment: A controlled study. Clin Orthop 199:17–27, 1985

Canale S, Kelly F: Fractures of the neck of the talus. J Bone Joint Surg 60A:143–156, 1978

Comfort T, Behrens F, Gaither D, et al: Long-term results of displaced talar neck fractures. Clin Orthop 199:81–87, 1985

DeLee JC, Curtis R: Subtalar dislocation of the foot. J Bone Joint Surg 64A:433–437, 1982

Franklin J, Johnson K, Hansen ST: Immediate internal fixation of open ankle fractures. J Bone Joint Surg 66A:1349–1356, 1984

Grob D, Simpson L, Weber G, et al: Operative treatment of displaced talus fractures. Clin Orthop 199:88–96, 1985

Harding D, Waddell J: Open fracture in depressed fractures of the os calcis. Clin Orthop 199:124–131, 1985

Harper MC, Hardin G: Posterior malleolar fractures of the ankle associated with external rotation-abduction injuries. Results with and without internal fixation. J Bone Joint Surg 70A:1348–1356, 1988

Hawkins L: Fractures of the neck of the talus. J Bone Joint Surg 52A:991–1002, 1970

Kellam J, Waddell J: Fractures of the distal tibial metaphysis with intra-articular extension — the distal explosion fracture. J Trauma 19:593–601, 1979

Limbird RS, Aaron RK: Laterally comminuted fracture-dislocation of the ankle. J Bone Joint Surg 69A:881–885, 1987

Lindsjo U: Classification of ankle fractures: The Lauge-Hansen or AO system. Clin Orthop 199:12–16, 1985

Monson ST, Ryan JR: Subtalar dislocation. J Bone Joint Surg 63A:1156–1158, 1981

Phillips W, Schwartz H, Keller C, et al: A prospective randomized study of the management of severe ankle fractures. J Bone Joint Surg 67A:67–78, 1985

Pozo JL, Kirwan E, Jackson AM: The long-term results of conservative management of severely displaced fractures of the calcaneus. J Bone Joint Surg 66B:386–390, 1984

Ruedi T, Allgower M: The operative treatment of intra-articular fractures of the lower end of the tibia. Clin Orthop 138:105–110, 1979

Shereff MJ: Fractures of the forefoot. In Greene WB, ed: Instructional course lectures. Park Ridge, Ill, American Academy of Orthopaedic Surgeons, 1990

Stephenson JR: Treatment of displaced intra-articular fractures of the calcaneus using medial and lateral approaches, internal fixation and early motion. J Bone Joint Surg 69A:115–130, 1987

Szyszkowitz R, Reschauer R, Seggl W: Eighty-five talus fractures treated by open reduction and internal fixation with five to eight years of follow up study of 69 patients. Clin Orthop 199:97–107, 1985

SECTION 6: HAND

Howard S. An
Douglas P. Hanel

48. Fingertip and Soft Tissue Coverage of the Hand
49. Tendon Injuries
50. Fractures and Dislocations of the Hand
51. Replantation
52. Wrist Injuries and Disorders
53. Nerve Injuries and Compression Neuropathies
54. Tendon Transfers of the Hand
55. Tenosynovitis, Osteoarthritis, and Rheumatoid Arthritis
56. Contractures and Reflex Sympathetic Dystrophy
57. Congenital Anomalies of the Hand
58. Tumors of the Hand and Amputation Surgery

48
Fingertip and Soft Tissue Coverage of the Hand

I. Fingertip Injuries
A. Anatomy
   1. Fingertip is defined as that portion distal to the insertions of the extensor and flexor tendons
   2. Volar pulp covered by the highly innervated skin that is attached to the phalanx by the fibrosepta
   3. Nailbed consists of the germinal matrix, which is responsible for growth, and the sterile matrix is responsible for nail adhesion
B. Classification
   1. Type: crush or sharp
   2. Allen's level
      a. Fingertip nail not involved
      b. Pulp and the nail to the distal phalanx
      c. Nail matrix and distal phalanx
      d. Base of distal phalanx
C. Treatment principles
   1. Restore sensation without tenderness and preserve tissue
   2. Maintain length
   3. Cosmesis
   4. Maintain joint motion
   5. Select surgery that is consistent with individual factors (eg, age, sex, occupation, hand dominance, nature of defects, and surgeon's experience)
D. Surgical options
   1. Healing by secondary intention
      a. For <1 cm defects or in children
      b. Technique requires thorough cleaning and apply sterile gauze with daily dressing changes until healed (3–5 weeks)
      c. This is simple and reliable technique but delayed healing or pyogenic granuloma may form
   2. Split-thickness skin graft (STSG)
      a. Epidermis with only part of the dermis (15–25/1000 inch)
      b. Indicated for small pulp defects
      c. Graft shrinkage reduces size of defect with STSG
      d. Requires vascularized pulp or tip will become pencil-tip shaped and the graft becomes unstable
      e. Technique
         (1) Harvest graft with dermatome or razor blade
         (2) Donor site: buttock, thigh
         (3) Anchor graft: suture and stenting techniques
         (4) Inspect in 7 days
      f. Disadvantages may be hypersensitivity or insensitivity, cosmetic problems, and skin texture or stability problems
   3. Full-thickness skin graft (FTSG)
      a. Epidermis and dermis without subcutaneous tissue
      b. FTSG is often preferred to give better cosmetic results, better sensory return, and better durability
      c. Direct closure of the donor site (groin or hypothenar areas)
      d. Technique: defat and suture in place, immobilize with a stent
      e. Slightly decreased rate of "take" and minimal shrinkage
   4. Composite grafts
      a. Consists of skin and bone (replacement of amputated part without revascularization)

    b. Injuries with sharp, clean amputations
    c. Gives good cosmesis and especially appropriate in children but success in unpredictable
5. Primary closure with shortening
    a. If <50% of distal phalanx, shorten bone, ablate germinal matrix, close primarily
    b. If 50% of distal phalanx present but exposed, will need local or regional flap for coverage (cannot shorten without resultant hook nail)
    c. Disadvantages: shortening and possibility of neuroma formation
6. Local flaps
    a. Volar V-Y (Atasoy, 1970): indicated for dorsal oblique types or transverse types of injury
    b. Kutler lateral flaps (Kutler, 1947, Fisher, 1967); best indicated for transverse amputations but less commonly used because of hypersensitivity or insensitivity
    c. Technique
        (1) Careful flap preparation
        (2) Undermining of flap and release of fibrosepta (flaps can be mobilized 10 mm)
        (3) Tension-free closure
7. Volar advancement flap
    a. Indicated for the thumb defects up to 1 cm
    b. Technique involves midlateral incisions with careful flap and neurovascular bundle dissection. Advance by interphalangeal (IP) flexion and may require proximal incision (Burow's triangles)
    c. Flexion contractures may occur (tolerated in thumb but not the fingers; therefore, do not use this flap on fingers)
    d. Damage to neurovascular bundle and neuroma is possible
8. Cross-finger flaps
    a. Types: dorsal cross-finger flap, reverse cross-finger flap, flag flap (for thumb), and palmar cross-finger flap (for thumb)
    b. Indicated for coverage of large (relatively) areas of skin and pulp loss with exposed bone
    c. Versatile and reliable and tissue is locally available
    d. Sensation improves with time; may attach digital nerve stump to dorsal cutaneous nerve found within the transferred flap
    e. Not indicated in rheumatoid arthritis patients and those >50 years of age because of flexion contracture
    f. Technique
        (1) Prepare recipient area and design flap from adjacent digit, use template to confirm design
        (2) Raise flap and suture in place: apply FTSG (never use STSG) to donor defect
        (3) Release and inset at 2–3 weeks
    g. Disadvantages are a defect on normal digit, possible joint stiffness, and may place hair-bearing skin on palmar surface of digit
9. Thenar flaps
    a. Mainly for palmar oblique and transverse amputations of the fingers
    b. Not advised in older patients because of flexion contracture
    c. Technique
        (1) Prepare digit, design along the digitopalmar crease, consider the H technique described by Melone
        (2) Close donor site defect primarily if flap is raised in digitopalmar crease (graft is rarely indicated)
        (3) Suture flap to involved digit and detach at 2 weeks
        (4) Radial digital nerve is at significant risk because it lies just deep to the flap that is raised
10. Neurovascular flaps
    a. Island flap is rarely used in fingertip injuries

     b. Isolated thumb pulp injuries in a clean wound
     c. Considerable expertise required
  11. Distant flaps
     a. Rarely used for fingertip injuries
     b. Indicated in multiple injured digits in those requiring specialized needs (ie, sensation)
     c. Prevent additional hand defects

II. Nailbed Injuries

A. If subungual hematoma is present, drain it. If ⅓ of nail, remove and examine matrix
B. In laceration, crush, or avulsion, remove nail and examine the nail matrix
C. Repair using absorbable suture
D. Replace nail or use silicone sheet spacer to make a nail template to keep the eponychium open
E. Graft nail bed deficits from toenail graft (split or full thickness) or use the undamaged area of remaining nail bed
F. If associated fracture, stabilize with K-wire, but remember this injury is an open fracture

III. Soft Tissue Coverage of Hand Defects

A. Assessment
  1. Tidy: incised, sliced, little contamination, or little tissue loss beyond margin of wounds
  2. Untidy: crush, avulsion, explosion, or heavily contaminated zone of injury far beyond margins of wound
  3. Timing: time delay between injury and treatment
  4. Mechanism of injury
     a. Type of machine
     b. Shape of punch press
     c. Hot vs cold rollers
     d. Injection, paint, oil, fluorocarbons, farm injury, penetrating injury
     e. Status of wound bed and vascularity
     f. Exposed structures
     g. Which structures need to be repaired?
     h. Need for secondary surgery
     i. Sensation and cosmetic concerns
     j. Hand function always supersedes cosmesis
B. Choice of coverage
  1. Primary vs delayed: other than bite wounds and farm injuries, very few hand wounds require delayed closure (if supple tissues are available close primarily)
  2. Free skin grafting
     a. Requires vascularized stable bed
        (1) Full thickness for all palmar wounds, all finger wounds
        (2) Split thickness for dorsum of carpal-metacarpal region (if at all possible, avoid meshing graft to avoid the "lizard skin" look)
  3. Local flaps
     a. Random pattern flaps
        (1) Vascular pattern lacks bias in any particular direction, and therefore lacks versatility
        (2) Skin arterial supply depends on multiple small perforating arteries from adjacent muscle, subdermal vessels from major arteries
        (3) Flap dissection and longitudinal dimension can be enhanced if flap is harvested with investing fascia (fasciocutaneous flap — Ponten)
        (4) Examples: advancement flaps, rotational flaps, transposition, Z-plasty
     b. Axial pattern
        (1) Direct cutaneous arteriovenous system superficial to or running within the investing fascia, supplies a large skin area. Vessel length becomes the determinant of flap length
        (2) Skin arterial supply depends on single identifiable vessel travel-

ing in a predictable area (or territory)
        (3) Examples: fillet, flag, Moberg
    4. Distant flaps
        a. Random pattern flaps
            (1) Cross arm
            (2) Abdominal flaps
        b. Axial pattern
            (1) Reliable vascular supply
            (2) Hairless skin
            (3) Donor site closed primarily
            (4) Hidden beneath clothing
            (5) Long pedicle allows some hand motion
            (6) Tubes can be formed to minimize raw surface area and assist in positioning the hand
            (7) Disadvantages: hand is usually dependent and the vessels of proximal pedicle lie deep to fascia and prevent thinning of flap at its base (particularly bothersome in the case of the groin flap)
            (8) Examples: deltopectoral, hypogastric, and groin flaps
        c. Musculocutaneous flaps
            (1) Consists of muscle with or without subcutaneous tissue and skin. Skin is supplied by muscular perforators. Muscle is supplied by dominant artery and venae commitantes
            (2) Examples: latissimus dorsi and gracilis
    5. Free flaps
        a. General considerations
            (1) Dominant artery and venae commitantes supply a territory of skin, muscle, bone, or combination thereof. Secondary venous drainage may come from subcutaneous veins
            (2) Rate-limiting factor: recipient vessels (may require distant vein grafts)
            (3) Microsurgical skills required
            (4) Should not attempt unless microsurgical success rate is >95%
        b. There are >30 territories described (the following are the most frequently used)
            (1) Cutaneous free flaps
                i. Cosmetically best
                ii. Limited ability to fill dead space
                iii. Examples
                    (a) Lateral arm (best used as ipsilateral and donor site conspicuous)
                    (b) Forearm (donor site very obvious and sacrifices radial artery)
                    (c) Dorsalis pedis (very high donor site morbidity)
                    (d) Groin (best donor site, difficult dissection in fat patients, pedicle does not exist in 12%)
                    (e) Scapular (very large flap, donor scar tends to spread)
            (2) Muscle
                i. Easily dissected
                ii. Most reliable pedicles
                iii. Can minimize bulk and donor site defect if harvested as muscle only
                iv. Excellent for filling dead space
                v. Examples
                    (a) Latissimus dorsi: work horse of free tissue transfer, can minimize bulk by splitting muscle and leaving the remainder innervated, can cover most any extremity defects
                    (b) Rectus abdominis: good for medium-sized defects, can be harvested with patient supine, "tummy tuck" incision minimizes donor site scar
                    (c) Gracilis: long and narrow (good for through and

through wounds), may have segmental blood supply (will lose distal third of muscle), can be innervated for functional muscle reconstruction
- (d) Tensor fascia lata (bulky, can use in lower extremity for vascularized tendon transfer)
- (e) Serratus anterior (last three slips can be harvested without compromising scapular function, may be innervated to simultaneously reconstruct thenar eminence skin and muscle loss)

(3) Osseous
- i. Not indicated for defects <10 cm
- ii. Must consider donor site defect
- iii. Examples
  - (a) Rib: no practical application in extremity surgery
  - (b) Iliac crest: can be harvested with skin used in head and neck reconstruction, very little "orthopaedic" applications, donor site morbidity quite significant
  - (c) Fibula: can be harvested with skin, used as skin marker for postoperative monitoring or coverage of small defects donor site morbidity, must preserve distal 1/4 of fibula to prevent ankle valgus

(4) Vascularized nerve
- i. Indications remain questionable
- ii. Examples: superficial radial nerve, sural nerve, saphaneous, ulnar nerves

(5) Composite digit
- i. Great toe transfer: thumb reconstruction in nonathlete
- ii. Toe pulp or toe wrap reconstruct digit without sacrificing complete digit
- iii. Second toe: better donor site morbidity can harvest simultaneously with third toe in order to reconstruct multidigit deficits

IV. Deep Thermal Injuries to the Hand

A. Assess extent and depth of burn, which relates to temperature and exposure time
B. Prevent progression of injury
  1. Cold thermal rapid rewarming at 42°
  2. Hot thermal requires early debridement
  3. Prevent bacterial superinfection
     a. Dressings
     b. Antibacterial agents: silver sulfadiazine
     c. Debridement to include full thickness and tangential thickness
C. Splint hand in position of safety with wrist slight extension metacarpophalangeal (MCP) flexion, and IP extension
D. Coverage: early and late
  1. STSG
  2. FTSG
  3. Flaps
     a. Groin pedicle flaps previous work horse
     b. More and more free flaps and forearm pedicle flaps are being used
  4. Late reconstruction consists of scar excision, reestablish web spaces, local and distant flaps, and FTSG

REFERENCES

Allen MJ: Conservative management of fingertip injuries in adults. Hand 12:257, 1980

Asko-Seljavaara S, Lahteenmaki T, Waris T, Sundell B: Comparison of latissimus dorsi and rectus abdominis free flaps. Br J Plast Surg 40:620–628, 1987

Atasoy E, Godfrey A, Kalisman M: The "antenna" procedure for the "hoo-nail" deformity. J Hand Surg 8:55, 1983

Atasoy E, Ioakimudis E, Kasdan ML, et al: Reconstruction of the amputated fingertip with a triangular volar flap. J Bone Joint Surg 52A:698, 1970

Barwick WJ, Goodkind DJ, Serafin D: The free scapular flap. Plast Reconstr Surg 69:779–785, 1982

Boyd JB, Taylor GI, Corlett R: The vascular territory of the superior and the deep inferior epigastric systems. Plast Reconstr Surg 73:1–14, 1984

Clayburgh RH, Wood MB, Cooney WP: Nail bed repair and reconstruction by reverse dermal grafts. J Hand Surg 8:594–599, 1983

Godina M: Early reconstruction of complex trauma of the extremities. Plast Reconstr Surg 78:285–292, 1986

Harii K, Ohmori K, Torii S: Free gracilis muscle transplantation with microvascular anastomosis for the treatment of facial paralysis. Plast Reconstr Surg 57:133–143, 1976

Katsaros J, Schusterman M, Beppu M, et al: The lateral upper arm flap: Anatomy and clinical application. Ann Plast Surg 12:489–500, 1984

Lister G, Scheker L: Emergency free flaps to the upper extremity. J Hand Surg 13A:22–28, 1988

Macht SD, Watson HK: The Moberg volar advancement flap for digital reconstruction. J Hand Surg 5:372, 1980

Maxwell GP, Steuber X, Hoopes JE: A free latissimus dorsi flap. Plast Reconstr Surg 62:464–466, 1978

McGregor MH, Jackson IT: The groin flap. Br J Plast Surg 25:3, 1972

Melone CP Jr, Beasley RW, Carstens JH Jr: The thenar flap. An analysis of its use in 150 cases. J Hand Surg 7:291–297, 1982

Saito H, Suzuki Y, Fujino K, Tajima T: Free nail bed graft for the treatment of nail bed injuries of the hand. J Hand Surg 8:171–178, 1983

Scheker LR, Kleinert HE, Hanel DP: Lateral arm composite tissue transfer to ipsilateral hand defects. J Hand Surg 12A:665–672, 1987

Seckel BR: Self advancing silicone rubber splint for repair of split nail deformity. J Hand Surg 11A:143–144, 1986

Shapiro J, Akbarnia BA, Hanel DP: Free tissue transfer in children. J Pediatr Orthop 9:590–595, 1989

Shepard GH: Treatment of nail bed avulsions with split thickness nail bed grafts. J Hand Surg 8:49–54, 1983

Tobin GR, Schusterman M, et al: The intramuscular neurovascular anatomy of the latissimus dorsi: The basis for splitting the flap. Plast Reconstr Surg 67:637–641, 1981

Urbaniak JR, Koman LA, Goldner RD, et al: The vascularized cutaneous scapular flap. Plast Reconstr Surg 69:772–778, 1982

Zook EG: The perionychium. In Green DP, ed. Operative hand surgery. New York, Churchill Livingstone, 1988

Zook EG, Guy RJ, Russell RC: A study of nail bed injuries: Causes, treatment, and prognosis. J Hand Surg 9A:247, 1984

Zook EG, Van Beek AL, Russell RC, et al: Anatomy and physiology of the perionychium: A review of the literature and anatomic study. J Hand Surg 5:528, 1980

49
Tendon Injuries

EXTENSOR TENDON INJURIES

I. Principles
A. Four zones
  1. Zone 1: distal to central tendon insertion
  2. Zone 2: from transverse portion of hood to central tendon insertion
  3. Zone 3: sagittal band at MCP joint
  4. Zone 4: proximal to MCP joint
B. In the fingers, the extensor tendons are flat and thin, have short excursion: accurate repair difficult but necessary
C. Adhesion is common and prevention is important

II. Zone 1 Injury (Mallet Finger)
(Fig 6-1)
A. Closed injury
  1. Splint distal interphalangeal (DIP) joint in extension for 8–10 weeks
  2. Continue night splints 4–6 weeks beyond full-time splints
  3. Proximal interphalangeal (PIP) flexion of 20°–30° relaxes lateral bands: therefore initial splint can incorporate PIP joint flexion (first 2 weeks postacute injury only)
B. Open injury or avulsion greater than 30% articular surface: primary repair of the tendon (K-wire fixation of the joint, not necessary to capture avulsed fragment)
C. Aggressive approach if subluxation is present
D. Chronic mallet deformity (>4–6 weeks): if no subluxation, it may be treated with splinting (may require 6–12 weeks). If subluxation present, reduce joint, reinsert tendon. Surgical procedures may be tendon reefing at DIP joint, Fowler operation (central slip release at PIP), or arthrodesis of DIP

III. Zone 2 Injury (Boutonnière Deformity)
A. Pathology
  1. Divided central tendon
  2. Torn triangular ligament
  3. Volar migration of the lateral bands
  4. Flexion of PIP and hyperextension deformities of DIP joints (due to relative shortening of lateral bands)
  5. Chronic deformity: contracture of oblique retinacular ligament and transverse retinacular ligament
  6. Lateral bands may also be lacerated in open injuries (active extension of PIP is lost)
B. Closed injury
  1. Splint PIP joint in neutral for 6–8 weeks
  2. Leave DIP (pulls lateral bands and torn central slip distally)
  3. At 4 weeks, allow motion in dynamic extension splint
  4. Assess weekly if PIP extension lag continues, may need to replace with static extension splint
  5. Total time of treatment may be 12–16 weeks
C. Open injury
  1. Primary repair, K-wire supplement
  2. If lateral bands are involved, will need to splint DIP joint
  3. If lateral bands not involved, leave DIP joint free and encourage motion at this joint
D. Chronic Boutonnière deformity
  1. Restoration of passive motion is absolute prerequisite

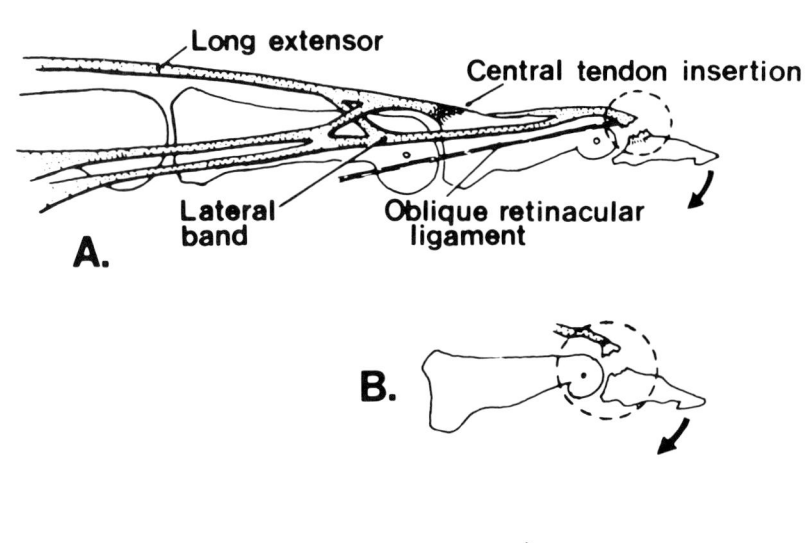

Figure 6-1. Mallet finger. **A.** Tendon avulsion. **B.** Avulsion fracture without significant joint involvement or subluxation. **C.** Joint incongruity and subluxation. (From Burton RI: Disorders of the extensor mechanism. In Evart CM, ed. Surgery of the musculoskeletal system. New York, Churchill Livingstone, 1983, p 269. Reprinted with permission.)

2. Numerous reconstructions are available (testimony to difficulty of this problem)
3. Procedures address four issues (in part or whole)
   a. Restoration of passive PIP and DIP motion (may require PIP joint capsular release and prolonged static and dynamic splinting)
   b. Extensor tendon tenolysis
   c. Central slip advancement
   d. Lengthening of extensor to DIP
4. Examples
   a. Littler: dorsal transposition and suture of lateral bands
   b. Eaton-Littler, Dolphin, Fowler, or Nalebuff: extensor division (lateral bands distal to central tendon insertion leaving oblique retinacular ligament intact, allowing the lateral bands to slide proximally (Fig 6-2)
   c. Matev: transposition of lateral bands to central tendon and opposite lateral band

IV. Zone 3: Extensor Injury Near Metacarpophalangeal Joint (Sagittal Bands and Transverse Fibers)

A. If PIP and DIP joints are also flexed in addition to MCP joint, intrinsic tendons are also likely to be lacerated in addition to central tendon and hood
B. Direct repair is usually indicated, followed by splinting

V. Zone 4: Extensor Injury Proximal to Dorsal Hood

A. Primary repair with suture
B. Tendon grafting (extensor indicis proprius [EIP] or extensor digiti quinti [EDQ]) for chronic laceration

VI. Swan-Neck Deformity

A. Conjoined lateral bands bowstring dorsally as the transverse retinacular and volar plate stretch, causing hyperextension of PIP and flexion deformity of DIP
B. May be secondary to chronic mallet, tight intrinsics, traumatically or congenitally

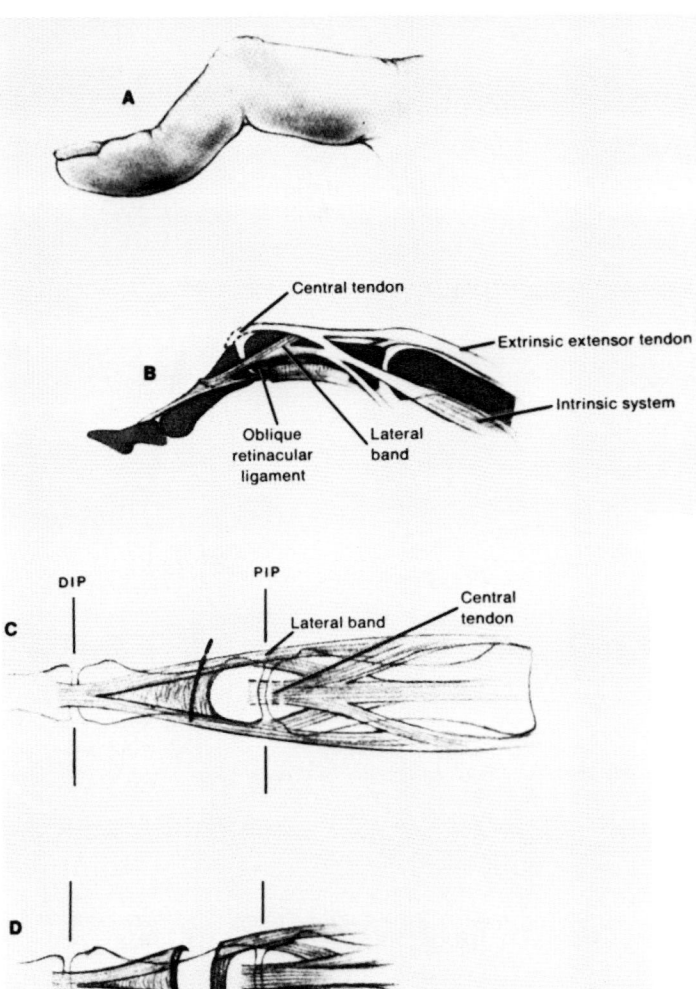

Figure 6-2. Boutonnière deformity. **A.** Flexion of PIP and hyperextension of DIP deformities. **B.** Central tendon is disrupted and the lateral band is migrated volarly. **C.** Eaton-Littler, Dolphin, Fowler, or Nalebuff utilizes partial extensor division (lateral bands distal to central tendon insertion leaving oblique retinacular legament intact, allowing the lateral bands to slide proximally. (From Burton RI: Disorders of the extensor mechanism. In Evart CM, ed. Surgery of the musculoskeletal system. New York, Churchill Livingstone, 1983, p 296. Reprinted with permission.)

lax volar plate, MCP joint volar dislocation as in rheumatoid hand, and loss of flexor digitorum sublimis (FDS) activity

C. Treatment
  1. If secondary to mallet finger, then fix the mallet
  2. If full range of motion (PIP and DIP) but locks as PIP joint extends or hyperextends, then do sublimis sling or spiral oblique retinacular ligament advancement (Fig 6-3)
  3. If secondary to intrinsic tightness, then do lateral band release

FLEXOR TENDON INJURIES

I. Anatomy

A. Zones (Fig 6-4)
  1. Distal to FDS insertion
  2. From MCP joint to FDS insertion ("no man's land")

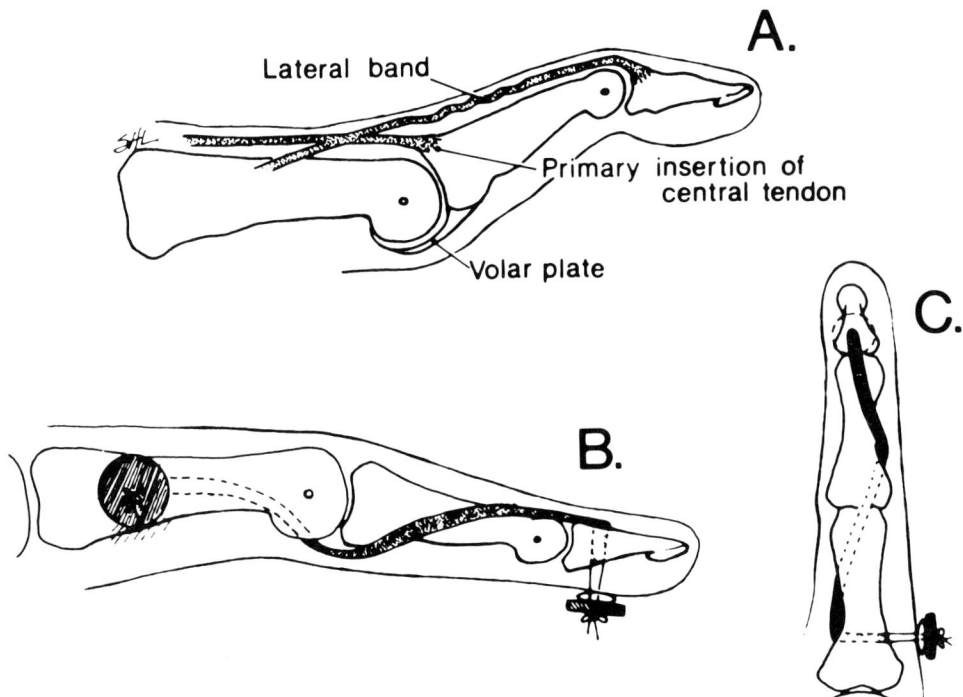

Figure 6-3. Swan-neck deformity. **A.** Hyperextension of PIP (laxity of the volar plate) and flexion of DIP (laxity of lateral bands) deformities. **B, C.** The palmaris longus is used to provide a tenodesis to correct both joint imbalance. (From Burton RI: Disorders of the extensor mechanism. In Evart CM, ed. Surgery of the musculoskeletal system. New York, Churchill Livingstone, 1983, p 283. Reprinted with permission.)

    3. From carpal tunnel to MCP joint
    4. Carpal tunnel
    5. Proximal to carpal tunnel
 B. FDS splits at A1 pulley for FDP to pass through (Camper's chiasma)
 C. Pulley system (Fig 6-4)
    1. Annular ligaments: A1 at MCP joint, A3 at PIP joint, A5 and DIP joint. A2 at proximal phalanx and A4 at middle phalanx are the most important and must always be preserved or reconstructed
    2. Cruciate ligaments: C1 between A2 and A3, C2 between A3 and A4, and C3 between A4 and A5
 D. Paratenon proximal to metacarpal neck and tendon sheath distal to the metacarpal neck

II. Blood Supply and Nutrition

A. Tendon: fibrils of collagen make up fascicles and loose connective tissues make up endotenon and epitenon
B. Covering
    1. Vascular paratenon for tendons without sheath
    2. Mesotenon (tendon sheath) along with annular and cruciate ligaments for nutrition, gliding and pulley function. The tendon sheath is composed of outer parietal and inner visceral layers that cover the synovial membrane (epitenon) of the tendon
C. Blood supply comes from
    1. Paratenons in tendons without the sheath
    2. Mesotenon, osseous insertions, and

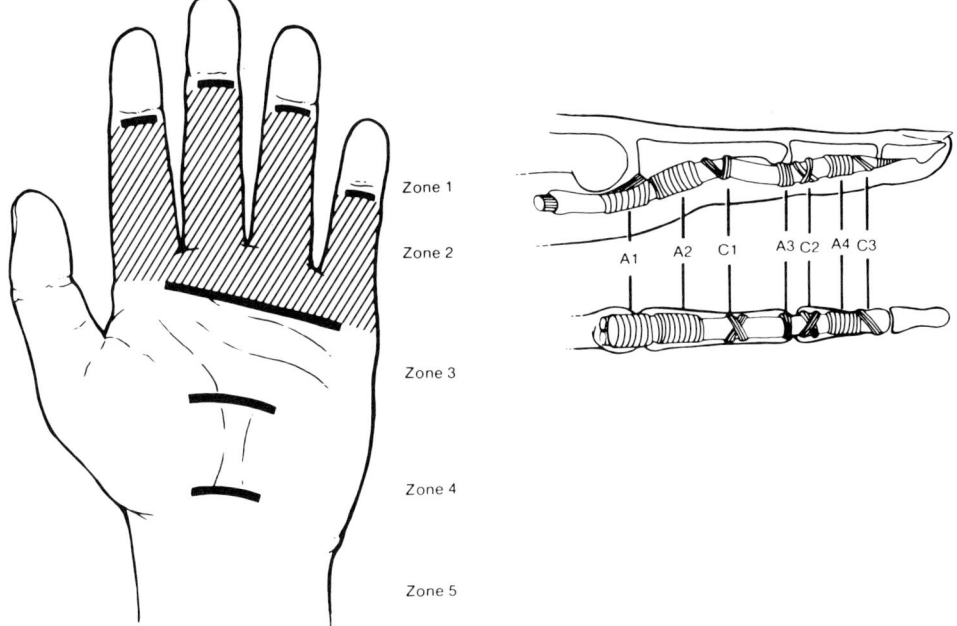

Figure 6-4. Zones of the flexor tendons and pulleys. Zone 1 is distal to FDS insertion. Zone 2 is the area of the flexor sheath. Zone 3 is the palm distal to the carpal tunnel. Zone 4 is the carpal tunnel itself, and zone 5 is proximal to carpal tunnel. The pulley system in the flexor sheath includes four annular and three cruciform pulleys. A2 and A4 pulleys are most important to preserve. (From Ezaki M: Hand Surgery. In: Bucholz RW, Lippert FG, Wenger DR, Ezaki M, eds. Orthopaedic decision making. Philadelphia, BC Decker, and St. Louis, CV Mosby, 1984, p 272. Reprinted with permission.)

synovial diffusion in tendons with the sheath
3. Vincula: vinculum longum superficialis, vinculum breve superficialis, vinculum longus profundus, vinculum breve profundus (the tendon in the midproximal phalanx is least vascular and more vascularity in the dorsal aspect of the tendon because of the vincular attachment)
4. Vascular pattern: very few vessels seen in the palmar third of the tendon

II. Tendon Healing
A. Tendons without sheath (paratenon covered)
   1. Inflammatory
   2. Fibroblastic: 3–14 days, "tendon callus" in 14 days
   3. Collagen organization: 3–4 weeks and tensile strength gradually increases until 12 weeks
   4. Densely scarred
B. Tendons with sheath
   1. Endotenon: collagen formation ("intrinsic")
   2. Epitenon: phagocytosis and differentiation of fibroblasts ("extrinsic")

IV. Flexor Tendon Repair
A. Primary repair, including zone 2
   1. Within 24 hours is ideal but up 21 days is acceptable, ie, results will be as good as staged repair

2. Relative contraindications
   a. Segmental tendon laceration
   b. Tendon advancement greater than 1 cm
   c. Associated skeletal injury necessitating prolonged immobilization
   d. Loss of pulleys
   e. Wound infection
   f. Extensive scarring
   g. Insufficient skin
B. Repair both FDS, flexor digitorum profundus (FDP) and the sheath
C. Preserve pulleys, especially A2 and A4
D. Atraumatic technique with loupe magnification
E. Core suture needs "grasping stitch" variation of Kessler technique
   1. Suture should pass within palmar third of tendon
   2. Suture locks by transverse limb passing superficial to longitudinal limb or by using a locking loop in corner
   3. Suture material: braided synthetic 3 or 4-0
   4. Epitenon suture: 6-0 monofilament provides alignment but not strength
G. Postoperative management
   1. Day one: bulky dressing (wrist at 30° and MCP at 70°–90° flexion)
      a. Elastic traction is attached to a nail suture and maintain involved digits in a flexed position at rest
      b. Actively extend IP joint fully 5–10 times every hour
   2. Day 3–7: hand is redressed in a light dressing in a thermoplastic dorsal blocking splint
      a. Elastic traction for controlled passive motion
      b. Actively extend IP joint fully
   3. Three weeks
      a. Discontinue forearm splint (attach digits to wrist band)
      b. Continue traction and IP extension exercise program
      c. Protect from full tendon tension from tenodesis effect
   d. Patients who do exceptionally well have a higher incidence of rupture; therefore, protect with traction beyond 6 weeks
   4. Six weeks: discontinue traction and continue exercise, initiate active flexion (no resistance exercise)
   5. Eight weeks: if flexion contractures are present, may institute extension splinting
   6. Ten weeks: graded resistive exercise and activity
   7. Twelve weeks: full activity

V. Staged Tendon Grafting (Hunter)
A. Frequently, three-stage procedures
   1. Stage I: tendon excision, rod placement, pulley reconstruction, soft tissue reconstruction, if necessary
   2. Stage II: replace rod with graft
   3. Stage III: tenolysis if necessary
B. Indications
   1. Excessive scarring of tendon bed
   2. Good passive range of motion
   3. Well-motivated patient
   4. Digits worth salvaging
C. Techniques
   1. Insertion of the rod (stage 1)
      a. Excise the damaged tendons
      b. Preserve or reconstruct pulley (A2 and A4)
      c. Secure distal juncture
      d. Achieve passive gliding
      e. Minimal proximal attachment (wrist or palm)
   2. Grafting (stage 2): 3 months later
      a. Donor tendons
         (1) Palmaris longus
         (2) Plantaris
         (3) Long toe extensors
         (4) EIP, EDQ
      b. Attach to implant distally and pull through
      c. Achieve proper tension (judge by tendodesis effect)
      d. Postoperative management: same as acute

D. Complications
   1. Synovitis around the rod
   2. Infection
   3. Rupture of the graft
   4. Too loose or tight tension of the graft
   5. Flexion deformity
   6. Adhesion of the graft

REFERENCES

Extensor Tendon Injury

Bowers WH, Hurst LC: Chronic mallet finger: The use of Fowler's central slip release. J Hand Surg 3:373, 1978

Burton RI: Extensor tendons-late reconstruction. In Green DP, ed. Operative hand surgery, ed 2. New York, Churchill Livingstone, 1986, p 2073

Dolphin JA: Extensor tenotomy for chronic Boutonnier deformity of the finger. Report of two cases. J Bone Joint Surg 47A:161–164, 1965

Grunberg AB, Reagan DS: Central slip tenotomy for chronic mallet finger deformity. J Hand Surg 12A:545, 1987

Kleinman WB, Peterson DP: Oblique retinacular ligament reconstruction for chronic mallet finger deformity. J Hand Surg 9A:399, 1984

Littler JW: The finger extensor system. Orthop Clin North Am 17:483, 1986

Littler JW, Eaton RG: Redistribution of forces in correction of boutonniere deformity. J Bone Joint Surg 49A:1267–274, 1967

Matev I: Transposition of the lateral slips of the aponeurosis in treatment of long standing "boutonniere deformity" of the fingers. Br J Plast Surg 17:281–286, 1964

Urbaniak JR, Hayes MG: Chronic boutonniere deformity — an anatomic reconstruction. J Hand Surg 6:379, 1981

Flexor Tendon Injuries

Armenta E, Lehrman A: The vincula to the flexor tendons of the hand. J Hand Surg 9A:210–217, 1984

Becker H, Orak F, Duponselle E: Early active motion following a beveled technique of flexor tendon repair. Report of fifty cases. J Hand Surg 4:454, 1979

Boyes JH, Stark HH: Flexor tendon grafts in the fingers and thumb: A study of factors influencing results in 1000 cases. J Bone Joint Surg 53:1332–1342, 1971

Cannon NM, Strickland JW: Therapy following flexor tendon surgery. In Strickland JW, ed. Hand clinics-flexor tendon surgery. Philadelphia, WB Saunders, 1985

Doyle JR, Blythe WF: Anatomy of the flexor tendon sheath and pulleys of the thumb. J Hand Surg 2:149, 1977

Gelberman RH, Amiel D, Gonsalves M, et al: The influence on the healing of flexor tendons: A biochemical and microangiographic study. Hand 13:120–128, 1981

Hunter JM, Salisbury RE: Flexor tendon reconstruction in severely damaged hands: A two-stage procedure using a silicone-Dacron reinforced gliding prosthesis prior to tendon grafting. J Bone Joint Surg 53A:829–858, 1971

Kleinert HE, Kutz JE, Ashbell TS, et al: Primary repair of lacerated flexor tendons in "no man's land." J Bone Joint Surg 49:577, 1967

LaSalle WB, Strickland JW: An evaluation of digital performance following two-stage flexor tendon reconstruction. J Hand Surg 7:411, 1982

Lister GD: Incision and closure of the flexor tendon sheath during tendon repair. Hand 15:123–135, 1983

Lister GD, Kleinert HE, Kutz JE, et al: Primary flexor tendon repair followed by immediate controlled mobilization. J Hand Surg 2:441–451, 1977

McClinton MA, Curtis RM, Wilgis EFS: One hundred tendon grafts for isolated flexor digitorum profundus injuries. J Hand Surg 7:224–229, 1982

Peterson WM, Manske PR, Lesker PA: The effect of flexor sheath integrity on nutrient uptake by primate flexor tendons. J Hand Surg 11A:413–416, 1986

Schneider LH: Staged tendon reconstruction. Hand Clin 1:109, 1985

Strickland JW: Flexor tenolysis. In Strickland JW, ed. Hand clinics-flexor tendon surgery. Philadelphia, WB Saunders, 1985

Strickland JW: Functional recovery after flexor tendon severance in the finger: The state of the art. In Strickland JW, Steichen JB, eds. Difficult problems in hand surgery. St Louis, CV Mosby, 1982

Strickland JW, Glogovac SV: Digital function following flexor tendon repair in Zone II: A comparison of immobilization and controlled passive motion techniques. J Hand Surg 5:537–543, 1980

Wade PJF, Muir IFK, Hutcheon LL: Primary flexor tendon repair: The mechanical limitations of the modified Kesseler technique. J Hand Surg 11B:71–76, 1986

Wilson RL, Carter MS, Holdeman VA, Lovett WL: Flexor profundus injuries treated with delayed two-staged tendon grafting. J Hand Surg 5:74, 1980

50
Fractures and Dislocations of the Hand

I. General Considerations
A. Soft tissue and neurovascular evaluation is important
B. Do not immobilize the uninjured areas of the hand if possible
C. Hand splinting should be close to the "position of function" (30° of wrist extension, 70° of MCP flexion, extension of IP joints and abduction and apposition of the thumb
D. Timing of healing and immobilization is about 3 weeks for phalangeal fractures and 4 weeks for metacarpal fractures (do not wait for x-ray healing before mobilization)
E. In open fractures, irrigation, debridement, and restoration of skeletal stability are done in order to manage soft tissue injuries
F. Simple dorsal dislocations of the fingers can be mobilized in 10 days, whereas volar dislocations should be immobilized for 3 weeks
G. Complications may be malunion, nonunion, joint stiffness, tendon adherence

II. Metacarpal Fractures
A. Index, long, ring, little fingers
  1. Index and long metacarpals are relatively fixed, whereas ring metacarpal has 20° and the little metacarpal has 30° of motion at the base
  2. Types: head, neck, shaft, base fractures
  3. Angulation: usually apex dorsal due to interossei force
  4. Treatment
     a. Head fractures: open reduction and internal fixation with K-wire for split or three-part fractures
     b. Neck fractures
        (1) Angulation up to 30° may be accepted for ring and little fingers but no more than 10° for the index and long fingers
        (2) Any rotation cannot be accepted
        (3) Closed reduction and gutter splint is applied and close follow-up
        (4) Start motion in 2 weeks and discontinue splinting in 4 weeks
        (5) Rarely, K-wire or open reduction is necessary
     c. Shaft fractures
        (1) Transverse fractures: correct angulation and dorsal displacement of distal fragment and plaster splint (K-wire or plate fixation if persistent displacement)
        (2) Spiral or long oblique fractures: up to 2–3 mm shortening may be accepted (interfragmentary screws in uncontrollable fractures)
     d. Base fractures: often due to crushing injuries and associated with fracture-dislocations at the carpometacarpal (CMC) joints (accurate reduction, particularly in the ulnar metacarpals is important to prevent post-traumatic arthrosis)
B. Thumb metacarpal fractures
  1. Intra-articular fractures
     a. Bennett's fracture: intra-articular fracture dislocation and proximal and radial displacement of the distal fragment by the abductor pollicis longus (APL)

b. Rolando's fracture: Y-shaped comminuted intra-articular fractures
c. Treatment: anatomic reduction
    (1) Percutaneous pin fixation under image intensification for Bennett's fracture
    (2) Open reduction and internal fixation for Rolando's fractures (if comminution is too great, either plaster or external fixation can be used and early motion)

III. Phalangeal Fractures

A. Fractures of the proximal and middle phalanges
   1. Displacement patterns
      a. Proximal phalanx: usually volar angulation (extensors' pull distal fragment dorsally)
      b. Middle phalanx: volar angulation for neck and dorsal angulation for base fractures
   2. Treatment
      a. Intra-articular fractures
         (1) Splinting if undisplaced fractures
         (2) Open reduction and internal fixation if displaced fractures (>10–15% articular involvement for base of the proximal phalanx and >20% for collateral ligament avulsion fractures)
         (3) Intra-articular fractures of the base of the middle phalanx is associated with dorsal subluxation and may require extension block splinting (K-wire fixation if >40% articular involvement)
      b. Shaft fractures
         (1) Undisplaced fractures: buddy tape or splinting
         (2) Displaced fractures require closed reduction and immobilization (if rotation and alignment cannot be maintained, internal fixation is indicated)
         (3) Oblique fractures of the proximal phalanx tend to rotate and transverse fractures of the proximal phalanx tend to angulation and may require pinning or internal fixation
B. Fractures of the distal phalanx
   1. More than 50% of hand fractures
   2. Types may be longitudinal, transverse, or comminuted
   3. Dorsal splinting of DIP is adequate in most cases
   4. Avulsion fracture of the extensor surface (mallet fracture)
      a. Continuous dorsal splint for 6 weeks
      b. Open reduction and internal fixation if >30% joint fragment, >2 mm displacement, incongruity articular surface, or volar subluxation
   5. Avulsion from the flexor surface: pull out technique to restore FDP

IV. Dislocations

A. CMC joint
   1. Dorsal more common than volar dislocation
   2. Usually associated with fractures
   3. Fifth metacarpal is the most common and the fourth and the fifth metacarpals may dislocate together
   4. Treatment: closed reduction and immobilization with plaster or pinning (open reduction is frequently necessary, particularly in late cases)
B. MCP joint
   1. Dorsal dislocations are more frequent
   2. Treatment
      a. Closed reduction for simple dislocation
      b. Open reduction for complex dislocation, in which the volar plate is interposed (either dorsal or palmar approach can be used) (Fig 6-5)
C. IP joint
   1. DIP joint dislocation
      a. Rare and always dorsal

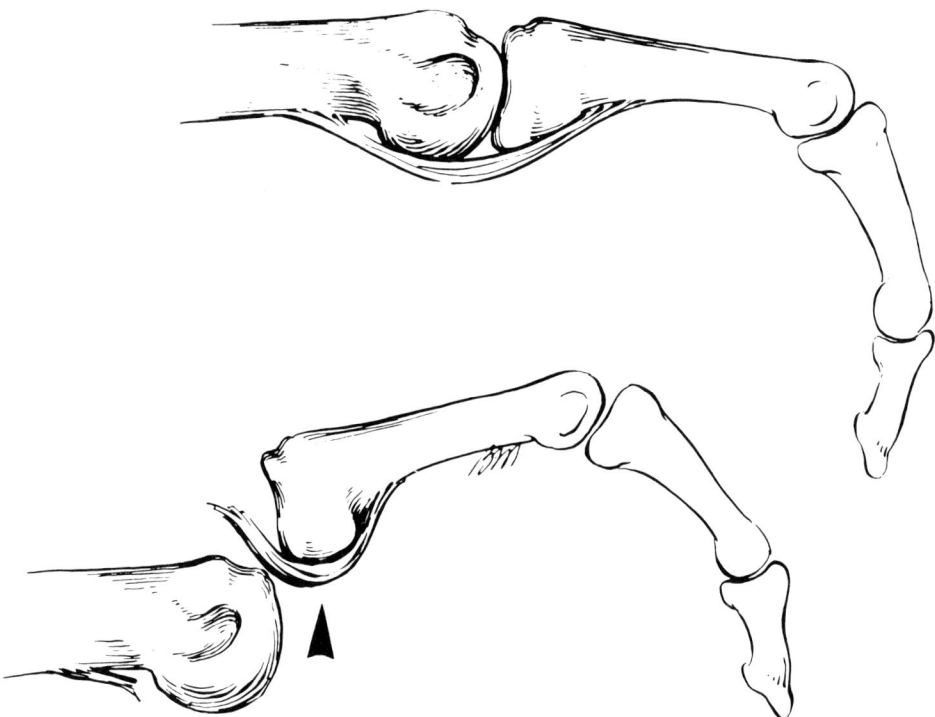

Figure 6-5. Metacarpophalangeal dislocation with interposition of the volar plate that prevents closed reduction. (From Green DP: Dislocations and ligamentous injuries in the hand. In Evart CM, ed. Surgery of the musculoskeletal system. New York, Churchill Livingstone, p.2:147, 1983, p 147. Reprinted with permission.)

   b. Closed reduction and prevent hyperextension for 3 weeks
   c. Open reduction or arthrodesis in chronic cases
  2. PIP joint dislocation
   a. Dorsal dislocation is more common
   b. Closed reduction and extension block splinting in acute cases (30° of flexion initially)
   c. Eaton volar plate arthroplasty or other techniques in chronic cases
   d. Volar dislocations are treacherous, associated with avulsion of extensor central slip
 D. Thumb
  1. Ulnar collateral ligament ruptures
   a. Also known as "gamekeeper's thumb"
   b. Stener lesion present in 75% of complete tears, which requires surgery (Fig 6-6)
   c. Surgery if >45° of ulnar opening, volar subluxation, and displaced fracture of the base of proximal phalanx with >10°–15° of articular involvement
  2. Radial collateral ligament ruptures
   a. Uncommon injuries
   b. Often missed initially
   c. Treatment
    (1) Immobilization for 4 weeks in acute cases
    (2) Reconstruction or arthrodesis in chronic cases

REFERENCES

Ali MS: Complete disruption of the collateral mechanism of proximal interphalangeal joints of fingers. J Hand Surg 9B:191–193, 1984

Barton NJ: Fractures of the hand. J Bone Joint Surg 66B:159–167, 1984

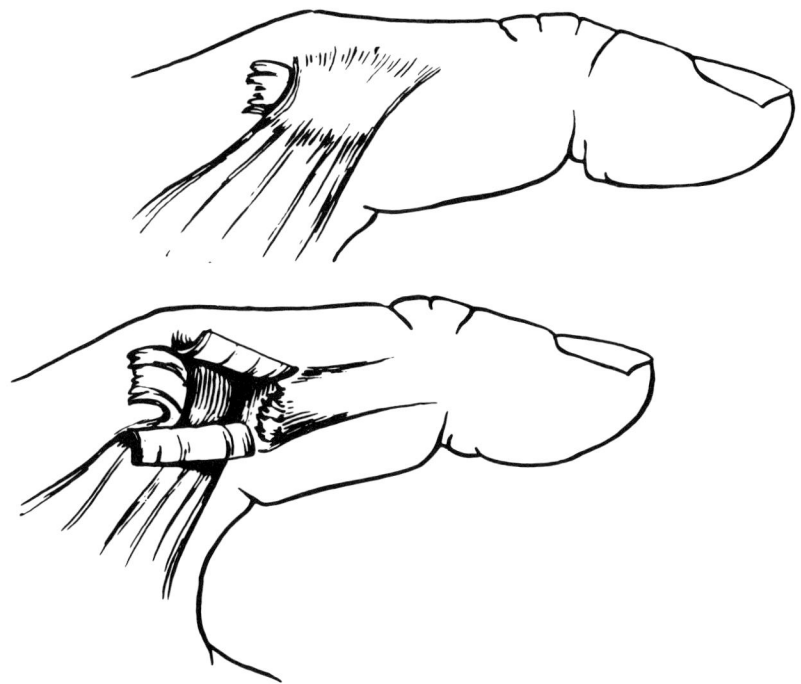

Figure 6-6. Stener lesion. The adductor aponeurosis is interposed between the two ends of the ruptured ulnar collateral ligament. (From Green DP: Dislocations and ligamentous injuries in the hand. In Evart CM, ed. Surgery of the musculoskeletal system. New York, Churchill Livingstone, 1983, p 162. Reprinted with permission.)

Barton NJ: Fractures of the phalanges of the hand in children. Hand 11:134–143, 1979

Belsky MR, Eaton RG, Lane LB: Closed reduction and internal fixation of proximal phalangeal fractures. J Hand Surg 9A:725–729, 1984

Bilos ZJ, Eskestrand T: External fixator use in comminuted gunshot fractures of the proximal phalanx. J Hand Surg 4:357–359, 1979

Black DM, Mann RJ, Constine RM, Daniels AU: The stability of internal fixation in the proximal phalanx. J Hand Surg 11A:672–677, 1986

Caffee HH: Atraumatic placement of Kirschner wires. Plast Reconstr Surg 63:433, 1979

Clendenin MB, Smith RJ: Fifth metacarpal hamate arthrodesis for post-traumatic osteoarthritis. J Hand Surg 9:374–378, 1984

Dray GJ, Eaton RG: Dislocations and ligament injuries in the digits. In Green DP, ed. Operative hand surgery, ed 2. New York, Churchill Livingstone, 1988, pp 777–811

Eaton RG, Malerich MM: Volar plate arthroplasty for the proximal interphalangeal joint: A ten year review. J Hand Surg 5:260–268, 1980

Fitzgerald JAW, Kahn MA: The conservative management of fractures of the shafts of the phalanges of the fingers by combined traction-splintage. J Hand Surg 9B:303–306, 1984

Freeland AE, Jabaley ME, Burkhalter WE, Chaves AMV: Delayed primary bone grafting in the hand and wrist after traumatic bone loss. J Hand Surg 9A:22–28, 1984

Freeland AE, Jabaley ME, Hughes JL: Stable fixation of the hand and wrist. New York, Springer-Verlag, 1986

Green SM, Posner MA: Irreducible dorsal dislocations of the proximal interphalangeal joint. J Hand Surg 10A:85–87, 1985

Green DP, Terry GC: Complex dislocations of the metacarpophalangeal joint. J Bone Joint Surg 55A:1480, 1973

Gross MS, Gelberman RH: Metacarpal rotational osteotomy. J Hand Surg 10A:105–108, 1985

Joshi BB: Percutaneous internal fixation of fractures of the proximal phalanges. Hand 8:86–92, 1976

Jupiter JB, Koniuch MP, Smith RJ: The management of delayed union and nonunion of the metacarpals and phalanges. J Hand Surg 10A:457–466, 1985

Lane CS: Detecting occult fractures of the metacarpal head: The Brewerton view. J Hand Surg 2:131–133, 1977

Lister G: Intraosseous wiring of the digital skeleton. J Hand Surg 3:427–435, 1978

McElfresh EC, Dobyns JH: Intra-articular metacarpal head fractures. J Hand Surg 8:383–393, 1983

Melone CP: Rigid fixation of phalanges and metacarpal fractures. Orthop Clin North Am 17:421, 1986

Minami A, An K, Cooney WP, et al: Ligament stability of the metacarpophalangeal joint. J Hand Surg 10A:255–260, 1985

Pritsch M, Engel J, Farin I: Manipulation and external fixation of metacarpal fractures. J Bone Joint Surg 63A:1289–1291, 1981

Riggs SA, Cooney WP: External fixation of complex hand and wrist fractures. J Trauma 23:332–336, 1983

Stern PJ: Preservation of digital length after traumatic bone loss. J Hand Surg 6:361–364, 1981

Vanik RK, Weber RC, Matloub HS, et al: Comparative strengths of internal fixation techniques. J Hand Surg 9A:216–221, 1984

51
Replantation

I. General Considerations
A. Definitions
1. Replantation: reattachment of a body part that has been totally severed from the body without attachments
2. Revascularization: reconstruction of blood vessels which have been damaged in order to prevent ischemia of a body part from becoming necrotic

B. Technical adequacy of microvascular repair is key to success
C. Factors that influence the selection process are the level of amputation, severity of injury, warm and cold ischemic times, age of patient, segmental injuries, general health of patient, vocation, and predicted rehabilitation (Urbaniak)
D. Good indications for replantations
1. Thumbs
2. Multiple digits
3. Metacarpal amputation (palm)
4. Wrist or forearm
5. Elbow or proximal must be sharply avulsed
6. Individual digit distal to FDS insertion
7. Almost any part of body in children
E. Bad indications for replantation
1. Crushed or mangled parts
2. Arteriosclerotic disease
3. Mentally unstable patients
4. Individual finger with an amputation proximal to the FDS insertion
5. Amputations at multiple levels
6. Ring avulsions are generally poor if replanted but better if revascularized
F. Overall success results should be 80–85% (viability)
1. Patient acceptance is generally good
2. Range of motion is about 50% normal
3. Sensibility recovers (two-point discrimination is ≤10 mm in 50% adults and ≤5 mm in most children)
4. Growth plate has normal growth in 80%

II. Amputated Part
A. Viability: 6 hours (warm), 12 hours (cool), up to 30 hours for digits (cool)
B. Preparation
1. Wrap the part with gauze moistened with Ringer's lactate or saline and place in a plastic bag surrounded by ice, or immersion in solution and placing on ice
2. Do not ligate or perfuse any vessels

III. Surgical Sequences and Technique
A. Sequences
1. Midlateral or Bruner incisions and isolate the neurovascular bundle
2. Debride and shorten and fix bone
3. Repair extensor tendon first then repair flexor tendons
4. Anastomose arteries, nerves, then veins (some authors prefer veins first)
5. Skin coverage
6. Temporary vascular shunt if ischemic time is prolonged
7. Fasciotomy and second look at 48 hours in major limb replantations
B. Surgical instrument
1. Loupes 3.5–4.5× for initial dissection
2. Operating microscope (20–40× power)
3. Microinstruments: spring-loaded scissors and needle holder, jeweler's forceps, microtipped dilator and irrigator, microclips, bipolar cautery, hemoclips, etc.
4. Needle and suture size
   a. Wrist: 130 μm, 8 or 9-0
   b. Palm: 100 μm, 9 or 10-0
   c. Proximal digit: 75–100 μm, 9 or 10-0
   d. Distal digit: 50–75 μm, 10 or 11-0

IV. Postoperative Period

A. Loosely closed wound with bulky dressing and elevation
B. Anticoagulation: individualized
C. No smoking and no caffeine
D. Monitoring
   1. Temperature probes
      a. Temperature <30° indicates a bad prognosis
      b. Temperature drop of >20° indicates trouble
   2. Oxygen saturation probes
   3. Clinically by color, capillary refill, and turgor
E. Failing replant
   1. Change position and inspect dressing
   2. Hydrate patient
   3. Heparin bolus and consider a regional block
   4. Return to operating room within the first 48 hours

REFERENCES

Belskey MR, Ruby LK: Double level amputation: Should it be replanted? J Reconstr Microsurg 2:159–162, 1986

Early MJ, Watson JS: Twenty-four thumb replantations. J Hand Surg 9B:98–102, 1984

Gelberman RH, Urbaniak JR, Bright DS, et al: Digital sensibility following replantation. J Hand Surg 3:313–319, 1978

Goldner RD: Postoperative management. Hand Clin 1:205–215, 1985

Jones JM, Schenck RR, Chesney RB: Digital replantation and amputation-comparison of function. J Hand Surg 7:183–189, 1982

Kleinert HE, Juhala CA, Tsai TM, et al: Digital replantation-selection, technique, and results. Orthop Clin North Am 8:309–318, 1977

Kleinert HE, Tsai TM: Microvascular repair in replantation. Clin Orthop 133:205, 1978

Kutz JE, Hanel D, Sheker L, et al: Upper extremity replantation. Orthop Clin North Am 14:873, 1983

Morrison WA, O'Brien BM, McLeod AM: Evaluation of digital replantation — a review of 100 cases. Orthop Clin North Am 8:295–308, 1977

Nunley JA: Microscopes and microinstruments. Hand Clin 1:197–204, 1985

Nunley JA, Koman LA, Urbaniak JR: Arterial shunting as an adjunct to major limb revascularization. Ann Surg 193:271–273, 1981

Schlenker JD, Kleinert HE, Tsai TM: Methods and results of replantation following traumatic amputation of the thumb in sixty-four patients. J Hand Surg 5:63–69, 1980

Tamai S: Twenty years experience of limb replantation-review of 293 upper extremity replants. J Hand Surg 7:549–556, 1982

Urbaniak JR: Replantation of amputated hands and digits. American academy of orthopaedic surgeons instructional course lectures. St Louis, CV Mosby, 1978, pp 15–26

Urbaniak JR: To replant or not to replant? That is not the question. J Hand Surg 8A:507–508, 1983

Urbaniak JR, Evans JP, Bright DS: Microvascular management of ring avulsion injuries. J Hand Surg 6:25–30, 1981

Urbaniak JR, Roth JH, Nunley JA, et al: The results of replantation after amputation of a single finger. J Bone Joint Surg 67A:611–619, 1985

Urbaniak JR, Steichen JB, Weiland AJ, et al: Microsurgical skills development laboratory manual. Park Ridge, IL, American Academy Orthopedic Surgeons, 1985

Weiland AJ, Villarreal-Rios A, Kleinert HE, et al: Replantation of digits and hands: Analysis of surgical techniques and functional results in 71 patients with 86 replantations. J Hand Surg 2A:1–12, 1977

Yamano Y: Replantation of the amputated distal part of the fingers. J Hand Surg 10A:211–218, 1985

52

Wrist Injuries and Disorders

I. Carpal Instability
A. Anatomy
  1. Carpal bones
     a. Two rows: proximal row (lunate and triquetrum) and distal row (trapezium, trapezoid, capitate, hamate)
     b. Columns concept (Navarro, 1921, Taleisnik, 1970)
        (1) Central: lunate and distal row (flexion and extension)
        (2) Lateral: scaphoid (rotation)
        (3) Medial: triquetrum (rotation)
  2. Intrinsic ligaments
     a. Volar radioscaphoid ligament: prime stabilizer of proximal carpal row (must be torn for rotatory subluxation of scaphoid to occur along with scapholunate ligament)
     b. Interosseous scapholunate ligament: torn in stage I, perilunate instability (rotatory subluxation)
     c. Volar radiocapitate and capitotriquetral ligaments: V-shaped volar ligaments (V-deltoid ligaments) from capitate create weak space of Poirier at capitolunate joint (these two ligaments are prime stabilizers of distal carpal row)
     d. Volar radiolunotriquetral ligament: provide sling for the lunate
  3. Collateral ligaments
     a. Radial collateral ligament: radial styloid to scaphoid tuberosity
     b. Ulnar collateral ligament: ulnar styloid to triquetrum
  4. Dorsal ligaments
     a. Dorsal radiocarpal ligament: from radius to triquetrum
     b. Dorsal intercarpal ligament: from triquetrum to trapezium
  5. Triangular fibrocartilage complex (ulnocarpal joint)
     a. Triangular fibrocartilage
     b. Meniscus homologue
     c. Ligaments (ulnolunate, ulnotriquetrum, lunotriquetrum)
B. Wrist motion
  1. Capitate: changing center of motion
  2. Radial deviation: scaphoid volar flexes and lunate volar flexes with it
  3. Ulnar deviation: triquetrum migrated distally and dorsiflexes lunate with it, scaphoid dorsiflexes
C. Pathomechanics and classification of carpal instabilities (Dobyns, Linscheid)
  1. Carpal instability dissociative (CID): complete ligament disruption with instability between bones of the proximal carpal row
     a. Proximal carpal row
        (1) Unstable scaphoid fracture
        (2) Scapholunate dissociation
        (3) Lunotriquetral dissociation
     b. Distal carpal row
        (1) Axial-radial (AR) dislocations
        (2) Axial-ulnar (AU) dislocations
        (3) Combined AR/AU dislocations
     c. Combined proximal and distal CID
  2. Carpal instability nondissociative (CIND): collapse pattern where the bones of each carpal row are still strongly attached to each other
     a. Radiocarpal CIND
        (1) Malunion of the distal radius
        (2) Radiocarpal ligaments rupture
        (3) Madelung's deformity
     b. Midcarpal CIND
        (1) Triquetrum-hamate-capitate ligament rupture

(2) Scapho-trapezium-trapezoid ligament rupture
(3) Combinations
c. Combined radiocarpal/midcarpal instability (capitolunate instability pattern)
3. Combined CID/CIND instability
D. Patterns of carpal instabilities (Fig 6-7)
1. Dorsal intercalated segmental instability (DISI)
a. Lateral column scaphoid-trapeziotrapezoid instability (lunate is dorsiflexed abnormally)
b. Scapholunate angle >60°
c. Capitolunate and radiolunate angle >15°
d. Associated with scaphoid fracture, dorsally angulated radius fracture, radioscaphoid and lunatocapitate and arthritis (scapholunate advanced collapse [SLAC] pattern: treatment is combination of biologic spacer and capitate-hamate-triquetrum-lunate arthrodesis)
2. Volar intercalated segmental instability (VISI):
a. Medial column lunate-triquetrumhamate instability (lunate appears abnormally palmar flexed)
b. Scapholunate angle <30°
3. Ulnar translocation: lunate is abnormally ulnarly displaced
4. Dorsal carpal dislocation
5. Radiocarpal translocation
6. Proximal carpal translocation
E. Progressive perilunate instability in acute trauma: mechanism of injury is wrist extension, ulnar deviation, and supination
1. Stage I: rotatory subluxation of the scaphoid or scapholunate dissociation
a. Radioscaphoid and scapholunate ligaments torn
b. Scapholunate gap (>3 mm) and foreshortened scaphoid
c. Ring pole distance <7 mm and "cortical ring" sign

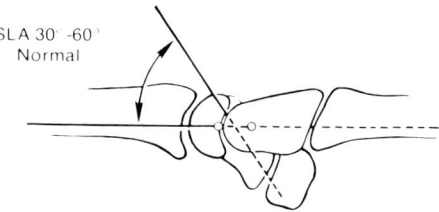
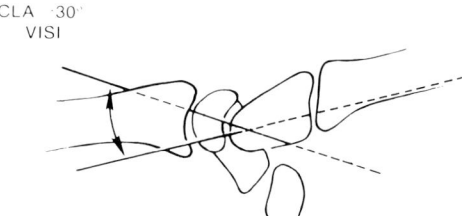
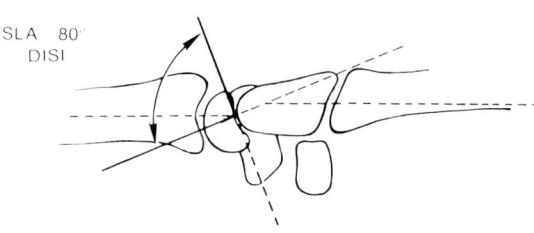

Figure 6-7. Diagrams showing scapholunate angle (SLA) and capitolunate angle (CLA). SLA is normally 30°–60°. In DISI, SLA becomes > 60° and in VISI, it becomes < 30°. CLA greater than 15° is abnormal. (From Ezaki M, Hand surgery. In: Bucholz RW, Lippert FG, Wenger DR, Ezaki M, eds. Orthopaedic decision making, Philadelphia, BC Decker, and St. Louis, CV Mosby, 1984, p 256. Reprinted with permission.)

d. Treatment: reduce with dorsiflexion, radial deviation with percutaneous pinning and cast for 6 weeks (open reduction and internal fixation may be necessary)
2. Stage II: midcarpal dislocation or perilunate dislocation (DISI pattern)
a. Lunatocapitate joint is disrupted with capitate dislocated on the lunate
b. If scaphoid is fractured, it is called transcaphoid perilunate dislocation
c. Treatment
(1) Closed reduction and pinning

(2) Open reduction and internal fixation are often necessary (dorsal and/or volar approach and stabilization of scaphoid, lunate, and capitate with three pins)
(3) Chronic: ligamentous reconstruction fails over time; therefore scaphoid-trapezium-trapezoid or scaphocapitate fusion is recommended
3. Stage III: triquetral-lunate dislocation
   a. Joint will usually reduce spontaneously and, if not recognized, will result in DISI
   b. Treatment: same as stage II
4. Stage IV: lunate dislocation (treatment same as above)

II. Scaphoid Fractures
A. General considerations
   1. Most common fracture of the carpal bones
   2. Vascular supply of the scaphoid: radial artery
      a. Artery to dorsal ridge of scaphoid: proximal 80%
      b. Volar radial branch: distal 20% (volar approach is less traumatic to proximal scaphoid)
   3. Diagnosis of acute fracture may be difficult and frequently not apparent on the initial x-ray (take repeat x-rays in 1–2 weeks)
   4. Bone scan may be utilized in doubtful cases

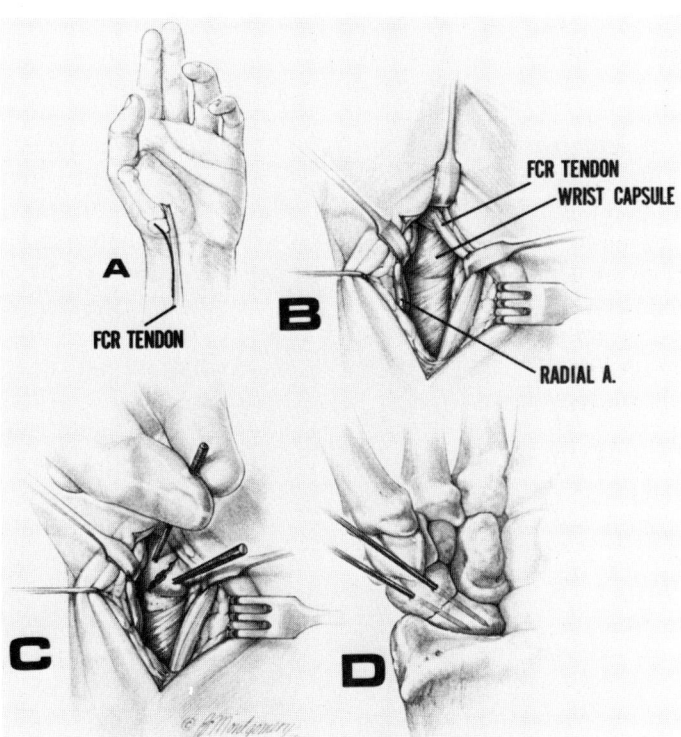

Figure 6-8. Open reduction through Russe-type incision and fixation with K-wires. Russe bone graft is placed in nonunion cases. (From Green DP: Dislocations and ligamentous injuries in the hand. In Evart CM (ed.): Surgery of the musculoskeletal system. New York, Churchill Livingstone, 1983, p 206. Reprinted with permission.)

B. Classification
1. Distal third: 10% incidence and rare avascular necrosis (AVN)
2. Middle third: 70% incidence and 30% AVN
3. Proximal third: 20% incidence and 100% AVN

C. Treatment
1. Acute, nondisplaced: thumb spica cast in slight volar flexion and radial deviation
   a. Distal fractures: 4–8 weeks of immobilization
   b. Middle fractures: 6–12 weeks of immobilization
   c. Proximal fractures: 12–20 weeks of immobilization
2. Acute, displaced
   a. Amount of displacement is controversial
   b. Most agree >2 mm
   c. Intercarpal relationship must be normal
   d. Internal fixation is recommended (ie, Herbert screw)
3. Delayed union or nonunion
   a. Must correct intercarpal relationships
   b. Options
      (1) Prolonged cast: 4–9 months
      (2) Electric stimulation
      (3) Volar Russe bone graft (Fig 6-8)
      (4) Herbert screw

III. Fractures of the Distal Radius

A. General considerations
1. Most common fractures seen about the wrist
2. Normal anatomy
   a. Volar tilt averaging 11°
   b. Radial-ulnar slope of the distal radius averages 23°
   c. The distance between the radial styloid and articular surface of distal ulna is 9–11 mm
3. Mechanism: compression with wrist dorsiflexed

B. Classification and treatment (Colles' fractures)
1. Frykman:
   a. Extra-articular (I) and with distal ulnar fracture (II)
   b. Intra-articular involving radiocarpal joint (III) and with distal ulnar fracture (IV)
   c. Intra-articular involving distal radioulnar joint (V) and with distal ulnar fracture (VI)
   d. Intra-articular involving both distal radiocarpal and radioulnar joints (VII) and with distal ulnar fracture (VIII)
2. Most important consideration is the status of the lunate sulcus (Jupiter)
3. Stable vs unstable
   a. Stable
      (1) Undisplaced: cast or splint
      (2) Displaced but stable after closed reduction
         i. Splint or long arm cast with the wrist in slight flexion and ulnar deviation (15°)
         ii. Slight supination to minimize deforming pull of brachioradialis but controversial
   b. Unstable (>20° angulation and 10 mm shortening, intra-articular and comminution — 4 parts: shaft, radial styloid, dorsal medial, palmar medial fragments)
      (1) Displaced and reduction lost after closed reduction
         i. External fixator (second metacarpal and radius)
         ii. Percutaneous fracture fixation combined with external fixation
      (2) Displaced and closed reduction not possible
         i. Open reduction and internal fixation
         ii. Usually dorsal approach
         iii. Multiple K-wires, screws, or plate, depending on fragment

size and bone graft as necessary combined with external fixator
C. Fracture of the distal radius with palmar displacement (Smith's fracture)
 1. Mechanism: either fall on back of the hand or falling on the fixed dorsiflexed hand with the forearm rotating into pronation
 2. Three types
  a. Type 1: extra-articular fracture with palmar angulation
  b. Type 2: intra-articular fracture with anterior subluxation of the carpus (identical to volar Barton's fracture)
  c. Type 3: extra-articular fracture with palmar angulation and translation of the distal fragment
 3. Treatment
  a. Type 1: closed reduction and long arm cast with the wrist in volar flexion and forearm in supination
  b. Type 2: Open reduction and volar plating
  c. Type 3: Open reduction and volar plating or possible percutaneous pinning
D. Dorsal rim fracture of the distal radius (dorsal Barton's fracture)
 1. Mechanism: dorsiflexed and pronation of the forearm with the fracture propagating to the dorsum
 2. Palmar radiocarpal ligament is torn
 3. Treatment: reduction and wrist in neutral to dorsiflexion about 30° and short arm cast
E. Fracture of the radial styloid (Chauffeur's or Hutchinson fracture)
 1. Avulsion fracture: radioscaphocapitate ligament or collateral ligament (small size)
 2. Treatment: long arm cast for 3 weeks and short arm cast for 3 weeks in slight ulnar deviation and supination (if >2 mm displacement, then percutaneous pinning)
 3. Associated injury: transstyloid perilunate dislocation
F. Injuries to the distal radioulnar joint (DRUJ)
 1. Dorsal subluxation of the ulnar head: long arm cast with the elbow 90° flexion and forearm in full supination
 2. Palmar subluxation: long arm cast with pronation
 3. Ulnar styloid fracture: short arm cast with ulnar deviation if minimally displaced and open reduction and K-wire reduction if cannot be reduced closely (if DRUJ is stable, fixation is not required)
 4. Triangular fibrocartilage tear/perforation
  a. Age dependent
  b. Diagnosis by arthrogram/arthroscopy
  c. Treatment
   (1) Presence of perforation alone is not an indication for treatment
   (2) Arthroscopy: symptomatic flap tears
   (3) Ulnar shortening: symptomatic DRUJ in a patient with ulnar neutral or positive ulnar variance
   (4) Hemiresection-interpositional arthroplasty: young persons with DRUJ arthritis
   (5) Resection (Darrach): older patients with DRUJ arthritis
   (6) Sauve-Kapandji procedure: alternate procedure

IV. **Kienböck's Disease**
A. Etiology
 1. Trauma (compression stress type of fractures)
 2. Devascularization-volar vessels
 3. Ulnar variance (negative)
B. Classification
 1. Stage I: small fracture lines
 2. Stage II: rarefaction along fracture lines

3. Stage III: sclerosis of the bone dorsal to fracture
4. Stage IV: collapse of lunate
5. Stage V: secondary arthritic changes of the radius

C. Treatment
1. Prolonged immobilization: poor results
2. Decompression: for first three stages
   a. Radial shortening
   b. Ulnar lengthening
3. Intercarpal arthrodesis: scaphocapitate fusion or capitate-hamate fusion with capitate shortening
4. Advanced cases with radiocarpal and intercarpal arthritis: consider proximal row carpectomy, wrist arthrodesis

REFERENCES

Alexander CE, Lichtman DM: Ulnar instabilities. Orthop Clin North Am 15:307–320, 1984

Almquist EE, Burns JF: Radial shortening for the treatment of Kienbock's disease. A 5 to 10 year followup. J Hand Surg 7:348–352, 1982

Armistead RB, Linscheid RL, Dobyns JH, Beckenbaugh RD: Ulnar lengthening in the treatment of Kienbock's disease. J Bone Joint Surg 64A:170–178, 1982

Axelrod T, Paley D, Green J, et al: Limited open reduction of the lunate facet in comminuted intra-articular fractures of the distal radius. J Hand Surg 13A:372, 1988

Beckenbaugh RD: Accurate evaluation and management of the painful wrist following injury. An approach to carpal instability. Orthop Clin North Am 15:289–306, 1984

Bieber EJ, Linscheid RL, Dobyns JM: Failed distal ulnar resections. J Hand Surg 13A:193, 1988

Cooney WP, Dobyns JH, Linscheid RL: Complications of Colles' fractures. J Bone Joint Surg 62A:613, 1980

Cooney WP, Dobyns JH, Linscheid RL: Fractures of the scaphoid: A rational approach to management. Clin Orthop 149:90–97, 1980

Evans G, Burke FD, Barton NJ: A comparison of conservative treatment and silicone replacement arthroplasty in Kienbock's disease. J Hand Surg 11B:98–102, 1986

Fernandes HJA, Koberle G, Ferreira GHS, Camargo JN Jr: Volar transscaphoid perilunar dislocation. Hand 15:276–280, 1983

Fernandez DL: Radial osteotomy and Bowers arthroplasty for malunited fractures of the distal end of the radius. J Bone Joint Surg 70A:1538–1551, 1988

Fernandez DL: A technique for anterior wedgeshaped grafts for scaphoid nonunions with carpal instability. J Hand Surg 9A:733–737, 1984

Gilula LA, Destouet JM, Weeks PM, et al: Roentgenographic diagnosis of the painful wrist. Clin Orthop 187:52–64, 1984

Glickel SZ, Millender LH: Ligamentous reconstruction for chronic intercarpal instability. J Hand Surg 9A:514–527, 1984

Gordon M, Bullough PG: Synovial and osseous inflammation in failed silicone-rubber prostheses. A report of six cases. J Bone Joint Surg 64A:574–580, 1982

Graner O, Lopes EI, Costa Carvalho B, Atlas S: Arthrodesis of the carpal bones in the treatment of Kienbock's disease, painful ununited fractures of the navicular and lunate bones with avascular necrosis and old fracture dislocations of carpal bones. Bone Joint Surg 48A:767–774, 1966

Green DP: Carpal dislocations and instabilities. In Green DP, ed. Operative hand surgery, ed 2. New York, Churchill Livingstone, 1988

Green DP: The effect of avascular necrosis on Russe bone grafting for scaphoid nonunion. J Hand Surg 10A:597–605, 1985

Green DP: Proximal row carpectomy. Hand Clin 3:163–168, 1987

Hastings DE, Silver RL: Intercarpal arthrodesis in the management of chronic carpal instability after trauma. J Hand Surg 9A:834–840, 1984

Herbert TJ, Fisher WE: Management of the fractured scaphoid using a new bone screw. J Bone Joint Surg 66B:114–123, 1984

Isani AI, Melone CP: Classification and management of intra-articular fractures of the distal radius. Hand Clin North Am 4:349, 1988

Jackson WT, Protas JM: Snapping scapholunate subluxation. J Hand Surg 6:590–594, 1981

Jones WA, Ghorbal MS: Fractures of the trapezium. A report of three cases. J Hand Surg 10B:227–230, 1985

Kleinman WB, Steichen JB, Strickland JW: Management of chronic rotary subluxation of the scaphoid by scapho-trapezio-trapezoid arthrodesis. J Hand Surg 7:125–136, 1982

Knirk JL, Jupiter JB: Intra-articular fractures of the distal end of the radius in young adults. J Bone Joint Surg 68A:647, 1986

Louis DS, Hankin FM: Arthrodesis of the wrist: Past and present. J Hand Surg 11A:787, 1986

Mayfield JK: Patterns of injury to carpal ligaments. A spectrum. Clin Orthop 187:36–42, 1984

Mayfield JK, Johnson RP, Kilcoyne RK: Carpal dislocations: Pathomechanics and progressive perilunar instability. J Hand Surg 5:226, 1980

Melone CP: Articular fractures of the distal radius. Orthop Clin North Am 15:217, 1984

Melone CP: Open treatment of displaced articular fractures of the distal radius. Clin Orthop 202:103, 1986

Neviaser RJ: Proximal row carpectomy for post-traumatic disorders of the carpus. J Hand Surg 8:301–305, 1983

Palmer AK, Wener FW, Eng MM, et al: Functional wrist motion: A biomechanical study. J Hand Surg 10A:39–46, 1985

Rand JA, Linscheid RL, Dobyns JH: Capitate fractures. A long term follow-up. Clin Orthop 165:209–216, 1982

Reagan DS, Linscheid RL, Dobyns JH: Lunotriquetral sprains. J Hand Surg 9A:502–514, 1984

Stark HH, Chao EK, Zemel NP, et al: Fracture of the hook of the hamate. J Bone Joint Surg 71A:1202–1207, 1989

Stern PJ: Transcaphoid-lunate dislocation: A report of two cases. J Hand Surg 9A:370–373, 1984

Swanson AB, Maupin BK, Swanson G deG, et al: Lunate implant resection arthroplasty: Long term results. J Hand Surg 10A:1013–1024, 1985

Taleisnik J: Fractures of the carpal bones. In Green DP, ed. Operative hand surgery. New York, Churchill Livingstone, 1988

Taleisnik J: The ligaments of the wrist. J Hand Surg 1:110, 1976

Trumble T, Glisson RR, Seaber AV, Urbaniak JR: A biomechanical comparison of the methods for treating Kienbock's disease. J Hand Surg 11A:88–93, 1986

Watson HK, Ballet FL: The SLAC wrist: Scapholunate advanced collapse pattern of degenerative arthritis. J Hand Surg 9A:358–365, 1984

Watson HK, Hempton RF: Limited wrist arthrodesis. The triscaphoid joint. J Hand Surg 5:320–327, 1980

Watson HK, Ryu J, Dibella A: An approach to Kienbock's disease: Triscaphe arthrodesis. J Hand Surg 10A:179–187, 1985

Nerve Injuries and Compression Neuropathies

BRACHIAL PLEXUS INJURIES

I. Anatomy of the Brachial Plexus

A. Anterior rami of the spinal nerves from C5 to T1. (Spinal nerves are bound to the transverse processes by prevertebral fascia)
B. Trunks: between the scalene muscles
  1. Upper trunk (C5, C6)
  2. Middle trunk (C7)
  3. Lower trunk (C8, T1)
C. Prefixed (C4 contribution) or postfixed (T2 contribution)
D. Cords: middle third of clavicle
  1. Lateral: formed by anterior divisions of upper and middle trunks
     a. Lateral pectoral nerve: pectoralis major
     b. Lateral head of median nerve
     c. Musculocutaneous nerve
  2. Medial: formed by anterior division of lower trunk
     a. Medial pectoral: pectoralis major and minor
     b. Medial brachial cutaneous
     c. Medial antebrachial cutaneous
     d. Medial head of median nerve
     e. Ulnar nerve
  3. Posterior: formed by posterior divisions of all trunks
     a. Upper subscapular: subscapularis
     b. Thoracodorsal: latissimus dorsi
     c. Lower subscapular: subscapularis and teres major
     d. Axillary: deltoid and teres minor
     e. Radial: triceps and extensors
E. Nerves from plexus itself
  1. Suprascapular: from upper trunk, innervates supraspinatus and infraspinatus
  2. Long thoracic: from C5, C6, and C7, and innervates serratus anterior
  3. Phrenic: from C4 and C5, and innervates the diaphragm

II. Classification

A. Open vs closed: open injuries are amenable to repair if the injury is by sharp objects and upper and middle trunks are involved
B. Closed (traction) injuries
  1. Supraclavicular injuries
     a. Supraganglionic
     b. Infraganglionic
  2. Infraclavicular injuries: cords and terminal branches
C. Neuropraxia, axonotemesis, or neurotemesis
D. Iatrogenic: surgical position with the arm abducted and extended
E. Brachial plexus injuries in contact sports
F. Thoracic outlet syndrome

III. Diagnosis

A. Clinical examination
  1. Differentiate preganglionic vs postganglionic
     a. Involvement of proximal muscles such as serratus (long thoracic nerve), rhomboids (dorsal scapular nerve), and diaphragm (C5 contribution) implies root avulsion or preganglionic lesion
     b. Horner's syndrome (meiosis, anhydrosis, ptosis) implies avulsion of T1 root

    c. Tinel's sign implies postganglionic lesion
  2. Trunk localization
    a. Upper trunk (C5, C6): loss of shoulder abductors, lateral rotators, and elbow flexors and supinator. Sensory loss over the radial aspect of arm, thumb, and index finger
    b. Middle trunk (C7): extensor of the elbow, wrist, and fingers and radial nerve sensory loss
    c. Lower trunk (C8, T1): combined median and ulnar nerve palsy except pronator teres (C6, C7)
B. Myelogram: traumatic pseudomeningoceles in preganglionic lesions
C. Axon reflex test: histamine is pricked to the skin
  1. Normal triple response (vasodilation, wheal, flare) in preganglionic lesion
  2. Vasodilation, wheal without flare in postganglionic lesion
D. Electromyography (EMG): 1 month after injury
  1. Denervation (spontaneous fibrillation at rest) rules out neuropraxia
  2. Denervation potentials of the paraspinal muscles indicate preganglionic lesion
  3. Afferent sensory tests are normal in preganglionic lesion because of intact dorsal sensory ganglion
E. Negative axon reflex and abnormal afferent sensory tests indicate postganglionic lesion in the sensory fibers but do not rule out motor root avulsion

IV. Treatment

A. Birth injuries
  1. Traction injuries secondary to fetal malposition, cephalopelvic disproportion, and use of forceps
  2. Incidence is decreasing (0.6/1000 births)
  3. Three types
    a. Upper plexus (Erb's palsy): C5, C6
    b. Entire plexus involvement
    c. Lower plexus (Klumpke's palsy): C8, T1
  4. Prognosis is varied (partial to full recovery)
    a. Contractures
    b. Posterior subluxation/dislocation of the shoulder
    c. A 30% incidence of posterior radial head dislocation of the elbow
  5. Treatment
    a. Observation and range of motion exercises
    b. Reconstructive surgery
    c. Early operative intervention is controversial
B. Open injuries
  1. Mostly upper trunk
  2. Lower trunk involvement with poorer prognosis
  3. Sharp lacerations should be explored and microsurgically repaired
  4. Gunshot injuries may be repaired electively 3 months later
C. Closed supraclavicular injuries
  1. Four common patterns with variable degrees
    a. C5 and C6
    b. C5, C6, and C7
    c. Entire plexus
    d. C8 and T1
  2. All preganglionic lesions and lower trunks postganglionic lesions are not amenable to surgical repair (early prognostication and tendon transfers should be planned)
  3. If myelogram and other tests indicate postganglionic lesions, 3–6 months of conservative treatment should be given and surgical exploration if no improvement
  4. Entire plexus involvement with flail and anesthetic arm
    a. No active treatment: sling and prevention of further injury and infection
    b. Above elbow amputation and pros-

thesis (arthrodesis of the shoulder may be done for stabilization)
D. Infraclavicular closed injuries
   1. Better prognosis for recovery and observation and documentation of improvement
   2. If the mechanism of injury involves high-energy force, neurotemesis is likely and early surgical exploration can be done
E. Surgical repair
   1. Surgical approach: from posterior sternocleidomastoid muscle toward clavicle and deltopectoral groove. Use nerve stimulator to aid in identification of the plexus. (Somatosensory evoked potentials can be utilized to identify preganglionic lesions)
   2. Intercalated autogenous nerve grafts
   3. Microscope, 8-0 sutures
F. Reconstructive surgery
   1. Shoulder
      a. Arthrodesis
      b. Tendon transfers for partial lesions (e.g., L'Episcopo procedure)
   2. Elbow flexion
      a. Steindler flexorplasty: weak
      b. Pectoralis major transfer
      c. Latissimus dorsi transfer
      d. Triceps (last resort)

PERIPHERAL NERVE INJURIES

I. General Considerations
A. Classification (Seddon)
   1. Neuropraxia: physiologic interruption from minor compression or contusion
   2. Axonotemesis: breakdown of axon and Wallerian degeneration
   3. Neurotemesis: complete anatomic severance
B. Anatomy
   1. Endoneurium: encases nerve fiber (axon and sheath)
   2. Perineurium: encases each fasciculus
   3. Epineurium: encases group of fasciculi or nerve
C. Rate of regeneration
   1. One to 3 mm/day
   2. A 30 day delay at suture line
   3. Additional delays occur at motor and sensory receptor organs
D. Factors in prognosis of nerve suture
   1. Age: better in children
   2. Time between injury and suture
   3. Proximal nerve lesions are generally worse than distal lesions
   4. Length of nerve gap
   5. Experience of surgeon
   6. Mechanism of injury (sharp injury better than avulsion)

II. Surgical Options
A. Epineurial repair: nerves with pure motor or sensory function or sharp injuries (may misalign the fascicles)
B. Group fascicular repair: mixed nerves, large nerves, particularly if partially severed nerves
C. Epineural plus group fascicular repair for major nerves (median or ulnar nerves at the elbow)
D. Fascicular repair: small peripheral nerves but potential for increased scar (digits)
E. Nerve grafting (group fascicular): presence of gap or too much tension

III. Primary Versus Secondary Repair
A. Advantages of primary repair
   1. One procedure
   2. Easier orientation of nerve
   3. No scar or retraction
   4. Electrical stimulation can be used to identify nerve fascicles within 72 hours
B. Advantages of secondary repair
   1. Extent of damage to the nerve will be easier to identify
   2. Less chance of infection
   3. Thickened perineum is easier to hold sutures

COMPRESSIVE NEUROPATHIES OF THE UPPER EXTREMITY

I. General Considerations

A. Pathoetiology: multiple etiologic factors, such as anatomic abnormalities, inflammation, tumors, trauma, metabolic and iatrogenic problems
B. Increased risk for entrapment neuritis elsewhere in patients with compressive neuropathy ("double crush")
C. Anatomic factor is of significance where the nerve passes through a potentially tight space

II. Median Nerve

A. Carpal tunnel syndrome
 1. Anatomically defined by scaphoid tubercle/trapezium radially, pisiform/hook of hamate ulnarly, and transverse carpal ligament volarly
 2. Many are of unknown etiology but inflammatory, trauma (overuse or occupational), tumors, or hypothyroidism may contribute to the pathogenesis
 3. Symptoms: sensory disturbance in the median nerve distribution, night pain in the same area, and clumsiness of the hand
 4. Signs: decreased sensation to light touch in the median nerve distribution, thenar weakness, thenar atrophy (late cases), positive Phalen's wrist flexion test, and positive Tinel's sign
 5. Differential diagnosis: diabetic neuropathy, cervical root impingement, pronator syndrome, and anterior interosseous syndrome
 6. Electrodiagnostic test
    a. Confirm the diagnosis, assess prognosis, rule out nerve entrapment elsewhere (latency >5ms)
    b. Ten percent false-positive and false-negative results (clinical correlation is therefore critical)
 7. Treatment
    a. Conservative: neutral wrist splint to prevent wrist flexion, nonsteroidal anti-inflammatory drugs (NSAIDs), steroid injections, vitamin B_6
    b. Surgical indications: established pain, numbness, weakness, and recurrence that are recalcitrant to conservative treatment
       (1) Incision in line with the ring finger metacarpal to avoid the palmar cutaneous branch of the median nerve
       (2) Transection of the transverse carpal ligament
B. Pronator syndrome
 1. Pressure by lacertus fibrosus, between the ulnar and humeral heads of the pronator teres, and proximal arch of the FDS
 2. Pain in volar forearm that increases with activity, sensory disturbance in the distribution of median nerve, including palmar triangle, pain with resistance of pronation, positive Tinel's sign at the forearm
 3. Treatment
    a. Conservative: splint 4–6 weeks
    b. Surgical release if no response: explore and release ligament of Struthers, lacertus fibrosus, pronator teres, and FDS arch
C. Anterior interosseous nerve syndrome
 1. Etiology is compression in the forearm by the superficialis sling
 2. Weakness of the flexor pollicis longus (FPL), FDP index, and pronator quadratus
 3. Treatment: splinting first and surgical release if no response

III. Ulnar Nerve

A. Guyon's canal syndrome
 1. Anatomically, roof is volar carpal ligament, lateral wall is hook of hamate

and insertion transverse carpal ligament, and medial wall is pisiform and attachments of pisohamate ligament
   2. Various clinical pictures, depending on the exact site of compression (sensory nerve, motor nerve to the hypothenar muscle, or deep motor branch to the interossei and adductor pollicis)
   3. Treatment
      a. Conservative: rest, immobilization, avoidance of repetitive trauma, steroids
      b. Surgery: decompression and external neurolysis
      c. If associated with carpal tunnel syndrome, carpal tunnel release may decompress the ulnar nerve
B. Cubital tunnel syndrome
   1. Many etiologies: trauma, external pressure, compression between two head of flexor carpi ulnaris (FCU), ganglion, cubitus valgus with tarda nerve palsy, arthritis, etc.
   2. Pain, sensory disturbance, weakness in the distribution of the ulnar nerve
   3. Differential diagnosis: thoracic outlet syndrome, C8-T1 root compression, compression at Guyon's canal
   4. Treatment
      a. Conservative: avoid leaning on elbow, splinting
      2. Surgical releases: many procedures and many advocates (results are variable, depending on authors)
         (1) Release the intermuscular septum proximally, and two heads of FCU
         (2) Anterior transposition
            i. Submuscular
            ii. Subcutaneous
         (3) Medial epicondylectomy

IV. Radial Nerve
A. Radial tunnel syndrome
   1. Fibrous bands, tendinous origin of extensor carpi radialis brevis (ECRB), tendinous origin of supinator (arcade of Froshe), and at distal edge of supinator at its exit
   2. Pain over extensor origin, particularly with middle finger extension with elbow and wrist extended, and with forearm supination
   3. Differential diagnosis: tennis elbow, C6 or C7 radiculopathy
   4. Treatment: surgical release if failure of conservative treatment
B. Posterior interosseous syndrome
   1. Entrapment at the proximal edge of supinator
   2. Other etiologies may be Monteggia fracture/dislocation of radial head, inflammation (rheumatoid arthritis), tumors, iatrogenic (surgery)
   3. Motor loss of radial nerve without sensory deficits (brachialis [BR], extensor carpi radialis longus [ECRL], ECRB, supinator are intact)
   4. Treatment: surgical decompression

V. Thoracic Outlet Syndrome
A. Between first rib, scalenus anterior, and scalenus medius
B. Pain, vascular symptoms, and sensory disturbance in the C7-T1 distribution
C. Elevated stress test (opening and closing hand with arm elevated for 3 minutes), Adson's sign (monitor symptoms and radial pulse while the arm is in abduction and extension)
D. Clinical diagnosis is not easy to make, and EMG and arteriography are necessary to help make the correct diagnosis
E. Treatment
   1. Conservative: correct posture, exercises
   2. Surgical: first rib resection, scalentomy in recalcitrant cases

REFERENCES

Brachial Plexus and Peripheral Nerve Injuries

Brunelli G: Neurolysis and free microvascular omentum transfer in the treatment of postactinic palsies of the brachial plexus. Int Surg 65:6, 1980

Carroll RE, Kleinman WB: Pectoralis major transplantation to restore elbow flexion to the paralytic limb. J Hand Surg 4:501–507, 1979

Frykman GK, Cally D: Interfascicular nerve grafting. Orthop Clin North Am 19:71, 1988

Jones SJ, Wynn-Parry CB, Landi A: Diagnosis of brachial plexus traction lesions by sensory nerve action potentials and somatosensory evoked potentials. Injury 12:376, 1981

Leffert RD: Brachial plexus. In Green DP, ed. Operative hand surgery. New York, Churchill Livingstone, 1988

Millesi H: Interfascicular nerve grafting. Orthop Clin North Am 12:287, 1981

Millesi H, et al: Further experience with interfascicular grafting of the median, ulnar, and radial nerves. J Bone Joint Surg 58A:209, 1976

Narakas A: Brachial plexus surgery in symposium on peripheral nerve injuries. Orthop Clin North Am 12:303–323, 1981

Omer G Jr, Spinner M: Management of peripheral nerve problems. Philadelphia, WB Saunders, 1980

Seddon HJ: Surgical disorders of the peripheral nerves. Baltimore, Williams & Wilkins, 1972

Spinner M: Injuries to the major branches of peripheral nerves of the forearm, ed 2. Philadelphia, WB Saunders, 1978

Sunderland S: Nerves and nerve injuries, ed 2. Edinburgh, Churchill Livingstone, 1978

Wilgus EFS: Nerve repair and grafting. In Green DP, ed. Operative hand surgery. New York, Churchill Livingstone, 1988

Compressive Neuropathies of the Upper Extremity

Broudy AS, Leffert RD, Smith RJ: Technical problems with ulnar nerve transposition at the elbow: Findings and results of reoperation. J Hand Surg 3:85–89, 1978

Bucher TPJ: Anterior interosseous nerve syndrome. J Bone Joint Surg 54B:555, 1972

Comtet JJ, Quicot L, Moyen B: Compression of the deep palmer branch of the ulnar nerve by the arch of the adductor pollicis. Hand 10:176–180, 1978

Dellon AL, Mackinnon SE: Radial sensory nerve entrapment in the forearm. J Hand Surg 11A:199–205, 1986

Eversmann WW Jr: Entrapment and compression neuropathies. In Green DP, ed. Operative hand surgery, vol 2. New York, Churchill Livingstone, 1988

Hagert CG, Lundborg G, Hansen T: Entrapment of the posterior interosseous nerve. Scand J Plast Reconstr Surg 11:205, 1977

Hill NA, Howard FM, Huffern BR: The incomplete anterior interosseous syndrome. J Hand Surg 10A:4, 1985

Insera A, Spinner M: An anatomic factor significant in transposition of the ulnar nerve. J Hand Surg 11A:80, 1986

Kelly TR: Thoracic outlet syndrome: Current concepts of treatment. Ann Surg 190:657–662, 1979

Kleinert HE, Hayes JR: The ulnar tunnel syndrome. Plast Reconstr Surg 47:21–24, 1971

Lanz U: Anatomical variations of the median nerve in the carpal tunnel. J Hand Surg 2:44–53, 1977

Leffert RD: Anterior submuscular transposition of the ulnar nerve by the Learmonth technique. J Hand Surg 7:147, 1982

Lichter RL, Jacobsen T: Tardy palsy of the posterior interosseous nerve with a Monteggia fracture. J Bone Joint Surg 57A:124–125, 1975

Lister GD, Belsole RB, Kleinert HE: The radial tunnel syndrome. J Hand Surg 4:52–59, 1979

MacDonald RI, Lichtman DM, Hanlon JJ, Wilson JN: Complications of surgical release for carpal tunnel syndrome. J Hand Surg 3:70–76, 1978

Moss SH, Switzer HE: Radial tunnel syndrome: A spectrum of clinical presentations. J Hand Surg 8:414–420, 1983

Phalen GS: The carpal tunnel syndrome. Clinical evaluation of 598 hands. Clin Orthop 83:29–40, 1972

Riordan DC: Radial nerve paralysis. Orthop Clin North Am 5:283, 1974

Roles NC, Maudsley RH: Radial tunnel syndrome. Resistant tennis elbow as nerve entrapment. J Bone Joint Surg 54B:499, 1972

Shea JD, McClain EJ: Ulnar nerve compression syndromes below wrist. J Bone Joint Surg 51A:1095, 1969

Spinner M: Injuries to the major branches of peripheral nerves of the forearm, ed 2. Philadelphia, WB Saunders, 1978

Stallworth JM, Horne JB: Diagnosis and management of thoracic outlet syndrome. Arch Surg 119:1149–1151, 1984

Taleisnik J: The palmar cutaneous branch of the median nerve and the approach to the carpal tunnel. An anatomical study. J Bone Joint Surg 55A:1212, 1973

54

Tendon Transfers of the Hand

I. General Considerations
A. Indications for tendon transfers may be for substitution (nerve injury), replacement (muscle-tendon loss), or balance (deformed hand)
B. Prerequisites are tissue homeostasis, passive joint motion, stable skeletal framework, and available donors
C. One should use as few transfers as necessary to meet the objective and a tendon transfer should have only one function
D. Assessment of patient's functional needs, expectations, and rehabilitation potential is important
E. Available donor tendon should be grade 4 or better because transfer causes grade to decrease by one. Adequate excursion, expendability, and straight line of pull are important
   1. Potential force of a muscle is proportional to its cross-sectional area
   2. Potential excursion of a muscle is proportional to its resting fiber length
F. Length and tension of tendon transfer should be that all joints must be able to go through a full range of motion (suture transfer under no tension at its resting length with origin of donor muscle closest to the insertion of its recipient tendon but at slightly greater tension if the antagonist is strong)
G. When needs exceed the possible donor muscles, alternatives such as tenodesis, capsulodesis, or arthrodesis should be considered
H. Timing of transfers is variable, except one should wait until there is good tissue homeostasis (early tendon transfers can be done to act as internal functional splint, active assist, or complete substitute)
I. Postoperative protection for 3–4 weeks, followed by active range of motion

II. Commonly Used Transfers
A. Radial nerve palsy
   1. Functional deficit: loss of thumb extension, finger extension, wrist extension (if lesion is proximal to elbow)
   2. "Standard" transfer
      a. Pronator teres to ECRB for wrist extension (Fig 6-9)
      b. FCU to extensor digitorum communis (EDC) for finger extension (Fig 6-10)
      c. Palmaris longus to extensor pollicis longus (EPL) for thumb extension
   3. Alternative transfers
      a. FDS (long) to EDC for finger extension and FDS (ring) to EIP and EPL for thumb and EPL extension (Boyes) (Fig 6-11)
      b. FCR to EDC for finger extension (Brand)
B. Low median nerve palsy
   1. Functional deficits: thumb abduction and opposition
   2. Tendon transfers (insertion is into the abductor pollicis brevis APB)
      a. FDS (ring), using FCU as pulley
      b. EIP around the ulnar side of the wrist, using ulnar border of the forearm as pulley (Fig 6-12)
      c. Palmaris longus (as an internal splint in middle aged patients when median nerve has been repaired, good palmar abduction but poor pronation)
      d. EDQ (rarely used)

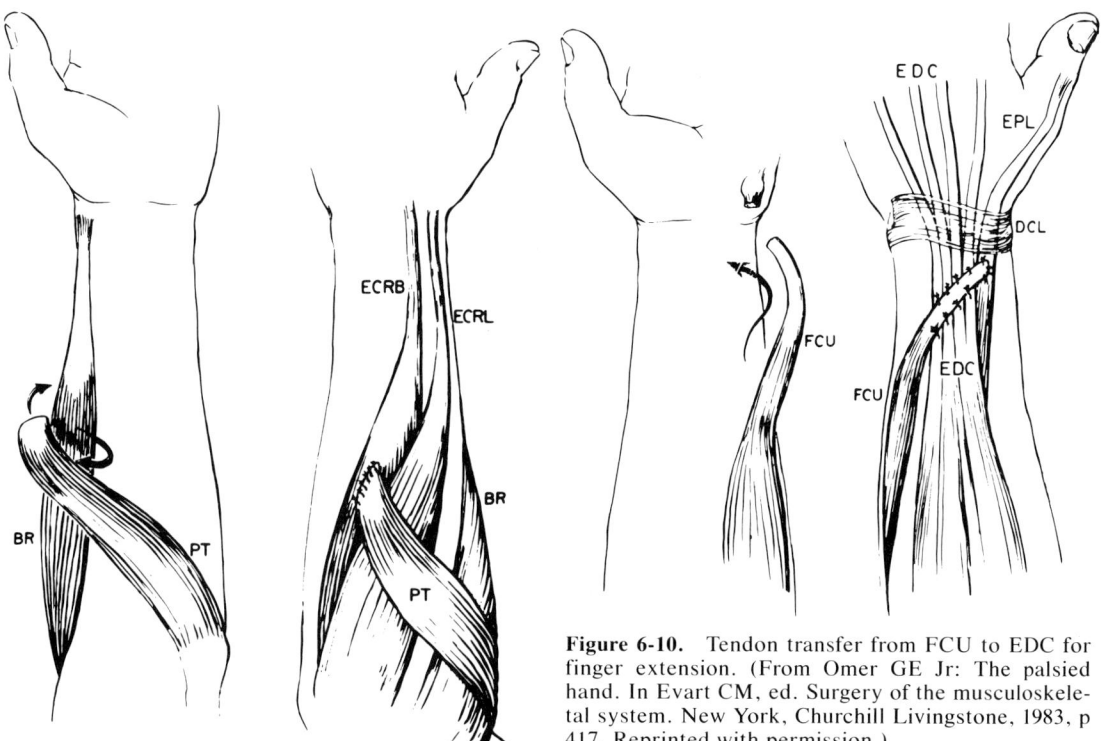

Figure 6-9. Tendon transfer from pronator teres to ECRB for wrist extension. (From Omer GE Jr: The palsied hand. In Evart CM, ed. Surgery of the musculoskeletal system. New York, Churchill Livingstone, 1983, p 413. Reprinted with permission.)

Figure 6-10. Tendon transfer from FCU to EDC for finger extension. (From Omer GE Jr: The palsied hand. In Evart CM, ed. Surgery of the musculoskeletal system. New York, Churchill Livingstone, 1983, p 417. Reprinted with permission.)

C. High median nerve palsy
  1. Functional deficits: thumb opposition, thumb interphalangeal flexion, and DIP flexion of index and middle fingers
  2. Tendon transfers
     a. Opponensplasty as low median nerve palsy
     b. Brachioradialis to FPL for thumb flexion
     c. FDP (ring and small) to FDP of index and long (side to side suture) for finger flexion power
D. Low ulnar nerve palsy
  1. Functional deficits: thumb adduction and index finger abduction, MCP flexion and PIP extension of ulnar digits. Loss of palmar arches and little finger abducted posture are also present
  2. Tendon transfers
     a. ECRB (plus graft), EIP, BR (plus graft), or FDS (long or ring) to adductor pollicis (AP) for thumb adduction
     b. Abductor pollicis longus (APL), EIP, ECRL to dorsal interossei
     c. Correct clawing ring and small fingers: FDS (ring) to radial digits lateral bands of ulnar two digits
E. High ulnar nerve palsy
  1. Functional deficits: loss of thumb abduction, index finger abduction, FDP of ulnar digits, and FCU function. Clawing is less because of weak finger flexors
  2. Tendon transfers
     a. Same tendon transfers for thumb adduction and index abduction in low ulnar nerve palsy
     b. Side to side suture to FDP of index and/or long fingers for FDP flexion of ring and small fingers

c. FDS of ring and little fingers should not be used as donors because these are the primary flexors of these digits

REFERENCES

Adams J, Wood VE: Tendon transfers for irreparable nerve damage in the hand. Orthop Clin North Am 12:403–432, 1981
Albright JA, Linburg RM: Common variations of the radial wrist extensors. J Hand Surg 3:134–138, 1978
Blacker GJ, Lister GD, Kleinert HE: The abducted little finger in low ulnar nerve palsy. J Hand Surg 1:190–196, 1976
Brand PW: General principles for restoration of muscle balance following paralysis in forearm and hand. In Chapman MW, ed. Operative orthopaedics. Philadelphia, JB Lippincott, 1988, pp 1369–1377
Brand PW, Beach RB, Thompson DE: Relative tension and potential excursion of muscles in the forearm and hand. J Hand Surg 6:209–219, 1981
Braun RM: Palmaris longus tendon transfer for augmentation of the thenar musculature in low median palsy. J Hand Surg 3:488–491, 1978
Brown PW: Reconstruction for pinch in ulnar intrinsic palsy. Orthop Clin North Am 5:323–342, 1974

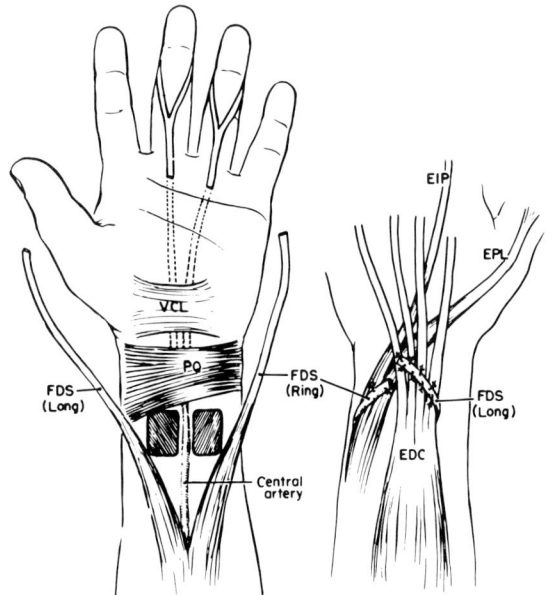

Figure 6-11. Boyes tendon transfer from FDS (long) to EDC for finger extension and FDS (ring) to EIP and EPL for thumb and EPL extension (Boyes). (From Omer GE Jr: The palsied hand. In Evart CM, ed. Surgery of the musculoskeletal system. New York, Churchill Livingstone, 1983, p 417. Reprinted with permission.)

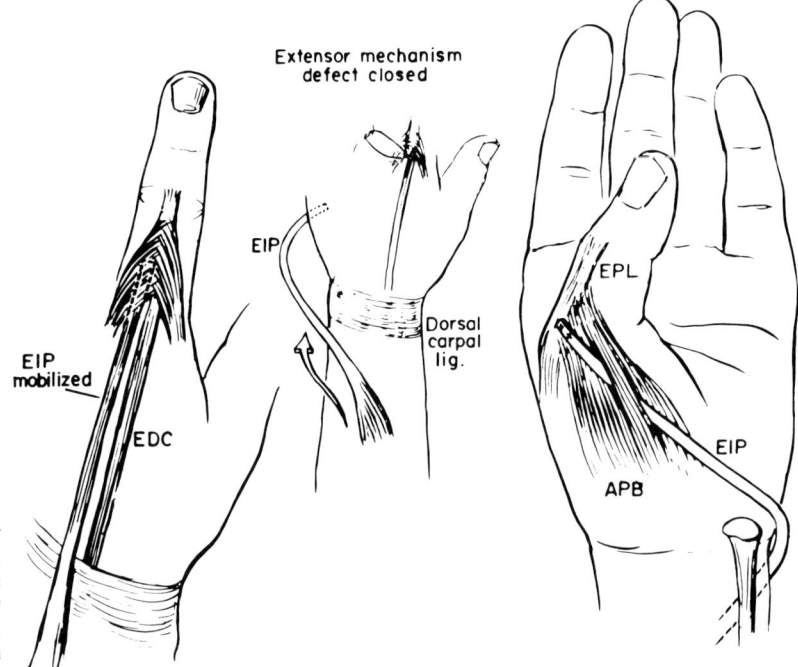

Figure 6-12. Opponensplasty by transferring EIP around the ulnar side of the wrist, using ulnar border of the forearm as pulley. (From Omer GE Jr: The palsied hand. In Evart CM, ed. Surgery of the musculoskeletal system. New York, Churchill Livingstone, 1983, p 414. Reprinted with permission.)

Brown PW: Zancolli capsulorrhaphy for ulnar claw hand. J Bone Joint Surg 52A:868, 1970

Browne EZ, Teague MA, Snyder CC: Prevention of extensor lag after indicis proprius tendon transfer. J Hand Surg 4:168–172, 1979

Burge P: Abducted little finger in low ulnar nerve palsy. J Hand Surg 11B:234–236, 1986

Burkhalter WE: Median nerve palsy. In Green DP, ed. Operative hand surgery, ed 2. New York, Churchill Livingstone, 1988, pp 1499–1534

Chuinard RG, Boyes JH, Stark HH, Ashworth CR: Tendon transfers for radial nerve palsy: Use of superficialis tendons for digital extension. J Hand Surg 3:560–570, 1978

Green DP: Radial nerve palsy. In Green DP, ed. Operative hand surgery, ed 2. New York, Churchill Livingstone, 1988, pp 1479–1499

Herrick RT, Lister GD: Control of first web space contracture. Including a review of the literature and a tabulation of oppenensplasty techniques. Hand 9:253–264, 1977

Kaplan EB, Spinner M: Normal and anomalous innervation patterns in the upper extremity. In Omer GE, Spinner M, eds. Management of peripheral nerve problems. Philadelphia, WB Saunders, 1980, pp 75–99

Labosky DA, Waggy CA: Apparent weakness of median and ulnar motors in radial nerve palsy. J Hand Surg 11A:528–533, 1986

Neviaser RJ, Wilson JN, Gardner MM: Abductor pollicis longus transfer for replacement of first dorsal interosseous. J Hand Surg 5:53–57, 1980

North ER, Littler JW: Transferring the flexor superficialis tendon: Technical considerations in the prevention of proximal interphalangeal joint disability. J Hand Surg 5:498–501, 1980

Omer GE: Combined nerve palsies. In Green DP, ed. Operative hand surgery, ed 2. New York, Churchill Livingstone, 1988, pp 1555–1567

Omer GE: Reconstruction of a balanced thumb through tendon transfers. Clin Orthop 195:104–116, 1985

Omer GE: Reconstructive procedures for extremities with peripheral nerve defects. Clin Orthop 163:80–91, 1982

Omer GE: Ulnar nerve palsy. In Green DP, ed. Operative hand surgery, ed 2. New York, Churchill Livingstone, 1988, pp 1535–1554

Pollock FH, Drake D, Bovill EG, et al: Treatment of radial neuropathy associated with fractures of the humerus. J Bone Joint Surg 63A:239–243, 1981

Riordan DC: Tendon transfers in hand surgery. J Hand Surg 8:748–753, 1983

Smith RJ: Intrinsic muscles of the fingers. Function, dysfunction, and surgical reconstruction. In AAOS instructional course lectures, vol 24. St Louis, CV Mosby, 1975, pp 200–220

Wissingers HA, Singsen EG: Abductor digiti quinti opponensplasty. J Bone Joint Surg 59A:895–898, 1977

Youm H, Thambyrajah K, Flatt AE: Tendon excursion of wrist movers. J Hand Surg 9A:202–209, 1984

55
Tenosynovitis, Osteoarthritis, and Rheumatoid Arthritis

TENOSYNOVITIS

I. General Considerations
A. Inflammatory or overuse conditions
B. Careful history and localized tender areas are frequently diagnostic
C. Tenosynovium is located in the flexor sheath, carpal tunnel, extensor compartments, and flexor carpi radialis (FCR) tunnel
D. General treatment: rest, splinting, NSAIDs, injections (synovectomy or surgical release in resistant cases)

II. Trigger Thumb or Finger
A. A1 pulley is most commonly involved
B. Clinical: triggering, locking, pain, and tenderness at base of the digit
C. Treatment: conservative first and surgical release of A1 pulley in resistant cases (take great caution not to injure the digital nerves)

III. DeQuervain's Disorder
A. Stenosing tenosynovitis of first dorsal extensor compartment
B. Multiple tendons of APL and septation between the APL and extensor pollicis brevis (EPB) is frequently present
C. Clinical: painful enlargement of first dorsal extensor compartment, limited wrist and thumb motion, positive Finklestein's test
D. Differential diagnosis: basal joint arthritis, scaphoid pathology, and intersection syndrome
E. Treatment
   1. Conservative treatment first
   2. Surgical release of the first compartment along the ulnar border in resistant cases
      a. Avoid damage to the superficial sensory branch of the radial nerve
      b. Must identify EPB (absent in 5%) and open sheath over both EPB and APL
   3. Preserve a volar-based retinacular flap to prevent palmar tendon subluxation

IV. Intersection Syndrome
A. Inflammation between opposing surfaces of APL and extensor carpi radialis
B. Clinical: pain and tenderness on the dorsal distal forearm with wrist movement
C. Treatment
   1. Conservative treatment is successful in the majority of cases
   2. Release of dorsal fascia over the musculotendinous juncture in recalcitrant cases

V. Flexor Carpi Radialis Tunnel Syndrome
A. Inflammation of FCR along the ulnar border scaphoid tubercle and trapezial crest
B. Clinical: wrist pain worse with flexion and extension of the wrist and joint tenderness on the radial volar region
C. Treatment
   1. Conservative initially
   2. Surgery if conservative management fails

a. Incision radial to FCR to prevent injury to palmar cutaneous branch of median nerve. Elevate the origin of thenar muscles (APB, flexor pollicis brevis [FPB]) and resect the scaphoid tubercle and trapezial crest
   b. Free FCR to insertion
   c. Brief immobilization and early active range of motion

VI. Extensor Carpi Ulnaris Tenosynovitis

A. Inflammation o f the sixth dorsal extensor compartment
B. Clinical: pain and tenderness over sixth dorsal compartment, particularly with wrist dorsiflexion and ulnar deviation
C. Differential diagnosis: distal radioulnar or ulnocarpal pathology
D. Treatment: conservative initially and explore sheath in recalcitrant cases

VII. Flexor Carpi Ulnaris Tenosynovitis

A. FCR overuse and inflammation
B. Clinical: painful palpation of the pisiform and painful with resistance to ulnar flexion
C. Differential diagnosis: pisotriquetral arthritis, ulnar neuritis
D. Treatment: conservative

OSTEOARTHRITIS OF THE HAND AND WRIST

I. General Considerations

A. Pathoetiology unknown: aging, trauma, immobilization, immune, or cartilageous problems
   1. Chronic loading of the joints
   2. Decreased lubrication of the joints
   3. Enzymatic destruction of the articular cartilage
   4. Increased subchondral blood supply
B. Common condition that affects older women predominantly
C. Common presenting complaints are joint stiffness, pain, or deformity
D. Joints commonly involved: DIP, carpometacarpal (CMC) joint of thumb, and PIP, in this order
E. Radiologic findings
   1. Joint space narrowing and juxta-articular erosion
   2. Subchondral bone hypertrophy
   3. Osteophyte formation
   4. Subchondral cyst formation
   5. Gross joint deformity
F. General treatment
   1. Conservative: NSAIDs, activity modification, and hand therapy, and splints
   2. Surgery
      a. Failure of conservative treatment
      b. Arthroplasty or arthrodesis when appropriate

II. Specific Joints

A. DIP joint
   1. Heberden's nodes and mucous cysts may be present
   2. Excision of mucous cysts with underlying osteophytes
   3. Arthrodesis
B. PIP joint
   1. Bouchard's nodes
   2. Debridement
   3. Arthroplasty using silicone implant
   4. Arthrodesis (30°–50° flexion)
C. CMC joint of the thumb
   1. Most common joint operated on in the hand for degenerative joint disease (DJD)
   2. Clinical: pain at the CMC joint, prominence at CMC, positive grind test
   3. Subluxation, fragments, and trapezium osteophytes, and hyperextension of MCP joint may develop
   4. Surgical treatment
      a. Staging
         (1) Stage I: thumb-CMC joint widened (effusion)
         (2) Stage II: slight narrowing, minimal sclerotic changes
         (3) Stage III: marked narrowing,

cystic changes, scapho-trapezial (ST) joint appears normal
            (4) Stage IV: as above, ST joint involvement
        b. Treatment
            (1) Stage I: NSAIDs, splints. If joint is hypermobile, do volar ligament reconstruction
            (2) Stage II: same as stage I (may require resection of trapezium-thumb articulation and tendon spacer)
            (3) Stage III: if ST joint is stable and not involved, do CMC arthrodesis or trapezium-thumb resection arthroplasty
            (4) Stage IV
                i. Excision of the trapezium
                ii. Stabilize the volar ligament
                iii. Replace trapezium with spacer (do not use Silastic in patients <60 years of age)
                iv. Must pay attention to amount of thumb MCP joint hyperextension (may require MCP arthroplasty or arthrodesis)
    D. Wrist
        1. SLAC
            a. Common degenerative arthritis of the wrist in relation to the scaphoid
            b. Typically progresses from the radial styloid to the distal scaphoid joint, radioscaphoid joint, and eventually at the capitolunate joint
            c. Radiolunate joint is always spared
            d. Treatment is combination of biologic spacer and capitate-hamate-triquetrum-lunate arthrodesis)
        2. Triscaphe DJD (trapezium-trapezoid-scaphoid): treatment is arthrodesis of triscaphe joint

RHEUMATOID ARTHRITIS OF THE HAND AND WRIST

I. Pathogenesis
A. Unknown antigens (Epstein-Barr virus [EBV], collagen II, immunoglobulins, etc.)
B. Inherited trait (HLA-DR4 type)
C. More common in females 25–50 years of age
D. Antigen-antibody interaction (immune complexes, complements, and rheumatoid factor)
E. Chemotaxis of inflammatory cells
F. Synovitis (lymphocytes and plasma cells) and pannus
G. Cartilage destruction (collagenase and protease from synovial cells and phagocytes)
H. Subluxation, dislocation, tendon rupture, deformity, and ankylosis

II. Examination and Diagnosis
A. Synovitis of wrist, MCP and PIP joints
B. Tendons: ruptures and trigger fingers
C. Deformities
    1. Wrist: dorsal ulnar head dislocation, volar carpal dislocation, and radial metacarpal shift
    2. MCP: volar and ulnar subluxation
    3. PIP: intrinsic tightness, swan neck, and Boutonnière deformities
D. Entrapment syndromes (especially carpal tunnel)
E. Complete evaluation of other joints

III. Indications for Surgery
A. Severe arthritic pain
B. Chronic synovitis not responding to medical treatment
C. Tendon ruptures
D. Deformities resulting in impaired function
E. Nerve decompression

IV. Goals of Surgery
A. Relieve pain
B. Correct deformity
C. Improve function

V. Staging Surgery
A. Timing of upper extremities vs lower extremities, depending on individual factors

B. Consider shoulder/elbow problems prior to hand surgery
C. Treat painful conditions first (carpal tunnel syndrome, trigger fingers)
D. Treat tendon ruptures immediately
E. Perform wrist stabilization, MCP arthroplasty, thumb arthroplasty or fusions, and DIP fusion of fingers when indicated. PIP arthroplasty or stabilization later

VI. Tenosynovitis

A. Synovial lined tendon sheath involvement
  1. Dorsal tenosynovitis: tenosynovectomy if no improvement after 4–6 months of appropriate medical management (rest, splints, medications, steroid injections)
     a. Straight dorsal incision
     b. Complete synovectomy of all six extensor compartments
     c. Extensor retinaculum under tendons for smooth gliding
     d. Repair tendons (side to side or tendon graft)
     e. Early postoperative motion
  2. Flexor tenosynovitis: palmar flexor tenosynovectomy if no improvement after medical treatment
     a. Carpal tunnel syndrome is frequently associated
     b. Trigger fingers
        (1) Diffuse synovitis or nodular thickening
        (2) If this does not respond to steroid injection, prompt surgery is recommended
        (3) Surgical treatment is synovectomy, excision of nodules, and may release one slip of FDS (do not release any annular pulley especially A1 because ulnar drift may worsen)
     c. Tendon ruptures: must identify the cause and remove
        (1) Extensor tendon ruptures: differentiate from MCP dislocation, subluxation of tendons to intermetacarpal heads, and posterior interosseous nerve compression
           i. EPL: EIP as donor transfer
           ii. EDC: distal tendon stumps to adjacent tendon (side-side repair, small and ring fingers are commonly affected)
           iii. Multiple tendons: FDS may be used as transfer
        (2) Flexor tendon ruptures
           i. FPL: most common flexor tendon involved, ruptures on the ridge of scaphoid-trapezium (tendon graft may be required)
           ii. FDP: side to side repair in zones 3 and 4, fusion of DIP joint in zone 2
           iii. FDP and FDS: side to side or FDS to FDP stump in zones 3 and 4, staged silicone rod tendon reconstruction or fusion of PIP and DIP for zone 2

VII. Wrist Involvement

A. Caput ulna syndrome
  1. Synovitis of ulnocarpal ligament
  2. Dorsal dislocation of ulna
  3. Volar subluxation of extensor carpi ulnaris (ECU)
  4. Treatment
     a. Tenosynovectomy
     b. Consider Darrach or Bowers procedures
     c. May perform Clayton's ECRL transfer to ECU ring and small fingers
B. Radiocarpal and intercarpal joints
  1. Synovitis around scaphoid
  2. Supination, radial angulation, and volar subluxation of the carpus
  3. Treatment
     a. Wrist arthrodesis
     b. Total wrist arthroplasty
        (1) With bilateral involvement, patients prefer at least one mobile wrist
        (2) Silicone space arthroplasty is

more reliable than total joint arthroplasty

VIII. Metacarpophalangeal Joint
A. Deformities: volar and ulnar subluxation and ulnar displacement of the extensors
B. Treatment
  1. Synovectomy
  2. Intrinsic release with or without crossed intrinsic transfer
  3. Silicone arthroplasty
     a. Must include ligament reconstructions, particularly the index finger (position in slight supination)
     b. Centralization or radialization of extensor mechanisms
     c. Well-directed and time-consuming postoperative splinting and therapy

IX. Swan-Neck Deformity
A. A 28% incidence
B. Hyperextension of PIP joint and flexion of DIP joint
  1. Flexor synovitis and stretching of palmar plate
  2. Stretching of transverse retinacular ligament and dorsal shift of lateral bands
  3. Increased flexor and intrinsic pull on MCP joint and increased extrinsic pull of extrinsic extensor tendon
  4. Contracture of collateral ligaments and joint destruction
  5. Reciprocal flexion of DIP joint
C. Types of swan-neck deformity
  1. Type I: PIP joint flexible
  2. Type II: PIP joint limited in certain position
  3. Type III: limited PIP joint
  4. Type IV: destructive PIP joint
D. Treatment
  1. Type I: synovectomy, flexor tendon tenodesis (sublimis sling), retinacular ligament reconstruction (Littler) and DIP joint fusion
  2. Type II: intrinsic release and MCP joint arthroplasty
  3. Type III: restore passive motion first (PIP joint manipulation, skin release, and lateral band mobilization) and may do fusion or arthroplasty later
  4. Type IV: PIP arthroplasty or fusion

X. Boutonnière Deformity
A. A 15% incidence
B. Flexion of PIP and hyperextension of DIP joints
  1. Dorsal synovitis and capsular distension
  2. Lengthening or disruption of central extensor tendon
  3. Attenuation of triangular ligament and volar displacement of lateral bands
  4. Increased extensor pull on distal phalanx
  5. Joint destruction and fixed contracture
C. Types of Boutonnière deformity
  1. Stage I: mild (passively corrected full mobilization)
  2. Stage II: moderate (passively corrected but limited motion)
  3. Stage III: severe (cannot passively be corrected and limited motion)
D. Treatment
  1. Stage I: synovectomy, extensor tenotomy (Dolphin, Fowler)
  2. Stage II: extensor tenotomy at DIP joint and shortening of central slip and mobilization of lateral band dorsally (Matev, Littler) after passive range of motion restored
  3. Stage III: PIP joint fusion or arthroplasty

XI. Thumb
A. Boutonnière deformity
  1. A 57% incidence
  2. Pathology begins at the MCP joint
  3. Flexion of MCP joint and hyperextension of IP joint
     a. Dorsal synovitis of MCP joint
     b. Attenuated extensor tendon and capsule
     c. Volar displacement of EPL and intrinsics

d. Volar subluxation of proximal phalanx
e. Reciprocal IP extension
4. Treatment
   a. Early: synovectomy and extensor rebalancing
   b. Late: MCP arthroplasty with IP fusion

B. Swan-neck deformity
1. A 90% incidence
2. Pathology begins at CMC joint
3. Hyperextension of MCP joint and flexion of IP joint
   a. Dorsal and radial subluxation of CMC joint
   b. Adduction of first metacarpal
   c. Volar synovitis of MCP joint
   d. Stretching of volar plate
   e. Hyperextension of MCP joint
   f. Reciprocal IP flexion
4. Treatment
   a. Hemiarthroplasty of trapezium or arthrodesis
   b. Extensor lengthening and volar tenodesis of MCP joint
   c. MCP arthrodesis or arthroplasty
   d. IP arthrodesis

REFERENCES

Tenosynovitis

Belsole RJ: DeQuervain's tenosynovitis: Diagnostic and operative complications. Orthopedics 4:899–903, 1981

Grundberg AB, Reagan DS: Pathologic anatomy of the forearm: Intersection syndrome. J Hand Surg 10A:299–302, 1985

Fitton J, Doldie W: Lesions of the flexor carpi radialis tendon and sheath causing pain at the wrist. J Bone Joint Surg 50B:359, 1968

Froimson A: Stenosing tenovaginitis. In Green D, ed. Operative hand surgery. New York, Churchill Livingstone, 1982

Pruzansky M: Stenosing tenosynovitis. In Chapman MW, ed. Operative orthopaedics. Philadelphia, JB Lippincott, 1988

Osteoarthritis

Ashworth CR, Blatt G, Chuinard RG, Stark HH: Silicone rubber interposition arthroplasty of the carpometacarpal joint of the thumb. J Hand Surg 2:345–357, 1977

Beckenbaugh RD, Linscheid RL: Arthroplasty in the hand and wrist. In Green DP, ed. Operative hand surgery, ed 2. New York, Churchill Livingstone, 1988

Braun RM, Rhoades CE: Dynamic compression for small bone arthrodesis. J Hand Surg 10A:340–343, 1985

Burton RI, Pellegrini VD Jr: Surgical management of basal joint arthritis of the thumb. Part II: Ligament reconstruction with tendon interposition arthroplasty. J Hand Surg 11A:324–332, 1986

Carroll RE, Hill NA: Arthrodesis of the carpometacarpal joint of the thumb. J Bone Joint Surg 55B:292, 1973

Carroll RE, Hill NA: Small joint arthrodesis in the hand. J Bone Joint Surg 51A:1291, 1969

Carter PR, Benton LJ, Dysert PA: Silicone rubber carpal implants: A study of the incidence of late osseous complications. J Hand Surg 11A:639–644, 1986

Clendenin MB, Green DP: Arthrodesis of the wrist. Complications and their management. J Hand Surg 6:253–257, 1981

Derkash RS, Niebauer JJ, Lane CS: Long-term follow-up of metacarpal phalangeal arthroplasty with silicone Dacron prostheses. J Hand Surg 11A:553–558, 1986

Dick HM: Wrist arthrodesis. In Green DP, ed. Operative hand surgery, ed 2. New York, Churchill Livingstone, 1988, pp 155–166

Easton RG: Replacement of the trapezium for arthritis of the basal articulations. J Bone Joint Surg 61A:76, 1979

Faithfull DK, Herbert TJ: Small joint fusions of the hand using the Herbert bone screw. J Hand Surg 9B:167, 1984

Froimson AE: Tendon arthroplasty of the trapeziometacarpal joint. Clin Orthop 70:191, 1970

Hill NA: Small joint arthrodesis. In Green DP, ed. Operative hand surgery, ed 2. New York, Churchill Livingstone, 1988, pp 121–135

Khuri SM: Tension band arthrodesis in the hand. J Hand Surg 11A:41, 1986

Kvarnes L, Reikeras O: Osteoarthritis of the carpometacarpal joint of the thumb: An analysis of operative procedure. J Hand Surg 10B:117, 1985

Lipscomb PR: Small joint arthrodesis in the hand. In Chapman MW, ed. Operative orthopaedics. Philadelphia, JB Lippincott, 1988

Swanson AB: Disabling arthritis of the base of the thumb. J Bone Joint Surg 54A:456, 1972

Swanson, AB, Swanson G deG: osteoarthritis in the hand. J Hand Surg 8:669, 1983

Watson HK, Ballet FL: The scapho-lunate advanced collapsed wrist. J Hand Surg 8:619, 1983

Watson HK, Ballet FL: SLAC wrist: Scapholunate advanced collapse pattern of degenerative arthritis. J Hand Surg 9A:358–365, 1984

Watson HK, Goodman ML, Johnson TR: Limited

wrist arthrodesis. II. Intercarpal and radiocarpal combinations. J Hand Surg 6:223, 1981
Watson HK, Hempton RF: Limited wrist arthrodesis. Part I: The triscaphoid joint. J Hand Surg 5:320, 1980
Watson HK, Vender MI: Intercarpal arthrodesis. Operative hand surgery, ed 2. New York, Churchill Livingstone, 1988
Wright CS, McMurty RY: AO arthrodesis in the hand. J Hand Surg 8:932–935, 1983

Rheumatoid Arthritis

Agee JM, Guidera M: Functional significance of the juncturae tendinae in dynamic stabilization of the metacarpophalangeal joints of the fingers. J Hand Surg 52A:896–906, 1970
Besser MIB: The conservative treatment of the swan-neck deformity in the rheumatoid hand. Hand 10:91–93, 1978
Bora WF, Osterman AL, Thomas V, et al. A free tendon graft for the treatment of the multiple extensor tendon ruptures at the wrist level in the rheumatoid patient. J Hand Surg 10A:434, 1985
Bowers WH: Distal radioulnar joint arthroplasty: The hemiresection-interposition technique. J Hand Surg 10A:169–178, 1985
Brase DW, Millender LH: Failure of silicone rubber wrist arthroplasty in rheumatoid arthritis. J Hand Surg 11A:175–183, 1986
Carvell JE, Mowat AG, Fuller DJ: Trigger wrist phenomenon in rheumatoid arthritis. Hand 15:77–81, 1983
Clayton ML, Ferlic DC: Tendon transfer for radial rotation of the wrist in rheumatoid arthritis. Clin Orthop 100:176–185, 1974
Clendenin MB, Green DP: Arthrodesis of the wrist — complications and their management. J Hand Surg 6:253–257, 1981
Ellison MR, Flatt AE, Kelly KJ: Ulnar drift of the fingers in rheumatoid disease. Treatment by crossed intrinsic tendon transfer. J Bone Joint Surg 53A:1061–1082, 1971
Eyring EJ, Longert A, Bass JC: Synovectomy in juvenile rheumatoid arthritis. Indications and short-term results. J Bone Joint Surg 53A:638–651, 1971
Fatti JF, Palmer AK, Mosher JF: The long-term results of Swanson silicone rubber interpositional wrist arthroplasty. J Hand Surg 11A:166–175, 1986
Ferlic DC, Smith CJ, Clayton ML: Medical considerations and management of rheumatoid arthritis. J Hand Surg 8:662–666, 1983
Ferlic DC, Smith CJ: Flexor tenosynovitis in the rheumatoid hand. J Hand Surg 3:364, 1978
Flatt AE: The care of the rheumatoid hand, ed 3. St Louis, CV Mosby, 1974
Fleisher A, McGrath MH: Rheumatoid nodulosis of the hand. J Hand Surg 9A:404–411, 1984
Gainor BJ, Hummel GL: Correction of rheumatoid swan-neck deformity by lateral band mobilization. J Hand Surg 10A:370–376, 1985
Granowitz S, Vainio K: Proximal interphalangeal joint arthrodesis in rheumatoid arthritis. A followup study of 122 operations. Acta Orthop Scand 37:301–310, 1966
Kessler I: Aetiology and management of adduction contracture of the thumb in rheumatoid arthritis. Hand 5:170–174, 1973
Kulick RG, DeFiore JC, Straub LR, Ranawat CS: Longterm results of dorsal stabilization in the rheumatoid wrist. J Hand Surg 6:272–280, 1981
Lamberta FL, Ferlic DC, Clayton ML: Volz total wrist arthroplasty in rheumatoid arthritis: A preliminary report. J Hand Surg 5:245, 1980
McCollum DE, Goldner JL, Rhangos WC, et al: Surgery of the hand in rheumatoid arthritis-indications, contraindications and expectations. J Bone Joint Surg 47A:1285, 1965
Mikic ZD, Helal B: The value of the Darrach procedure in the surgical treatment of rheumatoid arthritis. Clin Orthop 127:175–185, 1977
Millender LH, Nalebuff EA: Arthrodesis of the rheumatoid wrist: An evaluation of sixty patients and a description of a different surgical technique. J Bone Joint Surg 55A:1026, 1973
Moore JR, Valdata L: Tendon ruptures in the rheumatoid hand: Analysis of treatment and functional results in fifty patients. J Hand Surg 10A:433, 1985
Nalebuff EA, Feldon PG, Millender LH: Rheumatoid arthritis in the hand and wrist. In Green DP, ed. Operative hand surgery, ed 2. New York, Churchill Livingstone, 1988, pp 1655–1766
Nalebuff EA, Garrod KJ: Present approach to the severely involved rheumatoid wrist. Orthop Clinic North Am 15:369–380, 1984
Scott FA, Boswick JA: Palmar arthroplasty for the treatment of stiff swan-neck deformity. J Hand Surg 8:267–272, 1983
Shapiro JS: Wrist involvement in rheumatoid swan-neck deformity. J Hand Surg 7:484–491, 1982
Shapiro JS, Rodts T, Labanauskas I, Payne T: Early synovectomy versus late arthroplasty of the rheumatoid wrist: A comparative study. J Hand Surg 10A:430, 1985
Smith RJ, Atkinson RE, Jupiter JB: Silicone synovitis of the wrist. J Hand Surg 10A:47–60, 1985
Swanson AB: Flexible implant resection arthroplasty in the hand and extremities. St Louis, CV Mosby, 1973
Swanson AB, Herndon JH: Flexible (silicone) implant arthroplasty of the metacarpophalangeal joint of the thumb. J Bone Joint Surg 59A:362–368, 1977
Swanson AB, deG Swanson GL, Leonard J: Postoperative rehabilitation program in flexible implant arthroplasty of the digits. In Hunter JM, Schneider LH, Mackin EJ, Bell JA, eds. Rehabilitation of the hand. St Louis, CV Mosby, 1978
Swanson AB, Swanson deGroot G, Maupin BK: Flexible implant arthroplasty of the radiocarpal joint.

Surgical technique and long-term study. Clin Orthop 187:94–106, 1984

Taleisnik J: Subtotal arthrodeses of the wrist joint. Clin Orthop 187:81–88, 1984

Thirupathi RG, Ferlic DC, Clayton ML: Dorsal wrist synovectomy in rheumatoid arthritis — a long term study. J Hand Surg 8:848–856, 1983

Thompson JS, Littler JW, Upton J: The spiral oblique retinacular ligament (SORL). J Hand Surg 3:482–497, 1978

Torisu T, Masumi S, Aso K: Utilization of the extensor retinaculum in the radiocarpal joint of rheumatoid wrists. Clin Orthop 181:179–185, 1983

Vicar AJ, Burton RI: Surgical management of the rheumatoid wrist. Fusion or arthroplasty. J Hand Surg 10A:430, 1985

Contractures and Reflex Sympathetic Dystrophy

DUPUYTREN'S CONTRACTURE

I. Pathogenesis
A. Incidence
   1. Familial and genetic: more common in Northern Europe (Scandinavian and Celtic origin)
   2. More common in men (6:1) and 5th to 7th decades
   3. Higher in epileptics, alcoholics, diabetes, prolonged bed rest, chronic obstructive pulmonary disease, and smokers
   4. Trauma, vascular insufficiency, hypoxia
   5. Bilateral in >65%
B. Pathology: palmar fascia and cutaneous ligaments
   1. Nodule: perivascular fibroblasts (stage I)
   2. Contractile phase: myofibroblasts and increased adenosine triphosphatase (ATPase) (stage II)
   3. Advanced contracture: fibrocytes with type III collagens (increased cross-linking, insolubility, and hydroxylysine), ≥3 years (stage III)

II. Clinical Findings
A. Nodules (stage I, often painful, mostly ulnar two rays)
B. Contractures (Fig 6-13 A, B)
   1. MCP: pretendinous cord
   2. PIP: central cord and spiral cord (neurovascular bundle is displaced proximal, medially, and volarly) and retrovascular cord (DIP contracture also)
C. Dupuytren's diastheses
   1. More aggressive form
   2. Strong family history
   3. Early onset, bilateral, ectopic diseases (knuckle pads, dorsum of penis or Peyronie's disease, plantar fascia)
   4. Recurrence and prognosis worse

III. Treatment
A. Nodule: inject cortisone if painful (no surgery)
B. Surgery: fasciectomy of involved tissues
   1. Thirty degree MCP joint and 15° PIP joint
   2. Regional fasciectomy (primary closure, open palm technique, or skin grafting)
C. If carpal tunnel syndrome and Dupuytren's disease are coexistent, do them in separate stages
D. Amputation is an alternative in a severely contracted nonsalvageable small finger, including PIP joint

IV. Complications
A. Hematoma
B. Skin necrosis
C. Loss of finger flexion
D. Recurrrnce
E. Reflex sympathetic dystrophy
F. Infection

INTRINSIC CONTRACTURES

I. Etiology
A. Mallet finger: both extrinsic and intrinsic pull to PIP joint (tendency to hyperextend PIP to become swan-neck deformity)
B. Post-traumatic: three stages
   1. Early edema and ischemia secondary

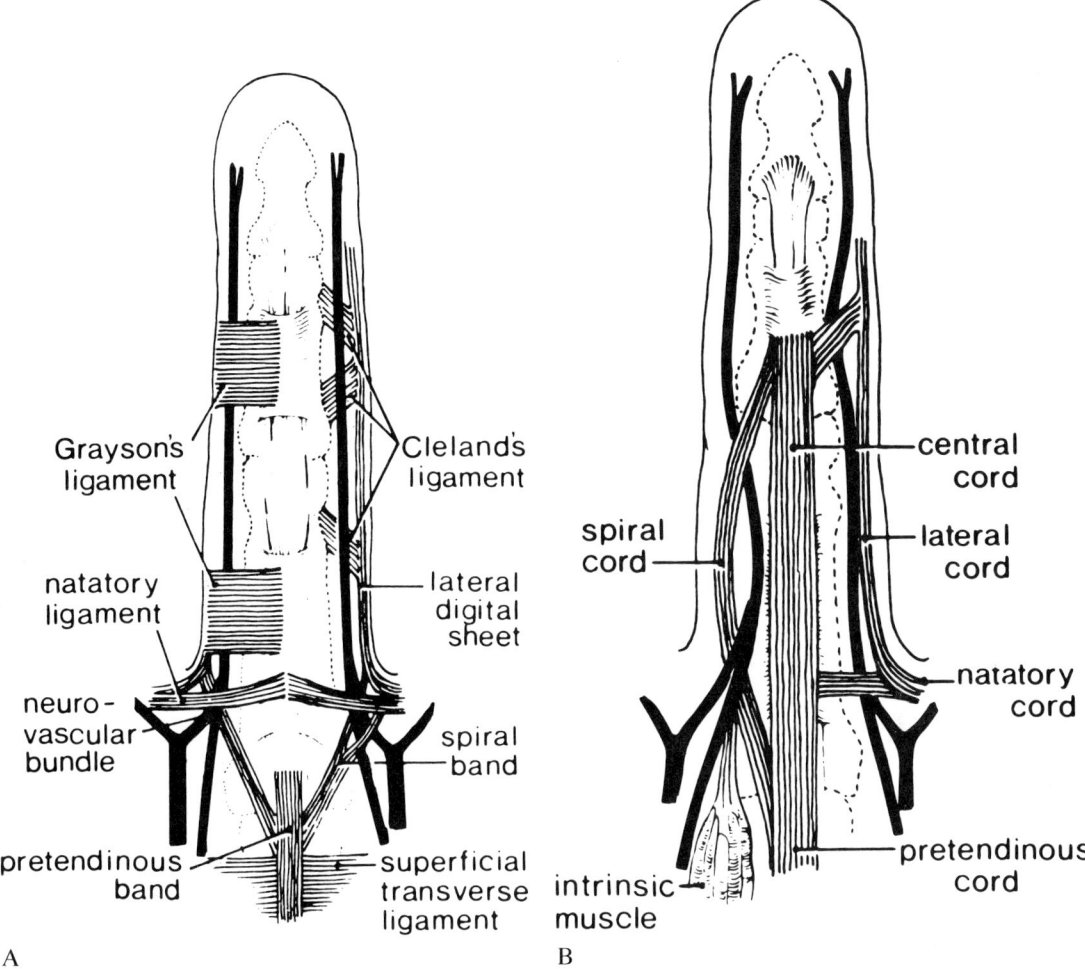

Figure 6-13. Dupuytren's contractures. **A.** Components of normal digital fascia that become diseased except for Cleland's ligament. **B.** The pretendinous band causes MCP contracture, and the spiral, central, lateral and retrovascular cords cause PIP contractures. (McFarlane RM: Dupuytren's disease. In Evart CM, ed. Surgery of the musculoskeletal system. New York, Churchill Livingstone, 1983, p 543. Reprinted with permission.)

      to trauma, immobilization, and compressive dressing
2. PIP extension contracture
3. Both MCP flexion and PIP extension contractures

C. Spastic: spastic interossei secondary to neurologic problems
D. Rheumatoid arthritis: subluxation of volar MCP joint and ulnar drift causing extrinsic overpull on the central tendon and/or intrinsic contracture result in swan-neck deformity
E. Lumbrical plus deformity: normally, relaxation of the lumbrical muscle occurs with FDP contraction to give PIP flexion, but if the lumbrical muscle is unable to relax, the contraction of the FDP transmit the force to the lumbricals to extend PIP and DIP (paradoxical extension). This phenomenon may occur in the following

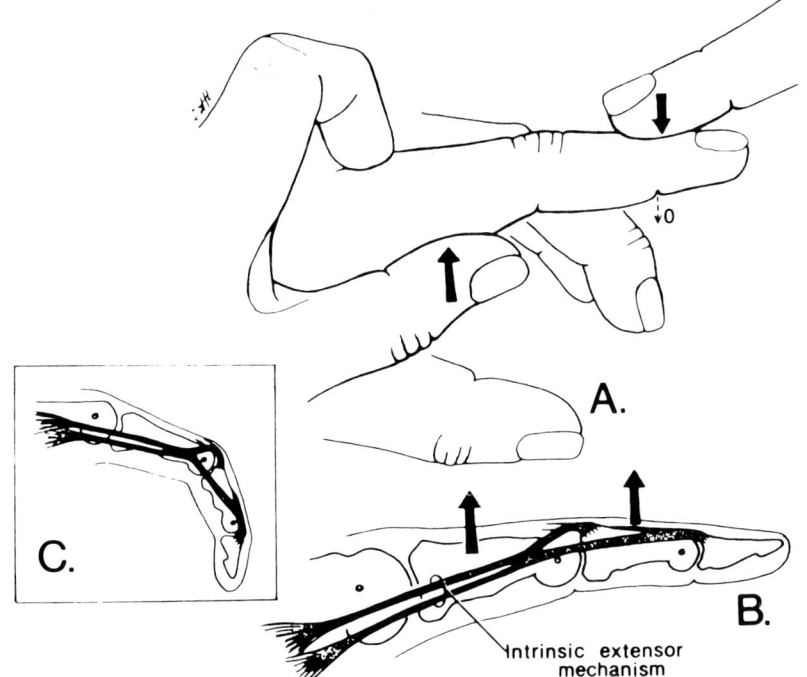

Figure 6-14. Intrinsic tight test. PIP joint flexion will be less when the MCP joint is extended than when it is flexed. (From Burton RI: Disorders of the extensor mechanism. In Evart CM, ed. Surgery of the musculoskeletal system. New York, Churchill Livingstone, 1983, p 281. Reprinted with permission.)

1. Lumbrical contracture
2. Too loose flexor tendon graft
3. Amputation or laceration of FDP distal to FDS

II. Clinical Findings

A. Intrinsic tightness (IT) test is positive: PIP joint flexion will be less when the MCP joint is extended than when it is flexed (Fig 6-14)
B. Deformity: MCP flexion and PIP and DIP extension of finger and thumb and adduction of the thumb

III. Treatment

A. Physical therapy: MCP extension and PIP and DIP flexion
B. Surgery
  1. Mallet finger: primary repair if acute and reconstruction (shortening and advancement of the terminal tendon) to prevent swan-neck deformity
  2. Post-traumatic: interossei and adductor release if compartment syndrome, distal intrinsic release for PIP extension contracture and proximal release or slide of interossei for late MP and PIP contractures
  3. Spastic: interossei muscle slide
  4. Rheumatoid arthritis: MCP arthroplasty and/or crossed intrinsic release or transfer. Intrinsic tenodesis (ulnar band) or spiral oblique retinacular ligament (SORL) transfer for swan-neck deformity
  5. Lumbrical: lumbrical radial lateral band release

COMPARTMENT SYNDROME AND VOLKMAN'S CONTRACTURES

I. General Considerations

A. Anatomy
  1. Forearm: volar flexor compartment, dorsal compartment, and mobile wad

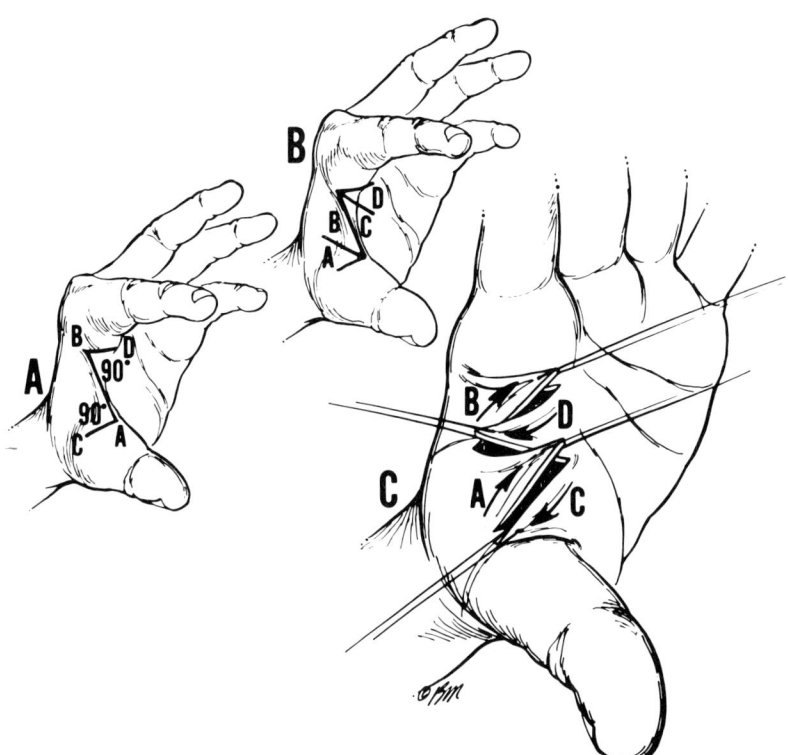

Figure 6-15. Four-flap Z-plasty to deepen the web space. (Dobyns JH, Wood VE, Bayne LG, et al: Congenital hand deformities. In Green DP, ed. Operative hand surgery. New York, Churchill Livingstone, 1982. Reprinted with permission.)

compartment (most commonly the volar compartment is involved, affecting the function of the median and ulnar nerves with flexor mass contracture and intrinsic paralysis of the hand)
  2. Hand: four dorsal interosseous compartments, three volar interosseous compartments, adductor pollicis, thenar, and hypothenar compartments
B. Etiologies: fractures, crush injuries, arterial ischemia, burns
C. Time is critical in that irreversible muscle and nerve damage after 8 hours
D. Most reliable signs of compartment syndrome are pain, particularly with passive muscle stretch and paresthesia. Pallor, pulselessness, and paralysis are late and useless findings
E. Diagnosis is made by clinical grounds and confirmed by wick catheter measurement (>30–40 mmHg)

II. Treatment
A. Remove external pressure, such as cast or dressings, and position the arm at the level of the heart (do not elevate)
B. Immediate fasciotomy from the elbow to the carpal tunnel for volar compartment
C. Longitudinal incisions for the hand compartments
D. Chronic Volkman's contractures
  1. Mild
    a. Usually localized involvement of FDP
    b. Splinting and range of motion therapy and occasional excision of infarcted tissue
  2. Moderate
    a. More flexor involvement
    b. Release nerve compressions, flexor-pronator slide, and tendor transfers
  3. Severe
    a. Severely contracted flexors and part of extensors

b. Flexor/pronator slide, intrinsic release, adductor release, thumb web deepening (Fig 6-15)
c. Tendon transfers if motors are available
d. Bony procedures may be necessary such as fusion, proximal carpal row carpectomy, etc.

REFLEX SYMPATHETIC DYSTROPHY (RSD)

I. General Considerations
A. Definition: dysfunctional state of the extremity with an abnormal amount of pain, swelling, stiffness, and discoloration, which occurs secondary to trauma to the extremity
B. Pathophysiology
  1. Increased sympathetic activity
  2. Abnormal vasomotor and skin trophic changes
  3. Signs and symptoms are more severe than the trauma or residual would suggest
C. Three factors are present to develop RSD
  1. Persistent pain (trauma or painful conditions)
  2. Diathesis (predisposition is essential, smoking has been shown to be a correlating factor, and as yet undefined genetic traits)
     a. Hypersympathetic reactor: increased sympathetic nerve activity. These patients have increased vasomotor instability with cold clammy hands, fainting, increased blushing, and lower pain thresholds
     b. Psychologic factors: emotionally labile, inadequate personality, passive aggressive, hypochondriacal personality
  3. Abnormal sympathetic reflex
     a. Trauma: normally sympathetic reflex produces a peripheral vasoconstriction until this effect is not necessary, then the reflex arc shuts itself off
     b. RSD: reflex arc is amplified and does not respond to feedback. This phenomenon produces vasoconstriction with tissue ischemia and increased pain causing a vicious cycle of increased sympathetic discharge called the sympathetic pain reflex
D. Clinical findings: severe burning pain, soft or endurated edema, stiffness, vasomotor trophic skin changes, and osteoporosis
E. Stages
  1. Stage I: burning pain, edema with skin changes. Bony demineralization occurs at 3–4 weeks
  2. Stage II: indurated edema and joint stiffness (3–9 months)
  3. Stage III: marked stiffness with joint contractures

II. Treatment
A. Early diagnosis and intervention are important
B. Remove aggravating factors: painful lesions, psychologic assessment and therapy, and decrease smoking
C. Eliminate abnormal sympathetic activity
  1. Drugs such as phenoxybenzamine, phentolamine, reserpine, or steroids
  2. Nerve blocks
  3. Stellate ganglion blocks or sympathectomy
  4. Hand therapy and splinting without causing pain
  5. Combination of treatment modalities and individualization

REFERENCES

Dupuytren's Disease
Albin R, Brickley D, Glimcher MJ, Smith RJ: Dupuytren's contracture: An active cellular process. J Bone Joint Surg 57A:726, 1975

An HS, Southworth S, Jackson WT: "Cigarette smoking and Dupuytren's contractures." J Hand Surg 13A:872–874, 1988

Beltran JE, Jimeno-Urban F, Yunta A: The open palm and digit technique in the treatment of Dupuytren's contracture. Hand 8:73–77, 1976

Chui HF, McFarlane RM: Pathogenesis of Dupuytren's contracture: A correlative clinical-pathological study. J Hand Surg 3:1, 1978

Hueston JT: Dermofasciectomy for Dupuytren's disease. Bull Hosp J Dis Orthop Inst 44:224–231, 1984

Hueston JT: Dupuytren's disease. In Flynn JE, ed. Hand surgery. Baltimore, Williams & Wilkins, 1982, pp 797–822

King EW, Exeter NH, Bass DM, Watson HK: Treatment of Dupuytren's contracture by extensive fasciectomy through multiple Y-V plasty incision. J Hand Surg 4:234, 1979

Legge JWH, McFarlane RM: Prediction of results of Dupuytren's contracture. J Hand Surg 5:608–616, 1980

Lubahn JD, Lister GD, Wolfe T: Fasciectomy and Dupuytren's disease. A comparison between the open palm technique and wound closure. J Hand Surg 9A:53–58, 1984

McCash CR: The open palm technique in Dupuytren's contracture. Br J Plast Surg 17:271, 1974

McFarlane RM: Dupuytren's contracture. In Green DP, ed. Operative hand surgery, ed 2. New York, Churchill Livingstone, 1988, pp 553–589

McFarlane RM, Jamieson WB: Dupuytren's contracture: Management of one hundred patients. J Bone Joint Surg 48A:1095, 1966

Tonkin MA, Burke FD, Varian JPW: Dupuytren's contracture: A comparative study of fasciectomy and dermofasciectomy in one hundred patients. J Hand Surg 9B:156–162, 1984

Watson HK, Light TR, Johnson TR: Checkrein resection for flexion contracture of the middle joint. J Hand Surg 4:67, 1979

Intrinsic Contractures

Flatt AE: Some pathomechanics of ulnar drift. Plast Reconstr Surg 37:295–303, 1966

Goldner JL: Intrinsic and extensor contracture of the hand due to ischemia and other conditions. In Flynn JE, ed. Hand surgery. Baltimore, Williams & Wilkins, 1966

Littler JW: Restoration of the oblique retinacular ligament for correcting hyperextension deformity of the proximal interphalangeal joints. In La main rheumatoide, groupe d'etude de la main. Paris, Expansion Scientifique Francais, 1966, pp 39–42

Parkes A: The "lumbrical-plus" finger. J Bone Joint Surg 53B:236–239, 1971

Shrewsbury MM, Johnson RK: A systemic study of the oblique retinacular ligament of the human finger. Its structure and function. J Hand Surg 2:194–199, 1977

Smith RJ: Balance and kinetics of the fingers under normal and pathologic conditions. Clin Orthop 104:92–111, 1974

Smith RJ: Intrinsic contractures. In Green DP, ed. Operative hand surgery, ed 2. New York, Churchill Livingstone, 1988, pp 609–631

Smith RJ: Surgery of the hand in cerebral palsy. In Pulvertaft RG, ed. Operative surgery. The hand, ed 3. London, Butterworth, 1977, p 215

Thompson JS, Littler JW, Upton J: The spiral oblique retinacular ligament (SORL). J Hand Surg 3:482–487, 1978

Tubiana R, Valentin P: The anatomy of the extensor apparatus of the fingers. Surg Clin North Am 44:897–906, 1964

Compartment Syndrome and Volkman's Contractures

Gelberman RH: Upper extremity compartment syndromes: Treatment; and Volkman's contracture of the upper extremity: Pathology and reconstruction. In Mubarak SJ, Hargens AR, eds. The compartment syndromes and Volkman's contracture. Philadelphia, WB Saunders, 1981

Gelberman RH, Zakaib GS, Mubarek SJ, et al: Decompression of forearm compartment syndromes. Clin Orthop 134:225–229, 1978

Ikuta Y, Kubo T, Tsuge K: Free muscle transplantation by microsurgical technique to treat severe Volkman's contracture. Plast Reconstr Surg 58:407, 1976

Matsen FA III: Compartment syndromes. New York, Grune & Stratton, 1980

Matsen FA III, Mayo KA, Krugmire RB, et al: A model compartmental syndrome in man with particular reference to the quantification of nerve function. J Bone Joint Surg 59A:648, 1977

Mubarek SJ, Owen CA: Compartmental syndrome and its relation to the crush syndrome: A spectrum of disease: A review of 11 cases of prolonged limb compression. Clin Orthop 113:81–89, 1975

Sorokhan AJ, Eaton RG: Volkmann's ischemia. J Hand Surg 8A:806, 1983

Sundoraraj GD, Mani K: Pattern of contracture and recovery following ischemia of the upper limb. J Hand Surg 10B:155, 1985

Tsuge K: Treatment of established Volkman's contracture. J Bone Joint Surg 57A:925, 1975

Whitesides TE Jr, Harada H, Morimoto K: Compartment syndromes and the role of fasciotomy, its parameters and techniques. American Academy Orthopaedic Surgeons, Instructional Course Lectures, St Louis, CV Mosby, 26:179, 1977

Reflex Sympathetic Dystrophy

An HS, Hawthorne K, Jackson WT: "Cigarette smoking and reflex sympathetic dystrophy." J Hand Surg 13A:458–460, 1988

Barnes R: The role of sympathectomy in the treatment of causalgia. J Bone Joint Surg 35B:172–180, 1953

Benzon HT, Chomka CM, Brunner EA: The treatment of reflex sympathetic dystrophy with regional intravenous reserpine. Anesth Analg 59:500–502, 1980

Bonelli S, Conoscente F, Movilia PG, et al: Regional intravenous guanethidine vs stellate ganglion block in reflex sympathetic dystrophy: A randomized trial. Pain 16:297–307, 1983

Charles ND: Skeletal blood flow: Implications of bone-scan interpretation. J Nucl Med 21:91–98, 1980

Christensen K, Jensen EM, Noer I: The reflex dystrophy syndrome response to treatment with systemic corticosteroids. Acta Chir Scand 148:653–655, 1982

Lankford LL: Reflex sympathetic dystrophy. In Omer GE Jr, Spinner M, eds. Management of peripheral nerve problems. Philadelphia, WB Saunders, 1980

Maurer AH, Holder LE, Espinola DA, et al: Three-phase radionuclide scintigraphy of the hand. Radiology 146:761–775, 1983

McKain CW, Urban BJ, Goldner JL: The effects of intravenous regional guanethidine and reserpine. A controlled study. J Bone Joint Surg 65A:808–811, 1983

Prough DS, McLeskey CH, Poehling GG, et al: Efficacy of oral nifedipine in the treatment of reflex sympathetic dystrophy. Anesthesiology 62:796–799, 1985

Schutzer SF, Gossling HR: Current concepts review. The treatment of reflex sympathetic dystrophy syndrome. J Bone Joint Surg 66A:625–629, 1984

57
Congenital Anomalies of the Hand

I. Concepts

A. Incidence
1. One in 3000 to 1/4000
2. Population dependent
   a. Polydactyly 3–4 times higher in blacks
   b. Syndactyly more common in whites

B. Development
1. Genetic: present at time of conception
2. Nongenetic or acquired: occurs during organogenesis 30–50 days after gestation
   a. Environmental teratogens: 10%
   b. Genetic: single dominant or recessive, 20%
   c. Chromosomal abnormalities: 10%
   d. Unknown: 60%

C. Genetics
1. Dominant (transmitted from generation to generation)
   a. Brachydactyly
   b. Central polydactyly
   c. Camptodactyly
2. Recessive (50% if heterozygotes mate)
   a. Usually more severe than dominant transmitted anomalies
   b. Arthrogryposis
   c. Thrombocytopenia: absent radius syndrome
3. X-linked
   a. Passed from mother to son
   b. Metacarpal synostosis

D. Environment
1. Drugs
   a. Heroin
   b. Phenytoin
   c. Thalidomide
   d. Alcohol
2. Radiation: questionable influence on limb buds

E. Surgery
1. Goals
   a. Functional extremity first and foremost
   b. Cosmesis: other than simple syndactyly, very few procedures result in cosmetically pleasing hand, must emphasize function as beauty
2. Timing of surgery
   a. If deformity progresses with age, then operate early
      (1) Radial club hand
      (2) Complex syndactyly
      (3) Delta phalanx
   b. Pollicization between 9 and 15 months
   c. Early surgery (prior to 24 months) associated with less psychologic stress for child
   d. Adult presenting for reconstruction of congenital hand deformity needs psychologic evaluation first

F. Classification
1. Failure of formation
2. Failure of differentiation
3. Duplication
4. Overgrowth
5. Undergrowth
6. Constriction ring syndrome
7. Generalized skeletal abnormalities

G. Treatment of common disorders
1. Failure of formation
   a. Transverse absence: 1/270,000
      (1) Forearm: short below elbow is most common, start prosthetics (passive) at 6 months, active prosthesis at 18 months, Krukenburg for bilateral blind patient
      (2) Carpal/metacarpal: excise nub-

bins; if wrist supple, use palmar plate; if metacarpals have functioning intrinsics, then lengthen metacarpal with distraction and deepen web space (or create a cleft)
- (3) Phalangeal
  - i. Partial: lengthen
  - ii. Complete: tendons attached to skin distally, consider toe phalanx transfer. Role of vascularized toe to hand transfer remains questionable
- b. Longitudinal deficiencies
  - (1) Segmental
    - i. Phocomelia (seal limb) is common in aborted fetuses
    - ii. Few indications for surgery
  - (2) Preaxial (radial): radial club hand
    - i. Associated with cardiac, hematopoietic, and gastrointestinal anomalies
    - ii. Unstable wrist: centralize hand over the ulna, osteotomy of ulna if necessary (Fig 6-16)
    - iii. Limited elbow motion is a contraindication to wrist surgery
    - iv. Pollicize early <1 yr so that child can develop a cortical representation for the new thumb. Note with absent radius there is anomalous anatomy. FDP is often absent and this can be a problem for the pollicized index
    - v. Casting and splinting of limited benefit. Teach parents stretching exercises
  - (3) Postaxial (ulnar): ulnar club hand
    - i. Not associated with other systemic anomalies
    - ii. Not unstable at the wrist
    - iii. Progressive ulnar deviation of the hand and radial head dislocation

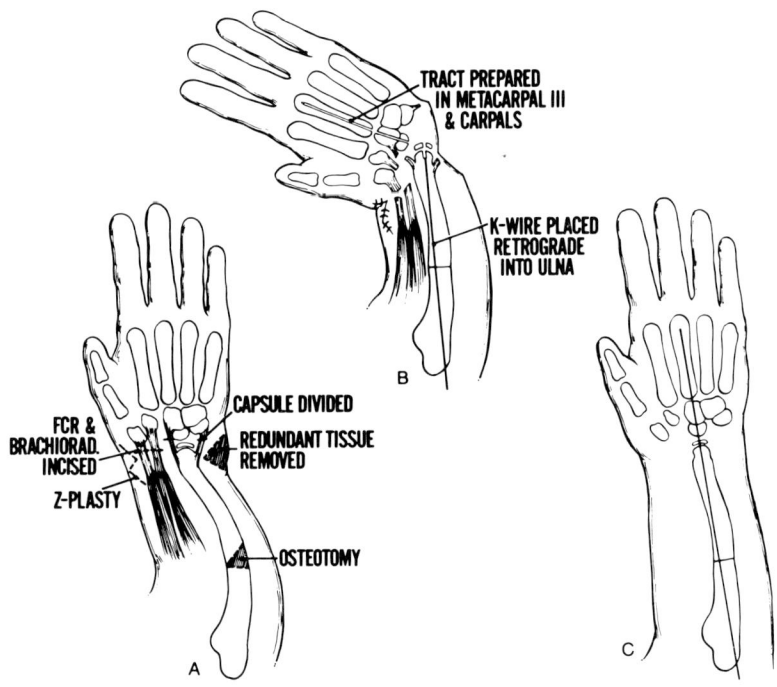

Figure 6-16. Technique of centralization of the carpus in the radial clubhand. Centralize hand over the ulna, osteotomy of ulna if necessary, and K-wire fixation. (From Dobyns JH, Wood VE, Bayne LG, et al: Congenital hand deformities. In Green DP, ed. Operative hand surgery. New York, Churchill Livingstone, 1982. Reprinted with permission.)

iv. Elbow abnormalities: instability, synostosis, and webbing
v. Surgical intervention of limited benefit
c. Central ray defects of the hand
(1) Typical cleft: V-shaped, familial, feet involved, central ray completely missing
(2) Surgery: closure of cleft, rotational osteotomy
(3) Atypical cleft: sporadic, U-shaped, usually only one extremity involved, usually has central metacarpals intact
2. Failure of differentiation: basic elements formed but final form incomplete
a. Synostosis: radioulnar most common, usually bilateral
b. Syndactyly
(1) Simple: skin only
(2) Complex: skin and bone
(3) Complete: involved out to the distal phalanx
(4) Incomplete: web extending beyond midportion of proximal phalanx but not complete
(5) Acrosyndactyly: tips fused together, but fenestrations present
(6) Syndromes associated with syndactyly
i. Poland's syndrome: unilateral short digits, syndactyly, hypoplasia of the hand and forearm, absence of the pectoralis major (sternocostal head). Not hereditary
ii. Apert's syndrome: acrocephaly, parrot beak nose, complex complete syndactyly involving all extremities, autosomal dominant
(7) Surgery
i. Separate functional digits
ii. Border digits at 6–9 months
iii. Index and middle digits 2–3 months later
iv. Will **always** need skin grafts, harvest FTSG from groin, foreskin, extra digits
v. Do not separate digits that will not improve function or cosmesis
c. Clinodactyly
(1) Curvature in radioulnar deviation
(2) Look at parents' hands for idea of final outcome
(3) Delta phalanx is special variant, usually requires osteotomy
d. Camptodactyly
(1) Flexion deformity
(2) Usually the small finger
(3) Autosomal dominant
(4) Some anatomic causes include aberrant lumbrical, FDS insertion, usually cannot identify causative factor
e. Flexed thumb
(1) Trigger: rigid flexed posture, may be snapped into extension (do not treat before age 1 year, may spontaneously resolve)
(2) Clasped: may be simple flexion contracture, which responds to splinting, or hypoplastic thumb, which requires reconstruction
3. Duplication
a. Radial duplication (thumb)
(1) Wassel classification: odd numbers designate partial duplication of phalanx, even numbers designate complete duplication
i. Bifid distal phalanx
ii. Distal phalanx completely duplicated
iii. Bifid proximal phalanx
iv. Proximal phalanx completely duplicated, most common is duplicate thumb
v. Bifid metacarpal
vi. Metacarpal completely duplicated

- vii. Any triphalangeal thumb in any location
- (2) Treatment must include parts from both thumbs, including preservation of ligaments, pulleys, realignment of flexor and extensor tendons
- b. Central duplication
  - (1) Appears to be complex syndactyly (radiographs demonstrate concealed central polydactyly)
  - (2) Treatment may result in the necessary ablation of two of the digits (single digital artery may be feeding three digits)
- c. Ulnar duplication
  - (1) Commonly seen in black population
  - (2) Commonly multiextremity involvement
  - (3) Treatment with ablation
4. Gigantism
  - a. Macrodactyly
    - (1) Neurofibromatosis, most common, enlargement of all elements, nerve oriented, ie, median nerve digits or ulnar nerve digits
    - (2) May be static (grows at linear pace) or progressive (grows at accelerated rate)
  - b. Other causes include hemangioma, lymphangioma
  - c. Treatment (reduction techniques)
    - (1) Epiphysiodesis
    - (2) Bone shortening
    - (3) Debulking
    - (4) Amputation
5. Undergrowth
  - a. Thumb hypoplasia
    - (1) Spectrum of problems runs from abduction contracture at thumb IP joint to complete absence of thumb
    - (2) Treatment is dependent on presence of thumb CMC joint; if missing, then reconstruction consists of ablation of thumb and pollicization of index; if present, may require reconstruction of ligaments, proper alignment of tendons (removal of aberrant insertions leading to pollex abductus deformity), first web space widening
6. Constriction band syndrome
  - a. Z-plasty revision of bands
    - (1) Most authors recommend correction of only 50% of the band at a time
    - (2) Others perform complete reconstructions without problems (Buck-Gramcko)
  - b. Acrosyndactyly
    - (1) Failure of differentiation versus the result of constrictive band syndrome
    - (2) Treatment is individualized: separation of complex syndactyly, phalangeal lengthening, transposition of parts to make functional units
7. Madelung's deformity (a generalized skeletal deformity)
  - a. Rarely obvious before adolescence
  - b. Females affected more often than males
  - c. Surgery indicated only for treatment of pain (not limitation in motion)

REFERENCES

Barot LR, Caplan HS: Early surgical intervention in Apert's syndactyly. Plast Reconstr Surg 77:282–287, 1986

Barsky AJ: Macrodactyly. J Bone Joint Surg 49A:1255, 1967

Blank CE: Apert's syndrome (a type of acrocephalo syndactyly) — observations on a British series of thirty-nine cases. Ann Hum Genet 24:151, 1960

Bora FW, Osterman AL, Kaneda RR, Esterhai J: Radial clubhand deformity. Long-term follow-up. J Bone Joint Surg 63A:741–745, 1981

Broudy AS, Smith RJ: Deformities of the hand and

wrist with ulnar deficiency. J Hand Surg 4:304, 1979

Buck-Gramcko DB: Cleft hands: Classification and treatment. Hand Clin 1:467, 1985

Buck-Gramcko DB: Congenital malformations of the hand: Indications, operative treatment and results. Scand J Plast Reconstr Surg 9:190–193, 1975

Buck-Gramcko DB: Hand surgery in congenital malformation. In Jackson I, ed. Recent advances in plastic surgery. London, Churchill Livingstone, 1981

Buck-Gramcko DB: Radialization as a new treatment for radial clubhand. J Hand Surg 10A:964–968, 1985

Burke F, Flatt AE: Clinodactyly. A review of a series of cases. Hand 3:269–280, 1979

Carroll RE, Green DP: Reconstruction of hypoplastic digits using toe phalanges. J Bone Joint Surg 57A:727, 1975

Cheng JCY, Chan KM, Ma GFY, Leung PC: Polydactyly of the thumb: A surgical plan based on 95 cases. J Hand Surg 9A:155–164, March 1984

Cleary JE, Omer GE: Congenital proximal radio-ulnar synostosis. Natural history and functional assessment. J Bone Joint Surg 67A:539–545, 1985

Dinham JM, Meggitt DF: Trigger thumbs in children. J Bone Joint Surg 56B:153, 1974

Dobyns JH: Segmental digital transposition in congenital hand deformities. Hand Clin 1:475–482, 1985

Dobyns JH, Wood VE, Bayne LG: Congenital hand deformities. In Green DP, ed. Operative hand surgery, ed 2. New York, Churchill Livingstone, 1988, pp 255–536

Frykman GK, Wood VE: Peripheral nerve hamartomas with macrodactyly in the hand: Report of three cases and review of the literature. J Hand Surg 3:307, 1978

Green WT, Mital MA: Congenital radio-ulnar synostosis: Surgical treatment. J Bone Joint Surg 61A:738, 1979

Hooper G, Lamb GW: Congenital fusion of the little and ring finger metacarpal bones. Hand 15:207–211, 1983

Ireland DCR, Takayama N, Flatt AE: Poland's syndrome: A review of forty-three cases. J Bone Joint Surg 58A:52, 1976

Johnson J, Omer GE Jr: Congenital ulnar deficiency. Natural history and therapeutic implications. Hand Clin 1:499–510, 1985

Kitayama Y, Tsukada S: Patterns of arterial distribution in the duplicated thumb. Plast Reconstr Surg 72:553–541, 1983

Light T, Ogden J: The longitudinal epiphyseal bracket: Implications for surgical correction. J Pediatr Orthop 1:299, 1981

Lister B: The hand: Diagnosis and indications, ed 2. New York, Churchill Livingstone, 1984

Maeda M, Matsui T: Camptodactyly caused by an abnormal lumbrical muscle. J Hand Surg 10B:95–96, 1985

Manske P, McCarroll HR Jr: Abductor digiti minimi opponensplasty in congenital radial dysplasia. J Hand Surg 3:552, 1978

McCarroll HR: Congenital flexion deformities of the thumb. Hand Clin 1:567–575, 1985

McFarlane RM, Curry GJ, Evans HB: Anomalies of the intrinsic muscles in camptodactyly. J Hand Surg 8:531–544, 1983

McMurty RY, Jochims JL: Congenital deficiency of the extrinsic extensor mechanism of the hand. Clin Orthop 125:36–39, 1977

Miura T: Congenital constriction band syndrome. J Hand Surg 9A:82–88, 1984

Neviaser RJ: Congenital hypoplasia of the thumb with absence of the intrinsic extensors, abductor pollicis longus, and thenar muscles. J Hand Surg 4:301–303, 1979

Nielsen JB: Madelung's deformity: A follow-up study of 26 cases and a review of the literature. Acta Orthop Scand 48:379, 1977

Peimer CA: Combined reduction osteotomy for triphalangeal thumb. J Hand Surg 10A:376–381, 1985

Sever JW: Congenital radio-ulnar synostosis. Surg Gynecol Obstet 24:203, 1969

Simmons BP: Polydactyly. Hand Clin 1:545–565, 1985

Simmons BP, Southmayd WW, Riseborough EJ: Congenital radioulnar synostosis. J Hand Surg 8:829, 1983

Smith RJ: Osteotomy for "delta-phalanx" deformity. Clin Orthop 123:91, 1977

Smith RJ, Kaplan EB: Camptodactyly and similar atraumatic flexion deformities of the proximal interphalangeal joints of the fingers. J Bone Joint Surg 50A:1187, 1968

Smith RJ, Lipke RW: Treatment of congenital deformities of the hand and forearm. Parts 1 and 2. N Engl J Med 300:344, 402, 1979

Streeter GL: Focal deficiencies in fetal tissues and their relation to intrauterine amputation. Contrib Embryol 22:1, 1930

Tada K, Kurisaki E, Yonenobu K, et al: Central polydactyly — a review of 12 cases and their surgical treatment. J Hand Surg 7:460–465, 1982

Tada K, Yonenobu K, Swanson AB: Congenital central ray deficiency in the hand — a survey of 59 cases and subclassification. J Hand Surg 6:434–441, 1981

Tsuge K: Treatment of macrodactyly. J Hand Surg 10A:968, 1985

Vickers DW: Langenskiold's operation (physolysis) for congenital malformations of bone producing Madelung's deformity and clinodactyly. J Bone Joint Surg 66B:778, 1984

Wassel HD: The results of surgery for polydactyly of the thumb: A review. Clin Orthop 64:175, 1969

Wood VE: Polydactyly and the triphalangeal thumb. J Hand Surg 3:436, 1978

Wood VE: Treatment of central polydactyly. Clin Orthop 74:196, 1971

Zancolli E, Zancolli E Jr: Congenital ulnar drift of the fingers. Hand Clin 1:443–456, 1985

58
Tumors of the Hand and Amputation Surgery

I. General Considerations
A. Tissue origin may be of skin, subcutaneous fat, fascia, tendon, muscle, blood vessels, nerve, cartilage, and bone (Table 6-1)
B. Classification
   1. Pseudotumors: tumorlike lesions
   2. Benign tumors
   3. Malignant tumors

II. Evaluation
A. History: age, onset, duration, and associated disease
B. Examination: size, location, neurovascular involvement
C. Imaging studies: plain x-rays, bone scan, computed tomography scan, magnetic resonance imaging, or arteriogram
D. Biopsy: excisional for benign tumors and incisional biopsy for large malignancies

III. Common Skin Tumors
A. Epidermoid inclusion cyst
   1. Common lesion
   2. Etiology: implanting epidermal cells into deeper tissues by trauma
   3. Pathology: squamous epithelium surrounding a central area of keratin and cholesterol
   4. Treatment: excision if symptomatic
B. Malignant tumors
   1. Squamous cell carcinoma
      a. Most common malignant tumor of the hand
      b. Variants: Bowen's disease, subungal epidermoid carcinoma, benign keratoacanthoma
   2. Basal cell carcinoma
   3. Melanoma
      a. Lentigo maligna melanoma
      b. Superficial spreading multiple melanoma
      c. Nodular malignant melanoma
      d. Acral lentiginous melanoma (melanoma under fingernail)

IV. Common Soft Tissue Tumors
A. Lipoma
   1. Incidence: more common in the proximal arm than hand and wrist
   2. Age: 3rd to 6th decades
   3. Location: most frequently thenar eminence
   4. Soft mobile nontender mass
   5. Treatment: excision for cosmesis and diagnosis
B. Benign giant cell tumor of the tendon sheath
   1. Most common benign neoplasm of the hand
   2. Age: 70% occur between 40 and 60 years
   3. Location: digits, especially volar index and long fingers
   4. Treatment: resection with portion of tendon sheath or capsule
C. Glomus tumor
   1. Incidence: rare
   2. Age: 30–50 years
   3. Location: 50% subungal
   4. Triad: pain, tenderness, cold sensitivity
   5. Treatment: complete removal
D. Ganglion
   1. Incidence: 50–70% of all hand tumors
   2. Female > male (3:1)
   3. Age: 70% between 20 and 40 years
   4. Etiology may be trauma, synovial herniation, degeneration, etc.

Table 6-1 Tumors of the Hand

Tissue	Pseudotumors	Benign Tumors	Malignant Tumors
Skin	Verruca vulgaris, sebaceous cyst, keloid, epidermoid cyst,* pyogenic granuloma	Keratosis, keratoacanthoma, dermatofibroma, eccrine poromas	Squamous cell,* basal cell,* melanoma,* Bowen's disease
Subcutaneous fat	Hematoma, seroma foreign body granuloma	Lipoma*	Liposarcoma
Fascia (fibrous)	Dupuytren's nodule, knuckle pads, fascitis	Fibroma, fibromatosis	Fibrosarcoma, malignant fibrous hystiocytoma, epitheliod sarcoma
Tendon	Synovitis, tendon cyst	Giant cell tumor,* xanthoma tendinosum	Malignant giant tumor of tendon sheath
Muscle		Leiomyoma	Leiomyosarcoma, rhabdomyosarcoma
Blood vessels	Aneurysm, arteriovenous fistula	Hemangioma, glomus tumor, lymphangioma	Hemangiosarcoma, Kaposi sarcoma
Nerve	Neuroma	Neurilemmoma (Schwannoma), neurofibroma, neurofibrolipoma, myoblastoma	Malignant Schwannoma
Joint	Ganglion,* mucous cyst*	Pigmented villonodular synovitis	Synovial sarcoma
Bone	Bone spurs,* carpal boss	Enchondromas,* osteochondroma, giant cell tumor, aneurysmal bone cyst, osteoid osteoma, bone cyst	Osteosarcoma, chondrosarcoma, Ewing's tumor, metastasis

*Common lesions

    5. Sixty percent arise dorsally (scapholunate region) and 20% arise volarly between radial artery and FCR

    6. Treatment: treat only if symptomatic (excision including the trap door in the joint capsule)

E. Mucous cyst
    1. Incidence: common, especially 50–60 years of age
    2. Ganglion of IP joints associated with DJD
    3. Identical to ganglion histologically

4. Treatment: excision of the cyst and part of osteophyte and capsule or arthrodesis if arthritic
5. Recurrence more common (28–36%)

V. Common Bone Tumors

A. Enchondroma
  1. Most common primary bone tumor of the hand
  2. Age between 2nd and 4th decades
  3. Typically, radiolucent lesion in the proximal phalanx
  4. Treatment: curettage with bone graft
B. Multiple enchondromatosis: Ollier's syndrome
C. Multiple enchondromatosis with angiomatosis: Maffucci's syndrome
D. Osteochondroma: seen in patients with multiple osteochondromas
E. Giant cell tumor: common in the distal radius

VI. Treatment Options for the Tumors of the Hand

A. Incisional or excisional biopsy
B. Marginal excision with or without bone graft
C. Wide local excision
D. Partial amputation of a digit
E. Ray amputation of a digit
F. Partial amputation of the hand
  1. Radial hemiamputation
  2. Ulnar hemiamputation
  3. Central hemiamputation
  4. Dorsal soft part hemiamputation
  5. Palmar soft part hemiamputation
G. Carpectomy: partial or total (allograft and fusion)
H. Excision of distal radius or ulna with or without replacement (osteochondral allograft)
I. Amputation: different levels

VII. Curettage and Bone Grafting

A. Benign cystic lesions
B. Pathologic fractures can be managed immediately or after fracture healing, depending on nature of the lesion
C. Dorsal approach for fingers: extensor apparatus and periosteum split longitudinally and oval window made, curettage and corticocancellous bone grafting

VIII. Amputation Surgery

A. General considerations
  1. Prime importance is function and maintaining length
  2. Cosmesis is important and critical to minimize scar and adjacent contractures
  3. Maintain sensibility and mobility but prevent neuromas
  4. Consider age and sex, occupation, hand dominance, attitude, avocation, and future reconstruction or prosthesis fitting
B. Surgical techniques
  1. If tendon insertion is absent, then sever tendon and allow it to retract. Do not suture flexors to extensors
  2. Release and allow appropriate retraction of tendons
    a. Quadragia: tethering of FDP on amputation stump, prevents full excursion of uninvolved tendons
    b. Lumbricale plus deformity: amputation distal to FDS insertion, paradoxical extension of PIP joint with increasing flexion effort
  3. Dissect nerves and perform sharp proximal transection with the nerve under tension so that it becomes proximal to the amputation site (consider sewing digital nerves end-to-end, Gorkisch)
  4. Contour articular condyles volar and laterally
C. Amputation levels
  1. Distal phalanx: requires shortening and contour of bone for primary closure, secondary intention closure, skin graft, or flaps
  2. Middle phalanx: shorten and contour bone, and preserve FDS insertion, and primary closure
  3. Proximal phalanx
    a. Primary ray resection for index only

b. Preserve central digits to prevent gap and little finger for grip strength
4. Ray resection
   a. Decreases torque strength of hand by 50%
   b. Index finger
      (1) It may be the primary procedure in selected patients
      (2) Neuroma of the radial digital nerve may be problematic
      (3) Begin early range of motion
   c. Long and ring fingers
      (1) Close gap for function and cosmesis
      (2) Correct angulation/rotation
      (3) Reconstruct web space
      (4) Ring ray resection: suture intermetacarpal ligament, and no transposition
      (5) Long ray resection: best results with transposition of index to third metacarpal and requires rigid internal fixation
   d. Little finger ray resection
      (1) Cosmesis only but best to retain for functional strength
      (2) Preserve fifth metacarpal base for the insertions of ECU and FCU
5. Thumb
   a. Reattach if possible
   b. Maintain length: may require flap coverage
6. Wrist: wrist disarticulation (adequate prosthetic fitting is available and pronation and supination is preserved)

REFERENCES

Tumors of the Hand

Andrew TA: Clear cell sarcoma of the hand. Hand 14:200–203, 1982

Angelides AC: Ganglions of the hand and wrist. In Green DP, ed. Operative hand surgery, ed 2. New York, Churchill Livingstone, 1988, pp 2281–2299

Angelides AC, Wallace PF: The dorsal ganglion of the wrist: Its pathogenesis, gross and microscopic anatomy, and surgical treatment. J Hand Surg 1:228–235, 1976

Archer IA, Brown RB, Fitton JM: Epithelioid sarcoma in the hand. J Hand Surg 9B:207–209, 1984

Averill RM, Smith RJ, Cambell CJ: Giant cell tumors of the bones of the hand. J Hand Surg 5:39–50, 1980

Barbieri CH: Aneurysmal bone cyst of the hand. An unusual situation. J Hand Surg 9B:89–92, 1984

Brason FW, Eschner EG, Sanes S, Milkey G: Secondary carcinoma of the phalanges. Radiology 57:864–867, 1951

Carroll RE: Osteogenic sarcoma in the hand. J Bone Joint Surg 39A:325–331, 1957

Creighton JJ, Peimer CA, Mindell ER, et al: Primary malignant tumors of the upper extremity: Retrospective analysis of one hundred twenty-six cases. J Hand Surg 10A:805–813, 1985

Dahlin DC, Salvadore AH: Chondrosarcomas of bones of the hand and feet. A study of 30 cases. Cancer 34:755–760, 1974

Dobyns JH: Hand reconstruction after tumor excision. In Evarts CM, ed. Surgery of the musculoskeletal system, vol 4. New York, Churchill Livingstone, 1983, pp 123–136

Doyle LK, Ruby LK, Nalebuff EG, Belsky MR: Osteoid osteoma of the hand. J Hand Surg 10A:408–410, 1985

Dryer RF, Buckwalter JA, Flatt AE, Bonfiglio M: Ewing's sarcoma of the hand. J Hand Surg 4:372–374, 1979

Enneking WF, Spanier SS, Goodman MA: The surgical staging of musculoskeletal sarcoma. Clin Orthop 153:106–120, 1980

Harkin JC: Differential diagnosis of peripheral nerve tumors. In Omer GE, Spinner M, eds. Management of peripheral nerve problems. Philadelphia, WB Saunders, 1980, pp 657–668

Harvey FJ, Bosanquet JS: Carpal tunnel syndrome caused by a simple ganglion. Hand 13:164–166, 1981

Holdsworth BJ: Nerve tumors in the upper limb. A clinical review. J Hand Surg 10B:236–238, 1985

Jokl P, Albright JA, Goodman AH: Juxtacortical chondrosarcoma of the hand. J Bone Joint Surg 53A:1370–1377, 1971

MacFarland GB: Soft tissue tumors. In Green DP, ed. Operative hand surgery, ed 2. New York, Churchill Livingstone, 1988, pp 2301–2322

Mackie IG, Howard CB, Wilkins P: The dangers of sclerotherapy in the treatment of ganglia. J Hand Surg 9B:181–184, 1984

Matev IB: Thumb reconstruction through metacarpal bone lengthening. J Hand Surg 5:482–487, 1980

McGarth MH, Watson HK: Late results with local bone graft donor sites in hand surgery. J Hand Surg 6:234–237, 1981

Mutale CB, Patil PS, Patel JB: Malignant fibrous histiocytoma of the second metacarpal. J Hand Surg 11B:149–150, 1986

Patel MR, Desai SS, Gordon SL: Functional limb salvage with multimodality treatment in epitheliod sarcoma of the hand: A report of two cases. J Hand Surg 11A:265–269, 1986

Peimer CA, Smith RJ, Sirota RL, Cohen BE: Epitheliod sarcoma of the hand and wrist: Patterns of extension. J Hand Surg 2:275–282, 1977

Rowland SA: Case report: Ten year follow-up of lipofibroma of the median nerve in the palm. J Hand Surg 2:316, 1977

Schenkar DL, Kleinert HE: Desmoplastic fibroma of the hand. Case report. Plast Reconstr Surg 59:129–133, 1977

Smith RJ: Complications of surgical treatment of tumors of the hand. In Boswick JA, ed. Complications in hand surgery. Philadelphia, WB Saunders, 1986, pp 286–293

Sugarbaker PH, Auda S, Webber BL, et al: Early distant metastases from epitheliod sarcoma of the hand. Cancer 48:852–855, 1981

Wu KK, Guise ER: Metastatic tumors of the hand. A report of six cases. J Hand Surg 3:271–276, 1978

Amputation Surgery

Beasley RW: Surgery of hand and finger amputations. Orthop Clin North Am 12:763, 1981

Burkhalter WE, Mayfield G, Carmona LS: The upper extremity amputee. Early and immediate post-surgical prosthetic fitting. J Bone Joint Surg 58A:46–51, 1976

Colen L, Bunkis J, Gordon L, Walton R: Functional assessment of ray transfer for central digital loss. J Hand Surg 10A:232–237, 1985

Gorkisch K, Boese-Landgraf J, Vaubel E: Treatment and prevention of amputation neuromas in hand surgery. Plast Reconstr Surg 73:293–299, 1984

James SL, Slocum DB: Upper extremity amputation. In Flynn JE, ed. Hand surgery, ed 2. Baltimore, Williams & Wilkins, 1975, p 348

Lister G: The choice of procedure following thumb amputation. Clin Orthop 195:45, 1985

Louis DS: Amputations. In Green DP, ed. Operative hand surgery, ed 2. New York, Churchill Livingstone, 1988, pp 61–119

Murray JF, Carman W, MacKenzie JK: Transmetacarpal amputation of the index finger: A clinical assessment of hand strength and complications. J Hand Surg 2:471–481, 1977

Neu BR, Murray JF, MacKenzie JK: Profundus tendon blockage: Quadrigia in finger amputations. J Hand Surg 10A:882, 1985

Parkes A: The "lumbrical plus" finger. J Bone Joint Surg 53B:236, 1971

Posner MA: Ray transposition for central digital loss. J Hand Surg 4:242, 1979

Rose EH, Buncke HJ: Selective finger transposition and primary metacarpal ray resection in multidigit amputations of the hand. J Hand Surg 8A:178–182, 1983

Steichen JB, Idler RS: Results of central ray resection without bony transposition. J Hand Surg 11A:466, 1986

Tubiana R, Roux JP: Phalangization of the first and fifth metacarpals: Indications, operative technique and results. J Bone Joint Surg 56A:447, 1974

Wilson RL, Carter-Wilson MS: Rehabilitation after amputations in the hand. Orthop Clin North Am 14:851–872, 1983

SECTION 7: SPINE

Howard S. An
J. Michael Simpson

59. *Congenital and Developmental Anomalies of the Cervical Spine*
60. *Scoliosis*
61. *Kyphosis*
62. *Spondylolysis and Spondylolisthesis*
63. *Cervical Disc Disease*
64. *Lumbar Disc Disease and Spinal Stenosis*
65. *Spinal Trauma*
66. *Tumors of the Spine*
67. *Arthritis of the Spine (Rheumatoid Arthritis and Seronegative Spondylitis)*

Congenital and Developmental Anomalies of the Cervical Spine

I. Developmental Anatomy

A. Atlas: neurocentral synchondrosis forms at 6–24 months and fuses at 4–6 years of age
B. Dens: two primary ossification centers coalesce at 1–3 months of age, and it is separated from the vertebral body by dentocentral synchondrosis, which fuses by 8 years
C. Normal variants: posterior bifid C1 arch, a bipartite superior articular surface of the atlas, pseudonotch of the atlas, absence or partial absence of the posterior arch of the atlas, backward "displaced" spinolaminal line of the axis, posteriorly tilted dens, pseudosubluxation of the axis (<10 years old), short C5, notched articular process of C7 and accessory ossicles

II. Evaluation

A. Clinical: limited range of motion, torticollis, facial asymmetry, and associated problems, such as scoliosis, renal anomalies, other head and neck deformities
B. Radiologic
   1. Flexion-extension view is very important to assess stability
   2. Cineradiography is occasionally helpful
   3. Tomogram, computed tomography (CT) scans or magnetic resonance imaging (MRI)
   4. Critical measurement on flexed lateral view
      a. Atlanto-axial interval: 4.5 mm (children) and 3.0 mm (adults)
      b. Space available for spinal cord (SAC): 13 mm
      c. Steel's rule of thirds: ⅓ spinal cord, ⅓ odontoid, ⅓ space at C1 level

III. Basilar Impression

A. General considerations
   1. Deformity of the bones at the base of the skull at the margin of the foramen magnum
   2. Odontoid is migrated cephalad
   3. Complications
      a. Neural compression
      b. Vertebral artery compression
      c. Obstruction of cerebrospinal fluid
   4. Types
      a. Primary: congenital associated with atlanto-occipital fusion, hypoplasia of atlas, bifid posterior arch of the atlas, odontoid abnormalities, and Klippel-Feil syndrome
      b. Secondary: developmental condition with softening of the base of the skull, associated with osteomalacia, rickets, Paget's disease, osteogenesis imperfecta, renal osteodystrophy, rheumatoid arthritis, neurofibromatosis, ankylosing spondylitis, and achondroplasia
B. Diagnosis
   1. X-rays (Fig 7-1)
      a. McGregor line: upper surface of the posterior edge of the hard palate to the most caudad point of the skull (>4.5 mm is abnormal)
      b. McRae: odontoid protrusion into

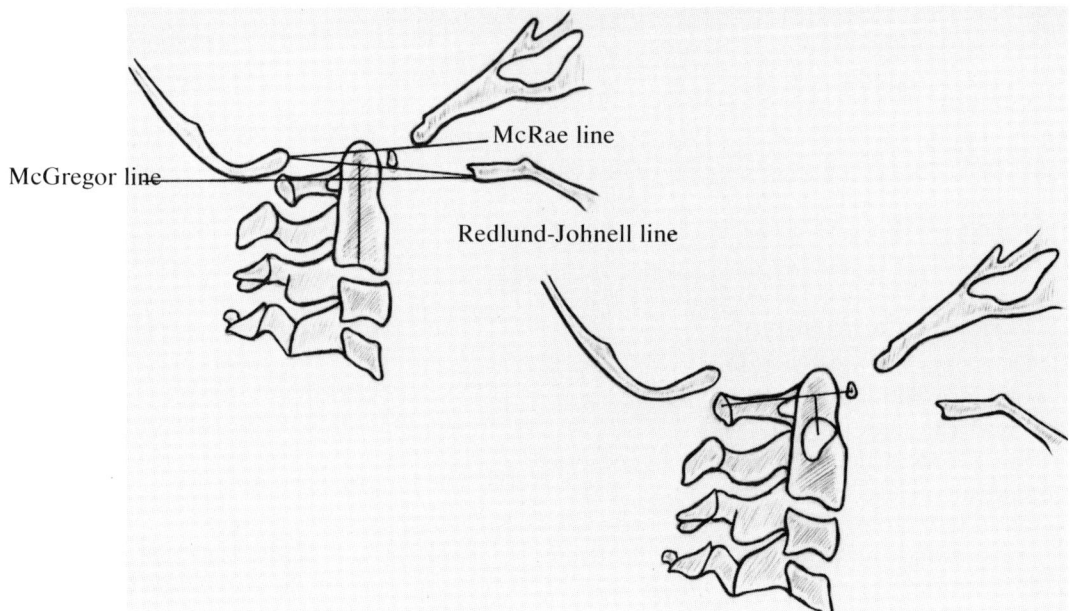

Figure 7-1. Various lines to determine vasilar invagination. **A.** McRae line from the posterior lip of foramen magnum to the clivus shows odontoid protrusion into the foramen magnum. Chamberlain's line is from the posterior lip of foramen magnum to the dorsal margin of the hard palate. McGregor line is from the upper surface of the posterior edge of the hard palate to the most caudad point of the skull (>4.5 mm of the odontoid cephalad to this line is abnormal). A vertical distance from the chamberlain's line to the inferior edge of C2 is abnormal if less than 33 mm (Redlund-Johnell method). **B.** Ranawat method is measuring the distance from the arch of C1 to the center of C2 pedicle (<13 mm is abnormal)

  the foramen magnum (key to neurologic problem)
  c. Chamberlain's line: from the posterior lip of foramen magnum to the dorsal margin of the hard palate
  d. Fischgold and Metzger: digastric grooves (anteroposterior [AP] view) >10.7 mm above tip of the dens
  e. Ranawat method: C1–C2 index or the distance from the arch of C1 to the center of C2 pedicle <13 mm is abnormal
 2. Clinical finding
  a. Short neck, asymmetrical face, torticollis
  b. Weakness, paresthesia, cranial nerve palsy, cerebellar signs (unsteady gait and nystagmus)
  c. Pain in the head and neck
  d. Vertebral artery compression with syncope and dizziness
  e. Cerebrospinal fluid (CSF) compression with hydrocephalus and seizures
  f. Commonly become symptomatic in 2nd and 3rd decades
 C. Treatment
  1. Posterior impingement: suboccipital craniectomy and decompression of the posterior ring of C1 and posterior stabilization
  2. Anterior impingement
   a. Hypermobile odontoid: occipitocervical fusion in extension
   b. If odontoid cannot be reduced, anterior excision of odontoid and stabilization in extension

IV. Klippel-Feil Syndrome
 A. General considerations
  1. Congenital fusion of cervical vertebrae

2. Failure of normal segmentation of cervical spine during weeks 3–8
3. Many associated anomalies: genitourinary (35%), central nervous system, cardiopulmonary, ophthalmologic, deafness, Sprengel's deformities (40%), upper extremity anomaly, scoliosis (60%)

B. Diagnosis
1. Clinical findings
   a. Triad: low posterior neck line, short neck, limited neck motion (majority have normal appearance with mild restriction of motion)
   b. Torticollis, facial asymmetry, and webbing of the neck
2. X-rays
   a. Plain x-rays: vertebral synostosis, flattening and widening of the vertebral bodies, and absent disc spaces or hypoplasia
   b. Tomogram (flexion and extension)
   c. Flexion and extension views
3. Complication: unfused segments become hypermobile and degenerative changes and instability may result particularly if
   a. Massive involvement with more than four segments
   b. Fusion of occiput to atlas and a C2–C3 fusion resulting in excessive mobility of C1–C2
   c. Fusion of C3–C4 with fusion of C5–C6 level

C. Treatment
1. Majority are asymptomatic, and symptoms appear in adult life
2. Conservative treatment for most patients
3. Fusion in selected unstable spines with spinal cord impingement

V. Congenital Anomalies of the Odontoid
A. Aplasia, hypoplasia, and os odontoideum (os odontoideum is most common, but hypoplasia is frequent in Morquio syndrome)

B. Etiology
1. Trauma: Salter I fracture with nonunion
2. Congenital: failure to fuse

C. Clinical finding: asymptomatic to atlantoaxial instability (pain, torticollis, neurologic symptoms and vertebral artery compression usually around 3rd decade)

D. Treatment
1. Conservative if stable
2. Surgery
   a. Surgical stabilization if >7–10 mm instability even without symptoms (atlanto-dens interval [ADI] with flexion-extension) and space available for spinal cord is <13 mm (SAC is distance between the posterior aspect of C2 to the nearest posterior structure, the foramen magnum, or posterior ring of C1)
   b. Consider surgery if neurologic signs or symptoms present
   c. C1–C2 fusion with wire fixation
      (1) Vertebral artery is proportionately closer to the midline in the child
      (2) Preoperative traction and reduction may be necessary
      (3) Postoperative halovest stabilization
   d. Occiput-C2 fusion is necessary if C1 ring is deficient

VI. Atlanto-occipital Fusion
A. General considerations
1. Failure of segmentation
2. Most commonly recognized anomaly of the craniovertebral junction
3. Prone to C1–C2 instability if associated with C2–C3 fusion or anomalies of the odontoid (70%)
4. Associated with dwarfism, funnel chest, pes cavus, syndactyly, cleft palate, and genitourinary anomalies

B. Clinical findings
1. Short neck, restricted neck motion, and torticollis

2. Fifty percent have relative basilar impressions secondary to diminished vertebral height of the atlas ring
3. Neurologic symptoms and signs, especially the odontoid is above the foramen magnum level (usually around 5th or 6th decade)
4. Tomograms and CT scan: anterior arch of the atlas is assimilated into the occiput
5. Flexion-extension view: ADI >3–4 mm and SAC <13 mm are significant
6. MRI: posterior encroachment by the foramen magnum on the upper cervical cord or medulla oblongata

C. Treatment
1. Nonoperative treatment: collar, brace, or traction
2. Occiput-C1–C2 fusion after traction and reduction if instability is present
3. Posterior decompression if necessary

VII. Torticollis (Wry Neck)

A. General considerations
1. Usually discovered in the first 6–8 weeks of life
2. Ischemia and contracture of the sternocleidomastoid muscle may be pathogenic (venous occlusion and fibrous replacement of tissue secondary to intrauterine position)
3. Head is tilted toward the involved side, and the chin is rotated to the opposite side
4. Associated incidence of congenital hip dislocation: 20%
5. Right side involvement: 85%

B. Clinical findings
1. Soft, nontender enlargement beneath the skin and resolves in 6–12 weeks
2. Contracture of the muscle follows with a decreased range of motion of the neck
3. Facial asymmetry and mild dorsal compensatory scoliosis may be present
4. Differential diagnosis
   a. Congenital cervical spine anomalies (ie, basilar impression, atlanto-occipital fusion, absent facet of C1, odontoid anomalies)
   b. Infection, tumor, trauma
   c. Extraocular muscle imbalance

C. Treatment
1. Stretching exercise, positioning and brace: 85–90% response within 1 year
2. Surgery after 1 year if persistent facial asymmetry, head tilting, and range of motion decreased
   a. Resection of a portion of distal sternocleidomastoid muscle heads (mastoid head in older child)
   b. Bipolar release or Z-lengthening
   c. Be careful of posterior auricular nerve and spinal accessory nerve

VIII. Atlantoaxial Instabilities

A. Etiologies
1. Inflammation: pharyngeal infection (Grisel's syndrome) and upper respiratory infection
2. Down syndrome: 25% incidence and boys >10 years of age are more at risk for myelopathy (rupture of transverse ligament)
3. Dysplasia: achondroplasia, spondyloepiphyseal dysplasia, Morquio syndrome, and Larsen's syndrome
4. Congenital anomalies

B. Treatment: C1–C2 fusion if neurologic symptoms present or >10 mm ADI

C. Rotatory subluxation may occur (left and right rotation CT scans are helpful)
1. Mild: collar and analgesics
2. Moderate: halter traction or tongs and collar
3. Fixed: C1–C2 fusion

IX. Absent Facet of C1

A. Torticollis
B. Gradually become fixed in the adolescent
C. Treatment: if deformity is unacceptable, fusion from occiput to C3 and halo stabilization

X. Other Cervical Spinal Problems in Children

A. Juvenile rheumatoid arthritis: atlantoaxial subluxation and subaxial instabilities may result in polyarticular or systemic onset types
B. Cervical kyphosis: incidence of postlaminectomy kyphosis is high in children
C. Disc calcification: self-limited disorder

REFERENCES

Burke SW, French HG, Roberts JM, et al: Chronic atlantoaxial instability in Down's syndrome. J Bone Joint Surg 67A:1356–1360, 1985

Canale ST, Griffin DW, Hubbard CN: Congenital muscular torticollis. J Bone Joint Surg 64A:810, 1982

Curtis BH, Blank S, Fisher RL: Atlantoaxial dislocation in Down's syndrome. JAMA 205:464–465, 1968

Dawson EG, Smith L: Atlanto-axial subluxation in children due to vertebral anomalies. J Bone Joint Surg 61A:582–587, 1979

Dyck P: Os odontoideum in children: Neurological manifestations and surgical management. Neurosurgery 2:93–99, 1978

Fielding JW, Hawkins RJ: Atlantoaxial rotatory fixation (fixed rotatory subluxation of the atlanto-axial joint). J Bone Joint Surg 59A:37, 1977

Fielding JW, Hawkins RJ, Ratzan SA: Spine fusion for atlantoaxial instability. J Bone Joint Surg 58A:400–407, 1976

Fielding JW, Hensinger RN, Hawkins RJ: Os odontoideum. J Bone Joint Surg 62A:376–383, 1980

Finerman GA, Sakai D, Weingarten S: Atlantoaxial dislocation with spinal cord compression in a mongoloid child. J Bone Joint Surg 58A:408–409, 1976

Kobori M, Takahashi H, Mikawa Y: Atlantoaxial dislocation in Down's syndrome: Report of two cases requiring surgical correction. Spine 11:195–200, 1986

Koop SE, Winter RB, Lonstein JE: The surgical treatment of instability of the upper part of the cervical spine in children and adolescents. J Bone Joint Surg 66A:403–411, 1984

Logan WW, Stuard ID: Absent posterior arch of the atlas. Am J Roentgol Radium Ther Nucl Med 118:431–434, 1973

McRae DL: The significance of abnormalities of the cervical spine. Am J Roentgol Radium Ther Nucl Med 84:3–25, 1960

Nicholson JT, Sherk HH: Anomalies of the occipitocervical articulation. J Bone Joint Surg 50A:295–304, 1968

Parke WW, Rothman RH, Brown MD: The pharyngovertebral veins: An anatomic rationale for Grisel's syndrome. J Bone Joint Surg 66A:568–574, 1984

Spierlings ELH, Braakman R: Os odontoideum: Analysis of 37 cases. J Bone Joint Surg 64B:422–428, 1982

Steel HH: Anatomical and mechanical considerations of the atlanto-axial articulation. J Bone Joint Surg 50:1481–1482, 1968

Winter RB, Moe JH, Lonstein JE: The incidence of Klippel-Feil syndrome in patients with congenital scoliosis and kyphosis. Spine 9:363–366, 1984

60
Scoliosis

I. Classification
A. Nonstructural: postural, hysterical, sciatic, inflammatory, compensatory
B. Structural (Scoliosis Research Society)
   1. Idiopathic (85%)
      a. Infantile (<3 years of age)
      b. Juvenile (3–10 years of age)
      c. Adolescent (10 years of age until maturity)
   2. Neuromuscular
      a. Neuropathic: cerebral palsy, syringomyelia, poliomyelitis, spinal muscular atrophy, Freidrich's ataxia
      b. Myopathic: arthrogryposis, muscular dystrophy, myotonia dystrophica
   3. Congenital: diastematomyelia, spina bifida, hemivertebra, wedge vertebra, unilateral unsegmented bar with contralateral hemivertebra, block vertebra
   4. Neurofibromatosis
   5. Mesenchymal disorders: Marfan, Ehlers-Danlos
   6. Rheumatoid disease
   7. Trauma (fracture, surgery, radiation)
   8. Extraspinal contractures (burns, thoracic surgery)
   9. Osteochondral dystrophies
   10. Infection
   11. Metabolic disorders
   12. Related to lumbosacral joint
   13. Tumors

IDIOPATHIC ADOLESCENT SCOLIOSIS

I. General Considerations
A. Etiology is unknown: there are numerous hypotheses, suggesting neuromuscular, hormonal, connective tissue, or labyrinth problems as part of pathoetiology
B. Genetic influence is strongly suggested: 5:1 female preponderance for curves >10, familial tendency (20 times greater in families), and sex-linked trait with incomplete penetrance and variable expressivity

II. Pathoanatomy
A. Lateral curvature
B. Vertebral rotation: spinous process is rotated toward concavity of the curve
C. Thoracic hypokyphosis
D. Typical types of curves
   1. Right thoracic with compensatory lumbar curve is most common (King type II)
   2. Double major curve (King type I)
   3. Right thoratic curve (King type III)
   4. Thoraco lumbar curve (King type IV)
   5. Double thoracic curve (King type V)

III. Natural History and Prognosis
A. Prevalence: 25/1000 (5%) >10° curves, and 4/1000 (0.4%) for >20° curves
B. Prognosis
   1. Greater the angulation and rotation, greater the tendency for progression: for example, there is 20% chance of progression in 20° curves, whereas 60% chance in 40° curves
   2. Younger age: more important factor than sex or family history (at puberty 90% spinal growth occurred but this is the time for highest risk of progression)
   3. Skeletal maturity is related to age (Risser sign)
   4. Shorter curves tend to progress more than longer curves
   5. Higher curves in the spinal column, the greater deformity and progression (ie, thoracic curves are generally worse than lumbar curves)

6. Stiffer curves in immature individuals and looser curves in mature individuals are worse
7. Females tend to progress more than males
8. Positive family history and slender spines may also be worse prognostic factors

IV. Diagnosis
A. Screening: school children between 10 and 14 years old
  1. There has been an overall increase in the number of referrals (about 3%)
  2. Of all referrals ⅓ have scoliosis (>10°)
  3. It has resulted in less surgery overall
B. History: age, sex, menarche, pain, and family history should be obtained
C. Physical examination
  1. Observation: shoulder levels, protruding scapula and ribs, inequality of breasts, waist, or pelvic line
  2. Measurements: rotational prominence on forward bending (rib hump, scoliometer), plumb line for decompensation, leg lengths, and thoracic lordosis
D. X-ray examination: Cobb angle, Risser sign (Fig 7-2), ring apophysis, rotation (Fig 7-3), and bone age

E. Pulmonary function test: >60° curves have decreased vital capacity

V. Management
A. Goals: straighten curve and maintain it
  1. Cosmesis often the primary concern from patient's point of view
  2. Respiratory function usually does not improve after surgery, but it may help to halt deterioration in larger curves
  3. Pelvic obliquity should be corrected if it becomes a functional problem
  4. Pain and neurologic problems are rare in adolescent idiopathic curves
B. Nonoperative treatment
  1. Observation: <25° in immature patients and <50° in mature patients (initially 3 months after the first visit and then every 6–9 months for curves <20°, looking for at least 10° change, and every 3–4 months for curves >20° looking for at least 5° change)
  2. Exercise: only as adjunct treatment, especially for patients with obesity, back pain, lumbar hyperlordosis, flexible kyphosis, trunk, and extremity muscle tightness
  3. Orthosis: curve >30°–45° (first visit) and >25° with documented progression

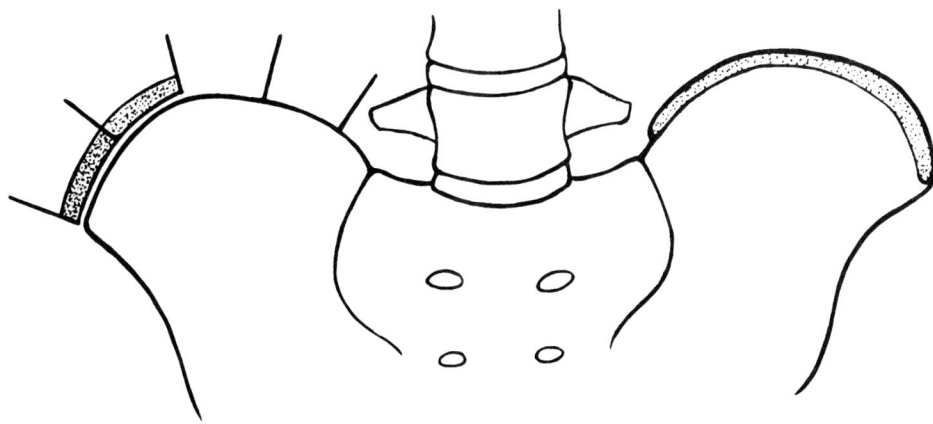

Figure 7-2. Risser signs by dividing excursion of ossification into four quarters. Risser sign of 4 is the end of spinal growth. (From Lonstein JE: Patient evaluation. In Bradford DS, Lonstein JE, Moe JH, et al, eds. Scoliosis and other spinal deformities. Philadelphia, WB Saunders, 1987, p 78. Reprinted with permission.)

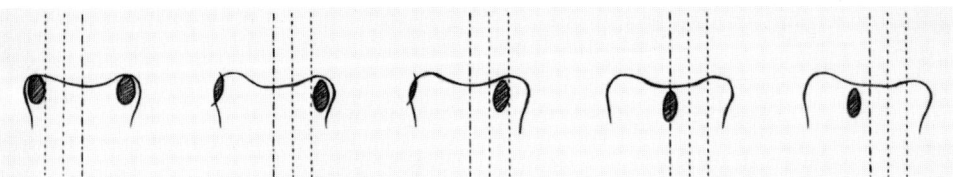

Figure 7-3. Vertebral rotation by noting the location of the pedicle. **A.** Grade zero **B.** Grade I, **C.** Grade II, **D.** Grade III, **E.** Grade IV. (From Lonstein JE: Patient evaluation. In Bradford DS, Lonstein JE, Moe JH, Ogilvie JW, Winter RB. Scoliosis and other spinal deformities. Philadelphia, WB Saunders, Inc 1987, p 74)

in immature patients (Risser 3 or less)
  a. Milwaukee or Cervicothoracolumbosacral Orthosis [CTLSO], Boston modules, or other TSLOs
  b. Underarm orthosis is appropriate for curves with the apex at or below T8 apex
  c. Orthosis is less effective for cervicothoracic curves and hypokyphotic thoracic curves
  d. Goal: prevent progression: 85% of compliant patients stop progression and improve (about 50% correction), but most return within 5° of original curve after brace treatment is ceased
  e. Decompensated curves respond poorly (50%)
  f. Curves >40° respond poorly
  g. Protocol: 23 hours a day until 2 years after menarche or Risser 4 or 5 and wean off in 1–2 years
4. Electrical treatment is less effective than bracing
5. Operative treatment: >40°–45° (thoracic)
  a. Choice of posterior fusion level (King)
    (1) Curve patterns
      i. Type I: S-shaped curve, where lumbar curve is larger and less flexible (fuse both thoracic and lumbar curve but not below L4)
      ii. Type II: S-shaped curve, where thoracic curve large and less flexible (fuse only thoracic curve down to the stable vertebrae) (Fig 7-4)
      iii. Type III: thoracic curve where lumbar curve does not cross midline (fuse thoracic curve down to the stable vertebra)
      iv. Type IV: long thoracic curve where L4 tilts into the curve (fuse the entire curve down to the stable vertebra, L4)
      v. Type V: double thoracic curves (fuse both curves)
    (2) Distal extent
      i. Should include Harrington stable zone: two perpendicular lines from the sacral pedicles
      ii. Should include neutral vertebra, which are nonrotated vertebrae
      iii. Generally, the distal vertebra is the stable vertebra by center sacral line
      iv. Do not fuse beyond L4 vertebrae (back pain problem later and flat back syndrome)
      v. Stopping at T12 may give junctional kyphosis
      vi. For type II curves, the caudal vertebra may need to include two vertebrae below the stable vertebra when using the Cotrel-Dubousset system in order to prevent decompensation
    (3) Flexibility index: fuse thoracic

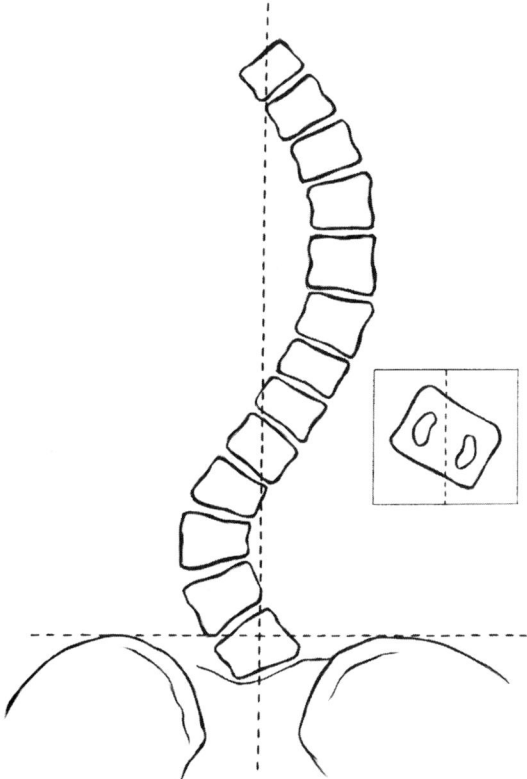

Figure 7-4. The center sacral line to establish the stable vertebra. (From King HA: Posterior scoliosis surgery. In Chapman MW, ed. Operative orthopaedics. Philadelphia, JB Lippincott, 1988, p 1985. Reprinted with permission.)

          only if lumbar curve is more flexible (type II curves)
       (4) Upper hook should be higher if sagittal deformity is present
       (5) Isolate short and flexible thoracolumbar or lumbar curves without kyphosis: anterior fusion with Zielke instrumentation or posterior Cotrel-Dubousset instrumentation is indicated, which accomplishes short fusion of only structural vertebrae
   b. Instrumentations
       (1) Harrington: distraction and compression but tend to flatten the spine
       (2) Drummond: combination of Harrington and Luque rods, which is safe with spinous process wiring
       (3) Luque: for paralytic scoliosis or for pelvic obliquity correction
       (4) Cotrel-Dubousset: derotation and sagittal correction
       (5) Anterior: Dwyer or Zielke (for thoracolumbar or lumbar curves) — contraindicated if kyphosis is present
       (6) Combined anterior and posterior procedure: done for large stiff curves (>80°) when bending x-rays fail to balance the spine
   c. Surgical technique
       (1) Donate 2–3 U of blood preoperatively
       (2) Cell saver during surgery
       (3) Spinal cord monitoring and wake-up test
       (4) Hypotensive anesthesia to decrease blood loss
       (5) Meticulous decortication, facet excision, and iliac crest autograft with or without allograft

VI. Idiopathic Infantile Scoliosis

A. Usually 2–3 months of age, males > females, and more common in England
B. Left thoracic curves: 90%
C. Prognosis
   1. Resolve spontaneously: 60–70%
   2. Progression
      a. Benign: >1 year onset, more double curves, and flexible
      b. Malignant: <1 year onset, thoracic curve, and rigid
D. Good prognosis if Mehta angle (rib-vertebral angle) is <20° and the convex rib does not overlap (phase I) the vertebral body on the posteroanterior (PA) radiograph
E. Treatment: splint or brace early (>30°) and subcutaneous rod without fusion if progressive

VII. Idiopathic Juvenile Scoliosis

A. Right thoracic pattern is most common
B. Variable progression: ⅓ are observed, ⅓ are braced, ⅓ require surgery
C. Brace if >30°
D. Surgery if progressive curve despite brace treatment, especially during puberty

VIII. Congenital Scoliosis (Fig 7-5)

A. Failure of segmentation or formation or both
B. Associate anomalies: genitourinary, dysraphism, heart, Sprengel's, Klippel-Feil, absent thumb, anal agenesis, etc.
C. Progress: 50–75% (especially cervicothoracic, high thoracic curves, during birth to 4 years, and at puberty about 5°–7° per year)
  1. Unilateral unsegmented bar is the worst (especially if contralateral hemivertebra)
  2. Multiple convex hemivertebrae are the next severe deformity
  3. Single hemivertebra: unpredictable progression
      a. Worse prognosis if fully segmented compared with semisegmented or nonsegmented types
      b. Incarcerated type, in which the hemivertebra does not produce scoliosis above and below, is generally better
      c. Hemivertebra at the thoracolumbar junction is generally worse
  4. Wedge vertebra: partial hemivertebra
  5. Block vertebra: bilateral symmetrical failure of fusion (no progression)
D. Treatment
  1. Orthosis is generally not indicated unless it is used for flexible or secondary curves only
  2. Surgery: posterior fusion in situ without instrumentation if progression is documented
      a. Unsegmented bar
        (1) Posterior in situ fusion in early cases
        (2) Late cases can be treated with anterior osteotomy, correction, and fusion both anteriorly and posteriorly

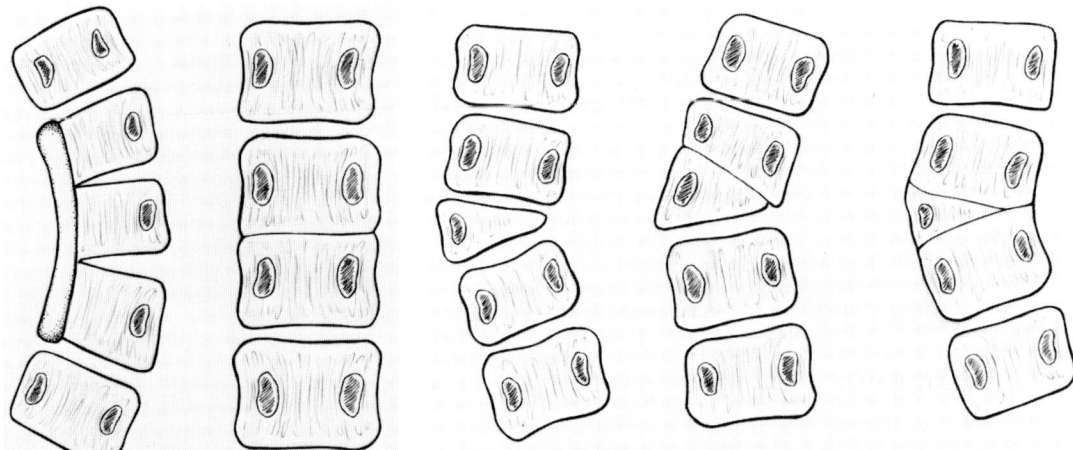

Figure 7-5. Types of congenital scoliosis. Far left: Unilateral unsegmented bar. Next left: Bloc vertebra. Center: Fully segmented hemivertebra. Next right: Semisegmented hemivertebra. Right: Nonsegmented hemivertebra. (Redrawn from Winter RB: Congenital spine deformity. In Bradford DS, Lonstein JE, Moe JH, et al, eds. Scoliosis and other spinal deformities. Philadelphia, WB Saunders, 1987, p 234. Reprinted with permission.)

b. Hemivertebrae: posterior fusion in situ in early cases. Anterior fusion for multiple hemivertebrae should be considered, since posterior fusion alone may not be adequate. Excision of hemivertebra is rarely done except in lumbosacral junction or for large stiff curves
c. Unilateral anterior hemiepiphysiodesis and posterior hemiarthrodesis may be considered if <70° curves, if <6 segments involved, <5 years old, and no significant lordosis or kyphosis
d. Diastematomyelia: excision of the bar and release of the tethered cord and fusion
e. If deformity is severe and includes lordosis, both anterior and posterior in situ fusions are recommended to prevent rotatory lordosis-scoliosis by posterior fusion alone (crankshaft phenomenon)

IX. Paralytic Scoliosis

A. Upper motor neuron diseases (cerebral palsy), lower motor diseases (poliomyelitis, spinal muscular atrophy, myelodysplasia), or muscle disease (muscular dystrophy)
B. Scoliosis is commonly a long C-shaped curve with associated pelvic obliquity and hip contracture
C. Rule out hydromyelia or tethered cord in progressive deformities in myelodysplasia patients
D. Treatment
  1. Orthosis (thoracic suspension or TSLO) if <50° to control curve before adolescence
  2. Spinal fusion to balance spine over leveled pelvis
    a. Posterior fusion with Luque rods and sublaminar wires and Galveston pelvic fixation (T3–T4 to ilium for nonambulatory patients with pelvic obliquity (Fig 7-6)

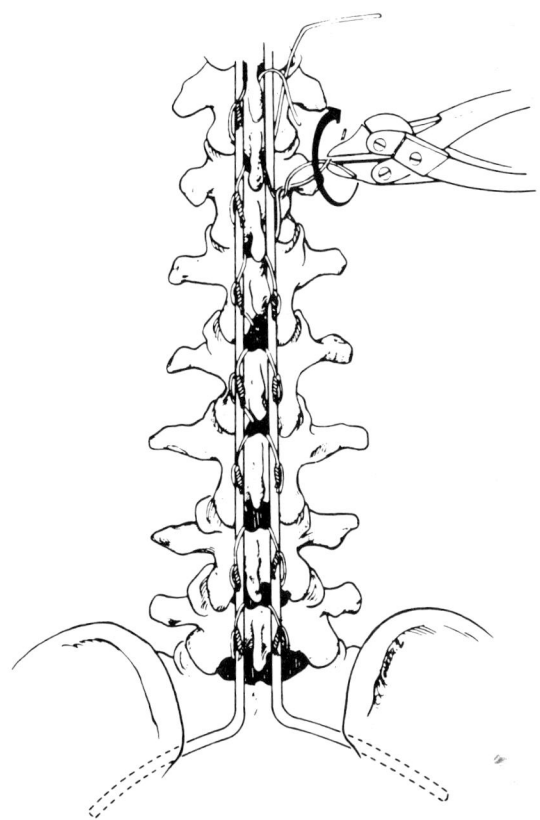

Figure 7-6. Galveston technique of Luque rods with sublaminar wires into the pelvis. (From King HA: Posterior scoliosis surgery. In Chapman MW, ed. Operative orthopaedics. Philadelphia, JB Lippincott, 1988, p 1985. Reprinted with permission.)

  b. Anterior release and fusion with or without instrumentation (Dwyer or Zielke), followed by posterior fusion with Luque rods for severe stiff curves and when preoperative traction x-rays do not balance the spine over pelvis
  c. Ambulatory patients without significant pelvic obliquity should be fused posteriorly without extending down to the sacrum
  d. Patients with musculodystrophy should have early instrumentation and fusion (usually at 20°–30°), because the incidence of progression is very high

X. Neurofibromatosis
A. Spinal deformity present: 20–25%
B. Types
   1. Nondystrophic: similar to idiopathic type
   2. Dystrophic: sharp angulated curves, scalloping of the vertebrae, rib penciling, large intervertebral foramen, and dural ectasia
      a. Scoliosis: early posterior fusion
      b. Kyphoscoliosis: anterior and posterior fusion
C. Paralysis may occur secondary to neurofibroma or kyphoscoliosis (myelogram or MRI should be done to rule out neurofibroma)

XI. Adult Scoliosis
A. General considerations
   1. Spinal deformity is more rigid and may also progress, especially if the curve is >50°, about 1° per year
   2. Spinal stenosis, disc disease, and osteopenia are associated problems: asymmetrical loss of disc height and vertebra may increase the Cobb angle
   3. Pain
      a. Location may be at the convex thoracic region, lumbar region due to facet degeneration on the concave side, or at the lumbosacral region
      b. Increased incidence of low-back pain if lumbar curve is >45°
      c. Rule out other sources of pain, such as abdominal aneurysm, renal calculi, tumors, disc disease, and spinal stenosis
   4. Sciatica: nerve root compression in the concavity of the curve may occur, which is best demonstrated by myelogram
   5. Respiratory compromise may occur in severe thoracic curves: dyspnea, pulmonary hypertension, and cor pulmonale
B. Evaluation
   1. Careful history and examination
   2. X-rays: plain x-rays, myelogram, MRI, or CT scan if sciatica
   3. Pain discography to localize site of pain
C. Treatment
   1. Conservative treatment: rest, nonsteroidal anti-inflammatory drugs (NSAIDs), and conditioning
   2. Brace is occasionally helpful for pain relief but not for sciatica, progression, and respiratory problems
   3. Surgery
      a. Indication: progressive thoracic or thoracolumbar curves >60° curves with unrelenting pain and sciatica, and progressive respiratory decompensation
      b. Techniques
         (1) Relatively flexible thoracic curves or balanced double major curves: posterior instrumentation and fusion with Harrington rod with sublaminar or spinous process wire fixation or Cotrel-Dubousset system
         (2) Rigid severe thoracic curves (>80°): anterior release and fusion followed by posterior fusion and instrumentation
         (3) Relatively flexible thoracolumbar or lumbar curves in younger patients: anterior fusion with Zielke instrumentation (no kyphosis, limited to T10 to L4), or posterior fusion and instrumentation with segmental fixation
         (4) Severe and rigid thoracolumbar or lumbar curves (≥75° and kyphotic): anterior release and fusion without instrumentation followed by posterior fusion and instrumentation
      c. Complication
         (1) Higher than adolescent spine, especially pulmonary problems
         (2) Pseudoarthrosis is less if two-staged anterior and posterior ap-

proach is used for severe deformities

(3) Flatback syndrome: loss of lumbar lordosis

REFERENCES

Pediatric Scoliosis

Allen BL Jr, Ferguson RL: The Galveston technique for L-rod instrumentation. Spine 7:276–284, 1982

Allen BL Jr, Ferguson RL: The Galveston technique of pelvic fixation with Luque-rod instrumentation of the spine. Spine 9:388–394, 1984

Allen BL Jr, Ferguson RL: L-rod instrumentation for scoliosis in cerebral palsy. J Pediatr Orthop 2:87–96, 1982

Andrew T, Piggott H: Growth arrest for progressive scoliosis: Combined anterior and posterior fusion of the convexity. J Bone Joint Surg 67B:193–197, 1985

Bergoyn M, Bollini G, Hornung H, et al: Is the Cotrel-Dubousset really universal in the surgical treatment of idiopathic scoliosis? J Pediatr Orthop 8:45, 1988

Bradford DS, Lonstein JE, Moe JH, et al: Moe's textbook of scoliosis and other spinal deformities. Philadelphia, WB Saunders, 1987

Bunnell WP: The natural history of idiopathic scoliosis before skeletal maturity. Spine 11:773–776, 1986

Carr WA, Moe JH, Winter RB, et al: Treatment of idiopathic scoliosis in the Milwaukee brace, long term results. J Bone Joint Surg 62A:599–612, 1980

Cochran T, Irstam L, Nachemson A: Long-term anatomic and functional changes in patients with adolescent idiopathic scoliosis treated by Harrington rod fusion. Spine 8:576–583, 1983

Denis F: Cotrel-Dubousset instrumentation in the treatment of idiopathic scoliosis. Orthop Clin North Am 19:291–311, 1988

Drummond DS, Guadagni J, Keene JS, et al: Interspinous process segmental spinal instrumentation. J Pediatr Orthop 4:397–404, 1984

Emans JB, Kaelin A, Bancell P, et al: The Boston bracing system for idiopathic scoliosis: Follow-up results in 295 patients. Spine 11:792–801, 1986

Fisher DA, Rapp GF, Emkes M: Idiopathic scoliosis: Transcutaneous muscle stimulation versus Milwaukee brace. Spine 12:987–991, 1987

King HA, Moe JH, Bradford DS, et al: The selection of fusion levels in thoracic idiopathic scoliosis. J Bone Joint Surg 56A:1302–1313, 1983

LaGrone MO, Bradford DS, Moe JH, et al: Treatment of symptomatic flatback after spinal fusion. J Bone Joint Surg 70A:569–580, 1988

Lonstein JE, Akbarnia BA: Operative treatment of spinal deformities in patients with cerebral palsy or mental retardation. An analysis of one hundred and seven cases. J Bone Joint Surg 65A:43–55, 1983

Lonstein JE, Bjorklund S, Wanninger MH, et al: Voluntary school screening for scoliosis in Minnesota. J Bone Joint Surg 64A:481–488, 1982

Lonstein JE, Carlson MJ: The prediction of curve progression in untreated idiopathic scoliosis during growth. J Bone Joint Surg 66A:1061–1071, 1984

Luk KDK, Leong JCY, Reyes L, et al: The comparative results of treatment in idiopathic thoracolumbar scoliosis using Harrington, Dwyer and Zielke instrumentation. Spine 14:275–280, 1989

Luque ER: Segmental spinal instrumentation for correction of scoliosis. Clin Orthop 163:192–198, 1982

McMaster MJ, David CV: Hemivertebra as a cause of scoliosis. A study of 104 patients. J Bone Joint Surg 68B:588–595, 1986

Mehta MH: The rib-vertebral angle in the early diagnosis between resolving and progressive infantile scoliosis. J Bone Joint Surg 54B:230–243, 1972

Moe JH, Kharrat K, Winter RB, et al: Harrington instrumentation without fusion plus external orthotic support for the treatment of difficult problems in young children. Clin Orthop 185:35–45, 1984

Moe JH, Purcell GA, Bradford DS: Zielke instrumentation (VDS) for the correction of spinal curvature. Clin Orthop 180:133–153, 1983

Ogiela DM, Chan DPK: Ventral derotation spondylodesis: A review of 22 cases. Spine 11:18–22, 1986

Osebold WR, Mayfield JK, Winter RB, et al: Surgical treatment of paralytic scoliosis associated with myelomeningocele. J Bone Joint Surg 64A:841–856, 1982

Sussman MD: Advantage of early spinal stabilization and fusion in patients with Duchenne muscular dystrophy. J Pediatr Orthop 4:532–537, 1984

Weinstein SL: Idiopathic scoliosis: Natural history. Spine 11:780–783, 1986

Weinstein SL, Ponseti IV: Curve progression in idiopathic scoliosis. J Bone Joint Surg 65A:447–455, 1983

Winter RB: Convex anterior and posterior hemiarthrodesis for congenital scoliosis; a preliminary report. J Pediatr Orthop 1:361–366, 1981

Winter R, Lonstein JE, Denis F, et al: Convex growth arrest for progressive congenital scoliosis due to hemivertebrae. J Pediatr Orthop 8:633, 1988

Winter RB, Lonstein JE, Drogt J, et al: The effectiveness of bracing in the nonoperative treatment of idiopathic scoliosis. Spine 11:790–791, 1986

Winter RB, Moe JH, Lonstein JE: Posterior spinal arthrodesis for congenital scoliosis. An analysis of 290 patients 5 to 19 years old. J Bone Joint Surg 66A:1180–1197, 1984

Winter RB, Moe JH, Lonstein JE: The surgical treatment of congenital kyphosis: A review of 94 patients age 5 years or older, with 2 years or more follow-up in 77 patients. Spine 10:224–231, 1985

Adult Scoliosis

Ascani E, Bartolozzi P, Logroscino CA, et al: Natural history of untreated idiopathic scoliosis after skeletal maturity. Spine 11:784–789, 1986

Bradford DS: Adult scoliosis. Current concepts of treatment. Clin Orthop 229:70–87, 1988

Byrd JA, Scoles PV, Winter RB, et al: Adult idiopathic scoliosis treated by anterior and posterior spinal fusion. J Bone Joint Surg 69A:843–850, 1987

Court-Brown CM, Stoll JE, Gertzbein SD: Thoracic facetectomy and bone grafting in the surgical treatment of adult idiopathic scoliosis. Spine 12:992–995, 1987

Cummine JL, Lonstein JE, Moe JH, et al: Reconstructive surgery in the adult for failed scoliosis fusion. J Bone Joint Surg 61A:1151–1161, 1979

Fabry G, Van Meklebeek J, Bocky E: Back pain after Harrington instrumentation for idiopathic scoliosis. Spine 14:620–624, 1989

Grubb SA, Lipscomb HJ, Coonrad RW: Degenerative adult onset scoliosis. Spine 13:241–245, 1988

Jackson RP, Simmons EH, and Stripinis D: Incidence and severity of back pain in adult idiopathic scoliosis. Spine 8:749–756, 1983

Kostuik JP, Hall BB: Spinal fusions to the sacrum in adults with scoliosis. Spine 8:489–500, 1983

Kostuik JP, Israel J, Hall JE: Scoliosis surgery in adults. Clin Orthop 93:225–234, 1973

LaGrone MO, Bradford DS, Moe JH, et al: Treatment of symptomatic flatback after spinal fusion. J Bone Joint Surg 70A:569–580, 1988

Lonstein JE: Adult scoliosis. In Bradford DS, Lonstein JE, Moe SH, et al. Moe's textbook of scoliosis and other spinal deformities, ed. 2. Philadelphia, WB Saunders, 1987 p. 628

Nuber GW, Schafer MF: Surgical management of adult scoliosis. Clin Orthop 208:228–237, 1986

Ogiela DM, Chan DPK: Ventral derotation spondylodesis (a review of 22 cases). Spine 11:18–22, 1986

Ponder RC, Dickson JH, Harrington PR, Erwin WD: Results of Harrington instrumentation and fusion in the adult idiopathic scoliosis patient. J Bone Joint Surg 57A:797–801, 1975

San Martino A, D'Andria FM, San Martino C: The surgical treatment of nerve root compression caused by scoliosis of the lumbar spine. Spine 8:261–265, 1983

Sponseller PD, Cohen MS, Nachemson AF, et al: Results of surgical treatment of adults with idiopathic scoliosis. J Bone Joint Surg 69A:667–675, 1987

Swank S, Lonstein JE, Moe JH, et al. Surgical treatment of adult scoliosis. J Bone Joint Surg 63A:268–287, 1981

VanDam BE, Bradford DS, Lonstein JE, et al: Adult idiopathic scoliosis treated by posterior spinal fusion and Harrington instrumentation. Spine 12:32–36, 1987

Weinstein SL, Ponseti IV: Curve progression in idiopathic scoliosis. J Bone Joint Surg 65A:447–455, 1983

61
Kyphosis

I. General Considerations
A. Anatomic: cervical kyphosis, thoracic kyphosis, thoracolumbar kyphosis, loss of lumbar lordosis, and lumbosacral kyphosis (spondylithesis)
B. Normal thoracic kyphosis: 20°–45°, mean, 34°
C. Normal thoracolumbar junction: 0°
D. Normal lumbar lordosis: 30°–50°
E. L5-S1 angle: 12°–14°

II. Biomechanics
A. Anterior column fails under compression and posterior column fails on tension
B. Posterior structures: lamina and ligamenta flava are relatively stronger than facets, capsules, and interspinous ligaments in resisting tension
C. Deformity increases the moment arm and further deformity may result
D. Eccentric loading affects cartilagenous growth of the vertebral end plates (compression decreases growth anteriorly and tension increases growth posteriorly, resulting in more kyphosis)

III. Classification
A. Postural
B. Scheuermann's disease
C. Congenital
   1. Defect of formation
   2. Defect of segmentation
   3. Mixed
D. Neuromuscular
E. Myelomeningocele
   1. Developmental (late paralytic)
   2. Congenital (present at birth)
F. Traumatic
   1. Due to bone and/or ligament damage
   2. Due to bone and/or ligament and cord injury
G. Postsurgical
   1. Postlaminectomy
   2. Following excision of vertebral body
H. Postirradiation: neuroblastoma and Wilm's tumor
I. Metabolic
   1. Osteoporosis
      a. Senile
      b. Juvenile
   2. Osteomalacia
   3. Osteogenesis imperfecta
   4. Other
J. Skeletal dysplasia
   1. Achondroplasia
   2. Mucopolysaccharidoses
   3. Neurofibromatosis
   4. Other
K. Collagen disease
   1. Marie-Strümpell disease
   2. Other
L. Tumor
   1. Benign
   2. Malignant
      a. Primary
      b. Metastatic
M. Inflammatory and infection

IV. Scheuermann's Disease (Juvenile Kyphosis)
A. General considerations
   1. Scheuermann first described radiologic manifestation of this disease in 1920
   2. Pathogenesis is unknown
      a. Genetic: familial tendency but no proof
      b. Collagen weakness and stunted ossification of the vertebral end plate is most likely mechanism
      c. Osteopenia, nutrition, and endocrine effects: increased incidence

in Turner's syndrome, nontropical sprue, and cystic fibrosis patients
            d. Mechanical, inflammation, and muscle weakness may be involved but there is no proof
        3. Pathology
            a. Thickened and contracted anterior longitudinal ligament
            b. Wedging of anterior part of the vertebral bodies
            c. Nucleus pulposus: protrusion anteriorly and into the bony spongiosa (Schmorl's nodes)
        4. Incidence: 0.4–8.3% of the population but only 1% seek medical attention
    B. Clinical findings
        1. Age: common during 12–14 years of age and equal sex ratio or slightly female preponderance
        2. Symptoms
            a. Deformity is the most common presenting complaint
            b. Pain: about 50% among those who seek medical attention but higher (78%) if the lumbar spine is involved
            c. Some patients develop lumbar spondylolysis later
        3. Examination
            a. Increased in thoracic kyphosis (rigid) and lumbar and cervical lordosis (compensatory), round shoulders, and head forward
            b. Muscle tightness and contractures, especially the hamstrings
            c. Associated with mild scoliosis: 30%
        4. X-ray findings
            a. Early: disordered endochondral ossification, irregular end plates, narrowing of intervetebral disc space, and Schmorl's nodes
            b. Intermediate: vertebral wedging and increasing kyphosis >45° (usually >5° and >2 vertebrae involvement)
            c. Late: degenerative changes such as osteophytes and facet hypertrophy
            d. Standing lateral and supine hyperextension views are helpful to assess the rigidity of the curve
            e. Widening of interpedicular space: spinal epidural cyst
    C. Differential diagnosis
        1. Postural round back deformity: modest kyphosis (40°–60°), flexible, and no radiologic changes
        2. Inflammation and infection: discitis, osteomyelitis, and spondylitis (ankylosing spondylitis, Reiter's syndrome, psoriasis, and inflammatory bowel disease)
        3. Trauma: multiple compression fractures
        4. Tumors: aneurysmal bone cyst, osteoid osteoma, osteoblastoma, eosinophilic granuloma, spinal cord tumors, and syringomyelia
        5. Congenital kyphosis (type 2) and dysplasia
    D. Types
        1. Thoracic type: most common
        2. Thoracolumbar or lumbar types: associated with more pain but less deformity
    E. Treatment
        1. Observation: mild deformity with minimal symptoms
        2. Brace: vertebral wedging >5° and curves between 45° and 65°, and 1–2 years of growth remaining
            a. Milwaukee brace if the apex is at or above T9
            b. Underarm TLSO: apex below T9 and thoracolumbar curves
            c. Curve correction and wedging improvement about 40% can be expected after 6–12 months, and the brace should be weaned until skeletal maturity but loss of correction is expected after several years
            d. Brace may have to be changed every 4–6 months until maximum correction is achieved
            e. Exercise, stressing pelvic tilt, ab-

dominal strengthening, spinal flexibility, and extension of the thoracic spine
3. Surgery
   a. Indication (rare)
      (1) Severe deformity after growth completion with unrelenting pain (usually >70° and >10° wedging, and resistant to bracing for 6 months)
      (2) Neurologic signs or symptoms
   b. Techniques
      (1) Posterior long fusion (partial facet excision and posterior and posterolaterally placed massive grafts) and instrumentations if the curve <70° and bending correction is achievable to 50°
         i. Large diameter double Harrington compression rods
         ii. Cotrel-Dubousset system
         iii. Luque rods but increased neurologic risks
      (2) Anterior fusion (transthoracic approach), followed by posterior fusion and instrumentation for curves >75° and bending cannot correct to 50° (better fusion rate)
   c. Postoperative regimen: cast or TLSO for 6–9 months until solid fusion
   d. Complications: pseudarthrosis and instrument failure (greater in posterior fusion alone), loss of correction, infection, pulmonary complications, and neurologic deficits (T5-T9 is the critical vascular zone)
   e. Postoperative correction is about 50%

V. Congenital Kyphosis
A. General considerations
   1. Types: may be single or multilevel
      a. Type I: failure of formation (hemivertebra)
      b. Type II: failure of segmentation (bar)
      c. Type III: combination of I and II
   2. Progression: about 7° per year
   3. Type I has worse prognosis for progression, paraplegia and upper levels are worse than lower levels, and type II is more benign without paralysis
B. Treatment
   1. Nonoperative treatment is futile
   2. Surgery
      a. Type I lesions
         (1) Posterior in situ fusion if <50° at 1–5 years and may augment posterior fusion 6 months later
         (2) Anterior and posterior fusion if >50° and older children (better correction and maintenance and less pseudarthrosis)
            i. Anterior decompression, release of all the tethering structures (anterior longitudinal ligament, disc and end plate to the posterior longitudinal ligament) — expose the spinal cord if advanced cases of cord compression but not necessary to expose it in milder cases
            ii. Intraoperative distraction and correction of the deformity
            iii. Rib, fibula, or iliac crest strut grafts (if the strut is placed >4 cm anterior to the spine, fracture of the graft is likely; therefore, vascularized rib may be used and pack additional bone in the space
            iv. Second-stage posterior fusion and compression instrumentation
            v. Postoperative immobilization: 6 months
      b. Type II lesions
         (1) Posterior fusion only if <55° in the older child

(2) Severe deformity: anterior osteotomy and correction and fusion may be tried, followed by posterior fusion
   c. Approach: rib should correspond to the upper level of deformity, and approach from the convex side if mild scoliosis is also present but approach from the concave side if severe scoliosis >60° and anterior decompression is planned
   d. Skeletal traction is contraindicated because it may cause paraplegia
   e. About 35°–40° correction can be expected
   f. Paraplegia can be a complication during correction of kyphosis

VI. Myelomeningocele
A. Congenital
   1. At birth: generally not recommended to correct the major spine deformity because of lack of bone stock and associated problems
   2. Posterior resection of kyphosis
      a. Two to three vertebrae proximal to the apex
      b. Posterior stabilization with Luque rods (Dunn or Galveston technique), followed by 6–9 months immobilization
      c. Better results if done before 3 years of age
B. Developmental or paralytic kyphosis
   1. Deformity is progressive, because the extensors of the spine (sacrospinalis and quadratus lumborum muscles) rotate anteriorly to increase flexion force
   2. Treatment
      a. Bracing for young patients and mild deformity
      b. Posterior fusion: long fusion to the sacrum
      c. Anterior release and fusion followed by posterior fusion with compression Harrington rods or Luque system for severe cases

VII. Paralytic Kyphosis
A. Poliomyelitis, anterior horn cell diseases (spinal muscular atrophy), cerebral palsy, Charcot-Marie-Tooth disease, muscular dystrophy, Friedreich ataxia, etc.
B. Lack of the extensor muscle strength
C. Natural history is progressive even after skeletal maturity
D. Treatment
   1. Spinal bracing until the patient is around 11–12 years old to achieve proper truncal height
   2. Posterior fusion with Luque instrumentation
   3. Two-staged anterior and posterior fusion in severe fixed deformities

VIII. Post-Traumatic Kyphosis
A. Acute or late secondary to severe compression fractures, burst fractures, or fracture-dislocations
B. More common in unstable fractures after conservative treatment
C. Symptoms: deformity, pain, and neurologic deficit
D. Treatment: combined anterior and posterior fusion

IX. Postsurgical Kyphosis
A. Usually after laminectomy for spinal cord tumors, syringomyelia, etc.
B. Fusion is recommended when extensive laminectomy is performed
C. Severe deformity is approached with a combined anterior and posterior fusion

X. Inflammatory and Infectious Kyphosis
A. Infection: tuberculosis and pyogenic osteomyelitis
   1. Thoracolumbar junction is most commonly affected
   2. Antibiotic treatment
   3. Anterior debridement and fusion if unresponsive to medical treatment, multiple level involvement, spinal cord compression

4. Progressive kyphosis needs anterior and posterior procedures

B. Inflammation: ankylosing spondylitis
1. Loss of lumbar lordosis and increased cervical and thoracic kyphosis
2. Primary location of disabling deformity should be assessed
3. Hip flexion contracture or joint disease should be corrected first and may prevent spinal surgery
4. Lumbar osteotomy: significant loss of lumbar lordosis and if relatively normal cervical and thoracic sagittal contour
   a. Plumb line of C7 should fall within the body of the sacrum after osteotomy
   b. Osteotomy is done at L3-L4 or L2-L3 junction and instrumentation and fusion (the angle of correction corresponds to the spine flexion deformity on standing)
   c. Apex of osteotomy should be anterior to the neural tube (at the junction of posterior longitudinal ligament and intervertebral disc)
   d. Combined anterior and posterior approach may be necessary
5. In severe kyphotic thoracic deformity, multiple posterior thoracic resection osteotomies can be done after anterior osteotomies
6. Osteotomy at C7-T1 junction with laminectomy from C6 to T2 is considered for primary cervical kyphosis

REFERENCES

Albanese SA, Bobechko WP: Spine deformity in familial dysautonomia (Riley-Day syndrome). J Pediatr Orthop 7:179–183, 1987

Bradford DS: Anterior vascular pedicle bone grafting for the treatment of kyphosis. Spine 5:318–323, 1980

Bradford DS: Juvenile kyphosis. Clin Orthop 128:45–55, 1977

Bradford DS, Ahmed KB, Moe JH, et al: The surgical management of patients with Sheuermann's disease. J Bone Joint Surg 62A:705–712, 1980

Bradford DS, Daher YH: Vascularized rib grafts for stabilization of kyphosis. J Bone Joint Surg 68B:357–361, 1986

Bradford DS, Ganjavian S, Antonious D, et al: Anterior strut-grafting for the treatment of kyphosis. Review of experience with forty-eight patients. J Bone Joint Surg 64A:680–690, 1982

Bradford DS, Moe JH, Montalvo FJ, Winter RB: Scheuermann's kyphosis. Results of surgical treatment by posterior spine arthrodesis in twenty-two patients. J Bone Joint Surg 57A:439–448, 1975

Bradford DS, Moe JH, Montalvo FJ, Winter, RB: Sheuermann's kyphosis and roundback deformity. J Bone Joint Surg 56A:740–758, 1974

Bradford DS, Winter RB, Lonstein JE, Moe JH: Techniques of anterior spinal surgery for the management of kyphosis. Clin Orthop 128:129–139, 1977

Bunch WH, Smith D, Hakala M: Kyphosis in the paralytic spine. Clin Orthop 128:107–112, 1977

Chou SN: The treatment of paralysis associated with kyphosis. Clin Orthop 128:149–154, 1977

Christofersen MR, Brooks AL: Excision and wire fixation of rigid myelomeningocele kyphosis. J Pediatr Orthop 5:691–696, 1985

Daher YH, Lonstein JE, Winter RB, Bradford DS: Spinal deformities in patients with Friedreich ataxia: A review of 19 patients. J Pediatr Orthop 5:553, 1985

Floman Y, Micheli LJ, Penny N, et al: Combined anterior and posterior fusion in seventy-three spinally deformed patients. Clin Orthop 164:110–122, 1984

Hall JE, Poitras B: The management of kyphosis in patients with myelomeningocele. Clin Orthop 128:33–40, 1977

Hensinger RN: Kyphosis secondary to skeletal dysplasia and metabolic disease. Clin Orthop 128:115–128, 1977

Herndon WA, Emans JB, Micheli LJ, Hall JE: Combined anterior and posterior fusion for Scheuermann's kyphosis. Spine 6:125–130, 1981

Heydemann JS, Gillespie R: Management of myelomeningocele kyphosis in the older child by kyphectomy and segmental spinal instrumentation. Spine 12:37–41, 1987

Hsu LC, Lee PC, Leong JCY: Dystrophic spinal deformities in neurofibromatosis. J Bone Joint Surg 66B:495–499, 1984

Leatherman KD, Dickson RA: Congenital kyphosis in myelomeningocele, vertebral resection and posterior spine fusion. Spine 3:22, 1978

Linseth RE, Stelzer L: Vertebral excision for kyphosis in children with myelomeningocele. J Bone Joint Surg 61A:699–704, 1979

Lonstein JE: Neurologic deficits secondary to spinal deformity. A review of the literature and report of 43 cases. Spine 5:331–355, 1980

Lonstein JE: Postlaminectomy kyphosis. Clin Orthop 128:93–100, 1977

Lowe GP, Menelaus MB: The surgical management of kyphosis in older children with myelomeningocele. J Bone Joint Surg 60B:40–45, 1978

Lowe TG: Double L-rod instrumentation in the treatment of severe kyphosis secondary to Scheuermann's disease. Spine 12:336–340, 1987

Luque ER: The correction of postural curves of the spine. Spine 7:270–275, 1982

Malcolm BW, Bradford DS, Winter RB, Chou, SN: Post-traumatic kyphosis. J Bone Joint Surg 53A:891–899, 1981

Mayfield JK: Severe spine deformity in myelodysplasia and sacral agenesis. Spine 6:498–509, 1981

McBride GG, Bradford DS: Vertebral body replacement with femoral neck allograft and vascularized rib strut graft. A technique for treating post-traumatic kyphosis with neurologic deficit. Spine 8:406–415, 1983

Moe JH: Modern concepts of treatment of spinal deformities in children and adults. Clin Orthop 150:137–153, 1980

Moe JH, Van Dam BE: In Bradford DS, Lonstein JE, Moe JH, et al, eds: Moe's textbook of scoliosis and other spinal deformities, ed. 2. Neurofibromatosis. Philadelphia, WB Saunders, 1987

Montgomery SP, Erwin WE: Scheuermann's kyphosis — long-term results of Milwaukee brace treatment. Spine 6:5–8, 1981

Montgomery SP, Hall, JE: Congenital kyphosis. Spine 7:360–364, 1982

Nerubay J, Katznelson A: Dual approach in the surgical treatment of juvenile kyphosis. Spine 11:101–102, 1986

O'Brien JP: Kyphosis secondary to infectious disease. Clin Orthop 128:56–64, 1977

Ogilvie JW: Spine deformity following radiation. Philadelphia, WB Saunders, 1987

Propst-Proctor, SL, Bleck EE: Radiographic determination of lordosis and kyphosis in normal and scoliotic children. J Pediatr Orthop 3:344–346, 1983

Riddick MF, Winter RB, Lutter LD: Spinal deformities in patients with spinal muscle atrophy. A review of 36 patients. Spine 7:476–483, 1982

Riseborough EJ: Irradiation induced kyphosis. Clin Orthop 128:101–106, 1977

Roberson JR, Whitesides TE Jr: Surgical reconstruction of late post-traumatic thoracolumbar kyphosis. Spine 10:307–312, 1985

Sachs B, Bradford D, Winter RB, et al: Scheuermann's kyphosis: Follow-up of Milwaukee-brace treatment. J Bone Joint Surg 69A:50–57, 1987

Speck GR, Chopin DC: The surgical treatment of Scheuermann's kyphosis. J Bone Joint Surg 68B:189–193, 1986

Stagnara P, De Mauroy JC, Dran G, et al: Reciprocal angulation of vertebral bodies in a sagittal plane: Approach to references for the evaluation of kyphosis and lordosis. Spine 7:335–342, 1982

Streitz W, Brown JC, Bonnett C: Anterior fibular strut grafting in the treatment of kyphosis. Clin Orthop 128:140–148, 1977

Taylor TC, Wenger DR, Stephen J, et al: Surgical management of thoracic kyphosis in adolescents. J Bone Joint Surg 61A:496–503, 1979

Tsou PM: Embryology of congenital kyphosis. Clin Orthop 128:18–25, 1977

White AA III, Panjabi MM, Thomas CL: The clinical biomechanics of kyphotic deformities. Clin Orthop 128:8–17, 1977

Whitesides TE Jr: Traumatic kyphosis of the thoracolumbar spine. Clin Orthop 128:78–92, 1977

Winter RB: Dwarfs. In Scoliosis and other spinal deformities. Philadelphia, WB Saunders, 1987

Winter RB, Moe JH: The results of spinal arthrodesis for congenital spinal deformity in patients younger than five years old. J Bone Joint Surg 64A:419–432, 1982

Winter RB, Moe JH, Bradford DS, et al: Spine deformity in neurofibromatosis. J Bone Joint Surg 61A:677–694, 1979

Winter RB: Congenital kyphosis. Clin Orthop 128:26–32, 1977

Winter RB, Moe JH, Lonstein JE: The incidence of Klippel-Feil syndrome in patients with congenital scoliosis and kyphosis. Spine 9:363–366, 1984

Winter RB, Moe JH, Lonstein JE: The surgical treatment of congenital kyphosis. A review of 94 patients age 5 years or older, with 2 years or more follow-up in 77 patients. Spine 10:224–231, 1985

Winter RB, Moe JH, Wang JF: Congenital kyphosis. Its natural history and treatment as observed in a study of one hundred and thirty patients. J Bone Joint Surg 55A:223–256, 1973

62

Spondylolysis and Spondylolisthesis

I. Etiology

A. Hereditary predisposition
 1. Familial tendency: more in dysplastic type compared with isthmic type
 2. More common in white males (6.4%) than black females (1.1%)
 3. Higher incidence among eskimos (up to 45%)
 4. Association with spina bifida of the sacrum
B. Stress fracture is definitely pathogenic
 1. Biomechanics
   a. Abrupt change in stiffness across the lumbosacral junction
   b. Pars interarticularis is strong but susceptible to fatigue fracture, especially with repeated extension forces
   c. Shear stress at the pars: physiologic flexion contracture of the hip and secondary hyperlordosis create pincerlike effect from the superior articular process of S1 and inferior articular process of the L4
 2. More common in males than females, probably due to the difference in their activity
 3. Higher incidence among football players, female gymnasts, and soldiers with heavy backpacks
 4. Lower incidence among nonambulatory patients

II. Classification (Newman) (Fig 7-7)

A. Dysplastic
 1. Congenital defect of superior S1 facet or inferior L5 facet without pars elongation or defect
 2. Higher incidence among family members
 3. More likely to be symptomatic and progressive
 4. Cauda equina compression or S1 root compression by inferior L5 facet may occur if the slip is >25°–30°
 5. Treatment consists of L5-S1 fusion in symptomatic cases and include L4 in severe slips
B. Isthmic
 1. Most common type due to stress fracture at the pars interarticularis
 2. Defect or elongation of the pars
 3. Acute fracture secondary to trauma is less common
C. Degenerative
 1. Instability of apophyseal joints and slippage, associated with lumbar spondylosis and disc surgery
 2. Most common at L4-L5 level followed by L3-L4 and L5-S1 levels
 3. Slip is rarely >30%
 4. Average age is around 65 years and more common in females
 5. Rotation component: one side slips more
D. Traumatic: fractures of the pedicle, lamina, or facet
E. Pathologic: osteogenesis imperfecta, Paget's disease, etc.

III. Clinical Findings (Isthmic Type)

A. Common from 7–20 years of age, and the onset usually coincides with adolescent spurt and progression occurs during 10–15 years of age
B. Most common at L5 over S1 vertebrae (95%)
C. Many are asymptomatic but low-back pain or L5 radiculopathy may develop

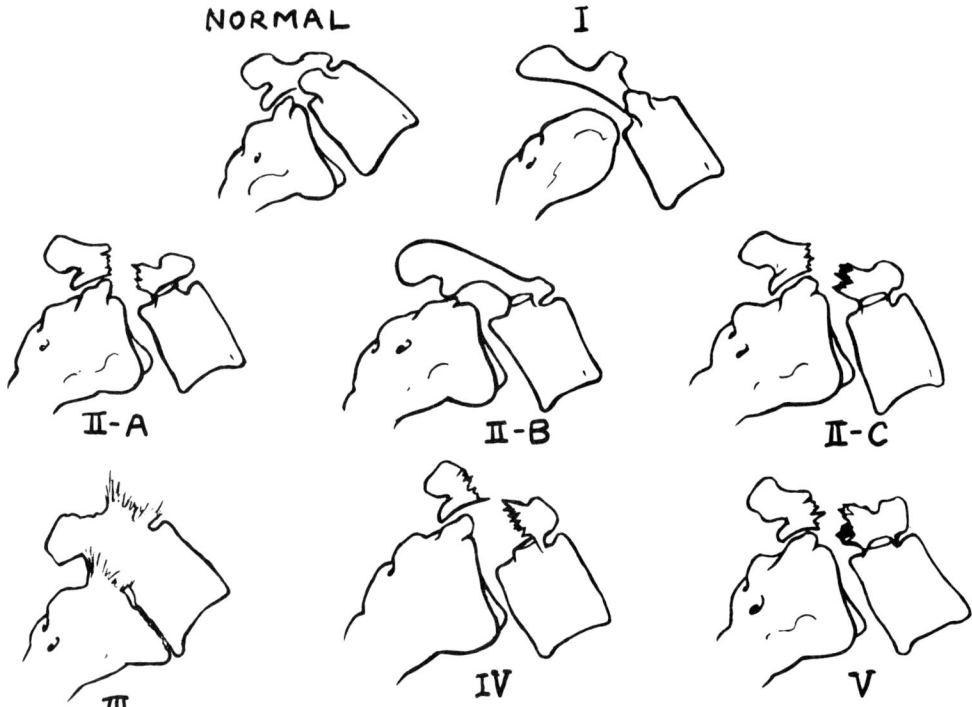

Figure 7-7. Newman's classification of spondylolisthesis. I: Dysplastic. II: Isthmic (**A.** break in parts interarticularis, **B.** elongated but intact pars, **C.** acute fracture). III: Degenerative. IV: Fractures other than pars. V: Pathologic. (From Bradford DS: Spondylolysis and spondylolithesis. In Bradford DS, Lonstein JE, Moe JH, et al, eds. Scoliosis and other spinal deformities. Philadelphia, WB Saunders, 1987, p 404. Reprinted with permission.)

D. Spondylolysis
 1. Incidence: 5% in general population and most commonly detected during 5–10 years of age
 2. Few are symptomatic and related to activities
 3. Differential diagnosis of low-back pain in children: disc space infection, osteoid osteoma, spinal cord tumor, herniated disc, rheumatoid spondylitis, muscle, and neurologic disorders
E. Physical examination: restricted forward flexion of the hips and back, tight hamstrings, flat buttock (vertical sacrum), lumbosacral kyphosis, compensatory lordosis, anterior protrusion of the pelvis, and pelvic waddle gait
F. Obstetric problem: pelvic outlet and midpelvis shallow in anteroposterior diameter

IV. Roentgenographic Findings

A. Defect at the pars interarticularis: "Scotty dog sign" on an oblique view
B. Grades and slip angle (Fig 7-8)
C. Trapezoidal L5 and dome-shaped sacrum tend to progress
D. Myelogram, CT scan, or MRI may be helpful in patients with radiculopathy to rule out concomitant herniated disc and to visualize the nerve roots
E. Bone scan is helpful if relatively recent stress fracture or acute fracture is suspected

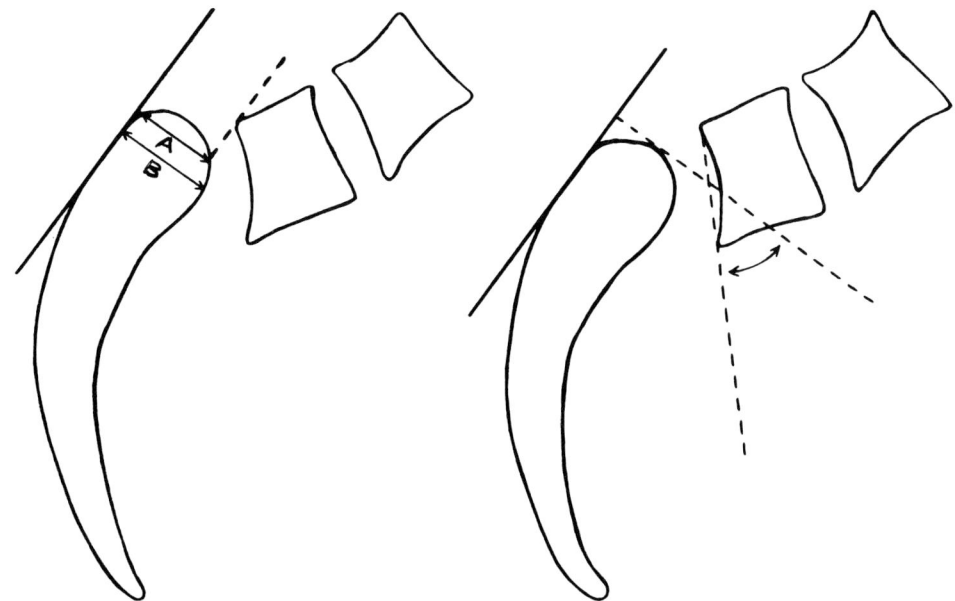

Figure 7-8. Slippage percentage and slip angle. (From Bradford DS: Spondylolysis and spondylolithesis. In Bradford DS, Lonstein JE, Moe JH, et al, eds. Scoliosis and other spinal deformities. Philadelphia, WB Saunders, 1987, p 410. Reprinted with permission.)

V. Prognosis

A. Progression is usually during 10–15 years of age (obtain x-rays every 6 months)
B. Females are more prone to a greater slippage
C. Slip >30% and 45° slip angle may give worse prognosis
D. Trapezoidal L5 and dome-shaped sacrum allow more slip

VI. L4 over L5 Isthmic Spondylolisthesis

A. Higher incidence of neurologic signs
B. Further slip may occur even after 20 years of age
C. There is a male preponderance
D. Sacralization of L5 is common
E. There is a tendency for small L4 transverse processes

VII. Treatment

A. Spondylolysis
 1. Restrict activities if symptomatic, followed by back and abdominal strengthening exercise and hamstring stretching
 2. Brace or cast: temporary if symptomatic and acute episode with positive bone scan
 3. L5-S1 fusion if unrelenting pain: rarely necessary
B. Spondylolisthesis
 1. Observation if <50% slip and asymptomatic
 2. Restrict activities, brace, and physical therapy if <50% slip and symptomatic
 3. Fusion if >50% slip with documented progression in the child or those with <50% slip who are symptomatic despite conservative treatment
    a. In situ posterolateral fusion: from tip of transverse processes to sacral alae
       (1) One-level fusion from L5-S1 if <50% slip and large L5 transverse processes
       (2) Two-level fusion from L4-S1 if

>50% slip or small L5 transverse processes
   b. No Gill decompression in the child
   c. Symptomatic relief can be expected up to 90%
   d. Pseudarthrosis up to 25% and more in two-level fusions
4. Repair of the defect with iliac crest bone graft supplemented with wire, screw or Cotrel-Dubousset pedicle screw with inferior laminar hook can be done in selected mild slip cases, involving L2 to L4
5. Adult spondylolisthesis
   a. Either isthmic or degenerative spondylolisthesis types
   b. Pain relief is the primary concern and conservative treatment for at least 6 months is necessary, as in other adult low-back pain patients (medications, exercise, brace, etc.)
   c. Observation if asymptomatic even if high-grade slip
   d. Myelogram, CT scan, or MRI scan to rule out herniated disc and spinal stenosis and localize sites of root compression in radiculopathy cases
   e. Surgery
      (1) Gill's procedure: removal of loose lamina alone is usually not adequate for complete decompression
      (2) Decompressive laminectomy with foraminotomy if radiculopathy and removal of the posterior portion of the sacrum if cauda equina involvement
      (3) Posterolateral fusion is required in most cases after decompression
      (4) Pedicular screws and plates may be considered to provide better stability
6. Severe spondylolisthesis (grade III or more)
   a. Goal
      (1) Prevent further slippage
      (2) Stabilization of unstable segments
      (3) Neurologic recovery or prevention of deficit
      (4) Pain relief
      (5) Cosmesis, posture, and gait improvement
   b. Treatment
      (1) Observation if asymptomatic
      (2) In situ fusion is standard
      (3) Decompression and fusion if neurologic symptoms present
      (4) Reduction, fusion, and instrumentation is dangerous in producing a neurologic deficit: one should only consider in patients with a high slip angle ($>45°$) and if preoperative flexion and extension films show mobility
         i. Cast reduction and fusion is relatively safer
         ii. Posterior laminectomy, decompression, and L4 to S1 fusion, reduction with instrumentation; this procedure has a high complication rate, particularly injury of the L5 nerve root

REFERENCES

Bell DF, Ehrlich MG, Zaleske DJ: Brace treatment for symptomatic spondylolisthesis. Clin Orthop 236: 192–198, 1988

Bohlman, HH, Cook SS: One-stage decompression and posterolateral and interbody fusion for lumbosacral spondyloptosis through a posterior approach. J Bone Joint Surg 64A:415–418, 1982

Boxall D, Bradford DS, Winter RB, Moe JH: Management of severe spondylolisthesis in children and adolescents. J Bone Joint Surg 61A:479–495, 1979

Bradford DS: Management of spondylolithesis and spondylolithesis. Instructional course lectures XXXII. American Academy of Orthopaedic Surgeons. St Louis, CV Mosby, 1983, pp 151–162

Bradford DS: Treatment of severe spondylolisthesis. A combined approach for reduction and stabilization. Spine 4:423–429, 1979

Bradford DS, Gotfried Y: Staged salvage reconstruction of grade-IV and V spondylolisthesis. J Bone Joint Surg 69A:191–195, 1987

Bradford DS, Iza J: Repair of the defect in spondylolysis or minimal degrees of spondylolisthesis by segmental wire fixation and bone grafting. Spine 10:673–679, 1985

Brown CW, Orme TJ, Richardson HD: The rate of pseudoarthrosis (surgical nonunion) in patients who are smokers and patients who are nonsmokers: A comparison study. Spine 11:942–943, 1986

DeWald RL, Faut MM, Taddonio RF, Neuwirth MG: Severe lumbosacral spondylolisthesis in adolescents and children. Reduction and staged circumferential fusion. J Bone Joint Surg 63A:619–626, 1981

Fredrickson BE, Baker D, McHolick WJ, et al: The natural history of spondylolysis and spondylolisthesis. J Bone Joint Surg 66A:699–707, 1984

Freeman BL, Donati NL: Spinal arthrodesis for severe spondylolisthesis in children and adolescents: A long-term follow-up study. J Bone Joint Surg 71A:594–598, 1989

Gaines RW, Nichols WK: Treatment of spondyloptosis by two stage L5 vertebrectomy and reduction of L4 onto S1. Spine 10:680–686, 1985

Garfin SR, Heller J: The operative reduction of spondylolisthesis. Indications, results, complications. Semin Spine Surg 1:125–132, 1989

Hanley EN Jr, Levy JA: Surgical treatment of isthmic lumbosacral spondylolisthesis. Analysis of variables influencing results. Spine 14:48–50, 1989

Harris IE, Weinstein SL: Long-term follow-up of patients with grade III and IV spondylolisthesis. J Bone Joint Surg 69:960–969, 1987

Hensinger RN, Lang JR, MacEwen GD: Surgical management of spondylolisthesis in children and adolescents. Spine 1:207–216, 1976

Horowitch A, Peek RD, Thomas JC, et al: The Wiltse pedicle screw fixation system. Early clinical results. Spine 14:461–467, 1989

Jackson AM, Kirwan EOG, Sullivan MF: Lytic spondylolisthesis above the lumbosacral level. Spine 3:260–266, 1976

Johnson JR, Kirwan EOG: The long-term results of fusion in situ for severe spondylolisthesis. J Bone Joint Surg 65B:43–46, 1983

Jones AAM, McAfee PC, Robinson RA, et al: Failed arthrodesis of the spine for severe spondylolisthesis. J Bone Joint Surg 70A:25–30, 1988

Kane WJ: Direct current electrical bone growth stimulation for spinal fusion. Spine 13:363–365, 1988

Lowe J, Libson JLE, Nyska IZM, et al: Spondylolysis in the upper lumbar spine. A study of 32 patients. J Bone Joint Surg 69B:582–586, 1987

Maurice HD, Morley TR: Cauda equina lesions following fusion in situ and decompressive laminectomy for severe spondylolisthesis. Four case reports Spine 14:214–216, 1989

McQueen MM, Court-Brown C, Scott JH: Stabilization of spondylolisthesis using Dwyer instrumentation. J Bone Joint Surg 68B:185–188, 1986

Nicol RO, Scott JHS: Lytic spondylolysis. Repair by wiring. Spine 11:1027–1030, 1986

Osterman K, Lindholm TS, Laurent LE: Late results of removal of the loose posterior element (Gill's operation) in the treatment of lytic lumbar spondylolisthesis. Clin Orthop 117:121–128, 1976

Pedersen AK, Hagen R: Spondylolysis and spondylolisthesis. Treatment by internal fixation and bonegrafting of the defect. J Bone Joint Surg 70A:15–24, 1988

Peek RD, Wiltse LL, Reynolds JB, et al: In situ arthrodesis without decompression for grade III or IV isthmic spondylolisthesis in adults who have severe sciatica. J Bone Joint Surg 71A:62–68, 1989

Pizzutilo PD, Mirenda W, MacEwen GD: Posterolateral fusion for spondylolisthesis in adolescence. J Pediatr Orthop 6:311–316, 1986

Saraste H: Long-term clinical and radiological follow-up of spondylolysis and spondylolisthesis. J Pediatr Orthop 7:631–638, 1987

Scaglietti O, Frontino G, Bartolozzi P: Technique of anatomical reduction of lumbar spondylolisthesis and its surgical stabilization. Clin Orthop 117:164–175, 1976

Steffee AD, Sitkowski DJ: Reduction and stabilization of grade IV spondylolisthesis. Clin Orthop 227:82–89, 1988

Van Dan Oever M, Merrick MV, Scott JH: Bone scintigraphy in symptomatic spondylolysis. J Bone Joint Surg 69B:453–456, 1987

Velikas EP, Blackburne JS: Surgical treatment of spondylolisthesis in children and adolescents. J Bone Joint Surg 63B:67–70, 1981

Verbiest H: The treatment of lumbar spondyloptosis or impending lumbar spondyloptosis accompanied by neurologic deficit and/or neurogenic intermittent claudication. Spine 4:68–77, 1979

Whitecloud TS, Butler JC, Cohen JL, Candelora RD: Complications with variable spinal plating system. Spine 14:472–474, 1989

Wiltse LL: Spondylolisthesis in children. Clin Orthop 21:156–163, 1961

63
Cervical Disc Disease

I. General Considerations
A. Epidemiology
   1. Protruded intervertebral disc: more common in males and those 30–50 years of age
   2. Cervical spondylosis is more common in older patients
B. Pathogenesis
   1. Disc degeneration with referred pain
      a. Water content of the disc decreases with aging
      b. Posture and mechanical effects (occupational, diving, lifting, etc) may be pathogenic
      c. Cigarette smoking may be a risk factor
   2. Prolapsed intervertebral disc
      a. Large central herniation may cause cord impingement
      b. Lateral disc herniation may cause impingement of the root below
   3. Cervical spondylosis
      a. Multilevel degeneration of the discs and loss of intervertebral disc heights
      b. Osteophyte formation, particularly at the neurocentral joints or joints of Luschka, and root or cord impingement may result
      c. Kyphosis or decrease in cervical lordosis may result due to the loss of anterior disc heights and due to zygapophyseal joint subluxation posteriorly
C. Clinical categories
   1. Discogenic syndrome with referred pain
   2. Central disc herniation with myelopathy
   3. Lateral soft disc herniation and radiculopathy
   4. Lateral hard disc (cervical spondylosis) with radiculopathy
   5. Cervical spondylotic myelopathy
   6. Combination of above

II. Clinical Findings
A. Cervical radiculopathy (Table 7-1)
   1. Pain: location and radiation, depending on the level involved
   2. Neurologic findings: numbness, paresthesia, weakness, reflex changes
   3. Exacerbated by neck extension and ipsilateral lateral bending, and relieved by neck flexion, deviation to the opposite side, and shoulder abduction
   4. Neck flexion frequently reproduces radicular symptoms in acute soft disc herniation cases
B. Cervical myelopathy
   1. Pain and paresthesia not typical and variable
   2. Neurologic findings: gait disturbance, clumsy hands, spasticity, hyperreflexia, sphincter disturbance, and motor weakness worsening with activity
   3. Exacerbated by flexion (Lhermitte's sign)
C. X-ray findings
   1. Pain x-rays
      a. Clinical correlation is poor >40 years of age
      b. Anteroposterior, lateral, and oblique views may show narrowing of the intervertebral disc space, degenerative changes in the zygapophyseal joints, neurocentral joints, and foraminal encroachment
   2. Myelography
      a. Acute disc herniation is depicted by extradural filling defect and obliter-

Table 7-1 Clinical Symptoms and Findings of Cervical Nerve Root Involvement

Nerve Root	Disc Level	Clinical Symptoms and Findings
C3	C2-3	Pain and numbness in back of neck, particularly around mastoid process and pinna of ear; no readily detectable weakness or reflex change
C4	C3-4	Pain and numbness in back of neck, radiating along levator scapula muscle and occasionally down anterior chest; no readily detectable weakness or reflex change
C5	C4-5	Pain radiating from side of neck to shoulder top and numbness over the deltoid muscle; weakness and atrophy of the deltoid muscle; no reflex change
C6	C5-6	Pain radiating down the lateral side of arm and forearm, often into thumb and index fingers and numbness of tip of thumb or on dorsum of hand over first dorsal interosseus muscle; weakness of biceps muscle and depression of biceps reflex
C7	C6-7	Pain radiating down middle of forearm, usually to middle finger, although index and ring finger may be involved; weakness of triceps muscle and depression of triceps reflex
C8	C7-T1	Pain radiating down medial aspect of forearm to ring and small finger and numbness of small and medial portion of ring finger; intrinsic muscle atrophy and weakness and no reflex change

ation of the nerve root sleeve at a single level
   b. Cervical spondylosis
      (1) Nonfilling of the nerve root sleeve at one or more levels and extradural filling defects in radiculopathy cases
      (2) Flattening of the spinal cord and obstruction of the contrast flow in myelopathy cases
      (3) Multiple indentations anteriorly opposite the disc spaces and posteriorly by enfolding of the ligamentum flavum in cervical spondylotic myelopathy cases
   c. Disadvantages: difficult to differentiate soft vs hard disc protrusions, difficult to determine the extent of intradural lesions, such as syringomyelia, and additional pathology is missed if complete myelographic block is present
3. Computerized tomography
   a. Postmyelogram CT scan is recommended in older patients
   b. Evaluate location of osteophytes and cord compression better than myelogram
   c. Cervical canal is <10 mm in absolute stenosis, and between 10 and 13 mm in relative stenosis
4. Magnetic resonance imaging (Fig 7-9)
   a. Particularly useful for spinal cord lesions, such as cord compression, syringomyelia, tumors
   b. Excellent imaging of an acute herniated disc
   c. Bony margins and osteophytes are less well visualized, than CT scans
   d. May replace myelogram and CT scan
D. Electromyography
   1. Adjunctive test with radiculopathy or myelopathy
   2. Not necessary to diagnose classic cervical radiculopathy

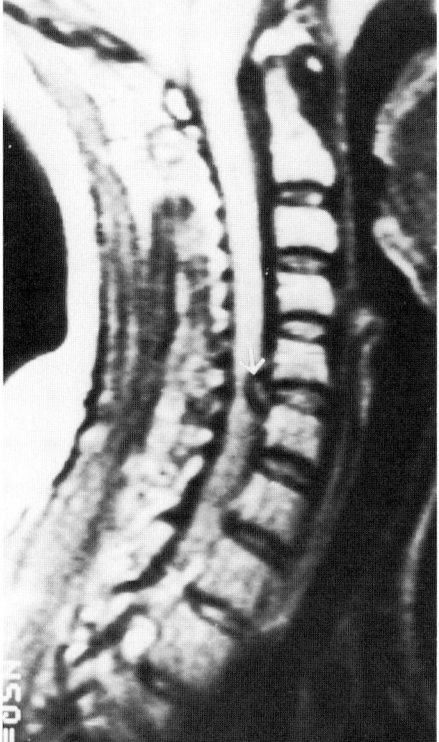

Figure 7-9. Sagittal magnetic resonance imaging of the cervical spine in a patient with a herniated C5-6 disc (arrow).

Table 7-2 Differential Diagnosis of Cervical Disc Disease

Neurologic
  Multiple sclerosis
  Amyotrophic lateral sclerosis
  Hydrocephalus
  Cervical cord tumors
  Syringomyelia
  Peripheral nerve entrapment neuropathies
  Brachial plexus injury or neuritis
  Thoracic outlet syndrome
Inflammatory
  Rhematoid arthritis
  Fibrositis (trigger point syndrome)
  Polymyalgia rheumatica
Neoplastic
  Metastatic disease
  Primary bone tumors
  Pancoast tumors
Infectious
  Vertebral osteomyelitis/discitis
Primary shoulder and upper extremity problems
  Subacromial bursitis
  Calcific tendinitis
  Biceps tendinitis
  Impingement syndrome of the shoulder
  Rotator cuff tear
  Glenohumeral arthritis
  Reflex sympathetic dystrophy
Cardiac ischemia

   3. Recommended to rule out other neurologic disorders, such as demyelinating diseases and peripheral neural entrapment syndromes or double crush phenomenon

III. Differential Diagnosis (Table 7-2)

A. Cervical radiculopathy
   1. Trauma: cervical sprain, traumatic neuritis (brachial plexus) and post-traumatic instability
   2. Tumors: superior sulcus tumor with C8 radiculopathy and Horner's syndrome and cord tumors
   3. Inflammatory conditions: neck and shoulder involvement
   4. Others: thoracic outlet syndrome, reflex sympathetic dystrophy, angina pectoris, and neurologic conditions

B. Myelopathy
   1. Trauma: post-traumatic instability
   2. Tumors: cervical cord tumors, bone tumors
   3. Neurologic conditions: demyelinating disease and anterior horn cell disease
   4. Congenital malformations

IV. Treatment

A. Conservative
   1. Soft collar, NSAIDs, and cervical pillow
   2. Traction is controversial
   3. Avoid narcotics and tranquilizers

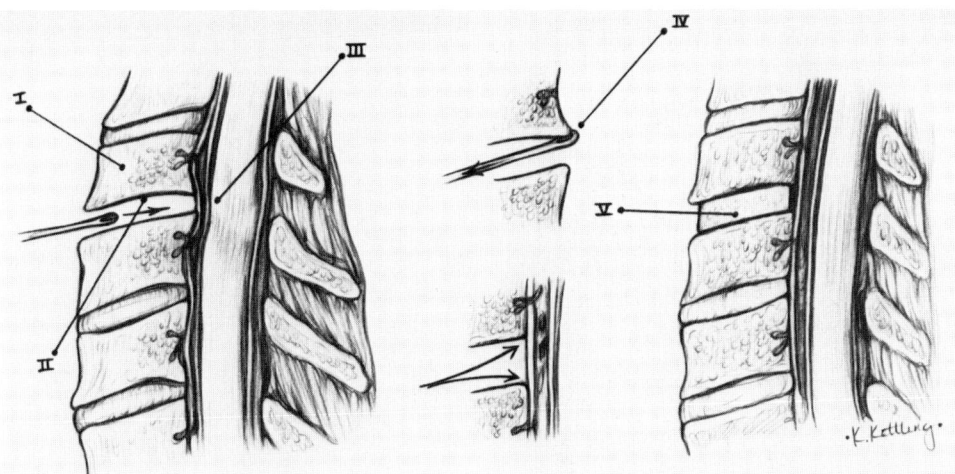

Figure 7-10. Anterior cervical discectomy and fusion. **A.** The annulus fibrosus, nucleus pulposus, and cartilaginous endplates (II) are removed. Vertebral body (I) and spinal cord (III) are shown. **B.** Removal of spurs may be required (IV). **C.** Bone graft (V) is inserted to distract the interspace (Modified from White AA, Southwick WO, DePonte RI et al: Relief of pain by anterior cervical spine fusion for spondylosis. J Bone Joint Surg 55A:523, 1973)

    4. Exercise and physical therapy modalities
    5. Infiltration of trigger points
  B. Operative indications
    1. Progressive signs of root or cord dysfunction
    2. Failure of conservative treatment to relieve pain
      a. Relief of arm pain or radiculopathy is predictable after surgery
      b. Neck pain alone should not be operative indication
  C. Surgical techniques
    1. Anterior approach
      a. Central soft disc herniation or bilateral radiculopathy at the same level should be approached anteriorly
      b. Unilateral soft disc or cervical spondylotic osteophyte causing radiculopathy may also be approached anteriorly (Fig 7-10)
      c. Spondylotic myelopathy at 1–3 levels
        (1) Discectomy and interbody fusion if cord compression is at the disc levels
        (2) Corpectomy and strut fusion if cord compression extends to the posterior vertebral margins (Fig 7-11)
      d. Stabilization after anterior procedures
        (1) Iliac crest bone or fibular strut grafts (Philadelphia collar is adequate after discectomy and interbody fusion, but halo vest is recommended following corpectomy and strut grafting)
        (2) Anterior plating is usually not necessary
      e. Complications
        (1) Neural injury (spinal cord injury, nerve root damage, dural tear)
        (2) Vascular injury (carotid artery, internal jugular vein, vertebral artery)
        (3) Vocal cord damage (recurrent laryngeal nerve injury)
        (4) Esophageal perforation
        (5) Tracheal injury
        (6) Horner's syndrome
        (7) Bone graft complications (extru-

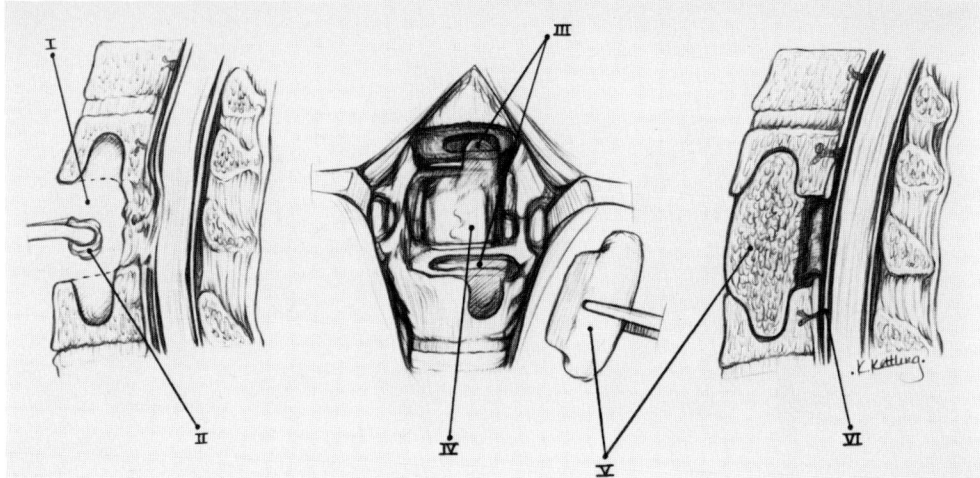

Figure 7-11. Vertebrectomy for cervical myelopathy. **A.** Removal of bone (II) from vertebral body (I) and osteophytes down to the posterior longitudinal ligament to relieve pressure on the spinal cord. **B.** Slots (III) to insert a tricortical iliac crest bone graft (V). Posterior longitudinal ligament or dura should be seen for adequate decompression. **C.** The bone graft extends from the upper endplate of the superior vertebra to the lower endplate of the inferior vertebra to be fused. There should be at least 5mm between the dura (VI) and the posterior part of the graft.

      sion, collapse, nonunion, donor site complications)
- (8) Infection
- (9) Wound problems (hematoma, drainage, dehiscence)
- (10) Anterior plate and screw fixation provides greater stability, but potential problems may be neural injury, esophageal injury, and hardware failure

2. Posterior approach (Fig 7-12)
   a. Unilateral soft disc or foraminal stenosis can be approached posteriorly by performing a partial facetectomy and foraminotomy with or without disc excision (Fig 7-13)
   b. Cervical spondylotic myelopathy due to multiple level disease may be treated by laminectomy and fusion or by laminoplasty (particularly for

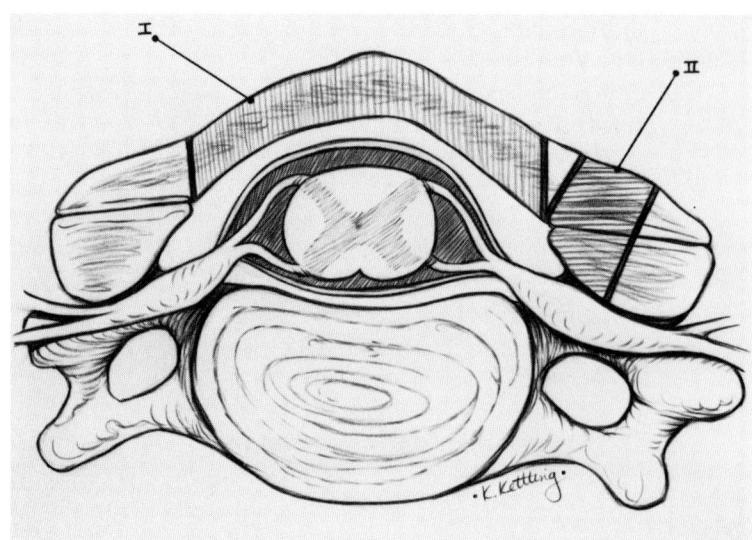

Figure 7-12. Illustration of laminectomy (I) and partial facetectomy (II).

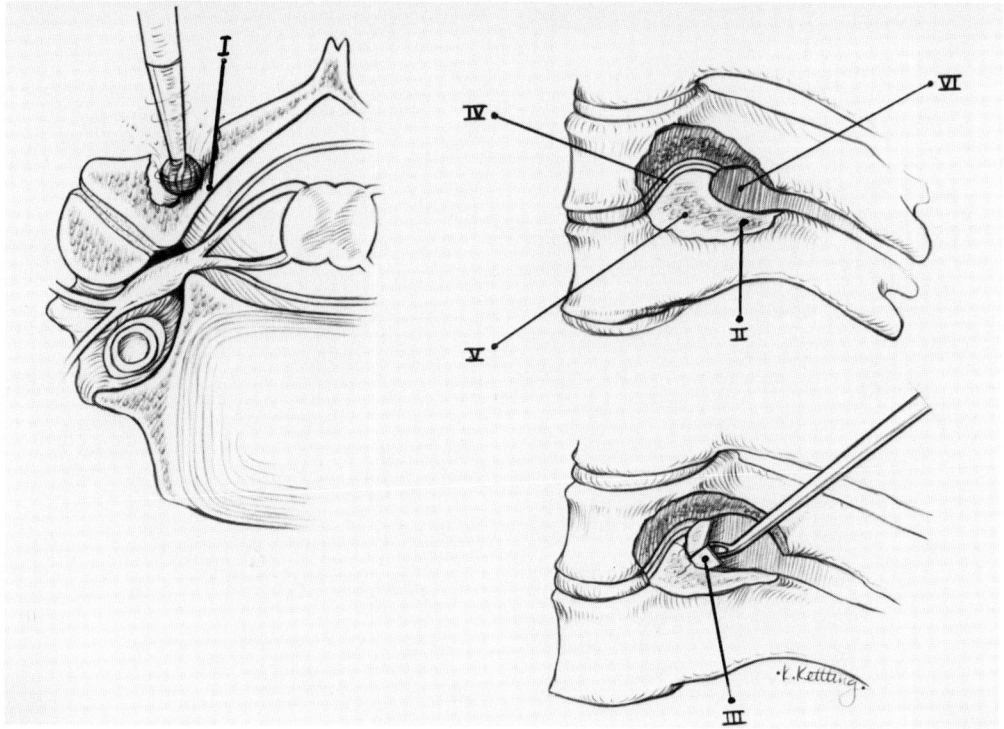

Figure 7-13. A partial facetectomy and foraminotomy for cervical radiculopathy. **A.** A diamond burr is used to thin the inner cortex (I). **B.** About 50% of facet (V), joint (IV), lateral portion of lamina (II), and the ligamentum flavum (VI) are removed. **C.** The thinned out bone (III) is removed with a currett.

congenital stenosis or ossification of posterior longitudinal ligament)
c. Posterior approach is preferred for more than three-level spondylotic myelopathy
d. Posterior stabilization after laminectomy
   (1) Wiring and facet fusion
   (2) Segmental instrumentation with Luque rod
   (3) Cervical posterior plating (Roy-Camille)
e. Complications
   (1) Neural complications: dural tear, nerve root deficit, spinal cord injury
   (2) Recurrence at the same or other levels
   (3) Instability after laminectomy

REFERENCES

Bohlman HH: Cervical spondylosis with moderate to severe myelopathy. Spine 2:151–162, 1977

Brown MD, Malinin TI, Davis PB: A roentgenographic evaluation of frozen allografts versus autografts in anterior cervical spine fusions. Clin Orthop 119:231–236, 1976

Bulger RF, Rejowski JE, Beatty RA: Vocal cord paralysis associated with anterior cervical fusion: Consideration for prevention and treatment. J Neurosurg 62:657–661, 1985

Callahan RA, Johnson RM, Margolis RN, et al: Cervical facet fusion for control of instability following laminectomy. J Bone Joint Surg 59A:991–1002, 1977

Clark CR: Cervical spondylotic myelopathy: History and physical findings. Spine 13:847–849, 1988

DePalma A, Rothman RH, Lewinnek G, Canale S: Anterior interbody fusion for severe disc degeneration. Surg Gynecol Obstet 134:755–758, 1972

Dillin W, Booth R, Cuckler J, et al: Cervical radiculopathy (a review). Spine 11:988–991, 1986

Ebraheim NA, An HS, Jackson WT, Brown JA: Internal fixation of the unstable cervical spine using posterior Roy-Camille plates: Preliminary report. J Orthop Trauma 3:23–28, 1989

Epstein JA: The surgical management of cervical canal stenosis, spondylosis, and myeloradiculopathy by means of posterior approach. Spine 13:864, 1988

Epstein JA, Carras R, Epstein BS, Lavine LS: Cervical myelopathy caused by developmental stenosis of the spinal canal. J Neurosurg 51:362, 1979

Fager CA: Posterolateral approach to ruptured median and paramedian cervical disk. Surg Neurol 20:443–452, 1983

Fager CA: Results of adequate posterior decompression in the relief of spondylotic cervical myelopathy. J Neurosurg 38:684, 1973

Flynn TB: Neurologic complications of anterior cervical interbody fusion. Spine 7:536–539, 1982

Gore DR, Sepic SB: Anterior cervical fusion for degenerated or protruded discs: A review of one hundred forty-six patients. Spine 9:667–671, 1984

Gore DR, Sepic SB, Gardner GM, Murray MP: Neck pain: A long term follow-up of 205 patients. Spine 12:1, 1987

Henderson CM, Hennessy RG, Shuey HM, Shackelford EG: Posterior-lateral foraminotomy as an exclusive operative technique for cervical radiculopathy: A review of 846 consecutively operated cases. Neurosurgery 13:504–512, 1983

Herkowitz HN: A comparison of anterior cervical fusion, cervical laminectomy, and cervical laminoplasty for the surgical management of multiple level spondylotic radiculopathy. Spine 13:774–780, 1988

Herkowitz H: The surgical management of cervical spondylotic radiculopathy and myelopathy. Clin Orthop 239:94–108, 1989

Hirabayashi K, Satomi K: Operative procedure and results of expansive open door laminoplasty. Spine 13:870–876, 1988

Hirabayashi K, Watanabe K, Wakano K, et al: Expansive open-door laminoplasty for cervical spinal stenotic myelopathy. Spine 8:693, 1983

Hukuda S, Mochizuki T, Ogata M, et al: Operations for cervical spondylotic myelopathy. J Bone Joint Surg 67B:609–615, 1985

Kikuchi S, Macnab I: Localization of the level of symptomatic cervical disc degeneration. J Bone Joint Surg 63B:272–277, 1981

Kimura I, Oh-Hama M, Shingu H, Yonago K: Cervical myelopathy treated by canal-expansive laminoplasty. J Bone Joint Surg 66A:914–920, 1984

LaRocca H: Cervical spondylotic myelopathy: Natural history. Spine 13:854, 1988

Lunsford LD, Bissonette DJ, Jannetta PJ, et al: Anterior surgery for cervical disc disease. Part 1: Treatment of lateral cervical herniation in 253 cases. J Neurosurg 53:1–11, 1980

Magnaes B, Hauge T: Surgery for myelopathy in cervical spondylosis: Safety measures and reoperative factors related to outcome. Spine 5:211, 1980

Mikawa Y, Shikata J, Yamamuro T: Spinal deformity and instability after multilevel cervical laminectomy. Spine 12:6–11, 1987

Miyazaki K, Kirita Y: Extensive simultaneous multisegment laminectomy for myelopathy due to the ossification of the posterior longitudinal ligament in the cervical region. Spine 11:531–542, 1986

Murphy F, Simmons JCH, Brunson B: Cervical treatment of laterally ruptured cervical discs: Review of 648 cases, 1939–1972. J Neurosurg 38:679–683, 1973

Riley LH, Robinson RA, Johnson KA, et al: The results of anterior interbody fusion of the cervical spine. Review of ninety-three consecutive cases. J Neurosurg 30:127–133, 1969

Robinson RA, Walker AE, Ferlic DC, et al: The results of anterior interbody fusion of the cervical spine. J Bone Joint Surg 44A:1569, 1962

Sim FH, Sivien HJ, Bickel WH, et al: Swan neck deformity. A Review of twenty-one cases. J Bone Joint Surg 56A:564–580, 1974

Simmons, EH, Bhalla SK: Anterior cervical discectomy and fusion. A clinical and biomechanical study with eight-year follow-up. J Bone Joint Surg 51B:225–232, 1969

Simeone FA, Dillin WA: Treatment of cervical disc disease: Selection of operative approach. Contemp Neurosurg 8(14):1–6, 1986

Simeone FA, Rothman RH: Cervical disc disease in the spine. Rothman RH, Simeone FA, eds. Philadelphia, WB Saunders, 1982

Teresi LM, Lufkin RB, Reicher MA, et al: Asymptomatic degeneration disk disease and spondylosis of the cervical spine: MR imaging. Radiology 164:83–88, 1987

White AA III, Southwick WO, DePonte RJ, et al: Relief of pain by anterior cervical fusion for spondylosis — a report of sixty-five patients. J Bone Joint Surg 55A:525–534, 1973

Whitecloud TS: Anterior surgery for cervical spondylotic myelopathy (Smith-Robinson, Cloward and vertebrectomy). Spine 13:861–863, 1988

Whitecloud TS, LaRocca H: Fibular strut graft in reconstructive surgery of the cervical spine. Spine 1:33–43, 1976

Whitecloud TS III, Seago RA: Cervical discogenic syndrome. Results of operative intervention in patients with positive discography. Spine 12:313–316, 1987

Williams JL, Allen MB Jr, Harness JW: Late results of cervical discectomy and interbody fusion: Some factors influencing the results. J Bone Joint Surg 50A:227, 1968

Williams RW: Microcervical foraminotomy. Spine 8:708–716, 1983

Yonenobu K, Fuji T, Ono K, et al: Choice of surgical treatment for multisegmental cervical spondylotic myelopathy. Spine 10:710–716, 1985

64

Lumbar Disc Disease and Spinal Stenosis

LUMBAR DISC DISEASE

I. General Considerations
A. Incidence: 80% of the general population will experience back pain and only 2–3% have sciatica
B. Age
   1. Mean age of onset: about 35 years
   2. Unusual <20 years and >60 years of age
   3. Herniated disc in children is rare but slippage of entire disc and vertebral end plate or "slipped vertebral apophyses" may mimic herniated discs
   4. Herniated disc in the elderly is also uncommon but may be associated with spinal stenosis
C. Sex ratio is equal but females present a decade later on the average
D. Natural history of low-back pain and sciatica
   1. Recovery in 50–60% in 1 week, 95% recovery in 3 months can be expected in patients with low-back pain, but about 50% recovery in 1 month and 75% recovery is expected in patients with sciatica
   2. Results after surgery are better than conservative treatment after 1 year but no significant difference 4–10 years later
   3. No loss of quality of surgical result by waiting until 3 months of observation except patients with cauda equina syndrome and progressive neurologic deficits
E. Epidemiologic factors contributing to low-back pain
   1. Certain occupations involving lifting heavy objects and heavy vibration
   2. Certain sports, particularly diving from a board
   3. Driving certain motor vehicles
   4. Large number of pregnancies
   5. Cigarette smoking
   6. Sedentary life-style
   7. Anxiety and depression
F. Socioeconomic impact: 30 billion dollars per year, but 80% of the cost is by chronic back pain patients, which make up only 10% of all back patients

II. Pathology
A. Intervertebral disc degeneration
   1. Degeneration or lumbar spondylosis
      a. Decreased water content (normally 88%, which decreases to 60% by 8th decade) and decreased proteoglycan content of the nucleus pulposus
      b. Narrowing of the disc space, which strains the facet joints posteriorly
      c. Osteophyte formation at the attachments of the longitudinal ligaments or annulus fibrosis and facet joints
      d. Traction spurs that are horizontally oriented due to segmental instability
      e. Of people over 55 years of age, 80% have degenerated disc changes by radiographic criteria
   2. Herniation
      a. Types
         (1) Protrusion: annulus tear
         (2) Extrusion: posterior longitudinal ligament tear
         (3) Sequestered: complete displacement with free disc fragment
      b. Locations (Fig 7-14)
         (1) Most common at L4-L5 and L5-S1 and rarely at high lumbar and thoracic regions

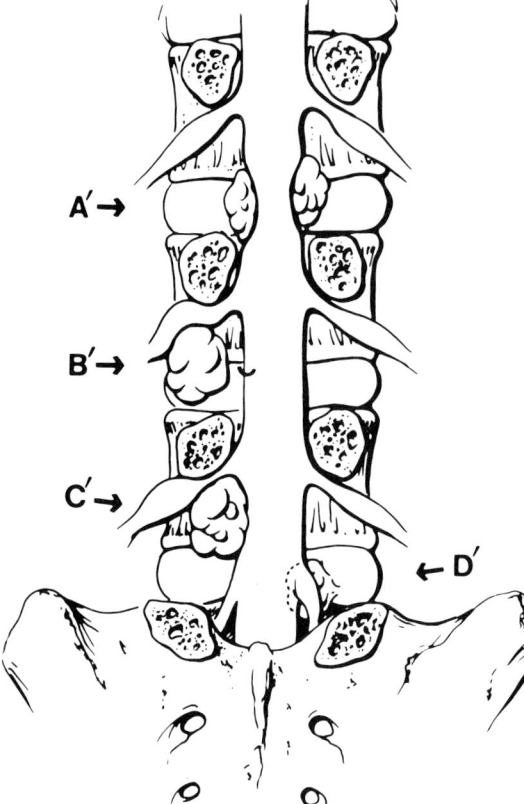

Figure 7-14. Pathologic variations of lumbar disc herniations. A': large central herniation; B': foraminal or far lateral herniation; C': left axillary herniation; D': classic posterolateral disc herniation. (From Stambough JL: Surgical techniques for lumbar discectomy. Semin Spine Surg 1:52, 1989. Reprinted with permission.)

      (2) Classically, posterolateral herniation with impingement of the nerve below (85% incidence)
      (3) Axillary herniations compress the nerve above (3% incidence)
      (4) Central herniation may cause back pain without radiculopathy or cauda equina syndrome (12% incidence)
      (5) Extreme lateral or foraminal herniation is more common in older patients, and relatively higher at L3 and L4 levels (5%)
      (6) Intradural herniation is extremely rare
      (7) Herniation at two different levels presenting at the same time is also uncommon
  B. Posterior joints
    1. Synovial reaction, cartilage destruction, osteophyte formation, capsular laxity, and subluxation
    2. Spinal stenosis: due to disc space narrowing, the facet joints undergo subluxation and hypertrophy, causing nerve root compression
  C. Nerve roots
    1. Anatomy
      a. Each nerve root exits below the pedicle and above the disc (ie, L5 nerve exits below the L5 pedicle and exits above the L5-S1 disc)
      b. Dorsal root ganglion lies in the intervertebral foramen, which may be the main source of pain
      c. Three branches: ventral ramus for motor function, sinuvertebral nerve to the annulus of the disc, and dorsal ramus for facets and posterior muscles
    2. Nerve root anomalies (Kadish and Simmons)
      a. Type I: intradural anastomosis
      b. Type II: anomalous origin of nerve roots
      c. Type III: extradural anastomosis
      d. Type IV: extradural division
    3. Furcal nerve: arise from L4 root and gives branches to femoral, obturator, and lumbosacral trunk (L4 compression may give referred pain to other areas)
    4. Vasculature
      a. Proximal and distal radicular arteries anastomosis in the proximal third of the root in the foramen, which may be a vascular-deficient area
      b. Intrinsic vasculature: interfascicular and intrafascicular vessels with com-

pensating coils and arteriovenous anastomosis allow considerable interfascicular motion and stretch of the root
      c. Thin pia allows exchange of metabolites with cerebrospinal fluid
      d. Mechanical compression causes vascular compression, which is manifested in neuroischemic claudication clinically
   5. Cysts or tumors such as synovial cyst, perineural cyst, or neurofibroma may mimic a herniated disc

III. Clinical Findings
A. History
   1. Sciatica
      a. Leg pain frequently becomes greater than back pain in large extruded or sequestered disc cases, but leg pain resolves with time in most protruded disc cases
      b. Leg pain is in a dermatomal distribution
      c. Pain is worse with sitting, coughing, sneezing, and forward bending
      d. Pain is usually alleviated by lying and rest
   2. Patients may have paresthesia and numbness in a dermatomal distribution
   3. Weakness or cauda equina syndrome may be presenting symptoms
   4. Mental status, drug history, industrial, or medicolegal status must be accurately determined
B. Examination
   1. Spasm and leaning posture, tenderness of the involved muscle in the leg, and decreased range of motion, particularly with flexion
   2. Root irritation: straight leg raising (SLR) tests
      a. Leseque SLR test: most important sign for detecting nerve root irritation
      b. Flip test: positive SLR lying down but negative SLR on sitting, which suggests malingering
      c. Contralateral SLR test is almost always pathognomonic of root impingement and suggests a sequestered disc fragment
      d. Reverse SLR should be done for L3 or L4 nerve root involvement
   3. Root compression signs: muscle weakness, wasting, sensory impairment, reflex changes
   4. Nonorganic tests for chronic pain (Waddell et al): three of five tests signify patients with malingering or other secondary gains
      a. Nonanatomic superficial tenderness
      b. Simulation tests (axial loading and rotation)
      c. Flip test
      d. Nonanatomic weakness and sensory findings
      e. Overreaction
   5. Pain drawing and Minnesota Multiphasic Personality Inventory (MMPI) test may be helpful in chronic back patients
C. Diagnostic studies
   1. Correlation with history and physical examination is most important
   2. Defer until 6–8 weeks after initial conservative treatment
   3. X-ray studies
      a. Plain x-rays: detect spondylolisthesis, tumor, infection, and spondylosis but nondiagnostic in herniated disc cases
      b. CT scan
         (1) Accurate for herniated disc and stenosis cases in 65–75%
         (2) Postmyelogram CT scan gives additional information in about 12%
         (3) Better than myelogram for foraminal disc herniation and for lateral recess stenosis
         (4) False-positive rates are high (36%)

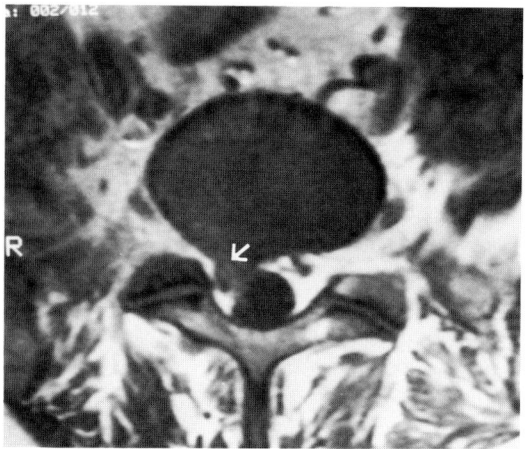

Figure 7-15. Axial magnetic resonance imaging of the lumbosacral spine in a patient with a herniated right L5-S1 disc (arrow).

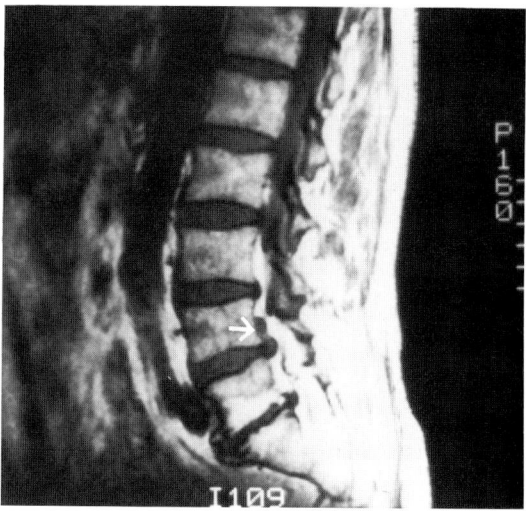

Figure 7-16. Sagittal magnetic resonance imaging of the lumbosacral spine in a patient with a sequestered L4-L5 disc with superior migration (arrow).

      c. Myelogram
        (1) Accurate for herniated disc and stenosis in 83%
        (2) Iohexol gives less side effects than metrizamide
        (3) False-positive rates are also high (37%)
      d. MRI is as good as myelogram or CT scan and is becoming the procedure of choice (false-positive rates are about 20% for herniated disc) (Figs 7-15, 7-16)
      e. Discography is rarely useful except to reproduce pain in discogenic syndrome patients without radiculopathy
      f. Bone scan if suspicious of tumor, infection or spondylolysis
    4. Electrodiagnostic tests are not routinely necessary except to rule out other neurologic disorders and if clinical correlation is not exact
    5. Injections of facets, root sleeves, or epidural space for certain diagnoses and for temporary pain relief

IV. Differential Diagnoses (Table 7-3)
A. Viscerogenic: kidney, uterine, prostate problems
B. Vascular: aortic aneurysm
C. Neurogenic: spinal cord tumors or cysts
D. Psychogenic: disability, medicolegal, and camptocormia
E. Spondylogenic
    1. Myofascial sprains and strains: iliolumbar syndrome, piriformis syndrome, quadratus lumborum syndrome, and fibrositis (trigger point syndrome)
    2. Inflammatory diseases: ankylosing spondylitis, Reiter's syndrome, inflammatory bowel diseases, and psoriatic arthritis
    3. Disc rupture, facet syndrome, spinal stenosis, and segmental instability
    4. Fractures especially osteoporotic compression fractures
    5. Neoplasms: myeloma, metastasis, and primary tumors
    6. Infections

V. Treatment
A. Conservative treatment
    1. Proven methods: patient education (decrease mechanical stress, and back school) and cardiovascular fitness pro-

Table 7-3 Differential Diagnosis of Low Back Pain

Congenital defects
  Facet tropism
  Lumbarization or sacralization
  Dysplastic spondylolisthesis
Neoplasms
  Metastatic tumors
  Primary bone tumors (benign and malignant)
  Intraspinal tumors (spinal cord and nerve root tumors)
Infections
  Osteomyelitis
  Epidural abscess
  Discitis
Inflammations
  Seronegative spondylitis (ankylosing spondylitis, Reiter's syndrome, psoriatic spondylitis, inflammatory bowel diseases)
  Sacrolilitis
  Isolated disc resorption
Metabolic diseases
  Osteoporosis or osteomalacia
  Paget's disease (Altman)
  Hyperparathyroidism
  Gout
Neurologic diseases
  Neuropathies
  Demyelinating diseases
  Transverse myelitis
Trauma
  Muscle strain
  Ligamentous sprain
  Compression fractures
  Spondylolysis and spondylolisthesis
Dengenerative diseases
  Herniated disc or annular tear
  Spinal stenosis
  Mechanical instability
  Internal disc disruption syndrome
Visceral diseases
  Genitourinary disorders
  Uterine and ovarian diseases
  Gastrointestinal disorders
  Vascular diseases and aortic aneurysm
Miscellaneous diseases
  Piriformis syndrome
  Iliolumbar syndrome
  Facet syndrome
  Quadratus lumborum syndrome
  Meralgia paresthetica
  Vertebral sclerosis
Postsurgical problems
  Osteolysis
  Arachnodinitis
  Instability
  Postfusion stenosis
  Recurrent disc herniation
Psychosocial problems
  Compensation or litigation involvement
  Drug addiction
  Hysterical conversion state

---

grams such as swimming and bicycling and appropriate back exercise
2. Unproven methods: prolonged bed rest, muscle relaxants, traction, braces, and manipulation
3. Avoid narcotics
4. Initial treatment usually consists of short duration of bed rest (1 week), NSAIDs, and gradual increase in mobilization and cardiovascular fitness exercises, such as walking, swimming, or bicycling, and back stabilizing exercise (successful in 80–90%)

B. Invasive treatment
1. Epidural steroids are not proven to be helpful but may be used for leg pain if NSAID's do not work
2. Chemonucleolysis is less used because of anaphylactic and neural complications
3. Surgery
  a. Indications of surgery
    (1) Failure of conservative treatments for at least 6 weeks
    (2) Radicular pain or neurologic deficits
    (3) Positive imaging studies that correlate with symptoms
  b. Laminotomy and discectomy without fusion is the gold standard treatment (Fig 7-17, Fig 7-18)
  c. Microdiscectomy may miss associated pathology, such as sequestered disc, facet impingement, and foraminal stenosis
  d. Percutaneous techniques are for non-

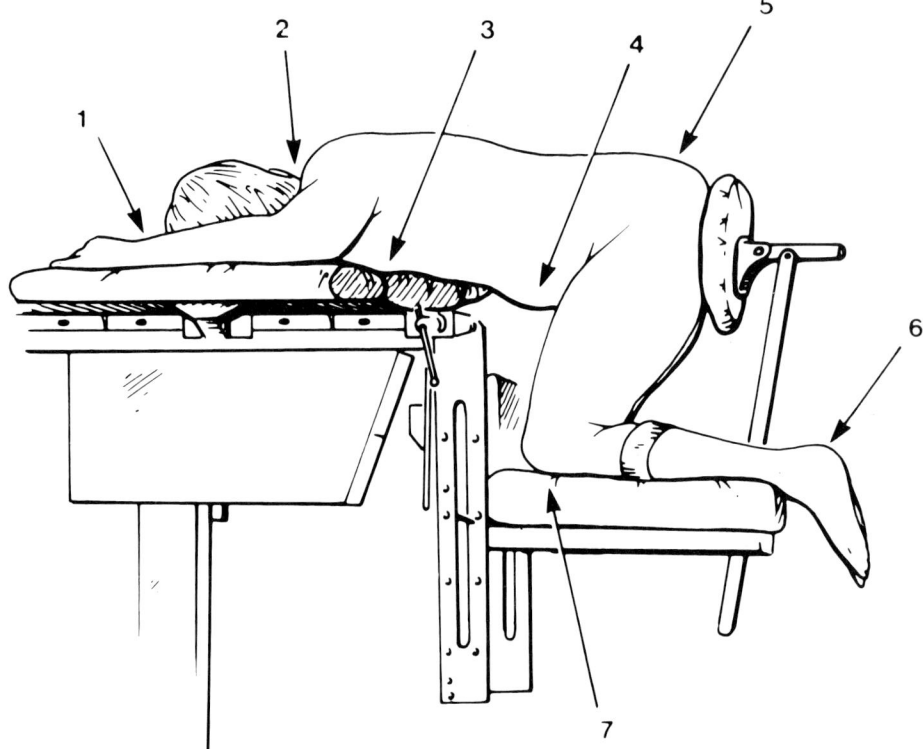

Figure 7-17. Position of the patient for lumbar disc and spinal stenosis surgery. The patient is prone in a kneeling posture. The arm is positioned at 90° or less of abduction (1), and the neck is not hyperextended (2). The ulnar nerves and axillae are padded (3). The abdomen is hanging free (4). The lumbar spine is slightly hyperextended (5). Antithrombotic stockings are worn (6). The patient rests on the chest and both knees, providing three-point stability (7). (From Stambough JL: Surgical techniques for lumbar discectomy, Semin Spine Surg 1:48, 1989. Reprinted with permission.)

   sequestered or contained herniated disc cases (results are inferior to laminotomy)
   e. Aggressive surgical approach should be taken if progressive motor deficit is noted
   f. Surgical emergency if cauda equina syndrome

SPINAL STENOSIS

General Considerations
A. Definition: narrowing of the spinal canal (central stenosis) or the lateral recess (lateral stenosis) with neural impingement that produces symptoms of radiculopathy
B. Spinal stenosis is an aging process, and therefore it is significant only if clinically symptomatic
C. More common after fifth decade

II. Classification
A. Congenital: usually developmental and central canal stenosis
   1. Idiopathic
   2. Achondroplastic
B. Acquired
   1. Degenerative stenosis
      a. Lateral stenosis: enlargement of superior facet
      b. Central stenosis: enlargement of inferior facet

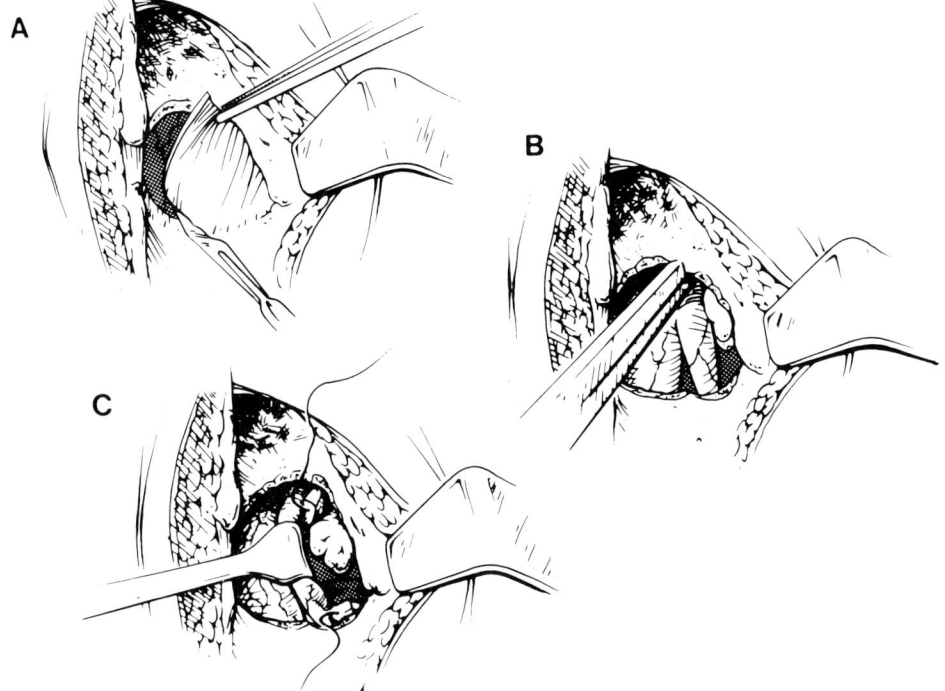

Figure 7-18. A. The interlaminar exposure starts with removal of the ligament flava. **B.** Further removal of laminar bone is done until the lateral portion of the nerve root is visualized with a punch working parallel to the lumbar nerve roots. **C.** The nerve root is protected by placing cotton surgical pads cephalad and caudad to the nerve root, and the nerve root is retracted medially to expose the herniated disc. (From Stambough, JL: Surgical techniques for lumbar discectomy. Semin Spine Surg 1:50, 1989. Reprinted with permission.)

2. Degenerative spondylolisthesis: L5 nerve is entrapped between the inferior facet of L4 and the posterior aspect of the body of L5
3. Combined: disc herniation, developmental and acquired stenosis may coexist
4. Iatrogenic: postlaminectomy, postfusion, post disc surgery
5. Post-traumatic changes
6. Miscellaneous: Paget's, fluorosis

III. Pathogenesis

A. Three joint complex: two posterior joints and the disc are all involved in the pathogenesis
B. L4-L5 level is usually first involved
C. Degenerative changes of the three joint complex secondary to repeated rotational and compression injuries
  1. Intervertebral discs develop circumferential and radial tears, internal disruption, and loss of disc height
  2. Posterior joints undergo synovitis, cartilage destruction, osteophyte formation, capsular laxity, and instability
D. Multilevel degenerative stenosis later

IV. Clinical Findings

A. Pain
  1. Variable
  2. Typically in the lower back, buttock, and the lower extremities
  3. Pain is worse with standing, hyperextension, and walking, but often relieved by rest, flexed posture, and sitting

4. History is the key in making the diagnosis of spinal stenosis
B. Claudication-like symptoms in 50%: rule out vascular claudication
C. Physical examination: paucity of objective findings, sciatic tension sign is usually negative, and neurologic deficits may or may not be present
D. Diagnostic tools
 1. Plain x-rays reveal spondylosis
 2. Electromyography (EMG) is 75% positive, but usually not necessary for making the diagnosis
 3. Myelography typically shows hourglass constrictions or complete block and root impingements
 4. CT scan is helpful in assessing canal dimensions, particularly of the lateral recess
 5. MRI is becoming more useful, but bony details are not as well demonstrated as on CT scans

V. Differential Diagnoses

A. Trauma (sprains, strains, compression fractures)
B. Infections (vertebral osteomyelitis)
C. Inflammatory disorders
D. Congenital defects (achondroplasia)
E. Metabolic (osteoporosis, Paget's disease)
F. Degenerative (disc herniation, facet syndrome)
G. Neoplasms (intraspinal, bone tumors, metastasis)
H. Neurologic disorders (peripheral neuropathies)
I. Circulatory (abdominal aortic aneurysm, vascular claudication)
J. Myofascial syndromes
K. Psychoneurotic problems

VI. Treatment

A. Conservative: NSAIDs, lumbosacral corsets, exercises, epidural steroids, and facet injection. Conservative treatment is not usually successful for severe spinal stenosis patients

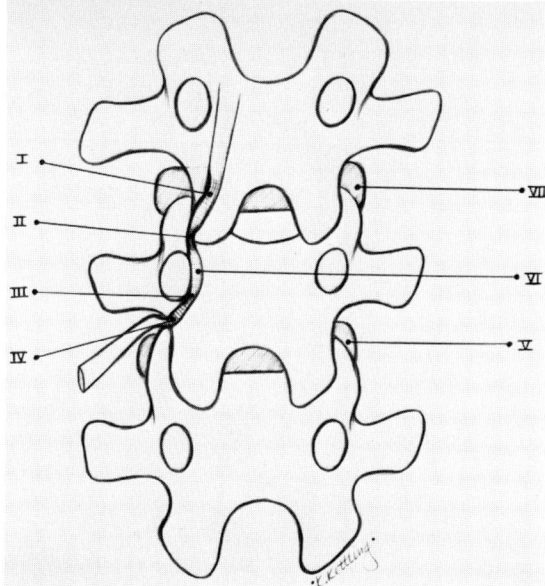

Figure 7-19. A nerve root may be impinged by many pathological processes. The most cephalad site is the posterolaterally herniated disc (I), followed by subarticular facet or lateral recess (II). The pedicular kinking may be pathogenic in disc collapse, scoliosis, or spondylolisthesis cases (III). Finally, foraminal stenosis (IV) by a far lateral herniated disc or facet subluxation may cause root impingement. The cephalad disc (VII), caudad disc (V), and the pedicle that bears the same number as the nerve root may involve in the entrapment of the spinal nerve.

B. Surgery if symptoms are significant to alter their quality of life
 1. Surgical techniques
  a. Positioning: kneeling with abdomen free with the spine in hyperextended position
  b. Control bleeding with bipolar cautery
  c. Headlight and magnifying glasses
  d. Correct level: expose the sacrum and take x-ray
  e. Decompression (Fig 7-19)
   (1) Central laminectomy
   (2) Lateral recess: remove overgrown superior facet by undercutting
   (3) Foraminal decompression: if the nerve root is tight after laminectomy and facet undercutting,

five additional sites may be responsible for nerve compression
  i. Superior facet against posterior vertebral body
  ii. Superior facet against pedicle
  iii. Superior facet or pedicle against bulging lateral annulus
  iv. Inferior facet and vertebral body (degenerative spondylolisthesis)
  v. Transverse processes of L5 and sacral ala (far out syndrome)
2. Fusion is usually not necessary unless more than a total of one facet excision has been performed or if spondylolisthesis has been present preoperatively

REFERENCES

Arnoldi CC, Brodsky AE, Cauchoix J, et al: Lumbar spinal stenosis and nerve root entrapment syndromes. Definition and classification. Clin Orthop 115:4–5, 1976

Aurori BF, Weierman RJ, Lowell HA, et al: Pseudoarthrosis after spinal fusion for scoliosis (a comparison of autogeneic and allogeneic bone grafts). Clin Orthop 199:153–158, 1985

Bell GR, Rothman RH: The conservative treatment of sciatica. Spine 9:54, 1984

Bell GR, Rothman RH, Booth RE, et al: A study of computer-assisted tomography. II. Comparison of metrizamide myelography and computed tomography in the diagnosis of herniated lumbar disc and spinal stenosis. Spine 9:782–787, 1984

Bernard TN Jr, Kirkaldy-Willis WH: Recognizing specific characteristics of nonspecific lowback pain. Clin Orthop 217:266–280, 1987

Bernini PM, Wiesel WW, Rothman RH: Metrizamide myelography and the identification of anomalous lumbosacral nerve roots. J Bone Joint Surg 62A:1203–1208, 1980

Booth RE: Spinal stenosis. In Anerson LD, ed. The American Academy Orthopaedic Surgeons: Instructional course lectures. St Louis, CV Mosby, 1986

Brodsky AE: Post-laminectomy and post-fusion stenosis of the lumbar spine. Clin Orthop 115:130–139, 1976

Brown CW, Orme TJ, Richardson HD: The rate of pseudoarthrosis (surgical nonunion) in patients who are smokers and patients who are nonsmokers: A comparison study. Spine 11:942–943, 1986

Burton CV, Kirkady-Willis WH, Yong-Hing K, Heithoff KH: Causes of failure of surgery on the lumbar spine. Clin Orthop 157:191, 1981

Cady LD Jr, Thomas PC, Karwasky RJ: Program for increasing health and physical fitness of fire fighters. J Occup Med 27:110–114, 1985

Cannon BW, Hunter SE, Picaza JA: Nerve root anomalies in lumbar disc surgery. J Neurosurg 19:208–214, 1961

Cauchoix J, Ficat, C, Girard B: Repeat surgery after disc excision. Spine 3:265, 1978

Crawshaw C, Fraxer A, Merriam WF: A comparison of surgery and chemonucleolysis in the treatment of sciatica: A prospective randomized trial. Spine 9:195, 1984

Crock HV: Observations on the management of failed spinal operations. J Bone Joint Surg 58B:193, 1976

Cuckler JM, Bernini PA, Wiesel SW, et al: The use of epidural steroids in the treatment of lumbar radicular pain: A prospective, randomized, double-blinded study. J Bone Joint Surg 67A:63–66, 1985

DePalma AF, Rothman RH: The nature of pseudoarthrosis. Clin Orthop 59:113–118, 1968

DePalma AF, Rothman RH: Surgery of the lumbar spine. Clin Orthop 63:162, 1969

Deyo RA: Conservative therapy for low back pain: Distinguishing useful from useless therapy. JAMA 250:1057–1062, 1983

Deyo RA, Diehl AK, Rosenthal M: How many days of bedrest for acute low back pain? N Engl J Med 315:1064–1070, 1986

Eismont FJ, Wiesel SW, Rothman RH: The treatment of dural tears associated with spinal surgery. J Bone Joint Surg 63A:1132, 1981

Fager CA, Freiberg SR: Analysis of failures and poor results of lumbar spine surgery. Spine 5:87–94, 1980

Feffer HL, Wiesel SW, Cuckler JM, Rothman RH: Degenerative spondylolisthesis. To fuse or not to fuse. Spine 10:287–289, 1985

Finnegan WJ, Fenlin JM, Marvel JP, et al: Results of surgical intervention in the symptomatic multiple-operated back patient: Analysis of sixty-seven cases followed for three to seven years. J Bone Joint Surg 61A:1077, 1979

Frymoyer JW: Back pain and sciatica. N Engl J Med 315:1090–1092, 1986

Frymoyer JW, Cats-Baril W: Predictors of low back pain disability. Clin Orthop 221:89–98, 1987

Frymoyer JW, Hanley E, Howe J, et al: A comparison of radiographic findings in fusion and nonfusion patients. Ten or more years following lumbar disc surgery. Spine 4:435–440, 1979

Frymoyer, JW, Hanley E, Howe, J, et al: Disc excision and spine fusion in the management of lumbar disc disease. A minimum ten-year follow-up. Spine 3:1–6, 1978

Frymoyer JW, Matteri RE, Hanley EN, et al: Failed lumbar disc surgery requiring second operation: A long term follow-up study. Spine 3:7, 1978

Frymoyer JW, Newberg A, Pope MH, et al: Spine radiographs in patients with low-back pain: An epidemiological study in men. J Bone Joint Surg 66A:1048–1055, 1984

Hazlett JW, Kinnard P: Lumbar apophyseal process excision and spinal instability. Spine 7:171, 1982

Herron LD, Trippi AC: L4-5 degenerative spondylolisthesis. The results of treatment by decompressive laminectomy without fusion. Spine 14:534, 1989

Holmes HE, Rothman RH: The Pennsylvania plan: An algorithm for the management of lumbar degenerative disc disease. Spine 4:15, 1979

Johnsson KE, Willner S, Johnsson K: Postoperative instability after decompression for lumbar spinal stenosis. Spine 11:107–110, 1986

Jones AM, Stambough JL, Balderston RA, et al: Long-term results of lumbar spine surgery complicated by unintended incidental durotomy. Spine 14:443, 1989

Kadish L, Simmons EH: Anomalies of the lumbosacral nerve roots and anatomical investigation and myelographic study. J Bone Joint Surg 66B:411, 1984

Kahanovitz N, Viola K, Muculloch J: Limited surgical discectomy and microdiscectomy. A clinical comparison. Spine 14:79–81, 1989

Kirkaldy-Willis WH: The relationship of structural pathology to the nerve root. Spine 9:49–52, 1984

Kirkaldy-Willis WH, Hill RJ: A more precise diagnosis for low-back pain. Spine 4:102–109, 1979

Knapp DR, Jones ET: Use of cortical cancellous allograft for posterior spinal fusion. Clin Orthop 229:99–105, 1988

Kostuik JP, Harrington I, Alexander D, et al: Cauda equina syndrome and lumbar disc herniation. J Bone Joint Surg 68A:386–391, 1986

Laasonen E, Soini J: Low-back pain after lumbar fusion. Surgical and computed tomographic analysis. Spine 14:210–213, 1989

Lee CK: Lumbar spinal instability (olisthesis) after extensive posterior spinal decompression. Spine 8:429–433, 1983

Lehmann TR, LaRocca HS: Repeat lumbar surgery: A review of patients with failure from previous lumbar surgery treated by spinal canal exploration and lumbar spinal fusion. Spine 6:615, 1981

Lehmann TR, Spratt KF, Tozzi JE, et al: Long-term follow-up of lower lumbar fusion patients. Spine 12:97–104, 1987

Nasca RJ: Rationale for spinal fusion in lumbar spinal stenosis. Spine 14:451–454, 1989

Nasca RJ: Surgical management of lumbar spinal stenosis. Spine 12:809–816, 1987

Onik G, Helms CA, Ginsburg L: Percutaneous lumbar discectomy using a new aspiration probe. AJR 144:1137–1140, 1985

Parke WW, Watanabe R: The intrinsic vasculature of the lumbosacral spinal nerve roots. Spine 10:508–515, 1985

Rothman RH, Bernini RH: Algorithm for salvage surgery of the lumbar spine. Clin Orthop 154:14, 1981

Rothman RH, Booth R: Failures of spinal fusion. Orthop Clin North Am 6:299–304, 1975

Rothman RH, Simeone FA: The spine, ed 2, Philadelphia, WB Saunders, 1982

Rothman RH, Tarlov E: Failed back surgery syndrome. JAMA 251:657, 1984

Spangfort EV: The lumbar disc herniation-A computer-aided analysis of 2504 operations. Acta Orthop Scand (Suppl) 142:52, 1971

Spengler DM: Current concept review. Degenerative stenosis of the lumbar spine. J Bone Joint Surg 69A:305–308, 1987

Spengler DM: Lumbar discectomy: Results with limited disc excision and selective foraminotomy. Spine 7:604–607, 1982

Spengler DM, Freeman CW: Patient selection for lumbar discectomy. Spine 4:129, 1979

Spengler DM, Freeman D, Westbrook R: Low back pain following multiple lumbar spine procedures. Spine 5:356, 1980

Stambough JL: Surgical techniques for lumbar discectomy. Semin Spine Surg 1:47–53, 1989

Tile M: The role of surgery in nerve root compression. Spine 9:57–64, 1984

Waddell G, McCulloch JA, Kummel E, Venner RM: Nonorganic physical signs in low-back pain. Spine 5:117–125, 1980

Weber H: Lumbar disc herniation: A controlled prospective study with ten years of observation. Spine 8:131–140, 1983

White AH, von Rogov P, Zucherman J, et al: Lumbar laminectomy for herniated disc: A prospective controlled comparison with internal fixation fusion. Spine 12:305–307, 1987

Wiltse LL, Guyer RD, Spencer CW, et al: Alar transverse process impingement of the L5 spinal nerve: The far-out syndrome. Spine 9:31–41, 1984

Wisneski RJ, Rothman RH: Microdiscectomy and percutaneous discectomy: Indications, history and results. In White AH, Rothman RH, Ray CD, eds. Spine surgery. St Louis, CV Mosby, 1987

Wisneski RJ, Rothman RH: The Pennsylvania plan II: An algorithm for the management of lumbar degenerative disc disease. American Academy Orthopaedic Surgeons: Instructional course lectures. St Louis, CV Mosby, 34:17–36, 1985

Witt I, Veswtergaard A, Rosenklint A: A comparative analysis of x-ray findings of the lumbar spine in patients with and without lumbar pain. Spine 9:298–300, 1984

65
Spinal Trauma

CERVICAL AND THORACOLUMBAR SPINAL INJURIES

I. General Considerations
A. Incidence: 10,000 new spinal cord injuries per year
B. Males and <40 years old: 80%
C. Motor vehicle accident most common
D. Midcervical spine (C5) most common

II. Patient Evaluation
A. Detailed history, mechanism of injury, associated injury must be sought
B. Neurologic evaluation
  1. Complete injury: no motor or sensory function below the zone of injury (C6 quadriplegia means three or more muscle function of wrist dorsiflexion)
  2. Incomplete injury: partial preservation of motor or sensory function below the zone of injury
    a. Anterior cord syndrome: motor paralysis, hypesthesia, no sensory (sharp/dull and temperature) function with preservation of posterior column (positional, proprioception, vibratory senses)
    b. Central cord syndrome: motor paralysis less in lower limbs than upper limbs with sacral sparing
    c. Brown-Sequard syndrome: ipsilateral motor paralysis and positional and vibratory sense and contralateral pain and temperature sensation loss
    d. Mixed syndrome: unclassifiable combination
  3. Spinal shock: hypotension without tachycardia (motor, sensory, and reflexes are absent but cannot determine complete injury until bulbocavernosus or other reflexes return, usually within 24 hours)
  4. Neurologic status (Frankel scale)
    a. A: no motor or sensory function below the level of injury
    b. B: sensation but no motor function
    c. C: motor function present but useless
    d. D: motor function present and useful
    e. E: normal motor and sensory
  5. Neurologic examination
    a. C4 (spontaneous breathing and shrug shoulders), C5 (deltoids and biceps), C6 (wrist extension), C7 (triceps and wrist flexion), C8 (finger flexion), T1 (intrinsics)
    b. L2 (iliopsoas), L3 (quadriceps), L4 (tibialis anterior), L5 (extensor hallucis longus [EHL]), S1 (gastrocnemius), S2 (bladder sphincter), S3 (anal sphincter)
    c. Sensory: C5 (upper outer arm), C6 (thumb), C7 (long finger), C8 (little finger) T1 (medial forearm), T10 (umbilicus), L1 (groin), L2 (anterior thigh), L3 (knee), L4 (medial malleolus), L5 (great toe), S1 (small toe), S2 (posterior thigh), S3-S5 (anal)
C. X-ray examination
  1. AP: spinous process alignment, lateral masses and open mouth view for C1 and C2
  2. Lateral:
    a. Must see C7-T1 (get swimmer's view if necessary)
    b. Normal soft tissue density is 4–5 mm at C2-3 level in adults and up to 20 mm at C5-C7

c. Loss of lordosis is an important sign
d. Vertebral alignment: >3.5 mm displacement and >11° (White's criteria) angulation are significant for instability
e. Spinal canal diameter: 17 mm (normal), <14 mm (stenosis), and spinal canal to vertebral body ratio <0.8 indicates congenital or developmental stenosis
f. Power's ratio >1 for determining anterior atlanto-occipital dislocation: distance between the basion and the spinolaminar line of C1 is divided by the distance between the posterior margin of the foramen magnum (opisthion) and the posterior margin of the anterior arch of C1 (Fig 7-20)
3. Obliques: intervertebral foramen and pedicles
4. Pillar view (hyperextension and 35° rotation): lateral masses between facets
5. Stretch test: >1.7 mm and 7.5° angulation on traction signifies posterior instability
6. Flexion-extension views: ligamentous injuries (initial or 3 weeks later and use White's criteria) (Fig 7-21)
7. Tomograms (best for odontoid fracture and facet fracture-dislocations)
8. CT scan shows middle column disruption, posterior element fractures, herniated disc, canal compromise
9. Myelogram: if unexplained neurologic deficit or for herniated disc or hematoma but less used with the advent of MRI

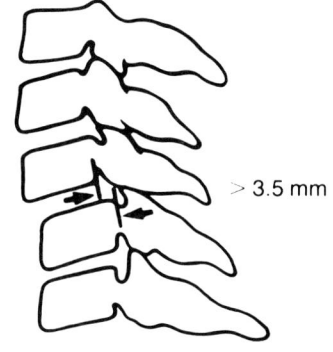

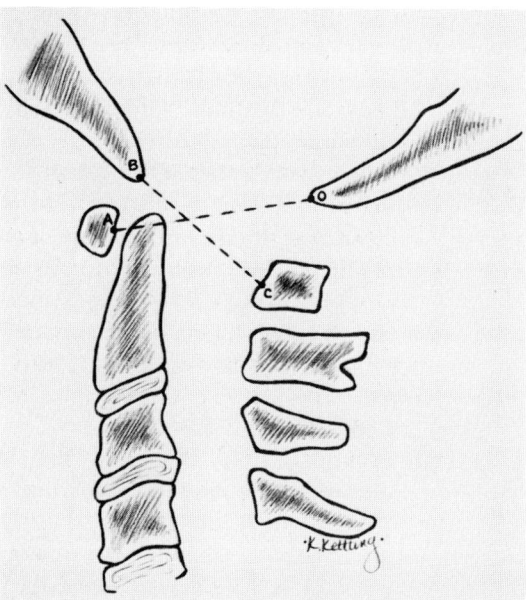

Figure 7-20. Power's ratio (BC/OA) greater than 1 to determine anterior atlanto-occipital dislocation: the distance between the basion and the spinolaminar line of C1 is divided by the distance between the posterior margin of the foramen magnum (opisthion) and the posterior margin of the anterior arch of C1.

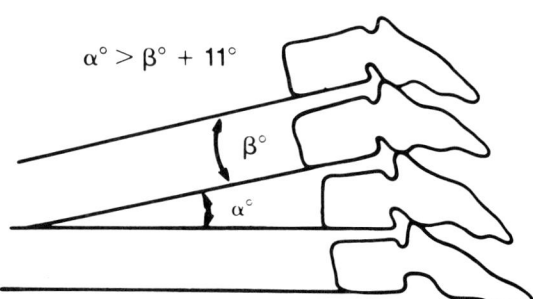

Figure 7-21. Criteria for cervical instability according to White and Panjabi. (From White AA III, Panjabi MM: Clinical biomechanics of the spine. Philadelphia, JB Lippincott, 1978. Reprinted with permission.)

10. MRI: prognosis after spinal cord injury can be somewhat predicted (distinguish between cord edema and hemorrhage) and soft tissue injuries such as herniated disc, hematoma, or ligamentous injury can be diagnosed. Syringomyelia is detected in late cases

III. Initial Management of C-Spine Injuries

A. Use of corticosteroids is controversial but should be administered early if used
B. Stryker bed is helpful
C. Prompt skeletal tong traction and reduction is important
D. Early rehabilitation is critical

IV. Specific Upper C-Spine Injuries

A. Occipital condyle fractures
   1. Diagnosis made with tomogram or CT
   2. Ligamentous injury, intracranial hematoma and neurologic deficit may accompany this injury
   3. Treatment: halo immobilization for 3 months and flexion-extension film is obtained. Occiput to C2 fusion if resultant instability
B. Occiput-C1 dislocation
   1. Violent, twisting, or flexion-extension force on the head
   2. Disruption of all ligamentous attachment
   3. Unstable and nearly always fatal
   4. Treatment: rigid immobilization in a halo body cast, followed by early occiput-C1-C2 fusion
C. C1-C2 subluxation: may be associated with odontoid or atlas fractures
   1. Rupture of transverse ligament
      a. Atlantoaxial interval: if 3–5 mm indicates rupture of the transverse ligament, >7–8 mm indicates all ligamentous disruption, and >10 mm causes spinal cord compression
      b. Treatment: C1-C2 fusion
   2. Atlantoaxial rotatory fixation: head is tilted toward the side of fixation and the chin and C2 spinous process are pointed toward the opposite direction
      a. Type I: rotatory fixation with no anterior displacement (65° rotation results in bilateral dislocation and cord compression of 7 mm)
      b. Type II: rotatory fixation with 3–5 mm anterior displacement (transverse ligament rupture and 45° rotation results in unilateral dislocation)
      c. Type III: rotatory fixation with >5 mm anterior displacement (all ligaments ruptured)
      d. Type IV: rotatory fixation with posterior displacement
      e. Treatment: reduction (traction) and C1-C2 fusion if unstable
D. Fracture of C1
   1. Types of fractures
      a. Posterior arch fracture: hyperextension injuries, associated with posteriorly displaced odontoid fractures or hangman's fractures (usually heals with halo immobilization)
      b. Lateral mass fracture: fracture line passes through the articular surface (usually heals with halo)
      c. Burst fracture of the ring (Jefferson's fracture)
         (1) Axial loading usually with breaks at two sites
         (2) Widening of lateral mass >7 mm indicates transverse ligamentous rupture (in this case, allow atlas fractures to heal first with halo immobilization for 2–3 months and C1-C2 fusion may be done if instability is >5 mm)
         (3) Treatment: cervical orthosis if nondisplaced; traction followed by halo jacket if displaced and limitation of rotatory movement for 8 weeks followed by cervical collar for 6–8 weeks (posterior C1-C2 fusion if nonunion.) Some propose occiput-C2 fusion, especially if both anterior and posterior rings have not healed)

E. Fractures of the odontoid (Fig 7-22)
1. Type I: rare avulsion fracture of the tip (stable and treatment is cervical collar)
2. Type II: fracture at the base of the odontoid
   a. Anterior displacement (flexion injury) is more common than posterior displacement (extension injury)
   b. Nonunion rate is 20–80% (especially >50 years of age, >4 mm displacement, and posterior displacement)
   c. Treatment
      (1) Halo traction to reduce it <4 mm and halo jacket for 12 weeks and cervical collar for 6 weeks
      (2) C1-C2 fusion: if delayed or nonunion or if the fracture cannot be reduced <4 mm, especially in the older patient (Gallie fusion for anteriorly displaced fractures and Brooks fusion for posteriorly displaced fractures)
      (3) Odontoid fractures associated with C1-ring fracture
         i. Consider posterior C1-C2 screw fixation or anterior odontoid screw fixation
         ii. Halo initially to let C1 heal then C1-C2 fusion if C2 nonunion develops
3. Type III: fracture through the body
   a. Nondisplaced: cervical orthosis or halo
   b. Displaced: halo body jacket for 3–4 months
F. Fractures through the pedicle of C2 (hangman's fracture)
1. Mechanism: probably extension injury followed by flexion
2. Types
   a. Type I: minimal displacement (<3 mm)
   b. Type II: significant displacement and angulation
   c. Type III: associated facet dislocation
3. Treatment
   a. Minimally displaced: halo jacket for 8 weeks
   b. Significantly displaced and angulated fractures: cervical traction for 3–4 weeks to reduce displacement and allow callus formation, followed by halo jacket for 2 months
   c. Facet dislocation or completely disrupted C2-C3 articulation: C2-C3 facet wiring and halo immobilization or posterior C2 pedicular screw fixation with C2-C3 plating
   d. Late instability or nonunion: ante-

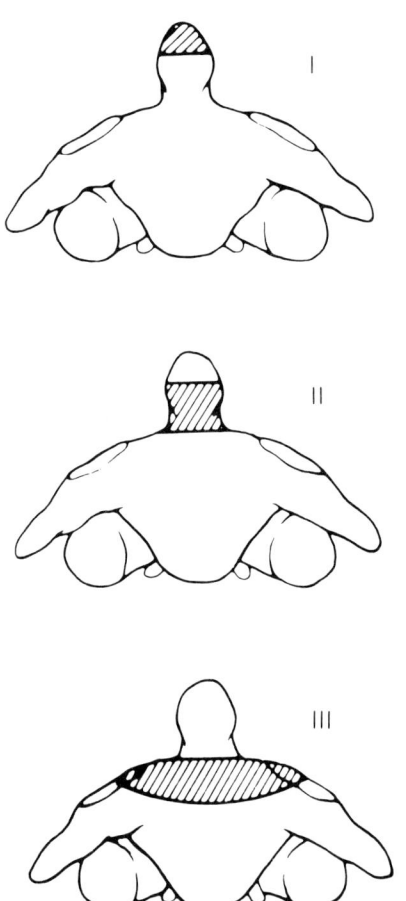

Figure 7-22. Anderson-D'Alonzo classification of odontoid fractures. (From Bucholz RW: Orthopaedic trauma. In Bucholz RW, Lippert FG, Wenger DR, Ezaki M, eds. *Orthopaedic decision making.* Philadelphia, B.C. Decker, and St. Louis, CV Mosby, 1984. Reprinted with permission.)

rior C2-C3 fusion or posterior pedicular screw fixation (C2-C3 plating)

V. Fractures and Dislocations of the Lower Cervical Spine

A. Classification (Allen) (Fig 7-23)
1. Distractive flexion (stage 1–4): perched facets, unilateral or bilateral facet dislocation
2. Vertical compression (stage 1–3): burst fractures
3. Compressive flexion (stage 1–5): compression fractures and tear drop fractures
4. Compressive extension (stage 1–5): fractures of the posterior elements and associated vertebral bodies
5. Lateral flexion (stages 1 and 2): uncommon
6. Distractive extension (stages 1 and 2): widening of the disc or retrolisthesis

B. White's diagnostic checklist (>5 is unstable)
1. Anterior elements: 2
2. Posterior elements: 2
3. Sagittal translation >3.5 mm or 20% vertebra: 2
4. Sagittal plane rotation >11°: 2
5. Positive stretch test: 2
6. Cord damage: 2
7. Root damage: 1
8. Abnormal disc narrowing: 1
9. Dangerous loading anticipated: 1

C. Facet fractures or dislocations
1. Unilateral (25%) or bilateral (50% displacement)
2. Associated disc rupture with anterior cord impingement may be present

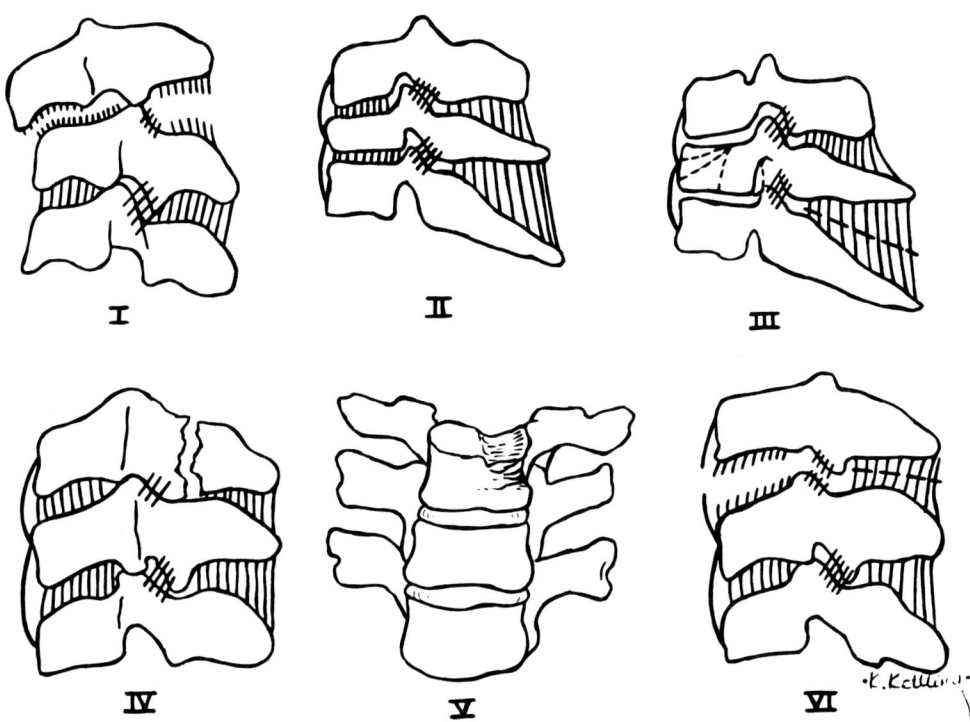

Figure 7-23. Allen-Ferguson classification of injuries of the lower cervical spine. I. Distractive flexion (stage 1 through 4): perched facets, unilateral or bilateral facet dislocation II. Vertical compression (stage 1 through 3): burst fractures III. Compressive flexion (stage 1 through 5): compression fractures and tear drop fractures IV. Compressive extension (stage 1 through 5): fractures of the posterior elements and associated vertebral bodies V. Lateral flexion (stage 1 and 2): uncommon VI. Distractive extension (stage 1 and 2): widening of the disc or retrolithesis

3. Treatment
   a. Unilateral: cervical traction for rapid reduction and primary fusion. If closed reduction cannot be done, then operative reduction and fusion with wiring followed by cervical orthosis for 3 months. Avoid manipulation under general anesthesia
   b. Bilateral: cervical traction for reduction (but avoid overdistraction) or operative reduction and primary stabilization with posterior wiring and fusion and cervical orthosis (Figs 7-24, 7-25)
   c. Facet dislocation with neurologic deficit: closed reduction or operative reduction followed by posterior wiring and fusion and cervical orthosis. Myelogram or MRI should be done to look for disc herniation. Anterior discectomy and fusion is also performed if anterior cord compression
   d. Facet fractures
      (1) Facet fracture with radiculopathy, removal of the fragment is done with fusion and stabilization
      (2) Facet fractures without neurologic deficits: halo immobilization if anatomically reduced and maintained, or early stabilization and fusion if displaced
D. Fractures of C3-C7 vertebral bodies
   1. Wedge compression fractures: cervical collar for 6 weeks if posterior elements intact and halo jacket if significant compression or posterior element disruption. Posterior fusion may be necessary in severe cases (>11° or 30% compression) or late instability cases
   2. Burst fracture (axial loading)
      a. Stable: minimal displacement with no ligamentous disruption or neurologic deficit (treatment is halo jacket)
      b. Unstable: posterior portion of the vertebral body is split off posteriorly into the spinal canal and the anterior portion is split off anteriorly. Middle mass is split sagittally, widening the interpedicular distance. Often there are associated lamina or pedicle fractures posteriorly (neurologic deficit depending on comminution)
   3. Tear drop fractures (axial loading with compression and rotation)
      a. Unstable: usually disruption of anterior ligamentous complex
      b. Posterior instability is frequently present (positive stretch test)
   4. Treatment of unstable burst or tear drop fractures (consider degree of instability and neural compression and treat all with initial tong traction)
      a. Fractures with no neurologic deficit: halo or posterior stabilization

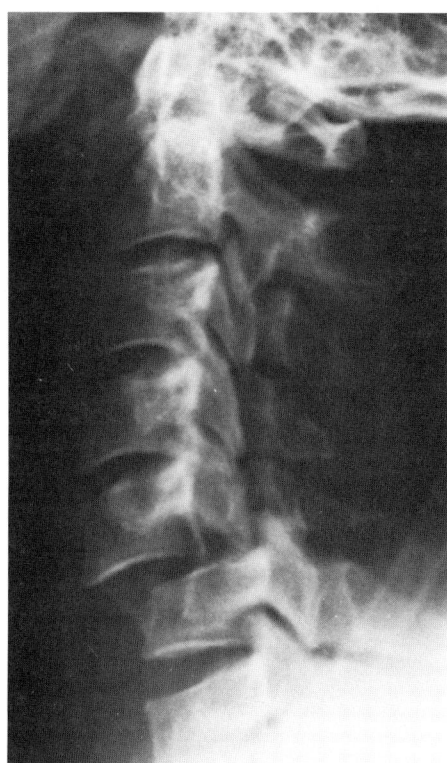

Figure 7-24. Bilateral jumped facets at C5-C6.

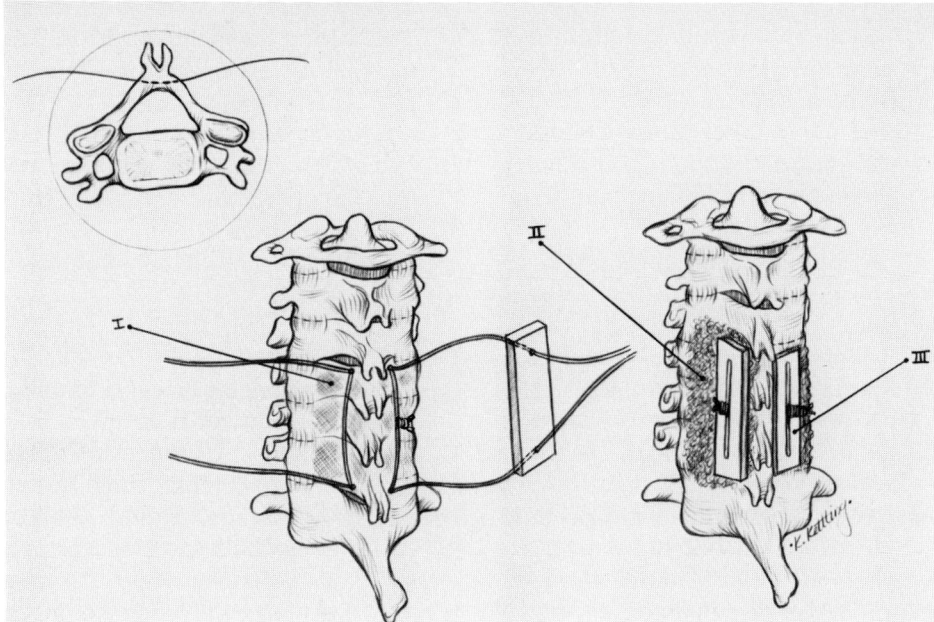

Figure 7-25. Posterior wiring and fusion, using cortical cancellous bone graft. **A.** Spinous process wiring **B.** Triple wires are used. Decorticate the posterior lamina (I). **C.** Corticocancellous bone grafts (III) are tightened down and additional cancellous bone (II) grafts are placed laterally. (Modified from Meyer PR: Surgery of the Spine Trauma Churchill Livingstone)

and fusion, or anterior strut grafting, depending on comminution and instability
  b. Fractures with partial neurologic deficit
    (1) Anterior decompression and strut grafting and posterior wiring and fusion (if associated posterior instability)
    (2) Anterior decompression, strut grafting, and plate and screw fixation (controversial)
  c. Fractures with complete neurologic deficit
    (1) Anterior decompression and strut grafting, particularly if root function at or a level below the injury is absent
    (2) Posterior wiring and fusion, followed by anterior decompression and strut grafting if associated posterior instability
  d. If posterior instability is present, either posterior wiring and fusion or anterior plate and screws are recommended in addition to the anterior decompression or fusion
E. Other cervical spine injuries
  1. Fractures of the spinous process (clay-shoveler's fracture)
    a. Flexion injury with avulsion fracture
    b. Stable injury and treated with cervical collar
  2. Hyperextension injury with retrolisthesis
    a. Patients >50 years and underlying cervical spondylosis
    b. Central cord syndrome or complete cord injury
    c. Retrolisthesis of upper over lower vertebra
    d. Treatment
      (1) Cervical collar if minimally displaced
      (2) Skeletal traction and anterior de-

compression and stabilization if cord compression
3. Soft tissue injury
   a. Extension: acceleration "whiplash"
      (1) Anterior longitudinal ligament, anterior musculature, and intervertebral disc
      (2) Symptoms: pain in the neck, referred pain to the head, shoulder, and arm, dysphagia, ocular symptoms, dizziness, and temporal mandibular problems
      (3) X-rays: prevertebral widening, widening of the disc space and posterior displacement
      (4) Twelve percent do not go back to work, and of those who are symptomatic 39% have x-ray evidence of disc disease
      (5) Treatment: brace acutely and may need surgery later if cervical spondylosis is problematic
   b. Flexion: (deceleration injury)
      (1) Muscle strain and greater auricular nerve stretch, interspinous ligament, capsular tear, posterior longitudinal ligament, and posterior aspect of the disc
      (2) X-rays: kyphotic angulation, anterior displacement of the vertebra, and facet widening
      (3) Treatment: conservative first and if instability by White's criteria, then posterior wiring and fusion

THORACOLUMBAR SPINE FRACTURES

I. General Considerations

A. Anatomic region
   1. Upper thoracic fractures (T2-T10)
      a. It takes high-energy injuries to fracture the thoracic spine, which is relatively stiff due to attachment to ribs
      b. High rate of spinal cord injury (80%) due to smaller canal diameter
      c. More unstable in flexion and kyphotic forces due to coronally oriented facets
   2. Thoracolumbar fractures (T11-L2)
      a. Most commonly encountered due to junctional instability and stress concentration
         (1) Loss of stabilizing forces by the ribs
         (2) Change from kyphosis to lordosis
         (3) Change of facet orientation
      b. Conus and/or root injury
   3. Low lumbar fractures (L3-L5)
      a. Larger vertebrae and resists more compression loading
      b. Facet joints are stronger and sagittally oriented
      c. Because of physiologic lordosis and the center of mass being closer to the vertebrae, kyphotic angulation is less likely to occur
      d. Neurologic injuries are less common due to larger canal diameter and the presence of nerve roots instead of the spinal cord
B. Spine stability (Denis)
   1. Three columns (Fig 7-26)
      a. Anterior column: anterior longitudinal ligament, anterior annulus fibrosus, and anterior half of the vertebral body
      b. Middle column: posterior longitudinal ligament, posterior annulus fibrosis, posterior half of the vertebral body
      c. Posterior column: pedicles, facet joints, lamina, spinous processes, and interspinous and supraspinous ligaments
   2. If the middle column is disrupted, then the spine is generally unstable
      a. Possible exception may be in thoracic vertebrae above T8, in which the spine may be stable due to its attachment to ribs
      b. Another exception may be in L4 or L5 region, where the intact posterior

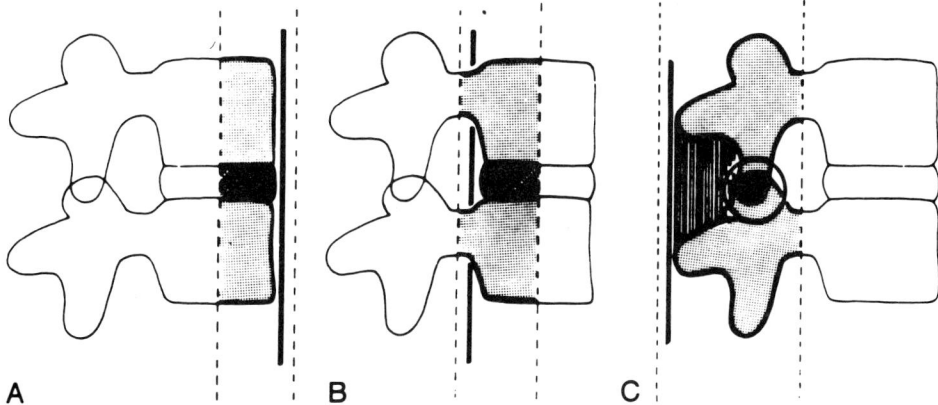

Figure 7-26. The three-column concept. **A.** Anterior column, including the anterior longitudinal ligament, the anterior annulus fibrosis, and the anterior part of the vertebral body. **B.** The middle column, including the posterior longitudinal ligament, posterior annulus fibrosus, and the posterior wall of the vertebral body. **C.** The posterior column, including the posterior bony complex, ligament flava, supraspinous ligament, interspinous ligament, and the capsule. (From Denis F: The three-column spine and its significance in the classification of acute thoracolumbar spinal injuries. Spine 8:317, 1983. Reprinted with permission.)

      column may still have significant weight bearing because of physiologic lordosis
   c. Distraction injuries where fractures occur through the cancellous bone are generally stable
3. Stability is not "black and white" but gray zone (Denis)
   a. Stable fractures: transverse process, spinous process, articular process, pars interarticularis, and compression fracture
   b. First degree instability: severe compression fractures and seat-belt injury
   c. Second degree instability: burst fractures with late neurologic involvement
   d. Third degree instability: fracture-dislocation and severe burst fractures with neurologic deficit
4. White and panjabi's check list (if >5, unstable)
   a. Anterior element disruption: 2
   b. Posterior element disruption: 2
   c. Relative sagittal plane translation >2.5 mm: 2
   d. Relative sagittal plane rotation >5°: 2
   e. Neurologic deficit: 2
   f. Disruption of costovertebral articulation: 1
   g. Anticipated dangerous loading: 2

II. Patient Evaluation

A. General assessment, including respiratory, cardiothoracic, abdominal, urologic, and head and cervical spine status
B. Neurologic assessment
  1. Neurologic status (Frankel Scale)
    a. A: no motor or sensory function below the level of injury
    b. B: sensation but no motor function
    c. C: motor function present but useless
    d. D: motor function present and useful
    e. E: normal motor and sensory
  2. Types (Holdsworth)
    a. Thoracic region: spinal cord injury (complete or partial)
    b. Lumbar region below L1: roots and/or cauda equina injury

c. Thoracolumbar junction
    (1) Complete division of the spinal cord and roots
    (2) Complete division of the spinal cord with escape of roots in varying degrees: most common
    (3) Incomplete division of the spinal cord with escape of roots in varying degrees
3. Physical and neurologic examination
    a. Palpation at the fracture site for posterior disruption
    b. Leg pain suggests nerve root compression
    c. Motor strength should be carefully assessed
    d. Sensory
        (1) Position and vibratory senses and deep pressure are preserved in anterior cord syndrome
        (2) Pain, touch, and temperature: contralateral loss in Brown-Sequard syndrome. Touch sensation (but not pain and temperature) may be preserved in central cord syndrome
        (3) Sacral sparing: anal sensation is preserved in central cord syndrome. Presence of rectal tone and sensation give better prognosis
    e. Reflexes
        (1) Presence of patellar or ankle reflexes initially after spinal cord injury may suggest better prognosis
        (2) Bulbocavernosus reflex indicates the end of spinal shock and complete cord injury is diagnosed
    f. Conus injury
        (1) S2, S3 upper motor neuron lesion
        (2) Frequently occult manifestation
        (3) Perianal sensation and tone are absent and bulbocavernosus reflex is absent
        (4) Inability to void and significant residual urine after voiding
        (5) Diagnosis aided by cystometrogram and MRI
    g. Cauda equina syndrome
        (1) Lower motor neuron lesion
        (2) Lower roots and bowel or bladder function affected
    h. Neurologic examination should be frequently repeated to document progression or improvement
4. Ascending paraplegia
    a. May occur in 3–4 days
    b. Transient or irreversible
    c. Possibly due to vascular compromise
C. Radiologic evaluation
    1. Plain x-rays: look for the posterior aspect of the vertebral body for retropulsion and translation. Kyphotic angulation should be measured
    2. CT scan is the best tool for evaluation of the middle column, especially with sagittal reconstruction
    3. Tomogram may be helpful in Chance type fractures
    4. Myelogram is rarely necessary unless physical examination and x-ray findings do not correlate (ie, suspected herniated disc and neurologic progression not accounted for by CT scan)
    5. MRI has replaced myelogram in trauma patients to evaluate the spinal cord and soft tissue disruption, especially of the posterior column
    6. Multiple level injuries are common

III. Classification
A. Holdsworth: two-column concept with anterior and posterior columns
B. Denis: Three-column concept
    1. Compression fractures
    2. Burst fractures
    3. Seat-belt type injuries
    4. Fracture-dislocations
        a. Flexion rotation
        b. Shear type
        c. Flexion distraction
C. Ferguson and Allen (mechanistic classification)

1. Compressive flexion
   a. Compression of anterior column
   b. Failure of posterior column in tension
   c. Failure of middle column in compression (burst fractures)
   d. Axis of rotation is posterior to the anterior longitudinal ligament
2. Distractive flexion
   a. All three columns fail in tension (seat-belt injuries)
   b. Axis of rotation is anterior to the anterior longitudinal ligament
3. Lateral flexion
   a. Minimal angulation if only the anterior and middle column injury
   b. Significant angulation when all three columns disrupted
4. Torsional flexion: unstable three-column injury with fracture-dislocation
5. Vertical compression: failure of all three columns under compression (axial loading burst fractures)
6. Translational: shear type fracture-dislocation
7. Distractive extension: all three columns fail in extension (rare)

IV. Treatment

A. General considerations
  1. Treatment depends on anatomic region, neurologic status, stability or mechanism of the injury, and patient's general status
  2. Anatomic
     a. Thoracic spine
        (1) Partial lesions: anterior decompression first and bone graft with or without posterior stabilization
        (2) Complete lesions
            i. Burst fractures: orthosis or posterior rodding if >40° kyphosis or early mobilization is important
            ii. Fracture-dislocations: posterior rodding and fusion
     b. Low lumbar spine
        (1) Intact neurologic status: Pantaloon cast or brace or posterior fusion if early mobilization is required
        (2) Neurologic deficit: posterior decompression and stabilization (short fusion techniques, such as transpedicular instrumentations)
     c. Thoracolumbar junction
        (1) Neurologic injuries: decompress or stabilize either anteriorly or posterolaterally
        (2) Intact neurologic status if unstable: posterior stabilization
  3. Neural recovery is possible by adequate decompression of the spinal cord in incomplete injuries even in late cases
  4. Laminectomy
     a. Contraindicated because it causes more instability, and manipulation or retraction of neural structures can cause further neural injury
     b. Exceptions are posterior element impingement and open fractures with bone fragment or bullet in the posterior aspect of the canal in incomplete injuries and spinal canal impingement in the low lumbar spine
  5. Corticosteroid treatment is controversial but should be administered early if used
  6. Timing of surgery is also controversial
     a. Immediate operative intervention probably gives the best chance for reduction and neural recovery, but clinically not proven. The following situations require early surgery
        (1) Progressive neurologic deficit
        (2) Unreducible dislocations
        (3) Debridement for open wounds or multiple trauma
     b. Early surgery (2–3 days)
        (1) Relatively easy reduction and decompression
        (2) Early mobilization of the patient, especially in the multiple trauma patient
        (3) Lack of time to assess the pa-

tient's general status and neurologic status
            (4) Potential operative complications of making the patient worse by spine manipulation
        c. Late surgery (10–14 days): chance for the spinal cord to recover from trauma and edema
    7. Skeletal traction and closed reduction and Stryker or motorized rotating bed in the initial period is helpful
    8. External immobilization
        a. Above T5: CTLSO
        b. T6-L4: Jewet hyperextension or TLSO braces
        c. L5-S1: Pantaloon cast
B. Neurologic status and stability
    1. Neurologically intact and spine stable
        a. Common in compression fractures, seat-belt type injuries, and burst fractures of the low lumbar spine
        b. Orthosis or body cast
    2. Neurologically intact and spine unstable
        a. Common in burst fractures and severe compression fractures
        b. Operative stabilization to prevent neurologic loss and early rehabilitation
        c. Conservative treatment is an option but the patient must tolerate long-term bed rest (1-2 months) and accept possibility of late deformity and neurologic deterioration
    3. Neurologically compromised and spine stable
        a. Burst fractures of the thoracic spine (T7 or above) and some pediatric fractures
        b. Surgical decompression (removal of disc or bony fragment) and stabilization in incomplete injuries
        c. Conservative treatment in complete cord injuries
    4. Neurologically compromised and spine unstable
        a. Burst fractures or fracture dislocations of the thoracic and lumbar spine
        b. Incomplete cord injuries: anterior or posterolateral decompression and stabilization
        c. Complete cord injuries: posterior stabilization and fusion
C. Specific treatment
    1. Compression-flexion injuries
        a. Anterior column injury alone usually does not give neurologic deficits
        b. Greater than 40% collapse, 20° angulation, and multiple compression fractures in the upper thoracic region give late kyphotic deformity
        c. Treatment
            (1) Anterior column failure: hyperextension orthosis
            (2) Middle column or posterior column failure: distraction or extension rod and fusion
    2. Distractive flexion (seat-belt type injuries)
        a. Chance fracture without subluxation or dislocation: hyperextension body cast
        b. Ligamentous flexion-distraction injury: compression rodding and short fusion
        c. Two-level injuries: closed reduction and casting or open reduction and short fusion with compression instrumentation
    3. Lateral flexion injuries
        a. Conservative treatment if only minimal angulation
        b. Distraction rod and fusion if significant angulation with three-column injury
    4. Torsional flexion injuries (fracture-dislocations)
        a. Frequently complete paraplegia
        b. Surgical posterior stabilization with fusion is necessary for early rehabilitation
    5. Vertical compression injuries (burst fractures)

- a. Neurologic involvement is frequent secondary to retropulsed fragment
- b. Treatment
  - (1) Neurologically intact
    - i. Conservative treatment with bed rest (1-2 months) followed by hyperextension cast may be offered
    - ii. Distraction rod and fusion for early rehabilitation
  - (2) Neurologically compromised
    - i. Anterior decompression and iliac tricortical graft stabilization with or without anterior instrumentation, and secondary posterior stabilization
    - ii. Posterior distraction systems such as Harrington rods or Cotrel-Dubousset with segmental wiring, and if adequate decompression is not obtained, either posterolateral or anterior decompression can be done
- 6. Translational injuries
  - a. Posterior stabilization and fusion
  - b. Segmental fixations are superior
- D. Spinal instrumentations
  - 1. Purpose
    - a. Stabilization to give early mobilization and better healing
    - b. Reduction to decrease late deformity and pain
    - c. Indirect decompression if no separate fragment in the canal
    - d. Temporary stabilization until fusion matures
  - 2. Indications
    - a. Unstable spines
    - b. Quadriplegics with early need for rehabilitation
    - c. Multiple trauma patients who require early mobilization
  - 3. Harrington distraction rods
    - a. Correction by distraction and hyperextension
    - b. Relies on tension of the anterior longitudinal ligament and good for resisting axial loads but weak in resisting torsion
    - c. Indicated for compression-flexion and vertical compression types
    - d. Usually three above and two below the site of fracture
  - 4. Modified distraction rods
    - a. Improve hook designs by Edwards (anatomic), bifid pedicle hooks or Jacobs' locking hooks
    - b. Square-ended contoured Moe rod for better rotational control and lordotic contouring
    - c. Edwards sleeves increase rod volume to direct anterior force in correcting kyphosis
    - d. Segmental fixations with sublaminar or Wisconsin wires increase torsional rigidity
    - e. Device for transverse traction link two rods to increase overall stability
  - 5. Harrington or Edwards compression rods
    - a. Relies on the stable middle column against compression
    - b. Indicated for distraction-flexion injuries or secondary posterior stabilization after anterior grafting
    - c. Avoid sublaminar wires with compression devices
  - 6. Luque rods with sublaminar wires
    - a. Better rotation stability but not good for resisting axial loading
    - b. Indicated for torsional flexion and translational injuries
  - 7. Cotrel-Dubousset system
    - a. Stiffer construct and can control axial loading, rotation, and translational forces
    - b. Can be used for all types of injuries
  - 8. Transpedicular instrumentation
    - a. Stiffest construct with shortest segment fusion
    - b. Most appropriate for lumbar fractures (L2 or below)

9. Anterior fusion with instrumentations
   a. May be primary treatment in fractures with incomplete neurologic deficit or secondary treatment after posterior instrumentation
   b. Great caution should be taken to protect vascular structures

REFERENCES

Cervical Spine Fractures

Allen BL, Ferguson RL, Lehmann TR, O'Brien RP: A mechanistic classification of closed, indirect fractures and dislocations of the lower cervical spine. Spine 7:1, 1982

Anderson LD, D'Alonzo RT: Fractures of the odontoid process of the axis. J Bone Joint Surg 56A:1663–1674, 1974

Bohler J: Anterior stabilization for acute fractures and non union of the dens. J Bone Joint Surg 64A:18, 1982

Bohlman HH: Acute fractures and dislocations of the cervical spine: An analysis of three hundred hospitalized patients and review of the literature. J Bone Joint Surg 61A:1119–1142, 1979

Botte MJ, Byrne TP, Garfin SR: Application of the halo device for immobilization of the cervical spine utilizing an increased torque pressure. J Bone Joint Surg 69A:750–752, 1987

Botte MJ, Garfin SR, Byrne TP, et al: The halo skeletal fixator. Clin Orthop 239:12–18, 1989

Brooks AL, Jenkins EB: Atlanto-axial arthrodesis by the wedge compression method. J Bone Joint Surg 60A:279–284, 1978

Burke DC: Hyperextension injuries of the spine. J Bone Joint Surg 53B:3–12, 1971

Clark CR, White AA III: Fractures of the dens. A multi-center study. J Bone Joint Surg 67A:1340–1348, 1985

Cotler HB, Kulkarni MV, Bondurant FJ: Magnetic resonance imaging of acute spinal cord trauma. J Orthop Trauma 2:1–4, 1988

Eismont FJ, Clifford S, Goldberg M, Green B: Cervical sagittal spinal canal size in spine injury. Spine 9:663–666, 1984

Evans DK: Dislocations at the cervicothoracic junction. J Bone Joint Surg 65B:124–127, 1983

Fielding JW, Cochran GVB, Lawsing JF, Hohl M: Tears of the transverse ligament of the atlas: A clinical and biomechanical study. J Bone Joint Surg 56A:1683–1691, 1974

Fielding JW, Francis WR, Hawkins RJ, et al: Traumatic spondylolisthesis of the axis. Clin Orthop 239:47–52, 1989

Fielding WJ, Hawkins RJ: Atlantoaxial rotatory fixation. J Bone Joint Surg 59A:37, 1977

Garfin SR, Botte MJ, Waters RL, et al: Complications in the use of the halo fixation device. J Bone Joint Surg 68A:320–325, 1986

Garfin SR, Shackford SR, Marshall LF, Drummond JC: Care of the multiply injured patient with cervical spine injury. Clin Orthop 239:19–29, 1989

Harding-Smith J, MacIntosh PK, Sherbon KJ: Fracture of the occipital condyle. J Bone Joint Surg 63A:1170, 1981

Herkowitz HN, Rothman RH: Subacute instability of the cervical spine. Spine 9:348–357, 1984

Hunter T, Dubo HI: Spinal fractures complicating ankylosing spondylitis. A long-term follow-up study. Arthritis Rheum 26:751, 1983

Johnson RM, Owens JR, Hart DL, Callahan RA: Cervical orthosis. Clin Orthop 154:34, 1981

Levine AM, Edwards CC: The management of traumatic spondylolisthesis of the axis. J Bone Joint Surg 67:217, 1985

Levine AM, Edwards CC: Traumatic lesions of the occipitoatlantal complex. Clin Orthop 239:53–67, 1989

Mazur JM, Stauffer ES: Unrecognized spinal instability associated with seemingly "simple" cervical compression fractures. Spine 8:687–692, 1983

Meyer PR: Surgery of the spine trauma. New York, Churchill Livingstone, 1989

Rorabeck CH, Rock MG, Hawkins RJ, et al: Unilateral facet dislocation of the cervical spine: An analysis of the results of treatment in 26 patients. Spine 12:23–27, 1987

Stauffer ES, Kelley EG: Fracture-dislocations of the cervical spine: Instability and recurrent deformity following treatment by anterior interbody fusion. J Bone Joint Surg 59A:45–48, 1977

Torg JS, Pavlov H, Genuario S: Cervical spinal stenosis with cord neuropraxia and transient quadriplegia in athletes. Surg Rounds Orthop 1:9, 1987

White AA, Johnson RM, Panjabi MM, Southwick WO: Biomechanical analysis of clinical stability in the cervical spine. Clin Orthop 109:85, 1975

Thoracolumbar Spine Fractures

Aebi M, Etter C, Kehl T, Thalgott J: Stabilization of the lower thoracic and lumbar spine with the internal spinal skeletal fixation system. Spine 12:544–551, 1987

Akbarnia BA, Forgarty JP, Tayob AA: Contoured Harrington instrumentation in the treatment of unstable spinal fractures. Clin Orthop 189:186, 1984

Bedbrook GM: Spinal injuries with tetraplegia and paraplegia. J Bone Joint Surg 61B:26, 1979

Benson DR: Unstable thoracolumbar fractures, with emphasis on the burst fractures. Clin Orthop 230:14, 1988

Bohlman HH: Current concepts review treatment of fractures and dislocations of the thoracic and lumbar spine. J Bone Joint Surg 67A:165, 1985

Bohlman HH, Eismont FJ: Surgical techniques of anterior decompression and fusion for spinal cord injuries. Clin Orthop 154:57, 1981

Bohlman HH, Freehafer A, Dejak J: The results of treatment of acute injuries of the upper thoracic spine with paralysis. J Bone Joint Surg 67A:360, 1985

Bradford DS, McBride GG: Surgical management of thoracolumbar spine fractures with incomplete neurologic deficits. Clin Orthop 218:201–216, 1987

Cammisa FP Jr, Eismont FJ, Green BA: Dural laceration occurring with burst fractures and associated laminar fractures. J Bone Joint Surg 71A:1044–1052, 1989

Cotler JM, Vernace JV, Michalski JA: The use of Harrington rods in thoracolumbar fractures. Orthop Clin North Am 17:87, 1986

Denis F: Spinal instability as defined by the three column spine concept in acute spinal trauma. Clin Orthop 189:65, 1984

Denis F, Armstrong GWD, Searls K, Matta L: Acute thoracolumbar burst fractures in the absence of neurologic deficit. Clin Orthop 189:142, 1984

Dewald RL: Burst fractures of the thoracic and lumbar spine. Clin Orthop 189:150, 1984

Edwards C, Levine A: Early rod-sleeve stabilization of the injured thoracic and lumbar spine. Orthop Clin North Am 17:121, 1986

Ferguson RL, Allen BL: A mechanistic classification of thoracolumbar spine fractures. Clin Orthop 189:77, 1984

Flesch JR, Leider LL, Ericksonn DL, et al: Harrington instrumentation and spine fusion for unstable fractures and fracture-dislocations of the thoracic and lumbar spine. J Bone Joint Surg 59A:143, 1977

Garfin SR, Mowery CA, Guerra J Jr, Marshall LF: Confirmation of the posterolateral technique to decompress and fuse thoracolumbar spine burst fractures. Spine 10:218–223, 1985

Gertzbein SD, Court-Brown CM, Marks P, et al: The neurological outcome following surgery for spinal fractures. Spine 13:641, 1988

Holdsworth F: Fractures, dislocations and fracture-dislocations of the spine. J Bone Joint Surg 52A:1534, 1970

Jacobs RR, Asher MA, Snider RK: Thoracolumbar spine injuries. Comparative study of recumbent and operative treatment in 100 patients. Spine 5:463, 1980

Kaneda K, Abumi K, Fujiya M: Burst fractures with neurologic deficits of the thoracolumbar-lumbar spine: Results of anterior decompression and stabilization with anterior instrumentation. Spine 9:788–795, 1984

Keene JS, Wackwitz DL, Drummond DS, Breed AL: Compression-distraction instrumentation of unstable thoracolumbar fractures: Anatomic results obtained with each type of injury and method of instrumentation. Spine 11:895–902, 1986

King AG: Burst compression fractures of the thoracolumbar spine. Orthopedics 10:1711, 1987

Kostuik JP: Anterior fixation for fractures of the thoracic and lumbar spine techniques, new methods of internal fixation results. Spine 8:512, 1983

Krompinger WJ, Frederikson BE, Mino DE, Yuan HA: Conservative treatment of fractures of the thoracic and lumbar spine. Orthop Clin North Am 17:161, 1986

McAfee PC, Bohlman HH: Complications of Harrington instrumentation for fractures of the thoracolumbar spine. J Bone Joint Surg 67A:672–686, 1985

McAfee PC, Bohlman HH, Yuan HA: Anterior decompression of traumatic thoracolumbar fractures with incomplete neurologic deficit using a retroperitoneal approach. J Bone Joint Surg 67A:89, 1985

McAfee PC, Yuan HA, Lasda NA: The unstable burst fracture. Spine 7:365, 1982

Olerud S, Karlstrom G, Sjostrom L: Transpedicular fixation of thoracolumbar vertebral fractures. Clin Orthop 227:45, 1988

Roy-Camille R, Saillant G, Mazel C: Plating of thoracic, thoracolumbar and lumbar injuries with pedicle screw plates. Orthop Clin North Am 17:147, 1986

Stauffer ES: Current concepts review: Internal fixation of fractures of the thoracolumbar spine. J Bone Joint Surg 66A:1136, 1984

Takata K, Inoue S, Takahashi K, Ohtsuka Y: Fracture of the posterior margin of a lumbar vertebral body. J Bone Joint Surg 70A:589, 1988

Weinstein JN, Collalto P, Lehmann TR: Long-term follow-up of nonoperatively treated thoracolumbar spine fractures. J Orthop Trauma 1:152, 1987

Willen J, Lindahl S, Norwall A: Unstable thoracolumbar fractures: Comparative clinical study of conservative treatment and Harrington instrumentation. Spine 10:111–122, 1985

66
Tumors of the Spine

I. Evaluation
A. History
 1. Pain is characteristically persistent, not relieved by rest, and worse at night
 2. Age is important; for example, consider metastasis and multiple myeloma in older patients, leukemia and neuroblastoma in young children, and eosinophilic granuloma and osteoid osteoma in older children
 3. Minor trauma causing fracture suggests pathologic fracture
 4. Neurologic: weakness, sensory changes, and gait difficulties
 5. Metastasis is frequently from breast, lung, prostate, kidney, and thyroid
 6. Metabolic bone diseases may mimic tumors: osteoporosis, Paget's disease
 7. Spinal infections can be confused with tumors
B. Examination should be thorough to evaluate the location of the tenderness and neurologic deficits
C. Laboratory and x-ray examinations
 1. Complete blood count (CBC), erythrocyte sedimentation rate (ESR), calcium, phosphorus, protein, alkaline phosphatase, serum protein electrophoresis, acid phosphatase and metastatic workup (chest x-ray, mammogram, etc.)
 2. Plain x-rays, bone scans, tomograms, CT scan, myelogram, and MRI
 3. Angiogram and embolization should be considered for vascular tumors (ie, renal cell tumors) and to assess the tumor in relation to major vessels and the feeding artery to the spinal cord

II. Biopsy
A. Closed biopsy: Craig needle (fluoroscopic or CT guided) is preferred for lesions in the lumbar spine
B. Open biopsy is preferred for cervical and thoracic lesions

III. Tumor Types (Table 7-4 to 7-6)
A. Benign bone tumors
 1. Osteoid osteoma
 2. Osteoblastoma
 3. Hemangioma
 4. Giant cell tumors
 5. Aneurysmal bone cyst
 6. Eosinophilic granuloma
B. Primary malignant tumors
 1. Multiple myeloma
 2. Chordoma
 3. Round cell sarcomas
 4. Chondrosarcoma
 5. Osteosarcoma
C. Metastatic tumors
 1. Breast
 2. Lung
 3. Prostate
 4. Kidney
 5. Thyroid
 6. Others (gastrointestinal, bladder, uterine, etc.)
D. Intraspinal tumors
 1. Intradural, extramedullary (meningioma, neurofibroma, etc.)
 2. Intradural, intramedullary (gliomas, ependymoma, etc.)
 3. Extradural (mostly metastatic tumors)
 4. Intraspinal cysts (perineural cyst, arachnoid cyst, syringomyelia, etc.)

IV. Treatment
A. Depending on accurate diagnosis
B. Radiation or chemotherapy for certain malignant tumors (ie, lymphoma, myeloma, metastatic tumors), and when the neural impairment is not due to bony elements or instability

Table 7-4 Benign Bone Tumors

Tumor	Age (yr)	Sex	Location	X-Ray	Treatment	Comments
Osteoid osteoma	<30	M>	Posterior elements	Nidus & sclerosis	Excision	Painful scoliosis
Osteoblastoma	<30	M>	Posterior elements	Radiolucent	Excision	Painful scoliosis
Hemangioma	>30	M=F	Body	Vertical trabeculae	None, radiation, or surgery	Most are asymptomatic
Giant cell tumor	>20	F>	Body & sacrum	Radiolucent	Excision (radiation?)	Recurrence is common
Aneurysmal bone cyst	<25	M=F	Posterior elements	Lytic & expansile	Excision (radiation?)	May involve next vertebra
Eosinophilic granuloma	<20	M>	Body	Radiolucent or collapse	Orthosis	Self-limiting process
Osteochondroma	10–20	M>	Posterior elements	Exophytic	Excision if symptomatic	Most are asymptomatic

Table 7-5 Malignant Bone Tumors

Tumor	Age (yr)	Sex	Location	X-Ray	Treatment	Comments
Multiple myeloma	>50	M>	Body	Osteopenia & collapse	Chemotherapy & radiation	Surgery if instability
Chordoma	30–70	M>	Sacrum, C1-2	Radiolucent destructive	Aggressive excision	Recurrence is common
Lymphoma	>20	M>	Body	Lytic or sclerotic	Radiation and chemotherapy	Non-Hodgkin's type
Neuroblastoma	<3	M>	Body	Osteopenia, destructive	Excision & chemotherapy or radiation	Rosette on histology
Chondrosarcoma	50–70	M=F	Body	Calcified & destructive	Excision	Chemotherapy or radiation not helpful
Osteosarcoma	10–20	M>	Body	Destructive	Debulk, chemotherapy and radiation	Rare de novo in spine
Metastatic tumors	>40	M,F	Body	Lytic or blastic	Radiation, surgery	Breast, lung prostate, etc.

Table 7-6 Intraspinal Neoplasms or Cysts

Tumor	Age (yr)	Sex	X-Ray	Treatment	Comments
Intradural, extramedullary					
Neurilemmoma (schwannoma)	30–40>	M = F	Circular filling defect on myelogram	Excision	Commonest intraspinal tumor
Neurofibroma			Circular defect, dumbell shape	Excision	Associated with neurofibromatosis
Meningioma	50–60>	F>	Circular defect with dural attachment	Excision	Eighty percent in thoracic spine
Intradural, intramedullary					
Ependymoma	20–60>	M>	Cord widening and dye defect	Excision	Fifty percent in the filum terminale
Astrocytoma	20–50>	M>	Cord widening	Excision (radiation?)	Higher grades worse prognosis
Cystic lesions					
Arachnoid cyst			Multiple dye defects	Excision if symptoms	Most common in thoracic
Syringomyelia	>20	M = F	Cord widening and MRI is positive	Laminectomy or syringostomy	Multiple causes
Perineural cyst			Cystic dilation of sacral roots	Observation, decompression	Most are asymptomatic

463

C. Surgery
  1. Indications
     a. Diagnostic reasons
     b. Excision for cure (benign tumors and primary malignant tumors)
     c. Unstable spine (by tumor invasion or following tumor resection)
     d. Neurologic deterioration
     e. Failure of previous radiation therapy
     f. Existence of radiation-resistant tumors
     g. Unremitting pain
  2. Surgical principles
     a. Excise the entire lesion if possible
     b. Approach anteriorly or posteriorly or both, depending on the location of the tumor
     c. Metastatic tumors are usually approached anteriorly, and second stage posterior stabilization is frequently necessary
     d. Use of bone grafts (autograft or allograft) is better than methyl methacrylate for long-term success
     e. Choose instrumentation that gives maximum stability
     f. Methyl methacrylate should be used as augmentation only
  3. Biopsy and surgical approaches
     a. Cervical spine
        (1) Biopsy
            i. Closed transoral approach for C1-C3 anterior lesions
            ii. Closed lateral approach with needle for C4-C7 anterior lesions
            iii. CT-guided approach may be more accurate and safer
            iv. Open biopsy may be preferred for posterior element lesions or anterior lesions if closed methods are deemed dangerous or if definitive treatment is planned after frozen section diagnosis
        (2) Excision and stabilization
            i. Posterior approach: autogenous bone graft with posterior wiring (alternatively, posterior plates, methyl methacrylate, or Luque sublaminar wires can be done)
            ii. Anterior approach: if the tumor involves the anterior body and compress the anterior cord (transoral or extended anterior approach can be used for C1-C3 and routine anterior approach for C4-C7 and iliac crest or fibular bone grafting with or without plates or methyl methacrylate)
     b. Cervicothoracic junction
        (1) Biopsy: open method is preferred unless CT-guided biopsy is used
        (2) Excision and stabilization
            i. Posterior approach: wires, plates, methyl methacrylate, or rods
            ii. Anterior approach: high transthoracic, sternal splitting, or supraclavicular approach
     c. Thoracic spine
        (1) Biopsy: open technique is preferable
            i. Transpedicular approach
            ii. Posterolateral: costotransversectomy
            iii. Transthoracic
            iv. CT-guided biopsy is preferred if closed method is chosen
        (2) Excision and stabilization
            i. Anterior approach: tumor resection and stabilization (bone graft with or without methyl methacrylate or plates may be used as augmentation)
            ii. Posterior approach: posterolateral resection of the tumor is possible, and posterior stabilization with various instrumentations can be done after or simultaneously with anterior procedures

d. Thoracolumbar or lumbar spine
   (1) Biopsy: closed technique with Craig needle using fluoroscopy (up to T11) or CT scan
   (2) Excision and stabilization
      i. Anterior approach: tumor resection and stabilization with bone graft with or without metal and cement
      ii. Posterior stabilization as needed (second-stage posterior stabilization should be done for lesions in the thoracolumbar region)

REFERENCES

Alexander AH: Chymopapain chemonucleolysis, discography, and needle biopsy technique. In Chapman's operative orthopaedics. Philadelphia, JB Lippincott, 1988

Bender, CE, Berquist TH, Wold LE: Imaging-assisted percutaneous biopsy of the thoracic spine. Mayo Clin Proc 61:942–950, 1986

Boland PJ, Lane JM, Sundaresan N: Metastatic disease of the spine. Clin Orthop 169:95–102, 1982

Capanna R, Albisinni U, Picci P, et al: Aneurysmal bone cyst of the spine. J Bone Joint Surg 67A:527–531, 1985

Ciappetta P, Celli P, Palma L, Mariottini A: Intraspinal hemangiopericytomas. Report of two cases and review of the literature. Spine 10:17–31, 1985

Clark CR, Keggi KJ, Panjabi MM: Methylmethacrylate stabilization of the cervical spine. J Bone Joint Surg 66:40–46, 1984

Danzig LA, Resnick D, Akeson WH: The treatment of cervical spine metastasis from the prostate with a halo cast. Spine 5:395–398, 1980

DeWald RL, Bridwell KH, Prodromas C, Rodts MF: Reconstructive spinal surgery as palliation for metastatic malignancies of the spine. Spine 10:21–26, 1985

Dunn EJ, Anas PP: The management of tumors of the upper cervical spine. Orthop Clin North Am 9:1065–1080, 1978

Dunn EJ, Anas PP: Tumors of the cervical spine. In Evarts MC, ed: Surgery of the musculoskeletal system 4:175–189, New York, Churchill Livingstone, 1983

Dunn HK: Tumors of the thoracic and lumbar spine. In Evarts MC, ed: Surgery of the musculoskeletal system 4:191–210, New York, Churchill Livingstone, 1983

Evarts CM: Diagnostic techniques: Closed biopsy of bone. Clin Orthop 107:100–111, 1975

Fidler MW: Pathological fractures of the cervical spine. J Bone Joint Surg 67B:352–357, 1985

Fielding JW, Pyle RN, Fietti VG: Anterior cervical vertebral body resection and bone grafting for benign and malignant tumors. J Bone Joint Surg 61A:251–253, 1979

Flatley TJ, Anderson MH, Anast GT: Spinal instability due to malignant disease. J Bone Joint Surg 65A:47–52, 1984

Friedlander GE, Southwick WO: Tumors of the spine. In Rothman and Simeone, eds. Spine. Philadelphia, WB Saunders, 1982

Fyfe IS, Henry APJ, Mulholland RC: Closed vertebral biopsy. J Bone Joint Surg 65B:140–143, 1983

Gladstein MO, Grantham SA: Closed skeletal biopsy. Clin Orthop 103:75–79, 1974

Goyal RN, Russell NA, Benoit, BG, Belanger JMEG: Intraspinal cysts: A classification and literature review. Spine 12:209–213, 1987

Harrington KD: The use of methylmethacrylate for vertebral-body replacement and anterior stabilization of pathological fracture-dislocations of the spine due to metastatic malignant disease. J Bone Joint Surg 63A:36–46, 1981

Hay MC, Paterson D, Taylor TK: Aneurysmal bone cysts of the spine. J Bone Joint Surg 60B:406–411, 1978

Himmelfarb YE, Sebes J, Rabinowitz J: Unusual roentgenographic presentations of multiple myeloma. J Bone Joint Surg 56A:1723–1728, 1974

Ker NB, Jones CB: Tumours of the cauda equina. J Bone Joint Surg 67B:358–362, 1985

Laredo J, Bard M: Thoracic spine: percutaneous trephine biopsy. Radiology 160:485–489, 1986

Lee CK, Rosa R, Fernand R: Surgical treatment of tumors of the spine. Spine 11:201–208, 1986

Light TR, Wagner FC, Johnson RM, Southwick WO: Correction of spinal instability and recovery of neurologic loss following cervical vertebral body replacement. Spine 5:392–394, 1980

Manabe S, Tateishi A, Abe M, Ohno T: Surgical treatment of metastatic tumors of the spine. Spine 14:41–47, 1989

McAfee PC, Bohlman HH, Riley LH, et al: The anterior retropharyngeal approach to the upper part of the cervical spine. J Bone Joint Surg 69A:1371–1383, 1987

Mick CA, Zinreich J: Percutaneous trephine bone biopsy of the thoracic spine. Spine 10:737–740, 1985

Moore TM, Meyers MH, Patzakis MJ, et al: Closed biopsy of musculoskeletal lesions. J Bone Joint Surg 61A:375–380, 1979

Nather A, Bose K: The results of decompression of cord or cauda equina compression from metastatic extradural tumors. Clin Orthop 169:103–107, 1982

Ottolenghi CE, Aires B: Aspiration biopsy of the spine. Technique for the thoracic spine and results of twenty-eight biopsies in this region and over-all results of 1050 biopsies of other spinal segments. J Bone Joint Surg 51A:1531–1544, 1969

Raycroft JF, Hockman RP, Southwick WO: Metastatic tumors involving the cervical vertebrae: Surgical palliation. J Bone Joint Surg 60A:763–768, 1978

Rodichok LD, Harper GR, Ruckdeschel JC, et al: Early diagnosis of spinal epidural metastases. Am J Med 70:1181–1188, 1981

Roscoe MW, McBroom RJ, St Louis E, et al: Preoperative embolization in the treatment of osseous metastases from renal cell carcinoma. Clin Orthop 238:302–307, 1989

Schaberg J, Gainor BJ: A profile of metastatic carcinoma of the spine. Spine 10:19–20, 1985

Sherman RMP, Waddell JP: Laminectomy for metastatic epidural spinal cord tumors. Clin Orthop 207:55–63, 1986

Siegal T, Tiqva P: Vertebral body resection for epidural compression by malignant tumors. J Bone Joint Surg 67A:375–382, 1985

Weinstein JN, McLain RF: Primary tumors of the spine. Spine 12:843–851, 1987

Wertheim SB, Bohlman HH: Occipitocervical fusion. J Bone Joint Surg 69A:833–836, 1987

Young RF, Post EM, King GA: Treatment of spinal epidural metastases. J Neurosurg 53:741–748, 1980

67
Arthritis of the Spine (Rheumatoid Arthritis and Seronegative Spondylitis)

RHEUMATOID ARTHRITIS

I. Cervical Spine Deformity

A. Atlantoaxial subluxation (AAS)
 1. Weak transverse ligament and synovitis of atlantoaxial and atlanto-odontoid joints
 2. Symptoms: neck pain, headache, and occasionally myelopathy (paresthesia, weakness, abnormal gait, and bowel or bladder difficulties)
 3. Increased atlantodens interval (ADI) (>3.5 mm is abnormal) and instability on flexion-extension view (tomogram or CT scan)
 4. MRI helpful to see the relationship between the spinal cord and soft tissues (ie, pannus) and bone
 5. Most subluxations are anterior, but posterior or lateral subluxations may occur
 6. Natural history
    a. Patients have a shorter life expectancy than the general population
    b. Subluxations can progress, but neurologic deterioration is not common
    c. Prognosis is worse if ADI >9 mm and atlantoaxial impaction is also present
    d. Once cervical myelopathy is established, the natural history without surgery is grave
 7. Treatment
    a. Conservative: neck collar and medications
    b. Surgery: myelopathy, unrelenting pain, or >7–9 mm ADI
       (1) Posterior atlantoaxial fusion (Fig 7-27)
       (2) Preoperative halo traction may be necessary in unreducible deformities
       (3) Halo immobilization for 3–4 months
    c. Surgical results are worse in patients with serious neurologic deficits; therefore early surgical intervention is indicated if there is progressive neurologic deficits and instability
B. Atlantoaxial impaction (AAI or basilar impression)
 1. Also known as cranial settling, upward migration of the odontoid, vertical subluxation of the axis, and pseudobasilar invagination
 2. Synovitis and cartilage destruction of occipitoatlantal and atlantoaxial joints
 3. Symptoms: occipital headache, myelopathy, or brainstem signs
 4. McGregor's line: >4.5 mm odontoid projection above the foramen magnum
 5. Ranawat's C1-C2 index: <13 mm is abnormal (Fig 7-1)
 6. Redlund-Johnell O-C2 index: <33 mm (men) and <27 mm (women) are abnormal
 7. Surgery
    a. Occiput-C1-C2 fusion
    b. Preoperative halo traction may be necessary in unreducible deformities
    c. Anterior transoral excision of the odontoid and pannus may be nec-

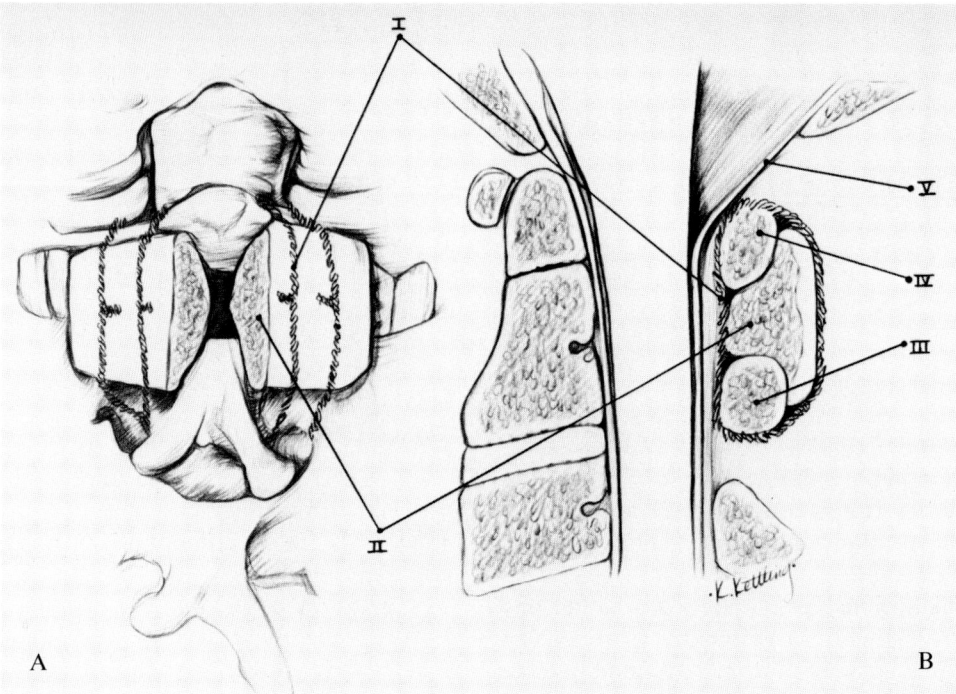

Figure 7-27. Brooks atlantoaxial fusion. **A.** Posterior view showing wires (I) and bone grafts (II). **B.** Lateral view showing dura (V), C1 arch (IV), and C2 (III) (Modified from Griswold, DM, et al: Atlantoaxial fusion for instability. J Bone Joint Surg 60A:285–292, 1978)

      essary in irreducible cases with anterior cord compression
- d. Resection of posterior foramen magnum and posterior arch of atlas may be necessary in posterior cord compression cases

C. Subaxial subluxation
1. Synovitis of facet joints, intervertebral discs (spondylodiscitis), and ligament involvement
2. Multiple level involvement and particularly common at C2-C3 and C3-C4 region
3. Subaxial problems
   a. Subluxation
   b. Subluxation below higher fusion
   c. Anterior spondylodiscitis with cord compression
   d. Compression from epidural rheumatoid granulation
   e. Subaxial hyperlordosis
4. Treatment: posterior fusion (myelopathy or >5 mm)

II. Spinal Deformity in Ankylosing Spondylitis

A. Loss of lumbar lordosis and increased cervical and thoracic kyphosis
B. Primary location of disabling deformity should be assessed
C. Hip flexion contracture or joint disease should be corrected first and may prevent spinal surgery
D. Lumbar osteotomy: significant loss of lumbar lordosis and if relatively normal cervical and thoracic sagittal contour
   1. Plumb line of C7 should fall within the body of the sacrum after osteotomy
   2. Osteotomy is done at L3-L4 or L2-L3 junction and instrumentation and fusion (the angle of correction corre-

sponds to the spine flexion deformity on standing)
3. Apex of osteotomy should be anterior to the neural tube (at the junction of posterior longitudinal ligament and intervertebral disc)
4. Both anterior and posterior procedures may be necessary
5. In severe kyphotic thoracic deformity, multiple posterior thoracic resection osteotomies can be done after anterior osteotomies
6. Osteotomy at C7-T1 junction with laminectomy from C6-T2 is considered for primary cervical kyphosis

REFERENCES

Brattstrom H, Elner A, Granholm L: Trans-oral surgery for myelopathy caused by rheumatoid arthritis of the cervical spine. Ann Rheum Dis 32:578, 1973

Breedveld FC, Algra PR, Vielvoye CJ, Cats A: Magnetic resonance imaging in the evaluation of patients with rheumatoid arthritis and subluxations of the cervical spine. Arthritis Rheum 30:624, 1987

Bryan WJ, Inglis AE, Sculco TP, Ranawat CS: Methylmethacrylate stabilization for enhancement of posterior cervical arthrodesis in rheumatoid arthritis. J Bone Joint Surg 64A:1045, 1982

Conaty JP, Morgan ES: Cervical fusion in rheumatoid arthritis. J Bone Joint Surg 63A:1218, 1981

Crockhard HA, Pozo JL, Ransford AO, et al: Transoral decompression and posterior fusion for rheumatoid arthritis with atlanto-axial subluxation. J Bone Joint Surg 68B:350, 1986

Ferlic DC, Clayton ML, Leidholt JD, Gamble WE: Surgical treatment of symptomatic unstable cervical spine in rheumatoid arthritis. J Bone Joint Surg 57A:349, 1975

Larsson SE, Toolanen G: Posterior fusion for atlantoaxial subluxation in rheumatoid arthritis. Spine 11:525, 1986

Lipson SJ: Cervical myelopathy and posterior atlantoaxial subluxation in patients with rheumatoid arthritis. J Bone Joint Surg 67A:693, 1985

Lipson SJ: Rheumatoid arthritis of the cervical spine. Clin Orthop 182:143, 1984

Lipson SJ: Rheumatoid arthritis of cervical spine. Clin Orthop 239:121, 1989

McMaster MJ: A technique for lumbar spinal osteotomy in ankylosing spondylitis. J Bone Joint Surg 67B:204, 1985

Meijers KAE, van Beusekam GT, Luyendijk W, Duijfjes F: Dislocation of the cervical spine with cord compression in rheumatoid arthritis. J Bone Joint Surg 56B:668, 1974

Menezes AH, Vangilder JC, Clark CR, El-Khoury G: Odontoid upward migration in rheumatoid arthritis: An analysis of 45 patients with "cranial settling." J Neurosurg 63:500, 1985

Morizono Y, Sakou T, Kawaida H: Upper cervical involvement in rheumatoid arthritis. Spine 12:721, 1987

Pellicci PM, Ranawat CS, Tsairis P, Bryan WJ: A prospective study of the progression of rheumatoid arthritis of the cervical spine. J Bone Joint Surg 63A:342, 1981

Rana NA, Hancock DO, Taylor AR, Hill AGS: Atlanto-axial subluxation in rheumatoid arthritis. J Bone Joint Surg 55B:458, 1973

Ranawat, CS, O'Leary P, Pellicci P, et al: Cervical fusion in rheumatoid arthritis. J Bone Joint Surg 61A;1003, 1979

Ransford AO, Crockard HA, Pozo JL, et al: Craniocervical instability treated by contoured loop fixation. J Bone Joint Surg 68B:173, 1986

Simmons E: Kyphotic deformity of the spine in ankylosing spondylitis. Clin Orthop 128:65, 1977

Simmons E: The surgical correction of flexion deformity of the cervical spine of ankylosing spondylitis. Clin Orthop 86:132, 1972

Smith PH, Benn RT, Sharp J: Natural history of rheumatoid cervical luxations. Ann Rheum Dis 31:431, 1972

Thomasen E: Vertebral osteotomy for correction of kyphosis in ankylosing spondylitis. Clin Orthop 194:142, 1985

Thompson RC, Meyer TJ: Posterior surgical stabilization for atlantoaxial subluxation in rheumatoid arthritis. Spine 10:597, 1985

Wertheim SB, Bohlman HH: Occipitocervical fusion: indications, technique, and long-term results in thirteen patients. J Bone Joint Surg 69A:833, 1987

SECTION 8: BIOMECHANICS AND BIOMATERIALS

Howard S. An
Jeffrey P. Schwab
David Skrade

68. Essential Concepts
69. Mechanics of Structures
70. Biomaterials
71. Biologic Tissues and Functional Biomechanics

68

Essential Concepts

I. Basic Definitions
A. Force: quantity necessary to accelerate a mass (Newton or m/s²) (see comparison of units in Table 8-1)
  1. Force: mass times acceleration ($F = ma$, Newton's second law)
  2. Weight: force produced by gravity ($W = m \cdot g$, where m = mass, g = acceleration due to gravity)
B. Mass: inertial quantity of matter (kg)
C. Moment: quantity necessary to accelerate an object angularly (also referred to as torque)
  1. Moment: magnitude of force times moment arm
  2. Moment arm: perpendicular distance between line of action of a force and center of motion that it tends to create (also referred to as lever arm)
  3. Couple: pair of equal and opposite parallel forces, applied at different points on the body, which produce a moment proportional to perpendicular distance between the line of action of forces
D. Mass moment of inertia: measure of resistance of an object to changes in angular velocity; analogous to mass in translational motion
E. Equilibrium: condition in which forces and moments on body are balanced
  1. Body is at rest, or in motion at a constant velocity (zero acceleration)
  2. $\Sigma F = 0$; $\Sigma M = 0$
  3. Often referred to as "static equilibrium"
F. Statics: study of external forces and moments on a body at rest
G. Dynamics: study of motion of, and external forces and moments on, a body in motion
  1. Kinematics: study of motion
    a. Translation: linear motion of a rigid body; every point on the body displaces an equal amount with respect to an external coordinate system, defined by vector quantities (magnitude, line of action, point of application, and sense)
      (1) Displacement: movement of an object from one position to another
      (2) Velocity: change in displacement per unit time
      (3) Acceleration: change in velocity per unit time
    b. Rotation: angular motion of a body relative to a line (axis of rotation); all points on the body maintain their distance from the axis of rotation
      (1) Angle
      (2) Angular velocity
      (3) Angular acceleration
  2. Kinetics: study of forces that cause motion
    a. Newton's laws
      (1) Inertia: body at rest tends to remain at rest, body that is moving tends to keep moving at a constant velocity
      (2) Force: mass times acceleration
      (3) For every action, there is an equal and opposite reaction
H. Dynamic equilibrium: analysis of kinematics and kinetics of a body in which inertial forces are considered
  1. Differs from "equilibrium" or "static equilibrium" because body does not have zero acceleration
  2. Newton's second law reformatted into: F (force) or $ma = 0$

Table 8-1 United States Customary Units and SI Equivalents

Entity	US Customary Units	SI Equivalent
Mass	1bm	0.4536 kg
Force	1bf	4.448 newtons (Nt)
Length	ft	0.3048 m
Velocity	ft/sec	0.3048 m/sec
Acceleration	ft/sec^2	0.3048 m/sec^2
Angle	deg	0.0175 rad
Moment/torque	ft-1bf	1.356 Nt-m
Mass, moment of inertia	1bm-ft^2	1.356 kg-m^2
Area, polar moment of inertia	ft^4	0.0086 m^4
Energy/work	ft-1bf	1.356 Nt-m = 1.356 J
Power	ft-1bf/sec	1.356 J/sec

I. Momentum
  1. Linear (translation): mass times velocity
  2. Angular (rotation): mass moment of inertia times angular velocity
J. Work: force times displacement along the line of force
K. Energy: amount of work done by a load on a body
  1. Strain energy: energy to deform an object
     a. Strain energy in elastic region is recoverable
     b. Resilient: higher recoverable strain energy
  2. Potential energy: energy stored in a structure as a function of position (with respect to gravity, height determines potential energy)
  3. Kinetic energy: energy a body possesses due to its motion (½ × mass × [velocity]^2)
L. Power: work or energy per unit of time

II. Types of Loading (Fig 8-1)

A. Compression: equal and opposite loads applied at opposite surfaces of a structure; causes shortening and widening (Poisson effect); force vector is normal to structural surface
B. Tension: equal and opposite loads applied at opposite surfaces, which tends to cause lengthening and narrowing of structure; force vector is normal to structural surface
C. Shear: forces applied perpendicular to surface of the structure
  1. Structure deforms internally in angular fashion
  2. Other types of loading will produce shear stress in some plane within the structure
D. Torsion: loading that causes a structure to twist about an axis
  1. Creates tension, compression, and shear stresses in different planes within the structure
  2. Shear stress is maximum furthest from axis of rotation
  3. Deformation is an angular deformation
E. Bending: load is applied to a structure at a point at which it is not directly supported
  1. Material on concave side is compression (material on convex side is in tension)
  2. Neutral axis is a line within structure where stresses and strains are zero
  3. Flexural unit stress: (M × c)/I, where M = bending moment, c = distance

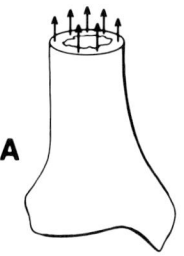

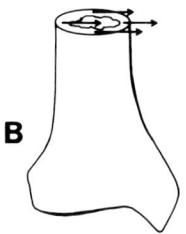

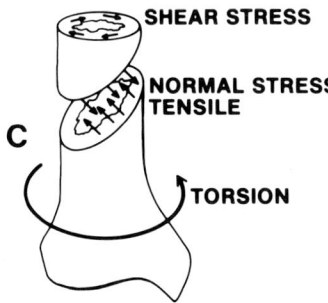

Figure 8-1. Loading in shaft of long bone. **A.** Tension. **B.** Shear. **C.** Torsion. (From White III AA, Panjabi MM: Clinical biomechanics of the spine. Philadelphia, JB Lippincott, 1978, p 501. Reprinted with permission.)

from neutral axis, and I = moment of inertia
F. Combined loading: application of two or more of the above loading types to a structure; is typical in vivo

III. Material Properties
A. Homogeneous: physical and mechanical properties are identical throughout the material
B. Isotropic: material for which the mechanical properties are independent of direction of loading
C. Anisotropic: material that has different mechanical properties, dependent on the direction of loading
D. Brittle: material that demonstrates little deformation before failure
E. Ductile: material that undergoes a relatively large deformation prior to failure
   1. Large plastic region on stress-strain curve
   2. Opposite of brittle
F. Hardness: measure of ability of a material to resist wear or local indentation or penetration

IV. Behavior of Materials
A. Stress: force/unit area; units of N/m^2 (Pascal), or lb/in^2
   1. Normal stress: stress perpendicular to the plane of a given cross-section
   2. Shear stress: stress applied parallel to the plane of a given cross-section
B. Strain: measure of deformation of a material (Fig 8-2)
   1. Normal strain: change in length divided by original length
      a. Deformation is perpendicular to plane of interest
      b. No unit
   2. Shear strain: angular deformation of a material
      a. Deformation is parallel to plane of interest
      b. Units are radians
C. Stress-strain curve: plot of stress vs strain of a material (Fig 8-3)
   1. Proportional limit (linear limit): point on stress-strain curve beyond which relation between stress and strain is no longer linear
   2. Elastic limit: up to this point on stress-strain curve, deformation is completely recoverable if load is removed; typically, is very nearly the same as proportional limit

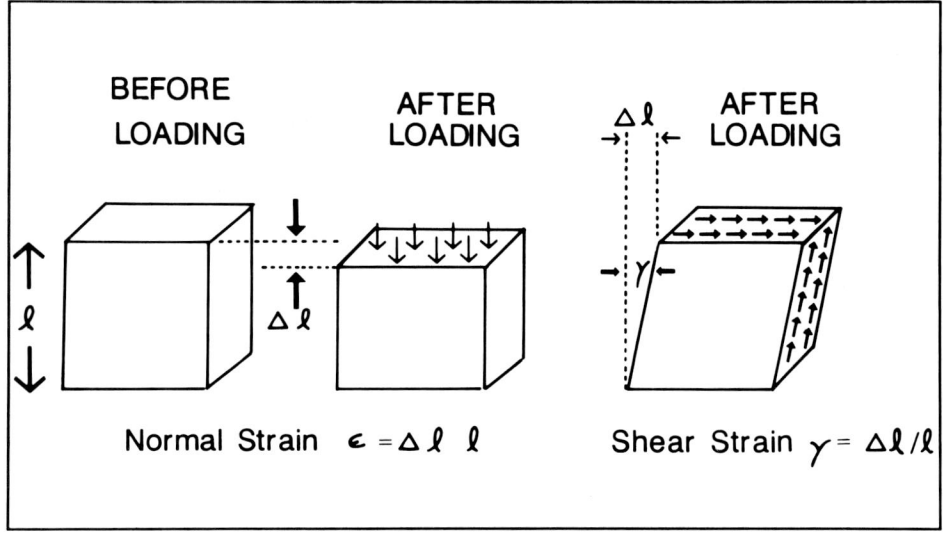

Figure 8-2. Strain. (From American Academy of Orthopaedic Surgeons: Orthopaedic science. A resource and self-study guide for the practitioner. Park Ridge, IL, 1986. Reprinted with permission.)

3. Yield point: point on stress-strain curve beyond which there is a marked increase in strain without a significant increase in stress
4. Yield stress: stress needed to produce a 0.2% permanent strain; convention that is used since yield point can be difficult to quantify exactly
5. Ultimate strength: maximum stress a material can withstand
   a. Often referred to as ultimate stress, ultimate yield point, ultimate tensile strength (UTS)
   b. For anisotropic material, UTS differs from ultimate strength in compression
6. Elastic region: area under stress-strain curve up to the elastic limit
7. Plastic region: area under stress-strain curve beyond elastic limit; deformation in this region is unrecoverable
8. Modulus of elasticity: ratio of stress to strain in tensile or compressive loading within the elastic region
   a. Also referred to as Young's modulus
   b. Units are N/m^2 (Pascals), or lb/in^2
   c. A determinant of a structure's stiffness, along with cross-sectional area, and length
9. Shear modulus: ratio of shear stress to shear strain
   a. Analogous to modulus of elasticity in tensile-compressive loading
   b. Also referred to as modulus of rigidity

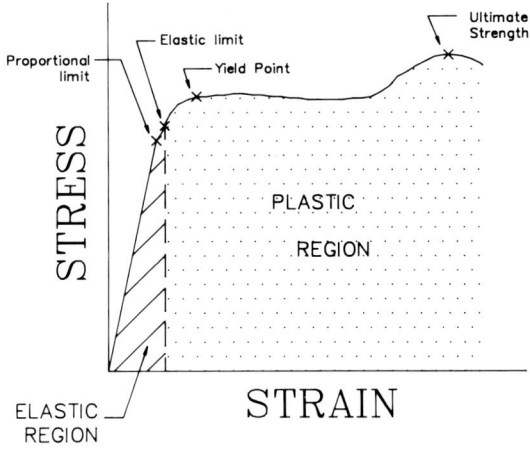

Figure 8-3. Plot of stress vs strain.

D. Strength: measure of a material's resistance to deformation; given in terms of stress

E. Fatigue: process in which failure of a structure is initiated by repeated loading to levels that are below ultimate strength (Fig 8-4)
  1. Endurance limit: stress to which a material can be loaded for an infinite number of cycles without failure
  2. Interdependency between number of cycles and level of stress needed for failure
  3. Dependent also on type of loading, structural geometry, and surface finish
  4. Corrosion contributes to fatigue
  5. Bone, as well as other biologic tissues, also subject to fatigue failure (often referred to as "stress fractures")

F. Fracture: failure of a structure by propagation of a crack

G. Toughness: energy to fracture for a given material; area under the stress-strain curve to failure

H. Fracture toughness: resistance of a material to propagation of a preexisting crack; more brittle materials, such as ceramics, typically have a low fracture toughness

V. **Rheology**
  A. Study of flow or deformation of matter
  B. Elasticity
    1. Property characterized in the ideal state by:
      a. Immediate deformation on application of a load
      b. Deformation fully reversible with load removed
      c. Linear relationship between stress and strain
    2. Referred to as "Hookean" materials (Hooke's law: $F = kx$, where F is applied force, k is stiffness constant, and x is displacement)
    3. Represented by a spring element
  C. Plasticity
    1. Property characterized in the ideal state by
      a. Zero deformation until a critical load is reached
      b. When critical force is reached, deformation is instant and continues as long as critical force is applied
      c. Deformation that does occur is permanent
    2. Represented by a block resting on a base with friction between the surfaces
  D. Viscosity
    1. Property characterized in the ideal state by
      a. Stress in the material varies with rate of deformation
      b. Time-dependent behavior
      c. Creep: with constant applied load, deformation continuously increases over time; effect is temperature dependent (Fig 8-5A)

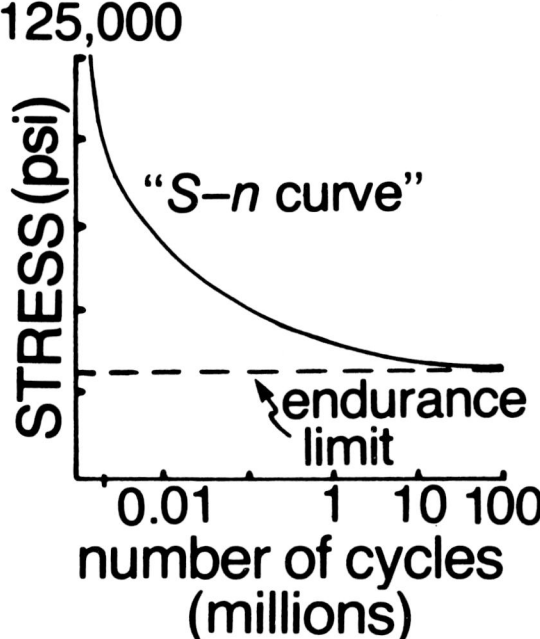

Figure 8-4. Cycling loading and fatigue stress. (From Cochran GVB: A primer of orthopaedic biomechanics. New York: Churchill Livingstone, 1982. Reprinted with permission.)

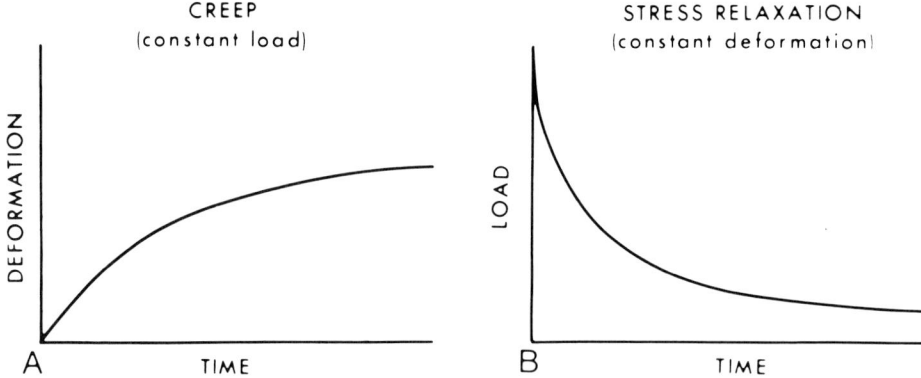

Figure 8-5. Creep and stress relaxation. **A.** Creep: with constant applied load, deformation continuously increases over time. **B.** Stress relaxation, with constant deformation, stress decreases continuously over time.

    d. Stress relaxation: with constant deformation, stress decreases continuously over time (Fig 8-5B)
    e. Deformation remains after load is removed
2. Differs from plasticity in that there is no critical load; any load causes deformation
3. Represented by a dashpot
4. Damping: refers to viscous effects; defined as the property that constitutes a resistance to changes in speed
5. Viscosity is quantified as the resistance of a material to flow deformation; this can apply to solids as well as fluids
    a. In solids, viscosity is ratio of shear stress to shear strain rate
    b. In fluids, viscosity is ratio of shear stress to velocity gradient
        (1) Velocity gradient: where two surfaces separated by a fluid are moving at a given velocity with respect to each other, velocity gradient is ratio of velocity to distance between the surfaces
        (2) Newtonian fluid: fluid for which viscosity is constant at a constant temperature; viscosity independent of velocity gradient
        (3) Non-newtonian fluid: fluid for which viscosity is dependent on velocity gradient
        i. Synovial fluid is an example; with higher velocity gradients, it is less viscous; this is important relative to joint lubrication; at higher speeds, or with smaller distance between joint surfaces, fluid is thinner (lower viscosity), and therefore provides better lubrication; however, it is also squeezed out from between the surfaces more easily
        ii. Thixotropic: changes in viscosity with changes in velocity gradient are time-dependent, ie, response to changes in velocity gradient are not instantaneous
E. Rheologic models
    1. Viscoelastic: substance whose properties are a composite of the ideal elastic element, and the ideal viscous element
        a. Biologic materials are viscoelastic, although plastic deformation (failure) also occurs
        b. Viscous component important in terms of creep, stress relaxation, and dependency on rate of loading

c. Viscoelastic models
   (1) Maxwell body: elastic element in series with viscous element
   (2) Kelvin body: elastic element in parallel with viscous element
   (3) Three-element model: Kelvin body in series with a second elastic element; this most accurately represents biologic tissues up to the point of failure

VI. Friction, Lubrication, and Wear
A. Friction: resistance between two surfaces sliding across one another
   1. Proportional to coefficient of friction between the two given surfaces, and normal force pushing the two surfaces together
   2. Static coefficient > dynamic coefficient
B. Lubrication: reduction of frictional forces between two bodies by introduction of substance between them
   1. Fluid film: lubricant material maintains separation between the two sliding surfaces (Fig 8-6)
      a. Hydrostatic: fluid film lubrication in which separation of two surfaces is maintained by external pressurization of the fluid film
      b. Weeping: one or both of the surfaces is porous; exudate from pores provides additional lubrication; an important form of lubrication with cartilage
      c. Hydrodynamic: separation of two surfaces is maintained by inflow of fluid film due to motion of the two bodies
      d. Squeeze film: motion of the two bodies tends to squeeze out the fluid film; lubrication decreases with time if the fluid is actually squeezed out
      e. Elastohydrodynamic lubrication: one or both surfaces is soft enough to be deformed by the fluid film; fluid film is trapped between the surfaces, thereby maintaining lubrication
   2. Boundary: chemical absorption of monolayer of lubricant molecules to surfaces of contacting bodies; in cartilage,

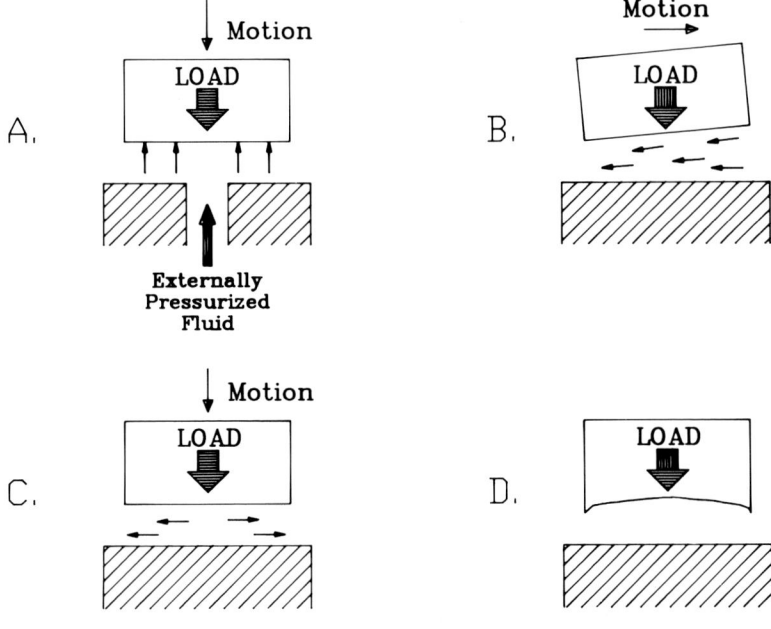

Figure 8-6. Types of fluid film lubrication. A. Hydrostatic. B. Hydrodynamic. C. Squeeze film. D. Elastohydrodynamic. Depiction of 6 degrees of freedom in three-dimensional space. (From American Academy of Orthopaedic Surgeons: Orthopaedic science. A resource and self-study guide for the practitioner. Park Ridge, IL, 1986, slide V, 10. Reprinted with permission.)

lubricant molecules are a hyaluronic acid protein complex
3. Mixed: combination of one or more of the above; for example, articular cartilage lubrication is boundary plus fluid film (elastohydrodynamic plus weeping plus squeeze film)

C. Wear: removal of surface material by mechanical action
  1. Types
    a. Interfacial: wear due to interaction of two surfaces
      (1) Adhesion: results if contact junction between two materials is stronger than material itself
      (2) Abrasion: soft surface scraped by hard surface
    b. Fatigue: wear due to deformation of contacting bodies; subsurface stress leads to surface wear
    c. Transfer: material from softer surface transferred to harder surface, changing nature of interface
    d. Third body: trapped wear debris or foreign particles between two bodies produces interfacial or fatigue wear
  2. Wear plays a role in fatigue failure

VII. Miscellaneous Terms

A. Biomechanics: study of form and function in biology using the principles of applied mechanics

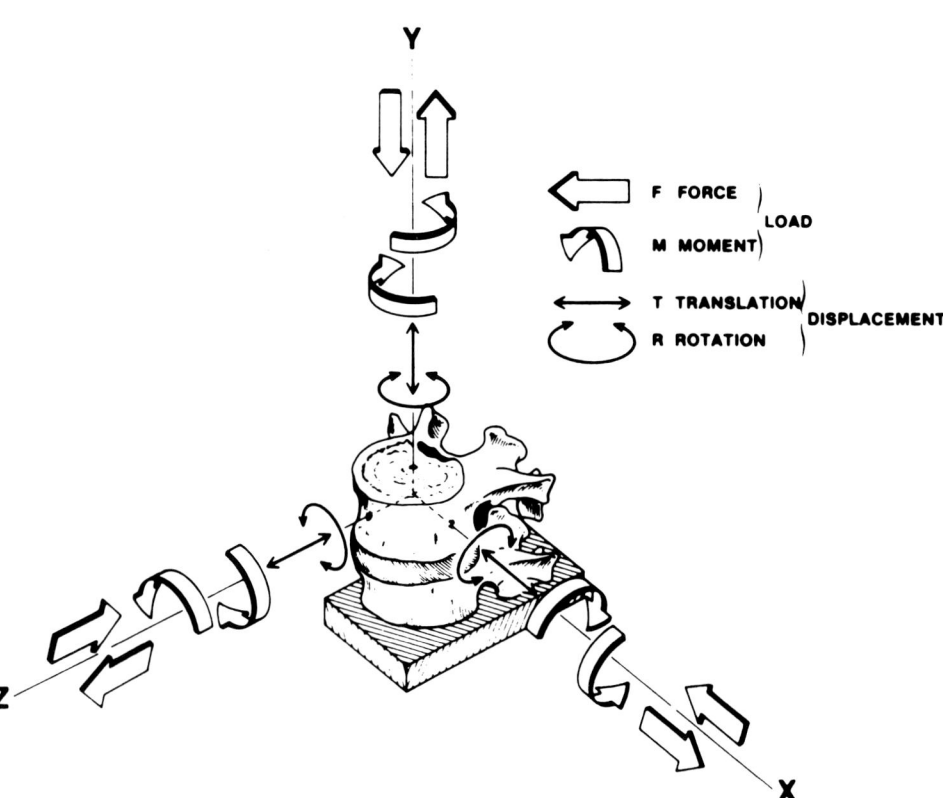

Figure 8-7. Degrees of freedom, consisting of translation along, or rotation about three mutually perpendicular axes. (From White AA III, Panjabi MM: Clinical biomechanics of the spine. Philadelphia, JB Lippincott, 1978. Reprinted with permission.)

B. Center of gravity: point at which a supported body is balanced about all axes
C. Center of mass: same as center of gravity
D. Centroid: center of a given area or volume
E. Degrees of freedom: number of unique variables needed to describe position of a body in space; in three-dimensional space, there are 6 degrees of freedom, consisting of translation along, or rotation about, three mutually perpendicular axes (Fig 8-7)
F. Scalar: mathematical quantity defined by magnitude only, for example, temperature
G. Vector: magnitude, line of application, point of application, and sense (direction along line of action)
H. Radius of curvature: radius of a circle that fits a given curve most closely

69
Mechanics of Structures

I. Definition of Structure
A. Structures are made of materials, but their behavior also depends on size, shape, and orientation

II. Moment of Inertia
A. Geometry of, or distribution of material in a structure; along with material properties, predicts behavior of a structure under loading
B. Area moment of inertia: measure of distribution of material in a cross-section of a structure with respect to some external reference (Fig 8-8)
 1. Determines bending stiffness and strength
 2. A times d^2, where A is area of a given unit and d is distance from a given axis
 3. Pertains to stress and strain within a structure under equilibrium
C. Polar moment of inertia: measure of distribution of material in cross-section of a structure with respect to an axis of rotation
 1. Determines torsional stiffness and strength of structure
 2. Pertains to stress and strain within a structure under static equilibrium

III. Bending Rigidity
A. Bending: load is applied to a structure at a point at which it is not directly supported
 1. Material on concave side is in compression; material on convex side is in tension
 2. Bending rigidity (bending stiffness): resistance of a structure to bending (Fig 8-9)
    a. Material furthest from neutral axis (extreme fibers) contributes most in resisting bending
    b. Stress is proportional to length raised to the third power
    c. For cylinders, stress inversely proportional to fourth power of the radius; for beams, stress inversely proportional to cube of thickness
 3. Flexural unit stress gives stress at a particular location within the structure; $\sigma = (M \times c)/I$, where M = bending moment, c = distance from neutral axis, and I = moment of inertia
 4. Neutral axis: defines region within a structure subjected to bending where stresses and strains are zero
 5. Cantilever bending: structure is fully supported at one location, and single load is applied at some other point; moment equals force times distance from support
 6. Three-point bending: structure loaded at three points, with single loading point on one side acting between two loading points on opposite side
 7. Four-point bending: structure is loaded so that two transverse forces are applied on one side, and two on the other
    a. Standard method for testing materials, as well as anatomic structures
    b. If forces are equal and arranged symmetrically, a pure constant bending moment exists between the two inner-most loading points
B. Load-deformation curve: depicts structural properties; can be derived based on structural geometry, and material properties (stress-strain curve)
 1. Deformation: changes in size or shape of a structure
 2. Load: forces and/or moments on a structure
 3. Stiffness: slope of load/deformation curve

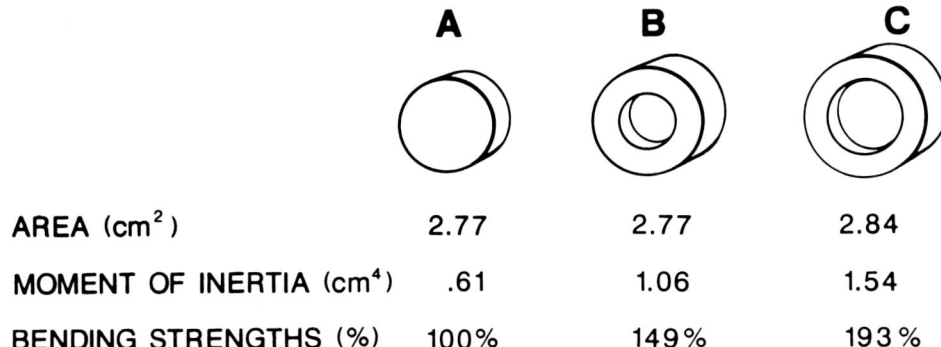

Figure 8-8. Moment of inertia for various cross-sections. This illustrates the drastic effects that geometry can have on bone strength, and, in particular, the advantage of having tubular shapes. (From American Academy of Orthopaedic Surgeons: Orthopaedic science. A resource and self-study guide for the practitioner. Park Ridge, IL, 1986, slide V, 34. Reprinted with permission.)

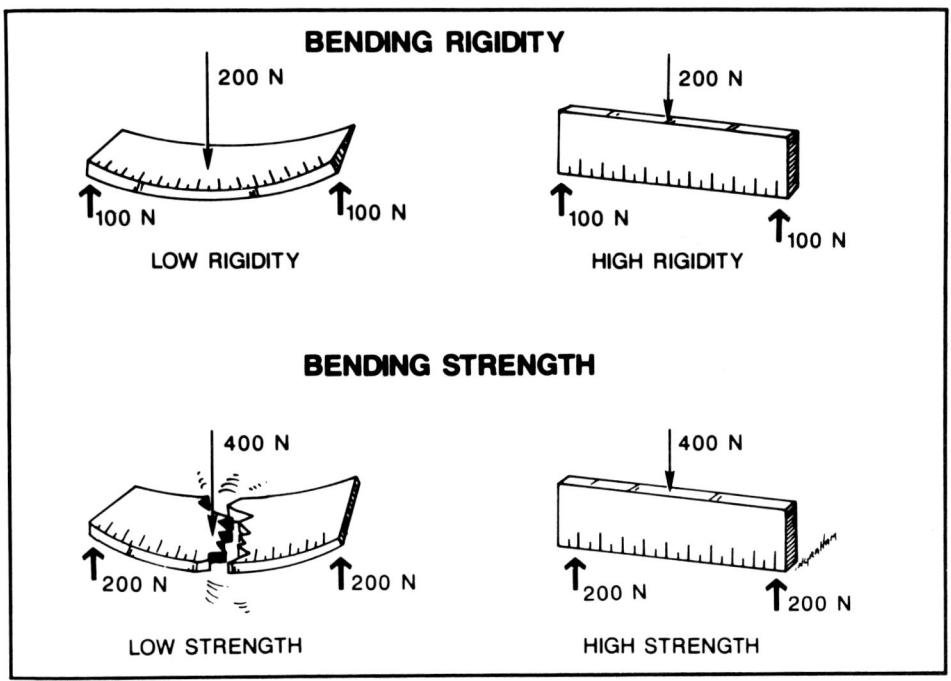

Figure 8-9. Bending rigidity (stiffness) of a structure under different directions of loading. (From American Academy of Orthopaedic Surgeons: Orthopaedic science. A resource and self-study guide for the practitioner. Park Ridge, IL, 1986, slide V, 33. Reprinted with permission.)

a. Stiffness: K = E · A/L, where E is modulus of elasticity, A is cross-sectional area, and L is length
  b. Also referred to as rigidity
 4. Hysteresis: energy lost or dissipated internally in loading and unloading of a structure; proportional to the degree of viscosity of a material

IV. Torsional Rigidity

A. Torque to produce a unit of angular deformation
B. Torsional rigidity equals (G · J)/L, where G = shear modulus, J = polar moment of inertia, and L = length
C. Materials furthest from axis of rotation most critical in resisting torsion; rigidity inversely proportional to fourth power of the radius
D. Analogous to stiffness (rigidity) for tension or compression loading

V. Miscellaneous Terms

A. Rigid body: collection of particles joined rigidly together; theoretically, there is no deformation; however, a body is often assumed to be rigid if its deformation is small relative to the motion or deformation being analyzed
B. Free-body analysis: method for characterizing forces on a body by isolating it from all its attachments, and assuming that it is in equilibrium
C. Combined loading: application of two or more loading types to a structure (ie, tension, compression, bending, torsion, shear); is typical in vivo
D. Principal planes: plane in which shear stress is zero; only normal stresses exist
E. Principal stresses: stresses normal to the principal plane
F. Buckling: bending produced by force along the long axis of a structure
 1. Mode of failure where ratio of length to width is approximately 10:1
 2. Loss of transverse trabeculae and thinning of longitudinal trabeculae in osteoporosis lead to buckling failure
G. Finite element analysis/method (FEA/FEM): numerical method for dividing a complex structure into smaller units for purposes of quantifying stresses and strains throughout the structure; used in orthopaedics because of complex geometries, and because of anisotropy of biologic materials

70
Biomaterials

I. Biomaterials
A. Types of materials (mechanical properties given in Table 8-2)
   1. Metals
   2. Ceramics: composed of a metal plus a nonmetal
   3. Polymer: man-made organic materials
      a. Consist of long chains of hydrocarbons
      b. May also include other nonmetals, such as N, O, Si, F
   4. Composites: any combination of these three types of materials
B. AISI: American Iron and Steel Institute; index system designates grades of steel
C. ASTM: American Society for Testing and Materials

II. Biocompatibility
A. Tolerance of host organism for an implant
B. Local host response: biologic reaction to implant in region of implantation
   1. Cellular and extracellular events consistent with early stages of wound healing
   2. Fibrous capsule is formed around implant
C. Systemic response: physiologic responses to an implant which are distant to the implant itself
D. Clastic response: cellular response to an implant in which local bone is destroyed
E. Neoclastic transformation: response to an implant in which mutagenic and possibly carcinogenic agents are elicited locally and at distant sites (due to chronic inflammatory cells at implant site or release of metal ions from implant)

III. Corrosion
A. Degradation of a material by chemical attack
B. Galvanic corrosion: due to contact between two metals with different oxidation potentials
   1. "Anodic" material is corroded
   2. Stainless steel most likely biomaterial to undergo galvanic corrosion
   3. Inclusion corrosion: type of galvanic corrosion due to impurity inclusions
C. Stress corrosion: surface layers produced by passivation crack due to high stresses; loss of passive layer accelerates corrosion
D. Intergranular corrosion: corrosion occurs along grain boundaries or crystal boundaries within the material
E. Crevice corrosion: occurs in a local defect, or crevice; crevice region depleted of oxygen, which accelerates corrosion
F. Pitting corrosion: same as crevice corrosion
G. Uniform attack corrosion: occurs in solution with high ionic conductivity, such as with typical physiologic solutions; hydrogen or oxygen-free radicals serve as acceptors for free metal ions (loss of free metal ions accelerates corrosion)
H. Fretting corrosion: micromovements between two components wears away passive layer, thereby accelerating corrosion
I. Passivation: process that occurs with a metal in an electrolytic solution; reactions occur that coat the metal surface (usually with a metal oxide), which prevents further release of metal ions into solution
J. Immunity: reaction between a metal and an electrolytic solution in which rate of release of free ions into solution is very low

IV. Metal Processing
A. Cast: molten metal poured into mold, then cooled

Table 8-2 Mechanical Properties of Various Biomaterials*[†]

Material	Ultimate Strength Tensile	Ultimate Strength Compressive	Yield Strength (Tension)	Modulus of Elasticity
Muscle	0.2	—	—	—
Skin	8	—	—	50
Cartilage (hyaline)	4	10	—	20
Fascia	10	—	—	—
Tendon	70	—	—	400
Bone, cortical	100	175	80	15,000
Bone, cancellous (without marrow)	2	3	—	1,000
Plaster of Paris	70	75	20	—
Polyethylene (UHMW - HDP)	40	20	20	1,000
Polytetrafluoroethylene (PTFE - Teflon)	25	—	—	500
Acrylic bone cement (PMMA: F-151)	40	80	—	2,000
Polyamide (nylon)	80	—	—	3,000
Aluminum (annealed, pure)	70	—	30	70,000
Titanium (cold-worked) (pure, F-67)	500	—	400	100,000
Titanium 6A1-4V (alloy: F-136)	900	—	800	100,000
Stainless steel (316, 316L)	>500	—		
Wrought, annealed (F-55, 56, 138, 139)	>850		>200	200,000
Wrought, cold-worked (F55, 56, 138, 139)			>700	200,000
Cobalt-chromium alloys				
Cast (F-75) (Co, Cr, Mo)	>450	—	>50	200,000
Wrought, annealed (F-90) (Co, Cr, W, Ni)	>300	—	>300	230,000
Wrought, cold-worked (F-90) (Co, Cr, W, Ni)	1500	—	1000	230,000
"Super alloys" (F562) (wrought, special heat-treated, cold working, etc.) (Co, Ni, Mo, etc.)	1800	—	1600	230,000

*This table gives a composite of values from a variety of sources. Data represent typical values rounded to facilitate recall. All materials listed have a broad range of values due to biologic, compositional, or manufacturing process variations. — indicates that a representative single value is not readily available. All values are in MPa (megapascals). 1 MPa = 145 psi.
[†]Adapted from Cochran GVB: A primer of orthopaedic biomechanics. Churchill Livingstone, New York, 1982.

    1. Problems with volume changes on cooling
    2. Voids and uneven dispersion of impurities weaken material mechanically
  B. Wrought or forged: shaping metal by blows or pressure from hammer, press, or machine
    1. Annealing: metal processing in which material is heated, then slowly cooled and shaped
      a. Increases ductility
      b. Reverses microstructural defects produced by prior metal-working
    2. Cold-working: forging a material at room temperature
      a. Increases strength and stiffness

METAL ALLOY SYSTEMS

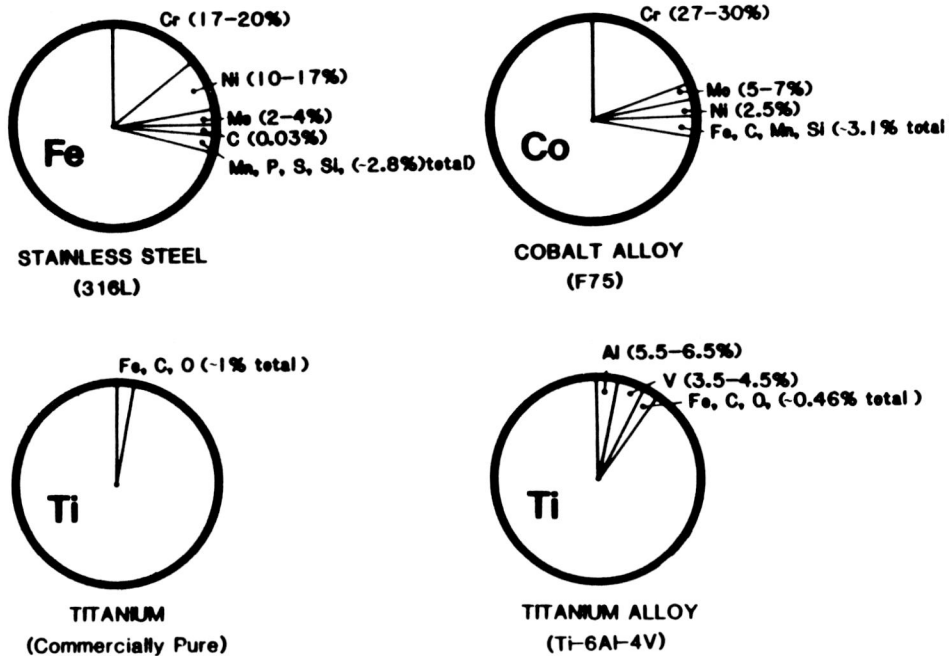

Figure 8-10. Composition of typical orthopaedic implants. (From American Academy of Orthopaedic Surgeons: Orthopaedic science. A resource and self-study guide for the practitioner. Park Ridge, IL, 1986. Reprinted with permission.)

    b. Reduces ductility
3. Hot isostatic press (HIP): liquid alloy atomized to powder, then powder is consolidated at high temperature and pressure
    a. Produces void-free solid, fine grain structure
    b. Increases strength

V. Metals (Fig 8-10)

A. Stainless steel
1. Composition: 60% Fe, 20% Cr, 15% Ni, 3% Mo, traces of others
2. Grades
    a. AISI 316, 316L, 316LVM
    b. Wrought, annealed (ASTM F-55, F-56, F-138, F-139)
    c. Wrought, cold-worked (ASTM F-55, F-56, F-138, F-139)
3. Properties
    a. Cr adds corrosion resistance by passivation
    b. C adds strength, but forms undesirable precipitate with Cr, which leads to crevice corrosion and fatigue fracture
    c. Ni adds strength and corrosion resistance
    d. Mo helps prevent crevice or pitting corrosion
    e. 316L: low C, more Ni
    f. 316LVM: vacuum-melted process; cleaner metal, resistance to fatigue
    g. Passivating process consists of dipping in nitric acid to generate oxide film on implant
    h. Surgical stainless is austenitic steel

(face-centered crystalline structure), as opposed to ferritic or martensitic
  i. Are either cold-worked or annealed
  j. Main problems with stainless steels: corrosion, fatigue fracture
B. Cobalt alloys
 1. Composition: 60% Co, 30% Cr, 7% Mo; traces of others
 2. Grades
  a. Cast (ASTM F-75)
  b. Wrought or forged (ASTM F-90)
  c. HIP: (ASTM F-562)
 3. Properties
  a. Highly resistant to corrosion due to Cr
  b. Highly resistant to fatigue fracture
  c. HIP or forging increases ductility and fatigue resistance
  d. Hexagonal crystalline structure
  e. Addition of Ni increases strength, but has corrosion and compatibility problems
C. Titanium
 1. Composition: pure Ti (ASTM F-67)
 2. Properties: lower stiffness, strength, and corrosion resistance than Ti alloys
D. Titanium alloys
 1. Composition: 90% Ti, 6% Al, 4% V; Ti-6Al-4V (ASTM F-136)
 2. Properties
  a. More corrosion resistance than stainless steel or cobalt alloys
  b. Lower modulus than stainless steel or cobalt alloys (less stress shielding)
E. Porous metals
 1. Composition
  a. Stainless steel, Co-Cr-Mo, or Ti in the form of beads or fiber mesh
  b. Void metal composites, with voids produced by vaporization of Mg microspheres from base alloy
 2. Beads or mesh bonded to solid substrate
  a. Sintering: beads bonded to each other and to substrate through heating process below melting point (fatigue strength of material decreased significantly due to heating process)
  b. Diffusion bonding: preshaped fiber metal pads bonded to substrate using heat and pressure (lower heat than with sintering; therefore mechanical properties not as drastically reduced)
  c. Plasma spraying: porous metal, in powder form, is propelled through a nozzle onto surface of the substrate solid
   (1) High energy arc at mouth of nozzle heats powder into a molten state
   (2) Substrate material is not actually heated, thereby reducing effects of porous coating process on substrate mechanical properties
 3. Properties
  a. Porous surface provides implant stability through ingrowth of bone into pores
  b. Must have strong initial fixation to minimize micromotion and allow ingrowth
  c. Pore size: 175 to 400 μm
  d. Fatigue life of implant reduced because of high temperatures in bonding processes or stress concentrations from beads and notches
  e. More difficult technique of implantation than with cemented implants
  f. Removal (revision) of porous metal implants can be very difficult
  g. Metal ion release activity not well known
  h. Porous implants not advised for patients with weak bone or patients who would otherwise have slow formation of new bone, such as elderly
  i. Ingrowth process not completely understood
F. "Super alloys"
 1. Composition: Co-Ni-Cr-Mo-Ti (ASTM F 562-578) (multiphase family of alloys)

2. Properties: increased fatigue strength and yield strength
3. Vacuum-melted and casted, then forged to preliminary formed parts

VI. Polymers
A. Polymethyl methacrylate (PMMA)
 1. Composition: $CH_2=CH\text{-}COOH$ (acrylic acid)
 2. Properties
    a. Cold-curing polymer
    b. Modulus about 10% of cortical bone
    c. Compressive strength about 50% of cortical bone
    d. Stronger in compression than in tension or shear
    e. Relatively brittle
    f. A viscoelastic material
    g. Used as a luting or grouting agent; not an adhesive agent
    h. Failure tends to occur at bone-cement interface
    i. Addition of antibiotic decreases strength
    j. Carbon additives increase strength, but intrusion properties are decreased
    k. Deleterious local tissue effects
       (1) Heat released on polymerization (67°C); tissue necrosis
       (2) Occlusion of nutrient metaphyseal arteries; tissue necrosis
       (3) Cytoxic effects
    l. Systemic effects
       (1) Hypotension following introduction of PMMA: peripheral vasodilation and myocardial depression
       (2) Methyl methacrylate monomer metabolized to methacrylic acid, which may diminish phagocytosis of leukocytes
 3. Cement technique
    a. Sets faster with high temperature and heat, but strength is decreased
    b. Larger cement mass decreases set time, but increases maximum temperature
    c. Slow beating under centrifugation or vacuum to decrease voids and absorb fumes
    d. Mixing time: 60–90 seconds dough time; several minutes from working time to setting time
    e. Early insertion of implant gives better intrusion and cohesion because of low viscosity, but may increase release of monomer, thereby increasing local cellular necrosis or systemic hypotension
    f. Pressurization important with cement plug and injection device
    g. Dry field without blood to prevent strength decrease secondary to voids or poor grouting
B. Polyethylene: Ultrahigh molecular weight (UHMWPE)
 1. Composition: polymerized ethylene $(CH_2=CH_2)$
 2. Properties
    a. Relatively tough and wear resistant
    b. Deformation and tensile cracking failure may occur
    c. Modulus and strength < bone
    d. Toughness, wear resistance, and strength a function of high molecular weight
    e. Role of creep in failure depends on the thickness (ie, acetabular component wear)
C. Polyester
 1. Textile band of braided polyethylene terephthalate
 2. Commercial name is Dacron (application as ligament substitution)
D. Polypropylene
 1. Ligament augmentation device
 2. Only outermost fibers show fibroplasia
 3. Strength and stiffness similar to UHMWPE
E. Polytetrafluoroethylene (PTFE)
 1. Braided fibers

2. Some ingrowth of fibrous tissues occurs into pores
3. Permanent implant for chronic instabilities
4. Commercial name is Gore-Tex

VII. Ceramics
A. Alumina
 1. Composition: aluminum oxide
 2. Properties
    a. Low tensile strength
    b. Brittle
    c. High compressive strength, modulus of elasticity
    d. Low coefficient of friction, and therefore high resistance to wear
    e. Inert; therefore good tissue compatability
B. Calcium phosphates
 1. Composition: hydroxyapatite (HA: $Ca_{10}(PO_4)_6(OH)_2$), tricalcium phosphate (TCP: $Ca_3(PO_4)_2$), or a mixture of the two
 2. Properties
    a. Low tensile strength, brittle
    b. High modulus, high compressive strength
    c. Inert, good tissue compatibility
 3. Typically used in porous form
    a. Micropores: pores within microstructure of material itself
    b. Macropores: granular form of ceramic; held with biologic or biocompatible "glue"; or granules sintered or plasma-sprayed to substrate solid
 4. Can be synthesized in vitro, or extracted from coral or bovine bone
 5. HA is essentially permanent, although it can be broken down and absorbed dependent on the incidence of crystalline defects; TCP can be absorbed in a matter of weeks or months
 6. Especially good biocompatability since bone mineral content formed in vivo is HA
 7. Porosity and biocompatability allow excellent bone ingrowth, referred to as "bioactive" material

VIII. Silicones
A. Spacer for nonweight-bearing small joints
B. Weak
C. Poor wear resistance
D. Silicone synovitis may be a problem

71
Biologic Tissues and Functional Biomechanics

I. Bone
A. Cortical bone
 1. Bone mineral: comprises about ⅔ of bone mass and responsible for stiffness of bone
 2. Organic bone matrix: comprises about ⅓ of bone mass and responsible for viscoelasticity of bone
    a. Type I collagen comprises 90% of the matrix
    b. Collagen oriented along the stress line in the lamellar cortical bone, which gives toughness and ductility
 3. In mature bone, the longitudinally oriented bone is strongest in compression, then in tension, and weakest in shear loading (Fig 8-11)
 4. Fatigue fracture: due to cyclic loading of magnitude and/or frequency, which is too great for bone to respond adequately through remodeling
 5. Viscoelasticity
    a. Depends on loading rate: faster the loading rate, the stiffer the bone, the higher total energy absorbed, the higher the ultimate strength to failure, and the lower the ductility
    b. At a higher loading rate, the bone is stronger than the ligament (midsubstance rupture of the anterior cruciate ligament occurs in a higher loading rate, but avulsion occurs in low loading rate injuries of the knee) (Fig 8-12)
B. Trabecular bone: about 25% as dense, 5–10% as stiff, and 5 times more ductile when compared with cortical bone
C. Compressive strength of bone is proportional to the square of density; stiffness is proportional to the cube of density
D. Aging
 1. Decreased density (less stiffness and strength), decreased strain to failure (more brittle)
 2. Larger diameter away from neutral axis maintains bending and torsional strength because of larger area and polar moments of inertia, but energy to failure is still less due to brittleness
E. Fracture geometry depends on loading and structural characteristics
 1. Bone fails on the tension side first, with propagation toward the compression side in an oblique track, resulting in "butterfly fragment" on the compression side
 2. Immature bone may fracture on the compression side first ("buckle fractures")
 3. Response in bending depends heavily on structural geometry with respect to a given load or the area moment of inertia (for example, the tibia is broader posteriorly, therefore bending in which the concavity is anterior will be better resisted than bending with a posterior concavity
 4. Torsional loading
    a. Internal rotation of the tibia gives stress at the lateral aspect first, resulting in a spiral fracture starting from distal lateral tibia, with the fracture line propagating proximally toward the medial side
    b. Higher the polar moment of inertia, the stronger and more resistant to

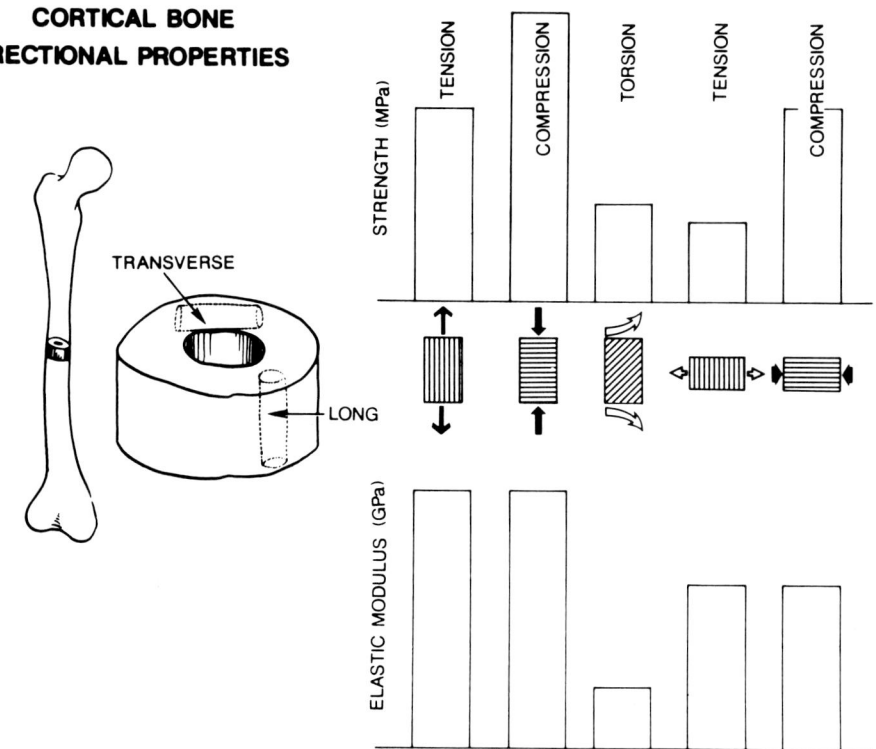

Figure 8-11. Directional properties of the cortical bone. (Longitudinally oriented bone is strongest in compression, then in tension, and weakest in shear loading.) (From American Academy of Orthopaedic Surgeons: Orthopaedic science. A resource and self-study guide for the practitioner. Park Ridge, IL, 1986. Reprinted with permission.)

      fractures; proximal tibia is stronger because of greater diameter and therefore greater polar moment of inertia (Fig 8-13)
   c. Higher rate of loading gives comminuted fracture; slower rate gives spiral fracture
F. Stress concentration (stress risers): discontinuity in a structure, such as a hole, notch, sharp corner, or sudden change in material property, causes high localized stress
   1. Stress riser on the tension side away from the neutral axis of bending is detrimental in internal fixation
   2. Rounder edge gives less stress than rectangle
   3. Section defects of cortical bone
      a. The presence of a hole (up to 20% of diameter) on the tension side of a bend weakens a tubular bone by 50% (Bechtol)
      b. No significant differences in strength among different sizes of defects up to 20%
      c. Fifty percent of torsional strength and 25% of normal capacity to absorb energy by a drill hole (Frankel and Burstein)
      d. Torque and angular deformation to failure are reduced to 30% and energy absorption capacity to 10% of normal by creating an open section in the tibia (ie, bone grafting)

Figure 8-12. Failure in bone-ligament-bone complex is dependent on rate of loading. (Cochran GVB: A primer of orthopaedic biomechanics. New York, Churchill Livingstone, 1982, p 169. Reprinted with permission.)

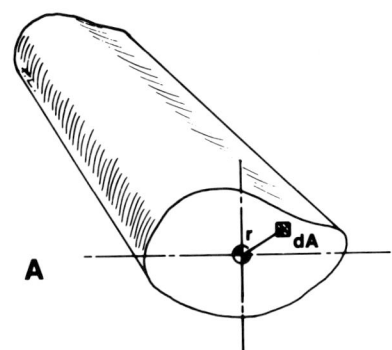

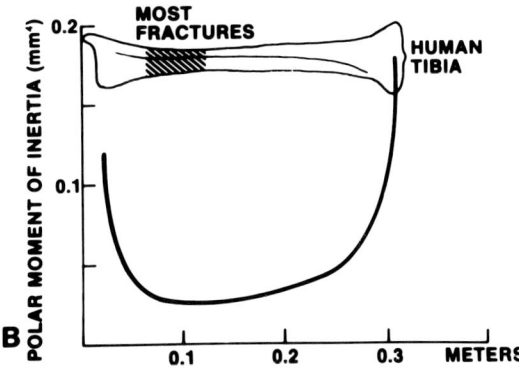

Figure 8-13. Effect of polar moment of inertia on location of torsional fractures of the tibia. **A.** Mathematical interpretation. **B.** Experimental values. (From White AA III, Panjabi MM: Clinical biomechanics of the spine. Philadelphia, JB Lippincott, 1978. Reprinted with permission.)

G. Bone remodeling: process in which living bone adapts to mechanical stresses placed on it
  1. Also referred to as Wolff's Law
  2. Changes in size (area), shape (area and polar moments of inertia), and structure (mineral content, orientation, and structure of collagen fibrils and crystalline calcium phosphate [CaP])
  3. Piezoelectric effects: changes in electrical properties of a crystalline material due to deformation
     a. Bioelectric phenomena involved in bone remodeling
     b. Basis for electrical stimulation of bone in fracture healing
  4. Stress shielding: plate, intramedullary rod, etc., implanted so that bone is not stressed enough; resorption of bone occurs
     a. Important consideration for orthopaedic implants
     b. Depends on material and structure of implant, properties of the bone, and configuration of bone/implant construct

II. Cartilage
A. Articular cartilage
  1. Extrusion of fluid from tissue during compression gives flow-dependent viscoelastic creep; rate of fluid loss and creep is dependent on the permeability of tissue
  2. At higher loading rate, the cartilage behaves like elastic material with a straight stress-strain line

3. At lower loading rate, the cartilage behaves more like viscoelastic material with S-shaped stress-strain curve
4. Lubrication is mixed: boundary plus fluid film (squeeze film elastohydrodynamic, weeping)
B. Meniscus: directional properties because of different fiber orientation
   1. Surface fibers are thinner and arranged randomly; interior fibers are thicker and arranged circumferentially
   2. Collagen fibers are strongest when loaded parallel to the fibrils; therefore menisci are stronger when loaded circumferentially because this is the orientation of the thickest and most uniformly organized fibers
C. Intervertebral disc
   1. Annulus fibrosus: collagen fibers arranged in oblique direction and provides greatest axial loading stability and 40–50% torsional stability
   2. Nucleus pulposus: type II collagen and mucoprotein gel act as a ball-bearing and changing center of rotation
   3. Intradiscal pressure
      a. Load on the disc is about twice the body weight for sitting
      b. Internal disc pressure is about 1.5 times overall load per unit area and the pressure decreases to half the applied pressure laterally but may be as high as 5 times applied pressure posteriorly
      c. Thirty percent lower disc pressure on standing, 50% lower lying on the side, and 80–90% lower lying supine compared to sitting
   4. Degeneration
      a. Shifts the instant center of rotation posteriorly and also decreases the height, both contributing increased stress to the facet joint
      b. Bulging of the disc depends on the intradiscal pressure and structural status of the annulus fibrosis

III. Ligaments and Tendons

A. Collagen fibers run in longitudinal direction
B. Stress-strain curve
   1. Toe: nonlinear and concave upward with fiber crimp being straightened
   2. Linear: steep increase in stiffness
   3. Failure: strain levels greater than bone
C. Tendon is stiffer and stronger than ligament; ligament more ductile than tendon (greater elongation to failure)
D. Bone-ligament complex: at fast strain rate, ligament fails; at slow rate, avulsion fracture occurs (Fig 8-12)
E. Decrease in elasticity and ductility with age
F. Viscoelasticity: higher rate of loading gives increased stiffness, strength, energy absorption, and ultimate elongation
G. Increased diameter of the ligament: stronger and stiffer
H. Increased length of the ligament: same strength but decreased stiffness

IV. Functional Biomechanics

A. Joint reaction force: force acting at joint surface due to internal or external forces on the associated limbs (Fig 8-14); joint reaction is resultant force vector of the additive internal-external forces
   1. Functional load (eg, ground reaction, object held in hand, etc.)
   2. Muscle or ligamentous loads and restraints at joint
   3. Inertial forces (applies only when there is limb acceleration)
   4. Joint friction forces (extremely small)
B. Instantaneous center of motion: at a given instant of time, the point about which a body rotates
C. Coupled movements: joint motion in which rotation or translation in one plane is accompanied by rotation and/or translation in another plane (eg, foot plantar flexion is accompanied by adduction and internal rotation

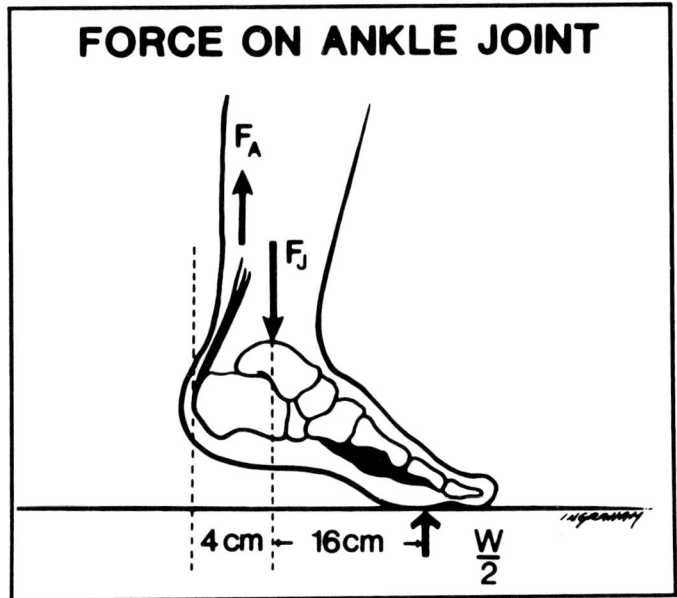

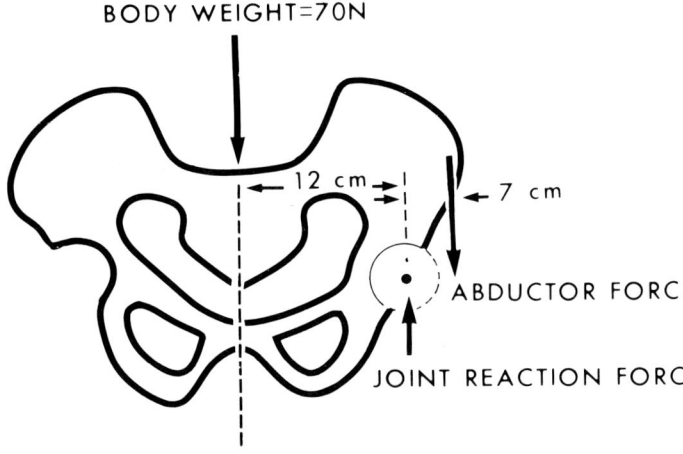

Figure 8-14. **A.** Simplified mechanical model for calculating ankle joint reaction force. F_A = Achilles tendon force; F_J = ankle joint reaction force. Because the muscle lever arm to reaction force lever arm is 1:4, there is a 3:1 negative mechanical advantage for the muscle force. It takes 4 times body weight of muscle force with one foot or 2 times body weight with two feet in order to raise the heel off the ground. The joint reaction force is the sum of muscle force plus the ground reaction force. (From American Academy of Orthopaedic Surgeons: Orthopaedic science. A resource and self-study guide for the practitioner. Park Ridge, IL, 1986. Reprinted with permission.) **B.** Calculation of the hip joint force. For moment equilibrium, the sum of moments are zero or (70 N × 0.12 m = abductor force × 0.07, abductor force is 120 N, and the vertical joint reaction force = 70 N + 120 N or 190 N. (From Mosely CF: Principles of biomechanics. In Cruess RL, Rennie WRJ, eds. Adult orthopaedics. New York, Churchill Livingstone, 1984, p 120. Reprinted with permission.)

D. Congruence: uniform fit between two articulating surfaces (if thickness of articular cartilage space is constant, then joint is congruent
E. Levers
   1. Class I: fulcrum between effort and load; eg, balance beam
   2. Class II: load between fulcrum and effort; eg, wheelbarrow
   3. Class III: effort between load and fulcrum; eg, elbow (Fig 8-15)
F. Muscle Activity
   1. Concentric muscle activity: muscle activation in which the length of the muscle is decreased
   2. Eccentric muscle activity: the muscle is active, but its length is increased
   3. Isometric muscle activity: muscle is

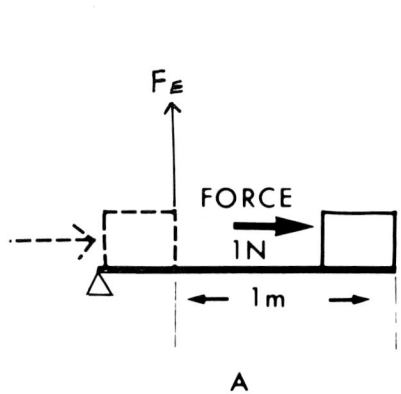 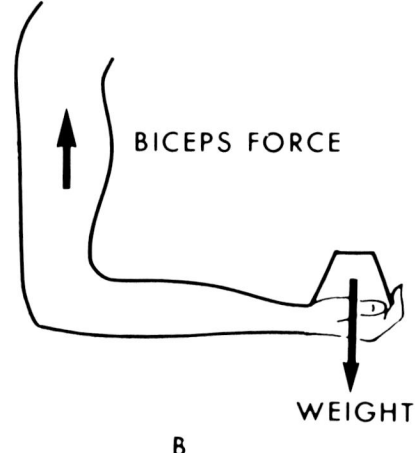

Figure 8-15. **A.** Class III lever, where the fulcrum is at one end, the effort is in the middle, and the resistance is at the other end. **B.** The joint reaction force = biceps force − weight.

active, and producing tension, but does not change length

REFERENCES

American Academy of Orthopaedic Surgeons: Orthopaedic Science. A Resource and self-study guide for the practitioner, Park Ridge, IL, 1986
Cochran GVB: A Primer of orthopaedic biomechanics. New York, Churchill Livingstone, 1982
Evans FG: Mechanical properties of bone. Springfield, IL, Charles C Thomas, 1973
Frankel VH, Burstein AH: Orthopaedic biomechanics. Philadelphia, Lea & Febiger, 1970
Frankel VH, Burstein AH, Brooks DB: Biomechanics of internal derangement of the knee. Pathomechanics as determined by analysis of the instant centers of motion. J Bone Joint Surg 53A:945–962, 1971
Frankel VH, Nordin M: Basic biomechanics of the skeletal system, ed 2. Philadelphia, Lea & Febiger, 1989
Frost HM: Orthopaedic biomechanics. Springfield, IL, Charles C Thomas, 1973
McLeish RD, Charnley J: Abduction forces in the one-legged stance. J Biomech 3:191, 1970
Murray MP, Drought AB, Kory RC: Walking patterns of normal men. J Bone Joint Surg 46A:335–360, 1964
Noyes FR, DeLucas JL, Torvik PJ: Biomechanics of anterior cruciate ligament failure: an analysis of strain rate sensitivity and mechanisms of failure in primates. J Bone Joint Surg 56A:236, 1974
Park JB: Biomaterials science and engineering. New York, Plenum Press, 1984
Torzilli PA, Mow VC: On the fundamental fluid transport mechanisms through normal and pathological articular cartilage during function. II. The analysis, solution, and conclusions. J Biomech 9:587, 1976
White AA III, Panjabi MM: Clinical biomechanics of the spine. Philadelphia, JB Lippincott, 1978

SECTION 9: ORTHOPAEDIC REHABILITATION

Kenneth M. Morrison
Howard S. An

72. Lower Limb Amputation
73. Lower Limb Prosthetics
74. Lower Limb Orthotics in Adults
75. Lower Limb Prosthetics and Orthotics in Children
76. Upper Limb Amputation Surgery
77. Upper Limb Prosthetics
78. Upper Limb Orthotics
79. Spinal Orthoses
80. Sports Orthoses

72

Lower Limb Amputation

I. General Considerations

A. Energy expenditure
   1. Significantly higher for dysvascular than traumatic amputee
   2. High expenditure, primary reason for failure of prosthesis in bilateral amputee
   3. Generally 15% increase for each joint level in traumatic amputee
   4. Expenditure more variable for dysvascular amputee; below knee amputation (BKA), 25%, bilateral BKA, 41%, above knee amputation (AKA), 65% increase in energy expenditure
   5. Bilateral dysvascular AKA will not use prosthesis
   6. Modify bilateral amputee wheelchair with rear wheels placed back to compensate for loss of legs as counterbalance
B. Risks for the dysvascular patient
   1. At 3 years, 25% of dysvascular amputees will have contralateral amputation
   2. At 3 years, 50% will have died

II. Determination of Appropriate Level in Ischemic Diseases

A. Doppler segmental pressure measurements
   1. Frequently erroneously elevated in diabetics secondary to arterial calcification
   2. Closely approximates arterial pressure measurements in atherosclerotic and normal patients
   3. Ankle pressure index (API) required to make serial readings meaningful. Normalized ankle measurements obtained. (API = ankle absolute Doppler pressure/arm Doppler pressure)
   4. API progressively decreases with advancing occlusive disease
B. Toe photoplethysmography
   1. More sensitive indicator of tissue perfusion, especially in diabetic patients because calcification not present in toes
   2. Described as toe/brachial pressure index
   3. Normal value: 0.8–0.9, <0.6 grossly abnormal
   4. Absolute pressures correlate well with success or failure of forefoot amputations
   5. More than 55 mm almost always results in successful healing of amputation
C. Segmental transcutaneous oxygen
   1. Sensitive indicator of local blood flow in area of test
   2. Oxygen tension >40 mmHg results in successful healing of amputation in almost all patients
   3. May be significantly affected by ambient temperature and skin preparation
D. Xenon-133 washout
   1. Good predictability of success of BKA with flow rates of >2.6 ml/min/100 gm tissue
   2. Very time-consuming examination
   3. Significantly affected by ambient temperature
   4. Not routinely available in most nuclear medicine departments
E. Bypass surgery
   1. Stenotic lesions as common in diabetic as nondiabetic
   2. Appropriate bypass surgery may double distal flow
   3. Must be performed prior to amputation in ischemic leg
   4. Often increases successful amputation by one level

III. Hip Disarticulation
A. Viability of flaps crucial to success
B. Difficult to fit usable prosthesis
C. Prosthesis often cumbersome, frequently discarded

IV. Above Knee Amputation
A. Much preferred to hip disarticulation, even if subtrochanteric because of improved sitting surface
B. Length of flap should be twice the radius of the stump
C. Perform myoplasty with repair of myofascia to myofascia over bone
D. Neuroma always forms, but result improved when nerve is buried in soft tissue by applying traction while transecting
E. Preferred level is 10–15 cm above knee joint to allow sufficient room for knee mechanism
F. Rigid dressing and pylon should be started as soon as wound is stable

V. Through Knee Amputation (Disarticulation)
A. Improved end bearing characteristics
B. Useful in growing child because growth plate continues to function
C. Knee level discrepancy unavoidable. Should be considered, especially in young female

VI. Below Knee Amputation
A. Ideal level is at the musculotendinous junction of the gastrocnemius (Fig 9-1)
B. Ideal bone length is 12.5–17.5 cm below knee joint
C. Stumps <5 cm below knee joint are not functional
D. Create long posterior flap with myofascial closure
E. Rigid dressing and pylon useful

VII. Syme's Amputation (Fig 9-2)
A. Amputation at the level of the tibial plafond with resection of the malleoli
B. Most satisfactory level in the lower extremity
C. Heel pad retained for end bearing
D. Most common causes of failure are posterior migration of heel pad and distal slough because dog ears trimmed
E. Results in bulky stump, may not be acceptable to women
F. Must be combined with a solid ankle, cushioned heel (SACH) foot

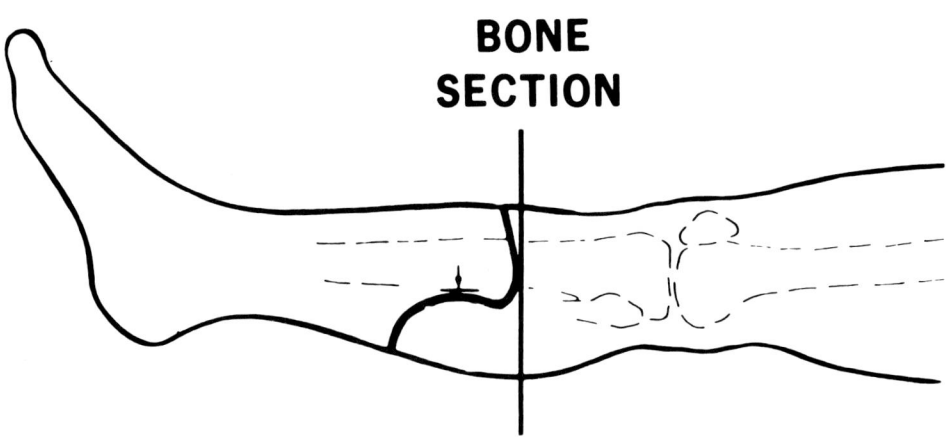

Figure 9-1. Ideal level is at the musculotendinous junction of the gastrocnemius about 12.5–17.5 cm below knee joint. (From Kostuik JP, Gillespie R, eds. Amputation surgery and rehabilitation. New York, Churchill Livingstone, 1981, p 67. Reprinted with permission.)

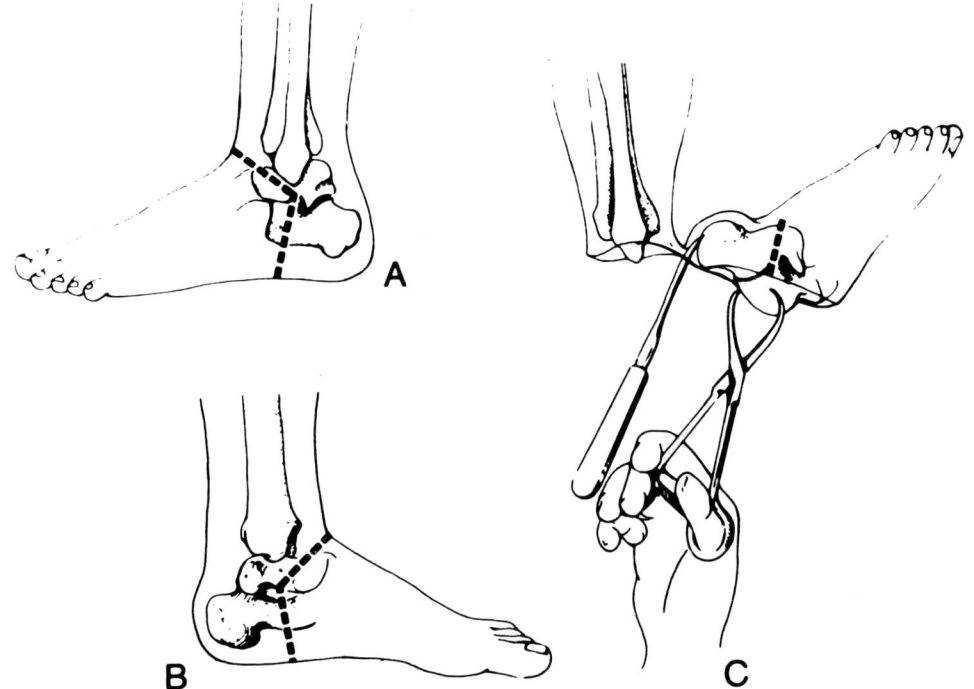

Figure 9-2. Syme's amputation. **A.** Lateral skin incision. **B.** Medial skin incision. **C.** Posterior tendo Achillis dissection. (From Kostuik JP, Gillespie R, eds. Amputation surgery and rehabilitation. New York, Churchill Livingstone, 1981, p 83. Reprinted with permission.)

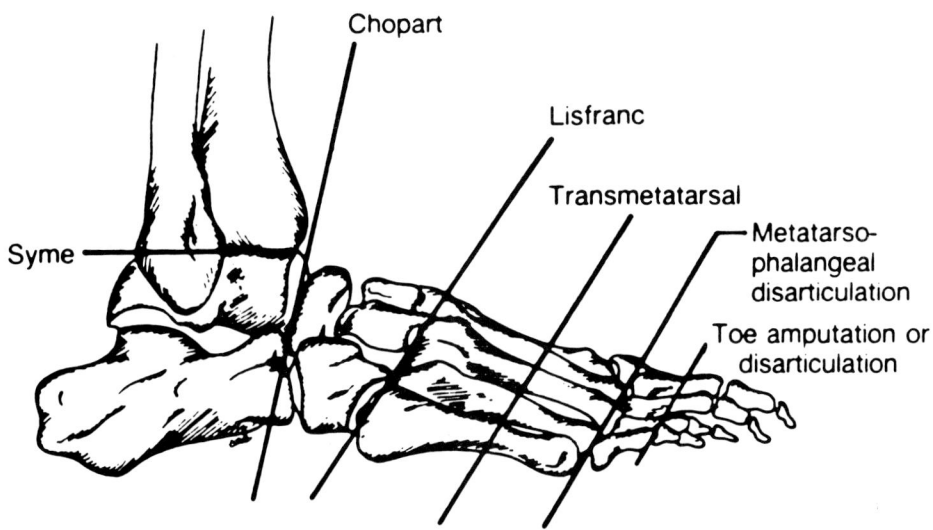

Figure 9-3. Bone division and joint disarticulation lines for foot amputations. (From Wagner FW Jr: Amputations of the foot. In Chapman MW, ed. Operative orthopaedics. Philadelphia, JB Lippincott 1988, p 1779. Reprinted with permission.)

G. Variations
1. Wagner: two-stage procedure for diabetics
2. Boyd: talectomy plus calcaneotibial arthrodesis
3. Piragoff: talectomy plus rotation of calcaneus and arthrodesis to tibia

VIII. Foot Amputation (Fig 9-3)
A. Requires careful evaluation of tissue viability, especially in diabetic
B. If forefoot amputation is too short, may result in plantar flexion deformity

73
Lower Limb Prosthetics

I. Early Postoperative Care
A. Rigid dressing should be considered first step in prosthetic fitting
B. Key is to prevent or control postoperative edema, minimize contractures, and deconditioning
C. Early pylon gait training and physical therapy shown to provide several advantages
   1. Decrease depression, improve patient's body image
   2. May improve likelihood of long-term prosthetic use
   3. Patients return to independent level of function more rapidly
   4. Hospital stay significantly shorter

II. Prosthetic Suspension and Sockets
A. Hip disarticulation
   1. Requires bulky suspension belt over iliac crests
   2. Usually provided with extension assist at "hip" to improve stability at toe off
B. Above knee amputation
   1. Belt suspension
      a. Often required for early amputee until stump has matured
      b. May be only alternative for very short stump
      c. Two types available
         (1) Silesian belt
            i. Suspends prosthesis during swing through
            ii. Provides resistance to rotation at heel strike
            iii. Frequently used with suction socket for short stump
         (2) Pelvic band (Fig 9-4)
            i. Usually fitted with a "hip" joint
            ii. Much more bulky, difficult to wear
            iii. Required for very short stump when medial or lateral stability cannot be achieved by socket design
            iv. Allows extension assist in patients with weak residual musculature
   2. Suction suspension (Fig 9-5)
      a. Skin contact required to maintain negative pressure during swing phase
      b. One-way valve removable to draw stump into socket
      c. Total contact socket required to prevent terminal congestion
      d. Contraindications
         (1) Excessively short or flabby stump
         (2) Severe scarring
         (3) Mental impairment
         (4) Upper extremity involvement
   3. Socket design
      a. Quadrilateral "total contact"
         (1) Distributes majority of weight to ischial tuberosity, buttock, and periphery of stump, little to terminal stump
         (2) Proximal socket contoured to maintain prosthesis under "ischial seat"
         (3) Custom molded to enclose adductors, rectus, gluteus maximus, and vastus lateralis into rectangle
         (4) Similar to "H" socket used in the United Kingdom
      b. "CAT-CAM" socket
         (1) Contoured adducted trochanteric controlled alignment method
         (2) Wide anteroposterior (AP), narrow medial/lateral design used to help maintain stump in adduction for more stable stance
         (3) Ischium contained within socket

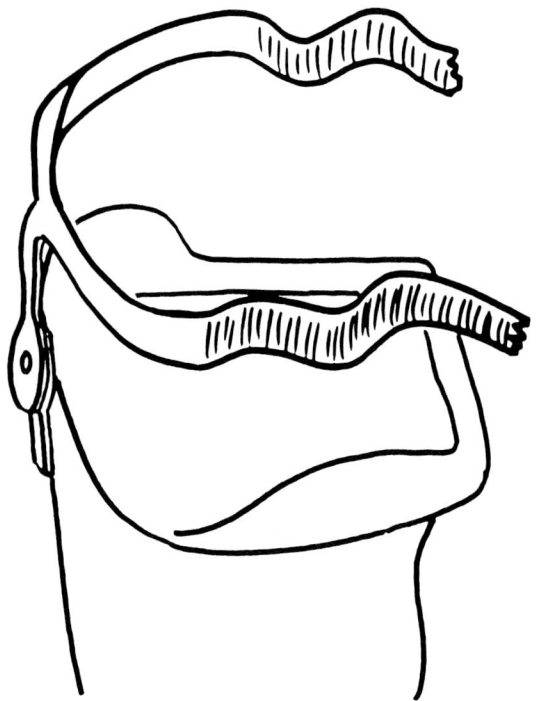

Figure 9-4. Hip suspension for the above-knee socket. (From Kostuik JP, Gillespie R, eds. Amputation surgery and rehabilitation. New York, Churchill Livingstone, 1981, p 276. Reprinted with permission.)

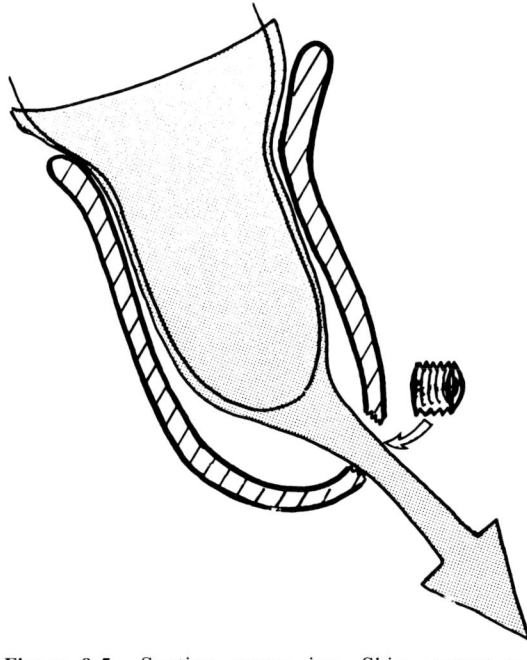

Figure 9-5. Suction suspension. Skin contact required to maintain negative pressure during swing phase, and one-way valve to draw stump into socket. (From Kostuik JP, Gillespie R, eds. Amputation surgery and rehabilitation. New York, Churchill Livingstone, 1981. p 277. Reprinted with permission.)

and not used as weight-bearing structure
C. Knee disarticulation
  1. Suspension
    a. Silesian belt
    b. Suction socket only if condyles trimmed
    c. Internal "waist" suspension around condyles if retained
  2. Early fitting with suspension strap (waist or shoulder) necessary for first prosthesis or until stump matures
  3. Socket design
    a. Quadrilateral socket frequently used; however, full end bearing possible if condyles retained
    b. Distal weight bearing tolerated to a greater degree
    c. Bulbous distal stump requires side entry into socket through "trap door" or "keyhole"
D. Below knee amputation
  1. Suspension
    a. Supracondylar strap (Fig 9-6)
      (1) Most commonly used for BKA
      (2) Loops over top of patella
      (3) May not provide sufficient stability with short stump
      (4) Uses retained knee joint for stability
    b. Thigh corset (lacer)
      (1) Older design, uncommon today
      (2) Still useful with short stump, severe ligamentous laxity, knee flexion contracture or massive obesity
    c. Supracondylar socket
      (1) Contoured to medial and lateral femoral condyles
      (2) Requires medial foam wedge to lock stump into prosthesis after insertion

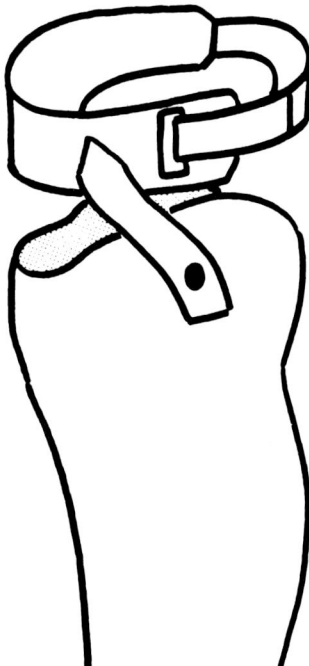

Figure 9-6. Cuff strap suspension for below knee amputation. (From Kostuik JP, Gillespie R, eds. Amputation surgery and rehabilitation. New York, Churchill Livingstone, 1981, p 282. Reprinted with permission.)

        (3) Poor cosmesis when sitting
     d. Suspension sleeve
        (1) Neoprene or latex sleeve grips prosthesis and thigh above knee
        (2) Occasional skin and hygiene problems in hot climates
        (3) Not useful with short stumps or ligamentous instability
  2. Socket design
    a. End bearing
      (1) Poorly tolerated in most patients
      (2) Rarely employed
    b. Patellar tendon bearing (PTB)
      (1) Becoming standard for industry
      (2) Preferred design because of intolerance to end bearing
      (3) Total contact design
      (4) Weight bearing over medial tibial flair, tibial tubercle and surrounding tissues, minimal end bearing

E. Syme's amputation
  1. Suspension: intrinsic, around retained malleoli
  2. Socket design
    a. PTB with some end-bearing characteristics
    b. Two types
      (1) Keyhole window
        i. Required to improve cosmesis and allow natural tapering of ankle
        ii. Some strength limitations
      (2) Windowless
        i. Lighter, more durable, easier to don, simpler design
        ii. Cosmesis poor
        iii. Requires inflatable cuff within prosthesis for suspension

III. Prosthetic Knee Mechanics

A. Mechanical
  1. Single axis, constant friction knee
    a. Friction clamp used to damp swing of knee
    b. Simplest and most durable design, most commonly prescribed
    c. Primary limitation is constant gait speed
  2. Polycentric knee: 4 bar linkage
    a. Axis moves with knee flexion to mimic natural knee
    b. Primary indications include knee disarticulation (unit folds under stump with knee flexion) and weak hip extensors (unit provides increased stance phase stability)
  3. Safety knee
    a. Automatically locks if weight borne on flexed knee
    b. Useful in blind patients, those with weak hip extensors and bilateral amputees

B. Hydraulic
  1. Allows variable cadence, more natural gait
  2. Resistance to extension in swing phase increases automatically as cadence increases

3. Primary limitations include increased cost and maintenance requirements
C. External hinge
   1. Applied to BK corset or thigh lacer and socket
   2. Useful with short stump, persistent knee flexion contracture, ligamentous instability of knee

IV. Prosthetic Foot Mechanics
A. SACH (Fig 9-7)
   1. Most commonly prescribed in United States
   2. Foam heel provides impact shock absorption
   3. No moving parts allows low maintenance cost and great durability
B. Single axis (Fig 9-8)
   1. Older style with single axis ankle joint and dorsi/plantar bumpers
   2. No provision for medial/lateral, transverse, and sagittal motion
   3. Generally replaced by SACH
C. Multiple axis (Greisinger)
   1. Provides motion comparable to ankle and subtalar joints
   2. Heavy, high maintenance requirements, more expensive than other alternatives
   3. Indicated for use on rough, uneven terrain
D. Seattle foot
   1. Essentially updated SACH with Delrin keel instead of wood
   2. Keel loaded at heel strike, released at toe off
   3. Outer foam cover replica of natural foot
   4. Useful for athletic patients
E. Stationary attachment, flexible endoskeleton (SAFE)
   1. Variation of SACH
   2. Keel is active only at toe off
   3. Functionally closer to natural foot
F. Flex-Foot
   1. Graphite or fiberglass leafspring includes shank of leg
   2. Very lightweight, durable
   3. Expensive (most expensive of all choices)
   4. Spring loading at heel strike provides pushoff
   5. Useful for athletic amputee
   6. Endoskeletal structure covered by foam outer cover

V. Prosthetic Shanks (Fig 9-9)
A. Endoskeletal
   1. Central metal tubing with foam outer cover for cosmesis

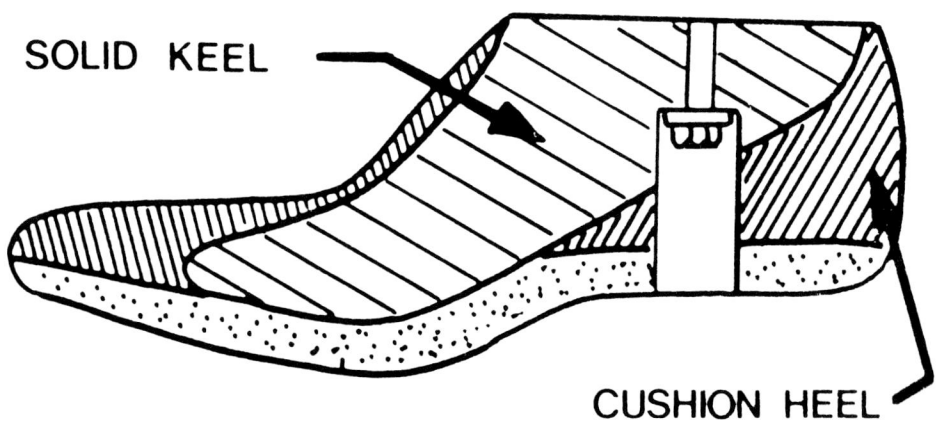

Figure 9-7. SACH prosthetic foot. (From Kostuik JP, Gillespie R, eds. Amputation surgery and rehabilitation. New York, Churchill Livingstone, 1981, p 289. Reprinted with permission.)

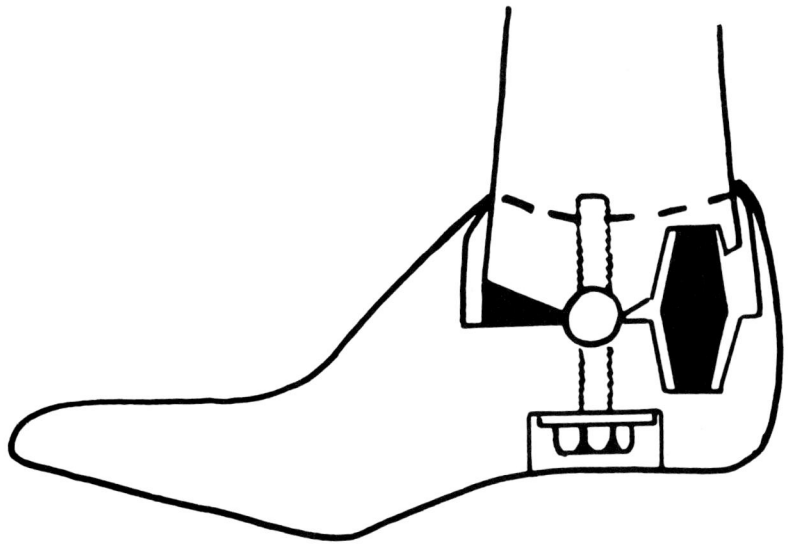

Figure 9-8. Single-axis foot with rubber plantar and dorsiflexion bumpers. (From Kostuik JP, Gillespie R, eds. Amputation surgery and rehabilitation. New York, Churchill Livingstone, 1981, p 290. Reprinted with permission.)

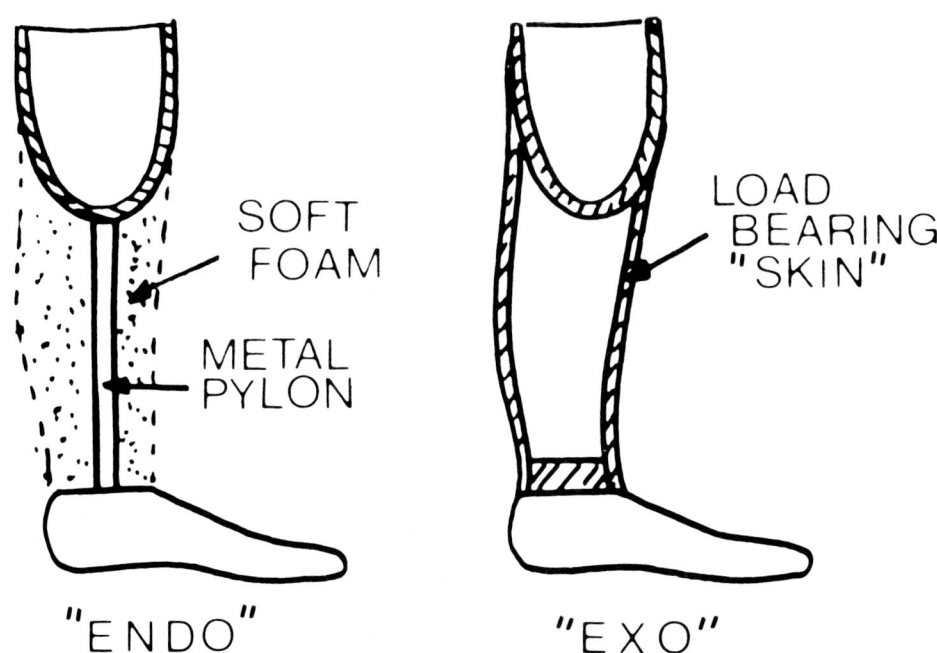

Figure 9-9. Endoskeletal and exoskeletal methods of prosthetic shank construction. (From Kostuik JP, Gillespie R, eds. Amputation surgery and rehabilitation. New York, Churchill Livingstone, 1981, p 291. Reprinted with permission.)

2. Most cosmetic of choices
3. Lighter but less durable than exoskeletal designs
4. Allows alignment after production

B. Exoskeletal
1. Hard outer shell with built-in socket
2. Less expensive, less cosmetic, more durable
3. Alignment cannot be changed after manufacture

74
Lower Limb Orthotics in Adults

I. Foot Orthotics
A. General considerations
1. Removable appliance placed within shoe. Extends from posterior border of shoe to metatarsal heads
2. Contoured to provide medial longitudinal arch support, midfoot, hind foot support, pressure relief from metatarsal heads as indicated

B. Indications and objectives
1. Arthritis (post-traumatic, osteoarthritis, rheumatoid)
   a. Prevent or limit motion
   b. Accommodate deformities
   c. Cushion impact loading
2. Arthrodesis
   a. Accommodate shortening, residual deformity
   b. Absorb impact loading
   c. Improve comfort, efficiency at toe off
3. Instability
   a. Accommodate deformity
   b. Support unstable intertarsal joints
4. Pes planovalgus
   a. Correct eversion
   b. Support medial longitudinal arch to relieve ligamentous strain
5. Plantar calcaneal bursitis, spurs, fasciitis
   a. Transfer weight to pressure-tolerant structures
   b. Support medial longitudinal arch

C. University of California Biomechanics Laboratory (UCBL) Orthosis
1. Rigid plastic insert constructed from mold of patient's foot in corrected position
2. Helps to maintain best possible position of calcaneus relative to talus
3. First choice for longitudinal arch support
4. Stabilizes intertarsal and tarsometatarsal joints

D. Heel cups
1. Prefabricated rigid plastic insert
2. Covers heel and surrounds posterior, medial, and lateral sides
3. Used to correct calcaneal valgus but may be of limited value because of short length

E. Sesamoid platform
1. Custom ¾ length orthosis
2. Useful in transferring pressure from first metatarsal head to shaft

II. Shoe Modifications
A. Indications
1. Pes planovalgus
2. Pes equinus
   a. Flexible
   b. Fixed
3. Talipes equinovarus
4. Pes cavus
5. Metatarsalgia
6. Metatarsus adductus
7. Hallux valgus, metatarsus primus varus
8. Hallux rigidus
9. Claw, hammer, mallet toes

B. Principles
1. Correct flexible deformities
2. Accommodate residual deformities
3. Transfer force from pressure-sensitive to pressure-tolerant areas

4. Help immobilize unstable or painful segments
C. Examples
1. Medial/lateral shoe wedge: used in adult to accommodate fixed deformity
2. Steel toe: inserted between layers of sole to decrease stress borne on metatarsal heads
3. Heel cushion relief: useful as adjunct in the management of plantar faciitis

III. Ankle-Foot Orthoses (AFO)

A. Primary function is to control alignment and motion of foot and ankle
B. Conventional orthoses (leather and metal)
1. Construction
   a. Metal upright attached proximally to calf strap, distally to shoe via metal stirrup or to shoe insert
   b. Ankle stops
      (1) Limit motion to predetermined range
      (2) Free motion ankle provides only medial/lateral constraint
      (3) Plantar flexion stop useful for equinus deformity
      (4) Dorsiflexion stop used in presence of weak dorsiflexors
   c. Ankle joint assists
      (1) Provide adjustable spring loading to compensate for specific deficit
      (2) May potentiate spastic dysfunction (cerebral palsy, stroke, other upper motor neuron disorders)
      (3) Contraindicated in joint instability
      (4) T-straps provide additional varus/valgus control
      (5) Double upright: most commonly employed and required if medial/lateral control is needed
      (6) Single upright: useful for mild dorsiflexion weakness with medial/lateral stability
2. Indications
   a. Spastic/flaccid paresis/paralysis of plantar/dorsiflexion
   b. Medial/lateral instability (severe)
C. Plastic orthoses (thermoplastic)
1. Construction
   a. Usually created from plaster model of extremity
   b. Prefabricated AFO available but not recommended for long-term use
   c. Polypropylene most commonly employed because of moldability, durability, and light weight
2. Indications
   a. Spastic/flaccid paralysis/paresis of dorsiflexion
   b. Mild/moderate, medial/lateral instability
   c. Need for improved cosmesis, decreased weight, interchangeable footwear
3. Contraindications
   a. Rapidly changing deformity (little adjustment possible)
   b. Unreliable patient (must be inserted into footwear)
   c. Severe weakness of plantar flexors (material will fail)

IV. Knee-Ankle-Foot Orthosis (KAFO)

A. Conventional (leather and metal)
1. Construction
   a. Identical to AFO with extension above knee with adjustable hinges
   b. Hinges single axis or polycentric
   c. Knee locks or posterior placement of hinges to increase stability at stance
   d. May be extended to ischium for ischial weight bearing
2. Indications
   a. Above with knee ligamentous instability
   b. Weak/absent knee flexors/extensors (spastic/flaccid)
   c. Long-term nonsurgical management

of limb deformities; prevention of pathologic femur fracture in structural insufficiency (may unload up to 50% of weight borne on extremity)
   3. Contraindications
      a. Absent active hip motion
      b. Obesity (adequate fit difficult)
      c. Poor cosmesis not acceptable
      d. Heavy weight not tolerated
   B. Molded KAFO (polypropylene)
      1. Construction
         a. Custom plaster mold of thigh-calf-ankle used in construction
         b. Anterior shell added to thigh component
         c. Conventional hinges added to knee to form hybrid
      2. Indications
         a. Same as conventional orthosis
         b. When light weight and cosmesis required
         c. Circumferential thigh mold allows use in management of long bone fractures
      3. Contraindications
         a. Same as conventional
         b. Obesity/rapid weight changes
         c. Skin intolerance to total contact

V. Hip-Knee-Ankle-Foot Orthosis (HKAFO)
   A. Construction
      1. Pelvic strap with single axis joint attached to conventional KAFO
      2. Conventional or molded available
   B. Indications
      1. Unilateral generally reserved for recurrent prosthetic hip dislocation
      2. Bilateral
         a. Pediatric paraplegia (spastic/flaccid)
         b. May be combined with cable system for LSU reciprocating gait orthosis
   C. Contraindications
      1. Unilateral: intolerance to bulk or weight of device
      2. Bilateral
         a. Traumatic adult paraplegia
         b. Intolerance to bulk or weight of device

Lower Limb Prosthetics and Orthotics in Children

I. Prosthetics
   A. Congenital lower limb deficiencies
      1. Unilateral at any level or bilateral BK should be fitted when infant pulls to stand (9–12 months)
      2. Training period usually lasts 2 weeks (longer if other limbs involved)
      3. Independent function with prosthesis usually occurs
      4. Bilateral AK ambulates better without prosthesis until age 6–8 years
   B. Traumatic lower limb deficiencies — see Chapter 74
   C. Following ablative surgery — see Chapter 74

II. Orthotics
   A. Angular and rotational deformities
      1. Denis-Brown splint: spreader bar with foot plates attached to shoes to maintain desired rotation
      2. A-frame orthosis: similar to Denis-Brown splint with thigh bands attached to create an A-frame
      3. Torsion shaft orthosis: tightly coiled adjustable spring attached from pelvic band to shoe
      4. Twister cables
      5. Use of all of above for torsional deformities very controversial. May induce secondary deformity in areas not requiring correction
   B. Positioning devices for congenital hip dislocation
      1. Freijka pillow
      2. Von Rosen splint: molded plastic splint incorporating shoulders, torso, and thighs to maintain flexion or abduction of the hips. Allows relatively little motion
      3. Ilfeld splint: plastic thigh cuffs bridged with metal crossbar. Allows greater motion
      4. Pavlic harness: chest strap, shoulder harness, anterior, posterior straps extend to booties to maintain abduction (posterior strap) and hip flexion (anterior strap). Allows greatest degree of activity. Usually tolerated well
   C. Positioning devices for Legg-Calvé-Perthes' disease
      1. Trilateral orthosis: ischial weight-bearing orthosis with single medial hinged upright. Maintains hip in abducted position and limits weight bearing
      2. Toronto orthosis: single central upright tube connected to bilateral thigh cuffs proximally, to spreader bars distally. Maintains abduction and internal rotation (similar to positioning in Petri casts)
      3. Scottish Rite orthosis: pelvic band and thigh cuffs bridged with hinges at hips. Hips maintained in abducted position with spreader bar but does not control internal rotation. Usually tolerated well
   D. Orthotics for myelomeningocele and other paralytic disorders
      1. Standing frame orthosis: prefabricated, adjustable frame designed to help improve trunk control and standing balance. Simple design. No movement allowed at hips or knees
      2. Parapodium: prefabricated standing frame with lockable hip and knee hinges

3. Reciprocating gait orthosis: bilateral HKAFO with cable system attaching hip joints. Extension of hip induces flexion of contralateral hip. Cable system also provides stability in stance by preventing simultaneous hip flexion
4. HKAFO, KAFO, AFO — see before

E. Shoe modifications
1. Heel wedges
   a. Usually 1/8–1/4 inch
   b. Medial tends to create heel varus, lateral heel valgus
   c. May also be used to accommodate fixed deformity
2. Thomas heel: medial extension of the heel to help support the medial longitudinal arch
3. Sole wedge
   a. Usually 1/8–1/4 inch
   b. Medial tends to supinate forefoot, lateral to pronate
4. Medial longitudinal arch support (scaphoid pad, navicular pad, "cookie")
5. UCBL orthosis: molded orthotic shoe insert used to control flexible combined hindfoot or forefoot deformities (see before)

76

Upper Limb Amputation Surgery

I. Surgical Indications
A. Trauma
  1. Most common indication, especially with severe burns, avulsion injuries or with associated massive soft tissue and neurovascular injury
  2. Replantation may be technically possible but may not provide a sensate, functional extremity
  3. Following brachial plexus avulsion or scapulothoracic dissociation, after an adequate trial of repair, elective amputation may be necessary to remove a useless, insensate limb
B. Tumor
  1. When limb salvage is not feasible or possible
  2. Amputation level should be selected very carefully to provide the most functional, but safe, level
C. Congenital abnormalities
  1. Functional considerations should take precedence over cosmesis
  2. Even small rudimentary or vestigial structures may have potential function and should be retained if possible
  3. Indications
      a. Poor function
      b. Absence of sensation
      c. Unacceptable appearance
      d. Pain
      e. Difficulty with prosthetic fitting
D. Uncontrolled infection: rarely indicated in uncompromised host

II. Single Finger
A. Distal to superficialis insertion: best level if choice available
B. Proximal to superficialis insertion
  1. Index through proximal phalanx or metacarpophalangeal (MCP) joint: oblique osteotomy of metacarpal often improves function and cosmesis
  2. Small through proximal phalanx or MCP joint: manage as index
  3. Long, ring fingers
      a. Primary ray resection often improves appearance of web space and function of hand
      b. Cosmetic replacements available but of limited value

III. Thumb
A. Retain as much thumb length as possible, even if to MCP joint
B. Must have sensate, painless skin cover

IV. Below Elbow
A. As important to retain elbow in upper extremity as knee in lower extremity
B. Wrist disarticulation not advised, despite improved pronation or supination, because of excessive length with terminal device
C. Ideal level is 4–5 cm proximal to radial styloid to accommodate prosthetic terminal device
D. Very short stump creates a difficult prosthetic fit but should be attempted

V. Above Elbow
A. Ideally, try to maintain a minimum of 60% of normal length of humerus. However, any length is preferable to disarticulation
B. Sixty percent of normal humeral length retains insertions of deltoid, pectoralis major, and latissimus dorsi

C. Maximum length is 5–6 cm proximal to condyles. Adequate room required for elbow joint mechanism
D. Exception is in children in whom retention of distal humeral physis is recommended when possible

VI. Surgical Technique for Above Elbow and Below Elbow Amputation
A. Create anterior and posterior flaps of equal length to provide a transverse terminal scar
B. Transect nerves and allow to retract to decrease the likelihood of neuroma formation
C. Approximate fascia of flexor and extensor muscle masses over cut end of bone
D. Rigid dressing advised to control postoperative edema
E. Early fitting of prosthesis (within 4 weeks) improves likelihood of prosthetic use and maintenance of bimanual activity

VII. Krukenberg Procedure
A. Divides radius and ulna in long forearm amputation
B. Provides mobile and sensate prongs
C. May be used to power prosthesis
D. Bizarre appearance limits application
  1. Blind amputee: improved tactile sense
  2. Bilateral amputee: bimanual activities enhanced

VIII. Shoulder Disarticulation
A. Preferred over four-quarter amputation because contour or shoulder retained
B. Use skin over deltoid to provide anterior and posterior scars
C. Prosthesis generally powered externally

IX. Four-Quarter Amputation
A. Functional prosthetic fitting usually very difficult to suspend
B. Prosthesis always externally powered
C. Patients prefer total cosmetic cap to improve contour of shoulder

77

Upper Limb Prosthetics

I. Components
A. Terminal devices
  1. Hooks
     a. Superior to hands for durability, ease of maintenance, prehension, grasping small objects, weight, and cost
     b. Voluntary opening
        (1) Dorrance split hook most commonly employed
        (2) Tension determined by number of rubber bands applied
     c. Voluntary closing
        (1) Sierra hook frequently used
        (2) More precise control of prehension
        (3) Usually self-locking when "grip" relaxed
        (4) More complex cycle of operation
  2. Hands
     a. Superior to hook in cosmesis and for grasping large, cylindrical objects
     b. Passive: essentially for cosmesis only, although may be used to stabilize objects in opposite hand
     c. Voluntary opening
        (1) Cable operation similar to hook
        (2) Utility, cosmesis and function vary with model
     d. Voluntary closing
        (1) Controllable prehension and automatic locking similar to voluntary opening hook
        (2) Several models available with variable degrees of function and cosmesis
  3. Externally powered
     a. Most powered by nickel cadmium batteries, gears and motors
     b. Microswitch control
        (1) Push-button controlled by movement of body part
        (2) May activate terminal device or elbow
     c. Myoelectric control
        (1) Activated by electromyographic (EMG) signal from forearm or arm musculature
        (2) Used to control elbow and/or terminal device, depending on level of amputation
B. Wrist units
  1. Used to attach terminal device to prosthesis and to control pronation and supination
  2. Allows interchange of terminal devices
  3. Fully passive function
  4. Friction wrist
     a. Variable position controlled by friction washer or forces applied to stud
     b. Preferred by bilateral amputees
  5. Locking wrist
     a. Position controlled by push-button or twist ring
     b. Not suitable for bilateral amputee
  6. Wrist flexion units: often chosen for bilateral amputee
C. Below elbow prosthesis
  1. Sockets
     a. Usually double walled
        (1) Inner wall total contact
        (2) Outer wall formed to match sound limb in length and contour
     b. Pronation or supination usually lost in all but very long stumps
     c. Split socket used for very short stumps
     d. Muenster prosthesis also used for very short stump

(1) Encapsulates olecranon and epicondyles into socket
(2) Hinges not used in design
(3) Suspensory device usually not required
 2. Hinges or elbow units
  a. Flexible
   (1) Primary function is socket suspension
   (2) Allow maximum active pronation or supination
   (3) Useful for wrist disarticulation and long below elbow
  b. Rigid
   (1) Usually steel to allow additional stability about the elbow
   (2) Single pivot or polycentric available
   (3) Pronation or supination controlled at wrist unit
  c. Step-up
   (1) Combined with split socket to allow increased active motion at elbow
   (2) Gear or double pivot device allows from 2:1 to 3:1 ratio increase
   (3) Significant loss of strength results and may require harness assist
 3. Harness and controls (Fig 9-10)
  a. Functions
   (1) Suspends prosthesis
   (2) Transmit shoulder flexion and scapular abduction to usable prosthetic motions
  b. Three types of harness
   (1) Figure-of-eight most commonly used
   (2) Chest strap used when heavy lifting required
   (3) Figure-of-nine used when little suspension required (Muenster type)
  c. Cable system transmits forces from shoulder and scapula to elbow and/or terminal device

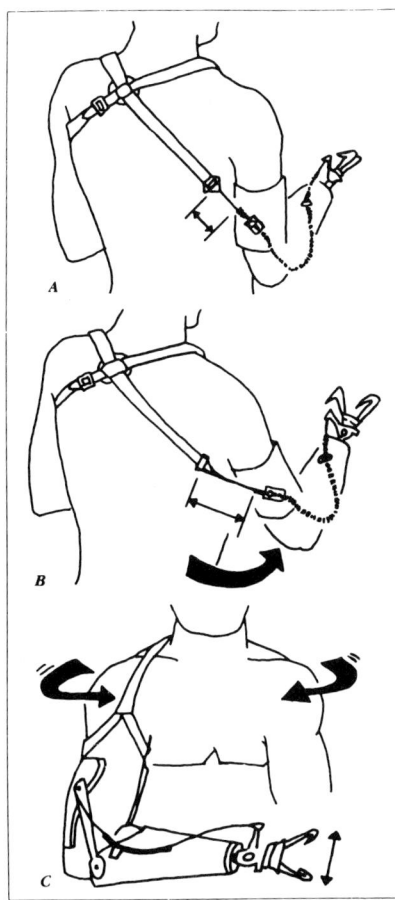

Figure 9-10. A. Single cable system for a below-elbow amputation B. Terminal device is opened by flexion of the shoulder and elbow C. Terminal device is also opened by adduction of both shoulders. (From Rodrigo JJ: Orthopaedic surgery: Basic science and clinical science. Boston, Little, Brown, 1986, p 536. Reprinted with permission.)

 D. Above elbow prosthesis
  1. Sockets
   a. Usually double walled
    (1) Inner wall total contact
    (2) Outer wall formed to match sound limb in length and contour
   b. Usually extend to acromion laterally, flattened to axilla medially
  2. Elbow units, two types
   a. External elbows (outside locking)
    (1) Used for elbow disarticulation or very long above elbow (AE)

(2) Flexed and locked by separate control cables (dual control system)
  (3) Lock system functions by alternator principle (tension/lock, tension/unlock)
  b. Internal elbows (inside locking)
   (1) Used for standard AE amputation
   (2) Control same as external elbow
 3. Harness and controls (Fig 9-11)
  a. Serves multiple functions
  b. Suspends prosthesis
  c. Transmits power for elbow flexion and locking, control of terminal device
  d. Figure-of-eight and chest strap designs most commonly used
 E. Shoulder prosthesis
  1. Terminal device, wrist unit, forearm section, elbow unit, same as before
  2. Humeral section: passive humeral rotation through "turntable" between socket and elbow
  3. Shoulder section
   a. Socket applied to remnant of shoulder and thorax
   b. Variable active or passive motion available, depending on shoulder remnant
  4. Harness and cable system
   a. Terminal device and elbow flexion controlled by scapular abduction
   b. Elbow locking or unlocking controlled by shoulder elevation
   c. Forequarter amputee uses opposite shoulder

II. Pediatric Upper Limb Amputees
 A. Benefits of early prosthetic fitting (6–8 months of age)
  1. Promotes balance in sitting, crawling, standing, and walking
  2. Accustoms child to normal length and symmetrical upper limb
  3. Stimulates bimanual function
  4. Incorporates prosthesis into body image
  5. Decreased tendency to depend on tactile input from end of stump

 B. Terminal devices
  1. Infants
   a. Baby mit, passive soft "hand"
   b. Used for gross bimanual holding
  2. Six to 8 months
   a. Voluntary opening, spring loaded, plastic coated, terminal device
   b. No cable system included
   c. Parent places object into device to teach prosthetic prehension
  3. At 15–24 months: control cable and harness added to prosthesis
  4. At 3–5 years: larger, more durable terminal device used
  5. At 5–15 years: cosmetic prosthetic "hand" and glove often preferred

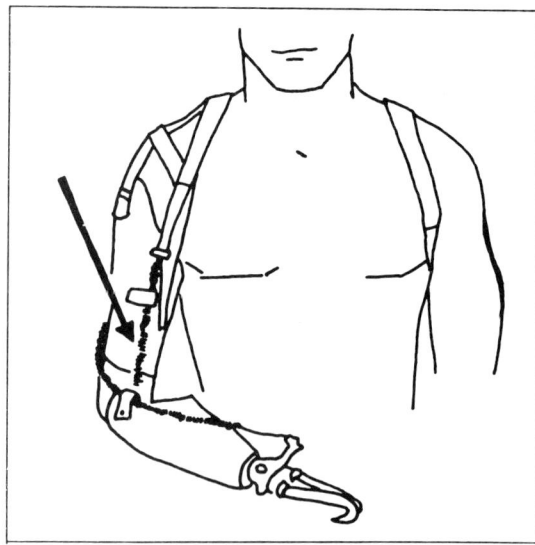

Figure 9-11. Double-cable system for above-elbow amputations. Anterior cable (arrow) controls the elbow-lock mechanism, and the posterior cable controls the opening of the terminal device. (From Rodrigo JJ: Orthopaedic surgery: Basic science and clinical science. Boston, Little, Brown. 1986, p 537. Reprinted with permission.)

78
Upper Limb Orthotics

I. Main Classifications
A. Static
   1. Immobilizes joint or body part
   2. Position and maintain correct joint alignment
   3. Protect recently injured or newly repaired tissues during healing
   4. Prevent tendon shortening and contracture caused by muscle imbalance
   5. Stabilize one or more joints to improve function in another
B. Dynamic
   1. Allows controlled motion in selected joints
   2. Neutralizes progressive deforming forces
   3. Substitutes for or supplements a weakened or paralyzed muscle
C. Functional
   1. Used to substitute for irreversible loss of function
   2. Maintains useful position of joint to maximize function of hand
   3. Activate or motor paralyzed or weakened joint function

II. Temporary Devices
A. Management of fractures and dislocations
B. Peripheral neuropraxia (median, ulnar, radial nerves)
C. Management of contractures with serial adjustments
D. Other soft tissue injuries
   1. Following tendon repair
   2. Conservative management of DeQuervain's, carpal tunnel syndrome

III. Semipermanent Devices
A. Usually requires a combination of dynamic and static splinting
B. Assistive device following tendon transfer following peripheral nerve injury
C. During acute and subacute phases of rheumatoid arthritis to protect and preserve joint and tendon function

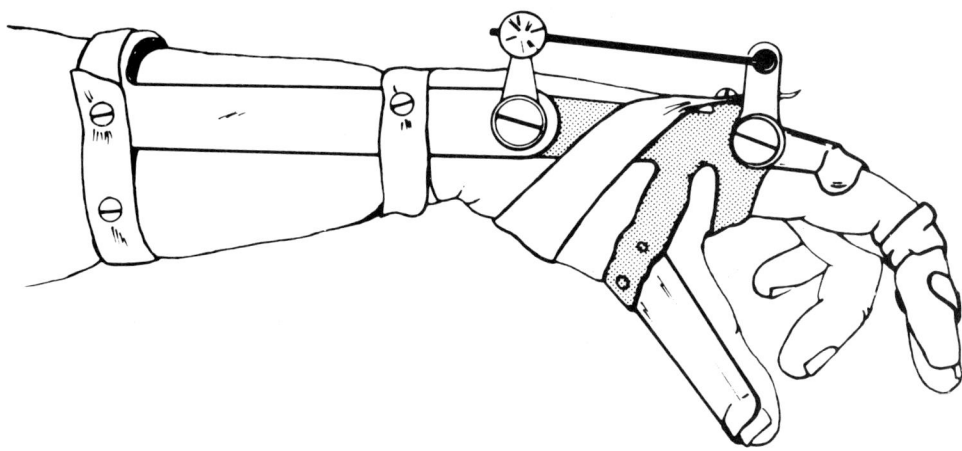

Figure 9-12. Rancho tenodesis orthosis or wrist-driven prehension orthosis to furnish prehension through reciprocal wrist extension and finger flexion motion or through tenodesis. (From Bunch WH, Keagy RD: Principles of orthotic treatment. St. Louis, CV Mosby, 1976, p 57. Reprinted with permission.)

D. Following joint replacement and tendon reconstruction in rheumatoid arthritis

IV. Permanent Devices
   A. Most commonly employed following permanent nerve, brachial plexus, or spinal cord injury
   B. Cord level
      1. C4 and above: only static splinting feasible
      2. C5
         a. Ratchet wrist-hand orthosis (WHO) (Fig 9-12)
         b. Extensor-driven WHO following tendon transfer
      3. C6: extensor-driven WHO
      4. C7: WHO or HO as a supplement to tendon transfer
   C. Brachial plexus
      1. Early positional splinting necessary to prevent contracture
      2. Permanent splint as deficit stabilizes
   D. Cerebrovascular accident/stroke
      1. Functional splinting usually less successful with cognitive impairment
      2. Useful for correction or prevention of contracture, pain management, and in decreasing spasticity

79
Spinal Orthoses

I. Flexible Spinal Orthoses
A. Sacroiliac corset
   1. Prefabricated, requiring alteration
   2. Useful in stabilizing minor sacroiliac disruptions and pubic diastasis
B. Lumbosacral corset (Fig 9-13)
   1. Most commonly used flexible spinal orthosis
   2. Prefabricated or custom-made
   3. Uses intra-abdominal hydrostatic pressure to reduce vertebral loading
   4. Rigid stays restrict spinal motion
   5. May be useful in conservative management of mechanical low-back pain
C. Thoracolumbosacral corset
   1. Uses intra-abdominal hydrostatic pressure to reduce vertebral loading
   2. Rigid stays restrict spinal motion
   3. Useful in inflammatory spondyloarthropathies (ankylosing spondylosis, psoriatic arthritis, Reiter's disease with spinal involvement)

II. Rigid Spinal Orthoses for Thoracic, Lumbar, and Sacral Spine
A. Uses intra-abdominal hydrostatic pressure to reduce vertebral loading
B. Restricts trunk motion
C. Modifies skeletal alignment
D. Most commonly used following limited in situ spinal fusion
E. May also be used to simulate fusion prior to procedure
F. Lumbosacral flexion-extension control orthosis (chairback brace) (Fig 9-13)
   1. Posterior lumbosacral rigid uprights attached anteriorly with straps
   2. Provides three-point stabilization of lumbosacral spine in flexion and extension
   3. Pelvic and thoracic bands restrict lateral motion to limited degree
G. Lumbosacral flexion-extension-lateral control orthosis (Knight)
   1. Lateral uprights applied to flexion-extension orthosis
   2. Restricts lateral motion to a greater degree
H. Thoracolumbosacral flexion-extension control orthosis, Taylor brace (Fig 9-14)
   1. Extension of posterior uprights to the thoracic spine
   2. Provides spinal support through intra-abdominal hydrostatic pressure and static uprights
I. Thoracolumbosacral flexion control orthosis (anterior hyperextension, Jewett brace) (Fig 9-15)
   1. Provides three-point stabilization with sternal, suprapubic, and thoracolumbar pads
   2. Prefabricated and requires adjustment
   3. Frequently used for thoracic wedge compression fractures
   4. May be employed in treatment of Scheuermann's disease instead of Milwaukee brace
J. Thoracolumbosacral orthosis (TLSO)
   1. Provides maximum orthotic immobilization
   2. Acts as total contact orthosis
   3. Custom formed of thermoplastic material (polypropylene) from plaster jacket mold
   4. Frequently used in conjunction with internal fixation following surgical stabilization of burst fractures, instrumentation, and fusion of idiopathic scoliosis or as an adjuvant to radiation therapy for tumors of the spine
   5. Useful in control of scoliosis with apex T_8 or below
L. Milwaukee brace (Fig 9-16)
   1. Specifically designed for the scoliotic or kyphotic child

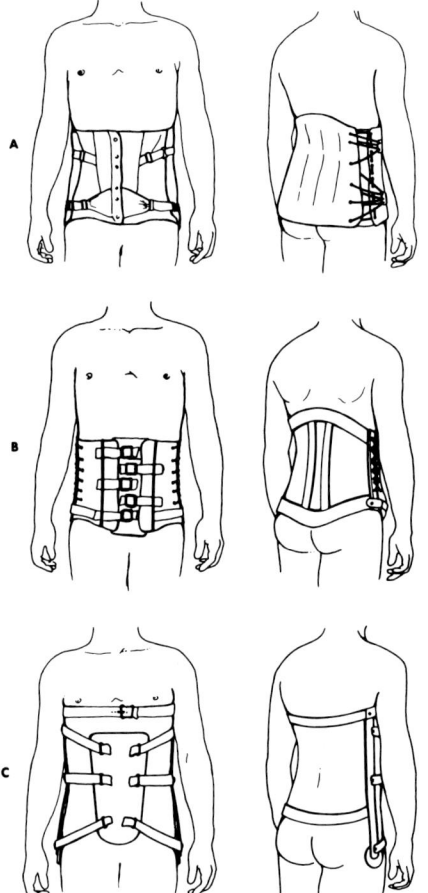

Figure 9-13. Lumbosacral orthoses. **A.** Flexible lumbosacral corset. **B.** More rigid chairback brace. **C.** Norton Brown brace. (From Bunch WH, Keagy RD: Principles of orthotic treatment. St. Louis, CV Mosby, 1976. Reprinted with permission.)

2. Scoliotic deformity is corrected by the force against the thoracic pad counteracted by the axillary sling and the lateral aspect of the pelvis
3. The thoracic pad is suspended from an outrigger-attached anterior upright and should be about 3–4 levels below the apex of the curve
4. The throat mold has replaced the original mandibular pad because of dental problems
5. This brace is quite effective in controlling flexible scoliotic or kyphotic curvatures in growing children

III. Cervical Orthoses

A. Flexion-extension control orthoses
  1. Soft collars
     a. Provide little control of motion
     b. Designed to remind wearer to limit head and neck motion, useful for minor soft tissue injuries
  2. Philadelphia collar
     a. Provides significant but limited control of flexion and extension
     b. Frequently used as immobilizer in transport of potential cervical spine injuries from the field
     c. Major function is as a reminder to wearer to limit head and neck motion
B. Flexion-extension-rotary control orthoses
  1. Sterno-occipital-mandibular immobilizer (SOMI) (Fig 9-17)
     a. Paired anterior uprights only
     b. Provides good control of cervical flexion and extension
     c. Rotational control significantly less than other "post" type appliances
     d. Useful for stable posterior element fractures and following anterior fusion
  2. Four-post appliance
     a. Anterior and posterior uprights
     b. Significantly greater control of rotation and lateral bending
     c. Useful in management of stable cervical spine fractures
  3. Halo vest
     a. Halo ring attached to skull through fixation pins
     b. Anterior or posterior uprights attach ring to body jacket
     c. Provides greatest degree of control in all planes
        (1) Only appliance to control upper cervical rotation significantly
        (2) Indicated for management of unstable cervical spine fractures (tear drop, burst, types II and III odontoid, hangman's, Jefferson fractures, facet dislocations)

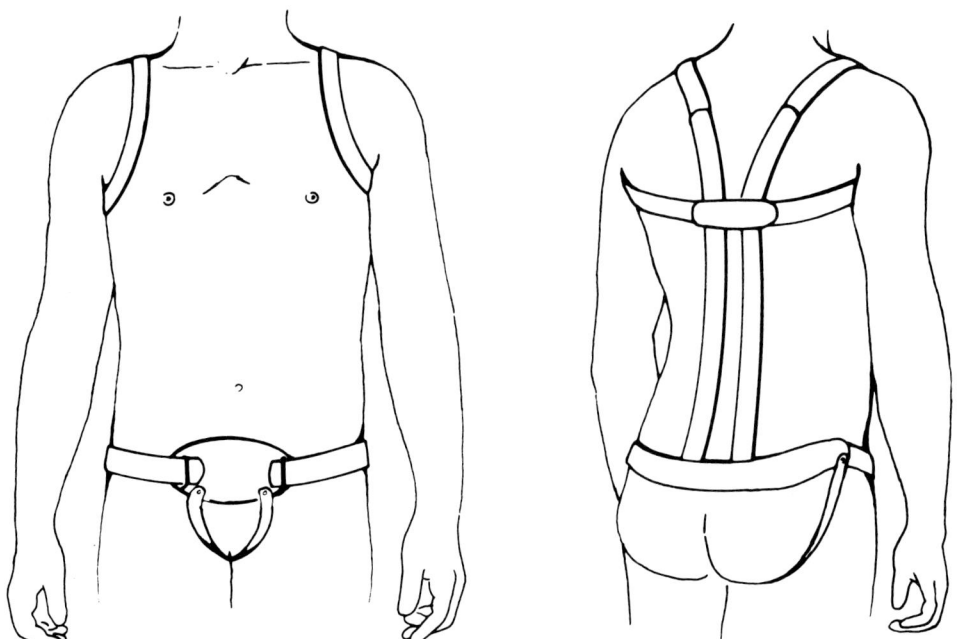

Figure 9-14. Taylor brace or thoracolumbosacral flexion-extension control orthosis with two posterior uprights to the thoracic spine. (From Bunch WH, Keagy RD: Principles of orthotic treatment. St. Louis, CV Mosby, 1976. Reprinted with permission.)

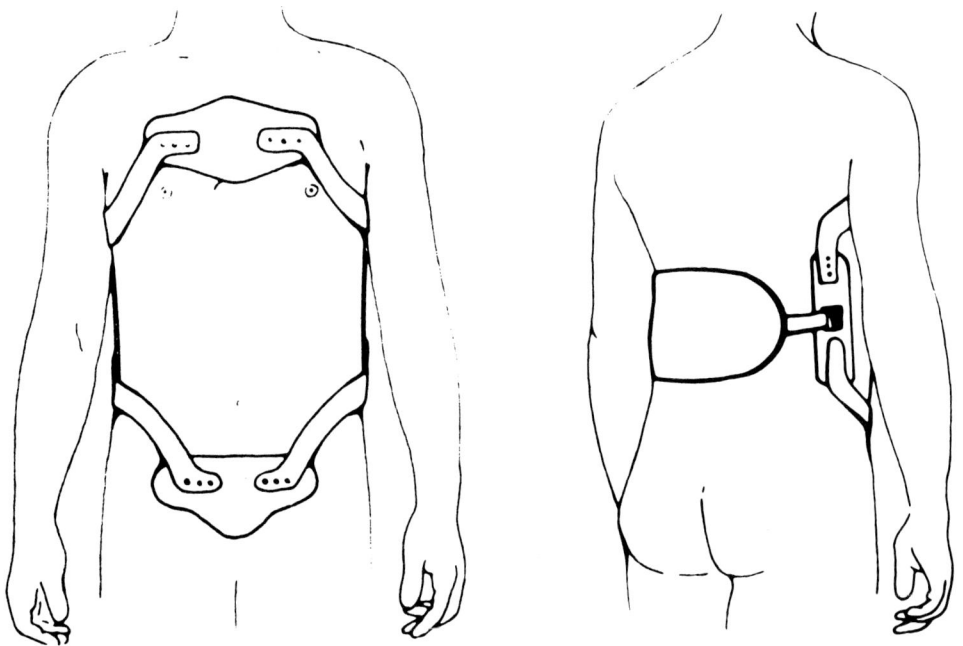

Figure 9-15. Jewett brace or thoracolumbosacral flexion control orthosis. (From Bunch WH, Keagy RD: Principles of orthotic treatment. St. Louis, CV Mosby, 1976. Reprinted with permission.)

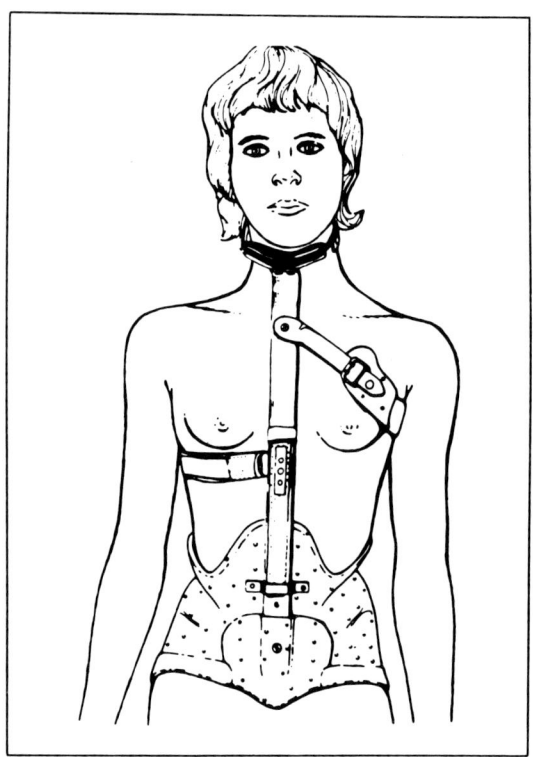

Figure 9-16. Milwaukee brace. The thoracic pad is suspended from an outrigger attached anterior upright and should be about 3–4 levels below the apex of the curve. (From Bunch WH, Keagy RD: Principles of orthotic treatment. St. Louis, CV Mosby, 1976. Reprinted with permission.)

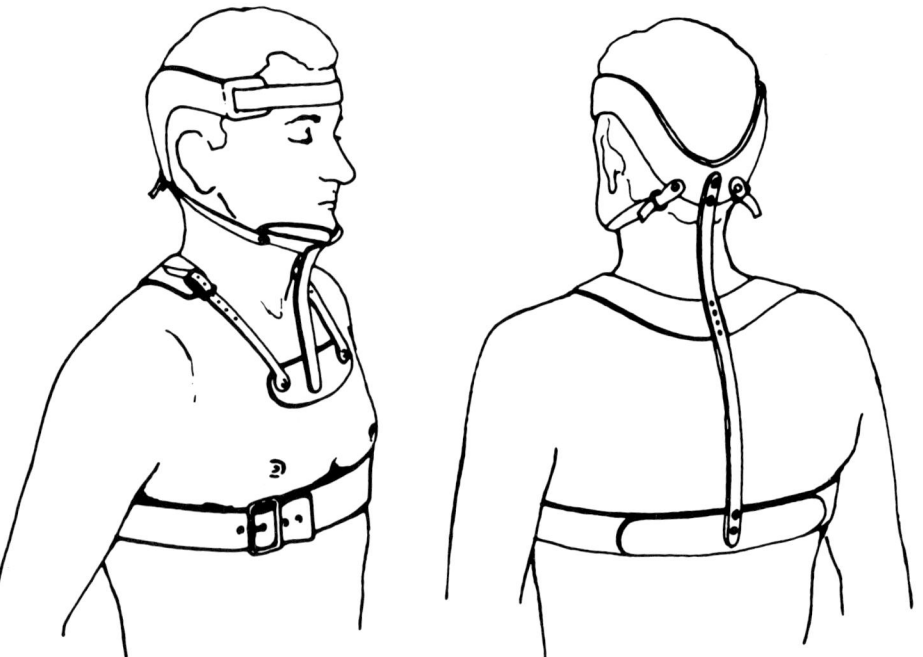

Figure 9-17. SOMI or cervicothoracic orthosis. (From Bunch WH, Keagy RD: Principles of orthotic treatment. St. Louis, CV Mosby, 1976. Reprinted with permission.)

80
Sports Orthoses

I. The Foot
A. Custom runner's orthotics obtained from positive casting of foot
B. May reduce abnormal pronation, pes planus (when associated with plantar fasciitis), pes cavus (may reduce "windlass effect" on plantar fascia)
C. Maintains the subtalar joint in neutral position and provides support for the medial longitudinal arch

II. The Elbow
A. Nirschl tennis elbow support
   1. Acts to disperse force from extensors
   2. Reminds wearer to limit resisted extension
B. Dynasplint
   1. Low load, constant tension, extension or flexion assist splint
   2. May help increase elbow range of motion following prolonged immobilization

III. The Knee
A. Postoperative knee bracing following repair/reconstruction may
   1. Improve cartilage nutrition
   2. Provide controlled isotonic rehabilitation
   3. Stimulate parallel collagen alignment
B. Mechanism
   1. Still controversial but thought to be a combination of skin proprioception and mechanical support
   2. Dynamic action much more significant than static
   3. No brace (custom or off the shelf) will provide significant static resistance to anterior or posterior translation of the tibia
C. Carbon Titanium (C.Ti.) brace
   1. Custom-made frame of graphite, nonelastic support straps, and pneumatic condylar pads
   2. May provide increased medial and lateral stability, limit anterior and posterior excursion of the tibia
   3. Rigid frame may also help give rotational control
D. Lenox Hill derotation brace
   1. Custom-made brace from casting of affected knee
   2. Useful in ligament-deficient knee or to protect ligament repair or reconstruction
E. Bledsoe
   1. Off the shelf brace
   2. Useful in postoperative management of cruciate or collateral ligament repair or reconstruction
   3. Much less expensive than custom braces
F. Dynasplint
   1. Low tension flexion or extension assist brace
   2. May be useful in management of contractures about the knee
G. Patellar support braces
   1. May have some value in treatment of patellofemoral maltracking
   2. Provides warmth and some proprioception

REFERENCES

Bunch WH, Keagy RD, Kritter AE, et al, eds: Atlas of orthotics, ed 2. St Louis, CV Mosby, 1985

Bunch WH, Keagy RD: Principles of orthotic treatment. St Louis, CV Mosby, 1976

Burgess EM, Matsen FA, Wyss, LR, Simmons CW: Segmental transcutaneous measurements of pO2 in patients requiring below knee amputation for peripheral vascular insufficiency. J Bone Joint Surg 64A:378, 1982

Corson JD, Jacobs RL, Karmody AM, et al: The diabetic foot. Curr Probl Surgery 10:721, 1986

Dallas Short Course: Orthotics and prosthetics. Dallas, University of Texas, 1986

Holstein P: The distal blood pressure predicts healing of amputations of the feet. Acta Orthop Scand 55:227, 1984

Kostuik JP, Gillespie R, eds: Amputation surgery and rehabilitation. New York, Churchill Livingstone, 1981

Kruger LM: Recent advances in surgery of lower limb deficiencies. Clin Orthop 148:97, 1980

Rosenfelder R: Infant amputees: Early growth and care. Clin Orthop 148:41, 1980

Shaperman J, Sumida CT: Recent advances in research in prosthetics for children. Clin Orthop 148:26, 1980

Sorbye R: Myoelectric prosthetic fitting in young children. Clin Orthop 148:34, 1980

Stokosa JJ: Prosthetics for lower limb amputees. In Haimovici H, ed: Vascular surgery: Principles and techniques. Norwalk, CT, Appleton-Century-Crofts, 1984

Swanson AB, Swanson G deG: The Krukenberg procedure in the juvenile amputee. Clin Orthop 148:55, 1980

Torg JS, Vegso JJ, Torg E: Rehabilitation of athletic injuries: An atlas of therapeutic exercise. Chicago, Yearbook, 1987

Wu Y, Keagy, RD, Krick HJ, et al: An innovative removable rigid dressing technique for below the knee amputation. J Bone Joint Surg 61A:724, 1979

Index

Page numbers in italics indicate references to tables.

Acetabulum, 35
  fractures
    anatomy, 305
    biochemistry, 305
    classification, 305–306
    management, 307–309
    radiographic examination, 307–308
Achilles tendonitis, 277
Achondroplasia, 187–188
Acquired immune deficiency syndrome, 107
Adamantinoma, 137–138
  diagnosis, 138
  pathology, 138
  treatment, 138
Adolescent hallux valgus, 152
Adult respiratory distress syndrome, 285
Aging, effect on cartilage, 86
Aitken classification, 181
Allografts, 80–81
Amputation surgery
  of hand, 398
  of lower limb, 499–502
  of upper limb, 514–515
Anaerobes, 106–107
Aneurysmal bone cyst, 123–124
  diagnosis, 124
  pathology, 124
  treatment, 124
Ankle
  arthritis, degenerative, 276–277
  blood vessels of, 50
  bones of, 50
  Charcot joint, 275
  fracture
    calcaneal, 329–330
    classification, 327
    talus, 330–331
    treatment, 327–329
  joint, 50
  muscles of, 50
  myelomeningocele and, 174
  nerves of, 50
  overuse disorders, 277–279
  rheumatoid disease, 275–276
  sprain, 278
  surgery of, 50–52
  see also Fibula; Foot; Leg; Tibia
Ankylosing spondylitis, 88, 468–469
Anomalies, see Congenital anomalies
Antibiotics, 98, 99
Arm, 7–10
  amputation
    above elbow, 514–515
    below elbow, 514
    four-quarter, 515
    Krukenberg procedure, 515
    shoulder disarticulation, 515
    surgery for, 514, 515

blood vessels of, 7
bones of, 7
muscles of, 7
nerves of, 7
surgery of 7–10
see also Elbow; Forearm; Hand; Humerus; Ulna
Arthritis
  of ankle, 276–277
  ankylosing spondylitis, 88, 468–469
  chrondocalcinosis, 90
  crystal-induced, 89–90
  enteropathic arthritis, 89
  gout, 89
  of hip, 238–245
  joint disorders, 91
  of knee, 246–254
  mixed connective tissue disease, 91
  ochronosis, 91
  pseudogout, 90
  psoriatic, 88–89
  Reiter's syndrome, 88
  rheumatic conditions, 90–91
  scleroderma, 90
  septic
    aspiration. 101
    clinical findings, 100–101
    pathogenesis, 100
    prognosis, 101
    treatment, 101
  seronegative, 88–89
  sicca syndrome, 91
  of spine, 467–469
  synovial chondromatosis, 91
  synovial diseases, 91
  synovitis, 91
  systemic lupus erythematosus, 90
  see also Osteoarthritis, Rheumatoid arthritis
Arthrogryposis multiplex congenita
  clinical findings, 179
  treatment, 179
Arthrodesis
  of hip, 238
  of knee, 252–253
  of shoulder, 224–225
Arthropathy, shoulder cuff tear, 219–220
Arthroplasty
  of elbow, 232, 232–233
  of hip, 238–243
Atlantoaxial instability, 406
  etiology, 406
  treatment, 406
Atlanto-occipital fusion, 405–406
  clinical findings, 405–406
  treatment, 406
Autografts, 80

Becker, muscular dystrophy, 175
Biceps, tendon rupture, 234

Biochemistry
  of cartilage, 83–85
Biomaterials, 485–490
  biocompatability, 485
  ceramics, 490
  corrosion, 485
  metal processing. 485–487
  metals, 487–489
  polymers, 489–490
  silicones, 490
  types of material, 485
Biomechanics
  concepts of, 473–481
    behavior of materials, 475–477
    definitions, 473, 480–481
    friction, lubrication, wear, 479–480
    material properties, 475
    rheology, 477–479
    types of loading, 474–475
  functional, 494–496
Bites, 103
Blount's disease, 157
Bone, 59–62
  of ankle, 50
  of arm, 7
  composition of, 59–60
  diseases of, metabolic, 63–69
    classification, 63
    Fanconi syndrome, 64, 66
    hyperparathyroidism, 65, 68–69
    hypophosphatasis, 65, 66
    osteomalacia, 63, 65, 66
    osteoporosis, 65, 67–68
    Paget's, 65, 68
    renal osteodystrophy, 64, 66
    renal tubular acidosis, 64, 66
    rickets, 63, 64, 66
  of elbow, 11
  fibrosarcoma of, 129
  of forearm, 16
  fractures of, 70–73
    electrical stimulation of, 72
    grafting, 71–72
    healing, 70–71
    nonunion of, 71
    surgery of, 71
    treatment of, 71–72
  function of, 59–62
  grafting, 79–81
    allograft, 80–81
    autograft, 80
  of hip, 35
  infarct of, 128
  of knee, 42
  of leg, 47
  lymphoma of, 134–135
  mechanics of, 491–493
  metastatic disease, 138–139
  mineralization of, 60–62
  remodeling of, 60–62

Bone (cont.)
  of shoulder, 3
  of spine, 27
  structure of, 59–62
  of thigh, 39
  tumors of, 123–124, 125–126
Bone grafting, 79–81
  allografts, 80–81
  autografts, 80
  of fractures, 71–72
Boutonnière deformity, 345–346, 380–381
Braces, see Orthoses
Brachial plexus
  anatomy, 4, 366
  injuries
    classification, 366
    diagnosis, 366–367
    treatment, 368
Bunionette, treatment, 272
Burns, of hand, 343
Bursitis, 233–234

Callus
  diagnosis, 273–273
  pathogenesis, 273
  treatment, 274
Caput ulna syndrome
  diagnosis, 379
  treatment, 379
Carpal bones
  anatomy, 359
  classification of instability, 359–360
  instability patterns, 360–361
  motion, 359
Carpal tunnel syndrome
  anatomy, 369
  diagnosis, 369
  etiology, 369
  treatment, 369
Cartilage, 82–92
  aging on, 86
  articular, 82–86
    biochemistry of, 83–85
    biomechanical functions, 85–86
    histology of, 82–83
    morphology of, 83
  immature, 86
  mechanics of, 493–494
  trauma to, 86
Catterall classification, 164–166
Ceramics, 490
Cerebral palsy
  classification, 170
  definition, 170
  pathoetiology, 170
  treatment, 170–172
Cervical disc disease, 428–434
Charcot joint, 275
Charcot-Marie-Tooth disease, 176–177
Children
  cervical spinal problems, 407
  deformities in, 154–157
  disorders of, 193–197
  fractures in, 198–212
  hallux valgus, 152
  orthotics in, 511–512
  prosthetics in, 511, 513
  scoliosis in, 408–412
Chondocalcinosis, 90
Chondroblastoma
  diagnosis, 120
  pathology, 120
  treatment, 120

Chondroma, periosteal
  diagnosis, 120
  pathology, 119
  treatment, 120
Chondromatosis, synovial, 91
Chondromyxofibroma
  diagnosis, 120–121
  pathology, 120
  treatment, 121
Chondrosarcoma
  diagnosis, 130
  pathology, 130
  treatment, 130
Chordoma
  diagnosis, 137
  pathology, 137
  treatment, 137
Clavicle, 3
Clawed toes, 271–272
  clinical findings, 272
  etiology, 272
  pathologic anatomy, 271
  treatment, 272
Clubfoot
  embryology, 145
  etiology, 145
  incidence, 145
  pathology, 145
  prognosis, 145
  salvage procedures, 146
  treatment, 145–146
  x-ray findings, 145
Collagen
  biosynthesis, 96
  disorders, 96
  types, 96
Compartment syndrome, 285–286, 386–388
  see also Volkman's contractures
Compressive neuropathies, see Neuropathies
Congenital anomalies
  of cervical spine
    absent facet of C1, 407
    anatomy, 403
    atlantoaxial instability, 407
    atlanto-occipital fusion, 405–406
    basilar impression, 403–404
    in children, 407
    evaluation, 403
    Klippel-Feil syndrome
    of odontoid, 405
    torticollis, 406
    treatment, 404
  of hand, 391–395
    classification, 391
    development, 391
    environment, 391
    genetics, 391
    incidence, 391
    surgery, 391
    treatment, 391–394
Congenital disorders, 181–185
Congenital hip dislocation, 158–162
Congenital vertical talus
  clinical findings, 148
  pathology, 148
  treatment, 149
  types, 147–148
  x-ray findings, 148–149
Connective tissue disorders, 91
  Ehlers-Danlos syndrome, 191
  homocystinuria, 191
  Marfan syndrome, 191
  osteogenesis imperfects, 190–191

Contractures, intrinsic, 384–386
Corns, 273
  pathogenesis, 273
  treatment, 273
  surgery for, 273
Coxa plana, see Legg-Clavé-Perthes disease
Coxa vara
  clinical findings, 181
  incidence, 181
  treatment, 181–182
  x-rays, 181
Cubital tunnel syndrome
  diagnosis, 370
  etiology, 370
  treatment, 370
Curly toe, 152
Cysts, of bone
  aneurysmal, 123–124
  unicameral, 125–126

Danis-Weber classification, 327
Dejerine-Sottas disease, 177–178
Desmoid, periosteal, 115
DeQuervain's disorder
  clinical findings, 376
  diagnosis, 376
  treatment, 376
Diabetes
  foot disorders and, 274–275
    classification, 275
    surgery, 275
    treatment, 275
Disc disease
  cervical
    clinical findings, 428–430
    diagnosis, 430
    epidemiology, 428
    pathogenesis, 428
    treatment, 430–433
  lumbar
    clinical findings, 437–438
    diagnosis, 438
    epidemiology, 435
    incidence, 435
    treatment, 439–440
Disc space infections
  clinical findings, 102
  treatment, 102
Dislocation
  of ankle, 320–333
  of elbow, 292
  of hand, 353–355
  of hip, 314
  of knee, 320
  of shoulder
    acute, 222
    overuse, 222–223
    recurrent anterior, 221–222
    subluxation, 222–223, 300–301
Dobyns classification, 359–360
Drugs, antimicrobial, 98
Dupuytren's contracture
  clinical findings, 384
  complications, 384
  pathogenesis, 384
  treatment, 384
Dwarfism
  diastrophic, 189
  metatropic, 189
Dysostosis
  metaphyseal, 188
Dysplasia
  chondroectodermal, 188
  epiphysealis hemimelica, 187

epiphysealis punctata, 187
metaphyseal, 189
progressive diaphyseal, 189

Ehlers-Danlos syndrome, 191
  orthopaedic treatment, 191
Elbow
  amputation of, 514–515
  antecubital region, 11–12
  arthritis
    arthrodesis of, 231
    arthroplasty, 232, 232–233
    biomechanics of, 231
    radial head replacement, 232
    stability of, 231
    synovectomy, 231–232
  bones of, 11
  dislocation of, 292
  fracture
    of humerus, 290–292
    of olecranon, 292–293
    pediatric, 202–205
    of radius, 293
  joint, 11
  muscles, 11
  palsied, surgical procedures, 236
  sports or overuse injury, 233–236
    biceps tendon rupture, 234
    olecranon bursitis, 233–234
    tennis elbow, 233
    throwing, 234–236
  surgery of, 12–15
  see also Arm, Forearm
Ellis-van Creveld syndrome, 188
Embolism, fat, 285
Enchondroma, 398
  diagnosis, 118
  pathology, 118
  treatment, 118
Engelmann's disease, 189
Enneking tumor staging, 110
Enteropathic arthritis, 89
Epidermoid cyst, 396
Epiphyseal fracture, pediatric, 198
Erysipeloid, 103
Evans classification, 312
Ewing's sarcoma
  diagnosis, 133–134
  pathology, 133
  treatment, 134
Exostosis, 118–119
  diagnosis, 119
  pathology, 119
  treatment, 119
Extensor carpi ulnaris tenosynovitis
  clinical findings, 377
  diagnosis, 377
  treatment, 377
Extremities, *see* Arm, Leg, Limb

Fanconi syndrome, *64*, 66
Fat embolism, 285
Felon, 103
Femur, 35, 38
  deficiency
    congenital, 182
    proximal focal, 181
  coxa vara, 181–182
  fracture of, 72
    anatomy, 310
    classification, 310, 316, 318
    diagnosis, 310
    pediatric, 208–209
    risk factors, 310–311
    treatment, 311, 316–317

growth pattern, 154
internal torsion, 155–156
normal variation of, 154
slipped capital epiphysis
  classification, 167
  clinical findings, 167
  complications, 168–169
  pathogenesis, 167
  prophylactic pinning, 169
  treatment, 167–168
  x-ray findings, 167
Fibromas
  desmoplastic
    diagnosis, 116
    pathology, 116
    treatment, 116
  nonossifying
    diagnosis, 114
    Jaffe-Campanacci syndrome, 115
    pathology, 114
    periosteal desmoid. 115
    treatment, 115
  ossifying
    diagnosis, 115–116
    pathology, 115
    treatment, 116
Fibrosarcoma, of bone
  diagnosis, 129
  pathology, 129
  treatment, 129
Fibrous dysplasia, 116–118
  diagnosis, 117
  pathology, 117
  treatment, 117–118
Fibula
  deficiency, congenital, 182
  fracture, pediatric, 210
  subluxation and dislocation, 278
Fingers
  amputation of, 514
  blood vessels of, 24
  extensor apparatus, 24–26
  ligaments, 24, 25, 26
  metacarpal fractures, 352–353
  nailbed, 341
  nerves, 24
  phalangeal fractures, 353
  sheaths, 24
  surgery of, 26
  tendons, 24, 25, 26
  tip of
    anatomy, 339
    classification, 339
    surgery, 339–341
    treatment, 339
  see also Hand
Flatfoot, *see* Pes planus; Tarsal
  coalition
Flexor carpi radialis tunnel syndrome
  clinical findings, 376
  treatment, 376–377
Foot
  adolescent hallux valgus, 152
  amputation, 502
  blood vessels of, 55
  bones of, 52
  callus, 273–274
    treatment, 274
  clawed toes, 271–272
  clubfoot, 145–146
  congenital vertical talus, 147–149
  corns, 273
  curly toe, 152
  diabetic, 274–275
  evaluation of, 154

fracture
  forefoot, 334
  pediatric, 210–212
  tarsometatarsal, 334
growth patterns, 154
hallux rigidus, 270–271
hallux valgus, 268–269
hammer toes, 271
interdigital neuroma, 272-273
joints, 53–54
ligaments, 53–54
malalignment, 156–157
mallet toe, 272
metatarsalgia, 273–274
  treatment, 274
metatarsus adductus, 146–147
muscles, 54–55
myelomeningocele and, 174
nerves of, 55
  diseases of, 272–273
normal variation of, 154
osteochondrosis, 152
oversue disorders, 277–279
pes cavus, 150–151
pes planus, 150
polydactyly, 152
problems of, 145–153
prosthesis for, 506–507
rheumatoid disease, 275–276
surgery of, 55–56
syndactyly, 152
tarsal coalition, 149–150
tarsal tunnel syndrome, 273
toeing out, 156
toe walking, 152
Forearm
  blood vessels of 16, 17
  bones of, 16
  compartments, 16
  fracture of, 72
  muscles of, 16, 17
  nerves of, 17, 17–18
  posterior, 17–18
  surgery of, 18–19
  volar, 16–17
  see also Arm; Elbow
Fractures
  of acetabulum, 305–308
  of ankle, 327–333
  calcaneal, 329–330
  of elbow, 290–294
  of femur, 316–317
  of foot and ankle, 278–279, 327–335
  of forefoot, 334
  healing and nonunion, 70–73
    clinical findings, 71
    grafting, 71
    healing, 70–71
    nonunion types, 71
    surgery for, 71
    treatment, 71–72
  of hip
    femoral neck, 310–311
    intertrochanteric, 311–313
    subtrochanteric, 313–3`4
  of humerus, 290–292, 295–297
  infections of
    nonunion, 105–106
    open, 105
  of knee, 318–321
  olecranon, 293–294
  pediatric, 198–213
    elbow, 202–205
    epiphyseal, 198
    femur, 208–209

Fractures (cont.)
  fibula, 210
  foot, 210–212
  growth mechanism injury, 198
  hand, 200
  hip, 207–208
  humerus, 205–206
  knee, 209–210
  partial physeal arrest, 198
  pelvis, 207–208
  radius, 201–202
  shoulder, 205–206
  spine, 206–207
  tibia, 210
  ulna, 201–202
  wrist, 200
  of pelvis, 302–304
  of radius, 287–289, 293, 362–363
  scaphoid, 361–362
  shoulder, 298–301
  of spine, 447–451, 452
  of talus, 330–333
  of tibia, 322–326
  ulna, 287–289
  of wrist, 361–363
Freiberg's disease, 76, 152
Frykman classification, 362

Ganglion, 396–397
Garden classification, 310
Gas gangrene, 106–107
Genetics, 141–142
  inheritance patterns, 141–142
Giant cell sarcoma
  diagnosis, 136
  pathology, 136
  treatment, 136
Giant cell tumor, 396
  diagnosis, 127
  pathology, 126
  treatment, 127
Glomus, 396
Goldner classification, 227
Gout, 89–90
Grafting, see Bone grafting
Gustilo and Anderson classification, 323–324
Guyon's canal syndrome
  anatomy, 369–370
  clinical findings, 370
  treatment, 370

Hallux rigidus
  clinical findings, 270
  definition, 270
  etiology, 270
  treatment, 270–271
Hallux valgus
  adolescent
    clinical findings, 152
    pathogenesis, 152
    treatment, 152
  pathoanatomy, 268
  severity classification, 268
  surgery, 268–269
  treatment, 268
Hammer toes
  clinical findings, 271
  etiology, 271
  pathologic anatomy, 271
  treatment, 271
Hand
  bones of, 22
  burns of, 343
  compartments, 24

congenital anomalies, 391–395
dislocations, 353–355
fingers, 24–26
fingertip injuries, 339–341
fracture
  metacarpal, 352–353
  pediatric, 200
  phalangeal, 353
infections of, 103
joints of, 22
muscles of, 22
nailbed injuries, 341
nerves of, 24
osteoarthritis of, 377–378
palmar, 23–24
rheumatoid arthritis of, 378
soft tissue
  assessment, 341
  coverage of, 341–343
surgery of, 26
tendon transfers
  indications, 372–374
tumors
  amputation surgery, 398–399
  bone, 398
  bone grafting, 398
  curettage, 398
  evaluation, 396
  skin, 396
  soft tissue, 396–398
see also Fingers
Hardcastle classification, 334
Hardinge technique, 38
Hawkins classification, 331
Hemangioma, 124
  diagnosis, 125
  pathology, 124–125
  treatment, 125
Hemophilia
  pathogenesis, 193
Herpetic whitlow, 103
Hip
  arthritis of, 238–245
  bones of, 35
  congenital dislocation, 158–162
    clinical findings, 158
    incidence, 158
    pathology of, 158
    treatment, 159–161
    x-ray findings, 158–159
  disarticulation at, 500
  dislocation, 314
  fracture of, 72
    femoral neck, 310–311
    intertrochanteric, 311–313
    pediatric, 207–208
    subtrochanteric, 313–314
  joint, 35
  infection of, 104
  muscles, 35–36
  myelomeningocele and, 183
  problems of, 238–245
  surgery of, 36–38
    arthrodesis, 238
    arthroplasty, 238–243
    osteotomy, 238
    replacement, 243–244
Histiocytoma, malignant fibrous
  diagnosis, 129
  pathology, 129
  treatment, 129
Histiocytosis X, 127–128
  diagnosis, 128
  pathology, 128
  treatment, 128

Histology
  of cartilage, 82–83
  of tumors, 113–114
Hohl classification, 319, 320
Homocystinuria
  clinical findings, 191
  treatment, 191
Humerus, 3, 7
  fracture
    complications, 296
    pediatric, 205–206
    prognosis, 296
    treatment, 290–292, 295–296
Hunter procedure, 350
Hunter's canal, 39
Hunter's syndrome, 186
Hurler's syndrome, 186
Hyperparathyroidism, 65, 68–69
Hypophosphatasia, 65, 66

Iliotibial band friction syndrome, 257
Impingement syndrome
  clinical findings, 217–218
  treatment, 218–219
Infarct, of bone
  diagnosis, 128
  pathology, 128
  treatment, 128
Infections
  orthopaedic, 98–108
    acquired immune deficiency syndrome, 107
    after arthroplasty, 104–105
    anaerobes, 106–107
    antimicrobial drugs for, 98
    atypical, 106
    disc space, 102–102
    fungal, 106
    gas gangrene, 106–107
    of hand, 103
    of joints, 104
    Lyme arthritis, 107
    necrotizing fasciitis, 107
    osteomyelitis, 99–100, 101–102, 105–106
    septic arthritis, 100–101
    tetanus, 107
    toxic shock syndrome, 107
    tuberculosis of spine, 103
Interdigital neuroma
  clinical findings, 272
  definition, 272
  diagnosis, 272
  etiology, 272
  incidence, 272
  treatment, 272–273
Intersection syndrome, 376
Intertrochanter fracture
  classification, 312
  stability, 312–313
  treatment, 313
Inheritance, patterns of, 141–142
Intrinsic contractures
  clinical findings, 386
  etiology, 384–386
  treatment, 386

Jaffe-Campanacci syndrome, 115
Joints
  arthrodial, 42
  ball and socket, 3, 35
  Charcot, 275
  disorders of, 91
  of elbow, 11
  of hand, 377–378

hinge, 42, 50
humeroulnar, 11
infected arthroplasty
  diagnosis, 104
  prevention, 104
  treatment, 104–105
of knee, 42–44
metacarpophalangeal, 380
radiocarpal and intercarpal, 379–380
radioulnar, 11
of shoulder, 3
of wrist, 378
Johner and Wruhs classification, 323
Juvenile rheumatoid arthritis
  onset, 193
  orthopaedic management, 193
  pauciarticular, 193
  polyarticular, 193
  treatment, 193

Kienböock's disease
  classification, 363–364
  etiology, 363
  treatment, 364
Klippel-Feil syndrome, 404–405
  clinical findings, 405
  complications, 405
  diagnosis, 405
  treatment, 405
Knee
  amputation, 500
  arthritis of, 246–254
  arthrodesis of, 252–253
  bones of, 42
  deformity, congenital, 184–185
  fracture
    dislocation, 320
    of femur, 318
    of patella, 318–319
    pediatric, 209–210
    of tibia, 319–320
  joint, 42–44
    infection of, 104–105
  ligaments, 42
  muscles, 44
  myelomeningocele and, 173–174
  osteoarthritis of, 246–252
  osteonecrosis of, 253
  prosthesis for, 505–506
  sports injuries, 258–265
  surgery of, 44–46
  see also Femur, Patella, Tibia
Kohler's disease, 76–77
Krukenberg procedure, 515
Kyphosis, 417–422
  biomechanics, 417
  classification, 417
  congenital
    treatment, 419–420
    types, 419
  inflammatory and infectious, 420–421
  myelomeningocele
    paralytic, 420
    postsurgical, 420
    post-traumatic, 420
  Scheuermann's disease, 417–419

Larsen's syndrome, 196
Lauge-Hanson classification, 327
Leg
  amputation
    above knee, 500
    below knee, 500
    hip disarticulation, 500
    level of, 499
    Syme's amputation, 500–502
  angular malignment, 156
  blood vessels of, 48
  bones of, 47
  compartments, 47
  deficiency, congenital, 181, 182, 183
  deformities, tibia, 183–184
  external rotation gait, 156
  femoral torsion, 155–156
  length discrepancy
    assessment, 196
    etiology, 196
    treatment, 196–197
  muscles of, 47–48
  nerves of, 48
  pain
    patellofemoral, 256
    in runners, 257–258
    prosthesis for, 503–05
    sports injuries in, 256–258
  surgery of, 48–49
  tibia vara, 157
  tibial torsion, 154–155
  see also Foot, Knee
Legg-Clavé-Perthes disease
  clinical findings, 163
  diagnosis, 163–164
  incidence, 163
  pathogenesis, 163
  prognosis, 165
  stages, 163
  treatment, 164–166
Letournel classification, 305–306
Ligaments, 96–97
  of hip, 35
  of knee, injuries, 259–265
  mechanics of, 494
  of shoulder
Limb, lower
  amputation of, 499–502
  othotics
    in adults, 508–510
    in children, 511–513
  prosthesis for, 503–507
    in children, 511–513
  sports injuries of, 255–265
  see also Foot; Leg
Limb, upper, see Arm
Linscheid classification, 359–360
Lipoma, 396
Lisfranc joint, 334
Liverpool technique, 38
Lyme arthritis, 107
Lymphoma, of bone
  diagnosis, 134
  pathology, 134
  treatment, 134–135

Maisonneuve's fractures, 327
Mallet finger, 345, 384
Mallet toe
  clinical findings, 272
  definition, 272
  etiology, 272
  treatment, 272
Marfan syndrome
  clinical findings, 191
  treatment, 191
Maroteaux-Lamy syndrome, 187
Mastocytosis, 128–129
Mechanics of structures, 482–484
Meleny's infection, 107
Melorheostosis, 190
Metabolic bone diseases, 63–69

Metacarpophalangeal joint
  deformities, 380
  treatment, 380
Metals, 487–489
Metastatic bone disease
  diagnosis, 138–139
  treatment, 139
Metatarsalgia
  diagnosis, 273–274
  pathogenesis, 273
  treatment, 274
Metatarsus adductus, 146–147
  clinical findings, 146
  pathogenesis, 146
  treatment, 146–147
Meyers and McKeever classification, 320
Moore technique, 38
Morquio syndrome, 186
Mucopolysaccharidoses, 186
Mucous cyst, 397–398
Multiple epiphyseal dysplasia, 187
Muscles
  abductors, 4, 35–36
  adductors, 4, 36
  of ankle, 50
  of arm, 7
  of elbow, 11
  extensors, 3, 11, 35
  flexors, 3, 11, 35
  of foot, 54–55
  of hip, 35–36
  of knee, 44
  of leg, 47–48
  pronators, 11
  rotators, 4, 36
  of shoulder, 3
  skeletal
    diseases of, 94–95
    physiology of, 94
    structure of, 93–94
  supinators, 11
Muscular dystrophy
  Becker, 175
  classification, 175
  Duchenne's, 175
Mycobacteria, 106
Myeloma
  diagnosis, 135
  pathology, 135
  treatment, 135
Myelomeningocele
  ankle, 174
  congenital, 420
  deformities, level and, 173
  developmental, 420
  foot, 174
  hip, 173
  knee, 173–174
  pathoetiology, 172
  spina bifida type, 172
  spine, 173
Myopathies
  congenital, 176
  inflammatory, 176
  myotonia, 175–176
Myotonia, 175–176

Necrotizing fasciitis, 107
Neer classification, 300
Nerves
  of arm, 7
  brachial plexus
    anatomy of, 4, 366
    injury of, 366–368

Nerves (*cont.*)
  injuries to, 95–95, 366–370
  of leg, 48
  peripheral injuries
    anatomy, 368
    classification, 368
    prognosis, 368
    regeneration, 368
    surgery, 368
  of shoulder, 4
  structure of
Neuroblastoma
  diagnosis, 136
  pathology, 136
  treatment, 136
Neurofibromatosis, 179–180, 414
  clinical findings, 179–180
  genetics, 179
  incidence, 179
  skeletal manifestations, 180
Neuroma, *see* Interdigital neuroma
Neuromuscular diseases
  cerebral palsy, 170–172
  classification, 174
  evaluation, 174
  muscular dystrophy, 175
  myotonia, 175–176
  spinal muscular atrophy, 178–19
Neuropathies
  compressive
    anterior interosseous nerve syndrome, 369
    carpal tunnel syndrome, 369
    cubital tunnel syndrome, 370
    Guyon's canal syndrome, 369–370
    median nerve, 369
    posterior interosseous syndrome, 370
    pronator syndrome, 369
    radial nerve, 370
    radial tunnel syndrome, 379
    thoracic outlet syndrome, 370
    ulnar nerve, 369–370
  hereditary motor and sensory, 176–178
    classification, *177*
Newman classification, 423
Noonan's syndrome, 196

Ochronosis, 91
Odontoid, congenetal anomalies
  clinical findings, 405
  etiology, 405
  treatment, 405
Olecranon
  bursitis, 233–234
  fracture, 292–293
Orthopaedic infections, 98–108
Orthoses
  spinal
    cervical, 522–524
    flexible, 521
    rigid, 521–522
    sports, 525–526
Orthotics
  lower limb
    ankle-foot, 509
    in children, 511–512
    foot, 508
    hip-knee-ankle-foot, 510
    knee-ankle-foot, 509–510
    shoe modification, 508
Osgood-Schlatter syndrome, 77
Osteoarthritis, 86–87
  of hand, 377–378
  of wrist, 378

Osteoblastoma
  diagnosis, 123
  pathology, 123
  treatment, 123
Osteochondritis dissecans
  clinical findings, 77
  treatment, 77
Osteochrondroma, 118–119, 398
Osteochondroses, 76–77, 152
  Freiberg's disease, 76
  Kohler's disease, 76–77
  Osgood-Schlatter syndrome, 77
  Panner's disease, 76
  Sever's disease, 77
  Sinding-Larsen syndrome, 77
  types, 76
Osteogenesis imperfecta, 190–191
  classification, 190
  clinical findings, 190
  pathogenesis, 190
  treatment, 190–191
Osteoma
  diagnosis, 121
  pathology, 121
  treatment, 122
Osteoid osteoma
  diagnosis, 122
  pathology, 122–123
  treatment, 123
Osteomalacia, 63, *65*, 66
Osteomyelitis
  acute hematogenous, 99–100
    clinical findings, 100
    pathogenesis, 99
    treatment, 100
  chronic, 106
    Cierny staging, 106
    physiologic class, 106
    treatment, 106
  vertebral
    biopsy, 102
    clinical findings, 102
    incidence, 101
    pathology, 101–102
    treatment
    x-ray findings
Osteonecrosis, 74–76
  of carpal scaphoid, 76
  of femoral condyles, 76
  of femoral head, 74–75
    diagnosis, 74–75
    histologic findings, 74
    pathogenesis, 74
    radiographic classification, 75
    treatment, 75
  of humeral head, 76
  of talus, 75–76
Osteopathia striata, 189
Osteopetrosis, 190
  tarda, 190
Osteopoikilosis, 189
Osteoporosis, *65*, 67–68
Osteosarcoma, 130–133
  diagnosis, 132
  pathology, 132
  treatment, 132–133
Osteotomy
  of hip, 238
Overuse disorders, of foot and ankle, 277–279

Paget's disease, *65*, 68
Pain
  of leg, in runners, 257–258
  patellofemoral, 256
Panner's disease, 76

Paronychia, 103
Patella fracture
  classification, 318–319
  treatment, 319
Pediatric conditions, *see* Children
Pelvis fracture,
  anatomy, 302–303
  classification, 303–304
  clinical findings, 303
  pediatric, 207–208
  treatment, 304
Pes cavus, 150–151
  clinical findings, 151
  pathogenesis, 151
  treatment, 151
Pes planus
  clinical findings, 150
  etiology, 150
  treatment, 150
  x-ray findings, 150
Physis, growth arrest, 198–199
Plantar fasciitis, 277–278
Polydactyly, 152
Polymers, 489
Posterior interosseous syndrome
  etiology, 370
  treatment, 370
Prader-Willi syndrome, 196
Principles of orthopaedic trauma, 283–286
Pronator syndrome, 369
  treatment, 369
Prosthetics
  lower limb, 503–507
    foot mechanics, 507
    in children, 511, 513
    knee mechanics, 505–506
    suspension and sockets, 503–505
Pseudoachondroplasia, 187
Pseudogout, 90
Psoriatic arthritis, 88–89
Pyknodysostosis, 189
Pyle's disease, 189

Radial tunnel syndrome
  diagnosis, 370
  treatment, 370
Radiography, of tumors, 109–110
Radius
  fracture, 287–289, 293, 362–363
    pediatric, 201–202
  replacement, 232–233
Reflex sympathetic dystrophy
  clinical findings, 388
  definition, 388
  etiology, 388
  pathophysiology, 388
  stages, 388
  treatment, 388
Reiter's syndrome, 89
Renal osteodystrophy, *64*, 66
Renal tubular acidosis, *64*, 66
Replantation, 357–358
  amputated part, 357
  postoperative period, 358
  surgical technique, 357
Rett syndrome, 196
Rheumatoid arthritis, 87, 385, 386
  of foot and ankle, 275–276
  of hand and wrist
    boutonnière deformity, 380, 380–381
    caput ulna syndrome, 379
    metacarpophalangeal joint, 380
    pathogenesis, 378
    surgery, 378–379

swan-neck deformity, 380, 381
tenosynovitis, 379
thumb, 380–381
wrist joints, 379–380
of spine
cervical deformity, 467–468
Rickets, 63, *64*, 66
Rockwood and Green classification, 322–323
Ruedi/Allgower classification, 327
Running injuries, 255–256

Salter classification, 164–166
Sanfilippo's syndrome, 186
Sarcoma
Ewing's, 133–134
giant cell, 136
Scapula, 3
Schatzker classification, 319
Scheie syndrome, 186–187
Scheuermann's disease
clinical findings, 418
diagnosis, 418
pathogenesis, 417–418
treatment, 418–419
types, 418
Scleroderma, 90
Scoliosis, 408–416
adult
evaluation, 414
treatment, 414–415
classification, 408
congenital
etiology, 412
progress, 412
treatment, 412–413
idiopathic adolescent
diagnosis, 409
management, 409–411
natural history, 408–409
pathoanatomy, 408
prognosis, 408–409
idiopathic infantile scoliosis
diagnosis, 411
prognosis, 411
treatment, 411
idiopathic juvenile, 412
neurofibromatosis, 414
paralytic
diagnosis, 413
treatment, 413
Seddon classification, 368
Seinsheimer classification, 313
Sever's disease, 77
Shoulder, 3–6
acromioclavicular disease, 220
adhesive capsulitis, 220–221
bones of, 3
brachial plexus, 4
cuff tear arthropathy
definition, 219
diagnosis, 220
history, 219
Milwaukee shoulder, 220
pathology, 219
radiographs, 219
treatment, 220
dislocation, 221–223, 300–301
entrapment neuropathies, 220
fracture
of clavicle, 298–299
of humerus, 298
pediatric, 205–206
of scapula, 299–300
glenohumeral arthrodesis, 224–225

impingement syndrome
clinical findings, 217–218
treatment, 218–219
inflammation and degeneration, 220
instability, 221–224
multidirectional, 224
posterior, 223–224
joint, 3
microtrauma, 222
muscles of, 3–4
nerves of, 4
overuse, 222
palsied, 227–228
replacement, 224–227
total, 225–227
surgery of, 4–6
palsied, 227–228
tendinitis, 220
Sicca syndrome, 91
Silicones, 490
Sinding-Larsen's syndrome, 77
Skeleton
dysplasias, 185–190
classification, 185
dwarfism, 185
see specific dysplasias
Smith-Petersen technique, 36
Southern technique, 38
Spina bifida types, 172
Spinal muscular atrophy
classification, 178–179
clinical findings, pathology, 179
Spinal orthoses, 521–524
Spinal trauma
cervical and thoracolumbar injuries, 445–452
cervical fractures, 447–452
evaluation, 445–447
management, 447
thoracolumbar fractures, 452–458
anatomy, 452
classification, 454–455
evaluation, 453–454
fractures, 452
stability, 452
treatment, 455–458
Spine, 27–34
ankylosing spondylitis, 468–469
articulation, 27–28
bones of, 27, 31
cervical, 27–31
congenital anomalies, 403–407
coccyx, 31–34
fracture, pediatric, 206–207
ligaments, 27–28, 31
muscles of, 28, 31–32
myelomeningocele, 172
nerves, 32
orthoses
cervical, 522
flexible, 521
rigid, 521–522
rheumatoid arthritis, 467–468
sacrum, 31–34
surgery of, 28–31, 33–34
thoracolumbar, 31–34
tuberculosis of, 103
tumors of, 460–466
Spondylitis, seronegative, 468–469
Spondyloepiphyseal dysplasia, 186
Spondylolysis and spondylolisthes
classification, 423
clinical findings, 423–424
etiology, 423
isthmic, L4 over L5, 425
prognosis, 425

roentgenographic findings, 424
treatment, 425–426
Sports injuries, 233–236
of foot and leg, 255–267
running, 255–256
Sports orthoses, 525–526
Staging of tumors, 110
Stenosis, spinal
classification, 440–441
clinical findings, 442–442
diagnosis, 442
pathogenesis, 441
treatment, 442–443
Structures
mechanics of, 482–484
bending rigidity, 482–484
definition of, 482, 484
torsional rigidity, 484
Subtrochanteric fracture
classification, 313–314
treatment, 314
Surgery
of ankle, 50–52, 277
of arm, 7–10
of elbow, 12–15, 236
of fingers, 26
of foot, 55–56, 275
of fractures, 71
of hand, 26, 378–379
of hip, 36–38, 238–245
of knee, 44–46
of leg, 48–49
replantation techniques, 357
of shoulder, 4–6, 227–228
of spine, 28–31, 33–34
of thigh, 40–41
of toes, 268–269, 270, 271, 272, 273
of tumors, 112–113
of wrist, 21–22, 378–379
Swan-neck deformity, 346–347, 380–381
treatment, 347, 381
Syme's amputation, 500–502
Syndactyly, 152
Synovial chondromatosis, 91
Synovitis, 91
Systemic lupus erythematosus, 90

Tailor's bunion, 272
Tarsal coalition
clinical findings, 149
incidence, 149
pathogenesis, 149
treatment, 150
x-ray findings, 149
Tarsal tunnel syndrome
clinical findings, 273
pathogenesis, 273
treatment, 273
Tendinitis, Achilles, 277
Tendons, 96
biceps rupture, 234
extensor injuries of hand
swan-neck, 346–347
zone 1, 345
zone 2, 345–346
zone 3, 346
zone 4, 346
flexor injuries of hand
anatomy, 347–348
blood supply and nutrition, 348–349
grafting, 35o
healing, 349
repair, 349–359
mechanics of, 494

Tendons (cont.)
  tibialis rupture, 278
  tumor of, 396
Tendon transfers of hand, 372–375
  indications, 372
  nerve palsy, 372–373
  radial nerve palsy, 372
  ulna nerve palsy, 373–374
Tennis elbow, 233
Tenosynovitis, 103, 379
  DeQuervain's disorder, 376
  extensor carpi ulnaris, 377
  flexor carpi radialis tunnel syndrome, 376
  flexor carpi ulnaris, 377
  intersection syndrome, 376
  trigger thumb or finger, 376
Tetanus, 107
Thigh
  blood vessels, 39
  bones of, 39
  Hunter's canal, 39
  muscles of, 39
  nerves of, 39
  septa of, 39
  surgery of, 40–41
Thoracic outlet syndrome
  diagnosis, 370
  treatment, 370
Throwing injury, of elbow, 234–236
Thumb
  amputation, 514
  boutonnière deformity
    diagnosis, 380
    incidence, 380
    treatment, 381
  swan-neck deformity
    diagnosis, 381
    incidence, 381
    treatment, 381
Tibia
  deficiency, congenital, 183–184
  deformity, angular, 183–184
  fracture
    anatomy, 322
    classification, 319, 320, 327
    complications, 325–326
    management of open, 324
    mechanism, 319, 322–324
    pediatric, 210
    pilon, 327
    treatment, 319, 324–325, 327
  growth patterns, 154
  internal torsion, 154–155
  normal variation, 154
  vara, 157
Tibiofibular syndesmosis injury, 278
Tile classification, 303–304
Toe walking
  clinical findings, 152
  diagnosis, 152

treatment, 152
Toes, see Clawed toes; Foot; Hammer toes; Mallet toe
Torticollis
  clinical findings, 406
  treatment, 406
Toxic shock syndrome, 107
Trauma
  to cartilage, 86
  infections after, 105–106
  multiple system, 283–286
    complications, 285–286
    orthopaedic management, 284–285
  reflex sympathetic dystrophy, 388
  see also Spinal trauma
Trevor's disease, 187
Trigger finger or thumb
  clinical, 376
  treatment, 376
Tuberculosis
  of spine, 103
Tumors, 109–140
  adamantinoma, 137–138
  aneurysmal bone cyst, 123–124
  bone infarct, 128
  chondroblastoma, 120–121
  chondosarcoma, 130
  chordoma, 137
  enchondroma, 118
  Ewing's sarcoma, 133–134
  exostosis, 118
  fibroma
    desmoplastic, 116
    nonossifying, 114–115
    ossifying, 115–116
  fibrosarcoma, of bone, 129
  fibrous dysplasia, 116–118
  giant cell sarcoma, 136
  giant cell tumor, 126–127
  of hand and amputation surgery, 396–400
  hemangioma, 124–125
  histiocytoma, malignant fibrous, 129
  histiocytosis X, 127–128
  lymphoma, of bone, 134–135
  mastocytosis, 128–129
  metastatic bone disease, 138–139
  myeloma, 135
  neuroblastoma, 136
  osteoblastoma, 123
  osteoma, 121–122
    osteoid, 122–123
  osteosarcoma, 130–133
  periosteal chondroma, 119–120
  of spine
    benign, *461*
    biopsy, 460
    bone, malignant, *462*
    cysts, *463*
    evaluation, 460
    intraspinal, *463*

surgery, 464
    treatment, 460–465
  treatment principles, 109–114
    age, 109
    biopsy, 110–112
    clinical, 109
    diagnosis, 111
    histology, 113–114
    location, 109
    radiographic, 109–110
    staging and grading, 110, *111*
  unicameral bone cyst, 125–126
Turner's syndrome, 196

Ulna
  fracture, 287–289
  pediatric, 201–202
Unicameral bone cyst, 125–126
Upper limb
  orthotics
    classification, 519
    devices, 519–520
  prosthetics
    components, 516–518
    pediatric, 518

Vertebrae
  disc space infections, 102–103
  osteomyelitis of, 101–102
Volkman's contracture
  anatomy, 386–387
  diagnosis, 387
  etiology, 387
  treatment, 387–388
Voorhoeve's disease, 189

Walton classification, 175
Watson-Jones technique, 36, 38
Web space abscess, 103
Werdnig-Hoffmann classification, 178–179
Winquist classification, 323
Wrist
  anterior, 20
  bones of, 20
  carpal instability, 359–361
  dorsal, 21
  fracture, pediatric, 100
  injuries and disorders, 359–365
  joints of, 20
  Kienböck's disease, 363–364
  muscles of, 20
  osteoarthritis of, 378
  radius fractures, 362–363
  rheumatoid arthritis of, 379–380
  scaphoid fractures, 361–362
  surgery of, 21–22
  see also Forearm, Hand
Wry neck, 406